Wouter J. Hanegraaff,
professor of History of Hermetic
Philosophy and Related Currents
at the University of Amsterdam.

Antoine Faivre,
emeritus professor of History of
Esoteric and Mystical Currents in
Modern and Contemporary Europe
at the École Pratique des Hautes
Études, Sciences religieuses
(Sorbonne), Paris.

Roelof van den Broek,
emeritus professor of History of
Christianity at the University
of Utrecht.

Jean-Pierre Brach,
professor of History of Esoteric
Currents in Modern and
Contemporary Europe at the
École Pratique des Hautes Études,
Sciences religieuses (Sorbonne),
Paris.

Dictionary
of Gnosis
& Western
Esotericism

Dictionary
of Gnosis
& Western
Esotericism

EDITED BY

Wouter J. Hanegraaff

IN COLLABORATION WITH

Antoine Faivre
Roelof van den Broek
Jean-Pierre Brach

VOLUME I

BRILL

LEIDEN · BOSTON

Published under the auspices of
the Chair of History of Hermetic Philosophy and
Related Currents at the University of Amsterdam.
For all information, including Bachelor and Master program:
www.amsterdamhermetica.com

Copperplate front cover: Jacob Böhme, *Alle theosophische wercken*. Amsterdam 1682
reproduced with kind permission of Bibliotheca Philosophica Hermetica, Amsterdam

Library of Congress Cataloging-in-Publication data

Dictionary of gnosis and western esotericism/edited by Wouter J. Hanegraaff; in collaboration with
Antoine Faivre, Roelof van den Broek, Jean-Pierre Brach.
    p. cm.
  Includes bibliographical references and index.
  ISBN 90-04-14371-8 (v. 1: alk. paper)—ISBN 90-04-14372-6 (v. 2: alk. paper)—
ISBN 90-04-14187-1 (set: alk. paper) 1. Gnosticism—Dictionaries. 2. Occultism—Dictionaries.
I. Hanegraaff, Wouter J. II. Faivre, Antoine, 1934– III. Broek, R. van den. IV. Brach, Jean-Pierre.
V. Title.

B638.D53 2005
135'.4'03—dc22

2004065465

ISBN 90 04 14371 8 (Volume 1)
ISBN 90 04 14372 6 (Volume 2)
ISBN 90 04 14187 1 (set)

PRINTED IN THE NETHERLANDS

CONTENTS

INTRODUCTION

Under the general heading "Gnosis and Western Esotericism", this Dictionary brings together a great range of historical currents and personalities that have flourished in Western culture and society over a period of roughly two millennia, from Late Antiquity to the present. By doing so, it intends not only to provide a comprehensive reference work, but also to question certain ingrained assumptions about the history of Western religion and culture, and promote new agendas and analytical frameworks for research in these domains. What is at stake in such a shift of perspective can best be illustrated by taking a short look at the main terminological conventions that have traditionally been dominant.

The term *Gnosticism* was originally a pejorative term, coined in the 17th century by the Cambridge Platonist Henry More. In adopting it as a purportedly neutral scholarly category, historians also largely took over the assumption that there had actually existed a distinct religious system which could be called Gnosticism, and which could be clearly defined in opposition to the early Christian church. In recent decades it has become increasingly clear, however, that any such reification of "Gnosticism" is untenable[1] and leads to historical simplications; the idea of a clear-cut opposition of Christianity versus Gnosticism in fact reflects heresiological strategies by means of which certain factions and their spokesmen sought (successfully, as it turned out) to cement their own identity as "true" Christians by construing a negative other: the adherents of "the Gnosis falsely so called", demonized as the enemies of the true faith. It is historically more accurate, however, to see the latter, who often adhered to mythological gnostic systems, as representatives of a much broader and variegated movement or type of religiosity 'characterized by a strong emphasis on esoteric knowledge (gnosis) as the only means of salvation, which implied the return to one's divine origin'.[2]

To this much broader movement of *Gnosis* in Late Antiquity belonged not only "Gnosticism", but also, in their own ways, Christians such as Clement of Alexandria and, notably, the currents that inspired the Hermetic literature. In the domain of *Hermetism*, too, scholarly research has long been influenced by artificial black-and-white distinctions based upon normative agendas. The great pioneers of this field, Walter Scott and André-Jean Festugière, sharply opposed a "learned" or "philosophical" Hermetism against a "popular" hermetism: the worldviews belonging to the former category deserved the respect of serious scholars, but although the "occult" and "superstitious" practices belonging to the latter (nowadays referred to more neutrally as "technical" hermetica) also needed to be studied, they were referred to with contempt as no more than 'masses of rubbish'.[3] A no less important bias concerned the almost exclusive focus of scholars like Festugière on the Greek and philosophical dimensions of the Hermetic literature, at the expense of their Egyptian backgrounds – an emphasis that echoes long-standing perceptions of Egypt as the homeland of paganism and idolatry pitted against Greece as the origin of Reason and Enlightenment. Progress in the study of Hermetism in more recent decades has essentially consisted in correcting these biases on the basis of careful philological and source-critical research. The central importance of Egyptian religion for understanding the Hermetic literature is now no longer in any doubt; and it has become clear that the "philosophical" and "technical" Hermetica are in fact products of one and the same pagan intellectual milieu in Graeco-Roman Egypt, and must therefore be seen as closely connected.[4]

---

[1] See notably Michael Williams, *Rethinking "Gnosticism": An Argument for Dismantling a Dubious Category*, Princeton: Princeton University Press, 1996; and the entry "Gnosticism I" in this Dictionary.

[2] See entry "Gnosticism I" in this Dictionary.

[3] W. Scott (ed.), *Hermetica*, I, Oxford, 1924, 1.

[4] See notably Jean-Pierre Mahé, *Hermès en Haute-Égypte* (Bibliothèque Copte de Nag Hammadi, Section "Textes",

In the context of Late Antiquity, and notably in Hellenistic Egypt, we are therefore dealing with a complex type of religiosity based on the pursuit of gnosis or salvific esoteric knowledge. This phenomenon cannot be reduced to either Gnosticism or Hermetism but includes both; and it may manifest itself in pagan, Christian, as well as Jewish contexts. Moreover, with respect neither to Late Antiquity nor to later periods is it possible to study the history of these currents in isolation from that of the so-called *occult sciences*. This fact adds considerable complexity to the domain covered in this Dictionary, since it implies a large overlap between theories and practices focused on "gnosis" and pertaining primarily to the domain of religion, and others pertaining more obviously to that of science. That much attention is given in the present reference work to astrology, alchemy and *magia naturalis* does not reflect any wish to recast these disciplines as essentially religious currents focused primarily on gnosis and spiritual pursuits, or to deny their grounding in natural philosophy and science. On the contrary, the intention is to highlight the complexity of the relations between science, natural philosophy, cosmology and religion in the period from Antiquity through the 17th and even 18th centuries, against the tendency of earlier generations to deny this complexity in the interest of simplifying "religion versus science" oppositions. Thus, for example, the attempt (associated with C.G. Jung and his school) to present alchemy as not a scientific but a spiritual pursuit is no less reductionistic than the tendency of positivist historiography to ignore religious dimensions of alchemical literature as irrelevant. This Dictionary seeks to highlight the importance of the natural sciences for the study of "Gnosis and Western Esotericism" as well as the relevance of the latter to the history of science and philosophy; for only by multi- and interdisciplinary research that is attentive to all the various dimensions of these complex domains will it be possible to correctly assess their importance in Western culture.

Processes of acculturation by means of which a variety of originally "pagan" systems of ideas – such as e.g. those originating in hermetic, neoplatonic, and even aristotelian contexts – became integral parts of Christian culture during the Middle Ages and Renaissance are an obvious focus of interest for the study of "Gnosis and Western Esotericism". Major examples during the Middle Ages are the reception of Hermetic literature by a range of Christian theologians,[5] the strange phenomenon of ritual magic flourishing in the context of the medieval "clerical underworld",[6] and the revival of the "occult sciences" during the later Middle Ages as a result of a flood of translations from Arabic into Latin.[7] These developments provided the indispensable foundation for what has been referred to as the *Hermetic tradition* of the Renaissance, starting with Marsilio Ficino's epoch-making translation of the *Corpus Hermeticum* in 1463 (published in 1471, and with numerous reprints throughout the 16th century), in the context of his life-long project of recovering the supreme religious philosophy of the "divine Plato" and a long chain of *prisci theologi* who were believed to have preceded him. Since Ficino saw Plato as a religious author and read him through neoplatonic lenses, his new Christian-platonic philosophy was bound to give a new legitimacy to late-antique theurgy and related occult practices, incorrectly but influentially attributed to ancient authorities like Zoroaster and Hermes Trismegistus. The resulting mixture of hermetic, neoplatonic and occult traditions (all, of course, integrated within a Christian framework) was further enriched by a heady infusion of Jewish traditions: the so-called *Christian kabbalah*, pioneered by Giovanni Pico della Mirandola, Johannes Reuchlin and many other authors in

3 and 7), 2 vols., Quebec: Presses de l'Université Laval, 1978 and 1982; Garth Fowden, *The Egyptian Hermes: A Historical Approach to the late Pagan Mind*, Princeton: Princeton University Press, 1986.

[5] See entry "Hermetic Literature II" in this Dictionary.

[6] The term was introduced in the standard textbook by Richard Kieckhefer, *Magic in the Middle Ages*, Cambridge: Cambridge University Press, 1989 (ch. 7).

[7] Mention should be made here of the pioneering and still indispensable multi-volume work by Lynn Thorndike, *A History of Magic and Experimental Science*, 8 vols., New York: MacMillan & Columbia University Press, 1923-1958.

their wake, left an indelible mark on all later developments of the tradition. Thus the 16th century saw the birth of a new type of syncretic religiosity that could make its appearance in various confessional contexts, and was based on Jewish, Christian and pagan components. Traditional disciplines like astrology, *magia* and alchemy now came to be understood as integral parts of a comprehensive religious philosophy and cosmology on neoplatonic, hermetic and kabbalistic foundations, sometimes referred to as *philosophia occulta*. The innovative (al)chemical philosophy based upon the writings (real or spurious) of Paracelsus left a particularly strong mark on subsequent developments, as represented notably by the Rosicrucian current of the early 17th century and its continuations over the next centuries, and the Christian theosophical tradition linked to Jacob Boehme and his followers, that emerged around the same time and found multiple adherents until the early 19th century and beyond.

It is again due to ingrained ideological biases – ultimately grounded in the biblical and theological rejection of paganism as idolatry – rather than for scholarly reasons that this entire domain was severely neglected by academic research until far into the 20th century. In 1938 Paul Oskar Kristeller first called attention to the importance of the Hermetic literature for Renaissance culture, and Italian scholars began to study some of the sources[8] (although specialists still tended to look at the occult dimensions of Renaissance hermetism as an embarrassment which they preferred to ignore as much as possible);[9] but it was only in 1964 that the "Hermetic Tradition" was definitely put on the agenda of scholarly research – particularly in the context of the history of science[10] – due to Frances A. Yates's extremely influential *Giordano Bruno and the Hermetic Tradition*.[11] In a series of later books, notably *The Rosicrucian Enlightenment* (1972) and *The Occult Philosophy in the Elizabethan Age* (1979), she further explored the development of Hermetic philosophy and related traditions such as the "Christian kabbalah" and the Rosicrucian furore of the early 17th century. While Yates's work has been of the greatest importance in bringing these subjects to the attention of a wide audience, particularly in the anglophone world, her grand narrative of "the Hermetic Tradition" as a coherent and quasi-autonomous counterculture based upon magic and leading to science has been called into question by subsequent research: what is nowadays referred to as *hermeticism* (an umbrella concept that in fact comprises much more, as we have seen, than the hermetic literature only)[12] was by no means limited to some magical

---

[8] Paul Oskar Kristeller, "Marsilio Ficino e Lodovico Lazzarelli: Contributo alla diffusione delle idee ermetiche nel rinascimento", *Annali della R. Scuola Normale Superiore di Pisa, Lettere Storia e Filosofia* 2:7 (1938), 237-263, repr. in Kristeller, *Studies in Renaissance Thought and Letters* I, Roma, 1956. See discussion in Wouter J. Hanegraaff, "Lodovico Lazzarelli and the Hermetic Christ: At the Sources of Renaissance Hermetism", in: Wouter J. Hanegraaff & Ruud M. Bouthoorn, *Lodovico Lazzarelli (1447-1500): The Hermetic Writings and Related Documents*, Phoenix: Arizona Medieval & Renaissance Texts & Studies, 2005.

[9] Paul Oskar Kristeller, "L'état présent des études sur Marsile Ficin", in: *Platon et Aristote à la Renaissance* (XVIe colloque international de Tours), Paris: J. Vrin, 1976, 63: 'grâce à l'oeuvre de Thorndike, de Miss Yates et d'autres, nous ne sommes plus épouvantés quand nous rencontrons des idées scientifiques bizarres ou des conceptions astrologiques, alchimique ou magiques chez les penseurs des siècles passés. Si nous découvrons des idées de ce genre dans l'oeuvre de Ficin, nous ne lui en faisons pas reproche, mais nous le plaçons simplement dans une vaste tradition intellectuelle qui avait été négligée et évitée trop longtemps par les historiens, et qui est représentée par une littérature étendue et difficile qui a encore besoin, même après les recherches récentes, d'un grand effort d'étude et d'exploration'.

[10] On this debate about the "Yates thesis" (inspired in particular by Yates's article "The Hermetic Tradition in Renaissance Science", in: Charles S. Singleton [ed.], *Art, Science, and History in the Renaissance*, Baltimore & London, 1967, 255-274), see e.g. Brian P. Copenhaver, "Natural Magic, Hermeticism, and Occultism in Early Modern Science", in: David C. Lindberg & Robert S. Westman (eds.), *Reappraisals of the Scientific Revolution*, Cambridge, 1990, and H. Floris Cohen, *The Scientific Revolution: A Historiographical Inquiry*, Chicago & London, 1994, 169-183.

[11] Frances A. Yates, *Giordano Bruno and the Hermetic Tradition*, London & Chicago: Routledge and Kegan Paul & University of Chicago Press, 1964.

[12] Hence the distinction made in this Dictionary between "Hermetism" (as referring to the philosophical Hermetica and their commentaries) and "Hermeticism" (as a concept referring to the entire syncretic mixture that emerged

subculture but was abundantly present in "mainstream" religious, philosophical and scientific discourse as well, and its great representatives were complex thinkers whose perspective can by no means be reduced to hermeticism and magic alone.[13] As a result, the simple and dramatic picture of a quasi-autonomous counter-tradition of "hermeticists" or "Renaissance magi" fighting against the establishment (theologians, rationalists, scientists) has given way to a less romantic but more accurate perception of "hermeticism" as a traditionally underestimated dimension of *general* religious and cultural developments in pre- and early modern Western society.

In a manner very similar to what happened in Late Antiquity, with the reification of "Gnosticism" as a distinct heretical system opposed to Christianity, the concept of a distinct system or tradition of "Hermeticism" (comprising, as we have seen, the entire mixture of hermetic literature, neoplatonic speculation, kabbalah, alchemy, astrology, and magic outlined above) seems to have emerged in the 17th century and to have been taken up especially in Protestant contexts.[14] It is mainly against this background that the proponents of the Enlightenment came to present it as the epitome of unreason and superstition. Once again, the process was one of cementing one's own identity by construing a negative "other": the very project of Enlightenment required a wholesale rejection of "the occult". But in this case, too, careful historical research reveals a much more complex picture. The more we learn about the relationship between the Enlightenment and phenomena such as Freemasonry and related associations (such as the Bavarian Illluminaten or the Gold- und Rosenkreuzer) or the variegated field referred to as 18th-century Illuminism, the clearer it becomes that the boundaries between reason and its "other" were in fact blurred and shifting, with many important figures finding themselves with one foot in each camp. As the historical evidence thus forces us to re-evaluate and problematize traditional concepts of the "Age of Reason", we also need to reconsider the effects of those concepts on subsequent historiography.[15]

The reification mainly by Protestant and Enlightenment authors of "Hermeticism" as a coherent counterculture of superstition and unreason, followed by its exclusion from acceptable discourse, forced its sympathizers to adopt similar strategies. From the 18th century on and throughout the 19th, as a by-product of secularization and the disenchantment of the world, one sees them engaged in attempts at construing their own identity by means of the "invention of tradition": essentially adopting the Protestant and Enlightenment concept of a hermetic or magical counterculture, they sought to defend it as based upon a superior worldview with ancient roots, and opposed to religious dogmatism and narrow-minded rationalism. Here, too, the process was a highly complex and ambivalent one, with hermetically-oriented authors making frequent reference to "reason", "science" or "historical facts" in order to defend the notion of an ancient and

in the wake of Ficino's translation of the *Corpus Hermeticum*, and that included many currents and ideas that are not actually derived from Hermetic sources).

[13] Wouter J. Hanegraaff, "Beyond the Yates Paradigm: The Study of Western Esotericism between Counterculture and New Complexity", *Aries* 1:1 (2001), 5-37.

[14] See in particular the polemics of Ehregott Daniel Colberg against what he referred to as "platonic-hermetic Christianity" (*Das Platonisch-Hermetisches* [sic] *Christenthum, Begreiffend Die Historische Erzehlung vom Ursprung und vielerley Secten der heutigen Fanatische Theologie, unterm Namen der Paracelsisten, Weigelianer, Rosencreutzer, Quäcker, Böhmisten, Wiedertäuffer, Bourignisten, Labadisten, und Quietisten*, 2 vols., Frankfurt & Leipzig: M.G. Widmann, 1690-1691), and the defense of the same currents by Gottfried Arnold (*Unpartheyische Kirchen- und Ketzer-Historie: Vom Anfang des neuen Testaments bis auf das Jahr Christi 1688*, Frankfurt a.M.: Thomas Fritsch, 1700). Note that the Roman Catholic Marin Mersenne already attacked the opinions of the 'platonists, rabbis and magi' earlier in the century (*Quaestiones celeberrimae in Genesim*, esp. the separate final section, entitled *Observationes et emendationes ad Francisci Georgii Veneti "Problemata"*, Paris, 1623). Mersenne clearly targets the entire compound (represented for him by authors such as Giorgio da Veneto and Fludd) that eventually came to be referred to as "hermeticism", but does not yet refer to it as such.

[15] Monika Neugebauer-Wölk (ed.), *Aufklärung und Esoterik* (Studien zum achtzehnten Jahrhundert, 24), Hamburg: Felix Meiner, 1999; Christopher McIntosh, *The Rose Cross and the Age of Reason: Eighteenth-Century Rosicrucianism in Central Europe and its Relationship to the Enlightenment*, Leiden, New York, Köln: E.J. Brill, 1992.

superior tradition of "magic and the occult" that had been present since hoary antiquity and had continued through the ages. The term *occultism*, a neologism first attested in 1842, was quickly picked up in these circles as an appropriate label for their own perspectives. Eventually the term has also come to be adopted by scholars, as a historical label for these same 19th-century circles and their 20th-century continuations.[16]

It is likewise in the first half of the 19th century that the term *esotericism* (French: "ésotérisme") emerged as well, having been coined by the Protestant historian Jacques Matter in his *Histoire critique du gnosticisme et de son influence* published in 1828. The term therefore did not originate as a self-designation by which certain religious authors or currents identified themselves or their own perspectives, but as a scholarly label applied *a posteriori* to certain religious developments in the context of early Christianity. To the present day, the term "esotericism" tends to be used by scholars in two different senses, that should be clearly distinguished: in a typological sense it refers to traditions of secrecy or (mainly among authors inspired by "religionist" agendas) to what is seen as the deeper "inner mysteries of religion" as opposed to merely external or "exoteric" religious observance, but in a strictly historical sense it functions, rather, as a general label for a series of specific currents in Western culture that display certain similarities and are historically related.[17] The term *Western Esotericism* in the title of this Dictionary refers to this second meaning. Particularly in French scholarship, "l'ésotérisme occidental" has long been used by scholars as the preferred umbrella term covering the entirety of currents and traditions that have been sketched above; and since the 1990s this terminological convention has rapidly been gaining ground in international academic discourse.[18] This process has been accompanied by a theoretical and methodological debate about definitions and demarcations, which is still in full development at the time of writing.[19]

Since the eventual outcome of these discussions is as yet far from clear, it would have been unwise to link the present Dictionary too specifically to one particular definition or theoretical approach. Such an attempt would, moreover, have been unnecessary, because – as in the study of "religion" generally – scholars in this domain often strongly disagree about abstract theoretical definitions although they in fact share a broad consensus about the historical phenomena covered by the term. Specialists may quibble about boundary issues, disagreeing about whether this or that specific current or personality should or should not be included under the broad labels "Gnosis" and "Western Esotericism", but experience shows that by and large they think of the same domain and the same currents when they are using these terms.

The major exception, which therefore needs to be addressed here, concerns the important question of "gnosis" and "esotericism" in the context of Jewish and Islamic culture. As for the Jewish context, it is significant that in his Hebrew publications Gershom Scholem preferred to speak not of Jewish mystics but of *ba'aley sod* (lit. "masters of the secret", translatable as "esoterics" in the typological sense referred to above);[20] accordingly,

---

[16] See entry "Occult / Occultism" in this Dictionary.

[17] See entry "Esotericism" in this Dictionary.

[18] See overview in Wouter J. Hanegraaff, "The Study of Western Esotericism: New Approaches to Christian and Secular Culture", in: Peter Antes, Armin W. Geertz & Randi Warne (eds.), *New Approaches to the Study of Religion* (Series "Religion and Reason"), Berlin, New York: De Gruyter, 2004, vol. 1, 489-519.

[19] See notably Antoine Faivre, *Access to Western Esotericism*, Albany: SUNY Press, 1994, 3-47; Wouter J. Hanegraaff, "Empirical Method in the Study of Esotericism", *Method & Theory in the Study of Religion* 7:2 (1995), 99-129; Antoine Faivre, "L'ésotérisme et la recherche universitaire", in: *Accès de l'ésotérisme occidental*, 2nd revised ed., II, Paris: Gallimard, 1996, 13-42; several contributions in Antoine Faivre & Wouter J. Hanegraaff (eds.), *Western Esotericism and the Science of Religion: Selected Papers presented at the 17th Congress of the International Association for the History of Religions, Mexico City 1995*, Louvain: Peeters, 1998; Monika Neugebauer-Wölk, "Esoterik und Christentum vor 1800: Prolegomena zu einer Bestimmung ihrer Differenz", *Aries* 3:2 (2003), 127-165; Kocku von Stuckrad, *Was ist Esoterik? Kleine Geschichte des geheimen Wissens*, Munich: C.H. Beck, 2004, 9-23.

[20] Joseph Dan, "In Quest of a Historical Definition of Mysticism: The Contingental Approach", *Studies in Spirituality* 3 (1993), 62-63.

the English translation of his classic introduction as *Major Trends in Jewish Mysticism* (1946) might be considered unfortunate. From both a historical and a theoretical perspective, excellent arguments could be adduced for including the entire domain of "Jewish gnosis and esotericism" within the context of the present Dictionary, and along similar lines one might argue in favour of including the domain of Islamic gnosis and esotericism, which likewise tends to be referred to as "mysticism".[21] The editors are aware of the cogency of the arguments that can be adduced in favour of a concept of "Gnosis and Western Esotericism" that fully and systematically includes the three great Religions of the Book; and they are acutely conscious of the fact that doing otherwise might be perceived by some readers as reflecting a Christianity-centered bias that incorrectly seeks to exclude Judaism and Islam from the domain of "European history of religions" or from "Western culture" as such. No such exclusion or marginalization is intended here. The decision to discuss the Jewish and Islamic dimensions as "influences upon" rather than as integral parts of Gnosis and Western Esotericism was made not for theoretical but for entirely pragmatic reasons. It reflects the fact that (partly due to linguistic barriers) the disciplines studying Jewish and Islamic "mysticism" have so far developed relatively independently and have already succeeded in achieving a certain degree of academic recognition, at least in comparison to the field here referred to as "Gnosis and Western Esotericism". With respect to the latter, it is true that many specific currents covered by the present Dictionary (particularly those pertaining to earlier periods) have long been subjects of serious academic study, but only very recently have conditions begun to be created – in the form of e.g. multidisciplinary conferences, academic institutions, monograph series, or academic journals[22] – that allow them to be seen in a larger historical context, so that their numerous historical interconnections are seriously explored and these various currents can be perceived as so many aspects of a much larger domain. Academic research into the later phases of the historical spectrum, from the Renaissance and *a fortiori* from the 18th century on, has been most seriously neglected by earlier generations (mostly due to the influence of the now discredited "secularization thesis" according to which these domains could not be anything more than marginal "survivals" that would eventually succumb to the pressures of rationalization and secularization);[23] and again it is only quite recently that this situation is beginning to improve.[24] By giving equal attention to these later and quite recent historical developments as to those belong-

---

[21] E.g. Annemarie Schimmel, *Mystical Dimensions of Islam*, Chapel Hill: University of North Carolina Press, 1975; Alexander Knysh, *Islamic Mysticism: A Short History*, Leiden, Boston, Köln: E.J. Brill, 2000.

[22] Large and successful symposia on Western esotericism have been organized in the context of the quincentennial congresses of the International Association for the History of Religions (I.A.H.R.) in 1995 (Mexico City), 2000 (Durban) and Tokyo (2005). Since 2001, E.J. Brill publishers brings out an academic journal *Aries: Journal for the Study of Western Esotericism*. Peeters publishers (Louvain) have been publishing a monograph series "Gnostica: Texts & Interpretations" since 1997. An America-based "Association for the Study of Esotericism" was recently established and organized a successful conference in 2004, and a Europe-based counterpart is in the process of being established. Finally, an academic chair for the study of Western Esotericism having existed since 1965 at the École Pratique des Hautes Études (Sorbonne) in Paris, a second chair connected with a complete subdepartment and teaching program (Bachelor and Master) was established at the University of Amsterdam in 1999 (see www.amsterdamhermetica.com).

[23] The decline of the classic secularization thesis, the "return of religion", and the concomitant emergence of new theoretical frameworks (e.g. rational choice theory) have been much discussed in recent years, and this is hardly the place for an overview of the debate and the pertinent literature. For an application to the study of Western Esotericism, see e.g. Wouter J. Hanegraaff, *New Age Religion and Western Culture: Esotericism in the Mirror of Secular Thought*, Leiden, New York, Köln: E.J. Brill, 1996/Albany: SUNY Press, 1998; and idem, "How Magic Survived the Disenchantment of the World", *Religion* 33:4 (2003), 357-380.

[24] A new interest in the relevance of 19th-/20th-century esotericism for understanding processes of modernization is demonstrated by e.g. Joscelyn Godwin, *The Theosophical Enlightenment*, Albany: SUNY Press, 1994; Corinna Treitel, *A Science for the Soul: Occultism and the Genesis of the German Modern*, Baltimore, London: John Hopkins University Press, 2004; Alex Owen, *The Place of Enchantment: British Occultism and the Culture of the Modern*, Chicago, London: University of Chicago Press, 2004.

ing to earlier periods, and thus establishing a "referential corpus" of primary and secondary texts pertaining to the complete historical spectrum, the present Dictionary hopes to contribute to the current academic emancipation of "Gnosis and Western Esotericism" as a comprehensive domain of research. Furthering collaboration with parallel disciplines focused on Jewish and Islamic "mysticism" is part of that development, and may well end up transforming our perception of all of them. As the hoped-for outcome of such a future development, perhaps one day the time will be ripe for a Dictionary even much larger than the present one, and which will fully include the Jewish and Islamic along with the Christian and secular dimensions of "Gnosis and Western Esotericism".

The above overview is based upon the premise that seemingly innocuous terminological conventions are often the reflection of hidden or implicit ideological agendas. Perhaps no other domain in the study of religion has suffered from such biases as seriously as the one to which this Dictionary is devoted, for it covers more or less all currents and phenomena that have, at one time or another, come to be perceived as problematic (misguided, heretical, irrational, dangerous, evil, or simply ridiculous) from the perspectives of established religion, philosophy, science, and academic research. Often these perceptions have led to serious distortions of the historical evidence, usually in the form of simplified pictures of complex realities and the creation of imaginary "enemies". The label "Gnosis and Western Esotericism" is proposed here as part of a deliberate attempt at overcoming such biases and moving towards a more neutral, accurate and balanced reading of Western history of religion and culture; but obviously it would be extremely naive to think that any terminology can be entirely free from such problems. The editors are acutely aware of the fact that usage of the terms "Gnosis" and "Western esotericism" is not limited to academic contexts, since both are also used in popular literature to promote various "spiritual" agendas and aspirations. Likewise they are painfully aware of the ironical fact that the very attempt at gathering an enormous variety of currents and personalities under one general umbrella might easily be mistaken, against all their intentions, for just another attempt at reification and simplification, suggesting the presence of some "universal gnosis" or abiding "esoteric truth".[25] Fortunately, however, the very contents of this Dictionary provide the best antidote against such misperceptions: rather than a repetitive series of variations on the same essential "truths", the reader will find here a dazzling variety of ideas and practices, reflective of ever-changing historical contexts and testifying to the remarkable creativity of the religious imagination. We hereby offer this reference work to our readers in the hope that it will inspire them not only (if it is permitted here to quote Gene Roddenberry's Star Trek saga) "to boldly go where no one has gone before", but also to re-visit seemingly well-charted territories and discover how much we still have to learn about them.

Wouter J. Hanegraaff
Amsterdam, September 2004.

---

[25] See discussion of a number of representative cases in Wouter J. Hanegraaff, "On the Construction of 'Esoteric Traditions'", in: Faivre & Hanegraaff, *Western Esotericism and the Science of Religion*, 11-61.

ACKNOWLEDGMENTS

The idea for this *Dictionary of Gnosis and Western Esotericism* was born in 1996, and over the following years the editors have incurred debts to many people who by their valued contributions have helped bring it to realization. In the first place, we want to thank Hans van der Meij, senior editor at Brill publishers, for suggesting the very idea of this reference work, for actively engaging himself in its conceptualization, and for steering and supervising the editorial and production process from the publisher's side. We are no less grateful to the other people at Brill's office, whose professional input has been widely instrumental in making that process run smoothly. In particular, we want to thank Alinda Damsma, Sanne Massier-Wagner, and Wilma de Weert. Thanks to all of them, over that period of more than eight years the collaboration between editors and publisher has been a most pleasant and constructive one.

From 1999 on, the subdepartment of History of Hermetic Philosophy and Related Currents at the Universiteit van Amsterdam functioned as administrative center for the editorial process. We want to thank its two successive secretaries, Andréa Kroon and Hilda Nobach, for their efficiency in mediating between authors, editors and publisher and for assuming the many administrative and other tasks that a complex process like editing a large Dictionary entails. Without their work this Dictionary would never have seen the light of day.

Many contributions to this Dictionary were written in a language other than English. We owe a great debt of gratitude to the translators: Joscelyn Godwin (French, Italian, German), Nicholas Goodrick-Clarke (German), Christine Rhone (French), and Mirjam Westbroek (Dutch). The first two of these are important scholars in the field, and have written a significant number of contributions to the Dictionary in addition to their translations. The latter were made possible in no small measure by a generous subsidy from the Foundation "Chair of History of Hermetic Philosophy and Related Currents", for which we are particularly grateful. Finally, the chief Editor of this Dictionary would personally like to thank the Foundation, its founder, and the Universiteit van Amsterdam: the present work would not have materialized had it not been for the unique academic context they have created, which has proved to be so stimulating in the study of Gnosis and Western Esotericism.

The Editors

LIST OF CONTRIBUTORS

Allen, M.J.B., University of California, Los Angeles, U.S.A.
  [Ficino]
Auffray, J.-P., Issirac, France
  [Newton]
Bara, J.-F., Paris, France
  [Astrology II]
Barthélemy, P., Bibliothèque Nationale de France, Paris, France
  [Sedacer]
Bechmann, R., Boulogne, France
  [Villard de Honnecourt and the Medieval Craft]
Bee, G., Universität zu Köln, Germany
  [Audians]
Benzenhöfer, U., Bonn, Germany
  [Paracelsus]
Bergé, C., Centre National de la Recherche Scientifique, France
  [Illuminism; Kardec]
Binet, A.M., Université Michel de Montaigne-Bordeaux III, France
  [Pessoa]
Blaufuß, D., Erlangen, Germany
  [Pietism]
Bolzoni, L., Scuola Normale Superiore, Pisa, Italy
  [Camillo; Mnemonics]
Bonner, A., Palma de Mallorca, Spain
  [Llull]
Bourguet, P., Université de Nancy 2, France
  [Rétif de la Bretonne]
Boyer, A., Paris, France
  [Boys des Guays]
Bozóky, E., Université de Poitiers, France
  [Bogomilism; Catharism]
Brach, J.-P., École Pratique des Hautes Études (Sorbonne), Paris, France
  [Charbonneau-Lassay; Correspondences; Intermediary Beings III; Magic IV; Number Symbolism; Patrizi; Postel; Viterbo]
Brann, N.L., emeritus Universities of Maryland and Tennessee, U.S.A.
  [Trithemius]
Breymayer, R., Universität Tübingen, Germany
  [Oetinger]
Broek, van den, R., emeritus Universiteit Utrecht, The Netherlands
  [Archontics; Borborites; Cerdo; Cerinthus; Clement of Alexandria; Elchasai / Elxai; Gnosticism I; Gnosticism II; Hermes Trismegistus I; Hermetic Literature I; Hermetism; Intermediary Beings I; Justin the Gnostic; Menander; Monoimus; Naassenes; Prodicus; Satornilus; Simon Magus]
Buntz, H., Buckenhof, Germany
  [Alchemy III]
Calvet, A., Paris, France
  [Arnau de Vilanova; Roquetaillade]
Caron, R., Lannion, France
  [Alchemy V; Canseliet; Fulcanelli]
Casadio, G., Università degli Studi di Salerno, Fisciano, Italy
  [Marcus the Magician]
Chanel, C., Lyon, France
  [Théon]

Charmasson, T., Centre de Recherche en Histoire des Sciences et des Techniques, Paris, France
  [Divinatory Arts]
Ciliberto, M., Instituto Nazionale di Studi sul Rinascimento, Florence, Italy
  [Bruno]
Coudert, A.P., University of California, Davis, U.S.A.
  [Alchemy IV; van Helmont, F.M.]
Counet, J.-M., Université Catholique, Louvain-la-Neuve, Belgium
  [Cusa]
Dachez, R., Université de Paris, France / Institut Maçonnique de France
  [Freemasonry; Haugwitz]
Dan, J., The Hebrew University of Jerusalem, Israel
  [Jewish Influences III; Reuchlin]
Deghaye, P., emeritus Université de Caen, France
  [Arnold]
Deveney, J.P., New York City, U.S.A.
  [Hermetic Brotherhood of Luxor; Randolph; Spiritualism]
Doel, M.J.E. van den, Universiteit van Amsterdam, The Netherlands
  [Imagination]
Edighoffer, R., emeritus Université Paris-III-Sorbonne-Nouvelle, Paris, France
  [Andreae; Bacon, F.; Comenius; Haslmayr; Lewis; Rosicrucianism I; Rosicrucianism II; Sincerus
  Renatus]
Edighoffer, S., Neuilly-sur-Seine, France
  [Fludd]
Ernst, G., Università degli Studi di Roma Tre, Rome, Italy
  [Campanella]
Fabry, J.L., emeritus Université de Caen, France
  [Eckartshausen; Hahn; Jung-Stilling; von Meyer]
Faivre, A., emeritus École Pratique des Hautes Études (Sorbonne), Paris, France
  [Asiatic Brethren; Bô-Yin-Râ; Cazotte; Christian Theosophy; Douzetemps; Dutoit-Membrini; Egyp-
  tomany; Etteilla; Fictuld; Foix-Candale; Hermes Trismegistus III; Hermetic Literature IV; Kirchberger;
  Lopukhin; Mouravieff; Naturphilosophie; Ritter; Schlag; Secrecy III; Tomberg; von Welling]
Faivre, J.-L., Classes Préparatoires aux Grandes Ecoles, Reims, France
  [Grand Jeu; de Nerval]
Fanger, C., Elmwood, Ontario, Canada
  [Albertus Magnus; Bacon, R.; Fortune; Intermediary Beings II; Magic III; Secrecy II]
Faracovi, O.P., Università di Pisa, Pisa, Italy
  [Astrology IV]
Federici Vescovini, G., Università degli Studi di Firenze, Italy
  [Magical Instruments; Michael Scot; Peter of Abano]
French, B., Ph.D. University of Sydney, Australia
  [Leadbeater]
Gantenbein, U.L., Universität Zürich, Switzerland
  [Paracelsus]
Gijsen, A. van, Universiteit van Antwerpen, Belgium
  [Astrology I]
Gilbert, R.A., Bristol, United Kingdom
  [Barrett; Hermetic Order of the Golden Dawn; Stella Matutina; Waite]
Godwin, J., Colgate University, Hamilton, U.S.A.
  [Ashmole; Bulwer-Lytton; Burton; Hall; Jennings; Mead; Music IV; Orientalism; Rudolf II]
Gomes, M., Emily Sellon Memorial Library, New York, U.S.A.
  [Olcott]
Goodrick-Clarke, N., University of Wales, Lampeter, United Kingdom
  [Ariosophy; Hartmann; Hermeticism and Hermetic Societies; Lanz von Liebenfels; von List]
Gorski, W.T., Northwestern State University, Natchitoches, U.S.A.
  [Yeats]

Gouk, P., University of Manchester, United Kingdom
[Music III]
Graf, F., Ohio State University, U.S.A.
[Magic II]
Greiner, F., Université de Reims, France
[Dorn; Flamel; Gohory; de Nuysement]
Groot, J.W. de, Universiteit van Amsterdam, The Netherlands
[Dinter]
Guimbard, C., Université de Paris-IV-Sorbonne, Paris, France
[Fedeli d'Amore]
Haage, B.D., Universität Mannheim, Germany
[Alchemy II]
Hakl, H.T., Graz, Austria
[Dürckheim; Evola; Fraternitas Saturni; Heindel]
Hammer, O.K., University of Southern Denmark, Odense, Denmark
[Astrology V; Essenes, Esoteric Legends about; Human Potential Movement; Jungism; New Age Movement]
Hanegraaff, W.J., Universiteit van Amsterdam, The Netherlands
[Champier; Correggio; Correspondences; Esotericism; Imagination; Intermediary Beings IV; Jewish Influences V; Kerner; Lazzarelli; Magic I; Magic V; New Thought Movement; Novalis; Occult / Occultism; Roberts; Tradition]
Holzhausen, J., Freie Universität Berlin, Germany
[Valentinus and Valentinians]
Hutton, S., Middlesex University, London, United Kingdom
[Cudworth; More]
Introvigne, M., C.E.S.N.U.R., Torino, Italy
[Cagliostro; Deunov; Fabré-Palaprat; Grail traditions; Huysmans; Kremmerz; Martinism: Second Period; Neo-Catharism; van Rijckenborgh; Rosicrucianism III; Sangro di San Severo; Satanism; Scaligero]
Janssen, F.A., Universiteit van Amsterdam, The Netherlands
[Lefèvre d'Étaples]
Jong, A.F. de, Universiteit Leiden, The Netherlands
[Music I; Secrecy I; Zoroaster; Zosimus]
Keller, C.-A., Université de Lausanne, Switzerland
[Reincarnation I]
Keller, J., emeritus Université de Strasbourg, France
[Saltzmann]
Kilcher, A.B., Universität Tübingen, Germany
[Jewish Influences IV; Kircher; Knorr von Rosenroth]
Klaassen, F., University of Saskatchewan, Saskatoon, Canada
[Magic III; Robert of Chester]
Kluveld, A., Universiteit van Amsterdam, The Netherlands
[Kingsford]
Kotansky, R., Santa Monica, U.S.A.
[Amulets]
Lancellotti, M.G., Università di Pisa, Italy
[Hymns and Prayers]
Laurant, J.P., École Pratique des Hautes Études (Sorbonne), Paris, France
[Barlet; de Guaïta; Lacuria; Lévi; Marconis de Nègre; Milosz; Papus; Péladan; Politics; Ragon de Bettignies; Saint-Yves d'Alveydre; Schuré; Schwaller de Lubicz; Sédir; Tarot]
Lazar-Ovtchinnikov, A., Paris, France
[Novikov]
Leicht, R., Universität Potsdam, Germany
[Jewish Influences I; Jewish Influences II]
Leijenhorst, C., Radboud Universiteit Nijmegen, The Netherlands
[Anthroposophy; Aristotelianism; Neoplatonism II; Neoplatomism III; Steiner]

Lelli, F., Università di Lecce, Italy
  [Pico della Mirandola]
Lemoine, M., Centre National de la Recherche Scientifique, France
  [Bernard Silvester; Morley; William of Auvergne]
Löhr, W.A., Universität Hamburg, Germany
  [Basilides; Carpocratians; Perates; Sethians]
Lory, P. École Pratique des Hautes Études (Sorbonne), Paris, France
  [Hermetic Literature III]
Lucas, P.C., Stetson University, Deland, USA
  [Cayce; Davis; Summit Lighthouse]
Lucentini, P., Università degli Studi di Napoli "l'Orientale", Italy
  [Hermes Trismegistus II; Hermetic Literature II]
Luscombe, D.E., University of Sheffield, United Kingdom
  [Dionysius Areopagita, Pseudo-]
Maillard, C., Université Marc Bloch, Strasbourg, France
  [Goethe; Jung]
Marie, G., Nice, France
  [Lavater]
Marquet, J.-F., emeritus Université de Paris-IV (Sorbonne), France
  [Schelling]
Mathiesen, R., Brown, University, Providence, U.S.A.
  [Britten; Byzantium]
May, G., Universität Mainz, Germany
  [Marcion]
Mayer, J.-F., Université de Fribourg, Switzerland
  ["I AM" activity; Lorber; Swedenborgian Traditions; UFO Traditions]
Mazet, E., Ecole Polytechnique, Paris, France
  [Chevaliers Bienfaisants de la Cité Sainte]
McCalla, A., Mount Saint Vincent University, Halifax, Canada
  [Ballanche; Fabre d'Olivet; de Maistre; Romanticism; Saint-Martin; Wronski]
Méheust, B., Université d'Amiens, France
  [Animal Magnetism]
Mercier-Faivre, A.-M., Université de Lyon-2, France
  [Court de Gébelin]
Mollier, P., Bibliothèque du Grand Orient de France, Paris, France
  [Neo-Templar Traditions]
Moore, J.H., London, United Kingdom
  [Gurdjieff]
Moran, B., University of Nevada, Reno, U.S.A.
  [Paracelsianism]
Morisi, A., Università di Roma "La Sapienze", Italy
  [Galatino]
Mussies, G., Universiteit Utrecht, The Netherlands
  [Moses]
Nahon, M., Saint Aubin de Médoc, France
  [Élus Coëns]
Needleman, J., San Francisco State University, CA, U.S.A.
  [Gurdjieff tradition; Ouspensky]
Neugebauer-Wölk, M., Universität Halle-Wittenberg, Halle, Germany
  [Illuminaten]
Newman, B., Northwestern University, Evanston, U.S.A.
  [Hildegard of Bingen]
Oort, J. van, Universiteit Utrecht / Radboud Universiteit Nijmegen, The Netherlands
  [Augustine; Mani; Manichaeism]

Otten, W., Universiteit Utrecht, The Netherlands
  [Eriugena]
Overton Fuller, J., Rushden (Northamptonshire), United Kingdom
  [Saint-Germain]
Pape, G. le, Verdelot, France
  [Cryptography]
Pasi, M., Universiteit van Amsterdam, The Netherlands
  [Crowley; Mathers; Ordo Templi Orientis; Westcott]
Pearson, B.A., emeritus University of California, Santa Barbara, U.S.A.
  [Cainites; Nicolaitans; Ophites]
Pearson, J.E., Cardiff University, United Kingdom
  [Neopaganism]
Perrone Compagni, V., Università degli studi di Firenze, Florence, Italy
  [Hermetic Literature II]
Pinchard, B., Université de Lyon-3, France
  [Dante Alighieri]
Pollet, J.-J., Université d'Artois, France
  [Meyrink]
Principe, L., John Hopkins University, Baltimore, U.S.A.
  [Alchemy I; Boyle; Starkey]
Quinn, W.W., Scottsdale, Arizona, U.S.A.
  [Guénon; Schuon]
Refslund-Christensen, D., Aarhus University, Denmark
  [Scientology]
Roodnat, A.A., Erasmus Universiteit, Rotterdam, The Netherlands
  [van Helmont, J.B.]
Roudaut, F., Université Paul Valéry, Montpellier III, France
  [Le Fèvre de la Boderie]
Rousse-Lacordaire, R.P.J., Institut Catholique, Paris
  [Abellio; Corbin; Mysticism]
Rudolph, K., emeritus Philipps-Universität, Marburg, Germany
  [Mandaeans]
Rudrum, A., Simon Fraser University, Burnaby, Canada
  [Vaughan]
Santucci, J.A., California State University, Fullerton, U.S.A.
  [Bailey; Besant; Blavatsky; Theosophical Society]
Schuchard, M.K., Atlanta, Georgia, U.S.A.
  [Falk]
Sebti, M., Centre National de la Recherche Scientifique, France
  [Avicenna]
Sedgwick, M., American University in Cairo, Egypt
  [Neo-Sufism]
Shaw, G., Stonehill College, Easton, U.S.A.
  [Neoplatonism I]
Smoller, L.A., University of Arkansas, Little Rock, U.S.A.
  [Pierre d'Ailly]
Snoek, J., Ruprecht-Karls-Universität, Heidelberg, Germany
  [Essenes, Esoteric legends about; Illuminés d'Avignon; Pernety]
Spector, S., Queens College, New York, U.S.A.
  [Blake]
Stuckrad, C.K.M. von, Universiteit van Amsterdam, The Netherlands
  [Astrology III]
Summerfield, H., emeritus University of Victoria, Canada
  [AE]

Szőnyi, G.E., University of Szeged, Hungary
  [Dee; Hamvas]
Tambrun-Krasker, B., Centre National de la Recherche Scientifique, France
  [Plethon]
Teeuwen, M., Constantijn Huygens Institute for Text Editions and Intellectual History (KNAW), The
  Hague, The Netherlands
  [Music I; Music II]
Telle, J., Universität Freiburg im Breisgau & Universität Heidelberg, Germany
  [Khunrath]
Thomas, D.L., Roma, Italy
  [Reghini]
Tilton, H., Ludwig-Maximilians-Universität, Munich, Germany
  [Maier]
Toth, L., Paris, France
  [Gnostic Church]
Travaglia, P., Istituto Universitario Orientale, Naples, Italy
  [al-Kindī]
Trompf, G.W., University of Sydney, Australia
  [Macrohistory]
Valente, M., Università di Roma, Rome, Italy
  [Agrippa; Witchcraft]
Valette, P., Institut Universitaire de Formation des Maîtres, Picardie, France
  [Schubert]
Var, J.F., Chilly-Mazarrin, France
  [Martinism: First Period; Pasqually; Philippe; Willermoz]
Vasoli, C.E., Accademia Nazionale dei Lincei, Rome, Italy
  [Giorgio]
Versluis, A., Michigan State University, East Lansing, U.S.A.
  [Baader; Bourignon; Gichtel; Law; Lead(e); Novalis; Poiret; Pordage; Ziegler]
Voss, K.-C., Fatih University, Istanbul, Turkey
  [d'Orléans]
Weeks, A., Illinois State University, Normal, U.S.A.
  [Boehme; Weigel]
Willard, T., University of Arizona, Tucson, U.S.A.
  [Heydon]
Williams-Hogan, J., Bryn Athyn College of the New Church, Bryn Athyn, U.S.A.
  [Swedenborg]
Zander, H., Humboldt Universität, Berlin, Germany
  [Reincarnation II]
Zanier, G., Università degli Studi di Trieste, Italy
  [Iatromathematica]

LIST OF ENTRIES

Abellio, Raymond
AE
Agrippa, Heinrich Cornelius
Albertus Magnus
Alchemy
   Alchemy I: Introduction
   Alchemy II: Antiquity-12th Century
   Alchemy III: 12th/13th – 15th Century
   Alchemy IV: 16th – 18th Century
   Alchemy V: 19th – 20th Century
Al-Kindī, Abū Yūsuf Yaʿqūb ibn Isḥāq
Amulets
Andreae, Johann Valentin
Animal Magnetism / Mesmerism
Anthroposophy
Archontics
Ariosophy
Aristotelianism
Arnau de Vilanova
Arnold, Gottfried
Ashmole, Elias
Asiatic Brethren
Astrology
   Astrology I: Introduction
   Astrology II: Antiquity
   Astrology III: Middle Ages
   Astrology IV: 15th – 19th Century
   Astrology V: 20th Century
Audians
Augustine
Avicenna
Baader, Benedict Franz Xaver von
Bacon, Francis
Bacon, Roger
Bailey, Alice Ann
Ballanche, Pierre Simon
Barlet, François-Charles
Barrett, Francis
Basilides
Bernard Silvester
Besant, Annie
Blake, William
Blavatsky, Helena Petrovna
Boehme, Jacob
Bogomilism
Borborites
Bourignon, Antoinette
Bô-Yin-Râ
Boyle, Robert
Boys des Guays, Jacques François Etienne le
Britten, Emma (Floyd) Hardinge
Bruno, Giordano

Abano, Peter of → Peter of Abano

Abellio, Raymond (ps. of Georges
Soulès), * 11.11.1907 Toulouse,
† 26.8.1986 Nice

At the end of World War II and a development
that had led him from the left wing of the Socialist
Party, through Deloncle and Déat's collaboration-
ist parties, to the Resistance Movement, Georges
Soulès, a trained engineer, left politics for esotericism. He did so under the influence of Pierre de
Combas, a man well versed in esoteric traditions,
whom he met in 1943. Considered one of the great
French prose writers of his time, Soulès published
his works from 1946 until his death under the
pseudonym Raymond Abellio; they comprise a
play, novels, autobiographical writings and theoretical essays. By means of these various genres he
has developed an all-encompassing system for
interpreting the world and history, sustained by elements from the various esoteric traditions to which
Pierre de Combas had introduced him, and by the
Husserlian phenomenology that he encountered in
the 1950s.

In 1965 Abellio published his book *La Structure
absolue* (The Absolute Structure) which may be
considered the key to his philosophical system. The
"structure" in question is partly inspired by arithmological traditions [→ Number Symbolism] and
"kabbalistic" gematria [→ Jewish Influences V],
along with other influences such as the *I Ching*, the
→ Tarot, and → astrology; and partly it is inspired
by Edmund Husserl's phenomenological philosophy. The structure is visually presented as a sphere,
similar in some respects to the one presented by →
René Guénon in his *Le Symbolisme de la croix*
(1931), and which can be described as follows.
First, a horizontal cross (four angles of 90 degrees).
Second, a vertical line which runs across that cross,
passing through its middle. Third, the cross and the
line are enclosed within a sphere whose center is the
point of intersection between the horizontal cross
and the vertical line. By the same token, the sphere
has six poles (the four extremities of the cross, and
the two extremities of the vertical line); the point of
intersection is not a pole proper, but is considered
as important as the poles themselves. This three-
dimensional figure is supposed to provide important insights into any domain (science, metaphysics,
philosophy, psychology, history, etc), and into the
relationships between them, provided that whenever one uses it, the poles have been properly
"qualified" in accordance with the kind of enquiry
one has chosen to carry out (i.e., the terms or

notions one has decided to impart to each of the six
poles, whenever one makes use of the sphere, must
have been chosen in a pertinent way). Ontologically, as it were, the basic idea that underlies the
figure may be summarized as follows. The two lines
of the horizontal cross represent two dualities. The
extremities of the one line stand respectively for
our sense organ(s) and our body; the extremities of
the cross's other line stand respectively for the
"object" and the global "world" (the object "de-
taching" itself, in husserlian terms, from the
"world"). As a result we have two dualities, which
are said to be "turning" or "moving" around; but
not only horizontally, for they are also constantly
either tending upward toward the upper part of the
horizontal line (the "assumption" toward unity) or
descending along its lower part (descent toward
multiplicity). As for the center of the sphere, it
stands for the "transcendental Self".

This structure Abellio claims to be "absolute"
because he considers it to be applicable – in the
context of a doctrine of "universal interdependence" or universal → correspondences – to all areas
of reality, including even history. It is supposed to
reveal the "invisible history", or "metahistory", of
civilizations, interconnected with psychology, politics, physics, biology, etc., as well as of the transcendental Self of the human being. Two main
elements are said to distinguish the Abellian absolute structure from the Husserlian scheme. First,
the fact that he considers his notion of "interdependence" and "intersubjectivity" to be the starting point of the gnostic experience to be achieved,
not as its end. Second, his notion of "intensifying
dialectic", by which he means the dynamic movement to be imparted to the sphere, it being understood that, as already noted, its poles have been
properly "qualified".

Abellio's essays, works of fiction and autobiographies all must be understood in the context of
this dynamics. They are reflective of an ongoing
process whose final term he calls the "assumption"
(Abellio readily uses Christian terminology: baptism, communion, assumption, etc.) of the world's
multiplicity into the "inner Man". Man is thus supposed to be able to achieve the complete unification
of that multiplicity, a unification that will end up
providing the subject with a "gnostic consciousness", also called "second memory", by the same
token leading to the "transfiguration of the world".
History – the real one as well as Abellio's historical
fictions – then comes full circle, the past being connected to the future in a present beyond time.

The various literary genres that comprise Abellio's work are closely interconnected. They all tend

toward the same spiritual goal: the emergence of a transcendental Self. The essays proceed analytically and tend to use autobiographical material. The autobiographical work describes the genesis of the novels and of the essays, and integrates various theoretical elements. Abellio considers the novel to be the most complete form of writing, because it is the most synthetic one. It is not strictly analytical like the essay – it shows more than it demonstrates –, and it is not unfinished like the autobiography. This is why Abellio ascribes to his novels, which are meant to be 'a call to the reader's active awareness' (*Visages immobiles*, 11), a particularly potent initiatic value. Due to this primacy given to novelistic fiction and its supposed power of initiation, Abellio's work occupies a place apart in 20th-century esotericism: it is certainly one of the rare cases where novelistic material is presented as the catalyst for a gnostic "transmutation of consciousness". Indeed, although Abellio announced the "end of esotericism" through disoccultation (*La fin de l'ésotérisme*, 1973) and systematically distanced himself from the esoteric authorities of the past, his thought presents all the elements typical of Western esotericism: the notion of a transmutation of consciousness, the interdependence of various degrees of reality, a particular interest in natural phenomena, the creative → imagination, symbolic hermeneutics, and so forth. By virtue of this, he remains one of the more interesting figures in French esotericism in the 20th century. In addition to his fame as a writer, he is also noted as an epistemologist whose views continue to be instrumental in fostering interdisciplinary research and reflections.

Complete bibliography in: Antoine Faivre & Jean-Baptiste de Foucauld (eds.), *Raymond Abellio*, Paris: Albin Michel/Dervy, 2004, 391-420 ♦ Manuscript legacy: Bibliothèque Nationale de France, coll. E 38-b/370 ♦ Novels: *Heureux les Pacifiques* (1946), Paris: Flammarion, 1979 ♦ *Les Yeux d'Ézechiel sont ouverts* (1949), Paris: Le Livre de Poche, 1968 ♦ *La Fosse de Babel* (1962), Paris: Gallimard, 1984 ♦ *Visages immobiles*, Paris: Gallimard, 1983 ♦ Autobiography: *Ma dernière mémoire*, vol. I, Paris: Gallimard, 1971; vol. II, Paris: Gallimard, 1975; vol. III, Paris: Ramsay, 1980 ♦ Essays: *La fin du nihilisme*, Paris: Fernand Sorlot, 1943 ♦ *Vers un nouveau prophétisme* (1947), Paris: Gallimard, 1963 ♦ *La Bible, document chiffré*, Paris: Gallimard, 1950 ♦ *Assomption de l'Europe* (1954), Paris: Flammarion, 1978 ♦ *La structure absolue*, Paris: Gallimard, 1965 ♦ *La fin de l'ésotérisme*, Paris: Flammarion, 1973 ♦ *Approches de la nouvelle Gnose*, Paris: Gallimard, 1981 ♦ *Manifeste de la nouvelle Gnose*, Paris: Gallimard, 1989.

Lit.: Antoine Faivre, "Raymond Abellio and the Western Esoteric 'Tradition'", in: Faivre, *Theosophy, Imag-ination, Tradition: Studies in Western Esotericism*, Albany: State University of New York Press, 2000, 229-248 ♦ Antoine Faivre & Jean-Baptiste de Foucauld (eds.), *Raymond Abellio* (Cahiers de l'Hermétisme), Paris: Albin Michel/Dervy, 2004 (with detailed bibliography by Nicolas Roberti-Serebriakov) ♦ Marc Hanrez, *Sous les signes d'Abellio*, Lausanne: L'Âge d'Homme, 1976 ♦ J.-P. Lombard (ed.), *Raymond Abellio* (Cahiers de l'Herne, no. 36), Paris: L'Herne, 1979 ♦ *La Structure absolue: Raymond Abellio. Textes et témoignages inédits*, journal *Question de 72* (1987) ♦ Christine Tochon-Danguy, *Les Romans de Raymond Abellio: Une interprétation imaginaire de la crise contemporaine*, Lille: Ed. du Septentrion, 1997 ♦ Nicolas Roberti-Serebriakov, *Georges Soulès à la lumière d'Abellio, Raymond Abellio à la lumière de Soulès: Etude philosophique, historique et psychocritique d'un gnostique français*, thèse de Doctorat, E.P.H.E., Sciences Religieuses, Paris: Sorbonne, 2003.

J É R Ô M E   R O U S S E - L A C O R D A I R E

AE (ps. of George William Russell), * 10.4.1867 Lurgan, † 17.7.1935 Bournemouth

Theosophist, poet, prose author, artist, journal editor, officer of the Irish Agricultural Organisation Society, and member of the Irish Convention of 1917. George William Russell is best known by his pen-name *AE*, which he adopted after a compositor was unable to read more than the first two letters of Æon, the Gnostic word for a higher being with which he signed a letter to the editor of the Theosophical journal *Lucifer* in 1888. Russell was born into a Protestant family in the north of Ireland, and from adolescence onwards he experienced visions of superhuman beings and of scenes from the past and future, visions of which he sought explanations in exoteric and esoteric literature. Soon he came to believe that he possessed memories of previous lives. Around the age of twenty, he was drawn towards the teachings of Madame → Blavatsky, and he joined the Dublin Theosophical Lodge about 1890. Thereupon he embarked on seven years of intense study and systematic meditation. During this period, he made his living as a retail cashier and shared a house, at least intermittently, with other zealous Theosophists. Among these, from 1895, was Violet North, whom he married in 1898. On one wall of the house, he painted a still surviving mural of visionary figures, and in 1894 he published *Homeward: Songs by the Way*, the first of his many collections of poetry. By the following year, having decided that ancient Irish mythology embodied Theosophical doctrine, he was becoming an enthusiastic patriot. In 1896 he deduced from a vision that there was about to appear in Ireland an avatar who would recreate the nation after the imminent crumbling of the British Empire, and for the rest of his life he hoped to see in the flesh the face that had risen before his inner eye. From 1895 to 1896, he was the student of the visiting American Theosophist James Morgan Pryse (1859-1942), who knew Greek and expounded the esoteric meaning of the New Testament.

In 1897, Russell was persuaded by his intimate friend the poet → W.B. Yeats (1865-1939) to accept employment in the agricultural co-operative movement, which was designed to raise the Irish peasant farmers out of material and mental poverty. Russell believed that, like all human beings, they had fallen from a higher state into the cycle of → reincarnation, and he strove through this work to bring out the buried nobility within them. For more than seven years he persuaded poor men to help themselves by forming credit banks, planned schemes to ameliorate hardship, and shouldered administrative work. But his literary gift was not wasted, for in 1905 he was appointed editor of the *Irish Homestead*, the weekly journal that existed to support the agricultural co-operative movement, and he held the appointment till the paper ceased publication in 1923. Meanwhile, disillusioned with the Theosophical Society, he left it in 1898 to found his own Hermetic Society [→ Hermeticism and Hermetic Societies], in which he taught his followers in Dublin at weekly meetings. He continued to publish poetry, assisted other poets, painted landscapes and visionary figures, and helped to found the Irish National Theatre. As a patriot who combined his nationalism with pacificism, he campaigned for complete self-government for a united Ireland within the British Empire. From 1923 to 1930, he edited the *Irish Statesman*, a weekly designed to foster the cultural and political life of the newly independent Irish Free State. In 1930, while lecturing in the U.S.A., he rejoiced in a brief reunion in Los Angeles with James Pryse. His wife died in February 1932, and eighteen months later, unhappy with the narrow-minded provincialism engulfing the Free State, Russell moved to London. He died in a nursing home in Bournemouth in 1935.

Russell's early esoteric writings were published in the *Irish Theosophist* from 1892 through 1897. His principal mystical book is *The Candle of Vision* (1918), which shows that his beliefs were as firmly rooted in his own visionary experiences as in the syncretism of Blavatsky's *The Secret Doctrine*. Towards the end of his life, disappointed that he had never encountered the Incarnation of his vision of 1896, he described the imagined impact of such a being in his romance *The Avatars* (1933). Even in his editorial articles in the *Irish Homestead*, evidence of his Theosophical world view occasionally peeps out. Thus his reference to 'the guardians of humanity' who will not allow the human race to flee permanently from nature into city life (Notes of the Week, 5.3.1911) refers to the Masters, perfected individuals who have ascended to a higher plane to watch over human life on earth. Similarly 'the secret Ruler of the World', who seems to be guiding farmers all over the earth into the co-operative movement, is the Planetary Spirit of Theosophy (Notes of the Week, 7.1.1911). Russell's recommendation that systematic thought should entail approaching any matter from three viewpoints – its relation to consciousness or the human spirit, to forces or energies, and to material things – is based on the Theosophical trinity of primal emanations from the Deity: the Logos or Divine Mind, the Light of the Logos or the Divine Energy, and the Archaeus or that aspect of the Divine from which matter evolves. Russell's poetry contains many comparable allusions couched under such seemingly vague phrases as "the Ancient One" (the Planetary Spirit) and "the Mighty Mother" (the Archaeus). In *The Interpreters* (1922), written during the Anglo-Irish War and the Irish Civil War, Russell traces socialism, nationalism and imperialism to their roots in the Logos, the Archaeus, and the Light of the Logos respectively.

Although Russell sought to spread the spiritual knowledge that he found in Theosophy and the science of penetrating to reality through inward meditation, he probably had more success in promoting the arts in Ireland, and he played a part in the widespread quest in the early 20th century for economic democracy as a means of stemming the rural exodus. Most of his poetry has faded, but his book *The Candle of Vision* continues to impress many readers.

Homeward: Songs by the Way, Dublin: Whaley, 1894 ♦ *The Earth Breath and Other Poems*, New York & London: John Lane, 1897 ♦ *The Divine Vision and Other Poems*, London: Macmillan, 1904 ♦ *Co-operation and Nationality: A Guide for Rural Reformers from This to the Next Generation*, Dublin: Maunsel, 1912 ♦ *Collected Poems*, London: Macmillan, 1913. Expanded editions: 1915, 1919, 1926, 1935 ♦ *Imaginations and Reveries*, Dublin & London: Maunsel, 1915. Expanded edition: Dublin & London: Maunsel & Roberts, 1921 ♦ *The National Being: Some Thoughts on an Irish Polity*, Dublin & London: Maunsel, 1916 ♦ *The Candle of Vision*, London: Macmillan, 1918 ♦ *The Interpreters*, London: Macmillan, 1922 ♦ *Voices* of the Stones, London: Macmillan, 1925 (poems) ♦ Vale and Other Poems, London: Macmillan, 1931 ♦ Song and Its Fountains, London: Macmillan, 1932 ♦ The Avatars: A Futurist Fantasy, London: Macmillan, 1933 ♦ The House of the Titans and Other Poems, London: Macmillan, 1934 ♦ The Living Torch (Monk Gibbon, ed.), London: Macmillan, 1937 (selections from the Irish Statesman) ♦ Letters from AE (Alan Denson, ed.), London, New York, Toronto: Abelard-Schuman, 1961 ♦ Selection from the Contributions to the Irish Homestead, 2 vols. (Henry Summerfield, ed.), Gerrards Cross UK: Colin Smythe, 1978 ♦ The Descent of the Gods Comprising the Mystical Writings of G.W. Russell "A.E" (Raghavan Iyer and Nandini Iyer, eds.), Gerrards Cross UK: Colin Smythe, 1988.

Lit.: W.Y. Evans Wentz, The Fairy Faith in Celtic Countries, London: Oxford University Press, 1911 (the unnamed mystic of pp. 59-66 is AE) ♦ Monk Gibbon, "A.E.", in: The Living Torch, 3-81 (see above) ♦ Diarmuid Russell, "Æ", Atlantic Monthly 171 (February 1943), 51-57; repr. in Selections from the Contributions to the Irish Homestead I, 1-10 (see above) ♦ Henry Summerfield, That Myriad-minded Man: A biography of George William Russell "AE" 1867-1935, Gerrards Cross UK: Colin Smythe, 1975.

HENRY SUMMERFIELD

Agrippa, Heinrich Cornelius, * 1486 Nettesheim, † 1535 or 1536 Grenoble

German Humanist and theoretician of → magic. Agrippa's family belonged to the middle nobility in Nettesheim, near Cologne. He studied in Cologne from 1499 to 1502, when he received the degree of magister artium, and later in Paris. During his studies in the latter city, Agrippa seems to have taken part in a secret circle or self-help society, the members of which were interested in studying res arcanae, and with whom he tried to remain in contact in later years. In 1508 he traveled to Spain, where he got involved in an adventurous military campaign to seize a fortified castle near Barcelona. From there he continued traveling, by way of Valencia, the Baleares, Sardinia, Naples, Avignon, and Lyon. Agrippa's family was by tradition in the service of the Roman Emperors, and thus in his early years as well as later he served as a captain in the army of Maximilian I, Holy Roman Emperor, who awarded him the title of Ritter or knight. His irregular career as a university professor began at the university of Dôle (Burgundy) in 1509, where he was given the opportunity to lecture on → Johannes Reuchlin's De verbo mirifico, and wrote his De nobilitate et praecellentia foeminae sexus (On the Nobility and Excellence of the Feminine Sex), partly no doubt in an attempt to win the favour of Margaret of Austria. Agrippa's lectures attracted much interest and earned him a doctorate in theology, but he was forced to leave the city in 1510, after having been attacked by the Franciscan prior Jean Catilinet for judaizing heresy. His study of Reuchlin's work first suggested to Agrippa the project of a radical restoration of magic. In the winter of 1509-1510 he discussed this with → Johannes Trithemius, to whom he dedicated the first draft of his De occulta philosophia (On the Occult Philosophy), which remained unpublished for the time being. Trithemius – whose own experiences had taught him caution – advised him to persevere with his studies but to 'talk about arcane secrets only with proper friends'.

Having left Dôle, Agrippa went to London, from where he wrote his Expostulatio super Expositione sua in librum De verbo mirifico (Opera II, 508-518) in an attempt to defend himself against Catilinet's accusations. He repeated his ideas about Reuchlin's De verbo mirifico, and affirmed that his Christian faith was in no way incompatible with his appreciation for Jewish thought and exegesis: 'I am a Christian, but I do not dislike Jewish Rabbis'. While in England, he met the Humanist and Platonist John Colet, with whom he studied the Epistles of Paul; and we know that in the following years he was working on a commentary on the Epistle to the Romans. Having returned to his hometown Cologne, at the Faculty of Theology he gave some religious disputations – unfortunately lost – on religious practices in the contemporary church.

From 1511 to 1518 Agrippa lived in northern Italy, and was involved in the conflict between the French and Imperial armies: first in the service of the Emperor Maximilian and later in the circles of William IX Paleologus. In these years he came into contact with Agostino Ricci and perhaps Paolo Ricci, and deepened his knowledge of the writings of → Marsilio Ficino, → Giovanni Pico della Mirandola, and the kabbalah [→ Jewish Influences III]. He took part in the schismatic Council of Pisa (1512), but his loyalty to the Roman Church is attested by a letter (Agrippa, Opera II, 710) in which Pietro Bembo, the secretary of Pope Leo X, thanks him and acknowledges his orthodox position. Afterwards he lived for several years in Pavia, where he lectured at the University. His first course was probably devoted to Plato's Symposium (1512), and in 1515 he lectured on Ficino's Pimander. Around the same time he composed the Dialogus De homine, which remained unpublished during his lifetime and has survived only in a fragmentary state; based upon Pico della Mirandola's Heptaplus, it is full of references to the → Hermetic literature. Agrippa married his first (Italian) wife in Pavia, and experienced here one of the happiest periods of his life.

As a consequence of the 1515 French victory at Marignano, where the duchy of Milan was reconquered and the imperial army defeated, Agrippa had to flee from Pavia. He had to leave behind many of his manuscripts, which were later recovered by one of his friends. He moved to Casale, where he wrote his *Liber de triplici ratione cognoscendi Deum* (Book on the triple way of knowing God) dedicated to his protector William Paleologus. As in earlier and later works, he refuted scholastic theology and emphasized faith rather than human reason as the exclusive way to approach God. His *Dehortatio gentilis theologiae*, probably written in this period, was based upon a convivial talk given by Agrippa to some friends a few years after his course on the *Pimander*. He significantly warned them, and all intellectuals, not to go too far in their admiration for the Hermetic writings and neglect the primacy of Christian revelation: 'if, by taking away secretly, so to speak, the rich spoils from their illegal possessors, the Egyptians, and by elevating yourselves with their riches, you enrich the Church of God, then I no longer advise against pagan literature, but I recommend it to you'. In Turin, his last Italian stay, he lectured on the Epistles of Paul in 1516: it was to be his last appearance in a university context.

After a short intermezzo at the court of Charles III, Duke of Savoy, Agrippa was employed in 1518 as public advocate and defense lawyer in the free imperial city of Metz. On the eve of the Reformation the religious and theological debate was explosive. Agrippa and his humanist friends followed the developments with great interest and often with sympathy for the Reformers, without going as far as supporting the schism. It is worth noting in this context how in *De peccato originale* (1518), as in some other writings, Agrippa addressed the problem of salvation: faith is central, while reason is accorded only a secondary role. Agrippa was quite original, furthermore, in suggesting that original sin had consisted in the act of sexual intercourse, and in holding Adam rather than Eve responsible for the Fall. In this same period he also got into a conflict with the Dominicans, Claude Salin in particular, over his support of → Lefèvre d'Etaples's *De una ex tribus Maria*. Lefèvre had argued against the popular opinion that Saint Anne had been married three times and had given birth to three daughters: Mary the mother of Jesus, and two other Marys who were considered to be mothers of Apostles. The conflict turned very nasty, with professional teachers sermonizing against Agrippa from the pulpit.

In his capacity of legal advisor to the magistrate of Metz, Agrippa played a crucial role in a famous witch trial in 1519, where he defended a woman accused of witchcraft and, as a result, got into great trouble with the Inquisition. The woman was accused because her mother was considered a witch, and the pact with the devil was believed to be hereditary; but Agrippa argued that the sacrament of baptism was stronger than the pact with the devil. He implicitly accused the inquisitor not only of acting contrary to human decency, the law, and the spirit of Christianity, but also implied that his implicit denial of baptism as a sacrament was heretical. Although Agrippa succeeded in saving the accused's life, his conflict with the Dominican authorities made his position in Metz untenable and forced him to leave.

Agrippa moved with his wife and child back to Cologne, where he stayed for a year, apparently without regular employment. Here his wife fell ill, and she died soon after, probably during the travel with her husband to Geneva, where Agrippa became a citizen and worked as a physician. He remarried a few months later, with a woman from Geneva who would bear him six children. They traveled to Fribourg early in 1523, where Agrippa continued to work as a physician and gained increasing recognition as a progressive thinker.

He made the mistake of leaving Fribourg in 1524 and accept a position in Lyon, as physician to Louise of Savoy, Queen Mother of France. Agrippa's expectations were disappointed, for the Queen forced him to write astrological prognostications – a practice he despised – and suspected him of being a partisan of Charles of Bourbon, who was fighting against the King on the side of the Emperor. The Queen's treasurers refused to pay him his salary, and the court ridiculed him behind his back; at the end of 1527 Agrippa finally left his employment, but his criticisms of the Queen later caused him to be imprisoned for a time. In spite of his troubles in Lyon, Agrippa managed to remain productive. He wrote a commentary to → Llull's *Ars Brevis* and a declamation *De sacramento matrimonii* (On the sacrament of marriage); and in september 1526 he completed one of his most important works: the declamation *De incertitudine et vanitate scientiarum et artium atque excellentia verbi Dei* (On the uncertainty and vanity of sciences and arts, and on the excellence of the word of God). Apart from his financial troubles, his wife was ill as well, and *De incertitudine* certainly reflects his depressed mood at the time.

In 1528 a new and more successful phase in Agrippa's life began, with his appointment in Antwerp as advisor and historiographer to the governor of the low countries, Margaret of Austria. He wrote speeches, historiographical works and a document with instructions about an expedition to the Turks. Among the increasing number of students who sought him out was Johann Wier (1515-1588), who would study with him for four years. At the Imperial Court Agrippa had an influential friend, Eustache Chapuys, an Erasmian humanist (later Charles V's ambassador in England) to whom he later dedicated his *Querela*. The first years in Antwerpen seem to have been relatively peaceful and happy for Agrippa. He was able to devote himself to studies in the occult sciences, and in 1529 managed to publish a volume of collected writings; they contained largely theological writings, but also a text on the treatment of epidemic disease. A second edition published in 1532 also contained treatises on monastic life and on the relics of Saint Antony. In August 1529 Agrippa's peace was interrupted when his wife died of the plague that was sweeping Antwerp. While most of the town physicians fled the city, Agrippa remained on his post, only to be accused by his colleagues later, for illegal practice.

Agrippa had obtained an Imperial Privilege to publish several of his works, including *De incertitudine*; but after it had been published, in 1530, Princess Margaret began to suspect him of heterodoxy and solicited the opinion of the Theology Faculty of Louvain. She died in December, before her suspicions could be confirmed by the theologians, but Agrippa's troubles were not over: Charles V's brother, Ferdinand, detested the contents of *De incertitudine* and wrote about it to the Emperor. The inquiry was continued, and the Louvain theologians judged parts of his work heretical. Agrippa wrote an *Apologia* in his defense, and a *Querela* against those who were attacking his good reputation with the Emperor; but meanwhile the Sorbonne theologians attacked and banned *De Incertitudine* as well, for favouring Lutheranism. As a result of this increasing hostility, including accusations of black magic, Agrippa's position at the court became unstable and he no longer received payment. In August 1531 he was briefly imprisoned for debt in Brussels.

In the same year appeared the first book of his *De occulta philosophia*, dedicated to the progressive Archbishop elector of Cologne, Hermann von Wied, who played an important role in supporting his work in spite of the opposition. However, the Inquisitor of Cologne, Konrad Köllin, denounced *De occulta* and its author as heretical before the City Council. In his response to the Council, Agrippa accused the theologians of hindering the reform of the Church with their battle against humanists such as Reuchlin and Erasmus (who in a letter to Agrippa praised *De incertitudine*, but did not want to get involved in the controversies). Against the witch-hunters, whom he claimed were more interested in their own profit than in matters of faith, he seems to have issued a pamphlet denouncing the dangerous misdeeds of the Dominicans; but we only know of this work thanks to a reference in Sisto da Siena's *Bibliotheca Santa*. Finally, Agrippa wrote a preface to a work by a Cistercian monk, Godeschalcus Moncordius, in which he opposed the Cisterciansian methods against those of the Dominicans.

According to Johannes Wier, Agrippa married a third time, but his wife (a woman from Malines) betrayed him and he repudiated her in 1535. From 1532 on he seems to have resided mainly in Bonn. In 1533 appeared the final and complete version of *De occulta philosphia*, as well as his commentary on Llull's *Ars Brevis*. Agrippa's last surviving letter dates from the middle of 1533, and for the final years of his life we are dependent on Wier's account. According to him, Agrippa went to Lyon, where he was briefly imprisoned by King Francis, but released thanks to the intercession of friends. He died in Grenoble in 1535 or 1536 and his body is – ironically – buried in a Dominican church.

In spite of his profound religiosity and his deep knowledge, Agrippa was always in danger of being considered a dangerous outsider by the representatives of mainstream Renaissance culture. He lived in an age marked by religious turbulence and never-ending wars. While he liked to adopt an attitude of being "above the parties", Agrippa did not hesitate to criticize Catholics and Lutherans alike. Nominally a Catholic, he appreciated Luther, whose attack against the abuses of the church and initiatives for reformation he claims were never intended to destroy the idea of the Church itself. Agrippa's epistolary reflects his ambiguity in this regard: in a letter to his friend Campeggi (*Opera* II, 1010-1012), he expresses his hope that the Church will soon be reunified and 'freed from the impiety of the heretics and the darkness of the Sophists' (that is to say: the scholastic theologians). The successive letter, dated 17 September 1532, is addressed to Melanchton and is famous because of its reference to 'that unconquered heretic Martin Luther' (a formulation repeated in *De incertitudine*, but in a less favourable context). Discussing Agrippa's relation to contemporary Reformation currents, Paola Zambelli (1967) has placed him in the context of the radical Reformation and the spiritualists, nicodemism in particular.

In the *De nobilitate et praecellentia foeminae sexus* (published in 1529) Agrippa argued, against the traditional misogynic perspective, that women are superior to men, even though the representatives of the public sphere from which they had long been excluded did not accept this point of view. At the beginning of the 15th century a feminist trend had emerged in France, Italy and Spain, contradicting the traditional idea of female inferiority, and the responsibility of woman for original sin; inspired by the Roman de la Rose, it presented women as good, noble and pure. The originality of Agrippa's treatise lies in his use of kabbalistic and neoplatonic sources [→ Neoplatonism], according to which woman is an immediate manifestation of the divine, a principle of original life. For Agrippa all the virtues of Nature were evident in woman, considered superior by him because of her proximity to the divine. The treatise is important for having introduced into France the Platonic and Ficinian cult of beauty, according to which woman is the mediator between the human and the divine. As to the question of why women were excluded, he argued that this had to do with social conditions, education, and the prejudices of the age: obstacles that could be removed.

Agrippa's most notorious work, his masterpiece, and the one which gave rise to his undeserved reputation as a black magician, is his *De occulta philosophia*, whose final version in three books was published in 1533. It is a systematic synthesis of "occult philosophy" or "magic" (Agrippa originally wanted to call it *De magia*): the first book treats of the natural magic relevant to the sublunar or elementary world; the second book discusses → number symbolism, mathematics, → music and → astrology as relevant to the celestial world; and the third book is largely Christian-kabbalistic, focusing on angelology and prophecy as relevant to the highest or intellectual world. Magic emerges from Agrippa's magnum opus as the most perfect science, by means of which one may come to know both nature and God. Prior to the final version of 1533, Agrippa's thinking as reflected in *De occulta philosophia* passed through several stages. The book has been called "a neoplatonic credo": the influence of Ficino and Pico is evident, but less famous authors such as → Lazzarelli play a significant role as well. The first version – an encyclopaedic review rather than a treatise – most clearly reveals Agrippa's profound dependence on his predecessors, Reuchlin in particular. The final draft, as pointed out by Perrone Compagni, reveals a more mature grasp of the subject and of his claims about spiritual rebirth as necessary for religious reform. The latter should take place step by step: one must progressively remove one's ties to the blinding theology (scholasticism in particular) that conceals the real meaning of the Holy Scriptures. Through continuous contemplation of divine things, the soul may free itself from the lure of the senses. In his dedicatory letter to Trithemius, Agrippa seeks to explain how magic, which the ancient philosophers considered the highest science, could have fallen into such disrepute; he argues that 'by a certain corruption of times and men', many dangerous errors and superstitions crept in, and false philosophers prefixed the title of "magic" to their heresies and wicked practices. It is now necessary to restore magic to its former state of the purest kind of religion; and from the Third Book one can deduce that Agrippa conceived of the latter largely in terms of Christian kabbalah.

In his other great work, *De incertitudine*, Agrippa seeks to show the relativity of all human knowledge, as compared to God's word as the only foundation of true certainty, by means of an incisive attack on all the sciences and arts. Echoing Erasmus' *Encomium Moriae*, Agrippa satiricizes various beliefs, deploring the superstitions that have ruined the original purity of the Christian Church. The work has been incorrectly interpreted as a revival of Greek scepticism; but actually, Agrippa's aim was to build a new concept of faith, based on divine revelation more than on Church interpretation, and to expose the blindness and arrogance of the school-theologians. The Bible should be restored to a leading role in Christian belief and practice. Marc van der Poel has located Agrippa within the Ciceronian tradition, and shows how *De incertitudine* can be considered the culmination of Agrippa's battle against the scholastic theologians.

There has been much scholarly debate about what might seem to be a contradiction between Agrippa's defense of the occult sciences in *De occulta philosophia*, and his description of all human sciences as "vain and uncertain" in *De incertitudine*. However, the contradiction can be largely resolved by recognizing how sharply Agrippa distinguished between reason and faith: he criticized the scholastics for ignoring this distinction and thereby confusing the study of created things with the study of divine things. The authority of God's revelation in the holy Scriptures 'cannot be grasped by any judgment of our senses, by any reasoning of our mind, by any syllogism delivering proof, by any science, by any speculation, by any contemplation, in short, by any human powers, but only by faith in Jesus Christ, poured into our soul by God the Father through the intermediary of the Holy Spirit' (*De incertitudine*, in *Opera*, 299). Divine matters are not a matter for debate but an object of faith; in contrast, we are permitted 'to philosophize, dispute, and formulate deductions by means of our intellect concerning all created things', as long as we do not put our faith and hope in them (*De originale peccato*, in *Opera*, 553). From that perspective, one understands how the occult sciences can be a legitimate object of study, even though they must be considered "vain and uncertain" as a basis for absolute religious certainty. Accordingly, *De occulta philosophia* ended with a discussion of how to live a religious life that may make one worthy of receiving divine revelations.

Many unsubstantiated rumours began to circulate about Agrippa already during his life. The most influential portrait was presented by Paolo Giovio (1483-1552) in his *Elogia virorum illustrium*, which describes him as a man with a powerful mind, through which he tried to destroy the *République des lettres*. The most enduring part of Giovio's portrayal concerns Agrippa's death and the legend of his black dog. Agrippa's love for animals and his passion for his dog (whom he called "monsieur") was interpreted by the Italian humanist as proof that the dog was no one else than the devil. Two later authors, Andreas Hondorff and André Thevet, accepted the story and contributed to its diffusion. The legend was disputed by Agrippa's pupil Johann Wier, in his *De praestigiis daemonum ac incantationibus* (1563). Wier also attacked the attribution to Agrippa of a magical text known as the "Fourth Book of Occult Philosophy", the contents of which seemed to confirm his reputation as a black magician. A different literary tradition, influenced by several thinkers from Rabelais to Apollinaire and Thomas Mann, and including → Goethe, looks at Agrippa as an archetype of the Faust figure.

As Pierre Bayle wrote in his *Dictionnaire*, despite his great knowledge Agrippa was considered *malheureux* because of his great curiosity, his all too free spirit, and his unstable mood. With his restless journeys, he indeed seems to embody the spirit of the Renaissance. It is regrettable, although perhaps not surprising, that this outstanding thinker has gone down in history as little more than a magician, for precisely Agrippa's ambivalent position with respect to various religious and intellectual issues central to his time, and the very ambiguity of his combination of magic and skepsis in the search for truth, make him a fascinating representative of Renaissance culture. In any case, his *De occulta philosophia* is considered the standard *summa* of Renaissance magic, and has exerted an incalculable influence on later magical and esoteric traditions.

H.C. Agrippa, *Opera*, with an introduction by Richard H. Popkin, Hildesheim-New York, 1970 ♦ *Declamation on the Nobility and Preeminence of the Female Sex* (Albert Rabil, ed.), Chicago & London: University of Chicago Press, 1996 ♦ *De occulta philosophia libri tres* (V. Perrone Compagni, ed.), Leiden, New York, Köln: E.J. Brill, 1992 ♦ *Three Books of Occult Philosophy* (reprint of the 1651 translation by "J.F.", ed. & annotated by Donald Tyson), St. Paul: Llewellyn, 1993 ♦ *Über die Fragwürdigkeit, ja Nichtigkeit der Wissenschaften, Künste und Gewerbe* (Siegfried Wollgast & Gerhard Güpner, eds.), Berlin: Akademie Verlag, 1993.

Lit.: Charles G. Nauert, *Agrippa and the Crisis of Renaissance Thought*, Urbana: University of Illinois Press, 1965 ♦ J.-F. Orsier, *Henri Cornélis Agrippa: Sa vie et son oeuvre d'après sa correspondance (1486-1535)*, Paris, 1911 ♦ Marc van der Poel, *Cornelius Agrippa: The Humanist Theologian and his Declamations*, Leiden, New York, Köln: E.J. Brill, 1997 ♦ Paola Zambelli, "A proposito del *De vanitate scientiarum et artium* di Cornelio Agrippa", *Rivista critica di storia della filosofia* 15 (1960), 166-180 ♦ Eadem, "Magic and Radical Reformation in Agrippa of Nettesheim", *Journal of the Warburg and Courtauld Institutes* 39 (1976), 69-103 ♦ Eadem, *L' ambigua natura della magia: Filosofi, streghe, riti nel Rinascimento*, 2nd ed. Venezia: Marsilio, 1996 ♦ Charles Zika, "Agrippa of Nettesheim and his Appeal to the Cologne Council in 1533: The Politics of Knowledge in Early Sixteenth-Century Germany", in: J.V. Mehl (ed.), *Humanismus in Köln*, Cologne, 1991, 119-174 ♦ Christopher I. Lehrich, *The Language of Demons and Angels: Cornelius Agrippa's Occult Philosophy*, Leiden, Boston, Köln: E.J. Brill, 2003 ♦ Vittoria Perrone Compagni, "'Dispersa intentio': Alchemy, Magic and Scepticism in Agrippa", *Early Science and Medicine* 5:2 (2000), 160-177 (= special issue: Michela Pereira [ed.], *Alchemy and Hermeticism*).

MICHAELA VALENTE

Ailly, Pierre d' → Pierre d'Ailly

Aor → Schwaller de Lubicz, René Adolphe

Albertus Magnus, * ca. 1200 near Lauingen, † 15.11.1280 Cologne

1. LIFE 2. WORKS 3. WORKS OF
QUESTIONABLE AUTHENTICITY 4. SAINT
AND MAGICIAN

1. LIFE

German philosopher and theologian, one of the most influential Aristotelian [→ Aristotelianism] synthesizers of the 13th century, Dominican friar, teacher of Thomas Aquinas (c. 1225-1274). Albert was born into a Swabian family of knights and joined the Dominican order when he was a student at Padua, receiving the habit from Jordan of Saxony in 1223. It seems likely that he was sent to Cologne to make his novitiate and study theology from the local *lector*. Later, probably in the early 1240s, he was sent to Paris to lecture on the *Sentences* under the Dominican Master Guéric of St.-Quentin (Dominican Master 1233-1245). In 1245, Albert succeeded Guéric as Dominican Regent Master, a position he held until 1248. During this period Albert met Thomas Aquinas, who arrived in Paris in 1245 during Albert's first year as Regent Master. In 1248 Albert returned to Cologne with Thomas to establish the first Studium Generale in Germany in association with the new Dominican cloister of Heilige Kreuz. He remained in Cologne as Regent Master of the Studium Generale from 1248-1254 (Thomas returned to Paris in the fall of 1252, becoming Regent Master there in 1256).

Among the earliest works certainly known to have come from Albert's hand are public lectures he delivered during this period as Master at Cologne on → Pseudo-Dionysius Areopagita's *De divinis nominibus* and (although he was engaged to teach theology, not philosophy) on Aristotle's *Ethics*, a work lately made available in translation by Robert Grosseteste (c. 1175-1253). Albert appears to have been unworried by the Parisian bans on Aristotle early in the century and the papal reiteration of the need to purge the Aristotelian corpus of error in 1231. An independent thinker whose interest in the natural sciences and Aristotelian philosophy were lifelong, Albert saw no essential conflict between science and theology, believing that philosophical truth, faithfully sought, could only support, not detract from, the truth of theology. By the mid-1250s, the acceptance of at least some of Aristotle's works into the official Parisian curriculum was likely influenced by the interest shown in the Aristotelian corpus by Albert, Thomas, and others of their contemporaries who

had taught at Paris and shared similar views on the need to maintain a productive relationship between philosophy and revealed truth.

In 1254, Albert was elected Prior Provincial of the Province of Teutonia. The province at that time included something over 50 priories, all of which Albert engaged to visit personally on foot (Dominicans being forbidden the use of horses or wagons). He resigned from this job in June of 1257 in Florence and by 1258 he had returned to Cologne to resume his position as *lector* at Heilige Kreuz. It was not long, however, before another set of arduous administrative duties imposed themselves. In 1259 Albert was requested by the Papal Curia to fill the position of Bishop of Regensburg (also called Ratisbon). Albert had already shown skill as a mediator of conflicts, and a diplomatic touch was needed for this post, since the unpopularity of the previous Bishop had resulted in a forced resignation, and the acephalous diocese was now torn by strife and bankrupt. After consideration Albert decided to accept the position against the advice of the Master General of his order, putting himself under direct obedience to the Pope. Though technically this move released him from obedience to the Master General, it is clear that Albert never ceased to regard himself as a Dominican, obeying the rules of the order so far as it was in his power to do so, and also that the order did not cease to consider him one of their own.

By 1261 the affairs of the Regensburg diocese had been sufficiently organized for Albert to feel able to hand his duties over to a locally chosen bishop. He headed toward Italy to deliver his resignation to the Pope, whose unexpected death resulted in a year's delay before the election of a new bishop could be confirmed under the auspices of the new Pope, Urban IV (1216-1264). Nothing is known with certainty of Albert's activities during the remainder of 1261 and 1262, though it is presumed likely that he remained in Viterbo to wait for the outcome of the election, renewing his acquaintance with Thomas Aquinas and others he had known in Paris. In 1263, Pope Urban IV appointed Albert Preacher of the Crusade in Germany, Bohemia and all German speaking lands. Dutifully undertaking the commission, Albert traveled through Germany and the Netherlands, laying down (one imagines with relief) his peripatetic preaching office on the death of Urban IV in October of 1264.

From 1264-1267 Albert retired to the Dominican cloister in Würzburg. There is evidence that he took part in mediation of local disputes while working to finish the corpus of Aristotelian para-phrases. In 1268 Albert was in Strasbourg resolv-ing a dispute at the request of Pope Clement IV (Pope 1265-1268), and in 1269 he was called back to Cologne by the Dominican Master to reside there as *lector emeritus*. In the last years of his life in Cologne he worked on his paraphrase of the pseudo-Aristotelian *Liber de causis* and several late theological works while being called upon at inter-vals to act as mediator and to consecrate churches and other ecclesiastical structures. The legend that he went to Paris in 1277 to register his protest against the rumored condemnation of the ideas of his disciple Thomas Aquinas (who predeceased him in 1274) is probably unfounded. Albert was over eighty years old when he died in Cologne on November 15th, 1280.

2. WORKS

Albert's corpus is substantial (his *Opera omnia* takes up 38 volumes in the Borgnet edition) and contains a roughly equal quantity of theological and philosophical writing, including lectures and commentaries on the Bible, on Lombard's *Sen-tences*, on the Pseudo-Dionysius, and a large and important body of commentaries on or "para-phrases" of Aristotelian works. In addition to the writings definitely known to belong to Albert, there are several treatises which were attributed to him through the later Middle Ages and Early Modern period, but which are now considered to be of questionable authenticity. The questions surround-ing attribution are not straightforward, since in some cases works unlikely to have been composed by Albert still seem to be under his influence. In one case (that of the *Speculum astronomiae*) the attri-bution to Albert is still a matter of active scholarly debate. These works will be dealt with in a separate section.

Of the authentic works of Albert, the Aris-totelian paraphrases are probably the most impor-tant, not only to subsequent natural philosophy, but also to the history of Western Esotericism. As Albert explains at the opening of the *Physica*, these works were undertaken at the request of his Dominican brothers who wished to have all of Aristotelian natural philosophy laid out for them in an accessible way. Albert tried to follow the order of Aristotle's works, using the Aristotelian titles but paraphrasing (rather than citing and comment-ing on) Aristotle's words, presenting additional information at appropriate points to clarify and supplement the Philosopher's ideas, and adding in new material where discussions of topics appeared to be left incomplete. The paraphrases thus ad-hered to the spirit of Aristotle (as Albert under-stood it) more than to the letter, not only because Albert freely included new material, but also because he was not shy about contradicting Aristo-tle's opinions when he felt they were inconsistent either with his personal experience or with facts he had learned from other sources.

In his understanding of the natural sciences, Albert drew on a broad range of material extend-ing from the Church Fathers to the works of Ara-bic philosophers, and including not only the major commentators on Aristotle, but also anonymous treatises on various natural subjects, works of image → magic, → alchemy, and other medieval Hermetica [→ Hermetic Literature II]. While skep-tical of the extraordinary claims of magical and alchemical texts, Albert's quest for information about the natural world included perusal of many such works, and he respected the facts they reported when these seemed consistent with his own general or experiential knowledge. He refers to alchemy and alchemical operations repeatedly in the *De caelo et mundo*, the *Meteora*, and in the *Mineralium libri V*, where Book IV is particularly concerned with alchemical categories, and → Her-mes Trismegistus is a frequently cited authority. In Book II of the same work, he discusses sigils and image magic, calling it 'that part of necromancy which is dependent on astrology' (Wyckoff, 127) (here and elsewhere in his philosophical writings Albert uses the word "necromancy" in the benign sense indicated by Charles Burnett). Consistent with the practice of many who compiled herbals and books of remedies, Albert included in his *De vegetabilibus* a final section (part VI) devoted to uses of plants less theoretically plausible, but pre-sumably empirically attested, which contains over a dozen references to magic arts and *incantatores*. Albert's works generally bear the stamp of a wide-ranging mind which enjoyed taxonomy and sys-tems of classification. He rejected no plausible source of information out of hand, and preferred, where he could, to reconcile attractive philosophi-cal systems rather than champion one at the expense of another.

For all these reasons Albert's paraphrases played an important part in putting the Aristotelian cos-mos together for subsequent thinkers. He was one of the earliest and most important writers to inte-grate Arabic Aristotelianism into Christian natural philosophy, and his influence on medieval and Renaissance thinkers following him was profound. Less idiosyncratic than friar → Roger Bacon, less of a rigorous Augustinian than Thomas Aquinas, his natural universe remains wide open to influences from the heavens. No doubt in part for this reason he is something of a favorite among the medieval *auctoritates* in the Early Modern period, praised by → Ficino, relied upon by Pomponazzi, an Aristotelian cornerstone of → Pico della Mirandola's 900 *Conclusiones*, and cited as an authority in over a dozen places in → Agrippa's *De occulta philosophia* (where, to give comparative examples, Thomas is cited in six loci and Roger Bacon only in three – not that the influence of any of these thinkers should be considered as strictly confined to loci where they receive citations). It was probably advantageous that Albert's diplomatic gifts, Christian life of service, and reputation for saintliness conspired to make his name eminently citable; there were few other medieval philosophers so friendly to Hermetic thinking whose names could so unimpeachably be used to adorn the esoteric claims of Renaissance philosophers.

3. WORKS OF QUESTIONABLE AUTHENTICITY

Works attributed to Albert but of doubtful or questionable authenticity include two Books of Secrets (the *De secretis mulierum* and the *Secreta* or *Experimenta Alberti* also called the *Liber aggregationis*), a *De mirabilibus mundi*, around thirty alchemical treatises, and the important bibliographic work known as the *Speculum astronomiae* which categorizes texts of image magic according to their dependence on astral influence. Some of these works have been shown to be dependent in whole or in part on Albert's authentic writings. Lynn Thorndike demonstrated that the *De secretis mulierum* – a gynecological manual that was used as a medical textbook – is in part a compilation of medical information extracted from Albert's paraphrase the *De animalibus* (possibly by a student or disciple of Albert's), and the *Experimenta Alberti* lifts some of its material from Albert's *Mineralium libri V* in its section on the uses of stones (though other sections of the work do not depend on Albert's authentic writings).

Concerning the treatises on alchemy, the most important both in terms of manuscript count and potential likelihood of correct attribution is the *Semita recta* or *Libellus de alchimia*, a version of which was included in the Borgnet edition of Albert's *Opera*. Concerning its attribution, Pearl Kibre suggests that 'its clear, concise, and well ordered account of the subject resembles Albert's treatment of other topics of natural science in his authentic compositions' (Kibre 1942, 500). It is a feature of all the earliest alchemical texts attributed to Albert (including the *Semita recta*, the *Alkimia*

minor, the *De occultis naturae*, and the *Compositum de compositis*), that they show a deference to his style, many of these works putatively composed (like the Aristotelian paraphrases) at the request of Albert's Dominican brothers who wish to have the scientific elements of alchemy explained to them in an accessible way.

The question of attribution of the *Speculum astronomie* is so difficult to resolve with any certainty that it is worth briefly summarizing the issues at stake. While objections have been raised concerning the work's attribution to Albert from the early part of the 20th century, some suggesting that it might have been composed by Roger Bacon, these objections were countered by convincing arguments in favour of Albert's authorship by Lynn Thorndike and subsequently by Paola Zambelli. In brief, the *Speculum* resembles Albert's thinking; it shows the same style of preoccupation with taxonomy; it refers to works he is known to have read. It is impossible to nail the attribution down as firmly as might be wished, however, because the manuscript tradition does not begin to attribute the *Speculum* to Albert until the mid-14th century, nor is it mentioned as Albert's work in any texts dating from prior to that time (though attributions after the mid-14th century are consistent; that is, no manuscripts of any period are known which attribute the text to anyone else). From the earliest period of the controversy it has been pointed out that certain statements in it are inconsistent with Albert's views as expressed elsewhere in his writings, but arguments from attitude can go both ways. As Thorndike pointed out early on, there is considerable inconsistency in any case between Albert's views as expressed in his authentic works; in general he tends to express himself more conservatively in his theological mode than he does in his philosophical mode (Thorndike 1955, 426).

More recently it has been argued by Bruno Roy that the *Speculum* is the work of Richard of Fournival – a suggestion more plausible than the arguments in favor of Roger Bacon (since it is known that the author of the *Speculum* consulted Richard of Fournival's library), but suffering from the same lack of certitude in the area of manuscript attribution as trouble the arguments in favor of Albert's authorship. Roy suggests that if Albert did not write the work, he may well have read it – something which is almost a necessary postulate for those who do not believe that Albert wrote it, given the fact that Albert mentions so many of the works that are listed in it. The debate cannot be conclusively settled except by the discovery of further manuscript evidence, but in the meantime, it remains as difficult to dismiss the idea of Albertine attribution as to prove it. The *Speculum* was an important touchstone for Renaissance Esotericism; many of the Albertine citations in Agrippa's *De Occulta Philosophia Libri Tres* are to this work.

4. SAINT AND MAGICIAN

Like other natural philosophers of his era, Albert was the subject of numerous posthumous legends which made him into a magical and alchemical adept. If all that was said of his reputation in this regard was not strictly justified by the facts, nevertheless there is some continuity between his real life and his reputation, just as some continuity is observable between his questionable works and his authentic writings. Albert had perused volumes of magical and hermetic writings as already noted, and had also observed alchemical procedures in laboratory conditions, as he mentions in several places in the *Book of Minerals*, though it is probably not true (as one manuscript suggests) that he was a teacher of alchemy who took Roger Bacon as a disciple. Albert was also known for working miracles of another sort, and in the end the growth of his reputation for sanctity outstripped the growth of his reputation for magic. It is interesting that a *Vita* composed in the mid 1480s with a view to his eventual canonization devotes about a quarter of its pages to the refutation of the exaggerated magical claims laid upon him. In 1484, the Pope gave permission to the Dominicans of Cologne to celebrate Albert's Feast on November 15 – a gesture that was equivalent to beatification, though Albert was not finally canonized until 1931.

Albertus Magnus, *Opera Omnia*, Auguste Borgnet (ed.), 38 vols., Paris: Vives, 1890-1899 ♦ *Book of Minerals*, Dorothy Wyckoff (trans.), Oxford: Clarendon Press, 1967 ♦ *Libellus de Alchimia ascribed to Albertus Magnus*, Sister Virginia Heines (trans.), Berkeley and Los Angeles: University of California Press, 1958 ♦ *The Speculum Astronomiae and its Enigma*, Paola Zambelli (ed.), Dordrecht: Kluwer Academic Publishers, 1992.

Lit.: Agostino Paravicini Bagliani, *Le* Speculum Astronomiae *une énigme? Enquête sur les manuscrits*, Turnhout: Micrologus Library, Sismel, edizioni del Galluzzo, 2001 ♦ Pearl Kibre, "Alchemical Writings ascribed to Albertus Magnus", *Speculum* 17 (1942), 499-518 ♦ idem, "Further Manuscripts Containing Alchemical Tracts Attributed to Albertus Magnus", *Speculum* 34 (1959), 238-247 ♦ Paolo Lucentini, "L'Ermetismo magico nel sec. XIII", in: Menso Folkerts and Richard Lorch (eds.), *Sic itur ad astra: Studien zur mittelalterlichen, insbesondere arabischen, Wissenschaftgeschichte. Festschrift für Paul Kunitzsch*, Wiesbaden: Harrassowitz Verlag, 2000, 409-450 ♦ Bruno

Roy, "Richard de Fournival, auteur du *Speculum Astronomiae*?", *Archives d'histoire doctrinale et littéraire du Moyen Age* 67 (2000), 159-180 ♦ Loris Sturlese, "Saints et magiciens: Albert le Grand en face D'Hermès Trismégiste", *Archives de Philosophie* 43:4 (1980), 615-634 ♦ Lynn Thorndike, *A History of Magic and Experimental Science*, 8 vols., New York: Columbia University Press, 1923-1958, vol. 2, 692-717 ♦ idem, "Further consideration of the *Experimenta, Speculum Astronomiae,* and *De Secretis Mulierum* ascribed to Albertus Magnus", *Speculum* 30 (1955), 423-427 ♦ J.A. Weisheipl (ed.), *Albertus Magnus and the Sciences: Commemorative Essays*, Toronto: Pontifical Institute of Medieval Studies, 1980.

CLAIRE FANGER

Alchemy I: Introduction

1. FROM ALCHEMY TO ALCHEMIES 2. THE "SPIRITUAL" INTERPRETATION 3. ALCHEMY AND THE SCIENTIFIC REVOLUTION 4. ALCHEMY AND CHEMISTRY

Alchemy is a subject of enormous intrinsic interest but one which has long proven difficult to grasp properly. The last thirty years, however, have witnessed a remarkable florescence of scholarly work on the subject, which has shed much new light on this obscure subject and brought forth significant revisions and advances in our understanding of it.

Whereas it was common just half a century ago for historians of science to dismiss alchemy out-of-hand as a "pseudo-science" or to deploy it merely as a foil against which to set the origins of modern science, the unsuitability of such attitudes has now become apparent among serious scholars, and such prejudiced readings of alchemy are in the process of passing away. An enormous amount of work, nevertheless, remains to be done in the field, for many aspects and developments of alchemy remain very incompletely understood. One important part of the remaining work is the continued dismantling of erroneous views of alchemy promulgated since the Enlightenment which have, despite their dubious qualifications and origins, deeply tinctured a major part of the literature on alchemy written during the 19th and 20th centuries. Four interrelated, and now increasingly rejected, features of these earlier treatments are identifiable: first, the notion or assumption that alchemy is a largely monolithic tradition, bearing little significant internal articulation or dynamic development over time or cultures; second, the concept of alchemy as an essentially or primarily spiritual, psychic, or self-transformative endeavor; third, the idea that alchemy ran counter to, was a non-participant in, or non-contributor to the scientific developments of the period characterized as the Scientific Revolution; and fourth, the belief that alchemy was something clearly distinguishable (in terms of goals, practices, and practitioners) from chemistry prior to the 18th century.

1. FROM ALCHEMY TO ALCHEMIES

The idea of alchemy as largely monolithic in character comes partly from the rhetoric of early modern alchemical writers themselves. Oft-repeated mottoes such as "the Sages all say one thing", the drawing of mythic histories and genealogies of alchemy to stress its supposed antiquity, and the desire of aspiring alchemists to uncover the secret knowledge known to and hidden by their predecessors (for example, preparing the Philosophers' Stone) conspire to give the impression of a tradition that remained largely constant over time, cultures, and practitioners. The ambiguity of alchemical writings, moreover, allowed for their broad reinterpretation by subsequent alchemists (and others) to create the appearance of a harmony of views among authors who, when treated critically, show very little actual agreement. In fact, the diversity and dynamism within historical alchemy is sufficiently extensive that historians have now begun to group individual authors and practitioners within "schools" and to see the differences among their practices and goals. Many alchemists, for example, were interested predominantly in bringing about metallic transmutation, generally by means of the Philosophers' Stone. Others, like → Paracelsus or Alexander von Suchten, downplayed this aspect of alchemy in favor of medicinal applications. Some emphasized productive processes of all sorts – distillation, refining, salt or pigment manufacture, etc. – along the lines of an early chemical industry. Some emphasized the theological implications of alchemical work, while others ignored this dimension entirely. Many writers and practitioners pursued several or even all of these goals, and this brief catalogue does not even mention the important intersections of alchemy over its long history with fine art, theatre, literature, religion, political and social movements, and many other areas of culture and society.

Even within any one of just the early modern European groups there exist diversities of theoretical, philosophical, or operational frameworks. We can speak of, for example, Mercurialists, who sought the matter for the Stone in common mercury, and contrast these with Sendivogians who sought for it in some sort of niter. Likewise,

Scholastic → Aristotelianism appealed as a system to some alchemists – like Geber and Gaston Duclo – while Neoplatonic [→ Neoplatonism] or other notions appealed to others. Some alchemists took a rigidly mechanistic view of their processes, while others adopted non-mechanical or vitalistic views, with yet others falling at all the possible gradations in-between. The critical point is that we cannot blithely extend the example of a single individual or group of individuals to make claims broadly about alchemy as a whole. While this situation renders a comprehensive understanding of alchemy far more difficult, it also makes it a far more interesting subject of study, and in fact, one less alien from other branches of human inquiry.

2. THE "SPIRITUAL" INTERPRETATION

The idea of a monolithic, constant, and ancient "tradition" within alchemy received a boost from the development of the spiritual interpretation of alchemy in the 19th century. A key event here was the publication of Mary Anne Atwood's *Suggestive Inquiry into the Hermetic Mystery* (1850). Atwood reduced all "true" alchemy to a quest for spiritual elevation operating through Mesmeric trances, the knowledge of which, along with → animal magnetism, she believed to be a secret tradition dating back at least to the ancient Greeks. Alchemical writers who apparently busied themselves with actual laboratory operations, were, according to Atwood, mere "literal souls" who failed to perceive the hidden truth of alchemy, and were not "real" alchemists at all; they were in fact, in her words, as "blind" as the chemists and other scientists of her day. Such a division – which plays upon a common rhetorical device employed in early modern alchemical texts where the wise author routinely differentiates himself from imposters and false alchemists – helped give rise to a putative division of alchemy into "esoteric" and "exoteric" aspects. These terms are still encountered today, but when they are applied to early modern alchemy their validity is questionable. There is no evidence that a majority, or even a significant fraction of pre-18th century European alchemical writers and practitioners saw their work as anything other than natural philosophical in character, as even the prolific occultist writer → A.E. Waite (1857-1942) was forced to admit toward the end of his career in 1926. Nonetheless, Atwood's treatise touched off a surge of interest in alchemy within the context of Victorian occultism [→ occult/occultism]. Although Victorian and subsequent alchemy is extremely interesting in its own right, its popularity has become an obstacle to understanding earlier alchemy because the spiritual interpretation's universal historical claims about the intent and content of pre-18th century alchemy are untenable.

It is important to clarify the distinction between 19th century occultist views of a self-transformative "spiritual" alchemy and the actual religious dimensions of pre-18th century alchemy. Many early modern alchemists stressed how alchemical truths and religious truths support and reveal one another. Likewise, the language of alchemy is full of religious terminology such as death and resurrection, glorification, and extensive parallels with Biblical texts, the life of Christ, and even the sacred liturgy. The power of fire or the Stone to purify metals is sometimes related to Christ's freeing men from sin. And of course, early alchemists frequently stressed the sanctity and divine favor needed for success. Yet such expressions of piety, as well as the synoptic, analogical view of the truths of the universe (whether natural or supernatural) typical of early modern thought (not just of alchemy) and the extensive use of religious imagery as a source of metaphor is widely different from the 19th century's identification of alchemy with Mesmerism, self-illumination, and psychic transformation. Indeed, the majority of alchemists (though not all) were at pains to stress that their art operated naturally upon natural substances. Even if among the broad diversity of alchemists one could identify a few who seem to promote a view more or less akin to the 19th-century interpretation, this feature could not be proposed as characteristic of alchemy since the majority of alchemists clearly did not hold it.

A major (and, in a critical historical sense, deleterious) outgrowth of the Victorian occultist fascination with alchemy is the psychological interpretation put forth by → Carl Gustav Jung. According to Jung, alchemy is not about physical (chemical) processes at all but rather about psychological developments occurring within the practitioner. The metaphorical language and strange phenomena filling alchemical tomes actually record hallucinatory 'irruptions of the unconscious' which are 'projected' from the alchemist's psyche onto the contents of his flasks. Despite the inherently unlikely character of this notion, it has had enormous influence on the understanding of alchemy even among otherwise sober historians of science. Besides the fact that there are few outside the ranks of avowedly Jungian analytical psychologists who continue to assent to Jung's views, recent scholarly investigations of alchemy have undermined Jung's

construct. In the first place, there is now no question that the vast majority of early modern alchemists were deeply involved in practical pursuits, which they carried out and interpreted with clear-headed, conscious thought. Studies of obscure alchemical language show how even some of the most bizarre metaphorical expressions and emblems can be comprehensively "decoded" into chemical operations. Some of these decoded processes have even been reproduced in modern chemical laboratories, providing occasionally evocative visual results – such as the growing of a spectacular "Philosophical Tree" from gold. The physical appearance of such results, taken together with the delight and fertility of early modern culture in drawing analogies and similitudes affords more immediate and more likely explanations for the origins of at least some alchemical imagery than the invocation of so shaky a construct as irruptions of a collective unconscious. Moreover, the inspection of private manuscript materials, for example the laboratory notebooks of George Starkey (1628-1665, alias Eirenaeus Philalethes, a favorite example for Jung), indicate clearly how he consciously encoded laboratory results in extravagant allegorical guise for public view while he maintained clear, precise expressions for private circulation, and even how he went about deciphering the metaphorical texts of his predecessors into chemical operations he could test practically in the laboratory. The affinity of Jung's interpretation with the 19th-century occultists' spiritual interpretation is clear in their common sundering of alchemy from practical chemical processes and their description of alchemical transformation as taking place within the practitioner; neither has withstood critical historical scrutiny.

3. ALCHEMY AND THE SCIENTIFIC REVOLUTION

Given the currency of spiritual and psychological interpretations of alchemy, it is not surprising that many in the early generation of 20th-century professional historians of science, especially those most influenced by positivist tendencies, denied to alchemy any place in the history or origins of modern science save perhaps as a counter-example. Their dismissal of alchemy often echoed sentiments voiced against alchemy in the 18th century, e.g. that it was entirely fraudulent, or that it was simply part of the "occult" (a word poorly defined in this context) which was supplanted by the progress of reason. Thus, influential figures like George Sarton cast alchemy into the scorned bin of "pseudo-sciences" alongside → witchcraft, black → magic, and necromancy, bedfellows alchemy had acquired predominantly by the writings of the 18th-century *philosophes*.

Yet the last three decades of the 20th century have witnessed a major shift in this perception. First, the profound alchemical interests and commitments of several thinkers recognized as key to the development of the physico-mathematical sciences central to master narratives of the Scientific Revolution were revealed. → Isaac Newton, → Robert Boyle, John Locke, and others were shown to have invested enormous time and energy in traditional alchemical pursuits. Other notable scholars such as Daniel Georg Morhof, Pierre Gassendi, and Olaus Borrichius are now known to have taken alchemy seriously and seen it as no less a part of natural philosophy than astronomy or natural history. Second, a closer, more contextualized study of individual alchemists has shown not only the inadequate – indeed, sometimes caricatured – portrayals of them current in the secondary literature, but also the significant contributions which alchemy has brought to the development of early modern science. For example, alchemy brought forth such principles as an emphasis on the determination and conservation of weight in chemical processes, well-developed and explanatory particulate matter theories, analysis and synthesis as tools for understanding nature, the power of human artifice to create new or improved products over natural ones, and perhaps even the notions of force key to Newton's physics.

4. Alchemy and Chemistry

The last of the obstacles to understanding alchemy which were mentioned at the outset can be seen as a parallel to the segregation of alchemy from the scientific mainstream (both in the 18th and the 19th to 20th centuries). This is the frequent division of alchemy from chemistry as if the two were only marginally contiguous. This division was made quite clearly by the work of Hélène Metzger in the 1920s, with alchemy as vitalistic and inherently "primitive" on the one side, and chemistry as mechanistic and "scientific" on the other. The division was recapitulated in Marie Boas' studies of Boyle and in quite a bit of historical writing down to the present. Yet until about the end of the 17th century, the terms alchemy and chemistry were used largely interchangeably, and did not carry their modern definitions and distinctions. The division between the two terms dates from around 1700, and is tied up with a number of

issues, including the professionalization and institutionalization of chemistry at this time and the desire to insulate the newly professionalizing field from the criticisms to which earlier transmutational endeavors had been prone. Thus "alchemy" then became equated with gold-making (and generally fraud), while "chemistry" encompassed most everything else which could previously have been called either alchemy or chemistry. The important point is that it is distorting and historically inaccurate to read our current distinction between the terms back into the 17th century and earlier, and thus to imagine the existence of "chemists" and "alchemists" as distinct groups at that time. Use of the archaic (and inclusive) term *chymistry* for speaking comprehensively about the undifferentiated alchemy/chemistry of the early modern period has been suggested as a solution. Likewise, for the sake of greater clarity, a revival of archaic, but more precise, terminology has also been advocated, for example, *chrysopoeia* (gold-making) and less commonly *argyropoeia* (silver-making) to describe metallic transmutational chymistry, *iatrochemistry* or *chemiatria* to describe medicinal applications, *spagyria* to label Paracelsian-inspired attempts to create more potent substances by analysis and resynthesis, and so forth.

Much work is still required (and on-going) to fill out our understanding of so difficult and diverse a field as alchemy. Such fresh understanding will be advanced when we avoid making unnecessarily broad statements about the intent and content of alchemy *as a whole*, and instead carry out studies which adequately localize alchemical thought – of whatever century – in its due context of time and place. In particular, the new understanding now being gained of pre-18th century alchemy (or "chymistry") requires the recognition and rejection of preconceptions arising from anachronistic and untenable interpretations which date from the 19th and 20th centuries.

Lit.: Mary Anne Atwood, *A Suggestive Inquiry into the Hermetic Mystery*, Belfast: William Tait, 1918 ♦ Herbert Butterfield, *The Origins of Modern Science, 1300-1800*, New York: Macmillan, 1952, 98 ♦ Betty Jo Teeter Dobbs, *The Foundations of Newton's Alchemy, or The Hunting of the Greene Lyon*, Cambridge: Cambridge University Press, 1975 ♦ eadem, *The Janus Face of Genius: The Role of Alchemy in Newton's Thought*, Cambridge: Cambridge University Press, 1991 ♦ Bernard Joly, "Alchimie et Rationalité: La Question des Critères de Démarcation entre Chimie et Alchimie au XVIIᵉ Siècle", *Sciences et Techniques en Perspective* 31 (1995), 93-107 ♦ Carl Gustav Jung, "Die Erlösungsvorstellungen in der Alchemie", *Eranos-Jahrbuch*

1936, Zürich: Rhein-Verlag, 1937, 13-111 ♦ idem, *Collected Works*, 20 vols., London: Routledge, 1953-1979, see vol. 9, pt. 2: *Aion*; vol. 12: *Psychology and Alchemy*; vol. 13: *Alchemical Studies*; vol. 14: *Mysterium Conjunctionis* ♦ Robert Halleux, *Les textes alchimiques*, Turnhout: Brepols, 1979 ♦ George Starkey, *Alchemical Laboratory Notebooks and Correspondence*, ed. and trans. Newman and Principe, Chicago: University of Chicago Press, 2005 ♦ Hélène Metzger, *Les doctrines chimiques en France du début du XVII*e *à la fin du XVIII*e *siècle*, Paris: Presses Universitaires de France, 1923 ♦ eadem, "L'evolution du règne métallique d'apres les alchimistes du XVII*e* siècle", *Isis* 4 (1922), 466-482 ♦ Daniel Georg Morhof, *Epistola de metallorum transmutatione*, Hamburg, 1673 ♦ William R. Newman and Lawrence M. Principe, "Alchemy vs. Chemistry: The Etymological Origins of a Historiographic Mistake", *Early Science and Medicine* 3 (1998), 32-65 ♦ idem, *Alchemy Tried in the Fire: Starkey, Boyle, and the Fate of Helmontian Chymistry*, Chicago: University of Chicago Press, 2002 ♦ Barbara Obrist, *Les débuts de l'imagerie alchimique dans les XIV*e*-XV*e *siècles*, Paris: le Sycomore, 1982 ♦ Lawrence M. Principe, *The Aspiring Adept: Robert Boyle and His Alchemical Quest*, Princeton: Princeton University Press, 1998 ♦ idem, "Apparatus and Reproducibility in Alchemy", in: Frederick L. Holmes & Trevor Levere (eds.), *Instruments and Experimentation in the History of Chemistry*, Cambridge, MA: MIT Press, 2000, 55-74 ♦ idem, "D.G. Morhof's Analysis and Defence of Transmutational Alchemy", in: *Mapping the World of Learning: The Polyhistor of Daniel Georg Morhof*, Wolfenbüttler Forschungen 91, Wiesbaden: Harrassowitz, 2000, 138-153 ♦ idem, "Diversity in Alchemy: The Case of Gaston 'Claveus' DuClo, a Scholastic Mercurialist Chrysopoeian", in: Allen G. Debus & Michael Walton (eds.), *Reading the Book of Nature: The Other Side of the Scientific Revolution*, Kirksville, MO: Sixteenth Century Press, 1998, 181-200 ♦ Lawrence M. Principe and William R. Newman, "Some Problems in the Historiography of Alchemy" in: Newman and Anthony Grafton (eds), *Secrets of Nature: Astrology and Alchemy in Early Modern Europe*, Cambridge, MA: MIT Press, 2001, 385-434 ♦ Arthur Edward Waite, *The Secret Tradition in Alchemy*, New York: Alfred Knopf, 1926.

LAWRENCE M. PRINCIPE

Alchemy II: Antiquity-12th Century

A. HISTORY
1. INTRODUCTION 2. THE ALCHEMICAL WORK 3. THE DOCTRINE OF THE ELEMENTS 4. ALCHEMICAL PRACTICE 5. ALCHEMICAL IMAGES AND SIGNS 6. ALCHEMY IN MEDIEVAL SCIENCE 7. HISTORICAL SURVEY OF ALCHEMY UP TO 1200 (A. THE BEGINNINGS IN HELLENISTIC EGYPT B. ALEXANDRIAN ALCHEMY C. BYZANTINE ALCHEMY D. ARAB ALCHEMY E. WESTERN ALCHEMY UNTIL 1200)

B. LITERATURE
1. INTRODUCTION 2. ZOSIMOS OF PANOPOLIS 3. ALEXANDRIAN AND BYZANTINE ALCHEMICAL LITERATURE 4. ARAB ALCHEMICAL LITERATURE 5. JABIR AND THE *CORPUS JABIRIANUM* 6. RHAZES 7. AVICENNA 8. THE *TURBA PHILOSOPHORUM* 9. IBN UMAIL 10. ALCHEMICAL LITERATURE IN THE LATIN MIDDLE AGES UNTIL THE END OF THE 12TH CENTURY

A. HISTORY

1. INTRODUCTION

Alchemy possesses both a practice and a theory. The theory can appear as a speculative nature-philosophy of Greek origin, or as a metaphorical code for processes of purification and initiation occurring both in the alchemical work and in the soul of the alchemist. Such recurrent metaphors of suffering, death and resurrection are rooted in the mysticism of ancient myths and mystery-cults. It is no accident that these stages of the alchemical work are already present in the first available alchemical text from the 3rd century A.D., the *Physika kai Mystika* of Pseudo-Democritos, which derives from Bolos of Mendes in the 3rd century B.C. A further variety of the concept "alchemy" concerns the alchemists' quest for the panacea, which heals both men and metals like a medicine. This medicinal aspect has its origin in Arab alchemy and becomes very significant in Western alchemy, where it influences → Jean de Rocquetaillade (Rupescissa) and then → Paracelsus and the Paracelsians [→ Paracelsianism]. The panacea can be produced from plant or animal matter, or from minerals alone.

One cannot simply speak of "alchemy", but must distinguish its practical, theoretical, nature-philosophical, mystical and medical aspects. Among alchemists there are, correspondingly, scientists, medical men and mystical seekers after truth, and even charlatans.

The West took over the concept of "alchemy" from the Arabic (*al-kimiya*) and its Latin forms include "alkimia", "alquimia", "alchimia" and "alchemia". The prefix "al-" is simply the definite article in Arabic, but the etymological root of "chimia" is controversial. Its attribution to a mythical hero or prophet cannot be taken seriously. Equally untenable is its application to one of the "sons of God" in Genesis 1 and Joshua 2, named as Chemes, Chimes or Chymes in the apocryphal Book of Enoch, as → Zosimos and Olympiodoros report. Even its derivation from the Egyptian word *keme* (black), denoting the black soil of Egypt and thus a metonym for Egypt itself, whereby alchemy would signify "the Egyptian Art", has not been widely accepted. Nowadays it is usually traced back to the Greek work *cheo* (to pour). Accordingly, *chymeia* or *chemeia* would mean the craft of pouring molten metal. In view of what we understand by "alchemy" today, it is possible that the Greek word *cheein* (pouring) became confused with the Egyptian *kem* (black) in Hellenistic Egypt.

If one looks for the Greek word *chemeía* in the usage of Hellenistic and Byzantine alchemists, one finds it to be disappointingly rare, for they prefer to speak of a "holy art". By contrast, the Latin word *chymia* is frequently encountered in the medieval West, moreover synonymously with the introduction of the Arabic term, thus "alchemy" (Lat. *alchimia*). Not until the advent of the modern period is *chymia* used for the more practical art to distinguish it from the more theoretical *alchemey*.

2. THE ALCHEMICAL WORK

Alchemy endeavours to produce noble metals, precious stones, the panacea, and above all the Philosopher's Stone. On the one hand, it seeks to do this by finding the right mixture (*Eukrasia*) of natural substances according to the ancient doctrine of elements and qualities. Alternatively, it adds the Philosopher's Stone, usually a powder or elixir prepared from an unknown substance, to the base metal. But first of all this unknown substance must be reduced to the *prima materia* (first matter). This occurs in the alchemical process, the "Great Work" (*opus magnum*) which passes through various stages. According to the colours that appear, these are called *nigredo* (black), *albedo* (white), *citrinitas* (yellow), *rubedo* (red) among others. This change of coloration may be observed when an amalgam of copper and mercury is heated. According to the amount of evaporating mercury, white, yellow, red, and with further heat, grey and black colours are seen, described by alchemists as the *cauda pavonis* ("Peacock's Tail"). These stages are described in various numbers and orders, but most often appear as follows:

1. Calcination, i.e. oxidation by heating. Metal oxides are thus known as "metal calcinates".
2. Solution, i.e. dissolution in sharp ("mercurial") liquids.
3. Putrefaction, i.e. decomposition. The solution in the closed vessel is gently heated in warm compost or a warm water bath to induce fermentation and thus stimulate digestion. The resulting black colour (*nigredo*) is seen as death,

depicted as the "black raven", which is shortly resurrected as the "white dove" (*albedo*).

4. Reduction, i.e. the recovery of the fugitive "spirits" during the calcination process by means of a fluid ("philosophical milk"), whereupon a yellow coloration (*citrinitas*) appears.
5. Sublimation, i.e. by adding the "spiritual" substance the matter in the glass vessel attains a higher level than the *prima materia*. This violent reaction is seen as the raging of the "red dragon". A red coloration (*rubedo*) occurs.
6. Coagulation or Fixation, i.e. the solidification of the elevated and purified matter according to the principle "solve et coagula".
7. Fermentation is only rarely mentioned, it means the addition of a small amount of gold ("yeast of gold") to accelerate the process.
8. *Lapis philosophorum*, i.e. the Philosopher's Stone, the *prima materia* elevated and purified into *ultima materia* (supreme matter). It is usually described as a heavy, dark red, shining powder. When heated, it acquires a waxy consistency (*ceratio*), but it solidifies again on cooling.
9. Multiplication, i.e. a greater amount of Stone can be made from a little of its residue.
10. Projection, i.e. the throwing or strewing of the Stone powder onto a base metal, which is thereupon allegedly transmuted into gold (silver in the Lesser Work). This process is also called *Tinctura* or "tingeing" (colouring) and is analogous to the application of the panacea or elixir in medicine.

It is thus evident that a base material is supposed to be reduced to *prima materia* and then ennobled. There are parallels for this in the individuation process described by → C.G. Jung as the development of a mature personality, as well as in the myths of Osiris and Isis, mystery-cults, → mysticism, and solar and cosmic symbols of eternity (e.g. the Ouroboros symbol). However, the processes described are only comprehensible against a background of nature-philosophy. Its basis is the nature-philosophy of Aristotle [→ Aristotelianism].

A thing only exists, when the "form" (*eidos*) is added to "matter" (*hyle*). "Matter" is the passive principle in things, "form" the motive, pure activity. One can even say that "matter" is pure potentiality (Gk. *dynamis*; Lat. *potentia*) which is realised through "form" (Gk. *energeia*; Lat. *actus*). Only formed matter is real as an individual thing and reality consists of such individual things making up "substance" (*ousia*). Aristotelian "form" means not just the external shape of things, but its essential form, its type. As an entelechy (*entelécheia*, something that contains or realises a final cause), it carries its own purpose within itself, which leads to the external form of the thing. In a universal hierarchy of purposes, each thing becomes "matter" again, once it reaches a higher essential form, as the seed becomes the tree. Ascending this hierarchy, the share of "matter" is constantly decreasing, while that of "form" increases, up to the purest, quite immaterial form of God. In this Aristotelian teleology, God is not only the end, but also the cause of the chain of movement, the first unmoved mover, who always maintains movement and in this manner continually shapes the world with a purpose.

The Aristotelian idea that all things are striving teleologically towards more complete forms exercised a fundamental influence in all alchemical theory. The associated notion of a passive *prima materia*, however, does not appear among alchemists as an Aristotelian metaphysical principle, but as a substance as among the Stoics and akin to the *apeiron* of the Pre-Socratic Anaximandros or the primal clay in Plato's *Timaios*.

Alchemy destroys a base metal by eliminating its specific nature, and then infusing the remaining matter with a new, nobler essence. The oldest Hellenistic literature describes the base metal as being cured of its "sickness" and restored to *prima materia*. Then one adds a tincture (colouring *pneumata*, "spirits"), which produces a white or yellow coloration as in silver and gold. This could be either a serious imitation of nature or mere trickery. Magical interpretations of metallurgical observations underlie these early attempts at transmutation, which went no further than coloration. The early metallurgists making alloys established that the alloy exhibited other properties than the molten metals. Copper and tin have a different colour and are softer than bronze, and likewise golden brass is produced from red copper and earthy zinc oxide.

The idea of a single ennobling agent, the best known being the *Lapis philosophorum*, is a further development in which ideas of natural → magic may have played a role. The production of the Stone through the stages of the Great Work (*opus magnum*) is also based on the notion of reducing an initial substance to *prima materia*, and then giving it a new, more perfect form. A small quantity of the Stone so produced is then projected onto the base metal, so that this loses its "sick" form and is transmuted into the *ultima materia* of the Stone, the latter acting as a yeast in a fermentation process. As a symbol of eternity and the eternal life of the gods among the Egyptians, gold alone among the metals possesses this perfect "form".

The idea of *prima materia*, summoned into being by the formative spirit and constituting all material existence implies that everything is one, as is expressed in the famous 11th-century Greek copy of a Hellenistic alchemical manuscript (No. 299, fol. 188 verso, Biblioteca Marciana, Venice). Here one sees the Ouroboros symbol, the snake or dragon consuming its own tail, signifying eternity, endless change and renewal, with the caption *hen to pan* (everything is one). If everything has arisen from the One and is one, then all things must be transmutable into anything.

Alchemical theory was thus based on these early procedures, first in Greek and later in Arab alchemy, together with the Aristotelian notion of being (prime matter being given form). To these ideas were added further theories drawn from Greek nature-philosophy.

3. THE DOCTRINE OF THE ELEMENTS

The Ionic nature-philosophers regarded each one of the elements as the primary substance. In his didactic poem *On Nature*, Empedocles of Agrigent (c. 500-430 B.C.) created the classical doctrine of the elements. Adopted by Aristotle, this doctrine dominated the natural sciences and medicine until the late Middle Ages. It holds that all things consist of the "four root powers", namely the elements Fire, Air, Water and Earth, in a particular mixture. Two basic forces, "conflict" and "love", separate them and bring them into new combinations. However, these four elements are not identical with the fire, air, water and earth of empirical experience. They are rather invisible basic materials, the principles of solidity (Earth), fluidity (Water), vaporosity (Air) and combustibility (Fire). Only their chief properties (solid, fluid, vaporous, burning), but in a mixed rather than pure form, can be seen in the empirical elements.

Using his basic doctrine of the elements, Empedocles sketched out a theory of matter in which the four philosophical elements were composed of imperceptible small parts, elementary corpuscles, theoretically divisible but immutable. Variations of this theory are found in Anaxagoras of Klazomenai (c. 500-425 B.C.) and Plato (427-348/7 B.C.).

Classical atomic theory is distinct from such corpuscular theories. It is rather a further variant of corpuscular theory, distinguishing itself in that the atoms are indivisible, differing in form and size and scattered through empty space. It derives from Leukippos from Miletus (mid-5th century B.C.) and Democritos from Abdera (c. 460-370 B.C.), who extended the theory.

Aristotle's criticism of corpuscular theories, especially the mechanistic conception of atoms as in Democritos, tended to inhibit their acceptance. Nevertheless, corpuscular theory can be seen in Epicuros of Samos (341-270 B.C.), Titus Lucretius Carus (c. 560-633), the leaders of the 12th-century schools of northern France like Adelard of Bath (c. 1070-after 1146), William of Conches (c. 1080-1154), and even Hugo of St. Victor (end of 11th century-1141) and likewise among Salerno doctors like Alfanus, archbishop of Salerno (d. 1085) and Urso (second half of 12th century). Scholastics, e.g. → Roger Bacon (c. 1219-c. 1292), even succeeded in deriving a kind of corpuscular theory from Aristotle (*Physics*, Book I, Chap. 4) and spoke of the smallest particles of all things (*minima naturalia*). Above all, corpuscular theory plays a role in the *Summa perfectionis* of the Latin Geber at the end of the 13th century, theoretically the most solid medieval alchemical text, and the one most widely read in this period. The scientific methodology of Aristotle is fundamentally empirical, but unlike the atomists he does not conceive of natural processes in a mechanical and quantitative manner, but as an interaction of principles and qualities. This physics of qualities dominates the theory of alchemy and medicine until the advent of modern science.

Aristotle supplements the fourfold scheme with a fifth element, the *quinta essentia*, "quintessence" or "ether", which constitutes the heavens and stars. This "ether", also known as *spiritus*, and as *pneuma* by the Neo-Platonists, regulates the correct mixture of the sublunar elements, when forming terrestrial things from *prima materia*.

The notion of an ideal mixture of elementary qualities is present not only in the preparation of the Philosopher's Stone but also dominates the Hippocratic and Galenic medicine of the Middle Ages. Ever since Hippocrates of Kos (c. 460-377 B.C.), and also evident in the *Corpus Hippocraticum*, rational medical treatment was directed towards the maintenance or restoration of health, conceived as *Eukrasia*, i.e. the correct mixture of the four cardinal bodily humours of blood (*sanguis*), yellow gall (*cholera*), black gall (*melancholia*) and phlegm (*phlegma*). By contrast, sickness was *Dyskrasia*, the wrong mixture. These basic components of humoral pathology, which prevailed during antiquity and the Middle Ages, already appear around 400 B.C. in the text *On the Nature of Man* (Chap. 4), by Polybos, known as the son-in-law of Hippocrates.

The perfect mixture of the elements, qualities and humours plays a prominent role in both the alchemy and medicine of the Middle Ages until Paracelsus' dethronement of humoral pathology. Both sciences are based on Pre-Socratic and Aris-

totelian nature-philosophy as well as on the fundamental view that everything is a unity. In Aristotle, the ether influences the sublunar world. From its Mesopotamian and Egyptian origins onwards, → astrology seeks to establish relations between the stars – principally the seven ancient planetary gods Moon, Sun, Mercury, Venus, Mars, Jupiter, Saturn – and terrestrial events and destinies. It has many connections with alchemy and medicine. Like magic, it sees divine and demonic forces at work everywhere. Such animistic notions are rooted in pre-scientific times and were passed on through the mythologies of the Babylonians, Egyptians, Greeks and others. Based on the idea of → correspondences, even the metals were matched, because of their appearance, to the planets and their powers: gold to the Sun, silver to the Moon, mercury to Mercury, copper to Venus, iron to Mars, tin to Jupiter, and lead to Saturn.

The earth with its "perfect" spherical form stands at the centre of the Aristotelian world-picture. Around it revolve the seven planets and, in a counter-rotation, the sphere of fixed stars. The earth is the primal mother Gaia, constantly giving birth to new things. Aristotle described the origin of the metals in his *Meteorology*, as being formed in the earth's interior from dry earthy and moist watery evaporations. With the exception of gold, all are imperfect due to an earthy mixture and their solidification without sufficient watery constituents. He attributes the fusibility of metals to the element of water, their solidity to the element of earth. In Arab alchemy, indeed already in the *Liber misericordiae* within the *Corpus Jabirianum* (8th-10th century), the composition of all materials, even metals, is traced back to the two principles of Sulphur and Mercury, which are in turn composed of the four elements. Sulphur, the principle of combustibility, consists of Fire and Air; Mercury, the principle of fusibility, of Water and Earth. These terms do not denote natural sulphur and mercury. From this time on, the Sulphur-Mercury theory dominates alchemy, only being briefly rivalled in the 14th century by the Pure Mercury theory. However, the latter is really only a variant of the Sulphur-Mercury theory, as it assumes that the principle of Sulphur is already contained in that of Mercury. The purest and finest substance of this Mercury gives permanence to the metals (and all things), while Sulphur corrupts them.

Animistic tradition regards everything as alive, as moved by demons and spirits and their energies (*dynameis*). In this view, Sulphur is represented as the Sun, masculine, and linked to the element Fire (hot and dry). Mercury is seen as the Moon, feminine, and assigned to the element Water. Their mixture is conceived as sexual intercourse. The Arab *Turba philosophorum* (9th-10th century) describes the elixir for producing gold as the union of masculine and feminine.

Through Arab alchemy based on its Greek predecessor, this dualistic conception of matter reaching far back to prehistoric and mythological sources was extended into a triad of body, soul and spirit, which was in turn related to all of creation and applied to the idea of the Philosopher's Stone. In the 16th century the triad appears as Salt, Sulphur and Mercury, denoting the principles of matter, in the work of Paracelsus (1493-1541).

Considered in the context of psychology and mysticism, alchemy expresses in word and image a supreme spiritual endeavour to reach a goal that moves ever further away, the more costly the efforts. Speaking in images, and leading to paradox, alchemy has much in common with mysticism, in respect of this process of endless purification leading towards a goal. In an objective sense, this goal is always receding and can only be perceived subjectively. The mystical search for the hidden god is paralleled by the quest for the hidden Philosopher's Stone or panacea in alchemy. The salvational quests of both mysticism and alchemy lead through purification and illumination by contemplation to the goal of *unio mystica* or the Philosopher's Stone, respectively. This search for salvation fills the greater part of all mystical and alchemical literature. Actual mystical experience, the apprehension of God, is vouchsafed to few. The union with God in female mysticism revolves around constantly new images of the sexual act (*conubium spirituale*). Thus Mechthild of Magdeburg has the Holy Spirit say to God that he should take the soul as a bride to a wedding bed. Similar metaphors are found concerning the combination of Sulphur and Mercury in alchemy.

However, their imagery can only be compared. They both spring from the common root of syncretic Hellenistic soteriology in late antiquity, as recorded in → Gnosticism, → Neoplatonism and the *Corpus Hermeticum*. As formulated in Greek nature-philosophy, alchemy does not recognise the direct spiritual intervention of man on matter, e.g. through spells or incantations, and is thus quite distinct from magic, although its theory shares much with the world-picture of *magia naturalis*. If magic seeks to dominate the material world through spiritual forces, alchemy seeks to understand the inner coherence of matter and, from this insight in the reaction of material substances, proceeds towards the mastery of the material world. But the mystical

path of salvation does not lead to any exercise of power in the material world; rather, it leads out of this world to an unworldly life of spiritual elevation and perfection in the search for God. The common Gnostic legacy in mysticism and alchemy is this spiritual path from material imperfection through purification and illumination to perfection. This is their only point of contact.

Leaving aside fraudulent alchemists, alchemy essentially has two aspects. Besides its theoretical superstructure, it develops its practice.

4. ALCHEMICAL PRACTICE

For the completion of the Great Work through four to twelve stages – preferably seven or twelve in number – instruments were used, known from illustrations in the papyri of late antiquity and medieval manuscripts. Laboratories in the West, where equipment developed by Arab alchemy was in use, were first established alongside the pharmacy in monasteries, as an extension of university pharmacies in the late Middle Ages, and at princely courts. Instruments included mortars (Lat. *mortuarium*, a vessel for pulverization), crucibles (Lat. *tigillum*), scales, scissors, tongs. The vessel for the performance of the Work was the aludel (Arab. *Al-utal*, Gk. *Aithalion*), occasionally known as a cucurbite (Lat. *curcurbita*), a convex vessel with openings above and below made from clay, glass, iron or copper; aludels could be arranged in a series, one upon the other. When it was hermetically sealed with clay to a still-head or alembic (Arab. *Al-anbiq*, Gk. *Ambix*, Lat. *caput mauri*, i.e. Moor's head), the apparatus could be used for sublimation or recurrent distillation. If a separation was performed by distillation, the alembic with its extended spout (Lat. *alembicus rostratus*) was placed upon the vessel containing the matter to be distilled. The distillate streamed through the spout into a receiving vessel (Lat. *receptaculum*). The retort (Lat. *retorta*, *cornus Hermetis* [horn of Hermes], *matrix* [womb]) combined the aludel and alembic in a single vessel. There was further technical development in the apparatus of the Work in the 14th and 15th centuries, demonstrating the practical gains for chemistry later on. The "Pelican" was a still that enables continuous distillation by returning a distillate to its residue for re-distillation. Cooling systems were also constructed.

The raw materials were heated according to requirements in various ways with lamps or candles, but usually with a furnace charged with wood or charcoal. If an even warmth was required, a basin of fermenting horse-manure was advised, occasionally the reflection or refraction of sunbeams, or a sand-bath (Lat. *balneum arenae*), a steam-bath (Lat. *balneum vaporis*), ash-bath (Greek. *Thermospodion*), or water-bath (Lat. *balneum Mariae*), frequently and wrongly attributed to Mary the Jewess in Egypt, allegedly the sister of → Moses.

The materials used by alchemists remained largely unchanged from the time of Rhazes (865-925) onwards. They were joined in Western alchemy by salpeter, alcohol, nitric acid and sulphuric acid. Rhazes lists the following materials in his major work *Kitab al-Asrar* ("The Book of Secrets"):

a) Four "Spirits", i.e. volatile substances: i. Mercury, recognised as a metal by the 14th century, ii. Sal ammoniac (ammonium chloride), iii. Auripigment, Arsenic (arsenic sulphide), iv. Sulphur,
b) Seven Bodies, i.e. the seven metals recognised by Rhazes,
c) Thirteen Stones,
d) Six Atraments, see Schneider (1962), 66,
e) Six kinds of borax (Arab. *Bauraq*, sodium triborate),
f) Eleven Salts,
g) Nascentia, i.e. ingredients from plants,
h) Viventia, i.e. ingredients from animals.

5. ALCHEMICAL IMAGES AND SIGNS

Already in Greek alchemical literature signs are found for substances (and even equipment), whose derivation is still largely obscure and which are often ambiguous. They are especially frequent in the later medieval and early modern periods. The use of planetary signs for the seven metals is of course self-evident. Furthermore there are pictograms (e.g. a retort), ideograms (e.g. the Ouroboros as a symbol for the unity and cyclical renewal of the cosmos as well as the cyclicality of the alchemical Work), and logograms (e.g. a death's head, derived from the term *caput mortuum* for the residue of distillation).

There were two channels for passing on the practical and theoretical knowledge of alchemy. On the one hand, there is an open (*aperte*) objective language as with Rhazes, and, on the other, an obscure (*tecte*), image-laden language as with Ibn Umail (c. 900-960). The latter involved cover-names (*Decknamen*) which came from Greek into Arabic and thence into Western alchemy, e.g. for chemical substances: "red rose" for the elixir used to make gold; for chemical properties: "eagle" for the evaporation of volatile substances; for the colours of the alchemical process: "raven" for black. These were useful as codes only as long as they remained

unknown to a broader public. Although polysemy (*aqua* is not only water but every fluid substance) already caused enough confusion for the user, there were further codes, anagrams and acrostics, creating an arcane language accessible only to a small circle of initiates. Not only single terms were veiled in concealed language, but there was also a prolific use of metaphor and allegory. From the 3rd to the 8th century, alchemy made use of many genres, including recipe, revelatory vision, allegory, riddle, didactic poems and letters, dialogue, commentary, and later debate (e.g. *Turba philosophorum*).

Traditional images of the world as a large organism (e.g. conception, birth, growth, maturity and death) were passed on. In addition, there were images based on Christian beliefs (e.g. Christ's Passion and Resurrection in *Buch der heiligen Dreifaltigkeit*) and, in the Renaissance, images from ancient mythology (e.g. → Michael Maier, *Atalanta fugiens* (1618), plates 23-24, 44-46).

The tendency towards → secrecy has clung to alchemy since its origins. Zosimos of Panopolis (c. 300), whose works represent the earliest alchemical documents, already warns alchemists against the greed of kings and humanity in general. Such demands for secrecy run like a thread through alchemical literature. Nevertheless there were occasional bans, ever since Diocletian (296) (LMA II, 331), which multiplied in the late medieval period, and there were always plenty of opponents. Selfish interests, e.g. commercial monopoly, played their part, and possibly even altruistic efforts to protect humanity from the misuse of dangerous knowledge.

6. ALCHEMY IN MEDIEVAL SCIENCE

Any attempt to classify alchemy among the medieval *artes* is confronted by the problem of its multifaceted nature. In its European beginnings, only → Daniel of Morley (c.1140-1210) dares to attempt such a classification in his *Liber de naturis inferiorum et superiorum*, moreover as a subdivision of astronomy in the Quadrivium, the four mathematical arts of the seven *artes liberales*. Dominicus Gundisalinus (12th century), using the Arabic classification of sciences, regards alchemy as *scientia naturalis* in his work *De divisione philosophiae*. Alchemy was never able to establish itself as a discipline at the medieval colleges and universities. However, until around 1300 it was discussed at a university level and had its place in the great encyclopaedias, such as the *Speculum naturale* of Vincent of Beauvais (c. 1190-1264), who not only described its practical merits, but also defined it as a science.

Alchemy could be regarded as a field of philosophy on the basis of its theory and called a liberal art or even a natural science, while its craft practice assigned it to the mechanical arts. To the medieval scholastics, however, it was neither a mechanical art nor a magical art forbidden by the Church.

7. HISTORICAL SURVEY OF ALCHEMY UP TO 1200

The following overview summarises some important aspects, facts and specialist works in the development of alchemy.

(a) Its beginnings in Hellenistic Egypt are characterised by the imitation of noble metals and pearls in temple science contained in the recipe literature of the Leiden and Stockholm papyri (c. 3rd century A.D.) and in Bolos of Mendes (3rd century B.C.), and passed on to Pseudo-Democritos (c. 300 A.D.).

(b) Alexandrian alchemy. Greek and Middle Eastern, especially Egyptian influences, combine in a syncretism, to be seen in all areas of knowledge in Alexandria, the greatest cultural centre of the Hellenistic world. Between 100 and 300 Greek nature-philosophy blends with mythology, Gnosticism and Neoplatonism in apocryphal works and such pseudepigraphic authors as → Hermes Trismegistus (although alchemy is least evident in the *Corpus Hermeticum*), Isis, Agathodaimon, Cleopatra, Mary the Jewess, Ostanes, Pammenes, Iamblichus, and Moses. In his major work *Physika kai Mystika*, Pseudo-Democritos (3rd century) not only transmits Bolos of Mendes and gives recipes for tinctures, but also provides a syncretic, mystical alchemy, abundant in metaphor with quotations from Ostanes and Pammenes; there is a commentary on this by Synesius (4th century). Alchemical allegory is first found in Zosimos of Panopolis (4th century), the earliest biographically documented alchemist, whose work found a wide readership, largely in commentaries, especially by Olympiodoros (6th century), and is accessible through Arab quotations.

(c) Byzantine alchemy begins with Olympiodorus, who displays a thorough familiarity with practice and equipment, and is continued by Stephanos of Alexandria (7th century), Heliodoros (8th century), Psellus (11th century) up to Nikephoros (13th century). Early texts of this Byzantine alchemy with its rich symbolism, specialist terminology and illustrations of instruments are collected in the famous Greek Codex 299 (11th century) in the Biblioteca Marciana, Venice. This served as a model for later copies. Byzantine alchemy not only develops the full range of its literary forms, mentioned above, but also elaborates its metaphorical codes.

(d) Arab alchemy derives directly from Alexandrian alchemy through translations from the Greek or Syrian. The doxographical *Turba philosophorum* reflects Greek nature-philosophy, mythology and magic. This is also true of the extensive *Corpus Jabirianum* (8th-10th century), attributed to Jabir (the Arab Geber, not to be confused with the Latin Geber of the 13th century), which first propounds the Sulphur-Mercury theory and also first uses plant and animal matter besides minerals for the production of the elixir. The Jabirian *corpus* is the first to contain the idea that the elixir can cure human diseases as a panacea as well as transforming base metals into noble ones. Although Jabir offers no fully developed system of iatrochemistry for producing remedies by chemical means, his work represents its beginnings. The twofold division of Alexandrian alchemy into a recipe literature and metaphorical, coded texts is now quite evident in an exoteric, pragmatic form of alchemy and its esoteric, image-laden, veiled counterpart. The esoteric literature of alchemy includes the *Tabula Smaragdina*, whose roots reach back to Hellenistic times, the basic esoteric text for all subsequent alchemists; the writings of the "Brethren of Purity from Basra" (10th century), which demonstrate a Gnostic influence; the *Epistola solis ad lunam crescentem* ("Tabula chemica") of Senior Zadith, i.e. Mohammed ibn Umail (c. 900-960) and others like the astrological-alchemical sections of the *Secretum secretorum* (10th century), a pseud-Aristotelian compendium of considerable influence. The exoteric aspect is initiated by Rhazes (865-925), especially with his *Liber secretorum* (not to be confused with the compendium *Secretum secretorum*), followed by others including al-Farabi (c. 873-950) and the great → Avicenna (c. 980-1037), who denied the possibility of transmutation in his *Book of the Remedy*, and anticipated iatrochemistry, the alchemical preparation of medicines, long before Paracelsus.

(e) Western alchemy until 1200. In early medieval Europe, artisan crafts combine with parts of alchemical practice, as described by Pliny the Elder (c. 24-79) in his *Naturalis historia*. An ennoblement of matter is not intended in any way, nor any forgeries, and there is no theory of transmutation. This is therefore not really alchemy, but rather metallurgy, glass-making, bell-casting, mosaic work and producing colours, as represented in the following works: *Compositiones ad tingenda musiva* (9th century), *Mappae clavicula* (9th-10th century), *Schedula diversarum artium* (or *De diver-*

sibus artibus) of Theophilus Presbyter (c. 1100), *De coloribus et artibus Romanorum* of Heraclius (11th century). This is the literature of the *artes mechanicae*, which later extends through other chemical fields to mining, pyrotechnics and distillation by the 15th century.

The history of Western alchemy in the medieval period begins with the reception of Arab alchemy after the 12th century. Its advent is marked by the translation of the alchemical doctrines of Morienus Romanus for the Umayyad prince Khalid (Halid ibn Yazid ibn Mu'awiya) († 704), both pseudepigraphic, by Robertus Castrensis (also Ketenensis), i.e. → Robert of Chester from Ketton in 1144. It bears the title *Liber de Compositione alchemiae quem edidit Morienus Romanus, Calid regi Aegytiorum: quem Robertus Castrensis de Arabico in Latinum transtulit*. Toledo in Spain became a centre of such translating activity, led by Gerard of Cremona (c. 1114-1187).

Important early translations (12th-13th century) are *De aluminibus et salibus* of Pseudo-Rhazes, both exoteric and esoteric in its symbolism of the Ouroboros, as well as *De congelatione et conglutinatione lapidum* (c. 1200), the geological section on the origin of metals in Avicenna's *Book of the Remedy*, by Alfred of Sarashel. A Latin edition of Rhazes' *Liber secretorum* is available from the 13th century onwards, and also of *Liber lumen luminum* (also known as *Liber claritatis*), pseudepigraphically attributed to Avicenna or Rhazes. The *Tabula smaragdina* is then also translated. Arab alchemy, the *ars nova*, was also available through translations and compilations made in Sicily, like the *Ars alchemiae* of → Michael Scot (c. 1180-1235).

Pseudepigrapha not only circulated under the names of Rhazes and Avicenna but also under those of → Albertus Magnus, Thomas Aquinas, ("Of Multiplication"), → Arnau de Vilanova, → Ramon Llull, of whom several were actually opponents of alchemy.

B. Literature

1. Introduction

Founded by Alexander the Great in 332 B.C., Alexandria was the intellectual centre of both Egypt and the whole Hellenistic world, with its Museion and famous library. Here the ancient Egyptian monotheistic religion blended with its thousand-faced personifications of the deity – the One and the Many. Here again ancient Egyptian temple wisdom encountered not only the Greek pantheon, philosophy and science, but also Judaism, Christianity, Gnosticism and Neoplatonism. Myths and cults co-existed, influencing each other and becoming interwoven. This contact between different cultures was not limited to the less educated classes but reached up to the learned elites of the Museion and the library. The ideas of Greek alchemy, which overarched traditional metallurgical practices, grew out of this rich cultural humus. The myth of Isis and Osiris provides an example of this Graeco-Egyptian syncretism, which corresponds with many elements of alchemical imagery and nature-philosophical thought.

The Isis-Osiris mythology essentially consists in a message of salvation known to the mystical tradition of all great world-religions: through the surrender of the temporal self (dismemberment), the inner person attains a higher, eternal life (Horus, Serapis). This idea of purification from the worldly and incomplete is present in the mystery-cults of antiquity, in mysticism and in the "solve et coagula" of alchemy.

Such parallels in the development of alchemical theory in Hellenistic Egypt might lead one to expect corresponding esoteric ideas in the oldest papyri. However, the findings are meagre. The metallurgical skills of ancient Egypt are documented, indeed at a late stage (3rd century), in the formulae of the Leiden (X) and Stockholm papyri. These are chiefly concerned with the counterfeiting of precious stones, pearls, silver and gold through alloys and imitations using colouring, with tinctures playing a major role. There is no trace of the spiritual elevation and clarification found in the mystery-cults and mysticism. Only all-too-human concerns are evident in the temple arts and industry. Here one discerns no philosophical endeavour to discover the innermost constitution of matter, but rather the frank admission of fraudulent tricks.

However, quite similar recipes for the production of gold and silver are found in the first alchemical writer known by name, Bolos of Mendes (3rd century B.C.), transmitted in the fragmentary *Physika kai Mystika* of Pseudo-Democritos (c. 300). Bolos/Democritos is said to have publicised the secret alchemical temple wisdom of the Egyptian priests, according to Zosimos of Panopolis. Similar recipes surface later on in the Latin *Mappae clavicula*. As our earliest source, Bolos already interprets the processes described in the recipes in terms of natural magic, ideas of sympathy and antipathy in the cosmos. These recipes deal with the imitation and transformation of natural substances based on the simple theory that the cosmos is a unity in which everything must be convertible into everything else. Here speaks a practically oriented alchemy, concerned with the mastery of nature.

Such an imitation of nature, where tinctures play a special role, should be distinguished from purely metallurgical and mineralogical techniques, as described by Pliny the Elder (d. A.D. 79) in his *Naturalis historia*, and which were used in the West for the purposes of casting bells, and producing stained glass and church ornaments in the early Middle Ages up to the 12th century. However, between the 1st and 3rd centuries, Alexandrian alchemy develops a unity of theory and practice by assimilating elements of the most diverse philosophical currents, especially Gnosticism and Neoplatonism, as well as the doctrines of purification and salvation in myths and mystery-cults. The enigmatic language of alchemy with its pseudonymous authors appears at the same time. It is significant that only pseudepigraphic and apocryphal authors, named after figures in Egyptian, Jewish and Greek mythology, religion and magic, feature in these first three centuries of alchemical literature.

Isis reveals the secrets of making gold and silver to her son Horus and gives recipes in the text *Isis the Prophetess to her Son Horus*. To the Egyptian queen Cleopatra, who is also credited with a pharmaceutical-cosmetic work and a gynaecological tract, was attributed the *Chrysopoeia* (Gold Preparation), a rich symbolic and metaphoric text in one of the most important collections of sources for Greek alchemy, the Codex 299 of the Biblioteca Marciana in Venice (11th century; Ploss 1970, 18), fol. 188 verso. On a single page the basic axioms of alchemy are combined with practice: three concentric circles form two rings, containing the words: 'One is the All and through it the All and in it the All and if it does not contain the All it is nothing', and 'The Serpent is One, he who has the Venom with two Compositions', beside it an image of the Ouroboros with the caption 'One is the All'. The practice of alchemy, emphasised by Mary the Jewess, is additionally represented by a double-funnelled alembic and a furnace. This Mary the Jewess, known to some alchemists as Miriam, the sister of Moses, known to Muslims as the Coptic Mary, the slave of Mohammed, who bore him a son, is another of these historically unidentifiable authorities. Her name is wrongly attributed to the "Balneum Mariae" (*bain-marie*), a tripod vessel, which is placed in the fire and filled with a mixture of oil, wax and sand in order to produce a higher temperature than boiling water. The *bain-marie* is likewise illustrated in Codex Marcianus 299, fol. 195 verso. Another alchemical author, Ostanes, the Persian magician, is equally intangible from a historical point of view. Bolos/Democritos describes himself as having been a pupil of Ostanes in *Phy-*

sika kai Mystika. Even the serpentine god Agathodaimon, literally "good spirit", whose symbol is the Ouroboros, appears as the author of a commentary to the Gnostic "Oracle of Orpheus", in which he discusses tinctures and the whitening and yellowing of metals. All these mythical grandees remain a constituent part of alchemical literature throughout its entire history. But none has attained a greater importance than Hermes Trismegistus, the "Thrice-Greatest Hermes", whose name has clung to the "Hermetic art", and even to such technical terms as the "hermetic seal" of a laboratory vessel in the alchemical work or the *aves hermeticae* for the "volatile", rising vapours in the process of distillation. This deity appears yet again as an exemplary product of Hellenistic syncretism in Egypt. The seventeen tracts of the *Corpus Hermeticum*, however, make no reference to alchemy. This suggests that Hermes Trismegistus entered the theory of alchemy owing to parallels with his cosmic philosophy of purification, redemption and immortality. The *Corpus Hermeticum* proclaims a specific kind of redemption, a liberation of the spirit by knowledge. Besides the theosophical *Hermetica*, there are also medical-scientific treatises, which deal with alchemy among other subjects. The alchemical *Hermetica* are mostly preserved as fragments. A longer one entitled "Anepigraphos", that is "untitled", attributes the preparation of silver, here called the "moon", to Hermes and Agathodaimon.

The influence of the *Hermetica* was enormous. In the first instance, this tradition was fostered in the Middle East, by the Sabaeans of Harran and the Muslims, together with other aspects of Greek philosophy and science. The best-known Hermetic text, the *Tabula Smaragdina* (Emerald Tablet), the "Bible of the alchemists", which began to circulate in the West from the 13th century onwards, is also attributable to Islamic engagement with the alchemical *Hermetica*. Its earliest source is in Arabic versions, for example the final part of the "Book of the Secret of Creation" (also known as "Book of Causes", 9th century) by Balinas, the Pseudo-Apollonios of Tyana. The intellectual world of the *Tabula Smaragdina* derives from the Hermetism of Graeco-Egyptian alchemy.

This condensed *summa* of Graeco-Egyptian alchemy shines like a precious stone imbedded in one of the recurrent legends of discovery. The work bears the motto *hen to pan*, the unity of everything. All things have proceeded from this One, whence it follows that everything can be transformed into anything. Macrocosm and microcosm correspond to each other and turn into each other. The Philosopher's Stone has the Sun (Fire, philosophical Sulphur, which bestows a gold colour) for its father, the Moon (Water, philosophical Mercury, which gives a silver colour and is the matrix of the Stone) for its mother. The wind (Air, the "Volatile" that is the rising vapour in a heated distillation still, or aludel, a Hermetic vessel known as the Philosopher's Egg) carries the Stone aloft like a seed, and the earth (Mother earth, in which the minerals grow, likewise the mercurial humus of the Stone) nourishes the Stone and brings it to maturity. Here are clearly delineated the basic substances of philosophical Sulphur and Mercury according to the Sulphur-Mercury theory, besides the operation of the four elements in the Philosopher's Stone: Fire, Water, Air and Earth. These individual components are not just listed, but dynamically related to each other according to *theorica*, thus producing a coded description of the alchemical Work, the *opus magnum*. The process of purification is clearly described, from the coarse to the subtle, up to pure fire (Gold), elevated above the earthly. The circulatory movement up to heaven and back to earth is indicated, just as the alchemical elaboration of the symbol of the unity of the universe in eternal change, the ancient Egyptian Ouroboros, expresses the circular processes of the alchemical *opus*.

After Augustine (354-430) had declared his disaccord with everything connected with Hermes (*De Civitate Dei* 18.23), interest in this literature was checked in the Christian West, until it was unleashed again by translations from the Arabic in Spain and Southern Italy during the 12th-century Renaissance.

Wolfram von Eschenbach created his epic poem *Parzival* in the first decade of the 13th century under the influence of the School of Chartres. Here Parzival's wise hermit uncle Trevrizent recalls the mystagogic figure of Hermes Trismegistus. He guides the protagonists towards inner purification, moreover on the Hermetic-Gnostic path of understanding oneself, the microcosm as well as the macrocosm. Wolfram's Hermetism is combined with alchemical knowledge.

2. ZOSIMOS OF PANOPOLIS

The first historical alchemist, Zosimos of Panopolis (Akhmim) in Egypt, who was active around A.D. 300, knew the *Hermetica*. Latin (Western) alchemy calls him Rosinus. The *Suda* ("Souda", c. 1000), the most important, comprehensive Byzantine encyclopaedia, credits him with an alchemical encyclopaedia in twenty-eight volumes entitled *Cheirokmeta* ("Handles"). Only Greek and Syrian fragments have survived, somewhat distorted in a Christian sense, for Zosimos was not a Christian.

There is also a series of Arabic quotations. We have particular knowledge of Zosimos from the commentary of the Byzantine alchemist Olympiodoros (6th century).

On the one hand, Zosimos was a practical alchemist. Like Mary the Jewess, he places great value on apparatus, e.g. his book *On Apparatus and Furnaces*, and many alchemical recipes of his have survived. On the other hand, he gives the first instance of alchemical allegory and a coded language, because he pleads that the alchemical art be kept secret and charges Bolos of Mendes with having made it public. An example of his enigmatic language would be the following "description" of the Philosophers' Stone in dichotomous paradoxes: 'This stone which isn't a stone, this precious thing which has no value, this polymorphous thing which has no form, this unknown thing which is known to all'. In one of his works, the "Commentary on the Letter Omega" which probably belongs among the twenty-eight books of the alchemical encyclopaedia, he debates with his sister Theosebeia, that a sage who has self-knowledge needs no kind of magic to influence something. In contrast, he allows everything to develop according to the necessity of nature and thus produces permanent "natural tinctures". Zosimos' portrait of the true alchemist, e.g. in the book "On the Treatment of Magnesia", displays obvious Hermetic features. Zosimos introduces not only Hermetism together with reminiscences of current myths and religions to alchemy, but also the allegorical encoding of his ideas concerning the redemption of the corporeal, transient existence, of metals as well as men, into the immaterial realm of the spirit. Zosimos' endeavours are most clear in his alchemistic "Dream" or "Vision", the title of his allegory of the alchemical work. In fact, this is neither a dream nor a vision, but Zosimos chooses to use the literary form of an allegorical dream. With his ideas of clarification and *metanoia*, linked to a serial progression through purification to illumination and perfection, Zosimos stands at the beginning of a tradition – at once mythical, mystical, religious, philosophical, scientific, metallurgical and alchemical – which has been repeated a thousandfold by alchemists ever since. Zosimos' dream allegory presents all these traditions so clearly, that one may speak of a didactic text, artfully divided into three parts, and intentionally written in a coded linguistic form.

3. ALEXANDRIAN AND BYZANTINE ALCHEMICAL LITERATURE

After Zosimos of Panopolis, Greek alchemy exhausts itself in the repetition of old theory, in the elaboration and development of imagery in literary formulations, as well as wearisome descriptions of practical work. However, this has left a valuable legacy. Greek alchemy has been handed down to us in collections of manuscripts, including the already quoted Codex Marcianus 299 (11th century), as well as the Greek Codices 2325 (13th century) and 2327 (15th century) of the Bibliothèque Nationale in Paris. All other Greek survivals derive from these manuscripts. Greek alchemy exhibits the following literary genres: recipe, allegory, riddle, revelatory vision, didactic poem or letter, a tract in dialogue, and commentary. The Greek alchemists of the 4th century, especially Pelagros, Dioscoros, and Synesius are not proven historical figures. Only Synesius, who directs his commentary on Pseudo-Demo-critos to Dioscoros, can be identified with some probability as the Neoplatonist Synesius of Cyrene (c. 370- c. 414), bishop of Ptolemais in 410-411.

The transition from Alexandrian to Byzantine alchemy took place in the 5th century. Olympiodo-ros, a pagan historian and alchemist from Thebes in Egypt, inaugurates this process. The work enti-tled "The philosopher Olympiodoros on Zosimos, Hermes and the Philosophers" is attributed to him. It exhibits Gnostic influence as well as a knowledge of practical alchemy, especially in the description of equipment, but contains nothing new otherwise. He broadly concerns himself with the philosophi-cal bases of alchemy, especially the Greek philoso-phers of nature, and repeatedly quotes extracts from Zosimos, described as the "Crown of the Philosophers".

The rhetorical and metaphorical expansion of alchemy, already present in Olympiodoros to an unprecedented degree, culminates in Greek alchemy with Stephanos of Alexandria (7th century). During the reign of emperor Herakleios (610-641) he taught philosophy, especially Plato and Aristotle, geometry, arithmetic, astronomy and → music. Besides a commentary on Aristotle and a work on astronomy, he composed an alchemical tract in nine lectures. In an eclectic fashion, he combined a mys-tical Christianity with ideas of the Pythagoreans, Platonism and other philosophical currents. He presents alchemy not as practical laboratory work but as an intellectual and spiritual process. He inter-prets the practice of alchemy in a mystical way as the clarification of the soul, following in Zosimos' tradition. He stylizes the transmutation of base met-als into gold as a symbol for the perfection of the human spirit through understanding in a Gnostic sense. He uses the ancient metaphorical tradition, but disguises its sexual symbolism, which occurs overtly in Cleopatra as coitus, pregnancy and birth.

In the ensuing period, Christian ideas and images as well as references to the New Testament become increasingly prominent in the metaphorical usage of Greek alchemy. Overall, the interest in practical laboratory work recedes, while the poetic and alle-gorical ornament increases. Poems of this "allego-rizing" tendency by Heliodoros, Theophrastos, Hierotheos and Archelaos have survived from the 8th and 9th centuries. The old practice of encoding continues, but also basic ideas, e.g. the composi-tion of all things from body, soul and spirit, as in Archelaos.

Now alchemy, ever since Zosimos, manifests in a mythologised and psychologised form. This trans-mutation was linked with notions of death and reawakening in the oriental mystery-cults, crowned by the Gnostic idea of redemption through knowl-edge. This combination of practical knowledge and the esoteric formulation of mythological, psychic and soteriological ideas is continued in this period by Salmanas (9th-10th century) and Psellus (11th century), through whom alchemical knowledge reached the Latin West. However, unlike the inno-vations which Arab alchemy introduced to the Christian West, Byzantine alchemy brought no new theoretical ideas.

4. ARAB ALCHEMICAL LITERATURE

Translations from Greek and Syrian into Arabic made by Syrian-speaking Nestorians in Nisibis and Edessa and the Sabaeans in Harran proliferated under educated rulers like Harun al-Rashid (c. 764-809) and Al-Ma'mun (787-833). Besides these cen-tres of learning, Greek science entered the Islamic world through the Academy of Gondishapur founded during the Sassanid dynasty (224-651) in west Persia and through Egyptian centres, espe-cially Alexandria.

Since the end of the 8th century there were also sufficient numbers of Muslim translators proficient in Greek. As far as alchemical literature is con-cerned, several Persian and even Babylonian-Assyr-ian ideas and concepts found in Arabic versions are attributable to their translation in Persian and Mesopotamian locations. The newly developing Arabic literature of alchemy relied on these trans-lations and so transmitted both authentic material, above all Zosimos, as well as pseudepigraphic works, which were not recognised as such. These included, for example, Thales, Pythagoras, Leukip-pos, Empedocles, Democritos, Socrates, Plato, Aristotle, but also "Agathodaimon", "Chimes", "Hermes" and Hermetic writings, such as the already cited *Tabula Smaragdina*, which originally stood at the end of "The Book of the Secret of Creation" by Balinas (Pseudo-Apollonios of Tyana), and further authorities like Cleopatra, Mary the Jewess, Ostanes and others. Such pseudepigrapha in Arabic alchemy have still not been adequately researched.

From the 8th century onwards, Islamic scholars enter the historical stage. Only several of the great number of Muslim alchemists, who produced original and representative work, can be given as examples. Arab historiography is problematic, as legend is not always distinguishable from historical truth. The most important historical source is the "Fihrist" (kitab-al-Fihrist) of Ibn [-Abi-Yakub]-an-Nadim (second half 10th century).

Ibn an-Nadim introduces the Umayyad prince Khalid (Halid b. Yazid b. Mu'awiya) at the turn of the 7th to the 8th century as the first Arab alchemist. He claims to have seen works by him and his alchemical testament to his son. There are similar reports by other Arab historians. It is still an open question whether the historical Khalid is identical with this alchemist. However, Khalid's principal importance is his legacy to the Christian West, as the dialogue of Khalid with his alchemy teacher Maryanus (i.e. Morienus Romanus) was the first alchemical text to be translated from Arabic into Latin by → Robert of Chester in 1144, later printed under the title *Liber de compositione alchemiae quem edidit Morienus Romanus, Calid regi Aegyptiorum: quem Robertus Castrensis de Arabico in Latinum transtulit*. It is true that Khalid is credited with several alchemical works, among them "The Paradise of Wisdom", a divan of alchemical didactic poems, which were frequently quoted later.

5. JABIR AND THE *CORPUS JABIRIANUM*

The reception of Greek learning swiftly led to remarkable achievements in Arab alchemy, first evident in the extremely influential *Corpus Jabirianum*. Evolving from the 8th to the 10th century, its authorship is attributed to Jabir (ibn Hayyan), who is the subject of much scholarly debate owing to scant historical evidence. In any case, this Jabir or Arab Geber must have been succeeded by the Latin Geber of the 13th century, who is credited with a text which was produced in Italy. Jabir provides evidence of himself as a historical personality in the 8th-9th century by repeatedly asserting that he is a pupil of Ja'far as-Sadiq and that he followed the latter in the content and structure of his writings. The Imam 'Abd Allah Ja'far al-Sadiq (c. 700-765) lived a reclusive life in Medina. He must have enjoyed a high reputation, because a great number of legendary pseudepigrapha have gathered around his name. In one such attributed work, "The Open

Letter of Ja'far as-Sadiq regarding the Science of the Art and of the Noble Stone", one encounters in Arab alchemical literature the earliest subdivision of the metals as of all things into the triad body, soul and spirit, which plays such an important role in → Paracelsus as "Salt, Sulphur and Mercury".

The *Corpus Jabirianum* is extremely voluminous and treats of all ancient sciences. Three thousand titles in total are known, of which many relate to chapter-headings. The most important writings of Jabir are the following:

- "The Compassion", also known as "The Foundation", appears to be the oldest work in view of its archaic terminology. Ja'far is not named in this work.
- "The Hundred and Twelve Books", which continue and offer a commentary on "The Compassion" have only survived in fragmentary form (thirty "books" are preserved). The description of the elixir as made not only of mineral but also from organic, that is animal and vegetable substances, is especially significant for the further development of alchemical ideas. Ja'far is named here.
- "The Seventy Books" contain the most uniform and systematic plan of Jabirian alchemy. Greek authorities are frequently quoted. Ja'far is named only once. This general survey of Jabirian alchemy also contains, like "The Compassion", the Sulphur-Mercury theory, which Jabir probably derived from Balinas (Pseudo-Apollonios of Tyana). Parts of the "Seventy Books" were translated into Latin by Gerard of Cremona as *Liber de Septuaginta* and then used widely in the Christian West.
- "The Ten Books of Rectifications" are concerned with improvements in alchemy by specific authorities. Such "rectifications" are written by various alchemical authors under the assumed names of Pythagoras, Socrates, Plato, Aristotle and Democritos among others.
- "The Books of the Balances", originally one hundred and forty-four in number, of which forty-four survive, deal not only with alchemy but also with → astrology, medicine, logic, physics, metaphysics, arithmetic, music, grammar and prosody. Jabir gleans insights from all these sciences for his special theory of "balance".
- "The Seven Metals", whose contents continue the discussion of the theory of "balance".
- "The Development of the Potential into the Actual" is concerned with the theoretical assumptions of contemporary natural science such as the doctrines of the elements and qualities,

astronomy, meteorology and "klimata", that is the latitudinal zones of the earth. Here one finds the fundamental questions of all Jabirian texts arising from such fields as medicine, alchemy, sympathetic influences, theurgy, → astrology, the science of balances and the artificial creation of life.

– "The Great Book of Properties" appears disordered in its seventy-one chapters, because in its composition fifty core chapters were supplemented by slightly abridged chapters. This book contains the important innovation of iatrochemistry, that is the alchemical preparation of medicines, so crucial for the further development of Western alchemy (→ Jean de Rocquetaillade, Paracelsus).

Concerning sources, it is evident that Jabir chiefly relies on Arabic translations of Greek pseudepigraphical literature, which he wrongly assumes to be authentic. This is usually the case with Pseudo-Socrates, Plato, Porphyry, Democritos, Agathodaimon and Pseudo-Apollonios of Tyana (Balinas). The only genuine quotations stem exclusively from Aristotle and Galen – Jabir is familiar with the humoral doctrine of medicine – as well as from the only real alchemist, Zosimos. Jabir's alchemical theory may be sketched as follows:

The foundation and touchstone of all traditional as well as discovered theory is experiment. Aristotle's doctrine of the elements, which derives from Empedocles of Agrigent, is combined in the *Corpus Jabirianum* with the doctrine of qualities in its early form as in Galen. The alchemist must endeavour to produce a state of equilibrium. The goal of transmutation is to achieve the same composition of the elementary qualities as obtained in gold. Jabir wanted to achieve this with elixirs. When preparing elixirs, the raw material should first be broken down into the four elements, e.g. by dry distillation, which are then added in an appropriate manner to the specific elixir with reference to the "lack" in the material which is to be transmuted. In this way, Jabir considers it possible to "heal" the "sick" matter or metal, by bringing its elementary qualities into the same equilibrium as of gold. For all that, quantitative thought enters alchemical theory here. In Jabir, the elementary qualities are carried by the two philosophical principles Mercury and Sulphur, from which the metals arise under the influence of the planets. Jabir's Mercury-Sulphur theory may have been prompted by the Arab encyclopaedia of his revered Balinas (Pseudo-Apollonios of Tyana), which was known as "The

Causes", "The Collector of Things", but mostly as "The Book of the Secret of Creation".

Jabir's basic conviction that natural events are ordered according to measure and purpose leads him to place no limits on the alchemist's ability to imitate the world-creating demiurge. Everything is possible, even artificial procreation, that is the homunculus. One merely needs to produce the right mixture of elementary qualities through elixirs. The innovation of the *Corpus Jabirianum*, as in "The Seventy Books", in the preparation of such elixirs for transmutation consists in the use, besides minerals, of organic, animal and plant substances: blood, hair, sperm, bones, lions' urine, poisonous snakes, foxes, oxen, gazelles, asses, as well as parts of olive, jasmine, onion, ginger, pepper, mustard, pear, anenome and aconite.

A further idea from the *Corpus Jabirianum*, which only blossomed fully in Western alchemy, was the use of the elixir in medicine as a remedy, even as a panacea. In the sixth maqala of "The Great Book of Properties", Jabir reports that he healed a thousand patients on a single day with the aid of the elixir. He also used it with success against snake bites and poisonings.

The *Corpus Jabirianum* is based on empirical results, but it does not achieve the level of Rhazes, especially regarding alchemical equipment and substances. The *Corpus Jabirianum* divides minerals into the following classes: 1) "spirits", that is volatile substances like sulphur, arsenic (arsenic sulphide, realgar, auripigment), mercury, camphor and salmiac (Sal ammoniacum), which was scarcely mentioned in earlier Arab alchemical literature, and whose production from organic substances, e.g. hair, is described in the *Corpus*. 2) Metals, namely gold, silver, lead, tin, copper, iron and "khar sini" ("Chinese iron", still unidentified). 3) Eight further groups of minerals. The empirical aspect of the *Corpus Jabirianum* also demonstrates highly practical techniques, e.g. the production of steel and refinement, dyeing, protection from corrosion, and the making of "gold" ink from marcasite for the illumination of manuscripts.

Apart from the corpuscular theory, Jabirian alchemy contains the principal ideas of all ensuing alchemy. The *Corpus Jabirianum* knows of the esoteric, metaphorical, occult as well as the exoteric aspect of alchemy. It offers both theory and empirical practice.

6. RHAZES

The great Persian physician and alchemist Rhazes (865-925) offers the most striking example of a thoroughly exoteric, sober, and practical alchemy. His full name is Abu Bakr Muhammad ibn Zakariyya al-Razi, that is "the man of Ray" (ancient Rhagae) near Teheran. Together with Jabir, the alchemist Rhazes exercised the greatest influence on Western alchemy. He based his thought largely on Jabir, but did not accept his theory of balance. He compiled his alchemical works in a list called "Pinax". Towards the end of his life he abridged his major work "The Book of Secrets" (*Kitab al Asrar*) as "The Secret of Secrets" (*K. Sirr al Asrar*) with an almost identical introduction. Here "secret" must be understood in the sense of technical knowledge. A collection of twelve further books belongs to the alchemical corpus of Rhazes, including "The Book of Propaedeutic Introduction" (written c. 900-910), which presents contemporary alchemy in a clear and systematic fashion like a modern introduction to chemistry.

Rhazes was chiefly devoted to practical alchemy and experiment. Although his thinking is far removed from the allegory of Greek alchemy or an Ibn Umail and is reticent in speculation, he follows the theory of Jabir in particular. He accepts the Aristotelian doctrine of elements, also the Mercury-Sulphur theory of Balinas realised by Jabir, regards "Sulphur" as non-inflammable oil and adds to Mercury and Sulphur a third constituent of a salty nature, a triad which is naturally reminiscent of Paracelsus. Like Jabir, he uses plant and animal products for the preparation of elixirs, with which the base, "sick" metals can be "healed" into gold, and furthermore systematically classifies all chemical substances into animal, vegetable and mineral. A corpuscular theory is manifest in Rhazes' "Book of Secrets", more sharply defined than its vague beginnings in the *Corpus Jabirianum*: bodies consist of the smallest indivisible parts, that is atoms. These are eternal and have a definite size. The qualities of the perceived elements, lightness, heaviness, colour, softness, hardness, depend on the density of the atoms, that is on the amount of the empty space between them.

Rhazes' ideas concerning the theory of matter later influenced the corpuscular theory of the Latin Geber towards the end of the 13th century. Armed with this theory, Rhazes describes the alchemical work in precise terms: distillation, calcination, solution, evaporation, crystallisation, sublimation, filtration, amalgamation, ceration, i.e. a process for making substances into a waxy solid. For the transmutation, the substances are purified by distillation and calcination. They are then amalgamated. Following their purification they are next prepared in a waxen state, without any evolution of fumes. There follows the solution in "sharp waters", not generally acids (lemon juice, sour milk), but rather alkaline and ammoniacal solutions. Finally, a coagulation or solidification was performed to produce the elixir.

7. AVICENNA

After Rhazes came → Avicenna (980-1037), i.e. Abu 'Ali al-Husain ibn Abdullah ibn Sina, the supreme medical authority among Islamic doctors. Like Rhazes, he was widely educated in many fields including alchemy – although he wrote no work on the subject and was no alchemist. However, his name was used pseudepigraphically for a number of alchemical books. His most important philosophical work, a kind of Aristotelian encyclopaedia dealing with the sciences of logic, physics, mathematics and metaphysics, bears the title *Book of the Remedy*, which refers to the recovery from ignorance. Here he treated of the natural generation of the metals and thundered his famous invective against the alchemists, which the Latins quote as "Sciant artifices", i.e. "The alchemists should know . . ." Avicenna took a position contrary to Jabir's belief in limitless feasibility. The products of nature are better than those produced artificially. Alchemical art never measures up to nature. For this reason, neither can it transmute base into noble metals. Like Jabir, but as an opponent of the art of making gold, Avicenna signposts the purpose of alchemical elixirs as remedies in human medicine, a challenge first fulfilled in the Christian world.

8. THE *TURBA PHILOSOPHORUM*

The *Turba philosophorum* or "Convention of Philosophers" (as adepts called themselves) has enjoyed the greatest favour among alchemists up to modern times, despite or possibly because of its obscure language, which has still not been adequately explained up to the present day. The *Turba* first appears in manuscripts of the 12th century, a Latin edition was first printed at Basle in 1572, and the first German translation by Paul Hildenbrandt appeared at Frankfurt in 1597. Surviving fragments of the lost Arabic original bear the title "The Book of the Convention". The doxographic work, written in Arabic around 900, is entirely based on Greek alchemy. The *Turba* quotes entire passages from Pseudo-Democritos and Olympiodoros. There are also textual parallels with the first book of the *Refutatio omnium haeresium* by the Church father Hippolytus (3rd century), in which nine of the *Turba* discussants appear. There are no references to Arab alchemists nor any mention of the Mercury-Sulphur theory. The text is manifestly an Arab edition of an original Greek work.

The Latin edition presents the *Turba* in a fictional narrative framework as the report of Archelaos, called "Arisleus", on the "Third Pythagorean Synod", to which Pythagoras allegedly invited his pupils across the world. Pre-Socratic philosophers, their identity masked by gross distortions of their names, speak predominantly in debate with the convention: Anaximandros, Anaximenes, Anaxogoras, Empedocles, Archelaos, Leukippos, Ekphantos, Pythagoras and Xenophanes, besides Socrates and Plato.

There is little in the *Turba* relating to alchemical procedures. The four elements must be mixed. Only then can they combine in new substances. Thus, "our copper" must first be transmuted into silver, before one can proceed with the preparation of gold. Coded names obstruct further interpretation. The author of the *Turba* has clearly not practised alchemy himself, as indicated by his recommendation of alchemical literature instead of experiment – a statement he puts in the mouth of Parmenides in the eleventh chapter. There is a wide gap here with the thought of Jabir and Rhazes, and the scholars of Salerno and Chartres in the 11th and 12th centuries.

9. Ibn Umail

The most prominent representative of allegorical alchemy is Abu 'Abdullah Muhammad ibn Umail at-Tamimi (c. 900-c. 960), whom the Latin writers called Senior Zadith Filius Hamuel. He wrote two influential major works besides various poems. The first is entitled *The Book of Silvery Water and Starry Earth*, while its Latin translation is known as *Tabula chemica* or *Senioris antiquissimi philosophi libellus*. Both express Ibn Umail's allegorical and encoded manner of expression. In this book he claims to be interpreting the secrets of alchemy, revealed to him when visiting the temple in Sidr Busir. He particularly enlarges on the alchemical doctrines of ancient, pre-Islamic authorities, including Zosimos, Mary the Jewess and the *Hermetica*, as well as the *Turba philosophorum*. Among Islamic alchemists he quotes only Jabir, occasionally engaging in polemics against him, and appears well acquainted with several books of the *Corpus Jabirianum*. He either knows nothing of Rhazes, which is hardly conceivable, or else he wishes to ignore him as the leading exoteric authority. He is wholly indebted to metaphorical Greek alchemy and closes his eyes to the achievements of Islamic alchemy.

In his introduction he refers to his second major work, "Epistle of the Sun to the Crescent Moon", in which he gives poetic expression to his alchemical insights at the temple in Sidr Busir. There are ninety strophes and a total of 448 verses of "extraordinary wooden doggerel" about the sun, the great elixir and the half-moon, namely mercury. The first work is presented as a commentary on the poetic, second work.

The "Epistle" also exists in a Latin version under the title *Epistola Solis ad Lunam crescentem*. This second work of Ibn Umail was used in the late medieval period as a source for a widely circulated, anonymous German poem, which was integrated into the Latin and German editions of the *Rosarium philosophorum*. Its contents revolve around the relationship dictated by nature between Sol and Luna, seen in sexual terms as the love-play of cock and hen.

In retrospect it is evident that Arab alchemy knows both theory and practice, the esoteric aspect with its metaphorical language and the exoteric with its struggle to understand matter and experimentation expressed in sober, objective language. There are divergent opinions concerning the possibility of transmutation, with Jabir and Rhazes pro and Avicenna contra. Innovations include the preparation of the elixir from plant and animal substances, the doctrine of the correct mixture of the four elements, the medicinal use of elixirs as remedies, even as a panacea, and the Mercury-Sulphur theory in particular, as well as practical improvements in instruments, especially distillation apparatus.

From the 12th century onwards, Arab alchemy produces only commentators and compilers. The Christian West begins to absorb the greatest and momentous wave of ancient science, in the 11th century in southern Italy, especially at Salerno, and in the 12th century in Spain, notably at Toledo. This was primarily mediated by Arabic sources, and to a lesser extent, especially in southern Italy, by Greek sources. In this way alchemy came to Europe as an *ars nova*.

10. Alchemical Literature in the Latin Middle Ages until the end of the 12th Century

The natural philosophers of the School of Chartres, "physici" as they called themselves, sought to understand God's corporeal world in a rational manner. Both William of Conches and Adelard of Bath rebuked the ancient scientists, who had neither studied the writings of the *physici*, nor recognised the natural virtues (*vires naturae*), nor trusted their own reason (*ratio*). William's critique shows that this was not a mere rationalist impulse derived from the *Timaeus*, but reflected a wider receptivity to new knowledge: he implied that there were still hidebound scientists who relied on the elementary doctrine of the old *Timaeus* (of Chalcidius), when Constantinus Africanus was now available as a source.

William of Conches therefore supplements his knowledge of the doctrine of elements, in this case the corpuscular theories, with influences from Salerno, particularly Galen's doctrine of the elements in the *Liber regalis* of 'Ali ibn Al-Abbas al-Magusi (*Lat.* Haly Abbas, d. 994), entitled *Liber pantegni* (The Whole Art) in the translation of Constantinus Africanus (1010-1087). His widely diffused "Philosophia mundi" offers a systematic treatment of all existence based on this corpuscular theory.

Constantinus Africanus, the first major and world-renowned translator of Greek-Arabic science into Latin, is synonymous with Salerno as the oldest university centre of Europe and the foremost centre for the reception of Arabic scientific and medical literature. This leading school of medicine cultivated a tradition of rational scientific thought united with observation and experiment in the spirit of Hippocrates and Galen. At the same time as Constantinus, Alphanus of Salerno (c. 1015-1085) translated the tract *Peri physeos anthropou* of Nemesios of Emesa (5th century) from Greek into Latin under the title *Premnon physicon*. Like Constantinus, he was concerned with establishing a corpuscular theory of matter as the basis of Western medicine, because the text offers one of the most extensive descriptions of the Platonic atomic theory in the Middle Ages. It was widely disseminated.

The networking, from the 10th century onwards, of educational centres, especially of Salerno in southern Italy with those in northern France, was flanked and eventually superseded by the reception and assimilation of translations from the Arabic at Toledo in Spain soon extended throughout Europe.

From the end of the 12th century, Latin writers had access to the leading authors of Arab philosophy, → al-Kindi, al-Farabi, Avicenna and al-Ghazali, as well as the giants of medicine like Rhazes with his compendium *Ad Almansorem* and especially Avicenna's *Canon medicinae*. Much was introduced from other fields, including the *Hermetica*, superstitious material, and not least alchemy, presented as the *ars nova* by Robert of Chester. Alchemy therefore owes its existence in the West to this 12th-century wave of reception and assimilation. The gradual Arab-Latin transla-

tion of Aristotle's complete works was especially epoch-making.

Arab science was introduced into the West by the enormous translating activity of Gerard of Cremona (1114-1187) and his circle in Toledo. His pupils compiled a list of 71 of his translations. Among these are three alchemical titles: Jabir (Jabir ibn Hayyan), *Liber divinitatis de LXX* (Berthelot 1906), Pseudo-Rhazes, *De aluminibus et salibus* (Ruska 1935) and Pseudo-Rhazes, *Liber lumen luminum* (Lippmann 1954, III, 27). In addition, there are Rhazes' "Book of Secrets" and pseudepigraphic texts like Pseudo-Avicenna's *De anima in arte alkimie* or the treatises on alchemy in the *Secretum secretorum*, the Arab encyclopaedia of Pseudo-Aristotle.

The reception of Arab alchemy in Europe commences with the same story of Morienus Romanus for the Umayyad prince Khalid, which marked the Islamic reception of Greek alchemy. Robertus Ketenensis (Robertus Castrensis), i.e. Robert of Chester (from Ketton) translated it in 1144 as *Liber de compositione alchemiae* and introduced in its foreword "alchymia" as a hitherto unknown art into Europe. He and his friend Hermann of Carinthia were studying alchemy while staying near the Ebro in Spain. Both men were influenced by the School of Chartres.

The number of early translations of alchemical writings from Arabic into Latin was not that great, and the well-received "Book of Alums and Salts" represents the foundation text of alchemy in the West, combining theory, allegory and practice. The Arab original was probably written in Spain in the 11th or 12th century. Its contents are as follows: the unknown author generally follows the line of Jabir and Rhazes, but also quotes from a poem attributed to Khalid and, not unexpectedly, appends the Mercury-Sulphur theory. However, he repeatedly reverts to his own experiments. The work is predominantly practical and treats the basic substances according to Rhazes's classification: sixteen chapters on spirits (mercury, arsenic, sulphur, sal ammoniac), forty-nine on bodies, i.e. metals (gold, silver, iron, lead, tin, copper), eight on stones and twelve on salts. This sober and objective chemical exposition is, however, mixed with the use of cover-names and esoteric, allegorical codes. In his description of mercury, for example, empirical observation initially prevails. But then analogy is invoked to conclude that the mercurial spirit penetrating another metal, which it clearly is able to tincture by giving it a different appearance, may also be able to act as an elixir by clarifying this other metal into silver ("white") and gold ("red").

This description is known as the Pure Mercury

theory, already encountered among other theories of the transmutation of metals in Jabir's *Liber de septuaginta*. But then the language grows more obscure and a series of cover-names ensues ("water of life", "colouring herb"), as found in the *Turba philosophorum*, followed by a list of the properties of mercury deriving from its twofold nature. This twofold nature is conveyed by an image, entirely in the style of Ibn Umail's allegorical alchemy or the *Turba philosophorum*. The snake impregnating itself, giving new birth from itself, when its time has come, unites the opposites of masculine and feminine in itself and renews itself. This is an allegory of the Ouroboros symbol. The toxicity of the mercury vapours is emphasised and then an easily understood representation is given of red mercury oxide being slowly heated. A torrent of cover-names is used, as if to make the point. The ensuing allegorical dialogue between gold and mercury is traditional, as found in Jabir's "Book of Seventy". Once again, mercury is presented as the origin of all metals, even of gold, as well as its hermaphroditic nature. According to whether it is regarded as masculine or feminine, mercury should be wedded to the feminine (sister) or masculine (brother). This idea might appear to favour the Mercury-Sulphur theory rather than the Pure Mercury theory. However, as a hermaphrodite, mercury contains both principles, which can each enter into a new relationship and thus both theories can harmoniously co-exist. By means of arsenic and sulphur, mercury can thus transmute base metals into silver and gold.

The introduction of alchemy to the scholarly world of Europe in the 12th and 13th century immediately provoked controversy. Alfred of Sareshel (Alfredus Anglicus) stirred up opposition against the *ars nova* at the turn of the 12th and 13th century. He was a member of Gerard of Cremona's circle and was responsible for some of the new translations of Aristotelian writings from Arabic. In the fourth book of his translation of Aristotle's *Meteorologica* he added the meteorological section of Avicenna's *Book of the Remedy* under the title *De congelatione et conglutinatione lapidum* ("Concerning the Coagulation and Conglutination of Stones"), without acknowledgement. But this contains the "Sciant artifices", Avicenna's famous rejection of transmutation. With these first translations of the 12th century the entire Arab theory of alchemy together with its imagery and terminology entered the Latin West.

Aristotle, *The Complete Works of Aristotle: The Revised Oxford Translation* (Jonathan Barnes, ed.), 2 vols., 2nd ed., New Jersey: Princeton, 1985 (1st ed.,

1984) ◆ Plato, *Werke in acht Bänden: Griechisch und Deutsch* (Gunther Eigler, ed.), Darmstadt, 1972 ◆ Pliny the Elder, *Naturkunde, 37 Bücher, lateinisch und deutsch* (Roderich König and Gerhard Winkler, eds.), Munich, Zurich, 1973-1992 ◆ Plutarch, *Über Isis und Osiris* (Th. Hopfner, transl. and commentary), Prague, 1941 (Reprint Hildesheim, 1974) ◆ *Corpus Hermeticum*, see Copenhaver (1992) ◆ Calcidius, see Waszink (1975) ◆ Nemesius, *Peri physeos antropou*, see Fredrich (1894) ◆ Pseudo-Apollonios of Tyana, see Weisser (1980) ◆ Alfanus, *Nemesii episcopi premnon physicon sive "peri physeos anthropou" liber a N. Alfano archiepiscopo Salerni in Latinum translatus* (Carlos Burkhard, ed.), Leipzig, 1917 ◆ Jabir, *Jabir ibn Hayyan: Essai sur l'histoire des idées scientifiques dans l'islam*, vol. 1, *Textes choisis* (Kraus, Paul, eds.), Paris, Cairo, 1935 ◆ Ja'far (Ja'far al-Sidiq), see Ruska (1977) ◆ *Tabula Smaragdina*, see Ruska (1926) ◆ *Turba philosophorum*, see Ruska (1931) ◆ Ibn Umail at Tameme, Muhammad, *Kitab al-ma' al-waraqe wal-ard an-nagmeya (The Book of Silvery Water and Starry Earth)*, edition and translation, see Stapleton and Husain (1933) and Ruska (1936) ◆ Avicenna, *Avicennae de congelatione et conglutinatione lapidum*, see Holmyard and Mandeville (1927) ◆ Urso, *Der Salernitaner Arzt Urso aus der 2. Hälfte des 12. Jahrhunderts und seine beide Schriften "De effectibus qualitatum" und "De effectibus medicinarum"* (Curt Mathaes, ed.), med. Diss. Leipzig, 1918 ◆ William of Conches, *Dragmaticon. Ediert von Guilelmus Gratarolus: Dialogus de substantiis physicis*, Strasburg, 1567 (Reprint Frankfurt am Main, 1967) ◆ Wolfram von Eschenbach, *Parzival*, 2 vols. (Karl Lachmann, ed., Wolfgang Spiewok, transl.), Stuttgart, 1981 ◆ Dominicus Gundissalinus, *De divisione philosophie* (L. Baur, ed.), Münster, 1903 ◆ Vincent of Beauvais, *Speculum naturale*, Venice, 1494 ◆ Daniel of Morley, *Liber de naturis inferiorum et superiorum* (Karl Sudhoff, ed.), *Archiv für die Geschichte der Naturwissenschaften und der Technik* 8 (1917), 1-40 ◆ Geber, see Newman (1991) and Darmstaedter (1922) ◆ *Rosarium Philosophorum*, see Telle (1992) ◆ Michael Maier, *Symbola aureae mensae duodecim nationum*, Frankfurt am Main, 1617.

Lit.: P. Assion, *Altdeutsche Fachliteratur*, Berlin, 1973 ◆ A. Aurnhammer, "Zum Hermaphroditen in der Sinnbildkunst der Alchemisten", in: Meinel (1986), 179-200 ◆ J. Barke, *Die Sprache der Chymie*, Tübingen, 1991 ◆ M. Berthelot, *La Chimie au moyen âge*, 3 vols., Paris, 1893 (Reprograph. reprint Osnabrück, 1967) ◆ idem (ed.), "Geber – le livre des soixante-dix", *Mémoires de l'Académie des Sciences* 49 (1906), 310-363 ◆ idem, *Die Chemie im Altertum und im Mittelalter ... übertragen von E. Kalliwoda. Durchgesehen, eingeleitet und mit Anmerkungen von F. Strunz*, Leipzig, Vienna, 1909 (Reprograph. reprint. With a foreword by R. Schmitz, Hildesheim, New York, 1970) ◆ idem & C.E. Ruelle, *Collection des anciens alchimistes grecs*, 3 vols., Paris, 1888-1889 (reprint Osnabrück, 1967) ◆ H. Biedermann, *Materia prima: Eine Bildersammlung zur Ideengeschichte der Alchemie*, Graz, 1973 ◆ idem, *Handlexikon der magischen Künste*. 2 vols, 3rd ed., Graz, 1986 ◆ H. Birkhan, *Die* alchemistische Lehrdichtung des Gratheus filius philosophi im Cod. Vind. 2372, 2 vols., Vienna, 1992 ◆ H. Brunner, Grundzüge der altägyptischen Religion, Darmstadt, 1983 ◆ H. Buntz, "Deutsche alchemistische Traktate des 15. und 16. Jahrhunderts", Diss. Munich, 1968, accepted 1969 ◆ idem, "Das 'Buch der heiligen Dreifaltigkeit': Sein Autor und seine Überlieferung", Zeitschrift für deutsches Altertum 101 (1972), 150-160 ◆ R. Bütler, Die Mystik der Welt, Darmstadt, 1992 ◆ Ch. Butterworth & B.A. Kessel (eds.), The Introduction of Arabic Philosophy into Europe, Leiden, New York, Cologne, 1994 ◆ D. Chwolsohn, Die Ssabier und der Ssabismus, 2 vols., St. Petersburg, 1856 (Reprint Amsterdam, 1965) ◆ B.P. Copenhaver, Hermetica: The Greek "Corpus Hermeticum" and the Latin "Asclepius" in a new English translation, with notes and introduction, Cambridge, 1992 ◆ W. F. Daems, "'Sal-Merkur-Sulphur' bei Paracelsus und das 'Buch der Heiligen Dreifaltigkeit'", Nova Acta Paracelsica 10 (1982), 189-190 ◆ P. Diepgen, Das Elixier, die köstlichste der Arzneien, Ingelheim, 1951 ◆ E.J. Dijksterhuis, Die Mechanisierung des Weltbildes (H. Habicht, transl), Berlin, Heidelberg & New York, 1983 (Reprint of 1956 ed. De mechanisering van het wereldbeeld, Amsterdam ,1950) ◆ P. Dinzelbacher (ed.), Mittelalterliche Frauenmystik, Paderborn, 1993 ◆ R. Drux, (ed.), Menschen aus Menschenhand, Stuttgart, 1988 ◆ G. Eis, Vor und nach Paracelsus, Stuttgart, 1965 ◆ idem, Mittelalterliche Fachliteratur, 2nd ed., Stuttgart, 1967 ◆ M. Eliade, Schmiede und Alchemisten, 2nd ed., Stuttgart, 1980 ◆ R.J. Forbes, A Short History of the Art of Distillation from the Beginnings up to the Death of Cellier Blumenthal, Leiden, 1970 ◆ C. Fredrich, "De libro 'Peri physeos anthropou' pseudippocrateo", Phil. Diss. Göttingen, 1894 ◆ K. Frick, "Einführung in die alchemistische Literatur", Sudhoffs Archiv 45 (1961), 147-163 ◆ W. Ganzenmüller, Die Alchemie im Mittelalter, Paderborn, 1938 (Reprog. reprint Hildesheim 1967) ◆ K. Garbers & J. Weyer (eds.), Quellengeschichtliches Lesebuch zur Chemie und Alchemie der Araber im Mittelalter, Hamburg, 1980 ◆ M. Giebel, Das Geheimnis der Mysterien, Zurich & Munich, 1990 ◆ D. Goltz, J. Telle & H. J. Vermeer, Der alchemistische Traktat "Von der Multiplikation" von Pseudo-Thomas von Aquin: Untersuchungen und Texte, Wiesbaden, 1977 ◆ E. Grant (ed.), A Source Book in Medieval Science, Cambridge, Mass., 1974 ◆ B.D. Haage, "Das alchemistische Bildgedicht vom 'Nackten Weib' in seiner bisher ältesten Überlieferung", Centaurus 26 (1982), 204-214 ◆ idem, "Der Harmoniegedanke in mittelalterlicher Dichtung und Diätetik als Therapeutikum: Das mystische Leben in der Welt ohne die Welt im 'Armen Heinrich' Hartmanns von Aue", in: J. Kühnel et al. (eds.), Psychologie in der Mediävistik: Gesammelte Beiträge des Steinheimer Symposions, Göppingen, 1985, 171-196 ◆ idem, "Wissenschafts- und bildungstheoretische Reminiszenzen nordfranzösischer Schulen bei Gottfried von Straßburg und Wolfram von Eschenbach", Würzburger medizinhistorische Mitteilungen 8 (1990), 91-135 ◆ idem, Studien zur Heilkunde im "Parzival" Wolframs von Eschenbach, Göppingen, 1992 ◆ idem, "Wissenstradierende und gesellschaftliche Konstituenten mittelal-

terlicher deutscher Fachsprache", in: Th. Bungarten (ed.), Fachsprachentheorie. Bd. 1, Tostedt, 1993, 228-268 ◆ idem, "Ouroboros - und kein Ende", in: J. Domes et al. (eds.), Licht der Natur: Festschrift für Gundolf Keil zum 60. Geburtstag, Göppingen, 1994, 149-169 ◆ idem, Alchemie im Mittelalter, Zurich, 1996 ◆ R. Halleux, Les textes alchimiques, Turnhout, 1979 ◆ D. Harmening, Superstitio, Berlin, 1979 ◆ Ch. H. Haskins, "The 'Alchemy' ascribed to Michael Scot", Isis 10 (1928), 350-359 ◆ E.J. Holmyard, Alchemy, Harmondsworth, 1968 (1st ed., 1957) ◆ idem & D.C. Mandeville, "De congelatione et conglutinatione lapidum" being sections of the Kitab al Shifa, Paris, 1927 ◆ B. Joly, "Rhazes", in: Priesner & Figala (1998), 302-304 ◆ C.G. Jung, Studien über alchemistische Vorstellungen, Olten, 1978 ◆ idem, Psychologie und Alchemie, 5th ed., Olten und Freiburg i.Br., 1979 (2nd ed. within the collected edition of 1975; 1st ed., Zurich, 1944) ◆ G. Keil, "Die Frau als Ärztin und Patientin in der medizinischen Fachprosa des deutschen Mittelalters", in: Frau und spätmittelalterlicher Alltag: Internationaler Kongreß Krems a.d. Donau 2.-5.10.1984 (Sitzungsberichte der Österreichischen Akademie der Wissenschaften, phil.-hist. Kl. 473 1986), 157-211 ◆ R. Kieckhefer, Magic in the Middle Ages, Cambridge, 1989 ◆ H.M. Koelbing, Die ärztliche Therapie, Darmstadt, 1985 ◆ P. Kraus, Jabir ibn Hayyan: Contribution à l'histoire des idées scientifiques dans l'Islam, Cairo, vol. 1, 1943, vol. 2, 1942 ◆ K. Lasswitz, Geschichte der Atomistik vom Mittelalter bis Newton, 2 vols., Hamburg & Leipzig, 1890 (Photog. Reprint Darmstadt, 1963) ◆ J. Lindsay, The Origins of Alchemy in Graeco-Roman Egypt, London, 1970 ◆ E.O. von Lippmann, Entstehung und Ausbreitung der Alchemie, Berlin, vol. 1, 1919, vol. 2, 1931, Weinheim, vol. 3, 1954 ◆ LMA = Lexikon des Mittelalters, vols. 1, Munich & Zurich, 1977 ◆ F. Lüdy-Tenger, Alchemistische und chemische Zeichen, Vaduz, 1981 ◆ Z.R. von Martels (ed.), Alchemy Revisited: Proceedings of the International Conference on the History of Alchemy at the University of Groningen, 17.-19.4.1989, Leiden, New York & Cologne, 1990 ◆ M. Mertens, "Project for a New Edition of Zosimos of Panopolis", in: Martels (1990), 121-126 ◆ W.-D. Müller-Jahncke, "Homunculus", in: Priesner & Figala (1998), 182 ◆ R. Multhauf, The Origins of Chemistry, London, 1966 ◆ A.N. Nader, "Les alchimistes arabes du Moyen Age et leur conception de la nature", in: A. Zimmermann & A. Speer (eds.), Mensch und Natur im Mittelalter, Berlin & New York, 1991, 510-534 ◆ W.R. Newman, The "Summa perfectionis" of Pseudo-Geber: A Critical Edition, Translation and Study, Leiden, New York, Copenhagen & Cologne, 1991 ◆ idem, "Avicenna", in: Priesner & Figala (1998), 67 ◆ idem, "Alchemie, mittelalterliche/arabische", in: Priesner & Figala (1998), 26-29 ◆ B. Obrist, "Die Alchemie in der mittelalterlichen Gesellschaft", in: Meinel (1968), 33-59 ◆ B. Pabst, Atomtheorien des lateinischen Mittelalters, Darmstadt, 1994 ◆ Pauly = Der Kleine Pauly: Lexikon der Antike, 5 vols., Munich, 1975 ◆ M. Plessner, Vorsokratische Philosophie und griechische Alchemie in arabisch-lateinischer Überlieferung: Studien zu Text und Inhalt der "Turba *philosophorum"*, Wiesbaden, 1975 ◆ E.E. Ploss, H. Roosen-Runge, H. Schipperges & H. Buntz, *Alchimia: Ideologie und Technologie*, Munich, 1970 ◆ C. Priesner & K. Figala (eds.), *Alchemie: Lexikon einer hermetischen Wissenschaft*, Munich, 1998 ◆ J. Pruig, "The Transmission and Reception of Arabic Philosophy in Christian Spain (until 1200)", in: Ch. Butterworth & B.A. Kessel (eds.), *The Introduction of Arabic Philosophy into Europe*, Leiden, New York & Cologne, 1994, 7-30 ◆ H. Roosen-Runge, "Farben- und Malrezepte in frühmittelalterlichen technologischen Handschriften", in: Ploss *et al.* (1970), 47-66 ◆ J. Ruska, *Tabula Smaragdina*, Heidelberg, 1926 ◆ idem, "*Turba Philosophorum*", Berlin, 1931 ◆ idem, "Der Urtext der Tabula Chemica", *Archeion* 16 (1934), 273-283 ◆ idem (ed. & trans.), *Das Buch der Alaune und Salze: Ein Grundwerk der spätlateinischen Alchemie*, Berlin, 1935 ◆ idem, *Al-Raze's Buch Geheimnis der Geheimnisse, mit Einleitung und Erläuterungen in deutscher Übersetzung*, Berlin, 1937 ◆ idem, *Arabische Alchemisten*, Wiesbaden, 1977 (Reprint of the 1924 edition) ◆ H. Schipperges, "Die Schulen von Chartres unter dem Einfluß des Arabismus", *Sudhoffs Archiv* 40 (1956), 193-219 ◆ idem, *Die Assimilation der arabischen Medizin durch das lateinische Mittelalter*, Wiesbaden, 1964 ◆ idem, "Strukturen und Prozesse alchimistischer Überlieferungen", in: Ploss *et al.* (1970), 67-118 ◆ idem, "Die Rezeption arabisch-griechischer Medizin und ihr Einfluß auf die abendländische Heilkunde", in: P. Weimar (ed.), *Die Renaissance der Wissenschaften im 12. Jahrhundert*, Zürich, 1981, 173-196 ◆ idem, "Zum Topos von 'ratio et experimentum' in der älteren Wissenschaftsgeschichte", in: G. Keil & P. Assion (eds.), *Fachprosa-Studien: Beiträge zur mittelalterlichen Wissenschafts- und Geistesgeschichte*, Berlin, 1982, 25-36 ◆ idem, *Der Garten der Gesundheit: Medizin im Mittelalter*, Munich, 1985 ◆ idem, "Avicenna (980-1037)", in: D. von Engelhardt & F. Hartmann, (eds.), *Klassiker der Medizin*, Munich, 1991, vol. 1, 40-43 ◆ R. Schnabel, *Pharmazie in Wissenschaft und Praxis: Dargestellt an der Geschichte der Klosterapotheken Altbayerns vom Jahre 800-1800*, Munich, 1965 ◆ W. Schneider, *Lexikon alchemistisch-pharmazeutischer Symbole*, Weinheim, 1962 ◆ F. Sezgin, *Geschichte des arabischen Schrifttums*, vol. 4, Leiden, 1971 ◆ H.J. Sheppard, "Gnosticism and alchemy", *Ambix* 6 (1957), 86-101 ◆ A. Siggel, *Decknamen in der arabischen alchemistischen Literatur*, Berlin, 1951 ◆ P.H. Smith, "Hermetik", in: Priesner & Figala (1998), 176-177 ◆ H.E. Stapleton & M.H. Husain (eds. & trans.), "Three Arabic Treatises on Alchemy by Muhammad ibn Umail (10th Century A.D.): Edition of the Texts by Muhammad Turab Ale", *Memoirs of the Asiatic Society of Bengal* 12 (1933), 1-213 ◆ B.W. Switalski, *Des Chalcidius Kommentar zu Plato's Timaeus*, Münster, 1902 ◆ Z. Szydlo, "Hermes Trismegistos", in: Priesner & Figala (1998), 172-176 ◆ F. Sherwood Taylor, "The visions of Zosimos", *Ambix* 1 (1937), 88-92 ◆ idem, "The idea of the quintessence", in: E. Ashworth Underwood (ed.), *Science, Medicine and History: Essays on the Evolution of Scientific Thought and Medical Practice written in honour of Charles Singer*, London, New York & Toronto, 1953, 247-265 ◆ J. Telle, *Rosarium Philosophorum: Ein alchemisches Florilegium des Spätmittelalters*, 2 vols., Weinheim, 1992 ◆ idem, "Sol und Luna", VL, vol. 9 (1993), cols. 19-22 ◆ idem, "Aristoteles und Alexander über den philosophischen Stein: Die alchemistischen Lehren des pseudo-aristotelischen 'Secretum secretorum' in einer deutschen Übersetzung des 15. Jahrhunderts", in: Domes *et al.* (1994), 455-483 ◆ O. Temkin, "Medicine and Graeco-Arabic alchemy", *Bulletin of the History of Medicine* 29 (1955), 134-153 ◆ M. Ullmann, *Die Medizin im Islam*, Leiden, 1970 ◆ idem, *Die Natur- und Geheimwissenschaften im Islam*, Leiden, 1972 ◆ J.H. Waszink, *"Timaeus" a Calcidio translatus commentarioque instructus*, Leiden, 1975 (1st ed., 1962) ◆ U. Weisser, *Das "Buch über das Geheimnis der Schöpfung" von Pseudo-Apollonios von Tyana*, Berlin & New York, 1980 ◆ J. Weyer, *Graf Wolfgang II. von Hohenlohe und die Alchemie: Alchemistische Studien im Schloß Weikersheim 1587-1610*, Sigmaringen, 1992 ◆ idem, "Alchemie, antike", in: Priesner & Figala (1998), 22-25.

BERNARD D. HAAGE

Alchemy III: 12th/13th-15th Century

1. MAIN DEVELOPMENTS 2. LITERATURE

1. MAIN DEVELOPMENTS

The transition from Arabic to Western alchemy in the 12th and 13th centuries did not create an abrupt rupture. Its Hellenistic and Arabic foundations were adopted and developed further, leading to new theoretical speculation and more practical knowledge. Research on this period is still developing as the surviving manuscripts have not yet been thoroughly investigated and evaluated. Research is still needed to ascertain attributions and borrowings and to distinguish traditional theories and innovative ideas. Further biographical study would be necessary to investigate putative or legendary medieval authors, such as Basilius Valentinus, Bernhard von der Mark, → Nicolas Flamel, Vincentius Koffshki or Salomon Trismosin.

Medieval alchemy was not a natural science in the modern sense but a doctrine of nature, which tried to discover and apply the laws of nature through theory and experiment. Its fundamental assumption was a holistic concept, which united the macrocosm of the stars and the microcosm of man and nature. The teachings of authentic or legendary authorities such as Aristotle or → Hermes Trismegistus served as theoretical bases. New discoveries had to be harmonised with traditional teachings and this was a slow process. Speculation and practical experience formed a unity. Theory set the context and determined the direction of the work. Experiment either confirmed theory or occasioned new considerations.

The goal of the medieval alchemists was not just the exploration but the perfection of nature, regarded as a divine task or duty. This applied chiefly to the base metals which were classified as ill, impure or immature. They had to be purified and perfected into silver or gold, a goal achieved by stages of a longer process (*opus magnum*). They had to be destroyed in their outer form and reduced to a common prime matter (*prima materia*) from which they would arise renewed through the proper treatment and the favourable influence of the stars. The Philosophers' Stone (*lapis philosophorum*) played a varied role: it was either the additional ingredient which accelerated and brought about transmutation or it was the result of the process, and was then applied to other metals. It was not only ascribed healing powers towards inanimate nature but was regarded as an elixir, which could heal human diseases and prolong life. The desire to produce gold or silver was not the pre-eminent goal of serious alchemy and the intentional forgery of precious metals was opposed to it. The boundary between alchemy and related sciences such as astrology, medicine, or pharmacy was not a sharp one. Because the constellation of planets was allegedly responsible for the growth of metals and their properties, astrological knowledge was important for the alchemist. The link to medicine and pharmacy followed on a theoretical level, which set up an analogy between the alchemical process and the healing of the human body, or in practice, in which alchemy contributed towards the preparation of medicines.

Western alchemy began in the middle of the 12th century with translations from Arabic into Latin. The centres of this translation activity were Toledo in Spain, and the territories of Emperor Frederick II Hohenstaufen in southern Italy and Sicily. The most important translated works included the pseudo-Aristotelian book *Secretum secretorum*, the *Liber de Septuaginta* attributed to Jabir ibn Hayyan, the *Liber de Secretorum* of Rhazes, and a text entitled *De aluminibus et salibus*, also allegedly by Rhazes.

The development of alchemy was greatly influenced by the interest of two eminent 13th-century scholars. → Albertus Magnus also dealt with the growth of metals in his work *De mineralibus*. He evaluated alchemy as an activity, capable of changing the colour, weight or smell of matter. But he regarded this only as an apparent transmutation because its fundamental nature was immutable. → Roger Bacon came to a different conclusion, distinguishing between speculative and operative alchemy in his *Opus minus* and *Opus tertium*. While speculative reason could be given to explain the growth of matter from the elements, Bacon considered the principal task of operative alchemy as the preparation of medicines for the prolongation of life. Alchemy thereby became an established part of medieval knowledge, as represented in the encyclopaedias of Bartholomaeus Anglicus (*De proprietatibus rerum*, c. 1230), Thomas von Cantimpré (*De rerum natura*, c. 1240) or Vincenz von Beauvais (*Speculum maius*, c. 1250).

At this time, the first independent Latin monographs were written, but their authors are mostly unknown. These texts frequently appeared under the name of a famous scholar such as Thomas Aquinas (1224/25-1274), → Arnau de Vilanova (c. 1230-1311) and → Ramon Llull. The authors and their readers were evidently untroubled by the fact that these pseudepigraphic authors had written critically on alchemy or even been its determined opponents.

One work stands out within this growing literature, namely the *Summa perfectionis magisterii* (c. 1300), attributed to Jabir ibn Hayyan. Its author, whom scholarship knows as Latin Geber, may be identical with the Italian Franciscan Paulus de Tarento. His text dealt with applied alchemy but also provided new theoretical approaches. According to the Latin Geber, matter is composed of small and separate individual corpuscles. Even the four elements are composed of such corpuscles, but they exist in the elements as identical components. Quicksilver (mercury) and sulphur are composed from these elementary particles which then form the bases of other metals. Geber explained the variable chemical properties of individual substances by the size and density of the corpuscles. The possibility of an authentic transmutation of metals was supposed to result from the purification of the fundamental substances quicksilver and sulphur. Quicksilver or mercury thus acquired a special significance and Geber equated it with the *Lapis philosophorum*. Further texts bearing Geber's name were not necessarily written by the same author.

Among the authors influenced by the Latin Geber was Petrus Bonus (Pietro Bono or Buono), a physician and alchemist who probably came from Ferrara. The most important of his works is the text *Margarita pretiosa novella* (c. 1330). He aimed at creating a theoretical basis by presenting arguments for and against alchemy. He thereby distinguished between scientific knowledge in alchemy and divine illumination, which he equated with religion. This association was perhaps the reason for religious analogies with the alchemical process.

An important theoretical contribution came from the French Franciscan → Jean de Rocquetaillade (Johannes de Rupescissa), who is historically identifiable and also the author of prophetic books. In his *Liber de consideratione quintae essentiae omnium rerum*, he described the preparation of the quintessence of various substances which transcended the properties of the four elements. Through solution and multiple distillation, the substances were supposed to be separated and purified whereby their effectiveness was greatly increased. According to Rupescissa, this quintessence could be produced from minerals as well as from organic matter. He considered the preparation of alcohol through the distillation of wine as particularly important. This newly-won substance, liquid and flammable, united the contrary properties of the elements water and fire. Alcohol was moreover useful for preservation purposes and for the extraction of active ingredients from plants. The *Liber de consideratione quintae essentiae omnium rerum*, preserved in some hundred manuscripts, belongs to the most widespread alchemical works of the Middle Ages.

Western alchemy underwent an important expansion through its involvement with Christianity through several phases. It began with comparisons and analogies between the chemical process and the content of Christian doctrine. Alchemy thereby gained credibility and meaning, and confirmed Christian beliefs. A further stage involved the alchemical interpretation of Biblical passages, in which → Moses or Solomon were regarded as authorities, and Genesis, the Song of Solomon or the Apocalypse of St John were construed as alchemical allegories. This development began in the 14th century with Petrus Bonus and in the writings attributed to Thomas Aquinas (*Aurora consurgens*) and Arnau de Vilanova (*De secretis naturae, Exempla de arte philosophorum*). In these works the alchemical process was identified with the Passion and Resurrection of Christ and expounded in great detail. Later works like the *Buch der heiligen Dreifaltigkeit* continue these parallels between Christ and the Stone, which appears as an alchemical interpretation of the Christian Mass in the Hungarian Melchior Szebeni (*Processus sub forma missa*, before 1530). The close link with religion became an essential component of esoteric and theosophical alchemy in the 17th and 18th centuries.

The 15th century brought a further expansion of alchemy, evident in the growing number of manuscripts and the increasing use of vernacular languages. Latin still dominated, but works were translated into national languages and increasingly composed in the latter. The introduction of printing in the 15th century had actually not much impact, a fact that may be explicable by the persistence of secrecy concerning alchemical knowledge. Not until the 16th century did alchemical writings appear in print.

The focus of practical work was the alchemical process which was presented as a work of several stages in many and varied versions. The most frequently occurring numbers seven or twelve and details regarding the length of the process had more symbolic or astrological than practical significance. In principle any substance could serve as a starting point but metals were preferred and quicksilver or gold used frequently. According to the simplified principle of "Solve et caogula", the process began with the regression of the materials to their prime matter, which was supposed to be achieved through solution or combustion ("Solutio", "Calcinatio", "Putrefactio"). Next individual components had to be combined anew in several stages ("Coagulatio", "Coniunctio", "Fixatio"). The result was an improved substance, as a rule a precious metal. Changes of colouration corresponded to the individual stages, which passed through black ("Nigredo") through white ("Albedo") to red ("Rubedo"), using pictorial images as well as metaphors (raven, dragon, peacock, queen, king).

Even if the process never led to the desired goal, the work led to a continual growth of chemical knowledge through the countless experiments necessitating precise observation and notes. The vessels inherited from the Arabs were developed further, above all distillation aparatus. The alembic or aludel ("Cucurbit"), which served as a receiving vessel, was a broad full-bellied vessel made of clay or glass, later also of copper or iron. For distillation purposes, it acquired a helmet ("alembic") for collecting the distillate which was then conducted into a further vessel ("Rezipient", "Receptaculum") through a long, beak-shaped extension. This apparatus was gradually improved whereby the helmet was increased in surface area to assist cooling ("Rose Hat") or an arrangement for condensation ("Moor's Head"), before this was replaced by a cooling coil. Special distillation apparatus included retorts with a curved neck ("Pelican"), an arrangement with two reversionary tubes, permitting a continual circulation during distillation. An airtight ("hermetic") seal on the vessels by a special substance ("lutum sapientiae") prevented the escape of the distillate. Distillation required an even temperature for which one usually employed an air, water sand, or ash bath, but also sun beams, or the warmth produced by the fermentation of horse dung. The most important result of distillation was the extraction of alcohol from wine.

Another discovery was the preparation of alum from aluminous minerals, which was used for tanning leather and the blanching of wool before dyeing. Acids and alkalis were investigated and their properties thoroughly explored, leading to far-reaching improvements in pharmacy and metallurgy. It was first possible to separate gold and silver with the help of nitric acid. The most significant innovation of Western medieval alchemy was the preparation of gunpowder, already known in China.

Berthold Schwarz, a monk and gunsmith at Freiburg, first succeeded about 1370/75 in discovering the correct proportions for the explosive mixture of sulphur, salpetre and charcoal and using it in a weapon. This invention revolutionised weaponry for the next two hundred years. The production of canons and later firearms required a complete transformation in the equipment of armies, new military tactics and defensive fortifications. Chivalry lost its military significance, leading to major social changes.

The social and professional status of individual alchemists is difficult to establish owing to scant biographical data. However their circle must have been limited, considering the preconditions necessary for alchemy. These included literacy, proficiency in Latin, and access to manuscripts. Financial means were also necessary in order to acquire manuscripts, apparatus and chemicals, a room in which a laboratory could be set up, and a regular income to pursue the "Great Work" exclusively for months or even years. These preconditions were chiefly available at two locations: monasteries and princely courts.

There are biographical data for alchemists in both settings. Monks included Jean de Rocquetaillade, Ulmannus, the author of *Buch der heiligen Dreifaltigkeit*, Berthold Schwarz and perhaps the Latin Geber. Manuscripts and rooms were available and the monastic community provided board and lodging. Alchemists were also active at the medieval princely courts, and several princes were themselves alchemists. These include Friedrich I, Margrave of Brandenburg, Johann "the Alchemist", and Albrecht Achilles, but also Barbara von Cilli, the wife of Emperor Sigismund. It is debatable whether monarchs pursued alchemy as a result of philosophical and religious interests or with a view to riches. Alchemists first appear among the urban middle class in the course of the 15th century.

As alchemy spread, so did its criticism. This was directed less against its theoretical foundations,

which were hardly doubted, but rather against particular alchemists, who surfaced as "gold-makers" or deceived others with forged precious metals. The papal bull "Spondent quos non exhibent" (c. 1317) of Pope John XXII is one of the earliest bans, through which he possibly wished to restrict monastic alchemy. Over the next two hundred years bans followed from such princes as King Charles V of France (1380) and Kings Henry IV (1403/04) and Henry VI of England (1452), and from the cities of Venice (1488) and Nuremberg (1493). The town council of Nuremberg did not doubt alchemy itself but forbade its practice because people were deceived by it and injured by its practice. Many poets expressed criticism. In the *Divine Comedy* (1307-21) → Dante included the alchemists among the deceivers who must remain in the lowest circle of Hell and in Sebastian Brant's *Narrenschyff* (Ship of Fools, 1494), they appear as fools who deceive themselves. Brant quoted Aristotle as an authority who regarded the transmutation of metals as impossible. Neither bans nor criticism had any enduring effect.

The end of the Middle Ages represents a profound shift for alchemy as indeed for other sciences. The Renaissance interest in → Neoplatonism and → Hermetism had a positive influence on alchemy but there was a simultaneous but critical approach to traditional sciences. The work of → Agrippa von Nettesheim chiefly shows this. In his first great work *De occulta philosophia* (written 1510, revised and printed 1531) he advanced the doctrine that occult sciences such as alchemy → Astrology, Kabbalah [→ Jewish Influences] and → Number Symbolism could make an important contribution to knowledge of the world. But later he rejected all sciences, including alchemy, on account of their contradictions in his book *De incertitudine et vanitate scientiarum et artium.*

→ Paracelsus is a representative figure of this scientific upheaval. He adopted the Mercury-Sulphur doctrine of Arabic alchemy and complemented these principles with the principle of Salt, identified as the incombustible, non-volatile residue of the alchemical process. He distinguished between the "Alchemia transmutatoria", which he rejected and the "Alchemia medica" which he considered valid. He saw its real task as the preparation and application of medicine. In this process, "chemiatry" separated from alchemy and developed into pharmaceutical chemistry.

Other fields, previously part of alchemy, now became independent and practical sciences. These included the "Ars destillatoria", on which numerous printed books on distillation soon appeared.

Michael Schrick published the text *Nützliche Materie von mancherlay ausgeprannten Wässern* (1480). This was followed by the Strasbourg physician Hieronymus Brunschwig's *Liber de arte Distillandi de Compositis* and Philipp Ulstadt's distillation book *Coelum philosophorum* (1525), which foresook theoretical speculation despite its alchemical title.

One can observe a parallel development in books on pyrotechnics and mining and prospecting. They also omitted alchemical theories, limiting themselves to experiment and experience. Fundamental works in this respect were the books *De la pirotechnia* of Vannoccio Biringuccio (Venice 1540) and *Alchimi und Bergwerck* of Peter Kertzenmacher (1534). A complete compendium of chemistry and metallurgy was written by Georg Agricola in his posthumous work *De re metallica libri XII* (Basle 1556). This signalled the emergence of chemistry as an independent exact science. In 1597, the first chemistry textbook was published by Andreas Libavius, which still bore the title *Alchemia*, and in 1609 Markgrave Moritz of Hesse-Cassel established a "laboratorium chymicum publicum" at Marburg University, where the mathematician Johannes Hartmann taught the subject of "Chymiatrie".

Even if alchemy and chemistry separated from the 16th century onwards, medieval alchemy remained a vital tradition in numerous ways and formed the basis for the next three hundred years. The works written between the 12th and 15th centuries were distributed as manuscripts or as printed books, either as monographs or in collections such as the *Theatrum Chemicum* (1659-61), which comprised more than 200 texts. Medieval authors had an enduring influence and were frequently quoted in later works. The high estimate of medieval alchemy can be seen not least in the works of the 16th and 17th century being issued as those of legendary alchemists.

2. LITERATURE

The alchemical literature of the 12th to 15th centuries was largely written in Latin. It began with translations from Arabic, soon followed by independent monographs. An analogous process occurred two centuries later with translations from Latin into the vernacular languages. Vernacular language works ensued, often in collective volumes of manuscripts together with Latin texts. Latin was most important for the development of a professional vocabulary, as the vernacular adopted its words, concepts and translated terms. Individual survivals included words from the Greek (chem-

istry, elixir, theriac) or from the Arabic (alembic, amalgam).

Alchemical language is peculiar inasmuch as it has two forms of expression. Many prodedures in the experimental field were expressed in an objective and sober language, so making them comprehensible and easy to perform. These related to the special operations, substances and apparatus used in alchemical work. This discourse is scarcely distinguishable from the professional languages of other medieval sciences such as medicine or pharmacy. An arcane language prevails in other writings, with statements that are intentionally obscure and incomprehensible. Their use is paramount in theoretical and speculative alchemy but also in practice. The arcane language is typified by the polysemantic use of words like "water", which could simply mean water, but also an acid or quicksilver. An abundance of synonyms are also used for the same object, for instance, the Philosophers' Stone which has more than several dozen names. They extend from the names of substances (e.g. "Antimonium") to symbols ("Phoenix") and code names ("Rex regum", "Philosophical Gold").

The use of metaphors, personifications and allegories involving concepts and actions was particularly favoured. There were borrowings from the plant and animal world (dragon, wolf, serpent, rose, lily) and also from the correspondence of metals, planets and their deities, from ancient mythology and Christian symbolism. Texts in this arcane language often used an ecstatic tone, which approached the language of → mysticism. They were not only concerned with veiling alchemy and keeping its results secret. Whatever had to remain incomprehensible or meaningless to an uninitiated reader could give an expert in alchemy important information. The term "dragon" for quicksilver was not just a codename but also referred to the reactivity and toxicity of the metal.

The arcane language was also characterised by Number Symbolism, often expressed in geometrical forms. Every number and its corresponding form had a meaning. The number 1 (circle) embodied the Philosophers' Stone as the whole purpose of the Work. The number 2 signified polar opposites (male-female, solid-liquid). The favourite was number 3 (triangle) on account of its religious reference to the Trinity. This could stand for the fundamental Principles (Sulphur-Mercury-Salt), for the natural kingdoms (mineral-vegetable-animal), or for the progression of colours (black-white-red). The number 4 (square) stood for the four elements and their properties, the number 5 (pentagon) for the "Qunintessence" as an elaboration of the four elements. The number 7 signified the seven planets, the seven metals, or the seven stages of the Work. The phrase "squaring the circle" stems from this number symbolism.

A further characteristic of alchemical language is the use of signs for processes, substances, and apparatus. The oldest signs were the planetary symbols for gold and silver, followed by those for the other metals. Further signs developed as logograms or pictograms, made of letters and tironic notes. In contrast to modern usage, these signs were ambiguous as various signs could be used for specific concepts and the same signs did not always express the same content. There were more than 40 signs in use for quicksilver alone and over 30 for antimony, arsenic, gold, borax or *Weinstein* (tartar).

In terms of literary genres, medieval alchemy used recipes, prayers and riddles for shorter works, and tracts, allegories and didactic poems for longer works. The recipe was closely associated with the recipe literature of other sciences. Its title usually repeated the content in the form of a caption ("A recipe . . . to make"). The necessary ingredients often with their quantities are listed and the method of preparation is described briefly. The result is named at the end, followed by a prayer, formula, or exclamation ("Deo gratias"). Simple recipes were expanded into a description of the Work, its individual stages and observable changes of colour. They represent an attempt to describe a scientific event with some precision and resemble the tract.

The prayer was a special form of alchemical literature. It not only served to rebut charges of godlessness or heresy but showed the close connection between alchemy and the Christian faith. Most alchemists saw the collaboration of God as a precondition for the success of their work. Even riddles, often in rhyme, occur frequently in alchemy. The obscure statements of the arcane language, paraphrases or pictures provided sufficient material. It is probable that the cyphers using codenames, metaphors or secret scripts were understood as riddles.

Besides the recipe, the tract was the important genre of alchemical literature. It served the objective and discursive treatment of the theme but could also contain reflections and speculations. The simple treatise was accompanied by a letter containing a didactic conversation between two or more persons or giving answers to fictitious questions, a favourite device of scholastic philosophers.

Distinct from the tract, the allegory clothed alchemical theories or the course of the Work in a story which was understoood as a simile or para-ble. These stories often possessed the features of a tale and followed a similar pattern. They began with the death of a person or a couple (man and woman), who are then awakened through several stages to a new and better life.

A theme could also be handled in rhyme. Short and important statements were made more impressive through verse. Longer poems employed metric forms, even if the literary quality was often poor. The content of such a poem might be a synopsis of alchemical doctrines or a description of an alchemical process. The poetic form was particularly favoured in allegories, often fashioned as pictorial poems where verse and pictures accompanied each other.

While the illustration of Greek and Arabic manuscripts was limited to simple symbols and apparatus, the 14th century witnessed an increasingly elaborate illustration of alchemical writings. These images represented the practical work or the interior of a laboratory, a theme continued in painting from the 16th century onwards. They chiefly served to make the theory of alchemy and the Work more graphic. It was but a small step to transform the metaphors, personifications or allegories of the arcane language into images, reflecting the colourful phenomena of the alchemical Work.

To begin with, individual pictures had little connection with the text, but they developed further into pictorial sequences in which the alchemical process was reproduced in all its stages. Some examples are the poem *Sol und Luna,* and the prose text *Donum Dei. Sol und Luna* was a short German-language poem, probably dating from the 14th century and bound with the collective manuscript *Rosarium philosophorum* which was first printed in 1550. In its original form there were 78 verses and 20 pictures, which complemented one another. They tell the story of Sun and Moon as King and Queen who unite in a bath to form an Hermaphrodite, before they die and their soul leaves the body. After a heavenly dew has washed the corpse, the soul returns. A winged Hemaphrodite arises and the process repeats. S/he is reborn and finally appears as a crowned and enthroned royal couple.

The pictorial series *Donum Dei* was also composed around 1400. Despite many similarities with *Sol und Luna*, it is an independent work. Here again the pictures are the main focus while the text derives chiefly from quotations in ancient writings and simply forms the commentary. The process is represented in twelve stages, which occur in a glass flask and are additionally explained with flowers and colours. *Donum Dei* depicts the union of a

King and Queen, who are reborn after a phase of immolation and death.

The German-language didactic text *Splendor solis* was another favorite pictorial series composed of seven tracts with 20 pictures and longer text quotations. The author is named Salomon Trismosin about whom nothing certain is known. His traditional biography making him the teacher of Paracelsus is fictional. Most of the pictures have decorated borders displaying themes or concepts, for instance, alchemy is compared with "women's work" or "child's play" and appeared in 16th-century manuscripts as splendid folio miniatures. Meanwhile a picture sequence is interposed showing the alchemical Work passing through seven stages in the glass flask. Every stage is ruled by a planet and the pictures portray the character and professions of the "children" born under the corresponding planetary sign.

The breadth and literary variety of medieval alchemical literature is exemplified by four German-language works of the 15th century. The most remarkable work is the *Buch der heiligen Dreifaltigkeit*, which survives in numerous manuscripts, although it was never printed. The author was a Franciscan, who called himself a "virgin" and is named Ulmannus in several manuscripts. He wrote his book between 1410 and 1419 and dedicated it to Friedrich von Hohenzollern, later Margrave of Brandenburg, whom he probably met at the Council of Constance. He prepared a copy or an abridgement for Emperor Sigismund. The author possessed remarkably good chemical knowledge, perhaps from personal experience. The illustrated manuscripts show chemical vessels and furnaces. The *Buch der heiligen Dreifaltigkeit* offers an example of the Christ-Stone correspondence, represented in numerous pictures. The symbols of the Evangelists are used for the four elements; the Passion of Christ, his Resurrection and the Crowning of Mary are analogous to the alchemical Work. The book is also a religious document written in a passionate, evocative, and even ecstatic language where prose often gives way to verse. Ulmannus called his work a heavenly gift, that he wrote at God's command and which the Devil tried to hinder. He attributed incredible properties to the Philosophers' Stone: it is said to heal all diseases, give invisibility, and lend its owner the ability to float in the air and land again safely. Finally the book is related to prophetic and eschatological writings of the Reformation such as the *Reformatio Sigismundi*, which also indicates a relationship between the author and Emperor Sigismund. He clearly imagined that alchemy would produce the necessary financial and political resources to enable the Emperor to carry out a reform of Church and Empire.

The "Lamspring Figures" are among the great pictorial poems of the Middle Ages. The hitherto unidentified author probably lived in the second half of the 15th century in North Germany. His *Tractatus de lapide philosophorum* consists of 15 pictures explained in verse. The fundamental idea derives from Arabic alchemy, according to which the volatile components of a substance ("Spiritus" or "Anima") must be separated from the solids ("Corpus"), purified and then recombined as a new substance. Lamspring described this doctrine in two cycles. The first cycle consists of 10 pictures in which the separation of matter is portrayed by a pair of animals (fishes, lions, birds, wolf and dog, stag and unicorn) in a loose sequence. The crowned King and the fire-dwelling salamander represent the climax of this cycle. The last five pictures return to an allegory derived from the Arabic alchemist Alphidius. It describes how a father obtains for his son a guide who is to show him the whole world. Both climb a great mountain and from its peak contemplate Heaven and Earth. But the son yearns to return to his father, who consumes him in sheer joy. A divine shower of rain transforms the father first into water and then into earth, whence father and son arise anew. They have now become immortal and rule a great kingdom together with the guide. The final image resembles Christian representations of the Trinity. Lamspring's work became widely known through a printed Latin translation, published at Leiden in 1599, followed by further editions. The pictures can be found in several collections of the 17th century.

The cathedral dean and notary Johann Sternhals resident at Bamberg between 1459 and 1488 chose another literary form to present alchemical knowledge. His prose work *Ritterkrieg*, surviving as a manuscript and in printed editions (Erfurt 1595, Hamburg 1680), used a court case as the narrative frame for his tract, containing his alchemical experience over twenty years. In the trial, Gold ("Sol") appears before Mercury ("God and Judge") to accuse Iron as the "child of a whore" because it is of base descent. However, Iron can defend itself cleverly by proving that Gold is impure and listing many of its own advantages and achievements. Through the iron nails on the Cross, it had its own share in redemption. The Judge wants to pass no verdict but delegates the decision to the "Virgin Nature". But even she gives no metal preference, but admonishes both to modesty and harmony.

A more sober example is the manuscript didactic poem entitled *Der Stein der Weisen*, written by

Hans Folz, a Meistersinger resident in Nüremberg. Folz had acquired knowledge in many fields and repeats them in rhyme form as well as a plague regime and a balneological booklet. His poem on alchemy comprising 600 verses displays well-founded knowledge, but probably did not stem from personal experience. He appears to have studied specialist literature and quotes it extensively. The poem gives a survey of the theory and practice of alchemy, in which the various kinds of distillation and furnaces are described, even if the author considers one furnace and one vessel sufficient. The poem ends with directions for the preparation of the Philosophers' Stone.

Poetry as well as alchemical writings evidence the widespread and increasing interest in alchemy from the 14th century onwards. Already at the beginning of the 13th century there are occasional echoes in Wolfram von Eschenbach and Gottfried von Straßburg, although they indicate no precise knowledge of alchemy. The works of John Gower (1330-1408), William Langland (1332-1400) and Johann von Tepl (c. 1330-1414) contain brief references to alchemy, showing it to be a controversial part of contemporary knowledge.

Alchemy appears extensively in the continuation of *Roman de la Rose* (c. 1275/80), of Jean Chopinel (Jean de Meun). In his reflections on the relationship between art and nature, the poet also dilates on alchemy, saying that it is a real science only pursued properly by a few masters. He compares the transmutation of metals with the production of glass, in which potash produced by burning fern was used.

The role of alchemy is even more important in the work of the court poet Heinrich von Mügeln (c. 1320-1372). In his poem *Der meide kranz* (c. 1355) he describes a contest of the liberal arts in which "Alchemia" enters. She describes her special abilities, namely the production of colours and the transmutation of metals. However the Emperor-Judge does not give her the desired prize with the justification that he has seldom met a rich alchemist. Heinrich von Mügeln also deals with alchemy in one of his shorter poems, and quotes Geber as his authority.

A critical satire occurs in Geoffrey Chaucer's *Canterbury Tales* (c. 1480). In "The Canon's Yeoman's Tale" the pilgrims meet a canon and his servant. While the cleric remains silent and soon leaves the group, the servant speaks at length about their alchemical activities. He says he has worked seven years for his master, but the unsuccessful experiments have cost him his health and fortune. Alchemists can be recognised by their shabby clothing and the "pungent brimstone smell".

He readily reveals the results of the Work and their treatment. In a second Tale he reports how a canon won over a cleric to alchemy through lies and deception and ruined him. At the end he refers to the statements of ancient alchemists, who stress that the "Great Work" may only be performed by divine grace.

Jean Chopinel, Heinrich von Mügeln and Geoffrey Chaucer describe alchemy so precisely, that they were soon themselves quoted as alchemical authorities, while their verse – disconnected from the original work – enters specialist alchemical literature.

The works of medieval alchemy start to appear in print with few exceptions from the 16th century on, several as independent monographs but most as part of multi-volume collections such as *Theatrum chemicum* (6 vols, Strasbourg 1659-61), Jean-Jacques Mangets *Bibliotheca chemica curiosa* (2 vols., Geneva 1702) or *Eröffnete Geheimnisse des Steins der Weisen oder Schatzkammer der Alchymie* (Hamburg 1718). The pictures were often published separately. The two best-known works are → Michael Maier's *Atalanta fugiens* (Oppenheim 1618) and Daniel Stoltzius von Stoltzenberg's *Chymisches Lustgärtlein* (Frankfurt 1624). In both collections the pictures are explained by new verses, and in Maier's case by melodies and longer commentaries. By these means alchemical literature survived the Middle Ages and influenced authors from the 16th to the 18th century and also poets from the age of Baroque to the present.

Lit.: H. Buntz, "Die europäische Alchemie vom 13. bis zum 18. Jahrhundert", in: E.E. Ploss, R. Roosen-Runge, H. Schipperges, H. Buntz, *Alchimia: Ideologie und Technologie*, München: Moos, 1970, 119-210 ♦ B.D. Haage, *Alchemie im Mittelalter: Ideen und Bilder – von Zosimos bis Paracelsus*, Munich: Artemis & Winkler, 1996 ♦ C. Kren, *Alchemy in Europe: A Guide to Research*, New York: Garland, 1990 ♦ E.O. von Lippmann, *Entstehung und Ausbreitung der Alchemie*, Bd. 1 und 2, Berlin: Springer, 1919 and 1931, vol. 3, ed. Richard von Lippmann, Weinheim/Bergstr.: Verlag Chemie, 1954 ♦ C. Priesner and Karin Figala (eds.), *Alchemie: Lexikon einer hermetischen Wissenschaft*, Munich: C.H. Beck, 1998 ♦ J. Telle, *Sol und Luna: Literatur- und alchemiegeschichtliche Studien zu dem altdeutschen Bildgedicht*, Hürtgenwald: Guido Pressler, 1980 ♦ J. Telle (ed.), *Rosarium philosophorum*, 2 vols., Weinheim: Verlag Chemie, 1992 ♦ L. Thorndike, *A History of Magic and Experimental Science*, vols. 1-2 *(The First Thirteen Centuries)*, vols. 3-4 *(Fourteenth and Fifteenth Century)*, New York and London: University Press, 1923 and 1934.

HERWIG BUNTZ

Alchemy IV: 16th-18th Century

1. ALCHEMICAL THEORY AND PRACTICE
2. FROM ALCHEMY TO CHEMISTRY
3. SPIRITUAL ALCHEMY 4. ALCHEMICAL
LITERATURE

Not enough is yet known to write a complete history of alchemy in the early modern period. What can be said is that there was, at that time, an explosion of interest in the subject marked by the publication of an enormous number of alchemical texts. A relatively marginal pursuit in the Middle Ages, alchemy became more and more, over the 17th and 18th centuries, a mainstream occupation, influencing many scientists and philosophers as well as artists, poets, mystics, freemasons, theosophers, and spiritualists. Although scholars generally agree that alchemists contributed to the origins of early modern science, more work needs to be done to establish the precise nature of their contributions.

Up to the beginning of the 18th century the terms "alchemy" and "chemistry" were used interchangeably to describe activities ranging from practical laboratory experiments to mystical and psychological speculation. During the 18th century, however, the two words increasingly assumed their modern meaning in terms of two developments: first, metallic transmutation and gold-making (*chrysopoeia*) were identified as the distinctive goals of alchemy and dismissed by many as fraudulent activities, while "chemistry" was defined in broader terms as the science of analyzing and synthesizing substances; second, the mystical and spiritual aspects of alchemy flourished as never before, but they became increasingly separated from practical laboratory work. A clear distinction consequently emerged between gold-making and theosophical alchemy, on the one hand, and the science of chemistry on the other.

1. ALCHEMICAL THEORY AND PRACTICE

The traditional view that alchemy gave way to chemistry once occult, vitalistic theories of matter were replaced by the "mechanical philosophy" has been qualified by scholars who emphasize the existence and variety of both corpuscular and vitalistic theories throughout the medieval and early modern period and the difficulty of making a clear-cut distinction between the two. Like their ancient and medieval predecessors early modern alchemists accepted transmutation as an observable fact of life, and a diversity of alchemical schools arose with a wide variety of theories derived from Greek,

Arabic, and medieval sources to explain why it occurs and how the process could be duplicated in the laboratory. Although much more work on the theories of individual alchemists needs to be done before a complete picture of early modern alchemy will emerge, it is clear that from the 16th to the 18th centuries alchemists had at their disposal an array of theories that ranged from a view of matter as inanimate corpuscles moved by external forces to various vitalistic corpuscular theories in which non-material forces played decisive roles. Aristotle provided alchemists with a number of models to explain transmutation. The notion that matter was composed of the four elements – earth, air, fire, and water – convinced some alchemists that transmutation involved varying the proportions of the constituent elements in a base metal to emulate the proportions in gold. This could be accomplished through a potent transmuting agent known as the philosopher's stone. Aristotle expressed the same theory in another way. Each substance consisted of prime matter and a specific "form" that determined the characteristics of the substance, including the proportions of the elements it contained. Changing one substance into another on this model involved reducing a substance to prime matter and converting this into gold by means of the philosopher's stone.

Early modern alchemists also accepted the theory of Arabic alchemists from the school of Jabir ibn Hayyan (b. 721/2) that metals and minerals were formed from an "ideal" sulfur and mercury, sulfur accounting for flammability and mercury for the fusibility and volatility of substances. This theory originated in Aristotle's suggestion that the immediate constituents of minerals and metals were two "exhalations" formed below the surface of the earth, an "earthy smoke", which was later identified with sulfur, and a "watery vapor", identified with mercury (*Meterologica*, III, 6 378a). The 13th century author writing under the name Geber and mistakenly identified with Jabir viewed sulfur and mercury as complex, inanimate corpuscles, which united to produce different minerals and metals. Geber's corpuscular theory was also indebted to the notion of "least parts" in Aristotle's *Physics and Meterologica*, an idea developed in scholastic physics with the concept of *minima naturalia*. In his *Summa perfectionis* Geber claimed that the philosopher's stone was composed of "philosophical mercury", the tiny corpuscles of which were able to penetrate the pores of a base metal, transmuting it into gold. Diverse alchemical schools developed to explain the nature, preparation, and use of this mercury. The so-called "Mercurialist" school was the most popular of these during the 17th century and led → Boyle and → Newton, among others, to undertake experiments with mercury that may have contributed to their ill health. Geber's corpuscular theory influenced the later theories of Andreas Libavius (1540-1616), Daniel Sennert (1572-1637), and Gaston DuClo (c. 1630-?).

During the 16th century the sulfur/mercury theory was modified by → Paracelsus (1493/4-1541), who added a third element, salt. The salt, sulfur, mercury theory became characteristic of Paracelsians [→ Paracelsianism], who identified the tripartite nature of substances with the body, spirit, and soul and the Trinity. The vitalism and religious element inherent in Paracelsianism was not a novel aspect of alchemy. The tendency to view chemical processes in organic terms was characteristic of alchemy from its origin, but biological models became more prevalent from the Renaissance onwards as stoic, hermetic, neoplatonic, and kabbalistic influences became increasingly dominant. According to the Stoics each material entity contained its own specific "pneuma" or "seminal principle" (*logos spermatikos*), which molded formless matter in predictable ways. The idea that metals grow from seminal elements, or seeds, was reinforced by the neoplatonic concept of "seminal reasons" (*rationes seminales*), which contained blue-prints, so to speak, for constructing specific bodies from elementary matter. Augustine had posited that seminal principles existed in matter and germinated to produce different species of corporeal beings (*De Genesi ad litteram*). Paracelsians were particularly receptive to the idea that active forces, variously described as *archei* (from the Greek *archeus*, beginning, origin, first cause) or *semina* existed in bodies. The Danish Paracelsian physician Petrus Severinus and the Belgian Paracelsian → J.B. van Helmont accepted this idea, and their work influenced the corpuscular philosophy of Pierre Gassendi and Robert Boyle. This realization has led historians to appreciate the vitalistic elements persisting in 17th century "mechanical", "atomistic", or "corpuscular" philosophy. A notable example is the acknowlegment of the way Newton's alchemical studies contributed vitalistic elements to his concept of the forces of attraction, cohesion, and repulsion between material particles.

The obvious discrepancies between these various alchemical theories about exactly what and how many elements constituted matter was compounded by those like Etienne de Clave, Thomas Willis and Nicholas Lemery who postulated the existence of five elements: salt, sulfur, mercury, phlegm or water, and earth. Far from dismaying

most alchemists, however, this apparent confusion fit nicely with the ancient and basic alchemical doctrine of έν το παν, "One in all and all in one", derived from the neoplatonic conviction that every created substance developed from one divine source. This was the message of the *Emerald Table* (*Tabula Smaragdina*), a series of oracular precepts of unknown date attributed to the legendary founder of alchemy in the West, Hermes Trismegistus: 'As all things were produced by the one word of one Being, so all things were produced from this one thing by adaptation'. This text had enormous influence in the medieval and early modern period. The phrase "one in all" and "all in one" became an alchemical mantra. → Elias Ashmole's (1619-1692) heraldic motto was "ex uno omnia".

The practical operations necessary to produce the philosopher's stone and transmute base metal into gold were as varied as the theories upon which they were based. The enigmatic and secret nature of alchemical writing compounded the difficulty of knowing exactly what ingredients, procedures, and methods early modern alchemists employed. Although at odds about what to transmute and how to do it, they generally agreed that their work must follow a sequence of color changes from black to white to red, with occasional colors in between. The final red stage symbolized the advent of royalty, "the young king", or the philosopher's stone. Alchemists disagreed, however, about the nature and number of chemical processes necessary to produce these color changes. The most optimistic claimed the stone was made from one substance, in one vessel, in one operation, but this was a minority view. Salomon Trismosin describes seven processes in his *Splendor Solis* (16th century). George Ripley expanded this to twelve in his *Compound of Alchemy* (1591). In his *Dictionnaire Mytho-Hermétique* (1758), Dom → Antoine-Joseph Pernety associates each process with a sign of the zodiac.

2. FROM ALCHEMY TO CHEMISTRY

The traditional view that chemistry experienced a "postponed scientific revolution" (Butterfield) until the 18th century when Antoine-Laurent Lavoisier (1743-1794) overthrew the phlogiston theory has been questioned by historians who stress the evolutionary nature of developments in chemistry during the early modern period. According to this latter view, the transition from alchemy to chemistry extended over the course of two and a half centuries and occurred in two broad stages. During the first stage (c. 1500-1700) alchemists/chemists made considerable progress in identifying and classifying substances and reactions. In addition to making gold alchemists became increasingly interested in discovering medicines and commercial and manufacturing processes. During the second stage (c. 1700-1800), chemists like Herman Boerhaave (1668-1738) and Georg Ernst Stahl (1659-1734) distinguished between the chemical and physical properties of matter, focusing attention on the chemical molecule and its composition. Lavoisier built on the work of these predecessors. Nevertheless, his work was revolutionary inasmuch as he established new concepts (e.g. oxidation, vaporization) and new quantitative methods to determine chemical composition, all of which fragmented the scientific community.

During the 16th century the tradition of practical, laboratory alchemy can be found in the many works dealing with mining, metallurgy, smelting, glass making, distilling, dyeing, pharmacology, and other arts and crafts (H. Brunschwig, *Liber de arte distillandi*, 1500; G. Agricola, *De re metallica*, 1556; V. Biringuccio, *Pirotechnia*, 1540; P. Kertzenmacher, *Alchimia*, 1534). Andreas Libavius's *Alchemia* (1597) emerged from this tradition and has been described as the first systematic textbook of chemistry. These works are particularly useful for their detailed descriptions of the preparation and analysis of chemical substances and for illustrations of the variety of equipment used: alembics flasks, crucibles, baths, burners, bellows, and various kinds of furnaces producing different degrees of heat. Alchemical genre painting (H. Weiditz, D. Teniers, J. Steen, Rembrandt, A. van Ostade, G. Metsu) gives a clear indication of the array of apparatus in alchemical laboratories.

Somewhat akin to these works were treatises devoted to the so-called "secrets of nature", which were extremely popular in the 16th and 17th centuries. These offered procedures for such diverse things as transmuting metals, producing exotic plants and animals through grafting and cross-breeding, cutting, conserving, and cooking food, staving off baldness, eliminating wrinkles, and engendering beautiful children (J.B. della Porta, → C. Agrippa, A. Mizaldus, J.J. Wecker). Although these works described many processes of dubious worth, they were important inasmuch as their publication provided readers with information that could be tested.

Paracelsus was an important figure in the transition of alchemy to chemistry. Paracelsus and his followers broadened the scope of alchemy to encompass investigations of the composition, structure, properties, and reactions of matter. They were particularly interested in chemical medicines. As

experimenters, text-book writers, and systematizers, Paracelsians such as Daniel Sennert (1572-1637), Michael Sendigovius (1566-1636), and J.B. van Helmont (1579-1644) had a significant impact on medicine, pharmacy, and chemistry. Their interest in medicine led to the establishment of a school of "iatrochemisty", or medical chemistry that became an accepted part of the curriculum of medical schools during the 17th century.

While the idea that alchemy could shape and improve nature for human benefit had been an aspect of medieval alchemy, it gained greater prominence in the early modern period. From the second half of the 16th century the theme of restoration and renewal was an important component in the thought of an emerging number of Paracelsians and Pansophists, who combined alchemy, → magic, and the Kabbalah with Renaissance Hermetism. Characteristic of this genre were the *Rosicrucian Manifestos* (*Fama Fraternitatis*, 1614; *Confessio Fraternitatis*, 1615), which mix hermetic, neoplatonic, and alchemical themes into a potent proclamation of the dawning of a new age. While highly critical of alchemists whose only goal is gold-making, they emphasized the role of alchemy in prolonging life and health and employed alchemical symbolism to describe the spiritual and political regeneration of society. The conviction that scientific knowledge could restore man and the world to something approaching prelapsarian perfection is a common theme in the 17th century. → Francis Bacon (1561-1626) made this claim in *The Advancement of Learning*. In *The New Atlantis*, he envisioned a vast and well equipped scientific complex called "Solomon's House", which was dedicated to the investigation of nature for 'the relief of man's estate'. Bacon's ideas were championed by a number of English and continental millenarians and reformers who practiced alchemy. By emphasizing the crucial role played by human beings in improving and transforming nature, early modern alchemists contributed to the Enlightenment idea of scientific progress.

17th century alchemists/chemists such as J.R. Glauber (1604-70), Robert Boyle (1627-1691), J.J. Becher (1635-82), J.F. Helvetius (1625-1709), Hermann Boerhaave (1668-1738), and G.E. Stahl (1659-1734) made significant progress in understanding chemical reactions through experimentation and quantitative analysis. Although they continued to attempt transmutation, their work contributed to the growing fissure between alchemy and chemistry and illustrated the practical contributions alchemists made to manufacturing and commerce. Becher's career is instructive. He was one of many alchemists to enjoy the patronage of rulers and nobles (such as → Rudolf II, Elizabeth I, Henry IV, Louis XIII, and Landgraf Moritz of Hessen Kassel), who employed alchemists to shore up their power both symbolically and financially. Appointed by Leopold I as "Imperial Commercial Advisor", Becher proposed a variety of money-making schemes involving the manufacture of porcelain and chemicals, silk and wool weaving, wine and glass making, and the production of medicines. He also designed laboratories for testing alchemical claims and processes. A major factor in the transition of alchemy to chemistry was this kind of testing and the accumulation of negative evidence. Boerhaave, for example, performed an experiment in which he heated mercury at 100 degrees Fahrenheit continuously for fifteen years and six months. At the end of this period he rejected the sulfur/mercury theory, concluding that it was neither possible to transform ordinary mercury into the mercury of the philosophers by heat alone nor to fix mercury into anything approaching gold and silver. As more refined laboratory techniques and apparatus were developed in the 18th century, the testing of alchemical claims continued and they were increasingly found to be dead ends.

While there were notable advances in chemistry during the first half of the 18th century in terms of mineral analysis, metallurgical techniques, and the isolation of new substances such as phosphorus, there was still no clear idea of exactly what the elementary constituents of matter were. In investigating this question, the phenomenon of combustion received considerable attention. Alchemists had generally explained the transformations produced by heating and burning as a separation of bodies into the four elements of Aristotle, the three Paracelsian principles, or the five elements of Willis and others. Van Helmont was the first to challenge this assumption. He was followed by Boyle. Both discovered that different substances were produced during combustion and that many of these did not preexist in the material burnt. These observations were not correctly interpreted until Lavoisier. For the intervening hundred years the phlogiston theory suggested by Becher (*Physica subterranea*, 1669) and elaborated by his pupil Stahl provided the most popular explanation for combustion. Stahl maintained that when anything burned, phlogiston ("burning" in Greek) was released. The original substance could be restored if the lost phlogiston was recombined with the burnt residue. Stahl had the actual order of events backwards. What he described as a loss of phlogiston was actually a gain in oxygen, while the addition of phlo-

giston was in reality a loss of oxygen. Although mistaken, Stahl's suggested a plausible theory linking together a large number of facts, which suggested new experiments and led to new discoveries. These culminated in Lavoisier's experiments with mercury and his discovery of the role of oxygen in combustion. Lavoisier's work was made possible by the earlier discoveries of Joseph Black (1728-1799), Henry Cavendish (1731-1810), and Joseph Priestly (1733-1804), but he synthesized their findings into coherent theories that put chemistry on a firm quantitative basis. However, it was not until the elaboration of atomic theory in the following century by John Dalton (1766-1844) that alchemy and chemistry reached a final parting of the ways. The realization that each element had a specific atomic weight reflecting its structure and ability to react opened the way for modern theoretical chemistry.

Despite the denunciation of alchemy by such figures as Fontenelle (*Histoire de l'Académie des Sciences*, année 1722), Etienne-Francois Geoffroy (*Des supercheries concernant la pierre philosophale*, 1722), and Chevalier de Jaucourt ("Pierre philosophale", *Encyclopédie*, 1765), enthusiasm for alchemy continued in the 18th century. Reports of successful transmutation were given by such people as by James Price (1752-1783), a fellow of the Royal Society, and the respected German theologian J.S. Semler (1725-1791). Alchemy was studied and practiced especially in Germany, where it was closely connected to some forms of → Pietism and to the resurgence of Paracelsianism and → Rosicrucianism. Alchemical imagery and symbolism (combined with elements of → Freemasonry, → Hermeticism, Kabbalah, and pietistic Christianity) played a central role in the philosophy and rituals of the *Gold- und Rosenkreuz*, whose members were expected to engage in laboratory work in the hope of finding the quintessence or vital essence of the universe. Such a goal was clearly at odds with the rational, experimental, and essentially secular chemistry practiced by Lavoisier and his colleagues. This Rosicrucian order attracted a strong following throughout the German-speaking world as well as in Poland and Russia. It reached the height of its influence in the Prussia of King Frederick William II (1786-97), who was a member of the order, but by the end of the century it had all but disappeared. Leading figures of the late German Enlightenment such as the Marburg Professor of medicine F.J.W. Schröder (1733-1778), the anatomist S.T. von Sömmering (1755-1830), and his friend the naturalist Georg Forster (1754-1794) were drawn to alchemy and Rosicrucianism, although Sömmering and Foster eventually became disenchanted with both. → Goethe's "Pflantzen-lehre" drew partly on alchemical ideas. During his pietistic period (1768/69) he read Paracelsus, Basil Valentine, J.B. van Helmont, Eirenaeus Philalethes (George Starkey), and A.J. Kirchweger's *Aurea catena Homeri* (1723). Among the more flamboy-ant alchemists of the period were the Count of → Saint-Germain (1701-1784), Giuseppe Balsamo, better known as → Cagliostro (1743-1795), and his teacher, the enigmatic kabbalist, magician, and alchemist, → Samuel Jacob Chayyim Falk (c. 1710-1782). General Charles R. Rainsford (1728-1809), a member of the Royal Society who was involved with Falk, left hundreds of texts in five languages dealing with alchemy, Kabbalah, magic, medicine, and → astrology. Ebenezer Sibly (1751-99), who received a medical degree from Aberdeen Medical College, read Newton, Priestly, Lavoisier, Aristotle, → Hermes Trismegistus, → Khunrath, and Paracel-sus and attempted to combine them in *A Key to Physic and the Occult Sciences* (1792).

Although Alain Mothu has demonstrated that Paracelsian naturalism appealed to some libertine authors of clandestine literature in their fight against religion, for the most part the resurgence of alchemy in the 18th century constituted a backlash against aspects of the Enlightenment, especially the emphasis on reason to the exclusion of human spir-itual and emotional needs. It was a backlash that appealed increasingly to philosophers and theoso-phers rather than scientists. While the attempt to transmute base metal and produce the elixir remained legitimate laboratory objectives for some people, alchemy became increasingly detached from practical chemistry and more closely associ-ated with spiritual, theosophical, and philosophi-cal currents.

3. SPIRITUAL ALCHEMY

The tendency to interpret physical change in spiritual terms was part of alchemy from its incep-tion in the ancient world. Beginning in the Middle Ages and well into the 18th century parallels were drawn between alchemical processes and the mys-teries of Christianity (see e.g. George Ripley in the prologue to his *The Compound of Alchemy*: 'O Unity in the substance, and Trinity in the God-head . . . As thou didst make all things out of one chaos, so let me be skilled to evolve our microcosm out of one substance in its three aspects of Magne-sia, Sulphur, and Mercury'). The preparation of the philosopher's stone was described in terms of death and resurrection and equated with the death and resurrection of Christ; the constituents of the stone,

for example, the salt, sulfur, and mercury of the Paracelsians, were identified with spirit, soul, and body as well as the Trinity. The religious nature of many alchemical texts makes it difficult at times to distinguish those that describe actual laboratory processes from those employing alchemical lan-guage for purely spiritual ends. Nevertheless, there was a clear tendency among "spiritual" alchemists to distinguish themselves from those they disparag-ingly described as "puffers" or "sooty empirics". The English physician, alchemist, and Rosicrucian sympathizer → Robert Fludd (1574-1637) dis-missed the work of practical alchemists as "chy-mia vulgaris". Only their imagery and symbolism kept these alchemists in touch with the fire and the furnace.

The upsurge in spiritual alchemy coincided with the breakdown of religious unity during the Refor-mation. Alchemical symbolism provided an ideal framework for individuals seeking new schemes of salvation both for themselves and the world at large. The books written by → Jacob Boehme illus-trate how well alchemical symbolism served spiri-tual and theosophical ends. Boehme's writings fuse alchemical, Paracelsian, hermetic, and kabbalistic themes into a theosophical exhortation to spiritual rebirth. His collected works were republished six times between 1677 and 1769, and they influenced 18th and 19th century Romantics, philosophers, spiritualists, and theosophers.

Much of the spiritual side of western alchemy was rooted in the notion that the world was a bat-tle ground, in which the forces of evil (matter) bat-tled the forces of good (spirit). This idea came from a variety of sources, neoplatonic, kabbalistic, and Christian. Alchemists were sometimes presented as quasi-Gods in their laboratories, as saviors redeeming base matter, equating the philosopher's stone with Christ and identifying themselves with both (see e.g. Agrippa's discussion of Geber in *De Occ. Phil.* III, 36). One of the most daring appro-priations of Christian symbolism appears in the alchemical mass devised by Nicholas Melchior of Hermanstadt (*Theatrum Chemicum*, vol. 3). Abbot → Johannes Trithemius (1462-1516), → Valentin Weigel (1533-1588), A. von Francken-berg (1593-1652), → John Pordage (1608-1681), → Thomas Vaughan (1621-65), Angelus Silesius (1624-1677), Q. Kuhlmann (1651-1689), and → J.G. Gichtel (1638-1710) were among the 17th century authors who employed alchemical symbol-ism to describe spiritual transformations.

Although many alchemists were members of the clergy, their ventures into theology affronted a number of orthodox Catholics and Protestants.

There was a potential conflict between alchemy and mainstream Christianity that arose from the hermetic elements inherent in alchemy. Many alchemists believed that man not only has the power to become divine himself, but because he is a microcosm representative of the macrocosm, or world at large, he has the power to redeem matter as well. Not all alchemists embraced such extreme and heretical views. → Michael Maier (1568-1622), for example, was a committed Lutheran who believed the philosopher's stone was a gift of faith. But alchemy and alchemical symbolism could and did have unorthodox, even heretical implications. For example, the Catholic librarian and skeptic Gabriel Naudé (1600-53) criticized alchemy for both its impiety and obscurity. The Minim Marin Mersenne (1588-1648) and his friend Father Pierre Gassendi (1592-1655) accused alchemists of proposing a "chemical" religion in opposition to true Christianity. In 1625 the Sorbonne condemned Khunrath's *Amphitheatrum sapientiae* on the same basis, and the Inquisition initiated proceedings against J.B. van Helmont for attributing the healing powers of holy relics to magnetic virtues, akin to the lodestone and weapon-salve. Luther was one of the few Churchmen to praise alchemy both for its practical uses and its verification of Christian doctrine, but the bitter condemnation of Andreas Osiander (1498-1552) for his 'new alchemistic theology' reveals the hostile view of alchemy among many Lutherans. In 1690/91 the Lutheran theologian E.D. Colberg wrote a diatribe against the fanatical and unorthodox beliefs of those he derisively labeled "Alchymisterey" (*Das Platonisch-Hermetische Christenthum*).

Spiritual alchemy proliferated in the 18th century. Alchemical themes and symbols were integrated into Masonic and Roscrucian rituals, among such groups as the → Asiatic Brethren, the Lodge of the Amis Réunis, the → Illuminés d'Avignon, and various Rosicrucian orders in Germany. In *L'Étoile flamboyante* (1766) Baron de Tschoudy claimed that the goal of masonry and alchemy was identical. Among the most widely read works of spiritual alchemy were the collected works of Jakob Boehme, which were republished in Germany and England; J.P. Maul, *Medicina theologia, chymico- irenica et christiano-cabbalistica* (1713); the anonymous *Die edelgeborne Jungfrau Alchymia* (1730) of J.C. Creilung; → G. von Welling's *Opus mago-cabalisticum et theosophicum* (1735); A.J. Kirchweger, *Aurea Catena Homeri* (1723), which was translated into Frech in 1772 and reissued by the *Gold- und Rosenkreuz* as *Annulus Pla-*

tonis oder physicaklisch-chymische Erklärung der Natur (1781) and the *Compaß der Weisen* (1779). Scholars have noted the influence of alchemical ideas on → Romanticism, 18th-century philosophies of nature and history, and a wide variety of theosophical societies and organizations. → Novalis (1772-1801) read extensively in alchemical as well as theosophical literature. J.G. Herder's (1774-1803) philosophy of history was influenced by hermetic ideas. The vision of a golden age of social equality, political justice, and moral integrity characterizing the thought of Johann Albrecht Bengel (1687-1752) and his pupil → Friedrich Christoph Oetinger (1702-82) was fostered by alchemical expectations of universal restoration and renewal. Their work, along with that of Boehme, had a decisive influence on → F.W.J. Schelling's (1775-1854) "Naturphilosophie" as well as on G.W.F. Hegel's (1770-1831) philosophy. Hegel's friend → Franz van Baader (1765-1841), known as "Böhme redivivus", also utilized alchemical themes in his eclectic theosophy. → Martinez de Pasqually (1727-1774) founded the freemasonry rite of the → Elus-Coëns, which combined elements of alchemy and theosophy. He introduced → Louis Claude de Saint-Martin (1743-68) to the alchemical and theosophical idea of the God-man, who works in concert with God to restore humanity to its prelapsarian perfection. John L. Brooke has documented the widespread interest in alchemy in 18th century America and the influence alchemical ideas had in the later development of Mormon cosmology and theology.

4. ALCHEMICAL LITERATURE

The demand for alchemical literature reached its height during the early modern period and is reflected in the publication of numerous individual tracts and substantial collections of alchemical treatises such as *De alchemia opuscula* (1550), published by Cyriacus Jakob; G. Gratarolo, *Verae Alchemiae . . .* (1561); *Theatrum Chemicum* (1659-1661), published by L. Zetzner; the *Musaeum Hermeticum Reformatum et Amplificatum* (1678); Elias Ashmole, *Theatrum Chemicum Britannicum* (1652); J.J. Manget, *Bibliotheca Chemica Curiosa* (1702); Friedrich Roth-Scholtz, *Deutsches Theatrum Chemicum* (1728), and F.J.W. Schröder, *Neue Alcymistiche Bibliothek* (1771-1774) and *Neue Sammlung der Bibliothek für die höhere Naturwissenschaft und Chemie* (1775-1780). The Benedictine Antoine Joseph Pernety (1716-1801) published a key to alchemical symbolism in his *Dictionnaire Mytho-Hermétique* (1758). With *Les Fables Eygptiennes et Grecques dévoilées et réduites au même principle* he followed in the tradition of G.A Augurelli (1454-c. 1537), Salomon Trismosin (16th century), and Michel Maier (1568-1622), interpreting Greek and Egyptian myths in terms of operative alchemy. Alchemy was so popular in the early modern period that a new genre of literature emerged, the "transmutation history", which provided detailed eye-witness accounts of successful transmutations. Robert Boyle witnessed one such event and was afterwards so convinced of the possibility of transmutation that he was instrumental in obtaining the repeal of the English law against Multipliers (Henry IV, 1404) in 1689.

Reflecting its dual nature as both a laboratory science and a spiritual quest, alchemical literature appeared in a variety of forms ranging from straight forward descriptions of laboratory procedures to poems, autobiographies, dialogues, reports of alchemical meetings, catechisms, romances, parables, visions, prayers, and even the occasional play emphasizing its spiritual aspects (Knorr von Rosenroth's alchemical masque *Conjugium Phoebi et Palladis* [1677]) or ridiculing it as fraudulent (Ben Jonson's *The Alchemist*). Before the early modern period most alchemical texts were in Latin and restricted to the educated. The growth of vernacular alchemical literature made it accessible to a broader segment of society and helps to explain the proliferation of texts.

One of the major ways historians traditionally distinguished between alchemy and chemistry was on the basis of language. Alchemical texts were identified by their obscure, metaphorical style, chemical texts by their plain descriptions of chemical processes. However, more recent discussions have shown that it is not always possible to make such a sharp distinction. Many alchemical authors employed secret codes, anagrams, paradoxes, and allegories and deliberately confused readers by leaving out important words, including misleading information, employing exotic synonyms for the materials and processes discussed, and breaking off or changing the subject at crucial points to resume it in a seemingly unrelated place. Nonetheless, esoteric texts of this nature have been successfully decoded to reveal descriptions of actual chemical processes, and even in those instances when laboratory chemistry is clearly the subject of discussion alchemists tended to hide their message and even themselves under a veil of inscrutability. The works of Basil Valentine are a case in point. Whoever wrote these treatises hid under the pseudonym "mighty" or "valiant king" and tried to pass himself off as a monk living in the 15th century rather than someone (probably Johann Thölde) living in

the 17th. The use of pseudonyms and claims to belong to an earlier age are typical of alchemical authors. Both practices underline the claim that alchemy embodied a powerful secret wisdom originating in a divine revelation granted solely to the spiritually worthy. The texts attributed to Basil Valentine contain a mix of spiritual admonitions and obscure allegorical statements together with good laboratory directions for preparing such things as metallic antimony, hydrochloric acid, solutions of caustic alkali, acetates of lead and copper, gold fulminate, and many other salts. The author was also interested in the medicinal uses of compounds of antimony and mercury. Secrecy and obscurity is therefore not the hallmark of alchemical texts. Even Robert Boyle condoned secrecy in certain cases and purposely obscured reports of some of his alchemical experiments.

The propensity of alchemists to conceal their message was partly due to prudence. In an age before patents they were anxious to protect their chemical secrets and thus enhance their worth in the eyes of potential patrons. Alchemists were also cautious about expressing themselves too freely lest they be held hostage by avaricious men. Alchemical literature is filled with stories of imprisoned alchemists or those disguised to elude potential captors.

In addition to trying to protect themselves, many alchemists expressed themselves in ways that are obscure to the modern mind because they subscribed to what has been labeled "an emblematic worldview". They viewed the universe holistically: everything was related through a system of symbolic → correspondences linking the heavens to human beings, animals, plants, minerals, and metals. A prime example of this way of thinking appears in → John Dee's *Monas Hieroglyphica*. Dee considered this symbol a talisman embodying all the powers of the universe. By contemplating it, men would simultaneously absorb these powers and experience a spiritual transformation. For Dee, as for many alchemists, symbols offer direct access to hidden knowledge and a way to harness this knowledge for human advantage. In alchemy, a picture is literally worth a thousand words, which explains the popularity of alchemical emblem books, such as *Aurora consurgens* (15th century), *Splendor solis* (16th century), *Rosarium philosophorum* (1550), *Mutus liber* (1702), and the works of Michael Maier (1568-1622) and J.D. Mylius (1585-1628).

Alchemical emblem books reveal a worldview in which nature is alive, and human beings supply the model by which everything is measured. The creation of the philosopher's stone is envisioned as a birth resulting from the sexual union of male and female "seeds", depicted in the form of a King and Queen. Alchemical vessels are "wombs", inside of which the "Royal Child" develops. The chemical wedding and sexual union of the King and Queen are therefore central motifs in many alchemical texts. The beautiful sequence of illustrations in the *Splendor Solis* (16th century) depicts the drama of this carefully orchestrated birth. The conception and birth of the philosopher's stone is not, however, a straightforward affair. The chemical wedding requires the sacrifice, death, and rebirth of the couple, who are an extraordinary pair, for not only are they husband and wife, they are also mother and son, brother and sister, or father and daughter. This apparent endorsement of incest underscores the great alchemical truth that every created thing emanates from a single, divine soul-substance. This truth was illustrated by one of the most popular alchemical symbols, the *ouroboros*, or tail-eating serpent.

In the course of the 17th and 18th century the kind of symbolism characteristic of an emblematic worldview gradually gave way to less emotive and metaphorical descriptions of laboratory reactions for a variety of reasons. The great interest in alchemy encouraged the publication of an increasing number of textbooks in which laboratory operations were classified and substances and alchemical terms more clearly defined (for example, J. Beguin, *Tyrocinium chymicum* [1612]; N. Le Febvre, *Traicté de la Chymie* [1660]; C. Glaser, *Traité de la Chymie* [1663]; N. Lemery, *Cours de Chimie* [1675]. The defense of esotericism and secrecy became less useful and profitable as new career opportunities developed for court alchemists, textbook writers, university teachers, private tutors, public lecturers, and purveyors of chemical medicines, all of whom had an economic incentive to make their knowledge public. A new rhetoric of clarity and openness arose, and even though it was not always practiced, it reinforced the idea that knowledge of chemistry should be available to the educated public.

Lit.: S.G. Allen and J. Hubbs, "Outrunning Atalanta: Feminine Destiny in Alchemical Transmutation", *Signs* 6 (1980), 210-229 ♦ *Ambix* (The Journal for the Society for the History of Alchemy and Chemistry), published since 1937 ♦ W.B. Ashworth, "Natural history and the emblematic world view", in: D.C. Lindberg and R.S. Westman (eds.), *Reappraisals of the Scientific Revolution*, Cambridge: Cambridge University Press, 1990, 303-332 ♦ E. Benz, *The Mystical Sources of German Romantic Philosophy*, Allison Park: Pickwick Publications, 1983 [1968] ♦ F. Bonardel, *Philosophie de l'Alchimie: Grand Oeuvre et modernité*, Paris: Presses Universitaires de France, 1993 ♦ J.L. Brooke, *The Refiner's Fire: The Making of Mormon Cosmology, 1644-1844*, Cambridge: Cambridge University Press, 1994 ♦ *Cauda Pavonis* (The Hermetic Text Society Newsletter), published from 1982 to 2002 ♦ H. Butterfield, *The Origins of Modern Science, 1300-1800*, London: Bell, 1949 ♦ A. Clericuzio, "From van Helmont to Boyle: A Study of the Transmission of Helmontian Chemical and Medical Theories in Seventeenth-Century England", *British Journal of the History of Science* 26 (1993), 303-334 ♦ idem, "A Redefinition of Boyle's Chemistry and Corpuscular Philosophy", *Annals of Science* 47 (1990), 561-89 ♦ idem, "Robert Boyle and the English Helmontians", in: Z.R.W.M. von Martels (ed.), *Alchemy Revisited*, Leiden: E.J. Brill, 1990, 192-199 ♦ A. Clericuzio & P. Rattansi (eds.), *Alchemy and Chemistry in the 16th and 17th Centuries*, Dordrecht: Kluwer, 1994 ♦ N.H. Clulee, *John Dee's Natural Philosophy: Between Science and Religion*, London: Routledge & Kegan Paul, 1988 ♦ A.P. Coudert, *Alchemy: The Philosopher's Stone*, London: Wildwood House, 1980 ♦ *Chrysopoeia* (Journal de la Société d'Étude de l'Histoire de l'Alchimie), published since 1987 ♦ M. Crosland, "The Chemical Revolution of the 18th Century and the Eclipse of Alchemy in the Age of Enlightenment", in: von Martels, *Alchemy Revisited*, Leiden: Brill, 1990, 67-77 ♦ A.G. Debus, *The English Paracelsians*, London: Oldbourne Press, 1965 ♦ idem, *The Chemical Philosophy: Paracelsian Science and Medicine in the Sixteenth and Seventeenth Centuries*, New York: Science History Publications, 1977 ♦ idem, *Chemistry, Alchemy and the New Philosophy, 1550-1700: Studies in the History of Science and Medicine*, London: Variorum Reprints, 1987 ♦ idem, *The French Paracelsians*, Cambridge: Cambridge University Press, 1991 ♦ B.J.T. Dobbs, *The Foundations of Newton's Alchemy: or, "The Hunting of the Green Lyon"*, Cambridge: Cambridge University Press, 1975 ♦ idem, *The Janus Face of Genius: The Role of Alchemy in Newton's Thought*, Cambridge: Cambridge University Press, 1991 ♦ A. Donovan, "The Chemical Revolution: Essays in Reinterpretation", *Osiris* 4 (1988) ♦ R. Edighoffer, *Rose-Croix et société idéale selon Johann Valentin Andreae*, I-II, Neuilly-sur-Seine: Arma Artis, 1982-1987 ♦ A. Faivre, *Mystiques, theosophes et illuminés au siècle des Lumieres*, Hildesheim: G. Olms, 1976 ♦ idem, *Toison d'or et alchimie*, Milan: Archè, 1990 ♦ idem, *Theosophy, Imagination, Tradition: Studies in Western Esotericism*, New York: SUNY Press, 2000 ♦ K. Figala, "Newton as Alchemist", *History of Science* 15 (1977), 102-37 ♦ eadem, "Die exakte Alchemie von Isaac Newton: Seine 'gesetzmässige' Interpretation der Alchemie, dargestellt am Beispiel einiger ihn beeinflussender Autoren", *Verhandlungen der naturforschenden Gesellschaft in Basel* 94 (1984), 157-228 ♦ H. Gebelein, *Alchemie*, München: Eugen Diederichs Verlag, 1991 ♦ J. Godwin, *The Theosophical Enlightenment* (SUNY series in Western esoteric traditions), Albany: SUNY Press, 1994 ♦ J.V. Golinski, "Chemistry in the Scientific Revolution: Problems of Language and Communication", in: Lindberg & Westman, *Reappraisals of the Scientific Revolution*, 367-396 ♦ D. Goltz, "Alchemie und Aufklarung", *Medizin-historisches Journal* 7 (1972), 31-48 ♦ F. Grenier (ed.), *Aspects de la tradition alchimique au XVIIe siècle*, Paris: SEHA-Archè, 1998 ♦ O. Hannaway, *The Chemists and the Word: The Didactic Origin of Chemistry*, Baltimore: The Johns Hopkins University Press, 1975 ♦ Rudolf Hirsh, "The Invention of Printing and the Diffusion of Alchemical and Chemical Knowledge", *Chymia* 3 (1950), 115-41 ♦ E.J. Holmyard, *Alchemy*, London: Penguin, 1968 ♦ C.H. Josten, *Elias Ashmole (1617-1692)*, Oxford: Clarendon Press, 1966 ♦ idem, "A Translation of John Dee's *Monas Hieroglyphica* (Antwerp, 1654) with an introduction and annotations", *Ambix* 12 (1964), 84-221 ♦ D. Kahn & S. Matton (eds.), *Alchimie: Art, histoire et mythes. Actes du 1er colloque international de la Société d'Étude de l'Histoire de l'Alchimie*, Paris: Société d'Étude de l'Histoire de l'Alchimie, 1995 ♦ D. Kahn, *Hermès Trismégiste: La Table d'Emeraude et sa tradition alchimique*, Paris: Les Belles Lettres, 1994 ♦ E.F. Keller, *Reflections on Gender and Science*, New Haven: Yale University Press, 1985 ♦ S.T. Linden, "Alchemy and Eschatology in Seventeenth-Century Poetry", *Ambix* 31 (1984), 102-124 ♦ C. Lüthy, J.E. Murdoch, W.R. Newman (eds.), *Late Medieval and Early Modern Corpuscular Matter Theories*, Leiden: E.J. Brill, 2001 ♦ C. McIntosh, *The Rose Cross and the Age of Reason: Eighteenth-Century Rosicrucianism in Central Europe and its Relationship to the Enlightenment*, Leiden: E.J. Brill, 1992 ♦ G.A. Magee, *Hegel and the Hermetic Tradition*, Ithaca: Cornell University Press, 2001 ♦ S. Matton, "Alchimie et stoicisme: à propos de récentes recherches", *Chrysopoeia* 5 (1992-1995), 5-144 ♦ Z.R.W.M. von Martels (ed.), *Alchemy Revisited*, Leiden: E.J. Brill, 1990 ♦ C. Meinel (ed.), *Die Alchemie in der europaischen Kultur- und Wissenschaftsgeschichte*, Wiesbaden: Kom-mission bei O. Harrassowitz, 1986 ♦ C. Merchant, *The Death of Nature: Women, Ecology, and the Scientific Revolution*, San Francisco: Harper & Row, 1979 ♦ B. Moran, *The Alchemical World of the German Court: Occult Philosophy and Chemical Medi-cine in the Circle of Moritz of Hessen (1572-1632)*, Stuttgart: Franz Steiner Verlag, 1991 ♦ A. Mothu, "Une théosophie matérialiste clandestine au siècle des Lumières: les *Essais de quelques idées sur Dieu*", *Chrysopoeia* 5 (1992-1995), 751-798 ♦ W.R. Newman, "The Alchemical Sources of Robert Boyle's Corpuscular Philosophy", *Annals of Science* 53 (1996), 567-85 ♦ idem, "Alchemy, Domination, and Gender", in: Noretta Koertge (ed.), *A House Built on Sand: Exposing Postmodernist Myths About Science*, Oxford: Oxford University Press, 1998, 216-226 ♦ idem, *Gehennical Fire: The Lives of George Starkey, an American Alchemist in the Scientific Revolution*, Cambridge, MA: Harvard University Press, 1994 ♦ W.R. Newman and L.M. Principe, "Alchemy vs. Chemistry: The Etymological Origins of a Historiographic Mistake", *Early Science and Medicine* 3 (1998), 32-65 ♦ W. Pagel, *Paracelsus: An Introduction to Philosophical Medicine in the Era of the Renaissance*, Basel: Karger, 1983 ♦ idem, *Joan Baptista Van Helmont: Reformer of Science and Medicine*, Cam-

bridge: Cambridge University Press, 1982 ♦ R. Patai, *The Jewish Alchemists*, Princeton: Princeton University Press, 1994 ♦ C.E. Perrin, "The Chemical Revolution", in: R.C. Olbyt, G.N. Cantor, J.R.R. Christie and M.J.S. Hodge (eds.), *Companion to the History of Modern Science*, London: Routledge, 1990, 264-277 ♦ L.M. Principe, *The Aspiring Adept: Robert Boyle and his Alchemical Quest*, Princeton, NJ: Princeton University Press, 1998 ♦ idem, "Diversity in Alchemy: The Case of Gaston 'Claveus' DuClo, a Scholastic Mercurialist Chrysopoeian", in: A.G. Debus and M.T. Walton (eds.), *Reading the Book of Nature: The Other Side of the Scientific Revolution*, Sixteenth Century Essays & Studies, vol. 41, Kirksville: Thomas Jefferson University Press, 1998 ♦ L.M. Principe and W.R. Newman, "Some Problems with the Historiography of Alchemy", in: William R. Newman and Anthony Grafton (eds.), *Secrets of Nature: Astrology and Alchemy in Early Modern Europe*, Cambridge, MA: MIT Press, 2001, 385-434 ♦ J. Read, *Prelude to Chemistry*, Cambridge, MA: MIT Press, 1966 (1st ed., 1936) ♦ J. Ruska, *Tabula smaragdina: Ein Beitrag zur Geschichte der hermetischen Literatur*, Heidelberg: Carl Winter, 1926 ♦ P.H. Smith, *The Business of Alchemy: Science and Culture in the Holy Roman Empire*, Princeton: Princeton University Press, 1994 ♦ J. Telle, *Rosarium Philosophorum: Ein alchemisches Florilegium des Spätmittelalters*, Weinheim: VCH Verlag, 1992 ♦ J. Van Lennep, *Alchimie: Contribution à l'histoire de l'art alchimique*, Bruxelles: Crédit Commercial de Belgique, 1985 ♦ A. Versluis, "Alchemy and Christian Theosophic Literature", in: A. Faivre and W.J. Hanegraaff (eds.), *Western Esotericism and the Science of Religion* (Gnostica 2), Leuven: Peeters, 1998, 131-144 ♦ Klaus Vondung, "Millenarianism, Hermeticism, and the Search for a Universal Science", in: S.A. McKnight (ed.), *Science, Pseudo-Science, and Utopianism in Early Modern Thought*, Columbia: University of Missouri Press, 1992, 118-140 ♦ R.S. Westfall, "Newton and Alchemy", in: B. Vickers (ed.), *Occult and Scientific Mentalities in the Renaissance*, Cambridge: Cambridge University Press, 1984, 315-335.

ALLISON P. COUDERT

Alchemy V: 19th-20th Century

1. SURVIVALS INTO THE 19TH CENTURY
2. EMERGENCE OF THE CONCEPT OF "SPIRITUAL ALCHEMY" 3. THE LATE-19TH CENTURY REVIVAL 4. THE 20TH CENTURY

1. SURVIVALS INTO THE 19TH CENTURY

The decline of alchemy, already underway in the 18th century, reached its low point in the 19th, as testified by the miniscule number of treatises published throughout the latter period. Several factors explain this. The scientific revolution of the end of the 18th century had definitively separated chemistry from alchemy, to which it denied any scientific validity. Alchemical treatises were consequently given no serious consideration. Secondly, the end of the 18th century saw the death of several figures prominent in alchemy: Touzay-Duchanteau († 1788), → Etteilla (=Jean-Baptiste Alliette, 1738-1791), → Cagliostro (Giuseppe Balsamo, 1743-1795), Johann Daniel Müller (ps. Elias Artista, 1716-after 1786), → Dom A.-J. Pernety (1716-1796), J.-L. Salverte de Toux († 1797), Ebenezer Sibly (1751-1799), etc. General Charles Rainsford († 1809), Marie-Daniel Bourrée de Corberon (1748-1810), and → Francis Barrett († ca. 1810/15?) did not survive much longer. Typically, after a leader dies, the members of his group lose their enthusiasm for their object of study – in this case, practical alchemy. The dispersion of the members of the → Illuminés d'Avignon after the death of Pernety is a perfect example.

With the exception of a few isolated "adepts", most of whom published nothing in their lifetime, alchemy's survival at least up to the 1890s depended on its integration within larger bodies of doctrine. Around 1760, → Freemasonry had incorporated alchemical symbols and teachings into some of its high degrees. Rosicrucian currents [→ Rosicrucianism] (in the broad sense), from ∙ Michael Maier to the Gold- und Rosenkreuz, had always been closely related to alchemy. The theosophic current that started with → Jacob Boehme contained the seeds of a "spiritual" alchemy that was destined to play a major role in Western esoteric traditions; but with such diversity of conceptions that one should speak rather of "spiritual alchemies". Lastly, the current of → Naturphilosophie, limited to Germany, included elements and reflections of an alchemical nature.

During the transitional period (from the 19th to the 20th century), one short item among the events recorded in the press raised quite a stir. It was the announcement, in 1796, in the journal Reichsanzeiger (published in Gotha), of a secret society (the "Hermetische Gesellschaft" [→ Hermeticism and Hermetic Societies]) entirely devoted to the study of alchemical practice. The Hermetische Gesellschaft encouraged the readers to communicate with it, and among themselves, about the results of their alchemical experiments. The journal received many responses, so much so, that in 1799 both founders of the Hermetische Gesellschaft (Karl Arnold Kortum [1745-1824] and Friedrich Bährens [1765-1831]) withdrew from the Reichsanzeiger and created their own periodical, the Hermetisches Journal. Apparently, only two issues were published, in 1799 and 1802 respectively.

Notwithstanding, Kortum et Bährens remained very active, keeping up a lengthy correspondence with many people. They even granted diplomas, one of them to the theosopher and alchemist → Karl Von Eckartshausen, who had approached the Hermetische Gesellschaft in 1799. Kortum left the Society and was replaced in 1805 by a certain L.F. von Sternhayn, about whom little is known. Henceforth, the activities of the Hermetische Gesellschaft took on a more discreet character, but they seem to have continued up to 1810.

Apart from very general treatments such as → Barrett's The Magus (1801), the 19th century opened with Louis Gassot's publication in 1803 of La Philosophie Céleste (Bordeaux, An XI). He writes there of Unity, God, analogy, and alchemy in practical terms, also calling it "natural Philosophy", resulting in an interesting and original summa marked by borrowings from theosophy [→ Christian theosophy]. In England, The Lives of the Alchymistical Philosophers appeared anonymously in 1818. It is generally attributed to Barrett, though according to Francis King, John P. Kellerman (1779-18?) was probably the author.

A French alchemist, Cyliani, published Hermès dévoilé in 1832: a very short text written in romantic style. The anonymous author presents himself as an operative alchemist who attained the Great Work in 1831 'after spending 37 years at it', and states definitively 'that there are two ways, the dry way and the wet way' (see below, a propos Fulcanelli). If he himself followed the wet way, it was 'by preference' and 'by duty', although he was familiar with the dry way. In the 1960s, Bernard Husson revealed an unpublished manuscript (Récréations hermétiques, written after 1815) preserved in the Chevreul Collection (Paris, Musée d'Histoire Naturelle), which was 'very likely the most important source of Hermès dévoilé'.

In general, those who worked at alchemy and wrote about it were reluctant to offer the fruits of their labor for publication, with the result that several treatises of this period are known only in manuscript form (no census of them exists). One such is L'alchymie du Maçon (The mason's alchemy) by François-Nicolas Noël (1761-18?), dated 1813, of which Jean-Pierre Laurant writes that it is the work 'of an entire life of reflection, or the contribution of a group under the single name of Noël'. Other reasons, however, may have caused it to remain unpublished, along with the rest of Noël's work which includes the manuscripts Géométrie du Maçon (The mason's [plane] geometry), Physique du Maçon (The mason's physics), and Stéréométrie du Maçon (The mason's solid geometry).

The same case obtains with the *Compendium Hermeticum* (Hermetic compendium) by the theosopher Friedrich Herbort (1764-1833), who signs it with his initiatic name *Theodore a Silva*. This remained in manuscript until 1988. It belongs at the junction of several influences: theosophy (→ Saint-Martin was an important discovery in Herbort's life), Rosicrucianism (the society that Herbort founded in 1812, *Les Pélerins de Salem* [The pilgrims of Salem], had both masonic and Rosicrucian roots), Christian kabbalah [→ Jewish Influences III] and → mysticism (as a good theosopher, Herbort regarded the Bible as the authoritative Book). Herbort was a disciple of → Eckartshausen – himself the author of an alchemical treatise, *Chimische Versuche* (Regensburg 1801), and of a *Katechismus der Höheren Chemie*, published posthumously in 1819 – and very close to → Johann Friedrich von Meyer (1772-1849), with whom he corresponded for many years. Von Meyer himself left a small alchemical manuscript dated 1801, discovered and published by Jacques Fabry in 1988, which is in fact an exposition of the doctrine of his own master, Louis Schmid – of whom nothing further is known.

Another manuscript, dated Amiens, 1832 and now in the Biblioteca dei Lincei, Rome, is *Les arcanes ou secrets de la philosophie hermétique dévoilé . . . revu et corrigé par Lenain* (The arcana, or secrets of the Hermetic philosophy unveiled . . . revised and corrected by Lenain). Lazare Républicain Lenain (1793-ca. 1874) was also the author of *La Science Cabalistique* (Amiens 1823) and of a *Hommage à la Vierge Marie* (Homage to the Virgin Mary, Amiens, 1874).

The last important treatise of practical alchemy from the earlier 19th century was the work of Louis-Paul-François Cambriel (1764–ca. 1850), published in 1843 in the form of a *Cours de philosophie hermétique ou d'alchimie en dix-neuf leçons* (Course of Hermetic or alchemical philosophy in 19 lessons). Cambriel examines the sculptures and bas-reliefs of Notre-Dame Cathedral in Paris, which he says represent 'as clearly as possible all the work and the whole product or result of the Philosopher's stone'. In this, he was the successor of the alchemist Esprit Gobineau de Montluisant, the 17th century author of *Explications très curieuses des énigmes de Notre-Dame de Paris* (Very interesting explanations of the enigmas of Notre Dame of Paris).

2. EMERGENCE OF THE CONCEPT OF "SPIRITUAL ALCHEMY"

At mid-century, two works appeared almost simultaneously which would strongly influence the whole Western esoteric current. The first was *A Suggestive Inquiry into the Hermetic Mystery* (1850) by Mary Ann Atwood née South (1817-1910), daughter of Thomas South (ca. 1785-ca. 1855). Father and daughter, as joint authors, recall the main traits of alchemical history and develop their own vision, which is purely spiritual and greatly influenced by Boehme. They state that 'the Hermetic Philosophy is a process of experimentation into the Universal Spirit through man'. The method of experimentation, discreetly hinted at in Atwood's book and confirmed from other sources, was in fact the Mesmeric trance [→ Animal Magnetism]. Some additional documents, preserved by Atwood's friend Isabelle de Steiger (1836-1927), were incorporated into the second edition (1918), edited by Walter Leslie Wilmshurst (1867-1939).

The second seminal work was *Remarks upon Alchemy and the Alchemists . . .* (1857) by Ethan Allen Hitchcock (1798-1870). General Hitchcock was a graduate of West Point and a professional army officer until 1855, when he retired to devote himself to writing (though he returned to service for the Civil War and became President Lincoln's military advisor). He wrote that the previous year he had come across an old alchemical volume in a New York bookshop. It was a revelation to him: he continued to collect alchemical books and manuscripts, ancient and modern, often ordering them from London. He quickly became aware of modern European works, citing Hermann Kopp's *Geschichte der Chemie* (History of chemistry, 4 vols., Braunschweig 1843-1847), Louis Figuier's *L'Alchimie et les alchimistes* (Alchemy and the alchemists, Paris 1854), and the 2nd edition of Grove's *Correlation of Physical Forces* (London 1855). Hitchcock stated his theory briefly thus: 'My proposition is, that the *subject* of Alchemy was *Man*; while the *object* was the perfection of Man'.

The path opened by Atwood and Hitchcock had a powerful impact on the esotericism of the end of the 19th and beginning of the 20th century. The key to alchemy that they offered accorded with the Theosophical and Spiritualist [→ Spiritualism] doctrines so popular at this time. → A.E. Waite discussed it, cautiously at first, then in 1926 declared that the hypothesis was invalid. It entered the milieu of the → Theosophical Society through Dr. Alexander Wilder (1823-1908), who early on discovered Hitchcock's works on alchemy and → Swedenborg. Wilder was mostly responsible for writing the preface 'Beyond the Veil' for → H.P. Blavatsky's *Isis Unveiled* (1877), which mentions the alchemists. The theory also influenced the Viennese psychiatrist Herbert Silberer (1882-1922).

3. THE LATE 19TH-CENTURY REVIVAL

Alchemy revived at the end of the 19th century, most of all in France. Theoretical or spiritual alchemy played an important part in the groups founded by → Papus (Gérard Encausse, 1865-1916), but among his associates only → Stanislas de Guaïta seems to have practiced it. In the *fin-de-siècle* period, the man who most answered to the traditional image of the alchemist was Albert Poisson (1865?-1894). He abandoned his medical studies at quite a late stage in order to pursue alchemical research, and worked in the laboratories of the Faculty of Medicine in Paris. He devoted his leisure to seeking out alchemical books and manuscripts (of which some reappeared years later in the collection of Lionel Hauser), experimentation, writing, and editing ancient texts (→ Ramon Llull, → Albertus Magnus, → Roger Bacon, → Arnau de Vilanova, and → Nicolas Flamel, whose legend Poisson faithfully believed). By the end of his short life, Poisson had laid the foundation for a vast encyclopedia of alchemy, divided into several volumes of which four appeared. Beside *Cinq traités d'alchimie* (Five treatises on alchemy, 1893) and *Histoire de l'alchimie au XIVème siècle* (History of alchemy in the 14th century, 1893), his conceptions were most clearly explained in *Théories et symboles des alchimistes* (Theories and symbols of the alchemists, 1891). He writes: 'The matter of the Great Work was Gold and Silver, united to Mercury and prepared in a special fashion'. These materials, being respectively a Sulfur, a Mercury, and a Salt, prepared 'according to certain procedures', were placed in a glass vessel or Athanor. Then, Poisson explains, the cooking could begin; the matter's color changed in conformity with the length of cooking, and the appearance of red indicated the end of the experiment. One had then to 'communicate' to the matter thus obtained a greater 'power of transmutation', through an operation called 'fermentation'. The result, in theory, was the Philosopher's Stone.

This idea that gold and silver must form the prime matter, or components of it, was taken over by Poisson's successor and in a way his disciple, François Jollivet-Castelot (1874-1937) in his first major work, *Comment on devient alchimiste* (How to become an alchemist, 1897). This book, strongly influenced by contemporary occultism [→ occult / occultism], defended some fantastic theses, e.g. that alchemy 'came from the Temples of Chaldaean-Egyptian antiquity, and before that from the initiatic Colleges of Atlantis, of Lemuria, and of the Aryans (which takes us more than 40.000 years

into the past!)'. Jollivet-Castelot's exposition essentially followed Poisson's work, but included ideas from Tiffereau and did not disdain the scientific (or pseudo-scientific) discoveries of its time. Jollivet-Castelot worked tirelessly from the end of the 19th century until the 1930s, and edited several journals originating from a 'Société alchimique Française' (SAF) which he founded on Poisson's principles.

In Venice, Eduardo Frosine founded a "Società Alchemica Italiana" in 1909 on the model of the SAF. In London, the Alchemical Society was founded in 1912 'for the Study of the Works and theories of the Alchemists in all their aspects, philosophical, historical and scientific, and of all matters relating thereto'. Its presidents were John Ferguson and Herbert Stanley Redgrove (1887-1943). A.E. Waite, Isabel de Steiger, and J.B. Craven were among the vice-presidents, and published several articles in its *Journal of the Alchemical Society*; but both journal and society ceased all activity after two years, in 1914.

Some of the members of the → Hermetic Order of the Golden Dawn showed a genuine interest in alchemy. The Reverend William Alexander Ayton (1816-1908) joined the Order together with his wife in 1888; he was also a Freemason (1866) and a member of the → Hermetic Brotherhood of Luxor. A passionate devotee of alchemy, which he had practiced since about the 1850s, he was continually pursuing alchemical books and manuscripts, some of which he translated. Ayton corresponded with Frederick Leigh Gardner (1857-ca. 1930), author of a *Catalogue raisonné of Rosicrucian Books* (1903), and with Julius Kohn (ca. 1850-?), an Austrian émigré with whom Ayton exchanged or lent manuscripts, both for his personal use and for including elements in the Golden Dawn rituals.

Apart from W.A. Ayton, → A.E. Waite stands out as the other major representative of the Golden Dawn who took an interest in alchemy. He made many translations and editions of ancient texts (→ B. Valentine, → Paracelsus, E. Kelley, etc.), the publication of which was paid for by another devotee of alchemy, Lord Stafford. Waite's *The Secret Tradition in Alchemy* (1926) is still in print. An interest in alchemy is also evident in the works of the poet → William B. Yeats, likewise a member of the Golden Dawn (see e.g. *Rosa alchemica*, 1897).

In the 1920s, another Golden Dawn member, E.J. Langford Garstin (ca. 1893-1955), developed the principles of a spiritual alchemy in two books, *Theurgy* (1930) and *The Secret Fire* (1932), while in Italy → Julius Evola also expounded an exclusively spiritual conception of alchemy in his *La*

Tradizione Ermetica (1931), under the dual influence of → Arturo Reghini (1878-1946) and → René Guénon.

4. THE 20TH CENTURY

After World War I, alchemy experienced a resurgence, especially in the practical field, first in Europe then in the United States. An idiosyncratic English laboratory alchemist was Archibald Cockren (ca. 1880?-after 1960), a medical practitioner and author of *Alchemy Rediscovered and Restored* (1940). In this work he describes his alchemical procedures, including the making of 'philosophic gold', in semi-scientific terms, but without disclosing vital details such as the nature of the prime matter.

In France, the publication in 1926 of *Le Mystère des cathédrales* (The mystery of the cathedrals) first made known the name of → Fulcanelli, though to a fairly small public, since the book appeared in only 300 copies. The title announces the main theme: that the Gothic cathedrals of the Middle Ages were the vehicles for a Hermetic or overtly alchemical message, carved in stone by anonymous artisans. Fulcanelli treats the cathedrals of Paris and Amiens, and also two buildings in Bourges: the Palais Jacques-Coeur and the Hôtel Lallemand. Following Cyliani, he describes the two ways leading to the Great Work: one wet, also called 'long', which uses the 'vase of the art', requires 'uninterrupted work for 12 to 18 months', and starts from 'prepared natural gold, dissolved in philosophic mercury, which is then cooked in the glass vessel'. Fulcanelli writes that this is the way most often described in the treatises, and the most noble because of the rich materials it employs. The second way, called 'dry', is reduced to 'a single matter, a single vessel, a single furnace', in which one uses a crucible. It is considerably shorter, lasting one week, according to Basil Valentine, Salomon Trismosin, Philalethes, and Cyliani, among others.

Fulcanelli's disciple, → Eugène Canseliet (1899-1982), discovered alchemy in his adolescence through Cyliani's treatise. He supposedly met Fulcanelli in Marseille in 1915, and between 1921 and 1928 rewrote the texts given him for publication by Fulcanelli – or, as is widely believed, by the alchemist and artist Jean Julien Champagne (1877-1932). After the latter's death, Canseliet began to write independently, first in the form of articles for journals (1934 onwards), then his first book, *Deux logis alchimiques* (1945), which he began around 1935. For him, the alchemist responds to a divine call or 'vocation'. The Philosopher's Stone, crown of the alchemist's labors, is itself a 'gift of God'

(probably a reminiscence of the 15th century treatise *Donum Dei* attributed to George Aurach). Till the end of his life, Canseliet considered it his mission to maintain the tradition of practical alchemy. This he did with conviction, giving many interviews and devoting much time to answering innumerable enquiries, to the detriment of his own work and alchemical advancement.

Canseliet was friends with other alchemists, including André Savoret (1898-1977), author of an attempt to define alchemy (*Qu'est-ce que l'alchimie?* [What is alchemy?] Paris 1948) which is regarded today as the most concise introduction; José Gifreda, known as 'Magus Gifreda', doctor and engineer, who died in his native Barcelona in 1980, leaving a superb library; and, around 1948/1950, René Alleau and Bernard Husson († 1997).

In Germany, the writer, poet, and translator Baron Alexander von Bernus (1880-1965) discovered alchemy at the beginning of the 1910s. In 1912 he met → Rudolf Steiner. During World War I, through → Gustav Meyrink's agency, Bernus came into possession of a chest of alchemical texts including Christian August Becker's *Der Geheime Weingeist der Adepten (Spiritus Vini Lulliani s. Philosophici) und seine Medizinische Anwendung für Arzte und Chemiker* (The secret wine-spirit of the adepts . . . and its medicinal usage for doctors and chemists, Mühlhausen 1865). Already a rare book when Bernus discovered it, this guided him to an understanding of the mystery of Salt. In 1921, after several years of studying ancient treatises, he founded the Soluna laboratories and gradually developed about 30 tinctures. In 1936 he published the first edition of *Alchymie und Heilkunst* (Alchemy and the healing art), dedicated to the medicinal applications of alchemy. Other alchemists visited Bernus at Donaumünster, including Henri Hunwald (1908-1961) and René Alleau. The French writer Michel Butor, in *Portrait de l'artiste en jeune singe* (Portrait of the artist as a young monkey, Paris 1967), has written of his travels in Germany on the eve of World War II, and of his visit to Bernus, to whom he gave several books including those of Fulcanelli.

Following Canseliet, René Alleau (b. 1917) promoted alchemy within the Surrealist movement, to which he remained attached from 1946 to the present. In 1952 he gave lectures on alchemy and alchemical texts at the Geographical Society in Paris, attended first by André Breton (1896-1966) alone, then by many of the surrealists, brought there by Breton, who became his most assiduous auditors. In 1953 Alleau published an inspired work in the Fulcanellian tradition: *Aspects de l'alchimie traditionnelle* (Aspects of traditional alchemy). There he defended the idea of an alchemical theory that has remained essentially the same from antiquity to the present. The techniques of encoding and, in general, all the procedures of phonetic kabbalah, were intended to be incomprehensible except to those alchemists who possessed the keys. For Alleau, 'it is beyond doubt that the alchemical manipulations used material supports for an inner ascesis'. And he adds that 'the "mystico-moral" interpretations familiar from authors such as → Eliphas Lévi, → Péladan, → Guaïta, and Oswald Wirth' make no sense, because 'if one wants to reconstitute the mental chessboard of alchemical thought, one must admit . . . that this thought corresponds to an autonomous discipline, and that outside its framework no interpretation of its symbols can have any coherent sense'.

A very different path was followed by Armand Barbault (b. 1906), brother of the astrologer André Barbault and himself an astrologer as well. He was attracted as early as 1948 to plant alchemy – the elixir of life drawn from plants – although he was familiar with the principles of a more traditional alchemy that used only minerals and metals. Twenty years later he published the result of his experiments in *L'or du millième matin* (The gold of the thousandth morning, 1969). Barbault's plant elixir has been used successfully in the treatment of various illnesses and infections.

In the United States, especially from the 1940s onwards, Orval Graves († 1996), a member and librarian of the AMORC [Ancient and Mystical Order of the Rose Cross] and the Rose+Cross University, directed experiments for small-scale seminars, and published articles on alchemy and transmutation in *The Rosicrucian Digest*. One of the students at these seminars, Albert Richard Riedel (1911-1984), went on to play a prominent role in promoting alchemy in the USA under the pseudonym of 'Frater Albertus'. Born in Dresden, Riedel emigrated to the USA shortly after publishing *Drei Novellen* (Three short stories, 1932), and followed Graves's courses before developing his personal vision. In 1960 he published *The Alchemist's Handbook*, and simultaneously founded the Paracelsus Research Society. The activities of this group from 1960 to 1984 were enormous: the training of hundreds of pupils, most of whom were members of the AMORC or the Golden Dawn; the preparation of tinctures, publishing of numerous bulletins reserved for members (*Alchemical Bulletin Codex* 1960-1972; *Parachemy* 1973-1979; *Essentia* 1980-1984); and the publication by

Albertus of several ancient and modern texts, including *The Hermetic Art: The Teaching concerning Atomic Transmutation* (c. 1948), which was given to Albertus during a seminar in Austria in 1971. This very short treatise was by V.L. Volpierre (alias Nikolaus Burtschell, 1892-1952), an alchemist who had been in contact with Surya (alias Demeter Georgiewitz-Weitzer, 1873-1949) and who apparently published nothing else during his lifetime. The authorities to which Albertus largely refers are Basil Valentine (especially *Triumph Wagen Antimonii*, Leipzig 1604), Cockren's *Alchemy Rediscovered*, and Richard Ingalese (1863-ca. 1934).

Albertus had a surprising influence on Israel Regardie (1907-1985), who in *The Philosopher's Stone* (1938), under the influence of → C.G. Jung, had attributed a purely spiritual value to alchemy. His view of alchemy changed during the 1970s, when he frequented Albertus and other alchemists of the Paracelsus Research Society. The same years saw the emergence of the Scotsman Adam McLean (b. 1948), whose activities explicitly included the three realms of spiritual, soul, and physical alchemy. McLean's *Hermetic Journal* (1978-1992) and series of texts 'Magnum Opus Hermetic Sourceworks' (23 vols.) gathered contributions from former Golden Dawn members and from younger scholars and practitioners throughout the English-speaking world.

The FAR+C (Frères Aînés de la Rose Croix), led by Roger Caro (1911-1992) offered an "initiatic" teaching from the end of the 1960s through the next decade. Here Rosicrucianism and alchemy were closely associated with theology, notably in Kamala-Jnana's works: *Dictionnaire de philosophie alchimique* (Dictionary of alchemical philosophy, 1961), *Pléiade alchimique* (Alchemical Pleiad, 1967), and *Tout le Grand Oeuvre photographié* (The whole Great Work photographed, 1968).

Among Canseliet's many readers, after 1970 several took the plunge into practical alchemy combined with writing: Michel Binda (*La Vierge alchimique de Reims* [The alchemical Virgin of Reims], 1996), Jean Laplace († 1997), Séverin Batfroi (b. 1946, *Alchimie et révélation chrétienne* [Alchemy and Christian revelation], Paris 1976; *Alchimiques métamorphoses du mercure universel* [Alchemical metamorphoses of the universal mercury], 1977); Guy Béatrice (*Sainte Anne d'alchimie* [Saint Anne of alchemy], 1978; *Des mages alchimistes à Nostradamus* [From the alchemical magi to Nostradamus], 1982), Bernard Biebel, and Patrick Rivière (*Alchimie et spagyrie* [Alchemy and spagyrics], 1988).

Shortly after Canseliet's death in 1982, some works appeared under the name "Solazareff" (see Bibl.), advocating a practical alchemy following the 'dry way' of Fulcanelli and Canseliet, and devotion to the Virgin Mary. In the mid-1980s the Solazareff movement counted as many as 500 members or sympathizers, but no publication seems to have appeared since the mid-1990s. While the Fulcanelli-Canseliet school has been dominant in France and especially visible through publications, other schools exist, though in a more confidential fashion. This is the case with the "Philosophes de la Nature" (Philosophers of Nature), founded by Jean Dubuis in 1979, which also defends practical alchemy with a strong contribution from kabbalah. An American branch was founded, independent of the French one, which has ceased its activity in 1995.

Frater Albertus (alias Albert Richard Riedel), *The Alchemist's Handbook*, Salt Lake City: Paracelsus Research Society, 1960; rev. ed., 1974 ♦ idem, *From "One" to "Ten"*, Salt Lake City: PRS, 1966; reissued, with the unpublished Engl. trans. of *Praxis Spagyrica Philosophica*, Leipzig, 1711, York Beach: Samuel Weiser, 1998 ♦ idem, *Praktische Alchemie im zwanzigsten Jahrhundert*, Salt Lake City: PRS, 1970 ♦ idem, with the collaboration of Israel Regardie (eds.), *The Golden Manuscripts (Volpierre, The Hermetic Art, 1928; They made the Philosopher's Stone, Isabelle and Richard Ingalese, 1928; The True Book of the Learned Synesius, 1678; Circulatum Urbigerus, 1690)*, Salt Lake City: Para Publishing Co., 1973-1974; repr. Kila: Kessinger, 1992 ♦ idem, *The Alchemist of the Rocky Mountains*, Salt Lake City: PRS, 1976 ♦ René Alleau, *Aspects de l'alchimie traditionnelle*, Paris: Les éditions de Minuit, 1953; 1970² ♦ Mary Anne Atwood, *A Suggestive Inquiry into the Hermetic Mystery, with a Dissertation on the More Celebrated of the Alchemical Philosophers, Being an Attempt towards the Recovery of the Ancient Experiment of Nature*, London: Trelawney Saunders, 1850; new enlarged ed., ed. W.L. Wilmshurst, Belfast: William Tait, 1918; repr. New York: Julian Press, 1960 ♦ Armand Barbault, (under the pseudonym of Rumélius), *L'Elixir de longue vie et la pierre Philosophale*, Paris: Niclaus, 1948 ♦ idem, *L'or du millième matin*: Paris, 1969; Engl. trans., *The Gold of a Thousand Mornings*, London: Neville Spearman, 1975 ♦ Francis Barrett, *The Magus*, London, 1801 ♦ Alexander von Bernus, *Alchymie und Heilkunst*, Nuremberg, 1948²; 3rd ed., 1969; new expanded ed., 1994 ♦ idem, *Laboratorium Soluna. Handbuch mit einem Anhang: Das Mysterium der Heilung*, Schloß Donaumünster, 1949 ♦ idem, *Das Geheimnis der Adepten: Aufschlüsse über das Magisterium der Alchymie, die Bereitung der großen Arkana und den Weg zum Lapis Philosophorum*, Sersheim: Osiris-Verlag, 1956 ♦ Titus Burckhardt, *Alchemie: Sinn und Weltbild*, Olten: Walter Verlag, 1960; Engl. trans., *Alchemy, Science of the Cosmos, Science of the Soul*, London: Stuart & Watkins, 1967 ♦ Jorge Camacho, *Arcanes de la Philosophie Naturelle (Arcana Philosophiae Naturalis)*, Huelva: Fondation Pol François Lambert, 1998 ♦ L.P.-François Cambriel, *Cours de Philosophie hermétique ou d'alchimie en dix-neuf leçons, traitant de la théorie et de la pratique de cette science, ainsi que de plusieurs autres opérations indispensables, pour parvenir à trouver et à faire la pierre philosophale, ou transmutations métalliques, lesquelles ont été cachées jusqu'à ce jour dans tous les récits des philosophes hermétiques, suivies des explications de quelques articles des cinq premiers chapitres de la Genèse (etc.)*, Paris: Imprimerie de Lacour et Maistrasse, 1843; repr., ed. B. Husson, Paris: L'Omnium Littéraire, 1964 ♦ Eugène Canseliet, *Deux logis alchimiques en marge de la science et des arts*, Paris: Jean Schemit, 1945; 2nd rev. and aug. ed. Jean-Jacques Pauvert, Paris, 1979; 3rd ed., rev., recast, corr. and aug. by R. Caron, Paris: Jean-Claude Bailly, 1998 ♦ idem, *Alchimie: Etudes diverses de symbolisme hermétique*, Pauvert, 1964; 2nd aug. ed. Pauvert, 1978 and many reissues ♦ idem, *L'alchimie et son Mutus Liber*, Pauvert, 1967; repr. 1986; aug. ed., Bailly, 1996 ♦ idem, *L'alchimie expliquée sur ses textes classiques*, Pauvert, 1972; 2nd aug. ed., Pauvert, 1980 and many reissues ♦ idem, *Trois anciens traités alchimiques*, Pauvert, 1975; facs. repr. Paris: Fayard, 1996 ♦ idem, with Robert Amadou, *Le Feu du soleil: Entretiens sur l'alchimie avec Eugène Canseliet*, Pauvert, 1978 ♦ idem, *L'Hermétisme dans la vie de Jonathan Swift*, Montpellier: Fata Morgana, 1983 ♦ Archibald Cockren, *Alchemy Rediscovered and Restored*, London: Rider, 1940; Philadelphia: David McKay, 1941 ♦ Cyliani, *Hermès dévoilé dédié à la postérité*, Paris: Imprimerie de Félix Locquin, 1832; Paris: Chacornac, 1915; ed. B. Husson, Paris: L'Omnium Littéraire, 1964 ♦ Karl von Eckartshausen, *Chimische Versuche über die Radicalauflösung der Körper, besonders der Metalle von Hofrath von Eckartshausen*, Regensburg 1801 ♦ Julius Evola, *La Tradizione Ermetica*, Bari, 1931, 1948²; Engl. trans., *The Hermetic Tradition*, Rochester, Vt: Inner Traditions International, 1995 ♦ Fulcanelli (ps.), *Le mystère des cathédrales et l'interprétation des symboles ésotériques du Grand Œuvre*, Paris: Jean Schemit, 1926; 2nd aug. ed., Omnium Littéraire: Paris, 1957; 3rd aug. ed. with new preface, Jean-Jacques Pauvert: Paris, 1964 and many reissues; Engl. trans., *Fulcanelli, Master alchemist*, London/Jersey: Neville Spearman, 1971 (repr. Spearman: Suffolk, 1977); Albuquerque: The Brotherhood of Life, 1984, 2000² ♦ idem, *Les demeures philosophales et le symbolisme hermétique dans ses rapports avec l'art sacré*, Paris: Jean Schemit, 1930; 2nd aug. ed., with unpublished chapter and new preface, Paris: Omnium Littéraire, 1960, 2 vols.; 3rd augm. ed., Paris: J.J. Pauvert, 1965. Engl. trans., *The Dwellings of the Philosophers*, Boulder: Archive Press, 1999 ♦ [Pseudo]-Fulcanelli, *Finis Gloriae Mundi*, London: Liber Mirabilis, 1999 ♦ Edward John Langford Garstin, *Theurgy or the Hermetic Practice: A treatise on Spiritual Alchemy*, London: Rider and Co., 1930 ♦ idem, *The Secret Fire: An Alchemical Study*, London: The Search Publishing Co., 1932 ♦ Louis Gassot, *La philosophie céleste, Bor-*

deaux, An XI (1803) ♦ Emile-Jules Grillot de Givry, *Le Grand Œuvre: XII méditations sur la voie ésotérique de l'Absolu*, Paris: Chacornac, 1907, 1960² ♦ Richard Grossinger, (ed.), *The Alchemical Tradition in the Late Twentieth Century*, Berkeley: North Atlantic Books, 1991 ♦ Abel Haatan (alias Abel Thomas), *Contribution à l'étude de l'alchimie: Théorie et pratique du Grand Œuvre*, Paris: Bibliothèque Chacornac, 1905 ♦ Friedrich Herbort, *Compendium Hermeticum* in: J. Fabry (ed.), *Deux traités alchimiques*, Nice: Bélisane, 1988, 1-66 (unpublished German alchemical Ms. in facsimile, with French trans.) ♦ Ethan Allen Hitchcock, *Remarks upon Alchemy and the Alchemists, Indicating a Method of Discovering the True Nature of Hermetic Philosophy and Showing that the Search after The Philosopher's Stone had not for its Object the Discovery of an Agent for the Transmutation of Metals*, Boston: Crosby, Nichols, & Co., 1857; facs. ed., *Alchemy and the Alchemists*, Los Angeles: Philosophical Research Society, 1976 ♦ Emmanuel D'Hooghvorst, "Essai sur l'Art d'Alchymie", *Inconnues* 5 (1951), 3-44 ♦ idem, *Le Fil d'Ariane*, Paris: La Table d'Emeraude, 1996 ♦ idem, *Le Fil de Pénélope*, Paris: La Table d'Emeraude, 1998 ♦ François Jollivet-Castelot, *L'Hylozoïde: L'Alchimie. Les chimistes unitaires*, Paris: Chamuel, 1896 ♦ idem, *Comment on devient alchimiste: Traité d'hermétisme et d'art spagyrique*, Paris: Chamuel, 1897; facs. Le Tremblay: Diffusion Traditionnelle, 1995 ♦ idem, *Le Grand Œuvre alchimique*, Paris: Editions de L'Hyperchimie, 1901 ♦ idem, *Etudes d'Hyperchimie: Chimie et alchimie*, Paris: Emile Nourry, 1928 ♦ Manfred Junius, *L'Alchimia verde*, Rome: Edizioni Mediterranee, 1979; Engl. trans., *A Practical Handbook of Plant Alchemy*, New York: Inner Traditions International, 1985; reissued as *A Practical Handbook of Plant Alchemy. An Herbalist's Guide to Preparing Medicinal Essences, Tinctures, and Elixirs*, Rochester, Vt: Healing Arts Press, 1993 ♦ Lapidus (pseudonym), *In Pursuit of Gold*, New York: Samuel Weiser, 1976 ♦ Johann Friedrich von Meyer, *Smaragdene Tafel*, in: J. Fabry (ed.), *Deux traités alchimiques*, Nice: Bélisane, 1988, 1-8 (unpublished German alchemical Ms. in facsimile with French trans.) ♦ *Moderne Alchemisten: Alchemie im 20. Jahrhundert*, Sinzheim, AAGW, 2000 ♦ Augusto Pancaldi, *Alchimia Pratica*, Rome: Atanòr, 1983; new ed., Atanòr: n.p. 1997 ♦ Albert Poisson, *Théories et symboles des alchimistes: Le Grand-Œuvre suivi d'un essai sur la bibliographie alchimique du XIXème siècle*, Paris: Bibliothèque Chacornac, 1891; Paris: Editions Traditionnelles, 1969² ♦ idem, *L'alchimie au XIVème siècle: Nicolas Flamel, Sa vie – ses fondations – ses œuvres, suivi de la réimpression du Livre des figures hiéroglyphiques*, Paris: Bibliothèque Chacornac, 1893; repr. Paris: Gutenberg, 1981 ♦ Israel Regardie, *The Philosopher's Stone*, London: Rider, 1938; rev. ed., Saint Paul: Llewelyn Publications, 1970 ♦ Max Retschlag, *Von der Urmaterie zum Urkraft-Elixier* (1926), reissued in *Moderne Alchemisten: Alchemie im 20 Jahrhundert* ♦ idem, *Die Alchemie und ihr großes Meisterwerk: Der Stein der Weisen*, Leipzig: Hummel Verlag, 1934 ♦ Bernard Roger, *Paris et l'alchimie*, Paris: Alta, 1981 ♦ idem, *À la découverte de l'alchimie: L'Art d'Hermès à travers contes, légendes, histoire et rituels maçonniques*, Paris: Editions Dangles, 1988 ♦ Herbert Silberer, *Probleme der Mystik und ihrer Symbolik*, Vienna/Leipzig: Hugo Heller & Co., 1914; Engl. trans, 1917; repr. New York: Dover, 1971 ♦ Solazareff (pseudonym), *Introitus ad philosophorum lapidem*, n.p. 1984 ♦ idem, *L'Assation philosophique en voie sèche*, n.p., 1985 ♦ Thomas South, "The Enigma of Alchemy", *The Quest* 10:2 (1919), 213-225; repr. Edmonds, Wa: The Alchemical Press, 1984 ♦ August Strindberg, *Bréviaire alchimique: Lettres à Jollivet-Castelot*, Paris: Durville, 1912 ♦ G.W. Surya (alias Demeter Georgiewitz-Weitzer), *Der Triumph der Alchemie*, Leipzig, 1908 ♦ idem, *Hermetische Medizin, Stein der Weisen, Lebenselixiere*, Berlin-Pankow: Lanser Verlag, 1923 ♦ Théodore Tiffereau, *L'Or et la transmutation des métaux*, Paris: Chacornac, 1889, repr. Editions du Cosmogone: n.p., 1994 ♦ A.E. Waite, ed. R.A. Gilbert, *The Hermetic Papers of A.E. Waite: The Unknown Writings of a Modern Mystic*, Wellingborough: The Aquarian Press, 1987 ♦ Alexander Wilder, *New Platonism and Alchemy, A Sketch of the Doctrines and Principal Teachers of the Eclectic Alexandrian School; Also An Outline of the Interior Doctrines of the Alchemists of the Middle Ages*, Albany: Weed, Parsons, & Co., 1869; repr. Minneapolis: Wizards Bookshelf, 1975 ♦ Claude d'Ygé, *Anthologie de la poésie hermétique*, Paris: Montbrun, 1948; new ed., Paris: Dervy-Livres, 1976 ♦ idem, *Nouvelle assemblée des philosophes chymiques: Aperçus sur le Grand Œuvre des alchimistes*, Paris: Dervy, 1954; repr. Paris: Dervy, 1972; Paris: J.-Cl. Bailly, 1992.

Lit.: [Anonymous], *Ces hommes qui ont fait l'alchimie du XXème siècle*, Grenoble, 1999 ♦ Françoise Bonardel, "Alchemical Esotericism and the Hermeneutics of Culture", in: Antoine Faivre & Jacob Needleman (eds., in collaboration with Karen Voss), *Modern Esoteric Spirituality*, New York: Crossroad, 1992, 71-99 ♦ idem, *Philosophie de l'alchimie*, Paris: Presses Universitaires de France, 1999 ♦ Serge Caillet, *La Franc-Maçonnerie Egyptienne de Memphis-Misraïm*, Paris: Dervy, 2003 ♦ Richard Caron, "Notes sur l'histoire de l'alchimie en France à la fin du XIXème et au début du XXème siècle", in: R. Caron, J. Godwin, W.J. Hanegraaff & J.L. Vieillard-Baron (eds.), *Esotérisme, Gnoses et Imaginaire symbolique: Mélanges offerts à Antoine Faivre*, Louvain: Peeters, 2001, 17-26 ♦ Ithell Colquhoun, *Sword of Wisdom: MacGregor Mathers and the Golden Dawn*, London: Neville Spearman, 1975 ♦ I. Bernard Cohen, "Ethan Allen Hitchcock: Soldier – Humanitarian – Scholar. Discoverer of the 'True Subject' of the Hermetic Art", *Proceedings of the American Antiquarian Society* 61 (1951), 29-136; repr. Worcester, Ma: American Antiquarian Society, 1952 ♦ Jacques Fabry, *Le Bernois Friedrich Herbort et l'ésotérisme chrétien en Suisse à l'époque romantique*, Bern/Frankfurt a.M.: Peter Lang, 1983 ♦ idem, *Le théosophe de Francfort Johann Friedrich von Meyer (1772-1849) et l'ésotérisme en Allemagne au XIXème siècle*, Bern/ Frankfurt/New York: Peter Lang, 1989 ♦ Antoine Faivre, *Eckartshausen et la theosophie chrétienne*, Paris: Klincksieck, 1969 ♦ Juan García Font,

Historia de la alquimia en Espana, Madrid: Editora Nacional, 1976 ♦ Helmut Gebelein, *Alchemie*, Kreuzlingen/Munich: Heinrich Hugendubel Verlag, 1991; 2000² ♦ Robert A. Gilbert, *A.E. Waite: A Bibliography*, Wellingborough: The Aquarian Press, 1983 ♦ idem, *A.E. Waite, Magician of Many Parts*, Wellingborough: Crucible, 1987 ♦ idem, "The Rev. W.A. Ayton (1816-1908), in: *Revelations of the Golden Dawn: The Rise and Fall of a Magical Order*, Chippenham: Quantum, 1997, 149-158 ♦ Joscelyn Godwin, *The Theosophical Enlightenment*, Albany: SUNY Press, 1994 ♦ William T. Gorski, *Yeats and Alchemy*, Albany: SUNY Press, 1996 ♦ John Hamill, (ed.), *The Rosicrucian Seer: Magical Writings of Frederick Hockley*, Wellingborough: The Aquarian Press, 1986 ♦ Bernard Husson (ed.), *Deux traités alchimiques du XIXème siècle*, Paris: Omnium Littéraire, 1964 ♦ Didier Kahn, "Alchimie et Franc-Maçonnerie au XVIIIème siècle", in: *Mutus Liber Latomorum*, Paris: Jean-Claude Bailly, 1993, 25-38 ♦ Francis X. King, *The Flying Sorcerer, being the Magical and Aeronautical Adventures of Francis Barrett, Author of The Magus*, Oxford: Mandrake Press, 1992 ♦ Hans-Ulrich Kolb & Joachim Telle, "Schattenbeschwörung: Wirkungsgeschichtliche Noten zum lyrischen und alchemistischen Werk von Alexander von Bernus", *Heidelberger Jahrbücher* 17 (1973), 86-128 ♦ Herman Kopp, "Ueber den Verfall der Alchemie und die Hermetische Gesellschaft", *Denkschriften der Gesellschaft für Wissenschaft und Kunst in Giessen* (1847), 1-35 ♦ Jean-Pierre Laurant, *L'ésotérisme chrétien en France au XIXème siècle*, Lausanne: L'Âge d'Homme, 1992 ♦ idem, "*L'Alchymie du Maçon* de François-Nicholas Noël", in: Sylvain Matton (ed.), *Documents oubliés sur l'Alchimie, la kabbale et Guillaume Postel, offerts, à l'occasion de son quatre-vingt dixième anniversaire, à François Secret par ses élèves et amis*, Geneva: Droz, 2001, 439-455 ♦ Christopher McIntosh, *Eliphas Levi and the French Occult Revival*, London: Rider, 1972 ♦ Christine Maillard, "Résurgences de l'alchimie dans le premier tiers du XXᵉ siècle: Unité du réel et transmutation du sujet – sciences, psychanalyse, littérature", *Recherches Germaniques*, special no. 1, "Sciences, Sciences occultes et littérature" (2002), 111-147 ♦ Luther H. Martin, "A History of the Psychological Interpretation of Alchemy", *Ambix* 22 (1975), 10-20 ♦ Timothy Materer, *Modernist Alchemy: Poetry and the Occult*, Ithaca/London: Cornell University Press, 1995 ♦ Alain Mercier, "Auguste Strindberg et les alchimistes français Hemel, Vial, Tiffereau, Jollivet-Castelot", *Revue de littérature comparée* 1 (Jan.-Mar. 1969), 23-46 ♦ Hans Nintzel, "Alchemy is Alive and Well", *Gnosis* 8 (1988), 11-15 ♦ Charles Porset, "Les enjeux 'alchimiques' du Convent des Philalèthes", in: Didier Kahn & Sylvain Matton (eds.), *Alchimie: art, histoire et mythes*, Milan/Paris: Archè-SEHA, 1995, 756-800 ♦ *Der Rundbrief. An die Freunde der Alexander von Bernus Gesellschaft*, 1 (Jan. 1998) through 8 (May 2002) ♦ A. Porte du Trait des Ages, *F. Jollivet-Castelot: L'écrivain, Le poète, Le philosophe*, Paris: Eugène Figuière & Cie., 1914 ♦ Lawrence M. Principe & William R. Newman, "Some Problems with the Historiography of Alchemy", in: A. Grafton & W.R. Newman (eds.), *Secrets of Nature: Astrology and Alchemy in Early Modern Europe*, Cambridge, Ma: MIT Press, 2001, 385-432 ♦ Elmar Schenkel, "Exploring Unity in Contradiction: The Return of Alchemy in Contemporary British Writings", in: B. Korte & K.-P. Müller (eds.), *Unity in Diversity Revisited? British Literature and Culture in the 1990s*, Tübingen: Narr, 1998, 211-233 ♦ Heinrich Schipperges, "Das Alchymische Denken und Handeln bei Alexander von Bernus", *Heidelberger Jahrbücher* 24 (1980), 107-124 ♦ Franz Anselm Schmitt, *Alexander von Bernus, Dichter und Alchymist: Leben und Werk in Dokumenten*, Nuremberg, 1971 ♦ Mirko Sladek & Maria Schütze, *Alexander von Bernus*, Nuremberg: Verlag Hans Carl, 1981 ♦ Annelies Stöckinger & Joachim Telle, *Die Alchemiebibliothek Alexander von Bernus in der Badischen Landesbibliothek Karlsruhe: Katalog der Drucke und Handschriften*, Wiesbaden: Harrassowitz Verlag, 1997 ♦ Gerald Suster, *Crowley's Apprentice: The Life and Ideas of Israel Regardie, the Magical Psychologist*, London: Rider, 1989 ♦ Joachim Telle, "Dichter als Alchemiker: Vier Briefe von Gustav Meyrink an Alexander von Bernus", in: Hans-Günther Schwartz, Christiane von Stutterheim & Franz Loquai (eds.), *Fenster zur Welt: Festschrift für Friedrich Strack*, München: Iudicium, 2004, 357-379 ♦ Robert Vanloo, *L'Utopie Rose-Croix du XVIIème siècle à nos jours*, Paris: Dervy, 2001 ♦ A.E. Waite, *The Secret Tradition in Alchemy*, London: Kegan Paul, Trench, Trübner & C°, 1926; repr. London: Stuart & Watkins, 1969 ♦ Jost Weyer, "The Image of Alchemy and Chemistry in Nineteenth and Twentieth Century Histories of Chemistry", *Ambix* 23 (1976), 65-70 ♦ Walter Leslie Wilmshurst, "The Later Mysticism of Mrs. Atwood", *The Quest* 10/4, (July 1919), 487-507; 11/1-4 (Oct. 1919-July 1920), 31-53.

RICHARD CARON

Al-Kindī, Abū Yūsuf Yaʿqūb ibn Isḥāq, * 800? Kufa or Basra, † 866

Al-Kindī is considered the first Arabian philosopher. We know little about his life. He was born maybe at Kufa, maybe at Basra; in any case, it was in Basra that he studied languages and theology before moving to Baghdad, where he took active part in the rich cultural life of the city, under the protection of the ʿAbbāsid caliph al-Maʾmūn (813-833) and his successor, al-Muʿtaṣim (833-842). The ʿAbbāsid dynasty encouraged interest in the arts, science and philosophy, and the caliph al-Maʾmūn had founded the *bayt al-ḥikma* ("house of knowledge") in Baghdad in 830 A.D., where the first translations from the Greek were accomplished. It was in this centre that al-Kindī played an important role as chief translator of Greek philosophical works into Arabic and as an author of original philosophical works.

Greek writings provide one of the richest sources

of al-Kindī's own work. Aristotle's *Metaphysics*, in Arabic translation, was to become one of the major influences on his thinking. Al-Kindī himself worked on the translation of the *Theology* attributed to Aristotle but actually a summary of the *Enneads* IV-VI by Plotinus. Some of Proclus' works, amongst which the *Elements of Theology*, were translated into Arabic in al-Kindī's circle; and furthermore the writings of Hippocrates, Galen and above all Ptolemy are among the sources of al-Kindī's thought. In addition to Greek philosophy, the philosopher appears to have been influenced by that of India and Persia as well. Moreover the hermetic sect of the Sabāeans of Ḥarrān appears also to have had an impact on our philosopher, who sought to integrate astrolatrical and ceremonial elements of harranian origin within a scientific vision of reality.

Al-Kindī lived in an age of conflicting ideas in the Muslim world: the Ashʿarite school of thought represented orthodox Sunnite Islām in opposition to the Muʿtazilite, and the *Kalām*, theological science, was stimulated by the newly-available Greek philosophy. Al-Kindī accepted the fundamental elements of Muslim religion such as divine unity, prophetic wisdom, the creation of the world, and the oneness of God. Elements of Muʿtazilite doctrine are found in some aspects of al-Kindī's thought, for example concerning the relationship between philosophical truth and truth revealed by prophetic wisdom. Although al-Kindī underlined the importance of pure reason in knowledge of the "unique truth", he never gave priority to reason over revelation. Rather, he showed that the different methods by means of which one could reach philosophical truth require painstaking research, whereas revealed truth comes as a divine gift that requires neither effort nor time and is a quality peculiar to the prophets. That al-Kindī tended towards the Muʿtazilite doctrine is shown by his friendship with the caliphs al-Maʾmūn and al-Muʿtasim and likewise by his conflict with al-Mutawakkil (847-861), an opponent of the Muʿtazilites. This conflict caused al-Kindī to end up in a situation of political isolation, which would last until the end of his life.

Al-Kindī's interests were wide-ranging and varied: from natural to metaphysical philosophy, from medicine to → astrology and astronomy, from → music to → alchemy, from precious stones to meteorology. More than 260 works are attributed to al-Kindī in the *Fihrist*, the basic catalogue of Arabic works (written in the 10th century). Of these only a small part are still extant; for example the *Book on the first philosophy*, the *Epistle on the intellect*, the *Epistle on the substance of sleep and dream*, the

Discourse on the soul, the *Epistle on the reason why the ancients correlated the five geometric shapes to the element*, the essay *On the cause of the azure colour that is seen in the air towards the sky and is thought to be the colour of the sky*, the essay on *The true, first, perfect agent and the imperfect agent that is metaphorically so*, the essay *On definitions and descriptions of things*, the *Epistle on the difference of perspectives*, the *Epistle on the rays*, the *Book on the introduction to the science of the stars*, the *Epistle on knowledge of the strengths of compound medicaments*, and the *Book on the chemistry of perfume and distillation*.

The sheer quantity of al-Kindī's writings, the multiplicity of their sources, and his attempts to reconcile them with the dictates of the Islamic faith certainly do not make it easy to follow the development of his personal opinions. However, in his doctrine of rays, known in Latin Medieval culture by his treatise *De radiis*, the originality of al-Kindī's thought fully emerges. According to this theory, the four elements together with composite bodies and the planets make up a unified reality, in which all parts seem to be constituted by the very act of their continuous relationship: every object projects its own nature outwards, by means of "rays" which transmit that nature to other objects. According to al-Kindī, absolutely everything (elements, bodies, objects, planets, images, words, musical notes, souls, etc.) transmits rays. Thus the relationships between the stars, the elements and the composite bodies derive from and express the causal interactions which exist between the various levels of being; such relationships are made possible by the continuous radial flux which passes between them, for it is only by means of this flux that stars, elements and bodies can mutually connect. While accepting some aspects of Aristotelian cosmology, al-Kindī thus integrates them within a generalized context based upon the radical interconnectedness of all parts of the universe. Thus elements of → magic derived from the hermetic tradition (talismans, invocations and magical formulae, emblems and magical characters, animal sacrifices) are placed in a philosophical context based upon the concept of universal cosmic rays: the magician can use his knowledge of their relationships in order to attain a specific purpose.

Al-Kindī is also considered to have been the first to develop a doctrine of the "acquisition of the intellect", which was to have an enormous impact on the Islamic world and heavily influenced the philosophers al-Fārābī and → Avicenna. Al-Kindī believed that perfect knowledge occurred at the moment when the human faculty of reason joined the active intellect that originates from God: a theme which has continued to preoccupy Arab philosophers up to Averroes. Important works of al-Kindī were translated into Latin during the 12th century by Gerardo of Cremona, John of Seville, Robert of Ketton and Hugo of Santalla. In the Renaissance, al-Kindī was well known as a mathematician and physician. The *De Radiis* influenced the cosmologies of → Marsilio Ficino and → Giovanni Pico della Mirandola; and Gerolamo Cardano listed al-Kindī among the twelve greatest spirits. In Medieval and Renaissance culture, the doctrine of rays was interpreted as a rationale for magic.

Albino Nagy, "Die philosophischen Abhandlungen des Jaʿqūb ben Isḥāq al-Kindī", *Beiträge zur Geschichte der Philosophie des Mittelalters* 2:5 (1897) ◆ Muḥ ʿabd al-Hādī Abū Rīdah, *Rasāʾil al-Kindī al-falsafiyya*, Cairo: Dar al-Fikr al-ʿArabi, 1950-1953 ◆ Léon Gauthier, *Antécédents gréco- arabes de la psycho-physique*, Beyrouth: Imprimerie Catholique, 1938 ◆ Zakariyya Yūsuf (ed.), *Muʾallafāt al-Kindī al-mūsīqiyyah*, Baghdad: Matbaʿ at Shafiq, 1962 ◆ Michel Allard, "L'épître de Kindī sur les définitions", *Bulletin d'études orientales de l'Institut français de Damas* 25 (1972), 47-83 ◆ Marie Thérèse D'Alverny & Françoise Hudry, "Al-Kindi: De Radiis", *Archives d'histoire doctrinale et littéraire du Moyen Age* 41 (1974), 139-260 ◆ Michael R. MacVaugh, *Arnaldi de Villanova Opera medica omnia* (Luis Garcia Ballester & Juan Antonio Paniagua eds.), Barcelona, Granada: Seminarium Historiae Medicae Granatensis, 1975 ◆ Al-Kindî, *Cinq épîtres* (Centre d'Histoire des sciences et des doctrines: Histoire des sciences et de la philosophie arabes), Paris: Centre national de la recherche scientifique, 1976 ◆ Jean Jolivet & Roshdi Rashed (eds.), *Oeuvres Philosophiques et Scientifiques d'al-Kindī, L'Optique et la Catoptrique* (Islamic Philosophy Theology and Science 29), Leiden, New York, London: E.J. Brill, 1997 ◆ Gerrit Bos & Charles Burnett, *Scientific Weather Forecasting in the Middle Age: The Writings of al-Kindī*, London: Kegan Paul International, 2000.

Lit.: George Nicholas Atiye, *Al-Kindi, the philosopher of the Arabs*, Rawalpindi: Islamic Research Institute, 1966 ◆ Charles Burnett, "Al-Kindī in the Renaissance", in: Paul Richard Blum (ed.), *Sapientia amemus: Humanism und Aristotelismus in der Renaissance* (Festschrift Eckhard Kessler), München: Wilhelm Fink, 1999, 13-30 ◆ Cristina D'Ancona Costa, "Aristotele e Plotino nella dottrina di al-Kindī sul primo principio", *Documenti e Studi Sulla tradizione filosofica medievale* 3:2 (1992), 375-422 ◆ Ahmed Hasnawi, "Al-Kindī", in: Jean-François Mattéi (ed.), *L'Encyclopédie philosophique universelle*, Paris: P.U.F., 1992, 3.1, 655-657 ◆ Jean Jolivet, *L'intellect selon Kindī*, Leiden: E.J. Brill, 1971 ◆ Jean Jolivet & Roshdi Rashed, "Al-Kindī", in: Charles Coulston Gillispie (ed.), *Dictionary of Scientific Biography*, New-York: Scribner's, 1978 ◆ Rafael Ramón Guerrero & Emilio Tornero Poveda, *Obras filosóficas de al-Kindí*, Madrid: Editorial Coloquio, 1986 ◆ Emilio Tornero Poveda, *Al-Kindī: La transformación de un pensamiento religioso en un pensamiento racional* (Pensamiento Islamico 3), Madrid: Consejo Superior de Investigaciones Científicas, 1992 ◆ Pinella Travaglia, *Magic, Causality and Intentionality: The Doctrine of Rays in al-Kindī*, Firenze: Sismel-Edizioni del Galluzzo, 1999.

PINELLA TRAVAGLIA

Alliette, Jean-Baptiste → Etteilla

Amulets

1. INTRODUCTION 2. PAPYRUS (A. INSTRUCTIONS FROM FORMULARIES B. ACTUAL PAPYRUS AMULETS) 3. PHYLACTERIES [METAL AMULETS, LAMELLAE] (A. INSTRUCTIONS FROM FORMULARIES B. ACTUAL METAL PHYLACTERIES) 4. ENGRAVED GEMSTONES (A. INSTRUCTIONS FROM FORMULARIES B. ACTUAL GEMSTONES) 5. OTHER INSCRIBED MATERIALS 6. UNINSCRIBED MATERIALS 7. AMULETIC BUNDLES 8. AMULETS, GNOSTICISM AND THEURGY

1. INTRODUCTION

Amulets (Lat. *amuletum*; Gk. *phylaktērion*) are small devices usually worn on or attached to the body for protection and a variety of other purposes. In the ancient Mediterranean world, particularly during the later Roman Empire (ca. 2nd-5th cent. C.E.), a widespread industry of amulets proliferated. Amulets were comprised largely of inscribed texts written on a number of more or less permanent media (papyrus, metal strips, semiprecious gemstones, and occasionally organic materials). They display a great diversity as to type and manufacture, although a considerable stylistic uniformity in the industry is evident. Our major source for the use of amulets comes from the preserved collections of the Greek Magical Papyri, principally the longer formularies, or manuals, that give specific instructions for performing various magical rituals (*Papyri Graecae Magicae*[2] = *PGM*, with supplements in *Supplementum Magicum* = *SM*). Ancient Christian magical texts, mostly in Coptic (Meyer-Smith 1994), represent a natural development out of the older pagan traditions. Actual finds of amulets on papyrus, metal phylacteries (*lamellae*), gemstones, and other materials provide a resourceful supplement to our understanding of the interrelationship between the "the-oretical" formulas of the handbooks and the "applied" magic itself (cf. "Applied Magic": *SM* I, nos. 1-51; *SM* II nos. 52-66; "Formularies": *SM* II, nos. 70-100).

In addition to inscribed magical amulets (Kotan-sky 1991[a]), the manuals presuppose an extended tradition of "unlettered" amulets, organic or min-eral-based periapts (Gk. *periapton*, "tied onto; fas-tened on" [as an amulet]) used for healing and protection. Based on universal principles of sympa-thetic and antipathetic magic, these kinds of amulets have not usually survived, or when they have, are difficult to identify. Still, the side-by-side use of "uninscribed" versus "inscribed" amulets has continued unabated from antiquity down through the Middle Ages and even into modern times. Why amulets were required to be made or written on certain materials is in most cases unclear, although it is widely recognized that gold and silver, for example, was reserved for writing protective phylacteries, whereas lead was used for curses (gold and silver were popularly believed to be astral elements related to the sun [Helios] and moon [Selene], respectively; lead was the metal of Saturn). Distinctions were also made with certain gemstone materials. Hematite, for instance, the sesquioxide ore of iron (Fe 2 03), was commonly used for uterine amulets (Hanson 1995:290). Un-derstandably, some cross-overs exist in ambigu-ously defined arenas of magic (e.g., with victory spells where subjection of one's enemies is con-cerned [Kotansky 1991 (b)]). Numerous written rituals, too, are described in the magical papyri that do not involve the making of amulets, per se (writ-ten curses, divinatory spells, invocations, and so on). Here, the definition of what an amulet is can become blurred. Conversely, spoken charms to heal, and so on, are also commonly mentioned in the papyri without any specific mention of the ritual act of engraving a text (cf. *PGM* LXXIX, LXXX, LXXXI, for example; see further, below).

Important precursors to the written or "lettered" type of amulet in the magical papyri can be iden-tified in extant ancient Egyptian and Near Eastern sources. The texts of the papyri, although combin-ing elements from Egyptian, Babylonian (Persian), Greek, Jewish, and Roman beliefs, remain largely *sui generis*. Although any taxonomy is wrought with difficulties, extant magical texts, with few exceptions, can be readily identified as belonging to that class of text commonly referred to as "Graeco-Egyptian".

The primary function of amulets is both thera-peutic (healing) and apotropaic (protective). Speci-fic problems addressed may include the healing and curing of named diseases and medical complaints, as well as the warding off of danger and the general prophylaxis against harm. Ancillary roles of amu-lets may be subsumed under a number of acquisi-tional, or "talismanic" functions: the procurement of love, popularity, and favor (in virtually all areas of life); the winning of victory in legal and agonis-tic contests; and the requisition of all-around good luck. Sometimes within the papyrus record it is difficult to identify a written prescription as being "amuletic" in function. Spells for use in divination, incubation, and memory, for instance, would aim to acquire a kind of supernatural relationship (*cha-ris*) with a numinous power, or god, rather than serve to protect the body. Related to this are amulets prescribed for a number of more esoteric rituals, including special meetings with one's per-sonal *daimōn*, or "spirit-guide", to adopt the apro-pos → New Age terminology. Here the amulets procure the god's presence or otherwise protect the practitioner from any untoward presence of power. How all these "higher"-type rituals relate to the use of → magic in the late antique traditions of → Neo-platonism, theurgy, and → Gnosticism remains a desideratum. Little of this more "theurgic" use of amulets is detectable in the preserved amulets.

In the following survey, we shall examine each major categories of amuletic material – papyrus, metal phylacteries, and gemstones – and see first what the magic handbooks have to say about their use. Next we give an overview of the actual objects as the archaeological record has preserved them. A supplementary category of the organic amulets is also surveyed, including both *inscribed* and *unin-scribed* organic materials. This survey is intended to be representational and makes no claim at being comprehensive. The various corpora of magical texts are continually being expanded, and many pieces, both published and unpublished, have not been consulted. Comparatively poorly represented categories of materials (e.g., parchment, ostraka, engraved nails, etc.) are also not included and would require a separate study.

2. PAPYRUS

The ancient Greek magical formularies often detail the manufacture of actual amulets on papy-rus and other materials. Before the Daniel-Malto-mini editions, it was not always distinquished whether a published papyrus represented an exam-ple of an actual spell or amulet ("applied magic") or was merely a fragment from a handbook ("for-mularies"). With the larger codices (e.g., *PGM* IV, XII, XIII, XXXVI, etc.) this is seldom an issue;

however, with the smaller preserved fragments, one must be careful to differentiate between fragments of a handbook, however small, and actual amulets worn as personal objects. The telltale signs, of course, are whether the standard "personalized" formulas have been filled in or not (e.g. "so-and-so [NN] whom so-and-so bore" versus "Sophia whom Calpurnia bore"). Sometimes such distinctions were not carried out in actual practice. Many "applied" texts preserve fragments from formulary instructions, as if erroneously copied from their models by their scribes, a fact that proves that formularies were indeed used.

2. A. INSTRUCTIONS FROM FORMULARIES

The following spells specify a text to be written on a piece of "hieratic" or "new" papyrus, or the like. The formularies themselves often carry incipits or rubrics that name the medical complaint; otherwise, the nature of the written spell identifies the disease, using any variety of standard formulas. In some cases, a set of incantatory verses is recorded, but no mention of the actual writing of an amulet is specified. Here, it is entirely possibly that the incantation is merely spoken, although the purpose still remains "amuletic". In the *PGM* citations below, the context of the entire spell is given, not the precise reference to the amulet itself.

a. *Medical complaints*: discharge from the eyes (*PGM* VII. 197-98: magic word); breasts and uterus pain (*PGM* XXIIa. 9-10: Homer verse); a contraceptive (*PGM* XXIIa. 11-14: Homer verse, tied with hairs of mule); easy child birth (*SM* II. 94; written formula, on papyrus?); elephantiasis (*PGM* XXIIa. 15-17: Homer verse); fever (*PGM* VII. 218-21: magic names in "wing-formation"; *SM* II. 94: written formula, on papyrus?; *SM* II. 96: a magic formula for shivering); flux of blood (*PGM* XXIIa. 2-9: Homer verse); headache (*PGM* XX. 1-4; 13-19: Greek metrical verses; *PGM* LXV. 4-7 [migraine]: symbols; *Suppl.Mag.* II. 72: verses [written?]; cf. *Suppl.Mag.* II. 94); inflammation (*PGM* XX. 4-12: verses [written?]); scorpion sting (*PGM* VII. 193-96: inscribed "characters"; *PGM* XXVIIIa-c: set of three invocations; from a formulary? Cf. *SM* II. 89, but with no actual written amulet); uncertain (*SM* II. 80: formula to be worn around the neck: 'Protect so-and-so . . .' [frag.]; *SM* II. 84: fragmentary formulary for making amulets for various diseases [demons, epilepsy, prolapse of the uterus?], with no mention of writing). Similarly, *SM* II. 88 (against *erysipelas* and various skin eruptions) seems to preserve only spoken, not written, formulas.

b. *Favor and victory charms*: An invocation to Helios (no instructions for writing) preserves a standard formula for favor (*PGM* XXIIa. 18-27). Similarly, a magic name with a prayer for protection is called a 'Favor charm, a charm to dissolve a spell, a phylactery, and a victory charm' (*PGM* LXX. 1-4). This spell serves as an incipit for another, the 'Charm of Hekate Ereschigal against fear of punishment' (see Betz, 1980). Oddly, a "Charm to restrain anger and Charm for Success" mentions inscribing a papyrus 'to augment the words', but in fact invokes certain angels and magic names 'to protect me from every bad situation that comes upon me' (*PGM* XXXVI. 161-77). For a similar blurring of distinctions, another "phylactery", apparently to be written on papyrus but with no specifics, asks that 'favor' be granted from Ablanathanalba, but requests only protection from 'every evil thing' (*PGM* LXXI. 1-8).

c. *Other, Miscellaneous, and Uncertain Rituals*: The 100-lettered name of Typhon, inscribed for use in the powerful "Bear Charm", accomplishes any matter; it is used along with a phylactery of the plaited hairs from a *bear* (see below) (*PGM* IV. 1331-89); an inscribed papyrus *strip* is also used in a love divination (*PGM* IV. 1872-1927); the *hide* of an *ass*, a *leaf* of *flax*, along with an inscribed *papyrus* strip, are used in "Pity's *Spell of Attraction*" – in truth, a form of skull cup enquiry (*PGM* IV. 2006-2125); a *hieratic papyrus*, inscribed with a spell for protection against every evil demon(!), is used in a dream revelation as part of a larger spell of attraction (*PGM* IV. 2441-2621); the *blood* from the foot or hand of a pregnant woman is used to inscribe magic names on clean *papyrus* and tied to the left arm with *linen* as a phylactery in a rite to summon a god (*PGM* IV. 52-85); a *papyrus strip* engraved with magic names is washed off in water from seven springs and drunk in a memory spell (*PGM* I. 232-247); further, in a form of dream divination, requiring memory, a strip of *papyrus* inscribed with the Headless God is placed beside the head, with engraved laurel leaves (*PGM* II. 1-64); a phylactery against demons is presumably to be written on *papyrus* (*PGM* IV. 86-87); a new sheet of *papyrus* inscribed with a spell that subjugates demons, enchantments, and 'scourge which is from God' is used in the so-called "Stele of Jeu", apparently a type of ritual against demonic forces, perhaps those afflicting the Ascent of the Soul (*PGM* V. 96-172); an inscribed piece of *lead* (the usual material for *defixios* and other binding spells) is used to break a spell (*PGM* XXXVI. 178-87). Similarly, a triangular sherd found at the fork of a road is to be engraved to 'dissolve every enchantment' (*PGM* XXXVI. 256-64); a figure drawn on *papyrus* serves an uncertain purpose (*PGM* XXXVI. 264-74); a piece of *papyrus* with which a spotted lizard (?) has been picked up is engraved with five magic characters and placed under a table, for an unstated purpose (*PGM* LXIII. 21-24). Additional phylacteries, for which no writing material is mentioned, include a spell against night-mares and air-demons (*PGM* VII. 311-16), with an apparent variant (*PGM* VII. 317-18). Similarly, seven magical characters are used (written?) for protection in a "dismissal" formula in a revelation invoking Light; the bearer is to be 'healthy, free from terror and free from demonic attacks' (*PGM* LXII. 24-46). Noteworthy is the fact that a number of the preserved formulas above, although written against demons, appear in contexts other than healing or exorcisms. A recently published formu-lary, *P. Oxy.* LXV. 4468 (late 1st century C.E.) con-tains rites for a phylactery 'probably intended to protect from bad encounters (men or evil spirits?)' (Maltomini 1998:121). For rites combining papy-rus and other materials, see, further, section 5.

2. B. ACTUAL PAPYRUS AMULETS

a. *Medical complaints*: discharge (*SM* I. 26, 32); exorcism (*SM* I.24); discharge from the eyes (*SM* I. 26); fever (and shivering) of various kinds (*PGM* XVIIIv. 1-7; *PGM* XXXIII. 1-25; *SM* I. 2, 3, 4, 9, 10, 11, 12, 13, 14, 18, 19, 21, 22, 23, 25, 28, 29, 31, 34, 35); fever and headache (*SM* I. 14, 22; II. 92 [formulary?]); headache (migraine) (*PGM* XVI-IIa. 1-4; *SM* I. 32 [with discharge]); scorpion sting (*SM* I. 16); inflammation of the uvula (*SM* I. 1); healing (general) (*SM* I. 20, 30, 33, 36 [?]). It is clear from the actual papyrus amulets that fever-amulets predominate.

b. *Favor and victory charms, etc.*: a long Jewish invocation of six heavens, etc. for favor, influence, victory, and strength is an actual amuletic text in that it preserves the name of its bearer, Paulus Julianus (*PGM* XXXV. 1-42). Another favor charm (*charitēsion*) invokes a number of desirable attributes associated with Jewish (Solomon, etc.) and mythic Greek figures (Adonis, Kypris); it seeks favor, success, repute, beauty, love, charm, for the bearer (*SM* II. 63). Although it is non-personalized, its format suggests an "applied" amulet.

c. *Other, miscellaneous, and uncertain rituals*: An amulet with magic names and the formula 'protect the bearer' obstensibly serves for general protection (*SM* I. 15; general deliverance for Artemidora is also requested in an amulet naming Lord Serapis as "victor", *SM* I. 7); salvation is addressed in a non-specific formula (*SM* I. 27); another asks protection of a grave and mummified

body belonging to Phtheios alias Saioneis (*PGM* LIX: no writing mentioned [the text is fragmen-tary]). An image of Kronos, obtained from a vision of a star, is used for protection in a rite involving Isis/Providence (*PGM* LVII: to be copied on papyrus?). Finally, some papyrus slips are inscribed with magic names and/or symbols only (cf. *PGM* XVIIc. 1-14; *PGM* XXV. a-d; *PGM* LX).

3. PHYLACTERIES (METAL AMULETS, LAMELLAE)

Gold (Au), silver (Ag), tin (Sn), copper (Cu), iron (Fe), and lead (Pb) are all media described in the magical papyri for engraving amulets. Lead, and sometimes tin, are often used for a variety of non-protective rituals. These include *defixios* (curses), spells to arrest anger, restraining spells, and certain aggressive love-charms (cf. *PGM* VII. 411-16). Tin is also used in aggressive magic (cf. *PGM* VII. 459-61; 462-66). Although no actual amulets of tin have been recorded, it is important to recognize that many metals remain unanalyzed. Furthermore, most cases of leaden phylacteries turn out to be silver that has tarnished black. Similarly, copper is almost always mistaken for bronze (cf. *GMA* I. 32) because it oxidizes to a greenish patina. Generally speaking bronze, being an alloy of tin, copper, and other metals, is unsuitable for amulets, which require the use of only the "pure" metals and papyrus.

3. A. INSTRUCTIONS FROM FORMULARIES

a. *Medical complaints*: an inscribed *tin lamella* is used 'For Ascent of the Uterus' (*PGM* VII. 260-71: to be 'clothed in 7 colors'); a *tin* tablet is also used for sciatica (*SM* II. 74: engraved with *Iaeô*-formula and prayer for deliverance from pain in tendons, sinews, and bones); another is used for strangury (*SM* II. 94: magic name?), and possibly a second, as well (*SM* II. 96).

b. *Favor and victory charms*: A *gold* or *silver lamella* is engraved with a design of magic names and symbols for use in a charm to restrain anger; it works against 'enemies, accusers, brigands, pho-bias, and nightmares' (*PGM* X. 24-35: diagram of symbols and names); a *gold* leaf is inscribed with angel-names for good luck in part of the ritual called the "Sword of Dardanos", in truth a spell to attract the soul of another (*PGM* IV. 1716-1870); a *gold lamella* is also required for popularity and love (*PGM* IV. 2145-2240); and a "solar" (*gold*) amulet is inscribed with symbols and prayer in "Hermes' Wondrous Victory Charm" (*PGM* VII. 919-24). A *silver* leaf is required for favor and crowds and works for demons (*PGM* XXXVI. 275-83: names and symbols, used with frankincense); a strip of *tin*, inscribed in "Stele of Aphrodite" is to be used for friendship, favor, success, and friends (*PGM* VII. 215-18).

c. *Demon possession and the Evil Eye*: A *gold, silver, tin*, or piece of *hieratic papyrus* is needed for a phylactery against demons, phantasms, sickness, and suffering (*PGM* VII. 579-90: a "protective" formula). A *tin* tablet, inscribed with magic names and a spell of protection, is to be worn on a demoniac, following the exorcism (*PGM* IV. 1227-1264); a phylactery of *tin*, inscribed with magic names, is also used in the "Tested Charm of Pibechis for those possessed by demons" (*PGM* IV. 3007-86); and fragmentary rituals on a formulary against demoniacs includes the possible writing of a Solomonic formula, but no actual writing material is preserved (*SM* II. 94 [frag.]). A *tin lamella* is also inscribed for wrecking chariots (*PGM* IV. 2145-2240), but this genre belongs to the arena of aggressive magic.

d. *Other, miscellaneous, and uncertain rituals*: For divination, an inscribed *gold, silver* or *tin* leaf is needed in a foreknowledge spell (*PGM* III. 282-409: magic symbols only); an inscribed strip of *tin-foil*, crowned with myrtle, fumigated, and placed under the pillow secures a dream oracle (*PGM* VII. 740-55: magic names); both a *gold* and *silver lamella*, inscribed with vowels, are used in an initiation performed to the sun, in the "Book of Moses" (*PGM* XIII, see below); a strip of *tin* inscribed with a protective spell anticipates the visitation of a personal angelic being (*PGM* VII. 478-90), and a *gold* tablet, written as a "stele", delivers from death (*PGM* IV. 1167-1226). For general protection, a *silver* leaf is required (*PGM* III. 410-423: for memory); another *silver* one is used against a divine encounter (*PGM* IV. 154-285: inscribed with 100 letters with bronze stylus and strung with thong from ass-hide); again, a *silver* leaf in the "Slander Spell to Selene" gains protection against the deity (*PGM* IV. 2622-2707: magic characters). For victory (in courts, etc.) and for use in various favor and victory contexts a *silver lamella* is to be worn in one's garments (*PGM* XXXVI. 35-68). A "leaf" tied with linen and enclosed in a capsule with some substance of a black wolf is also mentioned in a fragmentary papyrus formulary (*SM* II. 81). Finally, an *iron lamella* is inscribed with Homeric verses for a variety of purposes (for runaways, as a counter-charm, in court, for favor, and various protective measures) (*PGM* IV. 2145-2240).

3. B. ACTUAL METAL PHYLACTERIES (*LAMELLAE*)

a. *Medical complaints*. The following examples represent what kinds of medical complaints and

issues are addressed on the actual inscribed amulets of gold, silver, and copper (Kotansky 1994 = *GMA* I; et al.). Their texts preserve a host of different prayers and formulas (see Kotansky: 1991a): 1) *Medical Complaints*: "elephantiasis" (*GMA* I. 18: *silver*. Graeco-Latin); eye complaints (*GMA* I. 31: *gold*, Latin; *GMA* I. 53: *gold*, for ophthalmia); epilepsy (with headache: *GMA* I. 57: *gold*, from Syria, 4th-5th cent. C.E.; Kotansky 1980; cf. Bevilacqua 1999: 18-27: *silver*); feet complaints (Jordan-Kotansky 1997: no. 339: *silver*); fever, using various types of formulas (*GMA* I. 56: *copper*, Hebrew-Greek. From near Kibbutz 'Evron, Israel; *GMA* I. 59: *silver*, from Oxyrhynchus, 3rd cent. C.E.) (see also the "Phylactery of Moses", below); headache (migraine) (*GMA* I. 13: *silver*, "Antaura" *historiola*); "wandering" of the uterus Beirut (*GMA* I. 51: *gold*, adjuration/exorcism formula), for which a rare Latin parallel on a lead sheet comes from Roman Britain (Tomlin 1997; see Aubert 1989; Hanson 1995; Betz 1998 for general studies). For health, see the gold plaque under "Favor and Victory Charms", and for sickness related to demons, see the section "Demonic Possession and the Evil Eye".

Multiple complaints: The so-called "Phylactery of Moses" (*GMA* I. 32: *copper*?), with its new fragment of Aquila (Deut. 32: 1-3), is a remarkable, albeit fragmentary, text that seems to preserve an initiatory rite for protection against all kinds of sorcery, binding-spells, evil spirits, as well as fever, the evil eye, and any apparition (*phantasia*). Similarly, a remarkably long Greek invocation of angelic spheres and realms (*GMA* I. 52: *silver*, Beirut), seems to be liturgical in nature. It seeks protection for Alexandra whom Zoe bore, from demons, compulsion of demons, sorcery, binding-spells, and various forms of love-magic. A kindred example seeks to protect the body, soul, and limb of Thomas, whom Maxima bore from all witchcraft (*goēteia*), sorcery (*pharmakeia*), curses, those who have died untimely and violently, and from every evil matter (Heintz 1996: *silver*). The so-called "Basilidian" *lamella* describes deliverance from 'the spirit of fever, all epilepsy, all hydrophobia, every evil eye, every violent sending of spirits, all poisoning' (Bonner 1950:100; et al.). A *silver* Greek-Aramaic bilingual text from Egypt preserves a lengthy incantation against a variety of demonic afflictions plaguing John, son of Benenata. The text preserves angelic invocations, fragments of various Biblical stories (*historiolae*) and citations to rid the bearer of every evil spirit, demon, dead person, and evil sorcery, along with quotidian fever and hectic fever (Kotansky-Naveh-Shaked 1992).

b. *Favor and victory charms*: A gold *lamella* from Thessalonika (2nd cent. C.E.) invokes "Aphrodite's Name" for favor and success (*GMA* I. 40); an Oxyrhynchus *silver* amulet requests 'favor, friendship, success, loveliness to him who bears the amulet' (*GMA* I. 60; 2nd-3rd cent. C.E.). Another, a long spell invoking a host of angel-names on a kind of house-amulet (from Phthiotis in Thessaly, 4th-5th cent. C.E.) requests victory and grace (*charis*); however, the context also mentions driving out demons, protecting 'the house and souls of John and Georgia', and 'turning away all harm from this house' (*GMA* I. 41: *gold*); an early *gold* amulet from Rome (ca. 1st cent C.E.), found near the tomb of the Scipios, carries the formula 'give a victory over the names written below' (*GMA* I. 28); a Christian *gold* plaque from Syria (5th-6th cent C.E.) is written for 'health and favor' (*GMA* I. 45); finally, a long spell on a *gold* leaf seeks protection for Proclus in a lawsuit before Diogenianus, the *dux* of Bostra in Arabia, and before Pelagius, the *assessor* (*GMA* I. 58; Kotansky 1991: 41-60); furthermore, an unedited phylactery in the former Amati collection appears to be a favor and victory charm (Bevilacqua 1989).

A relatively early silver *lamella* from Emesa, Syria (possibly, 1st cent. B.C.E.), cites a list of names related to that found in I Enoch, "Book of the Watchers". The spell requests that the divine names be "propitious" to the wearer (whether male or female) (*GMA* I. 48). Related to favor-magic is a *gold* spell from Nubia containing an invocation of Isis, Queen of Denderah, for fertility and conception (*GMA* I. 61). Similarly, a gold leaf from Zian (Tunisia, 2nd-3rd cent. C.E.) depicts a sword surrounded by magic names; it appears to invoke a kind of angel of "sexual frenzy" to drive a woman mad with love (*GMA* I. 62).

c. *Demon Possession and the Evil Eye*: A liturgical exorcism against the spirit named Phōath-phro is preserved on a *silver* piece from Antioch in Pisidia (*GMA* I. 35); a *gold* amulet from Amphipolis in Thrace includes magic formulas for protection against "every male and female demon" (*GMA* I. 38); the "Phylactery of Moses," mentioned above, protects against an evil spirit (*pneuma ponēron*), among other things a *bronze* (*copper*?) phylactery from Sicily (*GMA* I. 33), with its angelology, seems to also protect from an evil demon; a demon sent to 'menace' a named victim occurs on an unusual *gold* amulet from Rumania (*GMA* I. 24, Latin); a spell 'to drive away (*apelaunein*) every harmful and destructive spirit' occurs on a now lost *gold* amulet from Rome (*GMA* I. 25; cf. Bevilacqua 1991: 37f.). The same verb is found on a *silver* phylactery from Xanthos, using the formula, 'drive away every wicked demon, occurrence, happening, encounter, or evil eye, drive and chase them away' (Jordan-Kotansky 1996: addressed to the 'Holy Elements; Holy Characters'); a second, Christian, adjuration of Solomon and angels found at Xanthos (Jordan-Kotansky 1996) is probably *copper*, not *bronze*, and is contemporary with the piece mentioned above, despite the printed dates (III-IV? / IV-VI? Both are probably 4th cent. C.E.). A very difficult, fragmentary reading on a *gold* leaf found at Epiphania in Syria (4th-5th cent. C.E.), seems to preserve an adjuration of Pantokrator (*GMA* I. 47); a pair of phylacteries, one called a "Phylactery of the Living God" (*gold*), and the other "A Phylactery for every disease and sicknesses" (*silver*) were found together in the tomb of Abbagaza in Theodosia in the Crimea (*GMA* I. 65-66; 2nd-3rd cent. C.E.); similarly, from the Sea of Azov region of the Crimean Peninsula comes a *silver* "exorcism" of 'every spirit, *phantasma* (apparition), and every beast from the soul of this woman' (*GMA* I. 67); finally, a fragmentary *silver* leaf from Cyprus (4th cent. C.E.) invokes Jesus the Nazorean, his angels, and holy apostles in an apparent exorcism. In the later magic of the Byzantine period, lead seems to have become the standard material on which Christian exorcisms were copied (Manganaro 1994; cf. *GMA*, p. xvi).

d. *Other, miscellaneous, and uncertain rituals*: A list of magic names and "sovereign angels" are invoked to 'Save the one whom Atalante bore, Euphiletos' (*GMA* I. 39). This could be an amulet for protection in the afterlife (see below). General protection, too, is suggested by various formulas found on a number of phylacteries: 'Protect me, Alphianus' (*GMA* I. 2: *gold*, Segontium, Wales, 1st-2nd C.E.); a *silver* leaf from Badenweiler with mention of protection from "all danger" (*omni periculo*), perhaps written for a group (of litigants? *GMA* I. 7); a Greco-Latin *silver* charm for 'strength and life' writes to 'protect Justina whom Sarra bore' from unstated problems (*GMA* I. 8; near Poitiers, 4th cent. C.E.). A *silver lamella* from Amisos in Pontus may have been written for a lawsuit or unstated "matter" (*hypothesis*); it also guards against poison or witchraft (*pharmakon*, *GMA* I. 36). A pair of *bronze* hailstorm amulets (*GMA* I. 11) represent types of amulets that were not worn on the body but set up in fields.

A large percentage of the published magical *lamellae* preserve enigmatic texts with no indication of their specific purpose. These, for the most part carry nothing other than magical "charactēres",

vowels, and/or divine-names and angels: *GMA* I. 1;
3; 4; 5; 6; 9; 10; 12; 14; 15; 16; 17; 19; 20; 21; 22;
23; 26; 29; 30; 34; 37; 42; 43; 44; 49; 55; 63; 64;
cf. Parca 1997; Phillips 1997, etc. (*GMA* I. 54
seems to preserve some sort of unidentifiable astro-
magical fragment). Some of these more puzzling
texts with magic names or symbols may have been
written specifically for protection in the afterlife,
much like the spells of the Egyptian Book of the
Dead, Coffin Texts, and Pyramid Texts which
helped the deceased Pharaoh navigate specific per-
ils in the next world. Oblique references to Egyptian deities like Osiris Khentamenthes (in *GMA* I.
30), for example, may force us to rethink the thana-
tological context of many of these amulets. The
epithet of Osiris as Khentamenthes points to his
rulership of the "Western Half", the Realm of the
Dead in the Egyptian afterlife. In this respect, the
phylacteries may be continuing the tradition of the
"Orphic" gold leaves, texts deposited in late Clas-
sical-Hellenistic graves to assist the departed soul
in the next world. Among the corpus of phylacteries, there comes from Rome a late example of an
Orphic leaf used specifically as an "afterlife" talisman (*GMA* I. 27).

4. ENGRAVED GEMSTONES

Magical gems of semi-precious material (quart-
zes, jaspers, chalcedonies, hematites, among many
others) represent a special category of amulets
that owes its flowering to the early centuries of
the Common Era. The literature is quite extensive,
but the principal corpora include Bonner 1950;
Delatte-Derchain 1964; Philipp 1986. By the 2nd
century C.E., the manufacture of magic gemstones
began to increase exponentially. Magical intaglios,
unlike seal-rings, were written orthographically
and not in retrograde; hence, they were usually
worn openly so that their designs and lettering
could be read and interpreted. Although there is
some disparity between what the papyrus instructions inform us about the gemstone types, the difference has been overstated (e.g. in Smith 1979). It
is remarkable enough that the papyri describe, in
several instances, actual gemstone types, not that
every type known needs to be recorded in the
extant manuals.

In a number of cases, it appears that texts normally intended for writing on papyrus have also
been recorded on gemstone surfaces. There are also
longer spells, evidently copied from papyrus formularies, that address magic operations not falling
under the strict category of protective, healing
magic (i.e., they are not amulets). Examples are discussed in Bonner 1950, chapter VIII, and include

Spells to Restrain Wrath (*thymokatocha*), a Spell to
Cause a Separation (*diakopos*), Spells to Fetch a
Lover (*agogai*), and various spells intended to harm.

4. A. INSTRUCTIONS FROM FORMULARIES

The papyrus formularies describe magic gemstones in a variety of procedures, mostly ritualistic
rather than therapeutic. A full study is given in
Smith 1979, who suggests there may have existed
separate manuals just for gemstone magic. In *PGM*
IV. 1596-1715, in particular, the consecration and
empowerment of a phylactery or amulet (of stone
or other material), is described in detail. Other
examples of the use of engraved magic stones
include the following: A pebble numbered 3663
(the isopsephic value of the god Bainchōōōch) is
required in a direct vision spell (*PGM* IV. 930-
1114); a *magnet*, cut in form of a heart and
engraved with Hekate and vowels, is used in the
"Slander Spell to Selene" *PGM* IV. 2622-2707); a
lodestone carved with three-faced Hekate and
properly consecrated with natron, water, and
blood, is used in the "Prayer to Selene" (*PGM* IV.
2785-2890); a detailed description of how to carve,
consecrate, and use a scarab of 'costly green stone'
is provided in a rite to empower the practitioner
with powerful divinatory abilities (*PGM* V. 213-
303); similarly, a jasperlike agate, engraved with
Sarapis is used in some form of dream-divination
(*PGM* V. 447-58). For the "oblong" stone of
Heliorus, see section 5, below.

4. B. ACTUAL GEMSTONES

The preserved magic gems are characterized by a
rather canonical inventory of widespread designs:
the Anguipede-figure ("snake-legged cock-
headed" soldier), Chnoubis, Pantheos-deity, Harpocrates, Reaper-figure, and so on. Although these
are studied in the standard corpora, more thor-
ough-going treatments are also available (Post
1979: Anguipede). Scores of other minor types and
variations proliferate, as well, so that each stone, in
a sense, is unique. The gems types often carry more
or less standardized "undecipherable" magical
words, names, alphabetic series, using the Greek
alphabet alongside the strange system of magical
charactēres – a traditional magic "hieroglyphic"
system of entirely unknown origin and derivation.

a. *Medical complaints*: Inscriptions on a variety
of gemstones address the following representative
examples of medical complaints: colic (Bonner
1950: 62f. Delatte-Derchain 1964: 206); digestive
and stomach problems (Delatte-Derchain 1964:
67; 72; 149; Bonner 1950: 51-62, with reference to
certain ancient writers on stomach amulets and

the Chnoubis gems); fever (Bonner 1950: 67-68; Kotansky 1980); inflammation (Bonner 1950: 68); eye complaints (Bonner 1950: 69-71); liver-pain (Bonner 1950: 66; Delatte-Derchain 1964: 317); gout, or feet-problems (Bonner 1950: 75-76); hydrophobia (demonic) (Bonner 1950: 78); sciatica ("Reaper"-design gems with 'for the hips': Bonner 1950: 71-75; Delatte-Derchain 1964: 196-200: 'I work but don't strain'); scorpion sting (Bonner 1950: 77); wasting disease (*phthisis*: Bonner 1950: 78); uterine and related problems (Bonner 1950: 81-94, 183; Delatte-Derchain 1964: 245-258, of which the most common is the "Ororiouth"-type); and even inflammation of the uvula (Daniel-Maltomini 1989). Some types, of course, such as the Chnoubis-gems and certain "womb"-gems, rely more upon the glyptic design for their interpretation, although occasionally inscriptions support the interpretation. A more complete survey of all the gemstone literature for additional iatromagical inscriptions would make a useful study.

b. *Favor and victory charms (including "Good-luck" charms)*: Inscribed gems regularly request *charis* ("grace"/"favor") for the bearer, ostensibly for business, law-court, or other social settings, often on gems depicting Horus-Harpocrates (Bonner 1950: 48; Delatte-Derchain 1964: 97, 105, 153, with an example of a longer formula: "Give grace, beauty, victory to Sphyridas whom Thinousiris bore"). Some examples cross over into the arena of love and sexual magic (Delatte-Derchain 1964: 239, 242), but in all respects apply to social settings.

Perhaps related, though less social, are general requests for good luck, fortune, or that the god be "propitious," or "merciful," to the wearer (Neverov 1978: no. 47; Bonner 1950: 46f.; Delatte-Derchain 1964: 218). It is unclear whether the divine favor in these instances applies to everyday life, the afterlife, or both. In this respect, the widely attested formula 'protect (me)', written with various forms of *(dia)phylassō* (e.g., Bonner 1950: 45-47), 'protect me from all harm' (e.g. Delatte-Derchain 1964:137), or less often, 'help me' (e.g. Delatte-Derchain 1964: 144, 312), appear on the surface to be banal "good-luck" charms for day-to-day life; they may in fact have served, as well, as post-mortem amulets to be buried with the deceased.

Gems that carry commonplace religious slogans, acclamations, and epithets such as 'One God', 'One God Iao', 'One god who conquers all,' 'Isis conquers', 'Serapis conquers all', 'Great is the name of Serapis', 'Great is Nemesis', and so on (Bonner 1950: 46; 167-85; Delatte-Derchain 1964: 101, 160, 162, 287; 266, this last with a longer, liturgical formula) represent prayer-like requests for divine favor that may function apart from social contexts (victory over demons, bad planetary influences, etc.), or they may serve as abbreviated victory charms against human adversaries. A more careful study of these types would be useful. Various healing and protective formulas are also commonly found on Byzantine bronze pendants that carry similar slogans (Barb 1972). Included here should be the widespread proliferation of the "Seal of Solomon"/"Seal of God" types, depicting a militant figure mounted on horseback (Spier 1993; Delatte-Derchain 1964: 261-264; etc.).

c. *The Evil Eye and demonic possession*: Deliverance on gems from Envy (*Phthonos* or *Baskosynē*) and the 'much-suffering eye' is common (Bonner 1950: 96-99). Specific mention of protection from an evil demon is relatively rare on gems (cf. Bonner 1950: 95f.; Mastrocinque 1998; Kotansky 1991; 1995). The text of a long exorcistic formula, liturgical in nature, is preserved on a carnelian (Delatte-Derchain 1964: 316).

d. *Other, miscellaneous, and uncertain rituals*: A divination formula on a basalt tablet with vowels and magic names (*Mauar-/Mar-*permutations) and the formula 'reveal to me this very night, with truthfulness and remembrance' represents a rare example of a papyrus-type text written on a gem material (Tomassetti-Wuensch 1899). The warding off of drugs/poison, as well as health, headache, neckpains, and toothache on an agate marble provides another example of longer, papyrus-text spells written on stone (Neverov 1978: no. 50, p. 848). To this one may compare a hematite falcon amulet inscribed against evil (harm), the wrath of gods and demons, and sorcerers (*SM* I. 6).

Liturgical material from various more literary contexts, including hymnic or invocational fragments, are also found on gems and require independent analysis as a genre (Keil 1940; Bonner 1950: 181-185; Delatte-Derchain 1964: 98, 119, 140, 188, 381; Philipp 1986: 119; Bevilacqua 1991: 32 [for healing?]; Kotansky 1995; Kotansky-Spier 1995). Long inscriptions, too, written with Greek letters but preserving unintelligible sequences of text may indeed preserve known foreign texts, liturgical in nature, such as Egyptian or Hebrew. Some, too, may be corrupted forms of Greek (cf. Delatte-Derchain 1964: 337-342). The phenomenon of actual "fragments" of magic formularies being accidentally copied onto various amulets requires a systematic study (Blanchet 1934-1937 = Bonner & Youtie 1953 [1982]; Delatte-Derchain 1964: 98, 317; Philipp 1986: 119).

5. OTHER INSCRIBED MATERIALS

Here the use of ritual and amulet are sometimes indistinguishable. Small offerings or rituals involving organic and amuletic materials may be burned as protective gestures. In this sense the whole ritual of sacrifice and offering is prophylactic in nature.

Instructions from Formularies: A *circle*, on which one stands, is engraved with magic characters, while one is crowned with the *tail of a cat*, in a spell to acquire the "Shadow of the Sun" (*PGM* VII. 846-61); *eggs*, two "male", inscribed with myrrh ink, are used in a protective rite in a 'Meeting with your own daimon' (*PGM* VII. 505-28; cf. XII. 100); inscribed *eggs*, one placed in a latrine, the other buried in a house are also used in a favor charm (*SM* II. 97); a *Gothic ring* is inscribed with a formula to cure the eyes (*SM* II. 94); a *grape-vine leaf*, inscribed, for tumors (?), is boiled, etc. (*SM* II. 94); the *hide* of a *sheep*, one black, one white, one for the right and one for left arm, respectively, are each inscribed with magic names and Homeric verses in myrrhed ink (*PGM* IV. 475-829: "Mithras Liturgy"). The *hide* of an *ass* is also inscribed in a love-spell of attraction (*PGM* XXXVI. 361-71), although this is not an amuletic function, per se; the *hoofs* of a horse are inscribed with a spell in a "Victory charm for the races" (*PGM* VII. 390-93); the *hide* of a *hyena* is inscribed for coughs (*PGM* VII. 203-5; VII. 206-7); a seven-leafed *laurel* sprig is engraved with seven characters 'for deliverance' (from death?) in an Apollonian invocation (*PGM* I. 262-347); leaves of *laurel*, inscribed and held in the hand in an invocation serves for divine protection (*PGM* II. 1-64); a second garland of laurel, inscribed with magic names is also used for protection (*ibid.*); an alternative procedure (*PGM* II. 64-184) requires a twelve-leaf sprig, inscribed, along with a wool garland; a 12-leaf branch of *laurel* crown is inscribed with signs of the zodiac for protection in a dream divination (*PGM* VII. 795-845). Furthermore, for insomnia a leaf of *laurel* is inscribed with a magic names and placed under a pillow or mattress (*SM* II. 74); another *laurel* leaf is inscribed for insomnia (*SM.* II. 96). The leaf of a *Persea tree*, engraved with vowels protects against the manifestation of a god (*PGM* IV. 475-829: "Mithras Liturgy"). An *olive* leaf, inscribed on either side with a symbol for the sun and moon, heals fever (*PGM* VII. 213-14); an *olive* leaf is also used in a spell for *fever with shivering* (*SM* II. 81). *Linen*, the sacred fabric used for mummification, is required in several recipes instead of papyrus: In a certain "Charm for a Direct Vision", a piece of *linen* taken from a statue of Harpocrates is inscribed with a protective prayer, enclosed with an "everliving" plant, and entwined with Anubian thread (*PGM* IV. 930-1114); a *linen* rag, inscribed with characters, is used for hardening of the breasts (*PGM* VII. 208-9); a *linen* cloth is also used in a "Charm for a Direct Vision" (*PGM* VII. 335-47) and in a "Request for a Dream Oracle" (*PGM* VII. 359-69); these do not appear to serve amuletic functions. A *linen* strip, inscribed, and placed on the left side of the head while asleep obtains a Dream Revelation (*PGM* VII. 664-85).

Additional engraved materials from the recipes include the following: *mud* smeared on doorposts of a bedchamber, of which the right is then inscribed with a stylus with magic names and characters, is used in the form of an Apollonian divination (*PGM* II. 64-183); lime wood – inscribed with ink of vermillion with magic names and a prayer against aerial demons, angels, phantoms, ghostly visitations, and enchantments, and then enclosed in a purple skin and worn around the neck – protects the wearer against Selene (!) in a "slander spell" (*PGM* IV. 2622-2707); *oil*, invoked, and smeared on the body, is used for fever (*PGM* VII. 211-12); an *ostrakon* inscribed with a Christian *historiola* and placed on the right thigh, eases labor (*SM* II. 96); a *golden scepter* in a metrical "Prayer to Selene" is mentioned in an *historiola* of Kronos (*PGM* IV. 2785-2890: for steadfastness); a *scarlet parchment*, inscribed and plastered onto the side of the head, heals migraine headache (*PGM* VII. 201-2); the *rib of a young pig*, inscribed with a figure of Zeus and a magic name, is used to protect against a deity in the "Oracle of Kronos" (*PGM* IV. 3086-3124); a *seashell* is inscribed with a love charm (*PGM* VII. 300a-310), and another is used in a love-charm "to induce insomnia" (*PGM* VII. 374-76); these, properly speaking, are not amulets. A previously buried *skull of an ass*, inscribed with characters and a magic name (using the blood of a black dog) is used along with an *ass's tooth* (fastened with *silver*) and an *old lady's tooth* (fastened with *gold*) to protect the practitioner against the power of the goddess invoked (*PGM* XI.a 1-40); a *tassel*, attached to a garment, and invoked directly, is used as an amulet 'Against every wild animal, aquatic creature, and robbers' (*PGM* VII. 370-73); a *wick*, inscribed and used in 'another (Charm to induce insomnia)' (*PGM* VII. 376-84) is non-amuletic.

6. UNINSCRIBED MATERIALS (ORGANIC AMULETS: PLANTS, MINERALS, ANIMAL MATERIALS, ETC.)

The use of root- and other vegetal iatromagical remedies presumably goes back to prehistoric times. The following inventory of organic materials used as amulets stands in the same tradition of herbal remedies as that found in Theophrastus, Pliny, Dioscorides, Aelian, Aelius Promotus, Alexander Trallianus, the *Cyranides*, and many others.

The *eye of an ape* (or the *eye of a corpse* died violently), mixed with peony (Rose) and oil of lily, is required for an "Invisibility Spell" (*PGM* I. 247-262); a *bean*, with a small bug in it, can be worn as a contraceptive (*PGM* LXIII. 24-25); another contraceptive requires a *pierced bean* tied with *mule hide* (*PGM* LXIII. 26-28; cf. also *PGM* LXV. 1-4); the hairs of a *bear*, plaited into a cord and worn as a diadem, serves as a protective amulet in a "Powerful Spell of the Bear" (*PGM* IV. 1331-89); a *beetle* is used as an amulet for illness; (*SM* II. 78); the *whiskers* of a *cat* are used as a phylactery (!) while making a curse-spell using inscribed *lamellae* (*PGM* III. 1-164); a *falcon*, drowned in a honey-milk mixture and wrapped in a cloth along with ones's fingernails, hair, and an inscribed *papyrus* strip, is formed into a plaster of frankincense and old wine and then set up in a little juniper wood shrine in a rite to acquire one's own spirit-*daimon* (*PGM* I. 1-42); a rite involving a *falcon's head*, held in the right hand along with a black Isis band over the eyes, causes a real falcon to drop an oblong stone from the sky (*PGM* I. 42-195). This, in turn, is to be engraved as an amulet (with a lion-faced figure, Heliorus, and magic names) for protection in the use of another rite to acquire an assistant "spirit" guide; a *gecko* is used in a "Favor and Victory Charm" (*PGM* VII. 186-90); the eye of a *lizard* placed in a *goat* (?) *skin* may be used for eye affliction (*SM* II. 78: fragmentary); the *fat* of an *owl*, or the *eye* of a *nightowl*, along with the *ball of a dungbeetle* in unripe *olive oil*, is to be smeared on the entire body for protection in an "Invisibility Spell" (*PGM* I. 222-231); the heart of an *owl* may be used for eye affliction (*SM* II. 78: as above, fragmentary); *palm, palm fiber*, and male *date of palm* are used as a protective amulet in the "Charm of Solomon" (*PGM* IV. 850-929); three *peonies* wrapped around the left arm are used for general protection in a lamp spell to attract a woman (*PGM* LXII. 1-24); a white *rooster*, held in the hand with *twelve pinecones*, is used in an Invocation to the Sun (*PGM* III. 633-731); a *red rag* is possibly used for eye affliction (*SM* II. 78: as above); similarly, a *tick* from a black cow, in *goat* (?) *skin*, is used for eye affliction (*SM* II. 78: fragmentary, as above); a garland of *wool*, with alternating red and white strands is used in an Apollonian divination rite (*PGM* II. 64-184: as above, with mud); the *tooth of a hyena* is used in a

victory charm (*SM* II. 96); *wormwood*, ground up with *sun opal, a magnet-stone, heart of hoopoe*, and *honey*, aids memory in a divinatory rite (*PGM* II. 1-64); finally, in the rite above, requiring the white rooster, *wormwood* is held protectively in the right hand with a *snakeskin* held in the left as one invokes the sun (*PGM* III.633-731).

7. AMULETIC BUNDLES

In addition to these uninscribed, "organic" amulets, several passages in the papyri describe more complex amulets that involve a number of different operations, including the inscribing of papyrus texts and other objects. These can be largely described as "amuletic bundles" or "packets". For example, for business, a phylactery to be placed in one's shop is made up of a three-headed statuette of *Etruscan wax* that has been molded into a *sea falcon, baboon* and *ibis*; each of these figures is given certain divine attributes. This figure is then wrapped as an Osirian mummy, with a "heart" of *magnetite* and an inscribed hieratic *papyrus* placed inside. The whole is then set up onto an *iron* base, is installed in a miniature temple of *juniper* (at moonrise on the third lunar day), is given sacrifice and libation, is crowned with olive, and, finally, is invoked with the names written on the papyrus strip (*PGM* IV. 3125-71). Similarly, in *PGM* VIII. 1-63 a *baboon* figurine is carved of *olive wood* with the attributes of Hermes (= Thoth) and enclosed with an inscribed papyrus for good business and set up in a workshop; another such fetish is found in *SM* II. 97 (cf. further, the *skin of a mouse* kept in a workshop, for business, in the fragmentary *SM* II. 99). See further, *PGM* IV. 3172-3208; *PGM* V. 370-446. Related is the so-called Eighth Book of Moses (*PGM* XIII), a complex set of rites that obtains from the god a secret name that can be used in a variety of subsidiary magical rituals of the standard kind (healing, casting our demons, breaking spells, restraining anger, and so on).

8. AMULETS, GNOSTICISM, AND THEURGY

Although early collectors and savants often referred to the magic gemstones and *lamellae* as "Gnostic", such a designation has long fallen out of favor (cf. Bonner 1950: 1f.). No enduring connection between specific Gnostic groups and our preserved corpora of amulets has been conclusively established. An exception seem to be the amulets found among the ruins of the Manichaean houses at Kellis (Mirecki, et al. 1997), and this may point to a more widespread practice. Owing to the fact that many of the deities, angels, vowels, and magical *charaktēres* preserved in Gnostic documents (e.g., the Nag Hammadi texts) are the same as those found in the magical texts, the subject needs to be revisited (cf. Jackson 1989). Plotinus – disinterested in matters pertaining to theurgy – was one of those who complained that Gnostics composed magic incantations, presumably for the elevation of the soul past menacing demonic forces (*Enneads* II, 9, 14). In the *Books of Jeu* (ed. Schmidt-Mac-Dermot), adherents seal themselves with magic "characters" and invoke mystic names while holding an especially designed numerical pebble (*psēphos*) for just such protection in the higher dimensional realms (cf. Iamblichus, *De myster.* III, 14, 41, on the use of magic *charaktēres*). Further, among the Nag Hammadi Codices (NHC) there is persistent evidence of the use of magic names, symbols (*charaktēres*), angel-names, and vowels in common with the magical amulets (e.g. *Iaō, Sabaōth, Abrasax, Sesengenbarpharangēs, Akrammachamari*, etc.); cf. the *Apocryphon of John*, esp. NHC II, 15, 30-19, 10; *Gospel of the Egyptians*, NHC III, 52, 9-26, IV, 64, 2-23; the Hermetic *Discourse on the Eighth and the Ninth*, NHC VI, 56, 17-22 (a "magic" prayer; cf. 61,10-15). Also, the *Pistis Sophia*, esp. Book IV, presents the wholesale use of papyri incantations, presumably borrowed directly from magical handbooks. All this suggests that Gnostic groups would have written amulets to be used along with their magically invoked hymns (cf. *Gospel of the Egyptians* NHC III, 43, 20-44, 9; IV, 53, 17-54, 13, for mention of a secret name written on a tablet). It is also possible that they used amulets for specific healing rites (cf. the fever-amulets in *P.Kell.G.* 85-88).

Conversely, some of our preserved amulets may actually derive from Gnostic groups. The occurrence of some names and ideas peculiar to Gnosticism rather than to magic identifies the talismans as specifically Gnostic. The *Ialdabaōth*-gem discussed by Bonner (1950: 135-138) is certainly a Gnostic amulet, as he himself admits (see further, Kotansky-Spier 1995; Kotansky 1980, on *Elēlēth*, the principal Gnostic 'Light-Aeon', on a gold *lamella*; cf. Heintz 1996, on the *Pisandraptēs*, etc. on a silver *lamella* – a name found elsewhere only in the Gnostic *Apocryphon of John*, NHC II, 17, 16).

The issue of the mystic union (*systasis*) of the practitioner with his personal deity involves a kind of ritual common to both the "higher" forms of magical operations of the papyri and to specific theurgic undertakings (Eitrem 1942); however, what requires further study – contingent, of course, upon future discoveries in the field – is to what

extent the amulets used for these rites by either group would have looked the same. Additional research, therefore, may yield closer correlations between practitioners of magic and late antique philosophical schools, whether they be Gnostic, Neoplatonic, Hermetic, or Theurgic. Marinus of Neapolis, the successor of Proclus († 485), attributes to him the use of magic operations to control the weather, including the depositing of amulets (*phylaktēria*) for earthquakes (*Vita Procli*, 28; Eitrem 1942, 73). To what extent this kind of practice penetrated Neoplatonism is difficult to say, but it is indicative of the sort of overlap among competing philosophical systems common in late antiquity.

Lit. A. *General.* J.-J. Aubert, "Threatened Wombs: Aspects of Ancient Uterine Magic", *GRBS* 30 (1989), 421-429 ♦ H.D. Betz, "Fragments from a Catabasis Ritual in a Greek Magical Papyrus", *HR* 19 (1980), 287-295 ♦ idem, "Jewish Magic in the Greek Magical Papyri (*PGM* VII. 260-71)", in: *Antike und Christentum: Gesammelte Aufsätze* IV, Tübingen: Mohr Siebeck, 1998, 187-205 ♦ G. Bevilacqua, *Antichi iscrizioni augurali e magiche dai codici di Girolamo Amati* (*Opuscula Epigraphica* 2), Rome: Università degli Studi di Roma, 1991 ♦ idem, "Le epigrafi magiche", *Annali della Scuola Normale Superiore di Pisa*, serie 4:1 (1999), 65-88 ♦ S. Eitrem, "La théurgie chez les néo-platoniciens et dans les papyrus magiques", *SO* 22 (1942), 49-70 ♦ D. Frankfurter, "Amulets", in: G.W. Bowersock, et al. (eds.), *Late Antiquity: A Guide to the Post Classical World*, Cambridge: Harvard Univ. Press, 1969, 296f. ♦ H.M. Jackson, "The Origin in Ancient Incantatory *Voces Magicae* of Some Names in the Sethian Gnostic System", *Vigiliae Christianae* 43 (1989), 69-79 ♦ R. Kotansky, "Incantations and Prayers for Salvation on Inscribed Greek Amulets", in: D. Obbink & C.A. Faraone (eds.), *Magika Hiera: Ancient Greek Magic and Religion*, Oxford: Oxford University Press, 1991 [a], 107-137 ♦ idem, "Magic in the Court of the Governor of Arabia", *ZPE* (1991, 88 [b] 41-60 ♦ idem, "Greek Exorcistic Amulets", in: M. Meyer & P. Mirecki (eds.), *Ancient Magic & Ritual Power* (Religions in the Graeco-Roman World, 129), Leiden: E.J. Brill, 1995, 243-277 ♦ A. Mastrocinque, *Studi sul Mitraismo (Il Mitraismo e la magia)*, Rome: Bretschneider, 1998 ♦ P. Mirecki et al., "Magical Spell, Manichaean Letter", in: P. Mirecki & J. Beduhn (eds.), *Emerging from Darkness: Studies in the Recovery of Manichaean Sources* (NHMS 43), Leiden: E.J. Brill, 1997, 1-32 ♦ Louis Robert, "Amulettes grecques", *Journal des Savants* (1981), 3-44 ♦ J. Spier, "Medieval Byzantine Amulets and their Tradition", *JWCI* 56 (1993), 25-62.

B. *Magical Papyri.* K. Preisendanz & A. Henrichs (eds.), *Papyri Graecae Magicae: Die griechischen Zauberpapyri*, 2 vols., Stuttgart: Teubner, 1973-74 (= *PGM*) ♦ H.D. Betz, *The Greek Magical Papyri in Translation, Including the Demotic Spells*, I, *Texts*, Chicago: University of Chicago Press, 1986; 1992² ◆ R.W. Daniel, R. & F. Maltomini, *Supplementum Magicum*, I-II (Abhandlungen der Rheinisch-Westfälischen Akademie der Wissenschaften; Sonderreihe, Papyrologica Coloniensia, vol. 16.1/2), Opladen: Westdeutscher Verlag, 1990/1992 (= *SM*) ◆ F. Maltomini, "Magic, Religion and Astrology", in: M.W. Haslam, et al. (eds.), *The Oxyrhynchus Papyri*, vol. 65, London: Egypt Exploration Society, 1998, 103-129 (nos. 4468-4469) ◆ M. Meyer & R. Smith (eds.), *Ancient Christian Magic*, San Francisco: Harper Collins, 1994 ◆ William Brashear & Roy Kotansky, "A New Magical Formulary", in: Marvin Meyer & Paul Mirecki (eds.), *Magic and Ritual in the Ancient World* (Religions in the Graeco-Roman World, 141), Leiden, Boston: E.J. Brill, 2002, 3-24.

C. *Phylacteries (Lamellae).* R.D. Kotansky, *Greek Magical Amulets: The Inscribed Gold, Silver, Copper, and Bronze Lamellae*. Pt. I: *Published Texts of Known Provenance* (Abhandlungen der Nordrhein-Westfälischen Akademie der Wissenschaften. Sonderreihe Papyrologica Coloniensia XXII/1), Opladen: Westdeutscher Verlag, 1994 (= *GMA*) ◆ G. Bevilacqua, "Un filatterio gnostico inedito dai codici di Girolamo Amati", *Miscellanea greca e romana* 14 (1989), 287-298 ◆ idem, "Magica Varia dall' Antiquarium Comunale", *Bollettino dei Musei Comunali di Roma* 13 (1999), 18-30 ◆ C. Faraone & R. Kotansky, "An Inscribed Gold Phylactery in Stamford, Connecticut", *ZPE* 75 (1988), 257-266 (Taf. IX) ◆ F. Heintz, "A Greek Silver Phylactery in the MacDaniel Collection", *ZPE* 112 (1996), 295-300 ◆ D.R. Jordan & R. Kotansky, "Two Phylacteries from Xanthos", *Revue Archéologique* (1996), 161-174 ◆ idem, "A Solomonic Exorcism", in: *Kölner Papyri (P. Köln)*, Band 8 (Abhandlungen der Nordrhein-Westfälischen Akademie der Wissenschaften. Sonderreihe, Papyrologica Coloniensia, Sonderreihe Vol. VII/8), Opladen: Westdeutscher Verlag, 1997, 53-69, no. 338 ◆ idem, "A Spell for Aching Feet", in: idem, 70-81 ◆ G. Manganaro, "Iscrizioni Esorcistiche della Sicilia Bizantina", in: *Scritti classici e cristiani offerti a Francesco Corsaro*, Catania: Università degli Studi di Catania, 1994, 455-464 ◆ J. Naveh, R. Kotansky, S. Shaked, "A Greek-Aramaic Silver Amulet from Egypt in the Ashmolean Museum", *Le Muséon* 105 (1992), 5-24 ◆ R. Kotansky, "Two Amulets in the Getty Museum: A Gold Amulet for Aurelia's Epilepsy. An Inscribed Magical-Stone for Fever, 'Chills', and Headache", *J. Paul Getty Museum Journal* 8 (1980), 181-188 ◆ idem, "A Silver Phylactery for Pain", idem, 11 (1983), 169-178 ◆ M. Parca, "A Gold Lamella in the Joslyn Art Museum, Omaha (Nebraska)", *APF*, Beiheft 3, Band II (1997), 780-785 ◆ R. Phillips, "Son of Thoth' on an Unpublished Gold Lamella from Sidon", *Chronique d'Egypte* 72 (1997), 355-361 ◆ R.S.O. Tomlin, "*Sede in tuo loco*: A Fourth-Century Uterine Phylactery in Latin from Roman Britain", *ZPE* 115 (1997), 291-294 ◆ Roy Kotansky, "An Early Christian Gold *Lamella* for Headache", in: Marvin Meyer & Paul Mirecki (eds.), *Magic and Ritual in the Ancient World* (Religions in the Graeco-Roman World, 141), Leiden, Boston: E.J. Brill, 2002, 37-46.

D. *Magic Gemstones.* A.A. Barb, "Magica Varia", *Syria* 49 (1972), 343-370 (pls. XIX, XX) ◆ Campbell Bonner, *Studies in Magical Amulets, Chiefly Graeco-Egyptian* (University of Michigan Studies, Humanistic Series 49), Ann Arbor: University of Michigan/London: Geoffrey Cumberlege/Oxford: Oxford University Press, 1950 ◆ idem, "An Amulet of the Ophite Gnostics", *Hesperia Supplement* 8 (1949) 43-46 (pl. 8) ◆ C. Bonner & H.C. Youtie, "A Magical Inscription on a Chalcedony", *TAPA* 84 (1953), 60-66 [= *Scriptiunculae Posteriores* II, 676-82] ◆ A. Blanchet, "Une pierre gnostique apparentée peut-être à la 'Pistis Sophia'", *Mélanges Maspero, II: Orient grec, romain et byzantin*, Cairo: L'Institut Français d'archéologie orientale, 1934-1937, 283-287 ◆ A. Delatte & Ph. Derchain, *Les intailles magiques gréco-egyptiennes*, Paris: Bibliothèque Nationale, 1964 ◆ R.W. Daniel & F. Maltomini, "Una gemma magica contro l'inflammazione dell'ugola", *ZPE* 78 (1989), 93f. (Taf. III. a,b) ◆ Ann Ellis Hanson, "Uterine Amulets and Greek Uterine Medicine", *Journal of the History of Medicine* 7 (1995), 281-299 ◆ J. Keil, "Ein rätselhaftes Amulett", *Wiener Jahreshefte* 32 (1940), 79-84 ◆ R. Kotansky, "A Magic Gem Inscribed in Greek and Artificial Phoenician", *ZPE* 85 (1991 [c]), 237-238 ◆ idem, "Remnants of a Liturgical Exorcism on a Gem", *Le Muséon* 108 (1995), 143-156 ◆ R. Kotansky & J. Spier, "The 'Horned Hunter' on a Lost Gnostic Gem", *HTR* 88 (1995), 315-337 ◆ A. Mastrocinque, "Studi sulle gemme gnostiche", *ZPE* 122 (1998), 105-118 ◆ O. [Ya.] Neverov, "Gemmes, bagues et amulettes magiques du sud de l'URSS", in: *Hommages à Maarten J. Vermaseren: Recueil d'études offert par les auteurs de la serie Etudes préliminaires aux religions orientales dans l'empire romain* (EPRO 68), II, Leiden: E.J. Brill, 1978, 833-848 pls. clxvii-clxxvi ◆ Hanna Philipp, *Mira et Magica: Gemmen im Aegyptischen Museum der Staatlichen Museen Preussischer Kulturbesitz*, Berlin-Charlottenburg: Philipp von Zabern, 1986) ◆ P. Post, "Le genie anquipede alectro cephale: une divinité magique solaire. Une analyse des pierres dites Abraxas-Gemmen", *Bijdragen* 41 (1979), 173-210 ◆ Simone Michel, "Medizinisch-magische Amulettgemmen: Schutz und Heilung durch Zauber und edle Steine in der Antike", *Antike Welt* 26:5 (1995), 379-387 ◆ M. Smith, "Relations between Magical Papyri and Magical Gems", in: *Actes du XVᵉ Congrès Internationale de Papyrologie*, IIIe partie (Papyrologica Bruxellensia 18), Brussels: Fondation Égytologique Reine Élisabeth 1979, 129-136 ◆ G. Tomassetti, "Notizie epigrafiche", *Bullettino della Commissione Archeologica Comunale di Roma* [Ser. 5] 27 (1899), 292f. ◆ R. Wuensch, "Sopra uno scarabeo con iscrizione greca", *Bullettino della Commissione Archeologica Comunale di Roma* [Ser. 5] 27 (1899), 294-299 ◆ R.W. Daniel, "Some Magical Gems in the British Museum", *Zeitschrift für Papyrologie und Epigraphik* 142 (2003), 139-142 ◆ Simone Michel, *Die magischen Gemmen im Britischen Museum* (Peter & Hilda Zazoff, eds.), 2 vols., London, 2001.

ROY KOTANSKY

Andreae, Johann Valentin, * 17.8.1586 Herrenberg (Württemberg), † 27.6.1654 Stuttgart

Johann Valentin Andreae was the fifth son of a dean of the Lutheran Church. His grandfather was Jakob Andreae, Chancellor of the University of Tübingen and one of the principal authors of the Formula of Concord, which was to become the doctrinal basis of Lutheran orthodoxy. After losing his father at age 15, the young Andreae began a brilliant career as a student at Tübingen, became *Magister artium* in 1605, and following in his ancestors' footsteps, studied theology. During this time his career as a writer began, with two plays (*Esther* and *Hyacinth*), some writings on politics and → astrology, and the novel *Chymische Hochzeit Christiani Rosenkreutz* (The Chemical Wedding of Christian Rosenkreutz; see below) whose success has lasted to this day.

However, these brilliant beginnings were darkened in 1607 as Andreae entered an *atra tempestas* (somber tempest). It seems that his critical disposition incited him to write a lampoon against one of the close advisers to the Prince of Württemberg, which led to a judiciary inquest, interrupted his studies, and resulted in his being rejected as a candidate for ecclesiastical office. Between 1609 and 1611 he went on a long journey to Strasbourg, Lyon, Paris, and then Switzerland, where the Calvinist organization of the city of Geneva made a strong impression on him, and where he seems to have drafted the *Fama Fraternitatis* (Fame of the [Rosicrucian] Brotherhood) and the remarkable comedy entitled *Turbo* (Whirlpool). In fact, this Latin title evokes the turmoil or the vortex in which the young Andreae found himself swept away. In 1613, after a long trip to Italy, he was at last able to recommence his studies of theology. The following year he obtained a post as deacon (adjunct pastor) at Vaihingen; this was the same year of his marriage, and of the beginning of his correspondence with Johann Arndt.

During the Thirty Years War, his ecclesiastical and diplomatic career took on new impetus: he was named Dean at Calw and went on a mission in Austria to defend the positions of Lutheranism there. Also at Calw, he created the *Färberstift* (Dyers' Foundation), a charitable association whose goals included helping the poor and sick, giving grants to young students, creating a library, promoting the learning of foreign languages, financing apprenticeships, paying for the education of children from insolvent families, and supporting aid for the mentally and physically handicapped. This foundation

lasted until 1979. However, after the Battle of Nördlingen in 1634, Imperial troops completely devastated the town of Calw, leaving numerous casualties and causing grave epidemics. Andreae related this drama in *Threni Calvenses* (Calvian Lamentations), published in 1635. After the devastation, Johann Valentin Andreae's two daughters married notables of Calw and had so many offspring that an inquiry has established that in 1936, ten percent of Calw's high-school students were descended from the Andreae line.

After 1614, continuing his pastoral, social, and diplomatic activities, Andreae published a number of important literary and theological works, mostly written in Latin. Their common denominator was the desire to combat three principal scourges of his era in Württemberg: the blind rigor and sterile theological disputes of the Lutheran orthodoxy; the interference of temporal power in the life of the church; and the profound moral decadence of Christian society in his time. To fight these problems, and to propose a more authentic Christianity to his contemporaries, Andreae found a model in the *Vier Bücher vom wahren Christentum* (Four Books of True Christianity), published between 1605 and 1610 by the theologian Johann Arndt, who became Superintendent General of the Principality of Lüneburg in 1611. These "four books" were the Book of Scripture (the Bible), the Book of Life (Christ), the Book of Conscience, and the "Grand Universal Book of Nature". Arndt, whose texts contained extracts from mystics such as Tauler and Angela di Foligno, can be considered the pioneer of Protestant → Pietism, and he exercised a strong influence over Andreae. In Strasbourg, around 1615, Andreae published some extracts from Arndt's "Four Books" translated into Latin. In an apologue of his *Mythologia christiana* (Christian Mythology; 1619), Andreae applauded Arndt's emphasis on the necessity for Christians to actually lead their lives in accord with the faith they professed. The same year, Andreae dedicated his *Reipublicae Christianopolitanae descriptio* (Description of the Republic of Christianopolis) to Johann Arndt. In a hundred chapters, this work describes an ideal Christian society called *Caphar Salama* (in Hebrew, "village of peace"), built on a triangular island symbolizing the Holy Trinity. The inhabitants have realized in themselves the mystery of regeneration; in fact, they constitute the *Ecclesia in hac vita occulta* (Church concealed in this life) of which Luther wrote. Thus *Christianopolis* is a portrait of a city of regenerated Christians as Andreae, under Arndt's influence, imagined it. He continued to describe this city in the alchemical allegory of

Rosicrucian myth, in the *Invitatio Fraternitatis Christi* (Invitation of the Brotherhood of Christ; 1617-1618), in *Civis christianus* (Christian City; 1619), in *Christenburg* (1620), and in *Christianæ Societatis Imago* (Picture of Christian Society; 1620). In *Theophilus*, written in 1622 but not published until 1649, Andreae proposed the means of establishing the actual Christian City whose image he had so often portrayed. Three conditions were necessary: temporal authority must be favorable to its birth; education must develop moral integrity as well as culture; and each citizen must be *renatus* (born again). But Andreae did not delude himself; in *De Christiani Cosmoxeni genitura judicium* (Judgment on the Nativity of Christian Cosmoxenus), which appeared around 1615, he had presented this ideal citizen as a purely imaginary being.

To emphasize this contrast between the ideal city and the real world, Andreae was not content with presenting his readers with the image of an ideal Christian society. An important part of his work, beginning with the myth of the Rose-Cross [→ Rosicrucianism], is a satire on the oddities of his era. In 1617, he published in the fictitious place of *Helicone juxta Parnassum* ("Helicon on Parnassus", but in fact Strasbourg) about a hundred satirical dialogues under the title of *Menippus*, recalling the famous pamphlet of the *Satyre Ménippée* (Menippean Satire), published in France in 1594, paving the way for the triumph of Henri IV over the League. Menippos was a famous Greek Satirist of the 1st century B.C.E., who was imitated by Meleager, Varro, and Lucian, among others. Andreae situated himself in this tradition, criticizing the various orders of society of his time, and his satire created such a stir that one professor of philosophy at Tübingen, Caspar Bucher immediately published an *Antimenippus*, while Andreae himself resolved to have an expurgated version of his *Menippus* printed the following year.

One of the targets of Andreae's satire was the pretentious erudition of the savants of his era, the hollow eloquence of professors in need of more sense and less arrogance, who were nothing but *asinocreatores*, "donkey-makers" who did not know how to teach dialectic or rhetoric, while their pupils discovered Aristotle's Heavens, but not God's.

In the domain of religion, Andreae estimated in *Menippus* that the "Reformation" was nothing but a "Deformation" which had replaced a Pope with "*papelli*" (popelets), diminished the power of Peter's Keys, and made the Church dependent on a temporal power that preached the doctrine of Christ, maybe, but not the imitation of Christ or the cultivation of a pious life.

As an appendix to *Menippus*, Andreae published *Institutio magica pro curiosis* (Magical Institute for the Curious), which stated his position vis-à-vis the fantastic commentaries inspired by the Rosicrucian writings, notably the novel mentioned above, *Chymische Hochzeit Christiani Rosenkreutz*. It is a dialog between Curiosus, who hopes to be initiated into the secrets of → magic, and Christianus, who reveals to him that magic resides in the grand Temple of Nature illuminated by three torches: that of divine Providence, that of society, and that of the anatomy of the world. This satire, once again, is aimed at the false erudites of his time, imbued with Latin, theology, and abstract formulae. In retaliation, Andreae praised those who worked with matter, architects, geographers, and astronomers, astounding the young enquirer who longed for nonexistent mysteries.

Along with this satire, Andreae used a less scouring and more subtle method for opposing the follies of his era and the calumnies he had suffered, namely the literary device of fables and fiction. Such was the object of the work entitled *Mythologiæ christianæ sive Virtutum et Vitiorum vitæ humanæ imaginum Libri tres* (Three Books of Christian Mythology, or Image of the Virtues and Vices of Human Life), which appeared at Strasbourg in 1619. After the manner of Trajano Boccalini (1556-1613), who published the *Raguagli di Parnaso* (Reports from Parnassus) in 1612, An dreae presented his critique of society in the form of myths and fairy-tales. His goal was to better the people of his time with fables. In an apologue entitled *Lusus* (Manipulus V, 27), he imagines a dialog between Scurrilitas (Scurrility) and Lusus (Play). The first is negative, impudent, and mocking, while Play (to whom Andreae defers) only mocks religion, the state, and erudition when they display imposture and barbarity, 'in order to make it clear that one writes satires not for pleasure or from a taste for carping, but out of necessity, indicating a religious, honest, moderate, intelligent spirit, concerned for the future of society'.

As a supplement to the *Mythologia christiana*, Andreae published a dialogue entitled *Alethea exul* (The Exile of Truth), in which Alethea, interrogated by Philalethes about the mystery of the Rose-Cross, says that she has observed 'not without pleasure [*non sine voluptate*] a somewhat spiritual game [*lusum quendam ingeniosiorem*]', but that she has thereafter eclipsed herself so as to not be involved in an 'uncertain and dangerous affair [*rei incertæ et lubricæ*]'. This dialogue reveals Andreae's position in regard to the myth that he had at least helped to create. The character Christian

Rosenkreuz takes his name from the escutcheons both of Luther and of the Andreae family. Two later autobiographical writings by Andreae place the creation of the *Chymische Hochzeit* between 1603 and 1605. With an incontestable literary talent, the author describes the extraordinary dream-like adventure of Christian Rosenkreuz, witness to the alchemical reincarnation and union of *sponsus* and *sponsa* (bridegroom and bride), whom → Carl Gustav Jung later named the *animus* and *anima*. However, the text does not have any of the technical aspects of an alchemical treatise; it is a vivid account, punctuated with enigmas, mysterious episodes, and erotic allusions. But this is only what they appear to be, inasmuch as Christian, braving the ban against entering the basements of the royal palace, discovers Venus naked, for in fact she symbolizes the new invisible body of the soul. Spiritualized matter also appears in the description of the fountain of Hermes, at which the chosen ones drink. The water of Hermes is Mercury, the substance of all transformation, all redemption, both in man and in nature. This is why Christian Rosenkreuz, after having lived the regeneration of *sponsus* and *sponsa*, is called *Eques aurei Lapidis* (Knight of the Golden Stone). And if at the end of the novel he is supposedly condemned to become a gate-keeper at the royal palace, it is for the purpose of announcing to those who are worthy the re-descent of the soul into transformed nature.

The *Fama Fraternitatis*, which circulated across Europe in the form of manuscripts around 1610 and was printed in 1614 at Kassel, also magnifies the grandeur of the human-microcosm and cites → Paracelsus. Christian Rosenkreuz appears in this work as the heroic founder of an omniscient brotherhood capable of redeeming all of nature. Given Andreae's ambiguous declarations, the *Fama Fraternitatis* cannot be totally attributed to him. In the funeral oration for his friend Tobias Hess, who died in 1614, he evoked the deceased's liking for secret societies. As for the *Confessio Fraternitatis* (Confession of the Brotherhood), published at Kassel in 1615 in Latin and in German translation, its genesis is equally linked to Tobias Hess, for reasons that follow. A collection of essays entitled *Theca gladii spiritus* (Scabbard of the Sword of the Spirit) and published at Strasbourg in 1616 was attributed in the preface to Hess, whereas Andreae, twenty-six years later, admitted to having been its author. No fewer than twenty-eight sentences from the *Confessio Fraternitatis* figure in this collection beside extracts of other works of Andreae, such as *Invitatio Fraternitatis Christi* and *Bonæ Causæ Fiducia* (Trust in a Good Cause). From these docu-

mented elements we can conclude that the *Chemical Wedding* was authored by Andreae and that the *Confessio* resulted from Andreae's cooperation with Tobias Hess, whereas the *Fama Fraternitatis* is a collective work written by more than two authors. In the last chapter of the *Turris Babel* (Tower of Babel), a pamphlet published by Andreae in 1619, the author writes about numerous texts released under the name of the Rose-Cross: '. . . there are those which are . . . jokes . . .; some are poor ones, . . . some are pious and devout. . . . While I certainly repudiate even the company of the Brotherhood, you will never make me renounce the true Christian Brotherhood, that which under the cross exhales a perfume of roses'.

Andreae had attempted to realize this "true Christian Brotherhood" in many repeated efforts, and his vision of the Rosicrucian myth had been its literary and utopian translation, just as many other writings including *Christianopolis* (1619), *Christenburger Schlacht* (The Battle of Christenburg; 1620), *Christianæ Societatis Imago* (1620), and *Christiani Amoris Dextera porrecta* (The Extended Right Hand of Christian Love; 1620). These were no longer a matter of simple literary fiction, for Andreae had long dreamed of founding this Christian brotherhood under the patronage of Duke August of Brunswick (1579-1666). We recall that Johann Arndt, whose influence on Andreae has been emphasized above, exercised his pastoral activity in the Principality of Brunswick-Lüneburg. Moreover, at Tübingen Andreae had met a student related to the Lüneburg nobility, Wilhelm von Wense, born like him in 1586, but who died in an accident in 1641. In 1642, Andreae expressed his sorrow in a funerary oration in the honor of this friend. It was at Wense's instigation that August of Brunswick had been chosen as protector of the *Societas Christiana*.

Andreae had met Duke August for the first time in 1630. An important correspondence between the two men began in 1640, each one writing about 600 letters to the other. In one letter dated June 17, 1642, Andreae announced to August of Brunswick the arrival of the *Christianæ Societatis Imago* and the *Christiani Amoris Dextera porrecta*, and on July 26, the Duke acknowledged receipt of these 'lovely little treatises'. Scholars of Andreae had long thought that these works had disappeared, and as late as 1973 one specialist questioned whether the two treatises had truly been published, until the present author discovered the actual copies received and read by the Duke. The Christian society that they describe was placed under the protection of this nobleman, 'vir Pietate, Probitate et Litteratura Illustrissimus' (a man illustrious in piety, uprightness, and letters); its goal was to develop knowledge in the different domains of religion, the sciences, and society, which would then be concretized by the publication of an encyclopedia in the vernacular. Thus Andreae belonged in the line of learned societies such as the French Academy, the Royal Society, and the Fruchtbringende Gesellschaft (Fruit-Bearing Society) to which he was admitted in 1646, thanks to the recommendation of the Duke of Brunswick. By then in his sixties, he was admitted with the pseudonym of "*Fracidus*", a Latin adjective used to designated an overripe olive; the German version, "der Mürbe" (the Ripe One), was no more complimentary. However, the emblem that he was given, a tree covered in moss, and the motto "etiamnum viret" (he is still green), may have consoled him. Andreae declared to Philippe Heinhofer, a patrician of Augsburg and intermediary between him and Duke August, that he felt neither old nor weary. In 1650 he became Abbot and Prelate of Bebenhausen, the next year he was named Superintendent General (the equivalent of an archbishop), and he died in 1654 at Stuttgart.

Thanks to his brilliant invention of the Rosicrucian myth, Andreae's name is still cited in numerous contemporary works, from the United States to Europe and even Japan. Paradoxically, he seems to be less well known in the Christian milieu, except in the microcosm of Lutheran theologians. However, his writings played an important role in the evolution of Christianity after the Reformation. Whereas Luther, especially in *Von weltlicher Obrigkeit* (On Worldly Authority), established the so-called "theory of two realms", affirming that the Christian is simultaneously subject to two totally separate kingdoms, the spiritual in his religious life and the temporal in his societal life, and in consequence the notion of the ideal city was completely foreign to him, we have seen that Andreae never ceased to work in favor of a *respublica christiana*. Certainly he did not hesitate to castigate the princes whom he named idolaters, and in a satire entitled *Apap proditus*, he mercilessly criticized Caesaropapism. On the other hand, he praised in his *Theophilus* the sovereign who acted for the furthering of public religion in his state. That which he valued above all was the free manifestation of the *praxis pietatis* (devotional practice) within a Christian society. In this sense, he anticipated the first generation of Pietists, who, with Jakob Spener (1635-1705), reconciled the ecclesiastical structure with the *collegium pietatis* (college of devotion) and worked for the formation of *ecclesiolæ in ecclesia* (small churches within the Church). Finally, as the present author has shown in many studies dedicated to Andreae's work, his beautiful narrative of the *Chemical Wedding of Christian Rosenkreuz* is articulated around three axes: God, Man, and Nature. According to Antoine Faivre, it is to this triangle that theosophic thought applies itself. Theosophy, as taught in the lecture-halls of *Christianopolis*, is a school of humility and obedience, docile receptivity, a revelation directly infused by God. The itinerary of Christian Rosenkreuz, like those of Christian Cosmoxenus and the elect of *Christianopolis*, is the theosophic miracle of salvation.

Gesammelte Schriften, Stuttgart, 1995 sqq. (20 vols.), in process of publication ♦ *Christianopolis* (Ger. & Lat.), Stuttgart: Calwer Verlag, 1972 ♦ *Theophilus*, Stuttgart: Calwer Verlag, 1973 ♦ *Fama Fraternitatis – Confessio Fraternitatis – Chymische Hochzeit Christiani Rosenkreuz Anno 1459* (R. van Dülmen, ed.), Stuttgart: Calwer Verlag, 1976 ♦ *The Chemical Wedding of Christian Rosenkreutz* (J. Godwin, trans.), Grand Rapids: Phanes Press, 1991 ♦ *The Chemical Wedding of Christian Rosenkreutz Anno 1459* (E. Foxcroft, trans.), Montana: Kessinger Repr. n.d. ♦ *Rosicrucian Primer*, Edmonds WA: J.D. Holmes, 1994 ♦ *The Rosicrucian Manuscripts*, Woodbridge: Invisible College Press, 2002.

Lit.: Frances A. Yates, *The Rosicrucian Enlightenment*, London/Boston, 1972, chs. 3-5 ♦ John Warwick Montgomery, *Cross and Crucible: Johann Valentin Andreae (1586-1654), Phoenix of the Theologians*, 2 vols., The Hague, 1973 ♦ Richard Van Dülmen, *Die Utopie einer christlichen Gesellschaft: Johann Valentin Andreae*, Stuttgart-Bad Cannstadt, 1978 ♦ Roland Edighoffer, *Rose-Croix et société idéale selon Johann Valentin Andreae*, 2 vols., Neuilly-sur-Seine, 1982/Paris, 1987 ♦ idem, *Die Rosenkreuzer*, Munich, 1995 ♦ idem, *Les Rose-Croix et la crise de la conscience européenne au XVIIᵉ siècle*, Paris, 1998 ♦ idem, "Johann Valentin Andreae, précurseur du piétisme", *Positions luthériennes* 3 (2002) ♦ Christoph Neeb, *Christlicher Haß gegen die Welt: Philosophie und Staatstheorie des Johann Valentin Andreae*, Frankfurt/M., 1999 ♦ Martin Brecht, *J.V. Andreae und Herzog August zu Braunschweig-Lüneburg*, Stuttgart-Bad Cannstadt, 2002 ♦ Bernard Gorceix, "Introduction", in: *La Bible des Rose-Croix*, Paris: Presses Universitaires de France, 1970, I-LXIV.

ROLAND EDIGHOFFER

Animal Magnetism/Mesmerism

1. FRANZ ANTON MESMER 2. PUYSÉGUR 3. FRANCE 4. ENGLAND 5. UNITED STATES OF AMERICA 6. HYPNOSIS 7. ESOTERICISM AND MAGNETISM 8. RELATED DEVELOPMENTS 9. CONCLUSION

The cultural movements covered by the terms "mesmerism" and "animal magnetism" are so complex that a long treatise would be required to cover them fully. Here we shall only outline the main cultural currents, and describe the directions they have taken in France, Germany, the British Isles, and the United States of America.

1. FRANZ ANTON MESMER

Mesmer's major accomplishments are fairly well known. He was born on May 23, 1734 in Iznang, near Lake Constance. He studied theology and medicine, and in 1766 defended a thesis in which he asserted the influence of the planets on human maladies, which earned him the title of Doctor of Medicine. In 1767 he settled in Vienna to begin his career as a doctor, and the following year married Maria Anna von Posch, a rich widow from an influential family.

During 1773-1774 he first tried using magnets for medical purposes (an idea that came from England) in an attempt to cure one of his patients, Miss Österlin. The sick woman felt a sensation like a strange current passing through her, and her symptoms vanished. From this experience, Mesmer began to draw the first outlines of his theory. He believed that the magnets themselves were not solely responsible for the effect obtained, but that they had served to amplify and channel a "fluid" accumulated within his own body, which he had transferred to his patient through an act of will. He named this discovery "animal magnetism" (*Tiermagnetismus* or *tierischer Magnetismus*), a term that would soon become part of the current vocabulary. The theory he deduced from his discovery amounted to these principles: an impalpable fluid permeates the entire universe and connects human beings to animals, plants, objects, and to each other. All human maladies are caused solely by poor circulation of this fluid within the human organism. For healing, it is necessary to re-establish the equilibrium of the cosmic fluid. This is what the magnetizer does, as he projects his fluid by means of passes over the organism of the sufferer. However, the concept of animal magnetism is much more complex than one might think from this brief summary. It comprises: (1) a psychological, anthropological, and cosmological theory describing the intricate relationship between man and the universe; (2) the techniques practiced by the magnetizer to relieve his fellows; (3) the phenomena of magnetic somnambulism, described later; and (4) the cultural currents set in motion by Mesmer that would continue throughout the 19th century.

Mesmer's reputation as a doctor and healer soon began to grow. In 1775, Prince Elector Max Joseph of Bavaria invited him to assist in an investigation of séances of exorcism held near Constance by Father Johann Joseph Gassner, a priest who was attracting crowds and performing what appeared to be miraculous healings, laying on his hands to expel evil spirits. On November 23, 1775, after observing Gassner, Mesmer undertook to reproduce the same phenomena. He found that he could produce seizures in an epileptic patient merely by a touch of the finger, and could cause the sick to have apparent convulsions. On the strength of this, he concluded that Gassner was sincere, but did not understand what he was doing; his cures were real, but explainable by the effect of a mysterious agent, hitherto unknown: the "animal magnetism" that he, Mesmer, had just discovered. Thus mesmerism was born from an unlikely combination of efforts: the attempt to interpret exorcism from a rational standpoint; experimentation in magnetic medicine; and the first tentative theories of electricity and magnetism. What Mesmer did not admit was that he had found himself, in a way, in the same situation as Gassner. Essentially, while Gassner, as a religious healer, validated his power of suggestion using liturgical décor and the symbolic system that accompanied it, Mesmer drew on the prestige of science and the aura of mystery that always surrounds new discoveries.

Mesmer's reputation grew, but it also attracted difficulties that forced him to leave Vienna. In February 1777, he moved to Paris to promote his grand discovery there. He settled in a private mansion in the Place Vendôme, where he received patients from high society and charged them exorbitant fees for his services. A few initial successes in curing the maladies of influential people assured a continued influx of distinguished clients. He also gained the devotion of some zealous but self-seeking disciples, such as Dr. d'Eslon, personal physician to the Comte d'Artois (one of the King's brothers), and author of *Observations sur le magnétisme animal* (Observations on Animal Magnetism, 1780). Mesmer's residence became a fashionable haunt; ailing great ladies swooned there, and were seized by spectacular convulsions. Numerous healings were reported. But fashion became tinged with scandal. In 1784, on the demand of the King, an official committee was formed with the purpose of throwing light on Mesmer's controversial methods of treatment. The committee included several renowned experts, such as the chemist Antoine Laurent de Lavoisier, the astronomer Jean-Sylvain Bailly, and the American statesman Benjamin Franklin. The committee's verdict was paradoxical. Essentially, it affirmed that while the members could not objectively detect the fluid, some of the alleged cures were genuine. However, it did not encourage the practice, because in its view, Mesmer's success must be due only to the deceptive powers of the → imagination, which constituted a bad method of healing, especially in this era, when medicine was undergoing a complete revision at the hands of scientists. A confidential report was even given to the King, concerning the possible sexual undertones of magnetism.

Laurent de Jussieu, one of the committee members, challenged the commission's conclusions, writing a personal memorandum in which he asserted that the phenomena observed could not all be attributed to mere power of imagination, and suggested the action of an unknown power, which he called "*chaleur animale*" (animal warmth). 1784 was a year of apotheosis for Mesmer, but also the beginning of the end. Challenged by the official savants, he faced a revolt among his disciples. In 1785 he left Paris for an unknown destination. He spent his last years forgotten, and died in seclusion in 1815.

2. PUYSÉGUR

No sooner had the royal committee given its ambiguous verdict than the emergence of new, even stranger phenomena rekindled the debate. In April 1784 Armand Marie Jacques Chastenet, Marquis de Puységur, Colonel of Artillery and a prominent landowner, began to spend his spare time healing his employees by magnetizing them according to the principles of Mesmer's doctrine. He was called to the bedside of a young peasant suffering from an inflammation of the lungs. Suddenly and unexpectedly, he plunged his patient into a mysterious state of unconsciousness. The Marquis, along with his two brothers, had been among the first to subscribe to Mesmer's lessons, and while performing magnetic healing on this young man, he anticipated the effects that Mesmerian magnetism was known to produce – yawning, sweating, and convulsions, followed by an improvement of the state of health. But things did not develop in the way he expected. The patient's personality changed; a new self emerged, which seemed to overhang his waking consciousness. Furthermore, the young man appeared to be able to predict the course of his malady, to establish its stages, and to read the thoughts of his healer, even before they were fully formed.

Such a state of consciousness had not been reported by Mesmer, but it seems probable that he had encountered it. If he had not reported its existence, it was probably because it contradicted his materialistic assumptions. Be that as it may, Puységur established, in repeating the experiment upon more patients, that this state of consciousness could be reproduced fairly regularly, and that other somnambulists were equally capable of diagnosing maladies, reading thoughts, and perceiving events outside normal consciousness. By way of contrast with natural somnambulism (sleepwalking) known since antiquity, he named this new state "magnetic" or "artificial" somnambulism. The following year he published his observations in Paris and London, in a memoir that sparked an explosive chain of events. Magnetic somnambulists emerged all over France, and a vast argument on the subject began, which would occupy the educated world for most of the 19th century.

3. FRANCE

During the French Revolution and the First Empire, interest in magnetism entered a latent phase. Many of the aristocrats were forced into exile, and the public's attention was preoccupied by more pressing things. However, with the Restoration in 1815 and the return of many of the nobles, magnetism arose from its ashes. Puységur himself, who had stayed in France, resumed his studies and published some new works. In October 1825, Dr. Foissac, at the request of some medical students, directed a petition to the Academy of Medicine pleading for a re-examination of magnetism. He was not heard, but one of his colleagues, Dr. Husson, chief doctor of the Hôtel-Dieu, went to plead the cause before the Academy. When the report came that judgment had already been passed, Husson argued that it had been Mesmer's practices that had been judged – not somnambulism, of which Mesmer had been ignorant. The argument hit home, and in February 1826, Husson was made director of a new official commission. After five years of work, in June 1831, this commission produced an astonishing verdict, recognizing as genuine most of the somnambulistic phenomena alleged by the magnetizers.

The scandal surrounding the issue was such that the commission's report was printed but never distributed, and the anti-magnetists regained the lead. In 1837 Frédéric Dubois d'Amiens was chosen to head a new commission. Dubois was a young doctor who had become known four years earlier for a violent pamphlet in which he declared war on magnetism. Didier Berna, a physician and magnetizer, was chosen by the committee to coordinate its efforts, but the tension between him and Dubois was such that no agreement on protocols could be reached, and most planned experiments could not be performed. The committee gave a completely negative verdict in August 1837: none of the phenomena alleged by the magnetizers could be observed, and everything amounted either to trickery or to effects of the imagination.

In October of the same year, the conflict came to a head around a twelve-year-old girl from Montpellier, Léonide Pigeaire. Léonide, the daughter of a local physician, was reputed to be able to see through opaque objects. Her abilities had been attested to by many doctors, including Dr. Lordat, a well-known Montpellier physician, and her father had brought her to Paris to present her to the commission, which had defiantly offered a prize of 3.000 francs to anyone who could read text through an opaque object. Unfortunately, the protagonists could not even reach an agreement on the best method of hiding the text from the reader (a cowl or velvet blindfold fastened at the edges with sticky paper), and the test could not take place. Dr. Pigeaire lost by default, and Dubois d'Amiens' friends seized the opportunity to do away with magnetism in general. On June 15, 1842, after a turbulent session, the Academy of Medicine decided to have nothing further to do with animal magnetism, and not to accept any more papers on the subject.

But magnetism, defeated on the institutional level, continued to flourish in the culture. The doctors had retired from the scene, leaving the stage to writers, judges, theologians, and philosophers, who continued to think about and experiment with magnetism. Among their subjects was Alexis Didier, the famous somnambulist and most marvelous clairvoyant of the 19th century.

4. ENGLAND

During these times, the movement was spreading outside of France. In 1837, the magnetizer Dupotet, who had conducted the experiments for the Husson commission, exported magnetism for the first time to England, which had hitherto been preserved from the Mesmerian craze. After a brief period of mistrust, crowds flocked to his demonstrations. In 1840, he was joined by Charles Lafontaine, another renowned magnetizer. Soon the English developed a passion for mesmerism, and what had happened in France repeated itself, but more quickly. Dr. John Elliotson, a professor at University College in London and a rising star of British medicine, undertook with the aid of Dupotet to perform some public experiments upon two somnambulistic women, which unleashed passions and scandals. After a dazzling ascent, Elliotson suffered a brutal fall due to suspicions of fraud on the part of his somnambulistic subjects. Dropped by a number of his fellow magnetizers, he was forced to resign from his official functions. However, he continued to pursue the subject, later founding a high-level journal, *The Zoist*, which became the European authority on the subject of mesmerism.

Thus magnetism was expelled from the temples of the British Establishment, but, unlike in France, no official decree was issued to impede or limit its practice. And, just as in France, the subject impassioned writers and intellectuals, and gave rise to intense debates.

5. UNITED STATES OF AMERICA

Also in 1837, the Frenchman Charles Poyen left for the United States to propagate magnetism there. In this country, the resources of institutional protectionism were still in the embryonic stage, and therefore did not hinder the development of mesmerism as they had in France. Many reasons might explain its rapid success. For a nation with a mentality still firmly structured by religion, animal magnetism offered an understanding of the human spirit that was detached from theology but at the same time open to pneumatology. To a mentality obsessed with the concept of liberty, it offered the idea of an autonomous somnambulism. For a population disoriented by industrialization, it offered a method for mending social bonds.

Few official stumbling blocks hindered the spread of magnetism. Unlike in France, scientific hypnology did not set itself up to control magnetism and reject materials that could not be assimilated. Ultimately, it was the materialistic and utilitarian society, rather than institutional barriers, that stopped the spread of magnetism in America. The movement died out at the end of the 19th century.

6. HYPNOSIS

In 1843, James Braid, a Scottish doctor, proposed the term "hypnosis" to define a practice inspired by magnetism, but more limited in its effects and different in its conception. Braid had been inspired by Lafontaine's public demonstrations. According to the theorists of magnetism, it was the influence of the magnetizer that put the patient into a magnetic sleep. Braid, however, believed that the subject entered this state independently by means of auto-suggestion; there was no fluid, no occult influence of one human being on another; and consequently it did not matter by what method the sleep was attained. Braid remained reserved about the "higher magnetic phenomena" that the magnetizers claimed to produce, but he did not reject them, as is often thought. He contented himself with saying that he had not produced these results with his particular method. At first his method had little success, but after 1878, when the French medical institution decided to lift the decades-old academic taboo and accept the phenomena formerly called "magnetic", it became the obligatory reference. After its English reform, a change of terminology, a selection of phenomena deemed acceptable, and a materialistic remodeling of its phenomenology, what was formerly known as magnetism was accepted by so-called official medicine.

Around 1860, a few young doctors, including Eugène Azam and Paul Broca, had attempted to promote Braid's theory in France, but their attempts had remained isolated and without consequences. It was in 1878 that, under Charcot's leadership, hypnotism rocketed to success. First considered a useful tool for studying hysterics, the practice posed so many questions to psychology and medicine that it became, in the space of a decade, one of the biggest areas of research in the sciences of the mind. The medical establishment now began to embrace a part of what it had condemned fifty years before. Psychiatry, psychology, philosophy, and theories of art and education all found themselves appealed to by the question of hypnosis. Nevertheless, the phenomena that triggered this enthusiasm were nothing but an expurgated and attenuated version of the old magnetic phenomena. In Charcot's wake, though, physicians such as Julian Ochorowicz and philosophers such as Emile Boirac came to doubt the claim that hypnotism could completely explain away the phenomena produced by the old magnetizers.

At the end of the 19th century, under the impulse of these authors, animal magnetism made a new return to learned discourse, now colored by the scientific and materialistic orientation of that period. With this return was born the research program that the English named "psychical research" and the French, *métapsychique*: a problematic and controversial area of study, but one which aroused great theoretical hopes. Psychical research in Britain began around 1876 at Trinity College in Cambridge, thanks to the initiative of the philosopher Henry Sidgwick, an eminent professor of moral and political philosophy. *Métapsychique*, in France, was thus named in 1919 by the Nobel Prize-winning physiologist Charles Richet. Two decades of theoretical and experimental abundance followed, before the discipline gave way to the incoming tide of new ideologies that followed the Second World War.

7. Esotericism and Magnetism

This broad historical outline should not lead one to think that we are faced with a uniform current. In reality, the magnetic movement, in France, Germany, Britain, and America, has always contained multiple, and sometimes conflicting, schools of thought. In France, before the Revolution, the way mesmerism developed reflected the political and social instability of the era. In the years following the discovery of somnambulism by the Marquis de Puységur, the movement developed three principal divisions: on the "left" were the materialists, on the "center" the psycho-fluidists (Puységur's disciples), and on the "right" the esoterically oriented magnetizers. The materialists were disciples of Mesmer or of doctors who, like Dr. Jacques Pététin, wanted to rid themselves of the mesmerian "fluid" and preferred to talk of "vital electricity". In explaining the somnambulistic state, they emphasized the importance of this material vehicle that they thought produced it. The psycho-fluidists, disciples of Puységur and Deleuze, maintained that somnambulism revealed a hidden self and, although they were spiritualists, rejected all reference to entities outside of human consciousness; they saw the fluid only as a vehicle, and emphasized the *will* that set it in motion. The third category, finally, split into several branches. The importance of this last current, esoteric in nature, should not be underestimated.

The study of esoteric magnetism had its nucleus in the city of Lyon – rightly or wrongly reputed to be the esoteric capital of France. Its aristocratic adepts mixed the idea of progress with eschatological expectations, → mysticism, science, Christian esotericism, Jewish Kabbala [→ Jewish Influences], and → alchemy. The writings that they have left recall how simplistic our modern ideas of the Age of Enlightenment often are. They themselves were divided into several schools of thought. Some, like the Chevalier de Barberin, did not envisage entities external to human consciousness, but claimed to act directly upon the patient by will and prayer, without the mediation of any material fluid. Others, such as the famous Jeanne Rochette (whose "sleeps" were recorded by → Jean-Baptiste Willermoz), reported having contact with angelic entities during their trances.

If the esoteric branch of magnetism was born in France, it was in Germany that the movement reached its greatest development. The German mystics, philosophers, and writers carried magnetism to new metaphysical heights. It had an ideal terrain upon which to unfurl: the pre-romantic theologies of light and electricity, developed as early as 1765 by Prokop Divisch, → Friedrich

Christoph Oetinger, and Johann Ludwig Fricker. Most of the promoters of → *Naturphilosophie* (the "philosophy of nature") integrated magnetism into their theories and dedicated many studies to it, believing in the existence of a "universal connector" – the "inner sense" that, during the magnetic trance, put the somnambulist in communication with the whole of nature. One major example is → Gotthilf Heinrich Schubert, with his *Ansichten von der Nachtseite der Naturwissenschaft* (1808, Views from the Night Side of Natural Science) and *Die Symbolik der Traüme* (1814, The Symbolism of Dreams).

Other theorists sought to anchor the mysteries of somnambulism in physiology, in terms of theoretical oppositions between the cerebro-spinal system, the organ of diurnal thought and rationality supposedly dominant in men, and the ganglion system, the support of the nocturnal forms of life, that they believed to predominate in women. Around 1779, Eberhard Gmelin discussed his views in *Neue Untersuchungen bei den thierischen Magnetismus* (New Studies in Animal Magnetism, 1789). His views have caused many authors, such as Ricarda Huch, to affirm that most somnambulists were women or effeminate men.

There were many great German theorists of animal magnetism in the Romantic Era – for example, Dietrich Georg Kieser and Carl August von Eschenmayer, co-directors of the review *Archiv für den thierischen Magnetismus* (Archive for Animal Magnetism, 1817-1824). Kieser also wrote the important *System des Tellurismus oder thierischen Magnetismus* (System of Tellurism, or Animal Magnetism, 1826). Among the writings of Eschenmeyer figures *Mysterien des inneren Lebens, erklärt aus der Geschichte der Seherin von Prevorst* (Mysteries of the Inner Life, Explained by the Story of the Seeress of Prevorst, 1830). There were also Friedrich Hufeland, who tried to understand the sympathy between beings (*Über Sympathie*; On Sympathy, 1811); Johann Carl Passavant (*Untersuchungen bei dem Lebensmagnetismus und das Hellsehen*; Researches in Animal Magnetism and Clairvoyance, 1821); and Karl Friedrich Burdach, who in *Zeitrechnung des menschlichen Lebens* (Chronology of Human Life, 1829) maintained the existence of a transpersonal mental space to which the magnetic trance provided access.

The Swabian physician and poet → Justinus Kerner has a special place here; his name is bound up with that of the famous somnambulist Friederike Hauffe, the Seeress of Prevorst. This young woman is the archetype of the somnambule who, beset by various bodily ills, draws mystics,

writers, and doctors to her bedside. Living in a semi-permanent state of somnambulistic trance, Hauffe presented the whole gamut of magnetic endowments: the gifts of second sight and of precognition, predicting deaths, revealing maladies, prescribing remedies, and being extremely sensitive to certain substances. She even saw spirits of the dead and maintained a semi-permanent communication with them. The speeches she made during her altered states of consciousness included many ideas of a clearly theosophic character. They were recorded by Justinus Kerner in his book *Die Seherin von Prevorst* (The Seeress of Prevorst, 1829), which had a great impact, notably thanks to its publication in English in a translation by Catherine Crowe (*The Seeress of Prevorst*, 1845). But of all the Germans of this era, it was certainly → Franz von Baader who authored the most noteworthy writings devoted to the connection between animal magnetism and theosophy [→ Christian Theosophy] (cf. inter alia: *Über die Extase oder das Verzücktsein der magnetischen Schlafredner*; On Ecstasy, or the Rapture of Magnetized Sleeptalkers; 1817-1818). Compared with facts accumulated in France in the same era, the German magnetic body of work presents a striking and instructive difference. In effect, most of the French somnambulists famous for their clairvoyant gifts (notably Alexis Didier), exercised their second sight directly, without using supernatural entities as a relay. Their discourse while in a trance was turned towards earthly reality more than towards the celestial spheres or theosophical speculation, as tended to be the case in Germany.

8. RELATED DEVELOPMENTS

Connections between magnetism and spiritualism were drawn in the English-speaking world as well, although in this somewhat more materialistic culture the dominant approach was marked by positivism and a careful attention to scientific fact. In England, around 1838, Dr. Herbert Mayo, professor at King's College, London, experimented with magnetic somnambulists in the hope of counteracting the growth of materialism through proof of the existence of the soul and its independence from organic life. Around 1850, the experiments performed over distance with the famous Alexis Didier convinced him that the spirit was truly able to detach itself from the body. The Rev. Chauncy Townshend, a writer, painter, poet, and a friend of Dickens, also experimented with Alexis and published the result of his personal studies in *Facts in Mesmerism* (1844 – a work that would later inspire Edgar Allen Poe). Finally, in the United States of

America, the development of magnetism was marked by the exaltation of the individual typical of this young nation. Henceforth the somnambulists had no more need of magnetizers, but magnetized themselves. The American version of the "Magnetic Heroes" represented in France by Alexis Didier or in Germany by Friederike Hauffe appeared in figures like → Andrew Jackson Davis (*The Great Harmonia*, 1852) and Phineas P. Quimby, whose new interpretation of magnetic healing was at the basis of the movement of "mind cure" (→ New Thought).

9. CONCLUSION

For mainstream Western culture, animal magnetism was a shock and a challenge whose magnitude and effects are too often forgotten today. For the participants it brought great hopes, not only for a scientific breakthrough, but for a moral and social renovation and a deepening of spiritualist philosophy. For the movement's adversaries, it threatened to subvert reason and to pervert the social order; therefore it must be combated in every possible way. The result was a cultural battle that led to the repression of magnetism, and its eventual oblivion. While the phenomena of somnambulism have never been completely objectified or explained in a satisfying manner, they have certainly stimulated and/or disquieted all aspects of culture. Psychiatry, psychoanalysis, the psychology of altered states of consciousness, philosophy, the history of religion, ethnology, art, literature, and theories of education – all have been affected by this current and still bear its mark. And the questions posed by magnetism do not belong only to a movement that died out long ago; they remain highly pertinent even today.

The bibliography of animal magnetism is immense. It consists of a series of very diverse writings: brochures, pamphlets, theoretical studies, case studies, and accounts of séances. There are certainly over 5.000 titles in English, French, and German alone. The most complete bibliography is that of Adam Crabtree: *Animal Magnetism, Early Hypnotism, and Psychical Research, 1766 to 1925: An Annotated Bibliography* (Kraus International Publishers: New York 1988), but it is still far from covering all the relevant literature. The works mentioned below concern the essential episodes in the history of magnetism, but are meant only to serve the reader as a first orientation in this labyrinth.

Friedrich-Anton Mesmer, *Mémoire sur la découverte du magnétisme animal*, Geneva, Paris: Didot, 1779 ♦ Nicolas Bergasse, *Considérations sur le magnétisme animal, ou Sur la théorie du monde et des êtres organisés, d'après les principes de M. Mesmer*, The Hague, 1784 ♦ Jean-Sylvain Bailly, *Rapport des commissaires chargés par le Roi de l'examen du magnétisme animal*, Paris: Imprimerie Royale, 1784 ♦ Armand Marie Jacques de Chastenet, marquis de Puységur, *Mémoires pour servir à l'histoire et à l'établissement du magnétisme animal*, Paris, London: Dentu, 1784-1785 ♦ Laurent de Jussieu, *Rapport de l'un des commissaires chargés par le Roi de l'examen du magnétisme animal*, Paris: Veuve Harissart, 1784 ♦ Chevalier de Barberin, *Système raisonné du magnétisme universel*, Ostend: Société de l'Harmonie d'Ostende, 1786 ♦ Armand Marie Jacques de Chastenet, marquis de Puységur, *Recherches, expériences et observations physiologiques sur l'homme dans l'état de somnambulisme naturel et dans le somnambulisme provoqué par l'acte magnétique*, Paris: Dentu, 1811 ♦ Jacques-Désiré Pététin, *Electricité animale*, Paris: Bruno-Labbe et Gautier, 1808 ♦ Joseph-Pierre Deleuze, *Histoire critique du magnétisme animal*, 2 vols., Paris: Mame, 1813 ♦ Etienne d'Hénin de Cuvillers, *Le magnétisme animal retrouvé dans l'Antiquité, ou Dissertation historique, etymologique et mythologique sur Esculape, Hippocrate et Gallien; sur Apis, Sérapis et Osiris; suivie de recherches sur l'origine de l'Alchimie*, Paris: Barrois, 1821 ♦ Pierre Foissac, *Mémoire sur le magnétisme animal, adressé à MM. les membres de l'Académie des sciences et de l'Académie royale de médecine*, Paris: Didot, 1825 ♦ Justinus Kerner, *Die Seherin von Prevorst: Eröffnung über das innere Leben des Menschen und über Hereinragen einer Geisterwelt in die Unsere*, 2 vols., Stuttgart: J.G. Cotta, 1828 ♦ Frédéric Dubois (d'Amiens), *Examen historique et résumé des expériences prétendues magnétiques faites par la commission de l'Académie royale de médecine*, Paris, 1833 ♦ Joseph-Pierre Deleuze, *Mémoire sur la faculté de prévision*, Paris: Crochard, 1836 ♦ Didier Berna, *Magnétisme animal: Examen et réfutation du rapport fait par M.E.F. Dubois (d'Amiens) à l'Académie royale de médecine, le huit août 1837, sur le magnétisme animal*, Paris: Rouvier, 1838 ♦ Jean Pigeaire, *Puissance de l'électricité animale, ou du magnétisme vital, et de ses rapports avec la physique, la physiologie et la médecine*, Paris: Dentu et Baillière, 1839 ♦ Jules Dupotet de Sennevoy, *Le magnétisme animal opposé à la médecine: Mémoire pour servir l'histoire du magnétisme en France et en Angleterre*, Paris: Roret, 1840 ♦ Aubin Gauthier, *Histoire du somnambulisme chez tous les peuples, sous les noms divers d'extases, songes, oracles et visions, examen des doctrines théoriques et philosophiques*, 2 vols., Paris: Dentu et Baillière, 1842 ♦ James Braid, *Neurypnology or the Rationale of Nervous Sleep, Considered in Relation with Animal Magnetism, Illustrated by Numerous Cases of its Successfull Applications in the Relief and Cure of Diseases*, London: John Churchill, 1843 ♦ John Elliotson, *Numerous Cases of Surgical Operations without Pain in the Mesmeric State; with Remarks upon the Opposition of Many Members of the Royal Medical and Chirugical Society and Others to the Reception of the Inestimable Blessings of Mesmerism*, Philadelphia: Lea and Blanchard, 1843 ♦

Chauncey Hare Townshend, *Facts in Mesmerism, with Reasons for a Dispassionate Enquiry into it*, London: Longman, 1844 ♦ Charles Lafontaine, *L'art de magnétiser, ou le magnétisme animal considéré sous le point de vue théorique, pratique et thérapeutique*, Paris: Baillière, 1847 ♦ Joseph-Pierre Durand, called Durand de Gros, *Electrodynamisme vital, ou les relations physiologiques de l'esprit et de la matière démontrées par des expériences entièrement nouvelles et par l'histoire raisonnée du système nerveux*, Paris: Baillière, 1855 ♦ Jean-Martin Charcot, *Contribution à l'étude de l'hypnotisme chez les hystériques*, Paris, 1881 ♦ Julian Ochorowicz, *De la suggestion mentale*, Paris: Doin, 1887 ♦ Emile Boirac, *L'hypothèse du magnétisme animal d'après les recherches récentes*, Paris, 1895 ♦ Phineas P. Quimby, *The Quimby Manuscripts*, New York: Thomas Crowell, 1921.

Lit.: François Azouvi, "Sens et fonction épistémologique de la critique du magnétisme animal par les Académies", *Revue d'Histoire des sciences* (1976) ♦ Albert Beguin, *L'âme romantique et le rêve*, Paris: Librairie José Corti, 1939 ♦ Ernst Benz, *Theologie der Elektrizität*, Mainz: Akademie der Wissenschaften und der Litteratur, 1970 ♦ Christine Bergé, *L'Au-delà et les Lyonnais, Mages, médiums, et Franc-Maçons du XVIIème au XXème siècle*, Lyon: Lugd, 1995 ♦ Adam Crabtree, *From Mesmer to Freud: Magnetic Sleep and the Roots of Psychological Healing*, New Haven, London: Yale University Press, 1993 ♦ Robert Darnton, *Mesmerism and the End of the Enlightenment in France*, Cambridge, Mass.: Harvard University Press, 1986 ♦ Henri Ellenberger, *The Discovery of the Unconscious: The History and Evolution of Dynamic Psychiatry*, New York: Basic Books, 1970 ♦ Antoine Faivre, *Philosophie de la nature: Physique sacrée et théosophie XVIII-XIXème siècle*, Paris: Albin Michel, 1996 ♦ Robert C. Fuller, *Mesmerism and the American Cure of Souls*, Philadelphia: The University of Pennsylvania Press, 1982 ♦ Alan Gauld, *The Founders of Psychical Research*, New York: Schocken Books, 1968 ♦ idem, *A History of Hypnotism*, Cambridge: Cambridge University Press, 1995 ♦ George Gusdorf, *L'homme romantique*, Paris: Payot, 1984 ♦ Wouter J. Hanegraaff, "A Woman Alone: The Beatification of Friederike Hauffe (1801-1829)", in: Anne-Marie Korte (ed.), *Women and Miracle Stories: A Multidisciplinary Exploration*, Leiden, Boston, Cologne: E.J. Brill, 2001, 211-247 ♦ Bertrand Méheust, *Somnambulisme et médiumnité*, 2 vols., Paris: Les Empêcheurs de penser en rond, 1999 ♦ idem, *Un voyant prodigieux, Alexis Didier (1826-1886)*, Paris: Les Empêcheurs de penser en rond, 2003 ♦ Jean-Pierre Peter, "Un somnambule désordonné? Introduction to A.M.J. de Puységur", *Mémoires pour servir à l'histoire et à l'établissement du magnétisme animal*, Paris: Les Empêcheurs de penser en rond, 1999 ♦ Maria M. Tatar, *Spellbound: Studies on Mesmerism and Literature*, Princeton NJ: Princeton University Press, 1978 ♦ Alison Winter, *Mesmerized, Powers of Mind in Victorian Britain*, Chicago: University of Chicago Press, 1998.

BERTRAND MEHEUST

Anthroposophy

1. OCCULT PHYSIOLOGY 2. CHRISTOLOGY
3. PLANETARY EVOLUTION
4. REINCARNATION AND KARMA
5. THE SPIRITUAL PATH 6. THE
ANTHROPOSOPHICAL MOVEMENT

The term anthroposophy has been used by various hermetic and philosophical authors in the modern era, the earliest one being the English alchemist → Thomas Vaughan (1622-1666). In the 19th century the title was used by, among others, the philosopher Immanuel Hermann Fichte (1797-1879), son of the famous Johann Gottlob Fichte, and Robert Zimmermann (1824-1898), professor of philosophy at the university of Vienna. One of his students was → Rudolf Steiner, with whom the term anthroposophy is now usually associated. Steiner used the term to refer to his own esoteric doctrine, as distinguished from the older theosophy of the → Theosophical Society with which he broke in 1913. According to one of the definitions that Steiner has given of anthroposophy, it is 'a path of knowledge that connects the spiritual in man with the spiritual in the cosmos'. Steiner claimed that anthroposophy is not a matter of revealed religious doctrine, but of 'spiritual science' that one has to develop oneself: it does not teach 'the wisdom of man' but tries to awaken the 'consciousness of one's own humanity', not only as a key to understanding the macrocosmos but especially as a means of bringing about a spiritual transformation of daily life. This article gives a thematic survey of key topics in Steiner's anthroposophy. For information about Steiner's biography and the development of anthroposophy, see the article on Steiner.

1. OCCULT PHYSIOLOGY
One of the key elements of Steiner's anthroposophy is a spiritual or occult [→ occult/occultism] physiology of man. Steiner did not have one single physiological system, but developed several versions over the course of time. These different perspectives serve different purposes and for the most part they overlap only partially. They have their basis in the concept, provided in his book *Theosophy* (1904) and elsewhere, of a tripartition of body, soul and spirit. The human soul mediates between the eternal spirit or Self and the perishable physical body. In *Theosophy* and elsewhere, however, this tripartition is transformed into a fourfold distinction between physical body, etheric body, astral body and I, which is reminiscent of

Paracelsian medicine [→ Paracelsianism]. Macrocosmically, the physical body is what links us humans to the mineral world, while the etheric body links us to the plant world, the astral body to the animal world, and the I is uniquely human. The etheric body is roughly equivalent to what Aristotle calls the organic soul: it is responsible for growth and life, and is the bearer of heredity. As such it is essentially plastic, endowing the physical body with a specific form and shape. The astral body is sometimes simply referred to as "the soul" and is roughly equivalent to Aristotle's sensitive soul. It is the basis for interiority and subjectivity, giving rise to the whole range of emotions and desires, but also of unconscious impulses. Whereas the etheric body has a natural tendency towards unity and wholeness, the astral body is the principle of differentiation and specialization. Steiner sometimes compares the relation between these two "bodies" as that between the convex and the concave: the etheric body has the task of harmonizing and unifying the body, whereas the astral body carves out inner spaces, providing room for interiority. The I is Steiner's equivalent of the Aristotelian intellective soul. It is the eternal, imperishable Self that reincarnates in a new physical body and is the bearer of karma. It is not just our spiritual core which is added to the other "bodies", but in a quite Aristotelian fashion also functions as an entelechy, unifying, organizing and harmonizing our physiology, and giving our lives purpose and direction. In this connection Steiner speaks of the "I-organization", referring to the relation of the I to the several "bodies", as distinct from the I taken as an entity in itself. For instance, with respect to the physical body the I's activity can be seen in two typically human activities, namely speech and erect movement. In the case of the etheric body, the strength of the I and its grasp of the etheric body can be gathered from the way a child grows: harmonious growth is evidence for a strong grasp by the I, whereas irregular growth points to a weak one. The I can also pacify and harmonize the astral body, creating emotional stability and a sense of direction and purpose. From these examples it becomes clear that Steiner's I combines Schopenhauer's and Nietzsche's unconscious will and the Cartesian *cogito*. Clear and distinct awareness of the self is but one of the many functions exerted by the I, albeit a crucial one.

The human soul, according to Steiner, consists of several further subdivisions, the sentient soul (*Empfindungsseele*), the intellectual soul (*Verstandesseele*) and the spiritual soul (*Bewusstseinsseele*). These souls are the products of the I's transformation of, respectively, the astral body, the etheric body and the physical body. The sentient soul is the first stage of sentient and emotional life, in which the soul is completely absorbed by outer impressions and inner sentiments. The intellectual soul exhibits the first vestiges of thought activity by which we can turn outer impressions into clear perceptions and concepts, and can bring structure to our inner life. Thus, we create room for emotions such as sympathy, which go beyond the mere egoistic sense of self-preservation. This is why Steiner also refers to this soul as the sensitive-emotive soul (*Verstands-Gemütsseele*). The intellectual soul still has a sense of immediately belonging to the external world, without experiencing any ruptures. The spiritual soul, by contrast, emancipates itself from the external world. In this case, the I turns to sense perception coming from the physical body, experiencing a kind of alienation that can be remedied only by finding its spiritual core within itself. The spiritual soul, in other words, develops a high sense of self-consciousness that not only stands in opposition to the external world but also individualizes itself with respect to fellow human beings, loosening the collective ties of family, nation, religious community etc. Through self-consciousness, the spiritual soul is also able to take a more objective and less emotional stance towards external events, determining our actions by objective judgments rather than by sympathy and antipathy. In Steiner's view not only each human life but, as will become clear below, human culture as a whole as well, pass through these different stages.

Next to these three souls that present human beings have developed, Steiner also mentions three soul organs that will be cultivated in a distant future, but on which we can already partially work in our present stage of evolution, by means of spiritual exercises and moral conduct. Using theosophical vocabulary, Steiner calls these souls Manas or Spirit self (*Geistselbst*), Budhi or Life spirit (*Lebensgeist*) and Atman or Spirit man (*Geistesmensch*), which represent, respectively, the full transformation by the I of the astral body, the etheric body and the physical body. Steiner devoted special attention to the Spirit self, which can help us overcome the potential materialism and anti-social tendencies of the spiritual soul.

Next to his four-fold physiology, Steiner propounded a tripartition of soul activities, which also have an organic basis. Steiner divided the human organism into the region of the head or nervous-sense system (seat of the activity of thought), the heart-lung region or rhythmic system (seat of the activity of feeling) and the metabolic system (seat of the activity of will). This partition also has a macrocosmic counterpart, consisting in the three persons of the Trinity: Father (will), Son (feeling) and Holy Spirit (thought). This brings us to Steiner's Christology.

2. CHRISTOLOGY

Steiner vehemently campaigned against Adolf Harnack, David Friedrich Strauss and other representatives of contemporary Protestant *Leben Jesu Forschung* for robbing Jesus Christ of his divine status and reducing him to a mere prophet. For Steiner, Jesus Christ was essentially the divine Logos incarnate. Christ is the spirit of the sun who descended to the earth in order to redeem not only mankind but the earth in general. According to Steiner, mankind has fallen prey to the forces of evil, that have made him mortal and have thrown his diverse "bodies" into decadence. In order to re-vitalize humankind, Christ had to taste death himself and bring the ultimate sacrifice, thus becoming the "inner sun" or spirit of the earth and restoring its sense and purpose. According to Steiner, through the blood of Christ after the Crucifixion the whole earth began to shine. Though Steiner's emphasis on Jesus Christ's divine character could be called Gnostic [→ Gnosticism], he avoided docetism by affirming that Jesus Christ had really died in human shape and had risen from the dead. Nevertheless, he made a distinction between the human person Jesus, and Christ as the divine Logos. In fact, according to Steiner we can only legitimately speak of Jesus Christ from the Baptism in the Jordan onwards, which he sees as the moment in which Christ truly descended into Jesus and became man. Jesus' corporeal nature was a vessel which had been prepared over thousands of years. In an attempt to square the gospel according to Luke with the gospel according to Matthew, Steiner speaks of two children with the name Jesus and two pairs of parents called Joseph and Mary. He refers to the child of the gospel according to Luke as the Nathanic Jesus, after one of the sons of David, in whose bloodline he stood. He describes this child as Adam-Kadmon, the human nature that had not gone through the Fall; his very being was therefore complete innocence, which was only reinforced by the fact that Buddha had reunited himself with its astral body. On the other hand, the Solomonic Jesus – named after David's other son – had inherited the I of Zarathustra [→ Zoroaster]. When these children were twelve, the I of this second child merged with the other bodies of the first child, an event which according to Steiner is evi-

denced by the biblical story of Jesus teaching in the temple. The fact that his parents did not recognize him is explained by Steiner in the sense that the innocent child all of a sudden had turned into one of the wisest persons on earth. At birth, the first child was venerated by the shepherds who received Buddha's message of peace, while the second child was venerated by the three Magi, former pupils of Zarathustra who recognized their Master, offering him the results of his teachings: gold (transformed thought), incense (transformed feeling) and myrrh (transformed will). In this sense, Jesus reunited the two currents of shepherds or priests (descendants of Abel) and that of the kings (descendants of Cain).

Christ's task is to help man overcome evil, which according to Steiner has the two-fold character of Lucifer and Ahriman (after the Persian Ahura-Mazdao). Lucifer stands for the forces that try to lift man from the earth by accelerating normal development. He works through the powers of phantasy, → imagination, enthusiasm and sympathy. Lucifer is the devil who was responsible for the Fall, bringing us not only death and egoism, but also a sense of the self and of liberty, the possibility of taking decisions without the consent of God. Ahriman, by contrast, stands for the forces that fetter man to the earth by retarding normal development. Ahriman works through the powers of cold, materialist intellect, the will for power and domination, and antipathy. Whereas Lucifer tries to change men into bird-like, pseudo-angelic entities without any real connection to and concern for the earth, Ahriman attempts to change the earth into a machine, killing all vegetal, animal and individual human life. In a quite manichaeistic manner [→ Manichaeism], Steiner describes Christ's task as consisting not in eradicating this two-fold evil, but in transforming and redeeming it. Christ is the world-I that can find the balance and harmony between these two powers, using them for a good purpose. Steiner expressed this character in a huge wooden statue, the Representative of Mankind (*Menschheitsrepräsentant*), meant for the first Goetheanum and still on display in the present Goetheanum in Dornach, Switzerland. Christ there holds a middle position between the Luciferic and Ahrimanic forces. This explains why in some contexts, Steiner gives a very positive account of Lucifer as the light-bringer who has brought us knowledge and science, who presided over all pre-Christian initiation, the guide of the soul through the planetary spheres after death etc. Thanks to Lucifer man has become free, but thanks to Christ he can use this freedom in order to voluntarily do good, transcending the egoism that forms the shadow side of Lucifer's gift of freedom.

In this context, Steiner also developed his version of the distinction between higher and lower Self or "I". The lower self is the product of Lucifer, who is responsible for the ego-centred, daily consciousness that is tied to our blood. Christ inhabits our higher I; He is the universal I that purifies the egoistic forces of the blood and reunites humankind as a whole. Nevertheless, Christ is above all our example to emulate. With his help we humans can transform the earth into a "cosmos of love", restoring the gross, material earth to its original spirituality, freed of all gravity, decay and opaqueness. Thus we can create the new Heavenly Jerusalem of the Apocalypse. In this sense, Steiner was close to the Pelagianism of early modern spiritual → alchemy and to → Rosicrucianism.

Not unlike → Jacob Boehme, Steiner stressed the different characters and tasks of the three Persons of the Trinity, that not only pervades the natural world and human physiology (thought being connected to the Sprit, feeling to Christ, will to the Father) but is also reflected in the Celestial Hierarchies Steiner adopted from → Pseudo-Dionysius Areopagita. The first Hierarchy (Seraphim, Cherubim and Thrones) reflects the Father, the second (Dunameis, Kyriotetes, Exousiai) the Son, and the third (Angels, Archangels and Archai) the Holy Spirit. Steiner devoted special attention to the third Hierarchy, the "Hierarchies of personality" which stand closest to the human spirit. The Angels guide the individual person in accordance with his personal destiny, the Archangels are the leaders of nations and historical periods, while the Archai direct humankind as a whole. Among the Archangels, Michael occupies a central place. Steiner calls anthroposophy "Michaelic", referring to Michael's apocalyptic battle with the dragon. According to Steiner, St. Michael is the keeper of cosmic intelligence, which is formed by the diverse mutual relations between the planets, stars and Hierarchies. In order for us to become free, this cosmic intelligence has been bequeathed to man, who from the Greek period onwards has been able to develop human science and wisdom. Ahriman, the dragon that has been chased out of the heavens by Michael, tries to seduce us to use this intelligence for his own materialist, anti-human purposes. In answer, Michael challenges us to transform terrestrial intelligence into a new cosmic, Christianized intelligence that employs the powers of clear thinking in order to build a more just and harmonized world. He does not do so by direct inspiration but by appealing to our I that has to find an independent spiritual and moral path. Michael is the archangel guiding the present epoch, that according to Steiner started in 1879, the end of the so-called Kali Yuga or dark period, in which human kind could only with great difficulty gain access to the spiritual world.

3. Planetary Evolution

Steiner obviously had a very essentialist view of history, which, according to him, not only has well-defined periods, but also a clear sense and purpose. In fact, human physiology developed over eons in which the earth and our planetary system as a whole went through several phases, which Steiner calls Saturn-phase, Sun-phase, Moon-phase, the present Earth-phase and the future Jupiter-, Venus- and Vulcan-phases. Not only these names but also the description of the earth's planetary evolution itself have much in common with previous theosophical literature, especially the writings of → Mme Blavatsky. Steiner's description of the first three epochs of the earth phase owe a lot to theosophy as well. According to Steiner, Saturn, Sun and Moon are recapitulated during the respective phases of that he calls the Polarian, Hyperborean, Lemurian and Atlantean epoch. Steiner situates the biblical story of the Fall in the Lemurian epoch, in which Lucifer seduces the ancestors of man into using their I for their own, selfish purposes. They were thus able to cause enormous fires in their environment, which ultimately destroyed the mythical continent of Lemuria. Only a very small group was able to escape to the continent of Atlantis, where they became the ancestors of the fourth "root-race" of humankind, as Steiner refers to it, using theosophical vocabulary. Atlantis had planetary Oracles, places of initiation where a few chosen ones were taught about the evolution of the Cosmos and the importance of Christ therein. However, a few initiates became corrupt through the influence of Ahriman. They used their "mystery knowledge" in order to exploit and abuse the forces of nature for their own pleasure, which ultimately led to another gigantic backlash: according to Steiner the biblical story of the Flood is a legendary account of what really happened to Atlantis around the 10th millennium BC. Again, a small group of initiates were saved from the flood. Under the leadership of Manu, the great sun-hierophant, they founded the culture of the present 5th, post-Atlantean epoch of the earth phase. This epoch itself is again subdivided into several so-called "culture-epochs", namely the ancient Indian culture-epoch, the ancient Persian epoch, the ancient Egyptian epoch, the Greco-Roman epoch and the present spiritual soul epoch that started in the middle of the 15th century. Steiner situates the ancient Indian epoch before the origins of Vedanta philosophy, which is but a shadow of the wisdom of the Rishi's (the Indian masters described in theosophical literature). The Persian epoch is also situated well before the documented history of Zoroastrianism, which again is a reflection of the original wisdom of this period, in which man became more attached to the earth, inventing agriculture and founding cities. The Egyptian epoch is described by Steiner as the period in which the sentient soul was developed, for Egyptian culture was guided by its founding myths, spiritual images that pervaded daily life, and especially the sphere of life, death and the life after death. By contrast, the Greco-Roman epoch found its way out of the images of mythology into the clear thoughts of philosophy, marking the beginning of the epoch of the intellectual soul. Our present epoch, that of the spiritual soul, is determined above all by the development of natural science, by means of which we have been able to conquer and command nature, thereby alienating ourselves from the spiritual world. It is also the period in which old social, national and religious structures crumble, creating a void that has to be filled by the human I that acts in accordance with Christ.

The Death and Resurrection of Christ in the Greco-Roman culture epoch is thus the "midpoint" of planetary evolution, providing a remedy for the decay that had set in through Luciferic and Ahrimanic influences. From that moment on, humanity and earth in general have been able to make a U-turn, finding a new way up towards the New Jerusalem. Although this "U-shape" version of evolution going from original purity through decay and back again to a new form of purity is common to many forms of esotericism and especially prominent in modern theosophy, the central place accorded to the coming of Christ in the planetary evolution makes anthroposophy different from older theosophical accounts of planetary evolution, with which Steiner otherwise has a lot in common. In fact, apart from his esoteric perspective on the history of Persians, Egyptians, Greeks etc., Steiner also outlined an esoteric history of Christianity. Not unlike his theosophical predecessors Steiner more or less included all the known spiritual "Masters" in this history. For instance, he speaks about a "Council" taking place in the 4th century, in which participated the great esoteric leaders of the West: Manes, representing the I, Zarathustra, representing the astral body, Buddha, representing the etheric body, and Skythianos, representing the physical body. These four Masters mapped out the future development of Christianity from the perspective of the old initiatiory knowledge of the Egyptian and Greek mysteries, that had prepared Christ's coming. The basic question during this meeting was how the ancient secret knowledge could be saved and transformed in the light of Christ's redemptive act. These masters thus founded "esoteric Christianity", which according to Steiner appeared on earth in the form of the grail current (under the leadership of Percival) [→ Grail traditions in Western esotericism] and, subsequently, → Rosicrucianism under the leadership of Christian Rosencreutz.

Steiner thus showed himself as obsessed with the concept of evolution as all other members of the cultural elite in the 19th and early 20th centuries. In this connection he has often been accused of implicit or even explicit racism. His evolutionary logic, which is quite reminiscent of Hegel's philosophy of world history, implies that some "culture epochs", and also some races, are higher – closer to the nucleus of contemporary world development – than others. The vanguard of the present evolutionary epoch, for instance, is mainly to be found in Middle Europe, other nations being seen as less relevant or even as "decadent" survivals from earlier periods. Steiner's opponents point to a few very unfortunate passages which, for instance, speak of native Americans being decadent and more or less "ready" for the mass murder committed by the Europeans. Furthermore, Steiner speaks of the Jewish people as having fulfilled its mission and facing no other choice than either complete assimilation or extinction. This is not the place to draw a final conclusion about Steiner's alleged racism, but a full discussion should take into account some aditional factors: his explicit rejection of social Darwinism, his philosophy of freedom that speaks of the moral person acting on the strength of individual moral intuitions and breaking away from the collective morality of nation and religion, and his emphasis on the notion that we live in the epoch of the spiritual soul, in which the human I – which is common to all humankind – more and more comes to dominate the forces of race and religion that divide human beings. Moreover, Steiner actively combated antisemitism in his Berlin years and opened the newly founded Anthroposophical Society in 1923/24 for everyone, regardless of sex, race or religion.

4. REINCARNATION AND KARMA

In order for us to be able to experience planetary evolution and, above all, to further it, Steiner thought we need more than one life, in other words, we need to reincarnate. The theme of → reincarnation and karma is a central ingredient of Steiner's teachings, and underwent a fair degree of metamorphosis over the years. In fact, the last great lecture series before his death was devoted to yet another revision of his original conceptions. Karma, the law of cause and effects that connects our present life with previous ones is formed in the life between death and the new incarnation, to which Steiner devoted a lot of attention. His descriptions of the path of the soul through the diverse regions of the spiritual world has similarities with theosophical doctrines and pre-modern Western sources such as Macrobius and other Platonists. Again, however, Steiner's doctrine stands out not only for its highly systematic character but also for its attempt to integrate ideas about reincarnation and Karma within a Christian framework.

After death, the first body that we lose is the etheric one, which contains the memories of the past life. During the first three days after death, while this body is shed off, the soul re-experiences all the events of the past life in reverse other. Next, the soul enters the world to which Steiner refers by the theosophical term Kamaloka. Here, it is the astral body that is purged from its experiences in the past life. The Kamaloka confronts us with everything we have done out of egoism; it is the sphere of guilt, spite and retribution, showing us all the emotional and other damage we have caused in other people's souls. However, this almost Old Testament notion of tit for tat (in fact, Steiner says that the soul experiences → Moses as a kind of Guardian of this region) has been substantially transformed by Christ's Resurrection. The more we have lived our life with Christian love, the shorter this period will be. Moreover, Christ does not so much punish us four our failures as that he looks at them from the perspective of moral improvement.

Then, the I enters the lower and subsequently the higher Devachan – yet another theosophical term. The lower Devachan is basically the Platonic world of Archetypes, whereas the higher Devachan contains the cosmic intentions or thoughts behind these Archetypes. The higher Devachan stretches out over the Zodiac. Here we experience the "Sun at Midnight", the point between the upward movement after death and the downward movement towards a new incarnation. In this region Karma is formed in conjunction with the Celestial Hierarchies. Having worked through all of its past in the way up to the Sun at Midnight the I now goes back through the planetary spheres, forming its new bodies that contain the karmic consequences of the past life. In this connection, Steiner speaks about a three-fold karma: the karma of events that is linked with the physical body, the natural karma linked with the etheric body, and the karma of sympathy and antipathy linked with the astral body. The natural karma encompasses everything that has to do with health and disease, but also with the specific family or nation one has chosen to be born into etc.; sympathy and antipathy refer to our professional and other interests or affinities; whereas the karma of events refer to crucial experiences that shape or change our lives. In this context, Steiner does not tire of stressing that everything that happens to us has sense or purpose. Steiner essentially depicted a symbolic cosmos in which the Hierarchies continuously emit signs that gives us guidance for our actions, provided of course that we are able to read these signs. For instance, anthroposophists are supposed not to curse a train that gets broken on one's way to a highly important job interview, but to see it as a wake-up call by the Hierarchies, suggesting reflection on the question whether this particular job is really what one should be doing in life. This example also makes clear that karma according to Steiner is not just a matter of Leibnizian pre-established harmony, concocted in heaven, but is also the outcome of direct intervention by the Hierarchies in our daily lives.

Steiner urged anthroposophists to look for certain red threads running through a person's biography (including our own), with respect to the various forms of karma that in a next step can be explained in terms of karmic laws. For instance, in regard to natural karma, a certain susceptibility to smallpox is the result of one's past life's tendency to act without love or real interest. Actually, most of the many karmic laws that Steiner describes stretch out over various lives. Nevertheless, Steiner had anything but a deterministic or pessimistic outlook on karma. Again, the crucial fact here is the presence of Christ, whom Steiner calls "Lord of the Karma". Thanks to Christ, karma is no longer a deterministic cycle, from which we can only strive to escape as soon as possible. Karma and reincarnation are seen in the light of moral and spiritual perfectibility. Humans reincarnate in order to work on their own purification and especially on that of the earth. Christ thus transforms the karmic laws from laws of retribution for past sins, into possibilities for moral improvement. For instance, one may be confronted with a strong antipathy or open enmity by a certain person, which is the result of a negative act one has oneself committed against this person in a previous life. By trying not to respond by giving in to antipathy, fear or other negative emotions, but rather, by using the I to find common ground, one makes up for past sins. In this connection, Steiner also speaks of old or "moon"-karma and "new" or sun-karma. Thanks to Christ's presence in our I we can take the initiative to step beyond old karmic laws, creating a new and more positive karma that also extends to persons one has never met in previous lives.

Steiner tried to harmonize the doctrine of reincarnation and karma with the traditional theological doctrines concerning God's Grace and the forgiveness of sins. What Christ forgives or remedies is the objective consequences of our immoral acts: by committing sin, we not only hurt fellow human beings but also the spiritual sphere of the earth. Christ ensures that we are confronted with the subjective karmic consequences of our actions, in view of improvement, thereby preventing us from facing the objective effects that we would never be able to manage.

5. THE SPIRITUAL PATH

According to Steiner himself, all the doctrines discussed so far are the outcome of independent spiritual research, based on his innate clairvoyant capacities. In fact, Steiner emphasizes that he has found e.g. all the information concerning the dual biography of Jesus in the Akasha-Chronicle, the earth's planetary record in the spiritual world. Although Steiner taught all these doctrines to his followers, he certainly did not think that spiritual knowledge was confined to a few initiates or Masters. Quite on the contrary, scholars have described Steiner's esoteric doctrine as a "democratization" of spiritual experience as compared to older theosophy, even paving the way in this particular respect for the do-it-yourself-spirituality of the → New Age Movement. In many places in his work, Steiner gave indications for a systematic personal spiritual path that would lead to knowledge of the higher worlds. He gave particular meditations or mantras (especially in the form of the meditations intended for the First Class of his School of Spiritual Science) that could be used in order to develop the higher spiritual organs: imagination, inspiration and intuition. Imagination stands for a transmuted thought process, the so-called "vivid thinking" (*lebendiges Denken*) that transforms abstract thinking into dynamic spiritual images. Inspiration arises when we erase all imaginative elements and start "hear-ing" spiritually the spiritual forces that stand behind these images. It consists in a spiritualized process of feeling. Intuition, finally, leads to direct knowledge of spiritual entities and is brought about by a transformation of the will.

However, it is quite typical for Steiner that his concrete indications concerning the development of higher knowledge are outweighed by his consistent stress on the *conditions* for obtaining this knowledge. In works such as *Theosophy*, Steiner gives a whole series of so-called "side-exercises" (*Nebenübungen*) that are all geared to stimulating emotional and moral stability. Steiner never tired of emphasizing that meditation should not lead us away from our daily life, but is meant to give more depth to daily life itself. The basis of any meditational practice is our faculty of objective thinking, which prevents us from drifting off into a mystical fog of vague spiritual feelings. In his anthroposophical, post-philosophical career, Steiner stated that his own *Philosophy of Freedom* could and even should be used as a meditational text. He claimed that by developing imaginative, spiritual thought or *lebendiges Denken*, one should be able to gain independent confirmation of all the doctrines he had revealed to his followers.

Steiner thus had the same ambiguous attitude towards modern science as many other occultists of the 19th and early 20th century. On the one hand, science was viewed as a materialist threat to true humanity. On the other hand, there is the claim that anthroposophy is a spiritual science (*Geisteswissenschaft*), meeting scientific standards of objectivity, lack of prejudice etc. Nevertheless, there is an inherent tension within anthroposophy between Steiner's demand that one develop one's own spiritual capacities and conduct independent spiritual scientific research, on the one hand, and the need to come to terms with his revelations contained in the ca. 400 volumes of his *Gesamtausgabe*, on the other hand. Steiner frequently warned his followers that his texts should not be venerated as revelations, but should be used as heuristic tools in dealing with everyday experience. His occult physiology for instance, should be employed in categorizing empirical observation of a person's posture, way of walking etc.

6. THE ANTHROPOSOPHICAL MOVEMENT

The present Anthroposophical Society was founded under the Presidency of Steiner at the so-called Christmas Conference (*Weihnachtstagung*) of 1923/1924, as the successor of the earlier Society which Steiner did not lead himself (see →

Steiner). This Conference is still very important to contemporary anthroposophists, as Steiner not only laid the factual foundation of the Society but also the spiritual one; he did this in the form of the so-called Foundation Stone Meditation (*Grundsteinspruch*), which links tripartite man with the macrocosmos of the Hierarchies and the Trinity, and contains Steiner's version of the Rosicrucian Motto *Ex Deo nascimur, in Christo morimur, ex Spiritu Sancto reviviscimus* (we are born from God, we die in Christ and we are resurrected in the Holy Spirit). After Steiner's death in 1925, the Society soon became the scene of tremendous personal conflicts and disputes about the Society's future course. Moroever, very early on the Society was forbidden by the Nazis. Nevertheless, it survived all of this, resolved past conflicts, and witnessed a new period of growth in the 1970s and 1980s, especially thanks to the practical applications of anthroposophy such as Waldorf Schools, biodynamic farming, anthroposophical medicine, curative pedagogy (for the mentally handicapped) and various kinds of social initiatives, such as shops, enterprises and "green" and social banks. In this sense, what anthroposophists refer to as the Anthroposophical Movement is much wider than the membership of the Anthroposophical Society. Especially since the break with the Theosophical Society in 1913, anthroposophy and the later Anthroposophical Society have had a strongly – though not exclusively – Middle European, German-speaking character. In recent years, the Anthroposophical Society and Movement have had a wider international expansion, with more room for English-language conferences at the Society's headquarters in Dornach, Switzerland, official publications in English and a stronger presence in North- and South America and Asia. For more information on the Anthroposophical society, one may consult www.goetheanum.ch.

Lit. Geoffrey Ahern, *Sun at Midnight: The Rudolf Steiner Movement and the Western Esoteric Tradition*, Wellingborough, 1984 ◆ Daniel van Egmond, "Western Esoteric Schools in the Late Nineteenth and Early Twentieth Centuries", in: Roelof van den Broek and Wouter J. Hanegraaff (eds.), *Gnosis and Hermeticism from Antiquity to Modern Times*, Albany: SUNY Press, 1998, 311-346 ◆ Harald Lamprecht, *Neue Rosenkreuzer: Ein Handbuch*, Göttingen: Vandenhoeck & Ruprecht, 2004, 191-205 ◆ Christoph Lindenberg, *Rudolf Steiner: Eine Biographie*, Stuttgart, 1997 ◆ Renata von Maydell, "Anthroposophy in Russia", in: Bernice Glatzer Rosenthal (ed.), *The Occult in Russian and Soviet Culture*, Ithaca and London: Cornell University Press, 1997, 153-167 ◆ Helmut Zander, "Friedrich Rittelmeyer: Eine Konversion vom liberalen Protestantismus zur anthroposophischen Christengemeinschaft", in: F.W. Graf & H.M. Müller, *Der deutsche Protestantismus um 1900*, Gütersloh, 1996, 238-297 ◆ idem, "Anthroposophische Rassentheorie: Der Geist auf dem Weg durch die Geschichte", in: Stefanie von Schnurbein & Justus H. Ulbricht (eds.), *Völkische Religion und Krisen der Moderne: Entwürfe 'arteigener' Glaubenssysteme seit der Jahrhundertwende*, Würzburg: Königshausen & Neumann, 2001, 292-341 ◆ idem, "Die Anthroposophie: Eine Religion?", *Hairesis: Festschrift für Karl Hoheisel zum 65. Geburtstag* (Jahrbuch für Antike und Christentum, Ergänzungsband 34), Münster Westfalen: Aschendorff Verlag, 2002, 525-538.

CEES LEIJENHORST

Archontics

The Archontics were adherents of a Christian Gnostic sect [→ Gnosticism] of the 4th century, named after the archons, the rulers of the seven heavens, who played an important role in their system. The sect is only known through the refutation by its staunch opponent from the beginning, bishop Epiphanius of Salamis (*Panarion*, 40, to which the references below refer), from whom all information in later authors derives. Since it is not likely that these Gnostics called themselves after the evil planetary rulers they abhorred, their name may have been invented by Epiphanius himself, because of the great variety of names they used for the archons (40, 8, 7).

The founder of the sect was a certain Peter, a former Palestinian priest, who had been excommunicated because of his heterodox views, then lived for a long time in Arabia, and finally returned to Palestine where he, unrecognized, lived the life of a hermit. Epiphanius, however, who was head of a monastery in Eleutheropolis (ca. 335-ca. 365), discovered Peter's true identity from his secret teachings and expelled him from the church. But Peter remained in his cave and attracted many people. One of them was a certain Eutaktos from Armenia Minor (eastern Turkey). On his way home from a pilgrimage to Egypt he visited Peter and was converted to his Gnostic views, which happened to the end of Constantius' reign († 361). Back in Armenia, he succeeded in winning over many Armenians, especially rich dignitaries, to his heretical ideas (40, 1-8).

The Archontics made use of many books, of which they themselves had compiled two, the *Lesser Harmony* and the *Greater Harmony*. The former may have been no more than an abstract from the latter, since in 40, 2, 3 Epiphanius simply speaks of 'the book entitled *Harmony*'. They also used books that already circulated in heterodox circles, for instance the apocryphal *Ascension of Isaiah* and a work called *Strangers* (*Allogeneis*) (40, 2, 1-2). The latter certainly belonged to a special kind of literature of which they also had other specimens in their possession: works written in the name of Seth, or of Seth and his seven sons, who were called 'strangers' (*allogeneis*) (40, 7, 4). This is strongly reminiscent of the book *Allogenes* ("Stranger") which was used by Plotinus' Gnostics (Porphyry, *Life of Plotinus*, 16) and recovered in Cod. XI, 3 of the Nag Hammadi Library. The Archontics also held two prophets in high esteem, Martiades and Marsianos, who had been caught up into the heavens and had come down after three days. The name Marsianos may be no more than a variant of the name Marsanes, known, *inter alia*, from the title of another Nag Hammadi writing, *Marsanes* (Cod. X, 1). The books *Allogenes* and *Marsanes*, together with the *Three Steles of Seth* and *Zostrianus* (NHC VII, 5 and VIII, 1), form a group of late Gnostic works which combined traditional elements of Sethian gnosticism with Neoplatonic ideas [→ Neoplatonism], in particular those of Iamblichus. The Gnostics behind these books were no longer interested primarily in the origin of the bad material world and the soul's deliverance from evil but in the soul's experience of the divine through a ritual for heavenly ascent.

There are strong indications that the Archontics shared the same ideas and, therefore, were not an independent Gnostic group but a special Palestinian and Armenian brand of later Sethian Gnosticism [→ Sethians]. Their mythology and their interpretation of the first chapters of the Bible have much in common with Sethian writings such as the *Apocryphon of John* (NHC II, 1; III, 1; IV, 1; BG 8502, 2) and, in particular, the *Hypostasis of the Archons* (NHC II, 4). The *Harmony* explained that there are seven heavens, each ruled by a special archon and his band of angels. The soul has its origin in the eighth heaven, the abode of the high, good God, called the Father of All, and the Mother on high, also called the Luminous Mother, whence it descended into this world (40, 2, 3 and 8). The Archontics held that the soul is the indispensable food of the planetary rulers and their retinue: they cannot live without it since it comes from the moisture on high and provides them with power (40, 2, 7). The highest archon, Sabaoth, rules over the seventh heaven and is said to be the father of the devil (40, 5, 1). This feature of the myth might be due, however, to a misunderstanding of Epiphanius. In the *Hypostasis of the Archons* (NHC II, 95,

13-26), Sabaoth is the son of the devil who rebelled against his father and received authority over the seventh heaven as a reward. Just as the *Hypostasis*, the Archontics taught that Sabaoth was not as evil as the devil but far below the goodness of the highest God. He is identified with the God of the Jews and the non-Gnostic Christians (40, 5, 2).

Just as in the *Apocryphon of John*, the birth of Cain and Abel is due to the sexual union of the devil and Eve. In support of this view the Archontics cited John 8:44. They taught that both brothers desired their sister and that it was for that reason that Cain slew Abel. Seth, however, was born from the union of Adam and Eve, whereupon the power and the ministers of the good God caught him up lest he be killed too. After a long time he was brought down again, i.e. he was reincarnated, in such a state that neither Sabaoth, nor the authorities and principalities of the creator-god could prevail over him. On the contrary, he exposed their evil nature and solely recognized the unnameable power and the good God on high (40, 7, 1-3). In this way, Seth, the "Stranger" *par excellence*, became the Gnostic revealer and saviour.

The Archontics rejected the sacraments of the church in general and baptism in particular, as being instituted in the name of Sabaoth (40, 2, 6). They denied the resurrection of the flesh and only taught a resurrection of the soul by means of its heavenly ascent (40, 2, 5). If the soul has attained a state of Gnosis and has separated itself from the baptism of the church and the lawgiver Sabaoth, it is able to ascend to the eighth heaven of the Mother on high and the Father of All. It passes unharmed through the seven heavens, by virtue of its knowledge of the necessary passwords or words of defence to be said to the planetary rulers, a feature well known from other Gnostic texts (40, 2, 8). This was the core and kernel of the Archontics' doctrine of salvation. Their negative view of the material world led them to a docetic Christology, i.e. the doctrine that Jesus had only a carnal body in appearance (40, 8, 2). In accordance with their depreciation of the body, many Archontics practised sexual abstinence. Epiphanius had to admit this, but he immediately added that this was all feigned in order to deceive the simpler folk; according to him other Archontics 'polluted their bodies by licentiousness' (40, 2, 4).

The Armenian Archontics may have had some influence on the ideas of the Paulicians and other heterodox groups in Armenia and the Balkans and, through their intermediary, on those of the medieval Bogomils [→ Bogomilism] and the Cathars [→ Catharism] (dualism, rejection of water-baptism, use of the *Ascension of Isaiah*, the ascent of the soul to its heavenly origin, *et al.*).

K. Holl (ed.), *Epiphanius II: Panarion haer. 34-64*, 2nd. rev. ed. by J. Dummer, Berlin: Akademie-Verlag, 1980 ◆ Engl. trans. with notes in F. Williams, *The Panarion of Epiphanius of Salamis, Book 1 (Sects 1-46)*, Leiden: E.J. Brill, 1987; and B. Layton, *The Gnostic Scriptures: A New Translation with Annotations and Introductions*, Garden City, New York: Double Day & Company, 1987, 191-198.

Lit.: H.-Ch. Puech, "Archontiker", *RAC* I (1950), 633-643 ◆ M.E. Stone, "An Armenian Pilgrim to the Holy Land in the Early Byzantine Era", *Revue des Études Arméniennes* 18 (1984), 173-178.

ROELOF VAN DEN BROEK

Areopagite, Pseudo-Dionysius the
→ Dionysius Areopagita (Pseudo-)

Ariosophy

1. Lanz von Liebenfels's System
2. The Ordo Novi Templi 3. Rudolf
John Gorsleben 4. Herbert Reichstein
5. Ariosophy and the Third Reich

A dualistic-gnostic racial religion which attracted followers in Austria and Germany during the first half of the 20th century. The term "Ariosophy", meaning esoteric wisdom of the Aryan race, was first coined by → Jörg Lanz von Liebenfels in 1915. He earlier used the terms "theozoology" and "Ario-Christianity" and founded the Ordo Novi Templi (ONT) at Vienna in 1900 as a Christian gnostic order to celebrate an Aryan cult of pure race. → Guido von List, whose ideas on the occult heritage of the Aryans supplied further inspiration for Ariosophy, actually called his own doctrine "Wotanism" or "Armanism". During the 1920s and 1930s Ariosophy embraced the expanded ONT under the leadership of Lanz von Liebenfels, and an associated group of writers who combined theories of Aryan supremacy and racial purity with → astrology, numerology [→ Number Symbolism], kabbalism [→ Jewish Influences], graphology and palmistry.

Ariosophy elaborated a gnostic form of Christianity based on the divinity of the Aryans, supported by 19th-century anthropology, zoology and archaeology. Its doctrine also embraced ideas taken from the Theosophy of → Helena Petrovna Blavatsky. Ariosophy described a golden age (both prehistoric and medieval), when religious orders had governed racially pure Aryan societies on the basis of a racial gnosis. The Ariosophists claimed that an evil conspiracy of anti-Aryan agents (variously identified as inferior non-Aryan races of bestial origin, the Jews, or even the Church) had sought to undermine and ruin this pristine Aryan race by emancipating the non-German inferiors in the name of a spurious egalitarianism. The resulting racial confusion gave birth to the modern world with its wars, economic conflict, political uncertainty and the frustration of German world-power. The Ariosophists cultivated the esoteric knowledge and racial virtue of the ancient Aryans, in order to oppose the modern world and so prepare the way for a new pan-Aryan world order.

1. Lanz von Liebenfels's System
The doctrine of Ariosophy was first formulated by Jörg Lanz von Liebenfels, who entered the Cistercian novitiate as Frater Georg at Heilgenkreuz Abbey near Vienna in 1893. Here Lanz made good progress, taking his solemn vows in 1897 and assuming teaching duties in the seminary in 1898. However, Lanz harboured heretical ideas concerning the literally bestial nature of sin, an idea suggested to him by a tombstone relief showing a knight treading on a strange animal. Convinced that Christianity had betrayed its original racial doctrines, he left the order in 1899 and immersed himself in contemporary anthropological studies relating to the Aryan race, such as Carl Penka, *Origines Ariacae* (1883), Matthäus Much, *Die Heimat der Indogermanen* (1902), and Ludwig Wilser, *Die Germanen* (1904).

In 1903 Lanz published a long article 'Anthropozoon biblicum' in a periodical for biblical research. From his analysis of mystery cults described by Herodotus, Euhemerus, Plutarch, Strabo and Pliny, Lanz concluded that the ancient civilisations had practised an orgiastic cult involving sexual intercourse with small beasts or pygmies. Reliefs excavated at Nimrud in 1848 by the British orientalist Sir Austen Henry Layard showed such beasts (*pagatu, baziati, udumi*) being sent as tribute to the Assyrians. According to Lanz, the writings of the ancients, the findings of modern archaeology, and substantial sections of the Old Testament corroborated this terrible practice of miscegenation. He articulated a theology in which the Fall denoted the racial compromise of the divine Aryans due to wicked interbreeding with lower animal species, deriving from an earlier primitive branch of animal evolution. These persistent sins, institutionalized as satanic cults, led to the creation of several mixed races, which threatened the sacred and legitimate authority of the Aryans throughout the world, especially in Germany, where the Aryans were still most numerous. In 1905 Lanz published his fundamental statement of gnostic doctrine as *Theozoologie oder die Kunde von den Sodoms-Äfflingen und dem Götterelektron*, which again combined traditional Judaeo-Christian sources with the new life-sciences: hence theo-zoology. The first section of the book presented the evil realm by examining the origin and nature of the pygmies. The first pygmy, called Adam, spawned a race of beast-men (*Anthropozoa*), which gave rise to the various species of apes in the world. Quite distinct in origin were the earlier and superior god-men (*Theozoa*). Following Euhemerus and Saxo Grammaticus, Lanz believed that these superior forms of life were gods. Impressed by current scientific discoveries in electronics and radiology, Lanz saw electricity as a form of divine revelation and inspiration and attributed to *Theozoa* extraordinary sensory organs for the reception and transmission of electrical signals. These organs bestowed powers of telepathy and omniscience upon the *Theozoa*. True religion in Lanz's view consisted in endogamous cults of racial purity in order to maintain these divine powers and to counter the temptations of lecherous acts with the bestial apelings, pygmies and their crossbreeds.

Lanz's exegesis of the Old Testament led him to conclude that Jehovah, the God of Israel, was just such a prehistoric electrical being, who regularly manifested as a cloud, fire and lightning. The electrical nature of the Ark of the Covenant was evident, while 'God has both properties of electrical rays, he enlivens and he kills, he heals and he makes ill' (*Theozoologie*, p. 97). By contrast, the heathen deities of Israel were all throwbacks to the evil cults of bestiality. Moving on to the New Testament, Lanz also identified Christ as an electrical being, who came to redeem a fallen mankind from bestial miscegenation through a revival of the gnostic racial religion. According to Lanz, Christ was one of the last god-men but not God. Christ's miracles and magical powers and the transfiguration confirmed his electronic nature. Lanz substantiated this view with quotations from the apocryphal Acts of John and the Gnostic *Pistis Sophia*. Lanz interpreted the Crucifixion as the attempted rape of Christ by pygmies urged on by adherents of the bestial cults devoted to interbreeding.

In place of the originally distinct species of *Theozoa* and apes, there had developed several mixed races, of which the Aryans were the least corrupt. The marvellous electrical organs of the *Theozoa* had atrophied into the supposedly superfluous pituitary and pineal glands in modern man owing to miscegenation. Throughout all recorded history, the apelings and pygmies had sought to destroy the Aryans by dragging them down the evolutionary ladder by means of their promiscuity. The history of religion recorded a constant struggle between the bestial and endogamous cults. Besides Lanz's citation of Gnostic sources, his racial religion also betrays gnostic features. '[The gods] once walked physically on earth. Today they live on in man. The gods slumber in the racially degraded bodies of men, but the day will come when they arise once more' (*Theozoology*, p. 91). The entrapment of the divine electrical spark within racially inferior bodies transposes gnostic ideas into the modern discourse of physical anthropology and eugenics. Lanz claimed that a universal programme of segregation and breeding could restore these divine powers to the Aryans as the closest descendants of the god-men.

Lanz's radical interpretation of Scripture logically embraced the Judaeo-Christian notions of linear history, apocalypse and salvation. At the end of this manichaean temporal scheme stood the promise of final redemption. Lanz painted a grim portrait of modernity characterised by racial confusion, the decline of traditional elites, the emancipation and promotion of inferiors, and the rule of money. 'Why do you seek a hell in the next world! Is the hell in which we live and which burns inside us [the stigma of corrupt blood] not dreadful enough?' (*Theozoology*, p. 133). These "messianic woes" were the apocalyptic prelude to the millennium, when the ascendancy of the inferior races both in Europe and its colonial orbit would be reversed. Lanz fulminated against the (false) Christian tradition of compassion and social welfare and demanded that the state deal ruthlessly with the indigent. Women in particular were regarded as a special problem as they were supposedly more prone to the sexual attraction of racial inferiors. Socialism, democracy and feminism were the downfall of a racially pure world.

Lanz's millennium was a pan-German world-empire ruled by the aristocracy. As the original Aryan homeland, Germany had always been the nation of kings and heroes, while its Latin, Slav and Byzantine neighbours had fostered racial degeneration. Lanz claimed that traces of the holy electronic power still prevailed in the old princely dynasties of Germany. Provided their pedigree remained thoroughly noble, these aristocratic families were the closest living descendants of the former god-men. The princes had always cultivated genius, innovation and art at their castles and courts. In the modern age the racial inferiors constantly sought to compromise this progress by intermarriage and demands for a share in power. Lanz prophesied a millennium of aristocratic rule, underpinned by an aggressive programme of German imperialism to reconquer the world and vanquish the racial inferiors.

Lanz's religious ideas were strongly influenced by the political circumstances of Habsburg Austria at the turn of the century. Representative government had been introduced in 1867 under constitutional changes whereby the emperor shared power with a bicameral legislature, elected by a restricted franchise under which about 6% of the population voted. The franchise was widened in 1897 and universal male suffrage was introduced in 1907. The advance of representative democracy challenged traditional German dominance in the multinational empire of Germans, Czechs, Poles, Ukrainians and Slovenes. Lanz's hostility towards other races, his condemnation of democracy and call for the subjection of all nationalities in the empire to German aristocratic rule indicate his profound reaction to the political developments of his time. His political concerns were evident in his own journal *Ostara* (named after the pagan Germanic goddess of spring), which he began publishing in 1905. *Ostara*, subtitled "Library for Blonds and Fighters for Men's Rights", initially addressed the political and economic problems of the Habsburg empire from a racial and pan-German perspective. From 1908 until 1918 Lanz wrote seventy-one issues himself. Their stock themes were racial somatology, anti-feminism, anti-parliamentarianism, and the spiritual differences between the blond (higher) and dark (lower) races in sexual behaviour, art, philosophy, commerce, politics and warfare. The First World War was documented as an eschatological struggle between the blonds and the darks.

Theosophy was a further ingredient of Lanz's early doctrine. One of Lanz's contributors was the Theosophist, Harald Grävell van Jostenoode (1856-1932), who wrote two *Ostara* issues outlining a pan-German empire and a programme for the restoration of Aryan authority in the world. Lanz also made direct use of Theosophy in his *Bibeldokumente* series (1907-1908). The second number of the series, *Die Theosophie und die assyrischen "Menschentiere"*, gave an selective exegesis of → Helena Petrovna Blavatsky's major text *The Secret Doctrine*, newly translated into German between 1897 and 1901. He compared her occult anthropogeny favourably with the findings of modern palaeontology, incorporated the sunken continents of Lemuria and Atlantis in his own view of prehis-

tory, and recognised his *pagatu, baziati, udumi* of Assyrian lore in her account of prehistoric monsters. In Blavatsky's eighth stanza of Dzyan, verses 30-32, the early Lemurians first developed into two sexes but interbred with attractive, inferior females to produce monsters and demons. Lanz validated Blavatsky's scheme of five root-races (to date), concluding that the fourth root-race of Atlanteans had divided into pure and bestial sub-species, corresponding to the anthropoids and the anthropomorphic apes. The fatal sin of the former's descendants, the fifth root-race of the Aryans, had been persistent interbreeding with the latter's descendants.

2. THE ORDO NOVI TEMPLI

In 1900 Lanz founded the Ordo Novi Templi (ONT) to propagate his ideas of "theozoology" and "Ario-Christianity". His decision to organise his sect as a chivalrous male order in the Templar tradition [→ Neo-Templar Traditions] drew on his own monastic experience and the contemporary vogue of the grail-knight figure in neo-romantic music and literature (Richard Wagner, Erwin Kolbenheyer, Friedrich Lienhard). The Templars were closely associated with the Cistercian order. St Bernard of Clairvaux, the Cistercian founder, had composed the Templar rule in 1128 and later addressed a laudation to the knights for their martial championship of Christianity in the Holy Land. Lanz believed that the Templars represented a pan-Aryan initiative to create a 'Greater Germanic order-state, which would encompass the entire Mediterranean area and extend its influence deep into the Middle East'. The trial and brutal suppression of the Templars in 1312 signified to Lanz the triumph of the racial inferiors who were determined to undermine the racial cult. Armed with his gnostic-racial interpretation of Scripture, supposedly suppressed since the 14th century, Lanz refounded the lapsed military order for a new racial crusade.

The ONT combined Christian piety with modern notions of racial eugenics and pan-Aryanism in a gnostic religion of redemption through pure blood. In 1907 Lanz purchased Burg Werfenstein, a small medieval castle on the River Danube near Grein in Upper Austria, as the priory of the ONT, and developed a liturgy and ceremonial. The order rule described the ONT as a racial-religious association, which could be joined only by (male) persons of predominantly pure blood, who were blond-haired, blue-eyed and possessed of an "arioheroic" figure according to Aryan racial somatology outlined in *Ostara*. Brothers were admitted to the ONT in a hierarchy of orders, according to their degree of racial purity: Servers (SNT), persons less than 50% racially pure, or persons under twenty-four years who had not undergone a racial test; Novices (NNT) included all members aged over twenty-four years and being more than 50% racially pure, who had not yet been tested for advancement to the superior orders; these were Masters (MONT) and Canons (CONT) who possessed respectively 50-75% and 75-100% degrees of racial purity. The two highest orders of the hierarchy were Presbyter (pONT) and Prior (PONT). Any Master or Canon was eligible for promotion to Presbyter once he had founded a new house for the ONT. His rights included the saying of office and celebration of mass, but excluded the reception and investiture of brothers. A Presbyter whose chapter exceeded five Masters or Canons was eligible for installation as a Prior. Lanz devised vestments and heraldic devices for each order of the hierarchy, while brothers assumed an order-name upon reception, e.g. Fra Asmund MONT ad Werfenstein.

Order ceremonial was developed from 1908 onwards. Lanz composed devotional songs and verse and had the Werfenstein priory decorated with votive paintings of Hugo de Payns, founder and first Grand Master of the Templars, St Bernard embracing the suffering Christ, and images of the apelings or pygmies. In 1915-1916 Lanz published a New Templar breviary in two parts containing "Ario-Christian" psalms and canticles written by himself and other brothers. While based on traditional Christian texts, these texts reflected the dualist gnostic-racial doctrine with supplications to Christ-Frauja (a Gothic name for Jesus) for racial salvation and the sacrifice and extermination of the inferior races. Lanz also composed several ritual books. The basic text was the *Hebdomadarium*, which contained the three offices of matins, prime and compline for each day of the week. Each office had a space for readings relating to "Ario-Christian" doctrine from the *Festivarium NT*. This book of festival readings comprised three volumes: the *Legendarium* provided readings describing the historical and cultural traditions of the racial religion for matins on each day of the year. The materials for its 1400 pages were drawn from orthodox Christianity, modern science and the acts of the New Templars. The other volumes, the *Evangelarium* and the *Visionarium*, performed the same function in the prime and compline offices. These ritual books were supplemented by a hymnal (*Cantuarium*), a book of psalms, and an *Imaginarium NT* of devotional pictures. ONT liturgy fused the forms and beliefs of Catholicism with the racial gnosis.

The defeat of the Central Powers and the disintegration of the Habsburg empire in November 1918 confirmed Lanz's fears about the ascendancy of racial inferiors over the Aryans. In his view, the abdication of monarchs, revolutions, new national states, and inflation signalled the destruction of historic political entities and aristocratic elites, and the demoralisation of the upper and middle classes throughout Europe. Henceforth, anti-Semitism and a belief in a "Jewish-Masonic-Bolshevik" conspiracy underpinned his "Ario-Christian" religion. In the late 1920s he articulated a millenarianism based on cosmic periods of approximately 730 years within the Platonic Year. In the period 480-1210 society had been ruled by "spiritual-chivalrous orders" (Benedictines, Cistercians, Templars and Teutonic Knights). In the period 1210-1920 aristocratic rule was eclipsed by the rise of the masses. The Turks and Jews weakened the European polity and the spread of towns, capitalism, and the ideologies of nationalism and democracy encouraged the ascendancy of racial inferiors and the proletariat, culminating in Bolshevism and revolution. Lanz foretold that the period 1920-2640 would see the revival of hierarchies, patricians, and secret orders. He hailed the right-wing dictatorships of Spain, Italy and Hungary in the 1920s as precursors of the global counter-revolution.

During the late 1920s and 1930s Lanz continued to elaborate the doctrine of Ariosophy with numerous volumes of scripture and extensive booklet-series. His ten-volume *Bibiomystikon oder Die Geheimbibel der Eingeweihten* (1930-1935) was a major re-interpretation of the Bible in the light of the racial gnosis. In the booklets of his *Ariomantische Bücherei* and *Elekrotheologische Handschriften* series, Lanz outlined an "electrotheology" according to which divine "electrotheonic" beings (angels, grail-doves, muses, valkyries and norns) had physically represented the eucharist as a form of sexual sacrifice to breed up the "ario-heroic" race in prehistoric times. The bread and wine of the Christian mass symbolised the "electrotheonic" nature of Christ-Frauja, while the Holy Grail was actually a grail-dove. Lanz assimilated Orpheus, Moses, Pythagoras, Plato, Brahma and Apollonius of Tyana into his mystery-religion of electricity and race. He also wrote an esoteric key to the Gothic Bible of Ulfilas (*c.* 311-383), having identified Ariosophy with the Arian heresy which had flourished among the Germanic tribes during the great migrations.

Lanz's "History of Ariosophy" traced the racial

religion from Atlantis to the ancient world, through → neoplatonism and → gnosticism, to the reformed monastic and military orders of the Middle Ages, which represented a final climax of "Ario-Christian" civilization. The Moors in Spain, the Mongol invasions and the rise of the Ottoman Turks represented external racial challenges to the "Ario-Christian" domain of medieval Europe, which were matched by internal enemies. Lanz condemned the mendicant orders (Franciscans, Dominicans) for their plebeian spirit, intolerant dogmatism and hostility to the old monastic orders. By contrast with the "ario-heroic" culture of the Middle Ages, Lanz dismissed the Renaissance as a period of decline, characterised by increasing Jewish economic, political and cultural influence. The former strict ariosophical morality of Christianity was superseded by a universal doctrine of humanity which accelerated the rise of lower castes. Lanz regarded both the Jesuits and the Freemasons [→ Freemasonry] as revolutionary agents committed to cosmopolitanism, equality and liberalism, which favoured the dominance of racial inferiors.

In order to posit the underground continuity of Ariosophy, Lanz's "Ario-Christian" mystical tradition included → Hildegard of Bingen, Mechtild of Magdeburg, Meister Eckhart, Jan van Ruysbroeck and Thomas à Kempis. In the early modern period, these mystics were succeeded by → Jakob Boehme, Angelus Silesius, Nikolaus von Zinzendorf, and → Emanuel Swedenborg. In the 19th century, Lanz's roll of Ariosophical initiates included J.B. Kerning, the mystical Freemason; Carl von Reichenbach, the Viennese investigator of → animal magnetism; the French occultists → Eliphas Lévi, Gerard Encausse [→ Papus], and → Edouard Schuré; and the Theosophists Helena Petrovna Blavatsky, → Franz Hartmann, → Annie Besant and → Charles Webster Leadbeater. The tradition finally led to Guido von List, Rudolf John Gorsleben, and the contemporary mythologists of an Aryan Atlantis, Karl Georg Zschaetzsch, and Hermann Wieland.

Before 1914 ONT activity revolved around Lanz and some fifty brothers in Vienna and Werfenstein, but during the interwar years further order-houses were founded in Germany and Hungary, where Lanz resided after 1918. Wickeloh (near Uelzen, Germany) was established by Georg Hauerstein Jr. in 1925; Marienkamp-Szt. Balázs (near Lake Balaton, Hungary) founded by Lanz in 1926; Hertesburg (on the Darß peninsula, Germany), also founded by Hauerstein in 1927; Staufen (near Sigmaringen, Germany) founded by Friedrich Franz von Hochberg (1875-1954); Petena (near Waging am See, Germany), also founded by Hauerstein in 1935; Pilisszentkereszt (northern Hungary) in 1937. According to *Tabularium O.N.T.*, the regular order newsletter detailing receptions, chapters and donations, ONT activity reached its peak between 1925 and 1935, having established at least seven sites and received some three to four hundred brothers. In 1942 Hauerstein and Lanz founded the Vitalis New Templars (NT Vit) with Petena as its seat and archpriory. In contrast to the ONT, the NT Vit accepted female members. Order activity at Petena continued until 1973.

Besides providing the basis of ONT doctrine and liturgy, Ariosophy was also publicized during the 1920s by German esotericists interested in characterology and divination [→ Divinatory Arts]. In October 1925 Lanz began collaborating with the publisher Herbert Reichstein (1892-1944) on a new periodical devoted to Ariosophy initially entitled *Zeitschrift für Menschenkenntnis und Menschenschicksal* at Düsseldorf. Here Lanz summarized Ariosophy as a emanationist doctrine of "pan-psychic" energy, which animated the whole universe but found its most perfect manifestation in the microcosm of the blond-haired, blue-eyed Aryan. Ariosophy was concerned with the scientific study of the differences between the blonds and the darks with the aid of the esoteric sciences of palmistry, astrology, numerology, phrenology, kabbalism and heraldry (an idea taken from his colleague Guido von List). Lanz claimed that heraldic devices and names were hieroglyphs, in which the Aryan ancestors had recorded the history and karma of their families. Lanz thereby linked Ariosophy with the burgeoning interest in characterology and divination which had arisen in response to the anxieties and disruptions of postwar Germany. The chief contributors to the magazine were a Berlin group of esotericists known as the "Swastika Circle" and included Ernst Issberner-Haldane (1886-1966), a palmist; Frodi Ingolfson Wehrmann (1889-1945), an astrologer and ardent supporter of Guido von List's ideas about an ancient Germanic priesthood, who was also versed in numerology and the study of karma; Robert H. Brotz, a graphologist; and Wilhelm Wulff, an astrologer, whom Heinrich Himmler consulted during the last weeks of the Second World War.

3. RUDOLF JOHN GORSLEBEN

Rudolf John Gorsleben (1883-1930), also an ONT brother, made further contributions to Ariosophy. He had long been fascinated by the Edda and other secret survivals of the Aryan heritage, while his doctrine was also indebted to → occultism and

Theosophy. From 1920 Gorsleben published his own periodical *Deutsche Freiheit*, in 1927 renamed *Arische Freiheit*, which featured articles on the runes, crystals, number-mysticism and the Cheops pyramid. In 1928 this periodical amalgamated with Reichstein's characterological magazine under the new title of *Zeitschrift für Geistes- und Wissenschaftsreform* (entitled *Ariosophie* from September 1929). Through astrology, kabbalism and → magic, Gorsleben thought it possible to reactivate the occult powers inherent in each Aryan individual, thus enabling him to master the natural world. Gorsleben envisaged the advent of a new age, in which the Aryan would regain his former splendour and authority in the world. His major work *Hoch-Zeit der Menschheit* (1930) presented Atlantis, the megalithic stone circles of Europe, archaeological finds, astrology and mathematical theorems as evidence of the high civilisation of the Aryans. Their wisdom was held to have survived in a wide variety of cultural forms, including the runic shape of beams in half-timbered houses, coats-of-arms, countless symbols and words. These ideas of secret survival owed their inspiration to Guido von List and Philipp Stauff.

4. HERBERT REICHSTEIN

In December 1925 Herbert Reichstein began to publish a book-series, *Ariosophische Bibliothek*, to publicize Lanz's theories on subjects ranging from astrology to heraldry. By early 1926 Reichstein changed the name of his characterological institute to the Ariosophical Society, which fostered esoteric Aryan sciences of characterology and divination for the benefit of Aryans. Ariosophical characterologists were identified as heirs of the ancient Germanic priest-kings (*Armanenschaft*), rediscovered by Guido von List. Lecture-tours to major German cities were organized between 1928 and 1931, when Reichstein moved his operations to Preßbaum near Vienna to open an Ariosophical School as a conference centre for retreats and courses. Lanz von Liebenfels remained the intellectual leader of the Ariosophical movement throughout this whole period. Like Lanz, Reichstein practised name-kabbalism, based upon the Chaldean-Jewish notion of correspondences between letters and numbers: the sum of the numerical equivalents of the letters in a person's name disclosed information regarding his nature and destiny. After the Nazi seizure of power in Germany, Reichstein moved in April 1933 to Berlin, in order 'to be at the centre of the revival of a nationally awakened Germany'. There he published *Arische Rundschau*, a weekly newpaper which professed the struggle against

Judah, Rome, and Freemasonry in the context of ariosophical racism and occult predictions.

5. ARIOSOPHY AND THE THIRD REICH

Despite its esoteric and sectarian nature, Ariosophy had some influence on National Socialism in Germany. Philipp Stauff, a close friend of Guido von List and Lanz von Liebenfels, held high office in the Germanenorden, a secret quasi-masonic racist society founded in 1912 to counter Jewish influence in Germany. In 1917 the Bavarian chapter of the Germanenorden was taken over by Rudolf von Sebottendorff (1875-1945), who was also an admirer of List, Lanz von Liebenfels and Stauff. Under Sebottendorff's leadership the Germanenorden in Munich assumed the cover-name of the Thule Society and played a significant role in the Bavarian counter-revolution of April 1919. As early as autumn 1918 the Thule Society had fostered a political workers' circle. In January 1919 members of this group founded the German Workers' Party (DAP), which was renamed the German National Socialist Workers' Party (NSDAP) in February 1920. While the Thule Society and Germanenorden remained conspiratorial esoteric groups, the DAP embraced mass political activity. The use of the swastika as a Nazi party symbol may be traced back to the Germanenorden, Lanz von Liebenfels and Guido von List before 1914.

There is some evidence that the young Adolf Hitler read and collected Lanz's *Ostara* magazine while living in Vienna between 1908 and 1913. It is likely that he was impressed by Lanz's empirical studies of racial differences between the blonds and the darks, and the harmful influence of non-German races within the multinational Habsburg empire. Lanz's preoccupation with women as race-defilers, feminism and sexuality was mirrored by Hitler's concern that the Jews were seducing Aryan girls and drawing them into prostitution. Given his lifelong enthusiasm for Wagner's operas, especially *Parsifal*, Hitler would have identified with Lanz's notion of a knightly order committed to the holy grail of pure Germanic blood. Lanz's dualist-manichaean fantasy of a millenarian struggle between the blonds and the darks for racial and political world-supremacy could have laid the "granite foundation" of Hitler's own racist outlook for life.

Ariosophical ideas of a secret gnosis of the blood and occult survivals made a stronger impression on Heinrich Himmler and the SS, which cultivated the Aryan-Nordic heritage as an instrument of Nazi cultural policy. Karl Maria Wiligut [pseud. Karl

Weisthor, Jarl Widar] (1866-1946), an officer in the Habsburg army, had some contact with ONT brothers in Vienna around 1908, a link that was renewed in 1920-1921. Wiligut claimed to be descended from prehistoric Germanic sages of the Irminist religion. His purported ancestral-clairvoyant memory enabled him to recall the history of his tribe over thousands of years back to 78.000 BC. Richard Anders, an ONT brother and SS officer, introduced Wiligut to Heinrich Himmler, who decided to exploit this unique source on ancient Germanic religion and traditions. Wiligut's interest in the runes, symbols and other cryptic survivals of ancient Germanic priest-kings place him in List's tradition of the *Armanenschaft*. Wiligut was given officer rank in the SS, where he supplied rune-poetry and studies of cosmology and prehistory based on his family traditions. He also undertook land surveys of ancient Germanic sanctuaries, and was instrumental in the design of the SS *Totenkopfring* and the elaboration of Irminist wedding, spring, harvest and solstice rituals at the SS Staff College of Wewelsburg Castle. He also influenced Himmler's conception of the Wewelsburg as a SS vatican in a future revival of pagan Germanic religion.

During the Third Reich, Ariosophy was discouraged by the Nazis in common with other secret societies and lodge-like organisations. The ONT was suspended at Werfenstein and Vienna in December 1938, but activity continued at ONT houses in Germany and Hungary. Lanz continued to publish ONT material privately until his death in 1954. He was succeeded as Prior of the ONT by Theodor Czepl, who died in 1978. Czepl was succeeded by Walther Krenn who died in 1979, and Rudolf J. Mund held the office of PONT from 1979 until his own death in 1985. Owing to its racial and anti-Semitic content, Ariosophy remained a minute movement in postwar Austria. However, since the 1990s neo-Nazi groups have discovered an interest in List, Lanz von Liebenfels and the Thule Society.

Jörg Lanz-Liebenfels, "Anthropozoon biblicum", *Vierteljahrsschrift für Bibelkunde* 1 (1903), 307-316, 317-355, 429-469; 2 (1904), 26-60, 314-334, 395-412 ♦ idem, *Theozoologie oder Die Kunde von den Sodoms-Äfflingen und dem Götter-Elektron*, Vienna: Moderner Verlag, 1905 ♦ Selected titles from *Ostara: Bücherei der Blonden und Mannesrechtler*, first series, No. 1-89 (1905-1917): No. 26 *Einführung in die Rassenkunde* (n.d.); No. 33 *Die Gefahren der Frauenrechtes und die Notwendigkeit der mannesrechtlichen Herrenmoral* (1909); No. 35 *Neue physikalische und mathematische Beweise für das Dasein der Seele* (1910); No. 42 *Die Blonden und Dunklen im politischen Leben der Gegenwart* (1910); No. 43 *Einführung in die Sexual-*

Physik oder die Liebe als odische Energie (1911); No. 50 *Urheimat und Urgeschichte der blonden heroischen Rasse* (1911); No. 59 *Das arische Christentum als Rassenkultreligion der Blonden* (1912); No. 78 *Rassenmystik, eine Einführung in die ariochristliche Geheimlehre* (1915) ♦ *Ostara*, second series: No. 1 *Die Ostara und das Reich der Blonden* (1922) ♦ Selected titles from *Ostara*, third series, No. 1-101 (1927-1931): No. 2 *Der Weltkrieg als Rassenkampf der Dunklen gegen die Blonden* (1927); No. 3 *Die Weltrevolution als Grab der Blonden* (1928); No. 4 *Der Weltfriede als Werk und Sieg der Blonden* (1928); No. 12 *Die Diktatur der blonden Patriziates* (1929); No. 13/14 *Der zoologische und talmudische Ursprung des Bolschewismus* (1930); No. 101 Johann Walthari Wölfl, *Lanz-Liebenfels und sein Werk. 1. Teil: Einführung in die Theorie* (1927) ♦ Selected titles from *Ariomantische Bücherei*, No. 1-47 (1933-37): No. 3 *Der elektrische Urgott und sein großes Heiligtum in der Vorzeit* (1933); No. 5-10 *Praktische Einführung in die arisch-christliche Mystik*, I-VI Teil (1934) ♦ Jörg Lanz von Liebenfels, *Grundriß der ariosophischen Geheimlehre*, Oestrich i. Rheingau: Herbert Reichstein, 1925 ♦ idem, *Das Buch der Psalmen teutsch*, Düsseldorf-Unterrath: Herbert Reichstein, 1926 ♦ idem, *Das Sakrament der Ehe im Lichte der ariosophischen Theologie*, Düsseldorf-Unterrath: Herbert Reichstein, 1926 ♦ idem, "Die Geschichte der Ariosophie", *Zeitschrift für Geistes- und Wissenschaftsreform* 4 (1929), 1-5, 33-37, 65-69, 97-102, 177-182, 210-212, 237-240, 269-272, 302-305; 5 (1930), 4-9, 33-37, 68-73, 113-116, 137-146 ♦ idem, *Bibliomystikon oder Die Geheimbibel der Eingeweihten*, Pforzheim: Herbert Reichstein, 1930-1935 ♦ Herbert Reichstein, *Warum Ariosophie?*, Düsseldorf-Unterrath: Herbert Reichstein, 1926 ♦ idem, *Praktisches Lehrbuch der ariosophischen Kabbalistik*, Preßbaum: Herbert Reichstein, 1931 ♦ Rudolf John Gorsleben, *Hoch-Zeit der Menschheit*, Leipzig: Koehler & Amelang, 1930.

Lit. Wilfried Daim, *Der Mann, der Hitler die Ideen gab*, Vienna: Hermann Böhlau, 1985 ♦ Nicholas Goodrick-Clarke, *The Occult Roots of Nazism: Secret Aryan Cults and Their Influence on Nazi Ideology. The Ariosophists of Austria and Germany, 1890-1935*, New York: New York University Press, 2004 ♦ Ekkehard Hieronimus, *Lanz von Liebenfels: Eine Bibliographie*, Toppenstedt: Uwe Berg, 1991 ♦ Hans-Jürgen Lange, *Weisthor: Karl Maria Wiligut, Himmlers Rasputin und seine Erben*, Engerda: Arun, 1998 ♦ Rudolf J. Mund, *Jörg Lanz v. Liebenfels und der Neue Templer Orden*, Stuttgart: Rudolf Arnold Spieth, 1976 ♦ *Der Rasputin Himmlers: Die Wiligut-Saga*, Vienna: Volkstum, 1982.

NICHOLAS GOODRICK-CLARKE

Aristotelianism

From the second half of the 12th century the Latin West witnessed an enormous wave of translations of Aristotle's works from Arabic and Greek,

ARISTOTELIANISM   98

which reached its peak around the middle of the
13th century with William of Moerbeke. As a consequence, philosophers and theologians were faced
with the formidable task of reconciling this new
influx of pagan wisdom with Christian faith. They
did so in the institutional context of one of the most
enduring inventions of the Middle Ages, namely
the university. These new institutions developed
curricula dominated by the *Corpus Aristotelicum*.
Just like medieval Platonism [→ Neoplatonism:
Middle Ages], however, Aristotelianism is a complex historiographic category. The *Corpus Aristotelicum* not only comprised genuine works such
as the *Categories*, the *Physics*, the *Metaphysics* or
the *Nicomachean Ethics*, but also a wide range of
pseudo-Aristotelica, among which the *Theologia
Aristotelis*, the *Liber de Causis*, and the *Secretum
Secretorum*. Moreover, a number of commentaries
carried almost the same authority as Aristotle's
own text, such as those by Greek commentators
like Simplicius. By far the most prestigious of all
commentators was the Andalusian Arab Averroës,
whom the medievals simply referred to as *the* Commentator, analogous to Aristotle himself who was
known as *the* Philosopher (*Philosophus*). Aristotelianism not only determined the content of
medieval learning, but also the formal models by
which the teaching was structured. The boundaries
between the various disciplines, such as physics,
metaphysics, ethics and medicine, but especially
those between theology and philosophy, were settled using the criteria of Aristotelian philosophy of
science. Aristotle had defined science in terms of a
deduction of causal demonstrations on the basis of
self-evident principles that could only be intuited
and not demonstrated within each separate discipline. This proved to be an excellent model in safe-
guarding the disciplinary autonomy of theology,
while at the same time strengthening its rational,
scientific profile. The principles of theology were a
matter of revealed truth which could not be scientifically demonstrated but had to be accepted on
faith. Just like any other science, theology thus had
to work with indemonstrable first truths that could
not be provided by any other science. Equally, however, theology made use of Aristotelian logical procedures in order to deduce scientific truths from
these first principles. Medieval theology and philosophy employed what is known as the scholastic
method of determining questions by means of a
complex of *pro* and *contra* argumentations. This
method was put to use in the commentary tradition
on Peter Lombard's *Sentences*, the main textbook
of scholastic theology. In this model, philosophy,
the discipline that was taught at the medieval Arts

faculties, was subservient to theology, which
together with medicine, canon and civil law constituted the so-called higher faculties. However, not
all Masters of Arts were prepared to accept this
subordinate role of philosophy as *ancilla theologiae* (handmaid of theology). For instance, a group
of 13th century Parisian Masters known under the
collective name of Latin Averroists claimed full
autonomy for philosophy, even to the extent of
allowing philosophy to reach conclusions that
were not in conformity with faith.

   The disciplinary framework of medieval Aristotelianism might be one of the explanations for
why it had relatively few points of contact with →
Hermetism. In the 12th century, Hermetism had
mainly been associated with Platonism, which did
not make a sharp distinction between theology and
philosophy, especially metaphysics. → Hermes
Trismegistus was seen as part of a tradition of
pagan learning that had adumbrated important
elements of Christian faith, especially the dogma of
the Trinity. It is probably no coincidence that
Thomas Aquinas (1225-1274), one of the champi-
ons of medieval Aristotelianism, not only insisted
on the distinction between philosophy and theology (on whose collaboration he nevertheless insisted as well), but also vehemently rejected the
claim, expressed by Alan of Lille and others, that
Hermes had intuited the Trinity. With regard to the
definition of God in (pseudo-)Hermes' *Liber XXIV
Philosophorum* as the monad that generates a
monad in itself, Aquinas says that this statement
only pertains to the relation between God and His
creation (*Summa Theologica*, Part I, Question 32,
Article 1, ad 1). Natural reason can prove that the
world has been created by God, but we need the
revealed truth of Scripture in order to enlighten us
on what God is, most notably with respect to His
tri-une character. Parallel to this denial of Hermes'
prophetic gifts was the acceptance by Thomas
Aquinas and the majority of post-12th century theologians and philosophers of → Augustine's condemnation of Hermes' idolatry in *De Civitate Dei*
rather than Quodvultdeus' more positive account.
Finally, the very fact that Aristotle replaced Plato as
the great authority in philosophy may also explain
why many post-12th century philosophers and theologians were less attracted to Hermes, who had
been so closely associated with Platonism. It is
therefore no surprise that we find a large-scale
acceptance of Hermetic tenets only in philosophers
with overt Platonic or even anti-Aristotelian tendencies, such as Berthold of Moosburg. It seems
that the only philosopher who consistently tried to
reunite Aristotelianism, Platonism and Hermetism

was → Albertus Magnus. Obviously, there was one area in which Aristotelianism and Hermetism did meet, namely → alchemy. Alchemical literature of the Middle Ages made abundant use of the basic concepts of Aristotelian natural philosophy, such as hylemorfism, the potency-act distinction, and Aristotelian mineralogy. It is therefore no suprise that many alchemical tracts were attributed to (pseudo-)Aristotle. The connection between Aristotelianism and Hermetism can thus mainly be found outside the formal framework of the academic disciplines at the medieval universities.

In some handbooks we still find the once popular image that the philosophical innovations of the Renaissance were due to → Marsilio Ficino's translation of the *Corpus Platonicum*, while the Aristotelianism of the universities sank away into moribund sterility. Paul Oskar Kristeller, Charles Schmitt, Charles Lohr and others have shown that this conception is thoroughly misguided. To begin with, Aristotelianism was anything but moribund. Charles Lohr has established that (thanks to the invention of the printing press) the 16th century not only produced more translations of Aristotle's works than all the previous centuries taken together but also composed an immense amount of new commentaries. Moreover, recent studies have demonstrated that the Renaissance commentary tradition on Aristotle displayed a diversity and innovative potential that in certain of its aspects formed the bridge to the new philosophy and science of the 17th century.

One of the most interesting phenomena of the late 15th and 16th century is the Aristotelianism cultivated at the university of Padua. Since Padua did not have a theological faculty, the faculty of Arts was not constrained by any theological considerations and developed a secular Aristotelianism with a strong emphasis on natural philosophy, which among other things prepared the students for higher studies in medicine. The best known representative of this tradition was Pietro Pomponazzi (1462-1525). In his *De naturalium effectuum causis sive de incantationibus* of 1520 (published 1567), Pomponazzi accepts miracles and other wondrous events as long as witness reports were reliable. His main point is to develop a scientific explanation of these events along the lines of Aristotelian philosophy, which he combines with a strong version of Stoic determinism. Pomponazzi is prepared to accept the agency of angels and demons as an article of faith. Nevertheless, he argued, Aristotelian *philosophy* has to rule such agencies out, since angels and demons on account of their being immaterial do not have contact with physical objects, while all physical action must occur by direct contact. What does count as a viable explanation is, by contrast, the influence of the stars which determine completely the sublunar realm and in so doing also produce miracles and other wondrous events. In this context, Pomponazzi makes use of the Aristotelian notion of occult quality [→ occult/occultism], which designates an imperceptible, but nonetheless perfectly natural cause, such as stellar influence, the power of the imagination and hidden qualities of minerals and other natural objects. In so doing, Pomponazzi famously raised the scientific status of → astrology in the same way as the Bolognese philosopher Alessandro Achillini – who had briefly been his colleague at Padua – had raised the status of physiognomy and chiromancy in his *Quaestio de subiecto physionomiae et chiromantiae* (1503).

Nor was the philosophy that developed outside of the schools in all respects anti- or even un-aristotelian. True, when Ficino speaks of the venerable tradition of *pia philosophia* or *philosophia perennis* [→ Tradition] he is primarily thinking of the current that he takes to have been inaugurated by Hermes and so admirably continued by Plato. Nevertheless, Aristotle also had an – albeit modest – place in this typically Renaissance harmony model. Following the schemes of the ancient Neoplatonist commentators on Aristotle, Ficino depicts Aristotle as the best of the *physici*. As far as metaphysics is concerned, he recommends that one had better consult the Neoplatonists. However, for the lower realm of being Aristotle's physics is an excellent guide. Echoing humanist attacks on Peripatetic philosophy, Ficino states that his issue is not with Aristotle, but with his contemporary scholastic disciples, whose two competing sects, the Alexandrists (following Alexander of Aphrodisias) and Averroists haunt the universities (*Opera Omnia*, Basel 1576; reprint Torino, 1959, p. 1537). Albeit in opposite ways, both sects denied personal immortality, the very cornerstone of Ficino's philosophical speculation. There is, however, an undeniable presence of scholastic philosophy in Ficino's own philosophy, especially in his *opus magnum*, the *Theologia Platonica* (1469-1474). During his study at the university of Florence, Ficino must have imbibed quite a lot of Aristotelianism, especially in its Thomist form. Thomas Aquinas provided the building blocks of Ficino's metaphysical structure in the form of his dialectics of being and non-being, his distinction between matter and form, his view of causality and other central topics. But even more remarkable is the presence of Aristotelianism in Ficino's works on → magic, especially his *De vita libri tres* (1489). In the absence of an elaborated Hermetic or Platonist natural philosophy and in line with his appreciation of Aristotle's physics, Ficino uses the basic concepts of Aristotelian hylemorphism in order to explain the powers of → amulets and other magical devices. It has to be remarked, though, that he seems to be particularly dependent on Neoplatonic doctrines he found in → Avicenna's and Albertus Magnus's works. Brian Copenhaver has established that Ficino integrates the doctrine of substantial form as the imperceptible carrier of occult qualities, the notion of dispositive cause to account for the preparation of matter for the eduction of a form which is ultimately drawn from the celestial bodies, and other central tenets of Aristotelian hylemorphism.

An even greater presence of Aristotelianism can be discerned in Ficino's young friend, → Giovanni Pico della Mirandola, whom Ficino praises as one of the few who are still able to interpret Aristotle in the right, pious, way (*Opera Omnia*, p. 1537). Pico's *Conclusiones* were part of his grand project to reconcile all pagan and Christian learning. Though recent scholarship has established that Pico was far less unorthodox than his traditional portrayal, the fact remains that the Church of Rome was not particularly amused by the enthusiasm of this brilliant young man. In the *Apologia* (1487), which Pico wrote against accusations by Church authorities, he defended his conclusions regarding the eucharist and other theological topics by means of a wide display of scholastic theology and philosophy. In fact, it seems that Pico soon gave up on his attempt to integrate all available learning and limited himself to the less ambitious plan of reuniting Plato and Aristotle. The first result was his *De Ente et Uno* (1492), an exercise in metaphysical speculation about the convertibility of the the terms "being" (the highes genus for the Aristotelians) and "oneness" (the highest genus for the Platonists). This limitation also explains why Hermetism (to which in fact only nine out of the nine hundred *Conclusiones* had been devoted) disappeared increasingly from his works, and eventually gave way to an outspoken rejection in the unfinished *Disputationes adversus astrologiam divinatricem*. Here, Pico presents the wisdom of the Egyptians, which includes Hermetism, as a practical discipline of worship and not as theoretical science. Hermetism is at best a first inadequate sketch of the superior physics and metaphysics of Plato and especially Aristotle, since it lacks the defining characterisic of true science, namely rational argument (*Disputatio adversus astrologiam divinitatricem*, in *Opera Omnia*, Basel 1557;

reprint Hildesheim 1969, pp. 721-722). Interestingly, Pico thus seems to make room for scientific progress, contrary to the retrograde *ad fontes* of his mentor Ficino. In any case, Pico's *Disputations* contain a scathing attack on astrology, which is based on an anti-determinist version of Aristotelian philosophy. In line with Aristotle, Pico does admit stellar influence, but limits it to the lower faculties of the human soul. Stellar influence explains the behaviour of prophets, whose imagination is particularly susceptible. It cannot, however, determine man's free will, which is linked to the superior part of our soul.

With → Francesco Patrizi (1529-1597) Renaissance Neoplatonism gets a vehemently anti-Aristotelian twist. Like Ficino, Patrizi laments the spectacle of the division of academic Aristotelianism into two competing sects of which both deny the immortality of the human soul. In order to restore the unity of reason and faith, Patrizi presented a three-fold Hermetic-Platonist project. First, Patrizi developed a new edition of the *Corpus Hermeticum*, the *Chaldaean Oracles* and other *Hermetica*, which he attached to the second part of his enterprise, namely the *Nova de Universis Philosophia* (1591). In this all-encompassing philosophical system, he tried to explain the Hermetic "revelation" by means of philosophical, especially Platonist, arguments. Thirdly, the *Discussiones Peripateticae* (1581) takes up Ficino's idea of a philosophical concord and the tradition of *prisca sapientia*. Patrizi thoroughly revolutionized this notion. Usually, the idea of a basic philosophical concord was made plausible by showing the fundamental harmony of Aristotle's and Plato's philosophy. The *Discussiones* elaborate this programme in a radically polemical, anti-Aristotelian way. Patrizi attempts to demonstrate that everything valuable in Aristotle is downright plagiarism, whereas all his original contributions are mere humbug. Aristotle adopts all important themes of *philosophia perennis* in general, and of Plato in particular. By leaving his source unmentioned while at the same time explicitly criticizing Plato, Aristotle tried to achieve fame at the expense of his preceptor. The *Discussiones* condemn virtually all aspects of Aristotle's life and work. Among the allegations is that Aristotle was involved in a plot to kill Alexander the Great. Interestingly, Patrizi excludes Aristotle's logic and natural philosophy from his devastating criticisms. In fact, the first part of the *Nova de Universis Philosophia*, entitled *Panaugia* (All-encompassing Light) makes use of an "Aristotelian method". Here Patrizi points to the Aristotelian methodological *adagium* that in natural philosophy we should begin with experiential phenomena, which constitute the *primum quoad nos*, in order to gain knowledge of nature's causes, principles and elements, the *primum quoad natura*. The *Panaugia* is "Aristotelian" in the sense that it tries to develop an alternative to Aristotle's inference of the existence of the Immovable Mover on the basis of perceptible motion. This part of the *Nova de Universis Philosophia*, however, starts with perceptible *light* and gradually climbs to the source of all corporeal as well as incorporeal light, God. It unfolds a wide-ranging Neoplatonist light metaphysics, culled from traditional sources like Philo, Grosseteste and Ficino. In this sense the *Panaugia* exemplifies Patrizi's attitude towards Aristotelian philosophy, especially his physics and metaphysics: rather than a wholesale alternative, Patrizi propounds a complete reinterpretation of the traditional Aristotelian doctrines and their vocabulary along Platonist-Hermetic lines.

A final offshoot of Renaissance Aristotelianism blossomed at the German universities at the end of the 16th and beginning of the 17th century. After the Reformation the universities in the German lands had been reorganized according to confessional lines, i.e. following the Lutheran, Calvinist, and Roman-Catholic (mainly Jesuit) creeds. Paradoxically the strong confessional emphasis led to a much more liberal, very eclectic attitude towards Aristotle, whose philosophy always had to be measured against the canons of the diverse confessions. Hermetism was just one of the many elements that entered in the eclectic mixture that was taught at Protestant, especially Calvinist, universities and *Hohe Schulen*. The best-known representative of this tradition is Johann Heinrich Alsted (1588-1638), professor of theology and philosophy at the Academy of Herborn. Alsted combined solid Aristotelianism with Lullism, Hermetism and alchemy in his grand encyclopedic project that was aimed at restoring man's original dignity. This optimistic variety of Calvinism was to receive a devastating blow at the Council of Dordt and in the Thirty Years War which in most cases meant the closure of the more liberal universities. Alsted's eclectic and conciliatory programme can already be fathomed from his early *Physica Harmonica* (1616), which tries to reunite a number of different physics, in particular Mosaic physics (i.e. the account of the book of Genesis), Peripatetic physics and Hermetic physics (especially alchemy). The touchstone of this conciliatory programme is Mosaic physics: Alsted only accepts those elements of Peripatetism and Hermetism that can be squared with the biblical account. But the most impressive

synthesis of Aristotelianism and Hermetism can be found in his enormous *Encyclopaedia* (1630), which recalls the common Renaissance idea of a tradition of *prisca sapientia*, which according to Alsted includes the Indian Brahmans and Egyptian prophets, such as Hermes Trismegistus (*Encyclopaedia*; Herborn, 1630, p. 110). The *Encyclopaedia* not only lists a whole range of "Hermetic" disciplines such as astrology and the art of memory [→ Mnemonics], but also fuses Hermetism and Aristotelianism in its discussion of specific themes. An example is his description of prime matter, which Alsted deals with in the part devoted to physics. Alsted borrows the notion of matter as a *non-ens* from the Aristotelian tradition, combines it with the "Mosaic" idea of a primordial chaos, the notion of a vivifying world soul taken from the *Asclepius*, and a whole range of alchemical descriptions of matter which Alsted explicitly attributes to Hermes (*Encyclopaedia*; Herborn, 1630, p. 673). Alsted's *Encyclopaedia* is certainly not the only example of a synthesis between Aristotelianism and Hermetism at German universities. Other examples include Heinrich Nollius, professor of philosophy and medecine at the *Gymnasium Arnoldinum* at Steinfurt from 1616 to 1621. Given the influence of the textbooks by Alsted and others on modern philosophers such as Leibniz, we are forced to rethink the relations between Aristotelianism, Hermetism and modern philosophy.

Lit.: B. Copenhaver, "Scholastic Philosophy and Renaissance Magic in the *De Vita* of Marsilio Ficino", *Renaissance Quarterly* 38 (1984), 523-554 ♦ B. Dodd, "Aristoteles Latinus", in: N. Kretzmann et al. (eds.), *The Cambridge History of Later Medieval Philosophy*, Cambridge, 1982, 45-79 ♦ H. Hotson, *Johann Heinrich Alsted 1588-1638: Between Renaissance, Reformation, and Universal Reform*, Oxford, 2000 ♦ E. Kessler, "The Transformation of Aristotelianism during the Renaissance", in: J. Henry and S. Hutton (eds.), *New Perspectives on Renaissance Thought*, London, 1990, 137-147 ♦ E. Kessler et al. (eds.), *Aristotelismus und Renaissance: In Memoriam Charles B. Schmitt*, Wiesbaden, 1988 ♦ P.O. Kristeller, *The Philosophy of Marsilio Ficino*, Gloucester, Mass., 1964 ♦ C. Lohr, "The Sixteenth Century Transformation of the Aristotelian Natural Philosophy", in: E. Kessler et al. (eds.), *Aristotelismus und Renaissance: in Memoriam Charles B. Schmitt*, Wiesbaden, 1988, 89-99 ♦ C. Lohr, "Aristotelianism", in: H. Burkhardt et al. (eds.), *Handbook of Metaphysics and Ontology*, München, 1991, 40-50 ♦ J. Marenbon (ed.), *Aristotle in Britain during the Middle Ages*, Turnhout, 1996 ♦ M. Pine, *Pietro Pomponazzi: Radical Philosopher of the Renaissance*, Padua, 1986 ♦ A. Raspanti, *Filosofia, teologia, religione: L'unità della visione in Giovanni Pico della Mirandola*, Palermo, 1991 ♦ Ch. B. Schmitt, *Aristotle and the Renaissance*, Cambridge, Mass.,

1983 ♦ Ch. B. Schmitt, *The Aristotelian Tradition and Renaissance Universities*, London, 1984 ♦ Ch. B. Schmitt, *Reappraisals in Renaissance Thought*, London, 1989 ♦ Ch. B. Schmitt et al., *The Cambridge History of Renaissance Philosophy*, Cambridge, 1992 ♦ K. Schuhmann, "Giovanni Pico della Mirandola und der Hermetismus: Vom Mitstreiter zum Gegner", in: Piet Steenbakkers and Cees Leijenhorst (eds.), *Karl Schuhmann: Selected Papers on Renaissance Philosophy and on Thomas Hobbes*, Dordrecht, 2004, 135-176 ♦ F. Van Steenberghen, *Aristotle in the West: The Origins of Latin Aristotelianism*, Louvain, 1970² ♦ O. Weijers (ed.), *L'enseignement des disciplines à la Faculté des Arts: Paris et Oxford, XIIIᵉ-XVᵉ siècles*, Turnhout, 1997 ♦ M. Wilmott, "*Aristoteles Exotericus, Acroamaticus, Mysticus*: Two Interpretations of the Typological Classification of the 'Corpus Aristotelicum' by Francesco Patrizi da Cherso", *Nouvelles de la République des Lettres* 1 (1985), 67-95 ♦ P. Zambelli, "Aut diabolus aut Achillinus: Fisionomia, astrologia e demonologia nel metodo di un Aristotelico", *Rinascimento* 18 (1978), 59-86.

CEES LEIJENHORST

Arithmology → Number Symbolism

Arnau de Vilanova, * ca. 1240 Daroca (Lower Aragon), † 6.9.1311 Genoa

Vilanova was one of the most extraordinary figures of the Latin Middle Ages. Many questions on his personality remain unanswered even today, so much has legend and hearsay intermingled with reality. Arnau de Vilanova was born in Lower Aragon toward 1240. He became a Master of medicine and married in the 1260s. He then entered into the service of Peter III of Aragon as a doctor. During his years of intellectual formation, he took courses in Christian exegesis from the Dominicans of Barcelona and Brother Raymond Marti introduced him to Hebrew and rabbinical literature. His knowledge of Arabic was such that he translated several medical works by → Avicenna, Galen, and Albuzale into Latin. From 1289 to 1299, Arnau de Vilanova was the master regent of medical studies at the University of Montpellier. It was during this period that he composed most of his books on medicine. Besides his teaching, marked by Galenism, Arnau de Vilanova continued to assist, as a doctor and a counselor, princes (James II of Aragon, Frederick III of Sicily) and popes (Boniface VIII, Clement V). Although he enjoyed indisputable authority as a doctor, his religious and philosophical ideas were another matter, and they brought him many disappointments.

In 1292, he wrote a short work in which he set forth some of his key ideas. It was called *Introductio in librum Joaquim de semine Scripturarum*, and is a commentary on a book falsely attributed to Joachim de Flore. In particular, Arnau there defends the idea that any form of knowledge expresses a *mysterium* and consequently falls within the domain of prophecy as much as of knowledge itself. The mission of a doctor or an astrologer is not only restricted to giving treatments or designing horoscopes but also includes the task of truly working as a prophet in the exercise of his profession. Arnau de Vilanova had a reputation for spectacular healings. It is easy to imagine that in the eyes of some he was a perfect incarnation of that noble soul of whom Avicenna speaks in *De anima*, endowed with prophetic powers and whose gift is to heal the sick and transmute the elements. In his *Medicationis parabolae*, Arnau de Vilanova states that an effective remedy, a medicine, always proceeds from the Supreme Good. The doctor, he adds, who has received the grace of dispensing care, uses a symbolic language to arrive at the *occulta* from the *sensibilia*. The goal of medicine, indeed, is to start from observation of the *sensibilia* in order to rise to the government of the Almighty; but the *sensibilia* alone are no substitute for the intelligible and universal principles. Whence the introduction of mathematical calculations that helped Arnau build some of his medical theories; as in *Aphorismi de gradibus*, where, using the mathematical solutions put down by → al-Kindi, he tries to resolve the delicate question of the dosage of qualities in the composition of medicines. He repeated this approach in *De dosi tyriacalium*, in relation to dosing the simples that doctors used to make theriac.

His ideas on the necessity of a symbolic language and the permanence of the *occulta* (defined as the unexplained properties of natural objects, known either by chance or by revelation) are also basic to his views on → astrology. Astrology is basic to both a chemico-medical work such as *De aqua vitae simplici*, and a well-known therapeutic cure effectuated on the very person of Pope Boniface VIII. In *De parte operativa*, he declares that knowing the characteristics and arrangements of the Zodiac in order to liberate the astral influences makes it possible to accomplish marvels here on earth. Arnau strictly distinguishes such knowledge from magical practices, related to demons, which are misleading and ineffectual. Similar ideas (in particular the recourse to symbolic language) also underlie an alchemical text such as the *Tractatus parabolicus*, attributed to him, and from which → Jean de Roquetaillade drew inspiration in his *Liber lucis*. It remains unknown though whether Arnau himself practiced alchemy, and we do not know whether he personally composed treatises such as the *Tractatus parabolicus*, the *Defloratio philosophorum*, and the *Epistola super alchimia*; suffice it to say that some of them must have emanated from his secretariat. Arnau also composed an *Allocutio super significatione nominis Tetragrammaton* that consists of a reflection on the letters of *Yahweh* with the aim of proving the truth of the Holy Trinity by a method close to that of the Jewish Kabbalists. He states that the secrets of Holy Scripture are contained in Hebrew and Latin script. Such notions are supported by his views about the economy of dynamic salvation: he saw it as an active process in which, beginning with the Father and moving on through the Son, the Christian revelation is fulfilled in the age of the Holy Spirit, when all the enigmas of the Book will be resolved and the *renovatio* of the world will be accomplished. Here he is influenced by Joachim da Fiori and, even more pregnantly, by an abundant apocalyptic subliterature including, among others, the *Sermo sancti Methodi de regno gentium et in novissimus temporibus certa demonstratio*, the *Epistola ad Cyrillum*, the *Vaticinum Sybillae Erithreae*, and so on. The reading and study of such contemporaries as → Roger Bacon, → Ramon Llull and especially Pierre Dejean Olieu, the spiritual master of the Franciscans, complete his educational background – even if he mostly took his distance from them and followed his own path. Arnau de Vilanova was certain of the imminent manifestation of the Antichrist. Turning his personal revelations to advantage, with varying success he divulged his convictions, in the hope of being recognized as a theologian and prophet as much as a doctor. No doubt he sometimes succeeded in this. Frederick III of Sicily, for instance, disturbed by a dream, consulted Arnau to enlighten him and relieve him of his doubts and distress. Criticized, attacked by the Dominicans, and suspected of heresy, he was imprisoned and finally, unwilling to compromise his boldest concepts, was repudiated by his protectors. He found refuge with Frederick of Sicily, and died on 6 September 1311 off Genoa.

To most modern scholars, Arnau de Vilanova remains the exemplary representative of medieval Galenism. However, he was much more than that. If he never wastes an opportunity to vilify the enchanters and magicians, Arnau nevertheless refuses to consign the domain of knowledge to reason alone. His whole work pleads for the recognition of the intimate and illuminating revelations that experience (whether of a healing or a trans-

mutation) brings to light. For him, in the words of → Clement of Alexandria, 'without faith there is no gnosis'. A counselor to princes and popes, an ambassador, a traveling companion of the Spirituals, an exegete and theologian, a dream interpreter and active mystic, he is remembered as a sage versed in many areas of knowledge, closer to the magus and the heresiarch than to the philosopher, but also a friend of the poor, and a partisan of evangelical frenzy. An important corpus of alchemical, astrological, magical and medical works is generously attributed to him. Many have seen in him one of those high and mysterious medieval figures prefiguring Renaissance humanists such as → Marsilio Ficino.

Arnaldi Villanovani summi philosophi et medici excellentissimi Praxis Medicinalis, Lyon: Jean Stratius and Antoine Tardif, 1586 ◆ *Arnaldi di Villanova: Opera omnia* (Luis Garcia-Ballester, Juan A. Paniagua, Michael R. Mac Vaugh, eds.), Barcelona, 1975-1996 [8 vols. published] ◆ *Arnau de Vilanova, Obres catalanes*, I-II (Miquel Batllori, ed.), Barcelona: Barcino, 1947 ◆ Josep Perarnau i Espelt, "El text primitiu del *De mysterio cymbalorum Ecclesiae* d'Arnau de Vilanova, en appendix, el seu *Tractatus de tempore adventus Antichristi*", Arxiu de Textos Catalans Antics 7/8 (1988-1989), 7-169.

Lit.: Juan A. Paniagua, *Studia arnaldiana, trabajos en torno a la obra médica de Arnau de Vilanova, c. 1240-1311*, Barcelona: Fundacion Uriach, 1838, repr. 1994 ◆ Francesco Santi, "Orientamenti bibliografici per lo studio di Arnau de Vilanova, spirituale: Studi recenti (1968-1982)", *Arxiu de Textos Catalans Antics* 2 (1983), 371-395 ◆ Joseph Ziegler, *Medicine and Religion c. 1300: The Case of Arnau de Vilanova*, Oxford: Clarendon Press, 1998.

ANTOINE CALVET

Arnold, Gottfried, * 1666 Annaberg (Saxony), † 1714 Perleberg (Brandenburg)

Arnold studied theology in Wittenberg and afterwards worked as a private tutor in Dresden. In 1697 he became professor at the University of Giessen, where he stayed only one year. He then tutored in Quedlinburg (Saxony). From 1701 until his death, he exercised the pastoral ministry. Arnold died as a church inspector, but his work as a historian of Christianity has made him a major figure of German → pietism.

Arnold long hesitated about becoming a pastor, because he was reluctant to swear on the Augsburg Confession. He took a strong aversion to all clergy. However, this protégé of Spener, the founder of

Lutheran pietism, finally resigned himself to becoming a minister of "Babylon". He was to be mortified! Because he believed the true Church to be the inner Church, Arnold has been classed among the spiritualists: those who wanted to adore God in spirit and in truth, and not in temples made by human hands. But according to the doctrines that he sympathetically described, the inner Church is no more abstract than is the inner Man identifying with it. It is seen by him as a true communion of the faithful identifying with a single truth. It is secret for those who are not yet part of it. And in the end, it is the soul itself that becomes the true temple of God, at least for the few, and as long as the plenitude at the end of history has not yet arrived. The distinguishing feature of Arnold's Christian esotericism is precisely that it is not institutional. An invisible line thus separates those who are "converted" from the ordinary faithful, even when they all assemble in the same place for worship in the visible Church.

The "converted" are those Christians who have received the baptism administered by the Holy Spirit. This second baptism is not a visible sacrament. But through the grace that it dispenses, Man is born again, according to Jesus' explanation to Nicodemus. The Holy Spirit chooses to dwell in the heart of a person, who thereby becomes a "new Man". For him, the Holy Spirit is the presence of God incarnated by Wisdom. It is by this presence that Man is reconnected with God.

Created before humanity and the world, Sophia/Wisdom is the image of God. The sinner does not perceive her, but she shines in the heart of the regenerated Man. She is the thought of God, and the Man inhabited by the Holy Spirit is her mirror. She embodies the true doctrine written down in the Bible and in the teachings transmitted through the ages. The resulting gnosis, in the noble sense according to which Arnold understood it, is a synonym of holiness. A Man who is not "born from above" is necessarily a sinful person, the "old Adam", who cannot receive the Spirit of God. The holiness of the Man united with God is in fact the mirror of Wisdom. In his work as a historian of Christianity, Arnold was looking for the tradition of "true Christianity" in this sense, understood as the communion of the saints in Adam's posterity. This communion of saints is his version of the universal ministry, of which Luther had an idea, but of which the Lutheran clergy is merely a counterfeit.

Besides many poems and religious songs, often characterized by a baroque lyricism (see notably those in his collection *Göttliche Liebesfunken*, 1698), Arnold composed a good number of other works, among which we will here mention only a few that pertain to → Christian theosophy. First of all there is his monumental *Unpartheyische Kirchen- und Ketzerhistorie* (Impartial History of the Churches and Heresies, 1699-1700). It is clear from this work that the true Church also includes heretics. Without approving of them in every respect, Arnold generally argues in their defense. He categorizes many of them as belonging to the "witnesses to truth" that form a chain throughout the ages. They may be Catholic or Protestant. → Paracelsus, Schwenckfeld, → Weigel, and → Boehme have a place of honor among these reprobates, and Arnold's book contains extensive discussions of Boehmenist and neo-Boehmenist theosophy as well as of → Rosicrucianism; but Arnold in fact attempts to trace the entire lineage of mystical theology from the first centuries on. In this manner he creates a complete referential corpus of "true religion". Nobody before this *Impartial History* had ever attempted to provide such a systematic treatment of so many esoteric currents taken together. By doing so, the book in its turn came to exercise a notable influence on the further development of the very religious tendencies it described.

"Mystical theology" is supposed by Arnold to be communicated by inner channels; the converted person is instructed in it directly by the Holy Spirit. Nevertheless, Arnold also attempts to make it known through the human channel of writing; and this makes him, together with → Pierre Poiret (twenty years his senior) the great publisher of Christian mysticism in Protestant society. Arnold considered mystical theology, or *theologia regenitorum*, as a specific discourse. Although opposed to scholastic or dogmatic theology, and the confessions of faith of the visible Churches, he does explain mystical theology as a doctrine. He traces its history in two crucial works published in 1702: *Das Geheimnis der göttlichen Sophia* (The Mystery of the Divine Sophia) and *Historie und Beschreibung der Mystischen Theologie* (History and Description of Mystical Theology).

Wisdom, as Arnold explains in the former work, personifies the doctrine issued from the mouth of God before anything had been created. She is the divine intelligence, identified with the Word. From generation to generation, she is communicated to those people who are capable of receiving her. Priests who have no share in her revile the secret theology, but it perennially germinates and flowers in the spirit of the holy. It is always the same truth, whether found among Catholics or Protestants. It alone can end the quarrels between the theologians. Peace can reign among believers only through the communion of the saints. The book on the Divine Sophia pertains to Christian theosophical literature by its content and by the very nature of its theme. Arnold frequented the theosophers, and published, notably, the writings of → Gichtel in 1701, and the *Cherubinscher Wandersmann* by the theosopher poet Johannes Scheffler, *alias* Angelus Silesius. His form of writing and inspiration is nonetheless very different from that of Boehme or Gichtel. Compared with these theosophers, Arnold proves to be, in his work, "scholarly" and theological rather than properly visionary. Contrary to them, too, he is rather distant from any form of mystical naturalism – thus the idea of the creative → imagination, so prominent in Boehme or Gichtel, with all its implicit consequences, is almost absent from Arnold.

The young Luther, who glorified the 14th-century mystic Tauler, had once adhered to the tradition of "mystical theology". At the dawn of the Reformation he had published the *Theologica Germanica*, an anonymous treatise believed to have emanated from Tauler's associates. However, the Reformer had later turned away from these beginnings. Arnold attributed the decline of the Reformation to this reversal. In contrast, he saw in the doctrine of pure love, from Molinos to Madame Guyon, a flowering of mystical theology: the quietist heresy, flourishing in the context of German → Pietism, seemed to him to redeem Luther's mistake.

True Christianity according to Arnold unites only a small minority of the faithful here on earth. It must be considered first and foremost from the perspective of the end of time. Arnold nursed hopes for a universal restoration, or *apocatastasis*, at the end of a process of purification that would progressively extend, in the hereafter, to all of creation. Hell would come to an end. This concept of the *Wiederbringung aller Dinge* (re-establishment of all things) attracted quite a following at the time of Pietism, and was condemned in article twenty-three of the Augsburg Confession. It would reappear with Zinzendorf, but under the cover of a "secret theology", and was later incorporated to some extent into the theology of the Enlightenment period, which in the name of reason rejected the dogma of eternal suffering. In Arnold's time it was strictly prohibited.

Arnold's works have had a wide influence. Its later impact on the strictly esoteric plane of Christian theosophy aside, it must be noted that posterity has mainly retained its criticism of established religion and of the dogmas that bound the faithful. In reading the *Impartial History of the Churches and Heresies*, the young → Goethe would later conclude that an individual can create his own religion – an idea that greatly appealed to him. Arnold's opinion, however, was entirely different. For this fervent supporter of mystical theology, there could only be a single true doctrine, the one personified by Wisdom. The liberty of the Christian was that of the person who, freed from dogmas, had chosen the only true religion while completely renouncing his own will.

Unpartheyische Kirchen- und Ketzerhistorie, von Anfang des Neuen Testaments biss auff das Jahr Christi 1688, first edition: Frankfurt 1699 (I-II), 1700 (III-IV); reprint of the 1729 edition (Frankfurt), in 2 vols.: Hildesheim: Olms, 1967, and again 1999 ♦ *Göttliche Liebes-Funken aus dem grossen Feuer der Liebe Gottes in Christo Jesu entsprungen*, Frankfurt, 1698 ♦ *Das Geheimnis der göttlichen Sophia oder Weissheit, Beschrieben und besungen*, Leipzig, 1700; reprint Stuttgart-Bad Cannstadt: Frommann-Holzboog 1963 ♦ *Der richtigste Weg durch Christum zu Gott*; Frankfurt, 1700 ♦ *Historie und Beschreibung der Mystischen Theologie, oder Gottesgelehrtheit, wie auch deren alten und neuen Mysticorum*, Frankfurt, 1703; reprint Stuttgart-Bad Cannstadt: Frommann Holzboog, 1965, and again 1971 and 1969 ♦ *Pietist Selected Writings* (Peter C. Erb, ed.), New York: Paulist Press, 1983 (contains, 205-246, several texts by Arnold in English translation).

Lit.: Hermann Dörries, *Geist und Geschichte bei Gottfried Arnold*, Göttingen: Abhandlungen der Akademie der Wissenschaften in Göttingen, Philosophisch-Historische Klasse III/51, 1963 ♦ Erich Seeberg, *Gottfried Arnold: Die Wissenschaft seiner Zeit*, Darmstadt: Wissenschaftliche Buchgesellschaft, 1964 ♦ Pierre Deghaye, *La doctrine ésotérique de Zinzendorf (1700-1760)*, Paris: Klincksieck, 1969 ♦ Bernard Gorceix, "Le culte de la Sagesse dans l'Allemagne baroque et piétiste: A propos du *Mystère de la Sophie divine* du piétiste Gottfried Arnold (1700)", in: *Sophia et l'Ame du Monde* (A. Faivre, ed.), Paris: Albin Michel, 1983, 195-214 ♦ Dietrich Blaufuss & Friedrich Niewöhner (eds.), *Gottfried Arnold (1666-1714): Mit einer Bibliographie der Arnold Literatur ab 1714* (Proceedings of the Conference at the Herzog August Bibliothek in 1990), Wiesbaden: Harrasowitz Verlag, 1995 ♦ Frank Carl Roberts, *Gottfried Arnold as a Historian of Christianity: A Reappraisal of the Unpartheiische Kirchen- und Ketzerhistorie*, Ann Arbor (Mich.), Micr. Diss.: Nashville, 1973 ♦ Christa Habrich, "Alchemie und Chemie in der pietistischen Tradition", in: Hans Georg Kemper (ed.), *Goethe und der Pietismus*, Halle and Tübingen, 2001, 45-77.

PIERRE DEGHAYE

Ashmole, Elias, * 23.5.1617 Lichfield, † 18/19.5.1692 Lambeth

Antiquary. Son of Simon Ashmole, a saddler and soldier, and Anne Bowyer. Educated at Lichfield

Grammar School, then privately in London, where he qualified as an attorney (1640). After the sudden death of his first wife, Eleanor Manwaring (1603-1641) and the growing threats of civil war, he left London for Cheshire, the home of his in-laws. In 1644 Ashmole was appointed an army officer and Commissioner of Excise (taxes and customs collector) by the Royalist Parliament, which was then in exile in Oxford. Ashmole moved to Oxford and became a member of Brasenose College from 1644-1646, but did not take a degree. In 1646 he joined a masonic lodge in Lancashire, in one of the earliest known records of speculative → Freemasonry. Ashmole spent the years 1646-1649 avoiding political troubles arising from his royalist loyalty, and achieving financial security through marriage. His second wife was Mary Forster, formerly Lady Manwaring (1597-1668). During the Commonwealth period, Ashmole spent much time traveling with friends to country houses and parish churches, where he would copy inscriptions, records, and heraldic achievements. Out of this interest in genealogy and the dignities of ancestors came Ashmole's decision to research and compile a history of the Order of the Garter, Britain's first Order of knighthood.

With the restoration of Charles II (1660), Ashmole was well placed for royal favor. He was appointed Windsor Herald and Comptroller of the Excise, and became a founding member of the Royal Society (1660). In 1669 he was made honorary M.D. at Oxford. His third and happiest marriage (1668) was to Elizabeth Dugdale (1632-1701), daughter of his friend Sir William Dugdale, but no children were born alive to them. Ashmole inherited a large collection of ethnographical and natural curiosities from the estate of John Tradescant (1608-1662), the naturalist, gardener, and antiquary. In 1675 he offered this collection to Oxford University, and a purpose-built museum housing them (now the Museum of the History of Science) was opened in 1683. It was the first public museum in Britain. A fire in the Middle Temple (1679) destroyed much of Ashmole's library, his coin and seal collections, and all his notes on antiquarian subjects. However, at his death a substantial library of books and manuscripts remained, which was bequeathed to Oxford's Bodleian Library.

Ashmole was a late example of the Renaissance polymath. Although a member of the Royal Society, he never contributed any discovery or invention in the spirit of the new science. His sciences were the historical ones of heraldry, genealogy, and numismatics, and the natural ones of botany and medicine. His medicine was also antiquarian, being a blend of herbalism with old wives' cures based on the principles of sympathy and → magic. His magic was not mysterious or spiritual, but a practical application of the doctrine of → correspondences according to which he believed the universe to work. Ashmole made sigils and talismans in metals corresponding to the desired planetary influences, at the appropriate astrological times. Having learned goldsmiths' techniques, he would cast models of rats and insects, which he placed in his house and garden to repel vermin. His entire outlook on life was dominated by → astrology. When in London, he seldom missed the annual Astrologers' Feast. Among his closest friends were Sir George Wharton (1617-1681) and William Lilly (1602-1681), who did much to keep astrology alive and in the public eye during a period of waning belief. At every turn of events – personal, political, financial – Ashmole would draw a horary chart, connect it with the nativities of the people or events concerned, and attempt to predict the outcome for them.

Ashmole's regard for → alchemy was even less in tune with his times. He was not a practical, laboratory alchemist, but a profound student of alchemical literature, making an important collection of old English poems on the subject (*Theatrum Chemicum Britannicum*, 1652), including Thomas Norton's *Ordinall of Alchimy*. In his Preface to this anthology, Ashmole writes of the Philosophical Mercury and of the various types of Stone in terms that display his own belief in transmutation. His mentor in alchemy was William Backhouse (1593-1662), a landowning gentleman and a collector, who in 1651 adopted Ashmole as his philosophical "son". In 1653 Backhouse, believing himself to be near death, told Ashmole the true secret of the Philosopher's Stone, but no more is known than that. It seems most probable that the secret was spiritual, rather than chemical in nature.

Ashmole was also interested in the career and angelic conversations of → John Dee, and returned to this topic throughout his life. Intending to write a biography of the Elizabethan magus, Ashmole collected Dee's manuscripts and corresponded with his son, Dr. Arthur Dee (1579-1651). The biography was never completed, but in his other writings Ashmole propagated some lasting legends about Dee and his assistant Edward Kelley. Ashmole has done an invaluable service to historians in preserving the alchemical tradition through his editions, transcriptions, and the rich collection now in the Bodleian Library. The memory of the destruction of the monasteries and their records by Henry VIII, and the living example of Puritan vandalism, determined him in the duty of preserving all he could of the past. He was above all an antiquarian, and his philosophical convictions were partly those of a passing age. Perhaps his most lasting legacy was the idea of a museum, as a public collection of historical, exotic, and mind-expanding objects. Thus he is justly commemorated in Oxford's Ashmolean Museum, and in the countless other museums of which his was the prototype.

Lit.: Arthur Dee, *Fasciculus Chemicus: or Chymical Collections*, trans. James Hasolle (i.e. Elias Ashmole), London, 1650 ♦ C.H. Josten (ed.), *Elias Ashmole (1617-1692): His Autobiographical and Historical Notes, his Correspondence, and Other Contemporary Sources Relating to his Life and Work*, 5 vols., Oxford: Clarendon Press, 1967 (vol. 1 is a Biographical Introduction) ♦ idem, "William Backhouse of Swallowfield", *Ambix* 4 (1949), 1-33 ♦ Derek Parker, *Familiar to All: William Lilly and Astrology in the Seventeenth Century*, London: Jonathan Cape, 1975 ♦ Alan Pritchard, *Alchemy: A Bibliography of English-Language Writings*, London: Routledge & Kegan Paul, 1980 ♦ Matthew D. Rogers, "The Angelical Stone of Elias Ashmole", *Aries* 5:1 (2005) ♦ Frances A. Yates, *The Rosicrucian Enlightenment*, London: Routledge & Kegan Paul, 1972.

JOSCELYN GODWIN

Asiatic Brethren

Hans Heinrich von Ecker und Eckhoffen (1750-1790), a Bavarian Officer, established two of the various so-called "fringe-masonic" (in German: "winkel-maurerischen") Orders (or Systems) which flourished in the second half of the 18th century. The first, called the Ordo Rotae et Aureae Crucis (The Order of the Wheel and of the Golden Cross) was founded in 1776. When Adam Weishaupt had the idea of founding his famous Order of the → Illuminaten shortly afterwards, it was partly as a reaction against the esoteric orientation of the O.R.A.C. The latter did not attract many people and disappeared in 1779. Having been expelled in 1780 from another Order, the Gold- und Rosenkreuz (Gold and Rosy Cross) to which he also belonged, Ecker und Eckhoffen attacked it in a pamphlet published in 1781 (*Der Rosenkreuzer in seiner Blösse*). That year he moved from Munich to Vienna. Once in Vienna, he laid the foundations of a second System, the Orden der Ritter und Brüder des Lichts (Order of the Knights and Brethren of the Light). This was a new, albeit more elaborated version of the O.R.A.C. It soon took on the name of Die Brüder Sankt Johannes des Evangelisten aus Asien in Europa (The Brethren of Saint John the Evangelist from Asia in Europe), or Asiatische Brüder (Asiatic Brethren). In establishing Orders of his own (the O.R.A.C. and the Asiatic Brethren), Ecker und Eckhoffen had followed the trend shared during that period by many other Masons who claimed to possess the best esoteric knowledge. In establishing the Asiatic Brethren, he probably also wanted to take his revenge on the Gold- und Rosenkreuzer.

Like most Systems with higher degrees (or "higher grades"), the Asiatic Brethren recruited among Master Masons (which is the third degree of Freemasonry proper, and gives access to the higher ones) already initiated in a regular masonic lodge. The initiatory organization of the Asiatic Brethren was comprised of five degrees. The first two were designed as a kind of introduction to the following three, namely: 1) The Knights and Brethren of St. John the Evangelist from Asia in Europe. 2) The Wise Masters. 3) The Royal Priests, or "True Rosicrucians". The members of all degrees were supposed to "work" by themselves, outside the pale of the Asiatic Brethren lodge meetings proper, at kabbalistic interpretations of symbols, combinations of words and letters, etc.

One of the striking originalities of the Asiatic Brethren is that it seems to have been the first association of a masonic character in central Europe to recruit Jews. The pro-jewish attitude of the Asiatic Brethren is conspicuous in the Order's name itself, the term "Asia" referring to Jerusalem. Furthermore, the rituals were not designed by Ecker und Eckhoffen alone, but also by Jews supposedly well versed in Kabbalah, like Thomas von Schönfeld and Ephraim Joseph Hirschfeld. Schönfeld, a man of many parts, had been a follower of the Sabbatian movement (the cult of the 17th-century pseudo-Messiah Sabbatai Zvi). He had met Ecker und Eckhoffen in Innsbruck and then settled in Vienna (1785) in order to live close to him and actively participate in the workings of the Asiatic Brethren. In theory he was merely the archivist of the Order, but in fact he was instrumental in introducing kabbalistic elements and Jewish institutions into the rituals. For example, the supreme council of the Order was called the "Synedrion", i.e., Sanhedrin. The mingling of Christian and Jewish observances may have been easier for the Christian Brethren to accept than for the Jewish ones; but a number (albeit a small one) of Jews of the time belonging to the intellectual elite in Germany were imbued with the spirit of the Jewish Aufklärung, the Haskalah, and therefore prone to cast aside some norms of their faith. Furthermore, Schönfeld and Hirschfeld may have introduced some Sabbatian antinomian (both non-Christian and non-Judaical) elements into the Order's doctrine and rite; for example, according to the "Laws" of the Order its adepts were to partake of a festive meal including pork.

In the "instructions" of these rituals we learn that the Order is the continuation of a very ancient alchemical, theosophical and magical tradition transmitted over the centuries through various channels, not least the Knight Templars. Prevalent are a cosmogony and a cosmology of a theosophical character, blended with arithmology [→ Number Symbolism]. We find, among other mythical narratives, a vivid description of the original Fall, in which a "Son of the Dawn" (Luzifer) plays a major part. The symbolism of these rituals resonates with those of the Gold- und Rosenkreuz, which interpreted the first degree regular masonic symbols in an alchemical sense. Gershom Scholem has demonstrated that these texts borrow heavily from various sources (which they do not cite) belonging to Jewish kabbalistic literature, → Louis Claude de Saint-Martin's *Des Erreurs et de la vérité* (1775), and → Georg von Welling's *Opus mago-Cabbalisticum et theosophicum* (first published in 1718, complete editions in 1729 and 1785).

By 1785 the Asiatic Brethren were spreading rapidly far beyond Vienna, mostly in central Europe and Germany (Prague, Innsbruck, Berlin, Frankfurt, Hamburg). It is possible that it counted as many as several thousand members at that time. Quite a few were aristocrats or dignitaries of high ranks, like Duke of Liechtenstein, Count Joseph von Thun, a Minister of Justice in Austria, Prince Joseph von Linden, Prince Otto von Gemmingen, and Duke Ferdinand von Braunschweig. Nevertheless, since its inception in 1781 the System came in for its share of criticism and was attacked by rival fringe-masonic organizations with a similar esoteric orientation, such as the "Gold- und Rosenkreuz", which had gained a strong foothold in Berlin. This resulted into a flurry of published pamphlets: a quantitatively impressive body of literature, which is a welcome source of information for historians researching the esoteric organizations of that period. For example, when Ecker und Eckhoffen tried to present his System at the famous Masonic Convention of Wihelmsbad (in Hanau, 1782), his application was turned down, partly because he was discredited by his rivals, who presented him as a magician dealing with dangerous occult powers. Besides, the Masons at the Convent were for the most part Christians, and as such did not appreciate the fact that Ecker und Eckhoffen introduced Jews into Masonry. The success of the Asiatic Brethren aroused the special animosity of two prominent freemasons of the established rites,

Prince Johann Baptist Karl von Dietrichstein, Grand Master of the Austrian Lodges, and the famous masonic and Aufklärung figure Ignaz von Born. Partly due to their pressure, Joseph II passed a law (the "Freimaurerapatent", 11. Dec. 1785) imposing stricter controls on Masonic activity in Austria. As a result, the Asiatic Brethren and other similar higher degree Systems in Vienna dealing with esoteric matters like alchemy had to suspend their meetings.

Such events did not put an end to the Asiatic Brethren. Hampered in Austria, it continued to spread far and wide – albeit with unequal success –, particularly in North Germany (Hamburg, Hannover, Lubeck), Prague, Innsbruck, Berlin, Frankfurt, and Wetzlar. Prince Karl von Hessen Kassel became its official Grand Master in August 1786, which is why the same year the headquarters of the Order moved over from Vienna to Schlesvig. For some obscure reasons, Hirschfeld was expelled from the Order in 1790, but the texts he had written for the rituals stood him in good stead when he later used them in his book *Biblisches Organon* (1796), one of the most interesting theosophical works of the late 18th century.

After Ecker und Eckhoffen's death (1790) the Asiatic Brethren only maintained itself in an apparently limited number of lodges, but they were spread all over Europe throughout the first Empire. This survival was due in part to the never weakening efforts of Hirschfeld, and in Scandinavia to the tenacity of Karl A.A. Boheman. Furthermore, its discreet but enduring presence is documented well into the 20th century in a variety of similar Systems who took their inspiration from it. The → Hermetic Order of the Golden Dawn in England, Francesco Brunelli's Arcana Arcanorum in Italy, and even Theodor Reuss's original → Ordo Templi Orientis idea, were all more or less inspired by the Asiatic Brethren. Interestingly enough, the Asiatic Brethren, along with the Illuminaten (Adam Weishaupt's politically oriented fringe-masonic Order) has become the mainstay of 20th century antisemites who see both as the vehicle that spread the Jewish revolutionary plots and inspired the *Protocols of the Elders of Zion*.

Heinrich von Ecker und Eckhoffen, *Abfertigung an den ungenannten Verfasser* [= Friedrich Münter] *der verbreiteten sogenannten: Authentischen Nachricht von den Ritter- und Brüder-Eingeweihten aus Asien*, Hamburg, 1788 ♦ Ephraim Joseph Hirschfeld and Pascal Hirschfeld, *Biblisches Organon oder Realübersetzung der Bibel mit der mystischen Begleitung und kritischen Anmerkungen*, Offenbach (near Frankfurt am Main): Auf Kosten des Verfassers, 1796 ♦ [Frater a Scrutato],

Die Brüder St. Johannis des Evangelisten aus Asien in Europa oder die einzige wahre und ächte Freimaurerei, Berlin, 1803 ♦ Pokeasch Iwrim, *Beleuchtung einiger mystischen Allegorien und Hieroglyphen in nächster Berziehung auf den durch Bohemanns Missbrauch und die Bekanntmachung seiner Urkunden merkwürdig gewordenen Orden der Asiatischen Brüder*, Stade: Selbstverlag, 1804 ♦ *System des hochwürdigen, mächtigen und weisen Ordens der Ritter und Brüder des Lichts* (rituals of the O.R.A.C.), in: *Der Signatstern, oder die enthüllten sieben Grade und Geheimnisse der mystischen Freimaurerei . . .*, Freiburg im Breigau: Aurum Verlag, 1979, 3-147 (reprint of the Stuttgart: J. Scheible ed., 1866), with an introduction by Fritz Bolle, 1st ed. 1803.

Lit.: Konstantin Burmistrov, "Kabbalah in the Teaching of the Order of Asiatic Brethern", *Tirosh: Studies in Judaica*, III (Moscow, 1999), 42-52 ♦ Karl R.H. Frick, *Die Erleuchteten: Gnostisch-theosophische und alchemistisch-rosenkreuzerische Geheimgesellschaften bis zum Ende des 18. Jahrhunderts*, Graz (Austria): Akademische Druck- und Verlagsanstalt, 1973, 454-499 ♦ Jacob Katz, *Jews and Freemasons in Europe, 1723-1939* (The President and fellows of Harvard College), Cambridge (USA): Harvard University Press, 1970, Chapter III ♦ German translation of this Chapter: "Der Orden der Asiatischen Brüder", in: Helmut Reinalter (ed.), *Freimaurer und Geheimbünde im 18. Jahrhundert im Mitteleuropa* (Taschenbuch Wissenschaft 403), Frankfurt am Main: Suhrkamp, 1986 (first ed., 1983), 240-283 ♦ French ed.: *Juifs et Francs-Maçons en Europe (1723-1939)* (Histoires – Judaïsmes), Paris: Editions du Cerf, 1995 ♦ Christopher McIntosh, *The Rose Cross and the Age of Reason: Eighteenth-Century Rosicrucianism in Central Europe and its Relationship to the Enlightenment* (Brill's Studies in Intellectual History, 29), Leiden, New York, Köln: E.J. Brill, 1992, 161-177 ♦ Gershom Scholem, "Ein verschollener jüdischer Mystiker der Aufklärungszeit: E.J. Hirschfeld", *Year Book VII of the Leo Baeck Institute of Jews from Germany* (London) (1962), 248-278.

ANTOINE FAIVRE

Astrology I: Introduction

Astrology presupposes a relation between the positions and movements of the planets, stars and celestial orbs and zones on the one hand, and earthly events and/or human life on the other, and claims to explain this relation and predict future events in terms of the properties and relative positions of these heavenly agents. The most general idea behind this is expressed in the *Emerald Tablet* as "as above, so below".

The questions why such a relation should exist, how it works, how we can know it, and of what use it might be to human beings have been answered in rather diverse ways. Throughout the ages, the astrological view of the universe and of the nature of the relation between celestial and terrestrial phenomena has been essentially religious in nature, and it still is. Originally, astrology is supposed to have been mythical in character: the planets (traditionally including the sun and moon) and stars were thought to be living and divine beings, visible gods in the sky, whose great powers inspired awe and veneration. Gradually, the heavenly bodies became part of a hierarchical cosmology, in which the cause of their influences aquired a more transcendent character.

Basically, we might describe the most influential and long-lasting Western theories of celestial influence as either (more or less) "platonic" or (more or less) "aristotelian" in character; but in practice, the distinction is often problematic, as these views were often "harmonized". While both theories presuppose a transcendent and eternal Deity as the ultimate mover of the universe and regard man as a microcosmos, the "internal" organization of the universe is described in very different terms. The "platonic" universe is a living and animated organism, moved by the World Soul; the planets are "lesser gods", each of which performs his or her task by exerting a specific, innate influence on humankind by way of intermediaries. "Aristotelian" cosmology is more concerned with physical explanation of movement, light and influence of the heavenly bodies and orbs; although Aristotle does not explicitly discuss astrological theory as such, some of his views (especially from *De caelo* and *De generatione et corruptione*) could be used as a rational basis of astrological ideas. By way of Latin translations of Arab astrological literature, which was mainly aristotelian, these views gained great authorithy in Western Europe (Lemay 1962; 1987).

During the long period (12th- 17th/18th c.) in which celestial influence was part of the official Western European scientific paradigma, the why and how of these influences were seldom explained in a specific astrological context, as they belonged to the fields of cosmology, natural philosophy and metaphysics (Grant 1994, 569-617). Mainstream astrology had a rather practical approach; its theory was usually limited to an explanation of the qualities and influences of the planets, signs and other relevant elements according to astrological tradition, which claimed to be based on ages of experience and remained remarkably stable. Many texts are exclusively focused on methods of astrological interpretation and prediction.

Astrological statements are usually based on a diagram (chart, horoscope) depicting the state of the planets, stars and orbs for a specific place and time. This requires a detailed knowledge of the astronomical state of the heavens, which may be aquired by observation or (usually) by calculation on the basis of tables. For the interpretation of the figure, the astrologer could rely on traditional information about the meaning of the data. A chart may be drawn for several astrological purposes, of which the most prominent fields are: mundane astrology (revolutiones), horary astrology (interrogationes), natal astrology (genethlialogy) and elections of times (katarchen). *Mundane astrology* is concerned with general predictions about political power and changes of government, warfare, what will happen to nations, regions and classes of people. The charts from which these predictions were drawn usually represented the exact astronomical beginnings of solar years, seasons or months. Some were based on phenomena like eclipses, comets and conjunctions of the superior planets. *Astrometeorology* (astrological weather prediction) is a more specialized part of mundane astrology. Over long periods of time, general astrological predictions were popular as an indispensable element in almanacs. *Horary astrology* is based on the assumption that the heavens contain the answer to any question for the exact moment on which it is asked. The subject matter of the question decides in which of the *loci* or celestial houses the astrologer will find the answer. *Natal astrology*, which uses a person's natal chart to draw conclusions about his character and life, has always been and still is the most popular type of Western astrology. *Electional astrology* is concerned with choosing the most favourable moment for the beginning of an activity – a journey, a marriage, the building or buying of a house, and so on. Sometimes the "planetary hours" are observed: each planet rules one day of the week, and every hour of the day has its own planetary regent, which gives it a certain quality that makes it unfit for certain actions but excellent for others. The moon's phase, its zodiacal position, or the day of the lunar cycle are also considered important. Some parts of medical astrology, especially the choice of the right moment for medication, purging or bloodletting, are of this type, although the constellation at the moment that the patient fell ill is usually also taken into consideration. With regard to all these types of practical astrology, it is important to realize that they were not objects of belief, but constituted rational and systematic methods that were simply taken for granted as long as the concept of celestial influence was generally accepted. They became "pseudo-science" only at a time when this was no longer the case.

The main philosophical issue raised by astrology was the problem of free will and fate. Belief in astral determinism or fatalism, which was adopted by some of the ancients, was unacceptable in Christian Western Europe. The standard solution was found in limiting the influence of the planets and stars to man's "mortal" frame, which includes his body, passions and appetites, while asserting that it did not have power over his immortal and immaterial soul. The usual aphorism quoted in this context is *Vir sapiens dominabitur astris* ('the wise man will rule his stars'). Although this may be understood as 'the wise man is free from celestial influence', it could also be (and often was) interpreted as: 'the wise man will, by his self-knowledge, succeed to make the best of his potential as indicated by his birth chart'.

ANNELIES VAN GIJSEN

Astrology II: Antiquity

A. HISTORY
1. INTRODUCTION: ASTROLOGY, ASTRONOMY, AND METEOROLOGY 2. FROM A MESOPOTAMIAN SYSTEM TO HELLENISTIC FAITH 3. ASTROLOGICAL SYNCRETISM IN THE ROMAN EMPIRE 4. SOME ESSENTIAL ASTROLOGICAL TERMS AND NOTIONS 5. HITTITE AND INDIAN ASTROLOGY 6. CONCLUSION

B. LITERATURE
1. INTRODUCTION 2. "TECHNICAL" ASTROLOGICAL TEXTS (2A. FROM MESOPOTAMIA TO THE HELLENISTIC WORLD 2B. FROM THE ROMAN EMPIRE TO THE BYZANTINE PERIOD) 3. ASTROLOGY AS REVELATION: HERMETIC ASTROLOGICAL LITERATURE (3A. ASTROLOGY IN "POPULAR" HERMETIC WRITINGS AND THE NEW AIM OF SCIENTIFIC OBSERVATION 3B. ASTROLOGY IN THE "LEARNED" HERMETIC TREATISES) 4. CONCLUSION

A. HISTORY

1. INTRODUCTION: ASTROLOGY, ASTRONOMY, AND METEOROLOGY
The term "astrology", in its present sense, refers to a complex system of sidereal divination for the benefit of human affairs, but originally its meaning was more variegated. The term has long covered at least three different meanings: the present meaning, mentioned above, but also the scientific observa-

tion of the stars, that is, astronomy, and still earlier, the same observation of the stars for very practical purposes, in agriculture and in particular for weather prediction: meteorology.

The modern notion of astrology separated very slowly and confusedly from the two other notions. We could situate around the time of Aristotle the differentiation between the Greek terms astrology and meteorology, and only after the beginning of our era, the progressive differentiation between those of astrology and astronomy. However, the confusion of these two would persist practically until Kepler. Sometimes, to avoid such confusion, or to better define their methods, the technicians of ancient astrology attributed new terms to it (toward the 2nd century A.D.): "genethlialogy" and "apotelesmatica", which concentrate on the planetary influences studied at the birth of a subject, or again the "art of the Chaldaeans", referring to the most renowned source of ancient planetary divination.

2. FROM THE MESOPOTAMIAN SYSTEM TO HELLENISTIC FAITH

Elements of astrology, understood as astral observation from which predictions can be deduced, seem already to have existed as a complement to the Sumerian practice of haruspicy, but it was in Mesopotamia, toward the 2nd century B.C., that the elements of an astrological system were truly formed. It was founded on the idea of a sympathetic coincidence of the world, heaven and earth, and the realm of the gods; and on the obedience of each one, as part of the whole, to a pre-established destiny. Thus, for example, each celestial event, precisely observed, is considered as auspicious or inauspicious for the people, or for their leaders. A great number of such predictions, recorded on tablets, have been rediscovered in the library of Assurbanipal at Nineveh.

The greatest divinities were the stars, and the Mesopotamian sidereal cult, along with astrological practices, spread widely, from Nineveh to Babylon. In addition, there was developed a precise subdivision of time, which assigned the months and the days to the dominion of astral divinities. These still presided, in what was a rudimentary beginning of geography, over each of the four parts dividing Mesopotamia inside an ideal circle. Let us first note that the Moon, *Sin*, presided over the hierarchy of the planetary divinities, and the portents drawn from its observation were comparatively numerous. The Egyptian priests, in contrast, later followed by the Greek astrologers, gave primacy to the Sun. Finally, ancient astrology

owes the zodiac and its subdivision into "signs", which include the constellations, to Mesopotamian technique.

Celestial observation in Egypt, before the Hellenistic era, did not concern the influence of the stars upon a single individual, any more than it did according to the Mesopotamian method. Rather, it provided orientation, on the basis of the planetary movements and the horary tables of the risings and settings of stars, for the establishment of the ceremonial calendar of divine worship (favourable and unfavourable days, exact hours for services) and for the determination of sacred space by means of the cardinal points, needed to build the temples. We also owe to priestly Egyptian science the *Tables of the Thirty-Six Decans*, which mark the rhythm of the year and make it possible to calculate stellar risings.

Starting with the colonizing waves of Greeks moving to the East, from the eighth to the 6th century B.C., the amount of contact between the Chaldaeans and the Greeks increased, especially with Babylonia under Nabuchadnezzer. As early as that period, the Greeks began to draw from the oriental breeding ground all the astrological techniques that they were lacking. Moreover, an oriental understanding of the world began to permeate religious practices and even philosophical thought. Thus, the school of Pythagoras, probably connected with Orphism, drew inspiration from the sidereal cults of the East; it saw in numbers, which establish harmonious cosmic relationships, the essence of all things. The repercussions of this astral vision of the world, attributed to Pythagoras, continued well into the Roman Empire, in → Neoplatonism and in commentaries on Plato's *Timaeus*.

In the 3rd century B.C., in the *oikoumene* opened by the conquests of Alexander the Great, many Eastern Mystery religions spread through the Hellenistic world and found a favourable reception there. In their context, the astrological techniques became more than a means to an end. Revering Cybele, Attis, Atargatis, and Serapis, and especially Isis, to whom the faithful in quest of individual salvation adhered unanimously, these Mystery Religions had two faces. Their *exoteric* cult was open to everyone, and was often stamped with → magic; another, *esoteric* cult addressed a few initiates, and often involved a teaching of astrology, or even astrolatry.

Moreover, the weakening of civic religion in the Greco-Roman world favoured new individualistic aspirations, soon supported by certain tendencies in the Socratic, Platonic, and Stoic philosophies, and this opened up a terrain favourable to astral determinism. The discoveries of the Hellenistic scientists were numerous and genuine; they included the precession of the equinoxes, an outline of the heliocentric theory of the universe, and the exact measurement of the circumference of the Earth. Simultaneously, the Egyptian priest Manetho, at the court of the Ptolemaeans, and the "Chaldaean" historian Berosus, a protégé of the Seleucids, wrote histories of their civilizations that included astrology, notably in the genealogies. Berosus settled on the island of Cos at the beginning of the 3rd century B.C., where he opened a very famous and busy school of astrology. A true "astrological science" was born, whose mythical founding fathers were the "Hellenized Magi", Zoroaster, Ostanes, and Hystapes, whose "philosophy" and methods J. Bidez and F. Cumont have analysed.

From this period, we can date both a metamorphosis of astrology and its consolidation in the minds of people. It gained the sanctity of a faith in addition to its foundations as a science, while losing some of its traditional characteristics as a result of contact with the Greek spirit and the use of certain facts of astronomical discovery. It was also from the Hellenistic era on that astral divination was no longer applied solely to entire peoples and monarchs, but – responding to the new individualistic aspirations – came to include predictions for particular persons.

3. ASTROLOGICAL SYNCRETISM IN THE ROMAN EMPIRE

Astrological beliefs had not been absent in Rome before the imperial period, as shown by edicts condemning certain astrologers and practitioners of the occult sciences during the Republic. But it was due to the imperial conquests of the Orient, as early as the 1st century A.D., that astrology found a very broad following among all the classes of Roman society, including some of the emperors, such as Tiberius. Whole dynasties of astrologers, for example that of Thrasyllus, enjoyed celebrity. Yet, some sceptics raised their voices, such as the philosopher and scholar Carneades in the 2nd century B.C., or Lucian in the 2nd century A.D., the satirical poets of the Roman Empire, and the voices of Christianity.

The notion that the fate of living beings was absolutely determined by the laws of the planetary movements, and that humanity was completely subject to this sidereal fatality – the theoretical foundation of astrology – long ensured it a credible philosophical backing. Moreover, astrolatry, already practised in the Pythagorean school,

spread to Rome with the syncretic religion of the Syrian Baals and that of Mithra, a solar god who promised his worshippers heavenly immortality. Following the example of these religions, almost all the religions of salvation used astrological methods as a means of divination and as sacred elements of worship.

In accordance with the syncretism of the mystery religions, a kind of compendium of ideas came into being, characterized more by belief than by rationality, and the influence of which extended to the educated classes. Among the philosophical systems appropriated to serve as a substratum for these new forms of thought, Stoicism takes the first place. The Stoic notion of submission to fatality – but developed into a moral duty of renunciation –, its notions of a harmonious order of the world, universal sympathy, pantheism, and the migration of souls to the stars blended with the belief in sidereal divination and became a moral system propagated by a Syrian Stoic, Poseidonius of Apamea, teacher of Cicero. Indeed, the notion of universal sympathy, cornerstone of the Stoic system, made it possible to accept the influence of the stars on the natural elements (e.g. in the phenomenon of the tides, as demonstrated by Poseidonius) and even on human beings.

Thus the weakening of the critical spirit, which already inaugurated the era of the annotators and compilers at the turn of the Christian era, was as perceptible in astrological beliefs as it was in the writings that propagated them. This was true notably of two scholars of the 2nd century A.D., whose works have survived. The first, Vettius Valens of Antioch, fits the image of the scholarly compiler, more an astrologer and a priest than a scientist and an astronomer, although his work is cited with admiration by the Arab astrologers, such as Masallah in the 8th century A.D., and was much copied and annotated. His astrological tract, the *Anthologies*, is a didactic manual in nine books intended for his disciples, which methodically teaches how to set up a birth theme. The greatest merit of this work is that, although of Egyptian obedience, it attempts to reconcile the two rival astrological doctrines that were still mutually exclusive in the Hellenistic period: Egyptian (the tradition issued from the *Liber Hermetis* and from the teaching of Nechepsos-Petosiris) and Babylonian (the doctrine of the Chaldaean magi transmitted by Berosus).

His contemporary, Claudius Ptolemy, who also followed the Egyptian tradition, was a compiler equally lacking in originality. However, his famous *Tetrabiblos* or *Apotelesmatika* is a methodical work and more critical than that of Vettius Valens. It is also a precise pedagogical manual, which covers genethlialogy and the establishment of a birth theme and provides a meticulous classification of the fixed stars, the planets, the signs, and their aspects.

If we find in Ptolemy an aspiration to technicality, a "scientific" intent, such is not at all the case in Vettius Valens or his contemporaries. We already noted the sacred character of astrology as early as its Mesopotamian origins. Despite its pretensions as to the rigorous observation of the stars, at no time did it ever lose its religious aspect. The "Chaldaeans" who delivered predictions most often mixed their calculations with religious considerations. Firmicus Maternus, in his *Mathesis*, proclaimed the faith that motivated him and all his colleagues who were 'initiated' into the 'divine science'. Vettius Valens reminded his disciples of the necessary obedience to Fatality and the sacred rites (*Anthologies*, VII, 5 and IV, 2). Like a priest who initiates his mystes, he entreated them not to divulge his teaching (*ibidem*, VII, *prooimion*), for immortality will be assured to astrologers loyal to their faith.

Like Vettius Valens and his colleagues, and like the *Chaldaean Oracles* in the 2nd century A.D., the Neoplatonic philosopher Iamblichus granted astrology a prominent place in his *Mysteries of Egypt* (VIII, 4 sq.), not only as a technique of divination used in theurgy, but also as an essential part of hermetic metaphysical beliefs. Indeed, the astrological "revelation" of an astral cosmogony and of the sidereal influence on the world relates closely to the philosophical revelation of Hermetism and its moral substratum of a sympathy between the universe and humanity, the celestial and sublunar worlds. Furthermore, the principal aim of theurgic practice was to *influence* the invoked divinity, by any possible astrological and magical method.

Astrology, as a kind of knowing and as technique, thus became a favoured means of access to knowledge and gnosis, and hence a means of union with the divinity: the ultimate goal of Hermetic experience. The astrologer, or the magician, shared in the divine power, which he claimed came directly (through revelation) from the great Hermetic god Hermes-Thoth.

4. SOME ESSENTIAL TERMS AND NOTIONS FOR UNDERSTANDING THE ANCIENT ASTROLOGICAL SYSTEM

We have seen that the basis of astrology is the principle of solidarity between the celestial and the terrestrial parts of the universe: from this, the astrologers drew the conclusion of a necessary influence of the stars on human destinies.

The planetary aspects. Each star exercises a particular influence by its nature and position, and its aspects with respect to other stars exercise another influence. Certain planets are benefic (Jupiter, Venus, and the Moon); others are malefic (Saturn and Mars). Only the planet Mercury can have both qualities. Anthropomorphized and endowed with feelings, the stars stand in "opposition", "conjunction", or "exaltation" to each other, or in "depression" in a sign. They are part of a team or group, of the solar "sect" ("sect" of day, of the masculine gender: the Sun, Saturn, Jupiter and Mars) or of the lunar "sect" ("sect" of night, of the feminine gender: the Moon and Venus). The planet Mercury can again take part in both "sects", according to its situation. Likewise, human beings and animals, minerals and plants, as well as all parts of the known world, find a place in the solar or lunar "sect", within an organization of the world that considers itself rational and ordered.

The planets exercise determining influences, according to their relative positions. They can be in "opposition" or "squared" (two unfavourable aspects), or in "trine", "sextile", or "conjunction" (favourable aspects). The exact distribution of the parts of the human body under the rule of a planetary divinity and the signs of its "sect" is called *melothesia*. The geographical distribution of the regions of the *oikoumene* is called "chorography".

The zodiac and the birth theme. The Chaldaeans invented the band of celestial space that touches the solar or ecliptic orbit, which is inclined 24 degrees 27 minutes on the plane of the celestial equator. The two intersections of the ecliptic and the equator form the *equinoctial points* (in the signs of Aries and Libra); their opposing points are the *solstitial* or *tropical points* (in the signs of Cancer or Capricorn). On this circle are distributed the twelve signs, often zoomorphic, borrowed from Babylonian mythology; Greek tradition simply took over the figure of the zodiac and adapted it.

There are two principal systems of astrological divination. First there is the "apotelesmatic" or "genethlialogical" system, which informs the seeker about the most important events of his life. Second there is the system of "Initiatives", which defines the effects of a planetary configuration on a specific action to be undertaken.

To determine the events in the life of an individual, one must establish a "birth theme". This term is not equivalent to the modern sense of "horoscope". One establishes a birth theme by calculating the four points situated at the intersection of the planes of the horizon and the meridian for a given birth; four "Centers" are thus determined, and the planet and the sign that appear at these "Centers" reveal the subject's personality. There is first the "Horoscope", the "Ascendant point" (point I), which determines the beginning of the cycle of the twelve "Houses" and the thirty-six "Decans", each subdivision being dedicated to a particular area of human life; this is the point where the Sun was rising at the moment of the subject's birth, on the eastern horizon. Next are calculated the "Lower Culmination", "Imum Caeli" (IMC; point IV), the "Setting" or "Dysis" (point VII), and the "Upper Culmination" or "Medium Caeli" (MC; point X). These points are important in a birth theme and correspond with the subdivision of the "Houses".

5. HITTITE AND INDIAN ASTROLOGY

Hittite astrology did not originate from an invention proper to the peoples of Anatolia. The texts rediscovered at Boghaz-Köy, such as lists of portents derived from the aspects or the eclipses of the Moon, are all translations of Babylonian writings. We know that contacts were established very early between Mesopotamia and Anatolia, which permitted the Chaldaean culture to exercise a strong influence not only in all the → divinatory arts, but also in literature and in medical practice.

Likewise, even though the Pythagorean legend made the philosopher of Samos a disciple of the Brahmans, we may assume that Mesopotamian technique largely influenced Indian astrology, as early as the conquests of Alexander, and that, during the Hellenistic period, Graeco-Egyptian astrology blended with that of India.

Finally, both Hittite and Indian astrology, which lacked an originality specific to their culture, rarely practised individual divination; they devoted their calculations to the destiny of a whole country or of its rulers.

6. CONCLUSION

The system of apprehending the world suggested by astrological methods and their theoretical foundations was recognized, in Antiquity, from the Mesopotamia of the second millennium B.C. to the Hellenistic and Byzantine worlds, as a form of knowledge and often even as a sacred science.

The only discordant voices came from the intellectual elite. There was opposition to astrology from genuine astronomers and philosophers, and sometimes, for completely political purposes, even from certain rulers, hindered by astrological investigations in their desire for absolute power. Voices rose in opposition to astrology especially in the Graeco-Roman world, because this art pretended to appropriate the rational Greek spirit. It was held to be misguided because it proclaimed astrology as a science. Thus, Hipparchus, in the 2nd century B.C., wholly refuted the idea of using planetary observation to predict the future, even though he believed in the celestial nature of the human soul. Similarly, while Stoic philosophy, with which Hipparchus identified, was appropriated to serve as a "philosophical" substratum to astrology, the Stoics could not accept the divinatory formulas of the "mathematici" developed from stellar observation. The Cynical, Sceptic, and Epicurean philosophers also rejected any form of "astrological science"; Carneades, in the 2nd century B.C., ridiculed astrology and astrologers.

However, we have seen how much astrology was part of the mystery religions as early as the Hellenistic period, and how its methods served to discover the future in every area of life: birth, death, marriage, length of life, and so on. Even the juridical codes acknowledged it, if only to sanction its use as prescribed for magical practices. Frequently used in public life and political controversies, astrological consultation could also provide the name of a new emperor: the rulers, moreover, often availed themselves, as Augustus or Tiberius did, of personal astrologers. Thus, opposed and revered, science as well as faith, astrology conquered all of Antiquity despite discordant voices.

B. LITERATURE

1. INTRODUCTION

Astrological literature appears in the form of archeological documents (tablets and temple inscriptions) or texts (most often fragmentary). All are put under divine patronage, i.e. of a deified planet or a god already worshipped; the god most frequently invoked was → Hermes Trismegistus, associated with his Egyptian homologue Thoth, in a syncretic concern for venerable authenticity. Among the surviving texts we can distinguish between "technical" works and "mystical" revelations. The first not only deal with the simple ideological basis of sidereal divination, the belief in the sympathy of all the constituents of the universe, but also treat of the various "mathematical" ways to predict the future through the observation of the stars. The second group of astrological compilations, of later date, expresses the authors' faith in a revelation of a mystical nature and introduces astrological knowledge as a means of access to the union with the divine desired by the initiate. This is Hermetic astrology, more religious than "scientific".

2. "Technical" Astrological Texts
2a. From Mesopotamia to the Hellenistic World

Though one of the most ancient astrological documents known is a Babylonian tablet from the 2nd millennium B.C., most of the tablets conserved in the library of Assurbanipal at Nineveh are more recent and date from the 7th century B.C. The observations inscribed on these tablets are of a "scientific" nature: lists of planetary risings and settings, eclipses, and descriptions of planetary movements. However, the predictions drawn from them are very different from the strict deductions that one might perhaps expect, and all pertain to astrological method. These tablets already give a description of the zodiac, which Graeco-Roman astrology would later use and complete. However, the first birth theme (today incorrectly called "horoscope") conserved is more recent; it is Babylonian and dates from about 410 B.C., when Babylon was under the yoke of the Achaemenian Empire. Before this period, a similar astrological practice does not seem to have existed.

After the conquests of Alexander, toward the middle of the 3rd century B.C., we see an increasing interest in these individual themes in Babylon, while in Hellenistic Egypt we find them only from the last decades of the 1st century B.C., inscribed on papyrus. However, the best-known birth theme is Syrian, and it also dates from the 1st century B.C.: it is a pictorial document on the monumental tomb of King Antiochus I of Comagena at Nimrud-Dagh. Depicting a lion covered with stars, it is moreover a "theme of conception" (a royal theme par excellence) and it represents the situation of the planets, not at the birth of the king, but at the supposed moment of his conception, in the sign of Leo.

Finally, the Hellenistic period is especially rich in collections of pseudepigrapha that, under the name of legendary heroes or deities, dispense astrological and magical teachings of an encyclopedic character. Often, only the titles of these collections have survived.

Some astrological texts reflect a tradition strongly tinged with religiosity, issued from Greco-Egyptian circles of the Hellenistic period. They have come down to us as fragments, attributed to the pharaoh Nechepsos and his supposed confidant, the priest Petosiris. These tracts probably appeared in Alexandria toward 150 B.C. and could be inspired from somewhat earlier sources, even though Petosiris claims to represent the Hermes-Thoth revelation itself. In any case, the fragments transmitted to us, along with the citations of these tracts by many astrologers, such as Firmicus Maternus or Vettius

Valens, reveal them as a true sum of both astrological technique and texts considered as sacred. Their authors moreover present them as a heavenly revelation; it is, for example, a "divine voice" that grants Petosiris the privilege of knowing the essence and the influence of the stars on the world.

At the same period also appear other writings claiming the direct authority of Hermes Trismegistus; the most "scientific" one of them is the *Liber Hermetis*, of which there exists only a Latin translation. This work deals particularly with the "twelve *loci* of the sphere", gives a detailed list of decans, and introduces many practical exercises, notably to calculate the death date of a subject. Astrologers like Thrasyllus, Vettius Valens, and Firmicus Maternus used it extensively. In the 3rd century A.D., the philosopher and astrologer Iamblichus of Chalcis stated that the number of works inspired by the *Hermetica* exceeded fifty thousand (*Mysteries of Egypt*, I, VIII). Likewise, an anthology conserved under the name Pseudo-Manetho, whose beginning dates to about the 1st century B.C., with interpolations written until the 2nd century A.D., was also strongly influenced by the tradition of the *Hermetica*. It mixes the authority of Asclepius, Petosiris, and the Egyptian priest Manetho and mainly deals with the system of "Initiatives" (on a specific action to undertake) and the calculation of a subject's lifetime. Also well known during the Hellenistic period were collections of the → Iatromathematica of Hermes, which study medical astrology (predicting notably the outcome of an illness), and the *Salmeschoiniaka* (*Papyrus Oxyrhinchus* III, 128), which place the division of time and favourable dates into the astrological context of the thirty-six decans. However, these two types of text show almost no characteristics of astrological technique, but instead are reflections of Hermetic faith. They are left to us in a fragmentary state. W. Gundel has published some of them; others appear in the *Catalogus Codicum Astrologorum Graecorum*.

During the same period, a Babylonian astrological theory transmitted by the "Chaldaean" channel (chiefly the Syrian priests and perhaps the astrological school of Cos, where Berosus, whose work is lost, was teaching) came to enrich planetary divination. It was to become foundational to astrological doctrine by affirming the influence of the stars on the inhabited world, and particularly on humanity, as well as their divine nature. This was, it seems, the only original "Chaldaean" contribution to Hellenistic astrology. From the same "Chaldaean" tradition issued the apocryphal texts written under the pretended Persian authority of the "Hellenized magi", as J. Bidez and F. Cumont have called them: Pseudo-Zoroaster, Ostanes, and Hystapes. Many of these works were in the Library of Alexandria; sometimes we still have their titles or some references transmitted by Arab astrologers.

At the very beginning of the Christian era, a religious sect established on the shores of the Dead Sea at Qumran left us manuscripts written in Hebrew and Aramaic. Some contain birth themes established according to the Essene belief in the determinism of human life and its predestination to a "Destiny of Light" or a "Destiny of Shadows", and are strongly tinged with spirituality. On the basis of the time of birth, Essene astrology could determine the character of a being, then its destiny and spiritual evolution. Some themes, studied and published by A. Dupont-Sommer, are those of personalities of great moral qualities, one of whom is even supposed to have been an "Elect of God". If their style and form recall those of Chaldaean themes, these texts show us to what extent Essenian Judaism was open to the influences of the great spiritual and esoteric currents of the Hellenistic world.

2B. FROM THE ROMAN EMPIRE TO THE BYZANTINE PERIOD

The development of astrology in the Roman Empire was to a great extent connected with the success of Eastern religions, which supplanted civic religion. With the religion of Isis and its mystery cult, astrology found a prominent position. In Egypt, pictorial astrological literature was represented by the zodiacs decorating the temples of Denderah, Esnah, and Akhmim in Upper Egypt. These zodiacs are all from the Roman era, despite the claims by the priests and astrologers connected to the temples, who wanted to trace them back to remote Egyptian antiquity. They were copied from Hellenistic zodiacs, as also happened in other traditions and cultures (Indian or Chinese). The most complete (circular) zodiac is that of Denderah. On view at the Louvre in Paris, it shows the division into zodiacal signs and decans, with the constellations and the planets in the signs.

By the end of the 1st century B.C., senator P. Nigidius Figulus had already worked to disseminate astrological theories in Rome, even trying to reconcile the "Chaldean" and "Egyptian" doctrines in the light of neo-Pythagoreanism. Likewise, a Syrian philosopher, Posidonius of Apamea, a reputed scholar who was the teacher of Cicero and a commentator on Plato's *Timaeus*, broadly contributed to give astrology the support of Stoicism as a philosophical foundation. He was to inspire, among others, the theories of Ptolemy in his *Tetrabib-*

los. The rulers themselves, from Caesar to the Severi, furthered the influence of astrology on the minds of their subjects. These rulers included Tiberius and Hadrian, who believed in the power of the stars and employed the services of reputed astrologers, such as Balbillus or the "dynasty" of Thrasyllus. Some fragments of their astrological exercises are still extant in the *Catalogus Codicum Astrologorum Graecorum* (CCAG, VIII, 3); Balbillus, for example, has left us an original method to calculate the length of an individual's lifetime.

Similarly, the poet Manilius, who identified with Poseidonius among others, provides in the five chants of his *Astronomica* a description of the planets and the signs, their relationships and their influence on people. The court of Augustus or Tiberius seems to have commissioned this work of little originality. During the Empire, in an intellectual atmosphere that favoured commentaries and exegeses, most of the writings were astrological compilations and protreptic manuals for the purpose of training disciples. We have already mentioned the *Apotelesmata* of Pseudo-Manetho, of Petosirian persuasion, whose composition extended from the 1st century B.C. to the end of the 2nd century A.D. This collection displays analogies with the manuals of Claudius Ptolemy, Vettius Valens, and Firmicus Maternus. This is because they all borrow from the same earlier sources, those of the Hellenistic vulgate. From Ptolemy, a methodical theoretician and good pedagogue, we have inherited an influential tract on astronomy, the *Mathematical Syntax* or *Almageste*, which in thirteen books develops a geocentric vision of the world, despite the teachings of his master Hipparchus. His *Apotelesmatica*, or *Tetrabiblos* teaches in a critical and methodical manner all the areas of astrological technique (planets and signs, aspects, genethialogy, the art of establishing a birth theme, and calculations on the length of lifetime). His work influenced many later astrologers, such as Firmicus Maternus, Hephaestion of Thebes, Paul of Alexandria, Rhetorius of Egypt, Palchus, and even the Arab astrologers.

His contemporary, Vettius Valens of Antioch, left us *Anthologies,* a work in nine books, less critical than the *Tetrabiblos*. The collection, very mutilated, was a practical manual intended for his disciples. It is rather monotonous in its structure and form, mixing practical recipes with mystical injunctions to silence for students initiated into the "sacred science". Vettius Valens especially follows the tradition of Petosiris, but he has the recognizable merit of having attempted to reconcile the two rival astrological doctrines, "Egyptian" and "Chaldean", even though he was often content to compile rather than reconcile them. He remained, until the Middle Ages, an unrivaled master in both astrology and astral mysticism, held in great esteem by Antiochus of Athens, the Anonymous of 379, Hephaestion of Thebes, Palchus, Rhetorius, Theophilus of Edessa and many Arab astrologers. He would even be a subject, in the 16th century, of attentive study by → John Dee, the astrologer of Queen Elisabeth I of England.

We also still possess two works by an astrologer known as Firmicus Maternus, from the time of Constantine. The first, called *Astronomica*, is a paraphrastic commentary on the same work by Manilius. The second, *Mathesis*, is a compendium inspired by the *Orasis* of Critodemus and the *Hermetica*, and it describes in eight books the art of genethlialogy and of establishing a birth theme. The religiosity of the era and a syncretistic "mystical" theosophy strongly colours the whole work.

Besides the two summaries of Vettius Valens and Ptolemy, most of the other astrological tracts until the Byzantine period have survived in fragments, either as references in the better-conserved astrological manuals, or as astrological manuscripts. An inventory has been made, and the texts have been published, in the *Catalogus Codicum Astrologorum Graecorum* (*CCAG*; 12 volumes) by several philologists, including F. Boll and F. Cumont. This edition is still authoritative and cannot be neglected by anyone who wants to study ancient astrology.

In the "Chaldaean" astrological tradition, we must mention Critodemus, to whom Vettius Valens often refers, and who introduced Babylonian astrology in the 1st century A.D. His major work, the *Orasis* (the Vision), of which fragments remain (*CCAG*, VIII), often blends astrological description with speculations of a vague religiosity: astrology appears in it as a religion of salvation. Another work, contemporaneous with those of Vettius Valens and Ptolemy, has come down to us as fragments: the *Chaldaean Oracles*, a compendium of the "Chaldaean" theurgists attributed to a certain Julian the Theurgist, presented as a path to salvation through mystical union with cosmic and sidereal divinities.

From the 2nd century A.D. on, astrological literature was further distinguished by the works of Antiochus of Athens and Dorotheus of Sidon, who refer to "Egyptian" authority. In the 4th century came the contributions of the Anonymous of 379, as well as Hephaestion of Thebes, who was an uncritical compiler, and Paul of Alexandria, who restored Ptolemy. Finally, in the 6th century, Palchus, another disciple of Ptolemy and Rheto-

rius, produced a work that included many astrological citations and thus restored the two astrological traditions. All these tracts have come down to us as fragments, published in the *CCAG*.

3. ASTROLOGY AS REVELATION: HERMETIC ASTROLOGICAL LITERATURE

Within the philosophical and religious syncretism that characterized thinking from the Hellenistic period onward, the religions of salvation stimulated the individual to seek knowledge of the divine and revealed to him the means to arrive at it. The mystes often hoped to obtain a beneficent revelation from the divinity. This could be a metaphysical or teleological revelation, concerning the origin of the world and the fate of souls; it could be a proptreptic revelation, concerning a particular technique of astrology, → magic, → alchemy, or medicine; or a revelation concerning a specific life event, associated in this case with a prayer to obtain a favourable outcome.

From these individual requirements derived collections of different revelations: firstly, from about the 3rd century B.C., works concerning astrology, magic, and alchemy; secondly, more recent texts, toward the 2nd and 3rd centuries A.D., which reveal doctrines that are more philosophical and theological. In the first case we are dealing with a "popular" Hermetic literature, and in the second, with a "learned" one. If we use this classification derived from Festugière, we must nevertheless observe that the two groups of texts sometimes overlap; hence, we often find astrological observations in the "learned" treatises and, inversely, religious considerations in the "popular" ones.

3A. ASTROLOGY IN THE "POPULAR" HERMETIC TREATISES AND THE NEW AIM OF SCIENTIFIC OBSERVATION

We have already mentioned the *Liber Hermetis*, which is preserved in a Latin translation of a now lost Greek original (in a manuscript of 1431, cod. *Harleianus latinus* 3731). The original was written toward the 3rd century B.C. and attributed to Hermes-Thoth. It is a compendium permeated by the Hermetic faith in a divine revelation to the initiate, and intends to teach him an astrological doctrine and relevant exercises. The work treats of the fixed stars, the planets and their aspects, their positions in the zodiacal signs, the theory of the twelve houses of the sphere and examples of calculations to determine life events: birth, death, illnesses, etc. It also treats the theory of planetary "terms", gives a list of decans, and predictions on length of lifetime and violent deaths.

The astrological tracts on medicine (iatromathematics) and on botany, which are related to the former, are part of the "popular" hermetic writings and seem to date from the 1st century before our era. It should be remembered that the notion of "science" of the classical Greek era does not exist in these works. The "scientist" here is anything but "disinterested". He seeks to benefit from his observations and discoveries; he wants to know future events or become a master of nature through magic, by discovering the relationships of sympathy or antipathy that unite all the parts of the universe, including people. This explains the religious colouring and the appeal to mystery that "scientific research" often adopts as early as the end of the Hellenistic epoch.

Medicine was not exempt from this conception of the world and this perspective. Hermes' *Iatromathematica* (ed. Gundel) thus gives recipes for zodiacal and planetary melothesia by which the doctor can treat illnesses. Moreover, *The Sacred Book of Hermes to Asclepius on the Plants of the Seven Planets* (*CCAG*, VIII, 3, 153) puts the plants in close relationship with the decans, the zodiacal signs, the planets and the fixed stars. The book provides a list of recipes based on one or several plants, adapted to the patient's birth theme and the exact time of the beginning of the illness.

It was divine revelation again that enabled doctor Thessalus of Tralles, a religious author of the 1st century A.D., to be initiated by Asklepios himself into the knowledge of correspondences uniting twelve plants with twelve zodiacal signs and seven plants with seven planets (*CCAG*, VIII, 3, 163). After a spiritual preparation of fasting and silence and then a magical ritual presided over by an officiating priest, Thessalus entered into visual and oral communication with the god, who required secrecy from him in exchange for the revelation. We find again, as in all the Hermetic tracts, the mark of the same religious belief: truth can emanate only from the gods. Hence scientific research, considered as a quest for revelation and knowledge, must refer to them alone.

3B. ASTROLOGY IN THE "LEARNED" HERMETIC TREATISES

The teaching dispensed in the Graeco-Egyptian temples to groups of initiates should be primarily understood as religious knowledge. The corresponding ideas nourished a whole literature that flowered during the first three centuries of our era: it provided "revelations" in the form of dialogues on cosmogony, the gods, and the means of entering into communion with them. These "learned" treatises, such as the *Corpus Hermeticum*, the *Ascle-*

pius, and the text gathered in the *Anthology* by Stobaeus (→ Hermetic Literature I), evince the same religious and moral attitude as the so-called "popular" treatises. They are *logoi* of teachings revealing a cosmogonical aspect, or descriptions of the narrator's spiritual experience, affirming the regeneration of the mystes through initiation. All these texts, essentially "learned" and initiatory, contain numerous references to astrological theories and techniques. The most striking example is the fragment of Stobaeus (*CH*, III, fragm. VI, ed. Festugière) on the *Logos from Hermes to Tat*, explaining the doctrine of the thirty-six decans, in a description of the celestial world.

From the same perspective, *De Mysteriis Aegyptiorum* of Iamblichus of Chalcis, in the 3rd century A.D., defended the "Egyptian" doctrine and theurgic practices. In this work also, astrology was linked to hermetic astral theology (*De Mysteriis*, VIII, 4-7), and this system was taken up again in the Italian Renaissance, when → Marsilio Ficino translated and used the text. Thus, we can say that the division between the two literatures of hermetic astrology remained clearly intact in esoteric and exoteric teaching, but the analogies between them were evident in content and form. In content, "technical" and "learned" literature both purported to be apocalypses, revealed truths, often by the same god: Hermes Trismegistus, prophet of the word, was assimilated with the Egyptian god Thoth to gain greater authority. In their form also, the two types of literature are often related: based upon one faith, they both employ the language of the mystery religions, with the same divine invocations and the same conjurations to silence in the *Corpus Hermeticum* as in Vettius Valens.

4. CONCLUSION

We have seen that from the Mesopotamian world to the Byzantine era there existed a specific astrological literature, which varied according to its objectives and to the audiences addressed. But also literature itself, in the sense of literary creation and fiction, knew to make use of astrology: in the Graeco-Roman world, astro-theology blended with fiction to produce widely known works. The Greek and Latin novels are a good illustration of this: the *Aethiopica* of Heliodorus, the *Life of Apollonius of Tyana* by Philostratus, or Apuleius' novel *Metamorphoses*, assign a major role to the supernatural, and notably to the influence of the stars on humanity and the universe.

We have seen to what extent the "science" of astrology resulted in influencing all of Roman society, with satirists such as Martial or Juvenal, in the

1st century A.D., mocking the haste of their fellow-citizens to consult the stars and obey the rulings of the "mathematicians" for the smallest detail of their lives.

F. Cumont *et al.* (eds.), *Catalogus Codicum Astrologorum Graecorum*, 12 vols., Brussels, 1898-1953 (*CCAG*) ♦ E. Riess (ed.), "Fragmenta magica", *Philologus* 6 (1891-1893), 330-388 ♦ A. Dupont-Sommer, "Deux documents horoscopiques esséniens découverts à Qûmran, près de la Mer Morte", *Comptes rendus de l'Académie des Inscriptions et Belles Lettres* (1965), 239-253 ♦ J. Bidez & F. Cumont (eds.), *Les Mages hellénisés*, 2 vols.: I. *Introduction*, II. *Les Textes*, Paris: Les Belles Lettres, 1938 ♦ W. Gundel, "Neue astrologische Texte des Hermes Trismegistos: Funde und Forschungen auf dem Gebiet der antiken Astronomie und Astrologie", *Abhandlungen Bayerischen Akademie Wissenschaften*, München: Philol.-Hist. Abt., NF XII, 1936 ♦ A.D. Nock & A.J. Festugière (eds.), *Hermès Trismégiste*, 4 vols., Paris: Les Belles Lettres, 1945-1954 ♦ E. des Places (ed.), *Oracles Chaldaïques*, Paris: Les Belles Lettres, 1971 ♦ O. Neugebauer & H.B. van Hoesen (eds., with trans. and comm.), *Greek Horoscopes* (Memoirs of the American Philosophical Society, 48), Philadelphia: American Philosophical Society, 1959 ♦ P. Monat (ed. and transl.), *Firmicus Maternus, Mathesis*, 2 vols., Paris: Les Belles Lettres, 1992-1994; English transl. by J. Rhys Bram, *Ancient Astrology, Theory and Practice: Matheseos libri VIII by Firmicus Maternus*, Park Ridge, New Yersey: Noyes Press, 1975 ♦ E. des Places (ed.), *Jamblique, Les mystères d'Egypte*, Paris: Les Belles Lettres, 1966 ♦ G.P. Goold (ed. and trans.), *Manilius: Astronomica*, London etc.: Loeb Classical Library, 1977 ♦ F.E. Robbins (ed. and trans.), *Claudius Ptolemy, Tetrabiblos*, London etc.: Loeb Classical Library, 1948 ♦ W. Kroll (ed.), *Vettii Valentis Anthologiarum libri*, Berlin: Weidemann, 1908 (reprinted Dublin, 1973) ♦ D. Pingree (ed.), *Vettii Valentis Anthologiarum libri novem*, Leipzig: Teubner, 1986 ♦ J.-F. Bara (ed., transl., comment.), *Vettius Valens d'Antioche, Anthologies, Livre I* (EPRO 111), Leiden: E.J. Brill, 1989.

Lit.: A. Bouché-Leclercq, *L'Astrologie grecque*, Paris: E. Leroux, 1899 (reprinted Brussels: Culture et Civilisation, 1963, and Graz: Akademische Druck- und Verlagsanstalt, 1969) ♦ F. Cumont, "Zodiacos", in: Ch. V. Daremberg & E. Saglio (eds.), *Dictionnaire des Antiquités grecques et romaines*, vol. IX, Paris, 1877-1910 ♦ F. Cumont, *Astrology and Religion among the Greeks and Romans*, New York: Putnam, 1912 ♦ F. Cumont, *Les religions orientales dans le paganisme romain*, 4th ed., Paris: P. Geuthner, 1929 ♦ F. Cumont, "Astrologues romains et byzantins", *Mélanges de l'École française de Rome*, 37 (1918), 32-54 ♦ J. Bidez & F. Cumont, *Les Mages hellénisés*, 2 vols., Paris: Les Belles Lettres, 1938 ♦ A.-J. Festugière, *La révélation d'Hermès Trismégiste*, vol. I: *L'astrologie et les sciences occultes*, Paris: Gabalda, 1944 ♦ idem, *Hermétisme et mystique païenne*, Paris: Aubier-Montaigne, 1967 ♦ E. Riess, "Astrologie", in: G. Wissowa *et alii* (eds.), *Paulys Real-Encyclopädie der classischen Altertumswissenschaft*, vol. II, Stuttgart (1896), 1802-1828, vol. II ♦ Tamsyn Barton, *Ancient Astrology*, London & New York: Routledge, 1994 ♦ F. H. Cramer, *Astrology in Roman Law and Politics* (Memoirs of the American Philosophical Society 37), Philadelphia: American Philosophical Society, 1954 ♦ Marie Theres Fögen, *Die Enteignung der Wahrsager: Studien zum kaiserlichen Wissensmonopol in der Spätantike*, Frankfurt a. M.: Suhrkamp, 1993 ♦ Hans Georg Gundel, *Weltbild und Astrologie in den griechischen Zauberpapyri* (Münchener Beiträge zur Papyrusforschung und antiken Rechtsgeschichte 53), Munich: C.H. Beck, 1968 ♦ Hans Georg Gundel, *Zodiakos: Tierkreisbilder im Altertum. Kosmische Bezüge und Jenseitsvorstellungen im antiken Alltagsleben* (Kulturgeschichte der Antiken Welt 54), Mainz: Philipp von Zabern, 1992 ♦ Wilhelm Gundel, *Dekane und Dekansternbilder: Ein Beitrag zur Geschichte der Sternbilder der Kulturvölker* (Studien der Bibliothek Warburg 19), Glückstadt, 1936 ♦ Wilhelm Gundel & Hans Georg Gundel, *Astrologumena: Die astrologische Literatur in der Antike und ihre Geschichte* (Sudhoffs Archiv 6), Wiesbaden: Franz Steiner, 1966 ♦ James Herschel Holden, *A History of Horoscopic Astrology: From the Babylonian Period to the Modern Age*, Tempe: American Federation of Astrologers, 1996 ♦ John North, *The Fontana History of Astronomy and Cosmology* (Fontana History of Science), Hammersmith, London: Fontana, 1994 ♦ Kocku von Stuckrad, *Das Ringen um die Astrologie: Jüdische und christliche Beiträge zum antiken Zeitverständnis* (Religionsgeschichtliche Versuche und Vorarbeiten 49), Berlin & New York: Walter de Gruyter, 2000 ♦ R. Turcan, "Littérature astrologique", *Latomus* 27 (1968), 392-405.

JOELLE-FRÉDÉRIQUE BARA

Astrology III: Middle Ages

A. HISTORY
1. INTRODUCTION 2. ASTROLOGY IN ISLAMIC CULTURE (2A. THE EASTERN CENTERS 2B. AL-ANDALUS 2C. JEWISH ASTROLOGERS) 3. ASTROLOGY IN CHRISTIAN CULTURE (3A. LATE ANTIQUE INFLUENCES 3B. EARLY MIDDLE AGES 3C. THE TRANSLATORS OF THE 12TH CENTURY AND THEIR INFLUENCE)

B. LITERATURE
1. INTRODUCTION 2. ASTROLOGICAL LITERATURE UNDER MUSLIM INFLUENCE (2A. MUSLIM LITERATURE 2B. JEWISH LITERATURE 2C. MAGICAL LITERATURE) 3. ASTROLOGICAL LITERATURE UNDER CHRISTIAN INFLUENCE (3A. EARLY SOURCES 3B. THE 12TH-CENTURY TRANSLATORS AND THEIR IMPACT)

A. HISTORY

1. INTRODUCTION

It is a commonly held prejudice that the "middle" ages are a period of a mere transition from antiquity to the higher level of "modernity". In this view, it was the Renaissance that through its reference to antiquity woke up European culture from the deep sleep of the medieval period and helped making way for the triumph of enlightened rational science over magical-mystical speculation. This suggestive historical construction loses sight of the complex dynamics of this post-antique culture. Although it is true that parts of Christian theology in Rome and Byzantium aggressively attacked the religious and scientific traditions of antiquity, such an attitude should not be generalized. In fact, there are great differences from region to region and from ruler to ruler. Quite a few Christian sovereigns showed a remarkable interest in the sciences, and it was in the monastic schools of the high middle ages that the classical philosophical and scientific texts were tackled. Hence, the notion of a "medieval Enlightenment" (Flasch & Jeck 1997) is not too far-fetched.

Another prejudice that needs to be confronted is the idea of a "Christian occident". A more accurate picture of medieval culture will not be possible until (at least) the Muslim and Jewish traditions are taken into consideration, that fostered a complex pluralistic discourse and a transfer of knowledge. Those Christian courts that were unacquainted with Greek, Hebrew, and Arabic increasingly felt the need to catch up on Muslim science; as a result, from the 10th century onward Christian scholars became familiar with Arabic science, philosophy, and also astrology. Therefore, although the following overview is – for analytical reasons – divided into Christian and Muslim domains, the dynamic transfers between them must always be taken into account.

2. ASTROLOGY IN ISLAMIC CULTURE

Given the fact that the Qur'an castigates human worship of astral deities but describes the interpretation of astral signs as a fair means to understand God's will (see, e.g., sura 7:6-7), Muslim rulers from the beginning supported the development of the sciences in general and astrology in particular. Muslim culture – which soon reached from India and China to France and Spain – absorbed many different astrological traditions. Arabic science is therefore considerably more than the Arabs' science; an important achievement of Muslim scholars was the integration of Indian and Chinese astrology with the Babylonian and Hellenistic traditions that had been more or less canonized in the works of Ptolemy. In this regard, the Silk Road was an important place of exchange not only for goods but also for ideas, because Muslim, Manichaean, Jewish, Christian, and Chinese traditions were incorporated in new concepts.

2A. THE EASTERN CENTERS

Between the 8th and 10th centuries these traditions were actively collected and studied. The Abbassidian rulers of Baghdad in particular (Abū-Ja'far al-Mansūr, Hārūn al-Rashîd and 'Abdalla am-Ma'mūn) helped to create a scientific atmosphere which encouraged scholars of astrology to develop new theories and approaches. Under am-Ma'mūn the library of Baghdad reached the height of its influence; Greek manuscripts from Byzantium and Cyprus were collected and teams of translators provided text-critical Arabic editions. Thus, the majority of the extant classical astrological texts – including Ptolemy's works – were available in Arabic translation. In addition, a new genre was created that became a valuable tool for practicing astrologers throughout the middle ages. The so-called *zīj* is a kind of table that makes easily accessible the planetary constellations for a given time and helps the astrologers to figure ascendants and culminations, the horary movement of the stars, their average speed, the planets' retrograde phases, etc. (see North 1994 for a detailed description). At the same time, the quality of *astrolabes* was significantly improved, which led to a better foundation of calendrical calculation and astrological analysis.

Among the most important astrologers of the period were Ma'shallāh (Latin Messalah, a Jewish astrologer who calculated the foundation horoscope for Baghdad), Ya'qūb ibn Yshaq → al-Kindî, Ja'far ibn Muhammad Abū Ma'shar (Latin Albumasar, 787-886), Abū Abd 'Allah Muhammad ibn Ğabîr al-Battānî (c. 858-929), and Muhammad ibn Ahmad al-Birūnî (973-c. 1050). Latin texts from medieval and Renaissance provenance regularly refer to all of them as important scholars, but from the perspective of esotericism al-Kindî and his pupil Abū Ma'shar are without doubt the most influential. Al-Kindî put forward a rational and philosophical foundation of esoteric disciplines which comprised not only astrology but also → magic and other divinatory techniques. In his book *De radiis (stellarum)* (On the Rays of the Stars) he combined Platonism and → Aristotelianism and developed a metaphysical foundation of magic. Applying a Stoic concept of universal sympathy he argues that sympathy manifests materially in the "rays" between (celestial and sublunary) objects. From this al-Kindî deduces his thesis that a complete comprehension of the cosmos is possible, a thesis that is usually only attributed to Renaissance thought (see Travaglia 1999). But not only the stars send out "rays" but also every material object and even words and actions; therefore ritual, prayer, sacrifice, and magic are powerful ways of influencing the cosmos. This holistic explanation had a strong impact on e.g. → Roger Bacon's and → John Dee's philosophy of nature.

Abū Ma'shar grew up in Khurasan and was well acquainted with the doctrines of the Jews, Nestorians, Manichaeans, Buddhists, Hindus, and Zoroastrians who lived in that region. At the age of forty-seven he met al-Kindî and became his most important pupil. Abū Ma'shar's opus comprises many different texts of astrological provenance, but most influential was the *Introduction into Astrological Prediction* that he wrote in 848 in Baghdad and that became known to the Latin west as *Liber introductorius maior*. For Abū Ma'shar astrology is a mathematical science in the strict sense. In contrast to other – mainly Christian – astrologers who denounced horoscopic astrology and concrete prophecies as *astrologia superstitiosa*, he views these as an important subdiscipline of astrology. Therefore, the *Liber introductorius* gives a complete overview of all classical astrological techniques, including Indian parameters and traditions that Abū Ma'shar weaves into his doctrines. In another work, the *Zīj al-hazarāt*, he adds to the astronomical calculations a philosophical foundation of "hermetic" science. Astrology, he says, was once revealed to the humans by a divine source but was largely forgotten. He holds that his *zīj* was based on a text that had been hidden in Isfahan before the Flood and now was made known to the (learned) public by Abū Ma'shar.

Of particular significance for later astrologers was Abū Ma'shar's doctrine of Great Conjunctions. He elaborated the well-known ancient speculation about the importance of the threefold conjunctions of Jupiter and Saturn and applied it to the Shiite interest in the return of the Mahdi. Jews and Christians used this doctrine, for their part, to figure out the beginning of the messianic era or the return of Christ; this is but one example of how astrological doctrines fueled the apocalyptic discourse of Renaissance and Reformation Europe.

2B. AL-ANDALUS

In close contact with the eastern centers of the Islamic world from the 8th to the 15th century the western caliphates of the Spanish peninsula (*al-Andalus*) formed a second cornerstone of science and astrology. Already before the Muslims came to Spain there had been an astrological tradition, mainly based on the works of Isidore of Seville (see 3A below). But whereas earlier research was mostly interested in calendrical issues, from the 10th century onward new schools of astronomers at the emirate of Córdoba began to contest the hegemonic status of the east. The emir sent agents to Baghdad, Damascus, and Cairo to collect all extant literature; in the second half of the 10th century schools for mathematics, astronomy, and other arts were founded that systematized, commented, and elaborated this material. In Córdoba taught the astronomer al-Majritî († around 1007) who transferred the famous tables of al-Khwārismî to the meridian of Córdoba and adjusted the Islamic calendar. Al-Majritî instructed several well-known astrologers, and his example was followed by other centers of al-Andalus, from Seville and Valencia to Sargasso and Toledo.

As an example of how classical astrological techniques were further elaborated in medieval Islamic culture the teachings of Alcabitius (d. 967 in Aleppo) deserve mention. His *Liber introductorius* became a standard reference work for later astrology, after John of Seville had prepared a Latin translation in 1142. Alcabitius is important also with regard to his new system of dividing the twelve "houses" of the horoscope, i.e. the intermediate divisions between the Ascendant axis and the Medium Coeli axis. Referring to the classical methods of Porphyry and Rhetorius, the Alcabitius system remained in wide practice even after Campanus, Regiomontanus, and Placidus had proposed their new methods.

Of crucial importance for medieval astrology was the work of 'Alî ibn abî al-Rijāl (Latin Haly Abenragel or Albohazen Haly, c. 1016–1062). Whether or not he was educated in Baghdad is not clear. He worked as notary and court astrologer at the court of al-Mu'izz ibn Bādis in Tunis, where he wrote his main opus: a systematical description of all aspects of classical astrological knowledge in eight books. Although there are several different versions and collections of this work – the versions in Old Castilian and Latin were particularly influential in Europe –, it seems to be clear that the first three books treated astrology and astronomy in general, the fourth and fifth book described the casting and interpreting of horoscopes, the sixth was devoted to "revolutions" (i.e. to transits and related interpretations), the seventh to "elections" (i.e. to catarchic astrology), while the eighth book analyzed issues of mundane astrology and the turn of historical eras. Haly Abenragel makes extensive use of the old masters such as "Hermes", Dorotheos, Ptolemy, Ma'shallāh, and al-Kindî, and he not only presents their ideas but also discusses the pros and cons of their theories. That the Muslim astrologer was indeed regarded by later scholars as *Summus astrologus* or even as *Ptolemaeus alter* can be seen from the fact that his book was reprinted six times between 1503 and 1571.

2C. JEWISH ASTROLOGERS

From the beginning of the Muslim era the Spanish peninsula was characterized by a vivid exchange of Christian, Jewish, and Muslim religious traditions. In this situation, Jews had a particularly important position, because many of them were acquainted with several languages. Therefore, it comes as no surprise that the Christian king Alfonso X asked his Jewish physician Jehuda Moshe to prepare a translation of Haly Abenragel's work. Jews also worked as astrologers and wrote influential treatises in Hebrew (overview in Halbronn 1986). Among these are Abraham bar Chiyya (d. 1143), Abraham ibn Ezra (1098–1164) and Jehuda Halevi (1075–1141). Ibn Ezra published the most important astrological work of medieval Jewry, the *Sepher reshît hokhmah* (The Beginning of Wisdom), which was soon translated into French, English, and Old Castilian. In this book the author gives a concise introduction to nativities, horary astrology, elections, mundane astrology, and astrological medicine; its detailed reflections on the contemporary Aristotelian framework demonstrate the highest standard of medieval Spanish philosophy. In other books Ibn Ezra discussed astrological and theological issues with Jehuda Halevi, Solomon ibn Gabirol, and Abraham bar Chiyya, and he even proposed a calculation of the houses of the horoscope that resembled that of Placidus five hundred years later. Ibn Ezra wrote astronomical tables for Pisa (around 1143), and a London *zīj* that circulated around 1150 is also assigned to his authorship. The dominant position of Jewish scholars in medieval astrology continued until the Jews were expelled from Spain in 1492.

In the 13th and 14th centuries Spanish astrology spread over whole of Europe. The "Alfonsine Tables" gained wide currency due to their improved mathematical quality, and the use of astrolabes reached a new standard (see North 1994, 203-223).

3. ASTROLOGY IN CHRISTIAN CULTURE

Quite against a commonly held position, astrology flourished in regions under Christian control

as well. Christian astrologers tried to determine "licit" from "illicit" astrology, and several emperors drew on astrological techniques to legitimate their power in quite the same way as their Roman predecessors had done (see Stierlin 1988). This holds true for Charlemagne, Louis the Pious, Henri II, and the emperor Frederick II, to mention but the most important rulers.

3A. LATE ANTIQUE INFLUENCES

The classical astrological tradition had been preserved in Latin texts such as Firmicus Maternus and Manilius, and it was handed down to early medieval Christianity mainly by two authors: A.M.S. Boethius and Isidore of Seville. In his crucial work *Consolatio philosophiae* Boethius (c. 480–524) provided medieval culture with a well-versed description of classical philosophy and science. With regard to astrology, his contribution was important insofar as he reinforced → Neoplatonism and summarized the main arguments on the issue of determination, fate, freedom of will, and fatalism.

Boethius' influence was surpassed, of course, by the writings of Isidore of Seville (c. 570-636). His encyclopedic *Etymologiae* covered in twenty volumes the whole of classical science and culture, and his differentiation between *astrologia superstitiosa* and *astrologia naturalis* became the standard argument for medieval scholars to justify "licit" astrology. For Isidore, astrology is "superstitious" if it wants to predict the character and the fate of a native with reference to his or her horoscope; this branch of astrology had become superfluous with the victory of Christ. Although this branch is not necessarily wrong (like many others, Isidore speculated about the "Star of Bethlehem"), it is definitely illicit. The accepted branch of astrology – *astrologia naturalis* – is focused on meteorological and mundane aspects of nature, and it also includes astrological medicine. Isidore's claim that every physician needs to have an astrological education remained common in Christian culture right into early modern times.

3B. EARLY MIDDLE AGES

The main centers of Christian astrological research in early medieval times were the monasteries. Boethius' and Isidore's reception began with Beda Venerabilis (673-735) who applied their teachings to a reformulation of the Christian religious calendar. This resulted in a new genre of calendrical reckoning, the so-called *Computus* (Borst 1991). To the calendrical considerations were added country sayings and astrological rulings such as those of Firmicus Maternus. An important achievement of this new understanding was the calendrical reform of Charlemagne; his Imperial Calendar was in use until the 13th century (see Borst 2001). Among the monasteries that helped to establish a Christian astrology were the schools at Fulda, St. Gallen, Reichenau, and Regensburg. Later, in the 9th and 10th centuries, at the monastery of Santa Maria de Ripoll, monks compiled treatises on arithmetic, geometry, astronomy, and calendars, and translations of these documents circulated widely in western Europe. This is the explanation of why Hermann the Lame (1013–1054), a monk at Reichenau, was able to write his detailed description of the use of astrolabes – he simply knew the Ripoll texts. Hermann improved the Beda reckonings and in his book *De mensura astrolabii* transformed the Arabic lunar calendar of his Spanish sources into the Latin Julianic solar calendar.

How deep-reaching the cultural transfers between Christian and Muslim Europe were can be exemplified by the works of Gerbert of Aurillac (940-1003) who in 999 became Pope Silvester II (Lindgren 1976). Gerbert was educated in Barcelona in the *artes liberales* and was an expert of Arabic, mathematics, arithmetic, and → music. In his writings, he called for a reception of Arabic science in order to improve Christian culture, and he supported Arabic terminology and translations in the monastery schools, where Fulbert of Chartres, Hermann the Lame, or Walcher of Malvern were now studied in detail. In his book on the use of astrolabes – Gerbert had used one already in 989 in the monastery of Reims – he fortified Isidore's differentiation of natural and superstitious astrology. Through these activities, the knowledge of the astrolabe, which also made the casting of horoscopes much easier, became standard in Europe by the 11th century.

3C. The Translators of the 12th Century and their Influence

During the 12th century, most learned Christians felt the need to catch up with Muslim and Jewish science, and both with regard to literature and to art and iconography a considerable shift of astrological motives took place (Blume 2000). Isidore's differentiation was now further developed, e.g. by the scholastics Peter Abaelard (c. 1100-1140) at Chartres and Hugo of St. Viktor († 1141) in Paris, who taught that astrology can determine the *naturalia* (the natural causes) but not the *contingentia* (things that are dependent on chance and God's will). This was the official opinion of the Church for hundreds of years.

Adelard of Bath (c. 1080-c. 1150) was a key figure in the interference of Muslim and Christian astrology (see Hastings 1927, 20-42; Burnett 1987), because he actively reformulated astrological tradition. Adelard translated the tables of al-Khwārismî and speculated on Abū Maʿshar's theory of the growth and decline of empires and religions. At the end of the 12th century, astrology was a common issue of almost all monasteries, and astrological knowledge began to spread from the clerical realm to the courts, guilds, and other layers of society (Blume 2000).

Until the 13th century a vivid discussion about astrology developed among scholastic scholars, among them Gerhard of Cremona (1114-1187), → Bernard Silvester († after 1159), → Michael Scot († 1235/6), → Albertus Magnus, → Roger Bacon, Thomas Aquinas (c. 1225-1274), and → Ramon Llull (von Stuckrad 2003, 192-206). Albertus Magnus's *Speculum astronomiae* (written in the 1260s) became one of the most influential treatises on astrology in the high middle ages (Zambelli 1992; cf. Paravicini-Bagliani 2001). In order to establish astrology as an accepted science, he distinguished between (illicit) magical applications and scientific scrutiny. Furthermore, Albert described astronomy and astrology as two distinct branches of this science; whereas astronomy can be regarded as a mathematical discipline, astrology interprets these calculations and is able to predict future events. Since astrology leads every earthly matter back to its divine source, it necessarily leads man to God who is seen as the unmoved mover of everything that exists. With this argument Albert reacted to the scholastic critics of astrology and introduced astrology as an important discipline for the pious Christian.

Albert's position – and also Thomas Aquinas's, who likewise argued that astrology was based on reason and that reason determines the will – came under attack in the context of the (mainly French) Averroists. John Duns Scotus, among others, stressed the primacy of will over reason. Because this is also valid for God, God's will cannot be detected by reason. Hence, astrology is a transgression based upon human curiosity and the theological truths must be believed, not understood. A radically different position was held by Roger Bacon who saw → alchemy, astrology, and magic as the peaks of a natural science that was based on empiricism. Bacon – referring to Ptolemy, Haly Abenragel, Abū Maʿshar, and others – called on the Church to support an *Astrologia sana*, because no serious astrologer had ever claimed a fatalistic or deterministic astrology. In sum, all arguments were well established long before the "Renaissance" picked up these issues again.

B. LITERATURE

1. INTRODUCTION

By the end of the 4th century, the "classical" astrological literature of Greek and Roman provenance had reached the height of its influence and was spread widely over the ancient world. Ptolemy's *Tetrabiblos* were seen as the ultimate source of astrological reasoning (on the extant MSS see Boer 1961), but in addition to this scholarly kind of literature there also flourished a variety of philosophical, religious, or popular treatises that had their impact on later astrological discourse. Christian literature in particular – beginning already with Firmicus Maternus in the 4th century – questioned the legitimacy of astrology and developed a framework of interpretation that distinguished between accepted and illicit branches of this discipline. In other religious contexts, that is to say, in Jewish, "Gnostic", Hermetic, Manichaean, and later in Islamic traditions, Greek and Roman astrology was likewise reshaped and adopted in terms of a (more or less) monotheistic creed.

For the centuries to come, astrological literature can be divided roughly with regard to language. While the Latin west was more or less unaware of the standard astrological Greek works and referred to Latin sources, it was in the cultures under Muslim influence that those documents were not only preserved but also translated, and a rich astrological discourse was developed with a nature of its own. This situation changed only from the 10th century onward, when Christian scholars were becoming more and more acquainted with Muslim astrology and astronomy.

2. ASTROLOGICAL LITERATURE UNDER MUSLIM INFLUENCE

2A. MUSLIM LITERATURE

The first notable astrological author among the Arabs was *Theophilus of Edessa* (c. 695-785). Theophilus was a Greek who in his old age became court astrologer to the Caliph al-Mahdî († 785). He wrote four treatises on astrology in Greek, some excerpts from which are edited in the CCAG, that is to say the *Works on Elections for Wars and Campaigns and Sovereignty* (showing strong Indian influences already, it is the only extant Greek astrological literature devoted entirely to military astrology); *Astrological Effects*, depending on Indian astrology and Rhetorius' compendium of astrology;

Various [Kinds of] Elections, depending mainly on Dorotheos and Hephaestio of Thebes; and *Collection of Cosmic Beginnings*, a treatise on mundane astrology and annual and monthly predictions.

In the 8th century Indian astrologers such as Kankah were active at the courts of Baghdad and brought Hindu astrology to the Muslim west. Among those who absorbed these traditions, the Basra Jew *Ma'shallāh* (Latin Messalah, c.740-c. 815) stands out as the first real inventor of new approaches. He wrote more than twenty astrological treatises, the most important being *The Revolution of the Years of Nativities* (on Solar returns); *The Revolutions of the Years of the World* (on Aries ingresses); *Conjunctions*; *Letter on Eclipses*; *Reception of the Planets or Interrogations*; and *The Construction and Use of the Astrolabe* (Thorndike 1956; Spanish trans. by D. Santos). A summary of his book *On Conjunctions, Religions, and Peoples* is an outline of world history based on Aries ingress charts (referred to a fixed zodiac) and Jupiter-Saturn conjunctions (trans. and commentary by E.S. Kennedy and D. Pingree).

In the 9th century astrological theory and practice were elaborated by many influential experts. One of them was Ya'qūb ibn Yshaq → al-Kindî (c. 796-c. 870) who wrote hundreds of treatises on a variety of topics. With regard to astrology, three are particularly well known in the West, namely *De iudiciis astrorum* (The Judgments of the Stars; with works of other authors), printed in translation by Peter Liechtenstein, Venice 1507; *De pluviis, imbribus et ventis ac aeris mutatione* (Rains, Storms and Winds, and Change in the Air; again including pieces of other writers), printed in translation by Liechtenstein in 1507. His book *De radiis (stellarum)* (On the Rays of the Stars) with its combination of Platonism and → Aristotelianism influenced esoteric authors of the Renaissance, from → Roger Bacon to → John Dee.

Ja'far ibn Muhammad *Abū Ma'shar* al-Balkhî (Latin Albumasar, 787-886) is a key figure of Arab astrology in medieval times. Some fifty books are credited to him and his expertise in things astrological is enormous. His most famous works are *The Great Conjunctions* and the *Introduction into Astrological Prediction*. The latter was an encyclopedic treatment of all aspects of astrological theory and practice. It was translated as *Introductorius maior* by John of Seville (12th century), whose translation was never printed but is preserved in numerous MSS. Another translation by Hermann of Carinthia (as *Introductorium in astronomiam*) was published by Erhard Ratdolt at Augsburg in 1485 (repr. 1489). *The Great Conjunctions* – an

elaborate treatise on mundane astrology with special regard to the ("Great") conjunctions of Jupiter
and Saturn that change their position in one of the
four Trigons every 238 years – was also translated
by John of Seville and edited by Johannes Angelus
(Ernst Ratdolt: Augsburg 1489). Another book by
Abū Maʿshar was the *Kitāb al-ulūf* or *Book of the
Thousands*. Unfortunately, the original is lost, but
D. Pingree (1968) restored a substantial portion of
this work from later Arabic writers. The book
comprised Albumasar's outline of world history on
a framework of Aries ingresses and conjunctions,
but also an elaborate system of so-called "profec-
tions". Very popular in medieval and Renaissance
times was Abū Maʿshar's *Flores astrologiae* or
Liber florum, i.e. "The Flowers of Astrology" or
"Book of Flowers", translated by John of Seville
(Erhard Ratdolt: Augsburg 1488; repr. 1489 and
1495). The "Book of Flowers" is an anthology of
Albumasar's larger writings on mundane astrology.
Finally, his general treatise on the *Revolutions of
the Years of Nativities* must be mentioned. This
book on what today is called solar returns is preserved in the Arabic original and in Byzantine
Greek translation; the Latin translation made from
the Greek was falsely attributed to Hermes (*Hermetis philosophi de revolutionibus nativitatum
libri duo incerto interprete* (Two books of Hermes
the Philosopher on the Revolutions of Nativities
by an unknown translator; H. Wolf: Basel 1559).

Abū Bakr al-Hasan ibn al-Ḥashîb (Latin *Albu-
bater*, late 9th century) wrote an introduction to
astrology, a book on the revolutions of nativities,
and a very popular book on natal astrology. This
was translated around 1225 by Salio (or Solomon)
at Padua as *De nativitatibus* and published in an
astrological compendium at Venice in 1492 (ed.
and trans. D. Santos) and in another in 1493.
Divided into 206 chapters – some of them consisting of only one sentence – all aspects of astrological interpretation are tackled and illustrated with
one or more actual nativities.

Alcabitius (d. 967) or, less commonly, Abdilaziz,
became famous because of his system of house
divisions. But in his most important book, the
Introduction to the Art of Judgment of the Stars,
dedicated to the Sultan Sayf al-Dawlah (c. 916-
967), he also presented a complete description of
astrological theory and practice, numerous lists of
place names by climates and influences, and long
passages from Dorotheos and Maʿshallāh (see
AAASLT, 137-139). The Latin translation by John
of Seville, *Alchabitii Abdilazi liber introductorius
ad magisterium judiciorum astrorum* (1142), was
printed later more than a dozen times. Beginning

with Erhard Ratdolt's Venice edition of 1503, it
became common to print it along with the commentary of John Danko (14th century).

The writings of Muḥammad ibn Aḥmad *al-
Birūnî* (973-c. 1050), a leading scholar at the turn
of the millennium and the successor of al-Battānî
(c. 858–929), are important, not only because he
discussed Abū Maʿshar's system of Great Conjunctions and kept up correspondence with other
learned scholars – among them critics of astrology
such as Ibn Sina (→ Avicenna) – but also because he
spent a lot of time in India and incorporated further
elements of Indian astrology into his own system.
Al-Birūnî's works were not translated into Latin by
the 12th-century translators, but *The Book of Instruction in the Elements of the Art of Astrology*
(1029; trans. R. Ramsay Wright 1934) with its precise and coherent description of geometry, arithmetic, astronomy, and astrology nevertheless
influenced subsequent authors. In *Alberuni's India*
[sic] (2 vols., trans. Edward C. Sachau, Routledge:
London 1910) he gives a detailed account of life in
India in the early 11th century with special reference to Hindu astronomy and astrology. A treatise
on calendars with some information on astrology is
also available in English translation: *The Chronology of Ancient Nations*, trans. and ed. Edward C.
Sachau, London 1879; repr. Minerva: Frankfurt
a.M. 1984.

Next in the line of celebrated scholars was ʿAlî
ibn abî al-Rijāl (Latin Haly Abenragel or Albohazen Haly, c. 1016-1062). Particularly responsible for his fame is *The Outstanding Book on the
Judgments of the Stars*, which was translated into
Old Castilian as *El libro conplido en los iudizios de
las estrellas* at the court of Alphonso X the Wise
(1226-1284), first edited by Gerold Hilty in 1954.
Since the extant Castilian Madrid MS 3065 contains only the first five of the eight books, the Latin
translation that was made from a complete Castilian manuscript is important. It was first published
as *Praeclarissimus liber completes in judiciis astrorum* by Erhard Ratdolt, Venice 1485. The printed
book was as popular in Renaissance times as manuscript copies had been earlier. It was reprinted in
1503, 1520, 1523, 1525, 1551, and in 1571.

2B. JEWISH LITERATURE

Jewish scholars played a crucial role as translators of Arabic literature. Furthermore, they
wrote extensively in Arabic themselves and provided medieval (and Renaissance) Jewry with
detailed information on astrology in Hebrew. One
of the most influential figures was *Abraham ibn
Ezra* (1098–1164) who – in addition to Bible

commentaries and a Hebrew grammar – wrote more than fifty books on astrology and astronomy. In his works, he elaborates Arabic astrology into an own system of interpretation that meets Jewish interests. His best known astrological work is *Sepher reshît hokhmah* (The Beginning of Wisdom; 1148), which was translated into Old French by Hagin le Juif in 1273 (for English and French eds. see bibliography). There were also translations into Catalan that combined this book with other treatises of Ibn Ezra; the Latin translations were mostly made from the Catalan compilation. In *The Book of the Fundamentals of the Tables* Ibn Ezra proposed a division of the houses of the horoscope that were calculated in a similar way as Placidus developed it five hundred years later. The Latin version of this book was edited by José Millás Vallicrosa in 1947.

2C. MAGICAL LITERATURE

Another genre that must be mentioned belongs to the field of astrological › magic. The use of talismans and → amulets with astral symbolism flourished during the whole era under consideration, both under Islamic and Christian authority. Since it was important to produce and consecrate the images at a previously chosen time, this "applied astrology" forms a branch of electional astrology. There are a lot of medieval texts referring to planetary images, rings, and amulets (Robson 1931, ch. VII; Caiozzo 2003), a number of them being attributed to Hermes (Thorndike 1923–1958, vol. 1 and 2).

3. ASTROLOGICAL LITERATURE UNDER CHRISTIAN INFLUENCE

3A. EARLY SOURCES

For a long time, Latin Christian culture harked back to two influential works of late antiquity, that is to say, *De consolatione philosophiae* by A.M.S. Boethius (c. 480-524), written around 523, and the massive twenty-volume *Etymologiae* by Isidore of Seville (c. 570-636). Both texts served as major transmitters of late ancient philosophy and science into medieval Christian scholarship, only supplemented by Martianus Capella's *De nuptiis Mercurii et Philologiae* and Cassiodorus' *Institutiones*. The introduction of new techniques was limited to calendrical issues, until certain Christian monasteries became increasingly familiar with Arabic astronomy and astrology. This happened in the 10th and 11th centuries, when scholars such as Hermann the Lame (1013-1054; *De mensura astrolabii*) and Gerbert of Aurillac (940-1003, the later Pope Silvester II) introduced the Arabic art of using astrolabes into Christian culture.

3B. THE 12TH-CENTURY TRANSLATORS AND THEIR IMPACT

But it needed the effort of scholars from the 12th century to translate Arabic treatises into Latin and thus to provide a fair foundation for Christian experts to enter the discussion about astrology. Now, Ptolemy's works became available in Latin translations: the *Almagest* was translated anonymously in Sicily around 1160; Plato of Tivoli translated the *Tetrabiblos* in 1138 and the *Almagest* in 1160 (note Plato's order!); Gerhard of Cremona (c. 1114-1187) translated the *Almagest* in 1176. Two other translators of the time have already been mentioned: Hermann of Carinthia and John of Seville. The latter also wrote a short general treatise entitled *Epitome totius astrologiae* (The Epitome of All Astrology; ed. by Joachim Heller. Montani & Neuber: Nuremberg 1548); John's translation of the Arabic *watad* "peg" or "pin" into Latin *cuspis* was the origin of the English word "cusp" as designation of the point at the beginning of a celestial house.

In this overview, only a selection of important Christian authors who entered the stage in the 12th and 13th century can be discussed. An outstanding example of his age is Adelard of Bath (c. 1080-c. 1150), because he not only translated Arabic tables – his translation of a now lost book by al-Khwārismî (as *De numero Indorum*) is the closest to the original – and discussed the teachings of Abū Ma'shar but also wrote extensively on astrological magic and related topics. His *Ergaphalau* tackles the position of the science of the stars within a general division of knowledge and was probably meant to introduce a larger work on astrology (see Burnett 1987, 133-145).

Bernard Silvester wrote in 1147/48 an allegorical poem under the title of *Cosmographia*, which must be counted among the most important works of the high middle ages (today more than fifty manuscripts are still extant). The book, divided into *Megacosmos* and *Microcosmos*, adapts the teachings of Abū Ma'shar to a Christian context.

→ Michael Scot († 1235/6), who worked for the emperor Frederick II, translated al-Bitrujî's *De sphaera* (or *In astrologiam*) but was influential mainly due to his major work, *Liber introductorius* (Introductory book), which gives a history of astrology (from → Zoroaster to Gerbert of Aurillac) and provides his contemporaries with an extensive encyclopedic compendium of medieval knowledge about the science of the stars.

The Italian Guido Bonatti (Latin Bonatus, c. 1210-c. 1295) was perhaps the best known astrologer of the late Middle Ages. His comprehensive textbook *Liber introductorius ad iudicia stellarum* (Introduction to the Judgments of the Stars), written after his retirement from the court of emperor Frederick II, is a collection of ten separate treatises on various phases of astrology. It was printed as *Liber astronomicus* by Erhard Ratdolt, Augsburg, 1491. A contemporary of Bonatti's was Leopold of Austria, who wrote a compendium on astrology, *Compilatio Leupoldi ducatus Austrie filii de astrorum scientia* (Erhard Ratdolt: Augsburg, 1489).

→ Albertus Magnus' fame in matters astrological is based on his *Speculum astronomiae*. The "Mirror" does not only comprise a bibliography of books on astrology available at the end of the 13th century but also stands out as a highly sophisticated discussion of astrology in a scholastic context.

→ Roger Bacon accepts astrology as a valid science in his *Opus maius*, the shorter *Opus minor*, and in the *Opus tertium*, all of them being popular in the 13th century and influencing subsequent generations.

AAASLT: Francis J. Carmody, *Arabic Astronomical and Astrological Sciences in Latin Translation: A Critical Bibliography*, Berkeley & Los Angeles: University of California Press, 1956 ♦ CCAG: Franz Cumont et al. (ed.), *Catalogus Codicum Astrologorum Graecorum*, 12 vols., Brussels: Lamertin, 1898–1953 ♦ Manfred Ullmann, *Die Natur- und Geheimwissenschaften im Islam* (Handbuch der Orientalistik, Ergänzungsband VI, 2), Leiden: E.J. Brill, 1972 ♦ Fuat Sezgin, *Geschichte des arabischen Schrifttums VII: Astrologie – Meteorologie und Verwandtes bis ca. 430 H*, Leiden: E.J. Brill, 1979 ♦ Charles Coulston Gillispie & Frederic L. Holmes (eds. in chief), *Dictionary of Scientific Biography*, 18 vols., New York: Scribner, 1970-1990.
Individual authors: Abū Maʿshar: David Pingree, *The Thousands of Abū Maʿshar*, London: The Warburg Institute, 1968 ♦ David Pingree (ed.), *Albumasaris De revolutionibus nativitatum*, Leipzig: B.G. Teubner, 1968 ♦ Charles Burnett, Keiji Yamamoto & Michio Yano (eds./trans.), *Abū Maʿshar, The Abbreviation of the Introduction to Astrology*, Leiden: E.J. Brill, 1994 (includes the medieval Latin translation by Adelard of Bath) ♦ Abû Masar, *On Historical Astrology: The Book of Religions and Dynasties. On the Great Conjuctions* (Keiji Yatamoto and Charles Burnett, ed. and trans.), 2 vols., Leiden, Boston: E.J. Brill, 2000 ♦ *Albertus Magnus*: Stefano Caroti, Paola Zambelli et al. (eds.), *Alberto Magno, Speculum astronomiae*, Domus Galilaeana, 1977 ♦ *Al-Birūnî*: R. Ramsay Wright (trans.), *Abu'l-Rayhan Muhammad ibn Ahmad al-Biruni, The Book of Instruction in The Elements of The Art of Astrology*, London: Luzac & Co., 1934 ♦ *Albubather*: Demetrio Santos (trans.), *Albubather,*

Sobre las natividades, Barcelona: Edicomunicación, 1986 ♦ *Al-Mansūr*: Demetrio Santos (trans.), *Almazor, 150 proposiciones*, in: *Textos astrológicos*, Barcelona: Ed. Teorema, 1985 ♦ *Asim*: Ibn Asim, *Kitab al-anwa wa-l-azmina – Tratado sobre los anwa y los tiempos*, Arabic/Spanish, trans. and interpretation by Miguel Forcada Nogués, Barcelona: Consejo superior de Investigación y Ciencia, 1993 ♦ *Bernardus Silvestris*: Peter Dronke (ed.), *Bernardus Silvestris, Cosmographia* (Textus Minores 53), Leiden: E.J. Brill, 1978 ♦ *Bethen*: Demetrio Santos (trans.), *Bethen, Centiloquio*, in: *Textos astrológicos*, Barcelona: ed. Teorema, 1985 ♦ *Boethius*: Ludwig Bieler (ed.), *Anicii Manlii Severini Boethii Philosophiae Consolatio*, Turnhout: Brepols, 1957 ♦ *Bonatus*: Guido Bonatus, *The One Hundred and Forty-Six Considerations*, in: William Lilly (ed.), *The Astrologer's Guide* (1675), reprint London: Regulus, 1986 ♦ *Firmicus Maternus*: Wilhelm Kroll & Franz Skutsch (eds.), *Iulii Firmici Materni Matheseos Libri VIII*, Stuttgart: Teubner, 1968 ♦ *Haly Abenragel*: Escuela de Traductores de Sirventa (trans.), *Ali ben Ragel, El Libro Conplido en los iudizios de las Estrellas*, Barcelona: Indigo, 1997, see also the former edition from MS 3065 of the National Library in Madrid by Gerold Hilty (Madrid: Real Academia Española, 1954) ♦ *Hermann of Carinthia*: Charles Burnett (ed./trans.), *Hermann of Carinthia, De Essentiis: A Critical Edition with Translation and Commentary* (Studien und Texte zur Geistesgeschichte des Mittelalters, vol. XV), Leiden & Cologne: E.J. Brill, 1982 ♦ "Hermes": Demetrio Santos (trans.), *Hermes, Sobre las estrellas fijas*, in: *Textos astrológicos*, Barcelona: Ed. Teorema, 1985 ♦ Demetrio Santos (trans.), *Centiloquio*, in: *Textos astrológicos*, Barcelona: Ed. Teorema, 1985 ♦ *Abraham ibn Ezra*: Abraham ibn Ezra, *The Beginning of Wisdom*, trans. from the Hebrew by Rafael Levy & Francisco Cantera, Paris: Société d'édition "Les belles lettres", 1939 ♦ José Millás Vallicrosa (ed.), *Abraham ibn Ezra, El libro de los fundamentos de las Tablas astronómicas*, Madrid & Barcelona: Instituto Arias Montano, 1947 ♦ Raphael Levy, *The Astrological Works of Abraham Ibn Ezra*, Baltimore: The John Hopkins Press, 1927 ♦ *Isidore of Seville*: J.P. Migne (ed.), *Isidore of Seville, Ethymologiarum libri XX*, in: *Patrologia cursus completus, Series latinae*, vol. 82, 73ff., Turnhout: Brepols, 1969 ♦ *Raimundus Lullus*: Joan-Manuel Ballesta (trans.), *Ramón Llull, Tratado de Astrología*, Barcelona: Mercurio-3, 1991 ♦ *Maʿshallāh*: E.S. Kennedy & David Pingree (eds.), *The Astrological History of Māshāʾallāh*, Cambridge: Harvard University Press, 1971 ♦ Demetrio Santos (ed./trans.), *Messalah, Sobre la recepción de los planetas*, in: *Textos astrológicos medievales*, Madrid: Barath, 1981 ♦ David Pingree, *The Thousands of Abu Maʿshar*, London: The Warburg Institute, 1968 ♦ *Pietro d'Abano*: Graziella Federici-Vescovini (ed.), *Pietro d'Abano, Tradati di astronomia; Lucidator dubitabilium astronomiae; de motu octavae sphaerae et altre opere*, Padua: Programma, 1988 (1992²) ♦ *Ps.-Beda*: Charles Burnett (ed./trans.), *Ps.-Beda, De mundi celestis terrestrisque constitutione, A Treatise on the Universe and the Soul* (Warburg Institute Surveys and Texts 10), London: Warburg Institute, 1985.

Lit.: Elsmarie Anrich, *Groß Göttlich Ordnung: Thomas von Aquin – Paracelsus – Novalis und die Astrologie*, Tübingen: Hohenrain-Verlag, 1989 ♦ Francesco Barocelli & Graziella Federici-Vescovini (eds.), *Filosofia, scienza e astrologia nel Trecento europeo*, Padua: Poligrafo, 1992 ♦ Jean-François Bergier (ed.), *Zwischen Wahn, Glaube und Wissenschaft: Magie, Astrologie, Alchemie und Wissenschaftsgeschichte*, Zürich: Verlag der Fachvereine Zürich, 1988 ♦ Dieter Blume, *Regenten des Himmels: Astrologische Bilder in Mittelalter und Renaissance*, Berlin: Akademie Verlag, 2000 ♦ Emilie Boer, *Claudii Ptolemaei Opera quae extant omnia*, Leipzig: B.G. Teubner, 1961 ♦ Arno Borst, *Computus: Zeit und Zahl in der Geschichte Europas*, Berlin: Klaus Wagenbach, 1991 ♦ Arno Borst, *Die karolingische Kalenderreform*, Hannover: Hahnsche Buchhandlung, 1998 ♦ Arno Borst (ed.), *Der karolingische Reichskalender und seine Überlieferung bis ins 12. Jahrhundert*, Hannover: Hahnsche Buchhandlung, 2001 ♦ Rafael Gil Brand, *Lehrbuch der klassischen Astrologie*, Mössingen: Chiron Verlag, 2000 ♦ Charles Burnett (ed.), *Adelard of Bath: An English Scientist and Arabist of the Early Twelfth Century*, London: The Warburg Institute, 1987 ♦ Charles Burnett, *Magic and Divination in the Middle Ages: Texts and Techniques in the Islamic and Christian Worlds*, Aldershot & Brookfield: Variorum, 1996 ♦ Anna Caiozzo, *Images du ciel d'Orient au Moyen Âge: Une histoire du zodiaque et de ses représentations dans les manuscrits du Proche-Orient musulman*, Paris: Presses de l'Université de Paris-Sorbonne, 2003 ♦ Francis J. Carmody, *Arabic Astronomical and Astrological Sciences in Latin Translation: A Critical Bibliography*, Berkeley & Los Angeles: University of California Press, 1956 ♦ Patrick Curry (ed.), *Astrology, Science and Society: Historical Essays*, Woodbridge & Wolfeboro: The Boydell Press, 1987 ♦ Kurt Flasch & Udo Reinhold Jeck (eds.), *Das Licht der Vernunft: Die Anfänge der Aufklärung im Mittelalter*, München: C.H. Beck, 1997 ♦ Edward Grant, *The Foundations of Modern Science in the Middle Ages: Their Religious, Institutional, and Intellectual Contexts*, Cambridge: Cambridge University Press, 1996 ♦ Edward Grant (ed.), *A Source Book in Medieval Science*, Cambridge: Harvard University Press, 1974 ♦ Jacques Halbronn, *Le monde juif et l'astrologie: Histoire d'un vieux couple*, Milano: Archè, 1986 ♦ Charles Homer Haskins, *Studies in the History of Mediaeval Science*, Cambridge: Harvard University Press, 1927 ♦ James Herschel Holden, *A History of Horoscopic Astrology: From the Babylonian Period to the Modern Age*, Tempe: American Federation of Astrologers, 1996 ♦ Wolfgang Hübner, *Zodiakus Christianus: Jüdisch-Christliche Adaptationen des Tierkreises von der Antike bis zur Gegenwart*, Königstein: Hain, 1983 ♦ Richard Lemay, *Abu Ma'shar and Latin Aristotelianism in the Twelfth Century: The Recovery of Aristotle's Natural Philosophy through Arabic Astrology*, Beirut: The Catholic Press, 1962 ♦ Uta Lindgren, *Gerbert von Aurillac und das Quadrivium: Untersuchungen zur Bildung im Zeitalter der Ottonen* (Sudhoffs Archiv, Beiheft 18), Wiesbaden: Franz Steiner, 1976 ♦ Jean Marquès-Rivière, *Amulettes, talismans et pantacles dans les traditions orientales et occidentales*, Paris: Payot, 1938 ♦ Mark D. Meyerson & Edward D. English, *Christians, Muslims, and Jews in Medieval and Early Modern Spain: Interaction and Cultural Change*, Notre Dame: University of Notre Dame Press, 2000 ♦ John North, *The Fontana History of Astronomy and Cosmology*, Hammersmith, London: Fontana, 1994 ♦ Agostino Paravicini Bagliani, *Le Speculum Astronomiae: Une énigme? Enquête sur les manuscrits*, Sismel, Florence: Ed. del Galluzzo, 2001 ♦ Vivian E. Robson, *The Fixed Stars and Constellations in Astrology*, Philadelphia: J.B. Lippincott, 1931³ ♦ Julio Samsó, *Islamic Astronomy and Medieval Spain*, Aldershot & Brookfield: Variorum, 1994 ♦ Fuat Sezgin, *Geschichte des arabischen Schrifttums VII: Astrologie – Meteorologie und Verwandtes bis ca. 430 H*, Leiden: E.J. Brill, 1979 ♦ Henri Stierlin, *Astrologie und Herrschaft: Von Platon bis Newton*, Frankfurt a.M.: Athenäum, 1988 ♦ Kocku von Stuckrad, *Geschichte der Astrologie: Von den Anfängen bis zur Gegenwart*, München: C.H. Beck, 2003 ♦ S. Jim Tester, *A History of Western Astrology*, Woodbridge & Wolfeboro: The Boydell Press, 1987 ♦ Lynn Thorndike, *A History of Magic and Experimental Science*, 8 vols., New York: Columbia University Press, 1923–1958 ♦ idem, "The Latin Translations of the Astrological Works by Messahala", in: *Osiris* 12 (1956): 49-72 ♦ Pinella Travaglia, *Magic, Causality and Intentionality: The Doctrine of Rays in al-Kindi*, Sismel, Florence: Ed. del Galluzzo, 1999 ♦ Manfred Ullmann, *Die Natur- und Geheimwissenschaften im Islam* (Handbuch der Orientalistik, Ergänzungsband VI, 2), Leiden: E.J. Brill, 1972 ♦ Nicolas Weill-Parot, *Les "images astrologiques" au Moyen Âge et à la Renaissance: Spéculations intellectuelles et pratiques magiques (XIIᵉ–XVᵉ siècle)*, Paris: Honoré Champion, 2002 ♦ Paola Zambelli, *The Speculum Astronomiae and Its Enigma: Astrology, Theology and Science in Albertus Magnus and his Contemporaries*, Dordrecht etc.: Kluwer Academic Publishers, 1992.

KOCKU VON STUCKRAD

Astrology IV: 15th-19th Century

A. HISTORY

Throughout the Renaissance period, learned astrology enjoyed a flowering that did not fade until the end of the 17th century. The centers of this movement were the courts and the universities, where astrological studies developed in relation to those of astronomy and medicine. Essential to astrology's development were the multiple centers of Italy's political, cultural, and artistic life. At the University of Ferrara, Giovanni Bianchini (born in the first decade of the 15th century) taught and authored important astronomical tables. Also at Ferrara was Lucas Gauricus (1475-1558), whose inaugural lecture of 1507, *De astronomiae seu astrologiae inventoribus*, countered the anti-astrological theses of → Giovanni Pico della Mirandola.

Gauricus also taught at Bologna, spent time in Mantua, Rome, and Venice, and in Germany came into contact with the Wittenberg group. He was the author of a weighty series of works, among them a famous *Tractatus astrologicus* (1552), and was named Bishop of Civitate by Pope Paul III, whose pontificate he had predicted. At the Este court in Ferrara there was also Pellegrino Prisciani, counsellor of Prince Borso and inspirer of the astrological program illustrated circa 1470 by the frescoes of the Hall of the Months in Schifanoia Palace.

At the University of Bologna, astrology was practiced by Domenico Maria Novara, the teacher of Copernicus; by Gauricus; and by the mathematician and astronomer Johannes Antonius Magini (1555-1617), author of astronomical tables and of a comprehensive exposition of all astrology. At Mantua, Bartolomeo Manfredi was active, author of the *Libro del Perché*. In Tuscany under the Medici, Lorenzo Bonincontri (1410-1491) worked, teaching astrology there before moving to Rome, where he was summoned by Pope Sixtus IV, and published a commentary on Manilius in 1484. At Padua teachers included Valentin Nabod and Andrea Argoli, who was named Knight of Saint Mark by the Republic of Venice for his excellence as an astrologer, and was the teacher of Giambattista Zenno, the future astrologer of Wallenstein. At Milan, astrology was in great repute under the Sforza, especially Ludovico il Moro who was accustomed to shower his astrologers with gifts. At Rome, many popes were patrons of astrology, from Pius II (who publicly praised the predictions of Biagio da Cremona) through Sixtus IV (who had his privy astrologer in Bishop Paul of Middelburg), Leo X (who in 1520 instituted a chair of astrology at the University), and Paul III (whose personal astrologer was the Fleming, Albert Pigghe). At Naples, Bonincontri was long resident, called "nobilis astrologus" by Giovanni Pontano (1426-1503), the great humanist who was also devoted to astrology and treated its themes in his *De rebus coelestibus* and in his short poem *Urania*.

Spreading out from Italy, astrology enjoyed great success throughout Europe. At the French court, where Charles V the Wise (1364-1380) had founded an institution named after his astrologer "Collège de Maître Gervais", Louis XI (1461-1483) employed Galeotti and Angelo Catti; Simon de Pharès (1440-1495), author of the *Recueil des plus célèbres astrologues et de quelques hommes doctes*, was astrologer to Charles VIII; Cosma Ruggeri was in the service of Catherine de' Medici, who also used the services of Michel de Nostradamus (1503-1566) and Francesco Giuntini (1523-1580).

Catherine entrusted the education of her youngest son to Giuntini, a Florentine Carmelite and author of a monumental *Speculum astronomiae*. Antoine Mizauld (1510-1578), physician and astrologer, worked under Marguerite de Valois; Morin de Villefranche (1583-1650) was protected by Marie de' Medici and by the cardinals Richelieu and Mazarin.

Italian astrology was also welcomed in the German-speaking world. The Habsburgs were adepts and patrons of it: Frederick III (1440-1493) was constantly surrounded by astrologers, among them Johann Lichtenberger; it was for Maximilian I that Albrecht Dürer engraved the celebrated *Melencolia I*. Ferdinand I had the horoscope of his firstborn, the future Emperor Maximilian II, drawn up by the astrologer and historian Joseph Grünpeck. Charles V's astrology master was Petrus Apianus, and it was said that his decision to abdicate was connected with the appearance of the comet of 1555. Maximilian II patronized the astrologer Cyprian Leowitz (1524-1574), among others; → Rudolf II employed Tycho Brahe and Kepler. Teaching at the University of Vienna were the humanist and astrologer Georg Peuerbach (1433-1461), whose pupils included Johann Müller, called Regiomontanus (1436-1475), an astronomer-astrologer and the first publisher of a printed edition of Manilius; Stabius, who dedicated to the Emperor an astrolabe called *Horoscopion universale*; Martin Pegius, to whom is due the first astrological treatise in the German language, published in Basel, 1570; Petrus Apianus, author of a long treatise *Astronomicum Caesareum*, dedicated to Charles V; Johann Stoeffler, author of almanacs and ephemerides. Stoeffler's pupil Johann Schöner (1477-1547) was known as Carlostadius, and in 1545 published a great astrological opus with a preface by Melanchthon. Around Melanchthon at the University of Wittenberg there was an active group of astrologers including Schöner, Caspar Peucer (1525-1602), and Caro, who were also involved in the vexed question of Luther's horoscope, first calculated by Lucas Gauricus.

In the Low Countries, astrology was cultivated mainly at the University of Louvain, where Johannes Stadius (1527-1579) calculated the annual ephemerides from 1554 to 1606 and proposed a system of houses different from that of Regiomontanus; and at the University of Leiden, where Joseph Justus Scaliger (1540-1609) taught, author of a large commentary on Manilius. Learned astrology was less fortunate in England, where it was practiced without much renown in the 16th century by Leonard Digges and → John Dee; in

1603, Sir Christopher Heydon wrote *A defense of judiciary Astrology*. In contrast, during the 17th century worldly astrology was much used in England, especially in relation to political events. The chief exponent of this tendency was William Lilly (1602-1682), author of *Christian Astrology* (1647) and an outstanding expert on horary astrology.

Worldly astrology is the aspect of learned astrology that most leans toward popular astrology, which in the era of printing gave rise to a vast production of predictions, annual prognostications, almanacs, calendars, lunaries, and books of popular astrological medicine, often printed in many thousands of copies. Some of these genera were also cultivated by important astrologers, e.g. the prognostications of Lucas Gauricus and Girolamo Cardan (1501-1576). Paul of Middelburg's predictions of 1486 were especially popular: repeated in 1488 by Johann Lichtenberger, they treated the effects of the great conjunction observed in the sign of Scorpio on November 25, 1484. This conjunction was interpreted as announcing the proximate appearance of a false prophet and of a religion of great sanctity, which would lead to new laws suppressing the privileges of the nobility and succoring the miseries of the populace. This was taken in contrary ways by Protestants and Catholics, as the former saw Luther as the renovator, the latter as the false prophet. In this way, astrological prediction using the technique of the great conjunctions, favored by the Arab and late medieval astrologers, became linked with Christian prophetism, presenting itself as a tool for pinpointing the dates of the great events announced by biblical prophecies. Thus astrology took on a role of politico-religious agitation, as exemplified by the prophecy of Antonio Arquati *De eversione Europae* (1480); the predictions of the universal Flood, the first of them formulated at the end of the 15th century by J. Stoeffler, connected with the great conjunction in Pisces of 1524; the periodical diffusion of predictions relating to the death of popes and the election of their successors. This type of prediction was restricted in Catholic lands by the inclusion of astrological texts in the *Index librorum prohibitorum* of 1558, and by the papal bulls *Coeli et Terrae* (Sixtus V, 1586) and *Inscrutabilis* (Urban VIII, 1631). In contrast, from the second half of the 16th century astrology flourished in reformed Europe, even though Luther had regarded it with some scepticism, and Calvin had opposed it. Important astronomers such as Tycho Brahe continued to cultivate it, even in its predictive and prophetic modes.

Humanist philology contributed to the development of Renaissance astrology by discovering ancient texts unknown to the Middle Ages. There was Manilius's *Astronomicon*, found in 1417 by Poggio Bracciolini in the library of the Convent of St. Gall and first printed in Regiomontanus's edition of 1472. Humanism also caused the printing of new and more accurate editions of ancient, Arabic, and medieval texts, such as the *Mathesis* of Firmicus Maternus, printed in Venice in 1499; the *Opus continens X tractatus astronomiae* of Guido Bonatti, published in 1489; the *Tabulae astronomicae* of Alfonso of Castile (Venice 1492); the *Sphaera mundi* of Giovanni Sacrobosco (Venice 1478); the *Compilatio de astrorum Scientia* by Leopold, son of the Duke of Austria (Venice 1489); also Porphyry's Introduction to Ptolemy (Basel 1559), the Commentary on Ptolemy attributed to Proclus (Basel 1554), Arab astrological writings, the *Concordantia* of → Pierre d'Ailly (Augsburg 1490), and texts by → Peter of Abano.

Most importantly, the new translations of Ptolemy's *Tetrabiblos* (in Latin, *Quadripartitum*) and of the pseudo-Ptolemaic *Centiloquium* followed the principles of humanist philology in being no longer made from Arabic versions, but directly from the Greek. The first two books of the *Tetrabiblos* were translated by Joachim Camerarius (Nuremberg 1535), and a complete translation by Antonio Gogava (Louvain 1548) was followed by two more complete editions: one by Camerarius and the second by Melanchthon (printed Basel 1553). The *Centiloquium* was published in Naples in 1512 with a commentary by Pontano, and at Venice by Lucas Gauricus in 1542, using the translation of George of Trebizond. The reformist current of 16th-century astrology was due to these translations, as it tried to include in the humanist *restitutio litterarum* the rediscovery of the authentic nature of Ptolemaic astrology, considered as the highest expression of the art in antiquity. Thus Ptolemy became the tutelary divinity of a trend of study dedicated to purging astrology of Arab superstitions, recovering its genuine nature and removing any magical temptations. This trend found its greatest exponent in Girolamo Cardan (1501-1576) and spread all over Europe, numbering among its proponents the Italians Giovanni Pontano and Agostino Nifo (1473-1546), the Fleming Pigghe, and the German scholars gathered around Melanchthon at Wittenberg. At Paris there were Gervais Mastallerus of Breisgau, active at the College of Beauvais, and, to an extent, Pontus de Tyard. The Ptolemaic *Tetrabiblos* was the subject of many important commentaries. Beside that of Melanchthon, there were those published by Schöner in 1529, by Cardan in 1554, by Johann

Gartze, called Garcaeus (1530-1575) in 1576, by Conrad Rauchfuss, called Dasypodius, in 1578, by Giuntini in 1581, and the ones that remained in manuscript by Ristori and Nabod.

On the technical level, the exponents of the "Ptolemaic" current of astrology in the 16th and 17th centuries kept to the basic procedures of the art as codified in late antique astrology, as far as the theory of the planets, signs, houses, and aspects was concerned. This resulted in the abandonment of many of the references by astrologers who had written in Arabic, contemptuously defined by Cardan and → Campanella as *nugae araborum*, and a widespread revisioning of the technique of the great conjunctions. The latter, especially in Albumasar's version, had already been called into question by medieval astrologers like Ibn Ezra, and fiercely criticized in the most famous anti-astrological work of the Renaissance, the *Disputationes adversus astrologiam divinatricem* by Giovanni Pico della Mirandola (1496). The reference to an untrustworthy parameter such as mean planetary motion gradually disappeared, as did the use of the theory during the prediction of historical events. Astrologers began to place genethliac astrology and the examination of the individual nativity at the center of their studies, drawn on square-shaped diagrams and regularly reproduced in collections of natal horoscopes, which were very popular in this era.

New developments appeared in the procedure of setting up the houses (domification), absent in Ptolemy and mainly practiced by Arab astrologers such as al-Qabisi. The most important innovations in this field, discussed by the Flemish astrologer Gemma Frisius in his *De astrolabio catholico* (Antwerp 1556), were linked to domification *rationalis*, i.e., on a strictly geometrical basis, proposed by Regiomontanus, already delineated in a different version by John Campanus of Novara (1223-1296), and taken up at the end of the 13th century by Leo Hebraeus (Levi ben Gerson), and to domification *naturalis*, connected with the conception of astrology as an aspect of natural philosophy, proposed by Cardan and Magini and codified in the later 17th century by the Olivetian monk Placidus Titi (1603-1668). As for the so-called astronomical revolution, it did not in the least call astrological studies into question: they adopted a representation of the heavens in geocentric perspective, but were not necessarily connected with the geocentric system of the universe. Not by chance, many of the protagonists of the new astronomy also cultivated astrological studies, from G. J. von Lauchen, called Rheticus, to Coper-

nicus himself, and from Tycho to Kepler. Galileo in a letter to Dini, Kepler in *Tertius interveniens*, and Campanella in the *Astrologicorum libri* emphasized the independence of astrology from geocentricity and heliocentricity alike. What did take account of the new developments in astronomy were those fundamental tools of astrological work, the tables and ephemerides. The first to use the Copernican scheme in them was E. Reinhold, with the *Tabulae prutenicae* (1551). Francesco Giuntini embraced the planetary motions both from the geocentric point of view in the *Tabulae alphonsinae*, and following the heliocentric scheme of Copernicus. Henri de Boulainvillier proposed the use of planetary positions in heliocentric perspective in a book on practical astrology of 1701. Finally, logarithms, invented in 1619, were soon employed in astrological calculation: Kepler used them in 1624, and Bonaventura Cavalieri in *Nova pratica astrologica de far le direttioni . . . per via di logaritmi* (1639).

On the philosophical level, the Ptolemaic stream of astrology during the 16th and 17th centuries saw a revival of that linkage between astrological techniques and Aristotelian natural philosophy which Ptolemy himself had first sketched out. On this point, and also in its rejection of many Arab procedures, this orientation contrasted with the interpretation of astrology in a Platonic and Hermetic key, which found its archetype in the second book of *De occulta philosophia* (1533) by → Cornelius Agrippa of Nettesheim, himself indebted to important astrological pages of → Marsilio Ficino. While for Cardan, astrology formed a part of natural philosophy, for Agrippa it appeared as an instrument for penetrating the web of analogies that links the elementary world, the celestial world, and the divine world. This order of ideas was taken up by → Paracelsus (1493-1541) and → Robert Fludd (1574-1637) in their respective ways. Johannes Kepler (1571-1630) distanced himself from both of them, being a radical critic of Fludd's fantastic mathematics and at the same time reviving the Platonic idea of the cosmos as a perfectly ordered whole, created and directed by a spiritual principle through which everything is made according to harmonious geometrical proportions. On this basis, Kepler's theory of planetary aspects equated to the concords and discords in music (explained both in *Misterium cosmographicum* and in *Harmonices mundi*) constitutes one of the most relevant technical innovations of astrology in the modern age.

While Kepler's innovations found little response among astrologers, the welding of the procedures of the art and a natural philosophy of traditionally Aristotelian stamp was proposed again in the last two great *summae* of 17th-century astrology: the *Physiomathematica sive Coelestis philosophia* (1675) of Placido Titi, Professor of Mathematics at the University of Pavia, and the *Astrologia gallica* (1661) in 26 books by Jean Baptiste Morin (1583-1656), Professor of Mathematics at the Collège de France. Placido's work presented astrology as a natural science, assuming that all the significative factors used in it were purely physical realities defined after the categories of Aristotelian physics. In Morin's work, the *Primum mobile* was identified as the primary physical foundation of every event; the zodiac was linked to it, to whose signs a fixed meaning was ascribed on the basis of the planets that governed them in the supposed horoscope of the world. On this point Morin rejected → Campanella's opinion, which held that the zodiacal signs, representing the stations of the sun's course, should be assigned reversed meanings for births in the southern hemisphere.

In much of learned Europe at the end of the 17th century, natural philosophy was becoming linked more and more closely to the mechanistic image of the physical universe, of which René Descartes' work provided one of the most influential versions. The new climate rendered ever less credible the philosophical references to which much of modern astrology was bound, as witness the long and resentful polemic between Morin and Pierre Gassendi, and writings such as those of the astronomer Giovanni Montanari, *L'astrologia convinta di falso col mezzo di nuove esperienza e ragioni fisico-astronomiche* (Venice 1685). This set off a crisis in learned astrology, which was marked by the increase of prohibitions not only against the practice, but also the study of the discipline. In 1666, Colbert prohibited the Academicians from pursuing it; after 1670, astrology was no longer taught at the University. In 1682, Louis XIV extended the ban on astrological calendars to the whole of France; a *Reichstagsabscheid* of 1699 did likewise for the Germanic world. In 1708, in his report to the Académie des Sciences, Bianchini called the planisphere a testimony to human folly; in 1756, an ordinance of Maria Teresa of Austria banned astrological predictions and superstitious conjectures. In the Age of Enlightenment, astrology became ever more alien to cultivated circles: D'Alembert and Diderot's *Encyclopédie* defined it as unworthy of consideration by a man of reason. Voltaire was of the same opinion, as was the archaeologist Charles Dupuis, who equated astrol-

ogy with superstition in his three-volume work *Origine de tous les cultes* (1794).

In reaction to the excesses of a schematic rationalism, the secret societies reconsidered the motives of the Platonic-Hermetizing astrology of the 16th and 17th centuries. During the 18th century, these societies brought about a Hermetic revival with Neoplatonic and Gnostic elements; but astrology was not practiced among them, only studied from a symbolic point of view as an ethical and philosophical doctrine. The *Opus mago-cabbalisticum et theosophicum* (1735) of → Georg von Welling can be ascribed to this kind of orientation, while → Goethe's *Wilhelm Meister* also seems to acknowledge a symbolic and Hermetizing astrology. Goethe opened his own memoirs, *Dichtung und Wahrheit*, with an examination and commentary on his own natal horoscope. The interest in astrology also found a place in German → Romanticism, with a revival of its more strictly technical aspects. The most important exponent of this trend was Wilhelm Andreas Pfaff (1774-1835), who in an essay of 1816 entitled *Astrology* thus described the state of the art: 'Ignored, rejected, abandoned, the most ancient relative of heaven-dedicated Urania, that is, astrology, seeks to regain its own native land and its place among the sciences presided over by the Muses'. To Pfaff also is due a German translation of Ptolemy's *Tetrabiblos* (1822-23), which followed that which the celebrated astronomer J.C. Bode had published in 1795.

The spread of positivism stifled the incipient revival of astrological studies in almost the whole of Europe, with the marked exception of England, where at the same time as Pfaff's edition J. Ashmand had translated the *Tetrabiblos* into English, with an epigraph from Lord Byron and a dedication to Walter Scott. However, three editions of Ptolemy already existed in English: those of J. Whalley (1701), M. Sibly and J. Browne (1786), and J. Wilson (1820), while John Cooper had translated Titi's *Physiomathematica*. Using as its basic reference-points the texts of Ptolemy and Titi, English astrology developed throughout the century with close attention to the technical aspects of the discipline and to its empirical control. This direction differed from that of the esoteric astrology connected with the → Theosophical Society, founded in 1875, whose principal exponents were Sepharial and Alan Leo. From 1800 onwards, annual ephemerides were published under the title *Raphael's Ephemeris*. Among the new treatises on astrology in English were John Wilson, *Complete Dictionary of Astrology* (1819); John Worsdale,

Celestial philosophy or genethliacal Astrology (1824); Raphael (pseudonym of R.C. Smith), *Manual of Astrology*; Zadkiel (pseudonym of Lieut. Morrison), *Grammar of Astrology* (1834). Morrison founded in 1860 the Astrometeorological Society, and held that in genethliacal astrology the planets were to be considered as causes, but in horary astrology as signifiers. Zadkiel II (pseudonym of Alfred John Pearce) wrote *The Science of the Stars* (1881) and *Textbook of Astrology* (1897); George Wilde, *A Treatise of Natal Astrology* (1894). The latter work carried an Introduction by R. Garnett, librarian of the British Museum, who under the pseudonym of A.G. Trent distinguished astrology from theosophy, maintaining that 'Astrology is a physical and verifiable science or it is nothing'. The frequent use of pseudonyms by astrological authors is an evident symptom of the difficulty encountered by the discipline in getting legitimized in the eyes of the learned.

The same phenomenon was common in French culture of the late 19th century, in which astrology was cultivated mainly within the secret societies. Its principal representatives were the Abbé Constant, who wrote under the pseudonym of → Eliphas Levi, and the physician Gérard Encausse, who wrote as → Papus. In 1888 Papus launched the journal *L'Initiation*, while the occultist Eugène Jacob published under the pseudonym of Ely Star a work of Kabbalistic astrology, *Les mystères de l'horoscope*. At the end of the century, astrology began to attract the interest of astronomers such as C. Flammarion (who furnished a Preface to Jacob's work) and Père Nicoullaud, who in 1897 published under the pseudonym of Fomalhaut a *Manuel d'astrologie sphérique et judiciare*. The astrologer → F.C. Barlet and the bookseller-publisher Paul Chacornac became the masters of a new generation of students, including H. Selva and Paul Choisnard, who were also interested in the problem of the statistical control of the results of astrological work, along a direction of research destined to expand during the 20th century.

B. LITERATURE

The subdivision and ranking of the various branches of astrological study in the late Middle Ages followed the example of the *Speculum astronomiae*, attributed to → Albertus Magnus and inspired by Arabic models. This was radically altered in the Renaissance era, thanks to the rediscovery of the classics of ancient astrology, such as the astrological poem of Manilius; the fresh circulation of texts that had been little read in the Middle Ages, such as Firmicus Maternus's *Mathesis*; and above all the rediscovery of the true nature of Ptolemy's astrology. The latter was to be found in four books that have entered history under the name *Tetrabiblos* (in Latin, *Quadripartitum*), and which were now translated directly from the Greek.

The return to Antiquity that characterized the age of Humanism affected astrological culture essentially in the form of a return to ancient astrology, and especially to Ptolemy, prince of astrologers. An example of Ptolemy's changed role is the course followed by Girolamo Cardan, the great philosopher, mathematician, and physician. His father had set him on the path of astrological study *iuxta araborum principia* (after the principles of the Arabs), but then Cardan read the integral translation of the *Tetrabiblos*. This caused him to reorient his own studies, freeing himself from the *nugae araborum* and setting himself to write a detailed commentary on Ptolemy.

A new image of astrology now entered circulation, different from the medieval one: a technically more rigorous study, using the precise and sophisticated tools of astronomical mathematics, and ready to re-evaluate and, if need be, to discard formerly sacrosanct references and procedures. The first change was the individualization of the object of study, and the description of the relations between its internal members. The Middle Ages had understood astrology as a kind of knowledge intermediate between cosmology and natural philosophy, mainly oriented towards general events, both natural and historical; at the center of attention were the techniques of worldly astrology, often in the spectacular but debatable form of Albumasar's theory of the great conjunctions. Genethliacal examination, focusing on the drawing-up and analysis of individual horoscopes or birth-charts, had seemed a specialized and less relevant application of worldly astrology. Now this ranking was reversed. From the start of the Renaissance era, genethliacal astrology reclaimed its ancient primacy, together with an increased interest in techniques connected with divination and → magic, such as interrogations and elections. Interrogations would find their great new interpreter in the Englishman William Lilly, but Cardan tended to substitute for them procedures that answered questions on the basis of a chart drawn up not (as in the classical technique) for the moment at which the question was posed, but for the questioner's moment of birth. This type of questioning thus also fell within the field of genethlialogy. As for elections, closely connected with forms of astral magic, they found their place mainly in texts devoted to magic, such as *De occulta philosophia* (1533) by → Cornelius Agrippa, or connected with magic in various ways, such as → Tommaso Campanella's *De siderali fato vitando*.

Among the types of astrological literature that continued in a more medieval style, on the frontier between learned and popular astrology, were the calendars. These were full of astronomical, astrological, and liturgical information, explaining in simplified form the symbolism of planets and signs, and adding advice about agriculture and the conduct of life. In the same category were the annual prognostications, sometimes by illustrious astrologers such as Lorenzo Bonincontri, who published them for the years 1484-1491, and Cardan himself; the *Practicae*; and the predictions, both meteorological and prophetic, which determined the astrological procedures suitable for pinpointing the dates of the prophetic events. This category includes the predictions of Lichtenberger (who influenced Paul of Middelburg) regarding the effects of the great conjunction of 1484, and the numerous ones – 135 at least – about the epochal significance of the 1524 alignment of six planets in Pisces, mostly understood as announcing an imminent universal flood. Into this literature flowed the heritage of medieval conjunction lore, also present in Tycho Brahe but used ever more cautiously by astrologers. Already the object of criticism by medieval astrologers such as Ibn Ezra, and of a particularly fierce polemic by → Giovanni Pico della Mirandola, it was refuted, or at least revised, by Lucio Bellanti (*De astrologica veritate*, 1498), Agostino Nifo (*De nostrarum calamitatum causis*, 1505; *De falsa diluvii prognosticatione*, 1524), Pedro Ciruelo (*Apotelesmata astrologiae Christianae*, 1521), Cyprian Leowitz (*De coniunctionibus magnis*, 1564), and Johannes Kepler (*Discorso sulla grande congiunzione*, 1623). On the borderlines between astrology, prophecy, and esotericism falls the visionary work of Michel Nostradamus (1503-1560), very much criticized by the strict Ptolemaic astrologers, and famous for an edition of his *Quatrains* published in Lyon, 1555, in which there seems to be a description of the unusual death of Henri II, killed in a tournament in 1559, with surprising circumstantial detail (though a similar prediction had been made by Lucas Gauricus in 1552).

There has been much emphasis on the role in the history of astrology played by Giovanni Pico della Mirandola's *Disputationes* (1494). This monumental work in twelve books is a true *summa* of the late-medieval anti-astrological polemic, whose arguments were drawn on by Girolamo Savonarola for his *Tractato contra li astrologi*. Pico's work was certainly discussed at length by astrologers, and many of them wrote replies and refutations of it, from Pontano (*De rebus coelestibus*, 1519) to Bellanti (*De astrologica veritate*, 1498), from Cardan to Kepler. However, its impact on astrological studies from the Renaissance to the modern age came not so much from its arguments (which in the technical part of the work had simply amplified and radicalized doubts and objections already present among astrologers), as from the contact with the ancient sources of the discipline, and from a new vision of the tasks and methods of research, and of technical developments within the art. We have mentioned the role of the *Tetrabiblos*, which in the 15th century was translated directly from the Greek, in an edition of the first two books (translated by Camerarius) in 1535, then in a complete translation by Antonio Gogava in 1548. This work played a fundamental role in opening new perspectives for the discipline. It created a totally new image in which genethlialogy played the major part, while smaller parts were allotted to the procedures outside it. Interrogations, elections, and the conjunctions beloved of the Middle Ages gave way to a more sober worldly astrology, resembling that of the Greek master. The new general treatises on astrology often took the form of commentaries on Ptolemy, which became almost a literary genre in itself. An unpublished commentary by Conrad Herngartner dates back to the 15th century; the commentary by the Italian humanist and physician Giorgio Valla (1430-1499) was printed in Venice, 1502; Lucas Gauricus's *Paraphrases et annotationes* in 1539; Cardan's very important *Commentaria* in 1554; Conrad Rauchfuss's *Scholia in Claudii Ptolemaei quatuor libros Apotelesmaticos* in 1578; Francesco Giuntini's commentaries in 1581; Andrea Argoli's *Ptolomaeus parvus* in 1652; Placido Titi's commentary in 1658. Other commentators on Ptolemy were Nabod, Ristori, and Fantoni. As for the *Centiloquium*, that was the object of a commentary by Giovanni Pontano in 1512, and by Gauricus in 1540, who edited it from George of Trebizond's translation; however, doubts were beginning to form about the authenticity of this text, whose chief spokesman was Cardan. There was a great number of general expositions of the material, among the most important of which were *Tractatus praeclarissimus* (1514) by John of Glogau; *Enarratio elementorum astrologiae* (1560) by Valentin Nabod; *Astrologiae methodus* (1576) by Garcaeus; *Astrologicorum libri* (1629) by Tommaso Campanella; *Tractatus astrologicus* (1633) by Henry Rantzau; *Astrologia naturalis* (1645) by Dost von Glatz (Origanus); *Isagoge in Astrologiam* by Giovanni Antonio Magini; *Astrologia gallica* (1666) by J.B. Morin; *Physiomatematica* (1675) by Placido Titi. More typical of this era were the treatises devoted specifically to genethlialogy, sometimes virtual horoscope collections, such as *De iudiciis nativitatum* (1545) by J. Schöner; *Tractatus astrologicus* (1552) by Gauricus, which appeared in Italian the previous year; *Brevis et perspicua ratio iudicandi* (1558) by Leowitz; *Tractatus Astrologiae judiciariae de nativitatibus* (1540) by Gauricus; *Tractatus astrologicus* (1633) by the Danish nobleman Rantzau; *Liber de exemplis centum geniturarum* (1547) and *Liber duodecim geniturarum* (1554) by Cardan. The texts were increasingly illustrated with nativities, especially of famous men, with the object of confirming the worth of genethlialogy and of showing that the well-known events of their lives were in accordance with the astrological diagnosis.

From the middle of the 15th to the end of the 17th century, the Ptolemaic revival conferred on astrology, in the eyes of astrologers themselves, the character of a rational and coherent discipline, and moved the center of debate from the question, so much discussed in the Middle Ages, of its compatibility with Christian doctrine to that of its epistemological status and its position within the world of learning. It is not surprising that these two centuries saw the intensive production throughout Europe of a technical literature aimed at furnishing astrologers with the indispensable tools of their trade, which are ephemerides and the various types of tables. Among the most famous books of ephemerides are the *Tabulae astronomiae* or *Canones super Tabulas*, compiled in the middle of the 15th century by Giovanni Bianchini on the basis of the Alfonsine Tables, and printed in Venice in 1495 by Simone Bevilacqua, with a dedication to Lionello d'Este; *Tabulae prutenicae* (1551) by E. Reinhold; *Teoricae novae planetarum*, written in 1454 by Georg Peurbach, who revised Bianchini's tables by comparing them with Alfonsine ones; *Ephemerides novae* (1556) by J. Stadius; *Ephemeridum novum atque insigne opus* (1557) by Leowitz; *Ephemerides* (1582) by G.A. Magini; *Tabulae Rudolphinae*, with a *Sportula* for the astrologers, by Kepler. Among tables of other kinds were *Tabulae directionum* (1467) by Regiomontanus; *Tabulae bergenses* (1568) by Stadius; *Tabulae primi mobilis* (1609) by Magini.

The debate over the procedure of domification (division of houses) was very relevant at this time,

not least with regard to the various images of astrology current within the art. In the 13th century the geometrician Giovanni Campanus had proposed a system of houses *modo aequalis*, based on dividing the vertical into equal segments. At the end of the 15th century there was a revival by Regiomontanus and Schöner of domification *rationalis*, already proposed by Ibn Ezra, based on the division of the celestial equator. Cardan, in *De exemplis centum geniturarum* (1547) had adopted the equal method in a version considered to derive from Ptolemy, based on the division of the zodiac into equal segments; later he accepted the rational method, and finally returned to the equal one. Leowitz spoke for the rational procedure (*Brevis et perspicua ratio judicandi genituras ex physicis causis*, 1558). Magini adopted another method, again "in the manner of Ptolemy", based on the trisection of the diurnal arc. Finally Placido Titi proposed a "natural" system of houses that was not geometrical, with a proportional division of the diurnal and nocturnal arcs, in which each division corresponds to two hours of time. This is the Placidus method, still in use.

The panorama of 15th-17th-century astrological literature would be incomplete without mention of the many texts of astrological medicine that punctuate it. In them the ancient doctrine of zodiacal and planetary "melothesia" was revived for diagnostic and therapeutic purposes, following the most diffuse of → Marsilio Ficino's writings, the *De vita libri tres* (1489). The theory of critical days was very much used for studying the course and cure of illnesses. It was explained in texts such as *De diebus decretoriis* by Gauricus; *De ratione et usu dierum criticorum* (1555) by T. Bodier; *Amicus medicorum* (1614) by Jean Ganivet; *De astrologica ratione ac usu Dierum Criticorum* (1607) by Magini; *De diebus criticis* (1639) by Andrea Argoli; *De diebus decretoriis* (1665) by Placido Titi; *De annis climactericis* (1648) by Cl. Saumaise (Salmasius).

After having flourished for almost three centuries, European astrological literature suddenly diminished both in quantity and in quality when, at the end of the 17th century, the triumph of mechanistic physics distanced astrology from the university and from learned circles. The credibility of the discipline was impaired by the close connection made in many texts between its own techniques and a natural philosophy with Peripatetic roots, now become unpresentable in the learned world. The great *Lexicon mathematicum astronomicum geometricum* (Rome 1668) in which the Theatine monk Gerolamo Vitali, disciple of Titi, had gathered the fruits of three centuries of astrological labor, classifying all the Greek, Latin, and Arabic terms of the tradition, now appeared as the final homage to a defunct discipline and lay forgotten on the library shelves. From this moment until the second half of the 19th century, references to astrology, as also to alchemy and kabbalah, were used more in a symbolic sense than for any technical validity of the art. They appeared in the ambience of esotericism and secret societies, emerging now and then into the view of intellectuals like → Goethe and the German Romantics [→ Romanticism], who were discontented with a certain 17th-18th century schematic rationalism. One exception to this eclipse of astrological literature was the English environment, in which astrology, while not much in favor on higher cultural planes, still maintained a presence as a practice valued by the public, and fed by a technical literature oriented to the production of tables and ephemerides, which was especially prolific in the 19th century. In France, at the end of that century, there was a new wave of interest in astrology beyond the confines of esotericism: high-quality technical manuals were published, such as those of Fomalhaut and Selva, while Paul Choisnard laid the foundations for an approach to astrology as experimental and controllable research susceptible to the statistical method, thus opening the way to its 20th-century revival.

Simon de Pharès, *Le recueil des plus celebres astrologues* (J.P. Boudet, ed.), Paris: Champion, 1997 ♦ M. Ficino, *Scritti sull'astrologia* (O.P. Faracovi, ed.), Milan: Rizzoli, 1999 ♦ G. Pico della Mirandola, *Disputationes adversus astrologiam divinatricem* (E. Garin, ed.), 2 vols., Florence: Vallecchi, 1946 ♦ Pontus de Tyard, *Mantice: Discours de la verité de Divination par Astrologie* (S. Bokdam, ed.), Geneva: Droz, 1990 ♦ J. Calvin, *Advertissement contre l'astrologie judiciaire* (J. Millet, ed.), Geneva: Droz, 1983 ♦ G. Cardan, *In Ptolemaei Pelusiensis III de astrorum judiciis . . . commentaria*, in: *Opera omnia* (C. Spon, ed.), Lyon: Huguetan-Ravaud, 1663, vol. 5; reprinted Stuttgart, Bad Cannstatt: Frommann, 1966 ♦ G. Cardan, *Aforismi astrologici* (G. Bezza, ed.), Milan: Xenia, 1998 ♦ G. Cardan, *La natività del Salvatore e l'astrologia mondiale* (O.P. Faracovi, ed.), Milan: Mimesis, 2002 ♦ Placido Titi, *Tocco di paragone* (G. Bezza, ed.), Milan: Nuovi Orizzonti, 1992 ♦ G. Bezza (ed.), *Arcana Mundi: Antologia del pensiero astrologico antico*, 2 vols., Milan: Rizzoli, 1995 ♦ T. Campanella, *Opuscoli astrologici* (G. Ernst, ed.), Milan: Rizzoli, 2003.

Lit.: B. Soldati, *La poesia astrologica nel Quattrocento: Ricerche e studi*, Florence: Sansoni, 1906 ♦ A. Warburg, "Heidnisch-antike Weissagung in Wort und Bild zu Luthers Zeiten" (1920), in: G. Bing (ed.), *Gesammelte Schriften*, vol. 2, Leipzig-Berlin, 1932 ♦ L. Thorndike, *A History of Magic and Experimental*

Science, vols. 5-7, New York: Macmillan, 1941-1958 ♦ E. Garin, "Magia ed astrologia nella cultura del Rinascimento" (1950), in: *Medioevo e Rinascimento*, Bari: Laterza, 1954 ♦ W.E. Peuckert, *Astrologie*, Stuttgart: Kohlhammer, 1960 ♦ W. Knappich, *Geschichte der Astrologie*, Frankfurt a.M.: Klostermann, 1967 ♦ K. Thomas, *Religion and the Decline of Magic*, London, 1971 ♦ E. Garin, *Lo zodiaco della vita: La polemica sull'astrologia dal Trecento al Cinquecento*, Rome, Bari: Laterza, 1976 ♦ *Science, credenze occulte, livelli di cultura*, Florence: Convegno internazionale di studi, Olschki, 1982 ♦ S. Caroti, *L'astrologia in Italia*, Rome: Newton Compton, 1983 ♦ J. Halbronn, *Le Monde Juif et l'Astrologie: Histoire d'un vieux couple*, Milan: Arché, 1985 ♦ P. Zambelli (ed.), *"Astrologi hallucinati": Stars and the End of the World in Luther's Time*, 2 vols., Berlin, New York: De Gruyter, 1986 ♦ J. Tester, *A History of Western Astrology*, Suffolk: Boydell, 1987 ♦ *Divination et controverse religieuse en France au XVIe siècle*, Paris: Cahiers V.L. Saulnier no. 35, 1987 ♦ P. Curry (ed.), *Astrology, Science and Society*, Suffolk: Boydell, 1987 ♦ G. Ernst, *Religione, natura e storia: Ricerche su Tommaso Campanella e il tardo Rinascimento*, Milan: Franco Angeli, 1991 ♦ O.P. Faracovi, *Scritto negli astri: L'astrologia nella cultura dell'Occidente*, Venice: Marsilio, 1996 ♦ eadem, *Gli oroscopi di Cristo*, Venice: Marsilio, 1999 ♦ G. Zanier, *La medicina astrologica e la sua teoria: Marsilio Ficino e i suoi critici contemporanei*, Rome: Ed. di Storia e Letteratura, 1977 ♦ E. Weil, *La philosophie de Pietro Pomponazzi, Pic de la Mirandole et la critique de l'astrologie* (E. Naert and M. Lejbowicz, eds.), Paris: Vrin, 1985 ♦ G. Ernst, "Veritatis amor dulcissimus: Aspetti dell'astrologia di Cardano", in: E. Kessler (ed.), *Girolamo Cardano: Philosoph, Naturforscher, Arzt*, Wiesbaden: Harrassowitz Verlag, 1994, 157-184 ♦ P. Zambelli, *L'ambigua natura della magia*, Venezia: Marsilio, 1996 ♦ A. Grafton, *Cardano's Cosmos: The Worlds and Works of a Renaissance Astrologer*, Cambridge, Mass., London: Harvard University Press, 1999 ♦ N. Weill-Parot, *Les "images astrologiques" au Moyen Age et à la Renaissance*, Paris: Champion, 2002 ♦ Steven vanden Broecke, *The Limits of Influence: Pico, Louvain, and the Crisis of Renaissance Astrology*, Leiden, Boston: E.J. Brill 2003.

ORNELLA POMPEO FARACOVI

Astrology V: 20th Century

A. History

Although the sale of astrological almanacs flourished throughout the 18th and 19th centuries, in most Western countries the times were unpropitious for professional astrologers to expound on astrology as a worldview or interpret charts for clients. In the latter sense, there was thus a period of considerable decline throughout the West, with the partial exception of England where an astrological subculture continued to exist. By the turn of the 20th century, however, astrology had begun a process of revival. At the beginning of the twenty-first, astrology has regained a remarkably strong position in Europe and North America, especially in popular culture. Polls indicate that roughly a quarter of the population in several Western countries assent to the proposition that the position and movement of the planets against the backdrop of the heavens correlate with personality traits and/or events in one's life. Compared to previous epochs, 20th century astrology has gone through several major transformations. These can be viewed against the backdrop of a general definition of astrology.

Broadly speaking, astrology can be understood as a set of divinatory propositions and practices, sometimes associated with articulated world-views, which attempt to express specific modalities of human existence by means of a canonical language based on elements of celestial mechanics. Under this definition, astrology is an umbrella term denoting a potentially quite diverse set of rituals and doctrinal positions. In contemporary astrology, this diversity manifests itself in conflicting techniques, theories, world-views, and claims of what astrology can and cannot do.

The similarities between older and contemporary forms of astrology typically concern the generalities of this class of divination. Thus, older and newer astrologies share the assumption that there is a correlation between celestial and terrestrial phenomena (often expressed by astrologers in the formula "as above, so below"), and that certain individuals through appropriate training have acquired the skills necessary to unveil the details of this correlation. A commonly (although not universally) held belief in older as well as newer forms of divination is furthermore that astrology works because human life and the larger cosmos are interconnected through a network of non-material links.

The changes that have taken place throughout the 20th century can be briefly summarized in the following six points. (1) 20th-century astrology has joined forces with a variety of other belief systems that are particular to the late 19th and the 20th centuries. Thus, wide-spread forms of 20th century astrology have arisen through a syncretism with theosophically inspired → occultism and → Jungism. (2) Classical (traditional) astrology was associated with prognostication and specific claims about the correlation between celestial events and outward human behaviour. In present-day astrology there is a tendency to put main emphasis on behavioural dispositions, traits, and personality. (3) The coexistence of many independent practitioners, who can disseminate their ideas with rela-

tive ease due to factors such as cheaper printing technologies and the existence of popular media, has led to a considerable divergence of opinion. There is thus no agreement among astrologers e.g. on what symbols should be used in interpreting a chart (midpoints, asteroids, transplutonian planets, etc.), which of several fundamental but conflicting technical systems is valid (house divisions), how selected factors should be combined in chart interpretation, which factors should be accorded the greatest importance in the birth chart or, in the case of psychological astrology, what model of human personality is the most appropriate. The variety of interests within the astrological community has also led to the revival and development of many specialized forms of divination beside the interpretation of birth charts. These include various versions of mundane astrology (attempting to cast horoscopes for nations and organizations rather than individual people), financial astrology (which predicts e.g. fluctuations on the stock market), and even astrological traditionalism (which rejects the psychological interpretation of charts and attempts to go back to Renaissance and Mediaeval methods of predicting one's destiny). (4) Astrology has undergone ambivalent and conflicting forms of adaptation to the cultural context of modernity. The cosmological doctrines that went with pre-modern astrology – the geocentric model of the solar system, the Aristotelian distinction between sublunar and celestial worlds – are defunct. At the same time, the failure of more modern philosophical, astronomical and physical models to provide a plausible underpinning for astrological tenets has resulted in an at least partial allegiance to older theories of → correspondences, all the more remarkable in an epoch that has seen the adoption by many esotericists of theories of instrumental causality. However, these older theories are often unsystematically mixed with theories of mechanical causality, Jungian theories of synchronicity and other attempts at formulating explanatory models. (5) Astrology is no longer part of a culture of accepted claims. Thus, older forms of astrology were routinely invoked in political decision-making; in the contemporary West, the few cases when divination has been similarly used (as during the Reagan era) have caused considerable consternation and controversy. Furthermore, although older forms of astrology also met with criticism, this criticism was usually of an abstract and philosophical nature. Critics addressed topics such as the different fates of people born at the same time, the lack of a plausible modus operandi for astrological influences and the discrepancies between tropical and sidereal zodiacs. Modern opposition to astrological claims typically follows more empirically-oriented approaches. Contemporary skeptical responses typically point at the failure of astrologers in controlled experimental settings to correlate charts with personality profiles with any rate of success higher than chance. Conversely, several attempts have been made by astrologers to anchor their practices in empirical research; the most publicized of these attempts have been the statistical studies carried out by Michel Gauquelin (1928-1991). (6) Astrology is nevertheless practiced in a social context that bespeaks its positioning in contemporary society. Whereas practicing astrologers in pre-modern society characteristically plied their trade as independent agents, contemporary astrologers have the option of learning their craft through structured courses, to become members of organized bodies and to disseminate their ideas and advertise their practices through specialized journals. And whereas pre-modern astrology was treated as an arcane science in a male-dominated society, and was therefore dominated by male practitioners, contemporary astrology is integrated in a cultic milieu that is largely constituted by women, and is hence practiced by many women.

The revival of astrology began independently in England and in the USA. The key figure in England was Alan Leo (1860-1917), whose given name was William Frederick Allan. Leo, who had taught himself astrology, in 1890 became a member of the → Theosophical Society. In 1915 he founded an Astrological Lodge of the Theosophical Society. Leo was both a prolific writer and a very successful practicing astrologer. Numerous people became acquainted with astrology through Leo's textbooks.

In the USA astrology was to a large extent resuscitated from its slumber by Luke Dennis Broughton (1828-1898), who learned astrology in his native England and emigrated to America. He lectured and wrote extensively on astrology from the 1870s until his death, and introduced large numbers of people to the craft of chart interpretation.

The revival of astrology in countries such as France and Germany came a few years later, and was also largely ushered in by individual enthusiasts. In France, the astrological reawakening began during the last years of the 19th century with treatises published by → F.-Ch. Barlet (pseudonym of Albert Faucheux, 1838-1924) and Fomalhaut (pseudonym of abbé C. Nicollaud, 1854-1923). In Germany, Karl Brandler-Pracht (1864-1945) had a similar role in introducing astrology to the public around 1905. He was followed by a number of astrologers who attempted to create innovative versions of astrology. The most successful of these attempts, in terms of the number of adherents, is Alfred Witte's and Reinhold Ebertin's theory that the midpoints between the positions of the traditional symbols of the chart should be accorded an important role. In the 1930s, the situation of astrology in Germany was marked by the rise of national socialism. After a period of favor, when several high-ranking members of the Nazi party including Heinrich Himmler and Rudolf Hess were interested in the subject, astrology was repressed once the National Socialists came into power.

The astrology of the first decades of the 20th century largely continued to be event-oriented, each symbol generally correlated with physical features, places, specific fortunes and misfortunes. To the extent that it dealt with character, astrologers tended to use static and common-sense theories of personality. The key figure to effect the decisive turn towards incorporating more dynamic psychological models into astrology was Dane Rudhyar (1895-1985). Rudhyar, who was a follower and friend of → Alice Bailey's, became acquainted with → C.G. Jung's work in the early 1930's. His synthesis of psychology, theosophy and astrology was published as *The Astrology of Personality* in 1936. In a thoroughly spiritualized Jungian vein, Rudhyar saw the chart as a map to the particular path of individuation for the person concerned. The astrologer's function is very similar to that of a spiritual guide, who discerns for the client the meaning of being born at a particular time and place.

The prediction of events remained an important part of astrology well after the publication of Rudhyar's first volumes. However, the counterculture of the 1960s signified a major boost for astrology in general and its psychological and Jungian variety in particular. The awareness among the population at large was to a large extent heightened due to the concept of the advent of a new era in history, the Age of Aquarius (not least as popularized in the 1969 musical *Hair*). Among the astrological cognoscenti, Rudhyar, who had worked in relative obscurity for many years, became a major source of inspiration. Since the late 1960s, interest has exploded, measured in terms of the number of practicing astrologers, in the output of literature and the number of potential clients.

Whereas political constraints for the following two decades limited widespread interest in astrology to the Western world, the fall of the Iron Curtain has brought about yet another boost, since the 1990s entailed a surge of interest in the former East Bloc countries. The wider effects of globalization have spread modern Western, psychologizing forms of astrology well beyond the confines of Europe and North America, and have also introduced Indian and Chinese forms of astrology in the West.

At the same time, the very popularity of astrology in the last decades of the 20th century has given it the curious role of being a major catalyst behind the rise of organized skeptical movements. In 1975, 186 scientists signed a document against astrology which was published in the journal *The Humanist*. The following year, the *Committee for the Scientific Investigation of Claims of the Paranormal* (CSICOP) was formed largely as a response to the wide-spread support for astrology. Within the next few years, many similar skeptical organizations were created, most of which continue to devote considerable effort to debunking and combating belief in astrology. 20th century astrology thus has an indirect influence that goes well beyond the ranks of the "believers".

B. LITERATURE

The astrological literature of the 20th century is characterized by its scope and diversity. The vastness of the literature can be judged from the fact that at the beginning of the 21st century, catalogues of books in print list over three thousand astrology titles in the English language alone. The diversity is apparent from the fact that this literature ranges from elementary general introductions to highly specialized works, and covers many distinct branches of astrology, from the Jungian-inspired analysis of birth charts to various versions of mundane and predictive astrology. The following remarks can thus only give some ideas of the main trends of this literature.

Much astrology in the first decades after its revival at the beginning of the 20th century was characterized by the affinity of many of its practitioners with theosophy [→ Theosophical Society], and with the gradual transition from an event-oriented to a psychologizing practice. An important part of the literature on astrology of those decades is marked by this double affiliation. Among the "modern classics" of this genre one can single out *Esoteric Astrology* and other books written by the prolific Alan Leo (1860-1970) and *The Astrology of Personality* by Dane Rudhyar (1895-1985). Theosophically inspired astrology received its most extensive theoretical manifesto with → Alice Bailey's *Esoteric Astrology* (1950). However, predictive astrology represented a larger sector of the astrological literature during those first decades than it does today. Early 20th century handbooks on astrology, such as → Max Heindel's *The Mes-*

sage of the Stars (1913) and Oscar Schmitz' *Der Geist der Astrologie* (1922) thus devote considerable space to describing how a person's relation with career, money, marriage and health can be seen in the birth chart.

Whereas much of astrology in older periods was reserved for an intellectual elite that had the astronomical and mathematical knowledge necessary to erect a chart, astrology as it was revived in the early 20th century was a more popular practice. A distinct genre of 20th-century literature consists of elementary handbooks for mass-market distribution. Characteristic examples are Alan Leo's *Casting the Horoscope* (1902), and *Heaven Knows What* (1935) and *Astrology for the Millions* (1940) by Grant Lewi (1902-1951).

Since astrology was largely practiced by individuals in a loosely knit cultic milieu, the literature also soon evinced a considerable diversity of opinion. Among the literature presenting various technical innovations, a few sub-genres can be mentioned. In books such as *Applied Cosmobiology* Reinhold Ebertin (1901-1988) developed a distinct form of astrology, inter alia by assuming that midpoints between planets represented important forces in the chart. Another distinct direction in astrology are Sabian Symbols, in which every degree of the zodiac has its own meaning. This system of interpretation is the subject of Marc Edmund Jones' (1888-1980) *The Sabian Symbols* (1953).

Specific applications of astrology (other than interpreting the birth chart) were also revived and codified in founding texts. Charles Carter (1887-1968) published an influential text on mundane astrology, *An Introduction to Political Astrology* (1951). An early precursor of the attempts to analyze stock market fluctuations through astrology is J.M. Langham's *Planetary Effects on the Stock Market* (1932).

The revival of astrology coincided with a period of unparalleled success for the natural sciences. Already in the first years of the astrological revival, volumes were produced that attempted to ground the claims of astrology in empirical research. A pioneer in this field is Paul Choisnard (1867-1930). Among his titles one might mention *Influence astrale* (1901) and *Étude nouvelle sur l'hérédité* (1903).

Astrological literature of the latter decades of the century, i.e. after astrology made the transition from a specialized subculture into mainstream popular culture in the 1960s, shows characteristics similar to the aforementioned, but in radicalized form. Firstly, the psychologizing trend has become the dominant form of astrology. Much contemporary literature therefore takes for granted that astrology is a psychological art and thus a mode of understanding others as well as oneself, giving rise to titles such as *Relating* (Liz Greene 1978), *Astrology, Psychology and the Four Elements* (Stephen Arroyo 1975), *Relationships and Life Cycles* (Arroyo 1979), and *The Astrology of Self-Discovery* (Tracy Marks 1985).

Secondly, due to the widespread popularity of astrological beliefs, the existing customer base for literature on the subject is vast. A very large number of titles is thus published each year, making it possible for both broadly appealing subjects and niche interests to coexist on the market. The vast output of astrological texts can be loosely subdivided into genres. For the general public, there are mass-market books, e.g. the commercially highly successful best sellers *Sun Signs* and *Love Signs* by Linda Goodman (1925-1995). For the aspiring astrologer, new instructional texts are published each year, some of which are distributed by major, international publishing houses. Books for a more advanced audience tend to focus on specific interpretive issues. Thus, there are numerous books aiding the advanced practitioner to refine his or her understanding of the astrological houses, of specific planets or of characteristic configurations or events in the horoscope. Characteristic titles are *Saturn: A New Look at an Old Devil* (Liz Greene 1976), *The Twelve Houses* (Howard Sasportas 1985) and *Planetary Aspects* (Tracy Marks 1987). A considerable number of journals, ranging from mass circulation publications to specialized newsletters cater to the interests of those who have a long-term interest or are professionally involved in astrology. Closely related to these genres are astrological texts that are "literature" only by adopting a more inclusive definition. Among these there are the sun sign horoscopes in many newspapers and magazines. TV programs, Internet sites and advertisements in the media also contribute to making basic information on astrology a truly ubiquitous part of contemporary popular culture.

Thirdly, those who practice astrology continue to disagree on many issues. Present-day astrological literature therefore continues to be characterized by its diversity of opinion. The variety of doctrines on a number of technical issues has led to several distinct genealogies of traditions. Literature that presents specific interpretive choices can be subdivided accordingly. There are books linking astrology with Jungian thought. Among these, some of the most influential within the astrological community have been written by Liz Greene and Howard Sasportas, e.g. their joint production *The Development of the Personality* (1987). Others present a variety of esoteric or occult interpretations of the chart. Books linking → reincarnation and astrology can be placed in this category, e.g. *The Divine Plot: Astrology and Reincarnation* (Tad Mann 1986). The literature of yet another school, that of Uranian astrology, is distinct inter alia in that it hypothesizes the existence of eight planets unknown to astronomy. Yet another subgenre attempts to incorporate interpretations of major asteroids into the birth chart.

Fourthly, whereas all of the aforementioned are united by their interest in the natal charts of individual people, yet other genres of literature, each with multiple variations, concern distinct branches of astrology such as mundane astrology (the interpretation of the charts of nations and organizations), financial astrology, horary astrology (answering questions by interpreting the chart of the moment when the question was posed), electional astrology (choosing the appropriate moment to begin an activity through astrological considerations), and even astrological gardening (planting and harvesting according to astrological considerations). Thus, mundane astrology is the subject of volumes such as Nicholas Campion *The Book of World Horoscopes* (1992), whereas financial astrology is expounded in texts such as Henry Weingarten *Investing by the Stars* (1996).

Finally, astrology is no longer part of a culture of accepted claims. This fact has led to the rise of a new genre of literature on the subject. The booming interest in astrology has probably been the main impetus behind a genre of literature on astrology characteristic of the later part of the 20th century: the numerous attempts to carry out empirical studies of astrological claims. Excepting a few precursors, rigorous experimental studies of this kind have only been carried out since the mid-1950s. Two avenues of investigation have been followed. Firstly, there are statistical surveys examining whether chart factors can be correlated with specific individual traits. The most publicized and controversial of these are the studies of Michel Gauquelin (1928-1991), who in *The Cosmic Clocks* (1967) and numerous other books attempted to show that there was a statistically significant correlation between certain celestial events at birth and excellence in certain professions. Secondly, there is the skeptical literature that attacks astrology, typically along the line that astrologers consistently fail tests in which they attempt to match personality profiles with chart interpretations. A classic title in this genre is Roger Culver & Philip A. Ianna *Astrology: True or False? A Scientific Evaluation* (1988).

The implicit premise of such studies, whether

favorable or debunking, is that astrology is best analyzed by examining its relation with the empirical sciences; the polemics concern the question whether it is a valid science or a failed one. Almost entirely lacking from 20th century astrological literature are studies that treat contemporary astrology as a culturally constructed divinatory art. Considering the depth and finesse of the anthropological literature on e.g. African systems of divination, this lacuna is all the more remarkable.

Lit.: Patrick Curry, *A Confusion of Prophets: Victorian and Edwardian Astrology*, London: Collins & Brown, 1992 ◆ Shoshanah Feher, "Who holds the cards? Women and New Age astrology", in: James R. Lewis & J. Gordon Melton (eds.), *Perspectives on the New Age*, Albany: SUNY Press, 1992, 179-188 ◆ Suzel Fuzeau-Braesch, *L'astrologie*, Paris: Presses Universitaires de France, 1995 ◆ Ellic Howe, *Urania's Children: The Strange World of the Astrologers*, London: Kimber, 1967 ◆ James R. Lewis, *The Astrology Encyclopedia*, Detroit: Gale Research, 1994.

OLAV HAMMER

Audians

The Audians were adherents of a Christian sect, which flourished in the 4th century. Only a limited historical and geographical account of their activities can be gleaned from typically marginal references in the available sources (detailed survey in Puech 910/911). The scantness of concrete information is already apparent in the varying names for the group (Gk. *Audianoi, Odianoi*; Lat. *Haeresis Audiana*) as well as their founder (Gk. *Audios, Audaios*; Lat. *Audeus*; Syr. *Audi, Odi*). Moreover, no original documents of the Audians have survived. All information about the sect derives from the heresiological writings of major Church authors. The statements of Epiphanius of Salamis (*Panarion*, 70) and Theodore bar Konai (*Scholia*, 11,63) are particularly important in this respect.

Audius, the founder of the sect, was a Syrian from Mesopotamia, who lived during the 4th century. Statements concerning the period of his public activity vary widely; Epiphanius (*Panarion*, 70, 1) gives the most plausible date at the time of Arius (ca. 325 A.D.). Audius initially enjoyed great respect as an ascetic and opponent of the growing decadence of the clergy. His break with the Church probably followed soon after the Council of Nicaea. Audius rejected its edict on Easter, and his dissent was initially more schismatic than heretical. Audius had himself illegally consecrated bishop by a follower and founded communities, which

pledged themselves to extreme asceticism. He was thereupon banned by Constantine the Great to Scythia for several years. Afterwards he went on a long missionary journey, which led him into the Kingdom of the Goths, where he was successful as a missionary and monastic founder until his death. The persecution of all Christian communities by a Gothic ruler forced the Audians living there to flee back to the region where the movement had originated. There the sect swiftly declined in importance. In Epiphanius' time it was already small with an insignificant number of followers (*Panarion*, 70.15,5).

Little is known concerning the organisation and lifestyle of the Audians. Presumably the Audians were an initially orthodox ascetic movement, which wanted to restore the purity of the early Church and opposed any form of luxury. Afterwards, there arose an independent Audian church with its own episcopate, which assumed an increasingly heretical character, developed specific doctrines and elaborated its own apocryphal scripture, including a rich apocalyptic literature. Theodore bar Konai names an *Apocalypse of Abraham*, an *Apocalypse of John*, possibly identical with the so-called *Apocryphon of John* (= NHC II, 1 parr.), a *Book of Questions* and a so-called *Apocalypse of Strangers*, which is perhaps identical with the *Apokalypsis Allogenous* (Porphyry, *Vita Plotini*, 16), the text *Allogenes* (NHC XI, 3), and the *Allogeneis* of the → Archontics and → Sethians. This similarity suggests that the Audians shared many ideas with these groups. Moreover, the Audians presumably had various editions of the *Didascalia Apostolorum*.

Audian doctrines have syncretic features, chiefly indicating a proximity to Jewish and Judaeo-Christian views. As quartodecimans, the Audians retained the 14th Nisan as the time of Passover and thereby oriented themselves towards Jewish prescriptions (*Panarion*, 70, 9, 2-14, 4). There is also a markedly anthropomorphic image of God, based on a literal interpretation of Genesis 1:26: As God made man in his image, he also possesses a physical form. Accordingly, texts which endow God with attributes of the human body (e.g. Psalm 11:4; Isaiah 41:20) are understood in concrete terms rather than metaphorically (*Panarion*, 60, 2, 3-8). Here one sees an archaic, Judaeo-Christian conception of God with parallels in other early Christian texts, for example the pseudo-Clementine homilies (Stroumsa, 262).

The Gnostic views held by the Audians can be reconstructed in outline. Their cosmology and anthropology are characterised by a sharp dualism, expressed in the polar opposites of light and darkness. Darkness and seven other powers form the seven planetary archons, which function as creators of the world and man. The myth of human origin taken from Genesis is expanded: the progeny of a part of mankind resulted from Eve's sexual relations with the archons. The human body is governed by the seven archons and must therefore be overcome; for this reason any kind of sexual activity is condemned and the idea of a bodily resurrection rejected.

The Audians' exemplary fulfilment of an ideal disseminated by the Church coupled with diametrically opposed doctrines led Epiphanius to place the sect outside the usual heresiological scheme, a verdict which has persisted until the present day (Stroumsa 267: '... another case of Christian monks, apparently orthodox in their beliefs and praxis, but ... the carriers of radical, heretical teachings').

K. Holl (ed.), *Epiphanius III: Panarion haer.* 65-80 (2nd rev. ed. by J. Dummer), Berlin: Akademie-Verlag, 1980 ♦ translation with notes: F. Williams, *The Panarion of Epiphanius of Salamis*, Book 2/3, Leiden: E.J. Brill, 1994 ♦ A. Scher (ed.), *Theodor bar Konai, Liber Scholiorum*, vol. 2, 2nd edition = CSCO, Scriptores Syri, 26, Louvain: Peeters, 1954 ♦ Fr. translation: R. Hespel/R. Draguet = CSCO, Scriptores Syri, 188, Louvain: Peeters, 1982.

Lit.: H.-Ch. Puech, "Audianer", in: *RAC* 1 (1950), 910-915 ♦ J. Jarry, "Une semi hérésie syro-égyptienne: l'Audianisme", *Bulletin de l'Institut Français d'Archéologie Orientale* 63 (1965), 169-195 ♦ C. Scholten, "Audios", in: *LThK³* (1993), 1174 ♦ G.G. Stroumsa, *Barbarian Philosophy: The Religious Revolution of Early Christianity* (Wissenschaftliche Untersuchungen zum Neuen Testament 112), Tübingen: J.C.B. Mohr (Paul Siebeck), 1999.

GUIDO BEE

Augustine (Augustinus of Hippo),
* 13.11.354 Thagaste, † 28.08.430 Hippo Regius

Life and work of Augustinus of Hippo, the most influential Father of the Catholic Church in the West, were inextricably connected with the gnosis of → Manichaeism. In 373, as a young student of rhetoric in Carthage, he made his sudden change to the "religion of Light", which at that time was very attractive to intellectual circles both in Roman North Africa and, for example, Italy. From his nineteenth up to and even beyond his twenty-eighth year, Augustinus was a Manichaean Hearer (*auditor*). In the writings after his return to the Catholic Church (the definitive conversion to Catholicism took place in the autumn of 386), he was involved in a conflict with his former coreligionists and, at the same time, with his own Manichaean past. This period began with *On the Morals of the Catholic Church and the Morals of the Manichaeans* (started in 387) and came to a provisional conclusion with *On the Nature of the Good* (finished after 404). But also many excursions in his letters, sermons and major works like the *Confessions* (finished about 400) and the *City of God* (413-426/7) are definitely anti-Manichaean. Even towards the end of his life, in his writings against the Italian bishop Julian of Eclanum, Augustinus still had to struggle against the charge of being a Manichaean.

In many respects Augustinus's writings are unique sources for our knowledge of Manichaeism in the Latin West. Apart from the *Fragmenta Tabestina*, the remnants of a Manichaean codex in Latin found near the Algerian city of Tébessa in 1918, nearly all the other primary Latin sources came down to us via the works of Augustinus. Most important in this context are fragments of → Mani's *Treasure of Life* (via Augustinus's *Against Felix* and *On the Nature of the Good*; some other parts via Augustinus's pupil Evodius of Uzalis); fragments of Mani's *Foundation Letter* (mainly via Augustinus's *Against the "Foundation Letter" of Mani*); the *Capitula* of the Manichaean bishop Faustus (via Augustinus's *Against Faustus*) and the Letter of the Roman Manichaean Secundinus (preceding Augustinus's *Against Secundinus* in the manuscripts). The alleged Letter of Mani to Menoch, which the Italian bishop Julian of Eclanum brought to Augustinus's attention (see Augustinus's *Against Julian, an Unfinished Book* III,166 and 172-173), seems to be a (Pelagian?) falsification, though it gives proof of a profound knowledge of Manichaeism. From Augustinus's *Against Adimantus*, written to refute the disputationes of Mani's disciple Addā which seem to have been a collection of quotations from the Old Testament contrasted with selected New Testament texts, we get an impression of Manichaean biblical interpretation. Besides, Augustinus's *On the Morals of the Catholic Church and the Morals of the Manichaeans* and, not least, the 46th chapter of *On Heresies*, provide unique information on Manichaean myth, doctrine, ritual, and ethics.

To what extent Manichaeism exerted a lasting influence upon Augustinus has been a question since the attacks of Julian and other contemporaries. Apart from his marked and life-long anti-Manichaean attitude, more or less distinct positive Manichaean influences seem to have remained in (certain traits) of Augustinus's doctrine of the two cities (civitates), in his doctrine of sexual concupiscence, and in his appealing mystical spirituality.

Edition of Augustinus's main anti-Manichaean works by J. Zycha in CSEL 25, 1/2, Prague-Vienna-Leipzig: Tempsky-Freitag, 1891-1892 ♦ *De moribus ecclesiae catholicae et de moribus Manichaeorum*, recensuit J.B. Bauer, CSEL 90, Vienna: Hölder-Pichler-Tempsky, 1992 ♦ *De Genesi contra Manichaeos*, edidit D. Weber, CSEL 91, Vienna: Österreichische Akademie der Wissenschaften, 1998 ♦ F. Decret & J. van Oort (Latin text, French tr.), St. Augustinus, *Acta contra Fortunatum Manichaeum* (CFM, Series Latina II), Brepols: Turnhout 2004.

Lit.: F. Decret, *Aspects du Manichéisme dans l'Afrique romaine*, Paris: Études Augustiniennes, 1970 ♦ F. Decret, *L'Afrique manichéenne (IVe-Ve siècles)*, Paris: Études Augustiniennes, 1978 ♦ F. Decret, *Essais sur l'Église manicheénne en Afrique du Nord et à Rome au temps de saint Augustin*, Roma: Institutum Patristicum Augustinianum, 1995 ♦ J. van Oort, "Augustine and Mani on concupiscentia sexualis", in: J. den Boeft & J. van Oort (eds.), *Augustinina Traiectina*, Paris: Études Augustiniennes, 1987, 137-152 ♦ J. van Oort, "Augustine on sexual concupiscence and original sin", in: E. Livingstone (ed.), *Studia Patristica XXII*, Leuven: Peeters, 1989, 382-386 ♦ J. van Oort, *Jerusalem and Babylon: A Study into Augustine's City of God and the Sources of his Doctrine of the Two Cities*, Leiden: E.J. Brill, 1991, 33-47, 199-234 ♦ J. van Oort, "Manichaeism in Augustine's De ciuitate Dei", in: E. Cavalcanti (ed.), *Il "De ciuitate Dei": L'opera, le interpretazioni, l'influsso*, Roma-Freiburg-Wien: Herder, 1996, 193-214 ♦ J. van Oort, *Mani, Manichaeism & Augustine: The Rediscovery of Manichaeism & Its Influence on Western Christianity*, Tbilisi: Academy of Sciences of Georgia, 1996 (2001⁴) ♦ A. Hoffmann, *Augustins Schrift "De utilitate credendi": Eine Analyse*, Münster: Aschendorff, 1997 ♦ J. van Oort, "Mani and Manichaeism in Augustine's *De haeresibus*: An Analysis of *haer.* 46,1", in: R.E. Emmerick et al. (eds.), *Studia Manichaica*, Berlin: Akademie Verlag, 2000, 451-463 ♦ J. van Oort et al. (eds.), *Augustine and Manichaeism in the Latin West*, Leiden: E.J. Brill, 2001.

JOHANNES VAN OORT

Auvergne, William of → William of Auvergne

Avicenna (Abū ʿAlī al-Ḥusayn ibn ʿAbd Allāh ibn Sīnā), * ca. 980 Afsana near Buḫārā in Transoxiana, † 1037 Hamaḏān

1. LIFE AND WORK 2. AVICENNA'S THEORY OF KNOWLEDGE 3. AVICENNA'S LOST ESOTERIC TEACHING? 4. AVICENNA ON ALCHEMY

1. LIFE AND WORK

We know about Avicenna's life through an autobiography, completed by one of his disciples, Ǧūzǧānī (see critical edition Gohlman, ed.). Avicenna's father held a high position in the Samanid administration. A few years after Avicenna's birth, the family moved to Buḫārā, the capital of the Samanid's. In this intellectually active city, Avicenna received a very good education. He studied islamic jurisprudence (*fiqh*), medicine, and philosophical sciences: logic, mathematics, physics, and metaphysics. At seventeen, he was appointed personal physician of the Samanid Nūḥ ibn Manṣūr in Buḫārā; here he had the opportunity to complete his education, thanks to the extraordinary library of the Samanid ruler. After his father's death, he was also given an administrative position. A few years later, for reasons unknown to us, Avicenna left Buḫārā for Gorgānǧ in Ḫwārazm (999?-1012), where he came in the service of the Ma'munid Alī ben Ma'mūn. In the next years we find him in Ǧorǧān (1012-1014), Ray (1014-1015), and Hamaḏān (1015-1024), serving different rulers as a physician, and sometimes as a political administrator as well. Finally he went to Iṣfahān (1024-1037) where he stayed in the service of the Kakuyid ʿAlāʾ ad-dawla until his death, which happened during a trip with his master to Hamaḏān.

A philosopher, physician, and mathematician, Avicenna has left a large corpus that western intellectuals began to discover between the mid-12th and the late 13th century. His *magnum opus* is the encyclopedic *Kitāb al-Šifāʾ* (Book of the Cure), written between 1020 and 1027. It contains *Summae* (*Ǧumal*), i.e. collections on logic, natural science, mathematics and metaphysics. Each one is divided into several sections (*funūn*). A large part of the natural science collection, including the fifth chapter of the first treatise of Meteorology (which is itself the fifth section of the Natural science collection where Avicenna expresses his views on → alchemy), was translated into latin, like the whole of the metaphysics and a small part of the logic. The introduction to the Logic (*al-madḫal*) and a chapter from section 5 on proof (*al-borhān*), a large part of the first section of Natural science (*al-Samāʾ al-Ṭabīʿī*), the section 6 of Natural science which is the Treatise on the Soul (*Kitāb al-nafs*), and the whole Metaphysics were translated during the second half of the 12th century at Toledo. The names of the two translators of the Treatise on the Soul, the archdeacon Dominic Gundisalvi or Gundissalinus and Avendauth, an "israelita philosophus" are both mentioned in the letter dedicating the treatise to the archbishop John of Toledo. Several sections of Natural science, among which the fifth section on Meteorology, were translated at Burgos toward 1240 by Master John Gunsalvi and Salomon. A version of three chapters of this section had been separately translated at the end of the 12th century (see d'Averny 1952, 1957, 1970).

Using Aristotelian and Neoplatonic conceptual elements, Avicenna elaborated an original system of his own. His theory of knowledge is strictly rationalistic and has its source in his comprehensive philosophical system which is distinctly rationalistic as well. The principles of this system are not compatible with any kind of esoteric teaching. The emphasis on knowledge of what is internal (*bāṭin*) and as such not accessible to sense perception or to discursive thought, as opposed to what is external (*ẓāhir*) and visible – which is a fundamental character of mystical or esoteric thought in Islam –, is strictly alien to Avicenna's philosophical system. Below, we will see how Avicenna has nevertheless become important to the history of gnosis and Western esotericism.

2. AVICENNA'S THEORY OF KNOWLEDGE

The first Principle – i.e. God – in Avicenna's metaphysical system is a pure intellect (*'aql maḥḍ*). As such he has an uninterrupted intellection of himself and through his eternal thought of himself, he eternally and continually emanates the first intellect, which is the mover of the outermost sphere. The first intellect has an intellection of the first Principle and as a consequence of this intellection, a second intellect necessarily proceeds from it. It has itself as a second object of thought, insofar as it is a being that exists necessarily by reason of the first Principle, and it thereby emanates the soul of the outermost sphere. It also has itself as a third object of thought, insofar as it is a being which has a possible existence by reason of itself; and it thereby emanates the body of the outermost sphere. The process is the same for the second intellect, and so on, up to the tenth intellect. The power of the tenth intellect is not strong enough to emanate eternal beings, so it emanates both the substantial forms and the intelligibles (*Kitāb al-Šifā'*, Metaphysics, IX, 4). Each sphere of the Avicennian cosmos presents a triadic structure, an intellect, a soul, and a matter moved by the soul. Each element of this scheme is necessarily linked to the other and each effect can be rationally inferred from its cause. The pure intellect is the ultimate principle of all existents. Reality has an intelligible and a rational structure: the Avicennian rationalist theory of knowledge has its source in this metaphysical truth.

The last intellect of the cosmos, i.e. the active intellect, contains all the intelligibles and the goal of human activity is to acquire these. This is not possible as long as the rational immaterial soul is joined to the body; but the supreme bliss for this soul is to become like a perfectly polished mirror in which all knowledge is reflected. The destiny of the soul in the hereafter depends upon man's rational activity during his life. The highest state of human activity in this life and in the next is rational activity. A soul who has neglected this noble activity will suffer eternally. To obtain these intelligibles, the human intellect (which is a faculty of the rational soul) has to come into contact (*ittiṣāl*) with the active intellect. At birth, the human intellect contains no intelligibles : it is merely an empty potentiality for thinking, called "material intellect" (*'aql hayūlānī*), and belongs to every member of the species. Then, when it acquires the first intelligibles – i.e. theoretical propositions such as "the whole is greater than the part" – it is called "intellect *in habitu*" (*'aql bi-l-malaka*). When the human intellect obtains the secondary intelligibles which consist of universal concepts and derivative propositions – however without being into contact with the active intellect –, it is called "actual intellect" (*'aql bi-l-fiʿl*). Their acquisition normally requires the presence of the first intelligibles and the use of the thinking activity which requires the participation of the external senses (sight, smell and so on), as well as the internal senses (→ imagination, memory, and so on). The next stage, the "acquired intellect" (*'aql mustafad*) is no longer a stage of potentiality like the first three: at this level, the human intellect has established contact with the active intellect and receives the intelligible forms from it. The rationalist character of Avicenna's theory of knowledge is strengthened by two of his fundamental theses. 1) The "contact" between the sublunar and the supralunar realms is only an epistemic one. Avicenna rejects the possibility of an ontic union (the technical term for this used by the mystics is *ittiḥād*) between the human intellect and the transcendental principle of knowledge. 2) Some men possess "insight" (*ḥads*), which is an aptitude to acquire knowledge by establishing contact with the active intelligence without resorting to any kind of preparation (i.e. without using the thinking faculty), or to any teaching. When man establishes contact with the active intellect through insight, he obtains instantaneously the middle term in any syllogism. The knowledge of the intelligible world and of the reality as it is in itself is necessarily a syllogistic knowledge. When the capacity of insight reaches its highest level, it is called "holy intellect" (*'aql qudsī*). This capacity belongs only to prophets: it is the highest of the powers of prophecy and the highest level of the human faculties (*Kitāb al-Šifāʾ*. Treatise on the Soul, V, 5, p. 219). Thus, for Avicenna real knowledge is demonstrated scientific knowledge which follows a strict syllogistic process according to the rules established by Aristotle's logic. In Avicenna's comprehensive philosophical system, prophecy is conceived as a human experience, although an exceptional one, – it is studied in the sixth section of the Natural Science – interpreted in a rationalist manner without recourse to the religious theme of God's election. Moreover, the "mystic" (*al-ʿārif*) described by Avicenna in the *Išārāt wa-Tanbīhāt* (Pointers and Reminders) is the man who has purified his soul by asceticism and whose intellect has reached the level of "acquired intellect" (Goichon 1961, 486-489). The function of ascetic exercises, religious prescriptions such as fasting, prayer and so on, is only propaedeutic; they prepare the rational soul for establishing contact with the active intelligence.

Another important aspect of Avicenna's theory of knowledge is linked to his theory of imagination. The souls of the celestial spheres, being joined to a body, are endowed with a faculty of imagination which contains images of the particular things, while the intelligences of the celestial spheres contain only intelligible forms (*Kitāb al-Šifāʾ*, Treatise on the Soul, IV, 2, p. 158). By the medium of his imagination, man usually receives those images during the sleeping state while his senses are at rest. A brief survey of Avicenna's theory of the internal senses is necessary to understand this theory of imagination. To the five external senses, Avicenna adds five internal senses: (1) common sense, (2) retentive imagination, (3) compositive imagination, (4) estimation, (5) recollection. To be perceived, the sensible form grasped by the external senses must be imprinted in the common sense. When an image fashioned by man's compositive imagination is imprinted in the common sense, it is perceived as if it were a sensible form grasped by the external senses. Man's imagination receives the images from the celestial souls during the sleeping state and imitates them. Sometimes, the images framed are similar to those perceived during the visionary experience and sometimes they are not, when the imagination has been disturbed by the other bodily's faculties. In the first case, the result brings foreknowledge of the future and in the second case it is only a "confused dream". Some men have a strong imagination and a noble soul. Their imagination is not diverted by the activity of the senses and acquires through figurative images what the soul learns through intellectual prophecy.

Those men are prophets and their experience is the consequence of the prophetic imagination. The prophet transposes his particular vision into symbols and images accessible to everyone. But the status of those images is not clear: are they mere colourful duplicates of the intelligible forms or are they endowed with their own heuristic value? This unresolved point of Avicenna's theory of knowledge has given birth to different interpretations.

→ Henry Corbin has devoted to Avicenna's theory of imagination one of his important studies concerning the Islamic interpretation of the esoteric mystery of God's presence to man (*Avicenna and the Visionary Recital*). Corbin's interpretation has been highly influential among students of western esotericism but it presents some difficulties when we read it in the light of Avicenna's theory of emanation. According to Corbin's acute and in many respects inspired analysis, the islamic mystic and esoteric literature has produced an original answer to the question of the mystery of the possible meeting between man and the spiritual world. The meeting takes place in a world which is neither the world of sense perception nor the one of universal concepts, but an intermediary world called the *mundus imaginalis*. By his imagination, man participates in this world where it is given him to receive individual revelations which – although they are not sense perceptions –, have specific characteristics like smell, colour and sound. The *mundus imaginalis* is the nexus between the sensible world and the angelic world; its existence makes it possible for the mystic to meet an angelic entity which symbolizes his real nature. Henry Corbin confers a specific significance to three Avicennian recitals which he designates as "the visionary recitals' cycle", namely, *Ḥayy Ibn Yaqẓān* (Alive, the son of Awake), *Salāmān wa Absāl* and *Risāla-at-Ṭayr* (The Bird's Recital). He considers them to be the highly individual expression of a single visionary experience. They are not to be considered as allegorical recitals in the sense that the experience they describe could be expressed differently, for example through rational discourse. Rather, each Avicennian recital expresses an individual experience which has taken place in the *mundus imaginalis* through the medium of the faculty of imagination between the mystic (in this case, Avicenna) and an angelic entity who represents his real nature. Each symbol contained in those recitals is unique, being the trace of the authenticity of the experience. Each symbol is a "secret" offered by Avicenna to his reader in order to make him aware of his real nature. Thus, these recitals have an initiatic function which no other kind of discourse (allegoric or demonstrative) could assume.

For Corbin, Avicenna's recitals revolve around his pivotal doctrine of angelology, of which theory of knowledge and cosmology are only parts. Knowledge is an illuminative process, which leads the human soul to forsake the West and turn toward the East, i.e. toward the focus of its real nature. The angel's gift manifests itself as an inner epiphany of beauty and light invading the human soul and revealing to it its real nature. Knowledge is thus a gnosis, an initiatic process in which each soul experiences an absolutely unique relationship to the divine.

Corbin's interpretation of Avicenna's theory of imagination raises a fundamental question: is true knowledge an initiatic process, an absotutely individual relationship between a singular human soul and a celestial entity, or rather the reception by human souls of the intelligibles contained in the celestial intelligences through a single effusion, each soul receiving the amount of intelligibles it is ready to receive? To answer this question, we have to consider the structure of the process of emanation. In Avicenna's metaphysical system all reality emanates from God through the first intellect. God is the ultimate principle of both existence and intelligible thought. The flux coming from the supralunar realm is always identical to itself; only the disposition of the receptacles to receive it varies. This is a principle that Avicenna has always maintained. Thus, knowledge is one – i.e. it consists of all the intelligibles contained in the intellects of the celestial spheres – and continually emanates from the celestial principles. Only the disposition of men's intellect to receive it varies. The initiatic individual process between an angelic entity and a gnostic is hardly possible in such a rationalistic scheme where a unique flux continually and necessarily emanates from each celestial entity, each being like a mirror reflecting in his own way the supreme gift. Thus, it seems difficult to distinguish the experience related respectively in the three "visionary recitals" – which is an epistemic one – from the rational process of knowledge that man's intellect has to undertake to obtain eternal bliss as described by Avicenna in the *Kitāb al-Šifāʾ*.

3. AVICENNA'S LOST ESOTERIC TEACHING?

For a long time, western scholars have mistakenly believed that there had once existed a body of esoteric teaching by Avicenna, known as "Eastern philosophy". As shown by Gutas, the origin of this mistake goes back to the medieval Andalusian philosopher Ibn Ṭofayl († 1185) who borrowed the title *Ḥayy Ibn Yaqẓān* (Alive, the son of Awake)

from Avicenna's recital to elaborate the myth of the solitary philosopher. In his introduction, Ibn Ṭofayl had drawn a connection between Eastern philosophy and mysticism, and framed the following misleading subtitle: "On the Secrets of Eastern Philosophy". A modern western scholar, M.A.F. Mehren borrowed Ibn Ṭofayl's subtitle for his own edition and translation (into French) of some of Avicenna's treatises (*Rasāʾil Ibn Sīnā fī asrār al-ḥikma al-mašriqiyya*, the French title is *Traités mystiques d'Avicenne*) and this title has contributed to the idea that Avicenna had a mystical or esoteric teaching. In a well known paper from 1925, C.A. Nallino established, however, that in the part of his work named by himself "Eastern philosophy", Avicenna did not profess a teaching definitely distinct from the one contained in his systematic works. The fragment subsisting today in the manuscripts under the title *Kitāb al-mašriqiyyīn* (The Book of the Easterners) is a treatise on logic which contains no trace of an esoteric teaching (it is published under the name *Manṭiq al-mašriqiyyīn* by Ṣ. al-Naǧǧār). The "Easterners", as S. Pines (1952) has suggested, could be the name used by Avicenna to express his own interpretation of some philosophical issues raised by the Aristotelian philosophy. Thus, the idea of a lost avicennian esoteric teaching is incorrect.

4. AVICENNA ON ALCHEMY

Avicenna's views on Alchemy are expressed in the fifth chapter of the first treatise of his *Meteorologica* (i.e. the fifth section of the Natural Science of *Kitāb al-Šifāʾ*) known in the West as *Avicennae de congelatione et conglutinatione lapidum*. The Arabic title of this treatise is *Kitāb al-maʿādin wa-l-āṯār al-ʿuluwiyya*. In this treatise, Avicenna gives two different theories of the formation of metals. He accepts the mercury-sulphur theory, usually attributed to Ǧābir Ibn Ḥayyān (Geber; 8th-9th century), but he also maintains the Aristotelian theory which explains the diversity of metals by the theory of condensed vapors. It is the relationship between the four Aristotelian qualities – hot, cold, moist, dry – in the mercury and sulphur substance that determines the production of all metals: 'if the mercury is pure and if it be commingled with and solidified by the virtue of a white sulphur which neither induces combustion nor is impure, but on the contrary, is more excellent than that prepared by the adepts (*ahl al-ḥīla*), then the product is silver. If the sulphur, besides being pure, is even better than that just described, and whiter, and if in addition it possesses a tinctorial, fiery, subtle, and noncombustive virtue – in short, if is is superior to that which the adepts can prepare – it will solidify the mercury into gold' (ed. Holmyard and Mandeville). Avicenna believes that there is a specific difference between silver and gold; accordingly, it is impossible to transmute one metal into another one. Only the production of a "tincture" that makes a metal externally look like another one is possible. In this treatise, Avicenna clearly rejects the opinion of the alchemists who believe that the transmutation of metals is possible: 'As to the claims of the alchemists, it must be clearly understood that it is not in their power to bring about any true change of species' (*o.c.*, 41). In Zetzner's *Theatrum chemicum* and in Manget's *Bibliotheca chemica curiosa*, we find not only the *Avicennae De Congelatione et Conglutinatione Lapidum*, but also three other treatises attributed to Avicenna The first one is the *Liber Aboali Abincine de Anima in arte Alchemiae*. It was translated into Latin in the 12th century and was considered authentic. J. Ruska (1934) has definitly demonstrated however that it is a forgery composed in Spain in the 12th century. The second one is the *Declaration Lapis physici Avicennae filio sui Aboali*. This is likewise a forgery, as has been demonstrated by Ruska in the same article. The third one is the *Avicennae ad Hasen Regem epistola de Re recta*. Modern scholars do not agree about the authenticity of this treatise (the correct latin title of which is probably *Epistola Principis Albolaly cognominis Albinsceni ad Hakasen de Re Tecta*, as emphasized by Ruska). On the basis of the Latin translation, Ruska originally considered it a forgery. Some years later however, A. Atech published a critical edition of the Arabic version (in "Ibn Sīnā, Risālat al-iksīr") which allowed him to establish the treatise as authentic. Atech identified the minister to whom the treatise is dedicated as Abū-l-Ḥasan al-Sahl b. Muḥammad al-Sahlī or al-Suhaylī, who was minister at Gorgāng where Avicenna lived between 1002 and 1005). Moreover, as Atech notes, all the Arabic manuscripts attribute this treatise to Avicenna and two of them are very old (1192 and 1298). This treatise expresses the view on alchemy of the young Avicenna, who does not yet clearly reject the possibility of the transmutation of the metals as he will do later. H.E. Stapleton likewise believes that this treatise belongs to Avicenna's early manhood (Stapleton et al. 1962).

Kitāb al-Šifā' (Treatise on the Soul, ed. G.C. Anawati & S. Zayed), Cairo, 1974 ♦ *Ḥayy Ibn Yaqzān* and the *Risāla-at-Ṭayr* have been edited by M.A.F. Mehren in his *Traités mystiques d'Avicenne*, Leyde, 1889-1891 ♦ H. Corbin had translated the two treatises into French in his *Avicenne et le recit visionnaire*, Paris: Berg international (2th ed.), 1972 ♦ Of *Salamān wa Absāl's Recital* we have only an abstract made by Naṣīr al-Dīn al-Ṭūsī (1201-1274) in his commentary of the *Kitāb al*

išārāt wa-l-Tanbīhāt. For the arabic edition, see *Kitāb al-Išārāt wa-l-Tanbīhāt lī Abī 'Alī bin Sīnā ma'a šarḥ Naṣīr al-Dīn al-Ṭūsī* (S. Dunyā, ed.), 4 vols., Cairo, 1957 ♦ "*Manṭiq al-mašriqiyyīn*" (Ṣ. al-Naġġār, ed.), Cairo, 1982 ♦ *Avicennae De Congelatione et Conglutinatione Lapidum* (E.J. Holmyard & D.C. Mandeville, eds.), Paris: Geuthner, 1927 ♦ Avicenna, *Kitāb al-Išārāt wa Tanbīhāt* (French transl. by A.M. Goichon), *Le livre des directives et des remarques*, Paris: Vrin, 1961 ♦ *The life of Ibn Sina* (W.E. Gohlman, ed. & transl.), Albany, 1974.

Lit.: M.-Th. d'Alverny, "Notes sur les traductions médiévales d'Avicenne", *Archives* 19 (1952), 337-358 ♦ idem, "Les traductions d'Avicenne (Moyen Age et Renaissance)", in: *Avicenna nella storia della cultura medievale*, Accademia Nazionale dei Lincei 304 (1957), 71-87 ♦ idem, "Les traductions d'Avicenne: quelques résultats d'une enquête", *Correspondance d'Orient* 11 (Actes du V congrès international d'arabisants et islamisants), Brussels 1970, 151-158 ♦ S. Pines, "La philosophie orientale d'Avicenne et sa polémique contre les Bagdadiens", *Archives d'histoire doctrinale et litteraire du Moyen Age* 27 (1952), 5-37 ♦ J. Ruska, "Die Alchemie des Avicenna", *Isis* 21 (1934), 14-51 ♦ A. Atech, "Ibn Sīnā, Risālat al-iksīr", *Turkiyat Mecmuasi* (1952), 27-54 ♦ idem, "Ibn Sīnā ve Elkimya", *Ankara Universitesi Ilahiyat Fakultesi Dergisi* IV (1952), 47-62 ♦ H.E. Stapleton, R.F. Azo, M. Hidāyat Ḥusain and G.L. Lewis, "Two alchemical Treatises attributed to Avicenna", *Ambix* 10 (1962), 41-82 ♦ C.A. Nallino, "Filosofia 'orientale' od 'illuminatia' d'Avicenna", *Rivista degli studi orientali* 10 (1925), 433-467 ♦ G.C. Anawati, "Avicenne et l'alchimie", *Accademia nazionale dei Lincei* 41 (1971), 285-341 ♦ A. de Libera, *L'art des généralités*, Paris, 1999 ♦ D. Gutas, "Avicenna – V. Mysticism", *Encyclopaedia Iranica* (E. Yarshater, ed.), vol. III, London/New York: Routledge and Kegan Paul, 1985, 8 ♦ idem, *Avicenna and the Aristotelian Tradition*, Leiden/New York: E.J. Brill, 1988 ♦ H. Corbin *Avicenna and the Visionary Recital*, New-York: Pantheon Books, 1960 ♦ H.A. Davidson, *Alfarabi, Avicenna, and Averroes on Intellect*, New York/Oxford: Oxford University Press, 1992 ♦ A.M. Goichon, *Le récit de Ḥayy Ibn Yaqẓān commenté par les textes d'Avicenne*, Paris: Desclée de Brouwer, 1959 ♦ idem, *La philosophie d'Avicenne et son influence en Europe médiévale*, Paris, 1951 ♦ M.E. Marmura, "Avicenna – IV. Metaphysics", in: *Encyclopaedia Iranica* (E. Yarshater, ed.), vol. III, London/New York: Routledge and Kegan Paul, 1985, 73-79 ♦ P. Lory, "Islam", in: *Dictionnaire critique de l'ésotérisme*, Paris: PUF, 1988, 663-667 ♦ G. Nogales, "El misticismo persa de Avicena y su influencia en al misticismo espanol", *Cuadernos del Seminario de Estudios de Filosofia y Pensamiento Islamicos* II, Madrid, 1981, 65-88 ♦ G. Saliba, "Avicenna – VIII. Mathematics and Physical Sciences", in: *Encyclopaedia Iranica* (E. Yarshater, ed.), vol. III, London/New York: Routledge and Kegan Paul, 1985, 88-92 ♦ M. Sebti, *Avicenne: L 'âme humaine*, Paris: PUF, 2000.

MERYEM SEBTI

Aziz, Aia → Théon, Max

Baader, Benedict Franz Xaver von,
* 27.3.1765 Munich, † 23.5.1841 Munich

1. Life 2. Work 3. Baader's
Theosophy 4. Erotic Philosophy
5. Art 6. Social Philosophy
7. Science 8. Baader and Catholicism
9. Time 10. Natur-philosophie
11. Baader and his Contemporaries
12. Baader's Influence

Undoubtedly → Christian theosophy's greatest 19th-century German exponent, Baader is a grand unifying figure, joining in his writings the domains of science, religion, and literature, as well as the three main traditions of Christianity (Protestantism [particularly theosophy], Roman Catholicism, and Eastern Orthodoxy). A peerless aphorist, Baader is intellectually among the most stimulating, profound, and difficult of the theosophers. During his lifetime, Baader stood as at least the equal of, and arguably superior to his more well known philosophical contemporaries, many of whom were awed by his insights into nature and human culture, by his immense command over numerous languages, and by his uniting of religion and science and the arts. Even the most famous of his contemporaries were dazzled by their conversations with him; → Schelling reportedly said that for several hours after talking with Baader he was no longer certain what he himself thought.

1. Life

The son of a physician, Joseph Franz von Baader, Baader early on had awakened in him an inclination to study nature; already as a child, he had an extraordinary love of learning. At the age of sixteen, he and his older brother Joseph went to the Universät Ingolstadt, where his father wanted him to study medicine; in 1783, the two went to Vienna to continue their studies. Baader returned to Munich to assist his father in medical practice, but in 1786 decided to pursue his interests in natural science, in particular minerology and chemistry. He studied minerology at Freiberg, befriending such luminaries as Alexander von Humboldt, and spent four years in England beginning in 1792, where he witnessed the social effects of the industrial revolution, especially the appearance of a proletariat class. In 1796, he returned to Germany, where he rose through a series of successively higher administrative positions, in 1800 becoming a chief administrator for a group of factories. In the same year he married Francisca von Reisky, daughter of Baron von Reisky, who bore him two children, Guido (b. 1801) and Julie (b. 1804). Through various chemical experiments Baader developed a patented formula for glass fabrication that brought him a substantial income. During this period, he met with or became known to the major philosophical and literary figures of his day, including Tieck, → Novalis, → Schelling; he also studied the works of → Louis-Claude de Saint-Martin and → Boehme. In 1814, Baader wrote to the leaders of Austria, Russia, and Prussia, in the hope that he might be instrumental in forming a greater union between East and West, particularly in religious matters. During this time, he moved in very high circles in Russia and Germany, while also studying very intensely the works of Boehme, Saint-Martin, and related authors. His first published work was "Vom Wärmestoff" (On the Substance of Warmth), in 1786, which H. Grassl has termed 'the first fruit of Romantic speculation about nature' (40). In 1792, he published an article on the use of explosives, but for many subsequent years his primary intellectual work took place in journals, where he developed the comprehensive theosophic worldview expressed by 1815 in his seminal "Ueber den Blitz als Vater des Lichtes" (On the Lightning-Bolt as the Father of Light), followed in the next year by his "Sur l'Eucharistie" (On the Eucharist), and in 1817-1818 by writings such as "Ueber die Ekstase" (On Ecstasy) and "Sur la notion du temps" (On the Notion of Time). He maintained his connections with the Russian nobility, in particular with Alexander Galitzin. Baader taught at Ludwig-Maximilian Universität from 1826 onward, offering a series of philosophical lectures at Munich university, lectures which he wrote between 1828-1832 and in which he took issue with Schelling's philosophical views.

On 17 January, 1835, Baader's first wife died after a long illness. Baader was deeply affected by that loss, and shortly thereafter he lost his brother, Joseph, as well. In 1839, Baader married a young woman named Marie Robel, who was his junior by over four decades. Around this same time, he became engaged in a number of controversies concerning the relationships between Catholicism and Protestantism, on which he had views very much colored by his own deep study of the Protestant Boehme while remaining a lifelong Catholic himself. He also engaged in these late years, i.e. 1839-1840 in an intense polemic with Hegel, with whose views he greatly disagreed. In the summer of 1840, Baader's health began to fail, and he died in 1841 after a protracted illness.

2. WORK

Referred to as "Boehmius redivivus" [Boehme reborn] by August Wilhelm Schlegel – a complimentary designation still indissolubly linked to Baader's name – Baader was a great reader of Boehme, Saint-Martin, and Meister Eckhart, whose works he rediscovered for the modern era. Most famous as a theosopher, Baader's theosophic writings encompass an unusual range of subjects. Baader's collected works were edited by Franz Hoffmann and published posthumously (Leipzig 1851). The first several volumes deal with philosophy (the first with "speculative logic"; the second with metaphysics; and the third with nature-philosophy). The fourth volume, which includes his "Sätze aus der erotischen Philosophie" (Statements from the erotic Philosophy), and his "Vierzig Sätze aus einer religiösen Erotik" (Forty Statements from a religous eroticism), is organized around the concept of "philosophic anthropology". The fifth and sixth volumes center on the theme of social philosophy, while the remaining volumes (especially the seventh through tenth) deal with various aspects of religious philosophy. The eleventh volume includes Baader's journals, the twelfth his remarks on the writings of Louis-Claude de Saint-Martin, and the thirteenth his observations on the writings of Jacob Boehme. The fourteenth volume is devoted to Baader's thoughts on concepts of time; the fifteenth includes letters and a biography; completed by an index in the sixteenth volume. Baader's writings range even more widely than this overview would indicate, however, their scope including politics, social organization, natural science, literature, economics, and religion, revealing a remarkable catholicity and depth of thought.

3. BAADER'S THEOSOPHY

Baader explicitly placed himself in the theosophic current of Jacob Boehme, and indeed, a significant portion of his collected works is devoted to the explication of Boehme's writing. Christian theosophy in the Boehmean tradition is an esoteric current with the following characteristics: 1) a focus upon Wisdom or Sophia, 2) an insistence upon direct spiritual experience, 3) a spiritual cosmology 4) a spiritual leader who guides his or her spiritual circle through letters and oral advice. These four characteristics describe such figures as → John Pordage, → Jane Leade, Thomas Bromley, and Johann Georg Rapp, all of whom were members of and led Sophianic spiritual groups devoted to direct spiritual experience, and all of whom saw nature in a spiritual light. Theosophy drew upon and in many respects synthesized a variety of pre-existing spiritual currents in the West, including → alchemy, Sophianic mysticism, and a form of spiritual → astrology. Baader belongs to this current of thought, but his work is far more philosophical than that of visionary theosophers like Pordage. Baader's work is very much engaged with and part of the intellectual currents of his age; unlike theosophers like Pordage or Bromley, whose works consist largely in accounts of their own spiritual experiences, Baader gave many university lectures, corresponded and argued with all the main philosophers of his day, and in general was much more engaged with the society in which he lived than were the more reclusive theosophers like those mentioned above.

This said, Baader's work corresponds precisely with all four characteristics of theosophy. His work is certainly Sophianic, albeit in a much more intellectual form than with most theosophers. According to Baader's complex Sophiology, Sophia is 'the mirror and the eye of God, or the first idea of God' (15.447); Sophia corresponds to Plato's Idea, to the Indian idea of Maya, and to Jacob Boehme's *magie* (9.182, 219). Sophia is 'the heavenly Virgin', but not identical to the Virgin Mary (15.449). Baader also emphasized direct spiritual experience, or gnosis, which he held to be the center of Christianity. He drew explicitly upon the work of Meister Eckhart in this regard, whose work he rediscovered. Baader writes that 'True gnosis is a circle', and that 'the systematic character of gnosis [means that] every single concept leads to the Center, and the Center in turn to all other concepts' (14.160). Baader's work certainly emphasizes a spiritual cosmology or, as he puts it, cosmosophy, and much of his work has as its purpose the renewal of a proper relationship between humanity, nature, and the divine. His works include an ecological dimension that now seems strikingly prescient, but this ecological dimension is intimately linked to his spiritual cosmology that derives from Boehme and Saint-Martin. Finally, Baader himself may be seen as a spiritual leader who sought to guide others through his letters, essays, and lectures. His audience was not only a small group, however, but was national and international in scope. In this regard, he is unique as a public intellectual among theosophers.

4. EROTIC PHILOSOPHY

It is for his "Erotische philosophie" that Baader is undoubtedly best known. Baader wrote extensively on love and the erotic impulse, perhaps not least because he recognized that in the Christian tradition as a whole these themes were not adequately dealt with. In his *Sätze aus der Erotischen*

Philosophie, Baader begins by noting that religion and love are intimately connected, and that together they bring the highest happiness possible in life; but if they remain viewed only in the "chiaroscuro of reason" their significance remains far from realized. Baader argues that every union can take place only through a subjection: one cannot have an authentic union without the generosity of giving up, most of all, giving up one's pride. He points out that the word *Sünde* (sin) has the same root as *sondern* (to separate), and this reveals the underlying meaning of sin as the opposite of love. Love unites in mutual subjection; sin separates through individual pride. But this is not to say that separation does not have its place: Baader provides the example of a parent or of a lover with whom a sharp division eventually gives way to a reconciliation that results in a deeper love. In this example there is also an allusion to the relationship between the creature and God, the creature being separated from God only to be united more strongly in the end.

Baader offers a developed and profound theory of the androgyne as central to understanding the nature of humanity as well as of individual human lives and relationships. Male and female lovers are engaged in the process of realizing in one another the original spiritual androgyne: the man helps the woman to realize masculinity in herself, just as the woman helps man to realize femininity in himself. If the lovers are not engaged in this process, the woman becomes merely a serpent to the man, while he is in turn merely a luciferian proud spirit to her.

According to Baader, love entails service: even God serves his servants. And so, Baader continues, if you want genuine worldly power, be someone who can be loved and admired; for people will only serve well those for whom they have some admixture of love and admiration. The obverse of loving service is doctrinaire blindness: 'Since the negative spirit is doctrinaire and possesses peoples' intelligence, out of it emerges a crowd of coldblooded, parched and poisonous heart-rotting philosophic, religious, and moralistic systems, mostly worse than their originator, because they are more obsessed than possessed' (*Sätze* no. 31). Baader shares his denunciation of doctrinaire systems with other theosophers, like → Gichtel; most important in human relationships is the process of loving reconciliation and deeper union. The relationship between man and woman is analogous to and a reflection of the relationship between humanity and God.

5. ART

Baader's perspective on the arts is integrally united with his religious philosophy and spiritual anthropology. He profoundly dislikes the notion that art can be separated from religion, and at one point observes that 'beautiful art should have a religious aim, or can only be laughable, where it is not flat-out irritating' (SW II: 432). The task of the great artist is to unite the good, the beautiful, and the delightful, in this way awakening in us the sense of nostalgia (*Wehmut*) over a lost paradise, thus giving us a foretaste of the future indissoluble union of these three in paradise restored. To the degree that modern art is divorced from spiritual significance and does not recall paradise to us, it is degraded and even becomes a kind of self-parody. Art must be understood in a religious context; and in order to be great art, it must also be religious. As an example of the highest Christian art, Baader mentions images of the Madonna and of Christ that in turn reflect the virginal androgyne, the angelic nature prior to and above sexual differentiation. Great art, in Baader's view, represents the transcendence of sexual desire (as exemplified in heathen works of art). A great work of art reveals the integrated, virginal and transcendent nature of humanity. It reminds the individual lovers of how, when they will step before Christ, they will become integrated, whole beings, who realize the *Urbild*, the archetype of integrated humanity (SW III: 303-310).

6. SOCIAL PHILOSOPHY

Baader's social philosophy cannot be understood except in light of his integrated religious philosophy as a whole. If great art must be understood as a revelation or reminder of paradise and in relation to Baader's philosophy of spiritual eros, likewise society as a whole must be understood in the same light. In a striking passage entitled "Der Stammbaum der Liebe" (The Family Tree of Love), from his writings on the connections between *cultus* and culture (SW V:275-276), Baader observes how the divine love descends to humanity and spreads itself outward, horizontally, toward all humanity, as well as downward in order to raise up nature. In this is the origin of the religious *cultus* and hence of all culture. Humanity comes to realize its potential in culture, which in turn is inseparable from its spiritual meaning in the religious *cultus*. Baader conceives of society as existing in a triadic relationship of love: love for fellow humanity, love for God, and love for nature. He who does not love his brother does not love God or nature either. Thus Baader strongly criticizes modern rationalism, in which all three bonds are sundered. One cannot reverence nature alone, but only in relation to these three elements of the divine, humanity, and nature. The industrial and merely money-based economic worldview exists by virtue of sundering the bonds of inheritance and heritage, dissolving the proper relationship to nature and the land, and replacing it with mere exploitation. But a proper relationship with the land is a marriage-bond that joins past humanity with future humanity, and joins humanity, nature, and the divine in a profound unity that approaches and reflects paradise. In short: love is the foundation of a just and authentic society.

Baader's theosophic worldview requires a center and respects hierarchy, but does not support despotism. In a lecture on the freedom of the intelligence, Baader argues against both leftist and rightist political positions, the former being defined as a radical insistence on total individual freedom, the latter as stultifying traditionalism (SW I:133). Both of these, like an exclusively scientific viewpoint, represent false and deceptive kinds of freedom, for only through religious perception can one come to understand true freedom, which can be realized only insofar as one realizes that all power rests ultimately in God. Thus the concept of an enlightened monarchy was not foreign to Baader's writings. He saw great hope in the founding of Ludwig-Maximilian Universität in Munich, which he perceived as a sign of a possible new unity of secular and religious learning. This university was, of course, founded under the auspices of the Kaiser by that name, and hence Baader wrote that 'Only a monarch, whose heart burns for religious things, like his spirit and heart, entrusted with the depths of science and art, is gracious, only a monarch who pronounces particularly that he will not knowingly introduce the misuse of intelligence, and who is an enemy alike to unbelief and superstition, at the expense of his people knowing his religiosity, not that he should be religious at the expense of his knowledge – only under the protection and attention of such a monarch, I say, in a full, patriotic, proud and daring testimony, can the world-reconciling bond between the priests and the learned again begin to close!' (SW I:149-150).

Baader saw society as an organic whole – one might even say as an *anthropos*, with head, limbs, and so forth – and fought strenuously against nihilism and disharmony in society. In an organic society, religion and science would be reconciled under the sign of Sophia, or divine Wisdom. Drawing on such prominent mystics as Eckhart and Tauler, Baader insisted that a healthy society is one in which there is an integral unity with the divine, and an absence of selfishness, isolation, and arrogance. Everyone in such a society would be connected with its transcendent religious center and origin. Thus he wrote of the 'necessity of an inner conjoining of religion with politics, love being the organizing principle (as the organizer par excellence' (SW II:117).

7. SCIENCE

Since Baader was himself trained as a scientist, and worked in industry, his views on science and related questions take on a particular force: he sought to conjoin science and religion in himself and in his own theosophic perspective. In 1825, he published a text titled "Alles, was dem Eindringen der Religion in die Region des Wissens sich widersetzt oder selbes nicht fördert, ist vom Bösen" (Everything that opposes or does not further the penetration of religion into the region of knowledge is evil; SW VII:47ff.). Here he strongly denounced the separation of science and religion, insisting instead that the two must be joined together for the good of each. Those who cultivate the attempted suppression of science from religious viewpoints are as destructive, from Baader's perspective, as those who, on the contrary, seek from a scientific viewpoint to ignore and suppress religion. What should be promoted is a religious science or scientific religion: scientific inquiry guided by religious awareness. And Baader goes even beyond this idea to espouse the union of art and science with religion: the striving for the Kingdom of Heaven as an inner experience should be 'the focus for all outwardly effective creations of poetry and art of man, but also it should be . . . the principle of physics as the science and art of the illuminating Idea. Of which our so-called nature philosophy barely has an idea any more, because, having lost what the man of nature should be, science has also lost what the nature of man could and should be' (SW IV:215-216). Thus Baader's central organizing principle, here as throughout his work, is that of the reunion of the arts and sciences, reintegration of humanity as a whole, under the sign of the divine.

8. BAADER AND CATHOLICISM

A lifelong Roman Catholic, Baader nonetheless held somewhat unusual views regarding his own tradition. Most well known in this regard is his opposition to the institution of the papacy. Baader argued that a synodic or collegial structure was the best means of organizing the visible church, and that the papacy was merely an historical accretion, not an intrinsic part of Catholicism (SW V:399-404; V:369-382; X:53-88). He hoped for an eventual reunion of Eastern and Western Christianity, and saw a synodic or collegial organization as the best means toward this end (SW V:391-398; X:89-254). The majority of his essays on these topics date from the last two years of his life, but their themes occupied his attention from relatively early on. Like → Novalis, Baader hoped to see the whole of Europe united in a single overarching Christendom. But in spite of being deeply inspired (also like Novalis) by Boehmean theosophy, he opposed the purely inward trend of Protestant → Pietism, insisting on the necessity of an outward church (SW XII: 538ff.). In his essay "Ueber die sichtbare und unsichtbare Kirche" (On the visible and invisible church) Baader argued for the 'inseparability of the outer and inner churches', by which he meant the union of priest, scholar, and artist under the sign of gnostic realization (SW VII:211-222).

9. TIME

Throughout his work, Baader was much concerned with the nature and significance of time. In "Sur la notion du temps (On the notion of time, 1818)" he wrote that there are, in general, two classes of beings outside time: one is above it, the other below, the one paradisal, the other demonic (SW II:69). Life moves in a cycle of descent, continuation, and re-ascent. We ordinarily assume that eternity is an 'immoveable and starry present', whereas in fact it is, strictly speaking, completedness or completion; this is the true definition of eternity. Humanity has fallen from eternity into time. Following Saint-Martin, Baader distinguishes between eternal time and illusory time. Illusory time is what we ordinarily conceive of as time rushing past: it is peripheral and without any ultimate reality. Humanity cannot find God if it remains caught in this illusion-time, trapped in the peripheral. However, it can move from the peripheral to the center once again, for the peripheral illusion-time always carries traces of its transcendent origin. This allows the re-ascent, the reintegration of separated being into transcendence; and such reintegration brings about the restoration of humanity and nature to their original, virginal nature, which is the aim of all true religion. Philosophers like Kant are mistaken because their observations remain limited to illusion-time and do not recognize the primacy of love as the reintegrating principle. As a result, their philosophies are like autopsies on a loveless corpse: their observations are relevant only to fallen beings caught in illusion-time. By contrast, Baader insists that within time itself is the regenerative power of the divine Word, which we can awaken and which ultimately leads to the realization of a higher embodiment beyond mere illusory time.

Drawing on Saint-Martin and Boehme, Baader concludes that 'The original purpose of man was "to build paradise and to spread it first over the earth, and then over the whole universe" – that is, to turn back in or to enrapture the fallen outward-turned temporal beings (creatures) with the higher, eternal nature, the crown of their life, enrapturing them again in eternity. But man himself, turning outward from the eternal into this time, does not want to be revealed any more in God, but rather only in this creature, instead of being revealed again through God. And so he then sinks beneath these creatures' (II.119-120). Thus we see Baader's theosophic diagnosis of our condition, and its implied cure.

10. NATURPHILOSOPHIE

Baader's was the era of attempts at great syntheses of religion, science, philosophy, and the arts; and arguably the most complex of these was that of Baader himself. Faivre offers the following as characteristics of → Naturphilosophie: 1. A conception of Nature as a text to decipher by → correspondences; 2. A taste for the living concrete and for a plural universe; and 3. The identity of Spirit and Nature (1994, 83). It is in this latter regard that Naturphilosophie of this period led naturally to a fascination with → animal magnetism, a particular interest of Baader's. Indeed, Baader wrote quite a bit on animal magnetism, including on the idea that 'magnetic appearances are anticipations of posthumous conditions' (II.182; IV.47). In Baader's view, magnetism offered insight into the ways that spirit enlivens nature, as well as a way of revealing the ultimate unity of science and religion through an authentic Naturphilosophie that takes into account spiritual realities – as opposed to a rationalist philosophy of nature that renders nature merely a collection of objects to be exploited or manipulated. Baader criticized some contemporary nature-philosophers, for 'whoever . . . confuses himself with this external world will eventually end up believing that he is of the same (empty or inwardly null) nature that is is' (II.89-90). Baader wrote on Naturphilosophie in such essays as "On the Pythagorean Quaternity in Nature", where as early as 1798, he pointed out the importance of the triad and the quaternity in completing the triad (III.247, 267). Both Hegel and Schelling proposed triadic philosophic principles, but Baader saw them as incomplete even from a philosophical, let alone a religious perspective (XV.178ff.; IX.307). In other words, Baader opposed to some contemporary Naturphilosophers his own perspective that includes recognition of the divine aspects of both humanity and nature, and that did not render the natural world (and humanity) empty or void as he believed scientific rationalism did. Baader's religious Naturphilosophie separated his perspective from that of many of his contemporaries, including most notably Schelling and Hegel.

11. BAADER AND HIS CONTEMPORARIES

Even though he did not publish books, Baader was recognized by his contemporaries as a great philosopher. Novalis (Friedrich von Hardenberg) spoke very highly of him, as did Hegel, Schelling, Friedrich Schlegel, Jean Paul, Tieck, Fichte, and many others. Schlegel wrote in a letter that 'the most remarkable, the most intelligent, the most profound man I have seen in a long time is indeed Baader. He has made many things clear to me'. From all accounts, Baader was a brilliant speaker, and many have described how electrifying an intellectual encounter with him could be. This can still be seen in his aphoristic writings, even though many of his contemporaries lamented the fact that Baader could not write in as organized and lucid a manner as he spoke.

Among Baader's most important relationships was his friendship with Friedrich Wilhelm Joseph von Schelling. In 1806 Schelling broke with Fichte and Spinoza and, under the influence of Baader, turned to Boehme for inspiration. For more than a decade, the two were friends, Schelling being deeply affected by Baader's philosophy. However, in 1824 they broke completely, and during the remainder of Baader's life Schelling was extremely antagonistic toward his former friend, even seeking to block the publication of his *Sämtliche Werke*. Schelling felt personally affronted by several of Baader's critiques of contemporary philosophy, and put off by Baader's theosophy. Baader's *Bemerkungen über einige antireligiöse Philosopheme unserer Zeit* (Remarks about some anti-religious philosophemes of our time, 1824; II.443ff.) Schelling saw as a personal assault. Baader, for his part, said that Schelling had lost his creative spark many years before (SW XV:431ff.), and did not countenance what he saw as Schelling's pantheism. Baader saw Schelling's philosophy, like that of Hegel, as too limited and monodimensional. Baader claimed himself as 'the first one since the introduction of Cartesian philosophy who opened up again the insight into a more profound alliance between the knowledge of natural and divine things' (*Lettres inédites* IV.367). He saw Schelling as ignoring the hidden principles of nature as revealed by Boehme and before him by → Paracelsus; in Baader's view, Schelling did not understand the erotic transcendence of male-female polarity, so that his philosophy ends in dualism and ultimately "irreligiosity" (XV.438).

Another important figure Baader knew well was Hegel, and Baader's influence on him is important but remains relatively little-known. The two first met in Berlin in 1823/24, although Hegel had known Baader's work more than two decades before. Hegel was particularly influenced by Baader's *Fermenta Cognitionis* (SW XV:401ff.), even though in this work Baader criticizes some aspects of Hegel's thought. Unlike his relationship with Schelling, Baader's relationship with Hegel remained relatively cordial, in spite of the fact that Baader strongly criticized Hegel's idealism, his separation of spirit from nature and what Baader saw as his misunderstanding of the nature of God. In Baader's view, Hegelian philosophy pointed toward the resolution of duality in the triad, but in fact like Schelling's philosophy results in a dualism and an alienation from nature. Hegel, for his part, did write that their differences were minimal in the end, but this was by no means the view of Baader himself.

12. BAADER'S INFLUENCE

Since the 19th century, Baader has been surprisingly neglected even in Germany, let alone elsewhere in the world. This lack of interest can be attributed in part to the extraordinary complexity of his thought, as well as to the byzantine complexity of his sentences. His notorious prolixity is no doubt a major reason for his relative obscurity. Ramon Betanzos attributes the decline in Baader's stature in the 20th century to Baader's not having constructed a single elegant model of philosophy. Yet, as Faivre and Betanzos himself show, Baader's thought is in fact susceptible to being explained in a clear and organized manner.

Baader's main influence lies in Russian theosophy. Vladimir Solovyov and Nicolai Berdyaev remain the most important figures to have been clearly influenced by his theosophy and in particular by his erotic philosophy. → Leopold Ziegler is arguably the 20th-century figure who most clearly continues Baader's highly intellectual current of theosophy. A number of recent studies of Baader as well as works introducing Christian theosophy as a whole – chief among them the works of Antoine Faivre – are bound to spark a reassessment of Baader's importance.

Sämtliche Werke (Franz Hoffmann, et al., eds.), 16 vols., Leipzig, 1851-1860; Aalen: Scientia,1963 ♦ *Lettres inédites de Franz von Baader* (E. Susini, ed.) vol. 1, Paris: Vrin, 1942; vol. 2/3, Wien: Herder, 1951; vol. 5, Paris: Presses Universitaires de France, 1967 ♦ *Sätze aus der Erotischen Philosophie und andere Schriften* (Gerd-Klaus Kaltenbrunner, ed.), Frankfurt: Insel, 1991; repr. 1966.

Lit.: Ramon Betanzos, *Franz von Baader's Philosophy of Love*, Vienna: Passagen, 1998 ♦ Ernst Benz, *Die russische Kirche und das abendländische Christentum*, Munich: Nymphenburger, 1966 ♦ *Franz von Baader und Kotzebue*, Mainz: Akademie der Wissenschaften, 1957 ♦ Antoine Faivre, *Access to Western Esotericism*, Albany: SUNY Press, 1994, 113-146, 201-274 ♦ idem, *Theosophy, Imagination, Tradition: Studies in Western Esotericism*, Albany: SUNY Press, 2000, 93-95, 143-149 ♦ idem, *Eckhartshausen et la théosophie Chrétienne*, Paris: Klincksieck, 1969 ♦ idem, *Mystiques, théosophes et illuminés au siècle des lumières*, Hildesheim: Olms, 1976 ♦ idem, *Philosophie de la Nature: Physique sacrée et théosophie XVIII-XIX siècle*, Paris: Albin Michel, 1996, 25-180 ♦ idem, "Franz von Baader et les Philosophes de la Nature", in; Antoine Faivre & Rolf Christian Zimmermann (eds.), *Epochen der Naturmystik: Hermetische Tradition im wissenschaftlichen Fortschritt*, Berlin: Erich Schmidt, 1979, 381-424 ♦ Hans Grassl, *Aufbruch zur Romantik: Bayerns Beitrag zur deutschen Geistesgeschichte, 1765-1785*, München, 1968 ♦ Peter Koslowski (ed.), *Die Philosophie, Theologie und Gnosis Franz von Baaders: Spekulatives Denken zwischen Aufklärung, Restauration und Romantik*, Vienna: Passagen, 1993 ♦ Peter Koslowski (ed.), *Gnosis und Mystik in der Geschichte der Philosophie*, Munich: Artemis, 1988, 243-259 ♦ Willi Lambert, *Franz von Baaders Philosophie des Gebets*, Innsbruck: Tyrolia, 1978 ♦ Eugène Susini, *Franz von Baader et le Romantisme mystique*, 2 vols., Paris: Vrin, 1942 ♦ Arthur Versluis, "Christian Theosophic Literature of the Seventeenth and Eighteenth Centuries", in: W.J. Hanegraaff and R. van den Broek (eds.), *Gnosis and Hermeticism fom Antiquity to Modern Times*, Albany: SUNY Press, 1998, 217-234 ♦ idem, *Wisdom's Book: The Sophia Anthology*, St. Paul: Paragon House, 2000, 235-247 ♦ Gerhard Wehr, *Franz von Baader: Zur Reintegration des Menschen*, Freiburg: Aurum, 1980 ♦ Lydia Processi Xella, *Baader: Rassegna storica degli studi, 1786-1977*, Bologna: Il Mulino, 1977 ♦ idem, "La Dogmatica Speculativa di Franz von Baader", *Filosofia* 28 (1988), 73-88, 379-394 ♦ idem, *Filosofia erotica*, Milan: Rusconi, 1982.

ARTHUR VERSLUIS

Bacon, Francis (first Baron Verulam and Viscount St. Albans), * 22.1.1561 London, † 9.4.1626 Highgate

Bacon was the son of a renowned attorney. Gifted with rare precocity, he had a brilliant student career at Cambridge. While he was still young (1576-1579), Elizabeth I entrusted him with a diplomatic mission to France, then appointed him Queen's Counsel; he became a member of Parliament in 1584. In 1597, he published *Essayes or Counsels Civill and Morall*. After the Queen's death, her successor James I elevated Bacon successively to the positions of Attorney General (1613), Lord Keeper of the Seal (1617), Lord Chancellor and Baron of Verulam (1618), and Viscount St. Albans (1621). But in the latter year Bacon was accused of bribery, brought before a tribunal, fined

£ 40.000, and imprisoned in the Tower of London. Soon freed, he devoted the last four years of his life to writing various works, notably the utopia *New Atlantis*, published posthumously in 1627 after *Sylva sylvarum* (Forest of Forests), a natural history book that emphasized the necessity of practical experiments. It was in the course of one of these that Bacon met his death.

Fundamentally opposed to scholasticism, Bacon had emphasized scientific activities ever since his *Advancement of Learning* of 1605. As Thorndike has noted, and, following him, Rossi, Bacon's way of envisaging these activities, i.e., his "experimental science", was partly rooted in the "occult philosophy" [→ occult / occultism] of the Renaissance. Thus in *Sylva sylvarum*, Bacon stated that he considered it 'not natural history, but a high kind of natural magic'. This collection of fragments of what was intended to be a kind of grand encyclopedia of nature and the arts was destined to furnish the materials for the "New Science", as he hopefully called it. The influence on Bacon of the magical and alchemical traditions is perhaps nowhere more evident than in these texts. For example, he declares (as also in *New Organon*) that a spiritual or pneumatic body is contained in all substances. He believes in the transmutation of metals, for according to him a metallic spirit exists that is homogeneous and common to all, so that freeing a metal from its impurities amounts to rendering it in the pure state. Matter is reducible to two elements, mercury and sulfur; air can be transformed into water. Conformably with the occult philosophy of the Renaissance, Bacon thought that man is made to "scientifically" dominate nature, of which he is the 'servant and interpreter'. He was very interested in → astrology, which he treats at length in his *De augmentis scientiarum*. And he often says that he believes in the possibility of the indefinite prolongation of human life. Lastly, like many representatives of occult philosophy, he thought that the experimental methods used by the seeker should remain secret and known only to an initiated minority.

For all this, Bacon had no indulgence for → Paracelsus, whom he treats in *Temporis partus masculus* (The Masculine Birth of Time) as a monstrous hatcher of phantasms orchestrated by the trumpets of ostentation, and the author of many obscurities (among other reproaches, he includes that of believing in the magical power of the → imagination exercised at a distance). Bacon is no more tender towards → Cornelius Agrippa, whom he regards as a clown, nor towards Ieronymus Cardanus whom he sees as a spinner of cobwebs. His

basic objection to them is their taste for ostenta-
tious marvels, whereas according to Bacon, one
should not flaunt phenomena which give the
impression of being marvelous or admirable, but
instead study them with a mind motivated solely
by scientific curiosity. This is how he tried to modify the rules of → alchemy, to fit them to the needs
of a scientific technique. For example, in *New
Organon* (Book IV, § 4), where he appropriates the
goals of alchemy and makes use of its vocabulary,
he nevertheless sees himself as aloof from the
alchemists' subjective methods, especially their
constant recourse to ancient texts which they consider sacrosanct.

Many authors have tried to associate the person
and work of Bacon with the Rosicrucian current [→
Rosicrucianism], mainly basing their allegation on
his utopia *New Atlantis*, published as fragments a
year after his death, in which he presented the ideal
of a society that was both religious and extremely
advanced in knowledge. In the college called
"Solomon's House", an order of learned priests
pursues researches at a very high level in the artistic, scientific, and technological fields, for the service of humanity. This fictional account of a world
in which the progress of knowledge, experiment,
and technique would contribute to human happiness summed up the ideal that had possessed Bacon
all his life. In fact, this work has some analogies
with two other utopias: *La città del Sole* by → Campanella, and *Christianopolis* by → Johann Valentin
Andreae. The first of these utopias, written circa
1604 in the prison of the Holy Office, had been
published in Frankfurt in 1623, thanks to the dili-
gence of Tobias Adami, a relative of Andreae, who
had brought a Latin manuscript of it from Italy.

In *New Atlantis*, as in Andreae's *Christianopolis*,
the narrator and his companions survive a perilous
voyage to arrive at an unknown coast. For Bacon,
it is the place that harbored the last survivors of
ancient Atlantis. The mariners discover in the New
Atlantis a population imbued both with the ideas
of Kabbalah [→ Jewish Influences] and with the
earliest Christian convictions, which they derived
from a Bible that came to the island in a mysterious
cedarwood ark. Moreover, the New Atlantis is situated in a place called *Ben Salem*, whilst Andreae's
Christianopolis, which had appeared in 1619, is
built on the island of *Caphar Salama*. Beside these
two references to the Hebrew *shalom*, signifying
peace, there is the fact that Bacon's *Collegium*, the
site of study and research, is called "Solomon's
House". It is a center for experimental philosophy,
where new animal and vegetable species have been
created, and air travel and submarine navigation

have been invented. Certainly Andreae's *Christianopolis* also possessed amphitheaters reserved for
the advanced study of mathematics, physics, medicine, law, and astronomy, but the accent there was
on the Christian heaven and the mystical numbers,
whereas Bacon's Academy is essentially focused on
its experimental work, and looks forward to a triumph of science. Even so, Frances A. Yates saw in
the inhabitants of New Atlantis, who knew all the
languages of Europe, disciples of the Rose-Cross:
'Modern students of Bacon', she wrote, 'are not
familiar with Rosicrucian literature . . . But those
who read the *New Atlantis* before the *Fama* and the
Confessio . . . would have immediately recognized
the R.C. Brothers and their Invisible College in the
denizens of New Atlantis' (Yates 1972, 127). While
the correspondence between *New Atlantis* and the
two Rosicrucian texts is evident, the fact remains
that the influence of the latter on Bacon's work is
unproven, and that Yates's assertion can be questioned, to say the least.

Far bolder than Yates, some authors fascinated
by the Rosicrucians, or those who call themselves
Rosicrucians, have not failed to exploit the person
and work of Bacon for their own purposes. Most
notable are those who distinguished themselves in
the "Bacon-Shakespeare controversy", especially
from the middle of the 19th century onwards. This
controversy was re-launched during the occultist
period by W.F.C. Wigston in 1888 and 1891, then
by the widely-read writings of Alfred Dodd in
1931, and it even continues today. → Manly P.
Hall, who believed in this legend, compiled its
essentials in a chapter of his popular and oft-
reprinted folio volume, *An Encyclopedic Outline
of Masonic, Hermetic, Qabbalistic and Rosicrucian Symbolical Philosophy* (1928). An 'abundant
cryptographic proof' supposedly placed this theory
beyond all possible doubt. Hall invites the reader to
view a color-portrait of Shakespeare, then to super-
impose on it a semi-transparent page carrying the
portrait of Bacon, which according to Hall 'establishes beyond all cavil the identity of the two faces'.
It is Bacon 'who wrote into the Shakespearian plays
the secret teachings of the R.C. and the true rituals
of the Freemasonic Order'.

It was in fact easy to make of Bacon one of the
original inspirers of speculative → Freemasonry,
since he was already considered a Rosicrucian, and
Rosicrucianism as having been at the origin of
masonry. For example → Elias Ashmole, together
with a handful of other learned men including the
astrologer William Lilly, took the description of
New Atlantis as a model and created in London, in
1646, the "House of Solomon" whose name and

program were directly inspired by Bacon's work. But the program itself was just as much indebted to the "Rosicrucianism" of → Robert Fludd, interpreted in an atmosphere of alchemy, → astrology, medical → magic, etc. It was a small step from there to making Bacon the indirect inspirer, through Ashmole, of the Royal Society's creation. Finally the pre-masonic aspect of the "House of Solomon", as well as the widespread idea that speculative Freemasonry, which appeared in 1717, had emerged from the Royal Society, sparked a flurry of commentaries. After that it was no longer surprising to see Bacon's name listed on a frequent *corpus nominum* in many discourses of an esoteric type, in the company of other notorious and ancient (that is, 17th century) Rosicrucians. To Bacon was even attributed the title of "Imperator" of a Rosicrucian society that allegedly already existed in his time, and his portrait invariably figures in the grand gallery of esoteric worthies, as printed and distributed by societies like the A.M.O.R.C. Hall was a typical representative of this state of mind in not hesitating to assert that Bacon, 'if not actually the Illustrious Father C.R.C., referred to in the Rosicrucian manifestoes, . . . was certainly a high initiate of the Rosicrucian Order'. More than that, Bacon 'was a link in that great chain of minds which has perpetuated the secret doctrine of antiquity from its beginning' (Hall, CLXVI, CLXVIIIf.).

We are dealing here with very typical cases of the tendency to utilize historical personages and works for purposes of legitimization, no matter what violence is done to the objective facts of history. If in truth Bacon's thought has some of its roots in the occult philosophy of the Renaissance, we have seen that that does not make him an integral part of that tradition, in which he occupies a marginal position. Bacon's tenacious presence in the history of modern Western esoteric currents is essentially due less to the intrinsic content of his oeuvre than to efforts at appropriation. What is justified, following Thorndike and other commentators, is the idea that Bacon's influence contributed to developing in the English ruling classes of his time an 'amateurish interest' in the natural sciences and experimentation, which may have played a part in the foundation of the Royal Society, in which can be seen – and this time with justification – one of the sources of inspiration of speculative Freemasonry.

The Works of Francis Bacon, 14 vols., London, 1858-1874 (reprinted Stuttgart: Friedrich Frommann Verlag, 1963) ♦ *The Complete Essays*, New York, 1963.

Lit.: Alfred Dodd, *Francis Bacon's Personal Life-Story*, 2 vols., London: Rider, 1986 ♦ Manly P. Hall, *The Secret Teachings of All Ages: An Encyclopedic Outline of Masonic, Hermetic, Qabbalistic and Rosicrucian Symbolical Philosophy, Being an Interpretation of the Secret Teachings concealed within the Rituals, Allegories and Mysteries of all Ages*, San Francisco: H.S. Crocker Co., 1928 (1st ed.; illustrations by J. Augustus Knapp; see in particular CLXVf.) ♦ Edward D. Johnson, *Bacon-Shakespeare Coincidences*, London: Bacon Society Incorporated, 1959 (2nd ed.) ♦ L.C. Eiseley, *Francis Bacon and the Modern Dilemma*, Lincoln: University of Nebraska Press, 1962 ♦ Joshua C. Gregory, "Chemistry and Alchemy in the Natural Philosophy of Francis Bacon", *Ambix* 2 (1938), 98-111 ♦ William T. Smedley, *The Mystery of Francis Bacon*, London 1912 ♦ Frances A. Yates, *The Rosicrucian Enlightenment*, London: Routledge & Kegan Paul, 1972 ♦ L. Jardine, *Francis Bacon: Discovery and the Act of Discourse*, Cambridge: Cambridge University Press, 1974 ♦ Michèle Le Doeuff, "Bacon chez les Grands au siècle de Louis XIII", in: *Francis Bacon, lessico e fortuna*, Ateneo: Rome, 1985 ♦ idem, "Un rationaliste chez Augias: la théorie de l'imagination dans la Sylva Sylvarum", in: *Les Études Philosophiques*, Paris 1985 ♦ Paolo Rossi, *Francis Bacon: From Magic to Science* (Ital. orig. 1956), London: Routledge & Kegan Paul, 1968 (reprinted Chicago/London: University of Chicago Press, 1978) ♦ Lynn Thorndike, *A History of Magic and Experimental Science*, vol. 7, New York: Columbia University Press, 1958, 63-88 ♦ C. Whitney, *Francis Bacon and Modernity*, New Haven: Yale University Press, 1986 ♦ idem, "Hope in science", in: W.A. Sessions (ed.), *Francis Bacon's Legacy of Texts*, New York/London: AMS Press, 1990 ♦ W.F.C. Wigston, *Bacon, Shakespeare and the Rosicrucians*, London: G. Redway, 1888 (new ed. 1993) ♦ idem, *Francis Bacon, Poet, Prophet, Philosopher*, London: Routledge & Kegan Paul, 1891 (new ed. 2003).

ROLAND EDIGHOFFER

Bacon, Roger, * ca. 1215 place unknown, † ca. 1292 place unknown

English philosopher, educated at the Universities of Oxford and Paris (where he lectured on Aristotle in the 1240s), author of works on a broad array of topics including optics, semantics, physics, and theology. Bacon entered the Franciscan Order in the late 1250s, perhaps after returning to Oxford. Between 1265 and 1268, he compiled his encyclopedic and ambitious works, the *Opus Maius, Opus Minus* and *Opus Tertium*, undertaken for Pope Clement IV (Pope from 1265-1268) in the hope of persuading him to authorize a radical program of educational reform for theologians. The Pope's death in 1268 put an end to Bacon's hope of acquiring a papal aegis for his project. An entry in a late 14th-century chronicle of the Friars Minor asserts that Bacon was imprisoned in the late 1270s by the Minister General of the Order who condemned his doctrine for certain suspect novelties. While the precise nature of these novelties remains a matter for scholarly speculation, it is not implausible that he was indeed imprisoned; the 1270s were a decade of reaction against the influence of Arabic learning and Bacon's thought was connected to a number of potentially controversial issues. His writing (particularly in the three volumes commissioned by the Pope) reveals an opinionated and irascible personality, who was nevertheless a systematic thinker and important synthesizer of new ideas.

Bacon had a wide array of metaphysical enthusiasms and his interest in the new learning often tended to privilege its esoteric content. He was responsible for a careful edition, with introduction and commentary, of the pseudo-Aristotelian *Secretum secretorum*. Like most medieval readers, Bacon believed the *Secretum* to be the genuine work of Aristotle, hence deserving of careful attention. According to Bacon, all knowledge derived from and returned to a single paradigm which might eventually be reconstituted by taking into account both esoteric and exoteric faces of Aristotle's works. Bacon had an investment in the claims of the *Secretum* to reveal (enigmatically) the ancient wisdom delivered at the beginning of time to the Hebrew patriarchs and prophets, who had in turn transmitted it to the Egyptians, Chaldaeans, and others of the wise. This wisdom had fallen into desuetude until after the time of Muhammad, when (according to Bacon) it began to be recuperated by → Avicenna and Averroes and the other Arabic philosophers. The West was now in a position to reassemble the ancient wisdom of the prophets, but could do so only by attending to the new learning of the Arabs, balanced of course by an intensified study of Scripture.

The new learning included astrological and alchemical writings, and both disciplines played important roles in the curriculum advocated by Bacon in the works commissioned by the Pope. In the *Opus tertium*, Bacon urges the importance of a knowledge of → alchemy for medicine. Having derived a recipe for the philosopher's stone from an enigmatic description in the *Secretum secretorum*, Bacon held that this elixir (based on human blood, but with a rectified proportion of humours) could effect not only the transmutation of metals but also the prolongation of human life to the span enjoyed by the Old Testament patriarchs. In the chapter on mathematics in the *Opus maius*, Bacon urges the importance of the study of → astrology and stresses the need to know more about astral and other occult natural powers [→ occult / occultism] in order to combat the Antichrist, whose advent he

believed to be imminent, and who, as he believed, would know how to bring to bear the occult powers of art and nature against Christendom.

When he delivered the *Opus maius* to the Pope, Bacon included a copy of a shorter treatise, *De multiplicatione specierum*, which elaborates his understanding of the optical model of the propagation of species into a broad treatment of natural causation in general with attention to its grounding in mathematics. From Bacon's elaboration of the principle of multiplication of *species* (which he also referred to as forms, similitudes, images, intentions and rays), it is clear that he had a familiarity not only with the most important current writers on optics, but also with the *De radiis stellarum* of the Arabic philosopher → Al-Kindi. While the *De radiis* itself is not cited in the *De multiplicatione specierum* (for obvious reasons; its alternate title was *Theory of Magic Art*s, and is elsewhere mentioned by Bacon as a work containing much wisdom, but corrupted with falsity), its influence clearly underlies many of Bacon's more radical claims for occult powers and astral influences, most notably his varied and potentially controversial claims made *passim* in the *Opus maius* for the *virtus verborum*, the power of words. In the papal *opera*, too, as also in his famous "Letter on the secret works of Art and Nature and on the nullity of Magic", there is evident a strong concern with differentiating bad demonic magic power from legitimate occult natural powers – a concern not dissimilar to that manifested in other writers in the same century (like → Albertus Magnus, most notably in his *Speculum astronomiae*).

Bacon's effect on esoteric philosophy in later periods would appear to be largely indirect. His alchemical theory, basing the principle of the philosopher's stone in organic materials, seems to represent a kind of evolutionary dead end in the alchemical tradition, and other aspects of his thinking about the occult powers of nature apparently wield less influence than the originality of his ideas might sometimes seem to deserve. However, it is clear that his interests in these areas contributed to Bacon's later reputation, and (like several other medieval philosophers) he becomes the subject of some rather fantastic posthumous legends involving bronze heads and magic mirrors. → Agrippa, perhaps influenced by this legendary material, refers to Bacon as a dabbler in goetia, though others assert that he does not deserve this reputation. → Pico della Mirandola upholds him as being among the wise, an early champion of natural magic, while Bacon's standing remains prominent with → John Dee, who owned most of his works and annotated his famous *Letter*. Later, as most evidently may be seen in Lynn Thorndike's interpretation, he comes to be represented as urging the claims of experimental science against the superstitious fallacies of magic. Scholarly opinion is currently swinging towards giving the esoteric and magical content of his ideas a fairer representation.

Opus Maius, in: J.H. Bridges (ed.), *The Opus Maius of Roger Bacon*, 2 volumes and supplement, Oxford: Clarendon Press, 1897 ♦ *Opus Tertium*, in: J.S. Brewer (ed.), *Rogeri Bacon Opera Quaedam Hactenus Inedita*, London: Longman, Green and Roberts, 1859 ♦ "Epistola Fratris Rogerii Baconis de Secretis Operibus Artis et Naturae et de Nullitate Magiae", in: Brewer, o.c., 523-550 ♦ *Secretum secretorum cum glossis et notulis*, in: Robert Steele (ed.), *Opera hactenus inedita Rogeri Baconi* Fasc. V, Oxford: Oxford University Press, 1920 ♦ *De Multiplicatione Specierum, Roger Bacon's Philosophy of Nature*, David Lindberg (ed.), Oxford: Clarendon Press, 1983.

Lit.: Stewart Easton, *Roger Bacon and his Search for a Universal Science*, New York: Columbia University Press, 1952 ♦ Claire Fanger, "Things Done Wisely by a Wise Enchanter: Negotiating the Power of Words in the Thirteenth Century", *Esoterica* I (1999), 97-132 at http://www.esoteric.msu.edu/Archive.html Volume 1 ♦ Jeremiah Hackett, "Roger Bacon: His Life, Career and Works", in: Jeremiah Hackett (ed.), *Roger Bacon and the Sciences: Commemorative Essays*, Leiden/New York/Köln: E.J. Brill, 1997, 9-23 ♦ idem, "Roger Bacon on Astronomy-Astrology: The Sources of the *Scientia Experimentalis*", in: *Roger Bacon and the Sciences*, 175-198 ♦ George Molland, "Roger Bacon as Magician", *Traditio* 30 (1974), 445-460 ♦ idem, "Roger Bacon and the Hermetic Tradition in Medieval Science", *Vivarium* 31 (1993) 140-160 ♦ William R. Newman, "An Overview of Roger Bacon's Alchemy", in: *Roger Bacon and the Sciences*, 317-336 ♦ Irene Rosier, *La Parole comme Acte*, esp. Ch. 6, "Le pouvoir magique des mots", Paris: J. Vrin, 1994 ♦ Steven J. Williams, "Roger Bacon and the *Secret of Secrets*", in: *Roger Bacon and the Sciences*, 365-391.

CLAIRE FANGER

Bailey, Alice Ann, * 16.6.1880 Manchester, † 15.12.1949 New York

Born to Frederic Foster La Trobe-Bateman and Alice Hollinshead, Alice Ann La Trobe-Bateman is best known by the name she assumed when she married her second husband, Foster Bailey. She is chiefly remembered for three accomplishments. First, for serving as the amanuensis for her Tibetan master Djwhal Khul (known simply as The Tibetan or D.K.), the latter's teachings appearing in twenty-four books written from 1922 until the late 1940s, all of which reflect a Theosophically-based inter-

pretation of Humanity and the Cosmos. Second, for establishing an esoteric school known as the Arcane School in 1923. And third, as organizer (with her husband Foster Bailey) of two service activities known as "World Goodwill" and "Triangles".

Her religious upbringing was conservative Christian but with a "mystical" tendency. Although she came from a prominent family (the La Trobes), she led a life that was sometimes troubled in her youth (she had attempted suicide thrice by the age of 15), privileged (she claimed to have lived the life of a "society girl" up to the age of 22, living with her well-to-do grandparents and later, after their death when she was about eight years old, with her aunt), and service-oriented. Regarding the latter, having been stimulated by her upbringing to care for the poor and the sick, she attempted to put her fundamentalist Christian religious ideals into practice first by becoming a Y.M.C.A. worker and later, in her early twenties, by working as an evangelist to the British troops in the Sandes Soldiers Homes in Ireland and India. Despite this fundamentalist upbringing, Alice exhibited esoteric inclinations as well. According to her autobiography, this latter tendency first came to the fore in 1895, when at the age of fifteen, while with her aunt at Kirkcudbrightshire, Scotland, she experienced her initial contact with what she later came to see as a "Master of Wisdom": a member of that spiritually advanced hierarchy believed by Theosophists to disclose elements of the ancient wisdom to humans. The message of the Master – whose name she later discovered was Koot Hoomi or K.H. – was that she should work in the world on his behalf. A second event that she claimed to have occurred around the same time, and which she came to regard as significant, was her participation in a ceremony performed during the "Full Moon of May". The precise nature of this ceremony is unclear, but Alice claimed that it was held every year in a valley in the Himalayas, obviously implying an esoteric ceremony of some sort. Participation in this ceremony helped her realize her spiritual status, and perceive the unity of all existence as a 'divine and living whole' demonstrating 'the glory of the Lord'. For the next fifteen years or so, she led a tripartite life: first, that of evangelist and social worker following fundamentalist dogma; second, that of a budding mystic who retained a sense of the Hierarchy of Masters connected to inner spiritual planes; and third, from her late twenties to her mid-thirties, that of a woman involved in the world as the wife of a clergyman (Walter Evans) and mother of three daughters. The marriage, in 1907 or 1908, re-sulted in the couple traveling to the United States of America for reasons of her husband's seminary training. But the marriage soon disintegrated due to her husband's mental problems; his increasing violence, including occasional physical abuse of his wife, led to their divorce in 1915. Alice found herself without money, and was forced to make ends meet by working in a sardine cannery in Pacific Grove, California.

At this same time (1915), she first came into contact with the → Theosophical Society and its teachings. Having been exposed to the writings of → Helena P. Blavatsky, especially *The Secret Doctrine*, and those of → Annie Besant, she gradually mastered the Theosophical worldview that was to become basic to her understanding of the ancient wisdom as taught through her other Master, The Tibetan (Djwhal Khul), who appeared to her for the first time in 1919. These teachings included the following main points: (a) that there is a divine Plan in the universe; (b) that those who execute the Plan and who guide Humanity make up a Hierarchy of spiritual leaders led by the Christ; and (c) the Law of Cause and Effect and the law of rebirth (karma and → reincarnation). The "collaboration" with The Tibetan resulted in a vast corpus of teachings, beginning in 1922 with a volume called *Initiation, Human and Solar*.

A Treatise on Cosmic Fire (first published in 1925) provides a detailed description of how the macro- and microcosm have emanated from the "Boundless Immutable Principle", interpreted by the author as identical with the Parabrahm of H.P. Blavatsky's *Secret Doctrine*. On the macrocosmic level arise the three *Logoi*, described as the "Undifferentiated and Unmanifested", the aspect of "Duality of Spirit-Matter", and "Cosmic Ideation" (or the Universal World-Soul, the Creator). From the Logoi are manifested the universes, which in turn comprise "Manifesting Stars and Solar Systems". Three micro- and macrocosmic laws are associated with the three *Logoi* as cosmic functions: Synthesis (expressed as Will), Attraction (expressed as Love), and Economy (expressed as Intelligence). Seven centers of "logoic Force", also known as the seven planetary Logoi and the seven Rays, emanate from these Laws: Ray I (the Ray of Will or Power), II (Love-Wisdom), III (Active Intelligence), IV (Harmony, Beauty and Art), V (Concrete Knowledge or Science), VI (Devotion or Abstract Idealism), and VII (Ceremonial Magic or Order). These Rays, therefore, are manifestations or emanations of both the macro- and microcosm. By definition, a ray is 'a name for a particular force or type of energy, with the emphasis upon the qual-ity which that force exhibits and not upon the form aspect which it creates' (*Esoteric Psychology* I, 316). Applied to humanity and humans, the doctrine of rays is supposed to explain qualities of all of humanity, of the races, of cycles, of nations, of the soul, of the personality, and of the elements of the human mental, astral, and physical bodies.

Apart from the teachings of the Tibetan, which are published through the Lucis Trust – an entity created by Alice and Foster Bailey (who were married in 1919) in 1922 – the other main source through which Bailey's theosophy has been spread is the Arcane School, established by Bailey in April 1923 as a correspondence school designed to answer the questions raised by readers of her publications. As the name indicates, it is an esoteric school modeled after the original Esoteric Section of the Theosophical Society founded by Blavatsky. The seven principles or propositions of the Arcane School (described at the end of her *Unfinished Autobiography*) are: (1) it is a training school for disciples; (2) it is devoted to training *adult* men and women so that they may take their next step upon the path of evolution; (3) the School recognizes the Spiritual Hierarchy of the planet, and its instructions about the mode whereby that Hierarchy may be approached and entered; (4) it teaches that the 'souls of men are one'; (5) it teaches the necessity of *living* the spiritual life and rejects all claims to spiritual status; (6) it is non-sectarian, non-political, and international in its scope; (7) it claims to emphasize no theological dogmas, but teach only the Ageless Wisdom as recognized in all countries down through the ages. In addition to these principles, the essential teachings of the Arcane School are described as follows: (1) that the Kingdom of God, the Spiritual Hierarchy of our planet, is already invisibly present and will be materialized on earth; (2) that there has been a continuity of revelation down the ages and that from cycle to cycle God has revealed Himself to humanity; (3) that God Transcendent is equally God Immanent, and that through human beings, who are in truth the sons of God, the three divine aspects – knowledge, love and will – can be expressed; (4) that there is only one divine Life, expressing itself through the multiplicity of forms in all the kingdoms of nature, and that the sons of men are, therefore, ONE; (5) that within each human being there is a point of light, a spark of the one Flame – this is believed to be the soul, the second aspect of divinity, 'the *demonstration* of the divine livingness in each person which is our goal, and discipleship is a step upon the way to that attainment'; (6) that an ultimate perfection is possible for the individual aspirant and for humanity as a whole through the action of the evolutionary process (involving a 'myriad of developing lives, each with its place within the scheme . . . [leading] to those exalted spheres where the Lord of the World works out the divine Plan'); (7) that there are certain immutable laws governing the universe, and man becomes progressively aware of these as he evolves, these laws being expressions of the will of God; (8) that the basic law of our universe is to be seen in the manifestation of God as *Love*.

The ideas developed within the Arcane School led to the formation of two organizations that were founded to 'channel activity' in light of the teachings. The first, "Men of Goodwill" (later renamed "World Goodwill") was founded in 1932 in order to establish human relations based on the principle of "brotherhood" and non-discrimination with respect to race, religion, ideology, politics, and economic convictions. The second organization, "Triangles", was established in 1937, and operates according to a principle of networking that allows three individuals to 'link each day in thought for a few minutes of creative meditation'. "Triangles" is linked with "World Goodwill" as a microcosm of relationships established on a personal level, embodying a "spirituality" that purportedly bears no relation to any one religion. World Goodwill emphasizes an ethic based upon the 'Will to Good'. This Will is expressed in the esoteric philosophy of the Arcane School and the publications of the Tibetan through Bailey. Finally, all the teachings and service activities are encapsulated in the 'Great Invocation': 'From the point of Light within the Mind of God / Let light stream forth into the minds of men. / Let Light descend on Earth. // From the point of Love within the Heart of God / Let love stream forth into the hearts of men. / May Christ return to Earth. // From the centre where the Will of God is known / Let purpose guide the little wills of men – / The purpose which the Masters know and serve. // From the centre which we call the race of men / Let the Plan of Love and Light work out / And may it seal the door where evil dwells. // Let Light and Love and Power restore the Plan on Earth'.

Bailey's work has had a great influence on the development of contemporary esotericism. Although it is difficult to ascertain the number of individuals who have been exposed and influenced by her teachings, it may well be in the hundreds of thousands, if one judges from the publication records of Lucis Publishing Companies. Many of the teachings – such as those on spiritual evolution, the perfectibility of humanity, the unity of life, and

emphasis on "Love" – are closely related. These teachings, and the promise of a "New Age" – prominent not only in Bailey's publications but also reflective of the Zeitgeist of the 1920s and 1930s, and adopted and further popularized from the 1960s on – also contribute to her popularity: the earlier, England-based, utopian/millenarian phase of the → New Age movement was heavily influenced by Bailey's theosophy. In addition, Bailey's grand esoteric cosmology, rivaling those of Blavatsky, → Steiner, → Gurdjieff and → Ouspensky, helps add to her reputation as a significant thinker. As a result of the interest in this cosmology, a number of groups have developed in addition to the Arcane School and its sister organizations, including the Aquarian Educational Group, Arcana Workshops, the School for Esoteric Studies, the Tara Center, and Meditation Groups, Inc.

The Unfinished Autobiography of Alice A. Bailey, New York: Lucis Press Company, 1951 (1973) ♦ *Initiation, Human and Solar*, New York: Lucis Press Company, 1922 (1972) ♦ *Esoteric Psychology*, Two volumes, New York: Lucis Press Company, 1936 (1991) for volume I and 1942 (1970) for volume II ♦ *The Externalisation of the Hierarchy*, New York: Lucis Press Company, 1957 (1989) ♦ *A Treatise on Cosmic Fire*, New York: Lucis Press Company, 1925 (1979) ♦ *The Rays and the Initiations*, New York: Lucis Press Company, 1960 (1993) ♦ *A Treatise on White Magic*, New York: Lucis Press Company, 1934 (1979).

Lit.: Philip Jenkins, *Mystics and Messiahs: Cults and New Religions in American History*, Oxford and New York: Oxford University Press, 2000 ♦ J. Miller, "In Defense of Alice A. Bailey", *Theosophical History* 2 (1988), 190-206 ♦ Sir John R. Sinclair, *The Alice Bailey Inheritance*, Wellingborough Northamptonshire: Turnstone Press Limited, 1984 ♦ Steven J. Sutcliffe, *Children of the New Age: A History of Spiritual Practices*, London and New York: Routledge: Taylor & Francis Group, 2003.

JAMES A. SANTUCCI

Ballanche, Pierre Simon, *4.8.1776 Lyons, † 12.6.1847 Paris

The Ballanche family owned a publishing house in Lyons. An encounter with Juliette Récamier during her period of exile under Napoleon transformed Pierre-Simon's ambitions. Upon his father's death in 1816, Ballanche sold the business and moved the next year to Paris, where he devoted the rest of his life to private study and chaste devotion to Mme. Récamier. Ballanche held himself above the political factionalism of the Restoration era, believing that social and political harmony could be achieved only through an intellectual mediation of old and new values under a vision of a progressive Christianity. It was the elaboration of a progressive Christianity appropriate to the post-Revolutionary age that Ballanche set out to achieve in his works. Election to the Académie française in 1842 only partly assuaged Ballanche's conviction that his contemporaries had neither understood nor appreciated his teaching.

The intellectual career of the deeply, if heterodoxically, Catholic Ballanche began under the influence of → Joseph de Maistre and Louis de Bonald. Ballanche, however, influentially modified Traditionalism by adding to it an element of social progressivism. His work also displays familiarity with a wide range of esoteric thought, including → J. Boehme, → L.C. de Saint-Martin, the magnetizers Jacques Pététin and Johann Carl Passavant, and, above all, → A. Fabre d'Olivet, whom he knew personally.

Ballanche believed that the divine order underlying the material universe is discernible through the complementary mediations of symbolic imagination and primitive revelation. Ballanche's cosmos is the cosmos of → correspondences of the Illuminists: the material universe both veils the underlying spiritual reality and is a symbolic reproduction of it. The symbolic imagination of the poet-seer – exemplified in his *Vision d'Hébal* and discussed in Bk. VII of *Orphée* – intuits spiritual truths and translates them into material form (Ballanche is one of the founders of 19th-century symbolist poetics). Poetry is the intuitive faculty of penetrating the essence of beings and things. The direct and immediate contemplation of the unity and harmony of all things is a vision that lifts the seer out of time and space (Hébal's vision of the entire history of humanity lasts only as long as it takes a church clock to toll the Ave Maria). But this is the privilege of the few. Ballanche's philosophy of history, which is played out in time and space, is the story of the reintegration of all humanity.

As indicated by the titles of Ballanche's major works, *Institutions sociales* (1818) and *Essais de Palingénésie sociale* (1827-1831), the social order receives pride of place in Ballanche's philosophy of history. Social palingenesis, or social evolution, the providential law governing history, is the sequence of births, deaths, and rebirths of societies throughout the centuries of human history. Each new stage of social evolution effects the initiation of a greater proportion of humanity into knowledge of the primitive revelation and full participation in religion and society. Each social evolutionary advance must be won at the price of suffering because it is the means by which humanity expiates original sin. Social evolution will culminate in full religious and social equality for all humanity. This religio-social utopia, which Ballanche believes to be close at hand, will mark the completion of the terrestrial phase of the rehabilitation of humanity from the Fall.

While the doctrine of correspondences is fundamental to the nature of the world in which social evolution unfolds, the Illuminist themes central to the operation of Ballanche's philosophy of history are those of the identity of the fall and rehabilitation, redemption as the reintegration of lost unity, initiation, and magnetism [→ Animal Magnetism/Mesmerism]. Ballanche posits, prior to all history, a Primordial or Universal Adam. The Fall shattered the original unity of the primordial Adam by casting him into the world of time and space; into, that is, a process of succession and division that sundered the original unity into a multiplicity of individuals and generations. By entering into time and division (sexual and, even more fundamentally, social), humanity is able to expiate its sin over countless generations. The Fall transformed Universal Adam into social evolutionary humanity. And because social evolution is the means by which the lost unity of humanity will be restored, the means of overcoming the consequences of the Fall were produced in the Fall itself.

Social evolution operates by means of initiation, or the acquisition of responsibility. The content of primitive revelation has been transmitted through an unbroken chain of initiations down the ages. Initiation, for Ballanche, comprises the knowledge that the purpose of social life is the spiritual end of overcoming the effects of the Fall. Those in a given society who understand this are the initiators; those who do not are the initiateables. In the cosmogonic age (the first of three ages in Ballanche's philosophy of history), only isolated sages like Orpheus understood the rehabiliatory function of social life. The patrician age is so named because it marks the accession of the patricians to the knowledge that society is an instrument for the spiritual rehabilitation of humanity. History thenceforth chronicles the plebeians' slow acquisition of social responsibility and self-awareness. When, at the culmination of the plebeian age, the entire human race has come into possession of this knowledge, the initiation of humanity will be complete and social evolution will have accomplished its purpose. Each successive initiation represents a social evolutionary advance, the sum of which constitutes the rehabilitation of humanity.

Vision d'Hébal introduces Hébal as a Scottish chieftain endowed with second sight. Released from the limits of space and time and freed of his individuality, Hébal's consciousness is assimilated to the universal consciousness, he seizes immutable truths, and becomes the Universal Man living an infinite life. This description accords with contemporary theories (J.P.F. Deleuze and A.J.F. Bertrand) about animal magnetism. Allusions to magnetism, in fact, appear throughout *Palingénésie sociale*: Orpheus' account in Book II of *Orphée* of his poetic vision is strongly reminiscent of Hébal's vision; in *Prolégomènes*, Ballanche links magnetic somnambulism and linguistic capability as survivals of a primitive human faculty; and in *Orphée* he suggests that magnetism offers us the possibility of knowledge of the primitive instinctive faculties and suggests that these faculties will be reacquired as humanity evolves.

While it is sometimes difficult to tell what in Ballanche comes directly from Fabre d'Olivet, Saint-Martin, or Boehme, and what comes from these or other theosophical writers via intermediaries, the centrality of Illuminist themes demonstrates how deeply Ballanche's thought is indebted to the Western esoteric tradition. Nevertheless, Ballanche adapted his borrowings from → Illuminism by linking them to the history of social institutions. By reading historical events, not merely as signs of the process of the reintegration of the primordial Adam, but as the necessary and efficacious means of that reintegration, Ballanche historicized what he borrowed from Illuminism. Ballanche, finally, was not, properly speaking, an Illuminist: he never claimed to have experienced interior illuminations permitting him to penetrate the divine understanding; he did not consider himself a disciple of Boehme or any other Illuminist; and he was not initiated into any Illuminist society. Ballanche, moreover, seems less confident than the Illuminists that we can truly know the spiritual world; he does not deny the possibility of inspired theosophical knowledge, but restricts himself in his works to the historical demonstration of the terrestrial mission of humanity.

Essai sur les Institutions sociales dans leur rapport avec les idées nouvelles, Paris: Didot, 1818 ♦ *Essais de Palingénésie sociale: Prolégomènes*, Paris: Didot, 1827 ♦ *Essais de Palingénésie sociale. Orphée*, Paris: Didot, 1829 ♦ *Oeuvres complètes*, 6 vols., Paris: Bureau de l'Encyclopédie des connaissances utiles, 1833; repr. Genève: Slatkine Reprints, 1967 ♦ *La Vision d'Hébal* (1831) (A.J.L. Busst, ed.), Genève: Droz, 1969.

Lit.: Paul Bénichou, *Le Temps des Prophètes: Doctrines de l'âge romantique*, Paris: Gallimard, 1977, 74-104 ♦ Claude-Julien Bredin, *Correspondance philosophique et littéraire avec Ballanche* (Auguste Viatte,

ed.), Paris: Boccard, 1928 ♦ Joseph Buche, *L'Ecole mystique de Lyon 1776-1847*, Paris: Alcan, 1935, passim ♦ A.J.L. Busst, "Ballanche et le poète voyant", *Romantisme* 4 (1972), 84-101 ♦ Alfred Marquiset, *Ballanche et Mme. d'Hautefeuille: Lettres inédites de Ballanche, Chateaubriand, Sainte-Beuve, Mme. Récamier, Mme Swetchine, etc.*, Paris: Champion, 1912 ♦ Arthur McCalla, *A Romantic Historiosophy: The Philosophy of History of Pierre-Simon Ballanche*, Leiden, Boston & Köln: E. J. Brill, 1998 ♦ Arlette Michel, "Ballanche et l'épopée romantique", in: *Mélanges Jeanne Lods*, Paris: L'Ecole Normale Supérieure de Jeunes Filles, 1978, 876-886 ♦ Jacques Roos, *Aspects littéraires du mysticisme philosophique et l'influence de Boehme et de Swedenborg au début de romantisme: William Blake, Novalis, Ballanche*, Strasbourg: P.H. Heitz, 1951, 327-436 ♦ Auguste Viatte, *Les Sources occultes du romantisme*, 2 vols., Paris: Champion, 1928; reprint 1979, 214-242.

ARTHUR MCCALLA

Balsamo, Giuseppe → Cagliostro, Alessandro di

Barlet, François-Charles (ps. of Albert Faucheux), * 12.10.1838 Paris, † 24.10. 1921 Paris

A civil servant employed in the Registry, after law studies required by his father (librarian at the Bibliothèque de l'Arsenal), Albert Faucheux found in occultism [→ occult/occultism] the compensation for the scientific study he had been denied. First posted in Corsica, where he spent his free time in botanical studies, he then moved near Paris, where initiatic societies were flourishing in the 1880s, and concluded his career in 1899 as departmental director at Abbeville. He had meanwhile married Jeanne Bellchambers, an English singer and widow of a legal adviser, who protected his solitude – a little too much, so his occultist friends thought – and to whom he remained very attached until her death at the beginning of World War I. Thenceforth he lived an ascetic life in the Rue des Grands-Augustins, Paris, dividing his time between occultist societies and working on publications. There were few such societies to which he did not belong, his enthusiasm sometimes extending to frauds pure and simple (e.g., the *Centre ésotérique oriental de France* of Albert de Sarak). In addition to these activities, he regularly attended services in Notre-Dame Cathedral, the ritual of the Catholic Church having long fascinated him. This omnipresence made him a living archive of the occultist world; → Guénon owed him much of his own information on this subject. After having been one of the first members in France of → Madame

Blavatsky's → Theosophical Society, and apparently having belonged to the → Hermetic Brotherhood of Luxor, Barlet played an important role in a group descended from the latter, the Philosophie Cosmique of → Max Théon (Barlet took on the editing of its journal in 1901 and 1902). As a Gnostic bishop consecrated in 1890 by Jules Doinel (1842-1902), Barlet entered the Supreme Council of the Martinist Order [→ Martinism] of → Papus (1891), then became a directing member of the Ordre Kabbalistique de la Rose Croix of → Guaïta (1892). It was to → Saint-Yves d'Alveydre that Barlet, after a secular education, owed his interest in Judeo-Christianity, and in a Christianity conceived as the best possible object of study, which would open up to a vision of the synthetic and unitary world: that of synarchy. After the death of his master, Barlet published Saint-Yves' unfinished work, the *Archéomètre*, in Guénon's *La Gnose*. There was nothing in Barlet of the religious founder or the magus; he aspired to make occultism into a positive science, establishing laws and creating a pedagogy. → Astrology seemed to him the most suitable means for reconciling the demands of science with the attainments of tradition, but his publications were extremely varied.

Essai de chimie synthétique, Paris: Chamuel, 1894 ♦ *Principes de sociologie synthétique*, Paris: Chamuel, 1894 ♦ *Synthèse de l'esthétique*, Paris: Chamuel, 1895 ♦ *L'Art de demain*, Paris: Chamuel, 1897 ♦ *Ordre kabbalistique de la Rose-Croix*, Paris: l'Ordre, 1891 ♦ *La Tradition cosmique*, Paris 1903.

Lit.: Charles Blanchard, Louis Leleu, Paul Redonnel, Victor-Emile Michelet, Sédir, Georges Tamos, Emmanuel Delobel, Paul Chacornac, "Numéro exceptionnel consacré à la mémoire de F.-Ch. Barlet", *Le Voile d'Isis* 59 (1924) ♦ Jean-Pierre Laurant, *L'Esotérisme chrétien au XIXᵉ siècle*, Lausanne: L'Age d'Homme, 1992, chs. IV-V.

JEAN-PIERRE LAURANT

Barrett, Francis, * 18.12.1774 Marylebone, London, † probably ca. 1830 London

Barrett described himself, on the title-page of *The Magus*, the book on which his reputation rests, as a 'Professor of Chemistry, natural and occult Philosophy, the Cabala, &c., &c.' This was a somewhat grandiose claim for a man whose profession was that of apothecary and it brought derision from his contemporaries: the poet Robert Southey described him as a rascal who 'professes to teach the occult sciences' while being 'a greater rogue than Solomon'.

This jaundiced view was due in part to the notoriety Barrett had gained in 1802 from a series of unsuccessful attempts at balloon ascents that he had made, in front of very large crowds, first at Greenwich and subsequently at Swansea. Apart from these events little is known of Barrett's life. In his early adult years he travelled in the West of England and in South Wales. He was married at Barnstaple, Devon, in 1800 but returned to London where his son was born in 1801. Nothing certain is known about Barrett's career subsequent to the year 1802.

Equally uncertain is the source of Barrett's enthusiasm for occultism [→ occult/occultism], but in 1801 his one unquestioned work, *The Magus, or Celestial Intelligencer; being a complete system of Occult Philosophy*, was published at London by the prestigious publishing house of Lackington, Allen and Co. This compendium of the theory and practice of the occult sciences is largely derived from earlier books, notably the spurious *Fourth Book of Occult Philosophy* attributed to → Cornelius Agrippa, and the works of → Peter of Abano and → John Heydon. Barrett had access to copies of these and many similar texts from the library of Ebenezer Sibly, which had been acquired, after Sibly's death in 1799, by John Denley, a bookseller specialising in occult books and manuscripts. According to Frederick Hockley, Barrett had borrowed from Denley 'the whole of the materials' that he needed to write *The Magus* but had 'never recompensed him with a copy'.

But however many sources Barrett may have drawn upon, *The Magus* marked a departure in English occult literature. It was the first comprehensive survey of magic to be compiled by an avowed practitioner, and one who also gave 'private instructions and lectures' on the subjects contained in the book. The advertisement for this proposed institution, which was to be limited to twelve students, offered to initiate students into virtually every branch of the occult sciences. Barrett's original plans were much less grand. In the manuscript of *The Magus* (now in the library of the Wellcome Institute) he offered simply to correspond with interested readers, and it seems probable that the printed book, complete with engraved plates of talismans and Barrett's coloured drawings of the heads of demons, so impressed its author that he conceived the idea of a school of occult philosophy.

What success the school met with is unknown, but Barrett did have one apt pupil in the person of "Dr." John Parkins, an unsavoury astrologer, crystal gazer and author of two books on fortune-telling and folk-medicine, who set up a "Temple of Wisdom" at Little Gonerly in Lincolnshire. Barrett gave Parkins a manuscript on crystal gazing and associated magical practices, and it is clear from annotations by Parkins that he made use of it. But neither Barrett's "school" nor royalties from *The Magus* brought him financial security and Hockley's comment on his career is probably accurate: 'Barrett, notwithstanding his professorship of Magic, lived and died in poverty.'

One later book, the anonymous *Lives of Alchemystical Philosophers* (1815) has been frequently attributed to Barrett, but the weight of evidence is against this. His reputation thus stands or falls with *The Magus* which, despite its many faults, exercised a significant influence on the ideas and the writings of the many magicians and would-be Rosicrucians who flourished during the "occult revival" of the later 19th century. Nothing like it was published subsequently until members of the → Hermetic Order of the Golden Dawn began to produce their own editions and translations of magical and kabbalistic texts from 1889 onwards. That *The Magus* also was being regularly reprinted and is still being read late in the 20th century is a testament to the genius of its enigmatic author.

The Magus, or Celestial Intelligencer; being a complete system of Occult Philosophy, London: Lackington, Allen & Co, 1801 ♦ Surviving manuscripts by Barrett: Wellcome Library MS 1072 Holograph of *The Magus* (1800); MS 1073 *Direction for the Invocation of Spirits* (1802), Yale University Library, Mellon Collection MS 140 George von Welling, *Philosophy of the Universe*. Holograph transcription by Barrett of a translation into English of c 1780 (1801).

Lit.: Alison Butler, "Beyond Attribution: The Importance of Barrett's *Magus*", *Journal for the Academic Study of Magic* 1 (2003), 7-32 ♦ Ron Heisler, "Behind 'The Magus': Francis Barrett, Magical Balloonist", *Pentacle* 1:4 (1985), 53-57 ♦ Frederick Hockley, *The Rosicrucian Seer: Magical Writings*, Wellingborough: Aquarian Press, 1986 ♦ Francis X. King, *The Flying Sorcerer: Being the Magical and Aeronautical Adventures of Francis Barrett, Author of The Magus*, London: Mandrake, 1992 ♦ Timothy d'Arch Smith, *The Books of the Beast: Essays on Aleister Crowley, Montague Summers, Francis Barrett and Others*, Wellingborough: Aquarian Press, 1987.

ROBERT A. GILBERT

Basilides, 2nd century

1. BASILIDES ACCORDING TO CLEMENT OF ALEXANDRIA, ORIGEN, EUSEBIUS OF CAESAREA AND HEGEMONIUS 2. BASILIDES ACCORDING TO IRENAEUS 3. BASILIDES ACCORDING TO HIPPOLYTUS

Basilides was a free Christian teacher who presumably lived and taught in Alexandria during the reign of the emperor Hadrian (cf. Jerome, *Chronicle*, 201, 1f Helm). He had a son who became his disciple, Isidore. The ancient evidence about Basilides and his school can be divided into three groups: 1. the fragments and testimonies preserved by → Clement of Alexandria, Origen, Eusebius of Caesarea and Hegemonius (*Acta Archelai*); 2. the report of Irenaeus of Lyon, which influenced the heresiology of Pseudo-Tertullian, Epiphanius of Salamis and Filastrius of Brescia; 3. the report of Hippolytus of Rome. Scholarly opinion is divided as to the question whether 2. and 3. contain valid and authentic information. There is some scholarly consensus that 1., particularly the original fragments preserved by Clement of Alexandria, are authentic and might – where possible – be used as a touchstone for 2. and 3. A majority of scholars seems to accept 3. as genuine in one way or another. The view of the present author is that only 1. contains information about the teaching of Basilides and his early circle of disciples (perhaps only Isidore, but that remains unclear in Clement). 2 and 3 are either spurious, i.e. they are not by Basilides and his disciples, or reflect the views of later Basilideans. It is possible that Hippolytus or his source are using information derived from Irenaeus of Lyon and Clement of Alexandria.

1. BASILIDES ACCORDING TO CLEMENT OF ALEXANDRIA, ORIGEN, EUSEBIUS OF CAESAREA AND HEGEMONIUS

Basilides wrote *Exegetica* in 24 books (Agrippa Castor, in Eusebius, *HE* IV, 5, 7-8); this is probably a commentary on a gospel. The identity of this gospel is unclear. Origen mentions in passing that Basilides had written his own gospel (*Homilies on Luke* I, 2); and this claim, which is not confirmed by any other source, is not impossible. Perhaps Basilides had produced his own gospel "edition" upon which he then commented. There are indications that Basilides' gospel is based on the Gospel of Luke (see below). For Basilides' son Isidore, however, the use of the Gospel of Matthew is attested (see below). Three fragments of Basilides' *Exegetica* have been preserved, one in Clement and two in Hegemonius.

Clement of Alexandria presents in *Stromateis* IV, 81, 1-83, 1 a large fragment from the 23rd book of Basilides' *Exegetica*. It addresses the question of how the goodness and justice of God can be reconciled with the execution of persecuted Christians. Basilides rejects the answer that the deaths of

Christian martyrs are the work of the devil. For him, this is God's way of punishing the hidden sins of the Christians; it is a sign of the goodness of God that the Christians are not punished for any misdeeds but rather for their being Christians. Basilides defends the justice of God: if someone has not committed an actual sin, he may still undergo divine punishment, because he has the internal disposition to sin. Divine providence cannot be bad and unjust; every human being is sinful (Job 14:4 LXX), only God is just. It is striking how Basilides here combines two traditionally distinct ideas (cf. Philo of Alexandria): on the one hand, the goodness of a God who benefits his creatures, on the other hand, the justice of a God who judges and punishes. Basilides indicates that God guides human beings (*agein, periagein*); he seems to accept the Platonic and biblical concept of pedagogical and cathartic punishments (cf. Clement's remarks *Strom.*, IV, 83, 2; 88, 2).

Hegemonius quotes in *Acta Archelai* 67, 4-12 two fragments taken from the 13th book of Basilides' *Exegetica*. The first fragment is the beginning of the book indicating its contents: 'The parable of the rich man and the poor man demonstrates where the nature without root and without place which attaches itself to things might have come from'. Basilides' remark seems to allude to Luke 16:19-31. In view of the second fragment, the phrase 'the nature without root and without place' has to be understood as a periphrasis for "evil". It is, however, unclear how Basilides used Luke 16:19-31, in order to explore the nature of evil. In the second fragment Basilides pretends to relate the opinion of anonymous "barbarians" about the origin of good and evil in the world: in the beginning there were two ungenerated principles, light and darkness. Both existed for themselves, liked themselves, were perfect in themselves. Then, at a second stage, Light and Darkness took notice of each other: whereas Darkness desired the Light and pursued it, Light only looked at Darkness, but felt no desire to participate in it. In this way the ontological difference between good and evil was established. Still, by this look of Light at darkness, a reflection of Light was produced in the Darkness. Basilides concludes: 'Therefore there is nothing perfectly good in this world . . . because that which has been received in the beginning, was too little'. The visible creation is this mixture of darkness and light; it is bad, insofar as it falls far short of the perfectly good. It is difficult to tell whether this "cosmogony" reflects Basilides' own views. However, the fact that he adduces it is significant in itself: he emulates philosophers like Plutarch or Numenius

who also invoked exotic lore in order to explain the principles of this world (Löhr, 236-241). Moreover, the "cosmogony" of the barbarians is full of philosophical resonances: e.g. Darkness's pursuit of Light is erotic in the Platonic sense of the word. The "cosmogony" evinces no radical dualism, but is nevertheless more pessimistic about this world than either Plutarch or Numenius.

Apart from these three quotations Clement has several doxographical passages where he transmits various doctrines of Basilides. Since they are taken out of context, the precise meaning of these "doxai" is not always easy to determine. According to *Strom.*, IV, 86, 1, Basilides said that it is the will of God, firstly, to love everything – because everything has a relation to the totality of all things –, secondly, not to desire anything, and thirdly, not to hate anything. According to Basilides the sins that are forgiven by baptism are those that are committed involuntarily and in ignorance before baptism (IV, 153, 4). Basilides assumed an "Ogdoas" of which the virtues of Justice and Freedom were important elements (IV, 162, 1/perhaps an allusion to Ps. 84:11 LXX; 88:15 LXX; 96:2 LXX). "Election" (*ekloge*) is a favourite Basilidean self designation; Basilides – perhaps taking his cue from Gen. 23:4 – taught that the "election" is a stranger (*xenos*) in this world (IV, 165, 3). Basilides's faith is intellectual, is *noêsis*; he calls it (V, 3, 2) ' "faith", "kingdom" and a creation of good things, worthy to exist near the creator's being' (my translation follows a suggestion by R. Peppermüller), the 'unlimited beauty of an unsurpassable creation'. According to Basilides, Moses' temple (sic!, but cf. Hekataios of Abdera apud Diodorus Siculus, XL, 3) proclaims not the one God, but the one world (V, 74, 3); here Basilides probably follows an "interpretatio graeca" of Jewish religion (Löhr, 194f.). Basilides apparently taught the transmigration [→ Reincarnation] of souls (into both human beings and animals); Clement relates a "doxa" and Origen quotes a fragment where Basilides or his disciples use this doctrine in order to interpret two difficult passages from scripture, i.e. Deuteronomy 5:9 and Romans 7:9 (Clement, *Excerpta ex Theodoto*, 28; Origen, *Comm. on Rom.*, V, 1; cf. also Origen, *Comm. on Matth.*, ser. 38).

Clement mentions three writings of Isidore, the son of Basilides. *Strom.*, II, 113, 3-114, 1 quotes a short passage from Isidore's work *On the attached soul*. In this fragment Isidore relates an objection against the doctrine that the soul has attachments (*prosartemata*) which produce its passions: if you persuade others that the passions of bad people are caused by these attachments, they will have an excellent excuse for their misdeeds; they will say that they could not help misbehaving. But Isidore insists on human responsibility: we have to fight against these passionate attachments, 'we must prevail with the help of the rational part of the soul and rule over the lower creation within ourselves' (a possible allusion to Gen. 1:28; 9:1; cf. Philo, *Questions on Genesis*, II, 56). Shortly before this quotation, in *Strom.*, II, 112, 1ff., Clement presents a Basilidean "doxa" where the doctrine of the attachments is described in some more detail: the attachments are substantially spirits that have become attached to the souls according to an original confusion and mixture. This remark seems to indicate that the attachments derive from chaotic, primeval matter (a Platonic doctrine; Löhr 83, note 11). This first class of attachments seems to be responsible for human passions. To these are added a second class of attachments, i.e. spirits of a bastard and animal nature (wolves, monkeys, lions); they try to assimilate the passions of the soul to those of animals, ultimately even to those of plants and stones. This doxa is probably equally derived from Isidore's book. It is remarkable that Isidore tries to establish a difference between human passions and lower animal passions.

Strom., III, 1-3 contains three fragments of Isidore's *Ethica*, probably a writing dealing with moral problems. These fragments discuss the question of whether or not to marry: with reference to Matthew 19:11f. Isidore distinguishes between three kinds of eunuchs: those who have a natural aversion against women, those who refrain from sex either because of their conspicuous encratism or because they have been castrated, and those who wish to devote themselves fully to the kingdom of God and do not wish to be bothered by family cares. As regards those who find it difficult to live without sex, Isidore – interpreting I Cor. 7:9 – advises against a forced abstinence: if your prayer entirely focuses on celibacy you might get separated from Christian hope. If someone is too young or too poor and yet feels the need to marry, he should seek the support of his Christian brother. Isidore criticizes an attitude that avoids sin only out of fear. He concludes his discussion by quoting a Epicurean maxim (cf. Epicurus, *Ep. ad Men.*, 135; Fr. 456 Usener): for human beings, there are some things that are both necessary and natural; other are only natural. Clothing is both natural and necessary, but sex is only natural, not necessary. These fragments from Isidore's *Ethica* present an example of Christian pastoral advice. Like the pagan philo-

sophical schools, the school of Basilides and Isidore claimed to teach (Christian) philosophy as a way of life; theoretical instruction and practical advice went hand in hand. Like the pagans, Isidore taught his followers certain short maxims which they could recall and meditate at appropriate moments (Löhr, 116ff.).

Strom., VI, 53, 2-5: Clement quotes one fragment from the first and two from the second book of Isidore's treatise *Interpretations of the Prophet Parchor*. The identity of the Prophet is unclear (Löhr, 199, note 8). Clement's choice of quotations is meant to confirm his views on the 'theft of the Greeks': in the first fragment Isidore refers to a theory of Aristotle according to which all human beings use demons during their life time. Isidore designates this Aristotelian teaching as a "piece of prophetical learning" which Aristotle had purloined without acknowleding his source. The original context of this remark was perhaps a more extended discussion of the phenomenon of prophecy. The second fragment claims that the intellectual property of the Christians should not be attributed to any philosophers; the philosophers simply stole it from the prophets and attributed it to someone whom they spuriously claimed to be wise. In the third fragment this remark is illustrated with reference to a fragment of Pherekydes of Syros (cf. Fr. 68 Schibli); Isidore contends that Pherekydes' allegorical theology is derived from the prophet Cham. The last two fragments must be read as responding to a pagan theory according to which ultimate wisdom resides in an original true account of reality which is shared by ancient wise men such as Pherekydes, Linus, Musaios and Orpheus. The Platonist and critic of Christianity, Celsus, shared this theory (cf. Origen, *Contra Celsum*, I, 16); Isidore tries to top it by pointing to possible prophetic sources of the ancient pagan sages. With this claim he possibly exploited a tradition according to which Cham had been the ancestor of the Phenicians (Gen 10:6f.) and Pherekydes had been introduced to Phenician wisdom (Fr. 80 Schibli).

Apart from these three quotations from the writings of Isidore, Clement refers several times to opinions which he seems to attribute to the disciples of Basilides. In *Strom.*, II, 112, 1 the phrase 'those around Basilides' (*hoi amphi ton Basileidên*) seems to refer to Isidore only; the same applies to the phrase 'the pupils of Basilides' (*hoi apo Basileidou*) in *Strom.*, III, 1, 1. Perhaps, then, this is also the case in other passages where similar phrases are used in order to introduce Basilidean "doxai". In *Strom.*, I , 146, Clement relates different opinions among the Basilideans about the dates of the baptism and the death of Christ (perhaps the Basilideans speculated equally about his birth, cf. I, 145, 6). It is possible that Clement has read a Basilidean work where different chronological hypotheses were discussed. In *Strom.*, II, 10, 1 and 3, Clement relates Basilidean teaching about the correspondence between Christian hope and faith and the spiritual state/level of each Christian. In *Strom.*, II, 27, 2, he quotes a Basilidean definition according to which 'faith is an assent of the soul to those things that do not affect the sense perception because they are not present'. In *Strom.*, II, 36, 1, Clement paraphrases a Basilidean exegesis of Proverbs 1:7 which relates this saying to John the Baptist: when the Archon (i.e. John the Baptist) heard the saying of the servant spirit (that is the divine voice from heaven, the servant spirit being symbolized by the dove; cf. *Excerpta ex Theodoto*, 16), he was shaken and amazed. This amazement (*ekplêxis*) was called fear (*phobos*; cf. Diogenes Laertius, VII, 112) and this fear became the beginning of a wisdom that elects, selects, distinguishes and establishes everything in its proper place. 'This is because the ruler of everything brings forth not only the cosmos, but also the "election" [i.e. the Basilideans] by distinguishing it'. The revelation of Jesus as the Son of God at the river Jordan marks the beginning of a new dispensation, a re-creation of the world: from now on the Archon, a lower deity, is involved in the process of bringing the selves of the true Christians into their transcendent, celestial abodes.

2. BASILIDES ACCORDING TO IRENAEUS

Irenaeus of Lyons, *AH*, I, 24, 3-7, describes a Basilidean system, according to which the unbegotten and nameless Father begets a series of five emanations (Nous, Logos, Phronesis, Sophia and Dynamis). Sophia and Dynamis beget the primary powers, rulers and angels which in turn create the first heaven. From the primary rulers other powers and rulers derive which create a heaven modelled on the first one – and so on, until the number of 365 heavens is complete. The angels of the last, visible heavens have created everything that is contained in this world. They have distributed the earth and the nations amongst themselves, their chief is that angel that is reputed to be the God of the Jews. This angel wished to subject all other peoples to his people, the Jews. Provoked by this aggression, the other angels resisted him; likewise the other nations resisted the Jewish people. The highest God

watched the war between the angels and sent his first born Nous, who is Christ, in order to liberate the world from the rule of the angels. The Nous appeared as a man and performed miracles. He did not suffer, but instead of him Simon of Cyrene had to bear his cross (Mt. 27:32) and suffer, the Nous having exchanged his outward appearance with Simon of Cyrene. The powers crucified him out of ignorance (I Cor. 2:8). Since he is an incorporeal power and the intellect of the unbegotten Father he can change his outward appearance as he likes (cf. Peterson). By this mimicry he becomes invisible for the powers and angels in the 365 heavens and can ascend to his Father. All those who profess the crucified are still under the domination of the angels; those who deny him, on the other hand, are liberated from their oppressive power and have the true understanding of the dispensation of the unbegotten Father. This system probably has an apocryphal writing as its source. In spite of its negative evaluation of the created world, it is not dualistic: everything has the Father as its – albeit distant – source. Evil seems to be a function of the growing distance from the source. The emanations from the father describe a descent from the intellect to practical creative reasoning. The story of Christ's (i.e. Simon of Cyrene's) passion develops and glosses I Cor. 2:8 and Matth. 27:32; Irenaeus tries to suggest a connection between Christological Docetism and a Basilidean rejection of martyrdom: just as the Nous-Son became invisible for the powers and rulers, the believers should aspire to invisibility and the avoidance of martyrdom (I, 24, 6): 'You should know all, but no one should know you!' The Basilideans claimed a higher form of "gnosis": 'Not many people are able to understand this, only one in thousand, two in ten thousand' (cf. *Gospel of Thomas*, log. 23; other parallels, Löhr 265, note 40).

3. BASILIDES ACCORDING TO HIPPOLYTUS

Hippolytus of Rome, *Refutatio*, VII, 20-27/X, 14 gives a totally different account of the teaching of Basilides: according to him, Basilides and Isidore claimed that their doctrine derived from the apostle Matthias who had been privately taught by Jesus. The system starts with a piece of negative theology, the doctrine of the "non-existing" God. This God produces a "non-existing" world, i.e. he sows a seed that contains the cosmos. Everything else emerges from this world seed. Since the world seed was produced by the non-existing God, everything is produced out of nothing. The world seed contains a tripartite sonship: the first sonship, whose substance is light and subtle, ascends quickly to the God whose great beauty attracts everything. The second sonship needs the help of the "wing" of the Holy Spirit. But the Holy Spirit was unable to ascend to the height of the Father. The third sonship remains in the world seed; these are the pneumatic Christians. The system then distinguishes between the "hypercosmic" region, the boundary-spirit (i.e the firmament) and the cosmos. Below the firmament two archons with their corresponding sons emerge from the world seed: the Archon of the Ogdoas and the Archon of the Hebdomas. Then the gospel arrives in this world; it comes from beyond the firmament and is transmitted through the sons of the two archons. The archons are illuminated and understand that there is a world beyond them. Finally the process of downward illumination reaches Jesus, son of Mary. The world will continue to exist until the third sonship will have been formed and purified and will have followed Christ into the transcendent realm. The power for this transformation is conveyed by the light that shines from above. Once the whole tripartite sonship has been established in the hypercosmic region, God will cast a great ignorance over the whole cosmos and the two archons; all those souls that belong to this world will no longer come to know anything beyond it, all desire for the hypercosmic region will cease. Since desire means death, this will give them a kind of immortality. Thus the whole process of salvation history consists in the return of everything that was contained in the world seed to its natural position (like returns to like). The passion of Jesus Christ is interpreted accordingly: The death of Jesus is the beginning of the separation of all things; Jesus dissolves into his bodily, psychic etc. components which return to their natural positions.

Since this report has many parallels in other sections in Hippolytus' *Refutatio* where other "Gnostic" systems are reported, some scholars have concluded that Hippolytus' source for these reports was a forgery (Salmon, Stähelin). Even if that conclusion is unwarranted, we still need a theory to explain these parallels and to reconcile Hippolytus' report with the fragments found in Clement of Alexandria, Origen and the *Acta Archelai*. The Basilidean system according to Hippolytus exhibits several remarkable features: an extreme negative theology which possibly develops the information furnished by Irenaeus (or his source) that Basilides called the Father 'unnameable' (*innominatus*) (Irenaeus, *AH* I, 24, 4); an idiosyncratic version of the creation out of nothing which is hostile to both emanationism and a Pla-

tonic theory of creation; a peculiar theory of a tripartite sonship; the idea that at the end of salvation history God will bring over this world a state of ignorance. Some traits of the system seem to derive from Valentinian sources, but on the whole this is an original if uneven attempt to improve upon preceding versions of salvation history. However, as in the case of Irenaeus' report, there are no very strong reasons to attribute this system to Basilides and his early circles of disciples (Isidore).

Lit.: B. Aland, "Seele, Zeit, Eschaton bei einem frühen christlichen Theologen: Basilides zwischen Paulus und Platon", in: J. Holzhausen (ed.), *Psychê – Seele – Anima*, Festschrift K. Alt (Beiträge zur Altertumskunde, 109), Teubner: Stuttgart & Leipzig, 1998, 255-278 ♦ S.-P. Bergjan, *Der fürsorgende Gott: Der Begriff der PRONOIA Gottes in der apologetischen Literatur der alten Kirche* (Arbeiten zur Kirchengeschichte 81), Berlin, New York: Walter de Gruyter, 2002, 123-170. ♦ A.P. Bos, "Basilides as an Aristotelianizing Gnostic", *Vigiliae Christianae* 54 (2000), 44-60 ♦ H. Langerbeck, *Aufsätze zur Gnosis* (Abhandlungen der Akademie der Wissenschaften in Göttingen, Philol.-Hist. Klasse, Dritte Folge, Nr.69), Göttingen: VandenHoeck & Ruprecht, 1967 ♦ A. le Boulluec, *La notion d'hérésie dans la littérature grecque, IIe-IIIe siècles* (2 vols.), Paris: Études Augustiniennes, 1985 ♦ W. Foerster, *Gnosis: A Selection of Gnostic Texts* (trans. R. McL. Wilson), vol. 1: Patristic Evidence, Oxford: Oxford University Press, 1972 ♦ F. Legge (trans), *Philosophumena or the Refutation of all Heresies*, 2 vols., London, New York: MacMillan 1921 ♦ W.A. Löhr, *Basilides und seine Schule: Eine Studie zur Theologie- und Kirchengeschichte des zweiten Jahrhunderts* (Wissenschaftliche Untersuchungen zum Neuen Testament 83), Tübingen: Mohr, 1996 ♦ idem, "Isidor I (Gnostiker)", in: *Reallexikon für Antike und Christentum* 18 (1998), 977-982 ♦ E. Mühlenberg, "Basilides", in: *Theologische Realenzyklopädie* 5 (1980), 296-301 ♦ A. Orbe, "Los 'apéndices' de Basílides I/II (Un capítolo de filosofia gnóstica)", *Gregorianum* 57 (1976), 251-184 ♦ E. Peterson, "Alte Schulformeln und ihre Deutung", *Zeitschrift für die Neutestamentliche Wissenschaft* 23 (1924), 293-298 ♦ S. Pétrement, *Le Dieu séparé*, Cerf Paris 1984 ♦ G. Salmon, "The Cross-References in the 'Philosophumena'", *Hermanthena* 11 (1885), 389-402 ♦ H.S. Schibli, *Pherekydes of Syros*, Oxford: Oxford University Press, 1990 ♦ P. Schüngel, "Gnostische Gotteslehren", *Vigiliae Christianae* 53 (1999), 361-394 ♦ H. Stähelin, *Die gnostischen Quellen Hippolyts in seiner Hauptschrift gegen die Häretiker* (TU 6), Leipzig: Hinrichs, 1890 ♦ M. Tardieu, "Basilides", in: *Dictionnaire des Philosophes Antiques*, II, Paris, 1994, 85-89 ♦ Y. Tissot, "A propos des fragments de Basilide sur le martyre", *Revue d'Histoire et de Philosophie Religieuses* 76 (1996), 35-50 ♦ J.H. Waszink, "Basilides", in: *Reallexikon für Antike und Christentum* 1 (1957), 1217-1225.

WINRICH A. LÖHR

Bernard Silvester (Bernardus Silvestris),
* year and place of birth unknown,
† after 1159, place of death unknown

Little is known about his life. An educator in Tours, he died after 1159. He was the author of several works: *Experimentarius*, a book of spells, from Arabian sources; *Mathematicus*, a poem addressing the problem of destiny, in which he stated that 'blind chance stirs up the ridiculous troubles of humanity; our times are play, entertainment for the gods'; and a *Commentary* on Martianus Capella, in which he defined notably his hermeneutics. However, his principal work was the *Cosmography*, an allegorical novel, in which verse and prose alternate, and divided into two parts, the *Megacosm* and the *Microcosm*. Rather than attempt a complete analysis of this dense and complex work, let us concentrate on the major place that → hermetism occupies in it.

Bernard was, like the masters of Chartres (*v.g.* Thierry of Chartres, to whom his work was dedicated), an heir of Latin Platonism. From Macrobius he borrowed doctrinal elements and the idea that 'nature does not like to see itself exposed naked to every look', which justifies the recourse to 'fabulous narrative' (*narratio fabulosa*), an equivalent of Platonic myth. 'The veil (*integumentum*)', he says, 'is a discourse that contains a true meaning in a fabulous narrative. An example is the legend of Orpheus'. Bernard imitated the *prosimetrum* form of Martianus Capella's *De Nuptiis Philologiae et Mercurii*, which describes the seven liberal arts allegorically. He also borrowed from it the concept that knowledge is a prerequisite in the quest for wisdom. Bernard was sensitive, moreover, to the hermetic atmosphere of the *De Nuptiis*, in which arithmetical onomancy, theurgy, and divination [→ Divinatory Arts] are present alongside the liberal arts. At the term of an initiation *mysterium*, Mercury, that is, Thoth, representing the higher part of the human soul, saves the lower part, Philology, 'which loves reason'. Another major source for Bernard was the *Asclepius*. Bernard drew inspiration also from many classical authors: the great poets, notably Virgil, perceived as a pagan prophet, but also the astrologers such as Firmicus Maternus, Manilius, and Hygin. Among the medieval sources appear the *Liber de sex principiis* and certain Arabic astronomical treatises.

The construction of the *Cosmography* rests on a traditional concept: the correspondence between, on the one hand, the universe, the megacosm (or macrocosm), and, on the other, humanity, the microcosm. Its content consists of the story of the restoration of the universe, which Nature asked of Noys, who would gain satisfaction at the end of a long initiatory journey pursued from one end of creation to the other, including the different planets. A hermetic tone marks the characters in this novel, whether they belong to Christian theology or to pagan mythology. God is defined according to the Bible, as well as to the *Timaeus* and to Macrobius. He is both Tugaton (Good) and the luminous Trinity. His creation, which is the passage from material and spiritual oneness to the many, conceals a musical [→ Music] and numerical harmony [→ Number Symbolism].

Silva-Yle, matter, proves to have a mysterious duality. It is not only a formless chaos tending toward evil, but also a fertile principle and connected with God. Noys, despite his Nicean definition 'God born of God', is not Christ, but a feminine character, Wisdom and Divine Providence, at the same time as the cradle of life. Nature, a daughter of Noys, constructs the joining of the soul and the body, in parallel to the celestial order. Her sister, Urania, establishes mediation between the divine decrees written in the stars and the spiritual existence of humanity. Endelichia is the spouse of the World, thus its soul. Physis attends to organic life. Imarmene represents the continuity of a time that sees the historical development of matter. The latter is marked by the appearance of notable characters and events, agreeing with that which is written in heaven. Other characters play a role in the *Cosmography*: angels, demons, spirits of sexuality, ousiarchs of each planet operating between two worlds, and an ousiarch Panthomorphus who gives things their form.

The influence of the *Cosmography*, exercised already on medieval authors – Alain de Lille, Jean de Meung, Dante, and Boccacio –, has continued until our times, as the theologian C. S. Lewis refers to it explicitly in his symbolic science fiction novel, *Out of the Silent Planet* (1938). This success is explainable by the fact that Bernard, in assembling all the elements of European culture and spirituality in a poetic masterpiece, managed to create a true modern myth.

Cosmographia (P. Dronke, ed.), Leiden: E. J. Brill, 1978.

Lit.: Michel Lemoine, *Intorno a Chartres: Naturalismo platonico nella tradizione cristiana del XII secolo*, Eredità Medievale, Milan: Editoriale JACABOOK, 1998 ♦ B. Stock, *Myth and Science in the Twelfth Century: A Study of Bernard Silvester*, Princeton: Princeton University Press, 1972.

MICHEL LEMOINE

Besant, Annie, * 1.10.1847 London, † 20.9.1933 Adyar (Madras), India

A political and social activist and reformer, one of the outstanding British orators during the late 19th and early 20th centuries, whose main claim to fame today is her long and eventful tenure as the President of the → Theosophical Society (Adyar) from 1907 to her death in 1933, Annie Wood was born to William Burton Persse Wood and Emily Morris in 1847. Three quarters Irish by descent and, as she writes in her *Autobiography*, in her heart all Irish, she was to associate with the plight of the Irish under English domination, especially in her early years. In her later years, the plight of India and its natives was added to her concerns, which led her to advocate Indian Home Rule.

Wood's early education took an important turn at age eight (1855), when Ellen Marryat, perhaps a relative of Wood's now widowed mother, agreed to take Annie in her care. As an Evangelical Christian, Miss Marryat instilled in Annie not only Evangelicalism but also its emphasis on the uplifting of others less fortunate. After eight years with Miss Marryat, Annie returned to her mother, continued her studies, and met a young man who was soon to be ordained an Anglican priest, Frank Besant. They were married on December 21, 1867 and had two children over the next few years, Arthur Digby (b. January 16, 1869) and Mabel (b. August 28, 1870). Annie was soon to question orthodox Christian doctrine – especially the age-old issue about the existence of evil and misery in a world created by a God who is All-Good – when both infants contacted whooping cough in 1871. This doubt eventually led her to radically change her view of Christianity by denying the divinity of Christ. It was a position arrived at largely due to the influence of a clergyman, Revd. Charles Voysey, in 1872, a cleric who only a few years previously (1869) was himself charged with heresy by the Church. It is no wonder that Annie's association with Revd. Voysey caused much dismay with her husband.

The dual influence of Voysey and his associate, Thomas Scott – a free-thinker who sought to undermine the Church and whom Annie also met in 1872 – consolidated her acceptance of "heretical" doctrines, which she soon expressed in print. Her views and her refusal to accept her husband's admonition to return to the Church led to her eventual separation from Frank in 1873.

The following year introduced Annie, who exhibited atheist leanings by 1874, to the free-thinker and atheist Charles Bradlaugh and his National Secular Society through his newspaper,

The National Reformer. She joined the Society in August 1874, wrote extensively for the newspaper – so successfully that she eventually became its co-editor – and gave numerous addresses on behalf of the Society. During her tenure as co-editor, she advocated feminist causes, one of which was birth control, thus becoming the first woman to do so publicly.

By 1878, she assumed the office of secretary of the revived Malthusian League. One year earlier, she and Bradlaugh had reissued the 1832 pamphlet *The Fruits of Philosophy* by Dr. Charles Knowlton, through the auspices of their recently established (January 1877) Freethought Publishing Company. This led to Besant's and Bradlaugh's prosecution, still in 1877, under the Obscene Publications Act. The outcome was a verdict of "guilty", which was eventually reversed. The reversal of the judgement led Besant to write a series of articles on birth control in *The National Reformer* that was to be published in a pamphlet, *The Law of Population*.

In addition to her continued involvement with Bradlaugh and the National Secular Society, Besant became acquainted with socialism during the early 1880s. At first, she held negative feelings toward the movement, but by 1884 her opinion changed to the point where she decided, in January 1885, to join the Fabian Society, a decision that was carried out a few months later with a member of the society, George Bernard Shaw (1856-1950), sponsoring her. This was the beginning of a relationship – intellectual and perhaps romantic – that was to have an influence over her for some time. Her concern for the poor led her to convert to socialism, but it also led to her surrender her co-editorship of *The National Reformer*.

In 1887, economic conditions had deteriorated to a point where there were numerous demonstrations by the unemployed. One of the most famous sites of London, Trafalgar Square, was especially overridden with the unemployed and destitute, and thus became a rallying ground for the socialist groups. In November, all gatherings in the Square were banned, but an alliance of socialists, Irish, and radicals – together making up the Metropolitan Radical Federation – gathered nonetheless, with Besant as one of the leaders. The result was a clash between the demonstrators and the police known as "Bloody Sunday" (November 13), a *mêlée* that led to 300 people being arrested and 150 hospitalized.

A few days after, the Law and Liberty League was co-founded by Besant and William Thomas Stead, with Besant becoming the editor of its journal, *The Link*. The primary purpose of the League was to support free speech, to campaign for candidates who were in favor of free speech, and to champion the cause of the poor and downtrodden. By May 1888, a concrete cause presented itself with the unfair labor practice of the Bryant and May matchmaking firm. The working conditions at the factory were such that Besant and Herbert Burrows of the Social Democratic Federation instigated a boycott of the company and a strike by its workers. Both were successful. Subsequently the Matchmakers' Union was established, with Besant playing an active role both in the Union and in trade unionism generally. Later that year, her attention turned to poor children and their plight; she stood for a seat at the London School Board (the Tower Hamlets district) in 1888, won by a large margin, and remained in office for the following two years.

For all her activism in socialist causes, socialist philosophy, and socialist societies (she was by now a member of both the Fabian Society and the Social Democratic Federation), Besant felt there was a lack of adequate philosophy. Socialism was sufficient for solving economic problems, but not for realizing "the Brotherhood of Man", to use her expression. There was much talk at this time (1888) about the idea of Brotherhood, 'in which service to Man should take the place erstwhile given to the service of God', Besant remarked in an article in the February issue of *Our Corner*, a journal she had founded in 1883. But if socialism was insufficient, then where could such a Brotherhood be realized? Besant's attention was first drawn to the occult [→ occult/occultism] with the publication of A.P. Sinnett's *Occult World* in 1881, and to → Spiritualism from 1886 on; but it was her enthusiasm for the ideas contained in → Helena Petrovna Blavatsky's *The Secret Doctrine*, which Besant subsequently reviewed in 1889, that transformed her from socialism to Theosophy. Shortly after her review, which appeared in the *Pall Mall Gazette* in April, she joined the → Theosophical Society, on 10 May 1889, and thereafter visited Blavatsky in Fontainebleau. Blavatsky quickly recognized in Besant a potential asset to the Society, so much so that Besant quickly became Blavatsky's key disciple as a member of the Inner Group of the Esoteric Section and the co-editor of Blavatsky's magazine, *Lucifer*.

After Blavatsky's death on May 8, 1891, the Outer Head of the Esoteric Section (now called the Eastern School of Theosophy) passed to Besant, who was also the president of the Blavatsky Lodge in London, and to William Q. Judge, the Vice-President of the Theosophical Society. Judge was to be the head of the E.S.T. for America, Besant for the rest of the world, an arrangement that would not last longer than a few years. The arrangement ended in 1895, when Judge and a majority of members of the American Section decided to declare its autonomy from the Theosophical Society, thus leaving Besant as the most influential Theosophist with the possible exception of → Henry Steel Olcott.

Besant's visit to Ceylon (Sri Lanka) and India in 1893 to meet Olcott was the beginning of her lifelong love and devotion for India and its people. From 1896 on, she became a permanent resident of the country, engaging in many activities, the first of which was education. Besant's studies in Sanskrit and Hindu religion and philosophy resulted in her translation of the *Bhagavad Gītā* in 1895, with the assistance of the scholar Bhagavan Das. A year later, she conceived the idea of establishing a college for Hindu boys that would include instruction in Sanskrit. This idea came to fruition with the establishment of the Central Hindu College in Benares (now Varānasī) on 7 July 1898. The College was to have a profound impact on Indian education in the ensuing decades. A few years later (1904), the educational opportunity afforded to Hindu boys was extended to Hindu girls with the opening of the Central Hindu Girls' School, thus cementing the claim that Besant was one of the leading pioneers in the education of Hindus of both sexes.

From the mid-1890s on, Besant became associated with the increasingly popular lecturer and occult writer and investigator → Charles Webster Leadbeater. Although not herself a psychic, it was due to his influence that Besant's interests turned from religion to occult phenomena at this time. By 1895 a collaborative effort was begun to investigate a number of supra-physical phenomena, including → reincarnation and the astral plane. The results of these joint investigations were a number of co-authored books including *Occult Chemistry* (1908), *Talks on the Path of Occultism* (1926), *Thought Forms* (1901), and *The Lives of Alcyone* (1924). As early as 1898, their interest came to extend also to a Theosophical interpretation of Christianity, leading to Leadbeater's *The Christian Creed* of 1899 and Besant's *Esoteric Christianity* of 1901. The collaboration was temporarily halted by charges of immoral conduct brought against Leadbeater in 1906, which led to his resignation from the Theosophical Society in the same year. After Olcott's death in 1907, Besant was elected President of the Theosophical Society on June 28. By August, she and Leadbeater were again conducting occult investigations even before his formal reinstatement to the Society, which took place eighteen months later, in December 1908.

Leadbeater's reinstatement would soon lead to the defining moment in the history of the Theosophical Society, the discovery on Leadbeater's part of a young boy, Jiddu Krishnamurti, who was expected to be "overshadowed" by the Lord Maitreya, the World Teacher. Although talk of a Master of Wisdom who would appear amongst humanity goes back to H.P. Blavatsky, the discourse of a coming World Teacher, a Maitreya, Christ or Messiah – the identification of Maitreya and the Christ was apparently developed by Leadbeater – seems to have begun with Besant, in a rudimentary form around the turn of the century, and with Leadbeater in more developed form as early as 1901. By the end of 1908 Besant was quite explicit about a "Teacher and Guide" who would once again walk among humans. In April 1909, Leadbeater actually discovered a Brahmin boy whom he claimed would serve as the vehicle for the Teacher, the Lord Maitreya who would incarnate into him. The purpose of this coming was to prepare for the coming sixth sub-race of humanity and the still more remote sixth root race. For the next twenty years, especially after 1924, much of Besant's energy was devoted to furthering the cause of the World Teacher. All came to naught, however, when Krishnamurti dissolved the Order of the Star, the organization that was established to further the claims that he was the coming World-Teacher, by declaring in 1929 that "Truth is a pathless land" and by turning his back on Theosophy and its leadership.

In addition to the World Teacher taking possession of the body of Krishnamurti, a "World Mother" would also be manifested through an earthly vehicle: Mrs. Rukmini Arundale, the wife of George Arundale, who would later becomes Besant's successor as president of the Theosophical Society. The idea of the World Mother probably originated with Leadbeater, and was then taken up by Besant, who came to represent her as the 'embodiment of womanhood in the occult hierarchy'. Nothing much came of this new teaching, however, and by 1928 it had been forgotten.

Besant's emphasis on service to the Indian nation, in the context of which she attempted to promote a number of reforms (she encouraged inter-caste and interracial relations, championed the cause of the "outcasts" and "untouchables", and encouraged Indian women to engage in the public domain) eventually led her to get involved in the struggle for Indian independence. Although there is evidence of such activity as early as 1910, it was not until 1913 that she claimed to have come into contact with the Rishi Agastya, a Mahatma whom Theosophists believe is 'the Regent of India in the Inner Government'; this Master supposedly had instructed Besant, as his Agent, to 'form a small band of people, who were brave enough to defy wrong social customs, such as premature marriage'. Once engaged in this attempted reform, Besant established the Home Rule League in 1916, in imitation of the Irish Home Rule movement, and began to work for Indian self-government. As an outlet for her views, in 1914 she bought an old and established paper, the Madras *Standard*, and converted it into *New India*, which was 'to embody the ideal of Self-Government for India along Colonial lines . . .'. As a promoter of independence, she worked with many Indian leaders including the militant nationalist Lokamanya Bal Gangadhar Tilak (1856-1920) and the moderate former Theosophist Gopala Krishna Gokhale (1866-1915). It was during this time, between 1915 and 1919 that her political influence was at its height. Besant worked with all the great leaders of the independence movement, serving as President of both the Home Rule League in 1916 and 1917, and the Indian National Congress in 1917. By 1920, however, Mohandas Gandhi (1869-1948) had effectively assumed an ascendant position, eventually becoming the leader of the independence movement. His methods and goals were different from Besant's, and more attractive to the Indian population. Besant continued to participate in Indian self-rule throughout the 1920s, and supported the Nehru Report (named after Motilal Nehru [1861-1931]) of 1928, which advocated Dominion Status for India, in contrast to Motilal's son, Jawaharlal (1889-1964), who advocated complete independence. Besant did not live to see India receiving independence in 1947.

Throughout the 1920s, Besant became more involved with Krishnamurti and the Order of the Star in the East. After the dissolution of the Order of the Star (as it was called in the late 1920s) in 1929, Besant's health began to decline. On 20 September 1933 she died at the headquarters of the Theosophical Society in Adyar. She was cremated in the Garden of Remembrance on the Theosophical Society's estate, with a portion of her ashes placed in the Garden and a portion scattered over the Ganges at Benares.

An Autobiography, London: T. Fisher, Unwin, 1908 ♦ *Autobiographical Sketches*, London: Freethought Publishing Company, 1885 ♦ *Why I Do Not Believe in God*, London: Freethought Publishing Company, 1887 ♦ "The Army of the Commonweal", *Our Corner* 11 (Feb. 1888), 115-121 ♦ "Among the Adepts: Madame Blavatsky on The 'Secret Doctrine", The Blavatsky Archives [Internet] (1999), Tucson (AZ) [updated

2002, cited 2002 April, June]. Available from: http://
www.blavatskyarchives.com/besant1888.htm. First
published in *The Pall Mall Gazette* (London), April
25, 1889, 3 and reprinted in *The Theosophist* (Adyar,
Madras, India), August 1889, 696-698 ♦ *The Law of
Population: Its Consequences, and Its Bearing upon
Human Conduct and Morals*, London: Free-thought
Publishing Company, 1891 ♦ *The Bhagavad Gītā*
(1895), Adyar, Madras: The Theosophical Publishing
House, 1967 (11th Adyar edition) ♦ *The Ancient
Wisdom* (1897), Adyar, Madras: The Theosophical
Publishing House, 1939 ♦ *Sanātana-Dharma: An
Advanced Textbook of Hindu Religion and Ethics*,
Adyar, Madras: The Theosophical Publishing House,
1940 ♦ Besant and Charles W. Leadbeater, *Thought
Forms*, Adyar, Madras: The Theoso-phical Publishing
House, 1901 ♦ Besant and Charles W. Leadbeater,
Occult Chemistry (1908), Adyar, Madras: The Theo-
sophical Publishing House, 1951 (3rd edition, edited
by C. Jinarājadāsa) ♦ Besant and Charles W. Lead-
beater, *Man: Whence, How and Whither*, Adyar,
Madras: The Theosophical Publishing House, 1913 ♦
Besant and Charles W. Leadbeater, *The Lives of Alcyone*, 2 vols., Adyar, Madras: The Theosophical Publishing House, 1924 ♦ Besant and Charles W.
Leadbeater, *Talks on the Path of Occultism*, 3 vols.
(1926): vol. 1: "At the Feet of the Master" (6th ed.,
1971); vol. 2: "The Voice of the Silence" (6th ed.,
1973); vol. 3: "Light on the Path" (2nd ed., 1931).

Lit.: Arthur H. Nethercot, *The First Five Lives of
Annie Besant*, Chicago: University of Chicago Press,
1960 ♦ Arthur H. Nethercot, *The Last Four Lives of
Annie Besant*, Soho Square, London: Rupert Hart-
Davis, 1963 ♦ Anne Taylor, *Annie Besant: A Biography*, Oxford and New York: Oxford University Press,
1992 ♦ Catherine Lowman Wessinger, *Annie Besant
and Progressive Messianism (1847-1933)*, Lewiston,
N.Y./Queenston, Ontario: The Edwin Mellen Press,
1988 [*Studies in Women and Religion*, vol. 26] ♦ Rose-
mary Dinnage, *Annie Besant*, Harmondsworth: Penguin 1986.

JAMES A. SANTUCCI

Bibliophilus Irenaeus → Oetinger,
Friedrich Christoph

Bimstein, Louis Maximilian → Théon,
Max

Bingen, Hildegard of → Hildegard of
Bingen

Blake, William, * 28.11.1757 London,
† 12.9.1827 London

An engraver by trade, Blake was primarily a self-
educated graphic and literary artist whose work
reflects the attempt to confront contemporary

political and social problems through a philosophically based spiritualism. Although baptized and
buried in the Anglican Church, Blake was born into
a family of freethinkers, and himself attempted to
get back to the pure form of Christianity he
believed to have existed before it was corrupted by
organized religion.

Blake's life reflects the conflict between corporeal
and spiritual needs. He worked as a commercial
artist, engraving illustrations for popular books, including some by Mary Wollstonecraft (1759-1797),
Erasmus Darwin (1731-1802), and, notably, the
account of John Gabriel Stedman (1744-1797),
*Narrative of a Five Years Expedition against the
Revolted Negroes of Surinam* (1796). Yet, he was
always more interested in executing his own illuminated books, which reflect an increasingly strong
influence by the *prisca theologia* [→ tradition], a
pure form of theology that had developed as a
counterpoint to conventional religion. Attempting
to address the sometimes contradictory obligations
of his materialistic and idealistic needs, Blake experimented with novel paint formulæ and engraving
methods (explained to him, in a dream, by his
deceased brother Robert), all designed to make his
visions commercially viable. Unfortunately, none
of the innovations proved financially successful.

Throughout his life, Blake evinced a strong interest in spiritualism. As a child, he experienced religious visions, and as a young man, he circulated
among the mystics who frequented London in the
1780s. He met the neoplatonist Thomas Taylor
(1758-1835), as well as the artist Henry Füseli
(1741-1825); and he engraved the frontispiece for
Füseli's English translation of → Johann Kaspar
Lavater's *Aphorisms on Man* (1788). Intellectually,
he was attracted to the writings of → Emanuel Swedenborg, owning and annotating at least three of
Swedenborg's books – *Heaven and Hell, Divine
Love and Divine Wisdom*, and *Divine Providence* –
and was likely familiar with two others – *Earths
in the Universe* and *True Christian Religion*. In
addition, Blake and his wife both signed the register for the first General Conference of the New
Jerusalem Church in 1789. There is no clear evidence, however, that they attended any subsequent
meetings, and Blake was eventually disillusioned
enough to satirize Swedenborg's *Heaven and Hell*
in his own *The Marriage of Heaven and Hell*
(1790-1793), transforming Swedenborg's Memorable Relations into his own Memorable Fancies.
Renouncing, for a time, Swedenborg's influence,
Blake claimed that 'Swedenborgs writings are a
recapitulation of all superficial opinions, and an
analysis of the more sublime, but no further' (pl.
22, E 43).

From Swedenborg Blake turned to → Paracelsus, the 16th-century Swiss alchemist, and → Jacob Boehme, the 17th-century German visionary, whose works had been translated by the 18th-century English mystic, → William Law. Although Blake spent his entire life in England, he did leave London for a few years, spending 1800-1803 in Felpham, as a guest of minor poet William Hayley (1745-1820). Although the relationship with the practical-minded Hayley quickly deteriorated, the stay in the country afforded Blake access to an extensive library. More successful was the relationship with Thomas Butts, a minor bureaucrat whose patronage during the first decade of the 19th century enabled Blake to illustrate parts of the Bible and Milton, among other things. Later in life, in 1818, Blake was discovered by John Linnell (1792-1882) and John Varley (1778-1842), two young artists whose own interests in the occult helped reinvigorate Blake's final works.

These disparate interests all converge in Blake's own form of a *prisca theologia*, in which he uses a kabbalistic-like myth as the basis for unifying all of his spiritual interests. His thesis in the early tract, *All Religions are One* (1788), that 'The Religions of all Nations are derived from each Nation's different reception of the Poetic Genius which is every where call'd the Spirit of Prophecy', would lead inexorably to a rejection of any particular religious organization, the Swedenborgian New Church included. As he explained in *The Marriage of Heaven and Hell*: 'Till a system was formed, which some took advantage of & enslav'd the vulgar by attempting to realize or abstract the mental dieties from their objects: thus began Priesthood. / Choosing forms of worship from poetic tales. / And at length they pronounced that the Gods had orderd such things. / Thus men forgot that All deities reside in the human breast' (pl. 11).

Intellectually, Blake agreed with the basic assumptions of → Francis Mercurius van Helmont's delineation of the *prisca theologia*, that the universe is an organic, vital, evolving whole, and that humans, having been made in God's image, are to use their imagination to help restore the post-lapsarian world to its original perfection, through the exercise of their intellect and imagination. In the works leading up to *The Marriage of Heaven and Hell*, Blake applies his spiritual principles to contemporary problems. The early unpublished poem, *The French Revolution* (1791), focuses on the war in Europe; *Visions of the Daughters of Albion* (1793) considers English participation in the slave trade; and various lyrics in the collected *Songs of Innocence* (1789), and later, the combined *Songs of*

Innocence and of Experience (1794) explore different forms of social, religious, political and moral hypocrisy.

At the same time that he worked on these exoteric works, Blake also began exploring esoteric themes. *There is No Natural Religion*, the companion to *All Religions are One*, is a series of aphorisms that conclude with the Application: 'He who sees the Infinite in all things sees God. He who sees the Ratio only sees himself only. Therefore God becomes as we are, that we may be as he is'. He also began exploring the dimensions of gnosis in *The Book of Thel* (1789), a neoplatonic poem in which the soul ultimately chooses to stay in the 'vales of Har', Blake's name for what he sees as the debilitation inherent in pre-lapsarian Eden, rather than become part of the corporeal cosmos where, though contributing to the life cycle, she will die. Similarly, in the unengraved *Tiriel* (c. 1789), Blake merges exoteric and esoteric themes, condemning contemporary politics for being a function of the erroneous use of reason, as opposed to intellect. To complete this phase of his artistic development, Blake wrote two prophecies – *America* (1793) and *Europe* (1794) – in which he presents an apocalyptic interpretation of the American and French Revolutions.

In the mid-1790s, Blake began the decades-long process of rendering his kabbalistic *prisca theologia* into mythic form. During this period he completed the four "minor prophecies", in which he worked out specific details of his developing myth. In the first, *The Song of Los* (1795), Blake traces the progress of organized religion, attributed, in *The Book of Urizen* (1794), to the consolidation of the rational factor. The problem, as analyzed in *The Book of Ahania* (1795), is that once consolidated, reason became cut off from its spiritual component. Therefore, as suggested in *The Book of Los* (1795), the relationship between reason and vision had to be reconfigured. Of key importance to Blake's thought process at this stage was the commission, worked on in 1795-1796, to help illustrate the popular poem by Edward Young (1683-1765), *The Complaint, or Night Thoughts on Life, Death, and Immortality* (1742-45), an extensive meditation based on conventional Christian theology. Even though the commission eventually fell through, the detailed analysis required for the project forced Blake to confront point by point his own attitude towards exoteric theology.

During the next ten years, intermittently from 1796 until 1807, Blake attempted to consolidate his criticism into a full-scale epic that would counter the errors propagated by Young's *Night Thoughts*.

The Four Zoas – or *Vala*, as it was originally called – is the first major attempt to transform his *prisca theologia* into narrative form. Written, in many cases, on proof sheets from the Young project, *The Four Zoas* is an early revision and re-presentation of exoteric Christianity in an esoteric form, its nine "nights" corresponding respectively to the kabbalistic *sefirot* (emanations) from *Malkhut* (Kingdom) through *Hokhmah* (Divine Wisdom), tracing the *via mystica* back to *Keter Elyon*, the Supreme Crown. Even though the myth is populated by unique allegorical figures with originally coined names, its structure resembles Francis Mercurius van Helmont's system of Christian Kabbalism. A major collaborator with → Christian Knorr von Rosenroth (1636-1689) on the *Kabbala Denudata* (2 vols., Sulzbach, 1677-1684), van Helmont contributed the *Adumbratio Kabbalæ Christianæ*, a full-length Platonic dialogue between a Kabbalist and a Christian Philosopher, designed to demonstrate the congruence between the myth generated by Jewish mystic Isaac Luria (1534-1572) and Christianity. According to kabbalistic tradition, our existence is part of a larger cycle of creation, the purpose of which is to provide the opportunity for all souls to be purified. In the *Adumbratio*, van Helmont christianizes the myth, using the Bible to justify his transformation of the Jewish system. In order to add a specifically christological function, he expands what was originally a three-part structure – "Contraction", "the Breaking of the Vessels", and "Restoration" – into four phases: "The Primordial Institution", the Godhead's original intention for creation; "The State of Destitution", the fall, as caused by the breaking of the vessels, and the ensuing contamination of souls; "The Modern Constitution", corporeal existence in which both macrocosm (Christ) and microcosm (man) work, each on his own level, to effect the form of restoration; so that, finally, in "The Supreme Restitution", Christ can defeat the forces of evil and man can rise.

We do not know Blake's specific source for Kabbalism. However, in his major prophecies, he generated a universal *prisca theologia* which incorporates into a Lurianic/van Helmontian base all of his esoteric reading, including the neoplatonists, Boehme and even Swedenborg. The result was a four-fold myth about the nationalistic hero, Albion – 'His fall into Division & his Resurrection to Unity / His fall into the Generation of Decay & Death & his Regeneration by the Resurrection from the dead' (n. 1, 4:4-5). In this first attempt at an epic narrative, Blake seems incapable of delineating a non-conventional role for the Saviour.

Available only in a heavily revised manuscript, *The Four Zoas* reflects the creative process involved in the attempt to transform abstract theory into a fully realized myth. In its earliest form, originally entitled *Vala*, the epic was apparently intended to focus on the emanation of the spiritual component, her individuation signifying the consolidation of the force that would oppose true vision, and therefore lead inevitably to organized religion. As the poem evolved, however, Blake shifted his focus from the effect to the cause, from Vala to the four zoas, his name for the four psychological components that correspond to the four kabbalistic souls. In its final form, *The Four Zoas* depicts the initial disorganization of the four zoas, as Urizen (the Rational Soul) usurps the function of vision, causing Urthona (the Immortal Soul) to grow dark and to limp. Throughout the poem, the action delineates the process by which the zoas are ultimately realigned so that Albion can be regenerated. The problem is that at this point, the action leads almost inexorably to an external catalyst – Christian ransom – for its resolution. Although Blake would work on the poem for at least a decade, and would even complete its apocalyptic vision – 'The war of swords departed now / The dark Religions are departed & sweet Science reigns' (n. 9, 139:9-10) – he could never integrate within its action a christological function that was not inimical to the concept of free will.

Blake confronts that specific problem in *Milton*, a brief epic in which the historical John Milton – whose doctrine in *Paradise Lost* was the source, Blake believed, of subsequent theological misapprehensions – returns to correct his error. As a transmigrating soul, Milton has wandered in heaven for one hundred years, unhappy at the legacy he left on earth. Hearing, in the Bard's Song, the esoteric account of creation and fall, he identifies himself as the source of the exoteric misconception that has been promulgated on earth – 'I in my Selfhood am that Satan: I am that Evil One!' – and returns to correct his error: 'I go to Eternal Death' (14[15]:30, 32). Once there, he literally reforms Urizen so that Albion can rise, and all of creation can prepare for 'the Great Harvest & Vintage of the Nations'.

In delineating *gilgul*, the process by which the transmigrating soul returns to correct its error, Blake, like van Helmont before him, associates the kabbalistic *Adam Kadmon* (primordial man) with the christological function, though not as an external Saviour. Instead, he reconfigures Los, the personification that had been associated with the → imagination, into an internal Christ. Becoming what Blake will call 'the vehicular form' of Urthona (the Immortal Soul), Los is now depicted as having forgotten his originally intended function. But when Milton reforms Urizen, Los 'recollect[s] an old Prophecy in Eden recorded' (20[22]:57), and devotes himself to constructing Golgonooza, the lower Eden where transmigrating souls will be purified in preparation for the apocalypse. Instead of sacrificing himself for the sake of mankind, Los creates the structure through which the individual can, of his own free will, save himself.

If *Milton* creates the form of restoration, *Jerusalem*, Blake's final prophecy, enacts the process in the fullest sense. Consistent with the four-part structure delineated by van Helmont, Blake divides the action of *Jerusalem* into the four-part process 'Of the Sleep of Ulro! and of the passage through / Eternal Death! and of the awaking to Eternal Life' (4:1-2). Juxtaposing the corresponding actions of the macrocosm (*Adam Kadmon*/Los) and the microcosm *(Adam Rishon*/Albion), Blake divides his epic into four chapters, corresponding respectively to van Helmont's four sections. In his first chapter, Blake conveys the inverse of van Helmont's "Primordial Institution", portraying the prelapsarian state in terms of what was lost as a result of the fall, when Albion chose 'demonstration' over 'faith'. At the same time that Albion lapses into despair, the psychological state that prevents restoration of the microcosm, Los confronts his Spectre, the force of negation that attempts to deter him from effecting restoration on the macrocosmic level. In the second chapter, Blake depicts van Helmont's "State of Destitution", when 'Every ornament of perfection, and every labour of love, / In all the Garden of Eden, & in all the golden mountains / Was become an envied horror' (28: 1-3). Even though, in his spiritual blindness, Albion turns his back on the Divine Vision, still, Los labors at his furnace, renovating the form of religion so that Albion will be able to rise. Next, corresponding to van Helmont's "Modern Constitution", Albion, the microcosm, confronts the perversions of Christianity that were produced as a result of the fall, while simultaneously, Los, on the macrocosmic level, attempts to align the biblical tribes with Albion's sons, to prepare for the "Supreme Restitution", when Los will confront negation at its very source, as he 'alterd his Spectre & every Ratio of his Reason / . . . Till he had completely divided him into a separate space' (91:50, 52). Finally, 'Time was Finished! The Breath Divine Breathed over Albion' (94:18).

Through *Jerusalem*, which he worked on intermittently from 1804 until the 1820s, Blake was able to conceive a kabbalistic version of Christianity, one that enabled Albion to exercise the free will necessary to save himself, but without sacrificing the christological function of Los, who on the one hand, manipulated the form that Albion would actualize, and on the other, confronted the shards of negation that exist as an obstacle to cosmic restoration. Thus, it was through his verbal art that Blake was able to articulate his system. From that point on, however, he would focus on the visual art for its ultimate expression.

In his last works, Blake used the myth he had developed in the composite art as the standard against which to criticize and artistically revise the Bible and other religious works. He returned to the Book of Job, which he had worked on sporadically throughout his life, this time engraving plates that inverted the focus of the composite books. There, the pictures had been used to illustrate the verbal text; now, he uses words to illuminate what is primarily a visual text. In its completed form, Blake faults Job for constructing a rationalistic interpretation of religion, rather than experiencing God directly through the imagination. *The Ghost of Abel* (1822), a two-plate response to Byron's *Cain: A Mystery*, published in December 1821, is subtitled 'A Revelation In the Visions of Jehovah / Seen by William Blake'. For *Laocoön* (c. 1826-1827), his last illuminated work, Blake arranges a vast collection of aphorisms, using Hebrew and Greek, as well as English, all around a statue of Laocoön and his two sons, to convey the disparity between that which is taught and that which is true. Finally, on his deathbed, Blake worked on the 102-water color drawings that criticize and correct → Dante's *Divine Comedy*, demonstrating how organized religion had occluded the medieval Italian poet's true vision.

Tiriel (G.E. Bentley, Jr., ed.), Oxford: Clarendon Press, 1967 ♦ *The Divine Comedy* (David Bindman, ed.), Paris: Bibliothèque de l'Image, 2000 ♦ *The Illuminated Books* (David Bindman, gen. ed.), 6 vols., Princeton: The William Blake Trust and Princeton University Press, 1991-1995 ♦ *Illustrations of the Book of Job* (Malcolm Cormack, ed.), Richmond: Virginia Museum of Fine Arts, 1997 ♦ *The William Blake Archive* (Morris Eaves, Robert N. Essick and Joseph Visconti, eds.), www.blakearchive.org ♦ *The Complete Poetry and Prose* (David V. Erdman, newly revised ed.), Garden City, New York: Doubleday, 1988 ♦ *William Blake's Designs for Edward Young's "Night Thoughts": A Complete Edition* (John E. Grant, Edward J. Rose, Michael J. Tolley and David V. Erdman, eds.), 2 vols., Oxford: Clarendon Press, 1980 ♦ *The Four Zoas: A Photographic Facsimile of the Manuscript with Commentary on the Illuminations* (Cettina Tramontono Magno and David V. Erdman, eds.), Lewisburg: Bucknell University Press, 1987.

Lit.: Peter Ackroyd, *Blake*, New York: Knopf, 1996 ♦
Bryan Aubrey, *Watchmen of Eternity: Blake's Debt to
Jacob Boehme*, Lanham, Maryland: University Press
of America, 1986 ♦ G.E. Bentley, Jr., *Blake Records*,
Oxford: Clarendon Press, 1969 ♦ idem, *The Stranger
from Paradise: A Biography of William Blake*, New
Haven & London: Yale University Press 2001 ♦ Alli-
son Coudert, *The Impact of the Kabbalah in the Sev-
enteenth Century: The Life and Thought of Francis
Mercury van Helmont (1614-1698)* (Brill's Series in
Jewish Studies 9), Leiden: E.J. Brill, 1999 ♦ Morton D.
Paley, "'A New Heaven is Begun': Blake and Sweden-
borgianism", *Blake: An Illustrated Quarterly* 12
(1979), 64-90 ♦ idem, *The Traveller in the Evening:
The Last Works of William Blake*, Oxford: Oxford
University Press, 2003 ♦ Kathleen Raine, *Blake and
Tradition* (Bollingen Series 35.11), 2 vols., Princeton:
Princeton University Press, 1968 ♦ Sheila A. Spector,
*"Glorious incomprehensible": The Development of
Blake's Kabbalistic Language*, Lewisburg: Bucknell
University Press, 2001 ♦ eadem, *"Wonders Divine":
The Development of Blake's Kabbalistic Myth*, Lewis-
burg: Bucknell University Press, 2001 ♦ Joseph Vis-
comi, *Blake and the Idea of the Book*, Princeton:
Princeton University Press, 1993.

SHEILA A. SPECTOR

Blavatsky, Helena Petrovna, * 12.8.1831 Ekaterinoslav, † 8.5.1891 London

Undoubtedly one of the most fascinating, controversial, and influential women in the 19th century writing on the ancient wisdom tradition,
Blavatsky was born in the von Hahn family on
August 12, 1831 (or on July 31, according to the
old Julian calendar that was still current in Russia)
in Ekaterinoslav (Dnepropetrovsk), the Ukraine.
Descended from a prominent family of Russian,
French Huguenot, and German background, her
father, Col. Peter Alexeyevich von Hahn (1798-
1873), was a descendant of the medieval crusader
Count Rottenstern and a Captain of Artillery. Her
mother, Helena Andreyevna, *née* de Fadeyev (1814-
1842), was a woman of great literary talent who
wrote novels under the pseudonym of Zeneida
R__va. Because of her husband's position, the family traveled constantly. During an interlude in the
early 1840s following the death of her mother in
Odessa, young Helena was sent to live with her
grandparents (Andrey Mihailovitch de Fedeyev
and Helena Pavlovna Delgorukova) in Saratov,
where she remained until 1845. According to
accounts of this period, Helena already exhibited
traits of mediumship.

By age eighteen (1849) she married Nikofor
Blavatsky (1809-?), a man for whom she obviously
had little attachment, given that she left him after
only three months. From that time on she embarked on years of wandering, presumably in
search of esoteric truths and occult training, traveling to a number of destinations, including Constantinople – where the greatest concentration of
Sufi mystics resided – Greece, Egypt, and Eastern
Europe. While in Egypt (1849-1850), she met the
Copt occultist Paulos Metamon, a so-called magician who many years later (1871) was said to have
assisted Blavatsky in the establishment of the
"Société Spirite" in Cairo. It has been claimed
that Metamon was her occult teacher during these
early years of her travels. From Egypt, Blavatsky
left for Europe, traveling to Paris and London,
where she later claimed to have met her Master
for the first time in Hyde Park during the summer
of 1850.

From Paris, Blavatsky left for North America,
inspired by the novels of James Fenimore Cooper
and his descriptions of the Native Americans and
the promise of secrets possessed by the medicine
men or shamans. She arrived in Quebec, but was
ultimately disappointed with the group of Native
Americans with whom she met. After this meeting,
she commenced on a new plan, leaving for New
Orleans to investigate Voudouism, then on to
Texas, Mexico, and – for much of 1852 – to Central and South America. She then decided to go to
India, and together with two other companions –
one of them a Hindu she had originally met in Hon-
duras and whom she had selected to be her guru or
Master – they sailed first to Ceylon (Sri Lanka) and
then on to Bombay (Mumbai) sometime during the
latter part of 1852. During the same year she
attempted to enter Tibet through Nepal but failed
in her attempt. She then journeyed to south India,
Java, and Singapore and ultimately back to England. Her probable arrival there was in 1853, and
she remained until 1854. Sometime in the second
part of the year, she set out once again for the
United States, landing in New York, journeying
across country through Chicago to her final destination in San Francisco – traveling for part of the
journey in a covered wagon caravan – where she
remained until 1855.

Her next destination was India (Calcutta), which
she reached via Japan. During her second visit
there, from 1855 to 1856, she met with a German
acquaintance of her father (an ex-Lutheran minister by the name of Kühlwein) and two other companions, all of whom attempted to enter western
Tibet through Kashmir to Ladakh. If we trust the
account in A.P. Sinnett's (1840-1921) *Incidents in
the Life of Madame Blavatsky*, she alone among
her traveling companions was taken into Tibetan
territory by a Tatar shaman guide, albeit for only a
short time.

Blavatsky left India in 1857 for Europe (France and Germany) by way of Java, and finally ended up in Russia. The period from 1858 to 1863 she spent primarily with her family; and during a period of about a year she stayed with her husband, General Blavatsky, in Tiflis. We know that sometime around 1859 she became very ill and came close to death. This period in Russia is significant because the mediumistic or psychic powers she was said to have displayed since childhood now became particularly prominent; this, at least, is what we can deduce from the account of her sister, Vera Petrovna de Jelihowsky (or de Zhelihovsky, 1835-1895), who, when questioned on the subject, replied: 'I remember that when addressed as a medium, she (Mme. Blavatsky) used to laugh and assure us she was no medium, but only a *mediator* between mortals and beings we knew nothing about'. The types of phenomena that were produced during the time of Blavatsky's stay in Pskov are classified and described by Madame de Zhelihovsky as follows: '1) direct and perfectly clear written and verbal answers to mental questions – or "thought-reading"; 2) prescriptions for various diseases, written in Latin, and subsequent cures; 3) private secrets, unknown to all but the interested party, divulged, especially in the case of those persons who mentioned insulting doubts; 4) change of weight in furniture and of persons at will; 5) letters from unknown correspondents, and immediate answers written to queries made and found in the most out-of-the-way mysterious places; 6) appearance and *apport* of objects unclaimed by any one present; 7) sounds as of musical notes in the air wherever Mme. Blavatsky desired they should resound' (Sinnett, *Incidents*, 86). Blavatsky's exact whereabouts between 1863 and 1867 are not altogether certain, but it is reasonable to assume that she left her family and Russia around 1863 and traveled to Italy, the Balkans, Serbia, Egypt, and Persia (Iran). It was an eventful period because of her association with a revolutionary Italian society, the Carbonari, on the one hand, and a controversy surrounding her relationship to her adolescent ward, Yury, on the other. The child was apparently in her care since 1862, when she resided in Tiflis. Although he was the son of Baron Nicholas Meyendorff and an unknown mother, suspicion was placed on Blavatsky as being the actual mother by the sister-in-law of the Baron, who claimed that the latter had an ongoing affair with Blavatsky since she arrived in Russia in 1858. Yet, a medical examination in 1885 revealed that Blavatsky suffered from *Anteflexio Uteri*, 'most probably from the day of her birth', so it is unlikely that the child was hers.

When the boy died in 1867, she arranged, with the assistance of her long-time friend, Agardi Metrovitch, to have him buried in Russia. It was apparently this same Metrovitch who introduced Blavatsky to the cause of the Carbonari, but his identity and his relationship to Blavatsky remain unclear. According to Blavatsky herself, the two had been acquainted since 1850, and she probably knew that this revolutionary half-Italian had ties to the society that included among its membership Giuseppe Garibaldi (1807-1882) and Giuseppe Mazzini (1805-1872), and whose purpose was to break the hold of the Papacy over Italy. Blavatsky actively supported Metrovitch's cause, even to the extent of participating in the battle of Mentana (November 3, 1867). This battle was lost to the Papists and the French, and Blavatsky received multiple wounds, including being shot in the leg and right shoulder and stabbed near her heart.

Blavatsky's travels resumed in early 1868. She left Italy, traveling to India by way of Constantinople; this time she claimed that she was accompanied by her Master. After having reached India later in the year, she claims to have entered Tibet and resided both in Greater and Little Tibet, even staying at the home of the Master Koot Hoomi in Little Tibet and in Shigatse in southern Tibet, the latter close to Tashilhumpo, the residence of the Panchen Lama.

The first so-called Mahatma letter, or letter from the Master KH (Koot Hoomi), arrived at the home of Blavatsky's aunt, Nadyezhda Andreyevna de Fadeyev in 1870. It stated that Helena would be returning shortly to her family. This she did after journeying to Greece and Cyprus at the end of 1870, where she claimed to have met the Master Hilarion (Illarion). From Piraeus (Greece) she boarded the SS *Eunomia* for Cairo in July 1871. On route, the gunpowder magazine in the cargo hold blew up, causing many deaths. Blavatsky was rescued and brought to Alexandria, arriving in Cairo toward the end of the year. Here she made the acquaintance of Emma Cutting, who is known to Theosophists by her married name, Mme. Alexis Coulomb, and who would cause untold grief to Blavatsky thirteen years later.

While in Cairo, Blavatsky founded the "Société Spirite", a society that seems to have had a double agenda: a public and a private one. The first involved the public investigation of passive reception by mediums of spirit communications – a reflection of the → spiritualism that was practiced in the United States since 1848. There appears to have been another agenda, however, that was known only to certain individuals in the society (including Blavatsky and Metamon, the same Copt magician whom Blavatsky met in 1850). It involved conducting undisclosed occult practices that may very well have been similar to those practiced in the early → Theosophical Society. As far as Blavatsky was concerned, the importance of the "Société Spirite" lay in its private aspect. Within a few months, perhaps weeks, the formal society all but disappeared.

By April 1872, Blavatsky again left Egypt, traveling to Odessa to reunite with her family, but making a number of stops on the way. In March or April 1873 she traveled to Paris via Bucharest before finally taking a passenger liner to the United States, where she arrived on July 7, 1873. This journey marks the conclusion to her earlier life of travel and the beginning of the next major period of her life.

What are we to make of this extended period of travel by a girl who began her journeys as a recently married teenager and who later claimed to have resided in many of the most inaccessible places on earth, sometimes disguising herself as a man, once involved in a battle, meeting with practitioners of magic and the occult arts, and spending the better part of twenty years as a veritable gypsy? In psychological terms one might speak of travel compulsiveness, but if we take Blavatsky's own words seriously, this compulsion had a purpose. Most of what we know about this period originates from her own reminiscences, from the accounts of acquaintances who affirm having met her during the course of her travels, and from family members who left their own written recollections of her activities. Even if we assume an attitude of healthy skepticism regarding the question of whether all these accounts are to be trusted, it remains that much of it appears to have a basis in fact. Some of Blavatsky's adventures have been embellished by her, but it seems certain that she met many unusual people and acquired a vast store of esoteric and occult knowledge. Already as a child of fifteen, she claims to have been exposed to an occult library, consisting of several hundred volumes, belonging to her maternal great-grandfather, Prince Paul Vassilyevich Dolgorukov (1755-1837). In all likelihood, this was her first exposure to → alchemy, → magic, and kabbalah [→ Jewish Influences]. Combine this with the psychic abilities that her family claimed she exhibited, and we have the basic conditions for a theoretical as well as practical occultist. Blavatsky's interests appear to have driven her to seek more knowledge of esotericism and occultism, not just from written sources but also from living teachers. Who these teachers were,

and how they were related to the Theosophical "Masters" who were to play a highly important role in her life, remains a mystery to this day.

Why Madame Blavatsky came to the United States is open to speculation, but in keeping with her propensity for the mysterious, she claimed that she had been sent by her Lodge either to reveal the truth about modern spiritualism or to form a secret society. The events leading up to the foundation of what would become known as the Theosophical Society begin in 1874, with her introduction to Col. → Henry Steel Olcott (1832-1907). According to Olcott's account in his *Old Diary Leaves* (I, 1f.), their meeting took place in Chittenden, Vermont on October 14, 1874, during his investigation of the spirit or phantom phenomena allegedly occurring at the farmhouse of William and Horatio Eddy. Thus began a lifelong collaboration, sometimes rancorous and turbulent but always productive. Their initial interest involved the investigation of spiritualist phenomena, including the phantom forms at the Eddy brothers' home in Chittenden, and the reappearance (having first appeared as the spirit guide to Florence Cook in England) of the spirit "Katie King" in Philadelphia through the mediums Mr. and Mrs. Nelson Holmes. There is no doubt that Blavatsky defended → spiritualism in her early correspondence to the New York *Daily Graphic* and spiritualist papers. One example illustrating her high opinion of spiritualism and her belief that the United States was the cradle of that phenomenon appears in the *Spiritual Scientist*, in which she remarks that she 'came over here [the U.S.] from France with feelings not unlike those of a Mohammedan approaching the birth-place of his prophet'. Comparing these remarks in support of spiritualism, made in December 1874, to those made in February 1875, one can observe a marked change in attitude. In her correspondence of that month with Hiram Corson (1828-1911), a professor at Cornell University, she writes that for her, spiritualism is based not on the modern American variety that began in 1848 but on a much older one, originating 'from the same source of information that was used by Raymond Lully, Picus della Mirandola, Cornelius Agrippa, Robert Fludd, Henry More, etc. etc. etc.'. Thus she expressed for the first time her concept of an "ancient Spiritualism" or "occultism" [→ occult / occultism] that was later to become the foundation of her theosophy. To Blavatsky, American spiritualism was devoid of ancient wisdom, whereas "ancient Spiritualism" or occultism comprised 'a system that should disclose . . . the "deepest depths" of the Divine Nature, and show . . . the *real tie which binds all things together'*. In other words, what we see here is a shift from a form of spiritualism based merely upon investigation of "phenomena" but devoid of doctrinal content, towards one that claims to be rooted in the ancient wisdom of the Western esoteric tradition. Henceforth Blavatsky would continue to emphasize this tradition, while increasingly including Eastern (primarily South Asian) occult teachings as well. By July 1875 the first public statement of her views appears in a response to an article by HIRAF (an acronym for five authors) entitled "Rosicrucianism", which had appeared in the July 1 and 8 issues of the *Spiritual Scientist*. Blavatsky's response, entitled "A Few Questions to 'HIRAF'", appeared in the following two issues (July 15 and 22). For the first time, she presents a rather detailed exposition of her views on occultism and magic – presented by her as the practical and theoretical sides of the Ancient Wisdom. Because it is a response to → Rosicrucianism as interpreted by HIRAF, one important idea evident from this article is her acknowledgement of the existence of a number of "Brotherhoods" devoted to the "Wisdom or Occult tradition", going back as far as the Egyptian → Ophites and persisting through the "Fire-Philosophers" or Paracelsists and European alchemists.

Staying at 46 Irving Place in New York during much of 1875, Blavatsky attracted to her apartment a number of interested individuals curious to hear her views on occultism. From the early months of 1875, she was also involved in the writing of her first major work, *Isis Unveiled*. In addition to this creative activity, she experienced a rather tumultuous period involving domestic problems (her marriage with and divorce from a Russian citizen, Michael Betanelly, within the space of a few months) and a serious leg injury caused by a fall.

The meetings at her apartment led to the formation of the Theosophical Society later in 1875. On September 7, a lecture was given here by George Henry Felt (1831-1906) entitled "The Lost Canon of Proportion of the Egyptians". According to Felt's own account, he successfully proved the existence of 'elementals or intermediates, or elementary or original spirits' existing on various levels from 'inanimate nature through the animal kingdom to man'; furthermore, Felt affirmed that these beings were represented in the Egyptian zodiacs (i.e. the forms appearing there were not figments of the imagination but real creatures), and that they could be evoked by chemical means. This lecture incited Col. Olcott to suggest, in a note passed to Blavatsky during the meeting, whether it would 'not be a good thing to form a Society for this kind

of study?' Blavatsky agreed to the proposal, and the other members of the audience concurred, thus initiating the process of formally establishing a society which would soon come to be known as the Theosophical Society, which was to be organized on October 30 and 'constitutionally perfected' on November 17, 1875.

The second significant event that occurred during the New York years (1873-1878) was the publication of *Isis Unveiled* on September 29, 1877. A monumental work in scope, the text extended over 1268 pages in two volumes: the first volume called "The 'Infallibility' of Modern Science" and the second called "Theology". Originally entitled *The Veil of Isis* (which remains on the heading of each page), it had to be renamed once it was discovered that this title had already been used for an 1861 Rosicrucian work by W.W. Reade. Many years later, within a month of her death, Blavatsky revealed that the text was not written primarily for the general public but rather for the members of the Theosophical Society; and she added that much of the work was edited by Col. Olcott and Alexander Wilder (1823-1908) – an old acquaintance of Olcott's, and a member and later Vice-president of the Theosophical Society. Blavatsky writes in the Preface that *Isis Unveiled* 'is a plea for the recognition of the Hermetic philosophy, the anciently universal Wisdom Religion, as the only possible key to the Absolute in science and theology'. This Wisdom Religion is identified with magic, considered in ancient times 'a divine science which led to a participation in the attributes of Divinity itself'. Volume one is devoted to the hidden and unknown forces of nature, discussing subjects such as phenomena and forces (Chapter 2), elementals and elementaries (Chapter 7), cyclic phenomena (Chapter 9), psychic and physical marvels (Chapter 11), and the Inner and Outer Man (Chapter 10), all accompanied by a vast array of supportive and incidental knowledge – ancient and modern, Western and Eastern, esoteric and exoteric. Volume two discusses similarities of Christian scripture, doctrine, history, and personalities with non-Christian systems such as Buddhism, Hinduism, the Vedas, and Zoroastrianism, all based on the notion that they share a common origin referred to as the 'primitive "wisdom-religion"'.

Sometime during the writing of *Isis Unveiled* the idea came up (probably first in Olcott's mind) of a move to India, and eventually this plan was confirmed when the Masters' "Orders to make ready" to leave New York were recorded in his diary on May 24. Shortly thereafter (July 8, 1878) Blavatsky became a naturalized U.S. citizen.

Toward the end of the year, Blavatsky and Olcott departed from New York harbor to England, arriving from there in Bombay on February 16, 1879. Blavatsky was never to return to the U.S. again.

After their arrival in Bombay, accompanied by considerable publicity in the Indian newspapers, Olcott and Blavatsky settled in a home on Girgaum Back Road. One of the newspapers, *The Pioneer* (Allahabad), gave especially favorable accounts of the Theosophists because its editor, Alfred Percy Sinnett (1840-1921), had had an interest in the Theosophical Society and its founders as a result of his involvement with spiritualism. Sinnett's interest in Theosophy eventually led to his and Mrs. Sinnett's meeting the Theosophists for the first time in December 1879, thus resulting in Blavatsky's short-time involvement with *The Pioneer*. She contributed a number of letters, unsigned articles on Russian subjects, and an eleven-part translation of "The Travels of Colonel Grodekoff".

In October 1879, Olcott and Blavatsky initiated a monthly magazine designed as the main organ for the Society, *The Theosophist*, with an initial circulation of 400 copies. Prior to this event, however, far more ambitious plans were being developed. Olcott records in this diary entry of May 23, 1879, that Blavatsky began work on 'her new book on Theosophy', an undertaking that was to culminate in the publication of her greatest work, *The Secret Doctrine*.

In 1880, two significant events occurred. The first was Blavatsky's and Olcott's first tour of Ceylon (Sri Lanka), which resulted in both of them formally accepting the Five Precepts (*pansil*; Pali: *pañcasīla)* and presumably the Triple Gem as well. Thus they formally became Buddhists; although in Blavatsky's case one should perhaps say that she reaffirmed her Buddhism, since she already identified herself as a Buddhist during her New York residency in the 1870s. The outcome of this visit was the establishment of branches of the Theosophical Society in Ceylon and the initiation of a Buddhist revival that, through the sustained efforts of Col. Olcott, would continue to develop throughout the 1880s and 1890s.

In October 1880, a significant event took place: the receipt of the first of a long succession of letters from the Masters K.H. (Koot Hoomi) and M. (Morya) to Sinnett and others. K.H., M. and other Masters, believed to belong to an "Occult Brotherhood" in the East, were assumed to have given their philosophical and ethical teachings to the world through the medium of the Theosophical Society; they were also believed to have been the teachers of Blavatsky, who had first become their pupil (*chela*)

and who had received training and instruction during her visit to Tibet. From the first letter received by Sinnett on October 15, 1880 to the final letter of the series in 1886, 145 were written. The esoteric teachings contained in these letters were summarized by Sinnett in his book *Esoteric Buddhism* (1883).

The year 1884 was eventful for the Founders and for the Theosophical Society. Early in February Olcott and Blavatsky visited Europe – Blavatsky for medical reasons, Olcott on Society business and as an advocate for the Buddhist cause in Ceylon. While in England, Olcott had to intervene in a struggle that was causing considerable distress within the British Theosophical Society. The latter, formed in 1878, consisted in the early 1880s of a small, intellectual group of individuals whose president, George Wyld (1821-1906), attempted to establish an independent Society more in step with the teachings of Christianity and less with the "atheism" of Blavatsky and her anti-Christian views. Having failed, he resigned in 1882. A similar crisis within the Society developed over the next two years involving Mrs. → Anna Bonus Kingsford (1846-1888) and her close associate, Edward Maitland (1824-1897), resulting in the formation of the Hermetic Society [→ Hermeticism and Hermetic Societies]. Early in May, Olcott, Blavatsky and other members of the Theosophical Society assented to a series of meetings with a committee formed by the Society for Psychical Research (established in 1882) on the subject of psychic phenomena, including 'the phenomenal receipt of written documents' and 'the precipitation of Mahatmic writing within closed letters from ordinary correspondents while in transit through the mails'. Blavatsky was questioned in Cambridge in August 9th, and the S.P.R. committee was favorably impressed with her responses. Its 'preliminary and provisional' report came out in December 1884.

In the month following the interview, an explosive event in India lent support to the negative conclusions of a second S.P.R. Report, issued in 1885. These developments were to leave a permanent stain upon the reputations of the Theosophical Society and Blavatsky. Under the title 'The Collapse of Koot Hoomi', *The Madras Christian College Magazine* of September 1884 published the first part of an exposé containing fifteen letters purportedly written by Blavatsky to Emma Coulomb. The letters were intended to be proof of Mme. Coulomb's charge that Blavatsky had committed fraud. Blavatsky vehemently objected to the allegations, but did not bring charges against Mrs. Coulomb and her husband, Alexis, and the magazine.

This was because Olcott had convinced her to leave the decision to a special Committee comprising, among others, a number of prominent Indian legal experts and government officials. The Committee suggested not prosecuting the defamers due to the inherent legal dangers to plaintiffs in libel cases. This position was also supported by the delegates at the 1884 Annual Convention of the Theosophical Society, held in December.

Meanwhile, the S.P.R., which had concluded in its first report that there was some evidence that could not be discounted, decided to continue its investigation by sending an observer, Richard Hodgson (1855-1905), to India in November 1884. He remained there for three months, investigating the charges by the Coulombs; his goal was to determine 'the competency of the witnesses to phenomena, and to ascertain, if possible, the trustworthiness in particular of three primary witnesses, viz., Mr. Damodar K. Mavalankar, Mr. Babajee D. Nath, and Colonel Olcott'. Hodgson's conclusions, issued in December 1885, could not have been more damaging and devastating to Blavatsky and the Society. They included the following: (a) the letters to the Coulombs were written by Blavatsky, (b) the Coulombs were Blavatsky's accomplices in the production of fraudulent phenomena, (c) the primary witnesses to the existence of an Occult Brotherhood, including Blavatsky, had made false statements, (d) the Masters Koot Hoomi and Morya must be fictitious, since their handwriting resembled M. Damodar's and Blavatsky's, (e) no instance of phenomena was witnessed by Hodgson, (f) the objects of the Theosophical Society were political and Blavatsky was a Russian spy. Hodgson concluded with this statement: 'But acting in accordance with the principles upon which our Society [the S.P.R.] has proceeded, I must express my unqualified opinion that no genuine psychical phenomena whatever will be found among the pseudo-mysteries of the Russian lady *alias* Koot Hoomi Lal Sing *alias* Mahatma Morya *alias* Madame Blavatsky'. The S.P.R. Committee concluded: 'For our own part, we regard her neither as the mouthpiece of hidden seers, nor as a mere vulgar adventuress; we think that she has achieved a title to permanent remembrance as one of the most accomplished, ingenious, and interesting impostors in history'.

Blavatsky returned to India at the end of 1884, but within a month she became gravely ill, causing her to resign from the office of Corresponding Secretary of the Society on March 21. Shortly thereafter, she left India for the last time, traveling to Europe. After a sojourn of three months in Italy,

she decided to settle in Würzburg (Bavaria), in August 1885. By the end of the year, she was immersed in the writing of her *magnum opus*, The *Secret Doctrine*, aided by the recent arrival in Würzburg of Countess Constance Wachtmeister (1838-1910).

For the next two years, *The Secret Doctrine* was to be Blavatsky's major project. From Würzburg she moved to Ostend (Belgium) in July before being persuaded by some English Theosophists to settle in London. This she did in May 1887, residing first at the home ("Maycot") of Mabel Collins (1851-1927), the author of *Light on the Path*. Within a few days (on May 19), the Blavatsky Lodge was established, and within a few months (September), the magazine *Lucifer* was founded to provide 'some sort of public propaganda' before the publication of *The Secret Doctrine*, which took place a year later. If the contents of the magazine did not excite the general public, the title certainly did.

In September of 1887, Blavatsky and the Blavatsky Lodge moved to 17 Lansdowne Road, the focal point of Blavatsky's activities for the next two-and-one-half years before she relocated to 19 Avenue Road, St. John's Wood, London in 1890, which became the new headquarters of the Blavatsky Lodge as well as of the British Section and of European headquarters. The headquarters incidentally was the home of → Annie Besant (1847-1933), a recently recruited member (May 1889) and rising star of the Theosophical Society. Thirteen months after the establishment of the Lansdowne Road residence as headquarters of the Blavatsky Lodge (October 9, 1888), a second significant event occurred: the establishment of a new organization that was closely affiliated with the Theosophical Society. This organization, the "Esoteric Section of the Theosophical Society" (E.S.), had as its goal the promotion of 'the esoteric interests of the Theosophical Society'. Blavatsky became Outer Head (the Inner Heads were the Masters or Mahatmas), with the responsibility of giving esoteric teachings to a small group of students who desired chelaship. The E.S. was independent of the administration of the Theosophical Society, or in the words of Olcott, it was '*not* the T.S.; nor that its rules are binding only upon members belonging to that special school; nor that it would be violation of the T.S. constitution for it to interfere with their rights of private judgment; nor that the President-Founder is compelled to guarantee to every individual member, of whatsoever religion, race, sex, or color, his or her personal liberty of belief and speech'.

A few days after the founding of the Esoteric Section came the publication of *The Secret Doctrine*, consisting of two volumes with a total of 1474 pages. The first volume, *Cosmogenesis*, discusses cosmic evolution, expanding upon the contents of *Isis Unveiled*, while the second volume, *Anthropogenesis*, discusses the evolution of Humanity through a succession of Root Races, five of which have already appeared. Based on stanzas taken from *The Book of Dzyan* (seven in volume I and twelve in volume II), a work unknown to modern scholarship, said to be composed by an unattested people and in a language unknown to philosophy, *The Secret Doctrine* (SD) contains the following ideas: 1) There exists a single, Supreme, Eternal, Immutable, Unknown and Unknowable, Infinite Principle or Reality (SD 1:14); 2) There is a fundamental unity to all existence (SD I:120, 276); 3) The eternal, manifested Universe and everything within it is subject to the 'law of periodicity, of flux and reflux, ebb and flow' (SD I:17); 4) The evolution of nature – material and spiritual – reflects progressive development and not merely repetitive action (SD I:43, 277-78; II:653); 5) The evolution of the individual is not limited to one life but continues through innumerable lives made possible by the process of → reincarnation, i.e. the entrance of Self – the trinity of Spirit, Soul, and Mind – into another (human) body (SD II:302-306); 6) This evolution is brought about by the Law of Cause and Effect, or Karma – good actions leading to good consequences, bad actions to bad consequences – thus assigning full responsibility to the individual who performs the actions (SD I:639, 642-47; 7). The structural framework of the universe, humanity included, is by nature septenary in composition (SD II:605-41; 8). The cyclic, evolving universe is hierarchical in constitution, each component – for instance, the planets and the sun in our Solar System – consisting of seven constituents or globes, thus illustrating the correspondence between the microcosm of the human being and the macrocosm of the universe (SD II:68f., 434f.; 9). Human evolution on the Earth is taking place within seven Root Races, each of which is divided into seven sub-races. In our present state of evolution, we belong to the fifth sub-race (the Anglo-Saxon) of the fifth Root Race (SD I:610; II:1f., 86f., 300f., 434f., 688f.); 10) The individual is a microcosm, a 'miniature copy of the macrocosm' (SD I:274; 11). The universe is guided and animated by a cosmic Hierarchy of sentient beings, each having a specific mission (SD I:274-77).

Students of *The Secret Doctrine* soon began to ask questions about its contents. Blavatsky's responses during meetings of the Blavatsky Lodge

in the first half of 1889 led to the publication, in two parts, of the *Transactions of The Blavatsky Lodge of the Theosophical Society* in 1890 and 1891. They cover issues concerning the heart of *The Secret Doctrine*: the "stanzas of Dzyan" included in the first volume.

In July 1889, Blavatsky, while visiting Fontainebleau for rest and recuperation, wrote or "translated" excerpts from "The Book of the Golden Precepts", entitled *The Voice of the Silence*, allegedly part of the same series of texts from which the stanzas of the *Book of Dzyan* had been derived. Some stanzas she claimed to be pre-Buddhist, others Mahāyāna Buddhist in spirit. The first part, from which the title of the whole work is derived, highlights the progression of knowledge from the ordinary, waking (ignorant) state to the fourth or dreamless state of higher spiritual consciousness, until finally, in Blavatsky's words, your '*Self* is lost in SELF, *thyself* unto THYSELF, merged in THAT SELF from which thou first didst radiate'. The second part, "The Two Paths", refers to the '*Open PATH*', i.e. the path of the layman or the exoteric path, that 'leads to the changeless change – Nirvāna, the glorious state of Absoluteness, the Bliss past human thought'; and it distinguishes this from the second Path of 'RENUNCIATION', the 'Path of Woe', a '*Secret* Path [which] leads the Arhan to mental woe unspeakable' but which also leads to 'Paranirvānic' bliss. The third part, "the Seven Portals", purports to bring wisdom to the aspirant through 'a golden key that openeth its gate', which echoes in part the six *pāramitās* or perfections, discussed in great detail in the *Bodhicaryâvatāra* by the 8th century Buddhist poet Shāntideva.

The same month also witnessed the publication of *The Key to Theosophy*, a popular introduction to the "Wisdom Religion" or Theosophy. Among other subjects, it discusses the septenary nature of humanity and earth, reincarnation, post-mortem states, mind and ego, and gives information about the Theosophical Society and the Theosophical Masters or Mahatmas.

Although Blavatsky's writing career was open to criticism by non-Theosophist theologians, scientists, and academics, by far the most serious challenge to the credibility of her major contributions – *Isis Unveiled*, *The Secret Doctrine*, and *The Voice of the Silence* – came from a spiritualist, William Emmette Coleman (1843-1909), who claimed that she had plagiarized many of her teachings from sources such as Ennemoser's *History of Magic* and *Demonologia*, Dunlap's *Sod: The Son of Man* and *Sod: The Mysteries of Adoni*, King's *Gnostics*, and

Jacolliot's *Christna et le Christ* and *Le Spiritisme dans le monde*. Coleman listed a total of about one hundred secondary sources. Plagiarism has been an issue in Theosophy since the charges first appeared in the late 1880s. Blavatsky's methods of citing sources have been defended by Theosophists, but in all fairness no detailed investigation has even been conducted, nor have criteria been established to prove or disprove the allegations. Interestingly, many of the authors who were allegedly the victims of Blavatsky's plagiarism were alive when the charges were made, yet none indicted her.

A final assault on Blavatsky's character came from one of the leading American Theosophists, Elliott Coues (1842-1899). Having failed to retain a position of authority within the newly reorganized Theosophical Society in America in 1886, and having failed to enlist Blavatsky's aid in his efforts to gain control, Coues, in an article written by him appearing in the New York *Sun* in July 1890, attacked Blavatsky as an imposter and the Society for its teachings. This resulted in a lawsuit initiated in Blavatsky's name against both Coues and the *Sun*. The suit was terminated because of Blavatsky's death on May 8, 1891. Although Coues was unrepentant, the *Sun* did retract the story in a separate suit that W.Q. Judge, the General Secretary of the Theosophical Society in America, brought against the paper, and agreed to publish Judge's sketch of Blavatsky's life, entitled 'The Esoteric She', in the September 27, 1892 issue.

In the year before her death, Blavatsky took on additional administrative responsibilities when she became President of the newly established European Section. In *Lucifer* (July 1890), she declared that she would exercise 'the Presidential authority for the whole of Europe', thus effectively becoming the co-leader of the Theosophical Society and declaring independence from Adyar.

On April 26, symptoms of influenza appeared, and her condition grew steadily worse. Blavatsky's final days were described by Laura Cooper, who, with Claude Falls Wright and Walter Richard Old, witnessed her passing. Over one hundred notices appeared in the British press, in addition to numerous letters from Theosophists, all attempting to define Blavatsky's achievements. These achievements, according to the correspondents, were not to be located in her mediumship and psychic abilities, which may or may not have existed; rather, it was in her ability to synthesize with great erudition a vast expanse of knowledge and to articulate the knowledge that she believed to be the Ancient Wisdom of her Masters. Blavatsky's esoteric synthesis has served as a basic source for later esotericists,

literati, scientists, and entire movements, including the → New Age. Unlike most of her contemporaries, she is as visible today as any modern trendsetting guru, and she will most likely remain the most memorable and innovative esotericist of the 19th century.

H.P. Blavatsky, *Isis Unveiled*, 2 vols. (1877), Los Angeles: The Theosophy Company, 1982 ♦ idem, *The Letters of H.P. Blavatsky to A.P. Sinnett* (A.T. Barker, ed.) (1925), Pasadena: Theosophical University Press, 1973 ♦ idem, *Collected Writings*, 15 vols. (Boris de Zirkoff, ed.), Wheaton: The Theosophical Publishing House, 1950-1991 ♦ idem, "My Books", *Lucifer* 8:45 (1891), 241-247 ♦ idem, *H.P. Blavatsky teaches: An Anthology* (Michael Gomes, ed.), Adyar: The Theosophical Publishing House, 1992 ♦ idem, *The Key to Theosophy* (1889), Los Angeles: The Theosophy Company, 1973 ♦ idem, *The Secret Doctrine* (1888), 2 vols., Los Angeles: The Theosophy Company, 1974 ♦ idem, *The Voice of the Silence*, translated and annotated by "H.P.B." (1889), Pasadena: Theosophical University Press, 1976 ♦ Letter from Helena Petrovna Blavatsky to Elliott Coues (n.d.), repr. in *The Theosophical Forum* (October 15, 1933), 47-48 and reproduced at http://Blavatskyarchives.com/blacouesb.htm. ♦ Radda-Bai (ps. of H.P. Blavatsky), *From the Caves and Jungles of Hindostan* (1883-1886), transl. from the Russian by Mrs. Charles Johnston, Wheaton: The Theosophical Publishing House, 1975.

Lit.: Anon., *Transactions of the Blavatsky Lodge of the Theosophical Society*, Los Angeles: The Theosophy Company, 1923 (repr. from the original edition, 1890 and 1891; compiled from notes taken at the meetings of the Blavatsky Lodge of the Theosophical Society, from January 10th to June 20th, 1889) ♦ Anon., *The Theosophical Movement 1875-1950*, Los Angeles: The Cunningham Press, 1951 ♦ A.T. Barker (ed.), *The Mahatma Letters*, London: Rider, 1948 ♦ Daniel Caldwell (ed.), *The Esoteric World of Madame Blavatsky*, Wheaton: Theosophical Publishing House, Quest Books, 2000 ♦ Bruce F. Campbell, *A History of the Theosophical Movement*, Berkeley, Los Angeles, London: University of California Press, 1980 ♦ William Emmette Coleman, "The Sources of Madame Blavatsky's Writings", in: Vsevolod Sergeyevich Solovyoff, *A Modern Priestess of Isis*, London: Longmans, Green, and Col., 1895, Appendix C, 353-366 (also at http://Blavatskyarchives.com/colemansources1895.htm) ♦ Elliott Coues, "Attention Theosophists! A Little More 'Light on the Path' for Your Benefit", letter to the Editor, *Religio-Philosophical Journal*, May 11, 1889, 5 ♦ idem, "Blavatsky Unveiled!", The New York *Sun* July 20, 1890, 17 ♦ idem, "Through the Gates of Gold", letter to the Editor, *Religio-Philosophical Journal*, June 1 (1889), 5 ♦ Sylvia Cranston, *The Extraordinary Life & Influence of Helena Blavatsky: Founder of the Modern Theosophical Movement*, New York: G.P. Putnam's Sons, 1993 ♦ Michael Gomes, *The Dawning of the Theosophical Movement*, Wheaton: Theosophical Publishing House, 1987 ♦ idem, *Witness for the Prosecution: Annie Besant's Testimony on Behalf of H.P. Blavatsky in the N.Y. Sun/Coues Law Case*, Fullerton, CA: Theosophical History, 1993 [Theosophical History Occasional Papers, vol. I] ◆ Nicholas Goodrick-Clarke, *Helena Blavatsky* (Western Esoteric Masters 7), Berkeley: North Atlantic Books, 2004 ◆ Vernon Harrison, *H.P. Blavatsky and the SPR*, Pasadena: Theosophical University Press, 1997 ◆ Richard Hodgson, "Account of Personal Investigations in India, and Discussion of the Authorship of the 'Koot Hoomi' Letters", in: "Report of the Committee appointed to Investigate Phenomena Connected with the Theosophical Society", *Society for Psychical Research: Proceedings* 3 (1885), 207-400 ◆ William Quan Judge, *The Esoteric She: Articles on Madame Blavatsky's Life, Work and Teachings* (Daniel H. Caldwell, ed.), San Diego: Point Loma Publications, 1991 ◆ *Memoirs of H.P. Blavatsky*, compiled by Mary Neff, Wheaton: The Theosophical Publishing House, 1937◆ Henry Steel Olcott, *Old Diary Leaves*, 6 vols., Adyar: The Theosophical Publishing House, 1900-1941 ◆ Josephine Ransom, *A Short History of the Theosophical Society*, Adyar: The Theosophical Publishing House, 1938 ◆ idem, *Blavatsky as Occultist*, London: Theosophical Publishing House, 1931 ◆ Charles J. Ryan, *H.P. Blavatsky and the Theosophical Movement*, San Diego: Point Loma Publications, 1975 ◆ James Santucci, *La Società Teosofica*, Torino: Editrice ELLEDICI, 1999 ◆ A.P. Sinnett, *Incidents in the Life of Madame Blavatsky*, London: The Theosophical Publishing Society, 1913; repr. Arno Press, 1976 ◆ *H.P.B.: In Memory of Helena Petrovna Blavatsky*, by Some of her Pupils, London: Theosophical Publishing House, 1891.

JAMES A. SANTUCCI

Boehme, Jacob, * ca. 24.4.1575 Alt-Seidenberg, † 17.11.1624 Görlitz

1. LIFE 2. BOEHME'S PERSPECTIVE
3. AURORA 4. THREE PRINCIPLES
5. SUBSEQUENT WRITINGS 6. CONCLUSION

Shoemaker, Lutheran dissenter, and author of numerous writings that exercised a profound and lasting influence on German Spiritualism and → Pietism and its equivalents in other countries, on German literature and philosophy, as well as on mysticism and → Christian Theosophy.

1. LIFE

Despite a rich mythic and legendary overlay, the salient facts of Boehme's life are largely documented. He was born into a prosperous and respected Lutheran peasant family. As a young man, he was given the relatively thorough elementary school education that is reflected by his fine writing skills in German. He took up the shoemaker's trade

as an apprentice and journeyman before acquiring rights of citizenship as a master shoemaker in Görlitz in 1599. In that year, his unexceptional course of life appears to have become firmly established when he purchased a house and married the daughter of a prosperous butcher, out of which union the first of four sons was born in 1600. Although by his twenty-fifth year he was very much engaged in the normal life of his time, place, and station, he was religiously troubled and beset by deep melancholy. In 1600, the luminous experience which launched his career as a visionary author took place. In the famous version recounted by Franckenberg, the young shoemaker was seated in his shop when the gleam of light (presumably a reflection of the sun) in a tin or pewter vessel gave him the impression of looking into a concealed "center of nature", a sense that seemed confirmed during a walk out into the countryside. Boehme's own account in chapter nineteen of *Aurora* recollects a prior melancholy sense that God was remotely situated in the heavens above and that the poor human beings were abandoned in a harsh world down below, in which true piety was not required. Upon realizing that the "true heavens" were everywhere, he felt himself joyously embraced by divine love. This experience initiated his path to authorship and anticipated his themes of good and evil, divine presence, and natural or cosmic intuition.

The two parallel strands – involvement in the life of his times and apparent singularity of inspiration – traverse his career and constitute the central challenge to scholarship. Both as recounted in Franckenberg's early biography and recalled by Boehme himself, the experience of 1600 was a seminal one. From 1600 until 1612, he wrote and rewrote drafts of the book to which he gave the title *Morgen Röte im auffgang* (Morning Glow in the Ascendant). This work circulated beginning in 1612 as the 400-page fragment known by the equivalent title *Aurora*. Circulating in hand-copied manuscripts, *Aurora* caused a local and regional stir in these years of religious and political tension. When a copy of the manuscript came to the attention of the Lutheran chief pastor of Görlitz, Gregor Richter, the humble shoemaker was formally reprimanded by the city council for his unauthorized religious publication.

Authorial silence was imposed and apparently maintained until around 1618, when he resumed composing and circulating religious treatises. Thereupon began an uninterrupted authorial output that coincided with the first, Bohemian phase of the Thirty Years' War. Supporting himself and his family by mercantile activities, Boehme wrote and disseminated numerous tracts amounting to thousands of pages. *Beschreibung der Drey Principien Göttliches Wesens* (Description of the Three Principles of Divine Being, 1618), the initial treatise of this phase, is pivotal within his development. Most important among the writings that follow are *Vom dreyfachen Leben des Menschen* (On the Threefold Life of Man, 1620), *Viertzig Fragen von der Seelen* (Forty Questions about the Soul, 1620), *Von der Menschwerdung Jesu Christi* (On the Human Genesis of Christ, 1620), *Von sechs theosophischen Puncten* (On Six Theosophical Points, 1620), *De Signatura Rerum* (On the Signature of Things, 1622), and *Mysterium Magnum* (The Great Mystery, 1623). A number of longer works were written as responses to doctrinal controversies in which the author became involved: *Unterricht von den letzten Zeiten* (Teaching on the Final Times, 1620), *Schutz-Schriften wieder Balthasar Tilken* (Apologies against Balthasar Tilke, 1621), *Anti-Stiefel: Bedencken über Esaiä Stiefels Büchlein* (Anti-Stiefel: Remarks about Esaiä Stiefel's Booklet, 1621/22), *Von der Gnaden-Wahl* (On the Election of Grace, 1623), and *Von Christi Testamenten* (On the Testaments of Christ, 1623). The *Theosophische Sendbriefe* (Theosophical Letters, 1618-1624) document his interactions with the like-minded or with opponents and shed light on common experience at the start of the Thirty Years' War. A number of writings emerged as letters but can stand on their own as treatises. These include some essay-like tracts that exerted an influence on posterity, such as *Kurtze Erklärung von sechs mystischen Puncten* (Short Explanation of Six Mystical Points, 1620), a work that came to the attention of the young Schopenhauer and anticipated the latter's mature metaphysics of will. A single collection of mainly devotional tracts, *Der Weg zu Christo* (The Way to Christ, 1624), was printed during his lifetime. Its appearance in print touched off the final rounds of his conflict with Lutheran orthodoxy: his late controversy with the pastor of Görlitz which is documented in his *Schutz-Rede wieder Gregorium Richter* (Defense against Gregor Richter, 1624), as well as his journey to Dresden to answer questions from and direct an appeal to the new clerical and secular overseers of a Lusatian province conquered by Lutheran Electoral Saxony in 1620. Upon his death of natural causes at the age of forty-nine, his reputation was high, though contested; and it was soon to be spread abroad by friends including Franckenberg and Dr. Balthasar Walter. In the subsequent 17th century, Boehme's fame spread through much of Germany, as well as to Holland, England, France,

Russia, and America. He had a significant impact on sectarians, especially those of the Spiritualist or Pietistic type, and on religious authors, including the German Baroque poets Angelus Silesius and Quirinus Kuhlmann. Because of the richness of Boehme's thought and writing, it stimulated and influenced various strands of Christian mysticism, theosophy and dissent, including the English dissenters of the mid-17th century, the ecumenical and kabbalistic thought of → Oetinger, the French Christian philosophy of → Saint-Martin, and the mysticism of the Russian Berdyaev, among others. Boehme's influence declined in Germany after the 17th century. He was known during the Enlightenment in Germany, but was regarded less and less favorably. Leibniz could still write respectfully of various German mystics and Pietists including Boehme. Herder at least knew of him; but Hamann, whose own thought no doubt has considerable affinities with Boehme's, condemned him for his obscurities. Subsequent phases of his influence arose in the Romantic era [→ Romanticism] and around the beginning of the 20th century. Since this influence frequently resulted in a more distanced reinterpretation, it will be discussed below.

2. BOEHME'S PERSPECTIVE

Though massive, complex, and frequently inscrutable in detail and expression, Boehme's oeuvre reflects its historical origins and can be studied to highlight the source materials of its synthesis. The most fundamental origin and source is the Lutheran Reformation, with its elevation of scriptural and lay authority and its agony as the transfer of authority led to strife and confusion instead of to the harmony and renewal of spiritual life anticipated by adherents of the new faith. Before Boehme, conflicts within the Reformation had encouraged the antidoctrinal and sometimes mystical writings of → Paracelsus, Sebastian Franck, → Weigel, and others. Moreover, much of the history of German mysticism can be understood as an attempt to retrench articles of faith during the epochs in which these were undermined in their universality or in their apparent coherence by internal or external conflicts.

The Lutheran Reformation, in bestowing authority and spiritual autonomy on a Bible-reading lay priest, confronted the young Boehme with a set of contradictions which are worked out in his writings. If truth is integral and accessible, how do conflicts over doctrine arise and how can they be resolved? Given the premises of Lutheran theology that Boehme accepted, the answer could only lie in a more deeply and contextually enriched and spiritualized interpretation of the Bible. It could hardly seem satisfying to maintain a dual standard of two truths, according to which one truth was found in Scripture and another in the knowledge of nature or the experience of life. The injunctions to study nature, know thyself, and heed Scripture must all lead to the same luminous conclusion. This direction of thought correlated with Luther's teaching of divine omnipresence. This doctrine was formulated by Luther to justify his challenged doctrine of Christ's real presence in the bread and wine of Communion, but it was capable, independently of Luther's intentions, of being vivified in symbolic images and elaborated into a kind of religious metaphysics. The resultant metaphysics holds that the deeper core of truth that lies concealed beneath the outer letter is identical with the hidden substrate of nature and with the innermost core of the soul. The inner truths of nature, the soul, and Scripture are at root identical for the simple reason that the same hidden deity is present in all things created or eternal. By the same token, one and the same misapprehended truth had to lie at the root of all conflicting sources of authority, be they scriptural, natural-philosophical, existential-introspective, or even doctrinal. Doctrine – the province of a professional clergy (which Boehme despised as an instigator of religious strife) – fails to apprehend the deeper truth that is revealed by the Holy Spirit and witnessed in external nature and self-knowledge. Doctrine, as the province of the professional clerical class, is exclusionary and authoritarian. By contrast, the writings of Boehme, understood to be guided by the Holy Spirit and tutored by a nature construed as the visible symbol of God, were intended to be non-exclusionary and antiauthoritarian (though certainly their tolerant ecumenicism was doomed to fail almost from the start). Boehme's thought is understood by him as a deconcealment of a deeper truth that encompasses divergent doctrines in a broader harmony. Hence, the coherence of his underlying themes of nature theology, theogony, and theophany fulfills for him a dialectical progression from the simplicity of the divine source to a worldly multiplicity with its confusions, conflicts, and bifurcation of good and evil, to a resolution and synthesis, with a restored eschatological unity which is projected back onto a transcendent plane.

As an intellectual biotope, Görlitz was remarkably rich in humanistic, clerical, and alchemistic conveyers of knowledge and ideas. We can assume that Boehme's writings tapped into this rich soil. His ability to immerse himself in and draw on the half-clandestine circles is extraordinary, but not without equal in the history of knowledge. Interpreting Boehme is accordingly like interpreting other literature from a remote period. Its historical context is decisive. A hermeneutic approach crediting the author's divine inspiration is appropriately complemented by a sociohistorical approach which may ignore claims of special inspiration. As in Bible scholarship, skeptics and believers can proceed in fertile collaboration. It is only the interpretation that disregards the writings, or projects extraneous constructs onto them, that precludes a shared endeavor. In order to do justice to the express intention of Boehme's work, it is especially necessary to consider not only the originality of his theories but also their roots in the Reformation mainstream, since, for all his idiosyncracies, Boehme is overt in his allegiance to Lutheranism, distinguishing his faith from that of Calvinists, Catholics, and sectarians of several persuasions.

3. AURORA

Boehme's *Aurora* is seminal. The subtitle of this fragmentary work promises to bring to light the "Root or Mother of Philosophy, Astrology, and Theology", as well as a "Description of Nature". The work also undertakes to clarify the relationship of good and evil and promises to reveal eschatological dimensions. Not unlike Hegel's philosophy, the theosophy of Boehme aspires to encompass in essence everything known: as an evolving whole in which the work itself serves as a keystone and final proof, anticipating its own eschatological fulfillment. For Boehme, knowledge resides in the intuited parallels of Scripture, celestial and earthly nature, divinity, and humanity. "Philosophy" in his usage includes not only his intuitive grasp of nature, but also an increasingly informed borrowing from Paracelsus and alchemical philosophy [→ Alchemy]. → "Astrology" gives voice to an echo of the traditional planetary influences that go back to Ptolemy's *Tetrabiblos* (the "source spirits" with their equivalent qualities), as well as to an idiosyncratic understanding of the new heliocentric cosmology. "Theology" includes Boehme's unorthodox defence of his own Lutheranism, with its controversial doctrine of the real presence of Christ's body in the Eucharist, as well as the heterodox Spiritualism Boehme inherited from Valentin Weigel. Although it is certain that Boehme knew of the writings of both Weigel and Paracelsus, it is not known when the acquaintance began or based on which writings. Boehme's extensive contemplation of "the locus of the world" in *Aurora* suggests an early familiarity with Weigel's

Vom Ort der Welt (On the Place of the World, 1576). Boehme's sophiological speculation on the "Noble Virgin of Divine Wisdom" in *The Three Principles* echoes an epistolary exchange that took place between Weigel and the Görlitzer Abraham Behem, an older contemporary of Boehme. The teaching of the first Adam prior to the fall from grace could be of Kabbalistic origin, but it might also signal the influence of Gregor of Nyssa or → Johannes Scottus Eriugena. Though initially reluctant to acknowledge sources other than nature and the Holy Spirit, Boehme admits having studied (without satisfaction!) the works of many "high scholars". His first writing could hardly have been more frank in declaring its intention to harmonize divergent spheres of knowledge.

After the eschatological contextualization of its preface, the *Aurora*-fragment of 1612 begins by proclaiming that, if illuminated by God, one can research the divine being hidden in nature. This is done by means of a phenomenological reading of natural things: these are found to consist of "qualities" or "forces", which are in turn grasped in a reified form as source-spirits (*Quellgeister*), of which the author recognizes seven. The spirits or qualities vary somewhat in description but are sufficiently constant to give his thought its peculiar character. Turning attention to the manifest relations of the macrocosm of earth and the heavenly bodies, *Aurora* discovers in the solar system a visible symbol of the Trinity (a notion found also in Kepler's *Epitome of the Copernican Astronomy* in this same period). *Aurora* also accepts the symbolic and real centrality of the sun in the solar system. This counterintuitive image of things implies that the world is maintained in its stable condition by invisible forces. Therefore, the seven qualities or forces are elaborated into a microcosm of divine being, a kind of dynamic and nature-generating atom of all things and processes: the dry (saturnine) quality is superseded by the sweet quality and the bitter quality. A flash bifurcates the process or interaction of the qualities, giving rise to the qualities corresponding to water or fire. The fifth quality of love is followed by the sixth, known as "sound" (*Ton*) or "mercury" (*Mercurius*) and the seventh (*Corpus*). In the same way that the solar system or the revolving heavens can be said to be a created image of the uncreated God, the sequence of qualities is both manifest in time and a pattern of eternity. In making sense of this seemingly unmotivated sequence, it is helpful to notice how the individual qualities are linked with traditional planetary qualities in chapters 20 and 21. With slight variations, the seven qualities develop as the trunk of Boehme's inspiration, onto which most other terms of speculation are grafted and out of which the countless individual expressions of his thought branch off or blossom. In *Aurora*, the force-qualities appear in two very different substantive embodiments: as the world of the angels (who are either good in their obedience to God, or evil, as the spirits corrupted by obedience to the fallen Lucifer). The angels have anthropomorphic aspects that allow their world to serve either as a positive model for human society or as a warning against sinful pride, evil hostility, and wanton tyranny. In *Aurora*, the force-qualities are also generalized and understood as the metaphysical substance known as *Salitter*. Like the angels, *Salitter* exists in good and evil or eternal and fallen variants. *Salitter* is another name for *sal niter* or *niter*, a substance of interest to Paracelsus both for its chemical properties and eschatological implications, and about which the alchemists of Boehme's day were formulating sensational theories.

The avantgarde heliocentrism and alchemy of *Aurora* testify to its topicality with respect to the scientific culture of the time. The depiction of the angels as a utopia of freedom and ordered obedience to the sovereign deity echoes the political ambience of desperate optimism during the interval between the death of Rudolf II and the coronation of Matthias as the new Holy Roman Emperor (the compositional dates cited in the autograph manuscript coincide precisely with the months in question). It was a moment of hope against hope, when the long period of peace in Middle Europe and the ecumenical culture of Rudolphine Prague seemed poised between regression and fulfillment. However, the religious tensions and forces of intolerance were on the rise after the founding of the religious-confessional alliances which initiated the Thirty Years' War in 1618. Boehme's irenic utopia of the angels was only one of several reform-minded or antiwar tracts published during the second decade of the 17th century. The same decade saw the publication of the Weigelian or pseudo-Weigelian posthumous tracts against war and orthodoxy, as well as the Rosicrucian manifestoes [→ Rosicrucianism I].

4. THREE PRINCIPLES

When Boehme ended his mandated authorial silence on the eve of and in the first years of the war, his thinking and tone were more somber and esoteric than in 1612. References to persecution, war hysteria, and apocalyptic conflicts darken the exposition of his pivotal *Three Principles of Divine Being* of 1618. The "principles" of his title find

their way into his work at the beginning of this second tract as an interpretation of the Paracelsian *tria
prima* of Sulphur, Mercury, and Salt. In connecting
these three alchemical substances (found, according to Paracelsus, in all things) with three aspects of
the omnipresent trinitarian deity, Boehme was in
accord with the master's own statements of intention (though the latter were not widely known at
the time). However, the thematic and terminological incorporation of the *tria prima* by Boehme led
to an extraordinary complexity. His combination
of the three with his seven spirits or qualities could
be varied almost endlessly. He utilized these variations as a kind of code in terms of which his
discussion of the intractable problems of evil,
theogony, creation, and human freedom could be
treated. These were the universalized versions of
the historical questions of society and the individual in his time. Why did Christian faith lead to religious war? How could obedience to authority be
reconciled with spiritual autonomy? How could
the supreme source of authority for all Protestants,
the Holy Scriptures, be interpreted to reconcile
contending doctrines? How could scriptural
authority be reconciled with other sources of truth
or inner certainty? The resultant synthesis, though
surely daunting to modern readers, may have
seemed in its very intricacy the more compelling to
Boehme's thinking contemporaries in search of
alternatives to the inexorable cycle of intolerance
and warfare.

The Three Principles introduces the myths of the
androgynous Adam and the Noble Virgin of Divine
Wisdom into the evolving work. Prior to the hap-
less Adam whose fall is recounted in Genesis, God
had created an angelic Adam to be an eternal angel
in place of the fallen angel Lucifer whose fall
spoiled the region of the angelic realm that became
the place of the created world. This first Adam was
not mortal. "He" was neither male nor female: this
androgyny and perfection anticipate the state of
the reborn souls in heaven whose purpose is to subsist in eternal joy and glorify their Maker. The
female aspect of the first Adam was the Noble Virgin of Divine Wisdom. This is a female aspect of the
paradoxically trinitarian deity. It is possible that
Boehme's female deity owes something to the mar-
iological eternal virgin ("goddess") of Paracelsus's
Liber de Sancta Trinitate of 1524, but more likely
that she was borrowed from Weigel's evocation of
a divine "mother" who is instrumental in bringing
forth and increasing nature in his *Fourfold Interpretation of the Creation* (circa 1580). Boehme's
scriptural allusions link the Noble Virgin to the
personified Wisdom of the intertestamental apocrypha. But the author appeals to the reader's intro-
spection to recognize the truth independently of
sources. In *Three Principles*, the first Adam shows
signs of failure through his base desires of lust and
greed. God recognizes that no good can come of
this and remakes Adam as a mortal being, with an
external companion in Eve. God thus restarts
humankind on its long march to self-understand-
ing and redemption. The critical station upon that
path is the *now* of the book itself, a time in which
the new awareness and renunciation are to come to
the fore and recreate the primal work of perfection.
Near the end of the pivotal work of 1618, its
author appeals to his contemporaries to rally to the
chivalric cause of the Noble Virgin by opposing
religious war and hatred.

5. SUBSEQUENT WRITINGS

The works written after 1618, especially in his
most prolific year 1620, reveal signs of an increasingly formulaic composition. Boehme envisages a
single divine process that can be interpreted variously. The same process manifests itself as the articulation of the trinitarian deity within the "pure
divinity" or transcendent oneness of the Godhead;
as the creation of the finite world; as the resurgence
of life in nature; as the birth of an infant; or as the
spiritual rebirth of the beliver. The divine birth
takes place in eternity; however, it is reflected
everywhere in time. Theogony is mirrored in the
primal separation of the elements or planets out of
a primal chaos. The eternal divine birth is reflected
in the birth of each human being, and in the spiritual rebirth of the individual believer. Since time is
in eternity and eternity in time, the same pattern or
process can be discerned everywhere by the illuminated spirit. The birth agony of a mother and the
ordeal of a spiritual rebirth correspond to the inner
life of a nature that renews itself every springtime.
The death or suffering manifest in this process also
echoes the suffering and death of Christ. Furthermore, if the moment of redemption in the process
is not attained, the course and outcome remain
onesided, comparable to an alchemical transformation that goes wrong and spoils its ingredients.
The fallen nature of our world, its darkness and
death-riddled transience, are Lucifer's own kingdom. In this life, human beings simultaneously
inhabit two eternal worlds: the dark world which
is ruled by the wrath of God the Father and the
light world of the Son as Redeemer (represented
also by the Noble Virgin of Divine Wisdom), as
well as our world, which mixes light and darkness, much as the dual nature of Christ combines the divine and the human natures without

confounding them. Though Boehme deemphasizes the historical Jesus, his speculation is intensely Christocentric.

In his evolving oeuvre, his presentation of theogony becomes ever bolder and more intricate. Evil, though not part of the "pure divinity", appears to have a counterpart in a divine evolution that is eternal and trancendent, yet also projected into and realized by transient nature and humankind in history. It seems rather as if the contradictions of the age of religious war were to be accounted for theologically by dwelling on the deep mystery of God and the inevitability of evil. It is no doubt the case that the rational mind cannot resolve the paradox of a good and omnipotent God who nonetheless allows, or even causes, evil and suffering to arise; but the paradox generates ever more intricate conceptualizations of the divine process and of the complex depth of the world and human nature. In *Six Theosophic Points*, the "light world" rises out of the "dark world" of evil and suffering. Such aspects of the mature writings may lend credence to the opinion that Boehme's theosophy is gnostic in character. Yet much suggests that he understood his work as orthodox Christian and even Lutheran. The gnostic emphasis on secret knowledge and on salvation from a fallen realm in which the soul is in exile certainly seems for Boehme compatible with Christianity, even when the shadows deepen and the divine "light" recedes to the scope of the few truly faithful in a world ruled by the wrathful God's satanic instrument.

In his subsequent books (*The Threefold Life of Man* and *Forty Questions on the Soul*), the "dark world" or "fire world", ruled by the wrathful God, is counterpoised with the introspective search for the hidden God manifest in the innermost being of the soul. In *The Human Genesis of Jesus Christ*, an orthodox Christology is set forth by means of the coherence of Boehme's terms of speculation. In the dual natures of Christ, the same pattern of coherence is manifest as in the Virgin Birth in Maria, the eucharistic miracle of Christ's locally present flesh and blood, or the perfectability of the debased elements upon which alchemy attempts its transforming wonders. The Bible as a history of separate events and disparate persons is transcended in Boehme's speculative code as it reveals all things in all. The entirety of "our religion", writes the author at the beginning of chapter nine, resides in only three articles: the creation, fall, and rebirth or restoration. The three represent the eschatological aspect of the coherent pattern of all Boehme's thought.

Signatura Rerum and *Mysterium Magnum*

return to the exegesis of nature and Genesis (it is an article of faith that the book of the world and the first book of the Bible are correlative and cast light on one another). Boehme's work on the "Signature of Things" proceeds by spiritualizing alchemistic lore – and thus by decoding what was at its inception a product of religious analogy. Boehme's doctrine of the "signature of things" elevates a divinely inspired intuition over both doctrine and literalism. In the human realm, this suggests a morality of intention which militates against the doctrinally correct but inhumane conduct of the professional clergy during an era of religious war. The last extensive work, *Mysterium Magnum*, is an exegesis of Genesis that recapitulates his concepts and applies them in a verse-by-verse interpretation of the entire first book of Moses. In this long virtuoso performance, Boehme's speculative enterprise which had begun with speculation concerning Creator and creation comes full circle. Several lesser writings of his late period establish his eclectic liberality in incorporating sources such as the Kabbalah or the Weigelian speculation concerning the relations of subject and object (cf. *Betrachtung Göttlicher Offenbarung, Questiones Theosophicae*, 1624).

5. CONCLUSION

Boehme composed these later writings in a condition of rising optimism encouraged by the temporary decline of hostilities after the first, Bohemian phase of the war, and no doubt reinforced for him by his growing following of likeminded dissenters. Looking back, we recognize this period as one of momentary calm on the eve of the redoubled storm that would sweep his world aside; but to the author who died in 1624, the return of this relative calm under the coreligionist sovereignty of the conqueror of Lusatia, the Elector-Prince Johann Georg of Saxony, could not appear accidental. So it was in a state of rising expectation of new times that Boehme took the unique step of allowing a volume of mostly devotional writings to be printed and sold. This caused a storm of adverse reactions from various Lutheran clergymen. Their anger was transmitted and magnified by Pastor Gregor Richter of Görlitz, who again took his case to the city council. Matters were made worse when the latter was unable to respond decisively by curbing either the inflammatory sermons of Richter or the defiant protests of the author. With the support of his noble adherents, Boehme journeyed to Dresden and met with the high Saxon clergy. By his account, he was treated well. It is altogether conceivable that the Saxon clergy discerned in him a Lutheran loyalist by intention and an anti-Calvinist slandered by a Görlitz pastor whose own Melanchthonian leanings would have made him suspect. Even if the Dresden consistory did not pronounce the writings of Boehme unobjectionable, it is beyond dispute that their defenseless author was neither imprisoned nor reprimanded by these protectors of the faith who had shown little restraint in rooting out doctrinal deviation. In all events, the conclusion of Boehme's career is conducive neither to the Christian orthodox attempt to cast him as an outsider, nor to the heterodox attempt to reclaim him as the conscious founder of an alternative spiritual tradition. The history of Christianity or of Lutheranism is full of doctrines that are considered heretical and alien in one time or place but not in others. The posthumous vilification of Boehme's memory in Görlitz was brought about by the incendiary polemics of Richter.

Boehme scholarship needs to look beyond the frequent tendency to segregate the author in an esoteric tradition. Looking back at his work from beyond the "endtime" he envisaged, any appropriation risks misconstruing his intentions. His writings are certainly remote in origin and difficult to interpret; however, the same can be said of other authors in his or our own time. The complexity of Boehme's work is generated by its multiple simultaneous references to Scriptural exegesis, Christian doctrine, theology, philosophy, nature as macrososm and microcosm, alchemical theory, astronomy, meteorology, an introspective or humoral psychology, as well as his personal spiritual experience. Boehme's work is complex because it artfully strives to convey the sense that "all things are in all" (in accordance with its Lutheran tenet of divine omnipresence) and not least because he makes use of a symbolic code in treating his themes. He does this for a reason. The logical and discursive separation of things one from another (Creator from creature, heavens from earth, or wrathful Father from merciful Son) is the root of despair, doctrinal quarreling, and war. The symbolic terms into which he resolves the *separata* allow these to flow into and rise out of one another, perpetually quickened by the seven spirits and their qualities. However, this process is not undirected, nor is his ecumenicism relativistic. If nature and the human being are not redeemed, they must pass into the eternal hellish perdition that surrounds the righteous few in the fallen world of strife and suffering. God appears as an eternal free-flowing process, but God is only God by virtue of the free self-transcendance embodied in the Son (whereby the self-transcendance takes place in eternity, so that the gnostic implications are only apparent). Lucifer and the

evil spirits of our world are a spoiled son: the same evolutionary process gone bad. Adam and Christ are the dominant polarities of religious experience. Both are within the believer. The age of an eschatological enlightenment is near at hand. As the preface of *Aurora* makes evident, Boehme's work is to be a last flowering from the very root of the tree of knowledge. The sense of approaching chiliastic resolution is not bound to any date, but the historical darkness of Boehme's last years appears to him to foreshadow dawn, a belief eloquently expressed in several of the *Theosophic Letters* (esp. 41, 42). This means that to all other difficulties of his thought is added the unretrievable sense of a unique moment in the process of the world, a sense that informs his work. In presenting him as the intentional founder of a continuing tradition, one thus risks overlooking the informing chiliastic horizon of his theories.

Boehme's influence was, however, broad and far-reaching. The Pietists, dissenters, and mystics of the 17th and 18th centuries still maintained his sense of an all-informing chiliastic horizon. The German Romantics, who imagined themselves positioned at a similar, eschatologically exalted, turning point within the life of the world, made good use of him, having recognized, as did their Baroque precursors, the poetic and philosophical implications of his thought. The reception of the German Romantics alone ranged from → Novalis's *Aurora*-inspired vision of a resurgent springtime of nature and of a spirit realm in which all things are only by virtue of their correspondences with all other things and with God; to the early → Schelling's conceptual and terminological borrowings or → Franz von Baader's mysticism of love; to the grim finale of the Romantic period in Schopenhauer's pessimistic reevaluation of the Boehmian voluntaristic metaphysics and theory of the signatures. One of the most abiding virtues of Boehme's work is the poetic fecundity of its impact in Baroque or Romantic Germany, as well as England, Russia, France, or America. The reception of his writings could be facilitated by the understanding that one can appreciate the poetic beauty of his inspiration in the same way one encounters → Dante's great symbolic summa of high medieval knowledge – without embracing the beliefs on which it was founded.

Die Urschriften (Werner Buddecke, ed.), 2 vols., Stuttgart: Frommann-Holzboog, 1963; 1966 ♦ *Sämtliche Schriften* (Will-Erich Peuckert & August Faust eds.), 11 vols., a facsimile edition of *Theosophia Revelata: Das ist: alle Göttliche Schriften des Gottseligen und Hocherleuchteten Deutschen Theosophi Jacob Böhmes,*

Johann Georg Gichtel & Wilhelm Ueberfeld (eds.), Amsterdam, 1730, Stuttgart: Frommann-Holzboog, 1955-1961 ♦ *Werke* (F. van Ingen, ed.), Frankfurt a.M.: Deutsche Klassiker Verlag, 1997 ♦ For an overview of English translations, see Weeks, 1991, 247-248.

Lit.: Bo Andersson, *"Du solst wissen es ist aus keinem stein gesogen": Studien zu Jacob Böhmes "Aurora" oder "Morge Röte im auffgang"*, Stockholm: Almqvist & Wiksell, 1986 ♦ Ernst Benz, *Der Prophet Jakob Boehme: Eine Studie über den Typus nachreformatorischen Prophetentums*, Wiesbaden: Steiner, 1959 ♦ idem, *Der vollkommene Mensch nach Jakob Böhme*, Stuttgart: Kohlhammer, 1937 ♦ Werner Buddecke, *Die Jakob Böhme-Ausgaben: Ein beschreibendes Verzeichnis*, 2 Parts: 1. Originals, 2. Translations, Göttingen: Häntzschel, 1937, 1957 ♦ *Colloque Jacob Boehme* (Centre de Recherche sur l'Histoire des Idées de l'Université de Picardie), Paris: Vrin, 1979 ♦ Pierre Deghaye, *La naissance de Dieu, ou la doctrine de Jacob Boehme*, Paris: Albin Michel, 1985 ♦ A. Faivre & F. Tristan (eds.), *Jacob Boehme*, Paris: Albin Michel, 1977 ♦ Abraham von Franckenberg, *Historischer Bericht von dem Leben und Schriften Jacob Böhmens* (Sämtliche Schriften 10), Stutt-gart: Frommann-Holzboog, 1961 ♦ B.J. Gibbons, *Gender in Mystical and Occult Thought: Behmenism and its Development in England*, Cambridge: Cambridge University Press, 1996 ♦ Hans Grunsky, *Jacob Böhme*, Stuttgart: Frommann-Holzboog, 1956 ♦ Alois Maria Haas & Jan Garewicz (eds.), *Gott, Natur und Mensch in der Sicht Jacob Böhmes und seiner Rezeption* (Wolfenbüttler Arbeiten zur Barockforschung 24), Wiesbaden: Harrassowitz, 1994 ♦ Görlitz City Council, *Protokollband: Jakob-Böhme-Symposium 1974*, Görlitz, 1977 ♦ Serge Hutin, *Les Disciples anglais de Jacob Boehme aux XVIIe et XVIIIe siècles*, Paris: Editions Denoël, 1960 ♦ Alexandre Koyré, *La philosophie de Jacob Boehme*, Paris: Vrin, 1929, 1979 ♦ Ernst-Heinz Lemper, *Jakob Böhme: Leben und Werk*, Berlin: Union Verlag, 1976 ♦ Jean-François Marquet, "Alchimie et théologie chez Jacob Boehme", in: D. Kahn & S. Matton (eds.), *Alchimie: Art, histoire et mythes*, Paris/Milan: S.E.H.A. & Archè, 1995, 665-670 ♦ Andrew Weeks, *Boehme: An Intellectual Biography of the 17th-Century Philosopher and Mystic*, Albany: SUNY Press, 1991 ♦ Gerhard Wehr, *Jakob Böhme in Selbstzeugnissen und Bilddokumenten*, Hamburg: Rowohlt, 1971 ♦ Victor Weiss, *Die Gnosis Jakob Böhmes*, Zurich: Origo, 1955.

ANDREW WEEKS

Bogomilism

Bogomilism was a religious movement, condemned as heretical, which first appeared in the 10th century in Bulgaria. Its name comes from that of the first preacher of the sect, the pop (priest) Bogomil. The movement spread from Bulgaria to Constantinople and to different regions of the Byzantine empire (Macedonia, Thrace). Since the 12th century, the impact of Bogomilism is attested in the West.

Concerning the doctrinal origins of Bogomilism, scholarly opinions diverge. Medieval authors emphasized the characteristics it had in common with → Manichaeism, Paulicianism and Messalianism. The presence of the Paulicians, members of a dualist sect who moved from Asia Minor to Thrace around 975 A.D., could have favoured the birth of Bogomilism in Bulgaria. Essential components of Bogomilism are an anti-sacerdotal and anti-sacramental tendency, on the one hand, and dualistic beliefs, on the other.

The movement arose at the time of the czar Peter (927-969). Two important documents describe the heresy. The Letter of Theophylact, patriarch of Constantinople, written around 940, characterizes it as a mixture of Manichaeism and of Paulicianism. Indeed, according to this text, the beliefs of these new heretics correspond to those of the Paulicians: opposition between the creators of Good and of Evil, and between the visible and the invisible worlds; rejection of Moses' Law; association of the Prophets with Evil; a docetist Christology; rejection of the real presence in the Eucharist. In addition, they rejected marriage, which they considered a law of the demon.

The tract of the Bulgarian priest Cosmas (around 972) is a polemical text full of biblical quotations, written in order to convert the heretics to the orthodox faith. According to Cosmas, Bogomils attribute the creation of the visible world to the devil, whom some of them identify with a fallen angel, while others call him Mammon, because he ordered men to take women, to eat meat, and to drink wine. The heretics condemn marriage and call children "children of Mammon". They reject the cult of the cross and of the icons. For them, Christ's words about his body and his blood actually refer to the Gospels and the Acts of the Apostles. They understand Christ's miracles in the figurative sense. They do not hold in respect either the liturgy of the Church, or its hierarchy. They condemn the immorality of the priests. They do not accept the Old Testament and do not venerate the Mother of God. According to Cosmas, the Bogomils have their own prayers. They confess their sins to one another, and even women take part in this practice. They reject manual work, and revolt against the powerful.

In the 11th century, Bogomilism arrived in the Byzantine Empire. A letter of Euthymius, monk of Peribleptos (a monastery in Constantinople), written after his stay at Acmonia (in the Opsikion theme, in northwestern Anatolia) before 1025, relates the process against a heretic named John Tzurillas. He had preached in Thrace and around Smyrna, and then established his center of activity in a village of the Opsikion theme. According to Euthymius, the new heretics are called Phunda-giagitae ("bag-men") in the Opsikion theme, while in the Cibyrrhaeot theme (south-west of Anatolia) and in the West (Balkans) they are designated as Bogomils. They reject the Old Testement, the order of the priesthood, the cult of the saints, and the prayers of the Church except the Pater Noster; they do not venerate the cross, and do not practice communion and baptism. According to their cosmogony there are eight skies, seven of which were created by God; the eight one and all the visible world is the work of the devil, with the exception of the Sun and human souls. The devil had much difficulty in keeping the soul in Adam's body: he closed Adam's anus, then vomited in his mouth in order to block the exit of the soul. The heretics do not believe in the resurrection of the body, at the time of the Parousia and the Last Judgment.

At the same time, Michael Psellos describes the beliefs of the Euchites, who were apparently very close to the Bogomils. He makes use of informations given by a Thracian heretic. In their mythology the Godfather has two sons, and the elder son governs the terrestrial world.

At the beginning of the 12th century, Bogomilism had spread in Constantinople even among the aristocratic families. Much attention was attracted by an event that happened ca. 1100, an account of which is given by Anna Komnena (*Alexiad*). A heresiarch named Basil, who has preached his beliefs for more than forty years, was summoned to appear before the Emperor in his Palace in order to explain his teaching. Despite all attempts to convert him, he refused to renounce his convictions and was burned at the stake in the Hippodrome. Several of his followers were imprisoned.

The beliefs of the Byzantine Bogomils were described by the monk Euthymius Zigabenus in his *Panoplia dogmatica* (written between 1111 et 1118). He derives the Bogomils from the Messalian heresy, but mentions the Paulicians too. He begins by presenting the biblical canon of the heretics: they reject → Moses' books, and the God who appears here. They accept only the Psalms and the Prophets of the Old Testament. Their teaching concerning the Trinity is very particular: they assert that the Father engendered the Son, and the Son in turn engendered the Holy Spirit. The demon, or Satanaël, is the elder son of the Father, born before the Son and the Holy Spirit. He rebelled by pride against the Father and seduced part of the angels, but God expelled them from heaven. Then Satanael created the visible sky and earth, and the body of the first man. When he was trying to animate Adam's body, his breath, combined with moisture

that ran down from Adam, turned into a snake. Then Satanael asked God to send his breath of life to animate Adam's body. But later Satanael, in the shape of the snake, seduced Eva, and engendered with her Cain and his twin sister, named Calomena. But God punished him, depriving him of his divine shape and of his power of creation; however He permitted him to govern what he had created. God the Father sent his Word, Jesus Christ (whom the heretics also refer to as an archangel) down to earth. He slipped in through the right ear of the Virgin and then went out in the same manner; his body was immaterial, and physical only in appearance. Likewise it was only in appearance that he was crucified, died, and was resurrected. After having bound Satan, he returned to the Father. The heretics identify the God of the Old Testament with Satanael. They do not venerate icons, the cross and relics; they are against priests, who, according to them, are moved by demons. They think that demons live in everybody except the heretics themselves. They do not baptize with water but with the Holy Spirit, by laying the Gospel of John on the head of the initiate. Before becoming members of their sect, new believers have to practise purification rites and prayers. The heretics condemn the Eucharist and give a purely allegorical meaning to it. For them, the bread of the communion means the prayer of the Pater Noster, because it is a question of one's daily bread, while the chalice of blood means the new alliance. Reception of both is called the "Secret Supper". They assert that demons live in churches and Satan himself occupies the St.-Sophia of Constantinople! The only prayer they accept is the Pater Noster, which they recite seven times by day and five times by night. They assert that they have in themselves the divine Word or the Holy Spirit, and transmit it by preaching. According to them, at the time of death they leave the dirty clothes of the body, which will never be resurrected. They then assume the same immortal and divine shape as that of the Christ, and will enter the realm of the Father. The heretics gradually initiate new followers into their secrets. They give a particular interpretation to the Scriptures, frequently attributing an allegorical meaning to the text.

In the period of the 1240s, during the reign of John II Komnenos and of Manual Komnenos, the Bogomils were condemned several times. According to an anti-heretical treatise (of Anselm of Alessandria, ca. 1270), the people of the West – that is to say, of France – became familiar with the heresy in Bulgaria and Constantinople at the time of the second crusade. At the end of the 12th century, the Bogomil apocryphon intitled *Interro-*

gatio Iohannis, conserved only in two Latin versions, was adopted by the Italian → Cathars of Concorezzo. The contents reveal close similarities with the Bogomil beliefs described by Euthymius Zigabenus.

At the beginning of the 12th century there appears the nickname "Bougre" (Bulgare) as one of the names of Western Cathars. Anselm of Alessandria specifies in his tract 'because the French have let themselves be deceived by the Bulgares at Constantinople, one referred to the heretics in the whole of France as Bulgares'. In the middle of the 13th century, Raynier Sacconi gives a list of dualistic Churches in the West and the East. He asserts that all the Cathar Churches derive from two Eastern "orders": from that of Bulgaria and that of Drugunthia (the identification of which is very controversial; situated in Thrace or Macedonia). A third Eastern "order", that of Sclavonia, of which the center was situated in Bosnia, represented an intermediate tendency.

At the end of the 12th century, Bogomilism – referred to as Patarinism – appears in Serbia, where it is severely persecuted. But the heretics are able to take refuge in Bosnia under the protection of the ban Kulin. To the pope's alarm, Bogomilism prospers in Bosnia up to the Ottoman conquest (1463), even though from the middle of the 15th century king Stepan Thomas starts to persecute it. In 1462, he sends three aristocrats to Rome in order to refute theirs beliefs. At this occasion, the uncle of the inquisitor Torquemada writes up a list of the fifty errors of the "Manichaeans" of Bosnia. Under the Turkish domination, the Bosnian Patarins probably converted to Islam.

In Bulgaria, Bogomilism is again widespread during the 13th century. The synod of Trnvo condemns it in 1211, along with other sects. At this time, Bogomilism and Messalianism become synonyms. In 1238, the pope asks Hungarian king Béla IV for a military intervention in Bulgaria, which is full of heretics protected by Tsar John Asen. But the crusade cannot be organized: in 1241, the Tartars invade Eastern Europe.

In the Byzantine Empire, Bogomilism persisted up to eve of the Turkish conquest. It is particularly well attested in Thrace and in Macedonia in the 14th century. During the early 1320s the Bogomil heresy was present even on Mount Athos, coinciding with the growth of the Hesychast movement.

It has left very few traces in Russia, but in Russian and Slavonic apocryphal literature there are many themes and motifs that reflect a dualistic worldview and are close to Bogomil beliefs. For example, in the legend of *The Sea of Tiberiad* (conserved in Russian and South Slavic manuscripts, the most ancient of which are from the 15th and the 16th centuries), there occurs the motif of the world's creation with the help of Satan, combined with the motif of "cosmic diving": Satan, in the shape of an aquatic bird, brings up earth and a stone from the bottom of the water. God and Satan together create the earth, angels and demons from this matter.

Because of the unequal reliability of documents about Bogomilism and because of its wide diffusion in the Balkans and the Byzantine Empire during a period spanning six centuries, it is difficult to define its characteristics. Bogomilism was a many-faceted doctrinal heresy that contested orthodox religion and the Church and, in several historical contexts, could be the expression of political commitment.

J. & B. Hamilton, Y. Stoyanov, *Christian Dualist Heresies in the Byzantine World, c. 650-c. 1450: Selected sources translated and annotated*, Manchester/New York: Manchester University Press, 1998 ♦ J. Ivanov, *Livres et légendes bogomiles: Aux sources du catharisme*, Paris: Maisonneuve et Larose, 1976 ♦ H.Ch. Puech & A. Vaillant (eds.), *Le traité contre les Bogomiles de Cosmas le Prêtre*, Paris: Imprimerie Nationale (Droz), 1945.

Lit.: J. Gouillard, *La vie religieuse à Byzance*, London: Variorum Reprints, 1981 ♦ M. Loos, *Dualist Heresy in the Middle Ages*, Prague: Academia, 1974 ♦ D. Obolensky, *The Bogomils: A Study in Balkan Neo-Manichaeism*, Cambridge: Cambridge University Press, 1948 ♦ S. Runciman, *The Medieval Manichee: A Study of the Christian Dualist Heresy*, Cambridge: Cambridge University Press, 1947 ♦ F. Šanjek, *Les Chrétiens bosniaques et le mouvement cathare, XIIᵉ-XVᵉ siècles*, Brussels/Paris/Louvain: Nauwelaerts, 1976.

EDINA BOZOKY

Borborites

The Borborites or Borborians were adherents of a Gnostic sect that flourished in the 4th century and reportedly continued its existence at least until the 6th century. Epiphanius of Salamis, who has left us an extensive report on the Borborites (*Panarion*, 26), says that they were influenced by the teachings of the → Nicolaitans (*Pan.*, 26, 1, 3), who are discussed in *Pan.*, 25. They called themselves "Gnostics", but were also known as Phibionites, Stratiotics, Levitics, Secundians, Sokratites, Zachaeuses, Coddians and Barbelites (*Pan.*, 25, 2, 1; 26, 3, 7; also *Anacephlaleiosis*, 26). Since we only have Epiphanius' testimony, we do not know to what extent these Gnostic groups were really identical. The name Borborites means "Filthy people", which suggests that it was not a self-designation but a contemptuous quibble. *Anacephaleiosis*, 26, suggests what may have prompted it to Epiphanius himself or to others: 'Yet others call them Borborites. These people take pride in Barbelo, who is also called Barbero'. Therefore, another form of the name Barbelites ("Barbelo people") may have been Barberites, and that may have led to the nickname Borborites. Epiphanius' report makes it clear that the Borborites adhered to a "Sethian" form of Gnosticism [→ Sethians], comparable to that of the "Gnostics" in Irenaeus I, 29, and in the *Apocryphon of John* and related texts.

The Borborites made use of many books, which, except for a few quotations by Epiphanius himself, are completely unknown to us: *Noria*, about Noah's wife (cf. NHC IX, 2: *The Thought of Norea*), the *Gospel of Perfection*, the *Gospel of Eve*, the *Greater* and *Lesser Questions of Mary*, books of Jaldabaoth, books in the name of Seth (cf. NHC VII, 2: *The Second Treatise of the Great Seth*; NHC VII, 5: *The Three Steles of Seth*), *Apocalypses of Adam* (cf. NHC V, 5: *The Apocalypse of Adam*), the *Birth of Mary*, and the *Gospel of Philip* (a quotation, *Pan.*, 26, 13, 2-3, is not found in the *Gospel of Philip* of NHC II, 3). If Epiphanius is to be trusted, which will be discussed below, these books taught a curious Eucharistic ritual, in which instead of bread and wine male semen and female menstrual blood were offered up and eaten by the participants. With the semen on their lifted hands they said to the "Father of All": 'We offer you this gift, the body of Christ', and eating it: 'This is the body of Christ, and this is the Passover because of which our bodies suffer and are constrained to acknowledge the passion of Christ'. And doing the same with the menstrual blood they said: 'This is the blood of Christ' (*Pan.*, 26, 4, 5-8). The ideology behind this ritual seems to be that the divine element in human beings is located in their creative power and that, therefore, salvation is realized by the emission of the bodily fluids, which then are offered to God. In the section on the Nicolaitans, Epiphanius transmits a Gnostic myth about Barbelo, which seems to have been popular among the Borborites (*Pan.*, 25, 2, 2-4). According to this myth, she continually appears to the archons in beautiful form and 'through their lust-caused ejaculation robs them of their seed – to recover . . . her power' (*Pan.*, 25, 2, 4). Epiphanius refers to the Borborites when he says that some of the followers of Nicolaus said: 'We gather the power of Prunicus (i.e. Barbelo) from our bodies through their emissions' (25, 3, 2). In the section about the Borborites, however, he puts all stress on their unbridled licentiousness and promiscuity. They rejected fasting (26, 5, 8) and asceticism (26, 13, 1), but for-

bade procreation (26, 5, 12) and called the female members of the sect "Virgins" (26, 11, 9). To leave their "virginity" unimpaired, they practised coitus interruptus (26, 11, 9-11), and when a woman accidentally became pregnant they aborted the foetus and ate it (26, 5, 4-6), saying: 'We have not been deceived by the archon of lust, but we have gathered up the brother's transgression'. A special group, which they called "Levites", who may have been the same as the "Levitics", practised homosexuality (26, 13, 1). They found their views and practices confirmed by a curious exegesis of biblical texts, of which Epiphanius gives some examples.

For a correct assessment of the evidence presented above the all-important question is: How trustworthy is Epiphanius? At this point, scholarly opinion is divided and varies from almost complete acceptance of Epiphanius' reliability (Benko, Gero) to its almost complete rejection (Williams). Epiphanius claims to have come across this sect when he lived in Egypt, probably in Alexandria about A.D. 330. He had heard their teachings 'out of the mouth of practising Gnostics', who in fact were beautiful young women who tried to seduce and to convert him (26, 17, 4; 18, 2). But after reading their books and understanding their true intent, he reported them to 'the bishops' (probably the college of Alexandrian presbyters), and 'finding out which one were hidden in the church, . . . they were expelled from the city, about eighty persons' (26, 17, 9). He obviously did not participate in the sexual orgies of which he gives a detailed description. The instruction of the beautiful female adherents of the sect was apparently not very specific, since he understood their true intent only after reading their books. We may safely assume that he interpreted these books in the light of what he had heard or thought to have heard about the practices of the Borborites. In many Gnostic texts the divine element in human beings is called semen, which has to be gathered during the process of salvation, but this word is usually used in a metaphorical sense. However, it seems quite possible that some people took the word literally, which led them to practices as described by Epiphanius. Of course, his anti-heretical zeal may have given his fantasy free play, but that does not imply that his report is completely unreliable. Moreover, two Gnostic texts, which are earlier than Epiphanius' *Panarion*, explicitly condemn similar practices (*Pistis Sophia*, 147; *Second Book of Jeu*, 43). It has been objected that these texts are 'once again polemical accusations, not advocacy by practitioners' (Williams), but that does not exclude that there may have been some truth in these allegations. Religiously inspired sexual rituals, which from the outside look like sheer obscenities, are not uncommon in the history of religions.

According to a number of Syriac, Armenian, Coptic and Arabic sources, the Borborites survived tenaciously in the Christian Near East (Gero). They are reported to have lived in Southern Asia Minor, Armenia and Syria. In imperial legislation, they are mentioned from the 5th century onward: they are forbidden to build churches and to hold religious services. Unfortunately, these sources provide little information on the ideas and practices of these Borborites, and when they become more specific the influence of Epiphanius' report is unmistakable. The 6th-century author Barḥadbešabbā says that the Borborites believed that angels had created the world and that their central rite consisted of the ritual defilement of ten virgins by the priests of the sect. If one of these conceived, she was worshipped 'in the place of Mary' and her foetus was sacramentally consumed (Nau, 190f.): the child was apparently identified with the body of Christ and the woman with the Virgin Mary. There are other testimonies that some groups, which their opponents called Borborites, held the Virgin Mary in high esteem and even attributed to her a divine status. According to some she had a heavenly body, but according to others she was a heavenly power or even a goddess, so that she and her Son were two divinities by the side of God – a view already refuted in the Koran, Sura 5, 116. These views can be traced back to the 4th and the 5th centuries (van den Broek, 149-156).

The evidence presented above leads to the conclusion that the Borborites, who called themselves "Gnostics", most probably were an offshoot of the "Gnostics" who adhered to the system described in Irenaeus, Adversus Haereses, I, 29 and the Apocryphon of John. Their distinctive feature seems to have been a literal interpretation of the metaphor "semen" as indication of the divine element in humankind. There is no reason to push Epiphanius' testimony completely aside and to deny that the "gathering" of the divine sperm through sexual rituals apparently was an important element in their cult. But we need not to take Epiphanius' report at face value; on the contrary, we may assume that also in this case we have the same mixture of truth, hearsay, misunderstanding and sheer slander that so often characterizes his anti-heretical polemics. The strong emphasis Epiphanius lay on the sexual rituals of their cult has obviously obscured other aspects of their beliefs. One of these beliefs may have been the exaltation of the Virgin Mary to a divine status.

K. Holl (ed.), *Epiphanius I: Ancoratus und Panarion haer. 1-33*, Leipzig: Hinrichs, 1915; Engl. transl. with notes in F. Williams, *The Panarion of Epiphanius of Salamis, Book 1 (Sects 1-46)* (NHS, XXXV), Leiden: E.J. Brill, 1987; and B. Layton, *The Gnostic Scriptures: A New Translation with Annotations and Introductions*, Garden City, New York: Double Day & Company, 1987, 199-214 ♦ F. Nau (ed.), *La première partie de l'Histoire de Barḥadbešabba 'Arbaia* (Patrologia Orientalis 32, 2), Paris: Firmin-Didot, 1932.

Lit.: S. Benko, "The Libertine Gnostic Sect of the Phibionites according to Epiphanius", *Vigiliae Christanae* 21 (1967), 103-119 ♦ R. van den Broek, "Der Bericht des koptischen Kyrillos von Jerusalem über das Hebräerevangelium", in: idem, *Studies in Gnosticism and Alexandrian Christianity* (NHMS 39), Leiden: E.J. Brill, 1996, 142-156 ♦ L. Fendt, "Borborianer", *RAC* 2 (1954), 510-513 ♦ S. Gero, "With Walter Bauer on the Tirgis: Encratite Orthodoxy and Libertine Heresy in Syro-Mesopotamian Christianity", in: Ch.W. Hedrick & R. Hodgson Jr. (eds.), *Nag Hammadi Gnosticism and Early Christianity*, Peabody (Mass.): Hendrickson, 1986, 287-307 ♦ J. Jacobsen Buckley, "Libertines or Not: Fruit, Bread, Semen and Other Body Fluids in Gnosticism", *Journal of Early Christian Studies* 2 (1994), 15-31 ♦ M. Tardieu, "Epiphane contre les gnostiques", *Tel Quel* 88 (1981), 64-91 (French translation and commentary) ♦ M.A. Williams, *Rethinking "Gnosticism": An Argument for Dismantling a Dubious Category*, Princeton: Princeton University Press, 1996, 179-184.

ROELOF VAN DEN BROEK

Bourbon, Duchess of → Orléans, Bathilde d'

Bourignon, Antoinette, * 13.1.1616 Lisle (Flanders), † 1680 Franeker (Netherlands)

Bourignon was born to wealthy Catholic parents. Even as a child she spent much time in prayer and reclusion, and at four asked her parents in what country Christians lived, so that she might travel there, since she thought Christians lived in poverty and were not interested in worldly things. Although her father wanted her to marry a rich merchant, she left home in 1636, and spent some time in a convent. As she grew older, she mortified herself for seven years, wearing a shirt of horsehair and sleeping on a board, gave her clothing to the poor, and ate only what was necessary for life, even going so far as to mix ashes with her food to deny herself pleasure from it. She was of a middle stature, slender and delicate. She travelled extensively in Belgium, the Netherlands, and Germany, bringing a small wooden printing press with her; she also visited England and Scotland. Her works were placed on the Index of forbidden books by the Vatican; she was also condemned frequently by Protestants, including the Scottish Presbyterian general assemblies of 1701, 1709, and 1710. She died in Franeker, Holland, in 1680; her complete works were published in London in 1699.

Her major treatise, *Lumière du Monde* (Light of the World), was occasioned by M. Christian de Cort, Superior of the Fathers of the Oratory at Mechlin in Flanders, a man who regarded her as a spiritual teacher. She went to Holland for the printing of this book, and there encountered sectarians, including Jesuits, Jansenists, Lutheran and Calvinist Ministers, Anabaptists, Quakers, and Labadists, who attacked her as a visionary, a blasphemer, a heretic, and even as a sorcerer. She proposed a series of Rules from God, the first two of which are '1. Do all in good order, and in season; for I am a God of order: And Disorder comes from the Devil, and from Sin. 2. Never be eager in Temporal Affairs; but apply your mind to do well what you do, in quietness; for the wandering of the mind, and disquiet spoils all' (xix).

It is evident from this example of her writing that the works of Bourignon are much tamer than the invective poured out against her would seem to warrant. Her many treatises reveal the work of a very sincere and pious woman intent on spiritual practice. Bourignon, and her publisher → Pierre Poiret, were in fact at great pains to show their own orthodoxy, and for this reason she signed a confession of faith with five points, insisting on her belief in 'all that a true Christian ought to believe', dated 11 March 1675. Widely reprinted, her five points of public confession are: (1) I am a Christian, and I believe all that a true Christian ought to believe, (2) I am baptized in the Catholic Church, in the Name of the Father, in the Name of the Son, in the Name of the Holy Ghost, (3) I believe the Twelve Articles of the Creed, and I do not doubt of one Article of it, (4) I believe that Jesus Christ is True God, and that he is also True Man; as also that he is the Saviour and Redeemer of the World, (5) I believe in the Gospel, in the Holy Prophets, and in all the Holy Scriptures, both of the Old and New Testament.

Seeing herself as an orthodox Christian, in nearly every one of her works Bourignon attacked sectarianism, and in this one can see a bit more clearly why she was herself attacked. She launches into those who claim she is not Catholic – she will live and die a Catholic. But she so opposes sectarianism as to even attack those who take the name Catholic. Those who are Reformed, she writes, ought to reform themselves. Bourignon strongly critiques those who hypocritically take on a mantle of sanctity while remaining corrupt within. She attacks the corruption of established churches, and insists instead that 'La vraye Eglise consiste en l'assemblée des ames qui sont possédées par l'Esprit de Jesus Christ' (The true church consists in the assembly of souls possessed by the spirit of Jesus Christ) (III.294). She also attacked Quakerism in a separate treatise (*Œuvres*, vol. X).

The English translations of *Lumière du Monde* and some of Bourignon's other works, including *Confusion of the Builders of Babel* (1708), *An Admirable Treatise of Solid Vertue*, (1699) and *Collection of Letters* (1708) in turn inspired antimystic sentiments in England even as they later met with approval among non-sectarian spiritual circles like that of the Philadelphian Society. A very informative example of this antimysticism is to be found in a treatise by John Cockburn (1652-1729) entitled *Bourignianism Detected* (London 1698). 'They are not mean and ignorant Persons who follow this Woman', Cockburn wrote, 'they are some of the better sort, who have been reputed, Men of Sense, Learning, and Probity' (i-ii). Cockburn writes derisively that 'Our Quakers and Philadelphians, as well as the Quietists and Pietists abroad, are of the same kidney, and do all stand upon the same foundation; so that what overturns one, overturns all' (iii). Cockburn and others were particularly incensed at assertions of Bourignon's supernatural knowledge. Cockburn claims that she is in fact a messenger of Satan, a 'false prophet', and so forth (11, 25, passim). She was defended by George Garden and others against these charges, notably in Garden's work *An Apology for Antonia Bourignon* (1699).

Although she is occasionally cited as a Boehmenist, Bourignon did not strictly speaking belong to the theosophic tradition [→ Christian Theosophy], but instead represents a strain of Catholic quietist mysticism along the lines of Miguel Molinos. In Bourignon's work, as in quietist mysticism more generally, we see nothing of the visionary imagery that so characterizes the theosophic school. At the same time, quietist mysticism bears some similarities to theosophy in its emphasis on direct spiritual inspiration and on anti-sectarianism. The most complete study of Bourignon thus far is van der Does (1974).

Antoinette Bourignon, *Œuvres* (P. Poiret, ed.), 19 vols., Amsterdam (n.p.), 1679-1684 ♦ *La vie de demoiselle Antoinette Bourignon, écrite par elle-même*, Amsterdam, 1683 ♦ *Light of the World*, London: J. Burrough and J. Baker, 1696 ♦ *An Admirable Treatise of Solid*

Vertue, London: J. Burrough, and J. Baker, 1699 ♦ *Collection of Letters*, London: J. Burrough and J. Baker, 1708 ♦ *Confusion of the Builders of Babel*, London: J. Burrough and J. Baker, 1708.

Lit.: Mirjam de Baar, *"Ik moet spreken": Het spirituele leiderschap van Antoinette Bourignon (1616-1680)*, Zutphen: Walburg Pers, 2004 ♦ John Cockburn, *Bourignianism Detected: or the Delusion and Errors of Antoinia Bourignon*, London, 1698 ♦ Marthe van der Does, *Antoinette Bourignon, 1616-1680*, Amsterdam: Holland UP, 1974 ♦ George Garden, *An Apology for Miss Antonia Bourignon*, London: D. Brown, S. Manship, R. Parker and H. Newman, 1699 ♦ Serge Hutin, *Les Disciples anglais de Jacob Boehme aux XVIIᵉ et XVIIIᵉ siécles*, Paris: Editions Denoël, 1960 ♦ R.A. Knox, *Enthusiasm: A Chapter in the History of Religion*, Oxford: Oxford UP, 1950, 352-355 ♦ Gustav Krieg, *Der Mystische Kreis: Wesen und Werden der Theologie Pierre Poirets*, Göttingen: Vandenhoeck, 1979.

ARTHUR VERSLUIS

Bô Yin Râ (ps. of Joseph Anton Schneider, as of 1920 Joseph Anton Schneiderfranken), * 25.11.1876 Aschaffenburg, † 14.2.1943 Massagno (Switzerland)

Schneider studied at the Städelsche Art Institute in Frankfurt, from which he graduated in 1899, and at the art studios of the Municipal Theatre in Frankfurt (1896-1898). Hans Thoma, one of the leading German artists of the time, accepted him as one of his pupils. Later he also came to benefit from the advice and support of Max Klinger. In 1900-1901, he continued his studies at the Academy of Fine Arts in Vienna, and attended the Academy Julian in Paris before returning to Vienna. He then stayed in Berlin (1904-1908) and settled in Munich (1909-1915). While travelling in Greece from 1912-1913, he continued to paint (mostly landscapes), and in 1914 he began publishing his first writings, signed with the initials B.Y.R. Drafted in 1916, he was stationed in Görlitz, where he served as an interpreter in Greek, and met → Gustav Meyrink in 1917. In Görlitz he also founded a Jakob Boehme Society in 1920, exhibited his landscape paintings, and continued to work at his "cycles" – series of prose writings – like *Das Buch der königlichen Kunst* (The Book of Royal Art; 1913-1932). The first version of *Das Buch vom lebendigen Gott* (The Book of the Living God; 1919), his first book signed "Bô Yin Râ", is also the first of his writings published by Kurt Wolff (Verlag der Weissen Bücher, Leipzig) in the years 1920-1921. It is prefaced by Gustav Meyrink, whose novel *Der Golem* had appeared in 1915, also at Wolff's.

From then on Bô Yin Râ became a prolific writer. Most of his pieces are of small size, and he often put many of them together to constitute larger books. In the 1920s at least fifteen titles appeared, a number of them beginning with "The Book of . . ." like *Das Buch vom Jenseits* (The Book of the Afterlife; 1920/29), and *Das Buch vom Menschen* (The Book of Man; 1920/28). In 1923, the year when his *Okkulte Rätsel* (Occult Enigmas) appeared, he took up residence in Switzerland, at first in Horgen near Lake Zurich, then in Massagno near Lugano. As before, he continued to devote much time procuring new editions (enlarged or modified) of his former or more recent publications. In Switzerland he became acquainted with the publisher Alfred Köber-Stähelin, who from 1927 on published all his works. Among his last ones in the 1930s are *Ewige Wirklichkeit* (Eternal Reality; 1934) and *Geistige Relationen* (Spiritual Relations; 1939). At his death, Bô Yin Râ left a collection comprising forty books and two hundred paintings.

Bô Yin Râ is lavish in clues about post-mortem life which are sometimes reminiscent of → Swedenborg's. He explains, for instance in *Das Buch vom Jenseits*, that "life beyond" is in reality the very life we live on earth, only it is experienced by means of different senses. He occasionally touches upon the topic of → reincarnation, discussing under which conditions it may be possible. All his views on such questions are based on his belief in an intricate relationship between the Spirit's all-pervading radiant substance, and the concrete forms in which this substance manifests itself in material life. Nothing spiritual is ever devoid of form. It is a matter of using our creative → imagination to transform our external life and inner body after the picture of our spiritual life. Such a transformation is destined to prepare our life beyond, and can be achieved by artistic creation. His own paintings were supposed to play such a role.

In some of the writings which constitute the cycle *Hortus Conclusus*, discussions devoted to such topics are combined with a presentation of twenty of his paintings, for example, "Lux in Tenebris", "Birth of the External Cosmos", "Astral Luminescence", and "Inferno". These are meant to depict the very nature and dynamic structure of eternal life. His views here are reminiscent of those of the classical theosophical current (although he rarely quotes his predecessors), and he evinced a particular interest in → Jacob Bœhme.

Most of these works of art have a cosmological or cosmogonic character. In *Welten: Eine Folge kosmischer Gesichte* (Worlds: A Series of Cosmic Visions; 1924), a work introduced by a poem of → Giordano Bruno, he again presents twenty such paintings. His philosophy of nature, besides being scantily developed, does not call into question the theory of evolution. And when it comes to the evolution of mankind, he is content to explain that the progressive appearance of the human being as we now know him/her is the result of the influence of an eternal and active reality, exercised upon our ape-like ancestors.

Bô Yin Râ called himself a "Bote der Weissen Loge", a messenger of the White Lodge, claiming, like → H.P. Blavatsky and → Annie Besant before him, that he had received his revelations from a hidden Asiatic Master. As a matter of fact, he occasionally discusses the issue of the Blavatskyian Mahatmas, and his teachings are to some extent influenced by those of the → Theosophical Society, although he readily criticizes the latter, notably in *Mehr Licht!* (More Light!; 1921/1936), where he is also very critical of the Jewish Kabbalah [→ Jewish Influences]. The expression "White Lodge" (possibly linked to the name of Kurt Wolff's Publishing Company) seems to be meant in a metaphoric sense, and does not refer to any actually existing association. In any case, Bô Yin Râ's teachings are self-initiatory in character, devoid of any specific ritual.

Besides the "White Lodge" he oftentimes mentions (in particular in *Das Geheimnis* [The Secret]; 1923) a "Lichtgemeinschaft der Leuchtenden des Urlichts" (a Light Community of the Enlightening People of the Original Light). These "Leuchtenden" are the wardens of the "original legacy of mankind". The expression "die Leuchtenden" is very reminiscent of the "Lichtfähigen" (the people able to receive the Light) that → Eckartshausen had written about in *Die Wolke über dem Heiligthum* (1802). In a narrative set within *Das Buch der Gespräche* (The Book of Conversations; 1920), Bô Yin Râ tells us about his own initiation into this community of the "Leuchtenden", in Greece, but this description appears to be merely metaphorical.

A wide readership (there are countless new editions and translations) bears witness to Bô Yin Râ's continuing influence, which may be seen operating in various contemporary movements, particularly in neo-Rosicrucian groups [→ Rosicrucianism] such as the A.M.O.R.C. and the Lectorium Rosicrucianum.

Bô Yin Râ has been translated into at least fifteen languages. Since 1928 practically all of his works have been published and/or newly edited at Kober Verlag AG (Bern) in their original language, German, and many of them in English at the same publisher. Most of his works can be found in: *Nachlese: Gesammelte Prosa und Gedichte aus Zeitschriften*, 2 vols., Vol. 1: *Gesammelte Prosa und Gedichte aus Zeitschriften* (contains *inter alia*: *Über meine Schriften* [1930];

Warum ich meinen Namen führe [1927]; *Wer ist Bô Yin Râ?* [1924]). Vol. 2: *Gesammelte Texte aus Zeitungen und Zeitschriften (Aufsätze über Kunst; Abhandlungen; Besprechungen; aus den Zeitschriften Magische Blätter, Die Säule und Theosophie; Dankesadressen; Persönliche Erinnerungen)*, Basel: Kober Verlag AG, 1990 (1st ed., 1953) ♦ Among his works available in English are: *The Book on Life beyond* (1920/29), 1979 (2nd ed., 2002); *Spirit and Form* (1924), 2001; *The Meaning of this Life* (1927), 1998; *The Book on Solace* (1924), 1996; *The Book on Happiness* (1920), 1994; *About my Books, Concerning my Name and other Texts* (articles and shorter pieces), 1977; *Worlds of Spirit* (a compendium of texts and paintings), 2002; *The Book on Human Nature* (1920/28), 2000. *The Wisdom of St. John* (1924), 1975; All: Kober Verlag AG: Bern.

Lit.: Alexandre de Dánann, *Bô Yin Râ: De la Taychou Marou au Grand Orient de Patmos*, Milano: Archè, 2004 ♦ Otto G. Lienert, *Weltwanderung; Bô Yin Râ: Leben und Biographie*, Bern, 1994 ♦ Wolfgang Nastali, *Ursein – Urlicht – Urwort: Die Überlieferung der religiösen "Urquelle" nach Joseph Schneiderfranken Bô Yin Râ*, Münster: ATEdition, 1999 (2nd ed. revised) ♦ idem, "'Lebendiges Feuer': Die Überlieferung der ältesten Lichtbotschaft durch J.A. Schneiderfranken Bô Yin Râ", *Gnostika* 23 (2003), 45-55, and 24 (2003), 58-67 ♦ Rudolf Schott, *Bô Yin Râ: Leben und Werk* (1954), Basel: Kober Verlag AG, 1979 ♦ Otto Zsok, *Der religiöse Urquell: Dargestellt im Lichte des geistigen Lehrwerks von Joseph Anton Schneiderfranken Bô Yin Râ. Eine religionsphilosophische Studie*: Erzabtei Sankt Ottilien: EOS Verlag 2001.

ANTOINE FAIVRE

Boyle, Robert, *25.1.1627 Lismore (Ireland), † 31.12.1691 London

Boyle is a preeminent figure of the 17th century. He is best known as a natural philosopher, particularly in the fields of chemistry and physics, but his scientific work covers many areas including hydrostatics, medicine, earth sciences, natural history, and traditional → alchemy. His avid service to the Christian faith produced devotional and ethical essays, and theological tracts on the limits of reason and the role of the natural philosopher as a Christian. He also funded numerous missions and the translation of the Scriptures into several languages.

Boyle was born into one of the wealthiest families in Britain. He was the fourteenth child and seventh son of Richard Boyle, the Great Earl of Cork, by his second wife Catherine, daughter of Sir Geoffrey Fenton, secretary of state for Ireland. His education began at Eton at age eight where his studiousness was apparent. In October 1638, he and his brother Francis were sent on a Continental

Grand Tour with their tutor Isaac Marcombes. They travelled through France, Switzerland, and Italy. In 1642, owing to the Irish Rebellion, Francis returned home while Robert went to his tutor's home in Geneva to continue his studies. Boyle returned to England in 1644, and took up residence at his hereditary estate of Stalbridge in Dorset, where he began to write ethical and devotional treatises, many borrowing literary styles modelled after the French romances he enjoyed. In 1649 he began his first scientific experimentation, which instantly enthralled him. During these early years he was in contact with Samuel Hartlib, Frederick Clodius, Sir Kenelm Digby, and others. But probably most influential of all was his association with George Starkey (alias Eirenaeus Philalethes) who in the early 1650s tutored him in chemistry and introduced him to the writings and ideas of → Joan Baptista van Helmont. Helmontianian ideas would long prove important for Boyle's chemical thought.

In the winter of 1655-1656 he moved to Oxford, where he remained for twelve years. There he associated with the Philosophicall Club which included John Wilkins, Richard Lower, John Locke, and others interested in science, medicine, and anatomy. Much of Boyle's best-known work draws its origins from his Oxford period. In 1659, with the help of Robert Hooke, he built his famous air-pump, and studied the air, the vacuum, and pneumatics. In 1660 he acted as one of the founding members of the Royal Society. In 1668 he left Oxford and took up residence with his sister Katherine Jones, Vicountess Ranelagh, in London. There he lived and worked for the rest of his life – setting up an active laboratory, publishing at least one book nearly every year, receiving many visitors, and participating actively in the Royal Society. Throughout his adult life Boyle was sickly, suffering from weak eyes and hands, recurring illnesses, and probably one or more strokes. He was offered the Presidency of the Royal Society and the episcopacy but declined both. He died at age sixty-four after a short illness exacerbated by his grief over Katherine's death a week earlier. He left behind a huge accumulation of papers now at the Royal Society, and a bequest for the annual Boyle Lectures (in defense of Christianity) which continue to this day.

Boyle's work is characterised by its reliance on experiment and its reticence to formulate generalized theories. Boyle was particularly devoted to chemistry, arguing strongly for its usefulness in natural philosophy, and thus has sometimes been called the "Father of Chemistry". His chemistry was based on a largely (but not entirely) mechanical "corpuscularian hypothesis" – a sort of atomism which claimed that material substances were composed of one universal matter divided into miniscule particles ("corpuscules") and differentiated only by the accidents of shape and local motion. He opposed the doctrine of the *tria prima* as presented by contemporary Paracelsian chymists [→ Paracelsianism]. This opposition, together with Boyle's celebrity as a "heroic figure" of the Scientific Revolution and an exaggeration of the impact and importance of his *Sceptical Chymist* (1661) has lead to the simplistic conclusion that he opposed alchemy. In fact, Boyle maintained a life-long interest in and debt to traditional alchemy; while a few signs of this interest have long been known, many others have only recently been brought to light. Boyle's own secrecy regarding the subject, such as his extensive use of codes and ciphers in alchemical contexts, has contributed to the obscurity of his alchemical pursuits.

For example, Boyle believed in the reality of projective transmutation of the metals by means of the Philosophers' Stone. Indeed, Boyle endeavored to discover the secret of the Stone throughout his life, and claimed to have witnessed several transmutations. In the 1670s and 1680s he wrote a *Dialogue on Transmutation* which argued strongly in favor of the real existence of the Philosophers' Stone; only a fragment of this work was published, and that anonymously in 1678 as *A Degradation of Gold by an Anti-Elixir*. His early collaborative work on alchemical projects with Starkey/Philalethes provided him with a substance he believed to be the Philosophical Mercury necessary for making the Stone, and Boyle continued working with this substance for forty years, publishing a veiled account of it in the *Philosophical Transactions* in 1676. In 1689 he helped to effect the repeal of the Act against Multipliers, a 1404 statute outlawing transmutation. His interest in the repeal may stem from his belief that he had succeeded in preparing a transmuting powder – a "red earth" discussed after his death by John Locke and → Isaac Newton. He carried on extensive correspondence with alchemical practitioners throughout Europe.

Boyle considered his theological activities of at least equal importance with his scientific ones. His devotion to Biblical Christianity was the guiding principle of his life and work. Scientific study of God's creation was at heart a devotional activity; his last work, *The Christian Virtuoso* (1690) treats the interdependence of scientific and religious knowledge for the scientist. Boyle wrote on the literary style of the Scriptures, explored the limits of human reason, and urged readers to theological study.

Boyle also showed a keen interest in occult phenomena [→ occult / occultism], particularly → witchcraft, spirit invocation, second sight, and → magic. In 1658 he funded the English translation of the *Devill of Mascon*, an account by François Perrault of a poltergeist in Burgundy. He later supported Joseph Glanvill's mission of collecting and verifying witchcraft accounts. In dictating autobiographical notes to his friend and confessor, Gilbert Burnet, Bishop of Salisbury, Boyle spent a considerable fraction of the time describing accounts of occult phenomena – magic, spirit invocations, clairvoyance, and so forth – to which he had been witness or about which he had received what he considered reliable testimony. He also amassed such accounts of the supernatural into a collection which he apparently planned to publish as an adjunct to the "Strange Reports" appended to his *Experimenta et Observationes Physicae* (1690). Perhaps most curiously, Boyle seems to have believed that the Philosophers' Stone of the alchemists might not only be able to transmute base metals into gold, but also be a means for attracting and communicating with angels. These ideas are detailed in a fragmentary dialogue recently edited and published (Principe 1998), although their origins remain rather obscure. One cause behind Boyle's interest in supernatural phenomenon was his desire to demonstrate the reality of the supernatural realm with its spiritual activity and spiritual denizens. Proofs for the existence of spiritual entities and agencies promised to provide not only a refutation of the creeping atheism so feared by Boyle and others in the late 17th century, but also a counterpoint to the mechanical systems Boyle promoted in his natural philosophy, which, when taken to extremes, ran the risk of denying spirits, souls, and God.

The Works of Robert Boyle (Michael Hunter and Edward B. Davis, eds.), 14 vols., London: Pickering and Chatto, 1999-2000 ♦ *The Correspondence of Robert Boyle* (Michael Hunter, Antonio Clericuzio, and Lawrence M. Principe, eds.), 6 vols., London: Pickering and Chatto, 2001.

Lit.: R.E.W. Maddison, *Life and Works of the Honorable Robert Boyle, F. R. S.*, London: Taylor and Francis, 1969 ♦ John T. Harwood, *The Early Essays and Ethics of Robert Boyle*, Carbondale, IL: Southern Illinois University Press, 1991 ♦ Michael Hunter, *Robert Boyle: By Himself and his Friends*, London: William Pickering, 1994 ♦ idem, "Alchemy, Magic and Moralism in the Thought of Robert Boyle", *British Journal of the History of Science* 23 (1990), 387-410 ♦ idem, "How Boyle Became a Scientist", *History of Science* 33 (1995), 59-103 ♦ idem, *The Occult Laboratory: Magic, Science and Second Sight in Late 17th Century Scotland*, Woodbridge, UK: Boydell, 2001 ♦ Michael Hunter (ed.), *Robert Boyle Reconsidered*, Cambridge, 1994 ♦ Lawrence M. Principe, *The Aspiring Adept: Robert Boyle and His Alchemical Quest*, Princeton: Princeton University Press, 1998 [includes an edition of Boyle's previously unpublished *Dialogue on Transmutation* and *Dialogue on the Converse with Angels*] ♦ idem, "Robert Boyle's Alchemical Secrecy: Codes, Ciphers, and Concealments", *Ambix* 39 (1992), 63-74 ♦ idem, "The Alchemies of Robert Boyle and Isaac Newton: Alternate Approaches and Divergent Deployments", in: Margaret J. Osler (ed.), *Rethinking the Scientific Revolution*, Cambridge: Cambridge University Press, 2000, 201-220 ♦ idem, "Virtuous Romance and Romantic Virtuoso: The Shaping of Robert Boyle's Literary Style", *Journal of the History of Ideas* 56 (1995), 377-397 ♦ idem, "Newly-Discovered Boyle Documents in the Royal Society Archive: Alchemical Tracts and his Student Notebook", *Notes and Records of the Royal Society* 49 (1995), 57-70 ♦ Antonio Clericuzio, "A Redefinition of Boyle's Chemistry and Corpuscular Philosophy", *Annals of Science* 47 (1990), 561-589 ♦ Harold Fisch, "The Scientist as Priest: A Note on Robert Boyle's Natural Theology", *Isis* 44 (1953), 252-265 ♦ Rose-Mary Sargent, *The Diffident Naturalist: Robert Boyle and the Philosophy of Experiment*, Chicago: University of Chicago Press, 1995 ♦ Jan W. Wojcik, *Robert Boyle and the Limits of Reason*, Cambridge: Cambridge University Press, 1997.

LAWRENCE M. PRINCIPE

Boys des Guays, Jacques François Etienne le, * 1794 Châtillon-sur-Loing (now Châtillon-Coligny, Loiret), † 1864 Saint-Armand-Montrond (Cher)

Le Boys des Guays was the grandson of a special lieutenant in the bailiwick of Montargis (Loiret) who later became Procureur Général under the First Empire, and the son of a member of the military administration of Louis XVI. After earning a law degree, he became an advocate at the Royal Court of Paris, then decided for the magistracy, which he left in 1830 following his nomination as sub-prefect of Saint-Armand-Montrond. He was discharged from this office in 1831 because of his political opinions, marked by a liberalism that was deemed excessive. Nevertheless, for a brief period he exercised the functions of municipal councillor in that town.

In November 1834, during a ceremony in the Néo-Temple in Paris, Le Boys met a Monsieur Caudron, a reader of the works of the theosopher → Emanuel Swedenborg. Caudron gave Le Boys Swedenborg's treatise on *Heaven and Hell*, in which, he told him, Le Boys would find the explanation of the magnetic phenomena which had motivated his journey. After reading this work, supplemented by other works of Swedenborg's, Le Boys decided to dedicate the rest of his life to the propagation of "Swedenborgism" both in France and abroad. On November 18, 1837, this ardent neophyte opened a public cult in his house at Saint-Armand-Montrond, where at 3 o'clock every Sunday afternoon the local Swedenborgian community would assemble, consisting for the most part of craft professionals. Le Boys was assisted in his tasks by his wife, born Clotilde Rollet, and by his brother-in-law Eugène Rollet, future deputy of the Cher.

Beginning in 1838, Le Boys des Guays undertook the publication of the monthly periodical *La Nouvelle Jérusalem, revue religieuse et scientifique* (The New Jerusalem, religious and scientific review), which held the attention of its readers for ten years. At the end of this period it was forced to cease publication, as a result of severe financial difficulties. Also in 1838, Le Boys began his major work: the translation of Swedenborg's theological works into French, a task brought to completion in 1850. This "orthodox" disciple of the "New Jerusalem" also published analytical tables and indexes, finding the model for the latter in the index of Swedenborg's *Apocalypse Revealed*.

Le Boys des Guays had inserted in his periodical, by way of apologetics, *Les Lettres à un homme du monde qui voudrait croire . . .* (Letters to a man of the world who wants to believe). These were reprinted separately in 1852. After translation, they were presented to the public in England and North America, with several editions in English and German. Intended for future members of the New Church, these *Letters* aroused undeniable interest among the public.

Some of Le Boys des Guays' works benefited from the collaboration of Auguste Harlé (1809-1876), whose knowledge of the Hebrew language was of great advantage. This "indefatigable evangelist", as Marguerite Beck Block calls him, bore witness through his voluminous correspondence to a lasting concern for lending all his energies to the "New Jerusalem". He never ceased to enlarge his acquaintanceship, both in France and abroad, so as to help the New Church to expand. Some of his vis-

itors came from England and Russia. They could see for themselves that Le Boys' proselytism was founded in Swedenborg's doctrine of "uses", which notably emphasized the practice of the "true" and the "good".

Manuscript collection known as "Fonds Chevrier" (Correspondence of J.F.E. Le Boys des Guays and various documents). The collection is in the Bibliothêque Nationale de France, Paris.

Lit.: [Un Ami de la Nouvelle Eglise, i.e. Ed. Chevrier], *Histoire Sommaire de la Nouvelle Eglise Chrétienne fondée sur les doctrines de Swedenborg*, Swedenborg Society: Paris, London, New York, 1879 ♦ Marguerite Beck Block, *The New Church in the New World: A Study of Swedenborgianism in America* (Studies in Religion and Culture, American Religion Series V), New York: Swedenborg Publishing Association, 1984 ♦ Inge Jonsson & Olle Hjern, *Swedenborg*, Proprius Förlag: Stockholm, 1976 ♦ Jean-François Mayer, *La Nouvelle Église de Lausanne et le mouvement Swedenborgien en Suisse romande, des origines à 1948*, Zurich: Swedenborg Verlag, 1984 ♦ Karl-Erik Sjödén, *Swedenborg en France*, Stockholm: Almqvist and Wiksell International, 1985.

ANDRÉ BOYER

Britten, Emma (Floyd) Hardinge, * 2.5.1823 Bethnal Green (near London), † 2.10.1899 Manchester

1. LIFE 2. WRITINGS 3. THE ORPHIC CIRCLE 4. THE THEOSOPHICAL SOCIETY 5. IMPACT

One of the most influential figures in the early development of → Spiritualism in the United States and England, both as a medium and trance-lecturer and as a historian and theorist of that religious movement. A founding member of the → Theosophical Society and a member of its first Council. A powerful advocate for the revival of the study of → magic, and for its essential identity both with 19th-century mediumship and with medieval → witchcraft. A strong proponent of the mythological theory of Christian origins. A social reformer interested in marriage reform and in the abolition of slavery. Although her name and works are now largely forgotten, the combination of religious, magical, occult [→ occult / occultism], social and political ideals that she articulated has remained influential in the United States and Great Britain up to now, and has left its traces in several new religions, notably in Witchcraft (Wicca) and its cogeners.

1. Life

Britten wrote little about the first three decades of her life, which must therefore be painstakingly reconstructed from scattered data. She was the daughter of Ebenezer and Anne Sophia Floyd, and probably the granddaughter of a Baptist minister, William Williams. Her ancestors seem to have come from Somerset and Devon counties and more remotely from Wales. Even as a young child, Britten seems to have been a talented musician and vocalist, and also a visionary. Her father died when she was 11 years old. A year later she began to earn her living as a musician and vocalist, and also by serving as an entranced clairvoyant for the occult lodge that she calls the "Orphic Circle" (see below). It was probably aristocratic members of this lodge who enabled her to obtain some musical training in Paris in her late teens. In Paris, however, she damaged her singing voice; upon her return to England she turned to acting, which career she pursued (as a member of the Haymarket and the Adelphi companies) with modest success for almost a decade.

By 1850 Britten seems to have married E. Hardinge, a medical man, for in that year she began to appear on stage as Mrs. Hardinge. Also in 1850 she made or renewed her acquaintance with the enigmatic person whom she names "Chevalier Louis de B—", an intimate of the Orphic Circle. In 1853 she seems to have begun serving as a spirit medium for Dr. Hardinge, following the example of two American spirit mediums who were holding public seances in London at that time. In 1854, however, she seems to have left Dr. Hardinge, for she next appeared on stage in Paris and then in New York, where she met with little success. Early in 1856, therefore, she resumed her former career as a spirit medium.

During the years 1856-1857 Britten was employed by the Society for the Diffusion of Spiritual Knowledge to hold free public seances in New York as a test medium, and also to edit the society's journal, *The Christian Spiritualist*. After that journal ceased to be published (May 1857), one of the society's trustees arranged for her public debut as a trance-lecturer. As a trance-lecturer, she proved extremely successful. During the next eight years, 1857-1865, she gave numerous trance-lectures in most of the United States, and soon became one of the most influential advocates for the controversial new religion of Spiritualism. During these years Britten also held strong views on several other major controversies of that era, advocating the abolition of slavery, reforms in the legal and social position of women, and – most notably! – that the Bible should no longer be regarded as a divinely inspired book, but rather viewed as the confused remnants of myths and symbols from several very ancient religions that had venerated the sun, the human sex organs, and serpents.

In 1865 Britten returned to England for the first time in ten years. Among her first English trance-lectures was one advocating a revival of the study of ancient and medieval magic and witchcraft, which she supposed could shed much light on the phenomena of spirit mediumship. During the years 1865-1881 she shuttled back and forth across the Atlantic many times. In 1870, while in the United States, she married Dr. William G.P. Britten (ca. 1821-1894), like her a British subject. The years immediately after her marriage were ones of unusually diverse activities. Retiring for a while from the Spiritualist platform, Britten began to assist her husband in the practice of electrical medicine. Also, she and her husband edited and published two books for Chevalier Louis de B—, based on the doctrines and practices of the Orphic Circle: *Art Magic* (1876), a treatise on the history and theory of magic, and *Ghost Land* (1876), an occult biographical novel. In 1875-1876 she and her husband were two of the founding members of the Theosophical Society. In 1878 she returned to the Spiritualist platform, traveling overseas with her husband as far as Australia and New Zealand. In 1881 she and her husband returned to England for the last time, to spend their remaining years there.

2. Writings

Britten was a prolific writer from her early years onward. Even before coming to the United States, she had contributed articles on musical and other subjects to several journals. From 1856 until the end of her life she was a frequent contributor to many Spiritualist journals, using several pseudonyms as well as her own name. She also edited several Spiritualist journals. In addition to *The Christian Spiritualist* at New York (May 1854-May 1857), which she edited only during the last year of its publication, she founded and edited *The Western Star* at Boston (July-December 1872) and *The Unseen Universe* at Manchester (April 1892-March 1893). More significantly, she edited the English Spiritualist journal, *The Two Worlds*, for the first four years of its long existence (November 1887-February 1892).

Britten was also the author of two massive histories of Spiritualism, *Modern American Spiritualism* (1870) and *Nineteenth Century Miracles* (1883). She presented her critique of Christianity in *Six Lectures on Theology and Nature* (1860), and with somewhat greater sophistication in *The Faiths, Facts and Frauds of Religious History* (1879); these two works should be read in connection with Chevalier Louis de B—'s two books mentioned above, *Art Magic* (1876) and *Ghost Land* (1876).

Britten also wrote a few brief guides for Spiritualists, including *Rules to be Observed When Forming Spiritual Circles* (1870) and *On the Road; or, The Spiritual Investigator: A Complete Compendium of the Science, Religion, Ethics, and Various Methods of Investigating Spiritualism* (1878). Together with A. Kitson and H.A. Kersey she compiled a short manual for Spiritualist schools, *The English Lyceum Manual* (1887).

A small number of Britten's trance-lectures appeared as separate publications, beginning with two that she delivered at Boston in 1859 on *The Place and Mission of Woman* and on *Marriage*. They were shortly followed by her *Six Lectures on Theology and Nature*, delivered at Chicago in 1860. A series of trance-lectures that she delivered at London in 1865-1866 on various subjects was published under the title *Extemporaneous Addresses*. Britten also published a dozen of her short stories as *The Wildfire Club* (1861); many of them had first appeared in Spiritualist journals. And she was the author of a small book on the medical uses of electricity, *The Electric Physician; or, Self-Cure through Electricity* (1875). A few months after Britten's death, her sister, Margaret (Floyd) Wilkinson, edited and published the *Autobiography of Emma Hardinge Britten* (1900).

3. THE ORPHIC CIRCLE

As noted above, for several years in her teens Britten was employed as an entranced clairvoyant by the occult society that she calls the Orphic Circle (not its real name, see below). Among the members of this society were Philip Henry, the fourth Earl of Stanhope (1781-1855), Richard James Morrison, also known as Zadkiel the astrologer (1795-1874), the writer → Edward Bulwer-Lytton (1805-1873), and in later years perhaps also the explorer → Richard Burton (1821-1890). If not a formal member, the renowned occultist Frederick Hockley (1808-1885) was at least a welcome visitor, as was Chevalier Louis de B—.

The Orphic Circle admitted women as well as men to membership. Its members met as a lodge presided over by a Grand Master (one of whose titles seems to have been "Venerable") and were sworn to secrecy. The true name of the society was one of the society's secrets (though Britten is reported to have said on one occasion that it was a Rosicrucian society). At any given time it employed several young women and men (such as Britten had been) as entranced clairvoyants, also called *lucides* and *somnambules*. During its lodge meetings it undertook to project the double (i.e., to travel on the astral plane) and to invoke spirits into mirrors and crystals. It carried out these essential activities within a ritual practice that owed something to renaissance ceremonial magic as well as to mesmerism [→ Animal Magnetism] and that employed both hymns and specially prepared fumigations. However, it was not the members of the Orphic Circle themselves whose doubles were projected, or who saw and heard spirits in the mirrors and crystals, but the young entranced clairvoyants whom the society employed. Moreover, the spirits invoked into these mirrors and crystals were not, for the most part, spirits of dead men and women, but rather spirits that had never been human.

Such a synthesis of these three elements – Freemasonry, mesmerism and ceremonial magic – seems first to have been made at Lyon in the 1780s by a group of aristocrats and gentlemen. Among the most influential of these men were → Jean-Baptiste Willermoz and → Louis-Claude de Saint-Martin, both of whom were already members of the Order of the Elus Coëns, founded some decades earlier by Martines de Pasqually. From France this synthesis probably spread through aristocratic channels to England, where the Orphic Circle may have been just one of several groups formed to experiment with these new occult arts. The Orphic Circle seems already to have been in existence for some years when Britten began to work for it in 1835 or 1836; also she speaks of it as still in existence in the late 1880s, when most or all of its original members would have been dead.

The Orphic Circle clearly played an influential role in the development of magic and occultism in England during most of the 19th century; it is greatly to be regretted that so little is known of its history and membership, and only slightly more about its doctrines and practices. What is known so far comes exclusively from isolated comments that Britten made in several of her writings and from the two books and several articles published by Britten and her husband as the works of Chevalier Louis de B—. The true identity of the man behind that pseudonym, therefore, is of some historical interest. In the present author's monograph on Britten, it is argued that he is Ernest Christian Louis de Bunsen (1819-1903), second son of the renowned scholar and Prussian ambassador to England, Chevalier (later Baron) Christian Carl Josias de Bunsen

(1791-1860). Ernest de Bunsen was the author of a dozen substantial works in English and in German on the secret history of the world's great religions, on the occult symbolism and secret doctrine concealed in the Bible, and on the development of Christianity from a series of misunderstood myths and symbols originally pertaining to the cycles of heavenly phenomena, to sexuality and fertility, and to chthonic serpent worship. It remains to be seen whether this identification will stand the tests of further scholarly examination.

4. THE THEOSOPHICAL SOCIETY

Towards the end of 1875 a small group of occultists and Spiritualists met four times, twice in September at → H.P. Blavatsky's apartment and then twice in October at Britten's house in New York. At those four meetings the Theosophical Society was founded, its purposes determined, its organizational structure and bylaws devised and adopted, and its first officers elected. The society continued to meet twice a month from November 1875 to November 1876, generally in a rented meeting-room, but occasionally in a private home. Shortly after its formation the Theosophical Society adopted a policy of absolute secrecy about its activities. At this time it also seems to have begun a systematic program of occult training for its less qualified members, which was divided into three degrees (with a further six degrees said to be available "in the East"). However, in the following months several of its officers and most qualified members left New York for one reason or another, with the result that the society largely ceased to meet. Later its President (→ Henry Steel Olcott) and its Corresponding Secretary (Helena Petrovna Blavatsky), who both had moved to India in 1878, reestablished and revitalized it. Yet only a few of the founding members of the Theosophical Society took much part in its activities after 1878.

Just two of the founding members of the Theosophical Society were women, Britten and Blavatsky. Yet they not only had some of the strongest personalities, but also held some of the strongest credentials as occultists, in the fledgling society. Moreover, they seem to have held rather differing views concerning the purposes and program of the society. Blavatsky's views on this subject are well known from her voluminous writings, but Britten's must be inferred from scattered hints in her later articles and essays on occultism and in other texts (including the original records of the first years of the Theosophical Society). From all these sources it is very clear that Britten's views were strongly influenced by Chevalier Louis de B—'s views on the nature of magic in general and by his program for establishing a "school of the prophets" that would train qualified young people in a wide range of occult disciplines (clairvoyance, mediumship, crystalgazing, magnetic healing, prophesy, ministry, magic, etc.), all of which disciplines were to rest on an advanced understanding of animal magnetism and psychology (*Art Magic* [1876], chapters 10, 20, 23). Reflecting this divergence of views, the original printed *Preamble and By-Laws of the Theoso-phical Society* (1875) opened with two ambiguous paragraphs, carefully worded so as to accommodate each woman's point of view equally well.

In light of all this, it is likely that Britten enrolled herself and her husband as founding members of the Theosophical Society, and that she became a member of its Council, not because she greatly esteemed the occult skills, much less the personality and character, of H.P. Blavatsky, but rather because she hoped to shape the Theosophical Society into just such a "school of the prophets" as Chevalier Louis had programmatically delineated in *Art Magic*. She was unable to achieve her aims because she and her husband moved from New York to Boston in late April, 1876; because after November, 1876, the Theosophical Society ceased to meet regularly; and finally because from 1878 onward Olcott and Blavatsky in India – and in the United States William Quan Judge (1851-1896) – were able to take decisive personal control of the society's affairs and to reformulate its purposes and program as they alone saw fit. In consequence Britten ceased to take much part in the business of the Theosophical Society. Eventually she resigned from its Council, and later she publically criticized its new purposes and its methods of achieving them.

5. IMPACT

Britten lived and worked in close contact with esotericists, magicians and other occultists for nearly two-thirds of a century, with Spiritualists for nearly half a century, and with Theosophists for nearly a quarter of a century. By the end of her life, therefore, she had developed an extremely far-reaching network of acquaintances within these three overlapping groups of people, although it was largely limited to the United States and England. It is along this network that her direct and indirect influence made itself felt. Her original synthesis of religious, magical, occult, social and political ideas and ideals was an extremely powerful and attractive one in its day, and retains considerable power even now.

The impact of this synthesis was all the stronger because of the force and charm of Britten's personality and also because of the theory that she had developed in various articles to explain and justify her work in the world. According to this theory, true spirit mediums (seers, magicians, prophets, witches, magnetic healers – they are all much the same thing in her view) differed *physiologically* from the common run of humanity, and it was this difference that enabled them to see and do what most people could never see and do, but at the same time endowed and burdened them with special callings that most people never had. Such a medium or magician 'must be born so from his mother's womb' (in principle ordinary people can bring about the necessary physiological changes in their bodies by training and self-discipline, but that way is so slow, painful and difficult as to be beyond the capacity of most people). Britten strongly claimed to be such a born medium and magician herself, as evidenced by the early development of her special powers and the seemingly fortuitous training that she received in the Orphic Circle. Yet this meant that Britten had also been set apart from other women and men by Spirit Powers more real than the empty deities preached in various churches, to present to the world their controversial messages of religious and social reform and the revival of magic. The difficulty of such a calling was well expressed by her chosen motto, 'The Truth against the World!'

Emma Hardinge Britten, *Six Lectures on Theology and Nature*, Chicago: n.p., 1860 ♦ idem, *Modern American Spiritualism*, New York: American News Co., 1869 ♦ idem, *The Faiths, Facts and Frauds of Religious History*, Melbourne: G. Robertson, 1879 ♦ idem, *Nineteenth Century Miracles*, Manchester: W. Britten, 1883 ♦ "Chevalier Louis de B—" and Emma Hardinge Britten, *Art Magic; or, Mundane, Sub-Mundane and Super-Mundane Spiritism*, New York: The Author, 1876 ♦ eidem, *Ghost Land; or, Researches into the Mysteries of Occultism*, Boston: The Editor, 1876.

Lit.: Robert Mathiesen, *The Unseen Worlds of Emma Hardinge Britten: Some Chapters in the History of Western Occultism* (Theosophical History Occasional Papers IX), Fullerton: Theosophical History, 2001 [with an extensive bibliography of her published books and articles] ♦ John Patrick Deveney, *Astral Projection or Liberation of the Double and the Work of the Early Theosophical Society* (Theosophical History Occasional Papers VI), Fullerton: Theosophical History, 1997 ♦ Joscelyn Godwin, *The Theosophical Enlightenment*, Albany: SUNY Press, 1994, esp. 200-212, 251, 273-274, 303-304, 360.

ROBERT MATHIESEN

Bruno, Giordano (Filippo), * January/February 1548 Nola, † 17.2.1600 Rome

1. LIFE 2. PHILOSOPHY 3. MAGIC

1. LIFE

Filippo Bruno was born in Nola, near Naples, as the son of Giovanni Bruno, '*uomo d'arme*' (armiger), and Fraulissa Savolino. He first studied in Naples under the direction of Giovan Vincenzo Colle, known as "Il Sarnese", and the Augustinian father Teofilo da Vairano. In 1565 he entered the Neapolitan monastery of San Domenico Maggiore, taking the name of Giordano. Ordained priest in 1572, he completed his course of theological studies in 1575 with a dissertation on the *Summa contra Gentiles*. In June 1576 he was accused of having read and studied prohibited books. The seriousness of the accusation induced him to move to Rome, but after learning that the works he had surreptitiously used had been traced in Naples, he decided to quit the Dominican Order.

There then began a period of wandering through Italy: first to Savona, Turin, and Venice (where he published the small, lost work *De' segni de tempi* [On the Signs of the Times]), then to Padua and Brescia, where he appears to have cured a demoniac. In 1578 he passed into France, and after a stay at the monastery of Chambéry, moved to Lyon, then to Geneva. He was received by Gian Galeazzo Caracciolo, Marchese of Vico, and entered into contact with the Italian exile community. He worked as a proof-reader, and on March 20 matriculated at the University. In August 1578 Bruno was accused of defaming the Professor of Philosophy, Antoine de la Faye, and was arrested and brought before the Consistory Court. The incident caused him to abandon Geneva and return to France, where he stayed briefly at Lyon before settling in Toulouse. Here he obtained the title of "magister artium" (Master of Arts) and the post of "ordinary reader" in philosophy. The increasing bitterness of religious differences caused him to move to Paris, where he gave a successful course of lectures on the divine attributes. In addition, his courses on the Art of Memory [→ Mnemonics] aroused the interest of King Henri III, who, after having invited him to court to ascertain 'whether the memory he possessed and professed was [obtained] through natural art or through science', appointed him "extraordinary reader". In 1583 there appeared the works *De umbris idearum* (On the Shadows of Ideas), *Cantus Circaeus* (Circean Song), *De compendiosa architectura et comple-*

mento artis Lullii (On the Compendious Architecture and the Completion of the Lullian Art), and the comedy *Il Candelaio* (The Candlestick).

For motives that are not altogether clear, in 1583 he left France for England in the train of Michel de Castelnau, ambassador at the court of Elizabeth I. In the summer he held a course of lectures at Oxford, but on being accused of plagiarism, he was removed from the chair. In the same year appeared works on the subject of memory: *Ars reminiscendi* (The Art of Remembering), *Explicatio triginta sigillorum* (Explication of Thirty Seals), and *Sigillus sigillorum* (The Seal of Seals). Between 1584 and 1585 he composed the cycle of Italian dialogues: *La Cena de le Ceneri* (The Ash-Wednesday Supper), *De la causa, principio et uno* (On the Cause, the Beginning, and the One), *De l'infinito, universo et mundi* (On Infinity, the Universe, and the Worlds), *Lo spaccio della bestia trionfante* (The Expulsion of the Triumphant Beast), *La Cabala del cavallo pegaseo* (The Cabala of the Horse Pegasus), and *De gl'eroici furori* (On the Heroic Furies).

Returning to Paris in October 1585, he undertook a detailed critique of Aristotelian doctrines, first with *Figuratio Aristotelici Physici auditus* (The Shape of Aristotelian Physics), an original exposition of Aristotle's physical writings in a mnemotechnical and mythological vein, then with the harsh criticism of *Centum et viginti articuli de natura et mundo* (120 Articles on Nature and the World), a short work published under the name of his disciple Jean Hennequin, into which was incorporated the material used by Bruno for a public disputation at the College of Cambrai. To this period also belong the polemic with the Salerno geometrician Fabrizio Mordente, evidenced in *Dialogi duo de Fabricii Mordentis Salernitani prope divina adinventione ad perfectam cosmimetriae praxim* (Two Dialogues on Fabrizio Mordenti the Salternitan on the Divine Invention for the Perfect Practice of World-Measurement) which Bruno issued with the publisher Chevillot.

The worsening of the religious situation prompted him to move to Germany. He passed through Mainz, Wiesbaden, and Marburg, then between 1586 and 1588 stayed in Wittenberg. Matriculated as "doctor italicus" (Italian Doctor), he held private courses on Aristotle, commenting on the physical and rhetorical writings. A cycle of lectures on *Rhetorica ad Herennium* (Rhetoric to Herennius) was published in 1612 by Heinrich Alsted under the title of *Artificium perorandi* (The Art of Pleading). In 1587 Bruno published *De lampade combinatoria lulliana* (On the Lullian Combinatorial Lamp), *De progressu et lampade venatoria logico-*

rum (On the Progress and Hunting Lamp of the Logicians), and *Animadversiones circa Lampadem Lullianam* (Thoughts on the Lullian Lamp), and worked on the first version of *Lampas triginta statuarum* (Lamp of the 30 Statues) and *Libri physicorum Aristotelis explanati* (Aristotle's Books on Physics Explained), which were published posthumously in the edition of the *Opera* edited by Tocco and Vitelli. In 1588, after publishing a second edition of *Centum et viginti articuli*, entitled *Acrotismus Camoeracensis*, he left Wittenberg with the *Oratio valedictoria* (Farewell Oration).

Next he went to Prague, where he published *Articuli centum et sexaginta adversus huius tempestatis mathematicos atque philosophos* (160 Articles against the Mathematicians and Philosophers of this Time), dedicated to → Rudolf II, and *De lampade combinatoria R. Lullii* (On the Combinatorial Lamp of R. Lull). In 1589 he was in Helmstedt at the Academia Iulia: on the occasion of the death of Herzog Julius II von Braunschweig, founder of the Academy, he read an *Oratio consolatoria* (Consolatory Oration) that was printed in the same year. Beside this, he devoted himself to writing magical treatises: *De magia mathematica* (On Mathematical Magic), *De magia naturali* (On Natural Magic), *Theses de magia* (Theses on Magic), *De rerum principiis et elementis et causis* (On the Principles, Elements, and Causes of Things), and *Medicina lulliana* (Lullian Medicine). In 1590 he published at Frankfurt the trilogy of Latin poems, *De triplici minimo et mensura* (On the Triple Minimum and Measure), *De monade numero et figura* (On the Monad, Number, and Figure), and *De immenso et innumerabilibus* (On the Immense and Innumerable Things). Expelled from the city, in 1591 he went to Zurich, where he gave a cycle of lectures collected and published by his pupil Raphael Egli under the title *Summa terminorum metaphysicorum* (Summa of Metaphysical Terms). In the spring he returned to Frankfurt and published *De imaginum signorum et idearum compositione* (On the Composition of Images, Signs, and Ideas).

In August 1591 he was invited to Venice by Giovanni Mocenigo, who wished to learn the art of memory. On returning to Italy, Bruno stayed in Padua and Venice, and composed *De vinculis in genere* (On Bindings in General), *Praelectiones geometricae* (Geometrical Pre-elections), and *Ars deformationum* (The Art of Deformations). On May 23, 1592 Mocenigo denounced Bruno to the Venetian Inquisition; the philosopher was arrested and taken to the prison of San Domenico di Castello. On January 9, 1593 his trial began in

Rome. In 1599, at the end of a long and complicated legal proceeding, Bruno was invited to abjure eight heretical propositions, singled out by Cardinal Roberto Bellarmino. On December 21, Bruno's stubborn attitude precipitated the result of the trial: he was handed over to the secular arm and was burned at the stake in the Campo dei Fiori on February 17, 1600.

2. PHILOSOPHY

The pyre of Campo dei Fiori certainly marked the essential moment of creation for Bruno's reputation, and his myth. Beyond the myth, the "Nolan philosophy" turns out to have been based from the very beginning on a series of crucial motifs. Already in the first Parisian work, *De umbris idearum*, the exposition of mnemonic practice resolves itself into a lucid analysis of nature and man, in which Bruno underlines on the one hand the character of "vanity" and "shadow", and on the other, the capacity to grasp the "primal, true and good" even within the shadowed horizon of the manifested universe. In the Italian dialogues written in London between 1584 and 1585 (*La Cena de le Ceneri, De la causa, principio et uno, De l'infinito, universo et mundi, Lo spaccio della bestia trionfante, La Cabala del cavallo pegaseo*), the themes enunciated in *De umbris* flow together in a more profound theoretical context, deeply marked by fundamental theoretical acquisitions such as the doctrine of living matter and the "discovery" of Copernicus.

In the first Italian dialogue published in London, the *Cena de le Ceneri*, Bruno expounds the Copernican hypothesis in radical terms, showing how the doctrine of earthly motion presupposes the existence of a universe that is infinite, peopled by innumerable individuals and worlds, animated altogether and without distinction by a unique life-principle. The motion of the earth is in fact produced by the vital impulse that is innate in matter, and which drives every planet to revolve around its own sun, so as to draw life and nourishment from it: 'The cause of such motion', writes Bruno in *La Cena de le Ceneri*, discussing the earth's motion, 'is the renewal and the rebirth of this body, which cannot last forever under the same disposition. Just as things which cannot last forever through the individual (speaking in common terms) endure through the species, [in the same way,] substances which cannot perpetuate themselves under the same countenance, do so by changing their configuration. For the matter and substance of things is incorruptible and every part of it must be the subject of every form, so that every part can become every thing (insofar as it is able), and be every thing

(if not in the same time and instant of eternity, at least at different times, at various instants of eternity, successively and alternatively). For even though the matter as a whole is capable of all the forms at once, each part of the matter, nevertheless, is not capable of all the forms at once' (*Cena de le Ceneri*, dialogue V, in *Dialoghi filosofici italiani*, p. 119, trans. Gosselin & Lerner). Change and mutation thus characterize reality at every level: 'So, everything within its own kind has every [possible] alternation of dominion and servitude, of happiness and unhappiness, of that state we call life and that we call death, of light and dark, of good and evil. And there is nothing to which it is naturally appropriate to be eternal, except for the substance which is matter, to which it is no less appropriate to be in continuous mutation' (*Cena de le Ceneri*, dialogue V, in *Dialoghi filosofici italiani*, p. 120, trans. Gosselin & Lerner). The hierarchies and distinctions proper to the Aristotelian cosmos dissolve in view of the one living matter: there is no difference between the earth and the other planets. In the infinite universe, change figures as a fundamental structure of being at every level: man, like the worlds, is moved by a continual "transmutation".

Following the thread of this reflexion, Bruno touches on the delicate problem of the relationship between science and religion and defines the proper domains of each discipline, only to reaffirm vigorously the absolute autonomy of rational research. He observes, therefore, that a correct interpretation of Scripture must needs take account of the moral intentions of the prophets: 'those divine books which serve our intellect do not deal with demonstrations and speculations about natural matters, as if with philosophy. Rather, with a view to our understanding and feelings, the scriptures direct the practice of moral actions through laws. Having then this object before his eyes, the Divine Legislator did not bother, in addition, to discuss that truth which would not have helped the common people in turning away from evil and following good. Rather, he leaves this meditation to contemplative men, and speaks to the common people according to their way of understanding and speaking, so that they can understand what is most important' (*Cena de le Ceneri*, dialogue IV, in *Dialoghi filosofici italiani*, p. 91, trans. Gosselin & Lerner). Theologians and prophets work on the plane of civil communication in order to control peoples who are still barbaric: thus they have to use a simple and direct language that suits the nature and beliefs of the individuals they are addressing. Philosophers and scientists, on the other hand, are not proposing to educate the people, but addressing a few intellectuals in order to communicate a truth that is often in clear contradiction to the common way of thinking. Thus it is altogether wrong to confuse the language of science and the language of morals, using the sacred writings to confirm or reject a given physical theory: prophets and scientists are addressing different publics and pursuing different ends. Resuming this argument, Bruno would conclude in his dialogue *De l'infinito*: 'This is why theologians no less learned than religious have never opposed the liberty of philosophers, while the true philosophers of civil worth and of good custom have ever fostered religions. For both sides know that faith is required for the rule of the rude populace who must be governed, while demonstration is for the contemplatives who know how to govern themselves and others' (*De l'infinito, universo et mundi*, dialogue I, in *Dialoghi filosofici italiani*, p. 119, trans. Singer).

In the second dialogue published in London, *De la causa principio et uno*, Bruno's reflexion illustrates the theoretical core of the "Nolan philosophy" in the form of a vigorous debate between three speakers: he rethinks in fresh terms the problem of the matter of the universe, replacing the traditional notion of an inert receptacle of forms with the radically original image of a material principle endowed with life and inexhaustible vigor, from which new forms continually germinate. To this end, Bruno criticizes the Aristotelian distinction between potency and act, showing how the two terms are intimately linked: every act, in fact, can be explained only in relation to a pre-existing potency. But if that is true, then even the infinite act of the divinity appears linked inseparably to the infinite potency of matter. Emboldened by these theoretical premises, Bruno completely overturns the interpretation of matter, transforming it into an attribute of the divinity.

The cosmological problem of the first three London dialogues opens up in *Spaccio della bestia trionfante* to a closely-argued reflection of an ethical order that directly attacks the concept of religion. In the first three Italian dialogues, the phenomenon of religion appears as an instrument of government invented by the wise in order to control 'wild and ignorant peoples'. From this point of view, the reasoning of the *Spaccio* introduces a strongly original element: Bruno in fact defines the nature and function of civil law on the basis of the close link that joins human laws to the inaccessible divine truth. The point of departure of the argument developed in this work is the knowledge that the divinity never ceases to communicate with the world: thus the divine action is expressed either in the natural

universe, in the form of providence, or else in human society, in the historic forms of wisdom and laws: 'Above all things', Bruno writes, 'is situated Truth . . . That goddess who is joined to and close to Truth has two names: Providence and Prudence . . . Sophia is followed by her daughter, Law; and through Law, Sophia wishes to operate, wishes to be employed; through Law princes reign, and kingdoms and republics are maintained' (*Spaccio de la bestia trionfante*, dialogue II, in *Dialoghi filosofici italiani*, pp. 536-538, trans. Imerti).

In the light of the link which exists between human laws and the inaccessible divine truth, Bruno shows how the legislator's work is responsible for causing the principles that regulate the action of God in the universe to reverberate in the human community, selecting and favoring, beyond distinctions of titles, blood, and wealth, the action of those who can contribute in positive ways to social life. Civil law thus becomes the divine instrument that permits mankind to remove itself from the animal condition, to become, through community life and the practice of wisdom, the true "gods of the earth": 'the gods . . .' – as we read in the *Spaccio* – 'have instituted laws, not so much in order to receive glory, as to spread it among men. Thus the farther human laws and opinions are removed from the goodness and truth of Law and Judgment, the farther they remove themselves from regulating and approving that which is especially contained in the moral actions of men in relation to other men' (*Spaccio de la bestia trionfante*, dialogue II, in *Dialoghi filosofici italiani*, p. 542, trans. Imerti).

On this basis, Bruno reinstates the Machiavellian idea of civil religion and contrasts with the positive model offered by the Roman cult the sterile and inert preaching of Christianity. The political and religious crisis troubling Europe is thus no casual event, according to Bruno, but has deep theological roots and was born from none other than the reversal of values produced by Christianity, which put civil virtues in second place and exalted as supreme values humility, ignorance, and the passive obedience to the divine law. According to Bruno's interpretation, the seeds of decay introduced by Christian preaching culminated in Luther's Reformation, which represents the "evil angel" foreseen in the ancient Hermetic prophecy. Luther's theses, founded on the doctrine of predestination, have in fact severed every tie between divine justice and human justice: thus religion has lost its proper function of civil control and become a source of fanaticism and discord. The Reformers, Bruno writes, do not 'bring any fruits other than those used to suppress discussions, to dissipate harmony, to dissolve unity, and to cause children to rebel against their fathers, servants against their masters, subjects against their superiors; to cause schisms between peoples and peoples, nations and nations, comrades and comrades, brothers and brothers; to create division among families, cities, republics, and kingdoms' (*Spaccio de la bestia trionfante*, dialogue II, in *Dialoghi filosofici italiani*, p. 545, trans. Imerti).

In contrast to this politics centered on intolerance and violence, Bruno juxtaposes the enlightened action of Henri III of France, whom he evokes at the end of the dialogue as the model of the true "Christian prince", able to meet head on the deformities caused by Paul and Luther with an interpretation of Christianity in the spirit of civil law, resting on the values of peace and tolerance. In the closing passage of the *Spaccio*, Bruno adopts in secularized form the best inspirations of the Christian beatitudes, thus evoking themes on which he would long reflect. Analogous points recur in the preface to the *Articuli adversus mathematicos*, written in Prague in 1588. In this text, which may well be defined as Bruno's "profession of faith", the philosopher speaks one of the loftiest eulogies to freedom of thought: 'Everywhere', he writes, 'this law of love lies neglected, though so widely celebrated: this law born not of the malevolent demon of a single race, but in truth of God father of all, in that it conforms to the universal nature. It proclaims the love of the human race, whereby we should also love our enemies, hence not resemble the brutes and barbarians, but become the image of him who makes his sun shine on good and bad alike, and rains his grace on the just and the unjust. This is the religion that I follow without any controversy and prior to any disputation, whether by conviction of the soul, or through the ancient custom of my homeland and my people' (*La professione di fede di Giordano Bruno*, p. 69). Looking back to the tradition of Florentine → Neoplatonism and re-reading Erasmus, Bruno describes a model of religion that simplifies as far as possible its dogmatic and doctrinal apparatus and draws on the essential principles of the Gospels, interpreted ethically and free from any outside influence. Similarly in the civil realm, Bruno's religion serves as a place of unity, not of separation.

In the *Spaccio*, within an argument that dwells on the universal crisis, Bruno stresses the close connection of Christianity with decadence, and includes in his condemnation the whole Judeo-Christian tradition. He shows how the decadence of Europe has deep theological roots, derived from the reversal of values produced by Christianity, which, as we read in the *Cabala del cavallo pegaseo*, has put civil virtues in second place and exalted as supreme values "asinine" ignorance and the passive obedience to the divine law. Finally, in the *Eroici furori* Bruno takes up again themes and images from *De umbris* to show how, by moving out of the limit and the shadow, it is possible to forge a new relationship with the absolute truth, so as to transform an environment that is structurally finite and limited into an experience of the infinite.

As can be seen from this, it is the doctrine of matter and the closely connected theme of change that, for all the plurality of starting-points and motives that vary from time to time, constitute the axis on which Bruno's research rests: in this sense, it is significant that the theoretical positions of the *Dialoghi italiani* animate the speculation that unfolds in the three Frankfurt poems: *De triplici minimo et mensura*, *De monade, numero et figura*, and *De innumerabilibus, immenso et infigurabilibus*. These three works mark the stages of a rigorous speculative movement: in *De minimo*, Bruno focuses on the infinite atoms whose ceaseless collisions mark the cycles of natural life; in *De monade*, the doctrine of Lucretius blends with the idea of universal animation to highlight the one and only motive principle that operates in the inmost part of every being; in *De immenso*, in the course of a close criticism of Aristotle and Ptolemy, he reconstructs the salient points of the cosmology illustrated in the Italian dialogues.

3. MAGIC

Bruno constantly grafts magical reflections onto his philosophical arguments. As evidence of this, it is worth noting that most of the problems treated in the magical works find their theoretical basis in the reflections of a work written in the same period, but on a very different subject from → magic: the *Lampas triginta statuarum*. It is apparently paradoxical, not only because kabbalistic and Hermetic themes are almost entirely absent from this work, but because the few allusions to magic are without exception negative in tone: rather than exalting the abilities of the magus, Bruno aims to mock the blind credulity of those who open themselves to suggestions from another's will, to the point of becoming "vessels" and "instruments" of extraneous forces. Magical doctrines, having no contact with true wisdom, play a completely irrelevant role within a reflection that is supposed to describe the structure of the manifested universe, following a program symbolized by the figure of the "natural scale". The image which pervades the treatise in a series of close variations is not original in itself: it was sketched by Aristotle and filled out by the commentators of late Antiquity and the Middle Ages, who insisted on the hierarchical structure of the cosmos, in which every being is placed in an absolute ranking according to a rising scale that goes from the imperfection of matter up to the divine fullness, via ever-increasing degrees of perfection.

But Bruno rethinks the theme in a deeper way, modifying the traditional concept at two critical points. At the first level, Bruno dismantles the ontological structure erected by the Aristotelians by blending a series of elements taken from Aristotle's *Physics* with a conception of matter profoundly marked by the theoretical arguments arrived at in *De la causa*. At the base of the scale of nature, Bruno places not an imperfect and passive mass, but a matter animated by an insatiable desire for being, which compels it to make itself all and to become all. Between God and matter, or between the base of the scale and its summit, the only difference is given by the fact that matter can only act progressively, at different times and moments, to possess those infinite forms that coexist simultaneously in the divine plenitude. By placing the emphasis on matter and its "insatiable will", Bruno annihilates the hierarchical structure that is symbolized by the scale, which then becomes a simple metaphor for the "scientific method" described in the *Lampas*: to know nature it is not enough to grasp the profound unity underlying multiplicity, but one must first recognize the specific dignity of each being – for however small it is, it still participates in life and sense – and then comprehend one by one the relationships that unite it in infinitely varied ways to the other beings.

To describe such a process in imaginative form, Bruno takes one of the most suggestive personages of Greek mythology and shows through the figures of Thetis and Peleus the archetype of the action through which the human operator continually confronts the divine matter. Plunging deep into the rich fund of mythic material concerning Thetis, Bruno focuses on the long and laborious course which Peleus follows to conquer the goddess, alternating references to the episodes told in Apollodorus's *Bibliotheca* with direct quotes from the *Metamorphoses* of Ovid: the latter being a work which he obviously knew and loved, for he uses it frequently both in his Italian and Latin writings. If it is no surprise that one of the most detailed sections of the *Lampas* is full of references to Ovid, it is still significant that Bruno chooses to cite and to comment analytically only on those verses devoted

to the difficult conquest of Thetis. His choice is anything but automatic or indifferent, for his choice of passages is limited to those in which Ovid gives original expression to the mythological data, suppressing the heroic element so as to highlight instead the strength of desire that spurs Peleus on to find, beyond the succession of metamorphoses, the true face of the goddess.

In the *Lampas triginta statuarum*, Ovid's poem becomes the poetic figure of the long apprenticeship through which the "efficient cause" and the "operator" learn to imitate the inexhaustible cycle of natural metamorphoses, with a procedure that is never linear or pacific, but perennially liable to failure: this is evidenced, as Bruno reminds us, by Peleus's adventures, in which his laborious efforts to conquer the watery goddess often go in unexpected directions, resulting in consequences that are the opposite of what was foreseen. In this sense, one of the cardinal concepts of the chapter devoted to Thetis refers specifically to "labor", to the concentrated and meditated effort required by all operations in which man seeks to control the inner dynamism of the material substratum. Again, in an implicit polemic against those who maintain that human artifice inevitably exhausts the vigor of nature, Bruno insists that the gift of perfection, rare and extreme as it may be, can only arise out of human art. The myth of Peleus, who progressively dissolves the horrible metamorphoses of Thetis until he captures the goddess in all her splendor, show that absolute perfection, absent in nature, is always born from the informed work of an artifex, who, molding matter, directs it towards those "best forms" which nature never produces spontaneously, and which in any case are encountered only 'exceptionally', 'rarely', and 'in few individuals'.

It is thus in the relationship with matter, and specifically in the attempt to attain perfection, breaking up the inexorable rhythm of change, that Bruno sees the element that distinguishes the specific "fate" of man. And thus, having dissolved the ontological foundations of the scale of nature as traditionally understood, he returns to this image and introduces a second and significant variation on the ethical plane, to demolish any vision inspired by a rigid determinism and to celebrate, instead, the importance of human responsibility and action. In a rigorous speculative gesture, Bruno first reduces to a minimum the distance that separates man from the animal, and instead posits the maximum disproportion between the various destinies open to man. As the fruit of the metamorphoses of a unique and identical material, man is not superior by nature to other animate beings, with which he shares, albeit in different forms, sense and intellect. Nor does he stand out in his physical constitution, for animals exist, as Bruno reminds us, that have an affinity to him, such as the ape. Much less does man enjoy any superiority on the gnoseological level, because many animals – and here he cites the classic examples of the horse and the elephant – know how to reason most acutely. Thus the primacy of man is not a natural given: on the contrary, it is the fruit of the assiduous effort that carries man beyond his own natural limit, transforming him into a "sage" and a "hero". As Bruno recognizes, this is an extremely rare experience; however, it is only by virtue of this effort that access is gained to the highest class of living beings: beyond the plane of beings endowed with reason and intellect there is situated the "heroic" dimension, attained not by natural destiny, nor by divine beneficence, but only by conscious choice, after a long, laborious process of inner refinement.

Bruno is then able to use this carefully thought-out texture of variations for a profound rethinking of the concept of the scale of nature. In the *Lampas*, in fact, the symbol of the scale does not represent the finite steps of the descent of God into the sensible cosmos, because the communication between different levels of being is already guaranteed by matter, whose endless unfolding abolishes the traditional hierarchies. Nor does it allude to the orderly progression that goes from the animal to man, because the experience of man is configured in the very terms of a fracture with respect to his own natural role. Through these two important variants, the *Lampas* brings forth an extremely original image of nature: the universe is a living organism in which the incessant mutations of matter abolish every hierarchy and every order; combining with the work of man, it creates multiple orders that are different from those naturally given. The "scale of beings" is anything but stable and eternal (as Aristotle thought), but reveals a dynamic reality open to infinite mutations produced by the vitality of matter, which combining with the work of man opens up to diverse and unexpected forms and creates orders different from those naturally given. In the same way, the hierarchical order of beings can be subverted by the responsible action of man, who learns to know and to mold nature, and thereby learns to mold his own destiny, so that he can free himself from the animal condition and become wise and divine. From the speculations of the *Lampas* there emerges the primacy of knowing and of *praxis*, which allow one to comprehend and modify nature: and it is in the light of this knowledge that Bruno decides to proceed to a confrontation with magic.

In the magical art, the philosopher sees the paradigm of a non-dogmatic knowledge, which, through the model of a cosmos that is animate and woven of relationships and consonances, teaches him to recognize and value the infinite differences between things, and the infinite variety of human sentiments, suggesting the most efficacious strategies to act on the relationships between the various beings, to change and control the course of metamorphoses and the play of emotions. From the start, the attention to the role played by *fides* (faith) in magical operations bears witness to the precise will to naturalize magical *praxis*, depriving it of any linkage with astrological or theurgical doctrines: the fulcrum of the magical operation is thus identified within man and his passions.

In fact, in the most interesting and original of his magical writings, *De vinculis in genere*, Bruno distances himself from a hierarchical vision of magic and politics, to show how the action of the magus – similar to that of the politician – can result in good effects only if it succeeds in breaking down the consolidated hierarchies, recognizing the nature and specific dignity of the subjects which it addresses, and elaborating, in the light of an experience that is infinitely varied and dissimilar, the most effective techniques for acting on the multiform play of emotions and serving as vehicle for this *consensus* on which every kind of magic is basically rooted: 'It is necessary', Bruno writes, 'that he who would operate on reality by making use of bindings should possess in a certain way a universal theory of things, to be in the position of binding man, who of all things is so to speak the recapitulation. And this is so because – as we have said elsewhere – it is principally in the human species that one may discern the species of all things, especially through mathematics: thus some men resemble fish, others birds . . . Moreover, each man possesses a variety of customs, habits, intentions, inclinations, temperaments, and age, and, just as they imagine in the case of Proteus and Achelous that it is possible to take on a single material substratum capable of transmigrating into different forms, even so for binding one should continually use ever-varying kinds of knots' (*De Vinculis*, in *Opere magiche*, pp. 416-417).

And it is significant that at the heart of this reflection, Bruno revives the precise system of symbols that he used in the *Lampas triginta statuarum*, to show how every magical action is based on the play of attraction and repulsion which successively join the operator – the hero Peleus – to a specific material or a specific individual – the nereid Thetis – : 'that which is subject to binding is something profound and scarcely apparent to the senses . . ., it is subject to transformations moment by moment, behaving towards him who would bridle it no differently than Thetis when she tried to escape from Peleus's embrace: thus it is necessary to note the rhythm of its change, discerning beneath the preceding form the potentiality of the next one' (*De Vinculis*, in *Opere magiche*, pp. 447-449). Whoever wishes to throw bonds around individuals or people must thus decipher the cycle of metamorphoses, so as to discern beyond the apparent chaos the order that allows him to see, time after time, the most propitious moment to throw the bond: 'Therefore', Bruno concludes, 'after considering the subject's disposition and quality at the present moment, Peleus prefigures and predisposes the bindings for this Thetis, before she flees to take a definite form, knowing well that it is one thing to bind a serpent, another to bind a lion, and yet another, a boar' (*De Vinculis*, in *Opere magiche*, p. 449).

We are evidently dealing with a broad and articulate argument, in the course of which the philosopher recapitulates and elaborates in original fashion themes that were circulating in European culture, ranging from astrological concepts to Hermetic doctrines. The latter, which constituted an important point of reference for Bruno's thought, have been interpreted by F.A. Yates as the sole key for understanding the sense of his biographical and intellectual environment. Recent criticism has amply dwelt on the limits of this interpretation, but the thesis of the English scholar in her now classic study, *Giordano Bruno and the Hermetic Tradition*, has had the merit of shedding new light on aspects generally overlooked by interpreters; and the suggestive image of Bruno as "Hermetic magus" thus represents an essential stage in the philosopher's fortunes during the second half of the 20th century.

The passages from Bruno's works quoted in the text are from the following English translations: *The Ash Wednesday Supper* (ed. & tr. Hamden), Ct.: Edward A. Gosselin & Lawrence S. Lerner, Archon Books, 1977. ♦ *The Expulsion of the Triumphant Beast* (ed. & trans. Arthur D. Imerti), New Brunswick: Rutgers University Press, 1964 ♦ *On the Infinite Universe and Worlds*, (trans. Dorothea Waley Singer), in: D.W. Singer, *Giordano Bruno, His Life and Thought*, New York: Henry Schuman, 1950 ♦ Original editions of Bruno's works: *Opera Latine conscripta* (ed. F. Fiorentino [F. Tocco, H. Vitelli, C.M. Tallarigo]), Naples/Florence 1879-1891 ♦ *De umbris idearum* (ed. R. Sturlese), Florence: Leo S. Olschki, 1991 ♦ *Dialoghi filosofici italiani* (ed. and

intro. by M. Ciliberto), Milan: Mondadori 2000 ♦ *Opere magiche* (general ed., M. Ciliberto, ed. S. Bassi, E. Scapparone, N. Tirinnanzi), Adelphi: Milan 2000 ♦ *Opere italiane di Giordano Bruno* (ed. G. Aquilecchia, N. Ordine [et al.], appendices by L. Berggren, D. Mansueto, Z. Sorrenti), Turin: UTET, 2002.

Lit. For the bibliography of works by and about Bruno, the fundamental sources are V. Salvestrini, *Bibliografia di Giordano Bruno (1582-1950)*, 2nd ed., ed. L. Firpo, Florence: Sansoni, 1958 and M.E. Severini, *Bibliografia di Giordano Bruno 1951-2000*, Rome: Edizioni di Storia e Letteratura, 2002. A selective bibliography follows. E. Canone (ed.), *Giordano Bruno: Gli anni napoletani e la "peregrinatio" europea. Immagini. Testi. Documenti*, Cassino: Università degli Studi, 1992 ♦ L. Firpo, *Il processo di Giordano Bruno* (ed. D. Quaglioni), Rome: Salerno, 1993 ♦ V. Spampanato, *Il processo di Giordano Bruno con documenti editi e inediti*, Messina: Principato, 1921 ♦ G. Aquilecchia, "Lo stampatore londinese di Giordano Bruno e altre note per l'edizione della 'Cena'", in: idem, *Schede bruniane (1950-1991)*, Rome: Vecchiarelli, 1993, 157-207 ♦ G. Aquilecchia, *Le opere italiane di Giordano Bruno: Critica testuale e oltre*, Naples Bibliopolis: 1991 ♦ M. Ciliberto & N. Tirinnanzi, *Il dialogo recitato: Per una nuova edizione del Bruno volgare*, Florence: Leo S. Olschki, 2003 ♦ F. Tomizza, "Quattro varianti significative nel Dialogo I della 'Cena de le ceneri' di Giordano Bruno", *Rinascimento* 36 (1996), 431-456 ♦ G. Bruno, *Corpus iconographicum*: Le incisioni nelle opere a stampa, catalogue, graphic reconstruction, and commentary by M. Gabriele, Milan: Adelphi, 2001 ♦ M. Ciliberto, *Lessico di Giordano Bruno*, Rome: Edizioni dell'Ateneo e Bizzarri, 1979 ♦ C. Lefons (ed.), *Indice dei nomi, dei luoghi e delle cose notevoli nelle opere latine di Giordano Bruno*, Leo S. Olschki: Florence, 1998 ♦ M. Ciliberto, *Giordano Bruno*, Rome/Bari: Laterza, 1990 ♦ idem, *L'occhio di Atteone: Nuovi studi su Giordano Bruno*, Rome: Edizioni di Storia e Letteratura, 2002 ♦ A. Corsano, *Il pensiero di Giordano Bruno nel suo svolgimento storico*, Florence: Sansoni, 1940 ♦ T. Dagron, *Unité de l'être et dialectique: L'idée de philosophie naturelle chez Giordano Bruno*, Paris: Vrin, 1999 ♦ G. Gentile, *Giordano Bruno e il pensiero del Rinascimento*, Florence, 1920 (new ed., intro. by E. Garin, Le Lettere, 1991) ♦ G. Sacerdoti, *Sacrificio e sovranità: Teologia e politica nell'Europa di Shakespeare e Bruno*, Turin: Einaudi, 2002 ♦ F.A. Yates, *Giordano Bruno and the Hermetic Tradition*, London: Routledge & Kegan Paul, 1964 ♦ Hilary Gatti (ed.), *Giordano Bruno: Philosopher of the Renaissance*, Aldershot & Burlington: Ashgate, 2002.

MICHELE CILIBERTO

Bulwer-Lytton, Edward George
(Edward George Earle Lytton Bulwer), * 25.5.1803 London, † 18.1.1873 Torquay

Novelist and statesman. Youngest son of General William Earle Bulwer and Elizabeth Barbara Lytton. He first went by the name of Edward Bulwer. In 1838 he was created a baronet, and became Sir Edward Lytton Bulwer, Bt. In 1843, under the terms of his mother's will, he changed his surname to Bulwer-Lytton. In 1866 he was created 1st Baron Lytton of Knebworth, and was thereafter known as Lord Lytton.

Bulwer-Lytton's father died when he was four years old, leaving him to be raised by his mother in her ancestral home, Knebworth House, Hertfordshire. "Teddy" was a precocious child and, from an early age, a wide reader in his grandfather Lytton's library. As a boy, he came under the influence of the Rev. Chauncey Hare Townshend (1798-1868), an advocate of Mesmerism [⟶ Animal Magnetism], who remained a lifelong correspondent. After education at preparatory schools and by private tutors, Bulwer-Lytton attended first Trinity College, then the smaller college of Trinity Hall, Cambridge, and won the Chancellor's Gold Medal for his poem *Sculpture*. He spent two years in Paris (1825/26), developing into an elegant social figure with a dandified air, yet with a need for solitude and a keen, ironic eye that laid the foundations of his career as a novelist.

As a young man, Bulwer-Lytton was of a high-strung, romantic temperament. The first woman he loved was forced by her father to marry another man. Three years later she died, after confessing that she had always loved him. She remained an influence on him, appearing in his last novel, *Kenelm Chillingly*, as Lily Mordaunt. Later, while at Cambridge, he was involved with Lady Caroline Lamb (1785-1828), formerly Lord Byron's lover, who introduced him to the literary circles around the novelist and reformer William Godwin (1756-1836). After his return from Paris, she also introduced him to a beautiful, penniless Irish protégée of hers, Rosina Doyle Wheeler (1802-1882). After a stormy engagement, Bulwer-Lytton married Rosina in 1827. Bulwer-Lytton's mother was strongly opposed to the match, and cut off her son's allowance. Henceforth he had to earn his living by writing.

The Bulwers had two children, Emily (1829-1848) and Robert (1831-1891). For some years they kept up a brilliant social façade, but in 1836 they were legally separated. Rosina Lytton devoted the rest of her life to harrassing her husband, writing a novel that cruelly lampooned him (*Cheveley, or the Man of Honour*, 1839) and heckling him at his election meetings. His attempt to have her certified as insane only backfired on him by alienating the public and his son. It is not known whether Bulwer-Lytton had any later alliances, but he was close to Lady Blessington (1789-1849), who presided over a famous literary and social salon in Gore House, Kensington. Over a hundred of her letters to Bulwer-Lytton survive, dating from 1824-1849.

Bulwer-Lytton entered Parliament in 1831 as Liberal (Whig) member for St. Ives, Huntingdon, and a supporter of the Reform Bill. During the Prime Ministership of Lord Melbourne (Lady Caroline Lamb's husband), he caused a motion to be carried exempting the freed slaves in British colonies from a compulsory twelve-year apprenticeship. He left Parliament in 1841, to return as Conservative (Tory) Member for Hertfordshire from 1852-1866. His conversion was due to his friend Benjamin Disraeli (1st Earl of Beaconsfield, 1804-1881), who also had a career as a novelist. During 1858-1859 Bulwer-Lytton was Secretary for the Colonies, and presided over the incorporation of two important new colonies, British Colombia (Canada) and Queensland (Australia). After he was raised to the peerage in 1866 he sat in the House of Lords, but increasing deafness prevented him from debating. Although the conferral of a peerage satisfied a long-held ambition of the Lytton family, Bulwer-Lytton's last years were clouded by ill-health, depression, and unceasing troubles with his wife. Bulwer-Lytton left instructions that after his death he should be buried without Christian ceremony, next to his mother in unconsecrated ground. His son ignored these wishes, and took advantage of his father's fame to have him interred among the writers and politicians in Westminster Abbey.

Bulwer-Lytton's literary career was highly successful from the start. His first novel, *Pelham*, depicted the excesses of social life that he had witnessed in Paris, and is said to have started the fashion for masculine evening dress. His novels and plays, first published without disclosure of his authorship, assured him of a lifelong income and enabled him to lavishly restore his Tudor mansion, Knebworth. They also won him the friendship and respect of Charles Dickens (1812-1870), with whom he founded the short-lived Guild of Literature and Art (1854) for the benefit of poor authors. Bulwer-Lytton also edited literary magazines (*The New Monthly Magazine*, 1831-32; *The Monthly Chronicle*, 1841-?), and, less successfully, wrote poetry, including the epic poem *King Arthur* (1848). His baronetcy was awarded for services to literature. The subjects of his novels range over social satire and social criticism, crime, historical fiction, politics, science fiction, and the occult [→ occult/occultism].

Bulwer-Lytton's involvement with the occult began in the atmosphere of Mesmerism, or "magnetism", which was popular in the 1830s both as a social diversion and as a field of scientific research. Bulwer-Lytton's friend C.H. Townshend was an authority in the matter, and wrote *Facts in Mesmerism* (1840). Lady Blessington's salon was a hotbed of crystal-gazing, in which an entranced medium would speak messages read or seen in a crystal or glass. Here Bulwer-Lytton met the 4th Earl of Stanhope (1781-1855), previously guardian of Caspar Hauser (1813-1833) and a keen researcher into Mesmerism and crystal mediumship, and the painter John Varley (1778-1842), astrologer and friend of → William Blake. Bulwer-Lytton himself practiced geomancy (using dots drawn randomly on paper) and → astrology, making horoscopes and predictions for his friends. He foretold through geomancy the political career of Disraeli at a time (1860) when the latter was still better known as a novelist.

During the 1850s Bulwer-Lytton conducted researches and experiments in → spiritualism and Mesmerism, joining Lord Stanhope in séances with the American rapping medium Mrs. Hayden (1852). Bulwer-Lytton probably received → Eliphas Lévi on the latter's first visit to England in 1854. In 1855-1856, Daniel Dunglas Home (1833-1886) gave séances for Lytton in London and at Knebworth. Bulwer-Lytton was one of three persons present at Lévi's 1861 evocation of "Apollonius of Tyana" on the roof of a Regent Street store. But Bulwer-Lytton disappointed the spiritualist and the nascent occultist movements by refusing to lend his reputation to their causes. *The Spiritual Magazine*, 1867, reported him as saying: 'All the experiments I have witnessed, if severally probed, go against the notion that the phenomena are produced by the spirits of the dead; and I imagine that no man, who can take care of his goods, would give up his property to a claimant, who could bear cross-examination as little as some alleged spirit, who declares he is your father or friend, and tells you where he died, and then proceeds to talk rubbish, of which he would have been incapable when he was alive. I can conceive no prospect of the future world more melancholy, than that in which Sellaires and Shakespeares are represented as having fallen into boobies – or at best, of intellects below mediocrity'. Bulwer-Lytton expressed a similar opinion when he consented to be interviewed for the 1869 Report of the London Dialectical Society. His skepticism did not prevent him from using the themes of ceremonial → magic in his short story *The Haunted and the Haunters*, and of mediumship in his novel *A Strange Story*.

Contrary to later rumors and claims, Bulwer-Lytton is not known to have belonged to any secret society or Order. He was not a Freemason. The Societas Rosicruciana in Anglia (S.R.I.A.), apparently unaware of this, elected him their "Grand Patron" in 1872, but without his consent, for which the head of the Manchester College, John Yarker, humbly apologised. Most likely Bulwer-Lytton was "self-initiated" through following practices he found in books. He wrote to a friend: 'I know by experience that those wizard old books are full of holes and pitfalls. I myself once fell into one and remained there forty-five days and three hours without food, crying for help as loud as I could, but nobody came. You may believe that or not, just as you please, but it's true!' (*Life*, II, 32) It has been claimed, without evidence, that Bulwer-Lytton contacted the → Asiatic Brethren, the Fratres Lucis, and/or the "Jewish Lodge" in Frankfurt during his travels in Germany (1841-1843). In a letter to → Hargrave Jennings (1872) he stated that, unlike current pretenders to → Rosicrucianism, he possessed the 'cipher sign of the "Initiate"', and that the Rosicrucian Brotherhood still existed, only not under any name recognizable by outsiders.

Lacking concrete evidence, Bulwer-Lytton's reputation as initiate rests on his novel *Zanoni*, which is the most significant occult novel of 19th-century English literature. He made the initial sketches for it as early as 1825. Themes from it appeared in a short story, *The Tale of Kosem Kosamim the Magician* (1832), and about half of the text as *Zicci* (1838), but the metaphysical doctrines are fully developed only in the complete novel of 1842.

The story of *Zanoni* purports to be transcribed from a ciphered manuscript acquired from an old gentleman encountered in a London bookshop. Later it emerges that the old gentleman was the artist Clarence Glyndon, one of the protagonists of the story. How far this fictitious author's opinions are Bulwer-Lytton's own is uncertain. The narrative is set in the period of the French Revolution and the Terror (1791-1793). It gives a clear sense of discrimination between good occultism and bad. The narrator rejects Mesmer and → Cagliostro as profiteers, associating them with the errors of the *philosophes* and deists; he praises → Louis-Claude de Saint-Martin alone among the 18th-century lilluminates. The initiates of the story hate the

Revolution for its impiety, atheism, and dogma of *égalité*. They hold that the whole of the universe is a hierarchy, from the archangel to the worm, and that it is human inequality alone that holds out the hope of progress.

Besides Glyndon, the narrator, artist, and neophyte, the characters of *Zanoni* include two Chaldean initiates, apparently the only two left on earth of a high and ancient Order. This is not the Rosicrucians, but an older and more illustrious Order of which the Rosicrucians are a branch. It pays special respect to the teachings of the Platonists, the Pythagoreans, and Apollonius of Tyana. Evidently it is not Christian. The two initiates are Mejnour, the senior one, and Zanoni, who has been on earth for 5000 years. While sharing in the same occult knowledge and possessing the secret of indefinite life, these two contrast in character. Mejnour inhabits the body of an old man, with every earthly passion extinguished, in order to accomplish the transmutation of man into superman. He works at his plans with 'cabala and numbers', residing in Olympian calm behind the scenes and cycles of human history, indifferent to others' weal or woe as he is indifferent to his own. Zanoni is an equally mysterious character, but one who becomes less superhuman as the plot unfolds. There is much of the Comte de → Saint-Germain about him: Zanoni is also a cosmopolite, a 'noble traveler' who has seen the world (his servants come from India) and its history, a man who has achieved the elixir of life, who gives away priceless gems and stuns the public with his mystery and his wealth, coming and going as he pleases. Zanoni's choice is to enter the maelstrom of human passion, losing his occult powers in the process but gaining what his master Mejnour has rejected: love and death. The message of the work is that the love of human beings for each other, and their acceptance of death, are things of incalculable value, not to be surpassed even by the highest initiate.

The novel is an encyclopedia of ideas about the occult sciences. In pointing out the extreme ugliness of the French Revolutionary leaders, it supports the thesis of physiognomy. Herbalism is mentioned reverently, along with the general value of research into the mysteries of nature. The doctrines of universal sympathy, of secret affinities in nature, and of hierarchical planes of being permeated by an omnipresent Mind are essential to *Zanoni*. The multiple planes include those that can only be explored out of the physical body. Therefore ascesis is necessary to the aspirant, refusing the demands of the flesh in order to live in the soul and work with the imagination. The artist can do this as well as the mystic; a Platonic subtheme of *Zanoni* is the sacred nature of art, if only inspired by the "Ideal".

The world-view of *Zanoni* is of a universe populated by beings at every level: not just the physical series from galaxy to microbe that was currently exciting Victorian scientists, but an unseen hierarchy which could, by the proper means, be rendered perceptible. The lowest of them are the spirits of the four elements: the Gnomes, Undines, Sylphs, and Salamanders of → Paracelsus and of the *Comte de Gabalis*. No friends to humankind, these were believed by earlier magicians to be fiends, and their pacts with them to be drawn with the Devil. But no man can sell his soul, says Zanoni, for 'in every human creature the Divine One breathes; and He alone can judge His own hereafter, and allot its new career and home'. This immortal part of man is called by the Neoplatonic term *augoeides*, which manifests when 'the sphere of the soul is luminous, when nothing external has contact with the soul itself; but when lit by its own light, it sees the truth of all things and the truth centred in itself'. Thus man is tripartite, consisting of body, soul, and the *augoeides* or indwelling Divine Spirit. The magus can command the elemental spirits, but more importantly he can establish contact with higher beings. Zanoni twice summons a celestial apparition called Adon-Ai, from whom he has learned all his wisdom. Adon-Ai disputes with Zanoni at the point at which the initiate has decided to renounce his ascesis and embrace human love; when Zanoni is obdurate, the Son of Light smiles. On the second apparition of Adon-Ai, the spirit gives his blessing to Zanoni's decision, for by now Zanoni has also embraced human death, which Adon-Ai calls 'the sublimest heritage of thy race, – the eternity that commences from the grave'. Finally there is the famous "Dweller of the Threshold" whom both Glyndon the neophyte and Zanoni the adept have to face and overcome. This is a hideous personification of one's past thoughts and evil tendencies, which even if not perceived lures the aspirant towards disaster. The only way to conquer it, as Zanoni teaches Glyndon and demonstrates himself, is by overcoming one's fear and persisting in one's resolve to cling to virtue, come what may. Then two paths are open: one, the path to seraphic detachment such as Mejnour has achieved; the other, the path by which one becomes as a little child again, which is Zanoni's choice. *Zanoni* was Bulwer-Lytton's own favorite among his works. It was much read and discussed, especially in France and Germany, where many of Bulwer-Lytton's works were translated.

Bulwer-Lytton's late novel *The Coming Race* was influential in 20th-century science-fiction literature. It depicts a race with superior powers that has long lived beneath the surface of the earth. They have developed a force called "Vril" which they use for advanced technological and seemingly magical effects. In 1870, Lytton explained: 'I did not mean Vril for mesmerism, but for electricity, developed into uses as yet only dimly guessed, and including whatever there may be genuine in mesmerism, which I hold to be a mere branch current of the one great fluid pervading all nature'. Nonetheless, "Vril" has become a cliché of 20th century popular occultism, as has the notion of a hollow earth with its inhabitants.

Bulwer-Lytton's son Robert has sometimes been confused with him, especially by non-English writers, and merits a short note here. Edward Robert Bulwer-Lytton joined the diplomatic service in 1850 and served in Washington and many European capitals. In 1873, on his father's death, he succeeded to the peerage as 2nd Baron Lytton. From 1875-1880 he had the difficult task of Governor-General of India. In 1880 he was raised to an earldom and became 1st Earl of Lytton (but still also styled "Lord Lytton"). He served as ambassador in Paris from 1887 until his death there in 1891. The Earl of Lytton was a prolific poet under the name of "Owen Meredith". His friendship with → Saint-Yves d'Alveydre appears in his translation of the latter's *Le Poème de la Reine* (published 1892), and may be a symptom of a deeper involvement with French esotericists than can be documented. Saint-Yves's personal mythology (as expounded in *Mission de l'Inde*, 1886) gives an important role to India and to a subterranean race with superior technology.

Novels relevant to esotericism: *The Last Days of Pompeii* (1834), *Zicci* (1841), *Zanoni* (1842), *A Strange Story* (1862), *The Coming Race* (1871).

Lit.: James L. Campbell, *Edward Bulwer-Lytton*, Boston: Twayne publ., 1986 ♦ Sibylla Jane Flower, *Bulwer-Lytton: An Illustrated Life of the First Baron Lytton 1803-1873* (Lifelines 9), Aylesbury: Shire Publications, 1973 ♦ Joscelyn Godwin, *The Theosophical Enlightenment*, Albany: State University of New York Press, 1994, 123-130, 192-196 ♦ 2nd Earl of Lytton, *The Life of Edward Bulwer, First Lord Lytton*, London: Macmillan, 1913 ♦ Robert Lee Wolff, *Strange Stories and other Explorations in Victorian Fiction*, Boston: Gambit Inc., 1971, ch. "The Occult Fiction of Sir E. Bulwer-Lytton".

JOSCELYN GODWIN

Burton, Sir Richard Francis, K.C.M.G., * 19.3.1821 Elstree, † 20.10.1890 Trieste

Traveler and translator. Son of Lt.-Col. Joseph Netterville Burton and Martha Baker. Childhood in France and Italy, educated by private tutors. Learned several languages before attending Trinity College, Oxford (1840-1842; no degree). Burton was attracted to the occult while at Oxford, when the artist John Varley (1778-1842) drew his horoscope and introduced him to the kabbalah [→ Jewish Influences]. As an officer in the Army of the East India Company (1842-1849), Burton qualified as interpreter for six Indian languages and also studied Arabic, Sanskrit, Pushtu, and Portuguese. On his return he published four books about India. In 1853, disguised as an Indian healer and magician, he made the pilgrimage to Mecca and entered the Ka'aba. His book about this adventure ensured his fame. From 1854-1859 the East India Company supported Burton's expedition to Somalia, where he was badly wounded. In 1856 he served in the Crimea, then began a series of expeditions, partly supported by the Royal Geographical Society, to discover the source of the Nile. On his return in 1859 he was awarded the Founder's Gold Medal of the R.G.S. In 1860 he visited Utah and interviewed Brigham Young. In 1861 he married Isabel Arundell (1831-1896), and joined the diplomatic service. He served as British Consul at Fernando Po in Portuguese West Africa (1861-1863) and at Santos, Brazil (1865-1868), both posts giving him the opportunity for explorations of the interior. From 1869-1871 he was Consul at Damascus; from 1872-1890 at Trieste (1872-1890), varied by journeys to Iceland, India, Egypt, and West Africa. On 12.10.1878 he was elected a fellow of the → Theosophical Society in London. In 1886 he was made a Knight Commander of the Order of St. Michael and St. George. His body was buried in a marble replica of an Arab tent in the Catholic cemetery of Mortlake.

Burton was a many-faceted individual, driven by curiosity to risk his life and ruin his health in some of the most dangerous parts of the world. His superb talent for languages and his retention of all that he saw and learned made him the equal, and the envy, of professional scholars, and his translations of Oriental literature became classics. His intelligence, cynicism, and wit made him as many enemies as friends and his promotion was repeatedly blocked. He was a considerate husband to his devout Catholic wife, who had married him against the wishes of her aristocratic family. Burton frequently used his wife as a "magnetized" medium, asking her questions about absent persons or future events.

Burton's interest in altered states of consciousness led him to the use of hashish, opium, and other drugs. He was notoriously well-informed about the sexual practices of non-European peoples. Before his marriage, he took advantage of his postings to explore these in person, and contracted syphilis. He continued throughout his life to add to his encyclopedic knowledge on the subject, much of which is scattered in his twenty-three travel books. In Trieste Burton translated the poetry of Luis Vaz de Camoens (1524-1579/80), the erotic classics *Kama Sutra* and *Kama-Shastra, The Perfumed Garden of the Cheikh Nefzaoui, The Book of the Thousand Nights and a Night* (16 vols.), the *Pentamerone*, and Greek and Latin erotica. His translation of the "Arabian Nights" was glossed with a mass of erudition and a "Terminal Essay" on the sexual customs of the East that was a landmark in Victorian scholarship. Even more notorious was his book-length treatise *Human Sacrifice among the Sephardine or Eastern Jews* (1877), which has been blocked from publication to this day.

Burton had a sympathetic curiosity for all religions. In India he was inducted as an honorary Brahmin into the Nagar-Brahmin caste. In Karachi he was initiated as a Sikh, and underwent the long rituals to become an initiate of the Qadiri Order of Sufism. He probably had more knowledge of the religion and practices of Islam than any Westerner of his time. His published work, like that of the Theosophists, contributed to the growing appreciation of Oriental philosophy and culture in the later 19th century. Also Theosophical in spirit was his dispassionate acceptance of "occult" phenomena as evidence for the unknown powers of nature and of man, better understood in the East than in the modern West. In an address to the National Union of Spiritualists (1876) he asserted the existence of extra-sensory perception, but attributed it to unknown natural causes, rather than to spirits. As far as one can guess at Burton's private convictions, they were metaphysical rather than religious, perhaps resembling those of his admired Sufis, for whom all religions are but veils before reality. His deliberate flaunting of taboos and fearless pursuit of knowledge align him with the warrior current within the esoteric tradition.

Lit.: William Harrison, *Burton and Speke*, London: W. H. Allen, 1984 ♦ James A. Casada, *Sir Richard F. Burton: A Bio-bibliographical Study*, Boston: G.K. Hall, 1990 ♦ Mary S. Lovell, *A Rage to Live: A Biography of Richard & Isabel Burton*, New York & London: W.W. Norton, 1998 ♦ Edward Rice, *Captain Sir Richard Francis Burton*, New York: Charles Scribner's Sons, 1990.

JOSCELYN GODWIN

Byzantium

1. WHY SHOULD A STUDENT OF WESTERN ESOTERICISM PAY ATTENTION TO BYZANTIUM? 2. WHAT DOES "ESOTERIC" MEAN IN BYZANTIUM? 3. BYZANTINE ESOTERICISM VERSUS WESTERN ESOTERICISM 4. HELLENIC ESOTERICISM IN BYZANTIUM 5. ORTHODOX CHRISTIAN ESOTERICISM IN BYZANTIUM

Byzantium has been defined by Western scholars in many different ways, by many different criteria and for many specific purposes. The later Byzantines themselves, however, found their world easy to define. Its irreducible cultural *center* consisted of two things: the doctrines and practices of the Orthodox Church, on the one hand; and on the other, the Greek language. It was a Byzantine's mastery of the Greek language that distinguished him from the barbarian; it was his adherence to the Orthodox Church that distinguished him from the schismatic, the heretic, the pagan, and other such kinds of people.

But this was only the *center* of Byzantium, for Greek texts had also been translated into "barbarian" tongues. Thus Byzantium, more loosely defined, also encompassed other Christian peoples who were Orthodox in their doctrine and practice, but who had long celebrated the liturgy and read the Bible in languages other than Greek (notably, in Old Georgian and Old Slavonic). Moreover, in every culture there are always dissidents, and so Byzantium also contained individuals or groups of people who were not Orthodox, and others who were not even Christian.

Byzantium, so defined, first began to take shape during the fourth century CE on the territory of the Eastern Roman Empire. In the fifth century two major schisms divided the supra-national, multilingual Christian world into three disjunct communions: the non-Ephesian Church in Persia, the several non-Chalcedonian Churches in various lands of the East, and the combined Orthodox and Catholic Churches of Byzantium and Rome. In the seventh and later centuries Islam conquered large parts of the Byzantine Empire, as well as most of the lands where the non-Ephesian and non-Chalcedonian Churches were at home. In the eleventh century another schism broke the communion that had hitherto prevailed between the Orthodox Churches and the Roman Catholic Church, and the sack of Constantinople in 1204 by the Fourth Crusade widened this breach into a nearly unbridgeable chasm. Taken together, these developments massively reduced the linguistic and cultural variety of Byzantium, cutting it off from most of the Christian peoples that had long used Old Syriac, Old Armenian, Coptic, Old Ethiopic and Latin as their languages of liturgy and culture. On the other hand, Byzantium was able to extend its boundaries northwards, with the Christianization of Bulgaria in the ninth century, of Russia toward the end of the tenth century, and of other South Slavic realms in later centuries. In 1453, however, the last fortress of the Eastern Roman Empire, Constantinople itself, fell to an Islamic army, and the last Christian Emperor of Rome died fighting on its walls. Yet even after 1453 Byzantium continued to exist, albeit in attenuation, as a subjugated culture in Greek-speaking lands and as a transplanted culture in Orthodox Slavic lands.

1. Why should a Student of Western Esotericism Pay any Attention to Byzantium?

There are at least three answers to this question, each more compelling than the previous one. Firstly, most of the oldest foundation texts of Western esotericism – the dialogues and letters of Plato, the works of the Neoplatonic philosophers [→ Neoplatonism] and theurgists (above all, Iamblichus's treatise *On the Mysteries of the Egyptians*), the *Chaldaean Oracles*, the manuals of the Hellenic astrologers [→ Astrology] and alchemists [→ Alchemy], the *Corpus Hermeticum* [→ Hermetic Literature], the writings of pseudo-Dionysius the Areopagite, various Gnostic texts, and so on – were not only composed in Greek, but also have come down to us almost entirely through Byzantine channels of transmission, whether they are still extant in the original Greek or have now survived only in the form of old translations from lost Greek originals. Secondly, Byzantium never experienced – and never *needed* to experience – the Renaissance, the Reformation, the Counter-Reformation, or the Enlightenment. It is these four successive cultural movements that gave Western esotericism all of its present defining characteristics (as specified by Faivre 1994, 10-15), but the specified characteristics *cannot* serve to define Byzantine Esotericism. Thirdly, over many centuries profound and subtle differences in doctrine and practice developed between Christianity in Byzantium and Christian-

ity in Western Europe. In consequence, esoteric doctrines and practices came to occupy a different position and to play a different role in the Orthodox Churches of Byzantium than they did in the Catholic Church of Western Europe.

Because of these differences, one might legitimately ask whether Byzantine esotericism even exists. It does. Indeed, it is convenient to speak of *two* distinct Byzantine esotericisms. One of them may be termed *Orthodox Christian esotericism*. For over 1500 years this esotericism has been widely cultivated throughout the Byzantine world, especially in the great monasteries of the Orthodox Church such as those of Mt. Athos and Mt. Sinai. The other may be termed *Hellenic esotericism*. It has always drawn its inspiration directly from the pagan texts and traditions of Neoplatonic philosophy and theurgy. Therefore it has always been more or less problematic in Christian Byzantium. After the mandatory Christianization of all Byzantines in the sixth century, Hellenic esotericism seems to have been cultivated only sporadically, by a mere handful of highly educated Byzantines. Each of these two Byzantine esotericisms shares some important features with Western esotericism, although neither possesses all of the significant defining features of the latter (always here referring to Faivre's definition).

These differences between esotericism in Byzantium and esotericism in Western Europe enable a sensitive scholar to arrive at a deeper understanding of the latter by contrasting it with the former: light from the East often throws into very sharp relief, indeed, what could otherwise be only dimly seen in the West. Yet for this to occur, one must first become familiar with each kind of Byzantine esotericism on its own terms, not viewing it solely in terms of Western categories and theories.

One must also be careful to distinguish genuine Byzantine esotericism from various esoteric currents that have claimed to be Byzantine, but in fact have other historical roots. The most wide-spread of all these *pseudo-Byzantine esotericisms* are the ones pertaining to Sophia, the Wisdom of God. Though they are usually presented as genuine old esoteric traditions of the Orthodox Church, in point of historical fact they derive directly or indirectly from the work of the eccentric Russian lay theologian, Vladimir Sergeevich Solov'ëv (1853-1900), who combined Orthodox Christian esotericism with elements of two other traditions. One of these other traditions was Western-European Sophiology (cf. → Jacob Boehme or → Gottfried Arnold), which came to Russia through Freemasonic [→ Freemasonry] and Rosicrucian [→ Rosicrucianism] channels during the eighteenth century and had an enormous impact on Russian spirituality. The other tradition was Late Antique → Gnosticism, insofar as it had been recovered by nineteenth-century scholarship. Solov'ëv's synthesis of these three disparate traditions was presented with such skill and power, and satisfied the needs of its era so well, that it was believed to represent an authentic Byzantine esoteric teaching by many well-educated Orthodox laymen, and even by a few influential clerical theologians of the Orthodox Church.

2. WHAT DOES "ESOTERIC" MEAN IN BYZANTIUM?

To understand Byzantine esotericism in its own terms, we must begin with the word esoteric itself. In ancient Greek, the opposed adjectives ἐσωτερικός (esoteric) and ἐξωτερικός (exoteric) were relatively uncommon. The adjective ἐξωτερικός seems to have been the older of the two, originally meaning "exterior" or "foreign". It was derived from the adjective ἐξώτερος (outer), which was opposed to ἐσώτερος (inner); and those words in turn were derived from the twin adverbs ἔξω (outer) and ἔσω (inner). The adjective ἐσωτερικός seems to have been coined from ἐξωτερικός in order to create a pair of technical terms in philosophy. In philosophy, the use of these terms was originally limited to two contexts. They were used, first of all, to label the two orders into which the philosopher-magician Pythagoras (according to several later sources) appears to have divided his disciples: his exoteric disciples were those who might hear the master's teaching only in silence, never actually seeing him as he spoke from behind a curtain, whereas his esoteric disciples, tested by five years of silence, were privileged to go behind the curtain, to see Pythagoras himself and to speak with him (Hippolytus of Rome, Refutatio omnium haeresium I.2; Origen, Contra Celsum I.7; Iamblichus, De vita Pythagorica 17, 31, 32). Somewhat later, the writings of the philosopher Aristotle were said to have been divided into two classes: his exoteric writings were available for all to read, whereas his esoteric writings were restricted to members of his school (Clement of Alexandria, Stromateis V.9, cf. Lucian, Vitarum auctio 26, Aulus Gellius, Noctes Atticae XX.5; as it happens, Aristotle's exoteric writings survive only as fragments; it is his esoteric treatises that have come down to us). In each case, whether applied to pupils or to treatises, the two terms express an opposition between the outer, common world of the general public and the inner, restricted world of favored or accepted students. Even later,

Galen termed certain Stoic teachings esoteric (De Hippocratis et Platonis placitis III.4).

Under the influence of Christianity the opposition between ἐσωτερικός and ἐξωτερικός was subtly altered. Although neither word occurs anywhere in the Greek Bible – neither in the Septuagint Old Testament nor in the Greek New Testament –, St. Paul (II Cor. 4:16) speaks of ὁ ἔσω ἄνθρωπος (the inward man) and ὁ ἔξω ἄνθρωπος (the outward man), opposing the spiritual to the mundane; later, some pagans came to use the same phrases with similar meanings. Henceforth esoteric people in the original sense of the term – privileged students – are implicitly also distinguished by their deeper spirituality, and esoteric writings – treatises restricted to such students – are implicitly also writings that convey deeper spiritual truths; the exoteric, in contrast, are common and mundane. The Neoplatonists, too, used the terms in this broader sense, e.g. Iamblichus in his Protrepticus (1, 4, 21), as does Origen with reference to Christian doctrines in his Contra Celsum (III.37). Moreover, in another of his works Iamblichus divides doctrines into exoteric and esoteric, that is, into ῥητά (effable) and ἄρρητα (ineffable) (De communi mathematica scientia 18). This idea that the deepest spiritual truths are not only esoteric, but also ineffable, that is, they are inherently beyond the power of any language to express, colors all subsequent use of the term esoteric in Byzantium.

3. BYZANTINE ESOTERICISM VERSUS WESTERN ESOTERICISM

In Western Europe, too, there were texts and people, doctrines and practices that a Byzantine observer might have labeled esoteric. Even so, the borrowed words esotericus and exotericus seem to have been hardly ever used in Ancient and Medieval Latin. When they were used before and during the Renaissance, they seem to be have been used almost exactly as their Greek equivalents were in Byzantium, although perhaps sometimes without the Neoplatonic association between the esoteric and the ineffable.

Beginning with the Renaissance, however, the term esotericus came to be used more commonly in the West. Yet as its use grew, it acquired a new connotation, which the corresponding Greek word lacked: henceforth whatever was esoteric was necessarily opposed in one way or another to the prevailing judgement of the generally recognized experts. Thus in the West esotericists became proponents of rejected or forgotten knowledge (wrongly rejected or forgotten, they would claim), and Western esotericism eventually became – to lapse into contemporary jargon for a moment – a radical challenge to the "dominant paradigm" of its age, a form of "counter-culture". In the Byzantine world, by contrast, Orthodox Christian Esotericism always remained a fully integrated part of the "dominant paradigm", and never formed the nucleus of any Byzantine "counter-culture".

This contrast arose largely because of developments in Western Europe, not in Byzantium. During the final centuries of the Middle Ages, Aristotelian modes of knowledge and investigation came to dominate all the great universities and to shape the programs of education for all the learned professions. As a consequence of this, Platonic and esoteric modes of knowledge and investigation were widely rejected by these same universities and professions, and could be cultivated only outside of these institutions. Although the Renaissance challenged the dominance of Aristotle in the schools and professions, its challenge was only partly successful (chiefly in the liberal arts). Soon the Reformation and Counter-Reformation developed their own competing Protestant and Catholic forms of Aristotelian scholasticism. Also, from the late Middle Ages onward, the recovery of Roman law encouraged the development of powerful judicial institutions designed to investigate and repress all forms of deviance and dissidence. Individual or uncommon kinds of spirituality or → mysticism that had long been unchallenged now came to be severely repressed by the newly codified Protestant and Catholic orthodoxies, and this repression continued until the Enlightenment, which had its own radical views on the separation between Church and State. Despite its strong anti-ecclesiastical tendencies, the Enlightenment continued to reject Platonic modes of knowledge – along with → magic, occult philosophy [→ occult / occultism] and esoteric studies – as inconsistent with its own Cartesian principles, severely criticizing such things as works of deceit, delusion and folly. From this time onward, Western esotericism could only be cultivated as a radical challenge to the schools and professions, as a kind of counter-epistemology.

In Byzantium, however, everything was on a much smaller scale, especially during the latter centuries of its independence. Its schools and professions were less developed as institutions, Aristotle was never strongly privileged over Plato, and the line between Church and State was never as sharply drawn as it had long been in the West. Only among the very few Byzantine intellectuals who studied Hellenic esotericism after the sixth century does there seem to have been anything remotely like the Western impulse toward a counter-culture. It is because of this likeness that we shall examine Hellenic esotericism first.

4. HELLENIC ESOTERICISM IN BYZANTIUM

Hellenic esotericism drew its inspiration from the same Greek authors, texts and practices that originally nourished Western esoteric studies: from Plato, the pre-Byzantine Neoplatonists such as Plotinus, Porphyry and Iamblichus, the *Chaldaean Oracles*, the *Corpus Hermeticum* and the other writings ascribed to → Hermes Trismegistus, astrologers such as Ptolemy, and alchemists such as Theosebia and → Zosimos of Panopolis. In another key, it also used manuals of divination [→ Divinatory Arts], books of omens, treatises on the construction of → amulets and talismans, the recipes of the *Kyranides*, and even a few texts of demonic ritual magic such as *Solomon's Magical Treatise* ('Αποτελεσματικὴ πραγματεία Σαλομῶντος) a Greek work related to the Western *Clavicula Salomonis*), and the *Testament of Solomon*.

From the late fourth through the sixth century, of course, many highly educated Greeks not only remained pagan, but also studied the above-mentioned texts (and other texts of the same sort that have now been lost). Among these men and women were Maximus of Ephesus and his disciple the Emperor Julian, Plutarch the Neoplatonist and his daughter Asclepigeneia, and finally Proclus (cf. Marinus, *Vita Procli* 28). During those few centuries it was still lawful to be pagan in Byzantium, and pagans still could and did cultivate Hellenic esotericism, or even practice theurgy, without having to worry overmuch about the Church's censure.

Even after the sixth century, of course, some of these traditions survived in attenuated form, generally among less well educated Byzantines, who did not always know which notions and ideas about demons had been accepted by the Orthodox Church, and which had been rejected; or which exorcisms and small rites were permitted, which forbidden. Thus there arose what Richard Greenfield has termed 'alternative traditions of belief and practice' about demons, in contrast to the well-defined 'standard tradition' of the Orthodox Church; there are also alternative traditions for other rites and rituals. These alternative traditions, of course, were not clearly distinguished from the standard tradition by the masses, but what may surprise is the extent (as Greenfield has shown) to which even educated Byzantines combined the standard and alternative traditions during the last centuries of Byzantine independence. However, this was simply a matter of ignorance or confusion, not a deliberate foray into forbidden territory. Deliberate forays into forbidden territory remained rare, even in the late Byzantine period.

No more than a handful of named Byzantines are known to have made a serious study of Hellenic esotericism after the final repression of paganism in the 6th century. The best known are Michael Psellus in the eleventh century and Georgios Gemistos Plethon in the 15th. However, there must have been others whose names have not come down to us, but for whom the various extant manuscripts of the relevant Greek texts were copied during the last centuries of Byzantine independence.

Michael Psellus (1018-1081) was one of the greatest polymaths in all Byzantine history, even serving for a time as a sort of philosopher-in-residence to the Imperial court. His surviving works treat history, law, rhetoric, logic, Platonic philosophy, theology – and include not quite a dozen short theoretical tracts on demonology, the *Corpus Hermeticum*, the *Chaldaean Oracles* and theurgy! His principal sources seem to have been various works (some now lost) by Porphyry, Iamblichus and Proclus on these subjects. Indeed, Iamblichus's long work *On the Mysteries of the Egyptians* may owe its survival to Psellus's efforts, for he appears to have read it, and all extant manuscripts appear to descend from a single manuscript (now lost) that had been copied during or not long after his lifetime and also contained some of his treatises on esoteric themes. Yet despite his esoteric interests, Psellus remained thoroughly Christian in his own eyes, and in some of his writings justified such studies from a Christian perspective.

Georgios Gemistos Plethon (ca. 1360-1452) had many of the same esoteric interests as Psellus, but pursued them to a much more radical conclusion, for in his old age he went so far as to argue in favor of restoring Neoplatonic paganism and theurgy in place of Christianity. The work in which he made his strongest arguments for this, *On Laws*, was burned shortly after his death by order of Patriarch Gennadius II Scholarius, but significant fragments of it have survived (thanks in part to extracts made during Plethon's lifetime by several interested friends and students). Here and in other writings Plethon displays considerable interest in the *Chaldaean Oracles*, but the only source that he has for them is one of Psellus's commentaries on them. By the 15th century almost every earlier source – not only the complete *Chaldaean Oracles* themselves, but also various Neoplatonic commentaries on them – seems to have been lost.

When Plethon was almost 80 years old, he attended the great ecclesiastical council that met at Ferrara and Florence in 1438-1439. Although his impact on the council's proceedings was relatively slight, he was able to meet a number of Florentine scholars and statesmen, and to impress them greatly with his passion for Plato and the Neoplatonists. Cosimo de' Medici's Platonic Academy owes something to Plethon's inspiration, as does the program of Latin translations from the Greek that Cosimo de' Medici commissioned from → Marsilio Ficino. Ficino's translations, it should be noted, included the works of Plato and Plotinus, the *Corpus Hermeticum*, Iamblichus's *On the Mysteries of the Egyptians* (to which were appended translations of several short works by Porphyry, Proclus and Michael Psellus), and two of the works of pseudo-Dionysius the Areopagite (*The Divine Names* and *The Mystical Theology*) – in short, many of the most important Greek foundation texts of Western esotericism.

5. Orthodox Christian Esotericism in Byzantium

Although Hellenic esotericism developed somewhat in opposition to the prevailing norms of Byzantine culture, Orthodox Christian esotericism developed very much in agreement with these same norms, in sharp contrast to Western esotericism since the Renaissance. As noted above, this contrast owes much to specific developments in the cultural history of Western Europe. Yet the ease with which Orthodox Christian esotericism accommodated itself to the norms of Byzantine culture has a lot to do with certain characteristic features of the Orthodox Church, in particular, with some specific patterns of Byzantine liturgy and worship, with the privileged position that apophatic theology is given over cataphatic theology, and with the doctrine of *theosis*, or deification. We must consider these three points as we seek to present Orthodox Christian esotericism in its own terms.

One of the most significant characteristics of the Orthodox Church, for our purposes, is that a priest does not celebrate the eucharist by or for himself alone, apart from any congregation. This is a point of eucharistic theology and canon law. However, it is also a matter of simple necessity, for the worship of the Orthodox Church in all its complex fullness is the cooperative work of several different classes of people, lay as well as ordained – priests, deacons, rectors, singers, laity, and so forth – and the prescribed texts are scattered among a considerable number of liturgical books, several of which must be used together during any service. In the course of an entire year's worship, most of the texts in these various books must be woven together in a very complicated pattern. This pattern, moreover, changes somewhat from year to year according to the date of Easter, which moves back and forth along a range of thirty-five consecutive days according to a complex cycle that lasts 532 years from start to finish.

Instead of liturgical work, what the Orthodox Christian – whether a priest or not – does in solitude is to pray. Even though a near-by church may happen to be unlocked and empty, the traditional place for private prayers remains one's home, one's room or one's monastic cell. Even a parish priest – who is a married man – will use his home for this purpose, and a priest-monk will use his cell (in the Orthodox Churches most monks are not priests).

There is nothing, therefore, anywhere in the traditional practice of the Orthodox Church that corresponds very well to a Catholic priest as he celebrates a Low Mass by himself from a Missal, or as he reads his daily office from a Breviary in private, or as he offers up his personal prayers before a consecrated altar in solitude. This Catholic pattern has greatly influenced Western esoteric practices, which as often as not employs a consecrated altar before which initiates work their esoteric rituals in private and in a somewhat priestly manner. In Orthodox Christian esotericism, however, this priestly pattern played no role: rather, the dominant pattern was that of a solitary monk at prayer in his unadorned cell. In principle, therefore, Orthodox Christian esotericism does not need either ceremonies or ceremonial objects as foci for its practice. Additionally, it is an esotericism of solitude that one ideally practices by oneself, not in a group. It operates, therefore, without temples or lodges, and its practitioners are not quasi-priests, much less members of some esoteric priesthood or consecrated order that answers to a higher authority than any institutional church. Indeed, such a person is not part of any secret institution or organization at all, but just a simple Christian man or woman who seeks in solitude and silence to attain the most esoteric *mysteries* (μυστήρια) of all, which are also Divine.

However, these mysteries are ineffable (ἄρρητα), that is, they lie far beyond the power of any language to express. Indeed, they are incomprehensible, that is, they lie far beyond 'all things that can be perceived and understood (αἰσθητὰ καὶ νοητά), that are not or that are' (pseudo-Dionysius the Areopagite, *Mystica theologia* I.1), and must therefore be experienced by other means than words, concepts or even ordinary percepts. To express these other means, the same author says that they are to be attained 'in the hyper-luminous darkness

of a hidden silence' (*ibidem*). Indeed, he even says that they are 'beyond all being (οὐσία) and knowledge (γνῶσις)', a matter of θεοσοφία (theosophy) as well as of θεολογία (theology) (*ibidem*).

This kind of theology, which leads the reader upward by means of denials rather than affirmations, is called *apophatic* (from Greek ἀπόφασις, denial), in contrast to the other kind, cataphatic theology (from Greek κατάφασις, affirmation). The two kinds loosely correspond to what in the West are usually called *negative* and *positive* theology, but the correspondence is not exact. If the Catholic Church (especially since Thomas Aquinas) has favored an Aristotelian sort of positive theology, and has used negative theology mostly to supplement positive results, it it otherwise in the East. The Orthodox Church, much less wedded to Aristotelian modes of knowledge, has long delighted in apophatic theology. In this one point it favors the Neoplatonists, although it otherwise diverges enormously from them in matters of doctrine and practice.

The best way into this 'brilliant darkness of a hidden silence' is precisely specified in several works by Gregory of Sinai (ca. 1265-1346) and especially in an anonymous treatise of unknown age sometimes titled *The Three Methods of Prayer* (the latter treatise is attributed to Simeon the New Theologian, but is not by him). The tradition of practice expounded in these works is at least as old as the 4th century. In the 14th century it became, for a few decades, a subject of great controversy, which called forth the brilliant writings of Gregory Palamas (ca. 1296–1359) on the theory behind the practices. The tradition later came to be called *hesychasm*, derived from Greek ἡσυχία, *tranquility, quietness* and ἡσυχάζειν, to practice hesychia (despite the similarity in their names, there is no close relation betwen hesychasm and Western quietism).

The first of pseudo-Simeon's three methods of prayer demands the careful cultivation of what some esotericists now call the imaginal world. The second demands an equally careful withdrawal from this same imaginal world and from the senses and the mental processes that nourish it. These two methods are emphatically *not* recommended. On the one hand, the careful cultivation of the imaginal indeed results in sensible visions, but sensible visions are always delusions, simply because they are *sensible* (αἰσθητά). This method is sure to produce a visionary whose desires have been inflamed and whose heart is exalted, and very often it will derange him in the end. On the other hand, a careful withdrawal from the sensible and imaginal worlds produces false impressions of the opposite character, for which there is no good name in English: let us call them "certainties" for lack of a better term. These "certainties", in contrast to visions, derive their form and content from understanding (νόησις) rather than from sense-perception (αἴσθησις). Just as visions are delusions simply because they are sensible, so "certainties" are delusions simply because they are *understandable* (νοητά). Sense-perception (αἴσθησις) and understanding (νόησις) are equally dangerous, are equally productive of delusions, and equally need to be transcended (cf. pseudo-Dionysius the Areopagite, as quoted above).

The third of these methods, and the only one which is free from the dangers of these two kinds of delusion, requires neither that one cultivate the imaginal world in one's heart nor that one uproot it. Instead, one fills one's heart with attentiveness and constant prayer, which soon crowd out the imaginal entirely. If at first this constant prayer may be verbal, with repetition it becomes automatic and then it soon ceases to need words or images at all. It is this absence of words and images alone that prepares the heart for the ineffable mysteries that lie 'in the hyperluminous darkness of a hidden silence', and that constitute the theosophy 'beyond all being and knowledge', to use the words of pseudo-Dionysius the Areopagite (in this tradition of practice, as in the Old Testament, the *heart* is the site of human knowledge and understanding, the place where words, concepts and percepts operate).

If this sounds easy to do in principle, it is extremely hard in practice, and usually requires the assistance of an experienced guide. One should not undertake it at all until one has first learned how to be free of every anxiety and care, how to keep one's conscience wholly pure, and how to take no thought for anything worldly, not even one's own bodily comforts and discomforts. Having learned how to do these three things, one can begin one's practice of attentiveness and constant prayer, aided by a simple specified stable posture and method of regulated breathing. At first one experiences delusions of sense-perception and understanding. When these delusions have all finally been dispelled, one next experiences empty, heavy darkness (which, perhaps, may be regarded as the last delusion). Persevering in one's practice, this darkness is replaced at last by an experience beyond all understanding and sense-perception, beyond all words and images, beyond all concepts and percepts, beyond all previous experience of the body and mind. It is said to be an experience of something that may be called φῶς, *light*, but even that word is

greatly inadequate to convey what is experienced: pseudo-Dionysius the Areopagite has coined the word ὑπέρφωτος, hyperluminous, to refer to it (*Mysica theologia* I.1).

This experience transforms one completely, in a way that is precisely specified by the Orthodox Church. One undergoes a process that is called *theosis* (θέωσις) in Greek, a word which means *becoming God*, but may conveniently – yet somewhat misleadingly! – be rendered as *deification*. According to the blunt words of Athanasius the Great, the Word of God 'became man that we might become God' (Athanasius of Alexandria, *De incarnatione Verbi* 54; cf. Irenaeus of Lyon, *Adversus haereses* IV.38-39, V.praef.). This is the ultimate goal of human life, which every member of the Orthodox Church is allowed to pursue from birth to death: an esotericism that is wholly integrated into Byzantine culture.

It is these ineffable mysteries, this hyperluminous realm that lies 'beyond all being and knowledge', it is this precisely specified, difficult method of practice that opens the way into these mysteries and that realm, and finally it is this possibility of becoming God, that constitutes the open secret of Orthodox Christian esotericism – an esotericism that is freely offered to every inquirer. Despite the brevity and simplicity of the present summary, it is an extremely rich and subtle tradition of doctrine and practice, which cannot easily be rendered in any other language than its original Greek. It is also Byzantium's single most interesting contribution to the esoteric currents and traditions of the world.

Lit.: Karel Svoboda, *La démonologie de Michel Psellos*, Brno: Spisy filosofické fakulty Masarykovy University 22, 1927 ◆ Irénée Hausherr, "La méthode d'oraison hésychaste", *Orientalia Christiana* IX, Rome: Pontificum Institutum Orientalium Studiorum, 1927, 97-210 ◆ Vladimir Lossky, *The Mystical Theology of the Eastern Church*, London: James Clarke, 1957 [in French, 1944] ◆ S.S. Averincev, "Kujasneniju smysla nadpisi nad konxoj central'noj apsidy Sofii Kievskoj" [Toward the Clarification of the Sense of the Inscription over the Concha of the Central Apse of St. Sophia of Kiev], *Drevne-russkoe iskusstvo: Xudozhestvennaja kul'tura domongol'skoj Rusi* [Old Russian Art: The Artistic Culture of Pre-Mongol Russia], Moscow: Nauka, 1972, 25-49 ◆ Hans Lewy, *Chaldean Oracles and Theurgy* (1956), Paris: new ed. Études Augustiniennes, 1978 ◆ G.E.H. Palmer, Philip Sherrard & Kallistos Ware (transl.), *The Philokalia: The Complete Text*, London: Faber & Faber, 1979-1995 ◆ C.M. Woodhouse, *George Gemistos Plethon: The Last of the Hellenes*, Oxford: Clarendon Press, 1986 ◆ Richard P.H. Greenfield, *Traditions of Belief in Late Byzantine Demonology*, Amsterdam: Adolf M. Hakkert, 1988 ◆ Alexander P. Kazhdan *et al.* (eds.),

The Oxford Dictionary of Byzantium, New York/
Oxford: Oxford University Press, 1991 (*s.vv.* Chaldean
Oracles, Dionysios the Areopagite (pseudo-), Divina-
tion, Exorcism, Gregory Sinaites, Hesychasm, Hesy-
chia, Iamblichos, Incantation, Magic, Magicians,
Mysterion, Mysticism, Neoplatonism, Palamas (Gre-
gory), Plato, Plethon (George Gemistos), Plotinos, Por-
phyry, Proklos, Psellos (Michael), Solomon, Symeon the
Theologian, Theurgy) ♦ Kallistos Ware, *The Orthodox
Church* (1963), London/New York: new ed. Penguin,
1993 ♦ Antoine Faivre, *Access to Western Esotericism*,
New York: SUNY Press, 1994 ♦ Henry Maguire (ed.),
Byzantine Magic, Washington D.C.: Dumbarton Oaks,
1995.

ROBERT MATHIESEN

Cagliostro, Alessandro di (ps. of Giuseppe Balsamo), * 2.6.1743 (?) Palermo (Sicily), † 26.8.1795 San Leo (Rimini)

A legendary Italian adventurer and magus, the
self-styled Alessandro Count of Cagliostro first
appeared in London in 1776. He claimed to have
been born in a noble Italian family in 1749, and to
have been initiated into the highest esoteric secrets
by a Master Althotas in Malta. In London, he rapidly gained popularity for his accomplishments as a
healer, and was initiated into → Freemasonry in
1777. He also managed to make some powerful
enemies, who accused him of being none other than
Giuseppe Balsamo, an adventurer born in Palermo,
Sicily, on June 2, 1743, who had disappeared in
1775, when the Sicilian police were about to arrest
him as a professional con man. In 1777, Cagliostro
established in Naples a new Masonic rite, the High
Egyptian Freemasonry. As extraordinary a traveller as he was a healer, Cagliostro moved in the
1770s and 1780s from England to Italy, and from
the Netherlands to Germany, Poland, and Russia.

In France, he was befriended by Louis René
Edouard Cardinal de Rohan (1734-1803). This
friendship facilitated Cagliostro's introduction at
the Court of the French King Louis XVI (1754-
1793), from which circles a number of dignitaries
were initiated into his Egyptian Freemasonry, the
Supreme Council of which was established in Paris
in 1785. In the same year, however, Cardinal de
Rohan was arrested in connection with the infa-
mous affair of the diamond necklace. The Cardinal,
more naive than dishonest, had been duped by
Countess Jeanne de La Motte (1756-1791) into
believing that Queen Marie Antoinette (1755-
1793) wanted him to purchase, on her behalf, a
diamond necklace of enormous value. The jewels
were subsequently stolen, and Cagliostro was
accused of being La Motte's accomplice. He was

arrested in 1785 together with Serafina Feliciani
(1754-1794), a young and beautiful Italian whom
Cagliostro claimed was his wife, the "Countess of
Cagliostro". The *affaire du collier*, about which not
everyone was convinced that Marie Antoinette was
completely blameless, played a role in the run-up to
the French Revolution.

Eventually, both Cardinal de Rohan and the
Cagliostros were found innocent at the 1786 trial,
although they both fell from favour, and were
counselled by the King himself to keep a low
profile. Increasingly controversial, Cagliostro lost
many followers, and tried to revive his Egyptian
Freemasonry in England, Germany, and Italy. In
1789, he was persuaded that Rome would be a
promising seat for Egyptian Freemasonry (the Vatican's prohibition of Freemasonry notwithstanding), and that he would probably be protected there
by the Order of Malta, amongst which he had some
friends and followers. In Rome, Cagliostro also
met Serafina's parents. He kept his distance from
them, however, because they were not the kind of
people a Count was supposed to associate with.
This upset both Serafina's family and the "Countess of Cagliostro" herself, who ended up writing to
the Pope and co-operating with the Papal police
who, in the meantime, were investigating Cagliostro as a Freemason and a heretic. After the French
Revolution, Rome's police were particularly nervous, and Cagliostro was arrested on December 27,
1789. Serafina, who would ultimately be Cagliostro's main accuser at the trial, did not escape
arrest herself; she was taken into custody at the
Convent of Saint Apollonia, where she underwent
a mild form of imprisonment until her premature death in 1794.

Cagliostro was found guilty in 1791 both of
Freemasonry and of heresy, as well as of past petty
crimes committed under the name of Giuseppe Balsamo. On April 7, 1791, a death sentence was
imposed on him, but Pope Pius VI (1717-1799),
following the recommendation of the Court's large
majority, commuted the sentence to life imprisonment in the fortress of San Leo, near Rimini. Conditions in the dreaded fortress-prison were extremely
harsh, and Cagliostro's physical and mental health
quickly deteriorated. He was a frequent victim of
hallucinations but, nonetheless, stubbornly refused, right to the end, to admit guilt and be converted. After five years of imprisonment, he died
at 3 a.m. on August 26, 1795. That, in any case, is
what the official documents said, but Cagliostro's
legend was so persistent that many did not believe
he was really dead. In fact, it was rumoured in certain occult and Theosophical milieus well into the

19th century that no prison could ever hold Cagliostro and that he was still alive as an immortal and ascended master. Followers also refused to believe that Cagliostro was actually Giuseppe Balsamo, but many contemporary historians would disagree with them.

Cagliostro's legend has been perpetuated in countless novels and several movies. He shows up frequently in popular literature, and even the immensely popular Arsène Lupin (the gentleman-thief created by French novelist Maurice Leblanc, 1864-1941) crossed swords with a Countess of Cagliostro, a fictional daughter of the adventurer. It is much more difficult to establish exactly how much the historical Cagliostro really contributed to modern Western esoteric tradition. He did not write much; during his lifetime, he only published ten memoirs in defence of various accusations made against him, none of them particularly rich in esoteric details. Marc Haven (pseudonym of medical doctor Emmanuel Lalande, 1868-1926) collected Cagliostro's rituals of High Egyptian Freemasonry and the related "catechisms", published in their most complete form only in 1948, after Haven's death. Most rituals were probably written down in 1784, when Cagliostro was in Lyon, France. Not everything here is original work by Cagliostro, since he liberally included portions of earlier rituals of high degree Freemasonry, a movement flourishing in 18th century France and Germany.

Different rituals were intended for men and women. Central tenets in the rituals included the existence of God and the immortality of the soul (firmly placing Cagliostro in the spiritualist camp within 18th century Masonic controversies, against rationalists and atheists). There was also a concept of the fall from grace of human beings, originally spiritual, into the darkness of the material world, and the need for a restoration. This restoration comprised three stages: spiritual, intellectual, and physical. Spiritual restoration would be achieved through charity and the love of God, although Cagliostro spoke of a "natural religion" and an "eternal Christianity" which was more kabbalistic than it was Christian in the conventional sense of the word. Intellectual restoration meant that humans could enter the "sanctuary of nature" through a "natural philosophy" (in the German sense of *Naturphilosophie*, and including → alchemy), theurgy, and a technique for invoking the names of God. Cagliostro also recommended the use of a small child ("dove" or "pupil"), who would gaze into a water mirror and obtain visions, which were then interpreted by the initiated. Finally, mention was made of a mysterious physical restoration,

which would grant the magus some visible advantages, but also carried a symbolic meaning.

Thrice restored, the initiated became an "elected master", capable of prodigious facts of both theurgy and healing. The initiated could also transfer powers magically to his or her own pupils. As a consequence, in Cagliostro's system, the members of High Egyptian Freemasonry themselves possessed the power to heal and to perform the evocation of various spirits, but these powers were derivative and dependent on their continuing link with the order's "Grand Copthe" (i.e. Cagliostro himself). As for Cagliostro, his powers were not presented as natural abilities, but as coming from God.

Marc Haven, whose interpretation of Cagliostro was mostly Christian and mystical, regarded his two "quarantines", or magical retreats of forty days, as the weakest part of the Italian magus' system. The 19th and 20th century occult milieu has been enormously influenced by them, however, and claimed that the quarantines were regarded by Cagliostro and his immediate disciples as his *Arcana Arcanorum*, or greatest secrets. The first of the two quarantines was a magical retreat of forty days devoted to rituals and prayers. After thirty-three days, the retreatant would begin to 'enjoy the favours of visible communications with the seven primeval angels and know the seals and the numbers of these immortal Entities'. After the fortieth day, he or she received the first 'Pentagon, that is the virgin paper, on which the primeval angels place their numbers and seals', together with seven other 'secondary Pentagons on which only one of the seven angels has placed its seal'. Through the Pentagons, the retreatant 'commands the immortals in the name of God', with the 'effect to bind or to command the aerial spirits, and to effectuate many wonders and miracles'. This constitutes a typical theurgical ritual; Cagliostro's aim was to 'obtain the Pentagon and become morally perfect'. Although it also included original elements, parts of it were derived from the German Order of the Gold- und Rosenkreuz and from its schism (or, according to others, its "inner circle") known as the Order of the → Asiatic Brethren, founded by Baron Hans Heinrich von Ecker-und-Eckhoffen (1750-1790). The evocation of angels, or "guardian angels", on the other hand was quite common in 18th century occult movements. It may be concluded that Cagliostro's *Arcana Arcanorum*, in the first meaning of the term, included the theurgical evocation of one or more angels through talismans, seals, pentagons, and other techniques.

In the second quarantine, the second forty days, the intention was to 'become physically [rather than morally] perfect'. Although the texts of Cagliostro's quarantines in Manuscript No. 245 of the Biblioteca Nazionale in Rome, and in the version conserved at the library of Musée Calvet in Avignon, include some variants, the second quarantine in both versions required the retreatant to retire to a secluded place in order to 'seriously fast'. On the seventeenth day, he or she 'gives a small emission of blood' and 'begins to take certain white drops, that one cannot explain what they are made of', increasing the dose until on the thirty-second day, when, with 'another small emission of blood', the retreatant 'begins to take the first grain of *Materia Prima*'. The next day, 'a second grain of *Materia Prima* will produce a strong fever or delirium, and will cause the retreatant to loose his skin, hair and teeth'. After other rituals and practices, on the thirty-sixth day, the last grain of *Materia Prima* 'will cause the hair, teeth and skin to grow back', until the fortieth day when the retreatant 'returns home rejuvenated and perfectly recreated'.

All this might well seem, even to admirers of Cagliostro, an extremely bizarre practice destined, above all, to create sensation – an attitude not at all alien to the Italian magus. In reality, however, this is not the case. When we consider the second quarantine historically, with reference to its antecedents in the German Gold- und Rosenkreuz and within the context of a broader magical tradition (although some unclarities remain about it) it becomes possible to interpret the ritual at various levels. In fact the Gold- und Rosenkreuz, in a text entitled *Thesaurus Thesaurorum* (dated 1580, but certainly more recent), propagated a similar ritual. This, in turn, was interpreted (and probably practiced) in two different ways. At the level of "laboratory" alchemy, a "philosopher's stone" is obtained from the alchemical distillation of one's own blood, adding other components (in the *Thesaurus*, gold and urine), and consuming the result in the form of grains or drops. At the second level, of "internal" or sexual alchemy, the "laboratory" is the magician's body, and the main component is the male semen. Whether Cagliostro personally taught and practised both techniques is unclear, but certainly the text of the second quarantine makes sense only within the context of an already-existing occult tradition, and it was interpreted in both ways in the 19th and 20th century.

In the history of modern magical movements, Cagliostro's *Arcana Arcanorum*, as understood by a subsequent magical tradition in which the Italian magus is venerated as the founder, stands for three different things. Firstly, it indicates a theurgical system of evocation, by use of various techniques, of the Holy Guardian Angels, or other angels. Secondly, it means a practice of laboratory alchemy, in which dew drops, blood, gold and urine were variously combined. Thirdly, it means a practice of inner alchemy, i.e. of sex magic.

Cagliostro ultimately taught (to the obvious annoyance of his Catholic critics) that immortality was not for everybody. His system proposed a form of self-redemption in which the magical will of a person captured his or her own immortality, and achieved eternal life. It is here, rather than simply in his tragical larger-than-life adventures, that lies Cagliostro's continual fascination.

Lettre du comte de Cagliostro au peuple anglais pour servir de suite à ses mémoires, n.e.: Paris, 1786 ♦ *Lettre au peuple français, traduction d'une lettre écrite à M. . . . par M. le comte de Cagliostro, de Londres, le 20 juin 1786*, n.e.: Paris, 1789 ♦ *Mémoire pour le comte de Cagliostro, accusé, contre M. le Procureur général, accusateur*, Paris: Lottin, 1786 ♦ *Mémoire pour le comte de Cagliostro, demandeur, contre M.e Chesnon, et le Sieur de Launay, gouverneur de la Bastille*, Paris: Lottin, 1786 ♦ *Requête au Parlement des chambres assemblées signifiée le 24 février 1786 par le comte de Cagliostro*, n.e.: Paris, 1786 ♦ *Requête à joindre au mémoire du comte de Cagliostro*, n.e.: Paris, 1786 ♦ *Réponse à la pièce importante dans l'affaire De Launay*, Paris: Lottin, 1787 ♦ *Requête au Roi pour le comte de Cagliostro contre MM. Cheson et De Launay*, Paris: Lottin, 1787 ♦ *Deuxième requête au Roi pour le comte de Cagliostro contre M. Chesnon*, Paris: Lottin, 1787 ♦ *Rituel de la Maçonnerie égyptienne* (annoté par le Dr. Marc Haven et précédé d'une introduction de Daniel Nazir), Nice: Éditions des Cahiers Astrologiques, 1948.

Lit.: Marc Haven, *Le Maître inconnu: Cagliostro. Étude historique et critique sur la haute magie*, Paris: Dorbon-Aîné, 1912 ♦ [B. Marty], *Le Comte de Cagliostro* (catalogue of the exhibition organized by "Les Amis du Prince Noir"), Les Baux de Provence: Le Prince Noir, 1989 ♦ Denyse Dalbian, *Le Comte de Cagliostro*, Paris: Robert Laffont, 1983 ♦ Massimo Introvigne, "Arcana Arcanorum: Cagliostro's Legacy in Contemporary Magical Movements", *Syzygy: Journal of Alternative Religion and Culture* 1:2 (Spring 1992), 117-135 ♦ *Presenza di Cagliostro* (Proceedings of the Conference in San Leo, June 1991), Bologna: Centro Editoriale Toscano, 1994 ♦ Klaus H. Kiefer (ed.), *Cagliostro: Dokumente zu Aufklärung und Okkultismus*, Munich: C.H. Beck, 1991.

MASSIMO INTROVIGNE

Cainites

The Cainites are presumed adherents of a Christian gnostic sect named by several of the church fathers. They are associated with "Ophians" or → "Ophites" by Clement of Alexandria (*Stromateis*,

VIII, 17), Hippolytus (*Refutatio*, VIII, 20), and Origen (*Contra Celsum*, III, 13), but these authors provide no discussion of the sect's teachings. Tertullian (*De baptismo*, 1) refers to a female 'viper of the Cainite heresy' trying to subvert Christian baptism. The author of Pseudo-Tertullian's treatise, *Adversus omnes haereses*, a 3rd-century document possibly based on a lost work by Hippolytus, is the first to describe a system of teachings explicitly associated with the heresy of the Cainites (c. 2). But his account is manifestly dependent upon a system of teachings earlier described by Irenaeus (*Adversus Haereses*, I, 31, 1-2). Irenaeus adds to his account of the system of the "Gnostics" (I, 29) related material ascribed to unnamed 'others' (I, 30), to which he then appends a short account of beliefs held by still 'others' (*alii*, I, 31, 1).

These "others" are said to regard Cain as a superior being and to confess such other biblical anti-heroes as Esau, Korah, and the Sodomites, all of whom were protected by the intervention of Sophia. Judas is honored for accomplishing the 'mystery of the betrayal', and they use a document called the *Gospel of Judas*. Irenaeus claims to have access to writings of theirs that promote the destruction of 'Hystera' (the womb), associated with the creation of heaven and earth. They are also alleged to advocate the libertine behavior also attributed to the → Carpocratians (cf. *Adv. Haer*, I, 25). Each misdeed is associated with an angel ceremonially invoked, which they refer to as 'perfect knowledge'. This account, in context, can be taken as referring to a sub-group of the "Gnostics" earlier described by Irenaeus.

It is the author of the aforementioned Latin treatise, falsely attributed to Tertullian, who expressly attributes such teachings to a special group of heretics called "Cainites". In chapter 2 of his work, he gives an account of heretics he identifies as "Ophites", partially summarizing Irenaeus' account of the unnamed 'others' in *Adv. Haer*. I, 30. Later in the same chapter he refers to 'another heresy', that of the Cainites. In his account of the Cainites he closely follows Irenaeus (*Adv. Haer*. I, 31, 1), but he leaves out the material beginning with the reference to Hystera (I, 31, 2). Instead, he elaborates on the motivations of the betrayer Judas, one group claiming that Judas betrayed Christ because he was subverting the truth, the other saying that Judas betrayed Christ so that human salvation could be effected.

Epiphanius of Salamis has a lengthy description of the Cainites (*Panarion* 38, 1, 1-3, 5), manifestly based on Irenaeus and Pseudo-Tertullian, to which the bishop has added numerous vituperations.

Only a few extra details emerge: the Cainites honor the wicked, and repudiate the good. Cain's superiority to Abel is based on his having been begotten of a higher power. The angels invoked by the Cainites are the same ones who blinded → Moses, and protected Korah, Dathan, and Abiram (Num. 16). They use a book called the *Ascension of Paul*, which is also used by the "Gnostics" (or "Borborites", cf. *Pan.* 26).

Two questions emerge from these patristic accounts: 1. Is there any primary evidence that Christian heretics, of whatever sort, honored the biblical Cain? 2. Was there ever a sect of people who called themselves "Cainites"? In answering the first question, the primary evidence to which we must turn consists of that found in the Coptic sources making up the so-called "Nag Hammadi Library". It turns out that all of those texts that mention Cain at all portray him in a negative light: the so-called "Sethian Gnostic" texts [→ Sethians] (*Apocryphon of John* II, 10, 34; 24, 8-25 and parallels; *Hypostasis of the Archons* II, 91,12-28; *Gospel of the Egyptians*, III, 58, 15; cf. *Apocalypse of Adam*, V, 66,25-28 [Cain unnamed]), and Valentinian texts [→ Valentinus and Valentinians] (*Valentinian Exposition*, XI, 38, 24-27; cf. *Gospel of Philip*, II, 61, 5-10 [Cain unnamed]). Of these the passage comprising *Ap. John* II, 24, 8-25 requires further elaboration. There we read that the 'chief archon' Yaldabaoth, after the banishment of Adam and Eve from paradise, seduced Eve and begot in her two sons: Eloim-Cain, and Yave-Abel. The demonic origin of the biblical murderer Cain (but not of Abel) is a Gnostic interpretation of a Jewish exegetical tradition, interpreting the difficult passage in Genesis 4:1, the Hebrew text of which can be translated: 'I have gotten a man, namely Yahweh'. The Aramaic *Targum Ps-Jonathan* Gen. 4:1-2 contains an ancient exegetical tradition to the effect that Cain was the product of a liaison between the angel of death Sammael and Eve, who proclaims, 'I have acquired a man, the angel of the Lord'. The aforementioned passage in *Ap. John* reflects this Jewish tradition, but reinterprets it, although still presenting Cain in a negative light.

There is, however, one text which presents Cain in a positive light. The treatise *On the Origin of the World* contains an interesting passage which narrates the birth of 'the Instructor', who then enlightens Adam and Eve in paradise. The reference here is to the serpent of Genesis 3. The text goes on to state that Eve is the 'first virgin', who bore a son without her husband. In a hymnic passage featuring Eve, several 'I am' sayings end with the exclamation, 'I am the process of becoming; yet I have borne a man as lord' (II, 114,14-15). In this passage Cain and the 'Instructor'-serpent are virtually identified, and Cain is honored as the lordly revealer of gnosis. Thus, it turns out that there is primary Gnostic evidence for associating Cain with the gnosis requisite for salvation. Moreover, the specific association of Cain with the biblical serpent, in a positive evaluation, is found in Hippolytus' description of the teachings of the "Peratae" (*Refutatio* V, 16, 8-9).

As to the second question, whether there ever was a sect of people who called themselves "Cainites", a complete analysis of all of our evidence must lead to a negative answer. The "Cainite" sect is, finally, an invention of the church fathers. There were evidently some Gnostics who honored Cain, but none who called themselves "Cainites".

A. Rousseau & L. Doutreleau (eds.), *Irénée de Lyon: Contre les Hérésies*, vol. 1 (SC 264), Paris: Les Éditions du Cerf, 1979 (with French translation); Engl. translations: W. Foerster (ed.), *Gnosis: A Selection of Gnostic Texts*, vol. 1, Oxford: Clarendon Press, 1972, 41-43; B. Layton, *The Gnostic Scriptures: A New Translation with Annotations and Introductions*, Garden City, New York: Doubleday & Co., 1987,181 ♦ M. Marcovich (ed.), *Hippolytus: Refutatio omnium haeresium* (Patristische Texte und Studien, 25), Berlin/New York: De Gruyter, 1986 ♦ A. Kroymann (ed.), [Ps. Tertullian] *Adversus omnes haereses* (CC, ser. Lat. II, originally edited in CSEL 47), Turnhout 1954; Engl. translation: A Roberts & J. Donaldson (eds.), *The Ante-Nicene Fathers: Translations of the Fathers down to A.D. 325*, vol. 3, Grand Rapids, Michigan: repr. Wm. B. Eerdmans, 1963, 650-651 ♦ K. Holl (ed.), *Epiphanius II: Panarion haer. 34-64*, 2nd rev. ed. by J. Dummer, Berlin: Akademie Verlag, 1980; Engl. translation: F. Williams, *The Panarion of Epiphanius of Salamis, Book I (Sects 1-46)*, Leiden: E.J. Brill, 1987, 248-253 ♦ J.M. Robinson (ed.), *The Nag Hammadi Library in English* (3rd rev. ed.), Leiden: E.J. Brill, 1987.

Lit.: B. Pearson, "Cain and the Cainites", in: idem, *Gnosticism, Judaism, and Egyptian Christianity*, Minneapolis: Fortress Press, 1990, 95-107 ♦ C. Scholten, "Kainiten", *RAC* XIX (2001) [= fasc. 152, 2000], 972-982.

BIRGER A. PEARSON

Camillo, Giulio, * ca. 1480 Portogruaro (?), † 15.5.1543 Milan

Camillo was born around the year 1480 in Friuli, a region in the northeastern part of Italy, perhaps in the town of Portogruaro. It seems that the family originally came from Croatia (according to → Francesco Patrizi, both he and his father were also called "Delminio" after the ancient Dalmatian town of Delminium). After pursuing his literary studies in Venice and Padua, Camillo taught rhetoric and logic in several towns in Friuli and later in Bologna; he also spent long periods in Rome and Genoa. He is best known for his "theatre of memory" (see below), an ambitious project for the construction of a universal memory system [→ Mnemonics] which won the admiration of intellectuals all over Europe, although it eventually also became the object of criticism and ridicule. Francis I of France expressed an interest in the project, and so Camillo set off for France in 1530. The king agreed to finance the realisation of Camillo's theatre on the condition that the author reveal its secret to him alone. Thus encouraged, Camillo went to Venice to commission a scale model of his theatre in wood, which was seen and described by a friend of Erasmus, Viglio Zuichem, in February 1532. Between 1533 and 1538 Camillo remained in France, apart from trips to Italy as part of the entourage of Cardinal Jean of Lorraine in 1534 (for the election of Pope Paul III) and in 1536. As time passed and his remarkable theatre failed to materialise, however, Camillo began to lose favour at court; his enemies multiplied as the king's interest in the interminable project waned. In 1538, advanced in years, tired and in ill health, Camillo left France and returned home to Italy, hoping to find a new sponsor for his theatre. An attempt some years earlier to gain an invitation to the court of the new lord of Ferrara, Duke Ercole II d'Este, had already failed. Finally Camillo managed to attract the interest of Alfonse d'Avalos, the governor of Milan, and in 1543 he entered into his service. The universal theatre was destined never to be realised, however, for Camillo died unexpectedly on May 15th in Milan.

During his lifetime, Camillo had a wide circle of friends and admirers: artists such as Titian, Lorenzo Lotto and Pordenone, the architect Sebastiano Serlio, with whom he had maintained close ties, and writers such as Ludovico Ariosto, Pietro Aretino and Torquato Tasso, all of whom praised him in their works. We have seen that Camillo had began his career as a master of rhetoric, and he shared the classicist ideals of his friend Pietro Bembo (1470-1547), who believed that in order to write well one must imitate the great authors – Cicero and Virgil if one was writing in Latin, and Petrarch and Boccaccio if one was writing in Italian. According to Camillo, the imitation of great literary models was an attempt to capture the idea of eloquence that was present, even if in imperfect form, in the works of the greatest masters.

Thus, rhetoric would be transformed into a metaphysical art which could teach the user how to ascend from the particular to the universal and descend from the universal to the individual. Whoever mastered this art of rhetoric would be able to manipulate words and rhetorical artifices at will and subject them to an infinite variety of transformations. Camillo included rhetoric among the three arts of metamorphosis, together with → alchemy (the art of transforming physical objects) and deification (the art of transforming the human mind into a divine one).

To imitate his literary models and to create variations upon them, Camillo applied a series of procedures based on two principles: the first was the use of topical places, a traditional component of both rhetoric and logic; and the second was the Spanish philosopher → Ramon Llull's *clavis universalis*. In his analysis of a literary model, Camillo tried to identify the device or artifice used and break it down into its separate parts, each one of which could lead the user back to an original universal category (to *locus*, topical place). At this point the author would have before him all the possible combinations of arguments and artifices that might be used for his text. Thus, literary procedures also had a metaphysical dimension, and both were closely intertwined with the techniques of rhetoric.

From a philosophical point of view Camillo was fundamentally a syncretist; like → Pico della Mirandola, he was engaged in a search for the common elements that united different philosophical and religious traditions, the first principles that lay hidden between the lines of the text and which only a select few, versed in the neoplatonic, hermetic and kabbalistic traditions, were capable of reading. Camillo was less interested in abstract philosophical principles, however, than in the results that could be obtained by their application; the goal of his reinterpretation of philosophical traditions was to demonstrate that his theatre could actually work.

Camillo's theatre was conceived as a universal memory system, containing not only all the words and rhetorical artifices necessary to compose persuasive texts, but all of man's knowledge as well. He called it a "theatre" because its intent was to make visible the images which usually lay hidden in the mind. The basic scheme consisted of 49 loci generated by the permutation of two different orders; one acting in the vertical dimension (seven columns representing the seven planets); and one acting in the horizontal dimension (corresponding to the seven degrees of the cosmos). As the user passed from locus to locus and viewed the images placed in each, he could learn and "remember" the first principles of the cosmos, and see how they manifested themselves in the material world. The seven columns symbolised not only the planets but also seven of the ten Sefiroth, the secret names of God in the kabbalistic tradition. These passed across the seven degrees of the cosmos, and thus from the principles of the divine world to those of the natural world, of man and the arts and sciences. Camillo's theatre was designed to function on various levels: as a kind of data bank for those wishing to write poems or orations; as an easy-to-use encyclopaedia; or – on its most rarified and secret level – as a guide to the opus of alchemy and deification. We have seen that Camillo's theatre was never finished. We may read a summary description of it in his *Idea del theatro*, which was published posthumously (1550). To reconstruct the project in all of its parts and to understand its secret meanings, we must refer to several texts which have remained unedited for many centuries.

Giulio Camillo, *Della imitazione, Trattato delle materie che possono venir sotto lo stile dell'eloquente, La topica o vero della elocuzione*, in: Bernard Weinberg (ed.), *Trattati di poetica e retorica del Cinquecento*, vol. 1, Bari: Laterza, 1970, 159-186, 319-156, 357-408 ♦ idem, *L'idea del teatro e altri scritti di retorica*, Torino: RES, 1990 ♦ idem, *L'idea del teatro* (L. Bolzoni, ed.), Palermo: Sellerio, 1991

Lit.: Corrado Bologna, "Il *Theatro* segreto di Giulio Camillo: l'Urtext ritrovato", *Venezia Cinquecento: Studi di storia dell'arte e della cultura* 1 (1991), 217-274 ♦ Lina Bolzoni, *Il teatro della memoria: Studi su Giulio Camillo*, Padova: Liviana, 1984 ♦ Lina Bolzoni, *The Gallery of Memory: Literary and Iconographic Models in the Age of the Printing Press* (It. orig. 1995), Toronto: University of Toronto Press, 2001 ♦ Barbara Keller Dall'Asta, *Heilsplan und Gedächtnis: Zur Mnemologie des 16. Jahrhunderts in Italie*, Heidelberg: Universitätsverlag C. Winter, 2001, ch. 4 ♦ Paolo Rossi, *Logic and the Art of Memory: The Quest for a Universal Language* (It. orig. 1960), Chicago: The University of Chicago Press, 2000 ♦ Giorgio Stabile, "Camillo, Giulio, detto Delminio", in: *Dizionario biografico degli italiani* XVII, Roma: Istituto della Enciclopedia Italiana, 1974, 218-230 ♦ Mario Turello, *Anima artificiale: Il teatro magico di Giulio Camillo*, Aviani: Udine, 1993 ♦ Lu Beery Wenneker, *An Examination of "L'Idea del theatro" of Giulio Camillo, including an annotated translation, with special attention to his influence on emblem literature and iconography*, Ph.D. diss. University of Pittsburgh, 1970 ♦ Frances A. Yates, *The Art of Memory*, London: Routledge and Kegan Paul, 1966, chs. VI-VII.

LINA BOLZONI

Campanella, Tommaso, * 5.9.1568 Stilo (Calabria), † 21.5.1639 Paris

Tommaso Campanella, one of the most original philosophers of the 16th-17th centuries, tried to reconcile the natural philosophy of the Renaissance with a radical reform of the sciences and of society. He was born at dawn on September 5, 1568, at Stilo in Calabria (then under Spanish rule), to a very modest family: his father, Geronimo, was an illiterate cobbler. At fourteen, Tommaso decided to enter the Dominican Order because this seemed to him the best way to pursue his studies, for which he had shown a keen disposition from his earliest years. He gives rare glimpses of his youthful development in the *Praefatio* to his *Philosophia sensibus demonstrata*, written when he was not yet 21. Describing the period spent in the Dominican monasteries of Calabria, the young Campanella recalls how the Aristotelian teaching-texts seemed to him full of contradictions, and unable to offer convincing answers to the most important philosophical and metaphysical problems. Their reading had left him deeply unsatisfied, arousing in him more doubts than certainties. The teachers were unable to clear up his doubts, and the young student found himself in a parlous state of fear and loneliness, until the intuition dawned within him of a new philosophy, drawn not from books or from the minds of Aristotle and his commentators, but from the direct reading of the great "book of nature". He was accused of holding doctrines similar to those of a certain Telesio; but this judgment, intended as a severe censure, filled him with joy at having finally found a companion and a guide. He traveled to Cosenza, the home of Telesio, and was able to read the first edition of *De rerum natura iuxta propria principia*. From the first pages he felt the novelty and coherence of a doctrine which, in conformity with his own aspirations, derived its truth not from words written in books but from the direct examination of natural facts. Campanella was not able to meet Telesio in person (he had died in October 1588), but he paid homage to his bier in the cathedral and attached verses to the catafalque. It was an idealized encounter in which the young Dominican seemed to receive the spiritual legacy of the new philosophy; and in the sonnet no. 60 of the 89 poems which constitute the *Scelta di alcune poesie filosofiche* (1st ed. 1622), he did not fail to celebrate "Cosentine Telesio" who with his arrows had struck and slain Aristotle, the 'tyrant of the intellectuals', restoring to man the *libertas philosophandi* which is inseparable from the truth.

Campanella had written the eight disputations of the *Philosophia sensibus demonstrata* in the first eight months of 1589, to defend the Telesian philosophy from the attack on it by the Neapolitan jurist Giacomo Antonio Marta in his *Pugnaculum Aristotelis*. In his work, Campanella lays out a systematic criticism of Aristotle on the physical, cosmological, and metaphysical planes, in the light of the Telesian principles. These are integrated, in the first place, with motives derived from Plato's writings, from the Neoplatonic philosophers [→ Neoplatonism], and from the Hermetic tradition [→ Hermetic Literature] that had been made accessible through the Latin translation of → Marsilio Ficino; also with Campanella's knowledge of the medical works of Hippocrates and Galen, naturalists such as Pliny, atomists and Stoics – all the reading that had nourished him and rendered ever more intense his enormous appetite for knowledge. The *Philosophia* appeared in 1591 in Naples, to which Campanella had been transferred, residing in the palace of the Marchese Del Tufo. In the Viceroy's capital he was able to frequent aristocratic and intellectual society, especially the circle of Giovanni Battista Della Porta, author of celebrated works on natural → magic and physiognomy, whose palace was a place of pilgrimage for students from all over Europe. At Naples, however, the suspicions against Campanella grew, and in spring 1592 he was imprisoned in the convent of San Domenico, accused on the grounds that his exceptional knowledge had a diabolic origin, though the real imputation was that of supporting the "new" doctrines of Telesio against the scholastic and Aristotelian ones. Acquitted from the charges, before returning to Calabria Campanella went to Rome, then to Florence, where he was received cordially by the Grand Duke. However, the Duke did not confer on the young friar the hoped-for chair at a Tuscan university, having heard reports that were not altogether positive about him. During a stay at Bologna, the Inquisition caused the manuscripts of the works Campanella carried with him to be sequestered; he would see them again two years later in the Holy Office in Rome, when he was summoned to clear himself of the doctrines contained in them. Settling at Padua, he came to know Galileo, and this early meeting marked the beginning of a constant admiration and friendship for the scientist whose discoveries would contribute to the fall of the Aristotelian cosmos. There was no lack of disagreement between Campanella's and Galileo's doctrines, but as Campanella wrote in a late letter to Grand Duke Ferdinand II, 'the discord of intellects can cohabit with the concord of their wills'.

A fruitful period followed at Padua, as Campanella pursued his studies and wrote various works (all of them lost), until he became involved in another, more serious trial. He was arrested at the beginning of 1594, together with two friends, by order of the Inquisition. After a failed attempt to escape in the summer, he was transferred to the prison of the Roman Inquisition, where for some time the Florentine "heretic" Francesco Pucci and → Giordano Bruno had been incarcerated. In one of the sonnets of the *Scelta*, he compares the dark palace to 'Poliphemus's cavern', to the 'Labyrinth of Crete', and to the 'Palace of Atlas', in which, as though by fateful appointment, the free spirits meet who have abandoned the stagnant waters of conventional knowledge in order to venture boldly on the 'sea of truth'. Accused of having written a sonnet against Christ and a short atheistic work, *De tribus impostoribus* (which, he said, had been printed thirty years before he was born), and of having held Democritean doctrines, he was sentenced in 1595 'on the gravest suspicion of heresy' to make a solemn and public abjuration. At the end of 1597 he was consigned again to the Superiors of the Dominican Order, who enjoined him to return to Calabria.

On the return journey, Campanella spent some months in Naples, where he completed the *Epilogo magno*, in whose first five books he expounded his own system of natural philosophy, inspired by Telesian principles, while the sixth and last book treated ethics. The work, translated into Latin, became the *Physiologia*, the first of the four parts of the *Philosophia realis*, which would be published at Frankfurt in 1623; the other parts comprise *Ethica*, *Politica*, and *Oeconomica*, dealing with the conduct of home and family. The editions of Campanella's works which appeared at Frankfurt between 1617 and 1623, contributing greatly to his European reputation, were made possible thanks to the work of Tobias Adami, a German savant who during a stay in Naples between 1612 and 1613 had managed to make contact with the friar, then prisoner in the city jail, and had been given the manuscripts of his works.

The *Physiologia* develops Telesio's principles of natural philosophy, beginning with the affirmation that when the first Being, omnipotent, wisest and best, decided to create the world, defined as his 'statue' and 'image' of his infinite wealth, opened up a 'quasi-infinite' (*pene infinitum*) space in which to place it. This occurred at the beginning of that duration and vicissitude of things that we call Time, and which is the image of the Eternity from which it flows. Space, defined as 'primal substance,

or seat, or immobile and incorporeal capacity to receive every body', is homogenous ("high" and "low," "back" and "forward," "right" and "left" are human terms referring to located bodies). If the world did not exist, we would have to imagine it as void; but in fact it desires fullness and is invested with an attractive force such that it 'rejoices in sustaining beings' and abhors emptiness. The bodies, on their part, 'rejoice in mutual contact' and hate the void that separates them. In space, God collects matter, which is considered as a physical entity, lacking form, shape, and action, but fit to extend, divide, and unite itself and to take on every shape, just as wax can receive every seal. This is in clear contrast to Aristotle's and Averroes's conception, which defines matter as privation and a pure *ens rationis*. Campanella calls matter 'a second substance, the basis of forms, the passive principle of the composition of things'. Into this corporeal mass, God inserts heat and cold, two principles that are active and diffusive in themselves, incorporeal but unable to subsist without bodies. From their conflict – derived from the fact that each wants to dominate and occupy the greatest possible quantity of matter – originate the two first bodies or elements of the world: heaven, which is hottest, subtle, mobile, being formed from matter transformed into heat; and earth, made from matter rendered immobile, dark, and dense from cold. All the secondary beings take their origin from the fight between heaven and earth, heat and cold, and God uses the oppositions of the primal elements for the production of natural beings, which in their infinite multiplicity and diversity realize the infinite degrees of the primal, divine Idea.

Heaven, being unitary and not divided into spheres as in the traditional view, moves because it is hot, in virtue of its own intrinsic operation which conserves and vivifies it, without any need for recourse to extrinsic motivating intelligences. The motions of the heavenly bodies and the sun, extremely various and complex, transmit to the earth all these degrees of heat and light which constitute the essence of every single thing. In the light of these principles, Campanella explains every aspect of the natural world, from the celestial and meteorological phenomena to the formation of the waters, the constitution of minerals and that of plants, analyzing with particular attention animals and men. To explain the origin and the formation of these more complex organisms, he draws on a fundamental element of his philosophy: *spiritus*. This is made from material rendered extremely subtle by the solar heat; it is a sort of hot breath, which due to its subtlety and movement is capable of separating from the portion of matter in which it finds itself enclosed, and of acting upon it. Not being able to exhale from matter and return to heaven, as it would wish, the *spiritus* organizes and shapes matter from the inside in the best manner for its needs, and being aware of the dangers that threaten it from without, it constructs the bodily organs which are the instruments that guarantee its conservation and life.

On August 15, 1598, approaching his thirtieth birthday, Campanella returned to Stilo after a decade-long absence. The following year he became embroiled in the most dramatic events of his life, which would condition all the years to come. The reading of astrological [→ Astrology] and prophetic texts announcing a profound renewal of the Church; the appearance of signs in the heavens and of unusual natural events like eclipses, comets, earthquakes, invasions of locusts, torrential rains, and overflowing rivers; above all, the conditions of misery and injustice affecting the populace and the severe social and political disorder, convinced Campanella that with the end of the century there would come a period of tremendous changes. Thus a grand conspiracy was organized, of which he was the indisputed spiritual head, which proposed to turn the province into a republic, removing it from the tyranny of the King of Spain, while Campanella, regarded by his accomplices as a new legislator and Messiah, would promulgate 'new laws and restore every man to his natural liberty'. The plot failed at birth, for on August 10, 1599 it was denounced to the Spanish authorities by two of the conspirators. An army was immediately dispatched, leading to harsh repression. After frantic efforts to escape, Campanella was arrested, and in November four galleys reached the port of Naples laden with dozens of prisoners, some of them hanged to instill terror. Thus began the Neapolitan trials, whose course was much complicated by the double charge of rebellion and heresy against the accused, who were both laymen and ecclesiastics. In the 19th century the trials were reconstructed by Luigi Amabile, who has left an impressive documentation of these events that is still fundamental.

To avoid capital punishment, which could not be inflicted on the insane, Campanella resorted to the expedient of faking madness, which was ratified through the dreadful torture of the *veglia* [deprivation of sleep], which he evokes at the close of the *Città del sole* and in later pages, as proof of the freedom of the human spirit which cannot be forced or constrained even by the most extreme physical pressures. During his first period in prison he wrote his most famous short work, the *Città del sole*, in the form of a "poetic dialog" between one of Columbus's sailors and a knight, which has been seen both as the program of a failed insurrection and as its philosophical idealization. The work was published in Latin translation in 1623, in the Appendix to the third part of the *Philosophia realis* mentioned above, and in presenting it to the readers, Tobias Adami states that this ideal republic is superior to the model proposed by Plato in antiquity, or by Thomas More in recent times, because it is inspired by the great model of nature. In fact, the return to nature, understood as the expression of God's intrinsic "art" and wisdom, and the criticism of existing society, unjust and unhappy because divorced from that model, is the simplest and most convincing key to the reading of Campanella's utopia. It depicts a "political body" in which the parts are integrated so as to make a unitary organism, and the separate members, many and various according to their functions, are all coordinated for the common good. Political reflection is a primary and constant aspect of Campanella's thought, present from his youth until his last years of exile in Paris. He also treats other themes than those of utopia and prophecy, especially the relations between religion and politics, temporal and ecclesiastical power, and between the prospect of a universal monarchy and the reunification of humanity in 'one flock under one shepherd'. In his *Monarchia di Spagna* he emphasizes the universalist and providential function of the Catholic king, identified with the biblical Cyrus, liberator of the Church from the infidels and gatherer of the people in a single faith.

Campanella was sentenced to perpetual imprisonment in 1603, but in view of an exceptional astral event, the "great conjunction" of Jupiter and Saturn in the fiery sign of Sagittarius, he expected great changes and devoted himself to the practice of magic and demonic invocations, confident that he would soon be released. His hopes were dramatically disappointed. In June of the following year, after a plan of escape had been discovered, the prisoner was transferred to a harsher prison, the "pit" of Castel Sant'Elmo: an underground cell, damp and lightless, where he lived for the most dreadful years of his imprisonment. But it was from this darkness that came some of the most exalted and intense poetic compositions of that extraordinary songbook, the *Scelta*.

The composition of the *Senso delle cose e della magia* also dates from this period. Here Campanella expounds his vision of the natural world as a living organism whose single parts have life and sensibility. Every natural being aims at its own conservation, and to this end is endowed with "sense" according to various degrees and modalities. This sense is its capacity to distinguish what is positive and beneficial to its own life, which it thus pursues and seeks, from that which is perceived as negative and destructive, which is thus fled and avoided. Some beings, such as the heavenly bodies and light, possess a sense that is much more acute and pure than that of animals, while others, such as minerals and metals, have a more obtuse and obscure sense because of the weight of matter. As already said, the vital and cognitive functions in animal organisms are connected with the *spiritus*. Hot, mobile, passive, identified with the organic soul, the *spiritus* has its seat in the brain, whence it runs through the finest of nervous canals to fulfill its multiple vital and cognitive functions. As it enters, via the sense organs, into contact with external reality, it undergoes those modifications from which come all its passions and knowledge. All aspects of the cognitive process, from memory to → imagination, from discursive thought to the intellect itself, are attributable to the activity of the *spiritus*, which is capable of preserving the modifications and impressions it receives, of re-using them when similar situations occur, and of confronting and extending them.

The dimension of sensible knowledge is where the animal and the human levels can be compared, in order to learn their affinities and differences. Campanella rejoiced in the extraordinary powers of animals, which know how to achieve marvelous works and are endowed with forms of reasoning, language, natural prophecy, and perhaps even religiosity. But such analogies should not obfuscate or cast doubt on the difference and special quality of man, who is furnished with a *spiritus* far more refined and pure than the animal sort, capable of moving with agility between more spacious brain-cells, which allows him to construct far more complex chains of arguments. The true and radical difference between the two levels consists in the fact that man is also endowed with an incorporeal *mens*, divine in its origin, which constitutes and underlies his specific dimension and his excellence. His capacity to extend himself through thought and desire to infinity – and such a leap is not vain imagination, as Aristotle thought – proves that he is not the child of sun and earth alone, but of a pre-eminent and infinite cause. The connection of man with a supernatural world is confirmed by the fact that he can go beyond bodily possessions and the limits of natural self-preservation, turning, as philosopher and religious man, to higher possessions and ends. He can achieve higher forms of prophecy and ecstasy, not explainable by physiological or medical theories. Above all, man is endowed with a free will, thanks to which he can resist outside pressures, can value the objects of his choice, choosing the greater good even if no immediate advantage or utility results from it.

The fourth book of the *Senso delle cose* is devoted to natural magic. Della Porta, while listing the most curious occult properties of minerals, plants, and animals following the magical tradition, maintained that it is impossible to give a rational explanation for the relations of sympathy and antipathy, affinity and repulsion, that exist between natural entities. Campanella, on the contrary, proposes a re-reading and re-interpretation of this tradition in the light of the doctrine of the sense of things and of the *spiritus*. The magus is he who knows the specific quality of sense inherent in every entity, and is capable of using it in the appropriate way and of imposing specific alterations and passions on the *spiritus*. He knows how to potentialize the vital energies, suggesting food, drinks, ambiences, sounds, herbal and animal remedies which rejuvenate and increase them. He knows the secrets of generation and of diseases, and can arouse passions sufficient to achieve definite goals. Moreover, he knows how to explain strange phenomena such as the premonitions in dreams, seeing that the causes that prepare determined events are already present in the air (which is a shared "soul") and can be perceived before the events themselves occur. He knows the true and exact metamorphoses that take place in those who are bitten by a rabid dog, or in Apulian peasants bitten by tarantulas: the physical and psychological changes derive from the fact that the vital temperament in such unfortunates is hindered in its diffusion and dominance of their organism by the spirit of the animal which attacked them. Always resorting to the doctrine of sense, which in some cases may even persist in entities after their death, and to the capacity of the air to join persons and actions that are far apart and to preserve the passions in latent and dormant form, which can be reawakened on certain occasions, he can explain facts such as the bleeding of a corpse in the presence of its murderer. The same accounts for the possible efficacy of the "weapon salve", thanks to which it is believed possible to cure a wound by acting on the instrument that caused it, or the reason why (to cite a famous example repeated in every book on magic) a drum made of sheepskin shatters when a drum made of wolfskin is beaten, as an ancient terror reawakens in it.

Still in the pit of Sant-Elmo, Campanella composed the work that the German scholar Kaspar Schoppe suggested he call *Atheismus triumphatus*, and to which the author would also refer as *Anti-machiavellismo*. He intended to prove in it that religion is not a human invention, as politicians and supporters of state agendas maintain; it is not a useful fiction invented by priestly cunning and by rulers for maintaining their power, but a *virtus naturalis* that is intrinsic in man and in all of nature. Campanella also wrote the *Articuli prophetales*, in which, amplifying a document of his self-defense, he collected the texts of saints and prophets, literary writers and philosophers, astrologers and sibyls, which prove that it is legitimate to expect the coming of an epoch of renewal and the age of gold.

After being transferred to more comfortable prisons, during his long years of detention Campanella sent petitions and memoranda to popes and sovereigns in which he proclaimed his own innocence and pleaded for release, promising to undertake useful and marvelous tasks and books. Above all, he was dedicated to that grandiose work of reform and re-foundation of the entire encyclopedia of knowledge which had blazed within him since his early years. Beside the known works and numerous lost small works and texts, we mention the literary writings which were collected in the five parts of the *Philosophia rationalis* (Paris 1638); the *Theologia* in 30 books, finished in 1624 and left unpublished, whose publication, begun and continued by Romano Amerio, is still in progress; an *Astrologia* in six books, in which the author aims at freeing the doctrine from the superstitions of the Arabs, in order to re-establish it as a natural and conjectural doctrine; the *Medicine* in seven books, which was published at Lyon in 1635 thanks to the French savant Jacques Gaffarel, who had already prepared for the press an *Index* to the philosopher's works (Venice 1633), warmly emphasizing its novelty; and above all the most grandiose work which the author defined with justifiable pride as "the Bible of philosophy", the *Metaphysica*. The latter work, sketched in Campanella's youth and rewritten in subsequent years, finally appeared as an imposing folio edition of 18 books subdivided into three parts, published in Paris in 1638, a few months before the author's death. The work is extremely complex and various in its themes; here we must mention at least the distinction between knowledge *innata*, in virtue of which every entity knows and loves its own self, and knowledge *addita*, which derives from contacts and relations with the multiple objects of the external world. This latter knowledge can obfuscate the original knowledge that the soul has of itself, inducing a sort of self-forgetfulness in it; and the doctrine of the "primality", according to which the first, infinite Being is constituted from the infinite principles of Power, Wisdom, and Love, and all the sec-

ondary, finite entities which derive from it are constituted, as beings, from this very primality following their different modalities and proportions, and inasmuch as they are finite, from infinite degrees of non-entity. Nothingness does not exist either in God or outside him, but God makes use of it to give beings their distinction and finitude.

On January 13, 1611, after reading Galileo's *Sidereus nuncius*, Campanella wrote an elaborate Latin epistle to the scientist that reflects the emotions aroused by the extraordinary celestial messenger: a mixture of enthusiasm and perplexity, of praise and reservations. During the years that followed, he showed the greatest interest in Galileo's teachings about sunspots, floaters, and comets (and at the end of 1618 was able to observe those which spawned the debate of the *Saggiatore*). This fervid dialogue reached its climax in the drafting of the courageous *Apologia pro Galileo*. Written in 1616, when Galileo's teachings were arousing the first difficulties of a theological nature, and printed at Frankfurt in 1622, the *Apologia* was an act of great courage and intellectual honesty on its author's part, not only because Campanella took up this delicate question while he was in prison (and as he recorded later, his was the only voice in Europe that was raised in defence of the astronomer), but also because he was defending doctrines that were not his own. His image of a living and organic book of nature was, in fact, quite different from Galileo's idea of a book written in mathematical characters. Besides, Campanella had reservations about the Copernican doctrine, hard to reconcile with Telesian physics especially regarding the earth's motion. The *Apologia* is not so much a defense of the heliocentric system, as a defence of Galileo's *libertas philosophandi* and in general of the Christian scientist, whose first right and duty should be to set the reading of the book of nature above that of books by men. With great lucidity, Campanella touches on the nub of the problem, identifying it as the marriage of Aristotelianism with theology. Aristotelian philosophy does not contain a dogmatic and absolute truth, but, like every human doctrine, is modified and corrected in the light of reading the book of nature. When it no longer corresponds to experience, it should be discarded and replaced with a new doctrine that better reflects the data, exactly as Galileo has done, without fearing that this dismissal of Aristotelianism should have negative repercussions for theology.

After alternate hopes and failed promises, exhausting negotiations and delays, finally on May 23, 1626, after almost 27 years of prison, Campanella left Castel Nuovo, and a month later, by order of the Holy Office, was transferred secretly to

Rome and incarcerated in the palace of the Inquisition. The first period of his time in Rome was marked by disappointment and bitterness which even caused him to regret the last years of his Neapolitan imprisonment, due to the hostility towards his person and even more towards his books, pursued with ceaseless accusations and censures. But the most sensational episode of his Roman period was connected to Campanella's astrological skill, and the desire of Pope Urban VIII, secretly interested in such doctrines, to exploit it. The Pope wished to silence the rumors, already current in 1626 and becoming ever more insistent in the succeeding years, of his imminent death due to ill-omened astrological aspects. Campanella did not only reassure him about the length of his life, but, summoned to the papal palace, put into action those practices of natural magic described in the short work *De fato siderali vitando*. If the Pope seemed to gain reassurance from such counsels, the scandal exploded in 1629 when the book appeared in print at Lyon as the seventh and last volume of the *Astrologici*, risking compromising the Pope himself with accusations of superstitious practices. Campanella insisted that the work had been printed without his permission, as part of a plot organized by powerful enemies within his own Order who wanted to ruin him and destroy the Pope's favor towards him. Urban VIII hastened to promulgate in the first months of 1631 the most severe Bull *Inscrutabilis* against astrologers, and to imprison and put to death Don Orazio Morandi, abbot of Santa Prassede, in whose monastery astrological practices had become mixed up with political intrigues; but the scandal of the publication of *De fato* inexorably cooled Urban's sympathy for Campanella. It little helped that the friar hurriedly wrote an *Apologeticus* in defense of the astrological work, in order to demonstrate that the practices suggested in *De fato* were licit and natural.

In the political field, the Roman years saw Campanella's transference, at first cautious, then ever more obvious, to the French position. In a *Dialogo politico* he deplored the dissensions within the royal family, which risked enfeebling the energies of the whole nation, and praised the policies of Cardinal Richelieu. In his judgment, the Cardinal was not intent on egotistic personal power, as his enemies wanted to make believe, but on the reinforcement and centralization of the powers of the state, in order to make the nation stronger, more prosperous and coherent. But between 1633-1634 new and dramatic events brought the Roman period to a brusque end. In August 1633 one of Campanella's disciples, a young Dominican friar from Calabria called Tommaso Pignatelli, was imprisoned in Naples on the charge of having hatched an anti-Spanish plot. When the following year Pignatelli, condemned to death, was strangled in prison, the situation suggested an opportunity, approved by the Pope himself, for Campanella's expatriation to France. On the night of October 21 he fled from Rome as far as Livorno in the carriage of the French ambassador, François de Noailles. There he embarked for Marseilles, continuing stage by stage through Aix-en-Provence, where he was warmly welcomed by his erudite friend Nicolas-Claude Fabri de Peiresc, at whose house he was able to meet Pierre Gassendi. Resuming the voyage to Paris, on November 15 he stayed at Lyon, where he saw with satisfaction that the first four books of his *Medicina* had been printed, and reached the capital on December 1st.

Campanella was received warmly and sympathetically by Richelieu and Louis XIII, and enjoyed the favor of the learned. During his Parisian years he resumed his philosophical activity and devoted himself to the printing of his own *Opera omnia*, which despite innumerable obstacles began to appear, to his great satisfaction. During 1635-1636 he was involved in an intense resumption of political reflections, aimed at demonstrating that France, for all its difficulties and conflicts, was positioned in a rising phase of "waxing fortune", whereas the Hispano-Habsburg power was traversing the downward parabola of an inexorable decline. Nor did Campanella neglect the prophetic prospects, always dear to him. In a letter to the Grand Duke Ferdinand II, recalling his links with the Medicean house and his constant friendship towards Galileo, he affirmed his own faith that the messages of prophets survive their death: 'The coming century will judge us, because the present one always crucifies its benefactors, but then they are resurrected on the third day, or the third century'. On the occasion of the much hoped-for birth of the Dauphin, the future Sun King, which came on the same day as Campanella's own 70th birthday, he composed an inspired *Ecloga* in Latin. Taking up astrological and prophetic themes, he begs the Muse of Calabria to free him from old age, so that he can communicate his faith in the approach of a new epoch, in which the 'dark colors, signs of mourning and ignorance' will be shed, and immaculate hearts will put on white garments; an epoch in which 'impiety, fraud, lies, and strife will be exiled, the lambs will no longer fear the wolf, nor the herd fear the lion; the tyrants will learn to rule for the good of the people, and idleness will cease, after which hard labor will also cease; work shared by many in friendship will be play, for all will acknowledge one father and God'. Seized by dark presages at the approach of a solar eclipse, he tried to foil its threats, but died at dawn on May 21, 1639.

The only available resource for a complete description of Campanella's works and their complicated interrelations is still the volume by L. Firpo, *Bibliografia degli scritti di Tommaso Campanella*, Turin 1940. Because of the editions, discoveries of documents, and literature of succeeding years, both by Firpo himself and by other scholars, we must warn that this bibliography, while still valuable, needs many additions and corrections. There is an exhaustive compilation of Firpo's Campanella editions and studies in E. Baldini, "Luigi Firpo e Campanella: cinquant'anni di ricerche e di pubblicazioni", *Bruniana & Campanelliana*, II (1996), 352-358. This journal (from Year 1, 1995) should be consulted both for its updating of the editions and texts of Campanella since 1990, and for recent studies and documents about him.

Apologia pro Galileo/Apologie pour Galilée (text, trans., and notes by M.-P. Lerner), Paris: Les Belles Lettres, 2001 ♦ *La Città del Sole: Quaestio quarta de Optima Republica* (G. Ernst, ed.), Milan: Rizzoli 1996 ♦ *La Città del Sole* (ed. L. Firpo, new ed. by G. Ernst & L. Salvetti Firpo, Postface by N. Bobbio), Roma: Laterza, 1997 ♦ *Opera latina Francofurti impressa annis 1617-1630* (vol. I: *Prodromus philosophiae instaurandae, De sensu rerum, Apologia pro Galileo*; vol. II: *Realis philosophiae epilogisticae partes 4, Astrologicorum libri 7*) (facsimile ed. L. Firpo), Turin: Bottega d'Erasmo 1975, 2 vols. ♦ *Metaphysica*, Paris: [D. Langlois], 1638 (facsimile ed. L. Firpo), Turin: Bottega d'Erasmo, 1961 ♦ *Monarchie d'Espagne et Monarchie de France* (Italian & French trans., ed. G. Ernst), Paris: Presses Universitaires de France, 1997 ♦ *Opere letterarie* (ed. L. Bolzoni), Turin: Utet, 1977 ♦ *Philosophia sensibus demonstrata* (ed. L. De Franco), Naples: Vivarium, 1992 ♦ *Poesie* (ed. F. Giancotti) Turin: Einaudi, 1998 ♦ *Scritti letterari* in *Tutte le opere di Tommaso Campanella*, I (no other vols. appeared) (ed. L. Firpo), Milan: Mondadori, 1954 ♦ *Theologicorum libri* (ed. R. Amerio; from 1993, ed. M. Muccillo), Roma, 1949 ♦ *Tommaso Campanella* (ed. G. Ernst, Introduction by N. Badaloni) (series "Cento libri per mille anni", ed. W. Pedullà), Rome: Il Poligrafico e Zecca dello Stato, 1999; contains 16 texts by Campanella: pt. I, Scritti autobiografici e letterari: a selection of 14 *Lettere*; *Scelta di alcune poesie filosofiche*; *Syntagma de libris propriis et recta ratione studendi* (Latin & Italian); pt. II, Filosofia e natura: *Del senso delle cose e della magia, Apologia pro Galileo* (Lat. & Ital.), *De fato siderali vitando* (Lat. & Ital.), *Apologeticus pro libello "De Fato siderali vitando"* (Lat. & Ital.); pt. III, Pensiero politico: *Monarchia di Spagna; Città del Sole; Quaestio quarta de optima republica* (Lat. & Ital.); *Aforismi politici; Avvertimento al re di Francia, al re di Spagna e al sommo pontefice circa alli presenti e passati mali d'Italia; Aforismi politici per le presenti necessità di Francia; Dialogo politico tra un Veneziano, Spagnuolo e Francese; Due discorsi sullo stato ecclesiastico; Ultimi discorsi politici* ♦ *L'ateismo trionfato* (G. Ernst, ed.), 2 vols., I: edition of the unpublished Italian text; II: facsimile of the ms. Barb. lat. 4458, Pisa: Scuola Normale Superiore, 2004 ♦ *Lettere* (V. Spampanato, ed.), Bari: Laterza, 1927 ♦ *Lettere 1595-1638* (G. Ernst, ed.), Pisa-Rome: Istituto Editoriali e Poligrafici Internazionali, 2000 ♦ *Monarchie du Messie* (Latin & French trans., P. Ponzio, ed., V. Bourdette, trans.), Paris: Presses Universitaires de France, 2002 ♦ *Opusculi astrologici: Come evitare il fato astrale, Apologetico, Disputa sulle Bolle* (Lat. & Italian trans., G. Ernst, ed.), Milan: Rizzoli, 2003.

Lit.: Bruniana et Campelliana (from 1995), passim ♦ L. Amabile, *Fra Tommaso Campanella, la sua congiura, i suoi processi e la sua pazzia*, 3 vols., Naples, 1882 ♦ L. Amabile, *Fra Tommaso Campanella ne' castelli di Napoli, in Roma e in Parigi*, 2 vols., Naples, 1887 ♦ R. Amerio, *Il sistema teologico di Tommaso Campanella*, Milan, Naples, 1972 ♦ N. Badaloni, *Tommaso Campanella*, Milan, 1965 ♦ L. Blanchet, *Campanella*, Paris, 1920 ♦ G. Bock, *Thomas Campanella: Politisches Interesse und Philosophische Spekulation*, Tübingen, 1974 ♦ A. Corsano, *Tommaso Campanella*, Bari, 1961 ♦ G. Di Napoli, *Tommaso Campanella, filosofo della restaurazione cattolica*, Padua, 1947 ♦ F. Ducros, *Tommaso Campanella poète*, Montpellier, 1969 ♦ G. Ernst, *Religione, ragione e natura: Ricerche su Tommaso Campanella e il tardo Rinascimento*, Milan, 1991 ♦ eadem, *Il carcere, il politico, il profeta: Saggi su Tommaso Campanella*, Pisa-Rome: Istituto Editoriali e Poligrafici Internazionali, 2002 ♦ eadem, *Tommaso Campanella: Il libro e il corpo della natura*, Rome: Laterza, 2002 ♦ L. Firpo, *Ricerche campanelliane*, Florence, 1947 ♦ idem, *I processi di Tommaso Campanella* (E. Canone, ed.), Rome: Salerno, 1998 ♦ R. Hagengruber, *Tommaso Campanella: Eine Philosophie der Ähnlichkeit*, Sankt Augustin, 1994 ♦ J.M. Headley, *Tommaso Campanella and the Transformation of the World*, Princeton, 1997 ♦ A. Isoldi Jacobelli, *Tommaso Campanella: "Il diverso filosofar mio"*, Rome, 1995 ♦ M.-P. Lerner, *Tommaso Campanella en France au XVII siècle*, Naples, 1995 ♦ M. Mönnich, *Tommaso Campanella: Sein Beitrag zur Medizin und Pharmazie der Renaissance*, Stuttgart, 1990 ♦ L. Negri, *Fede e ragione in Tommaso Campanella*, Milan, 1990 ♦ P. Ponzio, *Tommaso Campanella: Filosofia della natura e teoria della scienza*, Bari: Levante, 2001.

GERMANA ERNST

Canseliet, Eugène Léon,* 18.12.1899 Sarcelles (France), † 17.4.1982 Savignies (France)

Eugène Canseliet, alchemist and writer, was born to a modest family of Belgian origin that settled in the Paris suburbs at the end of the 19th century. As a youth, he was interested in art, especially drawing, and competed for entrance into art schools. During World War I he attended that of Marseille, where his family had moved to protect him from the war. Canseliet never lost his passion for painting and drawing.

At Marseille he met → Fulcanelli, who, according to Canseliet's account, was already an old man; he made a habit of visiting him, listening to him, and running errands for him, while beginning to study the classic texts of → alchemy. At Fulcanelli's, Canseliet met Jean Julien Champagne (1877-1932), who is often presented as having been the real Fulcanelli. Champagne was a gifted painter, versed in practical alchemy, and close to some of the Parisian esotericists; he exercised a profound influence on Canseliet.

On returning to Paris from Marseille, Canseliet worked variously as an office employee, bookkeeper, etc., while continuing his alchemical studies. He visited Fulcanelli, who had returned to Paris after the Armistice in 1918, and Champagne, who from 1925 to 1932 occupied a room adjoining Canseliet's. Some paintings survive from this period of Champagne's life. Canseliet spent part of his income on acquiring old alchemical books, and those he could not obtain, he copied himself at libraries or in private collections such as Lionel Hauser's.

At the beginning of the 1920s, Fulcanelli invited Canseliet to a strange rendezvous. At the Sarcelles gas factory he asked his pupil to perform a transmutation, using materials that he himself provided. This operation, according to Canseliet, produced a small quantity of gold that was later cast into a ring. After this experiment, Fulcanelli handed Canseliet three manuscripts and entrusted him with preparing them for publication. The first, *Le Mystère des cathédrales et l'interprétation ésotérique des symboles hermétiques du Grand Œuvre* (The mystery of the cathedrals and the esoteric interpretation of the Hermetic symbols of the Great Work) appeared in June 1926 from Jean Schemit (1867-1945), a publisher specializing in erudite and artistic works. At Fulcanelli's request, Canseliet added a preface, and signed as "F.C.H." (i.e. Frère Chevalier d'Heliopolis), referring to a secret society of alchemists to which Fulcanelli had supposedly belonged. The illustrations that accompany Canseliet's redrafting of the text are all by Champagne.

Fulcanelli's second book appeared four years later: *Les demeures philosophales et le symbolisme hermétique dans ses rapports avec l'art sacré et l'ésotérisme du Grand Œuvre* (Philosophic residences

and Hermetic symbolism in its relationship to sacred art and the esotericism of the Great Work). But the third manuscript, entitled *Finis Gloriae Mundi* (The end of the world's glory) was taken back by Fulcanelli and kept from publication.

During the 1930s, Canseliet made lasting contacts and friendships, such as with the Christian alchemist André Savoret (1898-1977); Paul Le Cour (1876-1954), founder of the journal *Atlantis*, to which Canseliet contributed for the rest of his life; the polyglot philosopher Philéas Lebesgue (1869-1958); and Claude d'Ygé (alias Claude Lablatinière, 1912-1964). In 1945, Jean Schemit's widow honored her husband's promise and published Canseliet's first book. Although issued under difficult postwar conditions, the result was successful. From 1946 onwards, Canseliet lived in Savignies, near Beauvais.

In 1953, Canseliet was unexpectedly invited to make a journey by car from Paris to Spain. In Seville he was received by Fulcanelli, then aged about 114 by Canseliet's calculations. The purpose of this meeting, according to Canseliet, was for Fulcanelli to give his disciple advice and new information of a practical nature; in brief, to guide him in his research. Thenceforth Canseliet followed the so-called "dry way", re-reading in this spirit the works of Basil Valentine, → pseudo-Nicolas Flamel, A.T. Limojon de Saint-Didier, and Eirenaeus Philalethes (the "dry way" in alchemy is supposedly an accelerated process of obtaining the Philosopher's Stone that dispenses with the lengthy procedures of the more common "wet way", but is more difficult and hazardous).

In 1955, Canseliet began his collaboration with a new journal founded by Robert Amadou, *La Tour Saint-Jacques* (1955-1963). Other contributors included René Alleau (born 1917), Henri Hunwald (1908-1961), and Claude d'Ygé. Thanks to the latter, Canseliet was introduced to Jean Lavritch, owner of Omnium Littéraire (a branch of Editions des Champs-Elysées), a house specializing in esotericism and notable for publishing the journal *Initiation & Science* (1945-1963). In 1957 and 1960, Lavritch re-issued Fulcanelli's two books, augmented by Canseliet with new Introductions and two hitherto unpublished chapters. However, after differences arose between author and publisher, Canseliet was introduced to Jean-Jacques Pauvert, already well known for publishing the Marquis de Sade, André Breton, etc. Pauvert was convinced of the value of Fulcanelli's and Canseliet's writings, and agreed to publish them. The third edition of Fulcanelli's works (1964, 1965) and a volume of collected articles by

Canseliet (1964) met with immediate success. Thanks to Fulcanelli's literary qualities, but also to Canseliet's own writings, alchemy suddenly became respectable in the French literary world. The press and radio took hold of the phenomenon, and from then onwards, Canseliet was frequently solicited by journalists.

The 1970s were rich and active years for Canseliet. He wrote many articles, especially in *Atlantis*, then from 1977 in *La Tourbe des Philosophes*, a journal founded by Jean Laplace. He wrote several introductions, re-published Fulcanelli's works, completed his own *Alchimie expliquée sur ses textes classiques* (Alchemy explained on the basis of its classic texts), prepared augmented editions of his other books, published in facsimile the alchemical treatises he had copied in the 1920s, and co-authored a volume of interviews with Robert Amadou (see Bibliography). These efforts came to a dramatic close when Canseliet suffered a heart-attack in 1974. His long convalescence (during which he treated himself with dew) forced him to reduce his visits to Paris.

In his last years, Canseliet was busily giving interviews, answering the many letters he received, and ensuring that Fulcanelli's works remained in print; he also wrote his memoirs, which remained unfinished. His death, following a winter attack of influenza, left his work with no designated heir. It remains inseparable from that of his master, which in many respects it clarifies or completes. For nearly 60 years, this combined corpus has continued to have a strong influence, especially in France, where it has brought about a veritable renaissance of laboratory alchemy.

In the English-speaking world, Canseliet is best known as Fulcanelli's one and only disciple through Kenneth R. Johnson's biography of the latter; also through the publications of Frater Albertus (pen-name of Albert Richard Riedel). In an interview with Albertus (1976), Canseliet emphasizes the role of harmony in all alchemical endeavors: harmony with the material, with oneself, and with the cosmos. He mentions the difficulty of achieving the Great Work today because of pollution in the atmosphere and changes in the weather: these hinder the performance of alchemical operations, which are crucially timed by season, moon phase, and the state of the sky. Worst of all, he says, is the pollution of the human brain. A similar animus toward the modern age appears in his censure of the post-conciliar Catholic Church, particularly of its sanctioning cremation (Preface to 3rd ed. of *Le Mystère des cathédrales*, 31-33).

Unlike many 20th century interpreters, and even self-defined practitioners of alchemy, Canseliet insisted that it is first and foremost a physical activity requiring laboratory work. He had little tolerance for the symbolic interpretations of Gaston Bachelard, the pontifications of → René Guénon on the 'merely cosmological' and theoretical nature of the Hermetic tradition, and the psychologized alchemy of → Carl Gustav Jung (*L'Alchimie expliquée*, 75-90). On the other hand, he was ready to read alchemical wisdom into the literary works of François Rabelais and Jonathan Swift. The key to this reading lies in the supposed secret language of the alchemists, the *langue des oiseaux* (language of the birds) revealed by phonetic equivalents: thus the name of Swift's hero Gulliver conceals the words *gueule* (Fr., "throat") and *ver* (Lat., "spring"), which Canseliet eventually translates as 'the philosophic vase' (*L'Alchimie expliquée*, 109). Alongside this creative hermeneutics, Canseliet continued Fulcanelli's practice of discovering and interpreting symbolic programs found in the architecture of French buildings of the Medieval and Renaissance periods. Yet despite such a wealth of information, the essential mysteries are guarded: the aspiring alchemist must deduce for himself, with the help of prayer if lacking that of an accomplished master, the actual nature of the materials and what is practically to be done with them. In this respect, Canseliet's teaching contrasts with the tendency to openness and the setting of modest and accessible goals, as in the "alchemical" schools of Frater Albertus or of Jean Dubuis' "Philosophers of Nature".

Deux logis alchimiques en marge de la science et des arts, Paris: Jean Schemit, 1945; second ed. revised and enlarged: Paris: Jean-Jacques Pauvert, 1979; third ed., revised, reshaped and enlarged by R. Caron, Paris: Jean-Claude Bailly, 1998 ♦ *Alchimie: Etudes diverses de symbolisme hermétique*, Paris: J.J. Pauvert, 1964; second ed., enlarged, Paris: J.J. Pauvert, 1978 (followed by several new eds.) ♦ *L'alchimie et son Mutus Liber*, Paris: J.J. Pauvert 1967; republished 1986; Paris: enlarged ed., J.Cl. Bailly, 1996 ♦ *L'alchimie expliquée sur ses textes classiques*, Paris: J.-J. Pauvert, 1972; second ed., enlarged, Paris: J.J. Pauvert, 1980 (several new eds.) ♦ *Trois anciens traités alchimiques*, Paris: J.J. Pauvert, 1975 (new ed. in facsimile, Paris: Fayard 1996) ♦ *Le Feu du soleil: Entretiens sur l'alchimie avec Eugène Canseliet*, Paris: J.-J. Pauvert, 1978 (in collaboration with Robert Amadou) ♦ *L'Hermétisme dans la vie de Jonathan Swift*, Montpellier: Fata Morgana, 1983.

Lit.: Frater Albertus, *The Alchemist of the Rocky Mountains*, Salt Lake City: Paracelsus Research Society, 1976 ♦ idem, "An Interview with Eugene Canseliet", *Parachemy* 4:4 (1976), 366-371 ♦ "Hommage au

Maître Alchimiste Eugène Canseliet, F.C.H. 1899-1982", *Atlantis* 322 (1982) ♦ "Alchimie: Centenaire de la naissance d'Eugène Canseliet", *Atlantis* 398 (1999) ♦ Atorène, *Le laboratoire alchimique*, Paris: Trédaniel, 1981 ♦ Richard Caron, "Postface", in: E. Canseliet, *Deux logis alchimiques* (etc.), Paris: J.Cl. Bailly, 1998, 321-333 ♦ Judith Henry, *En hommage au plus grand alchimiste du XXème siècle, Eugène Canseliet F. C. H., et en souvenir de la plus touchante et fidèle amitié qu'il lui porta*, Paris: Editions Judith Henry, 1999 ♦ Jean Laplace, *Index général des termes spéciaux, des expressions et des sentences propres à l'alchimie se rencontrant dans l'œuvre complète d'Eugène Canseliet*, Paris: Editions Suger, 1986 ♦ idem, "En hommage aux 80 ans de M. Eugène Canseliet", *La Tourbe des Philosophes* 10 (1980).

RICHARD CARON

Carpocratians

The Carpocratians belong to the broad spectrum of Christian schools in the 2nd century that teach Christianity as a philosophy. Their founder, the Alexandrian Christian Carpocrates, was married to a lady called Alexandria who came from the island of Kephallenia in the Adriatic sea. They had a son called Epiphanes who received from his father an "encyclopaedic education", wrote some treatises and died at the age of seventeen. Clement reports that the deceased Epiphanes was given divine honours: a temple and a *mouseion* were erected in Same on the island of Kephallenia and every new moon a celebration commemorated his divinization (Clement of Alexandria, *Stromateis*, III, 5, 1-3). Clement does not assign a date to either Carpocrates or Epiphanes. Irenaeus of Lyons, however, who discusses the Carpocratians in *Adversus Haereses* (*AH*), I, 25, provides some elements of chronology. He refers to a Roman group that was headed by a certain lady called Marcellina. According to Irenaeus, Marcellina came to Rome in the time of bishop Anicetus and 'exterminated many'. Thus Irenaeus sees Marcellina as a contemporary of Polycarp (*AH*, III, 3, 4) and Valentinus [→ Valentinus and Valentinians], who, having come to Rome under bishop Hyginus, lived until the time of Anicetus (*AH*, III, 4, 3). Cerdo, who arrived in Rome under Hyginus (*AH*, I, 27, 1), is older, as is probably Marcion. Whether Irenaeus is correct in connecting Marcellina and her group with the Carpocratians is not quite certain: the pagan philosopher Celsus distinguished in his anti-Christian treatise the *True Doctrine* between 'Marcellians' as followers of Marcellina and 'Harpocratians' as followers of Salome (Origen, *Contra Celsum*, V, 62). Another contemporary of Marcellina is Hegesip-

pus who likewise came to Rome under bishop Anicetus. He wrote a work comprising five books; there he mentions the Carpocratians among the Christian sects that have sprung from the Jewish sects. He enumerates Menandrians, Marcianists (?), Carpocratians, Valentinians, Basilidians and Satornilians (Eusebius of Caesarea, *Historia Ecclesiastica*, IV, 22, 5). It is, of course, impossible to draw any chronological conclusion from the sequence presented by Hegesippus. We can only surmise that Carpocrates and his son lived in the first half of the 2nd century and that Marcellina came to Rome sometime after ca. 160 C.E. Justin Martyr who wrote between 150 and 160 C.E. nowhere mentions Carpocratians. The Roman group was probably still active when Irenaeus composed his *Adversus Haereses* about 185 C.E.

Irenaeus relates some further details about the Roman Carpocratians, the followers of Marcellina: they called themselves "gnostics" and tattooed the back of their right ear with a red hot iron. Moreover, they possessed images of Christ as a human being, executed in different materials, amongst them a portrait of Christ made by Pilate. They placed Christ's image among those of other philosophers like Pythagoras, Plato and Aristotle and paid them the kind of homage customary among pagans. This last piece of information is important because it suggests that the Carpocratians, like other philosophical schools, celebrated their founder as a divinized philosopher hero. This seems to confirm Clement's report mentioned above according to which Carpocrates' son Epiphanes was honoured as a deified philosopher-child prodigy in Same on the island of Kephallenia.

As to Carpocratian literature and doctrine, our knowledge is scarce and confined to the reports and quotations offered by Clement of Alexandria and Irenaeus of Lyons. Both writers evince a definite heresiological perspective: they wish to demonstrate that the Carpocratians are libertinists. Accordingly, they highlight those features of Carpocratian teaching that they consider as evidence for Carpocratian libertinism.

1. Epiphanes is the author of a work called *On Justice* of which Clement of Alexandria has preserved three fragments (*Strom.*, III, 6, 1-9, 3). There Epiphanes develops his concept of divine justice: divine justice is defined as 'community combined with equality' and as manifesting itself in the cosmic order. Every living being gets an equal share of e.g. light or food; no one has more than the other or something in which the others have no share. The law of divine justice is unwritten. Human laws that introduce private property violate this princi-

ple of divine justice. For example, the grapevines are for everyone; the idea that they are anyone's private property creates the thief. Epiphanes quotes Rom. 7:7: 'It is through the law that I got acquainted with sin'. The same applies to the union of male and female: since God has created the male with sexual desire in order to ensure the continuous existence of the human race, the commandment not to desire what belongs to your neighbour (including his wife) is absurd and ridiculous. Hence no one can lay exclusive claim to his own wife, for this would manifestly contravene the will of the divine creator.

In these fragments Epiphanes is not primarily interested in proposing the Platonic ideal of the community of wives. He rather presents an interesting example of a non-dualist rejection of the God of the Old Testament. Clement, *Strom.*, III, 5, 3 designates Epiphanes as the founder of the 'monadic gnosis'. Perhaps this means that Carpocrates – like Marcion's disciple Apelles (Eusebius of Caesarea, *Historia Ecclesiastica*, V, 13, 5) – assumes one principle rather than two. For him, God is, according to the platonic phrase, the 'creator and father of all' (Clement, *Strom.*, III, 7, 1; cf. Plato, *Timaeus*, 28 c3); his will manifests itself in the order of the kosmos. The Mosaic law is ridiculous. It does not even reveal, *pace* Marcion, a lower God who is legislator and creator. Here Epiphanes again seems to agree with Marcion's disciple Apelles who in his *Syllogisms* also tried to prove that the Old Testament with its many contradictions does not contain divine revelation.

2. It is not quite clear how the information Clement offers us about Carpocrates and Epiphanes can be combined with Irenaeus' report about the Roman (?) Carpocratians. There is some likelihood that Irenaeus is paraphrasing and summarizing an original document, but we cannot be sure whether Carpocrates himself or one of his followers is the author of this source. According to Irenaeus, the Carpocratians believed that Jesus was an ordinary human being, the son of Joseph. However, since his soul had not forgotten that in its pre-existence it had contemplated the sphere of the unbegotten father (cf. Plato, *Phaedrus*, 247c), it was exceptionally strong and pure. Therefore God the Father sent him a force that allowed him to escape the angels that have created this world and to ascend to God. The soul of Jesus received a Jewish education, but despised it. It was granted the power to eradicate those passions that it had acquired as a punishment for its sins. All those that, like Jesus, despise the angels that created the world will, like him, receive the power to do as he did.

Those human beings that are endowed with souls from the same sphere as that of Jesus can achieve the same or an even higher degree of perfection.

Here it is interesting to observe how the Carpocratians conceptualize Christ as a philosopher hero by proposing a Christian reinterpretation of the Platonic doctrine of the soul: according to them there are special souls that remember their preexistent state. However, the ascent to the highest God is not simply a function of that memory with its consequent strength and purity, but is rather dependent on the gift of a divine *dynamis* that allows them to escape the creator angels. To follow Christ, then, means to take part in the Carpocratian variety of the late antique "cult of learning" (Zanker), to imitate Christ the philosopher hero in one's own life.

Apart from this report concerning the main tenets of Carpocratian doctrine, Irenaeus has also preserved a Carpocratian exegesis of the parable in Luke 12:58-59 / Matthew 5:25-26 (*AH.* I, 25, 4; the text quoted by the Carpocratians is a mixture of Matthaean and Lukan readings). The Carpocratians identified the adversary with the devil who is one of the creator angels. The diabolical psychopompus leads the souls to the Archon, the first of the creator angels. He exercises the function of the judge and delivers the soul to a third angel, a bailiff, who imprisons the soul in a new body. Jesus' saying: 'You will not leave until you have paid back the last penny' is taken to mean that the soul will have to wander from body to body until it has 'carried out all the actions that are in this world'.

Irenaeus gives this Carpocratian gloss a robustly libertinist reading: according to him, the Carpocratians wish to suggest that the soul can only be liberated if it devotes itself to all possible misdeeds, blasphemies and debaucheries. If it realizes its total freedom in one life, it does not have to return into the body. This reading, however, presses the Carpocratians's doctrine too far: they probably read Jesus' saying as teaching the transmigration of the souls [→ Reincarnation], not as proposing a new ethics. Moreover, Irenaeus himself is doubtful as to whether it is correct to view the Carpocratians as endorsing libertinism (*AH*, I, 25, 5).

This Carpocratian exegesis must be seen in context: the so-called *Sentences of Sextus*, a collection of Christian ethical aphorisms that originated probably in Alexandria in the 2nd century, allude to the same parable (*Sent.* 39 Chadwick): after death the sinner will be punished by a demon 'until he has paid the last penny'. Origen agrees with the Carpocratians that the persons mentioned in the parable are to be identified as angels: the adversary is a personal demon that accompanies every human being tempting him or her to sin. The archon is the highest angel of every nation, the adversary tries to subject the human being in his care to him. Only those who practise the four cardinal virtues of wisdom, justice, courage and self-restraint can hope to get rid of their personal demon. The judge to whom the adversary escorts the human being is Christ himself who determines the appropriate punishment (Origen, *Homilies on Luke*, 35). Tertullian has read Irenaeus; in *De anima*, 35, he discusses the Carpocratian exegesis of Luke 12:58f. / Matth. 5:25f.

3. Finally, we must mention the fragment of a letter ascribed to Clement of Alexandria which the American scholar Morton Smith discovered in the Mar Saba monastery near Jerusalem (Clemens Alexandrinus, IV, ed. Stählin-Treu, XVII-XVIII). The letter is addressed to a certain Theodorus. It starts with a polemical injunction against the Carpocratians and informs us that Carpocrates had forced an Alexandrian presbyter to deliver to him a copy of the second, secret gospel of Mark. Carpocrates allegedly then altered this gospel and used it as the basis for his own teaching. The letter quotes fragments from the secret gospel of Mark that suggest that Jesus was involved in a homoerotic relationship. The authenticity of this letter is doubtful; it agrees with the heresiology of both Irenaeus and Clement insofar as it suggests that Carpocrates was a libertinist. However, neither Irenaeus nor Clement suggest homosexual libertinism.

Lit.: P. Boyancé, *Le culte des muses chez les philosophes grecs: Études d'histoire et de philosophie réligieuses*, Paris: De Bocard, 1937, 1972² ♦ F.J. Dölger, "Die Sphragis als religiöse Brandmarkung im Einweihungsakt der gnostischen Karpokratianer", *Antike und Christentum* 1 (1929), 73-78 ♦ H. Finé, *Die Terminologie der Jenseitsvorstellungen bei Tertullian* (Theophaneia 12), Bonn: Hanstein, 1958, 103-112 ♦ W. Foerster, *Gnosis: A Selection of Gnostic Texts* (R. McL. Wilson, trans.), vol. I: Patristic Evidence, Oxford: Oxford University Press, 1972 ♦ R.M. Grant, "Carpocratians and Curriculum", in: G.W.E. Nickelsburg (ed.), *Christians among Jews and Gentiles: Festschrift Krister Stendahl*, Philadelphia: Fortress Press, 1986, 127-136 ♦ A. Hilgenfeld, *Die Ketzergeschichte des Urchristentums, urkundlich dargestellt*, Leipzig: Fues, 1884 (repr. Darmstadt: Wissenschaftliche Buchgesellschaft 1963, Hildesheim: Olms, 1963, 1966) ♦ H. Liboron, *Die karpokratianische Gnosis: Untersuchungen zur Geschichte und Anschauungswelt eines spätgnostischen Systems*, Leipzig: Jordan & Grauberg, 1938 ♦ W.A. Löhr, "Epiphanes' Peri diakiosynês", in: H.C. Brennecke et alii (eds.), *Logos: Festschrift für Luise Abramowski zum 8. Juli 1993*, Berlin/New York: De Gruyter, 1993, 12-29 ♦ idem, "Karpokratianisches", *Vigiliae Christianae* 49 (1995), 23-48 ♦ Chr. Markschies, "Carpocrates", in: *Lexikon*

der antiken christlichen Literatur, Freiburg i.Br.: Herder, 1998, 119 ♦ S. Petersen, *"Zerstört die Werke der Weiblichkeit!" Maria Magdalena, Salome und andere Jüngerinnen Jesu in christlich-gnostischen Schriften* (Nag Hammadi and Manichean Studies XLVIII) Leiden, Boston, Köln: E.J. Brill, 1999 ♦ C. Scholten, "Karpokrates (K.) / Karpokratianer (K.ner)", forthcoming in *Reallexikon für Antike und Christentum*, 19 ♦ M. Smith, *Clement of Alexandria and a Secret Gospel of Mark*, Cambridge (Mass.): Harvard University Press, 1973 ♦ G.G. Stroumsa, "Gnostic justice and antinomianism: Epiphanes' On Justice in context", in: idem, *Barbarian Philosophy: The Religious Revolution of Early Christianity* (Wissenschaftliche Untersuchungen zum Neuen Testament 112), Tübingen: Mohr, 1999, 246-257 ♦ H. Usener, *Das Weihnachtsfest*, Bonn: Cohen, 1911², Bouvier, 1969³ (Repr. in: idem, *Religionsgeschichtliche Untersuchungen*, Hildesheim/New York: Olms, 1972), 30, 111-117 ♦ M.A. Williams, *Rethinking "Gnosticism": An Argument for Dismantling a Dubious Category*, Princeton: Princeton University Press, 1996, 167-169, 185-187 ♦ P. Zanker, *The Mask of Socrates: The Image of the Intellectual in Antiquity*, Berkeley-Los Angeles: University of California Press, 1995.

WINRICH A. LÖHR

Catharism

1. Introduction 2. Sources
3. History 4. Beliefs 5. Rituals
6. Hierarchy 7. Diffusion of Cathar
Beliefs 8. The End of Catharism

1. Introduction

Catharism was a dissident movement in medieval Western and Southern Europe, considered heretical by the Church. The name Cathar, which derives from the Greek *katharos* (pure), was first used in 1163, by the German monk Eckbert of Schönau. Heresiological literature also employed terms such as Neo-Manichaeans, Patarins (Italy), *Albigeois* (Langedoc, Lat. *Albigenses*), *Bougres* (Lat. *Bulgari*) and *Texerants/Tisserants* ("weavers"). Members of the sect called themselves "Good men" or "Good Christians".

The origin of Catharism is very controversial. Some scholars are convinced that → Bogomilism played a determinant role in the genesis of Catharism, since Bogomil and Cathar beliefs and rites are very similar. Others think that Catharism intensified dualistic tendencies within Christianity itself, and is in fact an attempt to return to the spirit of apostolic times. G. Volpe emphasized that the Cathars adhered to a religiosity that was close to the Gregorian Reform, characterized by nostalgia for primitive Christianity. R. Morghen put Catharism back in its contemporary Christian context, defining it as a reaction against the temporal ambitions of the Church, itself claiming to be a spiritual Church. Some scholars go even further: according to A. Brenon, who almost completely neglects its dualistic aspects, Catharism is an "ordinary Christianity". Today, a hypercritical approach of the sources sometimes even leads to doubts about the real existence of Catharism: some scholars present Catharism as a "construction by orthodoxy". According to this interpretation, partisans of a rigorous spiritual reform were incited by the Church to radicalize their ideas.

As far as the social aspects of Catharism are concerned, there was no question of marginality whatsoever. The Cathars penetrated all strata of urban and rural society and were often recruited from the middle class (merchants, lawyers, physicians, etc.). In the South of France, their protectors belonged to the chivalry of the castles, and in Italy members of the Ghibelline party were among their defenders. The involvement of women in the movement was important; they could also become Perfects, wholly initiated members of the sect.

2. SOURCES

Catharism is known through a considerable number of writings composed by its enemies and through only a few original Cathar documents. Among the indirect sources, anti-heretical treatises and "sommes" (summaries of heretical beliefs and practices for inquisitorial use) were written especially in Italy, from about 1200 onward. The acts of the inquisitional tribunals also give abundant information about persons, places, practices and beliefs. Finally, passages in historical writings, political correspondence and anti-heretical laws and decrees throw light on the historical circumstances of the development of Catharism and on the reactions it provoked.

Among the original Cathar sources, there are two rituals (one in Latin and one in Occitan), a theological treatise, *The Book of Two Principles*, attributed to John of Lugio, and another one, reconstituted from Durand of Huesca's anti-heretical treatise. A Latin apocryphon entitled *Interrogatio Iohannis* ("Questions of John"), used by the Italian Cathars in particular, has probably a Bogomil origin.

3. HISTORY

Since the 11th century, chroniclers mention Neo-Manichaeans, but they describe them so insufficiently that we cannot know whether we are dealing here with proto-Cathars or with partisans of a return to apostolic times, beyond the objectives of the actual movement of ecclesiastical reform. Catharism can be clearly identified only from the second half of the 12th century onward. From the 1160s onward, Cathars often appear in the documents because of the repression they provoked from the side of both civil and ecclesiastical authorities.

According the treatise of Anselme of Alessandria (*Tractatus de hereticis*, c. 1270), Western (French) people became acquainted with heresy in Constantinople during the Second Crusade. After returning to their country, they ordained there a bishop. Later on, the new heresy was diffused South of the Loire and in Lombardy.

Eckbert, abbot of Schönau, is the first author who described the Cathars with many details. In his *Sermons* (1163), he denounced Cathars who rejected the Catholic sacraments, marriage, the consumption of meat, and the intercession for the dead. He also revealed some of their beliefs, for example the creation of the human body by Satan, the negation of Christ's Incarnation, or the idea that human souls originated from rebelling angels.

The last three decades of the 12th century are characterised by a great expansion of Catharism. A document of which the authenticity is disputed gives an account of a heretical council at Saint-Felix-de-Caraman (between Carcassonne and Toulouse), held in 1167. On this occasion, a heretical dignitary, named Papas Nicetas (Niquinta), who went here from the East, confirmed the already existing episcopal boundaries in Languedoc and consecrated Cathar bishops. It is a fact that in 1177 a letter of Raymond V, count of Toulouse, sounded the alarm against the heresy. Religious missions first began in 1178, with the participation of Cistercian monks.

By this time, legal documents inform us about the Church's reaction against Cathars and other heretics, who are condemned to be deprived of their goods and to be reduced to servitude if they do not convert (council of Tours, 1163; council of Lateran, 1179). In 1184, at Verona, Emperor Frederick Barbarossa and Pope Lucius III take severe measures against heretics (banishment, infamy, civil incapacity). It is also the inauguration of the inquisitorial search for heretics. North of the Loire, the first heretics are burned at the stake (1172, Arras; 1182-1184, Campagne); in the realm of Aragon, kings Alphonse II and Peter II promulgate grave sanctions against heretics (1194, 1196).

Repression seems very efficient in the North, but in the North of Italy and in Languedoc the Cathar movement is still growing. According to the anti-heretical treatises, Italian Catharism was characterized by a great doctrinal diversity, which also reflected corresponding struggles for power. Pope Innocent III tried to impose anti-heretical measures in Lombardy, in Sicile and in Saint Peter's Patrimony, but, just as the Emperor Frederick II, he encountered fierce resistance in many cities of Lombardy and Venetia. Because of constant more or less exacerbated tensions between the partisans of the Emperor and the Pope (Ghibellines and Guelfs), the heretical communities persisted in Italian cities, where Cathars from Languedoc could take refuge until the end of 13th century.

But after the failure to convert the Cathars by preaching, Innocent III wanted to incite a military expedition in order to eradicate heresy in Languedoc, and he promised a crusade indulgence for participants. After the murder of his legate Peter of Castelnau (1208), the pope redoubled his efforts to organise a crusade in a Christian country. Though the French king Philippe Auguste did not participate in it personally, he allowed 500 knights to take the cross. The "Albigensian Crusade" began in the summer of 1209. Its first phase ended in 1215: at the IVth Lateran Council, Innocent III decreed that the town of Toulouse and the whole country which had been conquered would be conceded to count Simon of Montfort, the crusaders' commander-in-chief. But the political and religious resistance was revived by count Raymond VII. After a long series of struggles, the French king Louis IX imposed his conditions on Languedoc (Treaty of Paris, April 1229). In the same year, a council held at Toulouse specified the methods of religious repression, establishing the proceedings of inquisitorial inquiry. Shortly after this (1233-1234), the Papal Inquisition, an exceptional tribunal for the persecution of heretics, was created, for which Dominican friars became responsible. The last places of Cathar resistance fell in 1244 (Montségur) and in 1256 (Quéribus). The county of Toulouse was annexed to the French kingdom in 1271. Since the beginning of the Crusade, many people – Cathars and also their protectors – were arrested, imprisoned and burned.

Hunted by the Inquisition, the Cathars of Languedoc could still take refuge in Lombardy or in Aragon. The last Cathars were arrested round about 1320, during the meticulous enquiry of Bishop Jacques Fournier (future Pope Benedict XII), charged with the Inquisition in the diocese of Pamiers.

4. BELIEFS

Cathar beliefs are known through anti-heretical writings, depositions and confessions before the Inquisition and through two theological treatises and an apocryphal writing of the Cathars themselves.

The anti-heretical treatises invariably present Cathar beliefs in a systematic arrangement, emphasizing their contradictions with Catholic doctrine.

At the same time, they underline the diversity and divergences between the Cathar currents, opposing them to the unity of orthodox faith. Confessions and depositions recorded by the Inquisition indeed testify to varying features of Cathar myths and beliefs, which were almost exclusively orally spread. For Cathars, the principal preoccupation was the salvation of the soul. But they generally rejected the Catholic solution and emphasized the duality between Good and Evil, soul and flesh, proposing a new interpretation of the Holy Scriptures. Medieval heresiologists distinguished two principal currents within Catharism, which, already in 1849, the German scholar Ch. Schmidt designated as "absolute dualism" (radical current) and "mitigated dualism" (moderate current, closer to Catholic orthodoxy).

"Absolute dualism" characterized the Catharism of Languedoc and of the Church of Desenzano (near the lake of Garda) as well as that of the order of Drugunthia in the East (Macedonia or Thrace). According to this system, there existed from the beginning two realms: that of God, who is invisible and without evil, and that of the God of darkness, who is material and perishable. The equilibrium between them was broken by an intrusion of Satan into the divine world. The son of the God of darkness invaded the celestial court and seduced a part of the angels. Thrown out of heaven by God, together with his cohort, he created the material world and imprisoned the fallen angels in human bodies.

Moderate Cathars, who were particularly numerous in Italy (Church of Concorezzo) and more close to the Bogomils, believed that God had created angels and the elements of material world. Lucifer was an angel created by God, but moved by pride he raised a rebellion at the celestial court. Expelled to the world here below, with its still unorganized matter, he moulded the visible world and the body of the first human couple, with the permission of God. Like the radical Cathars, the moderate ones imagined that the evil creator had imprisoned two fallen angels in them.

The story of the fallen angels was spread in multiple variants and the modalities of Lucifer's promises were embellished with many imaginative details. In some versions, Lucifer imprisoned the angels after his fall, in order that they should forget their celestial origin. According to radical Cathars, the souls were condemned to migrate from one body to another (metempsychosis; → Reincarnation) until they arrived in the body of Perfects where they could be saved.

Christ played an essential role, but in comparison to Catholicism, there was an important difference: since they despised matter and flesh, Cathars could not agree with the dogma of the Incarnation. According to them, Christ had not a real but a phantom body. He went through Mary's body without taking on anything of her flesh. He did not suffer on the cross and did not bodily arise from death. All these beliefs restricted Christ's role; he was considered a messenger of God rather than the sacrificed Redeemer.

In the same way, the Cathars did not accept the dogma of the resurrection of the bodies after the Last Judgement. Concerning the fate of human souls, there were divergent opinions among the Cathars. The majority believed that all souls would go back to heaven; others thought that only the angels who had been forced to rebel but did not really sin would return to their celestial home. According to others, souls that could not be saved after nine incarnations would perish definitively.

The Cathars based their beliefs on the authority of the Bible. They made use of biblical texts that did not differ from those of the Catholic Bible. But they rejected the major part of the Old Testament, identifying the God of Genesis with Satan. Nevertheless, they accepted some books of the Old Testament, particularly the Psalms, the prophets, Job and the Books of Wisdom. Among the Gospels, they appreciated mostly that of John, of which they also made use in their rituals.

The Cathars had their own writings but most of them have disappeared. The treatise entitled *Book of Two Principles*, probably by John of Lugio, a radical Cathar, attributed the origin of the evil to the evil principle and denied free will as well.

The apocryphal *Interrogatio Iohannis* ("Questions of John"), used by Italian Cathars, is conserved in two Latin versions. According to Anselme of Alessandria, Nazarius, assistant ("greater son") of the bishop of Concorezzo, received this writing from the bishop and greater son of de Church of Bulgaria around 1190. The myths and beliefs expressed in this apocryphon are very close to those of the Byzantine Bogomils as they are described at the beginning of the 12th century. The text is qualified "secret" by Nazarius himself and also by the Inquisition: it means that its contents were reserved to initiated members of the sect. The apocryphon contains all major themes of sacred history, from the creation of the world to its end. Satan, head of the celestial powers, seduced by pride a great part of the angels, up to those of the fifth heaven; after their fall from the celestial world, God permitted Satan to organise matter for seven days. Satan arranged the visible world, and then he made the bodies of the first human couple, into which he introduced two angels. He seduced Eve in the shape of the snake. God authorised Satan, that is the God of the Old Testament, to reign for seven centuries. He deceived Henoch and → Moses, and sent John the Baptist to baptize in water. Christ was sent by God the Father to redeem humanity; his mother, Mary, was also an angel sent by God. Christ entered into Mary through her ear and came out in the same way. The apocryphon condemns baptism in water, emphasizes the special value of the Lord's Prayer and extols chastity. Its eschatology is essentially based on the New Testament. The Cathars also used the apocryphal *Ascension of Isaiah*.

5. RITUALS

Cathars recommended a return to the ritual of the first Christians and, at the same time, rejected the material components of the sacraments. For them, baptism in water did not have any value, and the Eucharist consisted of ordinary bread, without the real presence of Christ's body.

They practised their own rites: the daily breaking and blessing of bread, in the manner of the first Christians, and the monthly collective confession of faults (*apparellamentum*). Their principal rite, called *consolamentum*, was a spiritual baptism and an ordination of the "Perfects", who devoted themselves entirely to the Cathar faith, renouncing the pleasures of the world, and promising to observe chastity, truth, humility, obedience, and abstinence from meat of animal origin. When administering the *consolamentum*, the officiant laid the Gospel on the head of the new initiate and all the Perfects laid their right hand on his head or shoulder. The ceremony comprised also the sevenfold recitation of the Lord's Prayer and a lecture of St. John's Gospel.

6. HIERARCHY

The basis of the Cathar Church was formed by simple sympathizers, the "Believers", who could be married and have children, even though Catharism severely condemned procreation because of the imprisonment of the souls in human bodies. The Believers were necessary to support the Perfects in their mission, but also because they once could become Perfects themselves. One can imagine that many Believers waited until their last hour to renounce the pleasures of the world and to be "consolated" with the certainty of salvation. Only those who had received the *consolamentum* became full members of the Cathar Church. Before the systematic persecutions, these initiates or "Perfects" were wearing black clothing and for that reason were called "clothed heretics". Perfects had the mission to preach Cathar faith and to administer the *con-solamentum*, and they were travelling from place to place even during the persecutions. According to Cathar belief, souls could be saved only in the body of a Perfect; thus the Perfects played a decisive role in the process of salvation. But if a Perfect or a bishop committed a grave sin, he lost his spiritual power, and the persons whom he had consoled or ordained should be reconsolated or reordained.

The Cathar dioceses were administrated by bishops, assisted by a "greater" and a "lesser son". In Italy, dissensions between bishops and their orders often crystallized around doctrinal questions.

Ca. 1250, Raynier Sacconi, a former Cathar who had become inquisitor, established a list of Cathar Churches, specifying their doctrinal filiation. In Lombardy, he distinguished three orders: *Albanenses, Concorrenses and Baiolenses* (the two first ones corresponding to absolute and moderate Catharism, and the third to an intermediary current), and he specified that everywhere in Italy and in the Provence, the Cathars followed one of these currents. Raynier estimated that in his time there were 4000 Perfects in Italy.

7. DIFFUSION OF CATHAR BELIEFS

Even after the beginning of the persecutions, Catharism continued its proselytism. Nevertheless, the Cathars did not immediately reveal the core of their faith to their listeners and believers. Their preaching method was a progressive one and only the Perfects were initiated into all their secrets. According to Bernard Gui's *Handbook for the Inquisitor* and to testimonies registered by the Inquisition, the Cathar manner of preaching consisted of three steps. Firstly, they emphasized that their behaviour was in accordance with the evangelic ideal, even asserting that they held the position of the Apostles. Then they opposed their attitude to the bad way of life of the Roman Church, which was characterized by pride, cupidity, avarice, and dishonesty. Because of the moral decline of the Church, God had deprived catholic priests of their power to absolve sins and He had given it to the heretics. They underlined that nobody could be saved outside their sect. Having made their listeners sensitive to the problem of salvation, the Cathars began to reveal their beliefs, starting generally with their opinions about the sacraments. Anti-heretical treatises make mention of some of their "secret" beliefs. According to Eckbert of Schönau, new heretics could know the true doctrine only after 15 years. Some other authors enumerate several secret Cathar beliefs, for example that of the sin of Lucifer in heaven, the creation of four creatures by the evil God, Christ's body, and metempsychosis.

8. THE END OF CATHARISM

The Albigensian Crusade, the Inquisition and the anti-heretical measures progressively weakened the Cathar Church. In Italy, Catharism persisted without too much difficulty until the decline of the Ghibelline party (mid-13th century). After the 1280's, because of political changes and increased persecutions Catharism lost ground in the Italian towns. The last Cathar bishop (Cione di ser Bernardo) was captured in 1321. In Languedoc, a revival of Catharism can be observed between 1295 and 1310 in the mountains of Ariège, which came to an end with the action of the Inquisition in 1318-1325. The last Perfect, Guillaume Belibasta, was arrested and burned in 1321.

The disappearance of Catharism can also partly be explained by the introduction of new pastoral methods of the catholic Church, particularly by the activity of the Preaching Orders, i.e. the Dominicans and Franciscans. By involving laymen to a great extent in religious life, the Church also proposed to them new forms of piety and new structures (religious fraternities, new feasts, and processions) to practise them.

Collections of sources: R. Nelli, *Ecritures cathares*, Paris: Denoël, 1959 (new expanded edition by A. Brenon, Monaco: Editions du Rocher, 1995) ♦ W.L. Wakefield & A.P. Evans, *Heresies of the High Middle Ages*, New York/London: Columbia University Press, 1969 ♦ F. Zambon, *La cena segreta: Trattati e rituali catari*, Milan: Adelphi, 1997.
Editions of essential texts: L. Clédat, *Nouveau Testament traduit au XIIIe siècle en langue provençale suivi d'un rituel cathare*, Paris: Leroux, 1887, repr. Genève: Slatkine, 1968 ♦ I. von Döllinger, *Beiträge zur Sektengeschichte des Mittelalters*, 2 vols., München: Beck, 1890 (repr. Darmstadt: Wissenschaftliche Buchgesellschaft, 1968) ♦ J. Duvernoy, *Le Registre d'Inquisition de Jacques Fournier (1318-1325)*, Latin text: Privat: Toulouse, 1965; French trans.: Paris/La Haye: Mouton, 1977-1978 ♦ Ch. Thouzellier, *Livre des deux principes* (SC 198), Paris: Le Cerf, 1977 ♦ Ch. Thouzellier, *Rituel cathare latin* (SC 236), Paris: Le Cerf, 1977 ♦ E. Bozoky, *Le Livre secret des Cathares: Interrogatio Iohannis, apocryphe d'origine bogomile*, Paris: Beauchesne, 1980 (new ed. 1990).

Lit.: J.H. Arnold, *Inquisition and Power: Catharism and the Confessing Subject in Medieval Languedoc*, Philadelphia, 2001 ♦ M. Barber, *The Cathars in Languedoc: Dualist Heretics in Languedoc in the High Middle Ages*, Harlow: Longman, 2000 ♦ P. Biller & C. Bruschi (eds.), *Texts and the Repression of Medieval*

Heresy, York: Woodbridge & Rochester, 2003 ◆ A. Borst, *Die Katharer*, Stuttgart: Hiersemann, 1953 (new ed. Freiburg i. B., Basel, Wien, 1992); French trans.: *Les Cathares*, Paris: Payot, 1974 ◆ E. Bozoky (ed.), *Bogomiles, Patarins et Cathares, Slavica Occitania* (Toulouse) 16 (2003) ◆ E. Bozoky, "La part du mythe dans la diffusion du catharisme", *Heresis* 35 (2001), 45-58 ◆ A. Brenon, *Les archipels cathares: Dissidence chrétienne dans l'Europe médiévale*, Cahors: Dire, 2000 ◆ A. Dondaine, *Les hérésies et l'Inquisition, XIIᵉ-XIIIᵉ siècles: Documents et études*, London: Variorum Reprints, 1990 ◆ J. Duvernoy, *Le catharisme*, vol. 1: *La religion des Cathares*, vol. 2: *L'histoire des Cathares*, Toulouse: Privat, 1976 and 1979 ◆ A. Greco, *Mitologia catara: Il favoloso mondo delle origini*, Spoleto: Centro italiano di studi sull'Alto Medioevo, 2000 ◆ "Hérétiques ou Dissidents? Réflexions sur l'identité de l'hérésie au Moyen Age", *Heresis* 36-37 (2002) ◆ P. Jimenez, *L'évolution doctrinale du catharisme: XIIᵉ-XIIIᵉ siècles*, Thesis, Toulouse, 2001 (to be published: Paris Beauchesne) ◆ M. Lambert, *Medieval Heresy*, London: Blackwell, 1992 (2nd ed.) ◆ idem, *The Cathars*, Malden: Blackwell, 1998 ◆ R. Manselli, *Eresia del Male*, 2nd rev. ed., Naples: Morano, 1980 ◆ G.G. Merlo, *Contro gli eretici*, Bologna: Il Mulino, 1996 ◆ R. Morghen, *Medioevo cristiano*, Gius, Bari: Laterza, 1951 (5th ed. Roma: Laterza, 1978) ◆ R. Nelli, *Le phénomène cathare*, Paris/Toulouse: PUF/Privat, 1964 ◆ idem, *La philosophie du catharisme: Le dualisme radical au XIIIᵉ siècle*, Paris: Payot, 1975 ◆ M.G. Pegg, *The Corruption of the Angels: The Great Inquisition of 1245-1246*, Princeton: Princeton University Press, 2001 ◆ idem, "Historiographical Essay: On Cathars, Albigenses, and Good Men of Languedoc", *Journal of Medieval History* 27 (2001), 181-195 ◆ R. Poupin, *La Papauté, les cathares et Thomas d'Aquin*, Portet-sur-Garonne: Loubatières, 2000 ◆ idem, *Les cathares, l'âme et la réincarnation*, ibidem, 2000 ◆ M. Roquebert, *La religion cathare: Le mal, le bien, le salut dans l'hérésie médiévale*, Paris: Perrin, 2001 ◆ G. Rottenwöhrer, *Der Katharismus*, 4 vols., Bad Honnef: Bock und Herchen, 1982-1993 ◆ F. Sanjek, *Les chrétiens bosniaques et le mouvement cathare, XIIᵉ-XVᵉ siècles*, Brussels, Paris, Louvain: Nauwelaerts, 1976 ◆ H. Söderberg, *La religion des Cathares: Etudes sur le gnosticisme de la basse antiquité et du Moyen Age*, Uppsala: Almqvist & Wiksell, 1949 ◆ Y. Stoyanov, *The other God: Dualist Religions from Antiquity to the Cathar Heresy*, New Haven, London: Yale University Press, 2000 ◆ Ch. Thouzellier, *Catharisme et valdéisme en Languedoc à la fin du XIIᵉ et au début du XIIIᵉ siècle*, Paris: PUF, 1969 ◆ R. van den Broek, "The Cathars. Medieval Gnostics?", in: R. van den Broek & W.J. Hanegraaff (eds.), *Gnosis and Hermeticism from Antiquity to Modern Times*, Albany: State University of New York Press, 1998, 87-108 ◆ G. Volpe, *Movimenti religiosi e sette ereticali nella societa medievale italiana (secoli XI-XIV)*, Florence: Vallecchi, 1926 (5th ed. Florence: Sansoni, 1977) ◆ R. Weis, *The Yellow Cross: The Story of the Last Cathars 1290-1329*, London: Penguin Books, 2000 ◆ F. Zambon, *El legado de los cataros*, Madrid: Siruela, 1997.

Collections, Journals: Les Cahiers de Fanjeaux, Toulouse, Privat, annual publication since 1968 about medieval religious life in Languedoc; *Heresis*, international review published by the Centre of Cathar Studies, Carcassonne.

EDINA BOZOKY

Catharism, Neo– → Neo-Catharism

Cayce, Edgar, * 18.3.1877 Hopkinsville, Kentucky, † 3.1.1945 Virginia Beach, Virginia

Known to the American public as the "sleeping prophet", Edgar Cayce became an influential forerunner of New Age spirituality [→ New Age Movement] through the voluminous body of clairvoyant "readings" he left behind at his death in 1945. The transcripts of these trance sessions were catalogued and organized by the Association for Research and Enlightenment, the institution Cayce created in June 1931. Through the publishing initiatives of Cayce's son, Hugh Lynn Cayce, books discussing everything from alternative health therapies to the lost continent of Atlantis, and from the Dead Sea Scrolls to → reincarnation flooded the occult/metaphysical book market beginning in the 1950s, bringing a hodgepodge of Eastern and Western esoteric and alternative reality teachings to the American public.

Cayce's rural Kentucky early life inculcated into him the values of family loyalty, Bible study, and dedication to Christ. He was fascinated by the Bible and developed a habit of reading it from cover to cover each year. Cayce's biographers all relate stories of his budding clairvoyant abilities, including imaginary playmates, visions of deceased relatives, and the memorization of books he slept on. When he was thirteen, he had a vision of a beautiful woman to whom he confided that his deepest desire was to help the sick, especially children.

Cayce quit school early to help with the family finances. He worked as a farm laborer, bookstore clerk, and traveling salesman. His life took a sudden turn in 1900 when he came down with severe laryngitis that left him unable to speak or work for a year. He found a job as a photographer's assistant in Hopkinsville and resigned himself to his seemingly chronic disability. A traveling hypnotist heard about Cayce's condition and convinced him to be hypnotized. To the amazement of his family, Cayce was able to speak normally while in the trance state. Upon regaining normal consciousness, however, his disability returned. A New York specialist and a local amateur hypnotist convinced Cayce to diagnose his own condition while under hypnosis. This first "reading" claimed that his illness could be healed by suggesting, while unconscious, that blood circulation be increased to his throat area. The treatment was successful, and after some initial hesitation, Cayce began giving "health readings" for local people with intractable health problems. It was discovered that Cayce needed only the person's name and location in order to give the reading. He refused to accept payment for these services. One of the most remarkable of the readings was for a five-year-old girl who was suffering from convulsions and arrested mental development as a result of a spinal injury and influenza. After Cayce had diagnosed her condition, the girl was completely healed by means of osteopathic adjustments. Cayce married Gertrude Evans in 1903 and moved to Bowling Green, Kentucky. There he opened a photography studio with a partner.

Cayce gained national fame in 1910 after meeting Dr. Wesley Ketchum, a homeopath, who published a paper on Cayce in the American Society of Clinical Research. In October, the *New York Times* published an article summarizing the journal piece, and Cayce began receiving requests for readings from around the world. Cayce, Ketchum, and several others formed the Psychic Reading Corporation to handle these requests. Some of the therapies suggested in the readings were unorthodox, but most proved successful and Cayce's fame spread. In order to address the difficulty of finding doctors willing to carry out his unorthodox treatments, Cayce began formulating plans to build a hospital dedicated to his patients.

In 1923, Cayce gave his first reading mentioning → reincarnation. It would take much soul-searching before he could reconcile reincarnation with his Christianity, but eventually he was able to do this. Out of this development came the first "life readings", whose purpose was to assess a person's past lives in order to give guidance on the present life's course. It was out of the life readings that Cayce's teachings on meditation, dream interpretation, ancient civilizations such as Lemuria and Atlantis, spiritual development, and reincarnation would emerge.

Cayce moved his family to Virginia Beach, Virginia in 1925. He founded the Association of National Investigators in 1927 to conduct research on the information given in the readings. In 1928, with the assistance of a New York businessman named Morton Blumenthal, he opened the Edgar

Cayce hospital. Patients at the hospital obtained readings, diagnoses, and recommendations for treatment. Cayce's medical philosophy was that all schools of medicine should be consulted and that whatever was best for the patient should be employed to assist in the healing process. The hospital and Atlantic University, begun in 1930, were forced to close in 1931 because of the Great Depression. What remained was the Association for Research and Enlightenment, Inc. (A.R.E.), whose purpose was to both investigate and make public the information in the readings. The A.R.E. has survived until the present time and has been responsible for the worldwide dissemination of Cayce's peculiar mélange of theosophy, Eastern religions, mysticism, alternative healing therapies, dream study, and Christ-centered spiritual development.

Many skeptics came to Virginia Beach to debunk Cayce's work. One of them, a Catholic writer named Thomas Sugrue, became convinced of Cayce's authenticity and wrote *There is a River* (1943), the first and most popular Cayce biography. Coronet magazine published an article shortly thereafter on Cayce, "Miracle Man of Virginia Beach", and this greatly increased Cayce's notoriety and influence.

Cayce was besieged with requests for readings during World War II and felt a deep obligation to help all those who came to him for assistance. As a result of this overwork, he began to suffer from nervous exhaustion. In 1944, he suffered a stroke, and died on January 3, 1945. His wife died three months later. It was Cayce's loyal secretary, Gladys Davis, who assumed responsibility for cataloguing and indexing Cayce's 14.000 readings. Her work was not completed until 1971, by which time a new generation of spiritual seekers had discovered Cayce's legacy and joined the A.R.E. In time, the complete set of readings was made available on CD-Rom. The readings are also available for study at A.R.E. headquarters in Virginia Beach.

The present-day organizations that study and disseminate the Cayce readings include the A.R.E., the Edgar Cayce Foundation, Atlantic University (reactivated in 1985), the Health and Rejuvenation Research Center, and the Cayce/Reilly School of Massotherapy.

Lit.: Jess Stearn, *Edgar Cayce, the Sleeping Prophet*, New York: Bantam Books, 1968 ◆ Thomas Sugrue, *There is a River: The Story of Edgar Cayce*, New York: Dell Publishing Company, 1945 ◆ Herbert B. Puryear, *The Edgar Cayce Primer*, New York: Bantam Books, 1982 ◆ Jeffrey Furst, *Edgar Cayce's Story of Jesus*, New York: Coward-McCann, 1968 ◆ Phillip Charles Lucas, "The Association for Research and Enlightenment: Saved by the New Age", in: Timothy Miller (ed.), *America's Alternative Religions*, Albany: SUNY Press, 1995 ♦ K. Paul Johnson, *Edgar Cayce in Context: The Readings: Truth and Fiction*, Albany: SUNY Press, 1998 ♦ Sidney D. Kirkpatrick, *Edgar Cayce: An American Prophet*, New York: Riverhead Books, 2000.

PHILLIP CHARLES LUCAS

Cazotte, Jacques, * 17.10.1719 Dijon, † 25.9.1792 Paris

A Catholic all his life, Cazotte was educated at a Jesuit school in Dijon. He went on to study Law, and went to Paris in 1740, where he took up a position in the Administration of the French Fleet. In 1741 he published some original fairy tales (*La patte du Chat*), and in 1742 a number of fantastic "oriental" tales such as *Les Mille et une fadaises*, inspired by the French translation (by Galland, 1704) of the *Arabian Nights* (in French, *Les Mille et une nuits*). His professional duties obliged him to sojourn in various French harbours (such as Le Havre and Brest) between the years 1743 and 1747. Appointed in 1747 by the French Administration as "Contrôleur" in Martinique, he was to serve there only for a few months. Back in Paris he frequented the artistic and literary milieu, published ballads, and dabbled in music criticism, taking the side of Jean-Jacques Rousseau on behalf of French music (*Observation sur la lettre de Jean-Jacques Rousseau*, 1753). Later, he was sent to Martinique again, where he remained at his post from 1754 to 1759. He had married a native woman of the island, Élisabeth Roignan, and had two children by her. He was, however, plagued by financial problems, due in part to expenses he had incurred in a lawsuit against the Jesuits. Suffering ill health as well, he returned to France. But Cazotte's fortunes improved with the inheritance of his brother's estate. This provided him sufficient income to become a full-time writer. In this capacity, he and his family settled in Pierry, a village near Epernay, in Champagne in 1761. There, he wrote a long poem in twelve prose cantos intermixed with verse, entitled *Ollivier* (2 vols., 1763), followed by another romance, *Le Lord Impromptu* (1771), and what was to become by far the most popular of his works, *Le Diable amoureux* (1772). Other tales by Cazotte followed. Notable among them was a series of "oriental" works, entitled *Continuation des Mille et une nuits* (1788). Cazotte opposed the French Revolution during its earliest phases because he saw in it a great incarnation of Satan. Several personal letters he had written to friends

were seized in August 1792 by the revolutionary authorities. On the 18th of August in the same year he was imprisoned, but he made a brief escape thanks to the courage of his daughter. Captured again soon after, he was sentenced to death on September 24th, and guillotined on the following day.

Both *Le Diable amoureux* and some activities of its author pertain to the esoteric current called → Illuminism. The plot of *Le Diable amoureux* concerns a young man, Alvare, who has learned how to conjure spirits, and one night succeeds in summoning the Devil. The Devil appears, first with an ugly camel's head, then with the head of a spaniel, and finally with that of a young page who turns out to be a very attractive girl, with whom he quickly falls in love. Like Mephistopheles in the Faust story, she offers Alvare the power of ruling over 'mankind, all the elements and the whole of nature'. She says she can do so, thanks to a 'higher science', the knowledge of which she swears to teach him. In the end, Alvare never attains the promised powers, for although he wants to marry the lovely page, she suddenly vanishes and abandons him forever. This novel heralds the development of the literature of the fantastic and can claim to have inspired a number of poets. Indeed, its influence has been far-reaching and lasting, beginning with E.T.A. Hoffmann, → Gérard de Nerval and Charles Baudelaire, and proceeding through to Guillaume Apollinaire. The narrative of the invocation and corporal presence of a spirit – albeit a satanic one – attracted the attention of many readers of the time: not only people with refined tastes in literature, but also Illuminists fascinated with "theurgy" in relation to theosophical speculations.

In a long letter dated 6 February 1790 (see *Correspondance* ed. by Décote, 132), addressed to an unidentified correspondent, Cazotte explains that he had written *Le Diable amoureux* in a playful mood, inspired by stories he had heard from Freemasons [→ Freemasonry] dabbling in occult sciences [→ occult / occultism]. However, after its publication he was visited by numerous serious "seekers" after the secrets of the occult, who sought his advice because they believed him more knowledgeable than they were themselves. Some of these devotees of the occult suggested that he read *Des Erreurs et de la Vérité* (1775) by → Louis-Claude de Saint-Martin. Shortly thereafter, in 1777 or 1778, he agreed to be initiated into the Order of the → Elus Coëns founded by the theosopher and theurgist → Martines de Pasqually. The letter continues by relating how he eventually became disillusioned with the Martinists [→ Martinism], and joined the Marquise de La Croix in a crusade against them and the disciples of → Cagliostro. In the same letter he calls → Swedenborg 'the most extravagant of all visionaries'.

It is well documented, by two of his letters, that Cazotte did in fact belong to Pasqually's fringe-masonic and theurgic Order. Additionally, Saint-Martin's autobiography, *Mon portrait*, attests to him having known Cazotte personally, and gives details of Cazotte's initiation by the Elect Coën Duroy d'Hauterive. Finally, two documents listing the names of members of the Order also mention Cazotte. He seems to have been an Elect Coën until 1781 or so. Several possibly interconnected reasons may account for his decision to tender his resignation. He may have deemed Pasqually's teachings too great a departure from the tenets of his strict Catholic creed. He may have been disappointed with his own inability to conjure up angels. Or, again, he may have considered that → Freemasonry in general held certain political dangers, especially for the monarchy – a political stance he shared with his son, the Illuminist Scévole. Interestingly enough, the latter wrote in a letter to Cazotte, dated 15th July 1792 – the very day after the Revolution's Fête de la Fédération had taken place on the Champ de Mars – that a day earlier he had performed certain magical operations 'designed to put [the Champ de Mars] under the protection of the Lord'.

A previously unpublished text, brought to light in 1806 and written by the literary critic J.F. La Harpe, provides details about a story that circulated shortly after the Revolution. The setting is Paris at the beginning of 1788, at a banquet in the house of an unnamed member of the French Academy. A number of famous persons were present, among whom, besides La Harpe and Cazotte, were Nicolas-Sébastien Chamfort, Antoine-Nicolas Condorcet, Jean-Sylvain Bailly, and the Duchess of Gramont. All of them were rapturous about the great Revolution that was under way, because they felt that superstition and fanaticism would be replaced by enlightened philosophy. Cazotte jumped into the conversation, and addressed each guest face to face, predicting in detail his or her death by execution or suicide during the aftermath of the Revolution. True to his predictions, during the reign of the Terror, each of the guests died precisely as he had said they would. Over the past two hundred years, this text has been reproduced in various forms and commented upon many times. Scarcely two years after its first publication, → Johann Heinrich Jung-Stilling translated it into German in his famous *Theorie der Geister-Kunde* (Theorie of the Science of Spirits, 1808). In the extensive commentary which accompanies the translation, Jung-Stilling claimed to have met people who were able to attest to the accuracy of La Harpe's story, and went on developing the theory that Cazotte's prophecies were inspired by spirits with whom he communicated. 'Has there ever been', Jung-Stilling wrote, 'since the time of the Apostles any testimony more remarkable and more important bearing witness to the existence of the world of spirits and its action upon the visible world?' Sir → Edward Bulwer-Lytton contributed to the popularity of the prophecy by introducing it into *Zanoni* (1842), the most celebrated esoteric novel of the 19th century. The hero, Zanoni, is said to have been present at the banquet and prompted Cazotte to make the prophecy. Historians, however, tend to suggest that La Harpe only wanted to write an attractive literary piece that expanded on a tiny incident or even upon a simple rumour.

Published in 1852, → Gérard de Nerval's book *Les Illuminés* contains several chapters, each devoted to an Illuminé. Along with Cagliostro, → Rétif de La Bretonne, Quintus Aucler and others we find in this gallery the author of *Le Diable amoureux*. Nerval gives a slightly romantic biography of Cazotte, along with a lauditory presentation of his literary work. He dwells extensively on both the esoteric milieu to which Cazotte had belonged for some time, on *Le Diable amoureux*, and, not surprisingly, on the prophecy reported by La Harpe. In addition to that portrait drawn by the pen of the great Romantic, the place that → Eliphas Lévi devotes to him in his *Histoire de la Magie* (1860, Book V, Chapter 2) has contributed in no small measure to Cazotte's reputation as not only a poet and a novelist, but as mostly a man endowed with mysterious gifts.

Le Diable amoureux suivi de la Prophétie de Cazotte rapportée par La Harpe, de ses Révélations, d'extraits de sa correspondance ainsi que d'Ollivier et de l'Histoire de Maugraby (Georges Décote, ed.; Collection Folio Classique), Paris: Gallimard, 1981 ◆ *Jacques Cazotte Le Diable amoureux* (Annalisa Bottacin, ed.), Milan: Cisalpino/ La Goliardica, 1983 ◆ English: Cazotte, with Gérard de Nerval, J.L. Borges, *The Devil in Love, Followed by Jacques Cazotte: His life, Trial, Prophecy, and Revelations*, Venice: Marsilio, 1994 ◆ J.F. La Harpe, "Prédictions de Cazotte", in: La Harpe, *Œuvres choisies et posthumes*, Paris: Migneret, 1806 ◆ idem, *Correspondance de Jacques Cazotte* (Georges Décote, ed.), Paris: Klincksieck, 1982.

Lit. Georges Décote, "Note sur l'initiation de Jacques Cazotte", *Dix-huitième siècle* (1972), 229-236 ◆ idem, *L'itinéraire de Jacques Cazotte: De la fiction littéraire au mysticisme poétique*, Paris: Droz, 1984 ◆ Keeneth J. Fleurant, "Mysticism and the Age of Reason: Jacques Cazotte and the demons", *French Review* 49: 1 (1975), 68-75 ♦ Nadia Minerva, "Jacques Cazotte, *Il diavolo in amore*", *Spicilegio Moderno* (Parma-Milano: Ricci) 9 (1978), 201-202 ♦ idem, "Des Lumières à l'Illuminisme: Jacques Cazotte et son monde", *Transactions of the Fifth International Congress on the Enlightenment* (Oxford, The Voltaire Foundation) 3 (1980), 1015-1022 ♦ idem "Demonologia e profetismo in Jacques Cazotte", *Spicilegio Moderno* 15-16 (1981), 217-228 ♦ idem, "Démonologie tératologique et Lumières: Un aspect de l'imaginaire fantastique et de l'anti-philosophie au XVIIIe siècle", *Transactions of the Sixth International Congress on the Enlightenment* (Oxford, The Voltaire Foundation) (1983), 10-23 ♦ idem, "Diables et prophètes: Jacques Cazotte entre les Lumières et l'Illuminisme", in: Mario Matucci (ed.), *Lumières et Illuminisme*, Pisa: Pacini, 1985, 211-220 ♦ Jean Richer, *Aspects ésotériques de l'oeuvre littéraire*, Paris: Dervy, 1980, Chapter 3 ♦ idem, *La passion de Jacques Cazotte: Son procès*, Paris: G. Tredaniel/La Maisnie, 1988 ♦ Dietmar Rieger, *Jacques Cazotte: Ein Beitrag zur erzählenden Literatur des 18. Jahrhunderts* (Studia Romanica 15), Heidelberg: Winter, 1969.

ANTOINE FAIVRE

Cerdo, before 150

Cerdo was a Christian teacher who worked in Rome during the episcopate of Hyginus (ca. 136-142). The main sources for his life and teaching are the anti-heretical works of Irenaeus (ca. 180) and some later authors, who might be dependent on Hippolytus (ca. 220). Their information possibly derives from local Roman traditions but is very problematic. According to Irenaeus, *Adversus haereses*, III, 4, 3, Cerdo came under Hyginus 'repeatedly back to the church as a penitent: now teaching in secret, then doing penance, then again being convicted of heretical teaching on certain points and leaving the community of the brothers'. Though the same is told of more famous teachers such as → Marcion and → Valentinus (Tertullian, *De praescriptione haereticorum*, 30, 2f.: 'semel et iterum eiecti'), there is no reason to doubt the reliability of this report. It perfectly fits the evidence that the Roman church in the fourth and fifth decade of the 2nd century was still in a process of defining its theological identity and communal boundaries. Just as Valentinus and Marcion, Cerdo obviously considered himself a good Christian and wanted to be a member of the Church, but became a "heretic" because the church was closing its previously open border.

Of Cerdo's specific ideas very little is known. Irenaeus, *AH*, I, 27, 1, says that he was connected with the followers of → Simon Magus and makes him the forerunner and teacher of Marcion, which is repeated by Hippolytus, *Refutatio*, VII, 37. He is said to have taught 'that the god proclaimed by the law and the prophets is not the Father of our Lord Jesus Christ, for the one is known and the other is unknown, one is just and the other is good'. As a matter of fact, this is the core of Marcion's doctrine of the contrast between the ignorant but just God of the Jews and the God of love, the Father of Jesus Christ. The alleged connection with the Simonians is determined by Irenaeus' idea of a Gnostic genealogy and his wish to present Cerdo as a Gnostic. The later anti-heretical tradition, recorded by Pseudo-Tertullian, *Adversus omnes haereses*, 6, Filastrius, *Diversarum haereseon liber*, 44, and Epiphanius, *Panarion*, 41, who possibly all reflect the section on Cerdo in Hippolytus' lost *Syntagma*, has a lot to say about Cerdo The only reliable element in this tradition may be the information, transmitted by Filastrius and Epiphanius, that Cerdo came from Syria. For the rest these authors ascribe to Cerdo a complete Marcionite theology. He is said to have taught he doctrine of the two gods (including the rejection of the creator-god and the Jewish bible), the resurrection of the soul only and a docetic Christology. Moreover, he would have accepted as authoritative scripture the expurgated Gospel of Luke and some of the letters of the apostle Paul only. The doctrine of scripture is typically that of Marcion, but for the rest Cerdo is described in these sources as a full-fledged Gnostic.

This presentation of a rather obscure Christian teacher as a proto-Marcion and a Gnostic [→ Gnosticism] served an anti-Marcionite aim. In the 2nd and 3rd centuries, the Marcionite church became a forceful rival of the early-catholic church. It was in the interest of the anti-heretical writers to strip Marcion of his originality. Therefore, they tried to show that he was no more than an ordinary Gnostic and that even his most characteristic doctrines, about the two gods and about scripture, were not his own but had been borrowed from his teacher Cerdo.

This biased attitude of our sources makes it virtually impossible to come to firm conclusions about the nature of Cerdo's teaching, especially his doctrine of God. According to Irenaeus, Cerdo taught that the god of the Hebrew bible was just (*dikaios*) and Pseudo-Tertullian says that he was cruel (*saevus*). Both characteristics apply to the Jewish god as Marcion described him: he is just, but his justice is that of a despot. If it is true that Pseudo-Tertullian reflects Hippolytus' *Syntagma*, then we may assume that the latter also had described Cerdo's creator god in Marcionite terms.

Filastrius and Epiphanius, however, who also belong to the conjectured "Hippolytan" tradition, simply say that the lower god is evil (*malus, ponēros*), which makes him identical with the Gnostic Demiurge. This may be due to their intention to describe Marcion and his alleged teacher as ordinary Gnostics.

In the middle of the 2nd century there was a fierce debate on the interpretation of the Jewish bible in the context of the Christian message concerning Jesus the Saviour. The positions taken in this debate were strongly determined by the participants' assessment of the relationship between God, Jesus Christ and the creation. It is conceivable that Cerdo took a radical stance in this debate and in some way denied the authority of the Jewish bible for the Christian church, with a degradation of the Jewish god as its corollary. Since Marcion developed his radical "Gospel of the Alien God" from a similar starting point, in retrospect Cerdo may have been considered Marcion's teacher. It is unlikely, however, that the latter's very original doctrine of the two gods was no more than a further development of Cerdo's ideas.

A. Rousseau & L. Doutreleau (eds.), *Irénée de Lyon: Contre les Hérésies, Livre I* (SC 264), Paris: Les Éditions du Cerf, 1979 (with French trans.); Engl. trans., after the German trans. by W. Foerster, in: idem (ed.), *Gnosis: A Selection of Gnostic Texts*, Eng. trans. edited by R. McL. Wilson, vol. 1, Oxford: Clarendon Press, 1972, 44 ♦ A. Kroymann (ed.), [Ps. Tertullian] *Adversus omnes haereses* (CC, ser. Lat. II, originally edited in CSEL 47), Turnhout: Brepols, 1954; Engl. trans. by S. Thelwall in *ANCL*, vol. 18, Edinburgh: T&T Clark, 1870 (repr. in: *ANF*, vol. 3, Edinburgh/Grand Rapids: T&T Clark/W.B. Eerdmans, 1993) ♦ M. Marcovich (ed.), *Hippolytus: Refutatio omnium haeresium* (Patristische Texte und Studien, 25), Berlin, New York: De Gruyter, 1986; Engl. trans. by J.H. Macmahon, in *ANCL*, vol. 6, Edinburgh: T&T Clark, 1868-1869 (repr. *ANF*, vol. 5, Edinburgh/Grand Rapids: T&T Clark/W.B. Eerdmans, 1995) ♦ K. Holl (ed.), *Epiphanius II: Panarion haer. 34-64*, 2nd rev. ed. by J. Dummer, Berlin: Akademie Verlag, 1980 ♦ F. Williams, *The Panarion of Epiphanius of Salamis, Book I (Sects 1-46)*, Leiden: E.J. Brill, 1987 ♦ F. Heylen (ed.), *Filastri Episcopi Brixiensis Diversarum Hereseon Liber* (CC, ser. Lat., 9), Turnhout: Brepols, 1957.

Lit.: A. von Harnack, *Marcion: Das Evangelium vom fremden Gott. Eine Monographie zur Geschichte und Grundlegung der altkatholische Kirche*, 2nd. ed., Leipzig: Hinrichs, 1924 (reprinted: Darmstad Wissenschaftlichen Buchgesellschaft, 1960), 31*-39* ("Beilage II: Cerdo und Marcion"; with all relevant sources) ♦ D.W. Deakle, "Harnack & Cerdo: A Reexamination of the Patristic Evidence for Marcion's Mentor", in: G. May et alii (eds.), *Marcion und seine kirchengeschichtliche Wirkung – Marcion and his Impact on Church History*

(Texte und Untersuchungen zur Geschichte der altchristlichen Literatur, 150), Berlin-New York: de Gruyter, 2002, 177-190 ♦ G. May, "Markion und der Gnostiker Kerdon", in: A. Raddatz & K. Lüthi (eds.), *Evangelischer Glaube und Geschichte: Grete Mecenseffy zum 85. Geburtstag* (Aktuelle Reihe des Reformierten Kirchenblattes, 26), Vienna, 1984, 233-246.

ROELOF VAN DEN BROEK

Cerinthus, ca. 100

Cerinthus was a Christian teacher who lived in Asia Minor at the end of the first or the beginning of the 2nd century. The reports about his teaching are contradictory, and as a result modern scholars have described him either as an early Gnostic [→ Gnosticism] or as a primitive Christian who had been strongly influenced by Judaeo-Christian ideas.

Cerinthus appears as an arch-heretic in the first document that mentions his name, the so-called *Epistula apostolorum*, which was written ca. 150, most probably in Asia Minor. It claims to have been composed 'because of the false apostles Simon and Cerinthus' (1), who are 'enemies of our Lord Jesus Christ, who in reality alienate those who believe in the true word and deed, namely Jesus Christ' (7). That Cerinthus is mentioned here together with → Simon Magus does not necessarily imply that Cerinthus was considered a Gnostic too. But that he was seen as a serious heretic at an early date also emerges from a curious story told by Irenaeus, *Adversus haereses*, III, 3, 4, on the authority of Polycarp (ca. 150). The apostle John once went into the bathhouse at Ephesus and, seeing that Cerinthus was within, he rushed out of the bathhouse without bathing, exclaiming: 'Let us fly, lest even the bathhouse fall down, because Cerinthus, the enemy of truth, is within'. According to the same Irenaeus, John had 'proclaimed the Gospel' in order to refute the error that had been promulgated by Cerinthus (*AH*, III, 11, 1), but it seems possible that Irenaeus has simply inferred this from the bathhouse story. Irenaeus is also the first, in *AH*, I, 26, 1, to give more detailed information about Cerinthus' ideas. According to him, Cerinthus separated the creator god from the highest god and Jesus from Christ. The world was not made by the supreme God but by 'a certain Power', which was far removed from the 'Principality' that transcended the universe and of which the creative Power was ignorant. Cerinthus denied the virginal birth of Jesus and considered him the natural son of Joseph and Mary who surpassed all other human beings in righteousness, prudence and wisdom. At his baptism Christ descended upon Jesus, who from then on proclaimed the unknown Father. But at last Christ flew away from Jesus, who 'suffered and rose again while Christ remained impassible, being a spiritual being'. Hippolytus of Rome (ca. 220) has only one new element to add, namely that Cerinthus 'was trained in the education of the Egyptians' (*Refutatio*, VII, 33, 1; X, 21, 1: 'trained in Egypt'), which most probably was Hippolytus' own invention (Markschies, 59f.).

According to many New Testament scholars, the first Epistle of John can be read as an indirect source for Cerinthus' ideas, since there are indications that the opponents combated in this letter adhered to some kind of 'separation Christology' (see e.g. 1 John 2, 22; 4, 2f.). It is by no means certain, however, whether or to what extent this view was comparable to that ascribed to Cerinthus by Irenaeus. If the opponents of 1 John were actually Cerinthus and his disciples, one would expect a clear reference to Cerinthus' explicit separation between Jesus and Christ, which, however, is not the case.

Irenaeus and Hippolytus apparently saw in Cerinthus no more than an early Gnostic, but Eusebius, in his *Historia Ecclesiastica*, has preserved a tradition on Cerinthus that points in quite another direction. According to Gaius, a Roman anti-Montanist writer (ca. 200), Cerinthus appealed to revelations, 'said to be written by a great apostle' (probably the Apocalypse of John). He taught that 'after the resurrection the kingdom of Christ will be set up on earth, and that in Jerusalem the body will again serve as the instrument of desires and pleasures'. There would be 'a marriage feast lasting a thousand years' (Eusebius, *HE*, III, 28, 2). Bishop Dionysius of Alexandria (ca. 250), in a lost work called *On the promises*, related that according to some of his predecessors Cerinthus had written the Johannine Apocalypse himself. Dionysius denied this, but had to admit that Cerinthus had taught a radical millenarianism, which included the expectation that the millennium would be characterized by 'festivals and sacrifices and the slaying of victims' (Eusebius, *HE*, VII, 25, 3 and III, 28, 4-5). This would imply that Cerinthus expected that in the thousand years of Christ's kingdom the Jerusalem temple and its sacrifices would be restored, which points to a strong Jewish-Christian influence. Similar ideas are attacked in Origen's polemic against simple Jewish or Judaizing Christians who claimed that in the millennium 'their destroyed and collapsed city' would be rebuilt and that the resurrected would enjoy the pleasures of the body, including marriages and the begetting of children (*De principiis*, II, 11, 2). It is conceivable that Dionysius' description was coloured by Origen's polemic, but there are no compelling arguments to doubt the trustworthiness of the tradition that Cerinthus was a radical chiliast. This view is much more likely than the idea, suggested by Hill, that Cerinthus was not a millenarian himself but, just as → Marcion after him, expected a millenarian kingdom of the Jewish Messiah.

The millenarian expectation has its roots in Jewish eschatological speculations. It might simply have been because of this background that the chilast Cerinthus became depicted as a radical Jewish Christian. This picture is first found in the 4th century, in Epiphanius of Salamis (*Panarion*, 28), who remarkably enough does not make any mention of Cerinthus' millenarianism. Unfortunately, as so often, Epiphanius' report is a curious mixture of earlier literary traditions, hearsay, unwarranted assumptions and slander. He ascribes to Cerinthus everything he knows or thinks to know about the Jewish Christians and makes him a contemporary of the apostles and their main opponent in all the controversies with Jewish and Judaizing Christians that are reported in the New Testament.

Is it possible to harmonize the conflicting traditions concerning Cerinthus' teaching? The first observation to be made is that the expectation of a millennial kingdom of Christ on earth, characterized by marriages and procreation, is incompatible with the Gnostic view of the body and of matter in general. In the first two centuries, chiliastic expectations were widespread, especially, but by no means exclusively, among Jewish Christians. That Irenaeus does not mention Cerinthus' millenarian ideas may be due to the fact that he was a chiliast himself. Moreover, the idea ascribed to Cerinthus by Irenaeus that Jesus was the natural son of Joseph and Mary and that he was adopted as Son of God at his baptism in the river Jordan, was also a common Jewish Christian view. That Jesus allegedly proclaimed the Unknown God after his baptism may be no more than an inference by Irenaeus from his assumption that Cerinthus was an early Gnostic. At the turn of the 1st century AD, there was not yet a clearly distinguishable Christian Gnosticism over and against a non-Gnostic, ecclesiastical Christianity. As testified by the Johannine writings and Ignatius of Antioch, there was at that time, especially in Asia Minor, a fierce debate about the Christian interpretation of Jesus Christ and about the identity of the Creator. Most probably, Cerinthus took part in that debate from a Jewish-Christian position. The creation of the world by lower divine beings had already been discussed by Jewish and Greek theologians and philosophers. In the Gospel of John (1:3) it is ascribed to the Logos.

Cerinthus may have taught the more Jewish view that the world had been made by one or more angelic powers. With respect to Jesus, he apparently made a clear distinction between the human person Jesus and the divine Christ, the spirit who descended to him at his baptism. Cerinthus remains a shadowy figure, but it seems quite certain that his position in Irenaeus' catalogue of early Gnostics is unjustified.

All relevant texts with translation in A.F.J. Klijn & G.J. Reinink, *Patristic Evidence for Jewish-Christian Sects* (Supplements to Novum Testamentum, XXXVI), Leiden: Brill, 1973.

Lit.: Ch.E. Hill, "Cerinthus, Gnostic or Chiliast? A New Solution to an Old Problem", *Journal of Early Christian Studies* 8 (2000), 135-172 ♦ Klijn & Reinink, *Patristic Evidence*, 3-19 ♦ Chr. Markschies, "Kerinth: Wer war er und was lehrte er?", *Jahrbuch für Antike und Christentum* 41 (1998), 48-76 ♦ B.G. Wright III, "Cerinthus *Apud* Hippolytus: An Inquiry into the Traditions about Cerinthus' Provenance", *The Second Century* 4 (1984), 103-115.

ROELOF VAN DEN BROEK

Champier, Symphorien, * early 1470s Saint-Symphorien-le-Château, † 1539 or 1540 Lyons

French humanist, neoplatonist, physician, and author on medicine and occult sciences. Champier's father was a notary and apothecary. Symphorien studied for some time at the university of Paris, and next attended medical school in Montpellier, where he matriculated in 1495. Soon after, he was practicing medicine and teaching the liberal arts in the Dauphiné and probably the Bourbonnais. In 1498 he published his first book, *Janua logicae et phisicae*, largely devoted to Plato and Aristotle and their commentators → Lefèvre d'Étaples (a friend of Champier and a major influence on his thought) and → Marsilio Ficino. It was followed in the early years of the 16th century by two companion volumes concerned with moral advice to members of the aristocracy, that would remain his most well-known ones: the *Nef des Princes* (1502) and the *Nef des Dames* (1503). Both *Nefs* (ships) again show the strong influence of Ficino, and together with Champier's earlier work are among the first books that introduced Florentine Platonism in Renaissance France. The first contains French translations of editions and commentaries on Plato by Ficino, and the *Livre de Vraye Amour* (book four of the *Nef des Dames*) is largely based on Ficino's *De Amore*. Champier had hoped by

these books to find patronage at the Bourbon court, but without success.

In 1503 in Lyons Champier wrote a *Dyalogus . . . in magicarum artium destructionem* which discusses the origins and nature of → magic and divination [→ Divinatory arts], frenzies, dreams and visions, the magical effects of the → imagination, and the supposed activities of witches and demons, including incubi and succubi. From a pronounced Christian-orthodox perspective, and quoting multiple authorities, it attempts to separate truth from fiction in these matters, insisting that stories about demonic activities are often based upon delusion, and that many phenomena attributed to supernatural agency can in fact be explained along naturalist lines. In the same year 1503 Champier married a noble lady, Marguerite de Terraille, and returned to Montpellier to study for his doctorate in medicine, which he obtained in 1504. In the following years he published various small books on medical subjects, which together with his new title brought him increasing recognition.

The very titles of Champier's *De quadruplici vita* (1507) and *De triplici disciplina* (1509), two of his most important works, reflect the influence of Ficino's *De vita libri tres*, often referred to as *De triplici vita*. Like Ficino, Champier based his choice to combine medical with theological/philosophical discussion on the concept of *spiritus*, understood as the medium that joins body and soul and is therefore relevant to doctors as well as priests. In addition to Ficino, one notes a strong influence of → Giovanni Pico della Mirandola as well as his nephew Gianfrancesco Pico della Mirandola; and *De quadruplici vita* contained the first printed version of → Lazzarelli's Latin translation of the last three tractates of the *Corpus Hermeticum* (under the title *Diffinitiones Asclepii*; it does not contain the *Asclepius* itself, as one might infer from Walker 1958, 169). Indeed, Champier's books of 1507 and 1509 are largely compilations based on other authors' works, and are filled with references to authorities such as e.g. Pliny, Isidore of Sevilla, and platonic, hermetic and orphic sources. They are important not for any innovative ideas (Copenhaver [1978, 56] emphasizes Champier's 'undeviating unoriginality'), but for the role they have played in the transmission of the new Italian neoplatonic and hermetic philosophy to French intellectual circles. Champier is a typical example of how the *prisca theologia* associated with Ficino was received in France: with considerably more caution than in the Italian context, particularly regarding the dangers of → astrology, astral magic, and idolatry. While rejecting the notorious hermetic "god-making" passages (*Asclepius* 23-24, 37-38) as idolatrous, Champier believed them to be written by Apuleius, not → Hermes Trismegistus.

Around 1509 Champier was appointed as chief physician to Duke Antoine of Lorraine, whom he would henceforth follow on his many military expeditions. The year 1515 was of great importance to him: his Lord bestowed the order of chivalry on him, and he was honourably invited to join the medical college of Pavia. During this period and up to the end of his life he continued writing numerous books, most of them on medical subjects, and by the 1520s he had gained an international scholarly reputation. Having returned to Lyons, he became a member of that city's ruling council of twelve. Due to a tax recommendation that was taken badly by the populace, his house was sacked by a mob during the great *rebeine* (probably a food riot) of 1529 – an event that Champier believed was caused by heresy rather than economic despair. The last ten years of his life he kept writing and practicing medicine. He died in Lyons, leaving a daughter and two sons.

> *Liber de quadruplici vita . . .*, Lyon, 1507 ♦ "Commentarium in diffinitiones asclepij cum textu eiusdem" (from *Liber de quadruplici vita*), modern edition in: *Umanesimo e esoterismo*, Padova: Cedam, 1960, 248-289 ♦ *Dyalogus . . . in magicarum artium destructionem* (ca. 1503), modern edition with Engl. trans. in: Copenhaver, *Symphorien Champier* (see below), 243-319.

> *Lit.*: M.P. Allut, *Étude biographique & bibliographique sur Symphorien Champier*, Lyon: Nicolas Scheuring, 1859 ♦ Brian P. Copenhaver, "Lefèvre d'Étaples, Symphorien Champier, and the Secret Names of God", *Journal of the Warburg and Courtauld Institutes* 40 (1977), 189-211 ♦ idem, *Symphorien Champier and the Reception of the Occultist Tradition in Renaissance France*, The Hague, Paris, New York: Mouton, 1978 ♦ Margaret I. Holmes, "Italian Renaissance Influence in the Early 16th century, with Particular Reference to the Work of Symphorien Champier", M.A. thesis Univ. of London, 1963 ♦ idem, "A Brief Survey of the Use of Renaissance Themes in Some Works of the Lyonese Doctor, Humanist and Man of Letters Symphorien Champier", in: *Cinq études lyonnaises*, Geneva: Droz, 1966 ♦ A. Potton, "Études historiques et critiques sur la vie, les travaux de Symphorien Champier", *Revue du Lyonnais* 1 (1864), 7-32, 114-140 ♦ Cesare Vasoli, "Temi e fonti della tradizione ermetica in uno scritto di Symphorien Champier", in: *Umanesimo e esoterismo*, Padova: Cedam, 1960, 235-247 ♦ D.P. Walker, *Spiritual and Demonic Magic from Ficino to Campanella* (1958), repr.: University Park, Pennsylvania: Pennsylvania State University Press, 2000, 167-170 ♦ idem, *The Ancient Theology: Studies in Christian Platonism from the Fifteenth to the Eighteenth Century*, Ithaca, New York: Cornell University Press, 1972, esp. 66-83, 88-90, 106-117 ♦ Frances Yates, "The Fear of the Occult", *The London Review of Books, with the New York Review of Books* 26:18 (1979), 37-39.

WOUTER J. HANEGRAAFF

Charbonneau-Lassay, Louis, * 18.01.1871 Loudun, † 26.12.1946 Loudun

Born Louis Charbonneau (Lassay being a village near Loudun, wherefrom came several of his direct ancestors), he began his career as a member of a Roman Catholic congregation mostly dedicated to teaching, the "Frères de Saint Gabriel". On his own, as well as in the company of some competent local scholars, he was to gain proficiency in the historical disciplines which were later to occupy most of his intellectual activity: archeology, numismatics, sigillography, heraldry, folklore and local traditions of the areas surrounding his native Poitou. In 1921, having in the meantime been allowed back into laity and achieved for himself a solid scholarly reputation, he began to contribute to the Catholic monthly *Regnabit*, the main purpose of which was the enhancement of the symbolic and theological status of the devotion to the Sacred Heart. Most of his *Regnabit* articles are concerned with the many-faceted emblematics of Jesus Christ and illustrated with quaint, neomedieval woodcuts in his own hand; for the most part, these texts along with many others were later incorporated into his main work, *Le Bestiaire du Christ* (1940).

It was in a 1929 *Regnabit* article about the dove ('La colombe') as an emblem of Christ that Charbonneau-Lassay first disclosed the informations about certain "mystic-hermetic fraternities" ('fraternités hermético-mystiques') which have made him conspicuous in esoterically-minded circles to our day. Briefly told, our author claimed to be in contact with a few restricted *milieux* of scrupulous Roman Catholic orthodoxy, still in possession of materials pertaining to what he considered a valid expression of authentic Christian esotericism. Supposedly dating back without interruption to late medieval or early modern times, and having furthermore remained essentially secluded until then, the groups in question (mainly the "Chevaliers et Dames du Divin Paraclet" and "Estoile Internelle") had nevertheless taken the initiative, through the agency of their leader, Canon T. Barbot of Poitiers (1841-1927), of lending him some documents containing symbolic and "hermetic" elements, which he made use of in the book which was to become the above-mentioned *Bestiaire*. Somewhat later it was disclosed that Charbonneau-Lassay had in fact also been entrusted with the actual continuation of the first of these fraternities, that is, with its ritual transmission, which he bestowed on a few chosen individuals (mostly selected in parisian "guenonian" circles) just before the Second World War (this particular story is dealt with in specific studies mentioned below).

The original archives alluded to by our author being hitherto unavailable to scholars, it seems difficult (to say the least) to form a square opinion about the purely historical aspects of these fraternities, not to mention the exact nature and contents of their alleged esoteric teachings. Even as regards their real impact on Charbonneau-Lassay's work, we are in fact only made aware of it when he happens to explicitly quote these arcane sources along the way. It must, nevertheless, be kept in mind that he was in no way attracted to occultism [→ occult / occultism] as such, shared the rejection of → Freemasonry common to so many Roman Catholic writers of his time but, notwithstanding, looked favourably upon the practice of symbolism, which he conceived of as a convenient and lawful way of deepening one's understanding of the faith. For this very reason, he was – up to a point – an admirer (and personal friend) of → René Guénon, whom he had been instrumental in roping in for collaboration to *Regnabit* (1925-1927). To most occidental readers and members of the "traditionalist" French school, the main attraction of Charbonneau-Lassay's disclosures has been, however, to suggest a decidedly Christian alternative to Guénon's incitements to pursue one's quest for a ritual initiation preferably within a Sufi environment.

Le Coeur rayonnant du donjon de Chinon attribué aux Templiers, Paray-le-Monial: Secrétariat des Œuvres du Sacré-Cœur/Beaux Livres, 1922 (reprint Milano: Archè, 1975) ◆ *Simboli del Cuore di Cristo* (P.L. Zoccatelli, ed.), Roma: Arkeios, 2003 ◆ *Le Bestiaire du Christ*, Bruges: Desclée de Brouwer, 1940 (reprint Milano: Archè, 1974; english, spanish and italian trans.) ◆ *L'ésotérisme de quelques symboles géométriques chrétiens*, Paris: Editions Traditionnelles, 1967 (1994²) ◆ *Etudes de symbolique chrétienne*, Paris: Gutenberg Reprints, 1981-1986 (2 vols) ◆ *Il Giardino del Cristo ferito* (P.L. Zoccatelli, ed.), Rome Arkeios, 1995 ◆ *Héraldique Loudunaise*, La Roche Rigault: PSR, 1996 ◆ *Le Pietre misteriose del Cristo* (P.L. Zoccatelli, ed.), Rome: Arkeios, 1997.

Lit.: J.P. Brach, review of P.L. Zoccatelli, *Le lièvre qui rumine* (see below), *Politica Hermetica* 16 (2002), 269-274 ◆ idem, "L. Charbonneau-Lassay", in: J.-P. Chantin (ed.), *Les marges du christianisme: "sectes", dissidences, ésotérisme*, Paris: Beauchesne, 2001, 46-49 ◆ J.P. Brach & P.L. Zoccatelli, "Courants renaissants de

réforme spirituelle et leurs incidences", *Politica Hermetica* 11 (1997), 31-43 ◆ M.F. James, *Esotérisme, occultisme, franc-maçonnerie et christianisme aux XIX° et XX° siècles: Explorations bio-bibliographiques*, Paris: Nouvelles Editions Latines, 1981 (2 vols.), 68-71 ◆ S. Salzani & P.L. Zoccatelli, *Hermétisme et Emblématique du Christ dans la vie et dans l'oeuvre de Louis Charbonneau-Lassay (1871-1946)*, Milano: Archè, 1996 ◆ *Société Historique du Pays de Loudunois*, 1 (1998) ◆ L. Toth, "Le bestiaire du Christ", *Charis: Archives de l'Unicorne* 4 (2003), 49-62 ◆ P.L. Zoccatelli, "Louis Charbonneau-Lassay", in: J. Servier (ed.), *Dictionnaire critique de l'ésotérisme*, Paris: P.U.F., 1998, 287-288 ◆ idem, *Le lièvre qui rumine: Autour de René Guénon, Louis Charbonneau-Lassay et la Fraternité du Paraclet (avec des documents inédits)*, Milano: Archè, 1999; site internet: http://www.paraclet.org

JEAN-PIERRE BRACH

Chester, Robert of → Robert of Chester

Chevaliers Bienfaisants de la Cité Sainte

The Order of the "Chevaliers Bienfaisants de la Cité Sainte" (CBCS) is the "Inner Order" ("Ordre Intérieur") of the Rectified Scottish Rite, and its character and history cannot be understood without taking into account the history of its insertion in this masonic-chivalric System (or "rite"). The Rectified Scottish Rite was founded about 1780 by a group of French freemasons under the leadership of → Jean-Baptiste Willermoz (1730-1824) who intended to reform → Freemasonry, which they deemed had lost touch with its essential nature and aim. This reformation was carried out in the so called "Convent des Gaules" held in Lyons in 1778 and in the subsequent Convent of Wilhelmsbad held in 1782, and the foundation of the Order of the CBCS was part of it. The Rectified Scottish Rite, as it emerged from the Convent des Gaules, was (and has been up to now) an original system of Freemasonry consisting of two classes: a "symbolical" class and a chivalric one. The symbolical class comprises the three common degrees of "Craft" Freemasonry – Apprentice, Fellow Craft and Master Mason – plus a fourth and last degree called "Maître Ecossais de Saint-André". This is a synthesis of the essential contents of several French "higher degrees", namely the various degrees of "Ecossais" and the degree of "Chevalier d"Orient", the elements taken from these degrees (which are found independently in Royal Arch Masonry) being reworked according to the special perspective of the Rectified Scottish Rite. The Mason who has moved through the four symbolical degrees may then, if judged apt, be admitted in the "Inner Order", that is, the Order of the CBCS. He is first admitted in the quality of "Novice"; then, after the end of his novitiate, he may eventually be armed Knight after having made a profession of Christian faith, for the Order of the CBCS is a Christian Order of chivalry. The way this chivalric Order is related to the "symbolic" class is well marked in the ritual of the fourth degree. This ritual – and with it the whole symbolical teaching of the four degrees – culminates in a vision of the celestial Jerusalem; at the same time the candidate is warned that he has reached the end of his symbolical career, and that he is at the door of a new temple in which a new career may begin for him. The mention of the "Holy City" in the name of the Order of the CBCS thus refers to Jerusalem, which means both the terrestrial Jerusalem and the celestial one, of which the candidate in the fourth symbolical degree has had the vision.

This structure of the Rectified Scottish Rite as a masonic-chivalric system takes its origin from the previous but analogous German system which was called "Rectified Masonry" or (after 1764) "Strict Observance" (SO). This system was founded in the 1750s by Baron von Hund (1722-1776) and, after years of struggle with competing systems, it obtained a rather large extension and brilliant standing in Germany and in other European countries, having as its *Magnus Superior* the Duke Ferdinand of Brunswick. This system, like the Rectified Scottish Rite later, consisted of a masonic class and a chivalric one, the latter having the status of an "Inner Order". A notable feature of this chivalric Order is that it claimed to be a revival of the Order of the Knights Templar which, although suppressed by Pope Clement V under the pressure of the King of France Philip the Fair, was supposed to have survived in secret; and the SO went as far as contemplating an official restoration in itself of the said Order. By the time when the SO was expanding in Europe, Jean-Baptiste Willermoz was looking both for a convenient setting in which he could carry out his intended reform of Freemasonry and – already being a disciple of → Martinez de Pasqually (1727-1772) – for a source of further esoteric knowledge. He entered in connection with the SO in the early 1770s and obtained admission in it for himself and his team. In 1774 the SO "re-established" what was supposed to be the Templar Province of "Auvergne" (with headquarters at Lyons), and Willermoz along with eleven other French Brethren was admitted in the Inner Order, as Knight. A little later, the SO similarly re-established the "Templar" Province of "Occitania" with headquarters at Bor-

deaux, but this Province was not very active, while the brethren of Strasburg, belonging to the previously existing Province of "Burgundy", collaborated efficiently with Willermoz in the work of reforming Freemasonry, which he took up in the newly-established setting of the French branch of the SO. As we have already seen, this task was essentially carried out in the national Convent of Lyons of 1778 (gathering representatives of the Provinces of Auvergne, Burgundy and Occitania); it was the work of the French Brethren, to be confirmed and completed at the general Convent (which gathered representatives of all the Provinces of the SO throughout Europe) held at Wilhelmesbad in Germany in 1782. It is at the Convent of Lyons that the Inner Order received the new name of Order of the CBCS (or, more completely, "Ordre Bienfaisant des Chevaliers Maçons de la Cité Sainte", a name which makes explicit the connection of this chivalric Order with Freemasonry). The structure of the SO was conserved, but it must be emphasized that its spiritual content was changed considerably. On the one hand, Willermoz and his companions worked out new rituals and instructions which carried out, under the veil of symbols, a spiritual doctrine strongly influenced by Martinez de Pasqually's doctrine of the "reintegration of beings". On the other hand – and this concerns the Order of the CBCS more in particular – the claim to the historical and temporal succession of the Knights Templar was given up; only some kind of spiritual kinship was maintained (see below). Although this reformation was approved (not without difficulty) at the Convent of Wilhelmsbad, this did not have many consequences in Germany, because the Strict Observance did not survive the troubles of the wars of the French Revolution and of the Napoleonic wars. But the Rectified Scottish Rite – and in particular the Order of the CBCS – survived, and is now well alive in several countries, mainly in Switzerland (which was at one time the conservatory of the Rite extinct in other countries), Belgium and France.

The Order of the CBCS has a double aspect, an exoteric and an esoteric one. The exoteric aspect is expressed by the word "bienfaisant". Each member is bound, as he already was as a Mason, to practice beneficence in all its forms, but he is all the more vowed to this because he is also a Christian Knight. As such, he has vowed to defend the Christian religion; but at being admitted into the Order, he is taught that he no longer has to do so by the sword, as was the case for the medieval Knight: he must 'defend it by his speech, when in his presence it suffers undeserved attack; he causes it to be loved and respected by a mild and enlightened tolerance, by good morals, by a regular conduct and by the good examples he gives'. In one word, the exoteric content of the Order essentially consists in the same moral teaching as that of Freemasonry, but in a more explicitly Christian setting. It is interesting to notice, from an historical point of view, that this exoteric content is a synthesis, which intends to be harmonious, of Christian spirituality and of an Enlightenment humanism rid of its anti-christian aspects. But this remark is not of merely historical interest: for the CBCS, this synthesis is still valuable as a directive in one's present everyday life.

The esoteric aspect of the Order is in continuity with that of the symbolical degrees, which essentially consists in teaching, under the veil of symbols, a doctrine of the spiritual destiny of man, the main moments of which are the primordial state, the fall, and the reintegration – the present condition of man being located between the second and third moment. In the Inner Order, this symbolic teaching, which has culminated in the fourth degree of the symbolic class, has been brought to an end; the member of the CBCS, who is supposed to have assimilated the teaching with his intelligence and his heart, is vowed to make it work in his inner spiritual life as well as in his outer life, striving to obtain his personal reintegration and making a contribution to the universal one by using all the means which divine Providence and masonic initiation put at his disposal.

It is important to understand clearly the conception which the founders of the Order of the CBCS had of its relation with the Order of the Knights Templar. They assumed without restriction that the latter had possessed an important esoteric knowledge, and even that, after their suppression, they had transmitted that knowledge to lodges of operative masons, from which it later passed to speculative Masonry. This is what they kept of the current "templar legend". But the founders purified (so to speak) the legend in two ways. First, they did not insist on aspects of that knowledge which were especially attractive to many Masons – namely the art of making gold – but put the emphasis on the most spiritual aspects – those which concerned the essential term of masonic initiation, namely, according to their fundamental doctrine, the reintegration of all beings. On the other hand, as we have said, they renounced the claim, which had been that of the SO, to historical succession from the Knights Templar. This was partly due to prudence since, in France, such a claim would likely be judged subversive by the Crown, but it also had a deeper motivation, which is clearly expressed in the ritual of the admission to the novi-

tiate and in the corresponding instruction. The founders of the Order of the CBCS held that there is a transhistorical and hidden Order which goes back to the origin of the world, which carries the primordial and perfect initiation, and from which all historical Orders and all historical initiations are issued – whether chivalric or not (since at the level of that primordial Order this distinction is transcended). For that reason, a historical link with the Order of the Knights Templar was of no interest to them, the only important thing being the mystical link with the transcendent Order: 'Do not', says the instruction of the novitiate, 'mistake the sublime, secret, primitive and fundamental Order for the Order of the Knights Masons of the Holy City, nor for the Order of the Knights Templar. All are issued from this hidden Order; Masonry owes it its existence, and we are placed between the symbolic initiation and the perfect initiation, to help those whom the divine Providence calls to it to return back to this primitive Order'. This concept indicates to which level of transcendence the spirituality of the Order of the CBCS reaches. The place of the Order in this scheme must be carefully noted: it does not pretend to be able to confer the perfect initiation, and the only role it claims is to help each Knight to reach this level by himself, under the guidance of divine Providence.

Edmond Mazet, "Les actes du Convent des Gaules", *Travaux de la Loge Nationale de Recherche Villard de Honnecourt* 11 (2e semestre 1985), 57-106 ♦ Jean-François Var, "Les Actes du Convent de Wilhelmsbad", *Les Cahiers Verts* 7 (1985), 27-52.

Lit.: André Le Forestier, *La Franc-Maçonnerie templière et occultiste aux XVIIIe et XIXe siècles*, Paris et Nauwealerts, Louvain: Aubier-Montaigne, 1970 ♦ J. Webb, "The Scottish Rectified Rite", *Ars Quatuor Coronatorum, Transactions of Quatuor Coronati Lodge* n° 2076, 100 (1987), 1-5.

EDMOND MAZET

Christian Kabbalah → Jewish Influences III

Christian Theosophy

1. First Period (17th Century) 2. The Transitional Period (First Half of the 18th Century) 3. From Pre-Romanticism to Romanticism, or the Second Golden Age: 1750-1850 4. Effacement and Permanence (ca. 1850-2000)

For the historian of modern Western esoteric currents, "theosophy" is not to be understood in an essentialist sense, which would be based, for example, on its etymology (*Theo-Sophia*, wisdom of God), but in the sense commonly accepted within the academy. As such, it designates either a specific esoteric current in the wake of the emergence of modern Western esotericism from the end of the 15th century onward (e.g., neo-Alexandrian → hermetism, Christian Kabbalah [→ Jewish Influences], → Rosicrucianism, "spiritual" → alchemy, etc.), or matters pertaining to the much more recent history of the → Theosophical Society (established in 1875). It is in the former sense that "theosophy" is used in this article.

There is very little doctrinal unity among the representatives of the Christian theosophical current, but besides the fact that they are Christians they do share some common traits:

1. *The God/Human/Nature Triangle*. The inspired speculation of the theosopher bears simultaneously on God and the nature of God (intra-divine processes, etc.), on Nature (whether external, intellectual, or material), and on Man (his origin, his place in the universe, his role in the workings of salvation, etc.). Essentially, it deals with the relations between these three. Between the three components God–Man–Nature a complex network of relationships/correspondences is believed to exist, characterized by dramatic processes closely related to the narratives of Scripture; it is through "active imagination" that the theosopher believes he is capable of apprehending these → correspondences (see further below: 3).

2. *The Primacy of the Mythic*. The theosopher practices an ongoing, creative hermeneutic of authoritative religious texts (in most cases those pertaining to the Judaeo-Christian Revelation, i.e. the Bible), whereby he privileges the most mythic elements of the latter (for example, those found in Genesis, the vision of Ezekiel, the book of Revelation, etc.). Thus, great emphasis is placed on the roles of such characters as Sophia and the angels, which are present in the Bible, but to which they give further developments in "completing" the latter with stories about the Falls of Lucifer and of Nature, the adamic androgyne, etc.

As Pierre Deghaye has felicitously written, 'Theosophy is a kind of theology of the image'. One could speak here of a multi-faceted imaginary originating in the same primary material used by theologians (in the strict sense of the term), but which they usually present in a rather rational or conceptual mode.

3. *Direct Access to Superior Worlds*. According to the theosophers, man possesses in himself a faculty – generally dormant but always potentially present – that enables him to connect directly with the divine world or generally with superior beings, and that is able to "branch out" to them. This faculty is due to the existence of a special organ within us, a kind of *intellectus*, which is none other than our → imagination – understood in quasi-magical fashion as a force of creation as well as perception. Once achieved, this contact (1) permits an exploration of all levels of reality, (2) assures a kind of co-penetration of the divine and the human, and (3) gives our spirit the possibility of "fixing" itself in a body of light, that is to say, of effectuating a "second birth". Here we can see a rapport with the mystical experience (understood here as an experience of union, or as a quest for union with a personal God or the Godhead). However, the mystic *stricto sensu* purports to abolish images whereas, to the contrary, for the typical Christian theosophers the image signifies accomplishment.

None of these three traits is exclusive to theosophy, but the simultaneous presence of all three makes for the specificity of the theosophical discourse. Moreover, in terms of literary style the discourse of theosophy appears to adapt itself remarkably to the literary styles of its contemporary contexts. For example, in 17th-century Germany it espoused the baroque style, and in → Saint-Martin's writings (see below) either the style of the pre-Romantic writers (see his *l'Homme de désir*), or that of the philosophers of the Enlightenment (see his *Des Erreurs et de la Vérité*).

The theosophical current appeared at the beginning of the 17th century and went through four distinct periods: (1) The period from its appearance at the beginning of the 17th century and its development throughout that century, which may be called its first "Golden Age". (2) A modest, albeit specific and influential, prolongation lasting through the the first half of the 18th century. (3) The revival of theosophy in the pre-Romantic and Romantic eras, which can be considered a second "Golden Age". (4) The period of its decline from the mid-19th century onward.

1. FIRST PERIOD (17TH CENTURY)

The theosophical current is not without forebears. Born in Germany at the beginning of the 17th century, it has a great deal of affinity with → Paracelsianism. → Paracelsus, whose works had not been published until the end of the 16th century, had introduced a new, specific mode of reflection on Nature: a cosmology comprised of → magic, medicine, chemistry, experimental science and complex speculations about the networks of → correspondences uniting the different levels of reality in the universe. However, for the most part,

Paracelsus remained within the limits of an imma-nent philosophy of Nature (strongly tinged with alchemical notions). Subsequently, it fell to a few inspired thinkers to fit that cosmosophy into a more global vision, thus ensuring a transition from Paracelsian thought to theosophy proper. These thinkers, all of them Germans, can be seen as "proto-theosophers": → Valentin Weigel (1533-1588), → Heinrich Khunrath (1560-1605) and Johann Arndt (1555-1621).

Weigel, a Saxon pastor whose works were writ-ten from 1570 to 1584, may be considered one of the foremost direct precursors of German theoso-phy. He is the first, indeed, to have blended together the Rheno-Flemish mystical tradition, rather intellectual and abstract in character, and the colorful and concrete thought of Paracelsus. He was, indeed, very familiar with both. For example, his thoughts on the spiritual body of the new birth (a kind of celestial naturalism grafted onto the mys-tical tradition) introduced into the history of Ger-man thought the theme of the corporeality of the spirit, which the theosophers of the ensuing cen-turies (with the notable exception of → Sweden-borg) would develop. His influence upon → Friedrich Christoph Oetinger, → Franz von Baader and many others could hardly be overestimated.

Khunrath's *Amphitheatrum Sapientiae aeternae* (Amphitheatre of Eternal Wisdom; first ed. 1595) has most likely influenced → Jacob Boehme, not least with regard to the theme of the Divine Wis-dom (Sophia). As for Arndt, he formulated, particu-larly in Book IV (1610) of his *Vier Bücher vom wahren Christenthum* (Four Books on True Chris-tianity) what would come to be known as "mysti-cal theology". Arndt's system, not unlike Weigel's, brought medieval mysticism together with both the Paracelsian legacy and the alchemical tradition, and furthermore elaborated a theory about the possibility for the elected soul to acquire a "new body". Other names could be added to the list, like → Gérard Dorn (ca. 1530-ca. 1584), in whose alchemical writings we find a richly developed Phi-losophy of Nature – a visionary, highly elaborated *Physica* that in some essential aspects foreshad-owed that of Boehme.

With Jacob Boehme (1575-1624), a shoemaker from Görlitz in Silesia, the theosophical current acquired its definitive characteristics, the Boeh-mian work representing something like the early nucleus of what would constitute the "classical" theosophical corpus proper. One day in 1610, while contemplating a pewter vessel, he is said to have had an experience that determined his spiri-tual vocation. He had had the impression of grasp-ing at one stroke the networks of correspondences

and implications between different worlds or levels of reality (terrestrial, celestial, etc.). He then wrote his first book, *Morgen Röte im auffgang* (Morning-Glow Arising) also known as *Aurora*, which emerged from this enlightenment, and in which it is permissible to see the birth certificate, as it were, of the theosophical current strictly speaking. It was followed by many others, all written in German, but only *Der Weg zu Christo* (The Way to Christ) appeared during his lifetime, in 1624. From his abundant production, one of the most astonishing in Baroque German prose, mention should be made of *De tribus Principiis* (On the Three Princi-ples; written in 1619), *De signatura rerum* (On the Signatures of Things; written in 1621), and *Mys-terium Magnum* (The Grand Mystery; written in 1623), only the titles of which are in Latin. Even more strikingly than Weigel's and Arndt's, Boehme's system is a kind of amalgam between the medieval mystical tradition as continued in 16th-century Germany and a cosmology of the Paracelsian, alchemical type, along with some neo-kabbalistic ingredients. Not only Judaeo-Christian in charac-ter, but strongly Lutheran more specifically, given its historical, cultural roots, it presents itself as a visionary hermeneutic applied to biblical texts. Germanic in language, it is "barbaric" in character, in the sense that it owes practically nothing to ancient Greek or Latin "esoteric" currents such as Alexandrian → hermetism (a trait shared by Para-celsus too, for that matter). In contrast to medieval and even Neoplatonic concepts of the Divine, Boehme did not see the latter as static but rather envisaged it as a passionate struggle of opposing principles. His God is never *in esse*, but always *in fieri*, He is the Supreme Being who ontologically "sees" in His living mirror, i.e. the Divine Wisdom or Sophia, all the potentialities of the worlds He creates. The theme of Sophia leads into the major visionary avenues of Boehme's works, which are built up like a great Baroque cathedral: the Fall of Lucifer and Adam, the spiritual corporeality of the angels, the idea that all exterior form is language or *Figur*, the seven "spirit-sources" existing from all eternity, etc. This "prince of German theosophy", as he has often been called, contributed in large measure to the formation of a specific spiritual con-science in the general religious turmoil of 17th-century Germany.

Animated by Boehme's spirit and thinking, theosophy henceforth flourished in other countries as well. Its success at its beginnings was due to a number of factors. First, it emerged from Lutheran soil. Lutheranism allows free inquiry, which in cer-tain inspired souls could take a prophetic turn. Sec-ond, Lutheranism is characterized by a paradoxical blend of mysticism and rationalism, whence the need to put inner experience under discussion, and inversely to transform doctrinal discussions into inner experience. Third, at the beginning of the 17th century, less than a hundred years after the Reformation, the spiritual poverty of Protestant preaching and the dryness of its theology were sorely resented by some, whence a need for spiritual revitalization. The fourth factor which came into play presented itself as a challenge. Indeed, if in the milieus where theosophy was born there was a certain freedom vis-à-vis ministers of the cult, prophetic activity was nevertheless not well tolerated (Boehme was a scapegoat of the Lutheran minister in his town of Görlitz). Hence the "reformist" slant of the theosophers (in the general sense, not in the protestant one) – and of most esotericists, for that matter – , which was fostered as a reaction against the religious intolerance and theological feuds of the time. The fifth factor is linked to a strong desire among most intellectuals for a unity of sciences and ethics – a need to unify thought. The idea of a solidarity of thinkers, and of a "total" science, formed part of the spiritual and intellectual climate of the 17th century. Theosophy appeared to respond to that need, because of its globalizing character. It represents a tendency to integrate everything within a general harmonious whole. The same is true in the same period for → Rosicrucianism (see *Fama Fraternitatis*, 1614, and *Confessio*, 1615) and for the pansophic current linked to the latter. Pansophy also presented itself as a system of universal knowledge: → Amos Comenius (1592-1670) held that all things are ordained by God and classified according to analogical relations; knowledge of divine things is gained by starting from the concrete world, from the entire universe, whose "signature" or hieroglyphs it is first a matter of deciphering. Bound up with such a theosophical and pansophical program is the need of proposing an alternative worldview opposed to the emerging mechanistic view of the universe, i.e. to an epistemology that seemed to end up emptying the universe of its "correspondences" and living, spiritual complexity. Theosophy thus reaffirmed the place of the microcosm in the macrocosm; in so doing it was not "scientific" in the modern sense of the word, and never went beyond the project stage. Nevertheless, it appeared to many people as a promise, a hope, a new dawn of thought. Moreover, the poetic aspect of its discourses favored a co-penetration of literature and science, and by virtue of this indirectly contributed to the development of the popularization of science.

In the century under discussion, the main representatives of theosophy and some of their main writings are, in Germany (besides Boehme): → Johann Georg Gichtel (1638-1710), *Theosophia Practica* (Practical Theosophy; published in 1722, but written much earlier); Quirinus Kuhlmann (1651-1689), *Kühlpsalter* (1677); → Gottfried Arnold (1666-1714), *Das Geheimnis der göttlichen Sophia* (The Secret of the divine Sophia; 1700); Aegidius Gutmann (1651-1689), *Offenbahrung göttlicher Majestät* (Revelation of divine Majesty; see above) and Julius Sperber (? - 1616), *Exemplarischer Beweiss* (Exemplary Proof . . .; 1616). In the Low Countries, → Joan Baptista van Helmont (1618-1699*)*, *The Paradoxical Discourses concerning the Macrocosm and the Microcosm* (1685). In England, → Robert Fludd (1574-1637), *Utriusque Cosmi . . . Historia* (History of both Cosmoses; 1617/26); → John Pordage (1608-1681), *Theologia Mystica, or the Mystic Divinitie of the Æternal Invisibles* (1683); → Jane Lead (1623-1704), *The Laws of Paradise given forth by Wisdom to a Translated Spirit* (1695); → Henry More (1614-1687), the main "Cambridge neo-Platonist". In France, → Pierre Poiret (1646-1719), *L'Économie Divine, ou Système universel et démontré des œuvres et des devoirs de Dieu envers les hommes* (The Divine Economy . . .; 1687), and → Antoinette Bourignon (1616-1680), *Œuvres* (edited by Pierre Poiret in 1679 and 1684).

Many of these authors were prolific, and many of their works have not been cited here. With rare exceptions (like Fludd), they did not write in Latin but in the vernacular, their mother tongues being more advantageous than Latin for the expression of visions and feelings. And alongside writings proper, it is appropriate to call attention to the existence of a rich theosophical iconography – a "theosophy through images" – , which Khunrath's *Amphitheatrum* (see above) had inaugurated in a particularly lavish and radiant way, and which is also found beautifully exemplified in e.g. Gichtel's 1682 edition of the complete works of Boehme. More generally, this period is rich in esoteric engravings, a fact which is attested to by the numerous illustrated alchemical books published throughout the first half of the 17th century. Likewise, at the turn of the century, Freher (see further below) would draw a beautiful series of thirteen figures, also illuminating Boehme's works.

2. THE TRANSITIONAL PERIOD (FIRST HALF OF THE 18TH CENTURY)

During the second period an additional theosophical corpus was constituted, primarily in the German language. This continuity was favored by the same factors that were enumerated above with respect to the 17th century, because the same or similar questions continued to be asked on philosophical, political and religious levels. This new theosophical output was characterized by two main tendencies or families:

(1) A tendency that appears to qualify as traditional in that it is closely akin to the original Boehmean current. It was represented notably by the Swabian → Friedrich Christoph Oetinger (1702-1782), whose first book was dedicated to Boehme (*Aufmunternde Gründe zur Lesung der Schriften Jacob Böhmens*; Cheering reasons for reading the writings of Jacob Boehme; 1731), and whose production for the most part overflowed from this period into the third (see below, "Three Areas"). It is also represented by the English Boehmian → William Law (1686-1761), the author of *An Appeal to All that doubt*, *The Spirit of Prayer* (1749-1750) and *The Way to Divine Knowledge* (1752). A German who had emigrated to England, Dionysius Andreas Freher (1649-1728) proved to be one of Boehme's most inspired interpreters. His writings in English, and his translations from German into the same language, enjoyed a wide circulation. This was also the period of Gichtel's *Theosophia Practica* (1722), of *Le Mystère de la Croix* (The Mystery of the Cross; 1736) by the German → Melchior Douzetemps, and of *Explication de la Genèse* (Explication of Genesis; 1738) by the Swiss Hector de Saint-Georges de Marsais (1688-1755), who was akin to spiritual thinkers from the city of Berlebourg (the famous Bible of Berlebourg is an edition of the Bible that is rich in both theosophical and quietist commentaries).

(2) The second tendency was of a more paracelsian and alchemical orientation. Four German authors stand out here. → Georg von Welling (alias Salwigt, 1655-1727), *Opus mago-cabbalisticum et theosophicum* (1719, reprinted several times with additional chapters); A.J. Kirchweger (?-1746), *Aurea Catena Homeri* (The Golden Chain of Homer; 1723); Samuel Richter (alias → Sincerus Renatus), *Theo-Philosophica Theoretica et Practica* (Theoretical and Practical Theo-Philosophy; 1711); and → Hermann Fictuld (several works, among which *Aureum Vellus* [The Golden Fleece], 1749). Welling and Richter were extremely influential, mostly in Germany where they became part and parcel of the referential corpus of the neo-Rosicrucian fringe-masonic Rites in the second half of the century and well into the 19th.

With few exceptions, the theosophy of these two tendencies no longer evinces the visionary outpouring which characterized the beginning of the first period (exemplified by Gichtel, for instance).

Of course, we are dealing here with similar speculations about Scripture and Nature, but this dampened theosophy, more intellectual in character, hardly springs forth from a personally experienced *Zentralschau* ("central vision") like in Boehme, Gichtel, Jane Lead, etc. Not until the next period will such a personal "central vision", linked to strong intellectual speculation, reappear, in Saint-Martin and a few others. In any case, for the theosophers in the following decades, the new corpus produced during the second period would serve as a reference, albeit less than would the corpus of the first one.

During this second period, theosophy became the object of many discussions among scholars who were themselves, for the most part, aloof from the esoteric current, but who through their presentations contributed to ensuring its presence within the cultural and philosophical landscape of Europe. Among the forerunners of this critical output, mention should be made of two authors. Ehregott Daniel Colberg (1659-1698), a Protestant minister from Greifswald, attacked theosophy in his *Das Platonisch-Hermetisches* [sic] *Christenthum* (Platonic-Hermetic Christianity; 1690-1691, 2 vols., reprinted in 1710), also targeting Alexandrian Hermetism, Paracelsus, → astrology, → alchemy, etc. And Gottfried Arnold (1666-1714), a theosopher himself (see above), who authored *Unpartheyische Kirchen- und Ketzerhistorie . . .* (Unpartial History of Churchs and Heretics; 1699-1700, reprinted in 1729) and *Historie und Beschreibung der mystischen Theologie oder geheimen Gelehrtheit . . .* (History and Description of the Mystical Theology or Secret Knowledge; 1702). Arnold's first book contains a wealth of information (it remains an oft-consulted reference work on the subject of Western spiritual trends, not only on theosophy) and is something of a response to Colberg's book. Less critical of theosophy than Colberg and less laudatory than Arnold are Friedrich Gentzken (*Historia Philosophiae* [. . .]) (1724) and Johann Franciscus Buddeus (*Isagoge . . .*, 1729). More critical, but extremely knowledgeable and erudite is Jacob Brucker, a pastor of Augsburg, one of the founders of the modern history of philosophy, who authored a voluminous *Historia critica Philosophiae . . .* (1742-1744) in Latin, preceded by a shorter version in German, *Kurtze Fragen aus der philosophischen Historie . . .* (Short Questions from Philosophical History; 1730-1736). Never before had theosophy been made the object of such systematic treatment as was the case in these two treatises. A few years after Brucker's books, the great *Encyclopédie*, edited by

Denis Diderot (see vol. XVI, 1758, new ed. 1765, article "Théosophes"), dedicated a twenty-six-page entry to the subject. Diderot himself wrote the article, therein plagiarizing Brucker. The presence of theosophy in the *Encyclopédie* is all the more interesting as the word does not seem to appear in the dictionaries of the time.

3. FROM PRE-ROMANTICISM TO ROMANTICISM, OR THE SECOND GOLDEN AGE: 1750-1850

After a fifty-year period of latency, interrupted only by Swedenborg's writings (see below), theosophy once again began to come to life during the 1760s, and experienced a second Golden Age that lasted until the mid-19th century. Such a renewal was connected with the continuation and recrudescence of other esoteric currents (like Paracelsianism and Rosicrucianism), which, along with theosophy, constitute what is generally called → Illuminism, over the period ca. 1760 to 1820. Not a surprising occurrence, indeed, in a period pervaded by both optimism and uneasiness, a spirit of enterprise and one of meditation. Some specific factors can at least partly account for this renewal of theosophy. First, the increasing importance that was given to the idea of the "invisible" Church, understood by many people as the intimate experience of the believer, independent from any confessional framework. Man does not find God in any outward temple but only in the temple of his heart, which was often understood as an organ of knowledge. Second, a widespread interest in the problem of Evil, and more generally in the myth of the Fall and reintegration, which may be considered the great romantic myth *par excellence*. This myth was explicated through secularized art forms and in political projects, as well as in theosophical discussions. Quite a few masonic or fringe-masonic organizations became intent on "building the New Jerusalem" or "reconstructing Solomon's temple". Third, an interest in the sciences, not least in → animal magnetism, on the part of an increasingly wide public. Indeed, Newtonian physics had encouraged speculations of a holistic type, the main business being here to reconcile science and knowledge. Besides, experimental physics was popularized and introduced into the salons, in the form of picturesque experiments with electricity and with magnetism well suited for stimulating the imagination, because they hinted at the existence of a hidden life or an invisible fluid that traverses all the material realms. Eclecticism is inseparable from this third factor, a trait which also characterized the preceding period, which likewise had been fond of

curiosa and of anything likely to harmonize the data of knowledge. Within the theosophical scene that stretches over these eight decades or so, it is possible to distinguish three different areas (although these appear to be more or less interconnected).

(1) The first area is occupied by some authors located in the wake of the 17th century, in the sense that they are more or less Boehmian in outlook. Even when they do not claim allegiance with Boehme or even ignore him, their works generally bear on the same themes as his. → Martines de Pasqually somehow inaugurated the renaissance of European theosophy in this third period, with his *Traité de la Réintégration des Êtres créés dans leur primitives propriétés, vertus et puissances spirituelles divines* (Treatise on the Reintegration of Beings created in their original properties, virtues and spiritual and divine powers). Written in the 1750s and 1760s, it was read almost exclusively by the Freemasons [→ Freemasonry] who were the author's disciples and it remained unpublished until 1899. But during the period it had considerable influence, albeit mostly indirect.

Louis-Claude de Saint-Martin, one of Pasqually's disciples in the fringe-masonic Order of the → Elus Coëns, made some important elements of Pasqually's esoteric work known through his books *Des Erreurs et de la Vérité* (On errors and the Truth; 1775), and then *Tableau Naturel des rapports qui unissent Dieu, l'homme et l'univers* (Natural tableau of the connections that unite God, man and the universe; 1781). Saint-Martin's own theosophy took a different turn after he had come across the works of Boehme, in 1789-1791. He henceforth blended together Pasqually and Boehme, and considered himself mostly a follower as well as interpreter of the latter, by means of the translations of his works into French. But Saint-Martin's own works are no less original for that (*L'Homme de Désir* [The man of desire], 1790; *Le Ministère de l'Homme-Esprit* [The Ministry of Spiritual Man], 1802; *De l'Esprit des Choses* [On the Spirit of Things], 1802; etc.). Within the history of the theosophical output of that time, his originality is twofold. First, he was the most productive and creative theosopher of the period, authoring treatises, essays, poems, and a novel, and taking an active part in philosophical discussions with representatives of the Enlightenment. He was also the most original one; for example, his book *De l'Esprit des Choses* (2 vol., 1802) stands out as the only one in French which pertains to *Naturphilosophie* in the German sense of the term. Indeed, we find in it less visionary speculations than in his other works;

instead, it is mostly devoted to precise observations concerning animals, plants, natural phenomena, etc., along with theosophical interpretations of them. Second, Saint-Martin may be rightly considered the theosopher whose reception was the strongest throughout the 19th century in Europe, with the exception of Swedenborg's (see below). This was due not only to his literary qualities, but quite as much to the fact that he translated works of Boehme into French. These translations sparked a renewed interest in Boehme in Germany – where most cultivated people read French – and were influential on German → Romanticism, in particular, and German philosophy, in general. Conversely, Saint-Martin's major works were translated into German in the first half of the 19th century.

Among the other theosophers of some importance in the pre-romantic French-speaking area, mention should be made of at least two of them. → Bathilde d'Orléans, duchess of Bourbon, authored two works (*Opuscules, ou Pensées d'une âme de foi sur la religion chrétienne* [Opuscules, or thoughts of a believing soul about the Christian religion], 1811; *Correspondance entre Mad[ame] de B[ourbon] et Mr. R[uffin] sur leurs opinions religieuses* [Correspondences between Mme. De B. and Mr. R. on their religious opinions], 2 vol., 1812), strongly inspired by her friend Saint-Martin. She played the part of *inspiratrice* among various members and groups of the theosophical family. In Switzerland, → Jean-Philippe Dutoit-Membrini (alias Keleph Ben Nathan, 1721–1793), wrote *La Philosophie Divine, appliquée aux lumières naturelle, magique, astrale, surnaturelle, céleste, et divine* (The Divine Philosophy, applied to the natural, magical, astral, supernatural, celestial and divine lights; 2 vol., 1793), a book which owed little to Boehme and even less to Saint-Martin.

In German-speaking countries, within a new, abundant production a few names come to the fore. Friedrich Christoph Oetinger (see also above, second period) is one of the "Fathers" of Swabian → Pietism, but primarily the main German theosopher of the second half of the 18th century. He was also the most erudite in terms of esoteric literature in general. He was a great commentator on various theosophical works, like those of Boehme and Swedenborg, and of Kabbalistic works (*e.g., Lehrtafel [der] Prinzessin Antonia* [Educational Tableau of the Princess Antonia; 1763). → Karl von Eckartshausen, a native of Munich, was a polygraph (author of novels, short stories, political pamphlets, physical and alchemical treatises, etc.) whose most interesting theosophical writings were published posthumously (*Über die Zauberkräfte*

der Natur [About the Magical Powers of Nature], 1819; *Ueber die wichtigsten Mysterien der Religion* [About the most important mysteries of religion], 1823). → Johann Heinrich Jung-Stilling, in Marburg (*Blicke in die Geheimnisse der Naturweisheit* [Views into the mysteries of the wisdom of Nature], 1787), also stands in that wake, and so does → Frédéric-Rodolphe Saltzmann, in Strasbourg (*Alles wird neu werden* [All will become new],1802–1812), a disciple of Pasqually and Saint-Martin through → Jean-Baptiste Willermoz, to whose Masonic circle he belonged.

Later, and even more importantly, the Roman Catholic → Franz von Baader (1765–1841), a native of Munich (Professor at that University and a friend of both Friedrich Hegel and → Friedrich Wihelm Schelling), stands out as the most important theosopher of the 19th century. Furthermore, he is the best commentator on both Boehme and Saint-Martin. He is also the major representative (along with Schelling) of the romantic *Naturphilosophen*, and probably the most powerful and original thinker of them all. His publications range between 1789 and 1841. Interestingly, one sees the receptions of these thinkers operating in several directions: Saint-Martin has greatly contributed to Boehme's reception in Europe during the pre-Romantic and Romantic period. Furthermore, Saint-Martin's marked influence on Baader's thought (himself a highly influential philosopher) resulted in the introduction of both Boehme and Saint-Martin into German philosophy. To wit, the twelfth (published in 1860) of the sixteen volumes of Baader's *Sämmtliche Werke* (Complete Works) is entirely devoted to reflections on Saint-Martin, and is preceded by a long foreword by Friedrich von Osten-Sacken, which likewise has contributed to the Unknown Philosopher's reputation among German philosophers.

If Baader can rightly be taken as an accomplished theosopher within the German romantic *Naturphilosophie*, some other authors representative of the latter have shown to be deeply influenced by theosophy. For instance, Friedrich von Hardenberg (alias → Novalis, 1772-1801); Johann Wilhelm Ritter (1776-1810); → Gotttfried Heinrich von Schubert (1780-1860); Carl Gustav Carus (1789-1869); Carl August von Eschenmayer (1758-1852); Gustav Theodor Fechner (1801-1887), → Johann Friedrich von Meyer (1772-1849). As a matter of fact, the Romantic *Naturphilosophie* has features that connect it more or less directly to theosophy, namely: (a) a conception that Nature can be viewed as a text that must be deciphered with the help of correspondences, (b) the postulate that the universe is a living being comprised of several levels of reality, and (c) the affirmation of an identity, or at least a co-naturality, between Spirit and Nature.

(2) The second area, which cannot be said to be of a Boehmean kind, is original for at least two reasons. First, it can be summed up by evoking the name of one single author. Second, it seems to owe nothing to the theosophy that preceded it or was contemporaneous with it. The author in question is Emanuel Swedenborg (1688-1772), a learned Swedish scientist and renowned inventor who, in 1745, interrupted his properly scientific activities on account of dreams and visions, which had come to him quite suddenly and transformed his inner life. Henceforth, he gave himself up to the study of Holy Scripture and wrote his *Arcana Cœlestia* (Secrets of Heaven; 1745-1758), followed by many other books (like *De Nova Hierosolyma* [The New Jerusalem], 1758; *Apocalypsis revelata* [The Apocalypse Unveiled], 1766; *De coelo et ejus mirabilibus, et de inferno* [Heaven and its Wonders and Hell], 1758; *Vera Christiana Religio* [True Christian Religion], 1771).

If we consider the three main features of theosophy (see above: the triangle God-Man-Nature; the pre-eminence of the mythical; and the idea of direct access to the higher worlds), certainly we find all three to be present in Swedenborg's thinking. However, Swedenborg's theosophy differs from that of most other Christian theosophers by the following characteristics. First, it is devoid of dramatic elements. Second, we do not find the mythical figures that make the stories of "classical" theosophy. Third, and consequently, the entire framework of Fall and Reintegration of Eternal Nature by means of "alchemical" processes of transmutation (for example, the new birth or fixation of the spirit in a body of light) is absent. Swedenborg's universe is interconnected by innumerable correspondences, but given these three characteristics he sees them in a way which is different – more static – from that of most other theosophers. His works leave more an impression of meandering through a garden than of participating in a tragedy. Sophia is conspicuous by her absence; angels are merely the souls of deceased humans. But Swedenborg's views and works are of no less arresting interest for that. In terms of creative power he is the equal of Boehme and one of the most formidable thinkers of his century. Significantly enough, Oetinger and later Saint-Martin as well have been unsparing in harsh criticisms against Swedenborg, in whose theosophy they lamented the lack of notions like "spiritual corporeality", incarnation of the Spirit, and

the like. Jean-Jacques Bernard, in his *Opuscules Théosophiques* (1822), attempted to unite the theosophy of Swedenborg with that of Saint-Martin. As might be expected, the attempt fell rather short of being convincing, but the manner in which he tackled that task is nevertheless interesting. Indeed, it seems that the attempt was never seriously renewed. Be that as it may, the Swedenborgian theosophy, both more accessible and more "reassuring" than the ones otherwise prevailing, promptly met with tremendous success. Even more than the other aforementioned theosophical "areas", it influenced the works of such artists and writers as → William Blake, Charles Baudelaire, Honoré de Balzac, etc., and had a strong impact on initiatory societies in the Anglo-Saxon world and elsewhere. In terms of reception, it is certain that Swedenborg's success was very instrumental in overshadowing the other important theosophers, thereby limiting their reception in European culture.

(3) The third theosophical area of this period is occupied by a number of initiatory societies. Indeed, the last third of the 18th century witnessed a rapid proliferation of such organizations, particularly Masonic Rites (or "Systems") with "side degrees", otherwise called "higher grades" (i.e., those that include degrees above the three Masonic ones proper: Entered Apprentice, Fellow Craft, and Master Mason). In quite a few Masonic Rites of this kind, the side degrees borrowed from the literature of such esoteric currents as Kabbalah, Rosicrucianism, alchemy, and not least, theosophy. For this reason it is appropriate to speak of the presence of esotericism within → Freemasonry. That said, in making such borrowings, some of these Rites not only introduced theosophical elements into their rituals and instructions; not unfrequently they also engaged in publishing enterprises, thus contributing in no small measure to the dissemination of theosophical elements among the wider public. This is the case of the Order of the → Elus Coëns (established by Pasqually) whose teachings were in part made accessible through Saint-Martin's books. Other Masons, for example those who belonged or had belonged to the Rite called Rectified Scottish Rite (created in Lyon around 1768 by → Jean-Baptiste Willermoz) wrote books containing perspectives more or less inspired by that Order. Such is the case of Saltzmann (see above) and of → Joseph de Maistre (*Les Soirées de Saint-Petersbourg*, 1821). The Rectified Scottish Rite soon spread throughout Europe and Russia, and contributed strongly to propagating the theosophy of Saint-Martin and Pasqually among an ever

widening public. Russia occupies a peculiar place within that context. In Moscow, the publishing companies of Christian Freemasons like → Nicolas Novikov and → Vladimir Lopukhin, from the 1780s to ca. 1820, had many books of theosophy translated into Russian. In this connection, it seems appropriate to recall that the term "Martinism" [→ Martinism: First Period] in the Russia of that time has at least three connotations. It may refer either to Saint-Martin or Pasqually; to the Rectified Scottish Rite; or to a general and vague notion encompassing these three names together. That said, most Masonic Rites in Europe had hardly anything of a "Martinist" blend, despite their oftentimes strong theosophical inspiration at the level of the side degrees, which were rather inspired by the works of authors like Welling and Sincerus Renatus (see above, "Second period"). This is the case, for example, of the Order of the Gold- und Rosenkreuz, established around 1777 in Germany; of the Order of the → Asiatic Brethren, created around 1779; of the Order of the "Illuminated Theosophers", born around 1783, which was of a Swedenborgian type; and of the Ancient and Accepted Scottish Rite, created in France around 1804.

4. EFFACEMENT AND PERMANENCE (CA. 1850-2000)

During the second half of the 19th century (beginning with → Eliphas Lévi) appeared an esoteric current known as occultism [→ occult / occultism], which continued well into the 20th. One of its main characteristics is that it sought to combine the findings of both experimental science and the occult sciences cultivated since the Renaissance. Its representatives thereby wanted to demonstrate the emptiness of materialism. Occultism essentially restricted itself to the domain of "secondary causes", but its strong propensity for eclecticism caused it to touch on a number of diverse fields, including various earlier esoteric currents, among which theosophy. Hence the sometimes fluid boundary between occultism and theosophy. Such is the case, in France, with Albert Faucheux (alias → Barlet, 1838-1921) and Gérard Encausse (alias → Papus, 1875-1916). This is also why some theosophically inspired initiatory societies flourished, albeit in limited number, within the occultist current; for example, the Martinist Order [→ Martinism: Second Period] founded by Papus in 1891. As its name indicates, that Order was inspired by the works of Saint-Martin, and in that sense it was also close to the Rectified Scottish Rite (see above), which had continued to be very much practised in Masonic Obediences. Furthermore, a number of

the representatives of the occultist current edited books *of* or *on* theosophy. Pasqually's *Traité de la Réintegration* was published for the first time in 1899, edited by one of them. Papus edited texts by, and comments on, Saint-Martin and Pasqually.

Among works in Russian, those of some theosophically-tinged Orthodox philosophers are noteworthy: Vladimir Soloviev's (1853-1900) *Conferences on Theantropy* (1877-1878), *The Beauty of Nature* (1889), *The Meaning of Love* (1892-1894); and Nicholas Berdiaev's (1874-1945) *Etudes sur Jacob Böhme* (1930, in French). They are traversed by a sophiological inspiration and in some not negligible aspects stand in Boehme's wake.

There would be little to say about theosophy in the first half of the 20th century, besides the fact that it was (and still is, for that matter) present in the aforementioned initiatory societies. It was present, furthermore, through a few noteworthy authors, like → Leopold Ziegler (1881-1958) in *Überlieferung* (Tradition; 1948) and *Menschwerdung* (Humanization; 1948), and Auguste-Edouard Chauvet (1885-1955; *L'Esotérisme de la Genèse* [The Esotericism of Genesis], 1946-1958). As a matter of fact, the continuation of the theosophical current seems to have been (and still to be) hampered by the appearance of a new one, widely represented in the esoteric scene: perennialism (otherwise called the Traditionalist School) [→ Tradition], founded on the idea of a "primordial Tradition" overarching all the traditions of the world. It began to come to the fore with → Edouard Schuré's *Les Grands Initiés* (1889) and → Mme Blavatky's first works when the occultist current was flourishing. It made great headway in France as early as the 1920s with → René Guénon, and later on in the United States with → Frithjof Schuon. To a large extent due to the ever-growing influence of perennialism, the theosophical current (always understood here, of course, in the sense of Christian theosophy and its developments), which over the preceding hundred years had been fading away, practically dried up.

Guénon himself was not interested in the western theosophical corpus of the past, first, probably because of its Germanic roots (he was not a great admirer of German culture), and second, because he hardly dealt with the Western esoteric currents proper. It seems that the only text in which he portrayed modern western theosophy in positive terms consists of four lines only, in a book (*Le Théosophisme, histoire d'une pseudo-religion* [Theosophy: History of a Pseudo-Religion], 1921) which, as it turns out, is dedicated to a radical demolition of the Theosophical Society founded by H.P. Blavatsky –

part of whose roots are embedded in the occultist current and which has only tenuous connections with the theosophical one. In his introductory part, Guénon quotes as genuine theosophers Jacob Boehme, Johann Georg Gichtel, William Law, Jane Lead, Louis-Claude de Saint-Martin, and Karl von Eckartshausen. Obviously, the "classical" theosophical current only serves as a foil here. Guénon almost never mentioned it anywhere else, and was probably barely knowledgeable about it. Granted the difference in terms of contexts, it seems permissible to consider his influence to have been at least as instrumental as Swedenborg's had previously been, in overshadowing theosophy and thereby limiting its reception and continuation.

The Anthroposophical Society [→ Anthroposophy], originally a schism of the Theosophical Society, and founded by → Rudolf Steiner (1861-1925) in 1913, can be viewed as another competing movement by virtue of its goals and its large membership. Steiner's thought plunges its threefold roots into Early Rosicrucian literature, German Romantic *Naturphilosophie*, and the Theosophical Society of Mme Blavatsky, more than into the theosophical current proper.

Could the renowned Islamicist → Henry Corbin (1903–1978) be considered a Christian theosopher? For many years an active participant of the Eranos Conferences in Ascona, he was a philosopher and a savant interested not only in Islamic theosophy (Isma'ilyya, Shi'ism, Suhrawardi, Ibn 'Arabi, etc.), but also in the theosophy of the West. His scholarly work (for example, *L'Imagination créatrice dans le soufisme d'Ibn 'Arabi* [Creative Imagination in the Sufism of Ibn 'Arabi], 1958; *Terre céleste et corps de resurrection* [Celestial Earth and Body of Resurrection], 1960; *En Islam iranien* [In Iranian Islam], 1971-1972) is pervaded by an outspoken personal – religionistic – approach of a theosophical character. Corbin was the proponent of the idea of a "comparative theosophy" among the three great religions of the Book; but it is very telling that his main reference in terms of Western theosophy was, in line with the very nature of his Islamic preferences and his docetist slant, Emanuel Swedenborg.

Apart from Corbin, special mention should be made of an esotericist who, after having sojourned for a long time within the hothouse of the Anthroposophical Society and eventually left it, may be considered one of the rare contemporary representatives (and actually, an outstanding one) of the theosophical current. This is → Valentin Tomberg (1901-1973), a Russian of Baltic German origin, whose *Méditations sur les Arcanes Majeurs du Tarot* was written directly in French, published first in German in 1972 and then in several other languages, and represents one of the most outstanding books in 20th century Western esotericism.

In conclusion, the history of theosophy has had a development and a destiny similar to those of other esoteric currents. It appeared in a specific cultural milieu – the Baroque of the late Renaissance, late German Lutheranism – from which it cannot be divorced. Given the essentials of its specificity, its very nature disposed it to find a new impetus during the Enlightenment, then in the pre-Romantic and Romantic periods. Later on, it has survived through some epigones and only a few original thinkers as well; but its persisting influence within the esoteric landscape could and still can be seen operating in several directions, albeit mostly indirectly, in the form of its various migrations and derivations.

Lit.: Ernst Benz, *The Mystical Sources of German Philosophy* (French or. 1968), Allison Park: Pickwick, 1983 ♦ Pierre Deghaye, *De Paracelse à Thomas Man: Les avatars de l'hermétisme allemand*, Paris: Dervy/Albin Michel, 2001 ♦ Antoine Faivre, *Mystiques, théosophes et illuminés au siècle des Lumières*, Hildesheim: G. Olms, 1976 ♦ idem, *Philosophie de la Nature: Physique sacrée et théosophie, XVIIIᵉ-XIXᵉ siècles*, Paris: Albin Michel, 1996 ♦ idem, *Theosophy, Imagination, Tradition: Studies in Western Esotericism*, Albany: SUNY Press, 2000, 3-98 ♦ Antoine Faivre & Jacob Needleman (eds.), *Modern Esoteric Spirituality*, New York: Crossroad, 1992 ♦ Antoine Faivre & Rolf Christian Zimmermann (eds.), *Epochen der Naturmystik: Hermetische Tradition im wissenschaftlichen Fortschritt*, Berlin: Erich Schmidt, 1979 ♦ B.J. Gibbons, *Gender in Mystical and Occult Thought: Behmenism and its Development in England*, Cambridge: Cambridge University Press, 1996 ♦ Joscelyn Godwin, *The Theosophical Enlightenment*, Albany: SUNY Press, 1994 ♦ Bernard Gorceix, *La Mystique de Valentin Weigel (1533-1588) et les origines de la théosophie allemande*, Lille: Université de Lille, Service de reproduction des thèses, 1970 ♦ idem, *Flambée et agonie: Mystiques du XVIIᵉ siècle allemand*, Sisteron: Présence, 1977 ♦ Serge Hutin, *Les Disciples anglais de Jacob Boehme*, Paris: Denoël, 1960 ♦ Peter Koslowski (ed.), *Gnosis und Mystik in der Geschichte der Philosophie*, Zurich/Munich: Artemis, 1998 ♦ Arthur Versluis, *Theosophia: Hidden Dimensions of Christianity*, Hudson: Lindisfarne Press, 1994 ♦ idem, *Wisdom's Children: A Christian Esoteric Tradition*, Albany: SUNY Press, 1999 ♦ Auguste Viatte, *Les Sources occultes du Romantisme: Illuminisme, Théosophie (1770-1820)*, 2 vols., Paris: Champion, 1928 (several reprints) ♦ Gerhard Wehr, *Esoterisches Christentum von der Antike bis zur Gegenwart* (1975), rev. ed. Stuttgart: Klett-Cotta, 1995, 219-318.

ANTOINE FAIVRE

Church Universal and Triumphant →
Summit Lighthouse

Clement of Alexandria (Titus Flavius Clemens), † before 215

Clement was a Christian teacher who worked in Alexandria and left us some important writings, but about whose life only little is known. He was born in a pagan family, probably in Athens. After his conversion he studied with Christian teachers in Greece, Southern Italy, Syria and Palestine, and finally settled in Alexandria (ca. 180), where he became a pupil of Pantaenus, a non-Gnostic Christian teacher. According to Eusebius, *Church History*, VI, 6, Clement became Pantaenus' successor as head of the so-called Catechetical School, but that is by no means certain, since the existence of this ecclesiastical institution before 200 is far from being an established fact. Everything in Clement's preserved works suggests that he was an independent lay teacher and thinker, without any official connection with the Alexandrian church. About 203, under the pressure of a persecution, he fled from Alexandria to Asia Minor, where he died shortly before 215.

Clement may be called the first Christian scholar: he had a vast knowledge of Scripture and of Greek and Christian literature (more than 360 different quotations from Greek literary and philosophical works). His eagerness to show how learned a Christian could be sometimes tends to pedantry. He was well read in at least Homer and Plato, but, like many of his contemporaries, he knew most of the authors from whose works he is quoting only through anthologies and excerpts. Sometimes he obviously borrows a passage from another author's work without any notice. An interesting example of this procedure is his report on a procession of Egyptian priests who carry forty-two fundamental Hermetic books (*Strom.*, VI, 35-37; → Hermetic literature). The most important of his own works are: *Exhortation to the Greeks*, an apology which proclaims the supremacy of the Christian religion; *Paedagogue*, in three volumes, about Christian ethics; *Stromateis*, "Miscellanies" (lit. "Patchwork", "Carpets"), his most important work, in eight volumes; and *Excerpts from Theodotus*, quotations from the Valentinian [→ Valentinus and Valentinians] Gnostic Theodotus and others, with Clement's own comments.

In 2nd-century Alexandria, Christian intellectuals were almost exclusively found on the side of the Gnostics [→ Gnosticism]. Clement was a non-Gnostic Christian intellectual and he had to defend his position against Gnostics and pagan critics of Christianity on the one hand and simple ordinary church members on the other. The Gnostics held that faith (*pistis*) was in fact irrelevant and that only knowledge (*gnōsis*), in the sense of esoteric insight in things divine, led to salvation. Clement's answer was that every believer who had been baptised was saved and that, therefore, Gnosis was not necessary. With the help of Greek philosophical ideas about the activity of the mind he defined the concept of *pistis* and defended its indispensability. This was not only directed against the Gnostics but also against Greek intellectuals who reproached the Christians for accepting everything by faith and not on the basis of rational reasoning. The simple believers, for their part, held that faith was all-sufficient: the faithful had simply to accept on authority what was taught by the church, and, therefore, philosophical or Gnostic speculations were suspect and had to be avoided. Against them, Clement argued that faith is indeed sufficient and even indispensable for salvation, but that personal knowledge is better than belief on authority, since it brings the believer to a higher level of religious comprehension and makes spiritual growth possible. For that reason, Clement defended the use of philosophy in theological speculation. He even went as far as to sustain that Greek philosophy and the Old Testament were equal preparatory stages for the Christian message. His religious thinking was strongly influenced by Jewish Alexandrian philosophy (Philo), Middle-Platonism, and Christian Gnosticism. He shared with these currents the idea that the highest doctrines about God, the world and man cannot be revealed to everybody but should be reserved to a small circle of initiates who are worthy to comprehend them. In his *Stromateis*, Clement set himself the task 'to speak hidingly, to expose concealingly, and to point out silently' (I, 15, 1). From Philo of Alexandria he learned, *int. al.*, that by means of allegorical exegesis all kinds of philosophical and religious truths could be found in the divine scriptures. Middle-Platonism provided him with a philosophical framework that directed his thinking about God and Christ. Christ was for him the divine Logos, the Pedagogue and Teacher of mankind, who had revealed the divine truth, first and only partly to Greek philosophers and Hebrew prophets, and then completely when he himself became man in Jesus Christ. With Christian Gnosticism Clement was convinced that there existed a secret and esoteric Christian tradition alongside that which was openly transmitted by the Church: 'This knowl-

edge (*gnōsis*), handed down in unwritten form
from the apostles through a succession of teachers,
has come to a few people' (*Strom.* VI, 61, 3).
Clement attacked the Gnostics for their claim to be
the only true Christians and their rejection of faith
as a sufficient base for salvation, but he had also
much in common with them. He quotes many
Gnostic teachers from the 2nd century, and not
always disapprovingly. One of the scholarly problems of his *Excerpts from Theodotus* is the
difficulty to distinguish clearly between the Gnostic
quotations and Clement's own comments.

Clement's religious thinking culminates in his
description of the ideal Christian, the "True Gnostic", to which especially books VI and VII of the
Stromateis are devoted. A first and indispensable
characteristic of the true Gnostic is his moral perfection and detachment from worldly things
(strong influence of Stoic ethics). His knowledge
not only concerns God and good and evil, but also
the whole world: 'He possesses the most precise
truth about the world from its creation to its end,
having learned it from the Truth itself' (*Strom.* VI,
78, 5). It is a spiritual knowledge, which derives
from revelation and is to be found in the words of
the Logos, i.e. in the divine scriptures. Therefore,
an important part of the esoteric tradition is the
capacity to read the hidden meaning of Scripture by
means of allegorical exegesis. This provides the
Gnostic with a perfect knowledge of past, present
and future, and leads him to an ever-deeper understanding of the divine world and to the contemplation of God.

O. Stählin (ed.), *Clemens Alexandrinus*, I: *Protrepticus
und Paedagogus*, 3rd rev. ed. by U. Treu; vol. II: *Stromata Buch I-VI*, 4th rev. ed. by L. Früchtel, mit
Nachträge von U. Treu; vol. III: *Stromata. Buch VII
und VIII, Excerpta ex Theodoto. Eclogae propheticae.
Quis dives salvbetur. Fragmente*, 2nd ed. by L. Früchtel und U. Treu, Berlin: Akademie Verlag, 1960-1985;
with French translation: C. Mondésert, (ed.), *Le Pro-
treptique* (SC 2), 2nd ed., Paris: Éditions du Cerf, 1949
♦ C. Mondésert, H.-I. Marrou et al. (eds.), *Le Péda-
gogue*, 3 vols. (SC 70, 108, 158), Ibidem 1960, 1965,
1970 ♦ C. Mondésert, P.Th. Camelot et al. (eds.), *Les
Stromateis*, 7 vols. (SC 30, 38, 463, 278, 279, 446,
428), Ibidem 1951-2001 (Book III not yet published) ♦
F. Sagnard (ed.), *Extraits de Théodote*, (SC 23), Ibidem
1948 (2nd ed. 1970). English translation by W. Wilson,
in: *ANCL*, vols. 4 and 12, Edinburgh: T&T Clark,
1867, 1869 (repr. *ANF*, vol. 2, Edinburgh/Grand
Rapids: T&T Clark/W.B. Eerdmans, 1994).

Lit.: A. Choufrine, *Gnosis, Theophany, Theosis: Stud-
ies in Clement of Alexandria's Appropriation of his
Background* (Patristic Studies, 5), New York: Peter
Lang, 2002 ♦ A. van den Hoek, *Clement of Alexandria
and his Use of Philo in the Stromateis*, Leiden, New
York: E.J. Brill, 1988 ♦ S.R.C. Lilla, *Clement of
Alexandria: A Study in Christian Platonism and Gnos-
ticism*, Oxford: Oxford University Press, 1971 ♦
E. Procter, *Christian Controversy in Alexandria:
Clement's Polemic against the Basilideans and Valen-
tinians* (American University Studies, Series VII: The-
ology and Religion, 172), New York, Bern: Peter Lang,
1995 ♦ G.G. Stroumsa, *Hidden Wisdom: Esoteric
Traditions and the Roots of Christian Mysticism* (Stud-
ies in the History of Religion, 70), Leiden: E.J.
Brill, 1996 ♦ W. Völker, *Der wahre Gnostiker nach
Clemens Alexandrinus* (Texte und Untersuchungen zur
Geschichte der altchristlichen Literatur, 57), Berlin/
Leipzig: Akademie-Verlag/J.C. Hinrichs, 1952 ♦
D. Wyrwa, *Die christliche Platonaneignung in den
Stromateis des Clemens von Alexandrien* (Arbeiten
zur Kirchengeschichte, 53), Berlin & New York: De
Gruyter, 1983.

ROELOF VAN DEN BROEK

Comenius (Komenski), Jan Amos, * 28.3.1592 Niwitz (Moravia), † 15.11.1670 Amsterdam

Comenius' family belonged to the Fraternity
commonly known as the Moravian Brothers and
named *Jednota Bratska* in Czech, that is, Unity of
Brethren. From the 15th century, this *ecclesiola* had
greatly developed despite persecutions, and it had
received some of the Vaudois driven out of Brandenburg. After studying Latin and theology, Comenius went to Hess, in Herborn, then to the
Palatinate, in Heidelberg, and experienced the double influence of Calvinism and the millenarianism
professed notably by Johann Heinrich Alsted.
Returned in 1614 to Moravia, Comenius was
ordained pastor in 1616 and got married. However, the victory of Tilly, commander of the
Catholic League, at the White Mountain, over the
Bohemian army commanded by the Palatine Frederick V – the *Winterkönig*, king of Bohemia for a
single winter (1619-1620) – would change the
course of Comenius's life. Having lost his wife and
children, he was henceforth constrained to lead a
wandering life throughout Europe. In 1624, an
imperial edict issued a ban on all non-Catholic
priests and forced Comenius to take refuge in Lissa,
on the Silesian border, where he could enjoy the
protection of the powerful family of the Lezcynski.
He was able to remain there until 1641, surrounded by a community of Moravian Brothers, of
whom he was the bishop. It was there that his passionate interest in problems of pedagogy developed, which manifested in writings such as *Janua
linguarum reserata* or *Didactique, Conatuum*

Comenianorum Praeludia and *Conatuum pan-sophicorum dilucidatio*. Invited to London by Samuel Hartlib in 1641, he traveled to Sweden the following year, then to Elbing in Prussia. In 1643, Comenius published *Irenica quaedam scripta pro pace ecclesiae*, an ecumenical work before the term existed. After the peace of Westphalia, he fell under the influence of a visionary and went to Hungary with the idea of establishing a *Schola Pansophica* there. If he did not succeed in this, he at least completed an encyclopedic collection under the title *Orbis sensualis pictus* and an innovative method of teaching languages entitled *Scholus ludus seu ency-clopedia viva*. During the many conflicts between Poland and Sweden, Comenius, who had returned to Lissa, suddenly had to leave this city captured and destroyed by the Polish, because he had sided with the king of Sweden. He spent the last years of his life in Amsterdam and further published his *Opera didactica omnia* (1657), *De irenico irenico-rum* (1660) and his beautiful literary testament *Unum necessarium* in 1668.

Of the many works by this man of an often-tragic destiny, and beyond his priestly activities with the Moravian Brothers, we mainly retain his pedagog-ical innovations partly inspired by Ratichius (Wolf-gang Ratke, 1571-1635). In fact, his interest in didactics was only a means for him to arrive at the "general reform of the world" through "panso-phy", that is, a total science, universal knowledge making it possible to decode the "signatures" of the divine realities inscribed in the concrete world. Now, these ideas preoccupied a number of minds in the first half of the 17th century. The *Vier Bücher vom wahren Christentum*, completed in 1610 by Johann Arndt, and the different plans for Christian society proposed by the celebrated Swabian the-ologian → Johann Valentin Andreae (1586-1654) after the vogue of the Rosicrucian myth [→ Rosi-crucianism I], aimed to "reform the Reformation" toward a pansophic Christianity. The utopian story of *Christianopolis*, published by Andreae in 1619, described its pedagogical program. It is thus not surprising that Comenius should have seen himself as a disciple of Andreae who, according to him, had been able in his writings both to detect the ills from which the Church, the State and culture were suf-fering, and to suggest the appropriate remedies. Comenius had read the main works published by Andreae between 1616 and 1619. From 1628, Comenius and Andreae established an exchange of correspondence, which accompanied the sending of Comenius's *Christianae Societatis Imago* (1620) with a commentary that evoked both the "ludib-rium" of the *Fama Fraternatis* and its efforts,

engaged as early as 1614, to create a true *societas christiana*, with the purpose of "cleaning the Augean stables". Having been prevented from achieving this vast project, Andreae suggested to Comenius, in a letter of 16 September 1629, that he pick up the torch and promote an authentically Christian pansophy, one that is thus not content to ally the creator God with nature-philosophy. Comenius was indeed strongly subject to J.V. Andreae's influence, to the point of repeating in his *Labyrint sveta a raj srdce* (Labyrinth of the World and Paradise of the Heart), composed in 1622/23, entire passages from *Peregrini in Patria errores*. However, he granted the Christianization of pans-ophy a much broader sense in his plan to establish a universal alliance of Men of good will. His *Panegersia* aspired to the creation of a "Collegium Lucis ad fundandam Ecclesiam vere Catholicam philadelphiam" whose prelude he saw in the Rosi-crucian brotherhood. In his *Pansophiae templum ad ipsius supremi Architecti, Omnipotentis Dei ideas, normas legesque extruendum*, Comenius divided pansophy into seven parts, making it pos-sible for the mind to pass through successive stages from the knowledge of nature to the contemplation of the supreme God.

Opera didacta omnia, Praha: Academia scientiarum bohemoslovenica, 1957 ♦ *The Labyrinth of the World and Paradise of the Heart* (Classics of Western Spiritu-ality), Paulist Press, 1997 ♦ *Der Weg des Lichtes / Via lucis*, Hamburg: Meiner, 1997 (Dutch trans. Amster-dam: In de Pelikaan, 1992) ♦ *Grosse Didaktik: Die vollständige Kunst, alle Menschen alles zu lehren*, Stuttgart: Klett-Cotta, 1992.

Lit.: Martin Brecht, "'Er hat uns die Fackel über-geben . . .': Die Bedeutung Johann Valentin Andreaes für Johann Amos Comenius", in: *Das Erbe des Christ-ian Rosenkreuz*, Amsterdam: In de Pelikaan, 1988, 28-47 ♦ Klaus Gossmann & Henning Schröer, *Auf den Spuren des Comenius*, Göttingen: Vandenhoek & Ruprecht, 1992 ♦ Jaromir Cervenka, *Die Natur-philosophie des Johann Amos Comenius*, Hanu: Dausien, 1998 ♦ Richard Van Dülmen, "Johann Amos Comenius und Johann Valentin Andreae", *Bohemia: Jahrbuch des Collegium Carolinum* 9 (1968), 73-87 ♦ Carlos Gilly, "Comenius und die Rosenkreuzer", in: Monika Neugebauer-Wölk (ed.), *Aufklärung und Eso-terik*, Hamburg: Felix Meiners, 1999, 87-107 ♦ J.L. Criegern, *Johann Amos Comenius als Theologe: Ein Beitrag zur Comenius Literatur*, Leipzig-Heidelberg, 1881 ♦ Ludwig Keller, "Johann Valentin Andreae und Comenius", *Monatshefte des Comenius-Gesellschaft* I (1892 1893?), 229-241 ♦ J. Kvacala, *Johann Amos Comenius, sein Leben und seine Schriften*, Berlin, 1903-1904 ♦ idem, "Die pädagogische Reform des Come-nius in Deutschland bis zum Ausgange des 17. Jahrhunderts", in: *Monumenta Germaniae Paedagog-*

ica XXVI, Berlin, 1903 ◆ E. Pappenheim, *Johann Amos Comenius*, Berlin, 1892 ◆ Klaus Schaller, *Die Pädagogik des Johann Amos Comenius und die Anfänge des pädagogischen Realismus im 17. Jahrhundert*, Heidelberg, 1967 ◆ idem, *Comenius*, Darmstadt, 1973.

ROLAND EDIGHOFFER

Constant, Alphonse Louis → Lévi, Éliphas

Corbin, Henry, * 14.4.1903 Paris, † 7.10.1978 Paris

A philosopher by training, as early as 1925 Corbin developed a strong interest in Islamology, under the influence of Étienne Gilson, whose course on Latin Avicennism in the Middle Ages he took at the École pratique des Hautes Études (Vth section). A graduate in scholastic and general philosophy, with diplomas from the École pratique des Hautes Études and the École des langues orientales, librarian at the Bibliothèque Nationale, friend of, among others, Louis Massignon, Alexandre Kojève, Alexandre Koyré, Denis de Rougemont, and Joseph and Jean Baruzi, he concurrently studied and translated works by Sohrawardî, Karl Barth and Heidegger. From 1939 to 1945 he was at the French Institute of Archaeology in Istanbul, before joining the Franco-Iranian Institute of Teheran, where he created the Department of Iranology and then the collection of the Iranian Library. From 1949 he was a regular participant in the Eranos meetings in Switzerland, where he was in significant contact with → Carl Gustav Jung, Mircea Eliade, and Gershom Scholem. In 1954, having recently published *Avicenne et le récit visionnaire*, he was appointed Professor of "Islamism and Religions of Arabia" at the Vth section of the École pratique des Hautes Études. From the following year on, until 1973, he directed the Department of Iranology that he had created, and taught history of Islamic theology and philosophy at the faculty of literature of the University of Teheran. In 1958 appeared *L'imagination créatrice dans le soufisme d'Ibn 'Arabî*; in 1961, *Terre céleste et corps de résurrection*; in 1962, *Histoire de la philosophie islamique*; in 1971, the first two volumes of *En Islam iranien* and *L'homme de lumière dans le soufisme iranien*. In 1973 he became a member of the very recent Iranian Imperial Academy of Philosophy and founded the International Center for Comparative Spiritual Research, better known as the Université Saint Jean de Jérusalem. The same

year he published the last two volumes of *En Islam iranien*, and in 1977 *Philosophie iranienne et philosophie comparée*. He died on 7 October 1978. During all these years he was intensely active in the publication and translation of texts (besides Sohrawardî, Barth and Heidegger: Hamann, Heschel, → Avicenna, Sejestânî, etc.) and contributed to many periodicals, colloquia, and miscellaneous collections. Some of the latter contributions later appeared grouped together in posthumously published volumes.

Corbin's first text devoted to Iranian Sufism, and more particularly to Sohrawardî, was published in 1933 in *Recherches philosophiques*. Here he emphasized the connection established by Sohrawardî between an illuminative philosophy of Platonic inspiration, a hermeneutics of myth and an angelology – all tied together in a mystical experience of the assumption of Man into a higher reality. Most of his later works would relate specifically to this point, as developed by Ismaelian gnosis. At the same time, refusing categorization, he ceaselessly engaged and promoted a comparative approach, illustrated with particular clarity in his study 'Herméneutique spirituelle comparée' (1964) that is devoted to Swedenborgian theosophy [→ Swedenborg] and Ismaelian gnosis. Corbin explains here that the object of his hermeneutics is 'a *spiritual fact, . . . a* phenomenon of *understanding*'. He readily admits his debt to Heidegger, who provided him with the key to understanding first Shi'ite gnosis, and then 'the Christian gnosis and . . . the Jewish gnosis that are its immediate neighbors'. The task of spiritual hermeneutics is different from that of the historian, for it is not a matter of simply rediscovering and understanding the past, but of personally "taking charge" of it. For Corbin, this means interpreting historical materials in terms of "hierohistory", which he believes reveals 'the hidden esotericism under the phenomenon of the literal appearance . . . of the Holy Books' which is fulfilled in each believer. For Corbin, spiritual hermeneutics is thus a path of personal spiritual realization under the aegis of theosophy. This hermeneutics is considered to be equivalent to the Sufi *ta'wil*, and to reveal hidden and spiritual esoteric meanings to which correspond as many degrees of being as are felt by the hermeneut's own conscience. Thus Corbin is in fact concerned with what he calls, in commenting on Avicenna, an 'exegesis of the soul'.

Here we encounter a basic notion in Corbin's thinking: the → imagination. Drawing inspiration from Ibn 'Arabî and Sohrawardî as well as from → Ficino, → Bruno, → Boehme and Swedenborg,

Corbin draws a distinction between the imaginary, which is utopian and unreal, and the imagination, which is cognitive and creative. The imagination constitutes an autonomous world, the *Mundus imaginalis* or the imaginal, the place of theophanic apparition, vision, and prophecy; this is what he calls the "disjoined imagination". But it is also the response of the cordial and prayerful imaginative awareness of the subject, who perceives the imaginal in his beliefs and perceives himself through it as a moment of the theophanic imagination; this he calls the "conjoined imagination". By this double movement of the imagination, a union of subject and object (a *unio sympathetica*) and a reversal of interiority and exteriority are accomplished. The spiritual interiority supports the exteriority and, through its "magical" and creative operation, gives it body: 'In short, because there is imagination, there is *ta'wil*; because there is *ta'wil*, there is symbolism; because there is symbolism, there are two dimensions in beings'.

The centrality of this conception of the imagination as a faculty of *coincidentia oppositorum* and of *unio sympathetica* is not without its consequences for the notion of esotericism upheld by Corbin. He attaches a very special importance to the notion of *significatio passiva* as understood by Luther, and even makes it one of the main keys of his hermeneutics. It means that the divine attributes can be understood only insofar as they are in relationship with us, and insofar as the divine "*esto*", the "Be!", makes us be ('the being that we are has this same imperative, but in its *significatio passiva*!'). The two dimensions in each being are present in a docetist manner: '. . . the *mysterium conjunctionis* uniting the two terms is a theophanic union (from the Creator's viewpoint) or a theopathic union (from the creature's viewpoint), but in no case a "hypostatic union"'. Incarnation takes place only in a *caro spiritualis*, and not as "physical incarnation": '. . . the *subjectum incarnationis* is not God or man, but a middle term between the two, an extra-divine divine person, as well as an extra-human human person', in other words, the Angel, archetype of the person and self-revelation of the divine Being. Docetism is thus the foundation of the imagination, since by elevating material realities to the rank of an apparition it restores their value as image of the true spiritual reality – precisely that to which the hermeneut who follows the path of *ta'wil* aspires. Hence, Corbin clearly denies any esoteric potential to "orthodox" Christianity, for as a religion of Incarnation it closes the door to prophetism: '. . . the Incarnation is a unique and irreversible fact; it exists in the web of material facts; God has personally incarnated at a moment in history; this "occurs" in the chronology with definite dates. There is no more mystery, therefore no more esotericism necessary'. Esotericism even becomes impossible, as soon as dogmas are irremediably fixed, thus closing the door to 'any possibility of a new prophetic revelation dispensed by the Angels, but also [to] any initiative of a prophetic hermeneutics'. This docetist foundation of Corbin's spiritual hermeneutics is certainly the reason why he clearly favors, in the domain of Western esotericism, the figure of Swedenborg.

Given these foundations, although at one occasion he called on 'esotericists of all religions' to unite, Corbin in fact proved remarkably exclusive. In Christianity, only those who place themselves (or whom Corbin places) outside the dogmatic and institutional boundaries of the Great Church can be qualified as "esotericists" and can appeal to his ' "Inner Church" that requires no act of belonging for one to belong' and which is 'the community, the *omma*, of esotericists from everywhere and for always'. Along the same lines, Corbin also refers to the 'Church of John [that] can be neither secularized nor socialized, just like it is impossible to secularize and socialize the esoteric community of the Friends of God'. Thus, Corbin's definition of "esotericism" (understood, in terms of its etymology, as "interiorism") is, on the one hand, very comprehensive – even to the point of being applicable to phenomena completely different from esotericism in a historical sense – but, on the other, ultimately very restrictive as well. For in addition to his exclusion of Christian "orthodoxy" he also wants to demarcate himself from "pseudo-esotericisms" (undoubtedly the occultist currents, although he never names them explicitly). Since Corbin introduces into the heart of his approach a process in which the commentator identifies with his subject, he ends up creating a spiritual hermeneutics, not a hermeneutics of spiritualities. In studying and commenting on theosophers from East and West, he would clearly like, to some extent, to be a theosopher himself: '. . . one cannot remain a stranger [to the spirituality that] one wants really *to understand* and *to make understood*'. This method of hermeneutics, that Corbin claims to discover among the theosophers, he appropriates for himself to make of it, if not a universal method, at least a workable method for interpreting the religions of the Book (inasmuch as they are prophetic religions, that is, that they are 'professing the necessity of superhuman mediators between the divinity that inspires them, and common humanity'). Hence the comparatism that Corbin brings into play has as its prime vocation the rediscovery of the similarities and convergences that are revealed by the spiritual hermeneutics of each religion of the Book, and that are based upon the archetypes common to different spiritual worlds.

In this respect Corbin, since he makes the theosophers' approach into his own, deserves being studied as an esotericist probably more than as an "esoterologist". His perspective permits him to posit a very broad definition of esotericism (interiorism), while retaining from the actual history of esotericism only what agrees with his definition. Nevertheless, Corbin's contribution to the history of religions is undeniable: besides having been one of the principal initiators of Iranian studies in France, his works have greatly contributed to the legitimization of university research in esotericism. Moreover, his involvement in the Eranos meetings and his establishment of the "research community" called the Université Saint Jean de Jerusalem have undoubtedly stimulatd interdisciplinary studies in this area. Finally, while the methodological assumptions underlying his spiritual hermeneutics are certainly subject to criticism, his deepening of the notions of the imagination and the *mundus imaginalis* have contributed to the development of a criteriology of esotericism as heuristic as that of Antoine Faivre – who, on this point, recognizes his debt to Corbin while distinguishing himself from him in other respects.

Avicenne et le récit visionnaire, Teheran: Académie impériale iranienne de philosophie, 1952 (Paris: repr. Adrien Maisonneuve, 1954; Paris: Berg, 1979) ♦ *L'imagination créatrice dans le soufisme d'Ibn 'Arabi*, Paris: Flammarion, 1958, repr. 1977 ♦ *Terre céleste et corps de résurrection*, Paris: Buchet-Chastel, 1961 ♦ *Trilogie ismaélienne*, Paris: Adrien Maisonneuve, 1961 (repr. Lagrasse: Verdier, 1994) ♦ *Histoire de la philosophie islamique*, Paris: Gallimard, 1964, repr. 1986 ♦ *En Islam iranien*, Paris: Gallimard, 1971-1972, 1991 ♦ *L'homme de lumière dans le soufisme iranien*, Chambéry, Saint-Vincent-Saint-Jabron: Présence, 1971 ♦ *Philosophie iranienne et philosophie comparée*, Teheran: Académie impériale iranienne de philosophie, 1977, Paris: repr. Buchet-Chastel, 1985 ♦ *L'archange empourpré*, Paris: Fayard, 1978 ♦ *Corps spirituel et corps céleste*, Paris: Buchet-Chastel, 1979 ♦ *Anthologie des philosophes iraniens aux XVIIᵉ et XVIIᵉ siècles*, Paris: Bushet-Chastel, 1981 ♦ *Le Paradoxe du monothéisme*, Paris: L'Herne, 1981 ♦ *Temple et contemplation*, Paris: Flammarion, 1981 ♦ *Temps cyclique et gnose ismaélienne*, Paris: Berg, 1982 ♦ *L'homme et son ange: Initiation et chevalerie spirituelle*, Paris: Fayard, 1983 ♦ *Face de Dieu, face de l'homme: Herméneutique et soufisme*, Paris: Flammarion, 1983 ♦ *Hamman, philosophe du luthéranisme*, Paris: Berg, 1985 ♦ *L'alchimie comme art hiératique*, Paris: L'Herne, 1986.

Lit.: Adriana Berger, "Cultural Hermeneutics: The Concept of Imagination in the Phenomenological Approaches of Henry Corbin and Mircea Eliade", *The Journal of Religion* 66 (1986), 141-156 ♦ Tom Cheetham, *The World Turned Inside Out: Henry Corbin and Islamic Mysticism*, Woodstock: Spring Journal, 2003 ♦ "Henry Corbin et le comparatisme spirituel", *Cahiers du Groupe d'études spirituelles comparées* 8, Paris: Archè, 2000 ♦ Hans Thomas Hakl, *Der verborgene Geist von Eranos: Unbekannte Begegnungen von Wissenschaft und Esoterik. Eine alternative Geistesgeschichte des 20. Jahrhunderts*, Bretten: Scientia Nova/Verlag Neue Wissenschaft 2001, esp. 258-271 ♦ Christian Jambet (ed.), *Henry Corbin* (Les Cahiers de l'Herne), Paris: L'Herne, 1981 ♦ Christian Jambet, *La logique des orientaux: Henry Corbin et la science des formes*, Paris: Le Seuil, 1983 ♦ Seyyed Hossein Nasr (ed.), *Mélanges offerts à Henry Corbin*, Teheran: Institute of Islamic Studies McGill University, Tehran Branch, 1977 ♦ Seyyed Hossein Nasr, "Henri Corbin (1903-1978): Souvenirs et réflexions sur son influence intellectuelle vingt ans après", in: Richard Caron, Joscelyn Godwin, Wouter J. Hanegraaff & Jean-Louis Vieillard-Baron (eds.), *Ésotérisme, gnoses & imaginaire symbolique: Mélanges offerts à Antoine Faivre*, Louvain: Peeters, 2001, 783-796 ♦ Daryush Shayegan, "L'actualité de la pensée d'Henry Corbin", *Les Études philosophiques*, janvier-mars 1980, 61-72 ♦ idem, *Henry Corbin: La topographie spirituelle de l'Islam iranien*, Paris: La Différence, 1990 ♦ Jean-Louis Vieillard-Baron, "Henry Corbin (1903-1978)", *Les Études philosophiques*, janvier-mars 1980, 73-89 ♦ Steven M. Wasserstrom, *Religion after Religion: Gershom Scholem, Mircea Eliade and Henry Corbin at Eranos*, Princeton: Princeton University Press, 1999.

JÉRÔME ROUSSE-LACORDAIRE

Correggio, Giovanni da, * ca. 1451? Bologna?, † after 1503 place unknown

Apocalyptic prophet and hermetic messiah. We know about Correggio's activities from an anonymous "Epistola Enoch" and three dedicatory epistles written by his pupil → Lodovico Lazzarelli, and from scattered references in the works of contemporaries, including the famous abbot → Johannes Trithemius. Correggio's year of birth cannot be established with any certainty: all we know is that Lazzarelli describes him as being 'about thirty-three years old' in 1484, but this may reflect an attempt on Lazzarelli's part to emphasize parallels between the ages of Jesus and Correggio at the time of their public entrance in Jerusalem and Rome respectively (see below). Most probably Correggio was a bastard son of Antonio da Correggio (?-1474), which means he came from an old and powerful family belonging to the higher nobility. Although in his later life Correggio and his entire family were roaming through Italy and France while begging for their daily bread, he may have done this for spiritual reasons; there are indications that he had a house in Bologna, and suffered no serious financial problems.

Nothing is known about Correggio's life prior to his first appearance in Rome, on November 12, 1481. The cardinals were gathering for a consistory meeting, and Correggio appeared on the stairs of the papal palace holding up a Bible 'mystically closed with seven seals': an obvious reference to Revelation 5:1. He held an apocalyptic sermon and called for repentance. One of the bystanders was the young poet Lazzarelli, who followed him as his first pupil. Lazzarelli has left us a much more detailed description of Correggio's second appearance in Rome, on Palm Sunday, April 11, 1484. He first attracted a crowd by riding through the streets of Rome to the Vatican, clothed in rich garments and accompanied by four servants. Having left the city he changed his clothes, putting on a blood-stained linen mantle and a crown of thorns. Over his head was fixed a silver-plated disk in the shape of the crescent moon, with a text that identified him as God's or Jesus's servant Pimander and contained a quotation from the alchemical *Tabula Smaragdina*. Decked out with various symbolic paraphernalia, described in detail by Lazzarelli, he mounted a white ass and entered the gate of Rome, surrounded by his servants on horseback. He headed towards the Vatican, but made several stops to proclaim the coming judgment, identifying himself as 'Giovanni Mercurio da Correggio, the Angel of Wisdom Pimander'. People leaving the churches, with in their hands palm branches that they had received during high mass, started following him through the streets, thus greatly amplifying the similarity with Christ's entrance in Jerusalem. According to Lazzarelli's account, the guards at the gate of the St. Peter made way for him and allowed him to enter. Having dismounted, Correggio is said to have walked to the altar, offered up his mystical apparell and a paper entitled "The Eternal Gospel", prayed to God, and left the St. Peter. We know from the contemporary Jewish author Abraham Farissol that at one time Correggio was imprisoned in Rome. Although Lazzarelli describes him as freely entering and leaving the St. Peter, this is hardly credible. It is more likely that he was arrested at this particular occasion, without ever making it to the altar. He is said to have escaped from prison, and to have fled together with his friends and devotees. Back in Bologna he was imprisoned anew, on suspicion of heresy, but was apparently released.

In 1486 Correggio made another prophetic appearance, this time in Florence. He was on his way to the court of king Ferdinand I (Ferrante) in Naples, who had requested to see him, undoubtedly at Lazzarelli's suggestion. But Lorenzo il Magnifico ordered his arrest and imprisonment, and he was severely harrassed by a Franciscan inquisitor. Ferrante obtained his release, but we do not know whether Corregio ever made it to Naples. We then again lose track of him for several years, but sometime after 1492 he must have visited Rome with a considerable following, calling himself "the younger Hermes". In 1497 he preached in Venice; and in 1499 he passed through Cesena on his way from Milan, dressed in sackcloth and accompanied by his entire household, including his wife and five children. In 1501 he traveled to Lyon, still with his family, where he was granted an audience with king Louis XII, whom he impressed with his learning and with promises about sensational alchemical and magical secrets. Sometime later Correggio seems to have returned to Rome, where he claimed to possess an alchemical cure against the plague. His last writing was addressed to pope Julius II, and suggests that he was now in urgent need of a protector: 'Protect, protect me ... and I will protect you. Bestow your help on our Giovanni Mercurio ...'. And that is the last glimpse we have of Correggio: we do not know what became of him and his family, or where and when he died.

It is likely that Correggio started out as a Christian apocalyptic prophet, and that his striking self-proclamation as "Pimander", "Mercurio" and "the younger Hermes" reflects the influence of his pupil Lazzarelli. Lazzarelli believed that the great being Poimandres who appeared to Hermes in *Corpus Hermeticum* I was in fact no one else but Christ, who had now returned in the person of Correggio: the hermetic Christ. According to Farissol, in the years after 1484 Correggio referred to himself as 'Son of God, Mercurius, Trismegistus, Enoch and Methuselah', described himself as 'a son of God emanating from the Godhead with the divine spirit sparkling in him', and taught that 'whoever elevated himself and endeavored to gain perfection would attain ... the status of a son of God'. Corregio seems to have continued calling himself "Mercurio" to the end of his life, but his writings – several of which were published during his lifetime – show only scant hermetic references, and the later accounts contain no evidence that he kept presenting himself as Christ. In his meeting with king Louis XII in 1501 he presented himself, rather, as a great alchemist and magus, modeled after Apollonius of Tyana.

All Correggio's writings, written in a characteris-

tic excited and ponderous style, are heavily apocalyptic and frequently call on worldly and spiritual
leaders to take the lead in the final battle between
good and evil. His last works, notably his as yet
unpublished *De Quercu Iulii Pontificis sive de
lapide philosophico* (The Oak of Pope Julius, or the
Philosopher's Stone), show an increasing preoccupation with → alchemy: an aspect of his activities
that has not yet been studied in sufficient detail.
Likewise his indebtedness to Christian eschatological traditions, and to Joachimism in particular,
requires further investigation. It remains that Correggio's self-presentation as a hermetic messiah
makes him a striking example of how Christian
hermetism could be integrated in the popular
apocalypticism of the late 15th century.

Giovanni da Correggio, "Oratio ad sanctam crucem"
(Rome, 1499), modern edition with English translation
in: Wouter J. Hanegraaff & Ruud M. Bouthoorn,
*Lodovico Lazzarelli (1447-1500): The Hermetic Writ-
ings and Related Documents*, Phoenix: Medieval &
Renaissance Texts & Studies, 2005 ♦ "Exhortationes in
Barbaros Thurcos Scijthas Johannis mercurij corigien-
sis perornate" (Lyons, 1501; no modern edition) ♦
"Sonetto", modern edition with English translation in:
Hanegraaff & Bouthoorn, o.c. ♦ "Contra pestem
[etc.]" (n.p., n.d.), facsimile with English translation in:
W.B. McDaniel, "An Hermetic Plague-Tract by
Johannes Mercurius Corrigiensis", part I, *Transactions
and Studies of the College of Physicians of Philadel-
phia*, ser. IV, vol. 9 (1941–1942), 96-111 ♦ "De
Quercu Julii Pontificis sive de lapide philosophico"
(after 1503), British Library, ms Harley 4081 ♦
Lodovico Lazzarelli, "Three Prefaces" and "Epistola
Enoch", and Johannes Trithemius, fragment about
Correggio (1690): modern editions with English trans-
lation in: Hanegraaff & Bouthoorn, o.c.

Lit.: Wouter J. Hanegraaff, "Lodovico Lazzarelli and
the Hermetic Christ: At the Sources of Renaissance
Hermetism", in: Hanegraaff & Bouthoorn, *Lodovico
Lazzarelli* (quoted *supra*) ♦ Paul Oskar Kristeller,
"Ancora per Giovanni Mercurio da Correggio", in:
idem, *Studies in Renaissance Thought and Letters* 1,
Rome: Edizioni di Storia e Letteratura, 1956, 249-257
♦ idem, "Lodovico Lazzarelli e Giovanni da Correggio,
due ermetici del Quattrocento, e il manoscritto II. D. I.
4 della Biblioteca Comunale degli Ardenti di Viterbo"
(1960), repr. in: idem, *Studies in Renaissance Thought
and Letters* 3, Rome: Edizioni di Storia e Letteratura
1993, 207-225 ♦ W.B. McDaniel, "An Hermetic
Plague-Tract by Johannes Mercurius Corrigiensis", 2
pts., *Transactions and Studies of the College of Physicians of Philadelphia*, ser. IV, 9 (1941 & 1942), 96-
111, 217-225 ♦ Kurt Ohly, "Johannes 'Mercurius'
Corrigiensis", *Beiträge zur Inkunabelkunde*, n.F. 2
(1938), 133-141 ♦ David B. Ruderman, "Giovanni
Mercurio da Correggio's Appearance in Italy as Seen
Through the Eyes of an Italian Jew", *Renaissance
Quarterly* 28 (1975), 309-322 ♦ idem, "Observations

on a Christian Prophet and a Florentine Luminary:
Giovanni Mercurio da Correggio", in: idem, *The
World of a Renaissance Jew: The Life and Thought of
Abraham ben Mordecai Farissol*, Cincinnati: Hebrew
Union College Press, 1981, 35-56 ♦ Fabio Troncarelli,
"Il profeta di Correggio", in: Vincenzo de Caprio &
Concetta Ranieri (eds.), *Presenze eterodosse nel
Viterbese*, Archivio Guido Izzi, 1996, 9-26.

WOUTER J. HANEGRAAFF

Correspondences

1. INTRODUCTION 2. CORRESPONDENCES
FROM ANTIQUITY THROUGH THE
RENAISSANCE 3. CORRESPONDENCES SINCE
THE ENLIGHTENMENT

1. INTRODUCTION
The idea that reality consists of multiple "levels"
which in some manner mirror one another is
extremely widespread in all traditional societies: it
is basic to the various → divinatory arts, → magic,
and → astrology; but can also be found e.g. in the
architectural design of premodern villages, cities,
temples and court complexes; in the ways that the
orders of gods, angels or demons are imagined; in
systems of → number symbolism; and in various
cosmologies, including notions of the human being
as microcosm mirroring the structure of the
macrocosm. In the wake of Marcel Granet's *La
pensée chinoise* (1934) and the second volume of
Joseph Needham's *Science and Civilization in
China* (1956), the fundamental importance of
"correlative thinking" to traditional Chinese culture has come to be widely recognized by sinolo-
gists, but its role in other premodern cultures has
been curiously neglected, even to such an extent
that it is often considered to have been unique to
premodern China. In fact, however, correlative
thinking is ubiquitous in all pre-modern and even
early modern cultures, and its expressions (such as
e.g. the elaborate systematic tables of correspondences that can be found in Chinese, Indian, Mid-
dle-Eastern, Mesoamerican as well as in pre- and
early modern European contexts) are often strikingly similar. Rather than considering correspondences as a "doctrine" that can be traced back to
specific philosophical sources and authors, correlative thinking may therefore be considered a spontaneous tendency of the human mind; in fact,
neurobiological research suggests that its ultimate
foundations may lie in the way the human brain
uses "topographical maps" to organize data into
functional hierarchies (Farmer, Henderson &
Witzel 2000 [2002]). While taking this into

account, the following overview will be restricted to correspondences in Western culture specifically, and focus on the philosophical and theological frameworks that were developed here to account for and systematize correlative thinking.

Ancient and medieval cosmology was steeped in theology, in the sense that a primary importance was awarded to cosmogony and to an ontological perspective: philosophically considered either as a divine creation, or as an emanation of the highest Principle, the world was primarily understood as a reflection of the Godhead, meant to reveal its will and wisdom and, although closed and consisting of a finite (even if innumerable) number of components, expressing something of its supernal origin. Seen from such an angle, any interest in the universe (and/or its contents) was bound to assume the essential shape of an inquiry into the divine mysteries, conceiving of the world in terms of an ontological ladder leading back up to the divine sphere; or of a scrutiny of the symbolic "signs" which the natural world displays for the spiritual and moral edification of mankind.

The gradual development of these views into the notion of a "Book of Nature", complementing the "Book of Scripture" – that is to say, the emergence of a partially autonomous concept of "nature" (and consequently of "physics", or "natural philosophy") as such – required a concept of "secondary causes" mediating between God's will and its creation. The actual working of the universe (prior, of course, to the emergence of any sort of "mechanistic" insights, or to any concept of natural "laws") was maintained and regulated according to divine ordinance *by* and *through* these intermediary causes, whether they were regarded as angelic entities, celestial influences, numbers or otherwise. As is well known, this shift in philosophical outlook was inspired by the 12th-century commentaries on the book of *Genesis* and Plato's *Timæus* (stemming for instance from the School of Chartres, mainly Thierry of Chartres and William of Conches) and by the progressive assimilation, during the following century, of arabic and aristotelian cosmology by the Scholastics (commentaries of → Albertus Magnus on Aristotle's *Physics* and *De cælo*). Historically, these conceptions mediate in turn between the earlier perception of the world as theophany, and the later, Renaissance view of nature as a living garment or organic expression of the divine being. The same period also witnessed the gradual substitution of a mathematical paradigm for a metaphysical one within natural philosophy, partly owing to the emphasis on the idea of a cosmic numeric harmony.

2. CORRESPONDENCES FROM ANTIQUITY THROUGH THE RENAISSANCE

Theoretical formulations of correspondences reflect several tenets which, until (and well into) the Renaissance, were among the mainstays of the dominant world picture(s) of Western culture.

(1) The first is *the unicity of creation*, which implies that a perfect ontological continuity connects all levels of the universe, throughout the overall hierarchy of being. This theme of the "great chain of being", to which no precise historical origin may be assigned (it is present in Plato's *Ion* but certainly antedates Greek civilization), is perhaps one of the most important metaphysical foundations of ancient cosmological systems.

(2) Second comes *the doctrine of "participation"*, of platonic origin, in which "love" constitutes the universal link or bond between the constituents of the universe, in a horizontal sense as well (*Symposium*, 186b-188d). Frequently understood as more or less equivalent to the stoic scheme of *sympatheia/antipatheia*, the cosmic pattern of attraction/repulsion which determines the relations and interactions of all things, properties and beings within the world, it may be construed as some kind of "immanent determinism" permeating the cosmos, and as one of two main driving forces at work behind its active dynamisms.

(3) The second driving force, as well as the third tenet, consists in seeing *the universe as a living being*, endowed with an animating soul, and whose parts are utterly complementary and interdependent, exactly like the limbs of a body. Again, the unicity and "wholeness" of its structure is frequently understood as an organic image of the human body.

(4) This leads us to the fourth tenet, *the doctrine of universal analogy*. Through analogy, which refers to a primarily "vertical" perspective, all levels of existence within the hierarchy of being (or, for that matter, all things they comprehend) actually mirror each other, in the sense that the lower in ontological rank is considered as a "symbol" of the superior, essentially endowed with the same virtues, features and properties, the main difference between them being one of scale (or of "proportion", the original meaning of the Greek *analogia*). One of the most fundamental and widespread of these analogies is precisely that of the macrocosmos/microcosmos, which harks back to Plato's *Timæus* (although, in itself, it certainly dates from time immemorial and is also found in non-Western contexts, e.g. Taoism), envisaging the world as a "grand man" and man as a synthetic abridgement of the universe.

In a restricted sense, correspondences may be interpreted as the "horizontal" counterpart of the network of universal analogies; but according to a more encompassing understanding, they overreach from one natural realm or plane to another and, moreover, overlap quite frequently with analogies proper. Such ambiguities are rather common in this domain; one may think, for instance (and *mutatis mutandis*) of the equally ambivalent conception of the elements, often presented as both the foundations *and* the components of reality.

The network of correspondences appears as the outward expression of the hidden dynamics of *sympatheia/antipatheia*; as a system of "signs" canvassing the qualitative interactions of natural things and beings, and manifesting the manner of their distribution; as well as the practical means of their philosophical understanding, and of their magical or therapeutical use. Life and death, good and evil, illness and cure, and the general complementarity of natural qualities in bodies, result on the cosmological level from such a network, on the basis of which Plotinus described nature as "the great sorceress".

Correspondences were considered to possess in themselves a dual aspect, external and internal. The external one was based on plain outward resemblance in shape or characteristics – for example between a plant and a human limb, or between a given animal and a natural body, both being considered to stand under the dominion of the same astral influence and therefore to manifest (each in its own way) similar properties. The inner aspect refers to some internal "essence" of things, which is supposed to be at the root of all corporeal features, either of one single natural item or of a number of them, to which it is common. The external features, being visible, "manifest" the inner principle, and lead on to an easier and better knowledge of it.

Whenever such a "hidden" essence is being considered, the notion of "sign" – understood both in a natural and in a semantic way – is called upon to mediate between the internal and external properties. Yet the "sign" as such essentially denotes or indicates the presence of an invisible counterpart to the outwardly observable characteristics, whereas the term (and concept) of *signatura* (made famous by → Paracelsus [*Astronomia magna, Von der natürliche Dinge*] and, later, → Jacob Boehme [*De signatura rerum*]) applies to the very *relation* between occult [→ occult /occultism] and manifest, and constitutes an attempt to explain it in terms of the "imprint" or translation of an archetype into material reality. It must be noted that this relation

works, and therefore must be accounted for, in both directions: from the invisible to the visible, but from the visible to the invisible as well. The latter is the case when Paracelsus recommends close observation of "astronomy" as revealing the outward, visible manifestation, on a large scale, of what is hidden and inscrutable within man or natural things on a smaller scale, that is to say their inner essence and "occult qualities", thus postulating a fundamental connaturality of internal archetype(s) between the two orders. Occasionally *signatura* is taken to mean the mere external resemblance mentioned above between two different natural bodies, in which case it likewise points to a relation, albeit a different and more "superficial" one.

Conceptions of causality implied by the theory of correspondences are, again, nuanced, varied and ambiguous. Envisaged as depending on the cosmic network of sympathies and antipathies, correspondences may be understood in terms of a "preestablished harmony", or "immanent determinism", embedded as such in material reality and independent, for this reason, of causality in a strict sense. Yet, as we have seen, the doctrine cannot be cleared from astrological implications. In that context, the "occult" relation between celestial bodies and configurations and terrestrial beings may be interpreted – in line with the non-causal notion of "preestablished harmony" just mentioned – as purely dynamic and interactive, based on a common set of components (elements and qualities) held in common by the different realms; but it may also be seen as based on one of the many available conceptions of a physical, although invisible, astral influence (this might be referred to as a notion of "occult causality"), or as based on the presence of an invisible *archè* at work within all natural things (this may be referred to as "ontological" causality, with a cause being seen as transcending its effects, similar to the "essence" and its corporeal transcriptions, referred to above).

Seen from any such perspective (or from several of them at the same time), correspondences expressed an important understanding of how life was believed to be infused into the whole universe, and of the ontological intentionality which made it possible for "signs" to convey the properties of being along with those of structure, and fully reveal the invisible through the manifest (and vice versa).

3. CORRESPONDENCES SINCE THE ENLIGHTENMENT
The explicit worldviews and implicit assumptions that made it natural in pre-modern and early

modern contexts to think of reality in terms of correspondences gradually came to be compromised and called into doubt under the impact of the scientific revolution and, especially, of Enlightenment rationalism. Since the assumptions basic to the newly emerging world picture(s) were largely incompatible with correspondences, the nature and internal logic (in terms of its own guiding assumptions) of the latter was no longer understood; as a result, a new generation of scholars, in studying pre- and early modern cosmologies, found itself deeply puzzled by what seemed to them obvious "irrationalities" and "absurdities". Friedrich Max Müller's reference to the Brahmanas as 'the twaddle of idiots, and the raving of madmen', or E.B. Tylor's description of magic as a 'monstrous farrago' and a 'contemptible superstition' based upon incorrect thinking [→ Magic I], are only two well-known examples that demonstrate the failure of 19th-century scholars and intellectuals to understand correspondences in terms of its own premises. With respect to systems of correspondences in Western culture specifically, and with considerably more sophistication, 20th-century historians of science such as Brian Vickers (1984, 1988) have analyzed them as based upon a failure to recognize the distinction – formulated in terms of Saussurian linguistics – between signifier and signified; referring to Plato's *Cratylus*, Vickers correctly draws a parallel between correspondences and the concept of natural signs on the one hand, and modern scientific worldviews and the understanding of signs as conventional, on the other. In short, concepts of correspondences as based upon a non-causal connection, as well as notions of "occult causality" (see above), are deeply problematic from the alternative perspective of "instrumental causality" basic to modern scientific and rationalist worldviews; and the latter's implicit or explicit "nominalist" assumptions are no less incompatible with the "realist" ones that underly traditional correlative thinking.

→ Emanuel Swedenborg's famous "doctrine of correspondences" is a particularly good example of how traditional and modern notions clashed during the Age of reason. On the one hand, Swedenborg's doctrine is clearly based upon non-causal connections and formulated in a deliberate attempt at overcoming the limitations of instrumental causality, and his Biblical exegesis is grounded in an extreme version of linguistic realism; but on the other hand, Swedenborg thinks about correspondences along post-Cartesian lines, and about biblical exegesis in terms of a rationalist protestantism that relies exclusively on direct divine revelation for unveiling the real meaning of

linguistic signs (Hanegraaff 1996/1998; 2005). The result is a streamlined scholastic system that formally exemplifies traditional correlative thinking, but is curiously presented in Protestant and rationalist language.

While Swedenborg developed his system of correspondences with considerable intellectual sophistication, the same can hardly be said about most other authors who have defended or used it since the 18th century. Due to its incompatibility with the instrumental causality, rationalism and nominalism basic to modern science and philosophy, correspondences became a typical example of "rejected knowledge" seldom taken seriously by others than esotericists; and the latter, in turn, were mostly so influenced by the very worldviews to which they sought to find an alternative, that they unintentionally ended up interpreting correspondences in modern (rationalist, nominalist, quasi-materialist) terms. Tables of correspondences used by 19th- and 20th-century occultists (with → Aleister Crowley's volume 777, consisting largely of such tables, as perhaps the ultimate example) tend to be used quite pragmatically, on the nominalist assumption that its various terms – names of gods, angels, demons, colours, substances, numbers etc. – are mere conventional signs that can be rearranged or replaced by others according to the user's individual preferences (Hanegraaff 2003).

The major exception is → Carl Gustav Jung's theory of synchronicity. Explicitly presented as a principle of acausal connection between nature and the psyche (that is to say, as an alternative to a worldview based upon instrumental causality), and with many references to the major representatives of esoteric currents from antiquity to the Renaissance, it is in fact a sophisticated restatement of correspondences in modern psychological terms. In the general context of → New Age spirituality, Jung's theory has strongly contributed to a new popularity of correspondences – very seldom presented explicitly as a worldview, but broadly accepted in practice. Whereas 19th- and early 20th-century occultists were highly conscious of positivism and materialism as a serious threat that had to be countered by alternative worldviews, since the 1960s and increasingly since the 1980s one may observe a pragmatic attitude that implicitly assumes the presence of correspondences (for example in the use of → tarot or astrology) but seldom bothers to try and work out their theoretical implications or convince critics. In the wake of Jung himself, participants in the New Age milieu may sometimes invoke modern scientific theories, especially in the field of quantum mechanics, in support of correspondences or synchronicity; but such theories are seen less as "proof" than as additional confirmation of a perspective that would have been adopted in any case, with or without scientific support. Such a relaxed and pragmatic acceptance of correspondences may well reflect a post-modern relativism that fails to see why scientific naturalism should be more credible than a "spiritual" worldview of correspondences. This phenomenon may well be seen as confirmation of the perspective (referred to in the introduction) that sees correlative thinking as a spontaneous and perhaps neurologically-based tendency of the human mind, which may clothe itself in theories or worldviews, but ultimately does not need them to assert itself.

Lit.: Rudolf Allers, "Microcosmus: From Anaximenes to Paracelsus", *Traditio* II (1944), 319-407 ♦ M.L. Bianchi, "Occulto e manifesto nella medicina del Rinascimento: Jean Fernel e Pietro Severino", *Atti e memorie dell'Accademia toscana di scienze e lettere La Colombaria* 47 (1982), 183-248 ♦ idem, *Signatura rerum: Segni, magia e conoscenza da Paracelso a Leibniz*, Rome: Edizioni dell'Ateneo, 1987 ♦ George Perrigo Conger, *Theories of Macrocosms and Microcosms in the History of Philosophy*, New York: Columbia University Press, 1922 ♦ S.A. Farmer, *Syncretism in the West: Pico's 900 Theses. The Evolution of Traditional Religious and Philosophical Systems*, Tempe: Medieval & Renaissance Texts & Studies, 1998 ♦ Steve Farmer, John B. Henderson & Michael Witzel, "Neurobiology, Layered Texts, and Correlative Systems: A Cross Cultural Framework for Premodern Studies", *Bulletin of the Museum of Far Eastern Antiquities* 72 (2000 [2002]), 48-89 ♦ M. Foucault, *Les mots et les choses*, Paris: Gallimard, 1966, ch. 2 ♦ R. Gorris Camos (ed.), *Macrocosmo/Microcosmo: Scrivere e pensare il mondo nel Cinquecento tra Italia e Francia*, Fasano: Schena, 2004 ♦ Wouter J. Hanegraaff, *New Age Religion and Western Culture: Esotericism in the Mirror of Secular Thought*, Leiden etc.: E.J. Brill, 1996/Albany: SUNY Press, 1998, 424-429 ♦ idem, "How Magic Survived the Disenchantment of the World", *Religion* 33:4 (2003), 357-380 ♦ idem, "Swedenborg's *Magnum Opus* and its Reception", in: Emanuel Swedenborg, *Secrets of Heaven*, vol. 1, West Chester: Swedenborg Foundation, 2005 ♦ Arthur O. Lovejoy, *The Great Chain of Being: A Study of the History of an Idea* (1936), Cambridge, Mass./London: Harvard University Press, 1964 ♦ E.P. Mahoney, "The Metaphysical Foundations of the Hierarchy of Being according to Some Late Medieval and Renaissance Philosophers", in: P. Morewedge (ed.), *Philosophies of Existence, Ancient and Modern*, New York, 1982, 165-257 ♦ idem, "Lovejoy and the Hierarchy of Being", *Journal of the History of Ideas* 48 (1987), 211-230 ♦ G. Simon, "Porta, la physiognomonie et la magie: Les circularités de la similitude", in: M. Jones-Davies (ed.), *La magie et ses langages*, Lille: Presses de l'Université de Lille III, 1980, 95-106 ♦ idem, *Sciences et savoirs aux XVIe et XVIIe siècles*, Villeneuve d'Ascq: Presses Universitaires

du Septentrion, 1996 ♦ Kocku von Stuckrad, "Entsprechungsdenken als Grundform esoterischer Wirklichkeitsdeutung: Das Beispiel Astro-logie", *Spirita* 13:1 (1999), 12-17 ♦ C. Vasoli, "L'analogie dans le langage de la magie à la Renaissance", in: M. Jones-Davies, *La magie et ses langages*, o.c., 43-56 ♦ Brian Vickers, "Analogy versus Identity: The Rejection of Occult Symbolism, 1580-1680", in: idem (ed.), *Occult and Scientific Mentalities in the Renaissance*, Cambridge etc.: Cambridge University Press, 1984, 95-163 ♦ idem, "On the Function of Analogy in the Occult", in: Ingrid Merkel & Allen G. Debus (eds.), *Hermeticism and the Renaissance: Intellectual History and the Occult in Early Modern Europe*, Washington & London/Toronto: The Folger Shakespeare Library/ Associated University Presses, 1988, 265-292.

JEAN-PIERRE BRACH & WOUTER J. HANEGRAAFF

Court de Gébelin, Antoine (Antoine Court), * 1725 near Nimes, † 12.5.1784 Paris

Son of a pioneer of Protestant restoration in France, Antoine Court (1695-1760), Court is a figure typical of the late European Enlightenment. He lived in Lausanne until 1763, when he moved to Paris. In Switzerland he associated with Charles Bonnet and Isaac Iselin. The latter maintained relations with → Lavater and → Kirchberger, and was a member, like Court and Johannes Rudolf Frey, of the Economic Society of Bern; his theories on anthropology inspired Court de Gébelin and, after him, Chavannes. From that period on, Court de Gébelin had affiliations with a secret society connected to the "Order of the Knights of the Star", a para-Masonic order dedicated to the restoration of Protestantism in France. This so-called "Céphalegie" had been founded officially in 1749 by J.-Ph. Loys de Chéseaux, and was established in Paris, Berlin, and Dresden.

From 1763 on, Court de Gébelin played a major role in the Masonic lodges in Paris. In 1777, the Mother Lodge of the Philosophical Scottish Rite complimented him for his teachings on 'the most credible allegories contained in the grades of the Freemasons'. The general chapter of France probably used his work in 1784 for the thirty-first and the thirty-third degrees of the Scottish and Accepted Rite. Although not one of its founders, he was a member of the United Friends (Les Amis Réunis), probably from 1778 on. He was a twelfth-class Philalèthe and a commissioner to the archives (10 Feb. 1781), until his removal by Savalète de Lange (for absenteeism; actually illness) in 1783. His participation in the Lodge of Saint John of Scotland and his membership of the Elus Coëns (mentioned by Robert Amadou in an article "Court de Gébe-lin" in the *Encyclopédie de la franc-maçonnerie*) are disputed; he did correspond, however, with → Willermoz and → Saint-Martin. Court most distin-guished himself in the Lodge of the Nine Sisters (between 1778 and 1781), of which he was a very influential member, secretary, and eventually sec-ond supervisor (1778). He also founded the aca-demic offshoot of this lodge, the Museum of Paris (1780), whose president he remained until his death. Court became a patient of F.A. Mesmer and proselytized on his behalf (presenting a *Lettre sur le magnétisme* to the king, and joining the Société de l'Harmonie). He died while undergoing therapy with Mesmer, thus ruining all the good publicity he had provided him.

Court is especially known for his main work, *Le Monde primitif analysé et comparé avec le monde moderne* (The PrimitiveWorld Analyzed and Compared with the Modern World), published in nine volumes between 1773 and 1782. Strongly influenced by → Neoplatonism, this book aims to revive the ancient world and its lost harmony through rediscovery of the original, perfect lan-guage. This language, in which signs and things are perfectly related, is believed to be still in existence; it is hidden, but once revealed it will be accessible to everyone. By researching the common roots of all ancient and modern languages, Court believed he could recover the words of the original lan-guage, which are similar to onomatopoeia (in this he is clearly influeced by Warburton, Vico, and especially Charles de Brosses; he in turn influenced Nodier). His philological enterprise is supported by a decipherment of ancient traditions, which are seen as allegories; thus we see him interpreting myths (vol. I), calendars and rites (vol. IV), bla-zons, ancient history, and the → Tarot (vol. VIII). To prove his theories, Court relied on the Church fathers, the *Hieroglyphica* of Hor-Apollo, the → Hermetic literature, and his knowledge of kab-balah [→ Jewish Influences].

Court thus attempts to establish a link between ancient and modern knowledge, and between aca-demic and hidden learning; and in renewing the study of Antiquity, he seeks to revive an interest in the Egyptian mysteries (his French etymologies suggest an Isiacal origin for the city of Paris). Nonetheless his interpretations are most often marked by a rationalist and utilitarian approach. Numbers are considered figures of the universal harmony, marking the rhythm of time-reckoning; myths are stories about the invention of agriculture and astronomy. Until 1783 (*Lettre sur le mag-nétisme*), he was adamantly opposed to → astrol-

ogy. The Tarot is presented with great prudence as a game of the Egyptians, in which we find their 'civil, political and religious' ideas and an 'emblem of life'. He mentions its use by the Egyptians for purposes of divination [→ Divinatory Arts] only as a matter of curiosity and in referring to a text, which he reproduces at length, by another author (the count of Mellet, according to J.-M. Lhote). This rationalist tendency (or posture) seems to have progressively weakened under the pressure of various influences, such as that of Saint-Martin, who sought to win him over to his own worldview in their conversations at the time when Court was writing the final volumes of *Monde primitif*. Its first volume, on the one hand, and the *Lettre sur le mag-nétisme*, on the other, represent the two extreme poles of this evolution.

Finally, Court was an important link in the his-tory of the relationship between → Illuminism and Protestantism: vacillating between a strict interpre-tation of the Scriptures, on the one hand, and → Pietism, on the other, and likewise between a condemnation of prophetic inspiration (and of div-ination) and a conviction that the lineaments of the future are contained in the sacred texts, he affirmed that vestiges of all previous knowledge can be recovered by deciphering "the harmony of the world".

Le monde Primitif analysé et comparé avec le monde moderne, 9 vols., Paris: Valleyre senior, 1773-1782 (2nd ed. Chez Durand, 1777-1796) ♦ *Histoire naturelle de la parole, ou origine du langage, de l'écrit-ure & de la grammaire universelle, à l'usage des jeunes gens*, Paris: Valleyre senior, 1776 ♦ *Lettre de l'auteur du Monde primitif à Mrs ses souscripteurs sur le mag-nétisme animal, du 31 juillet 1783*, Paris: Valleyre senior, s.d., 1784) ♦ *Devoirs du Prince et du citoyen, ouvrage posthume pour servir de suite à la dec-laration des droits de l'homme*, Paris: Decaux, 1789 ♦ *Le Tarot* (extract from vol. 8), Jean-Marie Lhote (ed.), Paris: Berg International, 1983.

Lit.: *Bulletin de la Société de l'histoire du protestan-tisme français*, 1, 2 (1853), (1854), (1855), 56 (1864), 32 (1883), 45 (1896), 46 (1897), (1899), (1902), 58 (1909), 59 (1910), 75 (1926), (1928) ♦ Louis Amiable, *Une loge maçonnique d'avant 1789: la R. L. des 9 soeurs* (1897) (Charles Porset ed.), Paris: Edimaf 1989 ♦ Robert Amadou, "Court de Gébelin", in: E. Saunier (ed.), *Encyclopédie de la Franc-maçonnerie*, Paris: Librarie générale, 2000 ♦ Fernand Balden-sperger, "Court de Gébelin et l'importance de son *Monde Primitif*", *Mélanges Huguet*, Paris: P. André, 1940 ♦ Jacques Brengues, "Court de Gébelin à la lettre G, ou une linguistique maçonnique au XVIIIe siècle", *Annales historiques de la F.M.* 14 (Dec. 1975) ♦ Michael Dummet, Mann Sylvia, *The Game of Tarot: from Ferrrara to Salt Lake City*, London: Duckworth, 1980 ♦ Antoine Faivre, "Lettres inédites et commentées de J.R. Frey, Isaac Iselin, Court de Gébelin, 1778-1779", *L'Initiation* 37:4 (Oct.-Dec. 1963) ♦ Gérard Genette, *Mimologiques*, Paris: Seuil, 1976 ♦ Ronald Grimsley, "Court de Gébelin and *Le Monde primitif*", *Enlightenment Studies in honour of L.G. Crocker*, Oxford: Voltaire Foundation, 1979, 133-144 ♦ Wallace Kirsop, "Cultural networks in Pre-revolutionary France: Some reflexions on the case of Antoine Court de Gébelin", *Australian Journal of French Studies* 18:3 (Sept.-Dec. 1981), 231-247 ♦ Jean-Marie Lhôte (ed. and preface), in: Court de Gébelin, *Le Tarot*, Paris: Berg international, 1983 ♦ Anne-Marie Mercier-Faivre, *Un Supplément à l'Encyclopédie, le* Monde primitif *d'Antoine Court de Gébelin*, Paris: Champion, 1999 ♦ eadem, "L'astronomie du visible de Court de Gébelin", in: Lise Andriès (ed.), *Le Partage des savoirs XVIIIᵉ-XIXᵉ siècles*, Presses Universitaires de Lyon, 2003 ♦ eadem, "Les calendriers de Court de Gébelin: La danse du temps", in: Sylviane Rémi et Louis Panier, *Hommages à Michel Le Guern*, Lyon: PUL, 2005 ♦ eadem, "Le rêve des origines: Du protestantisme à la franc-maçonnerie", in: *Franc-maçonnerie et religion dans l'Europe des Lumières*, Paris: Champion, 1998, 57-76 ♦ eadem, "Le langage d'images de Court de Gébelin", *Politica hermetica* 11 (1997), 47-65 ♦ Daniel Robert, "Court de Gébelin: Son cours de religion et les débuts de son séjour en France", *Annuaire de l'Ecole pratique des hautes études*, 5ᵉ section: sciences religieuses, 77 (1970-1971), 31-63 ♦ Paul Schmidt, *Court de Gébelin à Paris*, theology thesis: St Blaise/Roubaix, 1908.

ANNE-MARIE MERCIER-FAIVRE

Crowley, Aleister (born Edward Alexander), * 12.10.1875 Leamington, † 1.12.1947 Hastings

One of the main figures in the history of English occultism [→ occult / occultism]. Despite his bad reputation and the controversies that have marked his life, his ideas have heavily influenced contemporary new religious movements of a magical [→ Magic] and neo-pagan bent [→ Neopaganism]. Crowley has left an enormous literary output, including almost any genre: from poetry and fiction to essay and autobiography. Apart from his occult interests and activities he is also remembered as a poet, mountaineer, and chess player of some talent.

The scion of a wealthy family of brewers, Crowley's early life and education were those typical of a member of the middle upper class in England of his time, but for the fact that both his parents were strict Plymouth Brethren (the fundamentalist evangelical sect founded by John Nelson Darby [1800-1882]). This element would play an important role in his future intellectual development. In fact, even if Crowley would eventually repudiate Christianity altogether, he always remained bound to the legacy of symbols and images of the Bible, especially its apocalyptic parts. Crowley seems to have been at ease with his parents' religious persuasion until 1887, when his father died prematurely. This event provides us with one of the keys for understanding Crowley's psychology, as it is probably at the origin of his unquenchable desire for revolt against traditional social and religious values. He had much admired his father, who, according to Crowley's later autobiographical account, does not seem to have held narrow views concerning his upbringing and education. But after his father's death, his mother and her family, whom Crowley accuses of sheer bigotry, began to have a much stronger influence over his life. This development, coupled with some unpleasant experiences he had in some of the schools he attended later, was certainly at the origin of his hatred of Christianity.

In 1895 Crowley entered the prestigious Trinity College, Cambridge, as an undergraduate student. Even though he did not conclude his studies, his university years would have a profound influence on him. In this period he publishes his first books of verses at his own expenses, which receive some favourable press reviews. He also begins to feel attracted by spirituality, and in particular by the occult. The turning point in his early life comes when, in 1898, he meets two members of the → Hermetic Order of the Golden Dawn (GD), who introduce him into the Order. He is initiated as a Neophyte in the Isis-Urania Temple of the GD, in London, in the autumn of that year. This is the first crucial event in Crowley's spiritual career. He dedicates himself with enthusiasm to the study of the teachings imparted by the Order, and rapidly climbs the initial steps of the Order's initiatic system. He also decides to follow the instructions contained in *The Book of the Sacred Magic of Abra-Melin the Mage*, a grimoire which had been edited and published in that same year by → S.L. Mathers, then the leader of the Order. In the context of the GD he meets two persons who will have a strong influence on him. The first one is Allan Bennett (1872-1923), who would later convert to Buddhism and become one of the first Buddhist missionaries in England. Bennett teaches Crowley the first rudiments of ceremonial → magic, and, during their experiments together, Crowley begins taking drugs in the context of magical practice – something that will remain an important aspect of Crowley's life in the subsequent years and, indeed, up to his death. The second important person is Mathers himself. In 1900 Crowley is directly involved in the feud which opposes Mathers, then living in Paris, to the London high-ranking members of the GD. He decides to side with Mathers and is therefore expelled, together with his mentor, by the London faction. The impact of the GD system on Crowley would remain fundamental, however.

The end of Crowley's experience in the GD marks the beginning of a period of travels around the world, which would last, with some interruptions, until 1906. He spends a long period in Mexico, and then in India, where, together with his friend Bennett, he discovers the practice of yoga and Buddhist doctrines. In 1902 he takes part in an important, but unsuccessful, expedition to conquer the K2, the second highest peak in the world. On his return to Europe he spends several months in Paris, getting acquainted with artists and intellectuals in the bohemian circles of Montparnasse. In 1903 he marries Rose Kelly (1874-1932), sister of his close friend, the painter Gerald F. Kelly (1879-1972). The couple then leaves for a long journey through the East. During their return journey occurs the second fundamental event in Crowley's spiritual career. In Cairo, in the Spring of 1904, he is reportedly put in contact, through the mediumship of his wife, with a præter-human entity named Aiwass. He receives from him the text of the *Book of the Law* (*Liber Legis*, also called *AL*), which he would later consider the sacred text of a new religion called "Thelema" (ancient Greek for "will").

After another unsuccessful expedition on the Kangchenjunga, in 1905, Crowley makes a long tour across southern China. During this travel he performs the ritual of the *Augoeides*, which is a continuation, in another form, of the ritual of Abramelin for the attainment of the knowledge of his Holy Guardian Angel. The ritual lasts thirty-two weeks, and has the peculiarity of being performed only in an imaginative – or rather "astral" – form. This means that Crowley, while travelling on horseback, imagines himself being in a magical temple and performing all the ritual acts necessary for this kind of working.

After his return to England, he publishes a collection in three volumes of his youthful works, mostly poetry (*Collected Works*, 1905-1907), a collection of essays (*Konx Om Pax*, 1907), and an important synthesis of his system of → correspondences, developed on the basis of the GD system (*777*, 1909). In this period he also meets an English officer, John Frederick Charles Fuller (1878-1966), who had spent a long time posted in India and had become interested in his works. Fuller writes the first critical work on Crowley, *The Star in the West* (1907), and in 1909 helps Crowley to found his

own magical Order, the A∴A∴ (the initials are usually interpreted as "Astrum Argentinum", or "Argenteum Astrum", i.e. Silver Star). In relation to this project, Crowley also starts the publication of a biannual periodical, *The Equinox* (1909-1913, 1919), which is presented as the official organ of his Order. In it he publishes its official teachings, but also poetry and fiction, both by himself and by other authors belonging to his circle. Also in 1909, together with his disciple Victor B. Neuburg (1883-1940), he "explores" the magical system of → John Dee, through an important series of invocations and astral travels in the desert of Algeria. The account of these magical experiences would be published in 1911 in *The Equinox* (I, 5) as "The Vision and the Voice".

Around 1910, rumours begin to find an echo in the press about Crowley's homosexuality and the alleged immorality of his Order's activities. It is the beginning of a campaign of vilification which will continue practically for the rest of Crowley's life, and will reach its climax after World War I. The A∴A∴ suffers from these exposures, and several members decide to resign. In the same period Crowley meets the journalist and occultist Theodor Reuss (1855-1923), a figure very active in the European fringe-masonic and occultist scene. Reuss wishes to launch a new fringe-masonic Order, whose main purpose is the teaching and practice of sexual magic: the → Ordo Templi Orientis (OTO). He asks Crowley for his collaboration and the latter accepts, in 1912, to create and run a British section of the Order under Reuss's authority. Crowley, now definitely convinced of his prophetic role in relation to Thelema, undoubtedly looks at the OTO as a convenient channel for the propagation of his new religious message. After having published, in 1912, the first two parts of his *Book Four*, where for the first time he systematically expounds his theories on magic, he begins in the following year to experiment with sexual magic, whose basic technique had been transmitted to him by Reuss.

Crowley spends the period of World War I in the United States. He has by then exhausted his financial resources, and at times finds himself close to destitution. He works as a journalist and editor for the German propaganda in America, an activity that will later cause him to be reproached for betraying his country. In this period he works with the American astrologer Evangeline Adams (1859-1932) on a project of writing a comprehensive treatise on → astrology. However, their collaboration ends prematurely, and Adams eventually, in the 1920s, publishes the result of their joint efforts under her own name. Crowley's astrological writings related to this project would not be published until 1974 (a more complete edition, restoring previously missing parts, has been published in 2002).

In this period, the number of his disciples (whether in the OTO or in the A∴A∴) has shrunk considerably. Among them, however, is the important figure of Charles Stansfeld Jones (1886-1950), who would come to play a significant part in the doctrinal development of Thelema, and would later (especially under the pseudonym of Frater Achad) gain some reputation as an author in his own right. Crowley himself writes, among several other works, the novel *Moonchild* (published in 1929), in which many figures of his past experience in the Golden Dawn are lampooned. In 1918 he meets Leah Hirsig, a schoolteacher, who will remain his lover and partner for several years afterwards. In 1919 he publishes the first volume of a new series of *The Equinox* (the so-called "Blue Equinox"), largely devoted to the OTO. Soon afterwards he leaves the United States and returns to Europe. In 1920 he settles in Cefalù, Sicily, where he establishes his "Abbey of Thelema", a sort of commune with Hirsig and other disciples, in which he tries to put into practice the principles of his new religion. It is a very productive period. He publishes another novel, *The Diary of a Drug Fiend* (1922); writes his enormous "autohagiography", *The Confessions* (partially published in 1929); and works on the third part of his *Book Four*, intended to be his *magnum opus* on magic (published between 1929 and 1930 as *Magick in Theory and Practice*). Crowley's experiment at the Abbey lasts only three years. In 1923 he is expelled by the Italian authorities, probably because of a renewed campaign of attacks in the English press. Subsequently he moves to Tunis, and later to Paris. In this period he also succeeds Reuss, who had died in 1923, as leader of the OTO. In 1925 there is a meeting in Weida, Germany, aimed at establishing his leadership of a German Rosicrucian movement, closely related to the German OTO, and led by the bookseller Hermann Tränker (1880-1956). But only a portion of the persons involved decide to follow Crowley and accept his new religious message. Among them are the businessman Karl Germer (1885-1962), who in the following years supports Crowley financially and will succeed him, after the latter's death, as head of the OTO.

During the years 1926-1929 Crowley's headquarters are mainly in Paris. Around 1928 two new young disciples join him, after having been in correspondence with him for some time: Israel Regardie (1907-1985) and Gerald Yorke (1901-

1983). They collaborate closely with Crowley until the early 1930s, when they part ways with him. Regardie would later become an influential author on magic and esoteric subjects in his own right, also contributing in the 1960s and the 1970s to the rediscovery of Crowley's ideas through new editions of his writings and an important study (*The Eye in the Triangle*, 1970). Yorke, for his part, would later become the owner of the largest collection of Crowleyana in the world (rare first editions, manuscripts and documents), thereby playing a fundamental role in the preservation of Crowley's intellectual legacy. His collection is now housed in the Warburg Institute, London.

In March 1929 Crowley is forced to leave France as well. He moves first to England, and then to Germany. In 1930 he makes a short trip to Portugal and meets the poet and esotericist → Fernando Pessoa, with whom he is on friendly terms, and whose esoteric ideas have been influenced to some extent by Crowley.

In 1932, at the eve of the nazi seizure of power in Germany, Crowley moves back to England. He will not leave the country again. In 1934 he is defeated in a libel suit against a publisher. Unable to pay the costs, he is declared bankrupt. He now lives almost entirely on the allowances sent to him by his disciples, especially the members of the only surviving body of the OTO at the time, the Agape lodge in California. But despite his material difficulties, he continues to write and publish extensively. Among the significant publications of this period, mention must be made of *The Equinox of the Gods* (1936), in which he narrates the events related to the revelation of the *Liber Legis* in 1904, and *The Book of Thoth* (1944), in which he expounds his personal interpretation of the → Tarot. This is also implemented by the design, made jointly with the artist Frieda Harris (1877-1962) of a new Tarot deck, which incorporates Crowley's peculiar symbolism and attributions. The deck would be published only posthumously in 1971. It has become one of the most widespread tarot decks in the world, frequently used also by persons who are not acquainted with – let alone accept – Crowley's philosophical or religious ideas.

Crowley spends the difficult years of World War II first in London, and then in various country retreats. His last resort is a boarding-house near Hastings, where he dies in 1947. Some other important works have been published after his death, such as *Magick Without Tears* (1954), written in his last years and containing an introductory exposition, in epistolary form, of his doctrine; the *Liber Aleph* (1961), a compendium of teachings originally written during the American period for his disciple C.S. Jones; and an edition of the *Confessions* (1969) including the hitherto unpublished volumes.

Because of his controversial reputation Crowley has often been dismissed, without adequate analysis of his works and ideas, as a mere quack or charlatan. One of the most popular misunderstandings has led to him being labelled a Satanist, which, if we exclude theological definitions of → Satanism, he was not (although he has certainly influenced contemporary Satanist movements). From a symbolical point of view, Satan plays no significant role in Crowley's ideas. His mythical and symbolical references went well beyond Christianity, and his aim was to propose a full-blown, original religious alternative to it. Despite the prominence of anti-Christian elements, his system can hardly be considered as a mere reversal of Christianity, as the classic definition of Satanism would require.

Crowley's doctrine, expounded in a large number of writings, is considerably more complex than it would appear at first sight. His works require careful study and analysis, especially as Crowley's literary style is sometimes – more or less on purpose – quite obscure. In the context of English occultism he was one of the very few authors to have received formal higher education in a traditional university, and all his life his cultural interests remained extremely wide and eclectic. As a result, he drew ideas and inspiration from many disparate sources, both Western and Eastern, and blended them into his own peculiar system. His Western sources include ceremonial magic, astrology, the Tarot, Kabbalah, Egyptian lore, John Dee's Enochian system, and → alchemy; his Eastern ones include yoga, Buddhism, Taoism, and the I-Ching. Two aspects stand out as fundamental in his work: magic (which, for various reasons, he chose to spell "Magick") and Thelema.

In a general sense, Crowley saw magic as a convenient term to define his doctrine as a whole, including Thelema. More specifically, Crowley understood magic mainly in two ways, both of which are far from uncommon in the context of occultist literature. The first one is mostly pragmatic in nature, and considers magic as a technique for achieving specific goals by means which cannot as yet be explained scientifically, but the results of which can (in theory at least) be tested in an empirical way. Gaining considerable sums of money or the effortless acquisition of extensive knowledge in a particular field could be mentioned as classic examples. Crowley's most famous definition of magic, which was subsequently adopted by a plethora of authors, is closely related to this idea:

"Magick is the Science and Art of causing Change to occur in conformity with Will" (*Magick in Theory and Practice*, 1929-1930, xii). According to this definition any intentional act could be defined as magical, which would of course seem to reduce the specificity of magic as a particular field of action. In reality, in referring to magic in this context Crowley usually had in mind a rather precise set of practices and ideas, based mostly on traditional ceremonial magic. He had learned their fundamentals during his membership in the GD, and considerably developed them on the basis of his subsequent experiences. In later years, his discovery of sexual magic led him to significantly change his understanding and practice of magic; in fact, sexual magic made most of the material apparatus of ceremonial magic superfluous. Sexual magical workings, based on notions of subtle physiology mostly borrowed from Eastern doctrines (in particular *haṭha yoga*), may use only the body of the magician as a magical tool, eliminating the need for external implements such as a temple or the traditional "weapons" of ceremonial magic. The aim of magic in this sense is not necessarily material in nature: magic can also be used to obtain communications from spiritual entities, or to explore the "astral plane" by means of the techniques of astral travel that Crowley had learned in the GD. The messages that he received through these magical practices often had a meaning that was specific to his own spiritual evolution (but they could also be on a grander scale and concern the evolution of mankind, as in the case of *Liber Legis*). By the same token, through these practices Crowley thought he could improve his knowledge of the symbolic network of correspondences, which are supposed to create a unifying link between all the parts of the universe. It is to be noted that, especially in relation to this first, pragmatic sense of magic, Crowley claimed to have a scientific, rational approach – again, something far from uncommon in the context of occultist literature.

The other sense in which Crowley understood magic was certainly seen by him as the most important, although it can be considered to be complementary to the first one. According to this second perspective, magic is not so much oriented towards immediate ends, but rather becomes a way to achieve what Crowley considered the supreme goal of one's life: spiritual attainment. Magic then loses its instrumental character, and becomes instead a practice and a worldview which encompass all aspects of a person's life. It is not so much a matter of different practices, but of a different interpretation of them. Traditional ceremonial and sexual magic could be used, in Crowley's vision, both for immediate purposes and as a means to achieve the ultimate spiritual goal. Ideally, in the latter case, the individual should fully dedicate himself to this pursuit, and be ready to sacrifice all his earthly possessions and affections for its sake. Crowley uses various expressions to define the aim of magic in this spiritual sense. In some passages he describes it as comparable to the mystical "union with God", but he also equates it with the ultimate goal of classic yoga practice, i.e. the ecstatic trance of *samādhi*. But perhaps his most famous definition describes it as the attainment of the "knowledge and conversation of the Holy Guardian Angel", a notion taken from the *Book of the Sacred Magic of Abra-Melin*. Among the members of the original (pre-1900) GD, Crowley was certainly the one most influenced by this book (which, it should be noted, was never a part of the official curriculum of this Order). He is probably also the only one who actually tried to put its instructions into practice. Crowley claimed to have attained the goal described in the book in 1906, and this was certainly a very important step in his spiritual career.

It has sometimes been assumed that his Holy Guardian Angel corresponded to Aiwass, the entity who had dictated to him the text of the *Liber Legis* in 1904, but this is not entirely correct and requires some qualifications. In fact, Crowley's notion of the Holy Guardian Angel evolved with time. At the beginning, it corresponded for him to the idea of "Higher Genius", "Higher Self", or "Augoeides" – a notion that was prominent in GD teachings and had been borrowed originally from theosophical literature. The Higher Self was not considered as an independent entity, but as the superior, spiritual element present in every human being. The aim of magical (or "mystical") practice was therefore to open one's consciousness to that higher part of oneself, which is normally not perceived by the non-initiate. Aiwass, on the other hand, was always seen by Crowley as a personal being, not necessarily discarnate, and completely independent from his own consciousness or psyche. In that sense Aiwass rather resembled the "Secret Chiefs" of the GD, or the "Mahatmas" of the → Theosophical Society. Subsequently, however, Crowley's ideas about his Holy Guardian Angel began to shift, and he came to identify it more and more with Aiwass. This evolution might be interpreted as a sign of Crowley's increasing personal identification with his own mission as the prophet of Thelema.

It is important to note that this "mystical" notion of magic is closely related to the idea of an initiatic path, which is another fundamental aspect of Crowley's magical doctrine. The stages through which the aspirant must proceed in order to achieve spiritual attainment correspond to the system of degrees in Crowley's own Order, the A∴ A∴, which was modelled on the one of the GD. But apart from the similarities, there were also significant differences between the two systems. One has already been mentioned: the added emphasis in Crowley's Order on Eastern doctrines and practices, especially yoga. Another difference lies in the fact that, in the original GD system, initiatic advancement was effected through a formal ceremony, akin to a masonic ritual. This made group meetings between members a common feature of the Order's activities. In Crowley's Order, on the other hand, this social aspect was increasingly reduced, the only form of contact between members being an individual relationship between the aspirant and his immediate superior in the Order's hierarchy. By the same token, initiation was supposed to take place mostly on the astral plane, which made the actual performance of a dramatic ritual less important than it was in the GD. But perhaps the most important difference between Crowley's Order and the original GD is that, in the latter, only the two first Orders which compose it (the GD proper and the Ordo Rosae Rubeae et Aureae Crucis [RR et AC]) were in principle accessible to members. It was assumed that the Third Order, including the three final grades of the system, was so elevated that only the "Secret Chiefs" could have access to it. But Crowley's ambition to reach the highest peak of initiation could hardly be restrained by this theoretical limitation. Therefore, not only did he introduce into his system a whole new doctrine concerning the import of these last degrees for the initiate; but he eventually claimed to have attained, in the early 1920s, the last degree, which he chose to call "Ipsissimus" (in the original GD system this grade had been left unnamed). For him, attaining this grade was equivalent to becoming a god. In this respect, an important element should be considered. The "union with God", or the knowledge of the Holy Guardian Angel, only correspond to an intermediate grade in Crowley's initiatic system, i.e. that of Adeptus Minor. After it, there remain several grades before the highest one is achieved. This would seem to imply that if the knowledge of the Holy Guardian Angel is the final goal of magic, as Crowley states on several occasions, the highest goal of initiation transcends it and goes much further. In reality Crowley was not particularly consistent on this point, and it can be concluded that magic, understood in its widest sense, included for him both the knowledge of the Holy Guardian Angel *and* the process leading to the highest step of initiation.

The other fundamental aspect of Crowley's doctrine is Thelema. Indeed, this complex religious element is what mainly differentiates Crowley from previous occultists. The doctrinal principles and beliefs fundamental to Thelema are combined with the practice of magic, so as to form an organic and coherent worldview. According to Crowley, the revelation of the *Book of the Law* in 1904 marked the beginning of a new "æon", i.e. a new cosmic age. The old age of Christianity, and more generally of paternalistic religions, symbolised by the image of the "Dying God" (borrowed from J.G. Frazer), was at its end. The new age is symbolised by the Egyptian god Horus, whose image as "son" is contrasted to that of his "father" Osiris (symbolising the previous age), and also to that of his "mother" Isis (symbolising a yet older, matriarchal age). The rebellious, individualistic, and iconoclastic energy of youth is therefore opposed to the decaying power of authority and tradition. The clearest example of an old-fashioned religion destined to swift extinction is of course Christianity, which for Crowley represents all that he rejects, both from a social and a moral point of view. Despite the prominence of images borrowed from the New Testament, Thelema and Christianity are seen as largely incompatible, and almost as exact opposites. Indeed, anti-Christian attacks are a recurrent theme in Crowley's writings. The negative charge of some biblical images (some examples of which will be given below) is reversed in Crowley's system, and becomes essentially positive.

The transition from the old to the new æon is concomitant with the activity of enormous cosmic energies, and is not supposed to take place quietly or peacefully. The effects of this cosmic storm on earth are a period of violence and wars, and Crowley saw a confirmation of his doctrine in various historical events that took place during his lifetime, notably the two world wars. As our planet enters the new æon, the old morality will expire, and will eventually be replaced by a new one based on Thelema.

The principles of this new religion are obviously taken from the *Liber Legis*, the holy scripture of Thelema. We mention here the three fundamental ones. The first is: "Do what thou wilt shall be the whole of the Law" (AL, I, 40). According to Crowley's interpretation, this principle does not justify the satisfaction of mere whimsical fancies or desires, and does not imply a notion of absolute individual freedom either. On the contrary, it implies that every human being is called to accomplish his/her "true Will", i.e. to follow his/her real nature and fulfil the role that the universe has assigned to him/her, whatever that may be. The second principle is: "Every man and every woman is a star" (AL, I, 3). The true Will of any individual is similar to the trajectory of a cosmic body, such as a star or a planet. If all human beings would follow their proper trajectory, conflicts would disappear, for they actually result but from ignorance of this trajectory. The ultimate goal of an initiate thus consists firstly in discovering his/her own true Will, and then in following its lead. It is at this point that magic plays a fundamental role in the system, since it is through magic that this process of discovery and accomplishment can be achieved.

Magical work also aims at the reunification of the opposites which, on a cosmic plane, are represented by a feminine and a masculine force, referred to respectively as Hadit and Nuit. The polarity between the two notions is not purely sexual: Hadit represents mostly the infinitely small, whose image is the geometrical point, full of still unfolded potentialities; Nuit represents the infinite space of the universe, whose image is the starry night sky. These macrocosmic notions appear already in the *Liber Legis*. Clearly of Egyptian origin, they correspond on a microcosmic plane with notions derived from biblical images, in particular the book of Revelation. Crowley in fact came to identify his role as prophet of Thelema with the image of the Great Beast described in Revelation, related to the number 666 (Rev. 13:1-18). Especially since the early 1920s, Crowley publicly used "The Great Beast 666" (or its Greek equivalent, "To Mega Therion") as his main alias. To complete the polarity, a female figure accompanies the male prophet figure; she is referred to as "Babalon" (obviously a slightly modified spelling of "Babylon") or the "Scarlet Woman", the prostitute who rides the Beast in Revelation (17:1-7). This role was actually fulfilled, during Crowley's life, by his partners. The two most significant "Scarlet Women" were undoubtedly his wife Rose and, later in his life, Leah Hirsig. Fundamental to the work of unification of these two poles, both on a macrocosmic and on a microcosmic level, is the third basic principle of Thelema: "Love is the law, love under will" (AL, I, 57). Love is seen by Crowley as the force that makes the union of the opposites possible. But this aspect of thelemite doctrine can also be considered the theoretical basis of sexual magic. The "Will" that controls love is in this case the concentration of the magician focused on the aim of the magical working during the sexual act.

What has been said so far concerning the basic tenets of Thelema should be complemented by another important element. It is possible to detect an influence on Crowley's doctrine of the solar-phallic theories which had become fashionable in England particularly in the second half of the 19th century. According to these theories, all religions had originally developed from the worship of the generative powers represented by the sun and the phallus. Most living religions supposedly still bore the remnants of this ancient legacy, and their symbolism could be interpreted accordingly. In Crowley's doctrine, great importance is given to the image of the Sun as giver of life, which corresponds on the human plane to the phallus. The correspondence between the two is completed by a strict analogy – certainly not original with Crowley – between light (radiated by the Sun) and semen (ejaculated by the phallus). Crowley, especially in his role as the "Great Beast 666" sees himself as a mediating figure between the two, incarnating a solar and phallic force at the same time. Finally, it must be noted that the prominence of the male-female polarity in Thelema does not in itself exclude other forms of sexuality than the heterosexual. In his personal development of sexual magic, Crowley made frequent use of practices based on homosexual intercourse, even if these could not be explained in terms of his doctrine of polarity.

No assessment of Crowley's importance in contemporary esotericism would be complete without a consideration of his legacy. Crowley's "Magick" and Thelema have both exerted an enormous influence on subsequent occultist and magically-oriented literature, so that it is sometimes impossible to understand aspects of the latter without an elementary grasp of Crowley's doctrine. Crowley's influence can be seen in the work of major authors such as → Dion Fortune, and that of his ex-disciples Israel Regardie and Kenneth Grant (b. 1923). Gerald Gardner (1884-1964), the founder of the neo-pagan movement known as Wicca, was certainly influenced by Crowley's writings on magic as well. The same can be said of the most prominent authors of contemporary Satanism, Anton Szandor LaVey (1930-1997) and Michael Aquino (b. 1946). The two magical Orders of which Crowley was the leader, the OTO and the A∴A∴, still exist today despite recurrent schisms, and are among the major vehicles for the transmission of his ideas.

Collected Works, 3 vols., Les Plaines: Yogi Publication Society, n.d. (1973; 1st ed.: 1905-1907) ♦ (ed.), The Equinox: The Official Organ of the A∴A∴: The Review of Scientific Illuminism, York Beach: Samuel Weiser, 1993 (vol. 1, 1-10; 1st ed.: 1909-1913); and 1992 (vol. 3, 1; 1st ed.: 1919) ♦ The Confessions of Aleister Crowley: An Autohagiography, London: Arkana, 1989 (1st ed.: 1929-1969) ♦ The Book of Thoth: A Short Essay on the Tarot of the Egyptians, York Beach: Samuel Weiser, 1986 (1st ed. 1944) ♦ Magick Without Tears, Saint Paul: Llewellyn, 1973 (1st ed.: 1954) ♦ Magick: Book Four Parts I-IV, York Beach: Samuel Weiser, 1997 ♦ Theodor Reuss and Aleister Crowley, O.T.O. Rituals and Sex Magick, Thame: I-H-O Books, 1999 ♦ Aleister Crowley and Evangeline Adams, The General Principles of Astrology, Boston, York Beach: Weiser Books, 2002.

Lit.: Massimo Introvigne, Il cappello del mago: I nuovi movimenti magici, dallo spiritismo al satanismo, Milan: Sugarco, 1990 ♦ idem, Indagine sul satanismo: Satanisti e anti-satanisti dal seicento ai nostri giorni, Milan: Mondadori, 1994 ♦ Richard Kaczynski, Perdurabo: The Life of Aleister Crowley, Tempe: New Falcon Publications, 2003 ♦ Alex Owen, "The Sorcerer and His Apprentice: Aleister Crowley and the Magical Exploration of Edwardian Subjectivity", Journal of British Studies 36 (1997), 99-133 ♦ Marco Pasi, Aleister Crowley e la tentazione della politica, Milan: Franco Angeli, 1999 ♦ idem, "L'anticristianesimo in Aleister Crowley (1875-1947)", in: PierLuigi Zoccatelli (ed.), Aleister Crowley: Un mago a Cefalù, Rome: Edizioni Mediterranee, 1998, 41-67 ♦ idem, "The Neverendingly Told Story: Recent Biographies of Aleister Crowley", Aries 3:2 (2003), 224-245 ♦ Israel Regardie, The Eye in the Triangle: An Interpretation of Aleister Crowley, Phoenix: New Falcon Publications, 1993 ♦ Kocku von Stuckrad, "Aleister Crowley, Thelema und die Religionsgeschichte des zwanzigsten Jahrhunderts", in: Brigitte Luchesi & Kocku von Stuckrad (eds.), Religion im kulturellen Diskurs: Festschrift für Hans G. Kippenberg zu seinem 65. Geburtstag, Berlin, New York: Walter de Gruyter, 2004, 307-321 ♦ Lawrence Sutin, Do What Thou Wilt: A Life of Aleister Crowley, New York: St. Martin's Press, 2000 ♦ John Symonds, The Beast 666: The Life of Aleister Crowley, London: Pindar Press, 1997 ♦ Hugh Urban, "Unleashing the Beast: Aleister Crowley, Tantra, and Sex Magic in Late Victorian England", Esoterica 5 (2003), 138-192 (www.esoteric.msu.edu/VolumeV/Unleashing_the_Beast.htm).

MARCO PASI

Cryptography

1. Introduction 2. Historical Backgrounds 3. Classification 4. An Example

1. Introduction

Cryptography in the context of Western esotericism can be understood simply as a means to preserve the confidentiality of a message (as in 18th-century → Freemasonry, which used ciphers deprived of any specific magical meanings as a means of communication). In its more specific sense, however, it aims at establishing a contact between the earthly realm and the heavenly one. Angels and men are supposed to use cryptography, understood in this sense, as a medium enabling them to achieve such contact or communication, especially since the physical and the spiritual worlds are different by nature. Therefore, cryptography has been considered the instrument as well as the necessary foundation for establishing connections between these two realms.

The methods used to encrypt or decrypt are always simple. They are usually based on mono-alphabetical substitution, i.e. the replacement of each letter within a message by a sign or symbol, while the order of the letters remains the same (as in the International Morse Code, for instance). This may be done by using either a simple list (as in e.g. → Martines de Pasqually's list of the 2.400 names of angels and archangels, see below), or a double entry chart (as in → John Dee's so-called "Enochian alphabet": the spirits, by means of a medium, indicate a cell in a matrix containing the letters of this alphabet). Such systems need to be simple in order to enable an instantaneous decipherment of the signs.

Cryptographic writings fall under the heading of → magic, inasmuch as they are rooted in the unifying system of the *philosophia occulta* [→ occult / occultism] as understood from the end of the 15th to the 17th century: a universe comprised of analogical mirrors in which all things endlessly reflect one another in a wide array of interrelations. In such a context, the sign drawn by the magus is intrinsically linked to the celestial entity invoked, or to the heavenly body of which it is the receptacle. The sign is considered to be, as it were, a written manifestation, or the direct expression, of an angel. For example, in Martines de Pasqually's system (18th cent.), the theurgist, in his "chamber of operations", drew on a linen carpet a sign or, as it is called in Martinesian parlance, a "hieroglyph", which was supposed to "correspond" to an angel and which was chosen among the 2.400 hieroglyphs of a list provided by Martines (this list is still extant in the legacy "Prunelle de Lière" at the Bibliothèque Municipale de Grenoble). If the operation was correctly performed, this hieroglyph or another one was expected to appear a moment later within the chamber, in a luminous form, to the eyes of the theurgist. If another hieroglyph appeared, this meant that, later on, the theurgist

would have to consult the list in order to find in it the hieroglyph which had appeared to him. During his next operation he would then use this second hieroglyph, because the latter apparently corresponded to the angel who had actually manifested himself to the theurgist in the chamber of operations. In sum, such glyphs are understood – in Pasqually's system as well as in other, similar ones – as signs to be drawn and used by the theurgist during the ritual, and as signs sent out by the angels invoked during that ritual.

The perspective under discussion might be called holographic in the sense that the entire correspondences network in question has a multi-dimensional character. A sign becomes the graph of a spiritual entity, that is, the latter's projection or coagulation into matter. Much prior to Pasqually, → Paracelsus, while describing a *magia caracterialis* in his *Astronomia Magna* (1571), claimed that engraved signs or characters have the same power as speech. The names or words formed by such cryptographic procedures are themselves considered to be vectors inseparable from the essence of the entities or the angels they refer to, and possessed of the latter's magical virtues and properties. In keeping with the concepts of *magia naturalis*, such cryptographic writings may be considered, therefore, as one application, among others, of the theory of signatures and universal → correspondences.

One of the most commonly shared ideas in such contexts is that the words (figures and characters) used in magic are all the more efficacious if they are drawn from the original divine language spoken by Adam in paradise. Commentators and magi alike, inspired by the belief in a *philosophia perennis* [→ Tradition], have lavishly written about this perfect language – a language capable of reflecting the very essence of things, and purported to be the genuine, true mirror of the innermost reality of our multi-layered universe. Along this line, the history of cryptography appears to have been closely bound up, particularly since the beginning of the medieval period, with that of the quest for a perfect and secret language. Here is a typical sample of this writing, the magic alphabet "Passing the River", based on the twenty-two Hebrew letters, included by → Agrippa in book III of his *De Occulta Philosophia*, (chapter XXX):

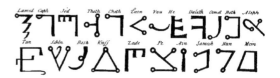

2. HISTORICAL BACKGROUNDS

A proposal for tracing the development of various forms and manifestations of cryptography in the West has been presented by Le Pape (1999). From the 10th to the 12th century, due to the numerous translations of hermetic and related writings from Arab into Latin, a domain for mutual fertilization between the three Scriptural Religions was created, which was instrumental in fostering esoteric and scientific ideas in general and, by the same token, the emergence of a *philosophia occulta* in particular (see e.g. the numerous Arabic magical alphabets reproduced in Hammer [1806]). The most interesting type of cryptographic writings to be found in this literature, and undoubtedly the most typical one, is known and referred to, in English, as "ring-letter writing(s)" (or ring-writing, ring-alphabet[s]; in French, *écriture[s] à lunettes*), since their baroque characters are partly made of tiny balls or rings. Such writings already appear in some Greek papyri of the 3th-5th centuries (see Ruelle [1913], in which few of the alphabets are complete, and Kenyon [1893], Nrs. CXXI-CXXV) but their sources might well be more ancient. They were widely disseminated during the Middle Ages, but occasionally at the expense of their actual purpose, since they came to be used without restraint in the fashioning of objects such as talismans. A series of small books, frequently ascribed to → Albertus Magnus (1206-1280), have punctuated their historical development. They are known as *Claviculae Salomonis* (see many examples in Thorndike [1923-1958] II, 279ff.), and have remained popular throughout the centuries. We find echos of them in Cornelius Agrippa's *De occulta philosophia* (1533), where planetary magic and demonic magic meet up again. In modern times this abundant heritage has undergone several modifications, and has been, as it were, polished and refined: the medieval "formulas" were, for the most part, rejected in favour of a more "noble" theurgy. For instance, Pasqually's cryptographic signs appear to be used mostly as instruments for attaining a redeeming personal gnosis, based on communication with angelic beings.

3. CLASSIFICATION

Within the esoteric context that interests us here, it is not so much the formal characteristics of cryptographic writings which matters, but rather their actual purpose, the needs they are supposed to meet. Hence the following classification is based upon a distinction between three main types of magical communication. It still remains, however, that a sharp borderline between such categories is not possible (as will become particularly clear in the case of the first category).

A. *Talismanic communication*. This category implies a communication with the celestial world from the perspective of the terrestrial, i.e., a communication based upon and subject to man's initiative. This appears to be the most frequently used type. For example, the signs engraved in talismans are closely linked to the nature of the celestial influences that one seeks to attract. The talisman, therefore, acts as a catalyst or receptacle for the radiance of the stars or of the angels. It is supposed to operate by means of identification, i.e. by assuming the characteristics of the celestial things to which it corresponds. This entails the necessity of knowing the affinities (patterns of sympathy and antipathy) which govern the relations between all parts of the universe, i.e. the ability of deciphering the book of Nature. Moreover, signs usually have to be engraved, and the talisman has to be prepared under the correct astrological constellation. The use of alphabets is here limited to selecting some of the signs necessary to a given magical operation; therefore we rarely find, in this context, a whole group of words or sentences. Alphabets used for this first type of communication are a common component of the so-called Solomonian literature (the numerous writings going under the name of *Claviculae Salomonis*, comprised, *inter alia*, of a number of small works attributed to Honorius or to Albertus Magnus). Likewise, the ring-alphabets known as those of Jupiter, Solomon, Syrianus or Brachmanicum (as documented in the writings of Joseph Hammer, Blaise de Vigenère, Cornelius Agrippa, → Athanasius Kircher) are typical of this means of communication; but many other alphabets used in the context of the other two types of communication occasionally appear here as well, since talismanic practitioners have erratically borrowed from various systems. Quite widespread in the Middle Ages, the golden age of "talismania", the ring-alphabets and the other alphabets mentioned here did not fall into oblivion but were still in use far beyond the 15th century.

B. *Natural communication*. This category involves communication from the celestial world to the terrestrial world. It is unilateral, not being the response to a request. The intermediate beings use, as it were, the supposed symbolic characteristics of the heavenly bodies, like comets, stars or planets, to build up words and messages that only the human beings in possession of a given secret alphabet will be able to decrypt, so that 'the Great Book of Nature be open for all to see though only a few can read it or understand it' (Rosicrucian

Confessio, 29). These messages, usually assumed to have been directly inspired by God, are mostly supposed to be the bearers of news concerning political events to come, but they can also refer to serious epidemics, such as the plague. Alphabets belonging to this type are called "Celestial writing" (*Scriptura Coelestis*, cf. Agrippa, *Occ.Phil.* III, 30), "Writing & Language of Heaven" (Ms Harley 6482 fol. 75), or *Malachim* ("Alphabet of Angels or Kings", as again in Agrippa, *Occ. Phil.* III, 30). The characters of these alphabets have sometimes the form of stars and are generally similar to the square Hebrew alphabet, but the extremities of these characters usually have the shape of rings. The relation between Celestial writing and stars is somewhat obscure in the *De Occulta Philosophia*, but two maps by J. Gaffarel (in his *Curiositez inouyes . . .*) indicate how to find the correspondence between each letter and each star (or constellation of stars, similar to the constellation of the zodiac) in the northern and southern hemispheres. Other authors have also reproduced the forms of these alphabets with great clarity. Among them are J.B. Hepburn (in his *Virga Aurea* [1616] he calls them *Super caeleste* and *Enochaeum*), Jacques Gaffarel, Athanasius Kircher or T. Bangius (*Caelum orientis et prisci mundi*, 1657). This group of alphabets is frequent in the Middle Ages and during the Renaissance, that is, in a period when the idea of a connection between the stars and their signs was rarely called into question. The ecclesiastical authorities sometimes took up arms against cryptographic views and practices, but could not deny that the star of Bethlehem bore witness to the role of a celestial object in helping humanity.

C. *Theurgic communication*. This type of communication is bilateral and therefore makes a dialogue possible. It left its mark in the 17th century in western Europe with a theurgy that turned out to be, so it seems, the most accomplished example of communication between angels and man. Here the angel, representative of the "subtle" realm, and Man, or part of the "gross" one, cooperates with a view to 'working out the miracles of one thing' (if it is permissible to make use here of the oft-quoted formulations of the *Tabula Smaragdina*) and establishing a kind of theurgical union in tune with heaven's harmony. Pasqually's system is a typical example of this form of "co-operative" theurgy in which the signs and hieroglyphs are used, as seen above, to invoke (and/or identify) each angel by his name. Further examples of this category are the alphabets called *Seraphicum* (in J.B. Hepburn, *Virga aurea* [1616], pl. I), *De transitu fluminis* (in Agrippa, *Occ.Phil.* III, 30; → Guillaume Postel,

Linguarum Duodecim Characteribus, 1538 etc.) or the series of alphabets referred to as "of Raphaël" (in Ms Harley 1921 fol. 56). Writings of this third type often appeared together in one single treatise (as is the case in books by A. de Balmis, 1523; Blaise de Vigenère, 1586; Julius Bartolocci, 1675-1694; Geoffroy Tory, 1529 or Athanasius Kircher, 1652-1654). An exceptionally long text, written in the *De transitu fluminis* alphabet, has been analysed and transliterated by M. Danon (1910). The alphabets that belong to this category enjoyed a broad success as early as the beginning of the Renaissance, and flourished at least as far as Martines de Pasqually's time.

4 . A N E X A M P L E

To illustrate the nature of cryptographic writings, let us take the seal of Saturn as Agrippa presents it (it was also reproduced by → F. Barrett, *The Magus . . .* II, 1, plate 3, along with much of the text of Agrippa's book, which contributed to its dissemination), and compare it with the letter "S" as it appears among the hieroglyphs of the aforementioned "Register of 2400 names" (Prunelle de Lière Ms in Grenoble) by Martinez de Pasqually. We see that these signs are similar, but not identical. The seal which can be found in Agrippa (*Occ.Phil.* II, 149) is, under the name of Saturn, accompanied by the magical square of that planet. This square is composed of the numbers 1 to 9, the sum value of each line of numbers being 15. The key to the construction of this seal as based upon a magical square was provided by → Louis-Claude de Saint-Martin (in *Des nombres*): by simply following the order of the numbers, one gets the seal. Different magical squares yield different seals:

| Agrippa / F. Barrett *the seal of Saturn* | M. de Pasqually hier. "S", n° 33 | Ms. BRI. Har. 6482 fol. 92 | Magic Square of Saturn |

This method only concerns the seals and is not true, of course, for ring-alphabets, since the latter are in the order of letters proper: they are transliterations.

The way these alphabets are organized, the number of letters, and their order, are very reminiscent of the Hebrew characters, and this is emphasized by the name given to each alphabet (frequently "old hebrew", e.g. Ms Harley 1921 fol. 58; "alphabetum hebraicum", e.g. Ms Harley 6030 fol. 15). Many Arabic authors (e.g. Ibn Wahshîya) tried to establish a correspondence between a ring-alphabet, the Hebrew alphabet, and the Arabic one. The problem that the Arabic alphabet has six more letters than the Hebrew, these authors usually solve by putting the remaining Arabic letters (which have no correspondance to the Hebrew alphabet) at the end of their ring-alphabet to get 28 letters, and trying to draw them in a style reminiscent of the graphism of the ring-writing. For example, if one compares the celestial alphabet of Agrippa to that of "Syrianus the philosopher" of Ibn Wahshîya (9th-10th cent., cf. Hammer, 36), one notices that the six Arabic letters unrelated to the Hebrew alphabet are gathered together at the end of the alphabet and are very similar to one another. In fact, the majority of cryptographic alphabets, whether they came from the Western world or from the Islamic one, have originated from adaptation of the Hebrew alphabet, over a period of more than one thousand years.

Cornelius Agrippa, *De Occulta Philosophia libri tres* (Perrone Compagni critical ed.), ♦ Anonymus [J.V. Andreae], *Confessio Fraternitatis* (modern ed. *Fama Fraternitatis/ConfessioFraternitatis Chymische Hochzeit* [Richard van Dülmen, ed.], Stuttgart: Calwer, 1973) ♦ Abraham de Balmis, *Grammatica hebraea*, Venice: Danielis Bobergi, 1523 ♦ Francis Barrett, *The Magus or Celestial Intelligencer, being a Complete System of Occult Philosophy in Three Books*, London: Allen and Co., 1801 (New York: facs. repr. S. Weiser, n.d.) ♦ Julius Bartolicci, *Bibliotheca magna rabbinica*, Rome: Ex. Typographia Sacrae Congreg. de Propag. Fide, 1675-1694 ♦ Jacques Gaffarel, *Curiositez inouyes, sur la sculpture Talismanique des Persans, Horoscope des Patriarches et lecture des Eftoiles*, Paris: Hervé du Mesnil, 1629 (pp. 633ff.) ♦ Frédéric-George Kenyon, *Greek Papyri in the British Museum*, London: Oxford University Press, 1893 ♦ Athanasius Kircher, *Oedipus Aegyptiacus hoc est Universalis Hieroglyphicae Veterum Doctrinae*, Rome: Ex typographia Vitalis Hascardi, 1652-1654 (I, 105; II, 217, 231, 278ff.) ♦ Prunelle de Lière, *Registre des 2400 noms*, MS Bibliothèque Municipale de Grenoble (France), Fonds Dauphinois, T.4188 ♦ Louis-Claude de Saint-Martin, *Des nombres* (Nicole Jacques-Chaquin, ed.), Nice: Belisane, 1983 ♦ Geoffroy Tory, *Champ Fleury auquel est contenu Lart & Science de la deue & vraye proportio des lettres Attiques . . .*, Paris: G. Gourmond, 1529 ♦ Blaise de Vigenère, *Traicté des chiffres, ou secrètes manières d'escrire*, Paris: Abel l'Angelier, 1636 (1586) ♦ idem, *Traité des comètes ou estoilles chevelues . . .*, Paris: Nicolas Chesneau, 1578 ♦ [Anonymous], *Picatrix* (David Pingree, ed.), London: The Warburg Institute, 1986 ♦ [Anonymous], Ms Harley 1921, London: British Library, compiled by Randle Holme (1627-1699), fol. 57, 58 ♦ [Anonymous], Ms Harley 6030, *Adversaria*, 1687, London: British Library, compiled by Humphrey Wanley, fol. 15, 16 ♦ [Anonymous], Ms Harley 6461, 16th cent. (?), London: British Library, fol. 53, 53 b ♦ [Anonymous],

Ms Harley 6482, 1714, London: British Library, Doc. of Dr. Rudd.

Lit.: E. Cazalas, "Le Sceau de la Lune de C. Agrippa", *Revue de l'histoire des religions* 114 (July-August 1936), 93-98 ♦ M. Danon, "Amulettes Sabbatiennes", *Journal Asiatique* (Jan.-June 1910), 331 ♦ Joseph Hammer, *Ancient Alphabets and Hieroglyphic Characters Explained*, London: W. Bulmer and Co., 1806 (repr. Retz: Bibliotheca Hermetica, 1976) ♦ Gilles Le Pape, "Ecriture à lunettes et théurgie", in: *Les cahiers de Saint-Martin* 7 (1988), 29-132 ♦ idem, "Les écritures à lunettes comme moyen de communication avec le monde des intermédiaires", *Politica Hermetica* 13 (1999), 68-87 ♦ idem, *De H.C. Agrippa aux "caractères" du Registre des 2400 noms du fonds Prunelle de Lière (Grenoble, fin du XVIIIe): Contribution à l'étude des écritures "à lunettes" dans les Temps Modernes*, unpubl. Ph.D. diss. École Pratique des Hautes Études: Paris, 1996 ♦ S. Liddell MacGregor Mathers, *The Book of the Sacred Magic of ABRA-MELIN the Mage*, New-York, London: Luzac & Co., 1898 ♦ idem, *The Key of Salomon the King (Clavicula Salomonis)*, London: George Redway, 1889 ♦ Karl Anton Nowotny, "The Construction of certain Seals and Characters in the Works of Agrippa of Net-tesheim", *Journal of the Warburg and Courtauld Intitutes* 12 (1949), 46-57 ♦ C.E. Ruelle, "La Cryptographie Grecque: Simples notes, suivies d'un Tableau général des Alphabets Secrets", in: *Mélanges offerts à M. Emile Picot*, Paris: Librairie Damascène Morgand, 1913, 2-3 ♦ Lynn Thorndike, *A History of Magic and Experimental Science* (1923-1958), repr. New York: The Macmillan Company, 1984.

GILLES LE PAPE

Cudworth, Ralph, * 1617 Aller (Somerset), † 26.6.1688 Cambridge

Cudworth was the leading philosopher of the group known as the Cambridge Platonists. He was born in Aller, Somerset, in 1617, the third son of Ralph Cudworth († 1624). He was educated at Emmanuel College, where he was elected to a fellowship in 1635. His contemporaries at the college included many of the Cambridge Platonists: Benjamin Whichcote, John Smith, Peter Sterry, Nathaniel Culverwell. Cudworth's friends at Emmanuel included Samuel Cradock, John Wallis and John Worthington, and the future Archbishop of Canterbury, William Sancroft. During the upheavals of the Civil War, Cudworth was appointed Master of Clare Hall and Regius Professor of Hebrew. In 1646 he gave a series of lectures on the Temple of Jerusalem and on 31st March 1647 he preached a sermon to the House of Commons. In 1654 he was elected Master of Christ's College, where his friend, → Henry More (1614-1687), was a fellow. In 1656 Cudworth advised

Cromwell on the readmission of the Jews to England. He retained his college and university appointments after the Restoration of monarchy and in 1662 was presented to a living in Hertfordshire by Archbishop Sheldon. In 1664 he preached a sermon at Lincoln's Inn. In 1669, he was involved in the expulsion from Cambridge of Daniel Scargill, a self-confessed Hobbist. But he received no preferment in the new ecclesiastical and political order, probably because of his earlier links to Cromwell, his latitudinarianism and his de-emphasis on the institutional aspect of religion. In his lifetime he published only one major book, his *True Intellectual System of the Universe* (1678). This was intended as the first part of a more extended treatise on liberty and necessity that was never completed. Two further parts were published posthumously: *A Treatise Concerning Eternal and Immutable Morality* (1731) and *A Treatise of Freewill* (1838). Two manuscripts on the same theme, "On Liberty and Necessity", remain unpublished to this day.

Cudworth's *The True Intellectual System of the Universe* is a compendious philosophy of religion in which he undertakes an anti-determinist defence of theism against atheism and materialism. In it he makes extensive use of *consensus gentium* arguments to demonstrate that the idea of God is natural to all mankind. In so doing he classifies all ancient thinkers as either theists or atheists, interpreting pagan polytheism as corrupt forms of monotheism. *The True Intellectual System* broaches a number of epistemological and ethical themes more fully treated in his unpublished writings "On Liberty and Necessity", and his posthumously published *Treatise Concerning Eternal and Immutable Morality* (1731), where he argues that mental reality transcends and precedes the physical world, and seeks to establish the certainty of knowledge and the existence of unchangeable moral principles. As the most fully worked out epistemology produced by any of the Cambridge Platonists *A Treatise Concerning Eternal and Immutable Morality* is the most important statement of innate-idea epistemology by any British philosopher of the 17th century. The natural philosophy espoused in his *System*, is a form of vitalistic atomism, which accepts Descartes' idea of body as inert extension, but explains movement and life in terms of the action of immaterial spirit. His most distinctive causal theory is his doctrine of "Plastic Nature", a vitalistic hypothesis framed to account for phenomena inexplicable in merely mechanical terms. Analogous to the Platonic doctrine of *anima mundi*, and the Stoic conceptions of

pneuma, "Plastic Nature" is conceived of as an incorporeal medium between God and creation designed to maintain the orderly day-to-day operations of nature and perform the directives of God, which it does unconsciously. By this theory Cudworth sought to oppose the mechanistic models of causality offered by contemporary thinkers like Hobbes, and to overcome two unacceptable features of Cartesianism: occasionalism and rejection of final causes.

As this example shows, Cudworth drew on both ancient and modern philosophy. Cudworth's extensive knowledge of ancient sources included both the philosophers of antiquity – especially those in the Platonic tradition, but also Aristotle – and the presocratic philosophers. He also believed that evidence of monotheism could be gleaned from the Orphic mysteries, Sibylline Oracles and writings of the ancient poets. Although he sided with Casaubon against → Kircher on the matter of the authenticity of the *Pimander* of → Hermes Trismegistus, he nevertheless argued that forged writings were evidence of some truth, because they would not have been credible had it not been for the presence of monotheistic beliefs among the ancient Egyptians. He also accepted the historicity of Thoth and the authenticity of other Hermetic texts [→ Hermetic Literature], notably the *Asclepius*. He rejected Casaubon's dismissal of the entire Corpus Hermeticum as forged, arguing that these texts were not part of a single book and that there were, in any case, non-extant texts known to the Fathers. Cudworth's view of both ancient and modern philosophy was shaped by his belief in the essential unity of philosophical truth, to which some philosophers came closer than others. Like his Renaissance forbears, Cudworth regarded all philosophy as belonging to a *philosophia perennis* [→ Tradition] and much of his intellectual energy was devoted to demonstrating the kernel of truth that was expressed in different ways by different thinkers. He explained philosophical diversity, both ancient and modern, as resulting from partial or distorted interpretations of the original truth, which he refers to as a "cabbala". To the extent that he believed that this original truth was contained in more or less obscure form within the writings of pagan thinkers, he accepted the existence of an occult tradition. In this he was influenced by the Platonic tradition of veiling mysteries from the uninitiated. He argued that Egyptian religion, in particular, had a double aspect, one part of it being secret and the other intended for public consumption. However, Cudworth did not believe in a separate esoteric wisdom that could only be accessed by unlocking the mysteries of the ancients. On the contrary, he held that the wisdom transmitted by the philosophers of the perennial tradition, and grasped dimly by others, was the original wisdom of Adam and Moses and that it was compatibile with the teachings of Christianity. The perennial philosophy to which Cudworth subscribed was, therefore, as much an ancient theology (*prisca theologia*) as an ancient philosophy (*prisca sapientia*). Cudworth did, however, subscribe to the view that by this means there had been a revelation to the pagans prior to the advent of Christ, as a *praeparatio evangeliae*, a claim which was sustained by the belief that the most virtuous pagans, like Plato and Pythagoras, had benefited from contact with the prophets of Israel or those who had been taught by them.

Although the idea of a perennial philosophy did not survive the critique of the early-enlightenment classical scholars like Richard Bentley, Cudworth's philosophical legacy continued long after his death. His English admirers included John Ray, John Locke, Lord Shaftesbury, Sir Andrew (Le Chevalier) Ramsay, Richard Price and Thomas Reid. He was also read by Leibniz and → Newton, and his doctrine of "Plastic Nature" became the focal point of a dispute between Bayle and Le Clerc (1703-1706). Through J.L. Mosheim's translation of his works (1733, reprinted 1773) Cudworth's writings were transmitted to the German Enlightenment.

Three treatises on "Liberty and necessity", London: British Library, Additional MSS 4978-82. ◆ *The True Intellectual System of the Universe*, London, 1678; facs. ed. Friedrich Frommann: Stuttgart-Bad Cannstatt, 1964 ◆ *A Confutation of the Reason and Philosophy of Atheism being an Abridgement or an Improvement of what Dr Cudworth Offered in his "True Intellectual System"* (ed. Thomas Wise), London, 1706, repr. 1732 ◆ *A Treatise Concerning Eternal and Immutable Morality* and *A Treatise of Freewill* (orig. 1731; 1838) (ed. S. Hutton), Cambridge: Cambridge University Press, 1996.

Lit.: G. Aspelin, "Ralph Cudworth's Interpretation of Greek Philosophy: A Study in the History of English Philosophical Ideas", *Göteborgs Högskolas Arsskrift*, 49 (1943) ◆ Ernst Cassirer, *The Platonic Renaissance in England* (orig. 1932), Edinburgh, 1953 ◆ Rosalie Colie, *Light and Enlightenment*, Cambridge: Cambridge University Press, 1957 ◆ Stephen Darwall, *British Moralists*, Cambridge: Cambridge University Press, 1992, 109-148 ◆ W.B. Hunter, "The Seventeenth-century Doctrine of Plastic Nature", *Harvard Theological Review* 4 (1950), 197-213 ◆ Martin Mulsow (ed.), *Das Ende des Hermetismus: Historische Kritik und neue Naturphilosophie in der Spätrenaissance.*

Dokumentation und Analyse der Debatten um die Datierung der hermetischen Schriften von Genebrard bis Casaubon (1567-1614), Tübingen: Mohr Siebeck, 2002 ◆ Jan Assmann, " 'Hen kai pan': Ralph Cudworth und die Rehabilitierung der hermetischen Tradition", in: Monika: Neugebauer-Wölk (ed.), *Aufklärung und Esoterik*, Hamburg: Felix Meiner, 1999, 38-52 ◆ J.A. Passmore, *Ralph Cudworth: An Interpretation*, Cambridge: Cambridge University Press, 1951 ◆ G.A.J. Rogers, "Die Cambridge Platoniker" and "Ralph Cudworth", *Ueberwegs Grundriss der Geschichte der Philosophie: die Philosophie des 17. Jahrhunderts*, vol. 3.1, Basle: Schwabe & Co., 1988, 245-6, 267-272, 285-290 ◆ G.A.J. Rogers, J.M. Vienne and Y.C. Zarka, *The Cambridge Platonists in Philosophical Context*, Dordrecht: Kluwer, 1997, 39-42, 93-100, 145-157, 173-196, 215-231 ◆ D.B. Sailor, "Cudworth and Descartes", *Journal of the History of Ideas* 23 (1962), 133-140 ◆ Dominic Scott, "Platonic Recollection and Cambridge Platonism", *Hermathena* 149 (1990), 73-97.

SARAH HUTTON

Cusa, Nicholas of (Niklaus Krebs), * 1401 Kues, † 11.8.1464 Todi

Born in 1401 in Kues, a small village on the banks of the Moselle not far from Trier, Nicolas Krebs studied the liberal arts at Heidelberg, law at Padua and theology at Cologne. He played an important part in the Council of Basel, which he joined in 1432 as a member of the conciliar party. This party considered the Pope to possess supreme authority in the Church, but to be nonetheless subject to the general Council, which better represented the community of the faithful and which hence had a greater legitimacy for promoting a true reform of the Church. Nicolas was disappointed by the narrow-mindedness of his side and by the loss of a legal case. In 1435 he joined the party of Pope Eugenius IV, who soon made him one of his foremost collaborators. As such, Nicolas was sent to Byzantium to appear before the Eastern Emperor and the Patriarch, who were to come to Italy with their entourage to seal anew the union of the Churches. The promised ships did not arrive, and Nicolas spent about six months in Byzantium, where one can imagine that he must have had fruitful conversations with the Greek scholars assembled there in view of the coming Council.

On his voyage back to Italy, Nicolas had his famous intuition of the "coincidence of opposites", according to which God, the infinite being, is above all oppositions and unites in himself the predicates that are judged incompatible in the finite world, such as being and non-being, absolute necessity and possibility, the *maximum* (the fact of encompassing all beings within himself) and the *minimum* (the fact of being contained in all beings). Thereupon Nicolas searched the philosophical and theological tradition for conceptual tools that would allow him to give an account of this discovery and explain its contents. He wrote several books, among which the most notable are *De Docta Ignorantia* (Learned Ignorance, 1440), *De Coniecturis* (Conjectures, 1443-5), *Idiota de Mente* (The Layman on the Mind, 1450), *De Visione Dei* (The Vision of God, 1453), *De Pace Fidei* (The Peace of Faith, 1453), and *De Non-aliud* (The Non-Other, 1462). The object of all of them was a dialectic approch to God, to the human mind and its capacity for knowledge limited by its finitude, and the consequences that result for the universe. Nicolas also had a great interest in mathematics, especially in the squaring of the circle, which he considered as the geometrical equivalent of the conjunction of opposites. His rich intellectual production came out of the little leisure time at his disposal, for he served the Pope with an intense diplomatic activity in the states of the Empire, to convince their rulers to support the papal point of view. In 1448 he was created Cardinal, with the title of the church of San Pietro in Vincoli. From 1450 to 1452, he was charged with the great legation throughout the Empire, for which he was given extensive powers to reform the Church, promulgate reforms, convoke synods, condemn the recalcitrant, grant indulgences on the occasion of the "Holy Year" of 1450, etc. After that he assumed pastoral duties as Bishop of Brixen before returning to Rome in 1458 and becoming in 1459 the Pope's Vicar General for the temporal world. He died on August 11, 1464.

Nicolas of Cusa passed rapidly into posterity as a man of universal knowledge. Beside his proven competence in civil and canon law, in philosophy and theology, he was seen as an expert in Greek and even in Hebrew, though he had only a very elementary notion of the latter. Likewise his competence in the scientific field, such as in mathematics and astronomy, has been largely overestimated. His mathematical works show that he did not surpass the level of a good amateur, and those more expert in this field, such as Toscanelli (1397-1482) or Regiomontanus (1436-1476) easily detected his limitations. His rich library, still preserved in the St. Nikolaus Hospital of Bernkastel-Kues, certainly contributed to this reputation; but owning a work in one's library does not necessarily mean that one has mastered its contents. The fact that Nicolas

was one of the first to incarnate the humanist ideal, according to which literature and the sciences determine a new relationship of man to the world and have value in themselves, also played a definite role here.

From *Learned Ignorance* onwards, his first great book of speculative theology, Nicolas belonged explicitly to the tradition of Pythagoras. He saw the latter as the first to have clearly perceived that man can only approach wisdom, without ever being able to attain it, for which reason Pythagoras was content with the title of "philosopher", and did not claim that of "sage" like his predecessors. Socrates, too, with his awareness of his own ignorance, is an especially pure illustration of true philosophy as Pythagoras conceived it. By promoting learned ignorance as the ideal of human knowledge, meaning a knowledge aware of its limits and of the element of unknowing that it carries within itself, Nicolas placed his own approach under the protection of these two illustrious figures.

Moreover, Pythagoras had regarded mathematics as the supreme instrument for knowing reality, and Nicolas also belonged unreservedly within this perspective. Numbers, produced by the human mind, are certainly not the very essence of things, but they approach the latter's secrets more closely than any other means [→ Number Symbolism]. Mathematical objects can represent higher realities, such as the theological verities; thus the coincidence of opposites that exists in God is imaged by the progression of geometric figures towards infinity. If a circle infinitely extended is identical to two straight lines, one can sense there the union and coincidence of realities which on the finite level remain opposed.

Nicolas also wrote a short eschatological treatise, *Coniectura de ultimis diebus* (Conjecture about the Last Days, 1448), which was much esteemed during the Renaissance. The life of Christ, to which Nicolas assigned 34 years, contains symbolically the whole subsequent history of the Church. Each year of Christ's life counts as 50 years in the life of the Church, which, having been born in A.D. 34, will last for 34 jubilees of 50 years each, and thus will end around 1734. Corresponding to the public life of Christ, preceded by the preaching of John the Baptist, will be an evangelical renewal becoming ever stronger from the 29th and 30th jubilees onwards. The persecutions suffered by Christ at the end of his life will also be repeated for the Church. This will be the triumph of the Antichrist: the Church will seem to be dead, but it will experience a resurrection before the actual return of its master. Given that Nicolas's prediction of the evangelical renewal corresponded in effect with the Protestant Reformation, one can easily understand the impact that this little treatise had on contemporary minds.

The treatise *Idiota de Mente* (The Layman on the Spirit, 1450) presents a humble workman who makes wooden shelters, but beneath his modest exterior possesses a very profound wisdom; a philosopher and a specialist in rhetoric come to him for initiation. He uses the simple gestures of his craft as analogies of the highest realities: God and his creative act, the human spirit as image of God, the status of numbers, mathematics as displaying the inner fecundity of thought. Nicolas is clearly criticizing here the book-learning of the scholastic thinkers; true knowledge is sometimes found among the ignorant, the fools, and those who are despised by the established intellectual or religious authorities.

In another short work, *Idiota de Staticis Experimentis* (The Layman on Static Experiments, 1450), Nicolas erects a general philosophy of measurement for natural phenomena. Using a simple balance, one can measure the different weights of waters from various origins: light and airy ones, good for habitation, or heavy, earthly, and noxious waters. One can draw up a table with the numerical characteristics of various waters and the specific mixture of elements that characterize them. One can do likewise for the metals, the airs, the humors, such as blood, urine, etc. The blood of a German is not exactly the same weight as that of an Italian, or an inhabitant of some other land. The blood and urine of an individual vary according to whether he is well or ill. A table of the ponderable differences of urine would certainly render great service to medicine by facilitating diagnosis. Evidently Nicolas grasped the idea of the functional variation of nature's measurable quantities, as revealing the hidden relations that things have with one another.

In 1453, Nicolas was deeply affected by the Turkish conquest of Byzantium and the disastrous consequences of wars waged for religious motives. He wrote one of his most penetrating books on this subject, *The Peace of Faith*, where he tries to show that all religious beliefs – Judaism, Islam, Zoroastrianism, paganism, philosophy (regarded as a religion worshipping Wisdom) – are founded on common assumptions. This common core can be explained as a faith that is the precondition of all religious confessions, and by this very fact unites them rather than opposes them. From this point of view, the differences between confessions amount to differences between rites, and do not call into question the common faith that unites them. For

Nicolas, this common faith is Christianity. It is not, however, a religion of reason – understood as the faculty of mind subject to the laws of traditional logic, and thus fit to grasp finite realities – which would be opposed to all the other religions that contradict reason; it is, rather, a religion of the *intellect*: the faculty of the spirit which is open to the conjunction of opposites, because it is higher than reason and situated at the principle of the latter, as light is to shadow. Even when the "rational" religions explicitly contradict some point of "intellectual" religion, they are implicitly admitting that it is part of their very conditions of possibility. Hence Christianity should not want to impose itself by force, because it is not opposed to other beliefs, being at another level than they. With *The Peace of Faith*, Nicolas made the most extensive contribution of the Latin Middle Ages to the problem of religious pluralism.

The central theme of Cusanus's thought, the "coincidence of opposites", may have given birth to the conviction that he was an "initiate" in the esoteric sense of the word. According to this principle, all affirmation about God is merely partial: it has to be completed and relativized by the contrary affirmation, because God unites in himself that which is incompatible in the finite. This often gives Nicolas's arguments a paradoxical aspect, being very respectful of the truth that some opinion may contain, but equally conscious of the necessity to integrate these diverse perspectives in a higher synthesis, which goes beyond the competence of reason, the latter being observant of the principles of non-contradiction and the excluded middle. Thus God is nowhere in the world, while being everywhere in it; the world has no limits, and thus may be called infinite, but on the other hand, being only a reflection of the true infinity which is God, it is better called indefinite; the cosmos has no clearly marked center or frontiers, but each point in the universe may be considered as both its center and its frontier.

Human thought can only divine this coincidence of opposites, without ever mastering it; that is why man's knowledge is always "learned ignorance". It is important to note that certain mystics believed that they could interpret Nicolas of Cusa as promoting a supression of intellectual activity in order to unite with God in ecstatic love, following the emotional interpretation of the *Mystical Theology* of → Pseudo-Dionysus by Thomas Gallus. But Nicolas clearly rejected this understanding of his doctrine: "learned ignorance" requires the intellectual recognition that God, "coincidence of opposites", is incomprehensible. There really is an authentic intellectual activity existing beyond the domain of reason, and one cannot reduce all mental activity to an emotional impulse alone. From this point of view, Cusanus is close (*Sermons dionysiens et eckhartiens*) to the way in which → Albertus Magnus and his Dominican disciples in Cologne (often miscalled the "Rhineland mystics") understood Pseudo-Dionysus's *Mystical Theology*: as a *divinization* of the intellect, and not as an annihilation of its activity.

Nicolai de Cusa Opera Omnia iussu et auctoritate Academiae litterarum heidelbergensis ad codicum fidem edita (publication in progress) ♦ *De docta ignorantia* (E. Hoffmann & R. Klibansky, eds.), Leipzig: Felix Meiner, 1932 ♦ *On Learned Ignorance*, Minneapolis, ²1985 ♦ *Apologia doctae ignorantiae* (R. Klibansky, ed.), Leipzig: Felix Meiner, 1932; Eng. trans. in: J. Hopkins, *Nicholas of Cusa's Debate with John Wenck: A Translation and an Appraisal of* De ignota litteratura *and* Apologia doctae ignorantiae, Minneapolis: Arthur Banning, 1988³, 43-66 ♦ *De coniecturis* (I. Koch, C. Bormann & I.G. Senger, eds.), Hamburg: Felix Meiner, 1972; Engl. trans. in: W.F. Wertz, *Toward a New Council of Florence: "On the Peace of Faith" and Other Works by Nicholas of Cusa*, Washington: Schiller Institute, 1995, 149-247 ♦ J. Hopkins, *Nicholas of Cusa: Metaphysical Speculations*, II, Minneapolis: Arthur Banning, 2000, 149-247 ♦ *Idiota De sapientia – De mente – De staticis experimentis* (R. Steiger & L. Baur, eds.), Hamburg: Felix Meiner, 1983; Engl. trans. *The Layman on Wisdom and the Mind* (trans. M.L. Fuhrer), Ottawa, 1989 ♦ J. Hopkins, *Nicholas of Cusa on Wisdom and Knowledge*, Minneapolis: Arthur Banning, 1996, 85-371 ♦ *De pace fidei* (R. Klibansky & H. Bascour, eds.), Hamburg: F. Meiner, 1970; Engl. trans. in: J. Hopkins, *Nicholas of Cusa's De pace fidei and Cribratio Alkorani*, Minneapolis: Arthur Banning, 1990, 31-71 ♦ J.E. Biechler & H.L. Bond (eds.), *Nicholas of Cusa on Interreligious Harmony: Text, Concordance and Translation of* De pace fidei, NY: Lewiston, 1990 ♦ *Sermons dionysiens et eckhartiens* (French trans. by F. Bertin), Paris: Cerf, 1998.

Lit.: V. Schultze, *Zahl Proportion Analogie: Eine Untersuchung zur Metaphysik und Wissenschaftshaltung der Niklaus von Kues*, Münster, 1978 ♦ J. Hopkins, *Nicholas of Cusa's Metaphysic of Contraction*, Minneapolis: Arthur Banning, 1983 ♦ P.M. Watts, "Pseudo-Dyonisius the Areopagite and three Renaissance Platonists: Cusanus, Ficino and Pico on Mind and Cosmos", *Supplementum Festivum: Studies in honor of Paul Oscar Kristeller* (J. Hankins, J. Monfasani & F. Purnell, eds.), Binghamton: State University of New York Press, 1987, 279-298 ♦ S. Meier-Œser, *Die Präsenz der Vergessenen: Zur Rezeption der Philosophie des Nicolaus Cusanus vom 15. bis 18. Jahrhundert*, Münster, 1989 ♦ D. Luscombe, "Denys the Pseudo-Areopagite in the Writings of Nicholas of Cusa, Marsilio Ficino and Pico della Mirandola", *Néoplatonisme et philosophie médiévale* (L.G. Benakis,

ed.), Turnhout: Brepols, 1997, 93-107 ♦ K. Flasch, *Nikolaus von Kues, Geschichte einer Entwicklung: Vorlesungen zur Einführung in seine Philosophie*, Frankfurt: Klostermann, 1998 ♦ S. Toussaint, "L'influence de Marsile Ficin à Paris et le Pseudo-Denys des Humanistes: Traversari, Cusa, Lefèvre d'Etaples", *Bruniana et Campanelliana* 5:2 (1999), 381-414 ♦ J.M. Counet, *Mathématiques et Dialectique chez Nicolas de Cuse*, Paris: Vrin, 2000 ♦ F.E. Cranz, *Nicholas of Cusa and the Renaissance*, Aldershot "Brookfield: Ashgate Variorum, 2000 ♦ P.R. Blum, "'Saper trar il contrario dopo aver trovato il punto dell'unione': Bruno, Cusano e il platonismo", in : E. Canone (ed.), *Letture Bruniane I-II del Lessico Intellettuale Europeo* ("Supplementi" di "Bruniana et Campanelliana"), Pisa, Roma: Istituti Editoriali e Poligrafici Internazionali, 2002, 33-47 ♦ M. Thurner (ed.), *Nicolaus Cusanus zwischen Deutschland und Italien*, Berlin: Akademie Verlag, 2002.

J.M. COUNET

Cusanus, Nicolas → Cusa, Nicholas of

Dante Alighieri, * 1265 Florence, † 1321 Ravenna

Exceptional poet and political figure involved in the dispute between the Guelphs and the Ghibellines, Dante took part in the *Dolce stil novo* movement alongside Guido Cavalcanti (ca. 1255-1300) and declared on several occasions that his poetic message addressed the mysterious → "*Fedeli d'amore*" (for ex. *Vita nuova*, III, 12). It is unknown whether these formed an ideal community of learned and loving poets or designated a secret society of an initiatory vocation. The characteristic of the work of Dante indeed consists in expressing this supposed initiatory dimension in the sole vocabulary of courtly poetry and the sorrows of love. Thus, in both his prose and his verse, and finally in the total work that is the *Divine Comedy*, he always speaks of love for a woman or for women, whose life and death mark the rhythm of the course of individual life as well as universal history and the entire cosmos. The esotericism of Dante could not employ any other basis or symbol.

After the death of the beloved woman, Beatrice (who cannot be reduced to Bice Portinari, a real woman whom Dante seems to have loved from late adolescence), came a successive series of tribulations. These mixed a political life of the first order, serious philosophical training in Florence and Bologna, and personal trials that were to culminate in exile. A mission in Rome to Boniface VIII in 1301, when Dante was Prior of Florence, proved to be a trap since he never returned to his hometown and was sentenced *in absentia* to exile and the stake. Only then did he find his definitive vocation in writing first the *Convivio*, a vast unfinished commentary on some of his *canzone*, and then the *Commedia* published in stages, whose last thirteen cantos would be known only after his death. We can consider, however, that every composition by Dante not only is a preparation for his mature work, but also is a specific and irreplaceable viewpoint on the final work. Thus, not a single line attributed to Dante fails to contribute to the development of a system of an unbelievable complexity that immediately provoked a wave of commentaries.

It would be superfluous, however, to dwell here on the function of the Florentine poet in Italian history and in the literary renaissance of the end of the Middle Ages. Nevertheless, if we define the work of Dante as the greatest poetic synthesis of Roman and Catholic civilization, we risk misunderstanding how such a sum could have served as a major source for an almost indefinite number of esoteric, revolutionary, or theosophical interpretations, always heterodox. Thus, we must move away from a general cultural evaluation of the work of the poet and enter into the complexity of his literature to detect the elements, in this apparently unequivocal celebration of a dogma, comprising subversion so profound and enigmatic that no clear-cut opinion on this subject can be formulated even today. Moreover, even if we return to the letter of the text, the debate remains far from easy, because most scholars since Bruno Nardi (1884-1968), who apply the rules of historiography to interpreting the work, restrict themselves to an interpretation of the literal sense and refuse for reasons of either psychological probability or epistemology to enter into any "esoteric" dimension.

Generally cited to justify this specific dimension is a verse that nevertheless seems more applicable to its immediate context than to the whole work: '*O voi ch' avete gl'intelletti sani, / Mirate la dottrina che s'asconde, / Sotto il velame delli versi strani*' (*Inf.*, IX, 61-63 [O you who have clear understanding, / Consider the doctrine that is hiding, / Under the veil of strange verses.]) Furthermore, we must not underestimate at least two major roads into the esotericism of Dante. First, as early as the beginning of book II (II, I, 2-12) of the *Convivio*, that is, when the commentary of the first *canzone* begins, Dante gives a complete theory of the different meanings of poetry. Far from merely repeating the traditional theory of the four meanings of Scripture, the author takes care to distinguish between the plurality of meanings of Holy

Scripture and the plurality of meanings appropriate to poetry (II, I, 4). Therefore, Dante indeed made during that period, that is, after the composition of the great allegorical *canzone*, a distinction between poetic fiction, regulated to produce a variety of meanings according to the understanding of the poet, and the work of God that is Holy Scripture. The latter would regulate, according to an infinite understanding, the meanings and the events in the real history of the world.

This system of meaning was to unfold throughout the four books of the *Convivio* and result in a development of exceptional depth, particularly in the use of the analogy between the liberal Arts and the Heavens. In this passage, whose importance → René Guénon has rightly emphasized in his *L'Esotérisme de Dante* (chap. II, regarding *Conv.*, II, XI, 9), Dante not only relates his words to the Heaven of Venus, but also announces the foundation of a completely analogous cosmos. The Crystalline Heaven identified with Ethics propels this cosmos, which finishes in the Empyrean Heaven identified with a kingdom of Peace foreign to any discursive content (*Conv.*, II, XIII-XIV, and René Guénon, *Autorité spirituelle et pouvoir*, chapter VIII).

However, this first construction does not suffice, because the famous Letter XIII to Cangrade della Scala, a name on which the esotericists have exercised their sagacity by finding in it the name of Gengis Khan and the symbol of the ladder, announces a revolution in the initial balance between poetry and theology. Some doubt the authenticity of this letter, but its breadth of vision can only be that of Dante or the group that inspired him. In its paragraphs seven and eight, we read that the poet of the *Divine Comedy* used theological allegory to his advantage: an allegory, that is, in which the literal meaning is not a fiction, but a reality like that which God assigns to the history that he is guiding. The poet is hence in the situation of an absolute Creator, whose visions are existences and whose allegories are as powerful as those of the Bible.

On this basis, the plurality of meanings in the work of Dante takes on a prophetic significance and makes the work a true universe, whose hidden meanings are as necessary and established as those governing Revelation. In this regard, we could nonetheless still speak of the wanderings of a poet or the hallucinations of an author, if another element of primordial importance did not invite us to cross to another level. In fact, the most enigmatic element permeating the work is indeed the worship of woman that commands his every statement.

Anyone looking at the assertions of Dante with the eye of Catholic dogma could only be struck by the strangeness of such allegory, always present and never clarified, all the more so as it penetrates to the very heart of the most sacred statements of dogma. The work of Dante, from this viewpoint, risks appearing as nothing less than an erotic parody of the religion of Christ, which no resurgence of Marian worship could justify in a simple manner. In this sense, the esotericism of Dante is invisible, because instead of hiding, it is present throughout, from the first line of the work telling of the meeting with Beatrice to the last, where the poet merges into universal Love. In a Catholic orthodoxy, Christ is the only mediator, but rather than acting primarily as a mediator, he represents the immediacy of the Trinitarian God, and the Virgin is the only intercessor. Within this context, a simple young woman from Florence, through the effect of her beauty, becomes the ultimate term of all joy and spiritual development. She becomes this to the point where she can epitomize the meanings of all civilization, whether it is a matter, as in the *Vita nuova* (chap. XXX), of the politics of the rulers of this world, or, as in the *Comedy*, of the destiny of the Church and the Empire (*Purg.*, XXIX-XXXIII). Dante continues along this line the undertaking to challenge the clerical order begun by the *Roman de la Rose*. It is not surprising that scholars attribute to the Florentine poet a manuscript of 232 sonnets, signed by a certain "ser Durante", rediscovered in Montpellier in the 19th century and proceeding from the library of Troyes. These sonnets, entitled *Il Fiore* (the collection appears in the complete works published by the *Società Dantesca italiana*), summarize the highlights of the *Roman de la Rose*. They convey a very strong protest against established society and the need to divert the dogmas of Catholicism in order to transmit a secret wisdom both highly erotic and profoundly heretical (for example sonnets V and XV). However, here we would have to reconsider all the poetry of Dante before the *Comedy* and especially the disturbing *canzone* to the woman "of stone" (the "*Rime pietrose*"), which crown the Dantean doctrine of *Fin Amor* (cf. *Il Fiore*, IV, 8).

This return of the pagan (and Virgilian) mysteries amidst Dantean condemnations of the '*puzzo del paganesmo*' (*Par.* XX, 125), the stench of paganism, has attracted the attention of interpreters, who have well perceived the risk involved in such an increase of religious mediations. Among them, certainly → Marsilio Ficino went the furthest in recognizing the need for a spiritual revolution in order to understand Dante's gift to Florence. The letter prefacing the great humanist commentary on Dante by Cristoforo Landino (1424-1498)

contains this same idea. Even if we consider this commentary a key to Florentine culture and the beginnings of the art of printing, it does not exclude the idea of a "poetic theology" of neo-Platonic origin, for which poetry is simply the "veil" of philosophical wisdom. This writing, which is primarily a celebration of the unity of Florentine culture, does not address the idea that Dante is esoteric *because heterodox*. It was only with the Romantic annotator of Dante, Gabriele Rossetti (1783-1854), that the thesis of the "esotericism of Dante", founded on the deliberate use of ancient mysteries, the allegorical worship of woman, Templarism (in particular because of *Purg.* XX, 93), and militant Ghibelline politics, found free and systematic expression. His immediate predecessor was probably Ugo Foscolo (1778-1827) and his well-known *Discorso sul testo della divina Commedia* of 1825. Foscolo, a great nostalgic poet of a paganism both Jacobin and virtuous, tried to show that the entire work of Dante stood in the service of a political and moral reform of Pythagorean origin, which Dante could express only indirectly, given the convictions of his time. That is why Foscolo proposed a primarily political coding of the writings of Dante. Influenced by → Freemasonry and → Rosicrucianism, Rossetti, on his side, suggested a similar interpretation, but he pushed the esoteric interpretation to a degree of complexity worthy indeed of a poet schooled in the Neapolitan baroque.

The works of Rossetti are little read, but they were plundered, in particular by his detractor Aroux. In explaining Rossetti's theses, Aroux intended to denounce the Romantic cult of Dante before the Roman authorities. He declared that Dante was a revolutionary and an atheist, heir to the Ghibelline doctrine of Frederick II (however condemned by Dante in Canto X of the *Inferno*). The book of Aroux, with his ambiguous vocation as both denouncer and continuator, was nevertheless very influential, because it was from reading Aroux, and not Rossetti, that Guénon would draw the first theses of his esoteric reading of Dante (*Esoterism of Dante*, chapter III). It remains that Rossetti, very influential in the symbolist culture through the works of his son and disciple, the painter Dante Gabriele Rossetti, could marshal with a sufficiently broad view and a peerless knowledge of Dante, although not without repetition and obsession, the most precise arguments in favor of the esoteric reading of the Florentine poet.

For Rossetti, Dante belongs to a millenarian tradition of primarily political protest against power, through a gnosis whose coding according to the terms of dominant ideologies serves only to divert the attention of censors, so that the "Faithful of love" – that is, of the love of this gnosis – may assemble to liberate humanity. However, this libertarian and naïve socialism would not retain us, if it did not lead to a permanently divided reading of the work. In this regard, Rossetti is decisive more by the attention he brings to bear on the intrinsic ambiguity of the work than by the unequivocal solution that he serves.

Let us retain, in this context, his interpretation of the overlapping of the letters C and O, in the first syllable of COMOEDIA, his meditation on the dual display of the earth and the sea in the *Quaestio terrae et aquae* (the last text of Dante known to us), and his relentless criticism of any psychological and sentimental interpretation of the platonic love for Beatrice. These approaches reappear in Valli, but without the breadth of vision and the humanist culture of Rossetti, or again in the poet Giovanni Pascoli, who attempted in his turn to decipher the work from the recurrent motifs of the eagle and the cross. Esoteric interpretations of Dante indeed proliferated, mixing → astrology, numerology [→ Number Symbolism], Templarism, Joachimism, → alchemy, and so on, as though modern readers were seeking in Dante the secret of a spirituality that was no longer accessible. It is from such a perspective that René Guénon contributed his analyses on the esotericism of Dante (which are not limited to the book by the same name), as did → Julius Evola, whose Ghibelline Dante adopts a magical and heroic tone, rather foreign to traditional thinking according to Guénon. To finish, let us not forget the nominalist tendency of Umberto Eco, who did not think of engaging his great novelistic machinery without declaring a merciless war on any esoteric interpretation of the Florentine poet.

The "adepts of the veil", as Eco ironically calls them, nevertheless have a promising future, since the writings of Dante keep resisting usual intertextual or psychological interpretations. There is in this work such a thirst for truth, such a power of conviction, and such an enigma concerning the symbols intended to manifest them, that it seems to summarize in itself all the forces of Western thought and the virtue of its peoples. There will always be authors who believe that commenting on Dante is not so much clinging nostalgically to a medieval ruin, as it is evaluating our own capacity to understand the forms and the resources of our spirit.

Lit.: *Comedia di Danthe Alighieri poeta divino con l'espositione di Christofhoro landino*, Firenze, 1481, 1537, etc ♦ Ugo Foscolo, *Studi su Dante*, in *Ed. nazionale delle Opere di Ugo Foscolo*, Vol. IX.1, Le Monnier: Firenze, 1979 ♦ Gabriele Rossetti, *Il mistero dell'amor platonico del medio evo derivato da' misteri antichi*, London, 1840; Milan: Archè, 1982 ♦ Gabriele Rossetti, *La Beatrice di Dante* (Maria Luisa Giartosio de Courten, ed.), Roma: Atanòr, 1988 ♦ Eugène Aroux, *Dante hérétique, révolutionnaire et socialiste: Révélations d'un catholique sur le Moyen Age*, Paris 1854, 1939 ♦ Giovanni Pascoli, *Minerva obscura*, Livorno, 1878 ♦ idem, *Sotto il velame*, Messina, 1900 ♦ idem, *Conferenze e studi Danteschi*, Bologna, 1914 ♦ Luigi Valli, *Il linguaggio segreto di Dante e dei Fedeli d'Amore* (1928) Milano: Luni editrice, 1994 ♦ René Guénon, *L'ésotérisme de Dante*, Paris, 1925; Paris: Gallimard, 1957 ♦ idem, *Autorité spirituelle et pouvoir temporel* (1929) Paris: Trédaniel, 1984 ♦ Julius Evola, *Il mistero del Graal e la tradizione ghibellina dell'Impero*, Rome, 1937 ♦ Philippe Guiberteau, *Le Banquet* (introduction, translation and notes by Philippe Guiberteau), Paris: Les Belles Lettres, 1968 ♦ Arthur Schult, *Dantes Divina Commedia als Zeugnis der Tempelritter-Esoterik*, Bietigheim: Turm Verlag, 1979 ♦ *L'idea deforme, interpretazioni di Dante* (Maria Pia Possato, ed.), Milano: Bompiani, 1989 ♦ Adriano Lanza, *Dante e la Gnose*, Rama: Edizioni Mediterranee, 1990 ♦ *Sotto il velame, terni e interpreti dell'esoterismo Dantesco*, Torino: Associazione Studi Danteschi e Traditionali, 2001 ♦ Bruno Pinchard (ed.), *Pour Dante*, Paris: Honoré Champion, 2001 ♦ Bruno Pinchard, *Méditations mythologiques*, Paris: Les Empêcheurs de penser en rond, 2002.

BRUNO PINCHARD

Davis, Andrew Jackson, * 11.8.1826 Blooming Grove, New York, † 13.1.1910 Watertown, Massachusetts

Writer, clairvoyant, physician, lecturer, reformer, and forerunner of → New Age spirituality, Davis can rightfully be called the major theologian and philosopher of 19th-century → Spiritualism in the United States. Although most of our information concerning his early life comes from an autobiography whose veracity is questionable, it is likely that he grew up in humble circumstances in rural New York state and was deeply dissatisfied with the conventional Presbyterianism and Methodism of his time. Davis showed little promise in the several apprenticeships – including as a shoemaker – he tried, but was rescued from a life of obscurity when a tailor named William Levingston asked him to serve as a subject for his experiments inmesmerism [→ Animal Magnetism] in 1843. Levingston had learned snippets of mesmerism from the traveling lecturer J. Stanley Grimes. Davis proved to be a natural trance performer and reportedly traveled clairvoyantly to remote places, conversed with spirits, diagnosed physical ailments, and read from books while blindfolded.

In 1844, Davis had a visionary experience in which he spoke with both the Greek physician Galen and the Swedish mystic and scientist → Emanuel Swedenborg. Galen gave him a magical staff constructed so as to represent symbolically the complete correspondence between the natural order and Galen's medical system. The Greek physician also proclaimed Davis's future mission as a clairvoyant healer. Swedenborg told him that he was to become a conduit for a coming revelation of wisdom and truth to humanity. Bolstered by this vision, Davis and Levingston opened a clinic where Davis practiced clairvoyant healing. While in a trance state, the young seer would visualize the inner organs of the sick person and prescribe cures. This shaman-like practice would be replicated and made famous by the "sleeping prophet" → Edgar Cayce, whose clairvoyant readings would become an important element in the emergence of New Age spirituality in the latter half of the 20th century.

By 1845, Davis had moved to New York City with Dr. Silis Lyon and the Universalist minister William Fishbough, both of whom were impressed with his clairvoyant abilities. The two arranged for a series of public lectures during which Lyon mesmerized Davis and Fishbough acted as a scribe. The one hundred fifty-seven talks Davis delivered in the trance state impressed a wealthy patron named Silone Dodge, who arranged for them to be published in 1847 under the title, *The Principles of Nature, Her Divine Revelation, and a Voice to Mankind, By and Through Andrew Jackson Davis, the "Poughkeepsie Seer" and "Clairvoyant"*. Although some scholars see the book as a derivative melange of Swedenborgian cosmology and Fourierist socialism, *The Principles of Nature* is significant for two reasons: (1) it became the first of an important genre of esoteric treatise – purportedly received in a trance state or from spirit beings, including, for example, → H.P. Blavatsky's *Isis Unveiled*, the *Oahspe Book*, the *Aquarian Gospel of Jesus the Christ*, the writings of → Alice Bailey, the *Urantia Book*, and the Seth material – that would provide the conceptual categories and dominant themes for such popular alternative spiritualities in the United States as Spiritualism, → New Thought, Christian Science, Theosophy [→ Theosophical Society], and New Age; (2) the book – which went through thirty-four editions – and its ideas helped provide a philosophical and theological underpinning for the nascent Spirititualist movement of the 19th century.

The Principles of Nature discussed the origin and development of the universe, the laws that governed the intercourse between spirits and humans, and various schemes for social reform. Among the book's primary ideas is that of eternal progress, whereby human beings, created in God's image, continue to evolve after death through six (Swedenborgian) spheres that surround the earth. Each sphere surpasses in beauty and wisdom the one which precedes it. Those spirits closest to the earth could communicate with embodied humans, and new cosmic spheres would appear for further development once all humans had progressed to the highest, or sixth sphere. Since deceased persons would move into the sphere that best corresponded with their moral stature, there was a strong incentive to live according to the highest moral code while on earth. This progressive view of human destiny resonated well with the optimistic and egalitarian tenor of 19th-century American society and provided a welcome alternative to the pessimistic Calvinist vision of selective salvation for the few and eternal damnation for the many. Davis's spiritual anthropology also paralleled that of Mormon founder Joseph Smith, who taught that humans had the opportunity to evolve into god-like beings and to rule their own planets and solar systems.

Davis continued to write books, pamphlets, and articles throughout his life and to support such Spiritualist periodicals as *The Univercoelum, Spirit Messenger*, and *Herald of Progress*. His most ambitious book, *The Great Harmonia*, was published in five volumes during the 1850s. This tome advanced Davis's grand scheme for societal transformation and made him a leading voice in the abolitionist, women's rights, lyceum, and marriage and health reform movements of the 19th century. His adamant support of abolition alienated him from the Spiritualist movement in the South.

Davis's Harmonial philosophy is an emanationist vision of the universe, with all creative power enthroned in a great spiritual sun and all natural phenomena reflecting eternal forms in the Divine Mind. By developing their spiritual senses in harmony with their physical senses, human beings could come to realize the → correspondences and relationships between the spiritual and the natural worlds and the divine laws and principles that order existence in both realms. Both societal and personal reform in this philosophy came about through a cultivation of harmony with nature, which was seen as the next highest level of existence emanating from the divine center. When persons recognized their places in the divine hierarchy of being, all would operate harmoniously as organs in a single whole, and mutual cooperation would lead to welfare for all living beings. The correspondences of this philosophy with → Neoplatonism, →

Hermetism, Swedenborgianism [→ Swedenborg], and Transcendentalism are obvious.

Davis's vision of children's education derived from his belief that those who died in childhood grew to maturity in the spirit world. The system of education in the "Summerland" for these children was called the lyceum. Davis believed that children held within themselves an image of perfect being and were therefore unlimited in their potentials. The mission of education was not to indoctrinate children into social conventions but to draw out their divine genius through conversation and discussion that was especially geared to each child's mentality and temperament.

In later life, Davis married a women's rights activist from Western New York, Mary Fenn Love. He also moved to distance himself from the physical phenomena associated with the spiritualist séance and to insist on the need for social reform in addition to spirit communication. When widespread fakery and quackery associated with mesmerism resulted in a New York law prohibiting mesmeric healers from practicing medicine, Jackson encouraged his colleagues to gain licenses from legitimate medical colleges. He himself enrolled in the United States Medical College in New York and graduated in 1883 with degrees in anthropology and medicine. Davis spent the last twenty-five years of his life treating patients regardless of their ability to pay from his clinic in Watertown, Massachusetts.

The Magic Staff: An Autobiography, New York: J.S. Brown & Co 1859 (repr. Pomeroy: Health Research 1972) ◆ Beyond the Valley: A Sequel to the Magic Staff: An Autobiography, Boston: Colby & Rich, 1885 ◆ The Great Harmonia, 4 vols., Boston: Benjamin Mussey & Co., 1850 ◆ The Principles of Nature, Her Divine Revelations, and a Voice to Mankind, New York: S.S. Lyon & William Fishbough, 1847 ◆ The Harmonial Philosophy: A Compendium and Digest of the Works of Andrew Jackson Davis, 2nd ed. 1923 (repr. Pomeroy: Health Research n.d.).

Lit.: Catherine Albanese, "On the Matter of Spirit: Andrew Jackson Davis and the Marriage of God and Nature", Journal of the American Academy of Religion 60:1 (1992), 1-17 ◆ Ann Braude, Radical Spirits: Spiritualism and Women's Rights in Nineteenth-Century America, Boston: Beacon Press, 1989, 34-41, 51-55, 71-76, 144-155, 181-182 ◆ Robert C. Fuller, Mesmerism and the American Cure of Souls, Philadelphia: University of Pennsylvania Press, 1982, 96-100 ◆ Frank Podmore, Mediums of the 19th Century, New York: New Hyde Park, University Books, 1963, vol. I, ch. 9.

PHILLIP CHARLES LUCAS

Dee, John, * 13.7.1527 London, † 26.3.1609 Mortlake

1. BIOGRAPHY: FROM HUMANISM TO MAGIC 2. MAGICAL SCIENCE: ASTROLOGY, ALCHEMY, "ARCHEMASTRIE" 3. DEE'S OCCULT PHILOSOPHY: ENOCHIAN MAGIC 4. OCCULTIST AND LITERARY RECEPTION

Humanist, mathematician, geographer, antiquarian, astrologer to Queen Elizabeth I. A cultural traveller on the Continent, including East-Central Europe. One of the most intriguing representatives of occult philosophy [→ occult/occultism] in the late-Renaissance period.

1. BIOGRAPHY: FROM HUMANISM TO MAGIC

Dee was born into a well-to-do textile merchant family which traced its origins to the nobility of Wales. From his father he inherited the intense ambition to fashion himself as a gentleman and conduct his life as near to the court as possible. A way towards this goal was a good education. He pursued university studies at St. John's College, Cambridge, where he received his BA in 1546 and his MA two years later. Among his college fellows he could count the children of the aristocracy newly created by the Tudors. Indeed these youngsters became the key politicians of the future Elizabeth I, and many of them proved to be important patrons of the aspiring scholar.

An interesting episode during Dee's school years was when he constructed a "flying scarabaeus" as a stage prop in a production of Aristophanes' The Peace. The invention later caused him much trouble, since the occasional charges of sorcery leveled against him would not fail to mention this act of "wizardry". Another important preoccupation, Dee's passionate love for books, also manifested itself during his student years: in 1544 he bought the first two volumes of his later legendary library.

After graduation Dee went to Louvain in order to learn about such areas of applied mathematics that were not available at home. He studied geometry and cartography with Gerard Mercator and Pedro Nuñez, and medicine and mathematics with Gemma Frisius. In 1550 he went to Paris where he met a great number of famous humanists, among others Pierre Mondoré, the librarian of the French king, Oronce Finé, professor of mathematics, Pierre de la Ramée, the innovator of logic, and → Guillaume Postel, a scholar of oriental languages who would later experience a magical-enthusiastic turn in his life similar to Dee's "enlightenment". It was in Paris that Dee held a famous lecture on Euclid's geometry, which he later remembered as follows: 'I did undertake to read freely and publiquely Euclide's Elements Geometricall, Mathematicè, Physicè, et Pythagoricè; a thing never done publiquely in any University of Christendome. My auditory in Rhemes Colledge was so great, and most part elder than my selfe, that the mathematicall schooles could not hold them; for many were faine, without the schooles at the windowes, to be auditors and spectators . . .' (*Autobiographical Tracts*, 7).

In the 1550s Dee lived in England as a tutor to children of aristocratic families, including the young king, Edward VI. Although the Catholic Queen Mary did not favour the ardent protestant Dee (he even found himself briefly in prison), this did not prevent the Doctor to propose to the Queen that she should establish a court library by collecting the manuscripts and valuable books dispersed as a result of the dissolution of the monasteries (cf. *Supplication to Queen Mary*). As his proposal remained unanswered, he himself saw to the establishment of a major library. During the next thirty years he devoted most of his income to purchasing books, maps, astronomical and other scientific instruments, until he had at his disposal England's largest private library, consisting of about four thousand volumes, as well as a scientific centre with an observatory and an alchemical laboratory (see the Introduction to *Dee's Library Catalogues*).

1558 was an important year in Dee's life. The accession of Elizabeth returned him to favour, and as a particular sign of this, Dee was entrusted the task of astrologically determining the day of the coronation. In the same year he constructed a mathematical table which was to help the sailors of the Muscovy Company to find the correct location of the North Pole. Most important of all, this year witnessed the publication of his first full-size scholarly book, the *Propaedeumata aphoristica*: a combination of mathematics and → astrology which claimed to provide an improved and corrected system for registering the stellar oppositions for the calculation of astrological charts.

From 1558 through the 1560s Dee's scientific interests broadened and changed: traditional mathematics and astrology were complemented by the neoplatonic-hermetic philosophy of the Florentine Academy also popularized by such "Renaissance magi" as → Francesco Giorgi da Veneto and → Heinrich Cornelius Agrippa. Beside these, another important influence on Dee was that of → Paracel-

sus. Dee was a pioneer in England in recognizing the importance of Paracelsus, and in these years he purchased a remarkably great number of books written by the German doctor or ascribed to him.

Between 1562-1564 Dee embarked on a long Continental journey, visiting Flanders, France, Switzerland and Germany. In Italy he edited an Arabic mathematical treatise with an Italian scholar; in Pressburg (Bratislava) he participated in the coronation of Maximilian II of Habsburg as king of Hungary, and, finally, in 1564 in Antwerp he wrote his major work, the *Monas hieroglyphica*, which appeared from the printing press of the Dutch Willem Silvius and was dedicated to Maximilian. This difficult work has become a basic text of occult-magical literature and is subject to ever new interpretations. In Holland he also came across a manuscript of → Trithemius' *Steganographia*, a work on the possibility of communication with angels. Later on Dee himself became a notable theoretician and practicioner of angel magic.

From the mid-1560s through 1583 Dee again stayed in England, enjoying a growing scholarly reputation and continuing to build his library. In 1578 he married Jane Fromond, who bore him many children and seems to have been a particularly supportive wife. Later that year he briefly travelled in Germany, 'to consult some famous doctors about the Queen's health', and met the German occultist scholar, Leonhard Thurneysser, in Frankfurt an der Oder. This is the time when he acquired his famous house in Mortlake, a village near London in the vicinity of Hampton Court. Four or five rooms were filled with the Doctor's library, and the place functioned as a "private academy" where not only pupils were frequent visitors but also members of the aristocracy, famous explorers, military leaders, members of the government, and occasionally even the Queen herself (on the "Elizabethan think tank" gathering at Dee's house see French 1572 and Sherman 1995, 29-53).

In 1570 Dee published his *Mathematicall Preface*, prefixed to Sir Henry Billingsley's translation of Euclid's *Elements*. Much more than a simple explanation of geometry, it is rather an elevated eulogy of the importance and usefulness of mathematics, including the magical sciences. Later in the same decade, in 1577, he published another important English work, the beautifully illustrated *General and Rare Memorials Pertayning to the perfect Art of Navigation*, which shows another face of the Doctor: the patriotic *homo politicus*, who was deeply concerned with England's advance as a sea power. Simultaneously he also compiled an ornate scroll, establishing the Virgin Queen's rights to the American territories: *Her Majesties title Royall*. It is clear that during these years Dee was much occupied not only with science and → magic but also with what Frances Yates has called "Elizabethan English imperialism", which combined the program of national expansion with religious associations, a reformed Tudor empire (Yates 1975, 84ff.).

Historians of science have noticed with regret that from the early 1580s Dee did not produce anything worthy of the attention of serious scientists. This is when his overtly esoteric period started, with ambitions and ideas that are highly intriguing to contemporary intellectual historians and historical anthropologists. Cultural historians have given various explanations for the development of Dee's interest in the occult. Recurring arguments are his disappointment with the natural sciences, his frustration about self-fashioning himself within the Elizabethan patronage system, and, finally, a growing preoccupation with one particular kind of magic, *scrying*, that led to his "angelic conversations".

According to the biographical evidence, this shift of orientation did not happen all of a sudden; rather, it was related to his changing scholarly and philosophical ideas, prompted, probably, by his discovery of Trithemius' *Steganographia* and the completion of the *Monas hieroglyphica*. What had started as an intellectual change in the 1560s, became a psychic reality by the late 1570s: his diaries relate more and more about strange dreams, sounds, and visions.

The angel magic Dee developed around this time comprised a kind of ritualistic seance during which, with the help of crystal balls and "scryers", he tried to obtain information from spirits and angels (on various techniques of scrying cf. Clulee 1988; Harkness 1999; Szőnyi 2004, Whitby 1988; on Dee's indebtedness to the medieval tradition of *ars notoria*, or Solomonic magic, see Clucas forthcoming). The "angelic conversations" could deal with various themes, ranging from dignified metaphysical questions to everyday problems, but it is important to emphasize that Dee's primary aim with angel magic was to gain a universal knowledge of natural philosophy. The first "full-scale" angelic conversation took place on 22 December 1581, with the help of a medium called Barnabas Saul. Events took a dramatic turn in 1582, when Dee met Edward Kelley, a wandering alchemist who proved to be a perfect medium for the scrying sessions. From this time on Dee needed the conversations on a daily basis and kept a detailed journal about their course, which survives today and is a

fascinating document of early modern esoteric mentality.

In May 1583 a Polish nobleman, Olbracht Łaski arrived in England, where he accomplished a noteworthy program, more cultural than political in nature. His guide was Sir Philip Sidney, the exemplary courtier and Renaissance poet. With him, Łaski witnessed → Giordano Bruno's debate with the Oxford philosophers at the ancient university, after which he was taken to Mortlake to meet Doctor Dee. The encounter determined the future life of Dee, Kelley, and their families. After participating in a few scrying sessions, Łaski suggested that the Englishmen go with him to Poland and try magic and alchemical transmutations there. Dee obtained the Queen's permission, and from 1583 through 1589 he lived on the Continent, pursuing the guidance of the angels as well as trying to gain profitable patronage at various Central European courts.

In 1584 Dee moved his "headquarters" to Prague where he secured an interview with Emperor → Rudolf II, hoping to gain a permanent position as court mathematician. When this failed, he repeatedly visited the Polish king Stephan Batory in Cracow, with the same purpose. After some conflicts during which he and his company were almost arrested by the Catholic Inquisition, and were subsequently expelled from the lands of Rudolf, they got permission to settle in Třeboň, on the estate of Vilém Rožmberk, a prominent Czech magnate and patron of arts as well as → alchemy and magic. There the angelic conferences continued with the occasional participation of the patron, who, however, was clearly more interested in the production of gold. Kelley, who had more experience with alchemical experimentations, soon overshadowed his master and finally Rudolf "borrowed" him back from Rožmberk.

In April, 1587 a rather controversial affair took place: the Doctor and Kelley – who then was trafficking between Prague and Třeboň – 'together with their wives, *nocte profundis*' made a covenant, following the instructions of Archangel Raphael: 'Note and remember that on Sunday the third of May, ann. 1587 (by the new account), I, John Dee, Edward Kelley and our two wives covenanted with God and subscribed to the same, for indissoluble and inviolable unities, charity and friendship keeping between us four, and all things between us to be common, as God by sundry means willed us to do' (*True & Faithful Relation*, 20-1 [new numbering]). As Fenton remarks, 'this new and strange doctrine' of marital cross-matching shows how far Dee was prepared to go in the pursuit of divine knowledge, but he also gives reasons why Kelley may have invented this shocking divine demand: possibly he wanted to bring the angelic conferences to an end – never expecting that Dee would accept the terms (*The Diaries of John Dee*, 209). Even this covenant could not mend the deteriorating relationship between master and medium. Kelley was building his own career in Prague while Dee obviously became homesick for England; in 1589 he finally petitioned Lord Rožmberk to give him permission to return home.

Back in England, Dee, now past sixty, reestablished himself in his Mortlake library, continued to enjoy the favour of Queen Elizabeth, and still had interesting encounters with men of learning, such as the mathematicians Thomas Harriot and William Digges, and the scholar Richard Cavendish. He also met influential persons – among them Walter Raleigh and the Archbishop of Canterbury – and maintained his Continental contacts by corresponding, among others, with Prince Moritz, Landgrave of Hessen-Kassel.

In 1592 Dee submitted an elaborate autobiographical memorandum to Elizabeth. This is known as the *Compendious Rehearsall* that aimed to convince the Sovereign about his knowledge, religious honesty, and strong loyalty to the Queen (see *Autobiographical Tracts*, 1-45). In return Elizabeth covered for him a bill of no less than £ 2306, related to his journey from Germany. In 1595 he received a wardenship in Manchester by Archbishop Whitgift, but he was never happy with that position. Up to 1605 Dee divided his time between Manchester and Mortlake with occasional visits to London. After the death of Elizabeth he sunk into oblivion and, in spite of several petitions, he never managed to attract the interest of James I – not even with his last considerable work, THALATTOKPATIA BPETTANIKH, *sive de Imperii Brytannici Jurisdictione in mari* . . . in which he suggested the extension of Britain's rights for the open seas (for details see Sherman 1995, 192-201).

Due to the plague of 1605 Dee lost his beloved wife and several of their children. Seventy-eight years old, he returned to Mortlake, never to leave the place again. Hard though it may be to believe, he still continued the angelic conversations, now with a medium called Bartholomew Hickman. And as if wanting to restart his life, the doctor still pondered yet another journey, probably to visit the Landgrave Moritz in Germany. The Archangel Raphael actually encouraged him: 'John Dee, thou hast been a traveller, and God hath ever yet at any time provided for thee in all thy journeys. He that hath commanded thee to take this journey in hand,

will provide for thee in Germany, or any other country wheresoever thou goest' (*A True & Faithful Relation*, 37 [new numbering]).

The last entry in the spiritual diaries is from September 1607, but we know from another notebook that Dee still conducted alchemical experiments between December 1607 and January the following year (Oxford, Bodleian, MS Ashmole 1486, cf. *The Diaries of John Dee*, 303). He died on 26 March, 1609, at the end of an extraordinary career that continues to present historians of science and culture with intriguing problems.

2. MAGICAL SCIENCE: ASTROLOGY, ALCHEMY, "ARCHEMASTRIE"

Dee's early career was dominated by mathematics; but already at that time, it was intertwined with mystical-occult concerns, the principal goal of which was to acquire perfect knowledge. His first important work was entitled *Propaedeumata aphoristica*: 'an aphoristic introduction . . . concerning certain virtues of nature' (1558). The work was dedicated to Gerard Mercator, the distinguished mathematician. Although based on the concepts of traditional → astrology, the book attempted to approach prognostication by a strictly scientific method. While the neoplatonist magi of the early Renaissance tried to gain control over the influence of the stars through talismanic magic and ritual incantations, Dee thought of accomplishing this task through mathematically constructed optical mirrors; and for this he needed an exact number of stellar constellations (Clulee, 1988, 39-70). While traditional astrologers usually settled for 120 constellations, Dee's book – which consists of 120 aphorisms – computed the number as 25341. The major setback of this result was that, centuries before the age of megacomputers, calculations with such a quantity could not be carried out. Dee tried to derive astrology from Nature alone, and avoid the danger of demonic intelligences, which haunted even his learned contemporary Giordano Bruno. Next to this seeming rationalism Dee also incorporated elements of the organic natural philosophy and the theory of macrocosmic/microcosmic → correspondences which provided an open gateway toward pythagorean → number symbolism as well as hermetic and magical ideas: 'The entire universe is like a lyre tuned by some excellent artificer, whose strings are separate species of the universal whole. Anyone who knew how to touch these and make them vibrate would draw forth marvelous harmonies. In himself, man is wholly analogous to the universal lyre' (*Aphorism* XI). In this passage, which seems to echo → Ficino, and elsewhere, the modern reader detects the author's longing for a transcendental and universal knowledge, the full vision of which was expanded in Dee's next work, the famous and much discussed *Monas hieroglyphica* (1564).

Dee himself defined the genre of this work as 'a magical parabole'. It consists of a lengthy introduction dedicated to Maximilian II, Holy Roman Emperor, followed by 24 very concise aphorisms or theorems. All these serve the interpretation of "the hieroglyphic monad", a mystical-magical sign, entirely the product of Dee's visual imagination. The monad incorporates the simplest geometrical elements: a circle with a point in its centre on top, two straight lines crossing each other in right angle under it, two touching semi circles at the bottom and all enclosed by an oval. Dee constructed it with the intention of condensing all the natural and supernatural → correspondences of the Cosmos into one single sign which would provide the beholder with a complete understanding of the created universe. In the Preface he emphasized that the monad was to be 'mathematically, magically, cabbalistically, and anagogically explained' (Josten ed. 1964, 155). The theorems elucidate the cosmic image on two levels. On one level, they explain how its elements and proportions express in a mystical but at the same time strictly "scientific" manner the ultimate cause of the World, the Oneness. The theorems make clear how all principal numbers can be derived from the geometrical elements in the core of the diagram. Dee also elucidates how these elementary figures can be used to generate all the signs of the planets as well as the metals, thus referring to the major spheres of the universe (macro- and microcosms).

On the second level the monad refers to the Magus, regarded as an experimenting scientist, emphasizing his potential to recreate the lost unity of existence. This layer of meaning stands in close relation to the alchemical significance which is alluded to by Dee when he identifies the two semi-circles with the Zodiacal sign of Aries, a fire sign bringing about the alchemical transmutation. This process naturally includes the spiritual transformation of the operating Magus as well. The oval frame of the image stands for the Egg of the Philosophers, the alembic in which the alchemical process is taking place. In the sign's basic pattern one can recognize the sign of Mercury, the key element of alchemy which at the same time has astrological importance. In *Theorem* XVIII, Dee calls attention to the interrelatedness of astrology and alchemy; he calls alchemy '*astronomia inferior*'.

In sum: considering the two layers of meaning we can see the hieroglyphic monad as an astrological cosmogram on the one hand, and as a talismanic summary of the alchemical transmutation on the other. The latter plane of reference entails the deification of man the Magus, i.e. the doctrine of *exaltatio*. The creation of the quintessential Mercury is nothing else but the liberation of the human spirit, the elevation of the operator's soul to the sphere of perfect knowledge. Dee's philosophical originality lies in the graphic construction of the monad (no identical diagram can be identified from earlier literature), while on the conceptual level he follows and elaborates the magical → neoplatonism of the Florentine Academy, primarily Ficino's *De vita*, which itself reaches back to Plato, Plotinus, Pythagoras, the Hellenistic "neoplatonici" and, last but not least, the lore of the *Corpus hermeticum*. Considering the possible employment of the hieroglyphic monad, one has to conclude that it was not simply meant to serve or illustrate a discursive and logical explanation; rather it was meant to conjure up a condensed mystical image, the purpose of which was to lead the meditating beholder to revelative illumination. The working of such revelative images might be compared to the Eastern practice of using mandalas (on the theory of revelative images see Gombrich 1972, 157-60; on interpretations of the Monad, see Clulee 1988, 75-143; Harkness 1999, 77-90; Josten in Dee 1964, 102-108; Szőnyi 2001 & 2004, Yates 1964, 148-150).

Although the *Mathematicall Preface* (1570) is usually considered to be a conservative summary of Dee's earlier scientific theories, in this work Dee in fact took a step further. This becomes clear when looking at his explanation of a discipline called "archemastrie". In the *Preface* Dee created a hierarchy of sciences which culminated in this discipline: 'This Arte, teacheth to bryng to actuall experience sensible, all worthy conclusions by all the Artes Mathematicall purposed, & by true Naturall Philosophie concluded. . . . And bycause it procedeth by Experiences, and searcheth forth the causes of Conclusions, by Experiences: and also putteth the Conclusions them selves, in Experiences, it is named of some, Scientia Experimentalis' (A.iijᵛ). This passage has often been cited by historians of science as proof that Dee was concerned with the experimental and practical disciplines and, what is more, advocated science in the vernacular; accordingly, he could be regarded as an important forerunner of the Scientific Revolution. But if Dee's "Scientia Experimentalis" is seen within the wider context of the *Mathematicall*

Preface, it becomes clear why such a conclusion must be regarded with caution. While introducing the chief auxiliary sciences of *Archemastrie*, Dee enlisted the following disciplines: 'the Science Alnirangiat, great Service. Under this, commeth Ars Sintrillia, by Artephius, briefly written. But the chief Science, of the Archemaster, as yet knowen, is an other OPTICAL Science: whereof, the name shall be told when I shall have some (more just) occasion, thereof, to Discourse (ibid.)'. Although Dee never seems to have given a clear definition of optics as he understood it, it has been suggested, by Clulee and others, that for him these sciences were part of magical activity rather than of experimental natural science. There is reason to suspect that optics meant "scrying" (crystal gazing), which by 1570 definitely entered the horizon of Dee's interest. And the purpose of this kind of optical magic, of course, was to attain a supreme superhuman knowledge.

Dee's burning desire to have a glimpse of the mysteries of Creation had a background similar to that of the Florentine neoplatonists and, later on, of Johannes Trithemius, Cornelius Agrippa, Paracelsus, Guillaume Postel, Giordano Bruno, and → Robert Fludd: it reflects the new self-consciousness of Renaissance Man who considered himself God's almost equal partner and who claimed his share of the secrets of Nature.

3. DEE'S OCCULT PHILOSOPHY: ENOCHIAN MAGIC

We have seen that, all along, Dee's career was characterized by the pursuit of perfect knowledge; and this ambition finally crystallized into his search for the *lingua adamica*, the antedeluvian perfect language, from the time of his construction of the hieroglyphic monad. It is only recently that Nicholas Clulee and Umberto Eco have perceived in the *Monas hieroglyphica* the germs of Dee's later explorations into the universal, angelic language (Clulee 1988, 71-116, Eco 1995, 186-189). In the *Theorem*s Dee manipulated the Monad in various ways (rotation, dismantling, combination and permutation of its elements), not unlike the way in which kabbalistic numerology works with the letters of the Hebrew alphabet. Already Guillaume Postel had suggested that the characters of the three sacred languages derive from a common geometrical base (Eco 1995, 188), and Dee entertained the same idea. It seems that he constructed the Monad not only as a mystical emblem for contemplation, but also as a "geometrical automaton" which could generate the alphabet of all languages and would thus represent the universal principle of

language (for a detailed analysis of the pertinence of the *lingua adamica* to Dee's thought see Håkansson 2001, 84-109 and Szőnyi 2004).

From this point on, Dee's thinking became more and more imbued with a spiritual-cosmic vision, and eventually he turned away entirely from the exact sciences. He became convinced that knowledge based on discursive logic and "booklearning" could not lead to the ultimate and universal comprehension for which he was striving. In 1584 he straightforwardly told this to Emperor Rudolf II, when the monarch gave him an audience in the Prague Hradčany: 'All my life I had spent in learning: but for this forty years continually, in sundry manners, and in divers Countries, with great pain, care, and cost, I had from degree to degree sought to come by the best knowledge that man might attain unto in the world: and I found that neither any man living, nor any Book I could yet meet withal, was able to teach me those truths I desired and longed for: And therefore I concluded with my self, to make intercession and prayer to the giver of wisdom to send me such wisdom, as I might know the nature of his creatures; and also enjoy means to use them to his honour and glory' (*A True & Faithful Relation*, 231). This speech confirms what he had admitted to his secret diary already in 1581, spelling out that after his failure to find 'radical truths' in the Book of Nature the only way for the scholar of universal wisdom remained to pray to God directly for an 'Extraordinary Gift . . .' (*Mysteriorum Libri Primus*, Sloane MS 3188, published by Whitby 1988, vol. 2).

This Gift was to be similar to Enoch's privileged knowledge, revealed to him by God, of the angelic language (see Gen. 5:24, Heb. 11:5, and the pseudepigraphical Books of Enoch). On the one hand Dee became convinced that Adam's language was a perfect medium to obtain directly from God the kind of knowledge he was craving (see Genesis 1:26-7 and 2:19), on the other he also shared the belief of many Renaissance philosophers that the Holy Scripture offered promise and hope for Man's regaining the dignity lost at the time of the Fall, provided the angelic language would be restored to humankind (see Psalm 8:4-6, Wisdom 7:15-21 and Sir. 17:3-7; the biblical background of Dee's angelic conversations was clarified by Whitby 1988, vol. 1). From these Biblical passages the early modern thinker could infer that by recovering this lost sacred language all his ambitions and desires concerning *exaltatio* could be fulfilled. This train of thought is the key to Dee's later scientific and philosophical investigations and there is ample evidence to think that he considered himself second only to Enoch to acquire the *lingua adamica*. Dee's solution was remarkably simple, yet rather unique among the "Renaissance magi": since science was unable to reconstruct the language of angels, one had to contact them and learn it from them directly.

Accordingly, Dee devoted the last decades of his life to this goal. Surprisingly, this scholar who was perfectly intimate with the subtle traditions of intellectual magic of his day, chose a rather primitive method of popular magic to contact the angels, namely scrying, or crystal gazing. This practice of divination [→ Divinatory Arts] was mostly used by village sorcerers in order to find lost property or call on the dead for advice. Inspired by Old Testament stories, Dee worked out a theory according to which the use of the "shew-stone" was to develop into the technology of a grandiose project leading to universal knowledge. His main problem was that personally he saw no visions in the shew-stone, so that he needed scryers, or mediums to communicate with the celestial beings. The sessions required two basic actors: the Magus and the Scryer. The Magus performed the conjurations, chants and prayers which prepared the evocation of Angels and spirits from the shew-stone. It was the Scryer who gazed at the ball, and the apparitions spoke via his tongue. In the case of the tandem of Doctor Dee and Edward Kelley, the Magus also acted also as a scribe, meticulously recording the actions. The most important requisite, thus, was the crystal ball, completed by other instruments, such as the Holy Table and some seals (on the choreography of the scrying sessions see Szőnyi 2004; these are also usefully introduced in Geoffrey James' thematically arranged selection of the spiritual diaries [Dee, James ed., 1994]). The Doctor firmly believed that he had succeeded in establishing the transcendental contact by the help of his medium. In his spiritual diaries he wrote down whatever Kelley dictated to him. Much of this material is still unpublished but the pioneering selection of Meric Casaubon (*True & Faithful Relation . . .*), which had been commissioned by Sir Robert Cotton, represents the character and the complexity of the document very well.

It is certainly not easy to distil the sense of Dee's speculations concerning the perfect language. In the 1970s an Australian linguist, Donald Laycock subjected the angelic language to the most thorough examination so far, and distinguished two layers in it. The specimen of the *lingua adamica* that was communicated through Kelley during the first scrying sessions (known as the *Liber Logaeth*) is rich in repetition, rhyme, alliteration and other patterns characteristic of poetry and magical charms. From this Laycock has concluded that Kelley must have been in trance, "speaking in tongues", when receiving these messages. As opposed to this, the Enochian language received later (*48 claves angelicae*, 1584, partly published in James 1994, 65-103) appears more like a real language, generated from set elements. In Dee's diaries there is a translation provided for these texts, which would allow speculation about its grammar. We also know that these texts were dictated to Kelley letter by letter, as opposed to the earlier trance-like flow of speech. As Laycock suggests, 'this is exactly the type of text produced if one generates a string of letters on some random pattern' (Laycock 1994, 40). Although the Enochian language appears to be very strange, it is not entirely impossible to reconstruct its morphology and syntax. Interestingly, according to Laycock, there is nothing strikingly un-English about the grammar, and he was able to compile an extensive dictionary of more than 2400 words, together with phonology and alphabet. About the transcendental validity of the angelic language, he sceptically suggested that the angels' 'limitations are those of Kelley; their occasional sublimities, those of Dee. If the true voice of God comes through the shewstone at all, it is certainly as through a glass darkly' (op. cit., 64).

The historian cannot avoid asking what we are to make of Dee's Enochian magic. While some practical occultists continue to use his keys and invocations even today, we should, rather, pinpoint Dee's importance in the context of Renaissance ideology, at the crossroads of the new science and the reformed religion. The spiritual diaries enable us to assemble an idiosyncratic mythology about the Fall of Mankind, the glorification of Enoch, and a burning desire for the dignity of man, i.e. *exaltatio* – a drive behind so many magical-esoteric programs. While Dee deserves only a minor place in the history of science, we might say that in the end – by turning directly to the angels – he created an almost perfectly consistent anti-theory of science, that still bemuses us with its coherence and faithfulness to its own premises. Rather than towards the rationalism of the Enlightenment, his system points in the direction of alternative intellectual developments of the Western esoteric tradition hallmarked by → Swedenborg, → Blake, → Yeats, Berdjaev and others.

4. OCCULTIST AND LITERARY RECEPTION

Apart from having a distinguished place in the history of early modern magic, Dee is important as an inspiring model for some modern occult trends as well as many works of literature and art.

The first to reconstruct and try out the Enochian system from Dee's surviving papers was → Elias Ashmole, who attempted a series of seances between 1671 and 1676. Following his example, → Wynn Westcott of the → Hermetic Order of the Golden Dawn included Enochian Calls as required materials for the Adeptus Minor degree. Furthermore, → Aleister Crowley took the Enochian system very seriously and published the (reinterpreted and developed) Calls in his occult journal, *The Equinox* (1909-1913). A further important development in the reception of Enochian magic is found in Anton Szandor LaVey's Church of Satan, developed in California in the 1960s; LaVey's *Satanic Bible* reproduces Crowley's Calls by changing words referring to "the Highest" to the name of "Saitan". Enochian magic features heavily in esoteric internet sites even today.

Dee's "literary career" begins with speculations that he may have been the model for Marlowe's Doctor Faustus or Shakespeare's Prospero (Yates 1979, 115-67). His name is first mentioned in Ben Jonson's *The Alchemist* and Butler's *Hudibras* in the 17th century, but the most exciting chapter of his literary fame has been unfolding since the early 20th century, and today it is in full bloom: in the 1920s the Austrian novelist → Gustav Meyrink – writer of the famous *Golem* – chose Dee as the main character of his novel *The Angel of the West Window*. In 1985 Simon Rees published a novel on Dee, entitled *The Devil's Looking Glass*. Three years later Umberto Eco gave a key episodic role to Dee in his *Foucault's Pendulum*. In 1992 the postmodern mystery writer Peter Ackroyd presented the Doctor as a creator of homunculi in his *The House of Doctor Dee*. The famous film director Derek Jarman not only commemorated Dee in his films *Angelic Conversations* and *Jubilee*, but he also painted Enochian topics and arranged his home garden on the basis of Dee's hieroglyphic principles. One could add to this list Stephen Lowe's play *The Alchemical Wedding* and the opera by John Harle and David Pountney, *Angel Magick*.

"A Supplication to Queen Mary . . . for the Recovery and Preservation of Ancient Writers and Monuments" (1556); London: BL, MS Cotton Vitellius C. VII. fol. 310 [published in *Autobiographical Tracts*, 46-7; and *Dee's Library Catalogue*, 194-195] ♦ *Propaedeumata Aphoristica . . . de praestantioribus quibusdam naturae virtutibus*, London: Henry Sutton 1558; Second edition, London: Reginald Wolfe, 1568; Modern edition by Wayne Shumaker in: *John Dee on Astronomy* ♦ *Monas hieroglyphica*, Antwerp: Willem Sylvius,

1564; Further editions: Frankfurt, 1591; in: Lazarus Zetzner, *Theatrum chemicum*, Strassburg: 1622, 2:191-230; Modern edition: "A Translation of John Dee's *Monas hieroglyphica*, with an Introduction and Annotations", trans. and ed. C.H. Josten [with facsimile of the original], *Ambix* 12 (1964), 112-221 ♦ *Mathematicall Praeface* [to *The Elements of Geometry of Euclid of Megara*, trans. Henry Billingsley], London: John Daye, 1570; Facsimile edition and introduction by Allen G. Debus, New York: Science History Publications, 1975 ♦ *A True and Faithful Relation of What Passed for many Years between Dr. John Dee (. . .), and Some Spirits . . .* (ed. Meric Casaubon) London: T. Garthwait 1659; Reprint: Glasgow: The Golden Dragon Press / The Antonin Publishing Co., 1974 and several other facsimile editions ♦ *Autobiographical Tracts* (ed. James Crossley), Manchester: Chetham Society Publications, vol. 24, 1851 ♦ *John Dee on Astronomy: "Propaedeumata Aphoristica" (1558 and 1568). Latin and English* (ed. and trans. Wayne Shumaker, intr. essay J.L. Heilbron), Berkeley, Los Angeles, London: University of California Press 1978 ♦ *John Dee: Essential Readings* (ed. and intro. by Gerald Suster), Wellingborough: The Aquarian Press, 1983 ♦ *The Heptarchia Mystica of John Dee* (ed. Robert Turner), Wellingborough: The Aquarian Press, 1986 (1rst ed.: Edinburgh: Magnum Opus Hermetic Sourceworks, 1983) ♦ *Mysteriorum libri*, 22 December 1581–23 May 1583, in: Christopher Whitby, *John Dee's Actions with Spirits*, New York: Garland, 1988, vol. 2, 1-408 ♦ *John Dee's Library Catalogues* [with facsimiles] (eds. Julian Roberts & G. Watson), London: The Bibliographical Society, 1990 ♦ *The Enochian Magick of Dr. John Dee* (ed. & trans. Geoffrey James), St. Paul, Min.: Llewellyn Publications, 1994 ♦ *The Diaries of John Dee* (ed. Edward Fenton), Charlbury, Oxfordshire: Day Books, 1998 ♦ Pseudo-Dee, *The RosieCrucian Secrets, Their Excellent Method of making Medicines of Metals also their Lawes and Mysteries* (ed. E.J. Langford Garstin), Wellingborough: The Aquarian Press, 1985.

Lit.: Stephen Clucas, "John Dee's Angelic Conversations and the *ars notoria*: Renaissance Magic and Mediaeval Theurgy", in: Clucas (ed.), *John Dee: Interdisciplinary Approaches*, Dordrecht, Boston, London: Kluwer, forthcoming ♦ Nicholas H. Clulee, *John Dee's Natural Philosophy: Between Science and Religion*, London: RKP, 1988 ♦ Umberto Eco, *The Search for the Perfect Language*, Oxford: Blackwell 1995 ♦ Peter J. French, *John Dee: The World of an Elizabethan Magus*, London: RKP, 1972 ♦ Eugenio Garin, *Lo zodiaco della vita*, Bari: Laterza, 1976 ♦ E.H. Gombrich, "*Icones symbolicae*: Philosophies of Symbolism and their Bearing on Art", in: Gombrich, *Symbolic Images: Studies in the Art of the Renaissance II*, London: Phaidon, 1972, 123-99 ♦ Håkan Håkansson, *Seeing the Word: John Dee and Renaissance Occultism*, Lund: Ugglan, 2001 ♦ Deborah Harkness, *John Dee's Conversations with Angels: Cabala, Alchemy, and the End of Nature*, Cambridge: Cambridge University Press, 1999 ♦ Donald C. Laycock, *The Complete Enochian Dictionary*, York Beach, Maine: Samuel Weiser, 1994 (1rst ed. London: Askin, 1978) ♦ William H. Sherman,

The Politics of Reading and Writing in the English Renaissance, Amherst: University of Massachusetts Press, 1995 ♦ Gy. E. Szőnyi, "Ficino's Talismanic Magic and John Dee's Hieroglyphic Monad", *Cauda Pavonis* 20:1 (2001), 1-11 ♦ idem, *John Dee's Occultism: Magical Exaltation through Powerful Signs*, Albany: SUNY Press, 2004 ♦ D. P. Walker, *Spiritual and Demonic Magic from Ficino to Campanella*, London: The Warburg Institute, 1958 ♦ Christopher Whitby, *John Dee's Actions with Spirits*, New York: Garland, 1988, vol. 1 ♦ Frances A. Yates, *Giordano Bruno and the Hermetic Tradition*, London: RKP, 1964 ♦ idem, *Astraea: The Imperial Theme in the Sixteenth Century*, London: RKP, 1975 ♦ idem, *The Occult Philosophy in the Elizabethan Age*, London: RKP, 1979.

GYÖRGY E. SZŐNYI

Deunov, Peter Konstantinov,
* 11.7.1864 Hadurcha (presently Nikolaevka) (Bulgaria),
† 27.12.1944 Izgreva (Bulgaria)

Deunov was born in a rural Bulgarian village in 1864, and went on to attend the American School of Theology and Science, run by American missionaries in the Danubian city of Svishtov. In 1888 he went to the United States, where he took courses at several Bible colleges and universities, including Boston University. He also became acquainted with several Theosophical and Rosicrucian bodies.

In 1895, Deunov returned to the Bulgarian city of Varna, where in 1896 he published his first book, *Science and Education*. According to his disciples, the Spirit of God descended onto Deunov on March 7, 1897 (Julian calendar), thus making him into one of the Masters of the White Brotherhood, Master Beinsa Douno. In the same year he founded the Society for Enlightening the Bulgarian People's Spirit, and started lecturing on his conversion experience and the White Brotherhood, gathering his first faithful disciples, including Penyo Kirov (1868-1918), Todor Stoimenov (1872-1952), and Georgi Mirkovich (1875-1950) around him. These three disciples attended the first "annual meeting" of the White Brotherhood, held on April 6, 1900 in Varna (Julian calendar: "Meeting of the Chain"). They were later joined by Maria Kazakova (1852-1908).

The Brotherhood spread to most Bulgarian cities, and in 1902 Georgi Mirkovich became the editor of the spiritualist [→ Spiritualism] magazine *New Light*, which changed its name to *Videlina*. Whilst at the start the Brotherhood maintained an interest in spiritualist phenomena, magnetism [→ Animal Magnetism], and phrenology, the focus gradually shifted to a Theosophical [→ Theosophical Society] doctrine, including references to secret Masters and the occult history of humankind, mostly derived from Madame → Blavatsky.

Deunov's very successful lectures in Sofia during World War I ultimately elicited a reaction from the Bulgarian Orthodox Church, accusing him of heresy; its leaders also persuaded the government to exile him to Varna. Deunov's insistence that the ancient Bulgarian heretics, known as → Bogomiles, were part of the White Brotherhood, certainly did not endear him to the Orthodox hierarchy. After the war, however, the Brotherhood met with renewed success, and in 1922 was able to open a school in Sofia, offering a "General Occult Course" and a "Special Occult Course" for the youth. The Orthodox Church reacted again by declaring Deunov "self-excommunicated", and excommunicating some of his leading disciples at the same time.

Under the authoritarian regime of the Democratic Union Party, which came into power in 1923, the large annual meetings of the Brotherhood were banned. Deunov continued his teaching activities, however, launching in 1924 the new magazine *Wheat Grain* (the first editor of which was Georgi Radev, 1900-1940), establishing in 1927 an ashram in Izgreva (near Sofia), and opening a school near the Rila lakes in 1929. In the 1930s, most of Deunov's efforts were focused on the teaching of Paneurhythmy, a discipline which encompassed music, songs and body movements.

In 1936, at the Izgreva ashram, Deunov was assaulted by a political opponent and suffered a brain haemorrhage. After his recovery, however, he supervised the spread of the Brotherhood in the West, and a center under the authority of the Bulgarian community was established in Paris in 1936 by Vittorio (1887-1976) and Annina Bertoli (1912-1989). In 1937, a Bulgarian disciple, Mikhail Ivanov ("Omraam Mikhaël Aïvhanov", 1900-1986), emigrated to France, where he established an independent Universal White Brotherhood. Although several of Deunov's disciples later accused Aïvhanov of having down-played the role of his master, misrepresenting himself as the founder of the Brotherhood, relations between the Bulgarian and the French branches have since become generally friendly, although they remain separate, and in several countries there are competing centers of both branches.

During World War II, bombing raids on Sofia forced the Brotherhood to move from Izgreva to the house of disciple Temelko Gyorev (1896-1990) in rural Murchaevo. Soon after the Soviet invasion of Bulgaria, they returned to Izgreva, where a weakened Deunov died on December 27, 1944. He had appointed no successor, and a Supreme Council took over the leadership of the Brotherhood, which achieved official government recognition in 1948.

Religious liberty was short-lived in the new Bulgaria, however, and state recognition was again withdrawn in 1956. The government then confiscated all of the Brotherhood's properties; several leaders were jailed and the Izgreva buildings were firstly nationalized, and then demolished in 1970. In the same decade of the 1970s, however, the Brotherhood cells, which had continued to operate underground throughout Bulgaria, won a certain degree of acceptance and some public meetings became possible again. In the 1970s and 1980s, expatriate disciples were also able to publish several of Deunov's works in both English and French. After the fall of communism, the Brotherhood again won legal recognition in Bulgaria in 1990, and started rebuilding a "New Izgreva" in 1995.

In the meantime, Deunov had become a popular name in neo-Theosophical and → New Age circles in the United States and Western Europe, and many who are not members of the Bulgarian Brotherhood (nor of its French counterpart established by Aïvhanov) today recognize Deunov as a significant master of Western esotericism. A smaller number of committed disciples still practice the exacting exercises of Paneurhythmy, and regard Deunov as more than simply a brilliant teacher; to them, he is the human embodiment of the White Brotherhood's Master, Beinsa Douno.

Beinsa Douno [P.K. Deunov], *The Master Speaks: The Words of the Great Universal Brotherhood*, Los Angeles & Paris: Sunrise Press & Le Grain de Blé, 1970 ♦ David Lorimer (ed.), *The Circle of Sacred Dance: Peter Deunov's Paneurhythmy*, Shaftesbury (Dorset)/Rockport (Massachusetts): Element, 1991.

Lit.: David Lorimer (ed.), *Prophet for Our Times: The Life and Teachings of Peter Deunov*, Shaftesbury (Dorset)/Rockport (Massachusetts): Element, 1991.

MASSIMO INTROVIGNE

Dianetics → Scientology

Dinter, Art(h)ur, * 27.6.1876 Mühlhausen (Alsace), † 21.5.1948 Offenburg (Baden-Württemberg)

Antisemitic author and one of the early members of Hitler's NSDAP. During the 1920s and 1930s propagator of an "Aryan" Christianity that was "cleansed" of Semitic influences and inspired by gnostic beliefs [→ Gnosticism].

Arthur Dinter was born as son of a Prussian customs official. His mother, Berta Dinter-Hoffmann, who like her husband originally came from Silesia, raised him as a Catholic along with his brother and three sisters, while his father contributed a nationalist perspective. Starting in 1895, Dinter studied physics at the universities of Munich and Strassbourg, receiving his doctorate at Strassbourg in 1903. After a brief career as teacher, he became dramaturg of a theatrical company in Alsace. In 1908 he founded, in Berlin, with two others, the *Theaterverlag des Verbandes deutscher Schriftsteller* (Association of German Dramatists). During these years Dinter developed his *völkisch* (nationalist and racist) and alternative religious sympathies, which would later make him into a propagator of "Aryan" Christianity. The racist philosophy of history of Houston Stewart Chamberlain's *Die Grundlagen des 19. Jahrhunderts* (The Foundations of the Nineteenth Century) – published in 1899 and frequently reprinted – was of paramount importance in Dinter's ideological maturation. His attempts to perform nationalist plays, in order to enhance nationalist feelings in the audience, met with resistance from the audience and colleagues and finally resulted in Dinter's removal from the Association.

From 1914 to 1916 Dinter served as an officer on the Western front. The traumatic experience of the defeat of Germany in 1918 increased Dinter's radical *völkisch* belief in the nefarious Jewish influence which had led Germany to disaster. After the war he joined the influential antisemitic *Deutschvölkischer Schutz- und Trutzbund* (German People's League of Self-Defence), in which he occupied a leading position.

Dinter gained notoriety after World War I as author of a trilogy of literary works (see bibliography). Between 1918 and 1928 more than 365.000 copies were printed. The first and best known part of this trilogy, *Die Sünde wider das Blut* (The Sin against the Blood), had been printed 260.000 times by 1934 and reached an audience of millions of people. In this extremely antisemitic novel Jews are portrayed as a demonic force, trying to subjugate the "Aryan" nations through "racial mixing".

In April 1923 Dinter met with Hitler in Munich and joined the NSDAP. Convinced of the idea that politics, religion and "race" are one, and that the political and moral regeneration of Germany had to be preceded by spiritual-religious regeneration, Dinter founded the *Geistchristliche Religionsgemeinschaft* (Spiritualistic Christian Religious

Community) in November 1927. In this community, later renamed *Deutsche Volkskirche* (German People's Church), Dinter preached his "Aryan" Christianity to his followers. The foundation of this community, intended as a *völkisch*-religious base for Hitler's NSDAP, led to a break with Hitler. Hitler wanted to keep the NSDAP away from sectarian influences, which would only curtail his ambitions of making the organization into a mass-party and hence would hinder his quest for power. Dinter was expelled from the NSDAP in October 1928. In 1937 all activities of the *Deutsche Volkskirche* – which by then had some 70.000 members – were banned by the National-Socialist authorities. In the spring of 1945, Dinter, who by this time had been completely forgotten, fled from the Red Army from Thuringia. Three years later he died in Offenburg.

Dinter's doctrine, which he called *Geistchristentum* (Spiritualistic Christianity), had clear gnostic characteristics. According to Dinter in the beginning there was a world of pure spiritual entities created by God. After a break in this divine sphere a great number of worlds came into being through emanations. The material cosmos is the lowest and most impure of these worlds. However, in this impure cosmos there still exists a part of the divine primeval light, that seeks reunification with God and the decomposition of matter.

The cosmos, according to Dinter, is inhabited by good (pure) and demonic (impure) spirits. Every spirit has the task, by way of a process of "self-purification" (the gnostic motive of self-deliverance), to return to God. In this divine movement the human individual is nothing more than a transitional phase in the process that has to lead to reunification with God. In Dinter's system human races are the carriers of the spirits; they are the vehicles the spirits use to achieve their aims. Good spirits will use the human body to purify themselves in order to finally return to God and transcend the cycle of birth, death and rebirth. Selfish and materialistic spirits, on the other hand, reincarnate only to satisfy their low, demonic urges.

According to Dinter the "Aryans" are the carriers of the good spirits, while the Jews are the embodiment of impure, demonic spirits. They are only after money and sex, and try to corrupt the "Aryans" in order to keep them from achieving their self-purification. This is also evident from the Jewish religion: according to Dinter the Old Testament is nothing but a set of rules created by a demonic God (Jahweh) to cheat and deceive the "Aryans". In Dinter's view Christ (an "Aryan" of absolute purity) came as a messenger from God to push aside the Old Testament and replace it by Christianity and to preach "spiritualisation" ("self-purification") or *Geistchristentum*. Christ's mission however was interrupted by the Jews, who crucified him and falsified his message. For the latter, Dinter holds Paul particularly responsible. It is clear that Dinter's view is heavily influenced by gnosticism; the ancient christian-gnostic view of Christ as a messanger from the benign, a-cosmic God who came to dethrone Jahweh, the demiurge, is evident in his message.

Dinter saw himself with his *Geistchristentum* as a reformer, a second Luther. According to Dinter, Luther had tried to restore idealistic, "Aryan" Christianity, and Dinter saw himself as the person called to "fulfill" Luther's Reformation. Dinter wanted to "cleanse" Christianity of Semitic influences in order to restore "true" Christianity in all its splendor and glory and bring closer the deliverance of "Aryan" humanity. Apart from Luther, Dinter also invoked → Marcion, the 2nd century Christian gnostic, whom he regarded as a precursor.

Dinter's efforts to instigate a total "religious revolution" and to make his church into the new national church were thwarted in the end because of the political realities of the National-Socialist state.

Art(h)ur Dinter, *Die Sünde wider das Blut: Ein Zeitroman*, Leipzig und Hartenstein im Erzgebirge: Verlag Matthes und Thost, 1918 ♦ *Die Sünde wider den Geist: Ein Zeitroman*, Leipzig und Hartenstein: Matthes und Thost, 1920 ♦ *Die Sünde wider die Liebe: Ein Zeitroman*, Leipzig und Hartenstein: Matthes und Thost, 1922 ♦ *Das Evangelium unseres Herrn und Heilandes Jesus Christus*, Langensalza: Emil Kabasch, 1923 ♦ *Das Geistchristentum: Monatsschrift zur Vollendung der Reformation durch Wiederherstellung der reinen Heilandslehre*, Nürnberg: Verlag der Geistchristlichen Religionsgemeinschaft, 1928-1936 ♦ *Die religiöse Revolution: Kampfblatt "Der Deutschen Volkskirche E.V."*, Leipzig: Verlag Deutsche Volkskirche, 1934-1936.

Lit.: Günter Hartung, "Arthur Dinter: Der Erfolgsautor des frühen deutschen Faschismus", in: Günter Hartung & Hubert Orlowski (eds.), *Traditionen und Traditionssuche des deutschen Faschismus*, Halle a.d. Saale: Martin-Luther-Universität Halle-Wittenberg, 1988, 55-83 ♦ Rodler F. Morris, *German Nationalist Fiction and the Jewish Question 1918-1933*, Chapel Hill: University of North Carolina, 1979, 196-444 ♦ Rodler F. Morris & George M. Kren, "Race and Spirituality: Arthur Dinter's Theosophical Antisemitism", *Holocaust and Genocide Studies* 6 (1991), 233-252.

JAN WILLEM DE GROOT

Dionysius Areopagita (Pseudo-), ca. 500

Dionysius Areopagita, a mystical theologian, was so named in the belief, which generally prevailed until the last century, that a body of writings in Greek was produced by Dionysius of Athens, the convert of the Apostle Paul (Acts 17:16-34). In fact, the writings were produced ca. 500 A.D. and probably in Syria. Scholars are not agreed on their author; one possibility is Peter Fuller, Patriarch of Antioch (471-488). The surviving *corpus* includes four treatises (*Celestial Hierarchy, Ecclesiastical Hierarchy, Divine Names* and *Mystical Theology*) and ten letters. Written in a lofty tone with a rich vocabulary and cosmic in scope, they largely represent a fusion of Christian angelology with the → neoplatonism of Proclus († 485) and others. Hierarchy is defined in the *Celestial Hierarchy* III.1 as 'sacred order, knowledge and activity assimilating itself, as far as it can, to the likeness of God (deiformity), and raising itself to its utmost, by means of the illuminations granted by God, to the imitation of God'. The object of hierarchy is assimilation and union of the soul with God. Parallels have been suggested by modern scholars between Dionysius's writing about divinisation through sacred knowledge and enlightenment and → Hermetism, but even if not strictly paralleled in or by "hermetic" literature *per se*, Dionysius believed that supradiscursive knowledge is capable of effecting an ontological transformation in man. For Dionysius, nine orders of angels in heaven and six orders of ministers in the church on earth are like mirrors which receive illumination from God and in turn mediate this illumination to the beings who come below them, with a view to purifying, enlightening, perfecting and thus uniting them with God. In *Divine Names* Dionysius proposes two types of theology: one affirmative, which arises from God's revelation of Himself to creatures but which entails the metaphorical use of names (such as Light or Beauty or Being) for the transcendent Thearchy; the other negative, which arises from the unknowability of God. In seeking deification or union with God, Dionysius starts with the sensible, created world and the material sacraments which provide symbols. But the inadequacies of human concepts and symbols when applied to God render the affirmative way inferior to the negative one, in which the human soul dispenses with the knowledge provided by the senses and by human reason, defines God by negatives (e.g. not light, not beauty, not being but beyond all these), and arrives through not knowing and not understanding at an ineffable union with Him. Because the negative way is superior, Dionysius also preferred dissimilar images of sacred realities (e.g. wild animals) to apparently similar ones (e.g. winged angels with human bodies and perfect faces), in order to highlight the illusory nature of the latter.

His writings, in Greek but translated into other languages (including Latin in the 9th century), have had a profound influence in both the eastern and western churches and were the subject of repeated commentaries in both. One direction to which they pointed was to debate about hierarchy and its role in society, both heavenly and human. But another direction was → mysticism within the traditions of the Catholic church. Mystical theology is the secret knowledge and incommunicable experience of God, non-intellectual and distinct from both natural theology and revealed theology. Two phrases of Dionysius enjoyed great fortune: the 'ray of darkness' and the 'cloud of unknowing' (*Mystical Theology,* chapter 1). His short treatise on *Mystical Theology* was especially influential during the late Middle Ages and in Spain and France during the 16th and 17th centuries. Thomas Gallus (d. 1246), Meister Eckhart (c. 1260-c. 1328), John Tauler († 1361), Ruysbroeck (1293-1381) and the Carthusian Denis Ryckel (1402-1471) drew generously from the *Mystical Theology* as did, in England in the mid-14th century, the author of *The Cloud of Unknowing* who, in addition, translated Dionysius's work into English under the title *Denis Hid Divinity*. St John of the Cross (1542-1591) analysed the successive stages through which the soul passes, of purgation, illumination, and union with God; similarities have been found between *The Cloud of Unknowing* (a work which John probably did not know) and his *Dark Night of the Soul.*

Unlike the medieval commentators, many Renaissance humanists understood that Dionysius was a neoplatonist. They also found connections between divinisation according to Dionysian teaching and traditions of secret → magic deriving from the kabbalah [→ Jewish Influences] and from → Hermetism. → Ficino, who re-translated some of Dionysius's works, is highly important in this context. He drew out more fully the similarities between Dionysius's negative theology and the teaching in the *Asclepius* that God has no name but also has all names, as well as the associations between the Sun's light and the Trinity and between the celestial spheres and the angelic powers. The connection between angelic intelligences and → astrology had long been familiar to the medieval scholastics, influenced as they were from the 13th century by → Avicenna. But Ficino, followed by → Giovanni Pico della Mirandola, → Cornelius

Agrippa, Hannibal Rosseli (fl. c. 1590) and → Giordano Bruno, fostered the association between astral powers, sun magic and the Dionisian hierarchies by turning also to Hermetic and kabbalistic sources.

J.P. Migne, *Patrologia graeca* 3 and 4 (Greek and Latin) ♦ *Dionysiaca: Recueil donnant l'ensemble des traductions latines des ouvrages attribués au Denys de l'Aréopage* (ed. P. Chevallier, OSB), 2 vols., Paris: Desclée de Brouwer, 1937-50 (This also contains the Greek text and a French translation) ♦ *Denys L'Aréopagite, La Hiérarchie céleste* (intr. by René Roques, study and critical edition by Gunther Heil, French trans. and notes by Maurice de Gandillac) (Sources chrétiennes 58 *bis*), 2nd ed., Paris: Les Editions du Cerf, 1970; French trans. with intr. and bibliography by Maurice de Gandillac (Bibliothèque Philosophique), 1945 ♦ English translation, *The Complete Works* (by C. Luibheid and P. Rorem) (Classics of Western Spirituality), New York: Paulist Press, 1987 ♦ Critical ed. by B.R. Suchla, G. Heil, A.M. Ritter, *Corpus Dionysiacum*, 2 vols. (Patristische Texte und Studien 33 and 36), Berlin: De Gruyter, 1990-1.

Lit.: Y. de Andia (ed.), *Denys l'Aréopagite et sa postérité en Orient et en Occident*, Paris: Institut d'Etudes Augustiniennes, 1997 ♦ A. Louth, *Denys the Areopagite*, London: Geoffrey Chapman, 1989 ♦ D. Luscombe, "Denys the Pseudo-Areopagite in the Writings of Nicholas of Cusa, Marsilio Ficino and Pico della Mirandola", *Néoplatonisme et philosophie médiévale* (L.G. Benakis, ed.), Turnhout: Brepols, 1997, 93-107 ♦ René Roques, *L'Univers dionysien: Structure hiérarchique du monde selon le Pseudo-Denys* (Théologie 29), Paris: Aubier, Editions Montaigne, 1954 ♦ René Roques, Maiul Cappuyns and Roger Aubert, "Denys (14) le Pseudo-Aréopagite", *Dictionnaire d'Histoire et de Géographie Ecclésiastiques* 14 (1960), cols. 265-310 ♦ René Roques, *Structures théologiques de la gnose à Richard de Saint-Victor* (Bibliotheque de l'Ecole des Hautes Etudes, Section des Sciences Religieuses 72), Paris: Presses Universitaires de France, 1962 ♦ P. Rorem, *Pseudo-Dionysius: A Commentary on the Texts and an Introduction to their Influence*, Oxford: Oxford University Press, 1993 ♦ S. Toussaint, "L'influence de Marsile Ficin à Paris et le Pseudo-Denys des Humanistes: Traversari, Cusa, Lefèvre d'Etaples", *Bruniana et Campanelliana* 5:2 (1999), 381-414 ♦ C. Vasoli, "L' 'Un-Bien' dans le commentaire de Ficin à la *mystica theologia* du pseudo-Denys", in: *Marsile Ficin: Les platonismes à la Renaissance* (P. Magnard, ed.), Paris: Vrin, 2001, 181-93 ♦ P.M. Watts, "Pseudo-Dyonisius the Areopagite and three Renaissance Platonists: Cusanus, Ficino and Pico on Mind and Cosmos", in: *Supplementum Festivum: Studies in honor of Paul Oskar Kristeller* (J. Hankins, J. Monfasani & F. Purnell, Jr), Binghampton (N.Y.): SUNY Press, 1987, 279-98 ♦ Frances A. Yates, *Giordano Bruno and the Hermetic Tradition*, London: Routledge and Kegan Paul, 1964.

DAVID LUSCOMBE

Divinatory Arts

1. DIVINATION AND THE CLASSIFICATION OF THE DIVINATORY ARTS IN THE MIDDLE AGES
2. PROGNOSTICS AND BOOKS OF LOTS IN THE MIDDLE AGES
(A. PROGNOSTICS B. BOOKS OF LOTS)
3. FROM THE 12TH CENTURY TO THE CONTEMPORARY EPOCH: THE PRINCIPAL DIVINATORY ARTS (A. PHYSIOGNOMY B. CHIROMANCY C. GEOMANCY D. SPATULOMANCY E. CATOPTROMANCY)

Divination, in general, is the art of divining the past, present, and future by means of various techniques. According to Cicero (*De Divinatione*) these can be divided into two main categories: "natural" or "intuitive" divination (*divinatio naturalis*) and "artificial", "inductive", or "reasoned" divination (*divinatio artificiosa*). For Cicero, the revelations bestowed by the gods on men in states of possession (*furor*) or in certain dreams belong to natural divination, whereas inductive or conjectural divination looks at sacred "signs" of whatever kind and submits them to interpretation, a procedure that requires a certain "art". Even though this aspect of interpreting sacred signs disappeared rapidly in the Latin West with the spread of Christianity, the distinction between natural, intuitive divination and artificial, inductive divination remains valid, most of the divinatory methods used belonging to the latter category. It must be emphasized that neither in the Middle Ages nor in later periods divination consisted of an established and coherent body of doctrine; rather, it consisted of a collection of "arts", or techniques, some of which are attested from the High Middle Ages onwards, and may appear to be legacies from classical Antiquity, whilst others did not develop until after the 12th century, with the diffusion of treatises translated either from Arabic or, much more rarely, from Greek.

Recent research into the divinatory methods used during the Middle Ages, and particularly those introduced from the 12th century onwards, presents us with a fairly accurate picture of the main techniques in use during that period, whereas this seems more difficult for the modern and contemporary periods. Therefore the emphasis here will be, first, on the conception and classification of the divinatory sciences in the Middle Ages; next, on the methods used in the High Middle Ages; and finally, on a certain number of techniques which have persisted with more or less success from the 12th century to the present. This study excludes

some techniques that enjoyed an important independent development and are no longer seen as
belonging to the field of divinatory arts, such as →
astrology, oneiromancy, and necromancy, the latter
being classified within the field of → magic.

1. DIVINATION AND THE CLASSIFICATION OF THE DIVINATORY ARTS IN THE MIDDLE AGES

The medieval concept of divination is essentially
based on the chapter that Isidore of Seville (circa
560-636) devotes to the magicians (*magi*) in his
Etymologies (*Etymologiae*, Book VIII, chapter IX
De magis). This chapter, the elements of which
recur in many medieval treatises, assimilates divination with magic, and as such has undoubtedly
been responsible for subsequent confusion between
magic and divination and for their common condemnation, as frequent in the Middle Ages as in the
modern era. However, the canons of the Church
Councils of the 4th, 5th, and 6th centuries, while
condemning both of them, often took care to distinguish between divination (*divinatio*) and the
magical art (*ars magica*). For example, the Synod of
Agde (506) included within the science of divination (*divinationis scientia*) auguries (*auguria*), lots
(*sortes*), and dreams (*somnia*).

Like the whole of the *Etymologies*, the chapter
De magis makes no effort at coherent organization,
but assembles information culled from various
ancient Greek and Latin authors: those of late
Antiquity, such as Tertullian (circa 155-220), or
Church Fathers such as → Augustine (354-430)
and Jerome (circa 342-420). As regards divination,
Isidore first adopts the distinction established by
Varro (116-27 B.C.) between four types of divination that make use of the four elements of earth,
water, air, and fire, respectively known as geomancy (*geomantia*), hydromancy (*hydromantia*),
aeromancy (*aeromantia*), and pyromancy (*pyro-
mantia*). Isidore's next paragraph borrows simultaneously from Augustine and Cicero. He states first
that those who practice divination are called diviners (*divini*), as if they were 'filled with God' (*quasi
Deo pleni*); assimilating themselves to divinity, they
fraudulently predict the future. Then, following
Cicero, Isidore distinguishes two types of divination, *ars* and *furor*, giving the definition of a series
of terms, some of which derive from divination,
others from magic, while most denote magical
and divinatory practices belonging to Antiquity:
haruspices (*aruspices*), augurs (*augures, auguria*),
auspices (*auspicia*), pythonesses (*pythones*),
astrologers (*astrologi, genethliaci, mathematici,*

horoscopi), and casters of lots (*sortilegi*). This last-
mentioned term belonged to the vocabulary of divination at least until the 10th century, and applies
to those who try to predict the future by consulting
books of lots. Thus in the 7th century (Council of
Narbonne, 619) and the 8th century (capitulary of
769) it is associated with the terms *divinatores*
and *divini* (diviners). The anti-divinatory literature
that developed after the introduction of Arab
astrology into the Latin West still continued to condemn, along with magic and astrology, which were
its main target, all the divinatory techniques
described by Isidore of Seville, sometimes adding
physiognomy, chiromancy, and geomancy. John of
Salisbury (circa 1115-1180), in his *Policraticus*,
adds nothing to Isidore's picture and invariably
sees in divination, as in magic, the work of
demons. Hugh of St. Victor († 1141), in his *Didas-
calicon*, distinguishes magical practices (*praestigia*
and *maleficia*) from the various divinatory arts,
and particularly from astrology. Mantics or divination (*mantice quod sonat divinatio*) itself contains five types (*species*): necromancy, which is
divination through the dead; geomancy, divination through the earth; hydromancy, divination
through water; aeromancy, divination through air;
and pyromancy, divination through fire. Hugh
divides mathematics (*mathematica*) into three
types: haruspicy (*aruspicina*), auguries, and horoscopes (*horoscopica*). In the 13th century, Thomas
Aquinas (1224/5-1274), especially in his *Summa
theologica*, likewise dissociates divination from
magic but invariably forbids its use, since for him
all divination proceeds from the operation of
demons. Again, in the 14th and 15th centuries,
neither Nicole Oresme (circa 1320-1382), in *Le
Livre de divinacions* (Book of divinations) written
around 1356, nor Laurent Pignon (circa 1368-
1449), in his treatise *Contre les devineurs* (Against
the diviners) written around 1411, deviate much
from this position.

These various classifications, which mostly refer
to the types of divination used in Greek and Latin
Antiquity, only cover a small part of the types that
were practiced during the Middle Ages. Setting
aside the treatises of astrology and oneiromancy
which are not our concern, the surviving texts of
the Middle Ages belong to two different traditions.
On the one hand we have a literature of prognostics in Latin or the vernacular, stemming from the
10th to the 15th century and mostly comprising
short texts, to which can be added a few books of
lots; on the other, actual treatises explaining the
methods of one or another divinatory technique, in
Latin or in a few cases in the vernacular, from the

12th century onwards. From the present state of research it appears that the only arts that were particularly studied, if not the only ones practiced, during the Middle Ages were physiognomy, chiromancy, geomancy, and to a lesser extent scapulomancy and catoptromancy.

2. Prognostics and Books of Lots in the Middle Ages

A. Prognostics

There are several different types of prognostics, nearly all constructed on the same model. The manuscript prognostics that begin with the 1st of January, of which the oldest go back to the 10th century, attribute their texts sometimes to the Venerable Bede, sometimes to Esdras, and in a slightly different version to → (pseudo) Dionysius Areopagita. These Latin texts, of which several French versions exist both in prose and verse, give information for each day of the week, from Sunday onwards, on which the year can begin; they give general indications on what the weather will be in each season, on the abundance of harvests and vintages, on the sicknesses that will afflict men and animals, and on events of collective import such as wars or epidemics.

On the same model, in the Latin and French manuscripts we also find prognostications for the coming year, sometimes attributed to Ezekiel, based on the day of the week on which Christmas falls, together with a short text on the significance of the winds that blow on Christmas Day, depending on the direction from which they come.

We also find prognostics in the Latin and vernacular manuscripts based on the day of the lunar month, following two types: either giving general indications of the actions to be undertaken, or avoided, on the 1st, 2nd, 3rd, etc. day of the lunar month, or, in addition to these, explications of the character and destiny of a man or woman (under two separate rubrics) born on these days, which refer more specifically to astrological physiognomy.

Another group of prognostics, in Latin and vernacular languages, concerns thunder, according to the day of the month or week when it is heard, and the direction from which it comes. These prognostics generally give indications of a meteorological and agricultural nature for the coming month or week. The quite numerous texts on "Egyptian Days", or more generally on "dangerous" days for undertaking some action, belong more to astrology.

B. Books of Lots

Among the surviving medieval books of lots, one can distinguish several types of work. Aside from the *sortes sanctorum* or *apostolorum,* based on choosing by lot passages from the Scriptures, of which few manuscripts exist, the books of lots or books of judgments all work on the same principle: a series of general questions (success of a voyage, outcome of an illness, conception or birth of a child, etc.) is linked to answers classed under rubrics of varying titles, e.g. proper names (generally with an Arabic sound), names of flowers, or animals. The manner of use is not always specified, and it seems that in certain cases the choice of an answer to the question depended on a throw of dice. There is another group of texts, often very brief, that are onomantic in character, in which the answer is obtained from the sum of numerical values attributed to the letters of the questioner's name, and from what remains after dividing this sum by a given number, the remainder referring to groups of prognostic tables.

We should also mention the medical-astrological spheres attributed to Pythagoras, Petosiris, or Apuleius, which are Greek in origin and were diffused in the West from the 9th century onwards, whose prediction system rests on numerological criteria. This type of treatise seems to persist in the modern age in the form of predictions in almanacs and booklets belonging to so-called "popular" literature. From the 12th century onwards, beside these books of lots and prognostics, we see the introduction and development in the Latin West of a certain number of divinatory methods whose transmission rests on an important tradition, first through manuscripts, then in print.

3. From the 12th Century to the Contemporary Epoch: The Principal Divinatory Arts

A. Physiognomy

Physiognomy belongs within the field of divination insofar as it claims to predict a person's destiny from his facial traits, the general look of his body, or the patterns of lines in his palm. Chiromancy, properly speaking, is only a subdivision of physiognomy, but treatises entirely devoted to this divinatory art have circulated since the Middle Ages. Physiognomy only developed in the West from the 12th century onwards, with the introduction of Greek and Arab science via the first Latin translations. Thus Western physiognomy stems from two different traditions, Greco-Latin and Arab.

Physiognomy was certainly born in Greece, the first treatises claiming Pythagoras or Hippocrates as its founder. Although the latter's works contain no physiognomy as such, they justify its use by their insistence on the close interdependence of the soul and the body. The first surviving treatise on physiognomy is attributed to Aristotle; those of Loxus and Polemon of Laodicea (or Palemon, 2nd century A.D.) are lost. There is in fact an Arabic translation of Polemon's treatise, probably made at the beginning of the 9th century, but neither this nor the abbreviated version made by the Jewish physician Adamantius in Alexandria during the 4th century was transmitted to the Latin West. The only treatises that reached the Latin West from classical Antiquity are that of Pseudo-Aristotle, translated directly from the Greek circa 1260 by Bartholomew of Messina at the request of King Manfred of Sicily, and an anonymous compilation attributed to Apuleius, probably translated from the Latin by the end of the 11th century. According to both Pseudo-Aristotle and Pseudo-Apuleius, the procedures for making a physiognomic judgment is to take account of a person's behavior, his resemblance to some animal, his belonging to one people or another, and also his sex, and then to examine in turn the various parts of his body, beginning with the legs and ending with the face.

The Arabic treatises form the second source of Western physiognomy. The Arabs were aware very early on of Polemon of Laodicea's treatise in a translation by an unknown author. Their physiognomy developed in two directions: the naturalist tradition, akin to medical interests, with the *Secretum secretorum* (Secret of Secrets) and part of the *Liber Almansoris* (*Kitâb al-firâsa*) of Rasis; and the astrological physiognomy represented in most of the treatises of astrology. Rasis devoted the second book of his *Liber Almansoris* to the study of the different temperaments and their signs. In the Latin translation by Gerard of Cremona (1114-1187), dating from 1187, this book contains 58 chapters. After showing how to diagnose the temperament by examining the color and shape of the face, the general aspect and that of the various members, Rasis reviews the characteristic physical signs of the different temperaments, then treats the signs of each member and draws up the portraits of several types of individual. The *Secretum secretorum* (also known under the title *Letter to Alexander*) is a compilation in Arabic that is probably quite late (11th-12th century), existing in both a short and a long version. Only the latter, translated into Latin by Philip of Tripoli at the beginning of the 13th century, contains a physiognomic section. Edited and

commented upon around 1257-1267 by → Roger Bacon, this work was attributed during the Middle Ages to Aristotle, probably thanks to → Albertus Magnus. Its physiognomic section is inspired both by Polemon and by Rasis: the goal of physiognomy is not the search for acquired characteristics, but for natural dispositions. The author reviews the general aspect of man and studies the signs of the different parts of the face and body. In addition, most of the Arab astrological treatises, such as those of Haly Abenragel or Abraham ibn Ezra, expound an astrological physiognomy: a physical and moral type, described at length, corresponds to each planet and to each sign of the zodiac.

The original production of the Latin Middle Ages rests mainly on four treatises: those of Pseudo-Apuleius, Pseudo-Aristotle, Rasis, and the *Secret of Secrets*. However, there are two works that predate these Latin translations: that of Gilles de Corbeil, physician to Philip Augustus, and that of → Michael Scot, whose *Liber phisonomie* (Book of physiognomy) probably derived from the Greek tradition via Arab sources. The most striking treatises are those of Albertus Magnus and, above all, of → Peter of Abano, completed towards 1295, who for the first time introduces astrology into the Latin physiognomic tradition; but we should also mention Michele Savonarola, who in the *Speculum physionomiae* (Mirror of physiognomy), circa 1450, prefaces his physiognomic study with an anatomical description of the relevant parts of the body.

The success of physiognomy did not wane in the modern and contemporary epochs. It was especially popular in the periods from the beginning of the 16th century until the second third of the 17th, and from the 1780s until the middle of the 19th century. The work of Bartholomaeus Cocles, *Chyromantiae ac physionomie Anastasis* (Awakening of chiromancy and physiognomy), published in Latin in Bologna, 1504, was translated into Italian in 1531, and into German, French and English in 1550. That of Giovanni Battista della Porta (1538-1615), *De humana physiognomia* (On human physiognomy), published in Latin in 1586, translated into French in 1655 and reissued in 1665 under the title *De la phisionomie humaine*, remarkable for its extent and its exhaustiveness, dominates an abundant 16th-century production. The principle at the heart of 16th-century physiognomy was that of the analogy between the human microcosm and the macrocosm, although there was a noticeable separation of physiognomy from astrology in the last years of the 16th century, after the papal bull *Caeli et terrae creator* of Sixtus V (1520-

1590) in 1586 condemned the divinatory sciences. The naturalist tradition stemming from Aristotle then overtook the astrological and divinatory tradition. This new tendency is illustrated in 1660 by the appearance of the treatise by Louis XIV's physician, Martin Cureau de la Chambre (1596-1669), *L'Art de connoistre les hommes* (The art of knowing men), which contains no astrological element whatever. But the major event in the history of physiognomy during the 17th century was the *Conférences sur l'expression des passions* (Lectures on the expression of the passions), a series of lectures given by the painter Charles Le Brun (1619-1690) before the Royal Academy of Painting and Sculpture. Le Brun no longer held that the face is the mirror resembling the soul, but saw it as the physical expression of its passions. Physiognomy suffered a decline in the 18th century, despite the success of the *Lettres philosophiques sur les physionomies* (Philosophical letters on physionomies) published in 1746, which rejected comparative or zoomorphic physiognomy. It revived at the end of the century with → Johann Caspar Lavater (1741-1801), whose four-volume *Physiognomische Fragmente zur Beförderung der Menschenkenntnis und Menschenliebe* (Physiognomic fragments for the furthering of the knowledge and love of man), published between 1775 and 1778 and translated into French as *Essais sur la physiognomie destinés à faire connaître l'homme et à le faire aimer*, met with success as well as hostility throughout Europe. Lavater's volumes, synthesizing all the tendencies and the whole history of physiognomy, remain the reference work in this field.

B. CHIROMANCY

Chiromancy has as its goal the prediction of the future or the divining of a person's character through studying the palm of the hand, and more particularly its lines. Although this technique is probably of ancient origin, either Greek or Latin, as attested by a number of references to texts attributed to Artemidorus, Pollux, or Suidas, no ancient treatise on chiromancy has been preserved in either language. The only known treatise in Greek appears in two manuscripts dating respectively from the 13th and 15th centuries.

In the Latin West, chiromancy did not appear before the middle of the 12th century. John of Salisbury, in his *Policraticus,* alludes to it as a new form of divination. Although chiromancy claims justification from the Bible (Job 37:7), its sources are of Arab origin, particularly a short work attributed to Rasis, *Knowledge of the Lines of the Hand.* Chiromancy is present in several medieval treatises

on physiognomy, but it also circulated in books devoted to it alone. Two of these, attributed to Aristotle, were printed in Ulm as early as 1490. Two others go under the name of Albertus Magnus, and numerous anonymous works show that the practice of this art was widespread. These treatises study only the three principal lines of the hand (life-line, median line, and mensal line), or the four lines (these, plus the base of the triangle), or else the four lines and the "mounts" that separate them. Most of these texts are very brief and technical, detailing the study of the various lines of the hand, the angles formed between them, and the mounts. The set of → correspondences established between the bodily organs and the lines of the hand allows for multiple interpretations. The interpretation becomes even more complicated when, certainly before the end of the 14th century, astrological correspondences enter this field (like that of physiognomy), relating the parts of the hand to the various planets. Some texts draw virtual portraits of people as a function of the importance of the line attributed to a certain planet.

During the 16th and 17th centuries, chiromancy was always associated with physiognomy. This was the case, for example, in Bartholomaeus Cocles's treatise *Chryomantiae ac physionomie Anastasis cum approbatione magistri Alexandri de Achillinis,* published in Bologna, 1504; and also in John of Indagine's *Introductiones apotelesmaticae in chyromantiam, physiognomiam, astrologiam naturalem, complexiones hominum naturas planetarum* (Astrological introductions to chiromancy, physiognomy, natural astrology, human complexions, and the natures of the planets) first published in Latin in Strasbourg, 1522, and frequently reissued. This work appeared in French in 1662 (*La Chiromancie et physiognomie par le regard des membres de l'homme*) under the name of Jean de Hayn. The case was the same with the treatise of Jean Bebot, published in Paris, 1619, *Instruction familière et très facile pour apprendre les sciences de chiromancie et physiognomie* (Familiar and very easy introducion for learning the sciences of chiromancy and physiognomy), and that of Martin Cureau de la Chambre, *L'Art de connoistre les hommes,* published in Amsterdam, 1660. However, Cureau's book was one of the last treatises of this type, associating physiognomy, metoposcopy (study of the forehead), and chiromancy, before Lavater, in his *Physiognomische Fragmente,* definitively separated chiromancy from physiognomy. Even so, chiromancy remained extremely widespread, and it certainly still ranks among the most popular divinatory methods.

C. GEOMANCY

Geomancy is a divinatory technique which took on, in the West, the name of one of the four types of divination defined by Varro after the four elements (see section 1, above). It was introduced to the Latin West in the 12th century by way of translations of Arabic works. It did not aim, as did ancient geomancy, at the interpretation of the earth's "movements", such as earthquakes and volcanic eruptions, but rather at knowledge of the past, present, and future through interpretation of a "theme", consisting of "houses" in which are placed "figures" formed by the combination of even and odd markings in four columns, each figure containing four to eight points. These figures, originally drawn on sand or earth on the basis of points cast at random with the finger or a stick, and later on paper with pen and ink, are sixteen in number, comprising eight couples of complementary or opposing figures: *Via/Populus, Conjunctio/Carcer, Fortuna Major/Fortuna Minor, Acquisicio/Amissio, Laeticia/ Tristicia, Puer/Puella, Albus/Rubeus, Caput/Cauda*. Certain qualities, properties, and meanings are attributed to each figure and to each house.

The first twelve geomantic houses, assimilated to the astrological ones, soon found the significations of the latter ascribed to them. Only the four last houses have strictly geomantic meanings, being called respectively the houses of the witnesses, of the judge, and of the over-judge. In geomantic treatises, the prognostications that answer the questions are generally grouped by houses according to their subject, and drawn from the combination of the respective properties and meanings of the figures and the houses.

The first Latin treatises are presented as translations of Arab texts, but it seems that their Arabic originals are lost. The oldest surviving text in Arabic is that of Abû Abdallâh az-Zanâti. Cited by Ibn Khaldûn in his 14th-century *Prolegomena*, this work, very likely dating from the 12th or 13th century, is in use to this day in the countries of the Maghreb and black Africa, as well as in Madagascar. There is also a tradition of Arab geomancy in Hebrew, certain Arab treatises only surviving in their Hebrew translations. These medieval translations seem to have been the work of the Jewish community settled in Spain, and especially in Toledo. Hebrew may therefore have played a role in the transmission of Arab geomancy to the Latin world. Arab geomancy is equally the probable origin of the development of geomancy in the Byzantine empire from the 13th century onwards, although the work of Nicholas of Otranto, for example, borrows much from the first Latin treatise on geomancy, that of Hugh of Santalla.

The first geomantic treatises in Latin, Hugh of Santalla's *Ars geomancie*, and the treatise known by its incipit as *Estimaverunt Indi*, which certain manuscripts attributed to Gerard of Cremona date from the 12th century and, as said, are presented as translations from the Arabic. They already explain the essentials of geomantic technique as it would be practiced in the West: the casting of points, formation of the "theme", significance of the figures and houses, elements of interpretation, examples of resolving geomantic questions. Astrology, closely associated with geomancy, is already present: the figures are connected to the planets and the signs of the zodiac; the meanings of the first twelve geomantic houses are those of the astrological houses; the geomancer is to take account in his interpretation of the aspects formed between the figures. The later medieval treatises, by Gerard of Cremona, Bartholomew of Parma, William of Moerbeke, John of Murs, and Rolandus Scriptoris, present few differences on a technical level, although the role of astrology tends to increase. Most of these Latin treatises were translated into the vernacular from the 14th century onwards: into German, French, Provençal, English, or Italian. Surviving inventories of medieval libraries bear witness to the existence of a large number of geomancies in the vernacular, showing that this divinatory technique was widespread beyond the restricted circles of the learned. Several original treatises appeared in the 16th century and even later, such as those of Christophe de Cattan in French, Bartholomaeus Cocles in Italian, → Heinrich Cornelius Agrippa, and → Robert Fludd; but eventually geomancy seems to have become no more than a curiosity for the erudite.

Beside these divinatory arts, which are in a sense the major ones and essentially derive from the written tradition, mention may also be made of some other divinatory methods whose practice has left few written traces, and whose importance is often difficult to evaluate: besides spatulomancy and catoptromancy (see below), examples are onychomancy (divination from the fingernails), crystallomancy, and pyromancy.

D. SPATULOMANCY

Spatulomancy (from Latin *spatula,* shoulderblade) is a divinatory technique practiced by interpreting the "signs" (lines, marks, grooves, etc.) found on the right shoulder-blade of a sheep. Its use is attested in many cultural areas and over very different epochs. In the Latin West, the first known

treatises were written in Arabic in Spain, then
translated into Latin in the first half of the 12th
century. We have four different Latin treatises, two
of which were translated by Hugh of Santalla, who
dedicated them before 1151 to Michael, Bishop of
Tarazona. This new technique then spread all over
Europe, but its practice does not seem to have given
rise to much literature.

E. CATOPTROMANCY

Catoptromancy, divination by the mirror, probably appeared in Greece as early as the 6th century
B.C., and was then diffused through East and West.
A. Delatte distinguishes two principal forms. In the
first, 'no appeal is made to any supernatural force,
and one is content to use the somehow magical
property possessed by reflective surfaces to foster
the imagination'. The hidden persons, things, or
events that form the object of the consultation
appear in the mirror before the eyes of the consult-
ant, the diviner, or a third party acting as medium.
In the second form of catoptromancy, the revelation 'is procured through signs or words from
supernatural beings – gods, angels, or demons –
whose appearance in the mirror is solicited by magical or religious rituals'. It is this second type that
developed in the Middle Ages and the modern
epoch, but without giving rise, so it seems, to the
writing of real treatises. The practice was mentioned and condemned as early as the 12th century
by John of Salisbury in his *Policraticus*. It was
again condemned by John XXII (Pope 1316-
1334) in 1318 and around 1326-1328; by the theological faculty of Paris in 1398; and by Sixtus V in
1586, in his bull *Caeli et terrae creator*. Although
Ronsard mentions it in one of his Hymns, from the
16th century onwards divination by the mirror
seems to have given way to divination by the crystal ball.

While it is possible to draw up a more or less representative account of the written tradition of divinatory arts in the medieval and modern periods, it
is far more difficult, given the current state of
research, to know which divinatory techniques
were really practiced, since their constant condemnation by the Church doubtless induced the "diviners" to dissimulate or at least to keep silent about
their activities in this field.

Mirella Brini-Savorelli, "Un manuale di geomanzia
presentato da Bernardo Silvestre da Tours (XII secolo):
l'*Experimentarius*", *Rivista critica di storia della
filosofia* 14 (1959), 283-343 ◆ Thérèse Charmasson,
Lectura geomantiae, in: *Hermetis Trimegisti astrologica et divinatoria* (*Corpus christianorum, Continuatio
medievalis*, CXLIV, C, *Hermes latinus*, IV: 4), Tournai:
Brepols, 2001, 349-397 ◆ R.A. Pack, "A Pseudo-Aristotelian Chiromancy", *Archives d'histoire doctrinale
et littéraire du Moyen Age* 36 (1969), 189-241 ◆ idem,
"Pseudo-Aristoteles chiromantia", *Archives d'histoire
doctrinale et littéraire du Moyen Age* 39 (1972), 289-
320 ◆ idem, "*Auctoris incerti physiognomia libellus*",
*Archives d'histoire doctrinale et littéraire du Moyen
Age* 41 (1974), 113-138 ◆ idem, "Almadel auctor
pseudonymous, *Definitate sex scientiarum*", *Archives
d'histoire doctrinale et littéraire du Moyen Age* 42
(1975), 147-181 ◆ R.A. Pack & R. Hamilton, "Rode-
ricus de Majoricis, *Tractatus chiromancie*", *Archives
d'histoire doctrinale et littéraire du Moyen Age* 38
(1971), 271-305.

Lit.: Charles Burnett, *Magic and Divination in the
Middle Ages: Texts and Techniques in the Islamic and
Christian Worlds* (Variorum Collected Studies Series
CS557), Aldershot, Burlington, Singapore, Sydney:
Ashgate, 1996 ◆ Thérèse Charmasson, *Recherches sur
une technique divinatoire: La géomancie dans l'Occident médiéval*, Paris, Geneva: Droz, Champion, 1980
◆ idem, "L'astronomie, la cosmologie, l'astrologie et
les sciences divinatoires", in: Daniel Poirion (ed.), *La
littérature française aux XIVe et XVe siècles*, t. I *Partie
historique* (Gründriss der Romanischen Literaturen
des Mittelalters, VIII, 1), Heidelberg: Carl Winter
Universitätsverlag, 1988, 320-335 ◆ Jean-Jacques
Courtine & Claudine Hauroche, *Histoire du visage:
exprimer et taire ses émotions, XVIe-début XIXe siècle*,
Paris: Rivages, 1988 ◆ Armand Delatte, *La catoptro-
mancie grecque et ses dérivés* (Bibliothèque de la faculté de philosophie et lettres de l'université de Liège
48), Paris, Liège: Droz, 1932 ◆ Anne Denieul-Cormier,
La très ancienne physiognomie et Michel Savonarole,
Paris, 1956 (extract of *La Biologie médiévale* 14,
1956) ◆ *Divination et controverse religieuse en France
au XVIe siècle: Colloque du Centre V.-L. Saunier,
Paris, 13 mars 1986* (Collection de l'École normale
supérieure de jeunes filles 35, Centre V.-L. Saunier 4),
Paris: École normale supérieure de jeunes filles, 1987 ◆
Toufic Fahd, *La divination arabe*, Leiden: E.J. Brill,
1966 ◆ Stuart Jenks, "Astrometeorology in the Middle
Ages", *Isis* 74 (1983), 185-210 ◆ Richard Kieckhefer,
Magic in the Middle Ages (Cambridge Medieval Text-
books), Cambridge: Cambridge University Press, 1989
◆ Melissa Percival, *The Appearance of Character:
Physiognomy and Facial Expression in Eighteenth-
Century France* (Modern Humanities Research Asso-
ciation: Texts and Dissertations 47), London: W.S.
Maney & Son, 1999 ◆ Lynn Thorndike, "Chiromancy
in Medieval Latin Manuscripts", *Speculum* 40 (1965),
674-706. ◆ idem, *A History of Magic and Experimen-
tal Science*, vol. 1, 2nd ed., New York: The Macmillan
Company, 1929; vol. 2, 6th ed., New York: Columbia
University Press, 1964; vols. 3-4, New York: Columbia
University Press, 1934 ◆ Jan R. Veenstra, *Magic and
Divination at the Courts of Burgundy and France: Text
and Context of Laurent Pignon's* Contre les devineurs
(1411) (Brill's Studies in Intellectual History, 83), Leiden, New York, Köln: E.J. Brill, 1998.

THÉRÈSE CHARMASSON

Dorn, Gérard, * ca. 1530-1535 Malines (Belgium), † after 1584 Frankfurt-am-Main

Dorn was one of the many followers of → Paracelsus who, like Petrus Severinus (1542-1602), Adam von Bodenstein (1528-1577) or → Jacques Gohory, contributed through their commentaries and translations to the dissemination of their German master's work in the scholarly circles of 16th-century Europe. Dorn's birthplace, by general agreement, seems to have been Malines in Belgium, but his frequent travels most often led him to reside in Germany, Switzerland or France. His biography remains known only in a fragmentary manner. Thus, everything about his childhood and his education is unknown. Of his student years, we know only that in 1559 he enrolled at the University of Tübingen where he probably studied medicine and where he may have met the Paracelsian Eisenmenger, known as Siderocrates (1534-1585). In 1565, he sojourned in Besançon, where he offered the manuscript version of his *Clavis totius philosophiae chymistae* to Cardinal de Granvelle (1517-1586), keenly interested in alchemy himself. Dorn was found again in Lyon the following year, where he published his *Clavis*, dedicated to Adam von Bodenstein (1528-1577), with whom he was probably associated and of whom he described himself as 'the very least disciple, just like of Theophrastus [Paracelsus] himself'. Shortly after the publication of the *Clavis*, in 1567, Gohory in his *Theophrasti Paracelsi . . . Compendium* lashed out against Dorn, accusing him of being unfaithful to the Paracelsian teachings. From 1568 to 1578, Dorn settled in Basel. He worked there for some time translating Paracelsus's writings into Latin on behalf of the publisher Petrus Perna. His dedications reveal his contacts, at that time, with some German princes such as Karl von Baden or Wilhelm IV von Hessen-Kassel, or the French ambassador Pierre de Grantrye. Owing to the latter, he further gained the protection of prince François de Valois (1555-1584), brother of King Henri III (1551-1589). Dorn reappeared three years later in Frankfurt-am-Main. He published there some ten more works before his death, in 1584 or shortly thereafter.

Dorn's abundant production reflects the diversity of his culture and of his centers of interest. The first version of his *Clavis* (1565) bears the stamp of an alchemical tradition principally represented by → Hermes Trismegistus, pseudo-Geber, → Jean de Roquetaillade, → Marsilio Ficino and G.A. Pantheus. However, his understanding of this alchemy is not a traditional one: over the transmutatory operations of the gold-makers, for whom Dorn shows mainly contempt, he prefers the search for a universal medicine based upon the therapeutic powers of the quintessence. His speculations also borrow from → astrology and → magic, the latter as understood by → Johannes Trithemius, as a form of wisdom leading to the understanding of physical and metaphysical things. According to Didier Kahn, Paracelsian influence in Dorn's work did not become manifest until the 1567 edition of the *Clavis*. This edition revealingly opens with a homage to the great German master, followed by two prefaces in which the author vows to be an ardent defender of medical alchemy against the traditional concepts of medical science, those of Galen in particular. This commitment to the Paracelsian cause led him to combine his works as a translator, commentator and lexicographer with polemics against others. Thus he published a severe *Admonitio* (1583) directed against Thomas Erastus (1523-1583), a commentary on *De vita longa* by Paracelsus (1583) and a *Dictionarium Theophrasti Paracelsi* (1584) that, because of its obscurity, aroused the wrath of the alchemist Andreas Libavius (1555-1616). His competence as an exegete also led Dorn to follow in the footsteps of the Italians Aurelio Augurelli (1456-1530) and Giovanni Bracesco (toward 1481-?) and take an interest in alchemical interpretations of pagan mythology (see his *Colloquium quo Titan Paterfamilias, Oceanitisque Mater, de sua prole consulunt*, 1568). In addition, it is noteworthy that, in making an effort at popularizing Paracelsus, Dorn moved toward a mystical and theosophical concept of alchemy. The second part of the *Clavis* already bears witness to this spiritual orientation: there he refers to the 'seven degrees of a speculative philosophy' that assimilate the operations of the great work with the different stages of asceticism. He reaffirmed this program of conjoining chemical work and moral accomplishment in his *Congeries Paracelsicae Chemiae* (1581), where the experiments performed in the laboratory are understood as the visible manifestations of a spiritual process developing in the intimate psyche of the alchemist. → C.G. Jung would later propose something similar in reference to the mechanisms of projection and transfer in his book *Psychologie und alchimie* (1944). It is interesting to note, finally, that Dorn gives the outlines of his wisdom in his *Monarchia triadis* (1577), where his speculations ally cosmology, operative research and → Christian theosophy.

The presence of many works by Dorn in the first volume of *Theatrum chemicum* (1602) reflects his importance in the history of alchemical literature. Certainly, the author of *Clavis* and *Congeries* appears as one of the major figures to carry the thinking of Paracelsus into the 17th century. A heir to the current of Renaissance *philosophia occulta* [→ occult / occultism] represented by Johannes Trithemius, Cornelius Agrippa, or → John Dee, his work moreover encouraged the emergence of an alchemical and Christian theosophy, whose main representatives are → Heinrich Khunrath, → Robert Fludd and → Jacob Boehme.

Clavis totius Philosophiae Chymisticae . . ., Lyon: heirs of Jacques Giunta, 1567 (German translation: *Schlüssel Der Chimistischen Philosophy . . .*, Strasbourg: Lazare Zetzner, 1602) ◆ *Veneni, quod Leo (nescio quis) Suavius in Theophrasticos evomere conatur, proprium in pectus eius . . .*, in: J. Gohory, *Theophrasti Paracelsi . . . Compendium*, Basel: Petrus Perna, 1568 ◆ *Chymisticum Artificium Naturae, Theoricum & Practicum . . .*, (Basel?): (P. Perna?), 1568 ◆ *Artificii Chymistici Physici, Metaphysicique, Secunda Pars & Tertia, quarum summarium versa pagella dabit . . .*, Basel: (P. Perna?), 1569 ◆ *Lapis metaphysicus aut philosophicus, qui universalis medicina vera fuit . . .*, (Basileae), 1570 ◆ *Monarchia Triadis, in Unitate, soli Deo sacra . . .*, in: Pseudo-Paracelsus, *Aurora Thesaurusque Philosophorum . . .*, Basel, 1577 (in French: *La Monarchie du Ternaire . . .*, Basel, 1577 and Paris: Gutenberg Reprint, 1981) ◆ *Anatomia corporum adhuc viventium . . .*, in: Pseudo-Paracelsus, *Aurora Thesaurusque Philosophorum . . .*, Basel, 1577 ◆ *Congeries Paracelsicae Chemiae de transmutationibus metallorum . . .*, Frankfurt: André Wechel, 1581 ◆ *Fasciculus paracelsicae medicinae veteris et non novae . . .*, Frankfurt, 1581 ◆ *De Naturae luce physica . . .*, Frankfurt: Cristoph Rab, 1583 ◆ *In Theophrasti Paracelsi Auroram Philosophorum, Thesaurum, & Mineralem Œconomiam, Commentaria . . .*, Frankfurt: Christoph Rab, 1583 ◆ *Dictionarium Theophrasti Paracelsi, continens obscuriorum vocabulorum . . . definitiones . . .*, Frankfurt, 1583 ◆ *De Duello animi cum corpore*, in: *Theatrum Chemicum*, Strasbourg: Zetzner, 1659, vol. 1, 472-484 ◆ K. Sudhoff, "Ein Beitrag zur Bibliographie der Paracelsisten im 16. Jahrhundert", in: *Centralblatt für Bibliothekswesen* 10 (1983), 385-391 ◆ idem, *Versuch einer Kritik der Echtheit der Paracelsischen Schriften*, vols. 1-2, Berlin: G. Reimer, 1894-1899.

Lit.: A.G. Debus, *The Chemical Philosophy: Paracelsian Science and Medicine in the Sixteenth and Seventeenth Centuries*, vol. 1, New York: Science History Publications, 1977, 74-75 ◆ M.T. Gnudi, "Dorn, Gerhard", in: C. Gillispie (ed.), *Dictionary of Scientific Biography*, vol. 4, New York: Charles Scribner's Sons, 1971, 169b-171a ◆ D. Kahn, "Dorn, Gerhard", in: C. Priesner & K. Figala (eds.), *Alchemie: Lexikon einer hermetischen Wissenschaft*, Munich: C.H. Beck, 1998, 112-114 ◆ D. Kahn, *Alchimie et paracelsisme en France (1567-1625)*, forthcoming from Editions Droz: Geneva ◆ idem, "Les débuts de Gérard Dorn d'après le

manuscrit autographe de sa *Clavis totius Philosophiae Chymisticae* (1565)", in: Joachim Telle (ed.), *Analecta Paracelsica*, Stuttgart: Franz Steiner, 1994, 59-126 ◆ J.F. Marquet, "Philosophie et alchimie chez Gerhard Dorn", in: J.C. Margolin & S. Matton (eds.), *Alchimie et philosophie à la Renaissance* (Actes du colloque international de Tours), Paris: Vrin, 1993, 215-221 ◆ Robert P. Multhauf, *The Origins of Chemistry*, London, 1966, 241-243 ◆ R. Partington, *A History of Chemistry*, vol. 2, London: Macmillan & Co., 1961, 159-160 ◆ L. Thorndike, *A History of Magic and Experimental Science* (1941), vol. 5, New York: Columbia University Press, 1987, 630-635.

FRANK GREINER

Douzetemps (or Douz[e]aidans), Melchior, * 1668/1669 place unknown, † after 1738 probably Offenbach am Main

Very little is known about Douzetemps's life: even his first name was not documented until 1984 (by R. Breymayer). This French Lutheran settled in Germany early in his life as a consequence of the revocation of the Edict of Nantes in 1685. His book (see below) gives the impression that he associated with people shaped by the spirituality of Quietism and → Pietism. He is reported to have met, in Aachen in 1730, a lady who was a disciple of Madame Guyon. She may have exerted a certain influence on him since, at that time, Quietism was making headway among German Lutherans.

In 1731 appeared a small text by Douzetemps, "Geliebte in dem Geliebten!" (Beloved in the Beloved!), to which R. Breymayer has recently called attention. It consists of 14 pages and was published in a collective volume *Bewährte und Harmonische Zeugnisse* (Warranted and Harmonious Testimonies). The authors seem to have belonged to the "Harmonisten", an irenic and pietistic group. The same year, a Saxon political agent had become aware of a letter in which Douzetemps had used the term "White Eagle", and as a result he was believed to be planning a conspiracy against the Polish Kingdom: for the heraldic arms of that monarchy contain such a bird. But actually, what Douzetemps had had in mind was nothing but the alchemical [→ Alchemy] "Mercurium Philosophorum", also called "White Eagle". Nevertheless, upon a request by the Count of Brühl who was in the service of Prince August II, Douzetemps, who was sixty-three at the time, was taken into custody around November, and imprisoned in the fortress of Sonnenstein near Dresden. He was released on 4 September 1732.

According to his own testimony in *Mystère de la Croix affligeante et consolante* he began writing that book – probably the only one he authored – after having spent ten months and thirteen days in the prison at Sonnenstein, 'deprived of paper, pen and ink'. On this point he may be exaggerating, since the book was published as early as 1732. He goes on to explain that he chose to write it in French rather than Latin or German because French was the most appropriate language for his work to be read by most of his friends.

The book has fifteen chapters, each of which ends with a short poem in Latin. It furthermore has an appendix of about 40 pages titled *Hortulus Sacer varii floris, coloris, odoris*, which is comprised of poems (some of which are alchemical, like "Lapis Transmutans"), also in Latin. According to Paul Chacornac, this *Hortulus* is inspired or even partly copied from *La Christiada* (1535), a work by Girolamo Vida.

The term "mysterium crucis" had always played a great role in systematic theology and Latin liturgy. It is not all that surprising that Douzetemps preferred that title rather than an esoteric, theosophical [→ Christian Theosophy] or alchemical one, since the majority of the discussions contained in the book are more "mystical" in nature, such as prayers, devotional meditations, etc. But these discussions are interspersed with many neo-kabbalistic, alchemical and theosophical passages which are really more "esoteric" in character. For example, Douzetemps devotes a long passage to the ontological meanings of the seven letters of IEHOVAH and their connections with one another. In so doing, he draws a series of triangles and other related geometrical figures from which a variety of crosses emerge. These are supposed to throw some light upon the mysteries of the Trinity and the Creation.

Chapter thirteen, titled "On the Wonders of the Cross within External Nature", and also the last chapter, resonate with Paracelsian [→ Paracelsianism] and Boehmian tones. Here we find a vivid evocation of the ontological role of the Sun, the "door of Light" situated at the very place where Lucifer stood before he fell. The Sun produces blood, sulphur, and everything that is oily; the Moon produces milk, salt, and everything that is watery. Such pages have a definite alchemical ring, enhanced both by the choice of technical terms like salpeter, niter, and vitriol, and by the names of the authors or works quoted, such as → Paracelsus, → Arnau de Vilanova, Basilius Valentinus, and, not the least, the *Aurea Catena Homeri* published in Frankfurt in 1723.

In French, the book was newly edited in Lausanne in 1786, then in 1791 at the same place upon the initiative of → Jean-Philippe Dutoit-Membrini. The latter highly praises Douzetemps in his book *La Philosophie divine* (Lausanne 1794), also partly a theosophical work. The edition of 1786 was reprinted in London in 1860 with a short, anonymous introduction in English. In April 1911, Alexandre Thomas, under the pen name Mandres, edited extracts from *Le mystère de la Croix* in the journal *La Gnose, revue mensuelle consacrée à l'étude des sciences ésotérique*. In the same journal and the same year appeared a series of articles by → René Guénon entitled *Le symbolisme de la Croix* which was published in 1931 as a book. The number of translations and testimonies in other languages bears witness to a rather discreet, but steady reception over a few decades. Johann Christoph Lenz, who was also a translator of → Swedenborg, translated it into German in 1782. The following year, the famous publicist Friedrich Nicolai, who had printed an edition of the Rosicrucian Manifestos in 1781 [→ Rosicrucianism], noted that esoteric philosophy was finding its way to Germany via French books like those written by Douzetemps and → Louis-Claude de Saint-Martin. At the end of his widely disseminated *Missiv an die Bruderschaft des Ordens des Goldenen und Rosenkreutzes* (1783), Nicolai wrote that *Le Mystère de la Croix* was 'one of the best Rosicrucian works'. In 1784, Johann Friedrich Kleuker quoted Douzetemps as an authority in his *Magikon*, which is for the most part a discussion of Louis-Claude de Saint-Martin's first two books.

The year 1786 saw the first Russian translation, edited by → Nicholas I. Novikov at the Typographic Society directed by → I. Lopuchin – two figures whose editorial activity consisted to a large extent of translations of books of an esoteric and more specifically theosophical character. At the time of Novikov's arrest the book was confiscated and burnt, in 1793, along with others of the kind, in compliance with Catherine II's edict on → Freemasonry and related matters. But as early as 1814, Alexander Labzin, an esotericist influenced by Novikov, procured a new edition in St. Petersburg which he prefaced under the initials Y.M. He used these initials in his introductions to quite a few other works as well, such as those of → Jacob Boehme, → Karl von Eckartshausen, Louis-Claude de Saint-Martin, Emanuel Swedenborg *et alii*. Theosophers occasionally quoted Douzetemps, albeit sometimes anonymously, like → Friedrich Christoph Oetinger in his *Lehrtafel der Prinzessin Antonia* (1763) and → Franz von Baader in *Fermenta Cognitionis* (Book II, 1823).

In view of the intrinsic interest, the context and the influence of the book, it would seem desirable that a critical, scholarly edition be prepared.

Melchior Douzeaidans [= Melchior Douzetemps], "Geliebte in dem Geliebten", *Bewährte und Harmonische Zeugnisse einiger unpartheyischer und in Gott verbundener Freunde . . .*, Frankfurt and Leipzig, 1731, 75-89 ♦ [Melchior Douzetemps], *Mystère de la Croix affligeante et consolante, Mortifiante & vivifiante, Humiliante & triomphante, de Jésus-Christ, et de ses Membres. Ecrit au milieu de la Croix au dedans et au dehors. Par un Disciple de la Croix de Jésus. Achevé le 12 d'Août, 1732. On y a ajouté quelques Poésies Latines sur divers sujets, composées aussi dans la solitude de Sonnenstein. Chara CrVX, MlhI DVX. Chère CroIX gVIDe assVré, Menez aV port azVré!*, Hombourg von der Höhe: Godefroy Memhard Imprimeur de la Cour et de la Chancellerie, 1732; Lausanne: New editions, 1786; Moscow and St. Peterburg, 1786; Lausanne: François Grasset, 1791; London and Edinburgh: William and Norgate, 1860, in French with an anonymous 'Introduction' in English (by C.J. Steward, according to P. Chacornac whose series of articles is quoted further below); Reprint of that English edition in French: Milan: Archè (Collection Sebastiani), 1975 ♦ Extracts (Mandres [Alexandre Thomas], ed.) in: *La Gnose, revue mensuelle consacrée à l'étude des sciences ésotériques* 4, 5, 6 (April-June 1911) ♦ Translations: [Melchior Douzetemps], *Das Geheimnis des betrübenden und tröstenden . . . Kreutzes Jesu Christi . . .*, trans. by L.Y.R. [= Johann Christoph Lenz], in Commission bei A.F. Böhme: [Frankfurt and] Leipzig, 1783 [recte: 1782]; Russian translation by A.M. Kutuzov and M.I. Bagryanski, ed. by N.I. Novikov *et alii*, Typographic Society of Moscow: I. Lopuchin, 1784; New edition of this Russian translation, ed. by Alexander Fedoroviitch Labzine, St. Petersburg, 1814.

Lit.: Reinhard Breymayer, "Ein radikaler Pietist im Umkreis des jungen Goethe: Der Frankfurter Konzertdirektor Johann Daniel Müller alias Elias/Elias Artista (1716 bis nach 1785)", *Pietismus und Neuzeit: Ein Jahrbuch zur Geschichte des neueren Protestantismus* 9 (1983), 192-196, 201 ♦ idem, "[Melchior] Douzetemps: *Le Mystère de la croix*, a critical review of the French edition of 1975", *ARIES (Association pour la Recherche et l'Information sur l'Esotérisme)* 2 (1984), 49-58 ♦ Paul Chacornac, "Un traité de mystique hermétique de Douzetemps", *Etudes Traditionnelles* n° 372/373, 63 (1962) 188-200; continued under the title "Le mystère de la Croix de Douzetemps", n° 374, 63 (1962) 259-265; n° 376, year 64 (1963) 59-72 ♦ *500 Years of Gnosis in Europe: Exhibition of Printed Books and Manuscripts from the Gnostic Tradition*, Amsterdam: In de Pelikaan, 1993, 242-243 (78a) ♦ Arthur Edward Waite, "Later Witnesses to the Life of Life", in: Waite, *Lamps of Western Mysticism*, New York: Blauvelt, 1973, 199-210 (1st London: ed. Kegan Paul, 1923).

ANTOINE FAIVRE

Dürckheim, Karlfried, Graf von Dürckheim-Montmartin, * 24.10.1896 Munich, † 28.12.1988 Todtmoos-Rütte

Dürckheim served in the First World War 1914-1918 and studied Philosophy and Psychology at Munich University from 1919 to 1923. After an educational stay in Italy from 1924 to 1925 he was Assistant of Felix Krüger (1874-1948), founder of "Holistic Psychology", from 1927 to 1931. He became university teacher in 1930 and was subsequently Professor of Philosophy at Breslau and Kiel Universities. From 1935 on he was staff-member in the office of Joachim von Ribbentrop (1893-1946), who was later to become foreign minister of the Third Reich, after which from 1937 he held a research assignment in Japan, where he received instruction in meditation (za-zen) and Japanese archery. In 1939 he briefly returned to Germany because of the death of his wife and his father. In 1945 he was interned by the American occupying power. During his imprisonment he decided to become a psychotherapist. In 1947 he returned to Germany, moving to Todtmoos-Rütte in the Black Forest in 1951, where he established the "Existential and Psychological Training and Encounter Centre" together with his former student Maria Hippius (born 1909), whom he married only as late as 1985. Dürckheim remained active as psychotherapist and international lecturer until his death.

Dürckheim had his first numinous experiences as a child. While under fire in the Great War, he sensed the 'indestructible' within himself and found it a 'liberating experience'. During his student years in Munich he enjoyed a large circle of friends including the poet Rainer Maria Rilke (1875-1926), the painter Paul Klee (1879-1940), and the sinologist Richard Wilhelm (1873-1930). In 1919 a chance encounter with the *Tao Te Ching* led to his first illumination, which he claims stayed with him all his life. He formed a meditation circle with friends and later studied the writings of Meister Eckhart, Lao-Tzu, and Gautama Buddha. During his ten-year stay in Japan, interrupted only once, Dürckheim met the famous Zen teacher Daisetz Teitaro Suzuki (1871-1966), which led to an intensive study of theoretical and practical Zen Buddhism. He saw all Japanese arts, from painting through fencing to the tea ceremony, as a path of self-attunement leading to the discovery of one's own "buddha nature". Most of Dürckheim's books can be traced to his existential experiences in Japan. They made his name well-known in the German-speaking world as well as in France, the Netherlands and the United States. His literary work comprises some 20 books, many of which are anthologies of lectures and journal articles. His influence on the contemporary spiritual scene was quite extensive and already 1954 he was invited by the Dutch Queen to hold a lecture on Zen Buddhism. In France Henri Hartung, a pupil of Sri Ramana Maharshi (1879-1950), and Gabriel Monod-Hertzen, a follower of Sri Aurobindo (1872-1950), worked with him. Dürckheim was also called the "spiritual father" of the so called Frankfurter Ring, a spiritual study centre where people like Frithjof Capra (b. 1939), Lama Anagarika Govinda (1898-1985), John Lilly (b. 1915), Raimundo Panikkar (b. 1918), George Trevelyan (1906-1996), and others came to teach.

Dürckheim's chief interest lay in relating Eastern wisdom to Western psychotherapy. He addressed the contemporary Westerner, whose spiritual and religious distress cries out for healing. He attributed this distress to the loss of spiritual meaning in all human activity, which focuses only on man and his worldly affairs while excluding God or "Divine Being". The inevitable result in Dürckheim's views is an achievement-oriented culture and a loss of tranquillity, a suppression of the feminine, and the decay of the spirit of community. The transcendent centre, which should provide a firm foundation of existence, is lost, and the individual is reduced to a purely rational unit of production. The resulting spiritual hunger cannot be assuaged by social, rational or economic measures. Dürckheim seeks to liberate the individual from his profane or mundane ego (*Welt-Ich*) and bring him into living contact with his true Self or Being (*Wesen*) beyond time and space. The transcendent Divine Being, present in each individual, thus manifests itself in the world, and the profane ego becomes transparent to its immanent transcendence. Dürckheim offers his "Initiation Therapy" as a means of supporting man on the path to wholeness and healing. His concept of initiation was borrowed from → Julius Evola, whom he studied and got to know personally. Dürckheim also read → René Guénon. According to Dürckheim man proceeds from his first initiatory experience of Being along a continuous process of development, without ever reaching a final goal. The state of being on the path, of becoming ever more transparent to the Divine Being, is the goal itself. Dürckheim is not concerned with the attainment of Nirvana as in Eastern religions. In his later works he describes this path as a way to Christ, whom he calls the eternal inner master. Dürckheim's work rests on four pillars:

1. Depth psychology, especially deriving from → C.G. Jung, which seeks to integrate the shadow on the path to the true Self. In this process the limits of the profane ego are surpassed and there is a breakthrough of Being on a transcendent plane.

2. "Personal Body Therapy" differentiates "the body one has" (*Körper*), important for health and vitality, from "the body one is" (*Leib*), the spiritual and mental life revealed by one's physical condition, gestures and expressions. The true or false inner attitude is outwardly reflected in the posture of the body. In an ideal case, the transcendent Being can even shine through the body. Various physical exercises (e.g. T'ai Chi, Aikido, cult dancing) promote this transparency. Dürckheim emphasizes the importance of being physically centred, allowing the physical centre, the inner centre of gravity, to come to rest in the *Hara* (belly). Firmness in the *Hara* brings certainty and thus alters the constitution of the whole person. This promotes new confidence and enables one to transcend more easily the limits and restrictions of the profane ego. Dürckheim also speaks of the subtle body and the aura.

3. "Creative Therapy" comprises artistic exercises such as dancing, singing, clay modelling and, most importantly, the method of "guided drawing" developed by Maria Hippius. The manifestation of Being is facilitated by creative action which, like the blockages which oppose it, derives from the unconscious.

4. Meditation also serves to open oneself towards the transcendent centre. Especially important is the practice of za-zen, sitting absolutely still in an erect position, whereby the belly and pelvic region provide a firm basis. Horizontals and verticals must be so ordered as to create the inner conditions for transcendence to manifest. Man should not actively seek God, but allow himself to be found by God. One should let go while breathing out, and open up while breathing in. The importance of meditation was evident at Dürckheim's Centre at Todtmoss-Rütte, where each day began with communal za-zen, another session following in the afternoon.

Initiation Therapy is primarily a path of practice and personal experience available to modern man who has lost his connection with traditional religion. Although Dürckheim has found a very positive reception in Christian circles, some theologians wonder whether Dürckheim's path may be too "subjective", representing an "autonomous ethic of self-realisation" which values personal "experience" over authentic "faith".

The Japanese Cult of Tranquillity (German orig. 1949), London: Rider & Company, 1960 ♦ *Im Zeichen der*

Großen Erfahrung, Weilheim: O.W. Barth, 1951 ♦
Durchbruch zum Wesen, Bern/Stuttgart: Hans Huber,
1954 ♦ *Hara, The Vital Centre of Man* (German orig.
1954), London: George Allen & Unwin, 1960 ♦ *Erlebnis und Wandlung*, Bern/Stuttgart: Hans Huber, 1956
♦ *The Way of Transformation* (German orig. 1961),
London: George Allen & Unwin, 1971 ♦ *Zen and Us*
(German orig. 1961), New York: E.P. Dutton, 1987 ♦
The Call for the Master (German orig. 1972), New
York: E.P. Dutton, 1989 ♦ *The Beyond Within: Initiation into Meditation* (German orig. 1976), Saint Meinrad: Abbey Press, 1992.

Lit.: Manfred Bergler, *Die Anthropologie des Grafen
Karlfried von Dürckheim im Rahmen der Rezeptionsgeschichte des Zen-Buddhismus in Deutschland*, Dissertation, Phil. Erlangen-Nürnberg, 1981 ♦ Alphonse
Goettmann, *Dialogue on the Path of Initiation* (French
orig. 1979), New York: Globe Press, 1992 ♦ Maria
Hippius (ed.), *Transzendenz als Erfahrung: Beitrag
und Widerhall. Festschrift zum 70. Geburtstag von
Graf Dürckheim*, Weilheim: O.W. Barth, 1966 ♦ Maria
Hippius-Gräfin Dürckheim, *Geheimnis und Wagnis
der Menschwerdung*, Schaffhausen: Novalis, 1996 ♦
Rüdiger Müller, *Wandlung zur Ganzheit: Die Initiatische Therapie nach Karlfried Graf Dürckheim und
Maria Hippius*, Freiburg, Basel, Wien: Herder, 1981 ♦
Christian Ottemann, *Initiatisches Christentum: Karlfried Graf Dürckheims Lehre vom "Initiatischen Weg"
als Herausforderung an die evangelische Theologie*,
Frankfurt am Main etc.: Peter Lang, 1990 ♦ Josef
Robrecht, Maria Hippius-Gräfin Dürckheim, Thomas
Arzt (eds.), *Der Mensch als Zeuge des Unendlichen:
Karlfried Graf Dürckheim zum 100. Geburtstag*,
Schaffhausen: Novalis, 1996 ♦ Rüdiger von Roden,
*Sich selbst zur Heimat werden: Übungen aus der
Initiatischen Therapie von Karlfried Graf Dürckheim*, Freiburg, Basel, Wien: Herder, 1987 ♦ Gisela
Schoeller, *Heilung aus dem Ursprung: Praxis der Initiatischen Therapie nach Karlfried Graf Dürckheim
und Maria Hippius*, München: Kösel, 1983 ♦ Sekretariat Rütte, *Im Zeichen der Wandlung: Dokumentation der Tagung zum 100. Geburtstag von Karlfried
Graf Dürckheim*, Existential-psychologische Bildungs-
und Todtmoos-Rütte: Begegnungsstätte, 1997 ♦ Gerhard Wehr, *Karlfried Graf Dürckheim: Ein Leben im
Zeichen der Wandlung*, München: Kösel, 1988.

HANS THOMAS HAKL

Dutoit-Membrini, Jean-Philippe,
* 27.9.1721 Moudon near Lausanne,
† 21.1.1793 Lausanne

Dutoit-Membrini studied Protestant theology in
Lausanne. Later, in 1750, during an illness, he had
a mystical experience in which he heard a voice
telling him: 'Thou shalt eat of the flesh of thy
Redeemer and drink of His blood'. Shortly after, he
vowed never to marry and steeped himself in the
writings of Madame Guyon, assisting with the

preparation of new editions of her works in forty
volumes (1767-1791 [in the Musée du Vieux Lausanne one can see his oratory, which contains a
chalice on which are inscribed the names of Jesus,
Mary, Joseph, and Madame Guyon]). Over many
years, he preached in the churches at Lausanne, but
in 1759 bad health compelled him to resign his clerical position. From then on he devoted himself
mostly to the study of mystical literature, gathering
about him a number of followers. The latter, like
Dutoit-Membrini himself, were part of a general
religious current that was widespread within the
Canton of Vaud. In that French speaking part
of Switzerland, many Christians distanced themselves from both Calvinist and Catholic influence
and created a kind of eclectic, irenic and esoterically tinged "mystical Church" of their own.
Before Dutoit-Membrini, Hector de Saint-Georges
de Marsais and then Fleischbein had played the
role of spiritual leader to this community in the said
Canton.

Dutoit-Membrini's "mystical" Christianity is
most marked, to the extent that it has an external
inspiration, by Quietism. His main book may be
compared to that of → Melchior Douzetemps' *Le
mystère de la Croix* (1732), in that it is replete with
passages of a theosophical character, which to a
large extent are presented in long footnotes. The
author is fully cognizant of the esoteric literature of
his time and frequently takes his stands with regard
to it. Especially in his book *La philosophie divine*
(1793), he expresses his views and personal experiences. Among his privileged conceptions is the
notion of "astral spirit", which is a third category
of knowledge, beside sensory perception and
divine illumination, made possible by the action of
the stars and planets upon us. Unfortunately, this
spirit is quickly spoiled and corrupted by the
venom of Lucifer and his kin, and made spurious
by other entities who are neither angels nor
demons. From this perspective, Dutoit-Membrini
is critical of both → animal magnetism and → Swedenborg's visions, which he finds highly dubious.
He has read *Des erreurs et de la verité* (1775) by →
Louis-Claude de Saint-Martin and is more indulgent toward this theosopher, whose views are to
some extent rather similar to his own, even though
he faults Saint-Martin for trusting his imagination
too much. He praises Douzetemps' book, but
advises readers not to take into consideration the
alchemical speculations contained therein. Dutoit-
Membrini's esoteric formulations also concern →
number symbolism (his book has a section on "the
numbers of the Cross" that echoes some of the
inferences of Douzetemps). Other speculations are

of an even more theosophical character, such as those he produces on the Elohim, the "nothingness beneath nothingness", Sophia, and Lucifer and Adam (their Falls and the terrible consequences thereof). Dutoit-Membrini's statements are delivered in tones reminiscent of → Jacob Boehme, whose follower he assuredly does not claim to be. In fact, he happens to stand more in the tradition of Saint-Georges de Marsais.

La philosophie divine was influential among his followers in the Canton of Vaud, for whom he wrote it in the first place. Beyond that circle, immediately after its publication, it became an authoritative reference among the people and authors belonging to, or touched by, the "illuminist" current [→ Illuminism]. Early in the 1790's, Dutoit-Membrini's book was discussed in letters exchanged between Saint-Martin and → Niklaus Anton Kirchberger. The publication of that correspondence in 1862 (English translation, 1863) once more called attention to Dutoit-Membrini among theosophically oriented readers.

Jean-Philippe Dutoit-Membrini, *De l'origine, des usages, des abus, des quantités et des mélanges de la raison et de la foi*, 2 vols., 1790 ◆ New version under the following title: Keleph ben Nathan [= Jean-Philippe Dutoit-Membrini], *La philosophie divine, appliquée aux lumières naturelle, magique, astrale, surnaturelle, céleste et divine*, 3 vols., 1793 ◆ Jean-Philippe Dutoit-Membrini, *La philosophie chrétienne*, s.l., 4 vols., 1800-1819 ◆ The Bibliothèque de la Faculté Libre de Théologie Protestante in Lausanne has recently transferred to the Bibliothèque Interfacultaire of the University of Lausanne the riches it contained in terms of still unpublished manuscripts by and on Dutoit-Membrini, many of which are still untapped by scholars.

Lit.: Charles Burger, *Un défenseur du quiétisme au 18ième siècle dans la Suisse française: Essai sur Jean-Philippe Dutoit-Membrini et sa philosophie divine*, Thèse de Doctorat, Strasbourg, 1868 ◆ Jules Chavanne, *Philippe Dutoit-Membrini, sa vie, son caractère et ses doctrines*, Lausanne, 1865 ◆ André Favre, *Un théologien mystique vaudois au XVIIIième siècle, Jean-Philippe Dutoit*, Genève, 1911 ◆ Auguste Viatte, *Les sources occultes du Romantisme*, vol. I: *Le pré-romantisme*, Paris: Champion, 1965 (1st ed. 1928), 112-119 (see also index of names, vol. II, 320).

ANTOINE FAIVRE

Eckartshausen, Karl von, * 28.6.1752 Haimhausen, † 13.5.1803 Munich

Eckartshausen attended school in Munich before going to study at the University of Ingolstadt, then directed by the Jesuits. They would have a lasting influence on his thought, and he later said that he had been guided 'along the ways of the marvelous' from the age of seven. An Aulic Councilor in 1776, he became a member of the Academy of Bavaria in 1777 and a secret archivist in 1784. His official functions, which he took very seriously, also provided him with a pretext for moralizing, preaching love of one's neighbor and tolerance. Married in 1778, he lost his spouse in 1780; in 1781 he remarried, with Gabrielle von Wolter, who would bear him eight children. After her death, in 1794, he married Theresa Weiss, with whom he had two children.

A conservative in politics, Eckartshausen was a theocrat, a monarchist, a friend of the Jesuits and a fierce enemy of the Bavarian → Illuminaten. At first he had mistakenly affiliated himself with this revolutionary and rationalist Order established by Adam Weishaupt, believing that he was dealing with a traditional initiatory society. Having left it, he strove to combat it. From 1780 to 1783, he mostly wrote juridical tracts but also took an interest in literature. He published theatre plays, pamphlets and brochures on the most diverse subjects. He defended the Jesuits against Nicolai, while identifying himself with an "authentic" *Aufklärung*. In the years 1784-1785 he published a number of "moral papers" (*Sittenblätter*) exemplifying the taste of the period for sentimental literature in the manner of Richardson. Intrigues and professional worries did not prevent him from becoming First Archivist in 1789.

From 1788 on he broke away from edifying literature and theatre plays, and devoted himself almost exclusively to esoteric thinking. Despite a certain taste for illusionism that recalls → Cagliostro, he was sincerely interested in → illuminism, → Christian theosophy, and speculative → mysticism, while opposing the pneumatological experiments of certain charlatans. His own experiments, which evoked the interest of the Prussian Court, were to some extent based on arithmology (or science of numbers symbolically understood [→ Number Symbolism]), which he believed gave access to the "principle of things". His *Zahlenlehre der Natur* (1794) is testimony to this research. Arithmology is the linchpin of his system; by means of it, this emulator of Pythagoras intended to resolve the Kantian opposition between *noumenon* and *phenomenon* and to achieve the synthesis of all knowledge. The ten Sephirot of the Kabbalah are considered the ten numbers of the Holy Names of God. No less than seventeen symbolic dreams were conducive, he tells us, to making him elaborate his complex arithmological system.

As fruits of this method, his works proliferated – he produced more than one hundred –, of which one of the best known, *Die Wolke über dem Heiligthum* (1802) would go through many translations and reprints. An indefatigable reader, he drew upon the Jewish and Christian Kabbalah [→ Jewish Influences] and was highly interested in → alchemy; in fact, he published works considered so outstanding that the Hermetic Society of Karlsruhe adopted them as basic manuals.

Eckartshausen's correspondence was gigantic. He exchanged letters with his friend Johann Michael Sailer (the ex-Jesuit who would become bishop of Regensburg), Conrad Schmid, Franz Joseph von Thun (the magician, and friend of → Johann Caspar Lavater), → Johann Heinrich Jung-Stilling, → Niklaus Anton Kirchberger, Friedrich Herbort, Johann Gottfried Herder, Friedrich Nicolai, → Franz von Baader, → Ivan Vladimir Lopukhin, and many others. With Ignaz Lindl he readily shared the dream of voluntary exile and emigration to Russia that characterized the *Erwecktenbewegung*. Through Tsar Alexander I, who highly valued his works, he became famous in Russia. His *Kostis Reise* (1795) resembles the initiatory roman à clef by Jung-Stilling, *Das Heimweh*. In his correspondence with Kirchberger (1793-1797), there is much talk of → Louis-Claude de Saint-Martin, the great master, after → Boehme, of → Christian theosophy. Eckartshausen claimed to have received secrets and theosophical revelations from an angel who spoke through the voice of a young woman. The revelations of Mme de la Vallière in Lyon seem comparable to these astonishing manifestations claimed by Eckartshausen, in which illusionism and a sincere belief in the intermediary world of angelic entities are constantly mixed. Just as striking is his claimed discovery of the secret of all possible inventions, through a contemplative path that is supposed to have given him access to the mysteries of the pneumatic world.

One finds in Eckartshausen the three panels of the theosophical triptyc: cosmogony, cosmology and eschatology. Moreover, he saw in the celebrated *Tabula Smaragdina* attributed to → Hermes Trismegistus the very image of the permanent exchanges that operate at the level of the three worlds (divine, angelic and human). Spirit and nature are two complementary forces that refer to a higher and unique reality. Like Boehme, he often treats of Sophia, the divine Wisdom who, at work in the creative process, is reflected in Christ, "Salt of Light" and revelation of Her splendor. However, Eckartshausen traces his system even more readily to the ten Sephiroth of the Kabbalah. Man is seen as an image of his creator. The divine Word is made manifest by the Son in the material world, which is the middle term between good and evil. In the myth of the "two Falls" he finds the solution to the problem of evil. Lucifer, the greatest of the angels, fell on account of his self-pride, thus introducing into the universe the first catastrophe. The primordial Adam, a spiritual being of immense virtues created to lead the rebel angels back to the narrow path, was unfortunately seduced by them. Attracted by the perspective of illusory material enjoyment, he fell as well, dragging along the whole of nature in this catastrophe and losing nearly all his spiritual faculties. However, within the opaque world in which it has come to be enclosed as a result of these falls, mankind is still capable of spiritual development. The Nature that surrounds us is full of divine signatures, and it is incumbent upon each one of us to decode them with a view to achieving our "regeneration". The latter would have been impossible without the redemption effectuated by the sacrifice of the Son of God. Christ has "raised up" Nature and Man, making them capable of a new spiritual birth (*Wiedergeburt*), and making possible the liberation of the paradisiacal substance enclosed in matter since the fall. The initiates, who practice 'the true royal and priestly science according to the Order of Melchisedech' – as Eckartshausen puts it –, will receive a luminous body on a regenerated earth.

A Catholic and a friend of the Jesuits, Eckartshausen nevertheless professed an ecumenism close to the notion of the "Inner Church" dear to → Ivan Vladimir Lopukhin. The process of regeneration described by him is considered compatible with his conception of the Roman Catholic Church, of which he remained a member all his life. He certainly considered religion to be a universal phenomenon, as attested by the mythologies of paganism and the great philosophers of Antiquity, notably Plato; but in the end, it is in the biblical revelation and in Christianity that religion finds its accomplishment. Jesus came to fulfill the Mosaic Law and redeem all of humanity through His blood. Jesus is all love, and Man must give Him life in the innermost part of himself. Against what he calls the Protestant error, Eckartshausen exalts not only the value of Catholicism and the necessity of worship and the sacraments, but also an attitude of the quietist type, similar to that of Fénelon or Madame Guyon. The heart of Man is the Temple par excellence. The true Christian community is thus the Inner Church always potentially present in the deepest part of the human heart. It does not require the believer to cut himself off from the world.

Man must act upon nature, knowing its laws. Eckartshausen shares with other *Natur-philosophen* of the pre-romantic period the idea that Nature is pervaded by a circular movement which is the result of two antagonistic forces, namely action/contraction, and/or active and passive states. There is no radical gap between spirit and nature because these two forces, which are both antagonistic and complementary, are at work within the four basic elements themselves, which function rather as a vehicle for them. As for Light, it is the organ of divine Wisdom (i.e., of Sophia, who engenders the elements). The initiate who possesses the right knowledge can act upon Nature, that is, pass from the material world to the world of the spirits. There is certainly some danger involved in dialogue with these entities: a secure inner sense is necessary, by means of which, through true → imagination (in the Paracelsian sense of the term), Man can be raised to the level of the higher forces to which his nature is indissolubly linked. "True → magic" has its foundation in the harmony of invisible links that interconnect God, Man and the universe. The calcinations of certain plants make it possible for an authentic magician to make their essence appear in aerial and etheric form. Transmutation is the goal of true alchemy, whose material foundation serves spiritual purposes. → Animal magnetism, of which Eckartshausen studied the theories and practices, could not but appeal to him, were it only because it was based on the idea of a universal fluid flowing through the whole cosmos.

The influence of Eckartshausen and his work extended to all of Europe and was especially perceptible in Germany, England, France and Russia. His system, which is nevertheless in no way innovative, is testimony to a scope and a depth of vision that command admiration. This richness makes him, next to Franz von Baader, one of the most representative gems of Christian theosophy in the last two decades of the German 18th century.

Karl von Eckartshausen, *Aufschlüsse zur Magie* (1788), facs. repr. Schwarzenburg: Ansata Verlag, 1978 ♦ *Gott ist die reinste Liebe*, Munich: J. Lentner, 1790 (trans. *God is the Love most Pure*, London: Hatchard, 1817) ♦ *Mistische Nächte*, Munich: J. Lentner, 1791 ♦ *Zahlenlehre der Natur*, Leipzig: G.E. Beer, 1794 ♦ *Probaseologie, oder praktischer Teil der Zahlenlehre der Natur*, Leipzig: H. Gräff, 1795 ♦ *Kostis Reise von Morgen gegen Mittag* (1795), repr. Andechs: Dingfelder-Argo, 1987 ♦ *Die wichtigsten Hieroglyphen fürs Menschen-Herz*, Leipzig: P.G. Kummer, 1796 ♦ *Die neuesten Entdeckungen über Licht, Wärme und Feuer*, Munich: J. Lindauer, 1798 ♦ *Entwurf zu einer ganz neuen Chimie*, Regensburg: Montag & Weiss, 1800 ♦ *Chimische Versuche*, Regensburg: Montag & Weiss, 1801 ♦ *Die Wolke über dem Heiligthum* (1802), Haarlem: repr. Rozenkruis Pers, 1979 (trans. *The Cloud upon the Sanctuary*, Edmonds WA: Holms, 1991) ♦ *Blicke in die Zukunft/ Ueber Sprache und Schrift/Ueber Verstand und Herz* (A. Faivre, ed. & intr.), Mullheim/Baden: Edition Ambra, 1997 ♦ *Ueber die Zauberkräfte der Natur/ Ueber die wichtigsten Mysterien der Religion* (A. Faivre, ed. & intr.), Mullheim/Baden: Edition Ambra, 1997.

Lit.: Diether Struss, *Karl von Eckartshausen, ein Trivialmystizist zwischen Aufklärung und Magie*, unpubl. Diss. Univ. Albert-Ludwig in Frieburg/Br., 1955 ♦ Antoine Faivre, *Eckartshausen et la théosophie chrétienne*, Paris: Klincksieck, 1969 ♦ See also the introductions by A. Faivre in the two volumes published by Ambra in 1977 (above).

JACQUES FABRY

Egyptomany

In modern times, ancient Egypt has inspired many works of literature, → music, and art. There are two distinct characteristics to Egypt in this context. First, it differs widely from the common European heritage of Greco-Roman culture, thus readily lending itself to mystery and appealing to a taste for exoticism. Second, its antiquity has caused it to appear in the Western imagination as the cradle or depository of a buried primordial or "traditional" knowledge; this applies especially to the Renaissance and the 17th century, when the Orient was still little known and the Far East even less so (Asia often being a synonym for Egypt). For these two reasons, many works of the esoteric type have been marked by Egyptophilia. Two postulates are found there, either implicitly or explicitly: first, that the hieroglyphs, pyramids, etc., are bearers of hidden meanings of a gnostic, initiatic, or soteriological nature; and second, that Egypt, having long been the most ancient known civilization, was closer to the primordial → Tradition. Moreover, → Moses was thought to have been initiated there, and → Hermes Trismegistus – often assimilated to Thoth – had left books that figured chronologically (for the Renaissance imagination) among the earliest manifestations of *prisca theologia* or *philosophia perennis*, whose scattered members now had to be reassembled. Following the second postulate, Egyptomania of the esoteric type belongs within a more general context: that of the place of the Orient in Western esotericism [→ Orientalism]. From the present perspective, it is an altogether secondary matter whether or not the esotericists' Egypt conforms to that of contemporary scientific Egyptology: it is above all Egypt as present in the esoteric → imagination that is relevant here for being studied on its own terms.

The *Asclepius,* one of the texts rich in Egyptian mysteries that belonged to the → Hermetic literature of 2nd century Alexandria, circulated in Latin throughout the Middle Ages; and in 1471 → Marsilio Ficino published his Latin translation of the recently discovered *Corpus Hermeticum.* The new current of Hermetism enjoyed a remarkable flowering for over two centuries. The Hermetic texts were believed to contain, in substance, the hidden wisdom of the Egyptian priesthood; and moreover, ancient Egypt was interesting from an esoteric point of view on account of its mythology – for while scrutinizing the hidden meanings of the latter (as well, incidentally, as that of the Greeks), some authors believed they were reading an encrypted account of the processes of the alchemical Great Work (e.g., → Michael Maier, *Symbola aureae mensae duodecim nationum,* and *Atalanta Fugiens,* 1617; → Dom Antoine Joseph Pernety, *Fables égyptiennes et grecques dévoilées,* and *Dictionnaire mytho-hermétique,* 1758). Neo-Alexandrian Hermetism and → alchemy are thus the two principal depositories of Egyptianizing esoteric discourse. The latter scarcely occurs in esoteric currents of the Boehmian type, i.e., in → Christian theosophy, nor in → Rosicrucianism, except for a few 19th and 20th century initiatic orders, such as AMORC. A learned Egyptologist with esoteric leanings appeared in the middle of the 17th century: the Jesuit → Athanasius Kircher (*Lingua aegyptiaca restituta,* 1643; *Oedipus Aegyptiacus,* 1652/1654), who was one of the prime movers of the great Egyptophile current that would follow. Kircher was soon followed in England by → Ralph Cudworth (*The True Intellectual System of the Universe,* 1678), who was also very widely read.

It was above all from the end of the 18th century that esoteric discourses and practices, apart from Neo-Alexandrian Hermetism and alchemy, began to find their inspiration in ancient Egypt. One can distinguish between pure speculation on the one hand, and the use of Egyptian symbols and themes in rituals, on the other. On the speculative level, J.G. Herder searched the ancient documents for their hidden meaning (*Ueber die älteste Urkunde des Menschen-geschlechts,* 1774/1776), and → Court de Gébelin, in his *Monde Primitif* (1773/1784) presented Egypt as the depository of the highest knowledge. In Book VIII of this encyclopedic work, he traced the origin of the → Tarot cards to this ancient civilization, followed in this by → Etteilla soon after. In another vein, Alexandre Lenoir (*Nouvelle explication des hiéroglyphes,*

1809) and A.P.J. Devismes (*Nouvelles recherches sur l'origine et la destination des pyramides d'Égypte,* 1812), then → Gérard de Nerval (*Voyage en Orient,* 1850), opened up new paths for the boldest speculations about the powers that the Egyptian priests were supposed to have wielded. Henceforth, the theme of the Great Pyramid never ceased to be repeated, especially after the publication of *The Great Pyramid* (1858) by John Taylor. → H.P. Blavatsky and her → Theosophical Society took up the torch of these speculations (*Isis Unveiled,* 1877), followed by → Edouard Schuré (*Les Grands Initiés,* 1889), and many others up to the present, including → Jan van Rijckenborgh, *De Egyptische oer-gnosis* (1960-1965). All of these belonged to the speculative domain.

As for the usage of Egyptian elements in rituals, hence in practice, one should first note the long-lasting influence of the Egyptophile and initiatic novel of Abbé Jean Terrasson, *Séthos, histoire ou vie tirée des monuments, anecdotes, de l'ancienne Égypte* (1731), which inspired the authors of many masonic and fringe-masonic rites [→ Freemasonry]. At least a dozen of the latter existed in the later 18th and early 19th centuries, including the "Architectes Africains", created by Friedrich von Köppen around 1767, the "Rite Hermétique", inaugurated around 1770, explicitly inspired by the teaching of → Hermes Trismegistus, and the "Egyptian Rite" of → Cagliostro, which dates from 1784. The beginning of the French Empire witnessed the appearance in Italy of the Rite known as Misraïm, imported to France by the Bédarride brothers (and not very Egyptian), followed in 1815 by the Rite known as Memphis – to which one might add that of the Mages of Memphis, created at the end of the 18th century. A number of present-day initiatic societies continue the trend, including the AMORC, founded in 1916, and the Theosophical Society, founded in 1875. Among the most popular contemporary examples of the esoteric fascination with Egypt are the novels *Einweihung* (Initiation, 1978) by Elisabeth Haich, and *Winged Pharaoh* (orig. 1937) by Joan Grant, both of them based on memories of previous Egyptian incarnations.

Lit.: Jan Assman, *Moses the Egyptian: The Memory of Egypt in Western Monotheism,* Cambridge Ma. & London: Harvard University Press, 1997 ◆ Jurgis Baltrusaitis, *La quête d'Isis: Introduction à l'égyptomanie,* Paris: Perrin, 1967 ◆ Gérard Galtier, *Maçonnerie Égyptienne, Rose-Croix et néo-chevalerie,* Paris: Le Rocher, 1989 ◆ Joscelyn Godwin, *Athanasius Kircher,* London: Thames & Hudson, 1979 ◆ Erik Hornung, *Das esoterische Ägypten,* München: Beck, 1999 ◆ Jean-Pierre Mahé, "La Renaissance et le mirage Egyptien", in: van den Broek & van Heertum (eds.), *From*

Poimandres to Jacob Böhme, Amsterdam: In de Pelikaan, 2000, 369-384.

ANTOINE FAIVRE

Eirenaeus Philalethes → Starkey, George

Elchasai/Elxai, ca. 100

According to Early Christian and Manichaean sources, Elchasai or Elxai was the founder of the sect of the Elkesaites and the recipient of a book of revelation. The main Christian sources about Elchasai are Hippolytus of Rome, who speaks of "Elchasai", and, independently, Epiphanius of Salamis, who always calls him "Elxai". Additional information comes from the Cologne Mani Codex and the Arabic writer Ibn an-Nadim. According to Epiphanius, *Panarion* 19, 2, 2, the name Elchasai means "Hidden Power" (Aramaic: *ḥail kᵉsai*), which is generally accepted by modern scholars. If Elchasai was a historical person, which has been doubted, he may have considered himself a manifestation of God, just as → Simon Magus claimed to be or was said to be a manifestation of the "Great Power". Epiphanius reports that Elchasai was of Jewish descent, had lived in the Trans-Jordan region at the time of the Emperor Trajan (98-117) and was the author of a book, 'ostensibly based on a prophecy or inspired by divine wisdom' (*Pan.*, 19, 1, 4). According to Epiphanius, the teachings of Elxai were adopted by several baptist sects in the Trans-Jordan area, the Jewish Osseans, the Jewish-Christian Ebionites, and the Sampseans, 'also called Elkeseans' (Pan., 19, 30, and 53, resp.). The reliability of Epiphanius' assertions is very difficult to assess, but there is no doubt that the Elkesaites were a baptist sect that took its origin somewhere east of the river Jordan and practised repeated purifying immersions. The Mesopotamian baptists among whom → Mani grew up also traced their rites back to Elchasai. In the Cologne Mani Codex, 94, 1-97, 17, Mani argues against the leaders of the sect that his refusal of ritual immersions and of agricultural work was in accordance with the teaching of 'Alchasaios, the founder of your Law', himself. In order to prove this surprising claim, he tells some stories about Elchasai, which actually support the Manichaean views but of which origin and meaning are disputed. In his work *Kitāb al-Fihrist*, IX, 1 (ca. 988), the Muslim scholar Ibn an-Nadim also deals with the baptists among whom Mani grew up. According to him, their founder was known as *al-ḥasīḥ*. Most scholars consider Epiphanius' information about Elchasai's background in the Trans-Jordan region more or less reliable. It finds some support in the fact that still in Epiphanius' lifetime there lived two highly venerated female descendants of Elchasai among the Sampseans (*Pan.*, 53, 1, 5-6; also 19, 2, 4-5). Other scholars, however, locate the beginning of Elchasai's career more eastward: in the Syrian-Parthian borderland (Strecker) or in Parthia (Northern Mesopotamia) itself (Luttikhuizen). This view is based on Hippolytus, whose report is rather cryptic at this point but nevertheless shows that there were Elkesaites who did not think of the Trans-Jordan region but of Parthia as the place of origin of Elchasai and his book (*Refutatio* IX, 13, 1). During the episcopate of Callixtus (217-222), a certain Alcibiades came from Apamea in Syria to Rome and propagated there the Elkesaite doctrines, basing himself on the book of Elchasai (Hippolytus, IX, 13, 1-4). He said that Elchasai had proclaimed his message in the third year of the Emperor Trajan (A.D. 101). This might be a mistake, for the book itself contained a prophecy that an eschatological war would break out in the third year after Trajan had subjected the Parthians (A.D. 116), which shows that at least part of it was written towards the end of Trajan's reign (Hippolytus, IX, 16, 4). The book had been revealed by an angel of enormous measures (height: 96 miles, breadth: 24 miles, etc.), who was called the Son of God. A female angel of the same measures, called the Holy Spirit, had accompanied him (IX, 13, 2-3). The same information is given by Epiphanius, *Pan.*, 19, 4, 1-2 (also 30, 17, 6-7 and 53, 1, 8) who says that the male angel was Christ, 'the great King' (this expression apparently came from the book, cf. below Hippolytus, IX, 15, 1). This vision suggests a Jewish-Christian background, for also in the *Ascension of Isaiah*, 9, 33-42 the visionary sees two glorious angels, the Lord, i.e. Christ, and the 'Angel of the Holy Spirit' (Stroumsa, Fossum). Other Jewish-Christian tenets are the prescription of circumcision and marriage and of praying toward Jerusalem, a life according to the Law, the rejection of the temple cult, the view that Christ was a normal human being, and the idea that Christ had repeatedly appeared in the course of history (Hippolytus, IX, 14, 1; Epiphanius, *Pan.*, 19, 1, 7 and 3, 5; 30, 3, 1-6 and 17, 5). According to Hippolytus, they claimed to have foreknowledge, practised → magic and → astrology (IX, 14, 2), and had to maintain → secrecy with respect to the content of the book of Elchasai (IX, 17, 1). In case of persecution they were allowed to deny with their lips what they believed in their heart (Origen in Eusebius, *Church History*, VI, 38; Epiphanius, *Pan.*, 19, 1, 8).

Hippolytus had personally combated the ideas of

Alcibiades (IX, 13, 4), since he recognized in his teaching the same heresy he repudiated in his opponent Callixtus, i.e. a second remission of sins. This remission was effected by a second baptism 'in the name of the great and most high God and in the name of his Son, the Great King' and could be administered 'as soon as he (the sinner) had heard this book' (IX, 15, 1). It seems possible that in Rome this baptism was interpreted as a second baptism for the Christians who converted to Alcibiades' Elkesaitism but that it originally meant the initiatory ritual for those who joined the sect. Origen also mentions the remission of sins for those who believe in the book (which, he says, reportedly had fallen from heaven), but he does not speak of a second baptism (Eusebius, *Church History*, VI, 38). According to Hippolytus, IX, 15, 1, it was meant for the remission of sexual sins in particular and had to be undergone fully clothed. During the ceremony seven witnesses 'written in this book' were called upon, i.e. heaven, water, holy spirits, angels of prayer, oil, salt and earth (IX, 15, 2). The same witnesses are also mentioned by Epiphanius, *Pan.*, 19, 1, 6, together with another series of witnesses (salt, water, earth, bread, heaven, ether, and wind). The seven cosmic powers were also called to witness at the reiterated immersions that were characteristic of the Elkesaites. People who suffered of consumption and those possessed of demons had to immerse themselves in cold water forty times during seven days (Hippolytus, IX, 16, 1). The book of Elchasai also gave instructions about how to act in case of the bite of a rabid dog, 'in which there is a spirit of destruction' (Hippolytus, IX, 15, 4-6). The person to whom this had occurred immediately had to run to a river or a spring in order to immerse himself fully clothed. It has been suggested that the rabid dog in fact refers to forbidden sexual desires (Peterson), which might be possible. Most probably, the oath that according to Hippolytus had to be sworn in that connection originally had nothing to do with the actual bite of a rabid dog or with sexual sin, but was spoken at the baptism that marked the admittance to the sect. It runs: 'I shall sin no more, I shall not commit adultery, I shall not steal, I shall not do injustice, I shall not be greedy, I shall not hate, I shall not break faith, nor shall I take pleasure in any evil deeds'. There are strong indications that the book of Elxai was originally written in Aramaic and translated into Greek at a later date. Epiphanius has even preserved a cryptic Aramaic sentence (*Pan.*, 19, 4, 3), which according to him was introduced by the words: 'Let nobody search for the meaning but only speak in prayer the following words'. This must be an addition of the Greek translation, since for Aramaic speaking people the meaning of the enigmatic words must have been clear: 'I bear witness to you on the Day of the Great Judgement'. This raises the question of how far the Greek translation differed from its Aramaic original. Its has been suggested that the book of Elxai originally was a Jewish apocalyptic writing that was christianized at a later stage (Luttikhuizen). Since we know very little of the beginnings and the history of the Elkesaite movement, this might be possible, but in view of the fact that all available sources already show a combination of Jewish and Christian elements, a Jewish-Christian milieu seems more likely. We know at least for sure that Jewish-Christian baptismal groups claimed Elchasai as their founder and held his book in high esteem. The man who became known as Elchasai, whether he called himself so or not, must have been a strong religious personality, who was able to amalgamate various religious ideas into a new and persuasive message of personal salvation. The Elkesaite movement has been characterized as a 'Gnostic Ebionitism' (Schoeps) or a 'syncretic-Gnostic Jewish Christianity' (Strecker). Its syncretic character is beyond doubt, but there are no indications that it adhered to typically Gnostic ideas, such as the separation between the supreme God and the creator or salvation through Gnosis.

All relevant texts with English translation in G.P. Luttikhuizen, *The Revelation of Elchasai: Investigations into the Evidence for a Mesopotamian Jewish Apocalypse of the Second Century and its Reception by Judeo-Christian Propagandists* (Texte und Studien zum antiken Judentum, vol. 8), Tübingen: Mohr, 1985.

Lit.: W. Brandt, *Elchasai: Ein Religionsstifter und sein Werk*, Leipzig, 1912 (repr. Amsterdam, 1973) ♦ J. Fossum, "Jewish-Christian Christology and Jewish Mysticism", *Vigiliae Christianae* 37 (1983), 260-287 ♦ F.S. Jones, Review of Luttikhuizen, *The Revelation of Elchasai* (see above), *Jahrbuch für Antike und Christentum* 30 (1987), 201-209 ♦ A.F.J. Klijn & G.J. Reinink, *Patristic Evidence for Jewish-Christian Sects* (Supplements to Novum Testamentum, vol. 36), Leiden: E.J. Brill, 1973, 54-67 (with texts) ♦ Luttikhuizen, *The Revelation of Elchasai* (see above) ♦ E. Peterson, "Die Behandlung der Tollwut bei den Elchasaiten nach Hippolyt", in: idem, *Frühkirche, Judentum und Gnosis*, Rom, Freiburg, Wien: Herder, 1959, 221-235 ♦ K. Rudolph, *Die Mandäer*, I: Prolegomena: Das Mandäer problem, Göttingen: Vandenhoeck & Ruprecht, 1960, 233-238 ♦ idem, "Die Bedeutung des Kölner Mani-Codex für die Manichäismusforschung", in: Idem, *Gnosis und spätantike Religionsgeschichte: Gesammelte Aufsätze*, Leiden: E.J. Brill, 1996, 667-685 (first published 1974) ♦ idem, "Jüdische und christliche Täufertraditionen im Spiegel des Kölner Mani-Codex", in: idem, *Gnosis und spätantike*

Religionsgeschichte, 686-697 (first published 1986) ♦
H.J. Schoeps, *Theologie und Geschichte des Juden-
christentums*, Tübingen: Mohr, 1949, 325-334 ♦ G.
Stecker, "Elkesai", *RAC* IV, 1171-1186 ♦ G. Stroumsa,
"Le couple de l'Ange et de l'Esprit: traditions juives et
chrétiennes", *Revue Biblique* 88 (1981), 42-61 (also
in: idem, *Savoir et Salut*, Paris: Editions du Cerf, 1992,
23-41).

ROELOF VAN DEN BROEK

Élus Coëns

→ Martinès de Pasqually bestowed upon the
Freemasons [→ Freemasonry] initiated into the
movement created by him in the second half of
the 18th century the title "The Order of the
Masonic Knights Élus Coëns of the Universe".
Adopting the name that the angel Gabriel had
given to Daniel (Dan. 9:23), he invited these
hommes de désir (men of aspiration) to partake in
the practice of a divine religion and exercise a
priestly function; they would participate in a
theurgic rite, involving invocations (referred to as
"operations") that sometimes resulted in a divine
"manifestation" from the higher planes. Like
Aaron who had been chosen by the Lord to be a
priest in His service (Ex. 40:13), they were – theoretically at least, for few of them seem to have really
experienced manifestations – chosen priests: elect
coëns or cohens (Kohen, plur. Kohanim, meaning
priests in Hebrew), according to the two spellings
used. In the 1760s, aristocrats of both the old and
the new nobility, well-to-do bourgeois who aspired
to spiritual ennoblement, and members of the
clergy, frequented the lodges. The Elus Coëns were
representative of all these different social groups
comprising the Masonic milieu.

Like many Freemasons – in a period when the
preeminence of reason over religious dogma began to be affirmed, which saw the publication of
the *Encyclopédie* between 1751 and 1772, and
the spread of new scientific knowledge within the
framework of scholarly societies and lodges – the
Élus Coëns were in search of the meaning of life
and its authentic religious and spiritual dimension;
they were in quest perhaps of the irrational and the
marvelous, perhaps of power, perhaps of the
absolute. In their own way they reflected the premises of → Illuminism. Having met Pasqually, they
followed his movement and his school, which
united theory and practice, study and exercises,
collective and individual theurgic work, discipline
of body and mind, and which sought to reintegrate
Man into the divine plan, of which he was believed
to have been a part but from which he had been
excluded through his errors and his faults.

Pasqually seems to have begun presenting his
ideas in Marseille, Avignon and Montpellier. Nevertheless, the first known archives place the beginning of his movement around 1760, when he was
in Toulouse. A Freemason, he held a patent from
1738, delivered by Charles Stuart to a certain Don
Martinez Pasqualis who was supposed to have
transmitted it to his eldest son, Joachim Don Mar-
tinez-Pasqualis. At the time, if some doubted the
authenticity of the patent, no one seems to have
disputed that he really was the son of this Mar-
tinez-Pasqualis. Some current research, however,
furnishes evidence of biographical contradictions.
However that may be, Pasqually proposed to the
members of a lodge in Toulouse a Masonic system
and theurgic exercises for entering into communication with the invisible. He did not manage to
achieve a convincing demonstration and was
expulsed. He succeeded, however, in gaining disciples, who maintained a Temple Coën after his
departure for Bordeaux in 1762. Pasqually enjoyed
a favourable reception in the only active lodge in
Bordeaux, the lodge *la Française*, and may even
have functioned as its master. He made disciples
there, or rather, "emulators": he preferred this
expression because it implied that a student does
not have to remain dependent on his instructor, but
may equal and even surpass him.

In 1765, the regiment of Foix arrived in the garrison at Bordeaux. A military lodge was constituted, the lodge Joshua, some of whose members
met with the lodge *la Française*. A few of them,
won over by Pasqually, were initiated as Élus
Coëns. These officers, who may have been more
readily available or more motivated than the other
emulators, played an important role in helping
Pasqually structure his movement into an Order
comprising ten "Scottish" grades, the highest of
which was that of a Master Réau-Croix, who was
entitled to direct a theurgic ceremony. For the
benefit of the new Élus Coëns and the new temples
set up in France and in the colonies, they copied the
rituals, the catechisms, and the instructions that
Pasqually refined, specified or modified as time
went by, as well as the grades. They also formed the
first tribunal for the Order in Bordeaux, instituted
to handle internal and external conflicts in the
Temple Coën. The secretariat, finally, was taken
charge of by one of them, a new officer who had
joined the regiment in Bordeaux and was to become
a recognized writer and Christian theosopher: →
Louis-Claude de Saint-Martin. The officers regularly
came to spend their winter quarters near Pasqually,
take notes of his instructions and comments, and
later communicate them to their absent comrades.

Little by little, these lessons in biblical exegesis were systematized in the form of a treatise which interpreted Old and New Testament texts in the light of Pasqually's theories: *la Réintégration et la Réconciliation de tout Être spirituel créé avec ses premières Vertus force et Puissance dans la jouissance personnelle dont tout Être jouira distinctement en la présence du Créateur* (The Reintegration and Reconciliation of every created Being with his original Virtues, Force and Power, in the personal delight of which each Being will partake in the presence of the Creator). Pasqually here reviews biblical themes from the perspective of various esoteric doctrines: kabbalah [→ Jewish Influences], → alchemy, → Rosicrucianism, gnosis, → hermetism, → astrology, and arithmosophy [→ Number Symbolism]. His sometimes "surprising" translations of Hebrew words are actually based on associations, and sometimes even on homonyms and puns. Interrupted in 1772 by Pasqually's departure to Santo Domingo, the treatise was not published until 1899. It is written without any interruption and must be seen as an edited transcription of notes taken during an oral teaching. Reminiscent of rabbinical oral teachings, it takes recourse to parables, symbolic stories, → correspondences, and analogies to transmit a correct understanding of the sacred texts. It also explains to the Élus Coëns the double fall into matter: God emanated "emancipated" spiritual beings – that is to say, endowed with free will – who had to practice a form of worship prescribed by the Divinity. But these beings sought to act as demiurges. As a punishment, the Creator enclosed them in a circumscribed material space; and Man, an androgynous being with a glorious body, was emanated and emancipated in his turn to guard them and help them regain their original state. But this Man-God, Adam, allowed himself to be seduced by the perverse angels and wanted, in his turn, to imitate God by creating spiritual beings. He fell, pulling the entire material world down with him. The whole work of reconciliation and reintegration in the heart of the divinity, as taught to Pasqually's "emulators", is based on the cult of worship initiated by the Creator, in which Men of Aspiration must render supreme honour to God. This cult requires moral, spiritual, even physical discipline: prayers, daily exercises, invocations, fasts and preparatory exercises for the theurgic meeting, and preparations for warding off negative forces, for purification, and for attempting to enter into contact with the higher spirits, with the angels, and indeed with Christ. During an "operation", the operator knew that he had succeeded in making contact if "manifestations" took place, in the form of "passes" that could be visually or auditorily perceived. These signs, referred to by Pasqually as *La Chose* (the Thing) showed the operator that he was on the path towards reconciliation with the Creator. Pasqually did not explain why he chose the term; but it is noteworthy that prior to Descartes, the unknown in an equation was called "the thing" and could be resolved only by trying out various operations; and also that → Pernety defined "the thing" as the work of the philosopher's stone.

One might ask what attracted Freemasons to the movement created by Pasqually. They may have been attracted by the spiritual exercises; by the strict and unusual daily discipline; by the human and theurgic qualities of this enigmatic man, whose personality deeply influenced some of them; or by his profound and original exegesis of the biblical texts, which had to be of interest to these men raised in Catholicism. They do not seem to have been shocked by the ideas of Pasqually, who in any case required them to continue following their religion. It is true though that a certain number of Élus Coëns became discouraged. One of the officers of the Regiment of Foix, Grainville (1728-1793), wrote in 1798 to an Élus Coën from Lyons, → Jean Baptiste Willermoz (who would become famous by creating a new Masonic movement, the Rectified Scottish Rite): 'We had a temple in the Regiment; we have let the stones fall away imperceptibly . . . now we would hardly be able to find three stones joined together, of the more than twenty-five that once were there'.

Despite Pasqually's efforts to establish the Order in France – he twice went to Paris, where he enjoyed some success with Masonic personalities such as Bacon de la Chevalerie (1731-1821), and set up his supreme tribunal that delivered patents –, the success of his Order really depended on his actual presence. However, constrained by financial problems, he could not regularly go to Paris and visit the Temples Coën open in France. He left for Santo Domingo in 1772, under conditions that are still somewhat unclear: perhaps they had to do with a small inheritance that he had to collect there, but more plausibly with a trial in which the Élus Coëns were involved in giving evidence, and that complicated his life in Bordeaux. After his departure, the order went downhill. Pasqually died two years later, leaving his wife's cousin, Caignet de Lester (1725-1778) as his successor, in Santo Domingo – no doubt hoping that the latter would keep the school alive until his son, born in 1768, could succeed him. Nevertheless, the "regent" soon died and the second successor, de Las Casas, officially closed the Temples Coëns in 1780.

The Élus Coëns were dispersed, but Pasqually had been able to create good contacts among the Réaux-Croix, who were accustomed to participating in the rites wherever they might be. If invited by the master of the Élus Coëns or by one of the "very powerful masters" (that is, a Réau-Croix), they would join the initiation rituals for the supreme grade in "sympathetic" cooperation (that is to say, at a distance), and might do the same in other rites, such as those at the equinoxes, considered favorable to theurgic work. Furthermore the Reaux-Croix made a vow of loyalty, which was respected by most of them. Already at Caignet de Lester's death, Saint-Martin made a tour of the centers that remained active: Lyons with Willermoz, Toulouse, where a new Temple Coën was open, Paris with Bacon de la Chevalerie, and Bordeaux, where the faithful remained in contact with Mrs. de Pasqually (17?-1813), admitted into the Order together with a few other women. With her was one of the most loyal members, a tonsured cleric called Abbot Fournié (1738-1825), who was a simple person but favored by "the Thing". He had been one of Pasqually's secretaries and was now given the assignment by his brothers to guide the education of the young Pasqually (1768-1838) who, in the minds of several Coëns and Willermoz in particular, was destined to make the Order rise again when the time would be ripe. But the Revolution caused them to lose trace of him, thus dashing their last hopes.

Pasqually and his Order, however, were not forgotten. In a new form, without theurgy, it was continued by Willermoz in Freemasonry; by Saint-Martin, whose writings served to disseminate some of Pasqually's ideas, and inspired many 19th century authors, such as Balzac (1799-1850); and finally by Abbot Fournié who, exiled in London, did not create a following there but wrote a treatise like his instructor. Many so-called initiatory movements today still claim to be inspired by the master of the Élus Coëns.

> Martinès de Pasqually, *Traité de la réintégration des êtres*, Paris, éd. Traditionnelles, 1988.

> Lit.: Johel Coutura, *Les Francs-Maçons de Bordeaux au 18ᵉ siècle*, Marcillac: éditions du Glorit, 1988 ♦ Louis-Claude de Saint-Martin, Robert Amadou, *Les leçons de Lyon aux élus coëns*, Paris: Dervy, 1999 ♦ Pierre Fournié Clerc tonsuré, *Ce que nous avons été, ce que nous sommes et ce que nous deviendrons*, Paris: Gutenberg Reprint, 1983 ♦ René Le Forestier *La Franc-Maçonnerie occultiste au XVIIIᵉ siècle & l'ordre des élus coëns*, Paris: La Table d'Emeraude, 1987 ♦ Michelle Nahon & Maurice Friot, "Martinès de Pasqually à Bordeaux", *Bulletin de la Société Martinès*

de Pasqually 7 (1997) & 9 (1999) ♦ Papus, *Martinès de Pasqually, sa vie – ses pratiques magiques – son oeuvre – ses disciples, suivi des catéchismes des élus coens*, Paris: Repr. Dumas, 1976 ♦ Michel Taillefer, "Les disciples toulousains de Martinès de Pasqually", in: *Le Temple cohen de Toulouse (1760-1792)* (Documents martinistes, 25), Paris: Cariscript, 1986 ♦ Dr Gérard Van Rijnberk, *Un thaumaturge au XVIIIᵉ Martinès de Pasqually*, Plan de la Tour: Editions d'aujourd'hui, les Introuvables, 1980.

MICHELLE NAHON

Encausse, Gérard-Anaclet-Vincent → Papus

Eriugena, Johannes Scottus, * 810 Ireland, † 877 France ?

Born in Ireland, where he may have been exposed to the Greek language, Eriugena first surfaces as a liberal arts teacher at the Palace school of Charles the Bald in Northern France around 850 C.E. Few details of his career are known. His knowledge of Greek was probably limited to the use of rhetorical terms. At the request of archbishop Hincmar of Reims he became involved in the ecclesiastical debate on predestination, although it seems he never held any ecclesiastical office himself. His treatise *On divine predestination* refutes the theory of a double predestination (to life and to eternal death) which had been put forth as the true Augustinian position by the monk Gottschalk of Orbais. Claiming that even this lofty religious matter ought to be settled before the forum of human reason, Eriugena argued that God's predestination equals a kind of divine prescience, thereby not undermining a human being's free will. Gottschalk's reasoning was judged faulty due to his poor knowledge of the liberal arts and his ignorance of the Greek language. Having received severe criticism from all sides for his radical intervention, Eriugena withdrew from public debate. Shortly after Charles the Bald commissioned him to translate some important Greek theological texts: *De hominis opificio* (On the Making of Man) by Gregory of Nyssa (ca. 331-395) and especially the important works by → Pseudo-Dionysius the Areopagite (ca. 500). A codex containing the latter had been donated to the Franks by the Byzantine emperor Michael the Stammerer and deposited in the monastery of St. Denis. Furthermore, Eriugena translated the so-called *Ambigua* by Maximus the Confessor (580-662), which is an attempt to harmonize passages in Gregory Nazianzus (ca. 329-390) and Dionysius. Due to his translation efforts his knowledge of Greek was much improved, while gradually broadening into a remarkable interest in and affinity with the basic structure of Neoplatonic philosophy [→ Neoplatonism].

Eriugena's training in the liberal arts and his knowledge of the Greek Christian-Platonic heritage stemming from his translation efforts come to fruition in his *opus magnum, Periphyseon* or *On the Division of Nature* (862-866), in which he synthesized eastern and western thought. While Eriugena believes that → Augustine (354-430) and Dionysius, his preferred western and eastern authorities, never contradict each other, he generally favours the Greek theologians as more astute. This reveals Eriugena's own affinity with Neoplatonic thought, with its emphasis on the dialectical process of *exitus* and *reditus*. Underneath it, there hides a transparently stratified cosmos, which is unified and diversified at the same time so as to bridge the abyss between Creator and creature. By adhering to the *exitus – reditus* model, Eriugena was able to overcome the static subject-object dichotomy of the Creator – creature model in favour of a more dynamic and organic view of the cosmos. For Eriugena, the preferred view of reality is to see God as belonging to nature, as *natura* encompasses both created and divine aspects, rather than seeing nature (i.e., creation) belonging to God. Moreover, the *exitus – reditus* model allows Eriugena to synchronize cosmic development and human self-awareness, as the end goal of his project is both rational and mystical (culminating in oneness with God).

In matters of scriptural exegesis, Eriugena naturally preferred the allegorical expositions of Origen and Ambrose over most literal or historical approaches, with the notable exception of the literal *Homilies on the Hexaemeron* by Basil of Caesarea (330-379), through which Eriugena gained access to the tradition of Greek natural philosophy. Eriugena's deepest intellectual debt is to Dionysius, whose characteristic preference for the so-called *via negativa* he implemented in his own thought, even though he claimed to have learned how to read Dionysius properly only with the aid of Maximus. From Maximus the Confessor he derived his specific interest in the interface between cosmology and anthropology which gives the *Periphyseon* its unique flavour. While Dionysius' *via negativa* taught him to polish human language so as to make it a fitting tool to analyze God's transcendence, Maximus gave him a sense of God's immanence, for the mystery of the Christian redemption embraces the entire cosmos. In conformity with

this, Eriugena developed a Christology in *Periphyseon* IV-V which highlights the event of the incarnation as a paradigmatic change in both human and cosmic history, as the entire cosmos will be redeemed. Rather than refining existing Christological terminology, Eriugena keenly brings out the paradisical quality of Jesus' human nature. At times, Eriugena's synthesis of western and eastern thought translates into an oscillation between eastern and western authorities, as is the case in his angelological analysis. While the angelology of Gregory the Great was generally dominant in the West, Eriugena propagated the angelic hierarchy of Pseudo-Dionysius instead (*Periphyseon* I, 444C). In this way the tradition of Greek angelology became an important influence in the West.

In the domain of → number symbolism Eriugena's eastern and western influences reinforce each other. Augustine's dialectical reflections on the triad, as God created everything *in pondere, numero et mensura* (cf. Wisdom 11:21), resonate nicely with the Dionysian tradition of negative theology in Eriugena's view of the universe as reflecting a created infinity and in his speculations on the divine monad in *Periphyseon* III.

Eriugena works with a wide array of sources as he unites Greek and Latin authorities. Next to the Bible, he had a mostly indirect knowledge of philosophical Neoplatonism and a direct knowledge of many Greek and Latin Church Fathers. He demonstrates a specific interest in the symbolism and scriptural allegories of paradise in *Periphyseon* IV. He equates the first man with *Nous* (the mind) and the first woman with *Aisthesis* (the senses), while the serpent represents their experience of *delectatio* (temptation). His views in this matter derive from Ambrose (339-397), through whom he is connected indirectly to the Middle Platonic tradition of Philo of Alexandria (20 B.C.-50 C.E.).

While it is unclear whether or not Eriugena had access to gnostic [→ Gnosticism] or hermetic sources [→ Hermetic Literature], his overall reasoning displays a definite mystical tendency. This is clear from his preference for the heretical notion of the *apokatastasis pantoon* at the end of the *Periphyseon*. In a more orthodox fashion it comes out in his commentary on Dionysius' Celestial Hierarchy, where he engages in the kind of light metaphysics that would re-emerge in Robert Grosseteste in the early 13th century. The famous dictum *omnia quae sunt lumina sunt* (Pseudo-Dionysius, *In Ier. Cael.* 1.1) is a phrase that has been much quoted in this context.

The *Periphyseon* seems not to have been read widely, as its idiosyncratic nature generally defied understanding. Ignorant indifference turned into hostility when the heretic Amalric of Bene used Eriugena's name to pass off some of his own teachings, for example on the absence of gender division in paradise. As a result, pope Honorius III ordered in 1225 that all copies of the *Periphyseon* be sent to Rome to be burned. When Thomas Gale published the first printed version of the *Periphyseon* in 1681, it was immediately put on the Index. Not until the early 20th century did the critical study of Eriugena's thought begin, following the publication of a seminal biography by M. Cappuyns in 1933. The work on modern editions is now nearly completed.

H.J. Floss (ed.), *Joannes Scotus: Opera omnia* (Patrologia Latina 122: 441-1222), Paris: J.P. Migne, 1853 ◆ J. Barbet (ed.), *Iohannes Scotus Eriugena: Expositiones in Ierarchiam coelestem* (Corpus Christianorum Continuatio Mediaevalis 31), Turnhout: Brepols, 1975 ◆ G. Madec (ed.), *Iohannes Scottus: De divina praedestinatione liber* (Corpus Christianorum Continuatio Mediaevalis 50), Turnhout: Brepols, 1978 ◆ I.P. Sheldon-Williams & L. Bieler (eds.), *Iohannis Scotti Eriugenae Periphyseon (De divisione naturae)* I-III, Dublin: Institute for Advanced Studies, 1968-1981 ◆ E. Jeauneau (ed.), *Iohannis Scotti Eriugenae Periphyseon (De divisione naturae)* IV, Dublin: Institute for Advanced Studies, 1995 ◆ E. Jeauneau (ed.), *Iohannis Scotti seu Eriugenae Periphyseon, editio nova* I-V (Corpus Christianorum Continuatio Mediaevalis 161-165), Turnhout: Brepols, 1996-2003.

Lit.: W. Beierwaltes, "Unity and Trinity in East and West", in: B. McGinn & W. Otten (eds.), *Eriugena: East and West*, Chicago & Notre Dame: University of Notre Dame Press, 1991, 209-231 ◆ M. Cappuyns, *Jean Scot Erigène, sa vie, son oeuvre, sa pensée*, Louvain/Paris: Universitas Catholica Lovaniensis, 1933 (repr. 1964) ◆ Deirdre Carabine, *The Unknown God: Negative Theology in the Platonic Tradition, Plato to Eriugena*, Louvain & Grand Rapids: Peeters & W.B. Eerdmans, 1995 ◆ eadem, *John Scottus Eriugena*, Oxford: Oxford University Press, 2000 ◆ Y. Christe, "Influences et retentissement de l'oeuvre de Jean Scot sur l'Art Mediéval: Bilan et Perspectives", in: W. Beierwaltes (ed.), *Eriugena Redivivus: Zur Wirkungsgeschichte seines Denkens im Mittelalter und im Übergang zur Neuzeit*, Heidelberg: Carl Winter Verlag, 1987, 142-161 ◆ Alois M. Haas, "Mystische Züge in Eriugenas Eschatologie", in: J. McEvoy & M. Dunne (eds.), *History and Eschatology in John Scottus Eriugena and his Time*, Leuven: Leuven University Press, 2002, 429-446 ◆ J. McEvoy, "Metaphors of Light and Metaphysics of Light in Eriugena", in: W. Beierwaltes (ed.), *Begriff und Metapher: Sprachform des Denkens bei Eriugena*, Heidelberg: Carl Winter Verlag, 1990, 149-167 ◆ idem, "Biblical and Platonic Measure in John Scottus Eriugena", in: McGinn & Otten, *Eriugena: East and West*, 153-177 ◆ B. McGinn, "The Entry of Dialectical Mysticism: John

Scottus Eriugena", in: *The Growth of Mysticism: Gregory the Great through the 12th Century*, New York: Crossroad, 1994, 80-118 ◆ D. Moran, *The Philosophy of John Scottus Eriugena: A Study of Idealism in the Middle Ages*, Cambridge: Cambridge University Press, 1989 ◆ W. Otten, *The Anthropology of Johannes Scottus Eriugena*, Leiden: Brill, 1991 ◆ Francesco Paparella, "La storia in Eriugena come autocoscienza divina", in: McEvoy & Dunne, *History and Eschatology* (see above), 39-57.

WILLEMIEN OTTEN

Esotericism

1. ESOTERIC 2. ESOTERICISM
3. TYPOLOGICAL AND HISTORICAL
MEANINGS 4. WESTERN ESOTERICISM

1. ESOTERIC

The adjective "esoteric" (ἐσωτερικός) has often been attributed to Aristotle, but in fact he uses only the word "exoteric" (ἐξωτερικός; see references in Riffard 1990, 65) and opposes it to "acroamatic" (from ἀκρόαμα, oral instruction). It is in a satire by Lucian of Samosata (2nd century C.E.) that the term "esoteric" makes its first appearance. Zeus and Hermes are selling various philosophers as slaves on the market, and claim that if you buy a disciple of Aristotle, you will get two for the same price: 'One seen from without, another seen from within . . . So if you buy him, remember to give to the first one the name of exoteric, and to the second that of esoteric' (*Vitarum Rustio* 26). In → Clement of Alexandria, the term "esoteric" is for the first time associated with → secrecy: 'the disciples of Aristotle say that some of their treatises are esoteric, and others common and exoteric. Further, those who instituted the mysteries, being philosophers, buried their doctrines in myths, so as not to be obvious to all' (*Stromata* V, 58, 3-4). Hippolyte of Rome first applied the terminology to the pupils of Pythagoras, who are said to have been divided into two classes, one exoteric and one esoteric (*Refutation of all Heresies* I, 2, 4), and the same claim is made by Iamblichus in his *Life of Pythagoras*. From here the adjective "esoteric", as referring to secret teachings reserved for a mystic elite, was taken up by later authors, such as Origen and Gregory of Nyssa. It appears in English in Th. Stanley's *History of Philosophy* (1687), as referring to Pythagoras' elite pupils, and in French in a Dictionary of 1752, where it denotes things 'obscure, hidden, and uncommon', orally transmitted by the Ancients to an elite (*Supplément* to *Dictionnaire universel françois et latin*, 1066).

2. ESOTERICISM

The substantive is of much more recent date: it first appears in French (*l'ésotérisme*) in Jacques Matter's *Histoire critique du gnosticisme et de son influence* published in 1828. Matter describes the → gnosticism of the 2nd century in terms of a syncretism between the teachings of Christ on the one hand, and Oriental, Jewish and Greek religio-philosophical traditions on the other. The gnostic 'theosophers of Christianity' had adopted the Pythagorean system of progressive initiation into the mysteries, with years of silent preparation: 'These ordeals and this esotericism existed throughout Antiquity, from China to Gallia . . .' (o.c., 83; and Matter again wrote about 'the esotericism of the gnostics' in an article in *La France littéraire*, febr./march 1834). → Jacques Etienne Marconis de Nègre adopted the neologism in 1839, writing that one of the principal points of the ancient priestly doctrine was 'the division of the sacred science in exotericism or external science and esotericism or internal science' (*L'Hiérophante . . .*, 16). And one year later Pierre Leroux spoke, again with reference to Pythagoreanism, of 'esotericism, the secret school, the religious and political sect, a kind of superior caste elevated to understanding by means of initiation' (*De l'humanité* [1840], II, 397). "Esotericism" was recognized as a new word, finally, in Maurice Lachâtre's *Dictionnaire universel* of 1852, where it is defined as 'From the Greek eisôtheô, the entirety of the principles of a secret doctrine, communicated only to affiliated members'. Perhaps it would have remained no more than an obscure technical term, had it not been popularized by → Eliphas Lévi in his influential books about → magic, from where it entered the vocabulary of occultism [→ occult / occultism]. Thus the theosophist A.D. Sinnett introduced the term into English with his *Esoteric Buddishm* (1883). Since the days of Lévi and Sinnett, various authors and currents have adopted the terms "esoteric" and "esotericism" as a self-designation, each one defining it according to their own preferences. For example, → Alice Bailey defines esotericism as the school of thought – her own – which recognizes 'that behind all happenings in the world of phenomena . . . exists the world of energies' (*Education in the New Age* [1954], 60).

3. TYPOLOGICAL AND HISTORICAL MEANINGS

As can be seen from the preceding overview, the term "esotericism" was not originally a self-designation by which certain religious authors or currents identified themselves or their own perspectives. Rather, it originated in Matter's work as a scholarly label, applied a posteriori to certain religious developments in the context of early Christianity. In current academic research the term is still used as a scholarly construct, according to two main perspectives that must be clearly distinguished.

a. According to *typological* constructs as commonly used in the context of religious studies, "esoteric" and "esotericism" refers to certain types of religious activity, characterized by specific structural features. Thus the term is commonly associated with the notion of "secrecy", and then stands for the practice in various religious contexts of reserving certain kinds of salvific knowledge for a selected elite of initiated disciples. As we have seen, this usage is in line with the original connotations of both the adjective and the substantive. In this typological sense, the term "esotericism" can be applied freely within any religious context, for concerns with secret knowledge reserved for elites can be found throughout history, and all over the world: in pre-literate and literate societies, from antiquity to the present, in east and west. The same is true for another, related typological understanding of the term, that associates it with the deeper, "inner mysteries of religion" as opposed to its merely external or "exoteric" dimensions. Such an understanding, which is also found among the proponents of perennialism [→ Tradition], is particularly congenial to religious studies of a "religionist" orientation (represented by scholars in the tradition of e.g. Mircea Eliade, → Henry Corbin, and → Carl Gustav Jung). Such approaches tend to promote the esoteric or "inner" dimension of religion as its true core, and oppose it to more "superficial", merely "exoteric" dimensions, such as social institutions and official dogmas. Traditionally, many scholars of Western esotericism as understood according to the second, historical usage of the term (see below) have had religionist leanings and therefore adopted this typological usage as well, resulting in considerable confusion about what they really meant by "esotericism".

b. According to *historical* constructs, "esotericism" is understood not as a type of religion or a structural dimension of it, but as a general label for certain specific currents in Western culture that display certain similarities and are historically related. For this reason, and in order to avoid confusion with typological usage, most scholars now prefer to speak of "*Western* esotericism". Although there is considerable debate about the precise definition and demarcation as well as the historical scope of Western esotericism (see below), there exists widespread consensus about the main currents that form its core domain. If restricted to the modern and contemporary period, the field consists in any case of the Renaissance revival of → hermetism and the so-called "occult philosophy" [→ occult / occultism] in a broadly neoplatonic context, and its later developments; → alchemy, → paracelsianism and → rosicrucianism; Christian kabbalah [→ Jewish Influences] and its later developments; theosophical [→ Christian Theosophy] and illuminist currents [→ Illuminism]; and various occultist and related developments during the 19th and 20th centuries, up to and including phenomena such as the → New Age movement. If the period is extended backwards so as to include late antiquity and the middle ages, it also includes → gnosticism, hermetism, neoplatonic theurgy, and the various occult sciences and magical currents that later fed into the Renaissance synthesis. From such a historical perspective, the question of whether the currents in question included initiations into secret knowledge or opposed some "inner" knowledge to mere "external" religiosity is irrelevant as a criterion for what does and does not count as "esoteric": emphases on secrecy and interiority can certainly be found within quite a few of the historical currents just listed, but they are absent in many others, and therefore cannot be seen as defining characteristics.

4. WESTERN ESOTERICISM

That at least some of the major currents such as listed above hang together, and should be seen as a field in its own right, seems to have been suggested first by the end of the 17th century. Ehregott Daniel Colberg attacked what he referred to as "platonic-hermetic Christianity" (*Das Platonisch-Hermetisches* [sic] *Christenthum*, 1690-1691), and not much later → Gottfried Arnold, in his famous "Impartial History" (*Unpartheyische Kirchen- und Ketzer-Historie*, 1699-1700) defended the "heretical" types of Christianity he saw as congenial to his own Christian-theosophical beliefs. In the following century, Jacob Brucker's massive *Historia critica Philosophiae* (1742-1744) likewise treated a range of currents that would nowadays be referred to as "Western esotericism", and straight lines from ancient gnosticism via → Jacob Boehme to German Idealism were drawn by the influential church historian Ferdinand Christian Baur (*Die christliche Gnosis oder die christliche Religions-Philosophie in ihrer geschichtlichen Entwiklung*, 1835). While authors like Colberg and Arnold approached the currents in question from a theological perspective, Brucker and Baur saw them mostly as examples of religious philosophy.

In the wake of the Enlightenment, mainstream 19th-century historiography seems to have largely neglected the domain nowadays referred to as Western esotericism. The specific currents belonging to it tended to be marginalized as the products of irrational *Schwärmerei* or as belonging to the prehistory of "real" science or philosophy (see e.g. the perception of → alchemy as proto-chemistry, or → astrology as proto-astronomy). It must be emphasized, however, that the portrayal of Western esotericism in 19th-century academic historiography has not yet been systematically investigated. Western-esoteric currents may in fact have received more serious attention from historians than might seem to be the case; there is reason to assume that often such research either did not make it into the main works of those historians whose names are still quoted today, or if they did, those works themselves often came to be quoted selectively by later generations, who concentrated in their turn on what they found most relevant and paid little attention to the rest. The progressive neglect of Western esoteric currents by 19th century historiography was undoubtedly aggravated by the fact that contemporary occultist authors such as → Éliphas Lévi or → H.P. Blavatsky *did* begin to write large "histories" of the field, in which their own fantasies took the upper hand over any critical approach to historical evidence. It is not hard to see that this new genre of popular occultist historiography was bound to make the field appear "tainted" in the eyes of academic historians, who therefore had all the more reason to avoid it: a scholar who published a book about Western esoteric currents was likely to be suspected of occultist sympathies by his colleagues, and in fact such suspicions remain common even today.

Important pioneers of the late-19th-century and early 20th-century academic study of Western esotericism are Carl Kiesewetter (whose *Geschichte des neueren Occultismus* [1891-1895] treated the occult sciences from → Agrippa to Du Prel), Auguste Viatte (whose 1927 study *Les sources occultes du Romantisme* [2 vols.] remains a standard reference on pre-Romantic and Romantic → illuminism even today) and Lynn Thorndike (whose massive *History of Magic and Experimental Science* in eight volumes [1923-1958] remains equally indispensable for anybody studying the history of → magic and the "occult sciences"). But the first 20th-century author to really conceive of Western esotericism in an integral fashion somewhat similar to how it is seen today seems to have been Will-Erich Peuckert, with his *Pansophie: Ein Versuch zur Geschichte der weissen und schwarzen*

Magie (1936; 2nd ed. 1956) followed by *Gabalia: Ein Versuch zur Geschichte der magia naturalis im 16. bis 18. Jahrhundert* (1967) and *Das Rosenkreutz* (orig. 1929, posthumously published in 1973). Peuckert began his *Pansophie* with the Florentine platonism and → hermetism of → Ficino and → Pico della Mirandola, and from there continued with the occult philosophy of the Renaissance, → Paracelsus and → Paracelsianism, → Christian theosophy and → Rosicrucianism.

While Peuckert's narrative gave special prominence to the historical antecedents of the figure of Faust as archetype of the magician, another and eventually more influential historiographical current emphasized, rather, the figure of → Hermes Trismegistus. The modern academic study of Renaissance hermetism was launched by Paul Oskar Kristeller, with a pioneering and influential article on Ficino and → Lazzarelli published in Italian in 1938 (repr. in *Studies in Renaissance Thought and Letters* I [1956], 221-247); and in 1955 appeared a first collection of Renaissance "hermetic" texts edited by E. Garin, M. Brini, C. Vasoli and P. Zambelli (*Test umanistici su l'Ermetismo*, 1955). Basing herself upon Italian researches along these lines, Frances A. Yates then published in 1964 her *Giordano Bruno and the Hermetic Tradition*, which definitively put the study of "the Hermetic Tradition" on the map of international academic research. Yates' "grand narrative" of hermeticism [→ Hermeticism and Hermetic Societies] created what was in fact the first comprehensive academic paradigm for the study of Western esotericism (although she herself did not use that term). It conceived of the field as based upon an intrinsically magical "hermetic philosophy" carried by great Renaissance "magi" such as Pico della Mirandola, → Giordano Bruno or → John Dee and continued (as argued in her later work) by the → Rosicrucianism of the 17th century; and this hermetic philosophy was presented as having given an essential impulse – perhaps *the* essential impulse – to the scientific revolution. This "Yates thesis" was highly provocative because it presented magic as the master-key to understanding the rise of modern science. Authors like Mary Hesse attacked it right away, arguing that scientific thinking had to be understood as emerging from its own internal history. The result was a vehement debate among historians of science and philosophy about the relevance of hermeticism to their domains of research. Once the question of a possible role of "hermetic" currents in the scientific revolution had been put on the agenda, there was a basis for investigating e.g. the importance of

alchemy in the work of great figures such as → Isaac Newton (as demonstrated by B.J.T. Dobbs, R.S. Westfall and others) and Robert Boyle (as demonstrated more recently by L. Principe), as well as many lesser ones. Nowadays Yates' thesis is no longer accepted in its radical form, and her interpretations are criticized in other respects as well, but it is nevertheless thanks to her that the study of hermeticism is now considered an acceptable pursuit in the context of history of science and philosophy.

A more problematic result of Yates' work, at least as far as academic scholarship is concerned, was the appropriation of what may be called the "Yates Paradigm" by a variety of more or less esoterically tinged "religionist" authors in the wake of the counterculture of the 1960s. It was easy for them to embrace hermeticism as a traditional counterculture rebelling against the forces of the establishment. Yates' narrative portrayed the Renaissance magi as emphasizing personal religious experience against the dogmas of the church, and trying to bring "the imagination to power" (*l'imagination au pouvoir*: the famous slogan of the 1960s student generation) against the cold "reign of quantity" associated with mechanistic science. As far as the religious (or "spiritual") dimensions of hermeticism were concerned, religionist authors interpreted them in the light of approaches associated with "Eranos" scholars such as → Carl Gustav Jung, Mircea Eliade, → Henry Corbin or Joseph Campbell (see Wasserstrom 1999; Hakl 2001), all of whom are themselves inspired by esoteric worldviews to a greater or lesser extent. The result was a religionist and often crypto-esoteric style of writing about esotericism that, predictably, tended to be treated with suspicion by scholars who insisted on academic rigor: once again, the agenda for the study of Western esotericism risked being dominated by apologists rather than scholars. With respect to post-18th-century developments, which fall beyond the scope of the "hermetic philosophy" covered by the Yates paradigm, the situation was even more unsatisfactory: as a rule, it can be said that serious studies in this domain (by e.g. James Webb, Joscelyn Godwin, Nicholas Goodrick-Clarke, Christopher McIntosh) have been published in spite of the academy rather than thanks to it.

It is only as late as the 1990s that the study of Western esotericism, under that title, has begun to be seriously recognized as an academic field of study in its own right. In these years the Yates paradigm, as well as its religionist interpretation from a countercultural perspective, has come to be challenged by a different one, introduced by

Antoine Faivre. Faivre defined Western esotericism as based upon a "form of thought" that could be recognized by the presence of four intrinsic characteristics, to which two non-intrinsic ones might be added. The intrinsic characteristics are (1) a belief in invisible and non-causal "correspondences" between all visible and invisible dimensions of the cosmos, (2) a perception of nature as permeated and animated by a divine presence or life-force, (3) a concentration on the religious → imagination as a power that provides access to worlds and levels of reality intermediary between the material world and God, (4) the belief in a process of spiritual transmutation by which the inner man is regenerated and re-connected with the divine. The two non-intrinsic characteristics – frequently but not always present – are (1) the belief in a fundamental concordance between several or all spiritual traditions, and (2) the idea of a more or less secret transmission of spiritual knowledge (Faivre 1994, 10-15; the definition was first formulated in a French publication in 1992).

The heuristic value of Faivre's definition is undeniable. Other than the Yates paradigm it can be seen as encompassing the entire period from the Renaissance to the present, while still clearly demarcating the field from non-esoteric currents. As a result, during the 1990s it has been adopted by many other scholars and has largely replaced Yates' grand narrative as the major paradigm in the field. Simultaneously, of course, various aspects and implications of it have come to be challenged. It has been suggested that the definition works best for the Renaissance "occult philosophy" and the late 18th/early 19th century Illuminist and Romantic context, but can only partly account for developments in the "spiritualist"/pietist context since the 17th century and the secularization of esotericism during the 19th and 20th centuries (Hanegraaff 1996, 2004); its restriction to modern and contemporary periods has been questioned, and it has been suggested that the limitations of Faivre's phenomenological concept of a "form of thought" could be overcome by a discursive approach (von Stuckrad 2004); and the nature of the relation of Western esotericism *sensu* Faivre to Christianity and to the other great religions of the book constitutes an ongoing subject for debate as well (Hanegraaff 1995, 2004; Neugebauer-Wölk 2003; von Stuckrad 2004). Undoubtedly these discussions will cause the present paradigm for the study of Western esotericism to further evolve into new directions. It is clear, however, that largely thanks to the emergence of the Faivre paradigm in the 1990s, Western esotericism is now increasingly recognized

as an area of research that deserves serious academic attention, and the implications of which are likely to transform our perception of Western religious history as a whole.

Lit.: Antoine Faivre, *Access to Western Esotericism*, Albany: SUNY Press, 1994 ♦ idem, *Theosophy, Imagination, Tradition: Studies in Western Esotericism*, Albany: SUNY Press, 2000 ♦ idem, "La question d'un ésotérisme comparé des religions du livre", in: *Henry Corbin et le comparatisme spirituel* (Cahiers du Groupe d'Etudes Spirituelles Comparées 8), Paris: Archè-Edidit, 2000, 91-120 ♦ Olav Hammer, "Esotericism in New Religious Movements", in: James R. Lewis (ed.), *The Oxford Handbook of New Religious Movements*, Oxford: Oxford University Press, 2004, 445-465 ♦ Wouter J. Hanegraaff, "Empirical Method in the Study of Esotericism", *Method & Theory in the Study of Religion* 7:2 (1995), 99-129 ♦ idem, *New Age Religion and Western Culture: Esotericism in the Mirror of Secular Thought*, Leiden, New York, Köln: E.J. Brill 1996/Albany: SUNY Press, 1998, 384-405 ♦ idem, "On the Construction of 'Esoteric Traditions'", in: Antoine Faivre & Wouter J. Hanegraaff (eds.), *Western Esotericism and the Science of Religion*, Louvain: Peeters, 1998, 11-61 ♦ idem, "Beyond the Yates Paradigm: The Study of Western Esotericism between Counterculture and New Complexity", *Aries* 1:1 (2001), 5-37 ♦ idem, "The Dreams of Theology and the Realities of Christianity", in: J. Haers & P. de Mey (eds.), *Theology and Conversation: Towards a Relational Theology* (Bibliotheca Ephemeridum Theologicarum Lovaniensis, 172), Leuven: Peeters, 2004, 709-733 ♦ idem, "The Study of Western Esotericism: New Approaches to Christian and Secular Culture", in: Peter Antes, Armin W. Geertz & Randi Warne (eds.), *New Approaches to the Study of Religion*, Berlin & New York: De Gruyter, 2004 ♦ Hans Thomas Hakl, *Der verborgene Geist von Eranos: Unbekannte Begegnungen von Wissenschaft und Esoterik. Eine alternative Geistesgeschichte des 20. Jahrhunderts*, Bretten: Scientia nova, 2001 ♦ Jean-Pierre Laurant, *L'ésotérisme chrétien en France au XIXe siècle*, Lausanne: L'Âge d'Homme, 1992, 19-48 ♦ idem, *L'ésotérisme*, Paris: Les éditions du Cerf, 1993 ♦ Monika Neugebauer-Wölk, "Esoterik und Christentum vor 1800: Prolegomena zu einer Bestimmung ihrer Differenz", *Aries* 3:2 (2003), 127-165 ♦ Pierre A. Riffard, *L'ésotérisme*, Paris: Robert Laffont, 1990 ♦ Kocku von Stuckrad, *Was ist Esoterik? Kleine Geschichte des geheimen Wissens*, Munich: C.H. Beck, 2004 ♦ Steven M. Wasserstrom, *Religion after Religion: Gershom Scholem, Mircea Eliade, and Henry Corbin at Eranos*, Princeton: Princeton University Press, 1999.

WOUTER J. HANEGRAAFF

Essenes, Esoteric legends about

The Essenes were a distinct group of Jews which, until the 20th century, was known only from a few descriptions in Greek and Latin texts. They are described by Philo in *Hypothetica* (11.1-18) and *Every Good Man Is Free* (12.75-13.91). Josephus writes of the Essenes in passages of several of his books. The most detailed description is found in *The Jewish War* (2.119-161). A shorter passage on them is included in *Jewish Antiquities* (18.18-22). Pliny the Elder wrote briefly about the Essenes in his *Natural History* (5.73). Since the discovery of the Dead Sea Scrolls at Qumran in 1947, the group associated with the scrolls was for the next five decades generally assumed to be the Essene community described by these Greek and Roman authors. This assumption has again been increasingly questioned during the 1990s (Boccaccini 1998).

Philo and Josephus describe the Essenes as an all-male order, divided into distinct classes and organized under officials to whom obedience was required. They are depicted as a tightly knit group following an austere and pious rule of conduct, living communally and strictly observing Mosaic law. Neophytes were initiated into the order and received three symbols of their new status: a hatchet, a loin-cloth, and a white garment. After a lengthy period of probation, the initiate swore an oath binding himself to piety, justice, a moral life and secrecy regarding the content of Essene teachings.

In his *Ecclesiastical History* (book II chapter 17), Eusebius of Caesarea (260-339) understands Philo's remarks on a group living in Egypt, whom he called Therapeutae, as describing forerunners of Christian monastic life. Through a mistaken identification of the Therapeutae and the Essenes, the latter group in time came to be used as an important topos in post-Reformation controversies concerning monasticism. A discussion developed about the acceptability of Christian monasticism, to which the Protestants were opposed. On the other side, it was especially the Carmelites – who claimed descent of their Order, through the Essenes, from Elia and Elisa – who defended the thesis that the Essenes were an early Christian monastic community. Several texts that claim that the Essenes were Christians also argue that Jesus had been one of that community, thereby giving monasticism even stronger rhetorical support.

The idea that Jesus had been an Essene was interpreted quite differently in Johann Georg Wachter's (1673-1757) influential *De primordiis Christianae religionis*, written in 1703 and revised in 1717. The Essenes are here described as a link in a long chain of transmission of "natural theology", i.e. a moral and philosophical deist tradition that had its ori-

gins among the Egyptians and included the kabbalah. Christianity is thus interpreted by Wachter as the outcome of a historical development and not of a revelation. Wachter's text was not published, but circulated widely in manuscript form. The first reference in print to his Essene hypothesis is found in Humphrey Prideaux *The Old and New Testament Connected in the History of the Jews and Neighbouring Nations* (1716-1718). Thereafter it becomes a common element in various Enlightenment critiques of Christianity as a revealed religion. It is also against this background that, from 1730 onwards, Masonic authors [→ Freemasonry] join into the discussion about the Essenes.

In 1730/1731, the anonymously published *A Defense of Masonry* appears to be the first Masonic text in which the Essenes are mentioned. They are described in terms that make them appear as Freemasons avant la lettre. By associating the two, the moral respectability of the Essenes as stressed in the ancient sources is used as a defense of Masonry. This pamphlet may at first have made little impact, but it was reprinted in the second edition of Anderson's widely disseminated *Constitutions* in 1738 (pp. 216-226, esp. 221).

A manuscript of a Masonic neo-Templar Order, the *Ordre Sublime des Chevaliers Elus*, dated 1750, radicalizes the parallelism by presenting the Freemasons as being, via several links, the ultimate historical descendants of the Essenes. → Jean-Baptiste Willermoz adopted this claim and in 1778 included statements to that effect in a text entitled *Instruction pour la réception des Frères Écuyers novices de l'Ordre bienfaisant de Chevaliers Maçons de la Cité Sainte*. These claims were repeated in successive versions of the text. From then on references to the Essenes are abundant in masonic literature.

By the end of the 18th century, diverse legend elements had been created that drew selectively on the characteristics of the Essenes as presented in the classical sources. From Masonic literature comes the image of the Essenes as a morally elevated brotherhood with secret initiation rituals and a set of symbols marking them off from the uninitiated. Wachter's book is the source of the legend element that makes the Essenes into covert rationalists, and places Jesus as a member of the Essene brotherhood. The Freemason Karl Bahrdt (1741-1792) is the first writer to have synthesized the various elements and to present for the public a detailed version of the legend. In *Briefe ueber die Bibel im Volkston* (1782), Jesus and several other central New Testament characters are presented as members of this initiatic order. The Essene faith is portrayed as a form of enlightened humanism, and the life and mission of Jesus are reinterpreted in rationalist terms. In Bahrdt's account, the Essenes spread their rational faith by staging fake miracles in order to convince the spiritually less enlightened masses. Jesus survived the crucifixion and was healed by Joseph of Arimathea and Nicodemus, who were also Essenes. Jesus then withdrew from public life and lived into old age. Karl Heinrich Venturini (1768-1849) fleshed out the details of Bahrdt's account in his four-volume novel *Natuerliche Geschichte des grossen Propheten von Nazareth* (1800-1802).

The main lines of the legend were later summarized in a widely spread anonymous text, *Wichtige historische Enthüllungen über die wirkliche Todesart Jesu* (1849), also known as the *Essäerbrief*. The author of this text was soon thereafter established as Philipp Friedrich Hermann Klencke (1813-1881), a medical doctor from Braunschweig. Although it consists of a summary of sections of Venturini's novel, Klencke's slender volume is purported to be a translation of a previously unknown Essene text in Latin. The text was vigorously attacked for being spurious, which led its author to publish several rejoinders on the same theme. The influence of the *Essäerbrief* can be judged by the fact that it went through numerous reprints since its first appearance, was translated into several languages and inspired several pastiches with similar themes.

19th-century esotericism was deeply influenced by the discovery of the Orient. From the early 19th century and onwards, attempts were made to explain the apparent similarities between Indian and Western forms of religion by claiming that there were historical links between the teachings of Jesus and Buddhism. This motif was combined with the Essene legend by the British author Godfrey Higgins (1772-1833). In his *Anacalypsis* (1833-1836), he presents a vast, speculative history of the human race and its spiritual development. The various religions of the world are placed into an overarching historiographic scheme, and are seen as reflexes of a perennial philosophy [→ Tradition]. The Essenes are included in this historiography in terms that recall all of the main themes encountered previously. The teachings of Jesus are at heart a set of moral precepts. Jesus was a member of the Essene order, a brotherhood that taught the same philosophy as the ancient Indians. Higgins surmises that the lost sacred writings of the Essenes may have been identical to the Vedas. Through the Essenes, this ancient wisdom was also passed on to both the Carmelites and the Freemasons. Several texts by later authors continue to give the Essenes various roles as links between diverse Eastern and Western traditions. Examples are Ernest de Bunsen *The Angel-Messiah of Buddhists, Essenes and Christians* (1880) and Arthur Lillie *Buddhism in Christendom or Jesus, the Essene* (1887).

Higgins' *Anacalypsis* is a major source of → Helena Blavatsky's worldview, and appears to have been the principal channel of transmission of the Essene legend into theosophical and post-theosophical currents. References to the Essenes are ubiquitous in the occultist literature, and the examples below are drawn from a large set of such accounts. The Essene legend thus also figures prominently in books by → Edouard Schuré, Otto Hanisch (founder of the Mazdaznan movement), → H. Spencer Lewis, → Manly Palmer Hall and many others. Whereas earlier accounts often claim that the Essenes were initiated into a more rational faith than that of the masses, many such late 19th and 20th century occultist versions of the legend present Essene initiatic knowledge as mysterious and esoteric.

Although the Essene motif is a minor one in Blavatsky's writings, mentions of the Essenes as a secret brotherhood and Jesus as an initiate into the wisdom of this group are scattered through her work. The Essenes are thus in *The Secret Doctrine* (vol. II: 111) seen as a group that taught the doctrine of → reincarnation, as supposedly did Jesus himself. In *Esoteric Christianity* (1902), second-generation theosophists → Annie Besant and → Charles Leadbeater expand on the topic of induction into arcane secrets, explaining that Jesus began his spiritual career in an Essene monastery but later continued to Egypt, where he received various further initiations.

→ Rudolf Steiner gives a wealth of details on the Essenes and their purported connection with Jesus, especially in *Das Matthäus-Evangelium* (1910) and *Aus der Akasha-Forschung: Das fünfte Evangelium* (1913). The Essenes were a brotherhood of initiates devoted to a complex process of spiritual development and clairvoyant investigation. Steiner also gives them a role as link between Buddhism and Christianity, but the connection is due to the intervention of spiritual entities rather than to any mundane historical transmission. Jesus is said to have entered the Essene community because he had acquired clairvoyant faculties similar to theirs. This fact came to the attention of some Essenes who lived in Nazareth, who admitted him to their order without requiring that he go through the usual initiatory rituals. Jesus stayed among them until his twenty-eighth year and was given esoteric knowledge in the form of visions.

→ Edgar Cayce associates the Essenes with Mount Carmel rather than Qumran, and states that they were part of a spiritual lineage established by Elijah. According to his readings, Mary and Joseph had previously come into contact with this group, and the initiations of Jesus were planned beforehand. The principal aim of being initiated among the Essenes was to receive instructions in → astrology, numerology, phrenology and the doctrine of reincarnation. Furthermore, in his past-life readings, Cayce often claimed that his clients had been acquaintances of Jesus and/or members of the Essene community. In time, a whole gallery of characters supposedly involved in this period of Jesus' life emerged from these trance sessions.

In the contemporary period, the writer most heavily reliant on the Essene motif was Edmond Bordeaux Szekely (1905-1979). In numerous books, notably *The Essene Gospel of Peace* (1974/75), Szekely portrayed the Essenes as links in the transmission of the perennial philosophy, but also as the forerunners of such modern preoccupations as holistic health and natural foods. Several organizations formed around the ideas and practices presented in Szekely's books, including the Essene School of Life and the First Christians' Essene Church.

The Essene legend entered the → New Age movement in the 1970s through compilations of Cayce's readings, as well as through channeled texts ascribed to discarnate entities such as Seth and Ramtha. From then on, the Essene motif is freely combined with other Jesus legends prevalent in the New Age milieu, not least his purported travels in Asia. As one example among many of this historical *bricolage*, New Age healer Diane Stein in her book *Essential Reiki* (1995) explains that the magi were in reality Buddhist monks who took Jesus on a tour of Egypt and India. Inspired by what he learned, Jesus became a member of an Essene order. He survived the crucifixion and lived near Srinagar until he died of natural causes at the age of 120 years.

Johann Georg Wachter, "De primordiis Christianae religionis", in: Winfried Schröder (ed.), *Freidenker der europäischen Aufklärung*, vol. 1:2, Stuttgart-Bad Cannstatt: Frommann-Holzboog, 1995 ♦ Karl Bahrdt, *Briefe ueber die Bibel im Volkston*, Halle: [s.n.], 1782 ♦ Karl Heinrich Venturini, *Natuerliche Geschichte des grossen Propheten von Nazareth*, Bethlehem (= Copenhagen): Schubothe, 1800-1802 ♦ Anon., *Wichtige historische Enthüllungen über die wirkliche Todesart Jesu*, Leipzig: Kollmann, 1849 ♦

Arthur Lillie, *Buddhism in Christendom or Jesus, the Essene*, London: Kegan Paul, Trench & Co., 1887 ♦ Rudolf Steiner *Das Matthäus-Evangelium*, Dornach: Steiner Verlag, 1910 ♦ idem, *Aus der Akasha-Forschung: Das fünfte Evangelium*, Dornach: Steiner Verlag, 1913 ♦ Edmond Bordeaux Szekely, *The Gospel of the Essenes*, London: Daniel, 1976.

Lit.: Per Beskow, *Strange Tales About Jesus: A Survey of Unfamiliar Gospels*, Philadelphia: Fortress Press, 1983 ♦ Gabriele Boccaccini, *Beyond the Essene Hypothesis*, Michigan & Cambridge: Eerdmans, 1998 ♦ Rainer Henrich, "Rationalistische Christentumskritik in essenischem Gewand: Der Streit um die 'Enthüllungen über die wirkliche Todesart Jesu'", *Zeitschrift für Kirchengeschichte* 106 (1995), 345-362 ♦ Reender Kranenborg, "The Presentation of the Essenes within Western Esotericism", *Journal of Contemporary Religion* 13 (1998), 245-256 ♦ Albert Schweitzer, *Geschichte der Leben-Jesu-Forschung*, Tübingen: Mohr, 1913 ♦ Siegfried Wagner, *Die Essener in der wissenschaftlichen Diskussion vom Ausgang des 18. bis zum Beginn des 20. Jahrhunderts* (Beihefte zur Zeitschrift für alttestamentische Wissenschaft 79), Berlin: Töpelmann, 1960.

OLAV HAMMER & JAN A.M. SNOEK

Etteilla (ps. of Jean-Baptiste Alliette), * 1.3.1738 Paris ?, † 13.12.1791 Paris ?

According to a long but spurious tradition, later refuted by Decker, Alliette was a barber and wigmaker. The truth of the matter is that, at least until 1768, he was a seed and grain merchant, like all the rest of his family members; and from 1768-1769 he was a print seller. In one of his books (1789) he refers to himself as a 'Professeur d'Algèbre', but this fancy title, although "confirmed" by his burial certificate, probably lacks any professional basis. In all likelihood, Alliette was more of a fortune-teller. In his publications, he freely advertised his rather expensive lessons and consultations in → Tarot, → astrology and healing. As early as 1772, in *Le zodiaque mystérieux* he gave a colorful description of how a spirit had appeared and spoken to him.

Alliette shared the fashion of his day for membership in esoteric societies and study groups. In this connection, he created in 1788 a "Société littéraire des interprètes du livre de Thoth", which aimed at using the seventy-eight Tarot cards as the structure of a universal language. On July 1st 1790 he also opened a "Nouvelle Ecole de Magie" (New School of Magic) in Paris. It seems to have attracted quite a few students. Lessons were offered on the Book of Thot (i.e., the Tarot of Marseille, see below) and many other related subjects. In his

Cours théorique published the same year, Alliette gave detailed commentaries on the essentials of the program of the "School".

At the latest, Alliette's interest in the Tarot dates from 1770, when his first book appeared: *Etteilla, ou Maniere de se Récréer avec le Jeu de Cartes Nommées Tarots*. Then, in 1783 and 1785, he published a series of four books ("Cahiers") under that same title. These contained many further developments of the ideas presented in the earlier book, and added fresh perspectives on them. Due to these publications, he stands out as the first author in the history of Tarot literature to have ever presented an esoteric interpretation of the Tarot of Marseille, or at least, such a detailed one. Alliette's initiative sparked a "tarotic" esoteric current of interest, which has never really diminished until the present time. Many Tarot decks posthumously published under his name are, however, of dubious provenance. In his "Cahiers", he informs his readers that the cards are not meant as a game, but as a tool for divination and meditation, and that he considers himself a restorer of their original meaning. He claims, for example, that the deck of Marseille (for this is what he means by "the Book of Thot") had been revealed by priests in ancient Egypt. With regard to this point in particular, it seems that only the Comte de Mellet was earlier in making a similar claim; it can be found in an article by him that was inserted into → Antoine Court de Gébelin's *Le monde primitif* (vol. XVII, 1781).

But Alliette goes much further than Mellet. In 1783 he assures us that the Book of Thot had been devised by a committee of seventeen magi, presided over by → Hermes Trismegistus himself in the 171st year after the Flood, some 3953 years ago. He was not content just to make this contribution, which strongly influenced the contemporary craze for Egypt [→ Egyptomany]. In *Le zodiaque mystérieux* (1772), and even more so later, in the fourth "Cahier" (1785), he claimed to have discovered strong connections between Tarot and astrology; in fact, this last "Cahier" is devoted to discovering → correspondences between the cards of the Tarot and the stars. He also occasionally drew upon what he knew of Jewish Kabbalah, notably when attempting to relate each trump card to a letter of the Hebrew alphabet. In 1786 and 1787 he published books dealing with other esoteric matters as well. First, there were two publications devoted to physiognomony; and second, a – better known – book on alchemy, *Les Sept Nuances de l'Oeuvre Philosophique-Hermétique*, in which he presents himself as a disciple of the Comte de → Saint-Germain. Alliette claimed that Saint-Germain, who was supposed to have died in 1784, was still alive. Alliette also boldly presents a full description of "le Grand Oeuvre" (the alchemical Opus Magnum) and gives impressive descriptions of what he calls the "hautes sciences" (that is to say, the "higher" or "occult" sciences) notably in his book of 1785 published under that title.

In 1787, when the Philalèthes were preparing their Masonic Convention in Paris, they decided to consult Alliette for his knowledge of → magic, despite the fact that he was not a Freemason. Alliette later became the object of some curiosity as a source of knowledge about esoteric literature, and was recognized as such by the fountainhead of the Occultist movement, → Eliphas Lévi, in his *Dogme et Rituel de la Haute Magie* (1858). Lévi wrote some critical commentaries on the works of Alliette, to whom he referred as 'the inspired whigmaker'. Thanks to Lévi we know that certain unpublished manuscripts of Alliette circulated in the first half of the 19th century: 'The writings of Etteilla', writes Lévi, 'have not all been printed, and some manuscripts of this father of modern cartomancers are in the hands of a Paris bookseller who has been good enough to let us examine them. Their most remarkable points are the obstinate perseverance and incontestable good faith of the author, who all his life perceived the grandeur of the occult sciences, but was destined to die at the gate of the sanctuary without ever penetrating behind the veil'.

Outside the circles of esoteric literature, Alliette inspired several authors of fiction. For example, Alexandre Dumas used him as a picturesque, albeit short-lived figure in one of his tales, 'L'Histoire merveilleuse de don Bernardo de Zuniga'. In a series of short stories by the same author, *Les mille et un fantômes* (1831) Alliette is cast in the role of an "illuminé" who knows "the secret of the elixir of life", is a friend of the Count of Saint-Germain, and has reached the age of three hundred years at the time of the French Revolution.

The bibliography of Alliette's works is fraught with technical difficulties. For more details see Decker et al. (infra) ♦ *Etteilla, ou Maniere de se Récréer avec le Jeu de Cartes Nommées Tarots*, Amsterdam and Paris: Lesclapart, 1770 ♦ *Maniere de se Récréer avec le Jeu de Cartes nommées Tarots*, Amsterdam and Paris: Chez l'Auteur, 1783-1785 (= "Cahiers" I, II, III, 1783; IV, 1785) ♦ Repr. of Cahiers I and II in one volume by Paris: Jobert, 1977 ♦ repr. of Cahier IV under the title *Etteilla: L'astrologie du livre de Toth* (Jacques Halbronn, ed.), Paris: Guy Trédaniel, 1993 ♦ *Fragments sur les hautes sciences, suivi d'une note sur les trois sortes de médecines données aux hommes, dont une mal à propos délaissée*, Amsterdam and Paris, 1785 ♦

*Philosophie des Hautes Sciences, ou La Clef Don-
née aux Enfans de l'Art de la Science & de la
Sagesse . . .*, Amsterdam and Paris: Chez l'Auteur, et
Nyon l'aîné, etc., 1785 ♦ *Les Sept Nuances de l'Oeu-
vre Philosophique-Hermétique, suivies d'un traité sur
la perfection des métaux, mis sous l'Avant-Titre
L.D.D.P* [= le dernier du pauvre], Paris: Ségaut, 1786
♦ *Apperçu* [sic] *d'un Rigoriste sur la Cartonomancie et
sur son Auteur*, Paris: Chez l'Auteur, 1786 ♦ *Jeu des
Tarots, ou Le Livre de Thot, ouvert a la Maniere des
Egyptiens, pour servir ici à l'Interprétation de tous les
Rêves, Songes, et Visions diurnes et nocturnes*, Mem-
phis = Paris: Veuve Lesclapart, Petit, et Samson, 1788
♦ *Livre de Thot: Les Sages ont ensemencé ce champ des
Sciences et des Arts, Pourquoi, Profanes, venez-vous y
jetter de l'Ivraie?* Paris: Chez l'Auteur, 1789 ♦ *Science:
Leçons Théoriques et Pratiques du Livre de Thot*,
Amsterdam and Paris: Chez l'Auteur, 1787 ♦ *Cours
théorique et pratique du livre de Thot, pour entendre
avec justesse, l'art, la science et la sagesse de rendre les
oracles*, s.l. 1790 ♦ *Dictionnaire synonymique du livre
de Toth, ou synonymes des significations primitives
tracées sur les feuillets du livre de Toth*, Paris: Chez
l'Auteur, 1791.

Lit.: Ronald Decker, Thierry Depaulis and Michael
Dummett, *A Wicked Pack of Cards: The Origins of the
Occult Tarot*, London: G. Duckworth, 1996, 74-115 ♦
Michael Dummett, *The Game of Tarot from Ferrara to
Salt Lake City*, London: Routledge & Kegan Paul,
1980, 105-110 ♦ Jacques Halbronn, "Recherches sur
l'histoire de l'astrologie et du Tarot", appendix to the
1993 reprint of Etteilla's *Cahier IV* (*supra*, 1-127) ♦
J.B. Millet-Saint-Pierre, *Recherches sur le dernier sor-
cier et la dernière école de magie*, Le Havre: Le Pelletier,
1859 ♦ Eloïse Mozzani, *Magie et superstitions de la fin
de l'Ancien Régime à la Restauration*, Paris: R. Laffont,
1988, 68-77 ♦ Charles Porset, *Les Philalèthes et
les Convents de Paris: Une politique de la folie* (Nouvelle Bibliothèque initiatique 18), Paris: H. Champion,
1996, 215, 294, 494, 523-525.

ANTOINE FAIVRE

Eugenius Philalethes → Vaughan,
Thomas

Eugenius Theodidactus → Heydon, John

Evola, Giulio Cesare (Julius or Jules),
* 19.5.1898 Rome, † 11.6.1974 Rome

Writer on philosophy, cultural and religious history, esoteric traditions and politics. Many details
concerning the circumstances of Evola's life remain
uncertain, since he neither discussed his private life
nor kept correspondence. Evola had probably
sprung from Sicilian landed gentry, was educated
as a Roman Catholic, but soon fell under the intel-

lectual sway of Arthur Rimbaud (1854-1891),
Friedrich Nietzsche (1844-1900), Carlo Michel-
staedter (1887-1910) and Otto Weininger (1880-
1903). He served in the First World War as an
artillery officer. Following demobilisation, he
underwent an existential crisis, compounded by
experiments with ether, which led to a transcendent
experience of the self. He became acquainted with
the Futurists Giovanni Papini (1881-1956), who
got Evola interested in Eastern wisdom and Meister Eckhart (c. 1260-1328) as well as Filippo
Tommaso Marinetti (1876-1944), who probably
introduced Evola to Benito Mussolini (1883-
1945). He next turned to Dadaism and became
friends with its chief representative Tristan Tzara
(ps. Samuel Rosenstock, 1896-1963). Evola's
paintings (exhibitions in Rome and Berlin), poetry
and theoretical writings established him as a co-
founder of Italian Dadaism. Evola broke off his
engineering studies shortly before graduation, as
he had no wish to become "bourgeois". He never
married nor practised a "bourgeois" profession. In
1922 he ended his provocative, artistic activity and
developed his own philosophy, which he called
"magical idealism" → after Novalis (Friedrich von
Hardenberg, 1772-1801). He brought his philosophical works to a conclusion around 1926. From
1924 onwards, he launched into an intensive study
of Western esoteric traditions (chiefly → alchemy
and → magic) and Eastern → mysticism (especially
Taoism and Tantrism) and established close contacts with the independent Theosophical group
Ultra in Rome, where he also lectured. In spite of
his personal friendships he became very sceptical of
Theosophy [→ Theosophical Society] and →
Anthroposophy. Thanks to the important Italian
esotericist → Arturo Reghini (1878-1946), Evola
made his first contact with the idea of an "integral
Tradition" (i.e. the idea that all essential religions
and cultures stem from a unified primal → Tradition of transcendent origin) in the sense of → René
Guénon (1886-1951), with whom Evola began to
correspond. In the period 1927-1929 he assumed
leadership of the magical initiatory Group of Ur,
in which esotericists such as Reghini and Guido
de Giorgio (1890-1957) participated, as well as,
anonymously, representatives of Italian intellectual
life including Emilio Servadio (1904-1995), the
father of Italian psychoanalysis, Aniceto del Massa
(1898-1976), art critic and writer, and the anthro-
posophically influenced poets Girolamo Comi
(1890-1968) and Arturo Onofri (1885-1928). In
the second year of Ur a dispute between Evola and
Reghini caused the end of its practical group work,
which was intended to influence politics spiritually

by the formation of magical chains and the creation of subtle energies. The reports of the group that remained around Evola were published under the name Krur. During this period Evola took up mountaineering, and became the first person to make certain Alpine ascents.

From 1925 onwards Evola had tried to intervene in the spiritual and political struggles of fascism in order to give it a sacral and imperial orientation. After the Group of Ur had dissolved, Evola immediately began to publish an intellectual and political periodical *La Torre*, which was discontinued by the order of Mussolini after ten issues, because Evola's spiritual imperialism was too intransigent. At this time Evola even had to protect himself against fascist hard-liners. His polemic *Imperialismo pagano* (1928) unleashed violent controversy in both fascist and the highest ecclesiastical circles. Around this time Evola became acquainted with the philosophers Benedetto Croce (1886-1952) and Giovanni Gentile (1875-1944), with whom he collaborated on the *Encyclopedia Italiana*. During the 1930s Evola adapted the Integral Tradition of Guénon in his own warrior fashion and made a profound study of alchemy, contemporary esoteric groups and the → Grail myth. In these years he undertook Traditionalist critiques of history and culture and wrote several of his most important books. He also traveled widely through Europe, to meet representatives of political currents corresponding to his own sacral, holistic, anti-liberal and anti-democratic ideas; these contacts include Edgar Julius Jung (1894-1934), the conservative revolutionary murdered by the National Socialists, Karl Anton Prince Rohan (1898-1975), the Roman Catholic monarchist founder of the *Europäische Revue*, and Corneliu Codreanu (1899-1938), founder of the Iron Guard in Romania. During a visit to Romania Evola met Mircea Eliade (1907-1986), the later historian of religion, who had adopted some of Evola's ideas and would remain in touch with him. He also had meetings with the constitutional lawyer Carl Schmitt (1888-1985) and the poet Gottfried Benn (1886-1956). At the same time Evola wrote widely for the contemporary press.

Evola had an ambivalent attitude to Fascism: on the one hand he hoped it would lead Italy back towards the pagan and sacral values of the Roman empire, but on the other hand he found it devoid of any transcendent foundation. With his spiritual ideas rejected by the Fascist bureaucracy, he turned to National Socialism, especially the SS, which he initially regarded as a military spiritual order. An acquaintance with Adolf Hitler (1889-1945) and

Heinrich Himmler (1900-1945) may have taken place but is not proven. By 1938, however, an official SS report dismissed Evola as a "reactionary Roman and fantasist", and recommended that his further activities be kept under observation. His efforts to bring the "two eagles" (Italy and Germany) closer together were frustrated by opposition in both countries. From the mid-1930s Evola made an intensive study of racial questions, in the hope of gaining official recognition and influence, as Mussolini had spoken positively about Evola's thesis of "spiritual" racism. Mussolini was interested in developing a counter-balance to the "materialistic biological" racism of National Socialism, but this came to naught as both Italians and Germans opposed it. During the Second World War, Evola studied Buddhism. In 1943 he was present in Rastenburg as multilingual confidant at the meeting of Mussolini and Hitler in the latter's headquarters, where a future German-backed government in Italy was discussed. Following the American invasion of Rome in 1944, Evola fled to Vienna, where he is said to have had an official assignment writing the history of secret societies. In 1945 he suffered a severe spinal injury during a Russian bombardment of Vienna, which left him paralysed in the legs for the rest of his life.

After three years in hospitals and sanatoriums, in 1948 Evola returned to Rome, where he immediately resumed writing. He soon became the intellectual focus of a small troop of mostly young disciples who sought to emulate his spiritual and political outlook. In April 1951 Evola was arrested, accused of being the "intellectual instigator" of secret neo-fascist terrorist groups and of "glorifying fascism". Complete acquittal followed after six months' investigative custody. Since the practical realisation of his ideas seemed impossible in the absence of party support, Evola's political orientation now changed in the direction of an "apoliteia", an attitude of disengagement from current politics. Studies of the links between sex and esotericism led to another of his principal works. Around the same time he produced countless periodical essays and numerous translations from the work of Mircea Eliade (1907-1986), Arthur Avalon (1865-1936), Daisetz Teitaro Suzuki (1877-1966), → Karlfried Graf Dürckheim (1896-1988), Oswald Spengler (1880-1936), Gabriel Marcel (1889-1973), Otto Weininger and Ernst Jünger (1895-1998). Together with his translations of Johann Jakob Bachofen (1815-1887), → Gustav Meyrink (1868-1932) and René Guénon during the 1930s and 1940s, these writings made Evola an important transmitter of wider European spirituality to Italy. In 1974 he died, propping himself up beside the window of his apartment in order to meet death upright, like his heroes. In accordance with his will, he was cremated. He expressly forbade a Roman Catholic funeral, and his ashes were lowered into a crevasse on Monte Rosa.

All Evola's creative work is characterised by his desire to surpass the merely mortal aspects of existence and his radical orientation towards transcendent principles, which he perceived as immanent at the same time. As early as his Dadaist phase he regarded art as 'a disinterested creation, which comes from the individual's higher consciousness'. He was unsatisfied by purely academic philosophy and sought a breakthrough to the completely different level of reality to which his own transcendent experience of the self had given him access. Based on the philosophy of German Idealism, chiefly represented by → Schelling (1775-1854) and Fichte (1762-1814), supplemented by Max Stirner's (1806-1856) solipsistic notion of the Ego, and by the ideas of French Personalism, as well as Nietzsche and Weininger, Evola arrived at the demand of an "absolute I", which – freed of any intellectual or material restriction – sees freedom, power and knowledge as an indivisible whole, and seeks to realise it. Teachings from Taoism, Hinduism, Tantrism, alchemy, magic, and Meister Eckhart are woven into this "magical idealism". Evola's "absolute I" is related to the Hindu *atman* (= *brahman*), and his notion of power corresponds to the *maya* of Tantrism, which subsumes both illusion and creative magic, as well as to the emptiness of the *Tao Te Ching*. The individual can find his only solid basis and his sole point of certainty in the transcendental I, the personality's deepest ground of being. However, philosophy should not remain an end in itself but must surpass itself and find its consummation in absolute action leading to higher levels. Evola's philosophy thus represents a propaedeutic for the attainment of transcendent initiatory realms. Thus it was only logical that his so-called philosophical phase should be followed by a magical phase.

From Evola's perspective magic has nothing to do with sorcery for gain or harm. He is concerned with a complete self-transformation and integration into transcendent realms, and with the higher dignity and freedom that result from it. This is supposed to happen by way of experiments 'according to those very principles of open-mindedness, scepticism and unflinching exploration which characterise the exact sciences'. Thus Evola prefers self-experiment and knowledge to faith, and represents a thoroughly modernist and post-Enlighten-

ment form of magic. Later in his life Evola speaks of a 'divine technology, traditional in the higher sense' and concludes with → Roger Bacon's definition of magic as "practical metaphysics". The writings of the "magical" Group of Ur therefore contain original texts from Tantrism, Buddhism, Taoism, ancient theurgy and especially alchemy, all of which in Evola's view are oriented towards transcendent self-realisation. Evola uses the concept of initiation to describe the quest and the conscious attainment of transcendent realms. This attainment is also connected with achieving continuous consciousness during sleep, and even beyond physical death. Evola believes neither in → reincarnation nor in the natural immortality of the human soul. Rather man must build up a "diamond body" around an absolutely stable centre of consciousness, which is capable of surviving the trauma of physical death and will replace the mortal body as a new vehicle in more subtle realms of existence.

Evola's emphasis on man's potential self-transformation through asceticism and discipline also explains why he recognized the same purpose in magic and alchemy. Alchemy as the royal art is not just a specialised knowledge concerning the transformation of metals, but a comprehensive physical and metaphysical system embracing cosmology and sacred anthropology, and aims at the spiritual transformation of men *and* metals. Evola championed a spiritual conception of alchemy before → C.G. Jung (1875-1961) and Mircea Eliade, who were both influenced by his view. Accordingly, he sees in the symbolic language of alchemy a universal code for all mysteriosophical fields: hence his equation of alchemy with Hermeticism in toto which was criticised by Guénon, who thought Evola likened alchemy too much to magic. Evola identified himself with the warrior *kshatriya* caste and similarly viewed the "Traditional sciences" in an activist and combative light. He thus differed markedly from Guénon, who emphasised the traditional primacy of the contemplative, priestly *brahmin* caste. Hence Evola's emphasis on the dynamic, magical and mutable aspects of the world, which also explains his controversial involvement in practical politics; and hence also his preference for activist Tantrism, whereas Guénon devoted himself to philosophical Vedanta. It is therefore an oversimplification to regard Evola merely as the Italian representative of Guénon. However, in common with Guénon, Evola rejected the Theosophy of → Helena Blavatsky (1831-1891), the Anthroposophy of → Rudolf Steiner (1861-1925), → spiritualism, and other contemporary neo-spiritualist groups. He was also definitely hostile towards the psychoanalysis of Sigmund Freud (1856-1939), and even more so towards Jung. In contrast to Guénon, Evola made positive statements on → Giuliano Kremmerz (1861-1930) and his Fratellanza Terapeutica Magica di Miriam, of which he was not a member, but whose doctrines influenced him. Likewise he was positive about the magical doctrine of → Aleister Crowley, with whom he was only superficially acquainted, and about → George Ivanovitch Gurdjieff (1877-1949). Nor does Evola's opinion of Christianity and → Freemasonry accord with that of Guénon, who recognised Traditionalist survivals in both institutions, which he therefore believed could lead to at least a virtual initiation. With the possible exception of fraternities completely hidden from us, Evola recognised no initiatory groups in modern times. Christianity, on the other hand he saw as a primary cause of spiritual decline in the West, because it preaches humility and submission rather than the self-determination of man. To Freemasonry he attributed an initiatory character only in its operative period, before the foundation of the Grand Lodge of England in 1717. Freemasonry had thenceforth turned into a speculative, purely rational association, devoted to the politics of the Enlightenment and thus acting in the sense of what Guénon referred to as "counter-initiation". Here one may detect the influence of Catholic world-conspiracy theorists extending from Louis de Bonald (1754-1840) and Leon de Poncins (1895-1975) to Evolas friend Giovanni Preziosi (1881-1945). In his own theory of world-conspiracy, probably derived originally from Guénon, Evola did not so much accuse specific human groups (Freemasons or Jews) of seeking to conquer the world. Rather he regarded them as the tools of extra-human spiritual powers.

In Grail mythology Evola sees a hidden initiatory mystery, and the Grail kingdom he regards as the specifically Western medieval manifestation of the Traditionalist idea of a supreme world centre under the "royal-spiritual" authority of a "world ruler". The quest for the Grail therefore symbolises "the desire to establish contact with this mysterious centre". In Evola's view, the Grail is a Nordic mystery on account of its links with Germanic and Celtic traditions as well as in its Hyperborean symbolism, and it also relates to the Ghibelline imperial tradition as opposed to papal supremacy.

In his works on culture and history, Evola uses the so-called "Traditional method". It accords greater importance to myths and symbols than to actual historical facts and highlights the intersection between sacred metahistory and profane history. Using Graeco-Roman and Vedic sources, Evola speaks of a Hyperborean centre located in the prehistoric Arctic where Nordic god-men ruled in a Golden Age. Due to cosmic catastrophes, they had to leave their homeland, as a result of which their heaven-oriented, solar and heroic-masculine world-view came to be over most of the world. A culture characterised by hierarchy, spiritual regality, ritual and initiation represented the primal Tradition which a man living by the Tradition should hope eventually to reinstate. On the opposing side stood the earth-oriented, lunar and matriarchal culture of the Southern peoples (here the influence of Bachofen is obvious), which led to wars but also to interbreeding with the Northern peoples. Thus the solar element in the West increasingly lost its vitality during a cyclical history of decline. A final efflorescence was felt in medieval Catholicism, as this was less Christian than inclined to sacral imperialism. The Renaissance and, above all, the French Revolution represented further stations of decline. Modernity would finally perish in a state of collectivism, lawlessness and materialism, as already prophesied in Indian religious texts (*Vishnupurana*). World history is therefore not an evolution but a downward devolution ending with the present iron (dark) age (*kali-yuga*). An authentic restoration of the Tradition will only be possible after the complete collapse of the modern world, because there can be no gradual transition between Traditional culture and modernity: we are dealing with two totally separated, *entirely different* concepts of time, values, and the sacred.

Evola made extensive studies of wisdom teachings from the East. He became acquainted with Tantrism, which is described by him as the only remaining regular path to transcendence in the *kali-yuga*, through the writings of Arthur Avalon (ps. John Woodroffe; 1865-1936), with whom he corresponded. Evola was particularly impressed by the active side of Tantrism as well as the practices of the left-hand path, which though highly sacred run contrary to customary moral and religious notions. That in Tantrism the divine female Shakti symbolises motion, energy and power, in contrast to the motionless male Shiva, influenced Evola own ideas of "sacred eros" to a high degree. The philosophy of Taoism was exemplary for the life-style of a sage in Evola's view, and "inactive action" (*wei-wu-wei*) was the best possible description of effective magic for him. In 1923, and again in 1959, Evola published two completely different translations of the *Tao Te Ching*, with commentaries by himself. He was also profoundly interested in the internal alchemy (*nei-tan*) of Taoism.

In Buddhism, Evola concentrated on the original teaching of Prince Siddhartha Gautama (c. 560-c. 480 B.C.) as well as on Zen. In contrast to the contemporary focus on pacifism and neighbourly love, Evola emphasised the warrior-like and aristocratic nature of early Buddhism pointing out that Gautama was not a brahmin but a member of the warrior caste (kshatriya). He also stressed the initiatory character of Buddhist asceticism, which as a "dry path" of non-identification and letting-go aims at the extinction of all "thirst" and the "great liberation" in the "void" (sunyata). Evola also published numerous essays in the periodical East and West edited by the Tibetologist Giuseppe Tucci (1894-1984), with whom he was acquainted for many years.

Evola regarded sex as virtually the only practical possibility open to contemporary man to experience something of the higher transcendental world. Only in the sexual act does man escape his all-encompassing profane ego and open himself to higher spheres. For Evola, male (= the unmoved spiritual mover) and female (= the malleable matrix) are transcendant categories, and the biological differences between man and woman are merely a reflection of these. Evola also refers to the Platonic myth of the androgyne whose division led to the two sexes which strive to regain their original unity. Sexuality offers the possibility of a breakthrough to transcendence through certain practices, in which man has to combine his inner masculinity with his inner femininity. The practices of kundalini yoga, Taoism, the → "fedeli d'amore" (Lieges of Love) as well as Arabic and European secret orders show the way in this direction.

Evola's political philosophy is based on hierarchical thinking and expressed in the "organic state". Its precondition is a centre founded on purely transcendental principles and permeating all areas of public life – without the need for violence, as in totalitarianism – by virtue of its superior spiritual power. The principal duty of the state is to lead its citizens towards transcendence, as in Plato. At the same time, Evola opposes the concept of nations and advocates a spiritual-monarchic imperial theory. Evola's notions of race derive from a tripartite division. From above to below he distinguishes between a "race of the spirit" (the various attitudes to sacral principles from fearful submission to an upright and self-relying relationship), a "race of the soul" (the various types of character from emotional to detached) and a "race of the body" (which covers the usual physical definition). As he dismissed the physical racial characteristics as the least important, he found himself in opposition to other racial theorists and increasingly lost influence among them.

Evola regarded Jewry primarily as a symbol of the dominance of materialism and economics in modernity. His statements range from polemical attacks and conspiracy theories to his warning 'not to make the Jews a kind of scapegoat for everything that Gentiles were really responsible for', ('Inquadramento del problema ebraico' in Bibliografia Fascista, XIV, No. 8/9, 1939, 717-728). One notes a certain tendency towards vulgarisation of these notions in his journalistic writings, as compared to his books. Due to his involvement with Fascism (Evola was never a party member, however), National Socialism and racism, Evola has been little read since the Second World War, except by keen opponents or supporters. Only since the early 1990s has he become more widely discussed as an artist and has he become the subject of numerous university dissertations. His uncompromising ideas have also been taken up by the underground youth music scene. Thus a compact disk was produced to honour Evola's centenary. Musical bands like Blood Axis, Alraune, Camerata Mediolanense, Allerseelen and Ain Soph composed and played themes inspired by Evola's writings. Practically all of his twenty full-length books, approximately 300 longer essays, and much of his collected journalism, numbering more than 1000 articles and countless reviews in newspapers and magazines, are in print. A growing number of translations has made Evola known outside of Italy as well – chiefly in France, but also, interestingly, throughout Eastern Europe. A foundation dedicated to his work in Rome is engaged in publishing definitive editions of his major writings, and in collecting and editing his scattered essays and biographical material.

Bibliographies: Renato del Ponte, "J. Evola: Una bibliografia 1920-1994", Futuro Presente 6 (1995), 28-70 ♦ Martin Schwarz, Bibliographie J. Evola, Wien: Kshatriya, 1999.
Selection of writings: Arte Astratta (Collection Dada), Zürich/Roma, 1920 ♦ Saggi sull'Idealismo Magico, Todi-Roma: Atanòr, 1925 ♦ L'Uomo come Potenza, Todi-Roma: Atanòr, 1926 ♦ Teoria dell'Individuo Assoluto, Torino: Fratelli Bocca, 1927 ♦ Imperialismo Pagano, Todi-Roma: Atanòr, 1928 ♦ Fenomenologia dell'Individuo Assoluto, Torino: Fratelli Bocca, 1930 ♦ La tradizione ermetica, Laterza: Bari, 1931 [The Hermetic Tradition, Rochester: Inner Traditions, 1995] ♦ Maschera e volto dello spiritualismo contemporaneo, Torino: Fratelli Bocca, 1932 ♦ Rivolta contro il mondo moderno, Milano: Hoepli, 1935 [Revolt Against the Modern World, Rochester: Inner Traditions, 1995] ♦ Tre aspetti del problema ebraico, Roma: Edizioni Mediterranee, 1936 [Three Aspects of the Jewish

Problem, Conway: Thompkins & Carion, 2003] ♦ *Il mistero del Graal e la tradizione ghibellina dell'Impero*, Bari: Laterza, 1937 [*The Mystery of the Grail*, Rochester: Inner Traditions, 1996] ♦ *Il mito del sangue*, Milano: Hoepli, 1937 ♦ *Sintesi di dottrina della razza*, Milano: Hoepli, 1942 ♦ *La dottrina del risveglio*, Bari: Laterza, 1943 [*The Doctrine of Awakening*, London: Luzac & Company, 1951; Rochester: repr. Inner Traditions, 1996] ♦ *Lo Yoga della Potenza*, Milano: Fratelli Bocca, 1949 [*The Yoga of Power*, Rochester: Inner Traditions, 1992] ♦ *Gli uomini e le rovine*, Roma: Edizioni dell'Ascia, 1953 [*Men Among the Ruins*, Rochester: Inner Traditions, 2002] ♦ *Metafisica del sesso*, Roma: Atanòr, 1958 [*The Metaphysics of Sex*, New York: Inner Traditions, 1983] ♦ *Cavalcare la tigre*, Milano: Scheiweiller, 1961 [*Ride the Tiger*, Rochester: Inner Traditions, 2003] ♦ *Il Cammino del Cinabro*, Milano: Scheiweiller, 1963 ♦ *Il fascismo*, Roma: Volpe, 1964 ♦ *L'arco e la clava*, Milano: Scheiweiller, 1968 ♦ *Meditazioni delle vette* (Renato del Ponte, ed.), La Spezia: Edizioni del Tridente, 1974 [*Meditations on the Peaks*, Rochester: Inner Traditions, 1998] ♦ *Lettere 1955-1974* (Renato del Ponte, ed.), Finale Emilia: La Terra degli Avi, 1996. Journals: *Ur* (Roma 1927-1928) ♦ *Krur* (Roma 1929); the three volumes of *Ur* and *Krur* have been reprinted in heavily revised versions 1955 and 1971 as Gruppo di Ur (ed.), *Introduzione alla Magia quale Scienza dell'Io*, Roma: Edizione Mediterranee [*Introduction into Magic*, Rochester: Inner Traditions, 2000 = only first volume of 1927] ♦ *La Torre* (February 1-June 15, 1930) ♦ *Diorama Filosofico*, regular supplement to *Il Regime Fascista* (February 2, 1934-July 18, 1943).

Lit.: Yearbook: *Studi evoliani* (Gianfranco de Turris ed.) since 1998, Rome: Fondazione Julius Evola ♦ Roma; Michel Angebert et al., *Julius Evola: Le visionnaire foudroyé*, Paris: Copernic, 1977 ♦ Mario Bernardi Guardi et al., *Delle rovine ed oltre: Saggi su Julius Evola*, Roma: Antonio Pellicani, 1995 ♦ Christophe Boutin, *Politique et Tradition: Julius Evola dans le siècle (1898-1974)*, Paris: Kimé, 1992 ♦ Francesco Cassata, *A destra del fascismo*, Torino: Bollati Boringhieri, 2003 ♦ Sandro Consolato, *Julius Evola e il Buddhismo*, Borzano: SeaR Edizioni, 1995 ♦ Nicola Cospito & Hans Werner Neulen (eds.), *Julius Evola nei documenti segreti del Terzo Reich*, Roma: Edizioni Europa, 1986 ♦ Gianni Ferracuti, *Julius Evola*, Rimini: Il Cerchio, 1984 ♦ Franco Ferraresi, "Julius Evola: Tradition, Reaction, and the Radical Right", *European Journal of Sociology* 28 (1987), 107-151 ♦ Marco Fraquelli, *Il filosofo proibito: Tradizione e reazione nell'opera di Julius Evola*, Milano: Terziaria, 1994 ♦ Francesco Germinaro, *Razza del Sangue, razza dello Spirito*, Bollati Boringhieri, Torino, 2001 ♦ Arnaud Guyot-Jeannin (ed.), *Julius Evola*, Lausanne: L'Age d'Homme, 1997 ♦ H.T. Hansen, "A Short Introduction to Julius Evola", *Theosophical History* 5:1 (January 1994), 11-22 ♦ idem, "Julius Evola's Political Endeavours", in: Evola, *Men among the Ruins* (see above), 1-104 ♦ Gian Franco Lami, *Introduzione a Julius Evola*, Roma: Volpe, 1980 ♦ Jean-Paul Lippi, *Julius Evola métaphysicien et penseur politique*, Lausanne: L'Age d'Homme, 1998 ♦

Roberto Melchionda, *Il volto di Dioniso: Filosofia e arte in Julius Evola*, Roma: Basaia, 1984 ♦ Antimo Negri, *Julius Evola e la filosofia*, Milano: Spirali, 1988 ♦ Renato del Ponte, *Evola e il magico "Gruppo di Ur"*, Borzano: SeaR Edizioni, 1994 ♦ Adriano Romualdi, *Su Evola*, Roma: Fondazione Julius Evola, 1998 ♦ Marco Rossi, "Julius Evola and the Independent Theosophical Association of Rome", *Theosophical History* 6:3 (1996), 107-114 ♦ Mark J. Sedgwick, *Against the Modern World: Traditionalism and the Secret Intellectual History of the Twentieth Century*, Oxford: Oxford University Press, 2004 ♦ Thomas Sheehan, "Diventare Dio: Julius Evola and the Metaphysics of Fascism", *Stanford Italian Review* 6:1-2 (1986), 279-292 ♦ Francesco Tedeschi & Fabrizio Carli, *Julius Evola e l'arte delle avanguardie*, Roma: Fondazione Julius Evola, 1998 ♦ Gianfranco de Turris, *Elogio e difesa di Julius Evola*, Roma: Edizioni Mediterranee, 1997 ♦ Gianfranco de Turris (ed.), *Omaggio a Julius Evola per il suo LXXV compleanno*, Roma: Volpe, 1973 ♦ Gianfranco de Turris (ed.), *Testimonianze su Evola*, Roma: Edizioni Mediterranee, 1973, enlarged edition 1985 ♦ Elisabetta Valento, *Homo faber: Julius Evola fra arte e alchimia*, Roma: Fondazione Julius Evola, 1994 ♦ Piero di Vona, *Metafisica e politica in Julius Evola*, Edizioni di Ar, Padova, 2000.

HANS THOMAS HAKL

Faber Stapulensis, Jacobus → Lefèvre d' Étaples, Jacques

Fabre d'Olivet, Antoine, * 8.12.1767 Ganges, † 27.3.1825 Paris

The immensely curious and massively erudite self-proclaimed Neo-Pythagorean Fabre d'Olivet was born to a wealthy Protestant family. As a young man, he came under the influence of Delisle de Sales, an Enlightenment rationalist with a penchant for historical speculation. Under Delisle's influence, Fabre d'Olivet wrote *Lettres à Sophie sur l'histoire* (1801), a resume of ancient and modern cosmogonic systems together with a history of civilizations. Fabre d'Olivet's other notable pre-theosophical work is *Le Troubadour: Poésies occitaniques du XIIIᵉ siècle* (2 vols., 1803-1804). This compound of poetry, a study, a dissertation on the Occitan languague, and a vocabulary was intended to revive interest in the poetry of the Troubadours and to defend the Occitan language. A mystification and celebration rather than scientific linguistics or philology, *Le Troubadour* closely resembles Macpherson's *Ossian*.

Fabre d'Olivet underwent a religious and vocational crisis between 1800 and 1805. He emerged as a theosopher. The key to his conversion seems to have been his discovery, the details of which are unknown, of a Unity that is the source and end of all diversity. → Tradition, or a primitive revelation granted to humanity by Providence, bears witness to this Unity. The existence of this Tradition, in turn, is demonstrated by the agreement of all cosmogonies. The homeland of the ancient wisdom was Egypt, from where it was transmitted to other peoples through initiation, most notably by → Moses, Pythagoras, and Orpheus.

Fabre d'Olivet's Illuminism, set out in a series of works published between 1813 and 1824, belongs to the esoteric tradition of thought that in its modern western form derives above all from → Jakob Boehme (1575-1624). He was an autodidact who acknowledged no master and belonged to no sect. Nevertheless, even if he never met → Saint-Martin, Fabre d'Olivet was in constant contact with his friends and disciples from 1800 onwards. Similarly, though he was never initiated into the Order of → Elus-Coëns, Fabre d'Olivet was thoroughly acquainted with the theurgic activities of → Martinès de Pasqually and → J.B. Willermoz. His principal works are *Les Vers dorés de Pythagore* (1813), *La Langue hébraïque restituée* (1810, published in 1816/1817), *Caïn: Mystère dramatique de Lord Byron* (1823), and *Histoire philosophique du genre humain* (1824; first published in 1822 as *De l'Etat social de l'homme*).

Vers dorés presents Fabre d'Olivet's theosophical views in the form of a commentary on his own translation of Pythagoras' *Golden Verses*. It is prefaced by a lengthy discourse, 'Sur l'essence et la forme de la poésie'. Pythagoras, for Fabre d'Olivet, is only a name for Tradition. Since all true knowledge derives from the primitive revelation, the universal truths may be found in all cosmologies and philosophies that have not separated themselves from Tradition. Fabre d'Olivet demonstrates the unity of the sacred tradition by correlating passages from Pythagoras with passages from other Classical writers, from Indian, Chinese, and Persian texts, and from modern philosophers. So, while it is true that → neopaganism and even Pythagoreanism itself were fashionable during the Empire, Fabre d'Olivet's "Pythagoreanism" is not a rejection of biblical religion but symbolic of the theosophical truths contained in the universal primitive revelation. And since Moses received the same Egyptian initiation as Pythagoras, the Pentateuch, correctly interpreted, contains the same doctrines as the *Vers dorés*, as Fabre d'Olivet set out to demonstrate in *La Langue hébraïque restituée*.

La Langue hébraïque restituée is Fabre d'Olivet's free translation and commentary on the first five books of the Bible. He believed that Hebrew, as one of the three primordial idioms of the language revealed directly to humanity by God, was a hieroglyphic language that veiled deep esoteric truths. The books of Moses, particularly Genesis, preserve this ancient wisdom, but it has been inaccessible until now because knowledge of the true esoteric meaning of Hebrew degenerated soon after Moses' death and has been lost since the Babylonian Captivity, except among the → Essenes. The Essenes, however, whom Fabre d'Olivet depicts as a small group of Alexandrian sages, were bound by oath to keep the ancient doctrines secret. When the Ptolemaic ruler of Egypt requested a translation of the Pentateuch for the great Library at Alexandria, the Essenes faced a dilemma: they did not want to flout the authority of the civil power, but religious law forbade communication of the divine mysteries. Their solution was to distinguish between the literal and the esoteric senses of the text. Thus they produced a literal translation, the Septuagint, in which the incommunicable mysteries remained veiled. Present-day versions of the Pentateuch are deficient and misleading because they reproduce only the literal sense of the ancient text. In *La Langue hébraïque restituée*, Fabre d'Olivet announced that he had rediscovered the esoteric meaning of Hebrew and reestablished the primitive theosophical cosmogony of Moses.

In 1811 Fabre d'Olivet claimed, in *Notions sur le Sens de l'Ouïe*, to have healed a deaf-mute named Rodolphe Grivel through the application of principles established in the as-yet unpublished *La Langue hébraïque restituée*. The Mosaic cosmogony, he asserted, contains the principles of all sciences, ancient and modern. The healing of Grivel vindicates the accuracy of his reconstruction of the primitive revelation. According to Léon Cellier's brilliant analysis, Fabre d'Olivet considered hearing, like the exercise of any sense, to be a manifestation of the volitive faculty. It follows that deafness may be cured by awakening the volitive faculty of the deaf person. Genesis 2:21 recounts that Eve was created from Adam's rib while Adam was in a deep sleep. In his commentary in *La Langue hébraïque* Fabre d'Olivet identifies "deep sleep" with magnetic sleep or somnambulism. Eve, in Fabre d'Olivet's system, corresponds to the volitive faculty. The Genesis passage therefore tells us that the volitive faculty is awakened through magnetized sleep. Fabre d'Olivet claimed to have healed Grivel's deafness by plunging the subject into magnetized sleep (Fabre d'Olivet was a practising magnetizer; he protested against the name → *animal* magnetism because it degraded what he considered to be a high spiritual phenomenon) and through the action of his own will awakened in the subject the faculty of hearing.

De l'Etat social de l'homme, reflecting in part the sense of historical evolution that Fabre d'Olivet acquired during the Bourbon Restoration, is an exposition of the 12.000-year history of the human race from earliest times to Bonaparte. Inasmuch as it is a philosophical history built on the cosmological principles set out in his earlier books, Fabre d'Olivet follows his Illuminist [→ Illuminism] predecessors in predicating history on cosmogony. He republished it two years later in the vain hope that the more fashionable title, *Histoire philosophique du genre humain*, would increase its sales. *Histoire philosophique* is prefaced by a lengthy 'Dissertation Introductive', which summarizes (and in places revises) the metaphysical foundation established in the earlier works on which the philosophical history is built. In it Fabre d'Olivet declares that conventional history is false because it has been written without knowledge of the true principles that govern the cosmos and history. If we are to understand the successive development of humanity, its moral faculties and their action, we must first grasp the metaphysical facts of the spiritual nature of humanity and its place in the hierarchy of the universe.

The cosmogonic drama of *Caïn* counters Byron's "blasphemous" version of the Genesis story by translating it together with a corrective commentary drawn from Fabre d'Olivet's own speculations on the meaning of Genesis in *La Langue hébraïque restituée*.

Fabre d'Olivet's epistemology takes up and purports to refute Kant's epistemological pessimism. Fabre d'Olivet's argument is based on a distinction between rationality and reason. Rationality, he says in *Vers dorés de Pythagore*, is a secondary faculty that corresponds to soul, the middle term of the triple nature of humanity as body, soul, and spirit; reason, or intellectuality, is a principal faculty that corresponds to spirit, the highest term of our triple nature. Fabre d'Olivet argues that Kant misled himself because, confusing rationality with intellectuality, he failed to understand the spiritual nature of reason. The result of Kant's error is a philosophy that first strips humanity of its spiritual faculties, then attempts to grasp spiritual truths with a faculty incommensurate with them, and finally, the attempt having necessarily failed, declares the spiritual truths to be unknowable. Fabre d'Olivet overcomes Kant's epistemological pessimism by redefining reason as an intuitive faculty capable of grasping the ontological Absolute.

Fabre d'Olivet's Illuminist drama is played out in a Boehmenist cosmos in which divine emanation bathes the universe in divine forces and humanity, created as primordial Adam, is a spiritual being of great power. Fabre d'Olivet identifies unfallen humanity with the Will, which, along with Providence and Destiny, is one of the three powers, or cosmogonic principles, of the universe. The Fall has obscured, but not effaced, this glorious identity. Fabre d'Olivet refers to humanity as the *règne hominal*; that is, the fourth kingdom, following the mineral, vegetable, and animal kingdoms. Nevertheless, he insists that the human essence is distinct from lower essences and that there is no continuity between the natural world and humanity. The *règne hominal*, in fact, is Fabre d'Olivet's name for the Universal Adam of the Illuminist tradition. Fallen humanity displays a triple nature, at once body, soul, and spirit, and lives a triple life, instinctive, passionate [*animique*], and intellectual (i.e., spiritual). These three lives, when they are fully developed, intermingle and are confounded into a fourth, or volitive, life. Through the exercise of the volitive life, which is proper to it, humanity gradually reintegrates primordial Adam and raises itself to the reattainment of its cosmogonic status. Humanity's (future) achievement of this status is the prerequisite for the reestablishment of harmony among the three cosmogonic principles of Providence, Will, and Destiny. The reestablishment of cosmogonic harmony, in turn, will create, replicating on the macrocosmic level the fourth life of humanity, a fourth power that is the very image or mirror of divinity and the realization of Fabre d'Olivet's version of Illuminist reintegration.

In his commentary in *Caïn*, Fabre d'Olivet interprets the Genesis narratives concerning the three sons of Adam and Eve as allegories of his cosmogonic principles. All future humanity was contained in prelapsarian Adam, in whose nature Will and Providence co-existed in perfect harmony. The Fall shattered the harmony within Adam's nature, precipitating both descent into the material universe of time and space and dispersal of the primordial Adam into the successive generations and myriad individuals of the human race. Adam's posterity divided his integrated nature: Cain embodied the faculty of Will and Abel that of Providence. This division was to be perpetuated in their descendants, creating in effect two races: *hommes volatifs*, who rely on their own powers, and *hommes providentiels*, who trust in God's love for humanity. Adam's sons and their respective descendants were intended to co-operate in the redemption of the human race. The free submission of human will to Providence would have quickly reintegrated primordial Adam, but Lucifer intervened. Knowing that he would not be able to dominate the providential race, Lucifer (actually a hypostatization of Will, and thus identical to Cain) persuaded Cain to kill his brother. Henceforth, Providence, annihilated by Will, no longer acts directly in the world. After the murder of Abel, Adam and Eve had another son, Seth. Seth, however, embodied, not Providence, but Fabre d'Olivet's third cosmogonic principle, Destiny, or blind fate. Human history is henceforth a struggle between *hommes volatifs*, the descendants of Cain who champion anarchic liberty, and *hommes fatidiques*, the descendants of Seth who preach submission to necessity. Caught in this dismal struggle, humanity calls out to Providence for assistance, but in vain since, save for rare exceptions like Orpheus, Moses, and Buddha, *hommes providentiels* no longer walk the earth. Nevertheless, though Providence no longer intervenes directly in human affairs, it still operates indirectly. Like Hegel's "cunning of reason", Fabre d'Olivet's Providence uses wilful human intentions to effect its own end of the redemption of humanity in the reintegration of Adam. Not only is God not responsible for evil in the world, but Providence ensures that, despite its best efforts to the contrary, humanity will be redeemed in the end. This is Fabre d'Olivet's version of theodicy, and indicates the central place the defense of Providence holds in his theosophical oeuvre.

Humanity may be a power in the cosmos, but since the Fall it is a power only in germ. Through the interaction of humanity with Fabre d'Olivet's other two cosmogonic powers, Providence and Destiny, humanity must develop its potential as Will. The essences of all species, including humanity's ontologically unique essence, were placed in them by God at the creation. Because the will of a being corresponds to its essence, individuals and species alike develop – that is, progressively realize the external characteristics appropriate to their preexistent essences – by means of the repeated exercise of the will. Fabre d'Olivet's fundamental image of development is the growth of a plant as the unfolding of what is contained in its seed (this is a variant of preformationism in which the voluntarism of Boehmenist Illuminism has been added to the organic language of biological preformationism). Fabre d'Olivet finds authority for this image in the Hebrew Bible (albeit in the theosophic version of Moses' teaching he himself "restored" in *La Langue hébraïque restituée*). The first word of Genesis, *bereshith*, according to Fabre d'Olivet, ought not be translated "in the beginning" but rather "*in principio*", "in principle", "in potential".

Creation signifies not the act of bringing something into being out of nothing but a process of bringing something from potential being into actual being.

History, for Fabre d'Olivet, is the progressive unfolding of what is already in humanity as its essence. The result is a teleological philosophy of history, in which the consequences of humanity's constitutive metaphysical principles are played out in time and space. In the 'Discours sur l'Essence et la Forme de la Poésie', Fabre d'Olivet addresses the relationship between the spiritual process of reintegration and the succession of historical events in his distinction between allegorical history and positive history. Positive history chronicles events that happened but that have no spiritual significance, whereas allegorical history arranges events that may never have happened into a dramatization of the spiritual destiny of humanity. Allegorical history alone, Fabre d'Olivet declares, is worthy of study. Fabre d'Olivet insists that history is meaningful only when it is explicitly subordinated to metaphysics; to, that is, the knowledge of its origin, end, and purpose.

As sketched in *Histoire philosophique du genre humain*, the development of humanity was at first subject to Destiny, but the divine germ humanity carries within itself – a spark of the divine will – develops, by reacting against Destiny itself, into an opposing volitional force whose essence is liberty. This is not a smooth or uniform process. Ever since the murder of Abel, history has been an incessant struggle between the human Will and Destiny. When the human Will sides with or yields to Destiny, centuries of decadence and oppression result. Conversely, the Will allied to Providence leads humanity toward perfection. For Fabre d'Olivet, theocracy is the political correlate of the principle of unity and thus the balance among the principles that Fabre d'Olivet desires can be attained only under theocratic government. *Histoire philosophique* concludes with a call for France, Europe, and ultimately the whole world, to form a single theocratic empire under the final authority of a Supreme Pontiff, thereby uniting at last the three cosmogonic principles in the ideal social structure. Cosmically speaking, the Will of humanity functions as a mediating power, entering elementary nature in order to bring harmony there and reuniting Destiny and Providence. The full development of the volitional germ constitutes the restored Will of the Universal Man, and thus the restoration of the *règne hominal* to its original and proper dignity as a cosmogonic principle. Through the action of human volition the *règne hominal* is reintegrated and the great ternary of Providence, Will, and

Destiny harmonized into the fourth principle that is the mirror of divinity.

Fabre d'Olivet's christology distinguishes him from most other Illuminists. He reduces Christianity to merely one manifestation of primitive revelation. And while he calls Jesus a divine man, he awards this title to all *hommes providentiels* (including Krishna, Odin, and Apollonius of Tyana). What makes Jesus great, in Fabre d'Olivet's opinion, is that he showed by his death and resurrection what the human will is capable of when it knows itself to be in conformity with the will of Providence. Similarly, all religions are true, and agree with each other, to the extent that they derive from the primitive revelation. Fabre d'Olivet is willing to concede that Christianity has changed the world on the moral or historical plane, but insists that Christianity has brought nothing new on the religious plane. Jesus, in Fabre d'Olivet's theosophy, ceases to be the unique and necessary Redeemer; Christ as saviour is replaced by the development of humanity into the cosmogonic *règne hominal* through the exercise of its will.

Fabre d'Olivet gathered around himself a group of disciples whom in 1824 he organized into a sect, *Théodoxie universelle*, whose ritual and theology he himself, as supreme Pontiff, provided. Fabre d'Olivet cast his new cult in the form of a masonic lodge except that he replaced the traditional masonic and architectural symbolism and paraphernalia with substitutes derived from agriculture (once again, the fundamental analogy between the soul and a seed). Fabre d'Olivet outlined the teachings of his sect in a work titled *La Vraie Maçonnerie et la Céleste Culture*, which remained unpublished until edited by Léon Cellier in 1953.

Fabre d'Olivet's posthumous reputation exceeded anything he had enjoyed during his lifetime. He was a figure of authority on a wide range of subjects for Illuminists of the 1830s and 1840s. Beyond Illuminism proper, he was an important influence on religio-social theorists of the Romantic period [→ Romanticism], most notably → P.S. Ballanche and P. Leroux. His fame reached its peak during the Symbolist period, when → Saint-Yves Alveydre offered an interpretation of him as a modern pagan that was taken up by the Symbolist poets, though it is impossible to point to a direct, decisive influence on any major poet.

Les Vers dorés de Pythagore expliqués, traduits en français, et précédés d'un discours sur l'essence et la forme de la poésie chez les principaux peuples de la terre, Paris: Treuttel et Würtz, 1813 (Paris: L'Age d'homme, 1978) ♦ *La Langue hébraïque restituée, et le véritable sens des mots hébreux rétabli et prouvé par*

leur analyse radicale, 2 vols. Paris: Barrois et Eberhard, 1815-1816 (Lausanne: L'Age d'homme, 1975) ♦ *Guérison de Rodolphe Grivel, sourd-muet: Notions sur le Sens de l'Ouïe*, Paris: Bretin, 1811; second edition: *Notions sur le Sens de l'Ouïe, en générale, et en particulier sur le Développement de ce Sens opéré chez Rodolphe Grivel et chez plusieurs autres enfants sourd-muets de naissance*, Montpellier: Picot, 1819 ♦ *Caïn: mystère dramatique de Lord Byron, traduit en vers français, et réfuté dans une suite de remarques philosophiques et critiques; précédé d'une lettre adressée à Lord Byron, sur les motifs et le but de cet ouvrage*, Paris: Servier, 1823 (Genève: Slatkine, 1981) ♦ *De l'Etat social de l'homme; ou vues philosophiques sur l'histoire du genre humaine*, 2 vols., Paris: Brière 1822; republished as *Histoire philosophique du genre humain*, 1824 (Paris: L'Age d'homme, 1974) ♦ *La Vraie Maçonnerie et la Céleste Culture* (Léon Cellier, ed.), Grenoble: Presses Universitaires de France 1953 ♦ English translations by L.A. Redfield (originally published New York and London: G.P. Putnam; reissued Kila, MT: Kessinger Publishers): *Social State of Man* (1915) ♦ *The Golden Verses* (1917) ♦ *The Hebraïc Tongue Restored* (1921) ♦ *Caïn* (1923) ♦ *The Healing of R. Grivel* (1927) ♦ *Mes souvenirs (1767-1825)* (G. Tappa & Cl. Boumendil (eds), Nice: Belisane, 1977 ♦ *Music Explained as Science and Art*, Rochester: Inner Traditions, 1987.

Lit.: Léon Cellier, *Fabre d'Olivet: Contribution à l'étude des aspects religieux du romantisme*, Paris: Nizet, 1953 ♦ Brian Juden, *Traditions orphiques et tendances mystiques dans le Romantisme français (1800-1855)*, Paris: Klincksieck 1971, 169-192 and passim.

ARTHUR MCCALLA

Fabré-Palaprat, Bernard-Raymond, * 1773 Cordes (Tarn), † 18.2.1838 Pau (Southern France)

Bernard-Raymond Fabré-Palaprat was the founder of modern neo-Templarism [→ Neo-Templar Traditions]. Although he styled himself a "medical doctor", he was actually educated in a Catholic seminary but was unable to complete his training there because of the French Revolution. He later worked as a pedicure performing small surgical operations (an activity not requiring a formal medical education at that time).

After the Revolution, Fabré-Palaprat joined Paris → Freemasonry in the lodge of the Knights of the Cross. In 1804, he and some of his Masonic companions declared that they had discovered, quite by chance and hidden in furniture which had belonged to Duke Louis-Hercule-Timoléon de Cossé-Brissac, who had been killed during the Revolutionary Terror of 1792, a number of documents "proving" the century-old theory, or legend, of a secret prosecution of the Order of the Knights

Templar (formally suppressed in 1307). The theory had many proponents in Masonic circles, but Fabré-Palaprat claimed not only to have found solid evidence for it, but also documents left by the last Grand Master in an uninterrupted line of succession dating back to the Middle Ages (namely, Cossé-Brissac himself), authorizing certain Masonic bodies to elect a new Grand Master after his death. Fabré-Palaprat concluded that the Knights of the Cross lodge held sufficient authority to appoint the Templar Grand Master, and had himself elected to the position in 1805.

Restoring the Order of the Temple was somewhat attuned to the imperial rhetoric of the time, and Napoleon I (1769-1821) himself even agreed to preside at one of its solemn ceremonies in 1808. Fabré-Palaprat's claims went beyond establishing yet another order of chivalry, however. Firstly, he proclaimed that modern Freemasonry had been founded by Templars, and that the Grand Master of the renewed Order of the Temple had authority over all the Masonic lodges throughout the world. In 1812, Fabré-Palaprat went still further, and claimed to have purchased from a Paris *bouquiniste* an original version of the Gospel of St. John entitled *Evangelicon*, together with an old commentary known as *Leviticon* or *Levitikon*. Historians today believe that these works, rather than forgeries authored by Fabré-Palaprat himself, were actually 17th or 18th century creations. Fabré-Palaprat, however, regarded them as ancient scriptures revealing the very truth about Christianity. They explained that Jesus Christ was not the Son of God, but a genial esoteric master educated in Alexandria. Before dying, according to the *Leviticon*, Jesus established an "Order of the East", with secret but unquestionable authority over the Church of the West. The first Grand Master of the Order of the East was John the Beloved; in the Middle Ages the Order ceased to exist under that name and became instead the Order of the Temple.

The implication was that Fabré-Palaprat, being the current Grand Master of the Order of the Temple, was both St. John's successor and head of the Order of the East, with full apostolic authority over the whole of Christianity. In 1812, Fabré-Palaprat was thus able to establish what was in fact a new religion, the so-called "Johannite Church", and to proclaim himself Sovereign Pontiff of that "John's Church", a body invested with full authority over "Peter's Church" (i.e. the Roman Catholic Church). Most neo-Templars regarded themselves as good Roman Catholics, and had no intention whatsoever of following Fabré-Palaprat into the Johannite Church. A schism followed in Fabré-Palaprat's Order of the Temple between the "Johannite" (also called "Palapratian") and the "Catholic" factions. Both continued as separate entities, with Fabré-Palaprat gathering his followers from among the most anticlerical of the French Freemasons of his time.

In 1831, Fabré-Palaprat met the defrocked priest Ferdinand-François Châtel (1795-1857), who had founded an anticlerical and overtly socialist "French Catholic Church" independent of Rome. Châtel joined Fabré-Palaprat's "Johannite" wing of the neo-Templar order and was consecrated by Fabré-Palaprat (on the basis of the authority he claimed to have as successor of St. John) as "Bishop" and "Primate of France" in the Johannite Church. Châtel was able to recruit other politically radical ex-priests, but his anti-Catholic excesses alienated even more neo-Templars, who left Fabré-Palaprat, outraged also by a "Johannite Mass" which Fabré-Palaprat (who had never been ordained a priest) publicly celebrated in 1834. The Johannite Church ultimately collapsed; Châtel continued to operate a "Radical French Church" for some years after that, but eventually abandoned all such projects altogether, and in his later years simply worked in a Paris drugstore. Fabré-Palaprat left Paris due to ill health in 1837 and died in Southern France in 1838.

After Fabré-Palaprat's death, the "Palapratian" and the "Catholic" wings of the neo-Templar order tried to merge by electing the British Admiral William Sidney-Smith (1764-1840), whom Fabré-Palaprat had appointed as Grand Prior for England in 1813, as Grand Master recognized by both branches. The merger proved short-lived, however, and the "Palapratian" (Masonic and anticlerical) and the "Catholic" branch of Fabré-Palaprat's Order of the Temple went their separate ways. Eventually, a "Catholic" wing in continuity with Fabré-Palaprat's initiative ceased to exist, and the "Palapratian" wing separated into several dozens of conflicting Orders and Priories.

Today, "Catholic" neo-Templar orders have again been established (some of them recognized by the Roman Catholic Church, which does not regard them as being in continuity with the Medieval Knights Templars, however, but as simple private associations), whilst more than a hundred "Palapratian" neo-Templar obediences, divided by a century-old history of schisms and separations, continue an independent existence with different degrees of success. A controversial figure throughout his life, Fabré-Palaprat stands at the gateway of modern neo-Templarism as such, and its endemic proclivity for division and schism.

Lit.: Léonce Fabre des Essarts, *Les Hiérophantes: Études sur les fondateurs de religions depuis la Révolution jusqu'à ce jour – 1re Série*, Paris: Chacornac, 1905 ♦ René Le Forestier, *La Franc-Maçonnerie templière et occultiste au XVIIIe et XIXe siècles*, 2 vols., repr. Paris: La Table d'Émeraude, 1987, 944-970 ♦ L. Dailliez & J.-P. Lombard de Comble, *Règle et Statuts de l'Ordre du Temple*, Paris: Dervy, 1996.

MASSIMO INTROVIGNE

Falk, Samuel Jacob,
* ca. 1710 Podhayce (Poland),
† 17.4.1782 London

Jewish Kabbalist known as the "Baal Shem of London" (master of the divine names). Scorned by rabbinic opponents as an ignoramus and charlatan, he was revered by mystical Jews as a healer and visionary. Through his association with occultist Freemasons [→ Freemasonry], his fame spread from England to the Continent, Scandinavia, Russia, and North Africa. Some Masons believed that he was the "Old Man of the Mountain", an "Unknown Superior" of illuminist Freemasonry – a belief that later fueled the anti-Semitic polemics of Edouard Drumont, Benjamin Fabre, and Nesta Webster. Scholem suggests that the youthful Falk was influenced by the antinomian Sabbatianism of Baruchia Russo, who interpreted Sabbatai Zevi's conversion to Islam in 1666 as a "holy sin", a necessary descent into the realm of evil (the *kellipoth*) in order to transform evil into good. Some radical devotées condoned public conversion to the dominant religion of one's region, combined with private adherence to Sabbatian beliefs. After moving to Fürth, Falk became well-versed in New Testament teachings, which he utilized in religious disputations with Christians, whose patronage he sought for his alchemical and magical exploits.

In the 1730's Falk visited aristocratic courts in Germany, where he dazzled witnesses with feats of kabbalistic healing, vision-inducement, angelic conjurations, treasure-finding, and political predictions. According to the *Mémoires du Comte de Rantzow* (Amsterdam, 1741), Falk was driven from Cassel by jealous Jesuits, who wanted him burned at the stake. In 1736 he found refuge with Baron de Donop and Count Alexander Rantzow, whose son George published Falk's startling pronouncements and magical feats. While boldly defending the superiority of the Jewish religion, Falk argued that 'the Jews are in ignominy, so that in a true sense they are the only Christians': moreover, their debasement will soon lead to their deliverance. His prediction of a universal war leading to a messianic consummation frightened Rantzow, who was ordered to abandon 'the pretended liberator of the Jews'.

Falk then fled to Holland, where he possibly met Moses Hayim Luzzatto, the great messianic kabbalist and suspected Sabbatian, whose writings he would long cherish. He also befriended Tobias and Simon Boas, wealthy bankers and Freemasons, who became his admirers and patrons. After Falk moved to London (ca. 1739-1740), Rantzow heard that 'the Portuguese Jews of the highest reputation rendered him honors as their prince and sovereign pontiff'. However, Parliament ordered the Jew's arrest but then released him on condition that he 'no longer Kabbalize'. A later Masonic colleague, General Charles Rainsford, reported that Falk was also censured for Kabbalistic indiscretions by certain Jewish authorities, who punished him and forced him to 'pass the rest of his life in solitude, without daring to communicate his knowledge, which he had the imprudence to make apparent for ostentation'.

As has been argued by the present author, over the next decades in London, Falk's path often crossed that of → Emanuel Swedenborg, the Swedish scientist and mystic, and the Papal Inquisition later linked their names as 'chiefs of the Illuminés'. During his residence in 1744-1745, Swedenborg was in contact with two unnamed Jews, who witnessed his visionary trance state and whom he defended as 'these good Israelites'. When he suffered an hallucinatory illness, he was treated by his 'intimate friend' Dr. William Smith, an eccentric Mason, who was studying Kabbala [→ Jewish Influences] with Falk. Until Swedenborg's death in 1772, whenever he visited London he lived in close proximity to Smith and Falk in their mutual neighborhood of Wellclose Square. In his diaries, Swedenborg referred to "Falker" (a surname also used by Falk), and his many descriptions of a Jewish magician in London bear striking similarities to those in the diary of Hirsch Kalisch, Falk's factotum. From their overlapping network of Masonic admirers (Rainsford, Thomé, → Cagliostro, etc.), a shadowy tradition of Falk-Swedenborg collaboration developed.

Though Falk remained a devout Jew, his ambivalent religious behavior provoked puzzlement among Jews and Christians alike. Their questions were intensified by the scandals erupting around other crypto-Sabbatians, such as Jonathan Eibeschütz, Jacob Frank, and Moses David, who were accused by orthodox rabbis of Sabbatian deception and debauchery. Frank, who publicly converted to Catholicism, was linked with Falk by some illuminist Masons. David, who participated in Falk's "brotherhood" in London in 1759, was associated with a secret Sabbatian sect on the Continent that attempted to combine Judaism with Christianity.

From 1764 on, Falk received financial support from the Goldsmid brothers, who moved from Amsterdam to London, became Freemasons, and gained great infuence in the Jewish and Christian communities. Now visited by diplomats and aristocrats from Europe, he attracted politically-minded Masons who hoped to gain his magical assistance for their causes. Prince Adam Czartorisky, leader of the Polish nationalists against Russian oppression, visited Boas and then Falk, and received their blessing and funding. The Duke of Chartres, Grand Master of the Grand Lodge of France, sought his support in London, and Falk consecrated a talismanic ring that would ensure Chartres's succession to the French throne. The Marquise de la Croix, protector of Jews in Avignon, and the Marquis de Thomé, founder of a Swedenborgian lodge in Paris, received Kabbalistic instruction from him.

But his most famous disciple was Joseph Balsamo, alias "Count Cagliostro," who in 1776 helped Falk develop the Egyptian Rite, which Cagliostro carried to lodges in Holland, France, Germany, Poland, and Russia, where – according to Catherine the Great – the Masons were infatuated with Swedenborg's teachings and thus welcomed Cagliostro, who possessed the secrets of Dr. Falk. In 1780 in Strasbourg, Cagliostro praised Swedenborg as a great man but stressed that the greatest Mason was the celebrated Falk of London. In 1782 at Wilhelmsbad, delegates to an international Masonic convention investigated Falk's kabbalistic influence on various *Illuminés* (questions which arose again at the *Philalèthes* conferences in Paris in 1783-1787).

During Falk's final year, Rainsford hoped to work with him on the development of a Judeo-Christian rite (the → "Asiatic Brethren"), dedicated to a transcendent form of kabbalism which did not require conversion from either religion. In October 1782 Rainsford sadly recorded, 'As to the Kabbalah, all is upset by the unexpected death of Dr. Falk'. However, the secretive order survived, and F.J. Molitor, a later Christian initiate, recorded in 1829 that the 'Asiatics' drew on the teachings of Sabbatai Zevi, Jacob Frank, and Dr. Falk, 'the *Baal Shem* of London'.

MS. Diary of Hirsch Kalisch in Jewish Theological Seminary of New York ♦ Commonplace Book of Samuel Falk in Jewish Museum in London. Hebrew edition published by Michal Oron, *Miba'al Shed Leba'al Shem: Schmuel Falk, Haba'al Shem Mi-Lon-*

don, Jerusalem: Mosad Bialik, 2003 ♦ Masonic and political documentation in Grand Lodge Libraries of London, Edinburgh, The Hague ♦ Rainsford MSS. in British Library and Alnwick Castle.

Lit.: [Jörgen L.A. Rantzau], *Mémoires du Comte de Rantzow*, Amsterdam: Pierre Mortier, 1741, 197-223 ♦ Caubet (ed.), "Les Philalèthes", *Le Monde Maçonnique* 14 (1873), 425, 474; 15 (1874), 164-165, 548 ♦ Hermann Adler, "The Baal-Shem of London", *Transactions of Jewish Historical Society of England* 26 (1902-1905), 148-173 ♦ Solomon Schechter, "The Baal-Shem, Dr. Falk", *Jewish Chronicle* (9 March l913), 15-16 ♦ Gordon Hills, "Notes on Some Contemporary References to Dr. Falk, the Baal Shem of London, in the Rainsford MSS. at the British Museum", *Transactions of Jewish Historical Society of England* 8 (1915-1917), 122-128 ♦ J.E.S. Tuckett, "Savalette de Langes, les Philalethes, and the Convent of Wilhelmsbad", *Ars Quatuor Coronatorum* 30 (1917), 131-171 ♦ Cecil Roth, *Essays and Portraits in Anglo-Jewish History*, Philadelphia: Jewish Publication Society of America, 1962, 139-164 ♦ Maria Trebiloni, "L'Esoterismo mistico e scientista di Bourrée de Corberon", *Annuario dell'Instituto Storico Italiano* 17-18 (1965-1966), 5-109 ♦ Emanuel Swedenborg, *The Spiritual Diary* (A.W. Acton, ed.), London: Swedenborg Society, 1977, 5620–5885 ♦ Gershom Scholem, *Kabbalah* (1974), New York: Dorset, 1987, 272-284 ♦ idem, *Du Frankisme au Jacobinisme*, Paris: Le Seul-Gallimard, 1981, 39 ♦ Raphael Patai, *The Jewish Alchemists*, Princeton: Princeton University Press, 1994, 454-462 ♦ Michal Oron, "Dr. Samuel Jacob Falk and the Eibeschuetz-Emden Controversy", in: Karl Grözinger & Joseph Dan (eds.), *Mysticism, Magic and Kabbalah in Ashkenazic Judaism*, Berlin & New York: Walter de Gruyter, 1995, 243-256 ♦ Marsha K. Schuchard, "Yeats and the Unknown Superiors: Swedenborg, Falk, and Cagliostro", in: Marie Roberts & Hugh Ormsby-Lennon, *Secret Texts*, New York: AMS, 1995, 114-167 ♦ idem, "Dr. Samuel Jacob Falk: A Sabbatean Adventurer in the Masonic Underground", in: Matt Goldish & Richard Popkin (eds.), *Jewish Messianism in the Early Modern Period*, Dordrecht: Kluwer, 2001, 203-227.

MARSHA KEITH SCHUCHARD

Faucheux, Albert → Barlet, François-Charles

Fedeli d'Amore

We owe the expression "Fedeli d'Amore" (faithful of love, Love's lieges) to → Dante Alighieri. In his *Vita Nuova*, the work in which he crystallizes his experience of human love, he records how after a dream-vision of his lady he decided to write a sonnet in which, he says, 'I would greet all the Faithful of Love' (*Vita Nuova*, III, 9), asking them to judge his vision. He may have meant by this expression a group of poets gifted with a higher intellective faculty, because in the same work he writes that some of his words whose meaning is uncertain should not be further explained; 'no one can resolve this uncertainty who is not as much a devotee of Love as I am; but those who are, will easily find the solution of these uncertain words' (*Ibid.*, XIV, 14). According to the commentary of the *Ottimo*, Dante the love-poet makes words mean something other than their usual meanings. Francesco da Barberino shares this claim to a hidden meaning: he reserves his *Documenti d'Amore* for initiated or enlightened readers, and at the end he presents a warrior with sword drawn to defend them, and to threaten any attempt at reading by the ignorant. The work is, in fact, obscure, and Francesco uses every artifice of double meaning in order to say in secret what he cannot evoke openly. Several of these poets give lyrical expression to the deep anguish felt at not being able to speak the truth out loud: '. . . I am not blind, yet I must act as though I were . . .', says Cecco d'Ascoli in his *Acerba*; '. . . I die, gazing at a beautiful face covered by a veil' (*L'Acerba*, 156). Dante, Francesco da Barberino, Guido Cavalcanti and Guido Guinizelli all celebrate in an enigmatic way the love of a woman they call *sapientissima* (wisest). The lyric poetry of the group well known under the sobriquet *Dolce Stil Nuovo* (sweet new style) is full of words like *dottrina* (doctrine), *intendimento* (understanding), *sapienza* (wisdom) and *intelligenza* (intelligence), the latter being the actual name of the woman whom Dino Compagni hymns in his eponymous poem.

Are the Faithful of Love simply the same as the poets of the *Dolce Stil Nuovo*, and is there a hidden meaning beneath the literal sense of their poetry? Is it a philosophical, theological, or political meaning? If we use the traditional scholastic division between matter and form, Love would be the outer form of the poetry, while the poem's soul would be an essential thought different from Love. In that case the loved ones whom the poet celebrates – *Madonna*, Beatrice, Giovanna, etc. – are masks for a significance which is not immediately grasped, but reserved for those gifted with a certain mental acuity. The starting-point of all poems in "stilnuovist" style is the love of a woman whose femininity is only the clothing for a profoundly abstract idea. The theme of the angel-woman (*donna angelicata*) allows the poet to objectify perfectly the Aristotelian and, later, the scholastic theory of potency and act. Applying the principle of analogy, the woman arouses in the man a love of the same nature as that through which God, the unmoved mover, is the source of movement. Every noble heart is virtually capable of realizing its perfection as a knowing being, with which divine wisdom has endowed it. Unlike the angels, who have immediate perception of the first principles, man starts from sense-data and rises, through a process of abstraction from the *signum formale* (formal sign) living in the subject as *intentio* (intention) or potency, to the very idea of divine beauty. The woman, as a vestige of the first creative Intelligence and mirror of divine Wisdom, awakens the capacity latent in every man of lifting himself, thanks to the principle of analogy, to the contemplation of the transcendent, which he perceives only through the Lady's beauty. To encounter beauty is to sense a beckoning presence. The loved one is a gift of God, *de sursum discendens* (descending from above), a creature whose reality manifests the divine Wisdom to human sight and intellect, and the loving of whom is an initiation into the mysteries of the Uncreated. The soul of Guido Guinizelli, arriving in the presence of his Creator, argues in its own defence that 'she had the appearance of an angel' (*Al cor gentile repara sempre Amore* [Love always cures the gentle heart], in *Poeti del Duecento* [Poets of the 13th century], 460). The love of this creature is an *amor sapientiae* (love of wisdom).

The most famous poem of Guido Cavalcanti, *Donna me prega* (*Ibid.*, 522), concentrates on this same theme of the passage from potency to act through the intercession of the phenomenon of love. At the request of a lady who is interrogating him on what "Love" is, he expounds a perfectly orthodox theory: love resides in that union of the possible and active intellects, the passage from potentiality to the effective actuality of knowledge. The scholastics even used for it the term "copulation'. In Cavalcanti's verse the love of a lady is none other than the love of *Sapientia* (Wisdom). It consists in a sort of stirring of the possible intellect (just as the beloved attracts the lover to her) towards its supreme beatitude, which is the actualization of all its potentialities of knowledge. The "tension" towards the woman is a metaphor for the aspiration towards the supreme intelligence of things that the being carries within itself. Cecco d'Ascoli says the same when, in his *Acerba*, he sings of that woman who gives form to the intellect, who existed before the beginning of all things, who grants light and salvation. A ray of the divine Wisdom, she is assimilated to the phoenix, symbol of the one and only wisdom that is reborn throughout the ages.

The endless quest for God is often described in

images borrowed from → alchemy. The love of
Madonna allows Francesco da Barberino, throughout his *Reggimento e Costumi di Donna* (Ladies'
behavior and customs), to tread a path through
various initiatic stages whose meaning may be
expressed as going from "faithful" to "intelligent",
from loyal belief to intellectual penetration. The
quest for the Lady is crowned by the award of the
philosopher's stone, whose 'reading by concentric
circles' (as Francesco puts it) permits him to realize
the communion of the knowing nature with the
realities intelligible by the human being. Intellect,
who awaits the poet at the portal of Madonna's
palace, is the possible intellect, held in tension by
this aptitude for knowledge that the reading of the
stone (pointing to the East) will illuminate, thus
permitting the passage from the virtuality of
knowledge to its actuality, which constitutes the
supreme beatitude. To attain beatifying Wisdom: is
that not to possess the rose which is brandished by
the strange figure with both male and female heads,
illustrated in Francesco da Barberino's *Tractatus
amoris et operum eius* (Treatise on love and its
works)? Its bodily union would then symbolize the
perfect fusion between the possible intellect (male)
and the active Intelligence (female). The millennial
dream of the transformation of base matter into
gold is realized on the spiritual plane.

All these poets of the *Dolce Stil Nuovo* share the
celebration of the love of a beautiful, pure, luminous lady, the quest for whom is basically the tireless pursuit of Wisdom. This belongs within a
venerable tradition, of which the Italian poets seem
to reflect two versions: the more "philosophical"
and Aristotelian version, interpreted especially by
Cavalcanti and by Dino Compagni in his poem
L'Intelligenza; and the more "mystical" version,
Platonic in essence, as expressed in the Song of
Solomon and in Catholic thought. Saint → Augustine and Richard of Saint Victor, for example,
incarnate the divine Wisdom in Rachel beloved by
Jacob; and the poetry of Guinizelli, Dante, and
Francesco da Barberino certainly resonates with
these mystical accents. Original sin, for them, has
thrown a dark veil over the human intellect and
prevented it from *scire recte* (knowing rightly). The
Redemption alone was able to draw man out of his
profound darkness, out of this *ignorantia* (ignorance), and make a part of the eternal verities again
accessible to human intelligence. Thus one can see
why the quest and love of the Lady allow the lover
to be reborn into the true life, the life of a regenerated nature, reconciled with God towards whom it
aspires as its ultimate perfection. The "Lieges of
Love", pilgrims on the path of transcendence that

leads to the Truth, did not only have a spiritual and
theological message to convey, but sought to bear
witness through their personal quest to man's
necessity of leaving the path through which he has
gone astray.

The esotericism of these devotees of Love consists in the multiplicity of meanings which Dante
himself evokes at the entrance to the city of Dys,
carefully distinguishing the apparent meaning of
his verse from its hidden meaning. Beneath the
quest for Wisdom, incarnated by a woman and
depicted in the Fedeli's cryptic language, these
poets concealed their profound aspiration to reach
God through personal and individual paths: the
way of mystical ecstasy, the contemplative way,
free from earthly constraints. In contrast to the
Church's worldly and deviant immanence, they
sought a transcendence that climaxes in meeting
God face to face.

During the 19th century and the beginning of the
20th, well before Dante's Catholic rehabilitation in
the encyclical *In praeclara* (1921), several Italian
writers followed in the footsteps of some Renaissance scholars (Corbinelli, → Postel) by supporting
the thesis that Dante's entire work holds a hidden
meaning. Often motivated by ideologies hostile to
the Roman Church, their various theses maintain
that Dante was masking an urgent call for reform,
especially Ghibelline or heterodox (e.g. Foscolo,
Rossetti, Caetani) or else mystical or sapiential
(e.g. Perez, Pascoli). These mysterious meanings
were supposedly both dissimulated and conveyed
by the secret language ('jargon') common to Dante
and the stilnuovist poets. This systematic argument
has been fiercely discussed and contested up to the
present day by a number of historians of medieval
Italian literature. It has also found defenders in
France (Delécluze, Aroux, Péladan, Vulliaud),
while Valli, Ricolfi and Alessandrini have taken it
further from a historical and stylistic perspective. It
is obviously a small step from there to representing
Dante's "secret doctrine" as essentially esoteric,
and the Fedeli d'Amore as an initiatic circle,
inspired by chivalry and especially by the Knights
Templar. The step was duly taken in 1925 by →
René Guénon, who was followed in turn, and to
various degrees, by authors both within and outside the Traditionalist current, e.g. (respectively)
J. Canteins or R.L. John. In an entirely different
spirit, this time academic, → Henry Corbin (1903-
1978) pointed out some remarkable parallels
between the "Fedeli d'Amore" of East and West,
based on the love poetry of certain Persian Sufis
(e.g. Ruzbehan, 1128-1209), whose esotericism
likewise presents human love as a "support" for

divine love, and as naturally destined to be transfigured ultimately into the latter.

> Cecco d'Ascoli, *L'Acerba* (B. Censori & E. Vittori, eds.), Ascoli, 1971 ♦ Dante Alighieri, *La Vita Nuova* (Maria Corti, ed.), Milan: Feltrinelli, 1993 ♦ Francesco da Barberino, *Tractatus Amoris et operum eius*, in: *I documenti d'Amore di F. da Barberino secondo i manoscritti originali* (F. Egidi, ed.), Rome, 1905-27 [4 vols.] (²1982; 5 vols.) ♦ idem, *Reggimento e costumi di Donna* (G. Sansone, ed.), Rome: Zauli, ²1995 ♦ *Poeti del Duecento* (Gianfranco Contini, ed.), Milan: Riccardo Ricciardi, 1960 ♦ *Poésie italienne du Moyen Age (XIIᵒ-XVᵒ siècles)* (H. Spitzmuller, ed.), Paris: Desclée De Brouwer, 1975 (bilingual ed. – only the 1st vol. appeared; ²1999).

> *Lit.*: M. Alessandrini, *Dante fedele d'Amore*, Milan: Atanòr, 1960 ♦ J. Canteins, *La Passion de Dante Alighieri*, Paris: Dervy, 1997 (²2003) ♦ idem, "René Guénon et l'ésotérisme médiéval toscan", *Connaissance des Religions* 65-66 (2002), 91-98 ♦ idem, *Dante: L'Homme engagé*, Milan: Archè, 2003 ♦ C. de Callataÿ-van der Mersch, *Le déchiffrement de Dante* (3 vols.), Leuven: Peeters, 1994-1997 ♦ B. Cerchio, *L'ermetismo di Dante*, Rome: Edizioni Mediterranee, 1988 ♦ A. Chastel, "Sur la poétique du Livre et du Nombre chez Dante", *Cahiers du Sud* 308 (1951), 13-19 ♦ H. Corbin, *En Islam iranien: Aspects spirituels et philosophiques*, Paris: Gallimard, 1971-1972 (4 vols.; vol. 3, 9-146) ♦ René Guénon, *L'ésotérisme de Dante*, Paris: Bossard, 1925 (many reprints) ♦ Philippe Guiberteau, *Dante et son itinéraire spirituel selon la VITA NOVA*, Paris: Librairie José Corti, 1983 ♦ R.L. John, *Dante Templare: Una nuova interpretazione della Commedia*, Milan: Hoepli, ²1987 (¹1946) ♦ A. Ricolfi, *Studi sui Fedeli d'Amore*, Rome: Soc. Dante Alighieri, 1933-1940 (2 vols.; ²1983) ♦ L. Valli, *Il linguaggio segreto di Dante e dei Fedeli d'Amore*, Rome: Optima, 1928-1932 (2 vols.; ²1994).

CATHERINE GUIMBARD

Ficino, Marsilio, * 19.10.1433 Figline, † 1.10.1499 Careggi (Florence)

1. LIFE AND WORKS 2. PRISCA THEOLOGIA 3. THEOLOGIA PLATONICA 4. ESOTERIC MEDICINE AND THE SPIRIT 5. DEMONOLOGY AND THE OCCULT 6. CONCLUSION

1. LIFE AND WORKS

Ficino, the eminent Florentine Platonist and one of the most learned and influential thinkers of his age, lived a somewhat uneventful life as a brilliant, networking scholar, patronized by the Medici, ordained in 1473, and elected a canon of Florence's cathedral in 1487 (his notable bust still adorns the south side of the nave). Originally destined for a medical career by his father, a doctor in the service of the Medici, and trained as an Aristotelian, he acquired, in addition to much medical learning, a rare mastery both of the difficult Greek of Plato, Plotinus, and Proclus, and of the ancient and medieval history of Platonic philosophy. Under the patronage of Cosimo de' Medici who gave him a villa at Careggi in 1463, Ficino set out to render all of Plato's dialogues into Latin, but interrupted this task almost immediately in order to translate the *Corpus Hermeticum*, under the title *Liber de potestate et sapientia Dei* but generally referred to as the *Pimander*, after the title of the first of the fourteen treatises known to him (Tommaso Benci subsequently produced a vernacular version). In 1464 he actually read his versions of Plato's *Parmenides* and *Philebus* to Cosimo on his deathbed. Eventually, with financing from Filippo Valori and other admirers, and having selectively consulted the renderings of various dialogues by such humanist predecessors as Leonardo Bruni, he published the complete Plato in 1484 (on a date coinciding with a conjunction of Jupiter and Saturn) and dedicated it to Lorenzo de' Medici. Ficino included prefaces (*argumenta*) for each dialogue, as well as a long commentary he had written by 1469 on the *Symposium* and entitled *De amore* (a vernacular version of which he also prepared). This became the seminal text of Renaissance love theory. Later he composed other magisterial Plato commentaries, some incomplete, on the *Timaeus*, *Philebus* (also the subject of a public lecture series), *Parmenides*, *Phaedrus*, *Sophist*, and on the Nuptial Number in book VIII of the *Republic*.

While continually revising his Plato during the 1470s, Ficino published the Latin text of his *De Christiana religione* in 1476 (which, as we now realize, was indebted to earlier anti-Jewish and anti-Moslem polemicists), as well as compiling his original philosophical masterpiece, an eighteen-book *summa* on metaphysics and the immortality of the soul, which he published in 1482. Indebted to → Augustine and Aquinas, it was nonetheless the fruit of his conviction that "Platonism" – actually → Neoplatonism, since he regarded Plotinus as Plato's most profound interpreter – was reconcilable with Christianity. He called it his *Theologia Platonica*, borrowing the title of Proclus's *magnum opus* to which he was considerably though secretly indebted; and then subtitled it, echoing both a Plotinian treatise and an early Platonizing treatise of Augustine, *De immortalitate animorum*.

In the 1480s Ficino turned again to Plotinus, with whom he had been familiar since the 1460s, and rendered the entire *Enneads* into Latin. For these he also wrote extensive notes and commentaries, publishing the whole in 1492 with a dedication to Lorenzo. Meanwhile he also worked on a three-book treatise on prolonging health, the *De vita*, having begun it apparently as part of his Plotinus commentary. It was full of encyclopedic pharmacological and other learning, and daringly combined philosophical, astrological, magical and psychiatric speculations. When it appeared in 1489, Ficino was threatened with a Curial investigation into its orthodoxy; but he fended this off successfully, if disingenuously, by asserting that he was presenting ancient views rather than his own. In the last years of his life he published translations of other Neoplatonic authors, including Iamblichus, Porphyry, Proclus, Synesius and the 11th c. Byzantine Psellus; he translated and commented on the works of → Pseudo-Dionysius Areopagita and embarked on a commentary on St. Paul's epistle to the Romans. Finally, he first supported but then vehemently attacked Savonarola.

Unlike most scholars, Ficino was able to exert a formative influence on his own age and on two subsequent centuries. Several reasons contributed to this. First, there was the intellectual fascination and novelty, bordering on unorthodoxy (even heresy, as we shall see), of his revival of Neoplatonism and the unfamiliar nature of what he had to say about the complementary roles of religion and philosophy in nurturing the spiritual and noetic life. His ecumenism, his delight in the notion that divine worship is natural and inherently varied, and his diverse interests, would align him with the very liberal wing of Christian theologians even today. Second, a revered teacher of the *signori* and their sons, he cultivated and sustained a learned and pastoral correspondence with well over a hundred pupils, friends, patrons, and admirers, many of them, including Lorenzo and various cardinals, in the highest offices of church and state, in Italy and abroad (this circle is often, if rather misleadingly, referred to as his Platonic Academy). His twelve books of letters in Latin (and there are others besides) range from elegant thank-you notes and witty compliments to philosophical treatises, and were later rendered into Italian. Finally, he was one of the first early modern intellectuals to enjoy the accelerated Europe-wide exposure made possible by the invention of the printing press. His works are now among the most splendid and valuable of the incunabula; and the *De amore* and *De vita*, along with the *Pimander* and Plato translations, became bestsellers.

Although Ficino had a humanist training and freely quoted the Roman poets, and although at one level he was a pious philosopher-apologist-

priest with a missionary goal, he was also the first of the Renaissance mages dedicated to the notion of a World Spirit and a World Soul. Apart from metaphysics, ethics and psychology, his interests embraced mythology (for him, poetic theology), → astrology, → magic, magical and figural numbers [→ Number Symbolism], demonology and the occult [→ occult / occultism], → music (especially harmonics) and musical therapy – interests which he found in Plato himself and therefore saw as authentic aspects of the Platonic tradition. While the depth of his technical understanding of later Platonism has rarely been equalled (his works of translation and interpretation bear witness to an enlightened and dedicated scholarship), his original philosophical, theological, and magical speculations constitute one of the enduring monuments of Renaissance thought and were enormously and diversely influential. The first edition of his own *Opera omnia* appeared in Basel in 1561, the second (and better) edition in 1576, and the third (a reprint, strangely, of the first) in Paris in 1641; and his *Platonis opera omnia* was printed a number of times too, as were other works or groups of works. Furthermore, dubious, spurious and lost works testify to his authority as an *érudit* and magus, as do many unpublished manuscripts.

2. PRISCA THEOLOGIA

The path to gnosis, though perfected by Plato, had a distant origin, and Ficino was one of the first Renaissance authors to champion the notion of a secret, esoteric, and (as Agostino Steuco would later call it) perennial wisdom that preceded and prepared the way for Christianity as the climactic Platonic revelation. As such it paralleled the Mosaic wisdom transmitted to the Hebrews by the Pentateuch, by the secrets of the Mosaic oral tradition later inscribed in the books of the kabbalah [→ Jewish Influences], and by the revelations of Moses' successors, the psalmists and the prophets. For symbolic and numerological reasons Ficino propounded the idea that Plato was the sixth in a succession of gentile sages, six being the sum of its integers and the product of its factors and thus, according to the arithmological tradition, the perfect number. It was also the number of Jupiter, of the days of biblical creation, of the links in Homer's golden chain from which hangs the pendant world (which the Neoplatonists interpreted allegorically), and of the six primary ontological categories in the *Sophist* (essence, being, identity, alterity, rest and motion). Indeed the hexad was such an authoritative category for charting the gentile succession of sages that Ficino had to adjust its members, since he had many more sages than slots available for them; but eventually he decided on → Zoroaster, → Hermes Trismegistus, Orpheus, Aglaophemus, Pythagoras, and Plato. This is remarkable on several counts. It omits such important figures as Socrates, Timaeus, Parmenides, and Empedocles whose dicta Ficino often quoted as Platonic. It also omits the sibyls whose authority he accepted and in whose company he included Diotima, Socrates' teacher in the metaphysics of love. And it insists in the Neoplatonic manner on Plato's Pythagorean wisdom, a wisdom embodied in the *aurea dicta* and *symbola* which Ficino found in Iamblichus's life of Pythagoras, translated into Latin, and published at the conclusion of his *Opera Omnia*.

Ficino knew Orpheus from the many fragments quoted in Plato's works and in the works of his commentators, and from the eighty-seven *Orphic Hymns* now thought to be products of later antiquity but that he and his contemporaries believed authentic. From early on, when he first translated them, he treated these *Hymns* as sacred but dangerous texts. Certainly they testified to Orpheus being the gentiles' David, and his songs, their psalms, and they listed the attributes of the deities they addressed in an aretology, a listing of virtues, hiding under a polytheistic rind a monotheistic core (a much revered prefatory palinode explained away the polytheism). But they also appeared to invoke demonic powers; and Ficino was careful to circulate only a few fragments in his Latin translation to some choice friends. Orpheus himself, though Plato's *Symposium* 179D condemns him as faint-hearted for his refusal to die for Eurydice (etymologized as "breadth of [the] judgment"), had been the master of incantation, the paradigmatic magus who bent the natural world to his will and whose music derived from the fundamental harmonies of the cosmos. Ficino was himself flatteringly addressed by various poet-friends as another Orpheus, and the figure of Orpheus was painted on an "Orphic" lyre he played in his Platonic hymn recitals – apparently to great effect, since onlookers describe him as both entranced and entrancing. At the onset of his career as a Medicean teacher and sage he seems indeed to have presided over a neo-Orphic revival. Orphic incantation became the key to his conception of Platonic or Platonizing poetry and, in general, of musical images and models, and the affective bearer, the perfect medium of philosophy.

Nonetheless Orpheus was subordinate to the two most ancient of the sages: first to Hermes Trismegistus, whose *Pimander* Ficino continually cited and whose *Asclepius* he knew from the Latin trans-

lation attributed to Apuleius, as well as from hostile notices in Augustine and more sympathetic ones in Lactantius. The two commentaries on these works, incidentally, which were eventually printed in Ficino's *Opera* interleaved with his own translation of the one and Apuleius' translation of the other, and which have long been attributed to him, were actually by his French disciple → Lefèvre d'Étaples (Faber Stapulensis). However, while Hermes' authority remained intact, Ficino retained a guarded approach to Egypt's religious tradition. This may have been partly because Egypt appears in the Bible as the land of exile even though → Moses could have taught or been taught by the Egyptian priests (and here determining whether Hermes was coeval with Moses or succeeded him was critical, though Ficino never entertained a later view that Hermes preceded Moses!). But Egypt was also known for its zoomorphic deities and pagan rites, and Hermes had devised a sacred, hieroglyphic alphabet utilizing animals, birds, and plants to convey his wisdom. The strange little myth of Theuth and Ammon in Plato's *Phaedrus* 274Bff may have played a decisive role here; for it portrays Ammon (Jupiter) rebuking Theuth (identified with Hermes) for inventing writing and thereby opening up the possibility of debasing or profaning teachings that should only be transmitted orally, in the fullness of time, by a master who had properly prepared his disciples for their reception and comprehension. An apotropaic story also attributed to Pythagoras, it created a dilemma for a committed interpreter such as Ficino, who was faced with voluminous texts of, and commentaries on, a wisdom that from the outset he felt impelled to explore and explain and yet considered sacred and thus needing protection from the eyes of the vulgar. It set private, esoteric teaching steadfastly against public exposition, and so went to the very heart of his commitment to educating and converting the elite of Florence.

Prior even to Hermes, however, was Zoroaster. Ficino must have derived this notion primarily from the controversial Byzantine, → George Gemistos Plethon, a Proclan revivalist who had made a great impression on the Florentines during the ecumenical council of Ferrara/Florence in 1438-1443 (the abortive attempt to reconcile the Roman and Greek churches). But he was also following the odd sympathetic references to Zoroaster in Plato's works, notably in the I *Alcibiades* 121Eff, and in the works of such Platonizing thinkers as Plutarch; and responding too to the authority of the *Chaldaean Oracles*, attributed to Zoroaster, a late antique compilation which he and others deemed authentic and whose derivative and eclectic Middle Platonism was therefore assumed to be the originary Platonism. For Ficino, however, Zoroaster's primacy was preeminently something that highlighted the centrality of the Epiphany and the Magi. The three wise Chaldaeans who had come from the East, following a star, were the followers of Zoroaster (whose very name in Greek has the word "star" in it, and who was supposedly the founder both of astronomy/astrology and of the magic associated with it). Thus they symbolized the coming of the ancient wisdom to the cradle of a new philosopher-king-magus: the new Zoroaster. Moreover, having set out from the very land from which Abram had departed, they symbolized the reunion of the two ancient branches of wisdom, the Hebrew and the Zoroastrian stemming from Noah's sons (since the Ark had come to rest allegedly in a province of Persia – and Persia, Chaldaea and Babylon were often confused). Insofar as Zoroaster was also, in Ficino's view, the discoverer of writing, since he used the stars and constellations, and not animals, birds, and plants, as the "letters" of his sacred alphabet, he was, in a way, the sage who had transcribed the wisdom of the stars, had brought the stars into men's language and had taught men to write with the stars. Hence the Magi were primarily astronomers and practitioners of a star-based magic, whose knowledge of the heavens had enabled them to find the Christ child and to worship him as the Zoroastrian, the supreme Platonic guardian in Bethlehem. Thus to Plato's Pythagorean, Orphic, and Hermetic predecessors, we should add Zoroaster as the original *priscus theologus*, the founder of the ancient gentile wisdom that Ficino himself was dedicated to reconciling with the theology of Abraham as perfected in Christ.

3. THEOLOGIA PLATONICA

The history of gnosis after Plato was also subject to revision by Ficino, since he believed that the Proclus-inspired writings nowadays attributed to the Pseudo-Dionysius of the late 5th century had been composed by the Dionysius mentioned in Acts 17:34 as an Athenian converted by St. Paul's preaching on the Areopagus, in other words by a thinker of the 1st century. Since one of the Dionysian treatises is a masterpiece of a negative theology inspired by the second part of Plato's *Parmenides* as interpreted by Plutarch of Athens, Proclus's teacher, this had the effect of transferring the fully fledged late Neoplatonism of Proclus back to the time immediately following the Ascension. Suddenly the opening of St. John's Gospel, the epis-

tles of St. Paul, and the Pseudo-Areopagitean treatises coalesced to form an impressive body of Christian-Platonic writing, a body that indeed signifies the perfection of the Platonic wisdom in the Christian revelation. Given the centrality of the *via negativa*, moreover, it had the effect of foregrounding Platonic dialectics as a mystical rather than a logical instrument, and thus of transforming the old Socratic scepticism or agnosticism into a kind of super- or supra-gnosis.

This pivotal misdating in turn impacted Ficino's perspective on the centuries we would now assign to the Middle Platonists, and led him to embrace the notion that the Ammonius Saccas who was Plotinus' teacher had been a Christian Platonist, and that the Origen whom Porphyry mentions as Plotinus' fellow disciple was the Christian heresiarch, author of the *De principiis* and *Contra Celsum*. Consequently, Plotinus emerges as a Christianized Platonist if not as a Christian. This was all-defining given the centrality of the *Enneads* in Ficino's own understanding of Plato, and his belief that Plotinus was Plato's beloved intellectual son 'in whom' – thus Ficino imagines Plato using the very words used by God according to the Gospels – 'I am well pleased'. After all, Ficino's supreme scholarly achievement was to render the fifty-four Plotinian treatises into Latin, and to devote his interpretational life to arguing that Plotinian and Christian metaphysics were almost one and the same, that Plotinus had written a *summa platonica* just as Aquinas would later write a *summa theologica*. Moreover, succumbing to a common temptation, Ficino read most of Proclus' subtle distinctions back into Plotinus, and thence into Plato, the *Hermetica*, the *Orphic Hymns*, and the *Oracula Chaldaica*, thus creating an ancient Platonic, but in effect Proclan, theology that had begun with Zoroaster but been perfected in the works of Plato, Dionysius, and Plotinus. Finally, since so much of Proclus had become incorporated into medieval theology by way of the Pseudo-Areopagitean writings – and, indeed, had become embedded in the Augustinian mystical traditions of the Middle Ages – Ficino was able to argue with conviction that the time was ripe for a Platonic revival that would unite wisdom and faith, philosophy and revelation, as they had once been united in the golden age, the pre-Noachian time of Enoch himself who had walked with God. Interestingly, this whole fabric is built on some fundamental mistakes in attribution and dating; but they were mistakes that the vast majority of Ficino's learned contemporaries shared. Thus Ficino was able to present a Neoplatonic view of the history of philosophy, and to propel that history back into the remotest past.

4. ESOTERIC MEDICINE AND THE SPIRIT

Ficino was also familiar with a number of ancient texts that he regarded as an integral part of the Platonic tradition but that were not strictly speaking philosophical (although they often included philosophical speculations and adduced philosophical premises). These included medical, pharmacological, and medical-astrological texts, some of them of Arabic provenance, that formed part of his intellectual training as a doctor – a role he never abandoned, since he regarded himself, in the Socratic sense, as a doctor of souls, a *medicus* even to the Medici. His *De vita libri tres* of 1489 is a treatise in three books on regimen, diet, abstinence, salves, beneficent powders and sprays, aromas, psychosomatic exercises, meditation and mood-elevation techniques, and astrological and demonological attuning. The third book in particular, entitled *De vita coelitus comparanda* ("On bringing one's life into harmony with the heavens"), is a rich and complex exploration of scholarly melancholy, holistic medicine and psychiatry. It makes continual reference to zodiacal and planetary influences, to stellar oppositions and conjunctions, to astrological election, to the theory of universal sympathies, and to synastry, the assumption that particular people are born under the same planet under the same astral configurations and are therefore star twins. Additionally, following → Albertus Magnus and Thomas Aquinas, Ficino treats of the therapeutic powers of talismans and → amulets when properly made and inscribed. Here he is drawing both upon Scholastic notions of acquired form and the hylomorphic structuring of corporeal and (contra Aquinas) incorporeal entities, and upon the Galenic and subsequently medieval notions of the vital, vegetable, and animal spirits that can be refined, like sugar, into the pure spirit. The spirit's health is the goal of all the various interlocking therapies, since the body will be well, that is, perfectly tempered, if the *spiritus* is well.

Ficino sees this spirit both as an image of the soul (like the meteor's tail) and as an envelope, vehicle, or aethereal body linking soul to body, the intellectual to the corporeal: it functions as the soul's chariot, first as the body in which we endure the cleansing purgatorial fires, and then as the glorified body of the resurrection and of paradise. Ficino believed that Zoroaster had been referring to this spirit or pneuma in such Chaldaean oracles as no.

104, which exhorts us not to add depth (that is, three-dimensional corporeality) to what is plane (that is, to the planar two-dimensional spirit); and no. 158, which asserts that even the pneuma (*idolum*) will be with us 'in the region of utmost clarity'.

Governing the amulets, talismans, salves and drugs, and the aethereal spirit alike are the astrological powers and influences, ever-changing in their dance; and governing these in turn are the musical consonancies and harmonies that rule the universe. Plato had described these in the *Timaeus*, in the famous passage on the two quaternaries of 1-2-4-8 and 1-3-9-27 (traditionally seen as a Greek *lambda*) used by his demiurge to create the mathematical-musical structure of the World-Soul. This Soul itself, in Ficino's speculative view, animated a World-Spirit that mediated between it and the World-Body; and to this Spirit our own spirit was originally attuned, and even united. An integral part of the healer's training therefore consisted in learning to understand a complex pneumatology with reference both to the cosmos (the great man, according to the famous Macrobian phrase), and to the human being, the little world. Indeed, rather than being a soul chained to or entombed in a body, according to the hallowed Platonic and Christian images, man is to be identified here with his spirit in this non-Pauline, quasi-medical sense: a spirit imaged as a talismanic inscription, an airy powder, an attar of roses, a musical chord, a diffused light, a planetary ray even, and subject to the influences of salves, songs, spells, incantations, and prayers. Ficino often responds to this world of "spiritual" therapies in fact not as a realm of insidious evil or of base matter but as a bountiful pharmacopoeia of lenitives and cures, a musical, a magical *concordia discors*.

It is this visionary dimension of Ficino's Aesculapian thought, with its many striking parallels to current → new age therapies on the one hand (to whose practitioners, however, his work is largely unknown), and on the other to features of Jungian depth psychology (see the work of James Hillman, Thomas Moore and others) that makes him, arguably more than → Paracelsus or Cardano, the most important speculative medical theorist of the Renaissance. Indeed, his arresting envisioning of the mind-body linkage and of our own demonic condition, and his holistic approach to health and to the importance of our inner sense of well-being and of well-being's power over the external world, make his general orientation, if not many of his specific ideas, enduringly attractive, and some would argue relevant.

5. DEMONOLOGY AND THE OCCULT

Other ancient or medieval texts Ficino studied carefully treat of aspects of arithmosophy and arithmology (Theon of Smyrna), oneirology (Synesius), angelology and demonology (Porphyry, Proclus and Psellus), and the occult (Iamblichus). Iamblichus in particular was an authority Ficino encountered at the onset of his Platonic studies; and among his first attempts at translating philosophical Greek were the four Iamblichean treatises that constitute a kind of Pythagorean handbook, dealing with Pythagoras' life and with various mathematical and numerological issues. The *De Mysteriis* probably served as his basic introduction to occult lore and to the notion of theurgy, of converting oneself and others – even wood, clay and stone statues – into gods.

While he identified the highest order or chorus of demons in ancient theology with the angels of Christianity, he also inherited a hierarchy of lower orders of demons who were principally beneficent spirits caring for the earth. Said by Hesiod to be thirty thousand in number, or divided into as many legions as there are stars in the night sky, with as many individual demons again in each legion, they were ruled by twelve princes in the twelve zodiacal signs. By virtue of their intermediate nature between the gods and men, they dwelt in the intermediate zone of the air, particularly of the upper or fiery region of air often identified with the aether; and their mandate embraced the airy realm of sleep and the production of omens, oracles and portentous dreams. Essentially airy beings, though they could be found throughout elemental creation, the demons were called by the ancients the *rectores* (helmsmen) and *exploratores* (spies or examiners) of men. They were apportioned and linked to the seven Ptolemaic planets, and assigned the guardianship and ministration of lunar, venerean, mercurial, solar, martian, jovian and saturnian entities (collective or individual) such as kingdoms, institutions, homes, places, people, animals, plants, and stones. The Jews, for instance, along with melancholics, were supposedly saturnian; all scribes, keen-scented dogs, and the city of Hermopolis, mercurial; Socrates, lions, and cockerels, solar; and so on. Their airy nature meant they were particularly sensitive to aromas, mists, fumes, and smokes. Thus the fumigation instructions accompanying many of the *Orphic Hymns*, quite apart from other invocatory dimensions, would make the chanting of such hymns attractive to the class of demons attending the deity who was the subject of the hymn, since they could materialize, if only momentarily, in the wafts of burning aromatics

ascending from the thuribels, hearths, altars, or lamps used for igniting fumigants. A solar demon for instance would be drawn to the eighth *Hymn to Helios*, which was sung to the smoke of incense and manna, a jovian demon to the nineteenth *Hymn to Zeus the Thunderer* sung to the smoke of styrax (while some of the hymns have identical fumigant instructions, the majority prescribe "aromatics" generally, and some lack any instructions at all).

However, as creatures essentially of light, the beneficent demons were most drawn to, and acted as mediums of, light: light scintillating from the faceting of gems and crystals, reflecting from pools and mirrors (natural or man made), refracting through lenses, beaming from lamps and lanterns, haloing clouds, and in shimmering mirages. Indeed the entire realm of optics was theirs, and necessarily so, given that Ficino thought of light as in some ways the spirit, or as linked to the spirit, of the natural world, its source being in the sun but its essence radiating through the length and breadth of the cosmos as life itself, as visible animation. In the *Platonic Theology* 8.13, citing the followers of both Orpheus and Heraclitus, Ficino actually calls light 'visible soul' and soul 'invisible light'. Hence the importance for him of Zoroastrian and Hermetic light worship or of light in worship, and the haunting significances of the reference to God in St. James' Epistle 1:17 as 'the father of lights' and of the noonday setting with the stridulating cicadas of Plato's *Phaedrus*. These harmonizing insects Ficino identified with demons, in the particular sense of men who had entered, after philosophizing for the requisite three millennia, a quasi immaterial, light-filled, demonic condition, being ruled entirely by their intelligences and about to repossess their glorified spirit-star bodies as their envelopes or vehicles. All light demons, whether erstwhile philosophers or planetary spirits, were benevolent, intellectual, even musical presences, higher pneuma-borne souls whom we will ultimately accompany in the universal cavalcade Jupiter leads across the intellectual heaven, thence to gaze from afar at the intelligible beings, the Ideas in their collectivity as both the unfolding or radiance of Beauty, and the enfolding or incandescence of Truth.

This demonological world is not confined, furthermore, to aromatic, musical or intellectual invocation in hymns or prayers at such threshold times as dawn, noonday, and dusk. For Ficino was also fascinated by ancient *idolum* theory. On the one hand, there was the materialist view, articulated most memorably by Lucretius, that effluvia or material images, idola, emanated from all objects, and were seen most obviously in mirrors (hence the Aristotelian story that mirrors bled in the presence of menstruating women). On the other hand, there were enigmatic references in Plotinus, Proclus, the *Orphica*, and the *Chaldaean Oracles*, to the idolum as the densest and most visible form of the spiritual body, to its being in some respects the shadow or other residual self. Plotinus' references to Homer's account of the shade, the idolum, of Hercules in the *Enneads* 1.1.12 and 4.3.27 were especially notable since they pointed to the readers' own demonic duality, their condition not so much as souls tied to bodies, but as higher souls tied to lower secondary souls, that is to say, to images or reflections of themselves. Life was seen now as the Platonic mirror, however distorting, to which Socrates alludes in the *Republic* 596DE when he speaks of the sophistical or "easy way" in which the created world might be reproduced catoptrically: 'You could do it most quickly if you should choose to take a mirror and carry it about everywhere. You will speedily produce the sun and all the things in the sky, the earth and yourself and the other animals'. Following Plotinus, Ficino interpreted this as an enigmatic reference to the World Body as it reflects the idolum of the World Soul, an idolum that is in turn identified with the twice-born Dionysus, lord of ecstasy and dance. Optics, accordingly, and its accompanying plane geometry, and especially (given the section in the *Timaeus*) the geometry of right triangles and the Pythagorean theorem that determines the squares and square-roots, the "powers" of their sides, became the key to understanding the nature of our reflected, catoptric demi-lives as Dionysian images tied to images, to idola and effluvia. It also became the key to understanding the demons and, by implication, our own ascending, philosophical, Apollonian selves, as beings who can pass like Alice through the terpsichorean illusions of the mirror plane into the world of intellectual, uranian light.

In such an ascent, man will again become the Hermetic and Orphic "spark", the "colleague" of a star that we once were, before our precipitation from Cancer, the Moon's constellation and "the gate of mortals", down through the nest of planetary spheres. As man ascends again towards Capricorn, Saturn's constellation and "the gate of the gods", he assumes the demonic, stellar, luminous body that is eternally his, and that Zoroaster had assumed when he devised an astral alphabet. For man, Ficino writes in a generic letter to the human race, is an earthly star enveloped in a cloud, while a star is a heavenly man (*Opera*, 659).

6. CONCLUSION

Ficino was voyaging through the straits of unorthodoxy out into the open seas of the ancient Gnostic heresies, including Manichaeism, that had been attacked by various Church Fathers, preeminently Augustine, and by Plotinus, Ficino's greatest Platonic authority next to Plato himself. That such esoteric and magical speculations did not get him into trouble is a measure of his personal diplomacy (testifying to his commitment to accommodation) and of the solidity and weight of his other philosophical and theological works. A century later → Giordano Bruno was burned at the stake for notions that were no more revolutionary. Ficino bequeaths us both the venerable Christian emblem of man as *viator* and the pagan emblems of him as a cicada, an Orpheus with his lyre strung to the planetary modes, a Hermetic seal, a Zoroastrian magus, a spark struck from the flint of dionysian matter, a starry charioteer in the *biga* of the soul. For his audacious attempt to reconcile Platonism with Christianity went far beyond Platonism: it became a life-long ecumenical quest to introduce into orthodoxy an encyclopedic range of unorthodox spiritual, magical, and occult beliefs keyed to the theme of the soul's ascent from the cave of illusion. That he had a profound posthumous impact upon western thought and culture for two centuries or more speaks to the European elite's continuing, if clandestine, interest in the exploration of many ideas that Plato himself would not have recognized and that had been censured and even persecuted by the Church. Ficino fervently believed, however, *a bono in bonum omnia diriguntur*. It is this credo, inscribed on the walls of his Platonic "academy" which gives to his labyrinthine pages a remarkable unity and generosity in the service of what was always a fundamentally Plotinian and therefore optimistic search for the "flower" in the mind, the oneness that is for him the object of both intellectual and spiritual ascent.

Opera omnia (Basel 1576; 1959), Paris, 2000 ♦ *De amore*, engl. transl. by Sears R. Jayne as *Marsilio Ficino: Commentary On Plato's Symposium on Love*, Dallas, Texas: Spring Publications, 1985 ♦ *De numero fatali*, ed. and transl. by Michael J.B. Allen, in: *Nuptial Arithmetic: Marsilio Ficino's Commentary on the Fatal Number in Book VIII of Plato's* Republic, Berkeley: University of California Press, 1994, Part Two ♦ *De vita*, ed. and transl. by Carol V. Kaske and John R. Clark as *Marsilio Ficino: Three Books on Life*, Binghamton, NY: Renaissance Society of America, 1989 ♦ *Epistolae I*, Florence: Sebastiano Gentile, Olschki, 1990; *Epistolae I, III, IV, V, VI, VII, VIII*, transl. Members of the Language Department of the School of Economic Science, London, 7 vols. to date, London:

Shepheard-Walwyn, 1975- ♦ *In Ionem*, ed. and transl. by Paola Megna, in *Lo Ione nella Firenze medicea*, Messina: Università degli Studi di Messina, 1999 ♦ *In Philebum*, ed. and transl. by Allen as *Marsilio Ficino: The Philebus Commentary* (1975; 1979); repr. Tempe: Medieval & Renaissance Texts & Studies, 2001 ♦ *In Phaedrum*, ed. and transl. by Allen as *Marsilio Ficino and the Phaedran Charioteer*, Berkeley: University of California Press, 1981 ♦ *In Sophistam*, ed. and transl. Allen in *Icastes: Marsilio Ficino's Interpretation of Plato's Sophist*, Berkeley: University of California Press, 1989, Part Two ♦ *Platonis Opera Omnia*, Florence, 1484; 2nd ed. Venice, 1491 ♦ *Plotini Enneades*, Florence, 1492 ♦ *Theologia Platonica*, ed. and transl. by Allen & James Hankins as *Marsilio Ficino: Platonic Theology* (The I Tatti Renaissance Library), Cambridge, Mass.: Harvard University Press, 2001-.

Lit.: Tamara Albertini, *Marsilio Ficino: Das Problem der Vermittlung von Denken und Welt in einer Metaphysik der Einfachheit*, Munich: Wilhelm Fink Verlag, 1997 ♦ Michael J.B. Allen, *The Platonism of Marsilio Ficino*, Berkeley: University of California Press, 1984 ♦ idem, *Plato's Third Eye: Studies in Marsilio Ficino's Metaphysics and Its Sources*, Aldershot: Variorum, 1995 ♦ idem, *Synoptic Art: Marsilio Ficino on the History of Platonic Interpretation*, Florence: Olschki, 1998 ♦ idem, "Marsilio Ficino, Demonic Mathematics and the Hypotenuse of the Spirit", in: Anthony Grafton & Nancy Siraisi (eds.), *Natural Particulars: Nature and the Disciplines in Renaissance Europe*, Boston: MIT Press, 1999, 121-137 ♦ Allen & Valery Rees, with Martin Davies (eds.), *Marsilio Ficino: His Theology, his Philosophy, his Legacy*, Leiden: E.J. Brill, 2002 ♦ Alessandra Tarabochia Canavero, "Tra ermetismo e neoplatonismo: l'immagine della Natura Maga in Marsilio Ficino", in: Linos G. Benakis (ed.), *Néoplatonisme et philosophie médiévale* (Actes du Colloque international de Corfou, 6-8 octobre 1995), Turnhout: Brepols, 1997, 273-290 ♦ André Chastel, *Marsile Ficin et l'art*, Geneva & Lille, 1954; repr. Geneva: Droz, 1996 ♦ Brian P. Copenhaver, "Hermes Trismegistus, Proclus, and the Question of a Philosophy of Magic in the Renaissance", in: Ingrid Merkel & Allen G. Debus (eds.), *Hermeticism and the Renaissance: Intellectual History and the Occult in Early Modern Europe*, Washington: Folger Shakespeare Library, 1988, 79-110 ♦ idem, "Hermes Theologus: The Sienese Mercury and Ficino's Hermetic Demons", in: J.W. O'Malley, T. M. Izbicki & G. Christianson (eds.), *Humanity and Divinity in Renaissance and Reformation: Essays in Honor of Charles Trinkaus*, Leiden: E.J. Brill, 1993, 149-182 ♦ idem, "Iamblichus, Synesius and the *Chaldaean Oracles* in Marsilio Ficino's *De Vita Libri Tres*: Hermetic Magic or Neoplatonic Magic", in: James Hankins, John Monfasani & Frederick Purnell (eds.), *Supplementum Festivum*: *Studies in Honor of Paul Oskar Kristeller*, Binghamton N.Y.: MRTS, 1987, 441-455 ♦ idem, "Lorenzo de' Medici, Marsilio Ficino and the Domesticated Hermes", Gian Carlo Garfagnini, *Lorenzo il Magnifico e il suo mondo: Convegno internazionale di studi, Firenze*

9-13 giugno 1992, Florence: Olschki, 1994, 225-257 ♦ idem, "Renaissance Magic and Neoplatonic Philosophy: *Ennead* 4.3-5 in: Ficino's *De Vita Coelitus Comparanda*", in Garfagnini (ed.), *Ficino e il ritorno di Platone* (see below), 351-369 ♦ idem, "Scholastic Philosophy and Renaissance Magic in the *De vita* of Marsilio Ficino", *Renaissance Quarterly* 37 (1984), 523-554 ♦ Arthur Field, *The Origins of the Platonic Academy of Florence*, Princeton: Princeton University Press, 1988 ♦ Gian Carlo Garfagnini (ed.), *Marsilio Ficino e il Ritorno di Platone: Studi e documenti*, 2 vols., Florence: Olschki, 1976 ♦ Eugenio Garin, "Immagini e simboli in: Marsilio Ficino", in: *Medioevo e Rinascimento: studi e ricerche*, Bari: Laterza, 1954, 2nd ed. 1961, 288-310 ♦ Sebastiano Gentile, Sandra Niccoli & Paolo Viti (eds.), *Marsilio Ficino e il Ritorno di Platone: Manoscritti, stampe e documenti*, Florence: Casa Editrice Le Lettere, 1984 ♦ James Hankins, *Plato in the Italian Renaissance*, 2 vols. Leiden: E.J. Brill, 1990 ♦ idem, *Humanism and Platonism in the Italian Renaissance*, 2 vols. Rome: Edizioni di Storia e Letteratura, 2003-2004 ♦ Teodoro Katinis, "Bibliografia ficiniana: Studi ed edizioni delle opere di Marsilio Ficino dal 1986", *Accademia* 2 (2000), 101-136 ♦ Robert Klein, "L'enfer de Ficin", in: E. Castelli (ed.), *Umanesimo e esoterismo: Atti del V convegno internazionale di studi umanistici*, Padua: Milan, 1960, 47-84 ♦ Sergius Kodera, "Narcissus, Divine Gazes and Bloody Mirrors: the Concept of Matter in Ficino", in: Allen & Rees (eds.), *Marsilio Ficino*, 285-306 ♦ Paul Oskar Kristeller, *Marsilio Ficino and His Work after Five Hundred Years*, Florence: Olschki, 1987 ♦ idem, *The Philosophy of Marsilio Ficino* (1943), Gloucester, Mass.: Peter Lang, 1964 ♦ idem, *Renaissance Thought and Its Sources*, New York: Columbia University Press, 1979 ♦ idem, *Studies in Renaissance Thought and Letters* I/III, Rome: Edizioni di Storia e Letteratura, 1956, 1993 ♦ Raymond Marcel, *Marsile Ficin (1433-1499)*, Paris: Les Belles Lettres, 1958 ♦ Gary Tomlinson, *Music in Renaissance Magic: Towards a Historiography of Others*, Chicago: University of Chicago Press, 1993 ♦ Stéphane Toussaint, "Ficino, Archimedes and the Celestial Arts", in: Allen & Rees (eds.), *Marsilio Ficino*, 307-326 ♦ Charles Trinkaus, *In Our Image and Likeness: Humanity and Divinity in Italian Humanist Thought*, 2 vols. Chicago: University of Chicago Press, 1970 ♦ Cesare Vasoli, *Quasi sit deus: studi su Marsilio Ficino*, Conte: Lecce 1999 ♦ D.P. Walker, *Spiritual and Demonic Magic: from Ficino to Campanella*, London: The Warburg Institute, 1958; repr. Notre Dame, Indiana, 1975, chapter 1 ♦ Edgar Wind, *Pagan Mysteries in the Renaissance*, rev. ed. New York: Norton, 1968.

MICHAEL J.B. ALLEN

Fictuld, Hermann, * 14.11.1700 (?) place unknown, † 1777(?) place unknown

Hermann Fictuld is the pen name used by an individual whose identity is disputed. In 1879 the historian of → Freemasonry Nettelbladt (Nettel-bladt, 766, n. 625) quoted a manuscript he had found (he did not say where), written by the freemason Baron Ernst Werner von Raven and partly devoted to the latter's relationship with Fictuld in the years 1768-1769. 'According to this manuscript', writes Nettelbladt, Fictuld's 'real name was Johann Heinrich Schmidt von Sonnenberg. Born on 7. March 1700. As early as 1716 he became the helpmate [Gehülfe] of a military surgeon in Temesvar (Hungria) and was instructed by him in → alchemy. Later, he became acquainted with Baron Prugg von Pruggenstein from Innsbruck, who gave him further teachings in this matter'. The end of Fictuld's preface to his *Cabala mystica naturae* disconfirms the date of birth given in Nettelbladt's manuscript, because Fictuld writes he finished that book 'on my birthday, 14. November 1739'. In this same manuscript, Raven also wrote that Fictuld had instructed the persons (among whom was Raven himself) desirous to send him letters to address them to 'Baron von Minsthoff, Langenthal, Switzerland'. Moreover, the anonymous author of *Sehr rare . . . Kunststücke* (Part III, Zittau/Leipzig, ed. of 1763, Preface) claimed that Fictuld's name was actually Hans Schmidt, that he was a physician from 'Huttwill' in the Canton of Bern, and that he recently made a lot of money at the Court of a Prince thanks to his teachings bearing on the Philosopher's Stone. Indeed, the idea that he was Swiss appears in another anonymous author who mentions the works of 'the still living Adept Hermann Fictuld in Switzerland' (*Kurtze Nachricht vom Auro Potabili*, Leipzig, 1767, 18).

The name "Minsthoff" (or very similar ones) mentioned by Raven is to be found in four other documents: 1) Duveen claims that on the last page of Fictuld's *Azoth et Ignis* (1749) he had seen 'printed 8 lines in cryptography', which revealed that Fictuld's real name was 'Johann Ferdinand von Meinstoff' or 'Meinstorff' (Duveen 214, 215; but Duveen's interpretation has not been checked as yet). 2) J.F. von Frydau wrote in his *Sendschreiben an einen . . . Prinz . . . in welchem von dem . . . Stein der Weisen gehandelt wird* (Quedlinburg/Leipzig, 1762) that Fictuld's *Probierstein* (1740) was written by 'H. Fictuld und Baron Meinstoof'. This ambiguous note might indicate that these were two different persons. 3) In a letter from → Friedrich Christoph Oetinger to L.F. Castell-Rehweiler (13. May 1763, in *Oetingers Leben und Briefe*), Oetinger mentions a 'Baron von Maienstof' who – the formulation is not clear – might be either Fictuld himself or someone close to the latter.

4) In 1779 the anonymous editor of the *Hermetisches ABC* (1779, III, 5, 251) claims to count Fictuld among the 'late wonderful and true wise men whom [he] liked very much' and says that his name was 'Meinstof' (spelt 'Weinstoof' in III, 251, which is possibly the source of the spelling used by Ferguson, see below) and that he came from Langenthal (hence, he adds, Fictuld was sometimes called Mummenthaler as a joke). Ferguson identified Fictuld as 'Weinstof' and wrote that he died in 1777 at the age of seventy-eight (Ferguson, I, 273). It would be interesting to know where Ferguson found this information concerning the date of Fictuld's death. Following Duveen, Breymayer and Häussermann (609) identify Fictuld as "Johann Ferdinand von Meinstorff". All these statements might contain some kernel of truth, and research into the German nobility archives may prove fruitful. In 1788 Johann Salomon Semler was of the opinion that the pen name was to be read 'HerMann F I C t V L D', as a chronogram for 1656, but Semler did not deduce anything further from this interpretation (Ferguson, I, 272 f).

Fictuld early developed a strong interest in → Rosicrucianism, and for years he toyed with the idea of giving birth to a new Rosicrucian society. In *Aureum Vellus* (written in 1747, published in 1749) he mentions the Rosicrucians with great praise, although at that time he had in mind mostly the Order of the Golden Fleece founded by Philip III the Good (in the same book, Fictuld goes as far as tracing the origins of Rosicrucianism not to Christian Rosenkreuz, but to Philip III). A manuscript dated as early as 1761 that is preserved in the Hungarian Archives of the Festetics family and considered by the historian of Freemasonry Abafi (*alias* Ludwig Aigner) to be the most important source of information for the first period of the "Gold- und Rosenkreuz", contains the rituals and statutes of a Society of the "Rosae Crucis". The account given in this document of the Order's founding is taken almost word for word from Fictuld's *Aureum Vellus* (Abafi, 81-85).

Besides, in the manuscript quoted above, Raven wrote that he received from Fictuld many letters (ca. 1767-1768) describing certain alchemical procedures. Raven was expected to compensate Fictuld financially for this information. In 1769 a certain "Br. O" replaced Fictuld as Raven's instructor. Raven describes how he quarrelled with this Brother, who in 1770 threatened to expel him from an 'association', which he occasionally refered to in his letters as 'the Society of the Ros[y] C[ross]'. Therefore, Raven's text provides evidence of the early existence in 1770 of a Rosicrucian society. The latter was probably the first version of the fringe-masonic Order of the "Gold- und Rosenkreuz" (The Gold and Rosy Cross, "officially" born in 1777). Furthermore, Raven reveals that in the late 1760s Fictuld had become an authoritative member of the aforementioned "Society of the Ros[y] C[ross]" in which he had formerly been a rather isolated 'instructor'. Be that as it may, it is strongly documented that later on, in the late 1770s and in the 1780s, Fictuld's books had become part and parcel of the bibliography strongly recommended by the Superiors of the Order of the Gold- und Rosenkreuz.

In addition to Raven, Fictuld exchanged letters with Friedrich Christoph Oetinger, and in his *Probierstein* (Touchstone) he devoted an entry to him that spread Oetingers's reputation as far as England (a fact noted with satisfaction by Oetinger). Fictuld even sent to him one of his works before publication, asking him for his advice. But Oetinger had some misgivings. He found Fictuld 'too little exercised in the spelling of [the letters of] the Holy Spirit, and too much attracted into the x and y of Nature' (*Oetingers Leben und Briefe*, letters to L.F. Castell-Rehweiler, 1763-1764).

Judging from the dates given in the prefaces to his works (written in German exclusively), Fictuld wrote from 1731 to ca. 1760. The first books deal not only with alchemy, but with → magic and Kabbalah [→ Jewish Influences] as well. As a matter of fact, all his publications correspond to the way he presented himself as early as 1750, namely as a 'Liebhaber der Theosophischen und Hermetischen Philosophischen Geheimnisse' (an amateur in the mysteries of theosophy, hermeticism and philosophy', see preface to his *Abhandlung von der Alchymie*, 1754). His writings fall into four main categories, which occasionally overlap in one and the same book. 1) Alchemy proper. He never tires of defending the alchemical worldview against its opponents and is lavish in descriptions of the procedures designed to prepare the Philosopher's Stone. Like many authors writing about this subject, he exhibits a wide knowledge of alchemical literature. His writings thereon often present themselves as conversations between "philosophers", a *topos* directly inspired by the classic alchemical work *Turba Philosophorum* (so much so that he gave this very title to one of his books). 2) Bio-bibliographical descriptions of authors who wrote on alchemy and/or philosophy of Nature. This second category is represented by the several editions of his book *Probierstein*, which claims to be (as the title indicates) a 'chemical and philosophical touchstone in which are tested the writ-

ings of the true Adepts as well as those of the misleading sophists'. 3) Arithmological and/or neo-kabbalistic speculations (for example, in *Cabbala mystica naturae*). 4) Writings which are mostly theosophical in character and which contain, for example, interpretations of Greek myths (in particular the Golden Fleece) and texts (like the *Emerald Tablet*), speculations on the Bible (preferably on the narratives on the original Falls, or on the Divine Wisdom), and developments of a Paracelsian orientation [→ Paracelsianism].

It is not surprising that *Aureum Vellus* (a big appendix [121-379] to *Azoth et Ignis*), which belongs primarily to the fourth category, was very influential among the "new Rosicrucians" since in it Fictuld discusses the chivalric Order of the Golden Fleece founded by Philip III the Good. This work is probably the only alchemical book entirely devoted to this Greek myth, which like many authors before him he interprets as 'a hermetic [= alchemical] alphabet'. But contrary to the interpretations of most of his predecessors his does not deal with alchemy alone. A theosophical inspiration runs through the whole work, notably in the long appendix which consists of a commentary of the *Emerald Tablet*. Here, and in his *Turba Philosophorum* (1763), Fictuld provides one of the most detailed interpretations of that text ever written.

Fictuld's language is oftentimes bombastic. At its best, it is reminiscent of the rococo style. But the vivid imagination he displays makes his books worthwhile reading. His erudition still provides a valuable resource for historians interested in late 18th century esoteric thought. Moreover, he typifies the kind of theo-alchemy (alchemy blended with theosophy, or the reverse) in Germany current at that time, interwoven with the inspiration of the so-called radical → Pietism. His works do not deserve the oblivion into which they have fallen. They merit a thorough scholarly study.

Wege zum Grossen Universal, oder Stein der Alten Weisen, s. l., 1731 ◆ *Chymische Schrifften, Darinnen in zwölff königlichen Palästen, von dem Stein der Weisen gehandelt wird . . .*, Nurenberg: J.C. Göpner, 1734 ◆ (Preface by Friedrich Roth-Scholtz), *Der längst gewünschte und versprochene Chymisch-Philosophische Probier-Stein, Auf welchem so wohl die Schrifften der wahren Adeptorum als auch der betrügerischen Sophisten seyn probiret worden . . .*, Frankfurt and Leipzig: M. Blochberger, 1740; New, enlarged version edited by Gottlieb von Weissenfels: Frankfurt and Leipzig: E. Lugenfeind, 1753 ◆ Third edition: Hilschersche Buchhandlung: Dresden, 1784 ◆ *Hermetischer Triumphbogen, auf zweyen Wunder-Säulen der grossen und kleinen Welt bevestiget . . .* (Consists of three texts which stand on their own: (separate title pages and paginations): a) *Der Allergrössten . . . Göttlichen Weisheit . . .* (a sort of introduction to the following two texts, b and c); b) *Cabbala mystice naturae . . . von dem Ewigen und Einigen Eins als dem Feu-rigen Liebes-Saltze . . .*; c) *Occulta occultissime*). E. Lügenfeind [!]: Petersburg, Copenhagen and Leipzig, 1741 ♦ *Azoth et Ignis, Das ist, das wahre Elementarische Wasser und Feuer Oder Mercurius Philosophorum. . . .* (Contains: *Aureum Vellus oder Goldenes Vliess Was dasselbe sey . . .*, Leipzig: M. Blochberger, 1749) ♦ *Hermetica Victoria, Das ist: Vollkommen Erfochteter Sieg und Triumph Des . . . Herma-phroditi . . .*, Leipzig: M. Blochberger, 1750 (written in 1747) ♦ *Abhandlung von der Alchymie, und deren Gewissheit*, Erlangen: J.C. Tetzschner, 1754 ♦ *Turba Philosophorum, das ist: Gesammlete Sprüche der Weisen zur Erläuterung der hermetischen Schmaragd-Tafel . . .*, s. l., 1763 (written in 1759) ♦ "Fürstliche und Monarchische Rosen von Jericho. Das ist: Moses Testament und Vergabung der Künsten und Wissenschaften . . .", in: *Neue Sammlung von einigen alten und sehr rar gewordenen Philosophisch und Alchymistischen Schriften*, part 3, Frankfurt and Leipzig, 1771. Written in 1760 (see Preface). This is a fake translation (actually, F. ist the author) ♦ Extracts from texts by F. are presented in vols. 3 and 4 of the anthology *Hermetisches A. B. C., deren ächten Weisen alter und neuer Zeiten vom Stein der Weisen* (C.U. Berlin: Ringmacher, 1778-1779; reprint Ansata: CH-Schwarzenburg, 1979).

Lit.: Ludwig Abafi-Aigner, "Die Entstehung der neuen Rosenkreutzer", *Die Bauhütte* 36, n° 11 (18. March 1893), 81-85; new version: "Die neuen Rosenkreuzer", *Latomia: Neue Zeitschrift für Freimaurer* 23 (1900), 69-78 ♦ Denis I. Duveen, *Bibliotheca Alchemica et Chemica*, Utrecht: HES Publishers, 1986, 214-216 ♦ Antoine Faivre, *The Golden Fleece and Alchemy*, Albany: State University of New York Press, 1993, 40-46, 81-85 ♦ John Ferguson, *Bibliotheca Chemica*, London: D. Verschoyle, 1954, vol. 1, 270-273 ♦ Karl R.H. Frick, *Die Erleuchteten: Gnostisch-theosophische und alchemistisch-rosenkreuzerische Geheimgesellschaften bis zum Ende des 18. Jahrhunderts*, Graz: Akademische Druck- und Verlagsanstalt, 1973, 314-317 ♦ *Friedrich Oetingers Leben und Briefe . . .*, Karl C.E. Ehmann (ed.), Stuttgart: J.F. Steinkopf, 1859 (see Oetinger's letters to Ludwig Friedrich Graf von Castell-Rehweiler, 13. May, 12. June and 9. September 1763, plus the letter just dated 1764) ♦ Christopher McIntosh, *The Rose Cross and the Age of Reason: Eighteenth-Century Rosicrucianism in Central Europe and its Relationship to the Enlightenment*, Leiden, New York, Köln: E.J. Brill, 1992, 46-48 ♦ C.C.F.W. Nettelbladt, *Geschichte freimaurerischer Systeme in England, Frankreich und Deutschland*, Berlin: E.S. Mittler, 1879 (reprint M. Sändig oHG: Walluf bei Wiesbaden, 1972), 517-519, 531-534 ♦ Friedrich Christoph Oetinger, *Die Lehrtafel der Prinzessin Antonia*, Theil 2, (Reinhard Breymayer and Friedrich Häussermann, eds.), Berlin/ New York: W. de Gruyter, 1977, 275, 609.

ANTOINE FAIVRE

Firth, Violet Mary → Fortune, Dion

Flamel, Nicolas, *ca. 1330 Pontoise, † 22.3.1418 Paris

Flamel's life, although destined to be legendary, had no outstanding features on the face of it. It was first that of a public writer, then of a comfortable artisan, the proprietor of a studio for the binding of manuscripts, on whom, as his ultimate professional honor, the University bestowed the title of *libraire-juré*, authorized copier of manuscripts. More than this busy career, Flamel's wife seems to have been the origin of his fortune. At her death in 1397, she bequeathed her husband a large sum of money and much revenue from rental properties. Flamel, at his death on 22 March 1417, left an impressive legacy: about 4000 gold crowns mainly intended for charitable works and pious gifts. Flamel's reputation as an alchemist would be born from this wealth, which was difficult to explain, but also from allegorical motifs painted on arcades that had been built at his orders, in 1389 and in 1407, at the cemetery of the Holy Innocents.

As noted by Didier Kahn, the first trace of the myth of Flamel the alchemist goes back to the end of the 15th or the beginning of the 16th century, when a French adaptation of *Flos florum* (a Latin treatise on → alchemy from the 14th century attributed to → Arnau de Vilanova) was published with the simple title: *Le Livre Flamel*. Subsequently, Flamel was incorrectly presented as the author of several other texts – notably the *Sommaire philosophique* (a French poem of the 15th century) and *Désir désiré* (1618, a French version of the *Thesaurus philosophiae* of Efferarius Monachus [14th century]) – and promoted as an authority in the field of hermetic research. The alchemical interpretation of the arches in the cemetery of the Innocents bolstered the idea that Flamel was an adept. Robertus Vallensis, their first exegete, in his *De antiquitate et veritate artis alchemiae* (1561) refers his readers, as regards the matter of pictorial illustration of the "mysteries of chemistry", to 'the enigma of Nicolas Flamel, who depicts two serpents or dragons, one winged, the other wingless, and a winged lion, etc.' and that one can 'see today in Paris at the cemetery of the Holy Innocents'.

It is in the *Livre des figures hiéroglyphiques* (1612) that the detailed story of Flamel as a maker of gold is found for the first time. An unknown publisher, Arnauld de la Chevalerie, published it twice in 1612 in a collection including *Trois traitez de la philosophie naturelle*. The questions of the dating and the real author of the text have not yet been resolved. If it ever really existed, the original Latin from which Arnauld de la Chevalerie claims to have made the translation has disappeared in any case. According to Robert Halleux, there are of this work 'no manuscripts prior to the edition', and it is 'now established that it can be dated to no earlier than the end of the 16th century', because of a citation of Lambsprinck published by Nicolas Barnaud in 1599. Claude Gagnon attributes the paternity of the book to the publisher himself, under whose pseudonym would be hiding, according to him, the writer Béroalde de Verville (1556-1626). The *Livre des figures* forms a triptych with clearly distinct parts. The first of them is equivalent to a sort of narrative preamble in which Flamel reports how a mysterious work fell into his hands, the book of Abraham, and continues to relate his difficulties in piercing its arcana, his initiation by a certain master Canches, and finally his realization of the philosopher's stone. Following this, he decided to have hieroglyphs painted on an arch, which referred to the alchemical art and would be helpful to those who would be able to decipher them. Next, these symbols are explained in two stages. First, in two introductory chapters the author sets forth his two keys of interpretation. One of them is theological; the other, called 'philosophical', is established 'according to the authority of Hermes'. The eight remaining chapters give detailed alchemical commentaries on the different motifs of the arch. The latter is illustrated separately on two full pages. It would seem that the Flamelian explications are made according to the rules of the ancient art of memory [→ Mnemonics] (Greiner 2000). This mnemotechnique result in a presentation of the two spheres of theology and of chemical experiments as closely associated operations belonging to the domains of the spirit and of matter respectively, thus furnishing the reader with a totalizing vision of the making of the philosopher's stone. As such the Book of pseudo-Flamel is primarily a testimony of the rise of Christian alchemy in France at the beginning of the 17th century.

Le Sommaire philosophique, in: *De La Transformation metallique, trois anciens tractez en rithme francoise*, Paris: G. Guillard & A. Warancore, 1561 ♦ P. Arnaud de La Chevalerie (ed.), *Les Figures hiéroglyphiques de Nicolas Flamel ainsi qu'il les a mises en la quatrième arche qu'il a bastie au Cimetière des Innocents à Paris . . . avec l'explication d'icelles par iceluy Flamel*, in: *Trois Traitez de la philosophie naturelle*, Paris: Vve M. Guillemot & S. Thiboust, 1612 ♦ *Thrésor de philosophie ou original du Désir désiré de Nicolas Flamel*, in: [M. Sendigovius], Paris: *Traicté du Soulphre*, 1618 ♦ *Le Grand Esclaircissement de la Pierre Philosophale, pour la transmutation de tous les Metaux*, Paris: L. Vendosmes, 1628 ♦ D. Kahn (ed.), *Nicolas Flamel, écrits alchimiques*, Paris: Les Belles Lettres, 1993.

Lit.: C. Gagnon, *Description du Livre des Figures Hiéroglyphiques attribué a Nicolas Flamel, suivie d'une réimpression de l'édition originale*, Montreal: Éd. de l'Aurore, 1977 ♦ idem, "*Le Livre d'Abraham le Juif* ou l'influence de l'impossible", in: D. Kahn et S. Matton (eds.), *Alchimie, art, histoire et mythes*, Paris/Milan: S.É.H.A./ARCHÈ, 1995, 497-506 ♦ F. Greiner, *Les métamorphoses d'Hermès: Tradition alchimique et esthétique littéraire dans la France de l'âge baroque (1583-1646)*, Paris: Honoré Champion, 2000, 252-266 ♦ R. Halleux, "Le Mythe de Nicolas Flamel ou les mécanismes de la pseudépigraphie alchimique", *Archives Internationales d'histoire des sciences* 33 (1983), 234-255 ♦ D. Kahn, "Flamel, Nicolas", in: C. Priesner & K. Figala (eds.), *Alchemie: Lexicon einer hermetischen Wissenschaft*, Munich: C.H. Beck, 1998, 136-138 ♦ D. Kahn, "Nicolas Flamel alchimiste?" in: *Nicolas Flamel: Ecrits alchimiques*, Paris: Les Belles Lettres, 1993 ♦ J. Rebotier, "La Musique de Flamel", in: Kahn & Matton, o.c., 507-546 ♦ E.F. Villain, *Histoire critique de Nicolas Flamel et de Pernelle sa femme*, Paris: G. Desprez, 1761 ♦ N. Wilkins, *Nicolas Flamel: Des Livres et de l'or*, Paris: Imago, 1993.

FRANK GREINER

Fludd, Robert, * 1574 Milgate House (Kent), † 8.09.1637 London

Fludd was born in his family manor. The fifth son of Sir Thomas Fludd, he would always remain very proud of his noble origins: we can see on the title page of his printed works that he has his university title preceded by Armiger or Esquire. We know little of his childhood. He was probably entrusted to a tutor for his basic studies; later he enrolled in Saint John's College, Oxford. While many students issued from the gentry considered their time at university as no more than a social necessity, Fludd prepared for his examinations in earnest and obtained his M.A. in 1598.

We have some information on his centers of interest during this period: he devoted part of his free time to → music and to what he called *mea astrologia* [→ Astrology]. This in fact allowed him, according to an anecdote included in 1617 in his masterly book *Utriusque Cosmi . . . Historia* (History of the Two Worlds), to unmask a thief. He was thus already known for his competence in the domain of astrology, but such research was considered neither blameworthy, nor, above all, in discord with the dominant religious tendencies at St. John's

College. In fact most of the clergy of the Anglican Church were trained at this university, where serious knowledge of the Scriptures was required of the students. Fludd shows his perfect knowledge of the Bible by the citations that he makes throughout his work. The basis of the philosophy then taught at the university was still Aristotelian. It is difficult to perceive whether the Neoplatonic [→ Neoplatonism] or hermetic [→ Hermetic Literature] currents had penetrated the university world, but what is certain is that Fludd knew the works of Petrus Ramus, a well-known anti-Aristotelian whose books were at St. John's.

After obtaining his M.A., Fludd left for travels on the continent that would last six years. He worked as a tutor in aristocratic families, for example for Charles de Lorraine and his brother, with whom he studied mathematics and various related sciences such as land surveying and establishing fortifications. This knowledge would fill part of the second volume of his *Utriusque Cosmi . . . Historia*, which also includes a treatise on geomancy, composed in Avignon for the Papal Vice-Legate, as well as a study on music.

When he could finally get to Italy, he stayed first in Livorno, and then in Rome. There he met a Swiss named Grutherus, who taught him engineering and the use of Paracelsian remedies [→ Paracelsianism]. One of them was the famous "weapon-salve" (based upon applying salve to the weapon that has caused a wound rather than caring for the wound itself; it was supposed to work on the basis of sympathy): a medication that later caused a controversy between Fludd and William Foster. In 1602, the traveler returned to Italy, and in Padua he met William Harvey, with whom he was to remain in contact and to whose discoveries regarding blood circulation he gave his full attention.

We have little information about his contacts in Germanic territory, but there is no doubt that he passed through the Court of the Elector Palatine at Heidelberg and that of the Landgrave of Hesse-Kassel. Fludd certainly turned this long stay abroad to advantage, by improving his knowledge in the areas that seem to have interested him from the period of his studies at St. John's College; and he found his medical vocation confirmed in an atmosphere where the theories of → Paracelsus were particularly in vogue.

Upon his return to England in 1605, Fludd enrolled at Christ Church College, Oxford, but it would seem that he encountered difficulties in conducting his medical studies. In fact, he was admitted to the London College of Physicians only in 1609. He was mainly criticized for his insolent attitude, that offended all the members of the Jury. The inflated idea that he had of his origins, combined with hypersensitivity, explains moreover the violence of his later reactions to any criticism of his theories, whether from Libavius, Mersenne, Gassendi, Kepler, William Foster or any other of his many critics. A few years later, however, Fludd was completely accepted in the college, and he was elected Censor in 1618 and 1627, and again in 1633 and 1634.

The exercise of Paracelsian medicine required Fludd to have an apothecary at his service, to manage his personal laboratory, where he prepared drugs for his patients and engaged in many alchemical experiments. He had a wide clientele. We know little about his method of therapy, except that he began by establishing his patient's horoscope, and that as a good disciple of Paracelsus he employed certain plants and chemical preparations. To this he added taking the pulse and examining the patient's urine: classical elements of diagnosis that he sets forth in his *Medicina Catholica* (I, b and II, b). His bedside manner was particularly appreciated: he attached much importance to the spoken word and to prayer.

Apart from these consultations, Doctor Fludd devoted his time to assembling all the writings that he had already partly composed at Oxford and during his travels, and that would eventually be assimilated into his voluminous work *Utriusque Cosmi . . . Historia*. The publication in 1617 of the first volume, about the macrocosm, did not fail to make quite some waves. Fludd had dedicated it to King James I, whom he qualified as Ter Maximus; but certain courtiers – Francis Bacon may have been one of them – called the monarch's attention to the often enigmatic illustrations contained in the work, and their occasionally obscure commentaries. As a result, James I, who was more or less obsessed with → witchcraft, asked the author to come and explain the meaning of his book. But if Fludd's theories certainly aroused *calomniators* (he himself uses this term), he also had many supporters and friends, in the country and on the continent, and the interview with James I went very well. The king's support for him was henceforth assured; and he even obtained a patent for his steel-making process and later the revenue from a property in Suffolk; these benefits were continued by the next monarch, Charles I.

Fludd's position was nevertheless made delicate due to his publication in 1616 of a work supporting the cause of → Rosicrucianism, entitled *Apologia compendaria, Fraternitatem de Rosea Cruce suspicionis et infamiae maculis aspersam, veritas*

quasi Fluctibus abluens et abstergens (Summary
Apology for the Rosicrucian Brotherhood, sullied
with stains of suspicion and infamy, but cleansed
with the Waters of truth). These "stains" came
from the work of a German Lutheran alchemist,
Andreas Libavius, who had attacked the *Fama*
(1614), the *Confessio* (1615) and the *Chymische
Hochzeit Christiani Rosencreutz* (1616). Libavius
accused their authors of heresy, attempted sedition,
and diabolical → magic. Fludd reacted violently;
according to him, the Brothers had no political
ambition but merely affirmed their attachment to
Christ and to a renovated religion. As for the marvelous things they promised, these could be obtained by means of natural magic, kabbalah [→
Jewish Influences] and astrology, all of them "arts"
that our doctor knew well and that he claimed were
in no way diabolical. In fact, Fludd himself did not
hesitate to apply as a candidate for joining the
Brotherhood. He thought that he could permit
himself to do so because he despised carnal and
worldly pleasures, wished to improve education,
and was motivated solely by thirst for wisdom.

As he had promised in the *Apologia*, he developed his arguments the following year, in 1617, in
a much longer work, the *Tractatus apologeticus
integritatem Societatis de Rosea Cruce defendens*
(Apologetic tract to defend the integrity of the
Rosicrucian Society). Several works that have long
been available only in manuscript, but have
recently been published – the *Declaratio brevis*
dedicated to James I (written probably as early as
1618) and *A Philosophicall Key* (written somewhat later) – show that when Fludd first heard of
the Rosicrucian manifestoes, he had already composed a large part of his *Utriusque Cosmi . . . Historia*; therefore if he broadly shared the ideas of the
Rosicrucians, he had nevertheless borrowed nothing from them for his work, and had never met any
member whatsoever of the Brotherhood.

Many critics have pointed out the complex nature of Fludd's thought, or at least its difficulty. But
fortunately he had a talent for illustrating his sometimes long and confusing discussions with engravings and diagrams, which were ironically referred
to as "hieroglyphs" by Kepler, but which have
certainly been responsible for the fact that his
name has survived in history. Because of their great
number and their quality, they first captured the
attention of bibliophiles, some of whom then
began to study the doctrine they were supposed to
illustrate.

The influence on Fludd of the Florentine Academy, especially → Marsilio Ficino and → Giovanni
Pico della Mirandola, is of the greatest importance;

this, together with many borrowings from the
Bible, is the foundation on which he built his entire
system of thought. Fludd's universe is based upon
the relationships of musical harmony (following
Pythagoras and Plato), with the purity of spirit progressively diminishing as it descends down to the
most material level. The arts, technology, science
and medicine are presented according to a similar
framework. Fludd's philosophy is first and foremost a religious one: it is "Mosaic', as he himself
calls it in his last work, *Philosophia Moysaica*, and
based on biblical interpretation. Fludd takes the
time to be explicit in this regard: if he might sometimes seem to deviate from the thinking of certain
Church Fathers, this is because Scripture often has
a double meaning, but he considers his works to be
always in line with orthodoxy. If, moreover, he cites
Plato, this is because he believes that this philosopher had knowledge of the work of → Moses; and
→ Hermes Trismegistus he believes to be in agreement with Moses as well. This was not the opinion
of the monk and mathematician Marin Mersenne,
who saw in Fludd's works a dangerous syncretism
of hermetico-kabbalistic origin that no longer had
anything in common with authentic Christianity. A
brutal controversy ensued between the two men
and their supporters, which lasted more than ten
years; the title of a short work by Fludd, *Sophiae
cum Moria Certamen* (Combat of Wisdom with
Madness), gives an idea of its violence.

The synthesis finally produced by Fludd contains
some original ideas, such as in particular his invention of a diagram of intersecting pyramids that
represents the descent of spirit (called *pyramis
formalis*) and the ascent of matter. Fludd was particularly proud of it and did not hesitate to include
it among the seven microcosmic arts, along with
prophecy, the art of memory [→ Mnemonics], chiromancy, etc. The figure on page 89 of *Utriusque
Cosmi Historia* (I, a), about the divisions of each of
the worlds, gives a perfect image of his conception
of the cosmos. First there is the *empyrean*, that is
the highest heaven, which is composed of three
parts corresponding to the divisions of the angelic
hierarchy; then follow the seven circles of the planets that move in the *etheric heaven*; and finally the
four parts of the elementary world, which are those
of the four elements, fire, air, water, earth. The
ascending pyramid stops at the edge of the superce-
lestial kingdom of God and the other pyramid
stops just before the circle depicting the earth.
These pyramids intersect the celestial regions at
precisely fixed intervals.

Intervals and proportions play a very great role
in Fluddian thinking, and immediately recall the

idea of the music of the spheres. The English doctor – who had been interested in music since his youth and who knew of Plato's heptachord and the Kabbalistic interpretation of the divine names – presents the world as organized according to the rules of a divine monochord; in fact, he used the term *Monochordum Mundi* as the title of his last reply to Kepler. The latter had accused him of using calculations and curves *hermetico more*, while he himself was studying only the planets, according to a rigorous mathematical method. In fact it was not enough for Fludd to apply his system to the whole macrocosm; he believed that Man's body and all his organs obeyed diapasons corresponding to the three heavens as well (*Utriusque Cosmi Historia* II, a 1, p. 275).

Fludd's God is unique and absolute: many of the figures in his *Utriusque Cosmi Historia* confirm this for us by enthroning the Hebrew tetragrammaton or the equilateral triangle at their summit. But, just as the Kabbalists distinguished a "luminous aleph" from a "tenebrous aleph" in the first letter of the Hebrew alphabet, Fludd sees in God a tenebrous aspect comparable to unorganized chaos, the expression of the divine *noluntas*, and on the other hand, an active state that brings the universe into being; this is the manifestation of the divine *voluntas*, so that this active state is necessarily good. The emblem on the title page of *Philosophia Mosaica* intends to express this duality and clarifies this aspect of his vision: the weatherglass, a sort of thermometer-barometer used to predict the weather, but that the doctor had invented above all for philosophical purposes. According to him, the expansion and the contraction of air which are made visible by the apparatus, are manifestations analogously related to the hot-cold antagonism, which is similar to that of light and shadows, both of which have issued from God. The movements of contraction and expansion immediately recall breathing: for Fludd all life on earth and in the cosmos depends on the divine breath. When God exhales, all the evil principles recede, but when He holds His breath, they can wreak havoc on humanity and the universe. Such is the manifestation of the divine *Voluntas* and *Noluntas*. Given the hierarchical structure of the cosmos as imagined by Fludd, beneficial effects are transmitted by the ministry of the angels who are active throughout the universe, but who can also become passive and "frozen" and thus make it possible for the opposing demons to act. The angels' mission is to govern the winds of the four cardinal points, whose effects are antagonistic. But even more than being the masters of the winds, the angels are in charge of

the stars and the planets, which have an influence on our earthly existence as well. We can understand how important it was for the doctor to set up a patient's horoscope before considering any therapy.

The question of the beginning of this universe also greatly interested Fludd. He claimed that before the Creation there had existed a *materia prima* or *hylè*, described by him as a 'dark cloud as black as pitch'; in response to critics who might see in it an entity coeternal with divinity, he hastens to quote Saint → Augustine, who compared this original state to silence in relation to speech. The first divine manifestation was light, and in this Fludd could claim the support of Moses, Plato and Hermes. The words *fiat lux* brought forth the highest heaven, the empyrean, filled with light that only the intellect can perceive. Then everything unfolded according to the hierarchical order, traversed by the pyramids described above. Noteworthy is the capital role of the primordial waters in the separation of the worlds; they are the vehicles of the creative light that splits the heavens in two, and then imposes order on matter, to constitute the three reigns of our world: animal, vegetable and mineral. This is not, of course, common water, but "alchemical water"; Fludd undoubtely alludes to it in his essay "Of the Excellensy of Wheat", which comprises the greater part of his *A Philosophicall Key* and which also appears in his *Anatomiae Amphitheatrum*.

When the first heaven and the lower heaven had been organized, God created the sun, which he made the seat of the quintessence. He placed it in the center of the intermediary heaven (or etheric) where it participates with both God and the Earth. In a way, it is the visible representation of God. What follows is borrowed by Fludd not from *Genesis* but from a myth of Orphic origin. In his *Tractatus Theologo-Philosophicus*, as in *A Philosophicall Key*, there appears a sort of demiurge, *Demogorgon*, flanked by *Eternity* (or Nature) and by *Chaos* who gave birth to *Litigium* (or Conflict), which is the source of so many evils that it had to be thrown down with *Chaos* into the tenebrous center of the earth. Nature brought another son into the world, Pan, to whom was entrusted the creation of the Microcosm, Man, who was created in perfect correspondence with the Macrocosm. His sensory organs are as many as there are planets; just as God is enthroned in the loftiest heaven, Man's intellect is in his head; in the middle part of his body is placed a little tabernacle, the heart, that provides blood to the members, just as the sun floods the macrocosm with its rays, giving it light, etc. Demogorgon needs only to blow part of his divine fire into him.

Fludd's Creator never abandons his creation. He intervenes ceaselessly, through the intermediary of Nature, which is in musical sympathy with him. Fludd tried to represent Nature in one of the first illustrations in *Utriusque Cosmi Historia* (I, a, pp. 4-5). She is the minister closest to God: connected to him by a chain, to her other hand is attached, also by a chain, a monkey that represents the microcosmic Art. In his later works, Fludd speaks less of Nature and more of the World Soul. He thinks that the kabbalists meant to describe the same principle with their *Metatron* who has dominion over the World, and in whom he sees (in his *Monochordum Mundi*) 'the Soul of the Messiah, or the Virtue of the Tetragrammaton, in which is the light of the Living God, and in which is the light of *Ensoph*, beyond which one cannot go'.

Fludd drew from all the sources available to him – the Bible and the kabbalah, music, astrology, alchemy, as well as technology – to construct his image of the universe. He can be seen as one of the last representatives of the Renaissance homo universalis. If some historians have seen in Fludd no more than an experimenter still too restricted by the bonds of alchemy, others will point out the importance he attached to the experimental foundations of his lengthy philosophical theories. Some of the debates stimulated by his work are still topical today.

Utriusque cosmi Majoris scilicet et Minoris Metaphysica, Physica Atque Technica Historia . . . Tomus Primus De Macrocosmi Historia., Oppenheim: Johann Theodor de Bry, 1617 (I, a) & 1618 (I, b) ♦ *Tomus secundus De . . . microcosmi historia . . .*, Oppenheim: Johann Theodor de Bry, 1619 (II, a, 1), 1620(?) (II, a, 2) & Francofurti, 1621 (II, b) ♦ *Anatomiae Amphitheatrum Effigie Triplici, More et Conditione Varia Designatum* [constitutes a sequel to *Utriusque . . .*], Frankfurt: Johann-Theodor de Bry, 1623 ♦ *Philosophia Sacra et vere Christiana Seu Meterologica Cosmica* [constitutes a sequel to *Utriusque . . .*], Frankfurt: Officina Bryana, 1626 ♦ *Medicina Catholica, seu Mysticum Artis Medicandi sacrarium . . .*, Frankfurt: William Fitzer, 1629 (I, a) & 1631 (I,b, II,a, II,b) ♦ *Philosophia Moysaica*, Gouda: Petrus Rammazenius, 1638 ♦ *Mosaicall Philosophy: Grounded upon the essential Truth or eternal Sapience, Written first in Latin, and afterwards thus rendered into English . . .*, London: Humphrey Moseley, 1659 ♦ "Truth's Golden Harrow" (C.H. Josten, ed.), *Ambix* 3 (1949), 91-150 ♦ "Declaratio Brevis" to James I (William H. Huffman & Robert A. Seelinge, ed. & trans.), *Ambix* 25 (1978), 69-92 ♦ "A Philosophicall Key", in: Allen G. Debus (ed.), *Robert Fludd and his Philosophicall Key*, New York: Science History Publication, 1979.

Lit.: Joscelyn Godwin, *Robert Fludd: Hermetic Philosopher and Surveyor of Two Worlds* (1979), repr. Grand Rapids: Phanes Press, 1991 ♦ William H. Huffman, *Robert Fludd and the End of the Renaissance*, London, New York: Routledge, 1988 ♦ *Robert Fludd: Essential Readings* (William H. Huffman, ed.), London: The Aquarian Press, 1992 ♦ Serge Hutin, *Robert Fludd (1574-1637): Alchimiste et Philosophe Rosicrucien*, Paris: Omnium Littéraire, 1971 ♦ J.B. Craven, *Dr. Robert Fludd (Robertus de Fluctibus): The English Rosicrucian. Life and Writings*, repr. Montana: Kessinger, n.d. ♦ Urszula Szulakowska, "Robert Fludd: The Divine Alchemy of the Eye of God", in: *The Alchemy of Light: Geometry and Optics in Late Renaissance Alchemical Illustration*, Leiden, Boston, Köln: E.J. Brill, 2000, 167-182.

SYLVIE EDIGHOFFER

Foix-Candale (= Foix de Candale), François, * August 1512 Bordeaux, † 5.2.1594 Bordeaux

Foix-Candale belonged to a family of the old Catholic nobility which provided some of the most ardent leaders of resistance to the Huguenots in the Southwest. He succeeded his brother as Bishop of Aire-sur-l'Adour near Bordeaux in 1570. Although that post remained merely formal, he was made Cardinal in 1587. Well versed in geometry, he acquired a reputation as a specialist in instruments of measurement. He used his castle of Puy-Paulin near Bordeaux as a "grand salon littéraire", gathering humanists, mathematicians, etc. Foix-Candale is considered one of the greatest humanists in Bordeaux in the second half of the 16th century, along with people like the historian Jacques Auguste de Thou, the publisher Simon Millanges, Joseph Scaliger and, of course, Michel de Montaigne (who, like Foix-Candale, had been a member of the Parliament of Bordeaux). His cousin Henri de Navarre (the future Henri IV) trusted him enough to send him in 1576 with a diplomatic mission to Elizabeth I of England.

Foix-Candale is an important figure in the history of Neo-Alexandrian → Hermetism, the ensemble of esoterically oriented commentaries (from the end of the 15th through the 20th centuries) of the Greek *Hermetica* in general, and of the *Corpus Hermeticum* (2nd and 3rd centuries) in particular. He first authored an edition (1566) of Euclid's *Elementa*, with commentaries which later inspired → John Dee. In that book, he stressed the necessity of the Pythagorean approach to numbers [→ Number Symbolism] and praised the idea, widespread in his time, that mathematics has a spiritual value. His last work (1584) does not deal with numbers but with the nature of the sacrament of the Eucharist. Even more than his first book, this one is strongly inspired by Hermetism.

In between his book on Euclid and his book on the Eucharist, he published three further texts. As noted by Frances A. Yates, all three mark 'new heights of ecstatic religious Hermetism' (1964, 173). They present themselves as editions, with his own commentaries, of treatises belonging to the *Corpus Hermeticum*. They consist of: (A) a Greek-Latin edition based upon the edition by Turnebus of 1554 (68 pp.), published in 1574; (B) a Greek-French edition of these texts (72 pp.), also in 1574; and (C) a book in French (759 pp. in folio), consisting for the most part of a new edition of them, published in 1579, but now accompanied by long philosophical expositions. His manuscript of this last book had been finished by 1572, but its publication was delayed due to the turmoil caused by the events of St. Bartholomew's Day. It is this last-mentioned book which made him most famous, because it is filled with his expositions of various aspects of Hermetism. It differs from the former two books in that it is much bigger, and Foix-Candale devotes much more space to his personal speculations than to purely philological considerations.

There are some similarities between this book of 1579 and the *Essais* (1580) of Foix-Candale's friend Michel de Montaigne. Both evince an extremely tolerant attitude in religious matters. This is a striking trait in a France then plagued by feuds between Protestant and Catholics, though it was a trait common in people for whom Hermetism was a staple diet. From a literary point of view, Foix-Candale's book consists of a long series of hardly interconnected discourses, written in a fluid style as the inspiration goes, very much like the *Essais*. The titles of most of Montaigne's essays are less an indication of what is to follow than a pretext for a free-wheeling association of ideas. Likewise in Foix-Candale's *Le Pimandre*, extracts from the C.H. serve as titles for expounding ideas which are oftentimes only tenuously related to these extracts or the titles. In this connection, another book, already a "classic" in esoteric literature, → Valentin Tomberg's *Meditationen . . .*, (1st ed. 1972) may also be compared to Foix-Candale's, in that each title of a chapter bears the name of a → Tarot card, though what follows is oftentimes somewhat removed from the symbolism of the card.

Foix-Candale's intellectual make-up was profoundly influenced by his study of Hermetic philosophy. At the beginning of his 1574 edition, in the dedicatory epistle to Emperor Maximilian II, he writes that → Hermes Trismegistus possessed knowledge of the divine equal to the apostles and the evangelists, and the rest of his epistle abounds in similar statements. Later, in his unpublished treatise on the Eucharist, he does not hesitate to rely upon Hermetic authority in defending the Roman Catholic doctrine of transubstantiation. Although he never seems willing to abandon or compromise his commitment to a Catholicism that would stimulate a religious reunion of all Christian confessions, he believes that Hermes Trismegistus was a contemporary of 'Saturn, King of Egypt' who preceded Abraham by several generations, and goes as far as claiming that Hermes' texts (the *Corpus Hermeticum*) are superior in form and understanding to the books of → Moses. He claims that Hermetic philosophy is a means of purification, that prepares one for the unifying experience of contemplating the divine. But in so doing he frequently seems to imply that salvation is made possible less by redemption and forgiveness of sins than by a spiritual "regeneration" – as he calls it – which is achieved through a form of gnosis. In this emphasis of salvation through knowledge ('piété avec cognoissance', 243), he goes even further than predecessors and contemporaries of a hermetic persuasion such as → Lefèvre d'Etaples, Gabriel du Préau, → Symphorien Champier, → Lodovico Lazzarelli or Philippe Duplessis de Mornay.

Foix-Candale does not extend to nature this notion of purification or "regeneration". Nature does not need to be regenerated, and man's "regeneration" does not take place through her. But nature is not lifeless for that: Foix-Candale sees her as a kind of big immortal animal. He holds long discourses on the Soul of the World, which range chronologically between Ficinian Platonism and the speculations of → Ralph Cudworth. He is lavish in his discussions of → astrology. Each star and planet has a power of its own which enables it to exercise a specific influence upon the sublunary world. The earth is replete with spirits or *daïmones* put in charge of carrying out the will of God and immersed within a very subtle matter. He speculates also about the kind of body that the angels may have, about their sex, about divine and human androgyny, etc. He believes in the existence of the elementals (spirits of the four elements) and even narrates how he himself met spirits or goblins somewhere in the mountains of southern France. As a matter of fact, his book contains certain reflections that have a Paracelsian character as he wrote when → Paracelcianism was just beginning to get known in France.

Like many other French Hermetists of the Renaissance (but contrary to most Italian ones), Foix-Candale is wary of the magical aspects of certain passages contained in the Hermetic writings, and above all in the *Asclepius*. Therefore he tends to underplay them or to blame them on the supposed "translator", the evil magus Apuleius. More generally, he is not interested in magical or theurgical practices. But → alchemy is for him a different matter, and his book contains expositions on this subject which should be put into the context of both his cosmological outlooks and the alchemical literature of his time. About his own activities in this domain he always remained very discreet, but he was himself an alchemist, or at least a spagyrist. He had a laboratory where he produced his medicines, including a panacea called "Eau de Candale" which has remained famous in France through the subsequent centuries. His neighbour and friend Michel de Montaigne mentions him in his *Essais* (II, XII) as someone engaged into the quest of the Philosopher's Stone, and the poet Agrippa d'Aubigné describes a tour of his laboratory in the company of himself and of Henri de Navarre. Except in his book of 1579, Foix-Candale did not publish anything on alchemy, but his knowledge was appreciated by specialists like → Clovis Hesteau de Nuysement and other theoreticians or practitioners of the Opus Magnum.

Foix-Candale's *Le Pimandre* of 1579 ranks among the most representative works to have been produced by the Neo-Alexandrian Hermetic current in the second half of the 16th century. More generally, it stands out as one of the most remarkable texts in Western esoteric currents since the early Renaissance, even until the present time. Surprisingly, it has not been newly edited since 1587. A third edition with philological and historical commentaries is badly needed.

Euclidis Megarensis Mathematici Clarissimi elementa . . ., Paris: Jean Le Royer, 1566; rev. ed. Jacques du Puys, 1578 ♦ *Mercurii Trismegisti Pimandras utraque linguae restitutus, D. Francisci Flussatis Candallae industria*, Bordeaux: S. Millanges, 1574 ♦ (reprinted in Paris in 1630) ♦ *Le Pimandre de Mercure Trismégiste Novellement Traduict De l'Exemplaire Grec Restitué en Langue Françoyse par François Monsieur de Foys de la famille de Candalle. A la Royne du Roy treschrestien Henry troisiesme*, Bordeaux: S. Millanges, 1574 ♦ *Le Pimandre de Mercure Trismégiste de la philosophie chrestienne, cognoissance du Verbe divin, et de l'excellence des œuvres de Dieu, traduict de l'exmplaire grec, avec la collation de . . . commentaires, par François Monsieur de Foix*, Bordeaux: S. Millanges, 1579; Paris: New ed. Abel l'Angelier, 1587 ♦ *Traicté du Saint-Sacrement par lequel plusieurs intelligences divines . . . sont esclaircies . . .*, 1584 (Manuscript Bibliothèque Nationale F. Mitterand in Paris: Fonds Français, 1886).

Lit.: Jean Dagens, "Le Commentaire du *Pimandre* de François de Candale", *Mélanges d'histoire littéraire offerts à Daniel Mornet*, Paris: Nizet, 1951 (see 21-26) ♦ idem, *Bérulle et les origines de la restauration catholique (1575-1611)*, Paris, 1952 (see 21-22) ♦ idem, "Hermétisme et cabale en France de Lefèvre d'Etaples à Bossuet", *Revue de Littérature Comparée* 1 (1961), 5-16 (see 6-7) ♦ Jeanne Harrie, *François Foix de Candale and the Hermetic Tradition in Sixteenth Century France*, doctoral diss. 1972, University of California, Riverside. Ann Arbor: University Microfilms International, 1975 ♦ eadem, "Duplessis-Mornay, Foix-Candale and the Hermetic Religion of the World', *Renaisssance Quarterly* 31:2 (1978), 499-514 ♦ Elaine Limbrick, "Hermétisme religieux au XVIè siècle: le *Pimandre* de François Foix de Candale", *Renaisssance and Reformation* 5 (1981), 1-14 ♦ Frances A. Yates, *Giordano Bruno and the Hermetic Tradition*, London: Routlege & Kegan Paul, 1964, 173, 179, 182, 406.

ANTOINE FAIVRE

Formisano, Ciro → Kremmerz, Giuliano

Fortune, Dion (ps. of Violet Mary Firth), * 6.12.1890 Bryn-y-Bia, Llandudno, Wales, † 8.1.1946 London

Occultist [→ occult / occultism] author, founder of the group which eventually became the Society of the Inner Light, originally conceived as an "outer court" of the → Hermetic Order of the Golden Dawn. Fortune was initiated into the Golden Dawn in 1919 (adopting the magical motto Deo non Fortuna, whence her pen name) but was subsequently evicted on account of personal conflicts with Moina Mathers (1865-1928, colleague and by then widow of → S.L. McGregor Mathers). Fortune continued to run the Fraternity of the Inner Light as an independent organization, still based on Golden Dawn principles, until her death (and for some years after it by the popular account). She was an amateur of psychology, a conscious and canny popularizer of occult ideas and methods, and a prolific author, both of textbooks on magic of a "how-to" variety, and of occult novels which depict the construction of magical rituals in such detail that the novels, too, have served as a set of ritual sourcebooks (both for post-Gardnerian Neopagan witchcraft [→ Neopaganism] and for ritual magicians more explicitly indebted to the magical tradition she founded). Her books continue to be popular among Neopagans and occultists and most of them remain in print.

By her own account Fortune came to occultism through the study of psychology. Some of her early experiences are chronicled in *Psychic Self-Defense* (1930), a remarkable book which is part anecdotal evidence, part do-it-yourself exorcism manual, part autobiography, and some part no doubt fiction. In its opening pages, Fortune describes an experience of being the victim of what at the time of writing she construes as a "psychic attack" by her employer, which took place when she was about twenty (or around 1910) and left her in poor health for some years afterwards. The effort to recover from this breakdown led her to take up the study of psychology, and subsequently, 'in order to understand the hidden aspects of the mind', occultism (*Psychic Self-Defense*, 19). In 1922 she published (under the name she reserved for her psychological writings, Violet Firth) a compendium of her lectures on psychology under the title *Machinery of the Mind*: a brief, popularizing digest of psycho-analytic ideas which (though useless as a commentary on Freud and of little interest to the practicing occultist) still gives insight into how easily then fashionable notions of psychology might be melded with the ideas of occultism. In later writings she continues to refer to the study of psychology as the thing which precipitated her into occultism, and it is likely that her ability to draw on the jargon of repressions, complexes, and mental pathologies did much to contribute to the popularity and accessibility of her books, inasmuch as her prose flows back and forth easily between esoteric and mystical language and a more modernizing, secular, and scientific rhetoric which tends to ease the fundamental alterity of the former.

Though the primary source for the shape and style of Fortune's magic was the Golden Dawn, other strands of influence include Christian Science (the religion in which she was raised) and Theosophy. Fortune's theosophical readings appear to have been important to the early development of her occult ideas, though she did not actually join the → Theosophical Society until 1924, acting upon instructions from the inner planes to do so. Soon thereafter she became president of the Christian Mystic Lodge of the Theosophical Society at her base of operations in London, 3 Queensborough Terrace. While she herself perceived a continuity between her activities under the auspices of the Theosophical Society and the Golden Dawn, not everyone felt comfortable with her dynamic personality and confident leadership. In 1927, having quarrelled with some of its other members

(whom she accused of corruption in the *Transactions* of the Christian Mystic Lodge), she resigned from the Theosophical Society. In the same time period she was evicted from the Golden Dawn due to the exacerbation of her psychic conflicts with Moina Mathers, and shortly thereafter she declared the existence of a new Fraternity of the Inner Light, which continued to operate, with her at its head, in the same location at 3 Queensborough Terrace. The newly declared fraternity initially involved the same core group of people who had previously attended meetings of the Christian Mystic Lodge; indeed throughout Fortune's conflicts with the larger societies there is a continuity to her own group provided not only by its incarnate membership but also by the inner planes masters with whom Fortune had been in contact since 1922 (two years prior to her membership in the Theosophical Society), who evidently commanded the interest and loyalty of those who had been working with her up to this point. Because Fortune's outlook tended to be broadly synthetic in any case, her personal conflicts never caused her to lose her sense of community with people involved in other forms and styles of occultism. Later on Fortune became familiar with → Aleister Crowley's writings, which for the most part she respected; of Crowley's *Magick in Theory and Practice* (1929) she declares that she approves the theory though condemns the practice (more mildly than many after her) as potentially dangerous for the neophyte ('The Occult Field Today', in *Applied Magic*, 60-64).

A colorful influence on her earlier writings is a teacher she does not name in any of her own works, but who is identifiable by external evidence as Theodore Moriarty (1873-1923), a charismatic figure, psychic, medium, Freemason and adept. It is unclear exactly when or where she met Moriarty; some experiences with him are retailed in *Psychic Self-Defense*, others recounted in the series of potboiling short stories ostensibly based on incidents at his "nursing home" for the psychically challenged which were first published in 1922 and collected into a volume as *The Secrets of Dr Taverner* in 1926. She describes the tales as 'studies in supernormal pathology', and comments that 'far from written up for the purposes of fiction, [they] have been toned down to make them fit for print' (*Secrets of Dr Taverner*, vii-viii). Despite the disclaimer, these tales fit into the genre of the horror story (as does also her first novel, *The Demon Lover*, published in 1927) more than that of the case study, though perhaps their chief interest lies in the attempt to couple the two genres.

In 1927 Fortune married Dr. Thomas Penry Evans (1892-1959), and the time period between her marriage and her death in 1946 saw the publication of some of her strongest and most popular writing, including *Sane Occultism* (1929), *Psychic Self Defense* (1930), *The Mystical Qabalah* (1935) and the novels *Winged Bull* (1935), *The Goat Foot God* (1936), and *The Sea Priestess* (1938). Perhaps her best novel, *Moon Magic*, was begun in the last years of her life though not published until 1956. The late novels have a similar pattern: the protagonist (an intelligent male, sexually deprived, and solitary), comes into contact with primordial spiritual forces through psychic experiences brought on by illness or disappointment; he meets a sensual, magically experienced and assertive woman, whom he assists in reconstructing or revitalising a ritual space (disused church or old priory, or, in the case of *The Sea Priestess*, an abandoned fort), after which the male and female protagonists work magical rituals to bring the cosmic forces which they have begun to channel into balance. Besides containing treasure troves of ritual ideas and techniques, these novels are overtly wish fulfillment fantasies, successful magical romances with gothic elements, and they continue to have a readership. Her own marriage, though it seems in some respects to adhere to the basic plot outline discoverable in the novels (she and Evans spent years constructing a ritual space and doing magic together there), may have had less satisfying results from the perspective of wish fulfillment: having fallen in love with a younger woman, Evans petitioned for and was granted a divorce in 1939.

As a writer, Fortune's gifts are generally more practical than philosophical. Above all she was a deft synthesizer of ideas, and her continued influence derives largely from her ability to bring difficult esoteric concepts into a lucid and readily accessible prose.

Dion Fortune (writing as Violet M. Firth), *Machinery of the Mind*, London: Allen & Unwin, 1922 ♦ Dion Fortune, *The Secrets of Dr Taverner* (1926), rpt. Columbus, Ohio: Ariel Press, 1989 ♦ *The Demon Lover* (1927), York Beach, Maine: rpt. Samuel Weiser, 1980 ♦ *Sane Occultism* (1929), rpt. with *Practical Occultism in Daily Life* (1935), London: Aquarian Press, 1987 ♦ *Psychic Self Defense* (1930), York Beach: Maine: rpt. Samuel Weiser, 1993 ♦ *The Mystical Qabalah* (1935), York Beach, Maine: rpt. Samuel Weiser, 1994 ♦ *The Winged Bull* (1935), York Beach, Maine: rpt. Samuel Weiser, 1988 ♦ *The Goat Foot God* (1936), York Beach, Maine: rpt. Samuel Weiser, 1980 ♦ *The Sea Priestess* (1938), York Beach, Maine: rpt. Samuel Weiser, 1978 ♦ *Moon Magic* (1956), York Beach, Maine: rpt. Samuel Weiser, 1978 ♦ *Applied*

Magic (1962), rpt. with *Aspects of Occultism* (1962), London: Aquarian Press, 1987.

Lit.: Janine Chapman, *The Quest for Dion Fortune*, York Beach, Maine: Samuel Weiser, 1993 ♦ Carr Collins & Charles Fielding, *The Story of Dion Fortune*, York Beach, Maine: Samuel Weiser, 1985 ♦ Gareth Knight, *Dion Fortune & the Inner Light*, Loughborough, Leicestershire, UK: Thoth Publications, 2000 ♦ Alan Richardson, *The Magical Life of Dion Fortune, Priestess of the 20th Century*, London: Aquarian Press, 1987.

CLAIRE FANGER

Fraternitas Saturni

The most important magical secret lodge of the 20th century in the German-speaking world. Unlike most secret occult groups, the Fraternitas Saturni has no legendary tradition. A Brotherhood of Saturn is said to have existed in Scandinavia at the turn of the 19th century and there may have been a group with a similar name in Warsaw under the leadership of → Jean-Marie Hoené-Wronski (1776-1853).

The Fraternitas Saturni was founded *de facto* in Berlin on May 8, 1926, by Eugen Grosche (order name Gregor A. Gregorius; 1888-1964) and four fratres, but the official date of foundation is Easter 1928. It derived from the Pansophical Lodge of the Lightseeking Brethren of the Orient-Berlin, also founded by Grosche. Grosche had functioned there, however, only as secretary, at the request of the pansophist Heinrich Tränker (order name Recnartus; 1880-1956). Tränker had been the first person to use the name of Pansophia for a strictly esoteric movement in Germany, and since 1921 he also acted as Grand Master of the O.T.O. (→ Ordo Templi Orientis) in Germany. The Pansophical Lodge was closed in 1926 due to a dispute between Tränker and → Aleister Crowley who, having been invited by Tränker to stay at his house, had come to Germany. Crowley's demand that all German groups under Tränker's aegis should submit to the Crowleyan world lodge A.A. (Argenteum Astrum) met with rejection. The dispute escalated and a majority of Lodge members (not including Tränker) were admitted to the newly-founded Fraternitas Saturni, which assumed the so-called Crowleyan Law of the New Aeon, while modifying it as follows: "Do what thou wilt, *is* (according to Crowley, *shall be*) the whole of the law. Love is the law, love under will, compassionless love". The specific Fraternitas Saturni formula "compassionless love" was added to emphasize the severe,

Saturnian character of the Brotherhood. The Fraternitas Saturni remained in contact with Crowley but was organisationally independent. Further members joined the Fraternitas Saturni in 1928 following the dissolution of the Orden mentalischer Bauherren (established 1922 in Dresden by Wilhelm Quintscher, 1893-1945), which also worked rites involving sex magic. It is not clear whether the National Socialist ban of the Fraternitas Saturni occurred in 1933 or as late as 1936. In 1936 Grosche emigrated to the Tessin, then to North Italy, from where he was expelled in 1943 and forced to return to Germany.

After the war, Grosche endeavoured to reassemble the former members of the Fraternitas Saturni. Initially he was living in the Soviet occupation zone, where he had problems on account of his esoteric interests. In 1950 he moved to West Berlin, where he tried to build up the Fraternitas Saturni as an umbrella organisation for various esoteric groups in the German-speaking world. He also contacted Hermann Joseph Metzger (1918-1990), who had newly-founded the O.T.O. and the Illuminati Order in Switzerland. While the collaboration with the O.T.O. soon lapsed, the Fraternitas Saturni quickly revived. In April 1950, the first issue of the long-standing monthly lodge periodical *Blätter für angewandte okkulte Lebenskunst* was published, which lay out the theoretical and practical basis of Fraternitas Saturni doctrine (typewritten carbon copies of important essays were already being sent to members in 1948-1950). On 18.3.1957, the anniversary of the death of the last Grand Master of the Knights Templar, the Fraternitas Saturni announced itself as the Grand Lodge of the Fraternitas Saturni at Berlin and officially registered itself as such. It supported outer courts (*Vorhöfe*) in several German cities. Grosche was nominated Grand Master. His death in 1964 unleashed a violent power struggle. Following the death of his successor Margarete Berndt (order name Roxane; 1920-1965), a triumvirate took over at Easter 1966. Thereupon Guido Wolther (born 1922, order name Daniel) became Grand Master. In order to attain a higher level of magical work, Wolther founded a new secret league within the Fraternitas Saturni, known as AMOS (Ancient and Mysterious Order of the Brotherhood of Saturn) and limited it to nine members. A strict "new training programme" followed, involving only "knowledge grades", which had to be really achieved rather than merely conferred as an honour. A new order periodical *Vita Gnosis* was founded and distributed only to members of those specific working grades. Because of this Wolther

fell out of favour and in 1969 Walter Jantschik (order name Jananda; born 1939) was elected Grand Master. But since he held only a lower degree (8°), further dissent followed. Shortly after this election, the internal order literature was made public. Dr Adolf Hemberger (1929-1991), Professor of Methodology and Scientific Theory at the University of Gießen, holder of an economics diploma and member of several occult groups, self-published essential parts of the secret records of the Fraternitas Saturni, thus unleashing a storm of protest. Jantschik meanwhile planned an "esoteric university" with higher degrees. But in 1969 a member who had only joined that same year was elected Grand Master, and henceforth the fraternity increasingly concerned itself with a general philosophy of life rather than with practical magic. From this time on, the history of the Fraternitas Saturni becomes tortuous. Splits, new foundations, dissolution and reunions follow in swift succession. Despite this decline, the lodge has survived (albeit possibly with interruptions) up to the present. Apart from various schismatic groups which formed and mostly disappeared over the years (Fraternitas Luminis, Fraternitas Uranis, Ordo Saturni, and an independent Frankfurt group *c.* 1962-63, already active when Grosche was still alive) the (original?) Fraternitas Saturni is once again magically active.

According to its own account the Fraternitas Saturni is a 'just, enlightened, perfect, secret, magical and ritual' lodge. "Just" (*gerecht*) means that the novice is expected to work on himself, in order to become a "square" (*winkelgerecht*; i.e. perfectly fitting like a brick in a building) member of human society and the Lodge. The Fraternitas Saturni is "enlightened" because its super-rational knowledge is mediated through the direct experience of magical rituals and not through logic. The Fraternitas Saturni is "secret" because public names and offices have no value inside the lodge. It is characterised as a Brotherhood because the members' bonds within it are supposed to continue beyond death. The Fraternitas Saturni accepts women and men on an equal basis. Woman however is regarded as the 'bleeding wound of the cosmos', and her "Moon powers" are the negative manifestation of Saturn. Man's task is to overcome these demonic energies.

The organisational structure of the Fraternitas Saturni shows a thirty-three degree system, resembling the Ancient and Accepted Scottish Rite and the Droit Humain, which carries Latin designations. After the Pronaos from the 1° to the 3° come intermediate grades, which lead to a Rosicrucian

Chapter from the 12° onwards. From the 21° onwards we have the High Degrees and finally the Highest Chapter from the 30° to the 33°. The Lodge Daimonium holding the 33° (the Gradus Ordinis Templi Orientis Saturni, abbreviated to GOTOS), functions as the spiritual head of the Lodge. The GOTOS, as an "egregor" (a subtle essence charged by group magical practices) in the sphere of Saturn, magnetically attracts and stores the power of the magical Chain of the Brotherhood. This GOTOS is compared to Baphomet, the Lodge Daimonium of the Knights Templar. The Fraternitas Saturni is administratively organized into the offices of Grand Master, Executive, (consisting of the Guardian of the Ritual, Secretary, and Archivist), Regional Masters, and Local Masters. A detailed Lodge Rule governs internal matters, admission and ejection, disputes, as well as the possibility of changing the rituals etc.

The use of hammer, spirit-level, set-square and plummet supply evidence of Masonic influence (trowel and dividers, and the columns of Joachim and Boaz are absent). In the context of the Fraternitas Saturni, however, their meaning is magical and not merely symbolic. There are no organisational links to regular → Freemasonry.

The Fraternitas Saturni describes itself as a 'pansophical society with a responsibility to train interested persons in the theory and practice of the pansophical sciences (occultism [→ occult/occultism], → magic, yoga, → mysticism, → astrology etc.) and to support them as assistant, guide and leader on the path to divine light'. The doctrines of the Fraternitas Saturni are very eclectic, in contrast to the O.T.O. groups, which mostly subscribe to the teachings of Crowley. Ancient Egyptian wisdom accompanies the magic of → Agrippa von Nettesheim; grimoires and → witchcraft (chiefly concerning plants and drugs) are used as well as Masonic symbolism. The Fraternitas Saturni uses Kabbalah [→ Jewish Influences] in the sense of Agrippa von Nettesheim and sees no problem in assimilating the doctrines of modern occult groups such as the → Hermetic Order of the Golden Dawn, the Adonistenbund, the O.T.O., or modern magicians like Franz Bardon (1909-1958). Astrology is especially important, as the relation of the self to cosmic powers is a basic assumption of the magician. → Ariosophy has exerted a certain influence (chiefly during the early years) because the Fraternitas Saturni uses ancient Nordic mysticism, magic and folklore for non-Christian wisdom teaching. There are also references to the glacial cosmogony (*Welteislehre*) of Hanns Hörbiger (1860-1931) in Fraternitas Saturni cosmosophy.

Ordinary → spiritualism is rejected because one's own will has to be surrendered. There is practically no reference to → Tarot. The emphasis of the doctrine naturally lies in magic, whereby the Fraternitas Saturni makes no distinction between "white" and "black" magic: everyone is free and responsible for his own karma. The invocation of so-called elementary and planetary spirits is given particular attention. Sex magic certainly belongs in the domain of Fraternitas Saturni knowledge, but contrary to current prejudice the Fraternitas Saturni is not exclusively a sex magical order. Whether the published sex magic rituals, such as the notorious 18° (Gradus Pentalphae), are actually worked or are merely a fantastic or "commercial" invention is unclear. The phallus is regarded as the earthly manifestation of the divine power of will and imagination; the vagina is the symbol for chaos as the creative ground of being; and the male seed is the vehicle of the divine spirit. Tantric practices are also taught, which are supposed to lead to a transformation of the powers of generation into spiritual energy. A period of chastity lasting up to 180 days is therefore prescribed before important rituals. Total abstinence is (theoretically) demanded for the highest degrees.

The teachings of the Fraternitas Saturni basically represent a Gnostic doctrine [→ Gnosticism] concerned with knowledge. Man is capable of discovering his inherent divinity through self-realization. The Fraternitas Saturni member does not seek to dissolve in the cosmos, but wants to fashion it. At the beginning of time darkness represented the more powerful primal element, but light was contained within it. A Logos was necessary in order for the light to dawn; and this Logos was Lucifer, the Light-Bringer. Lucifer is the demiurge, who created our visible world by breaking the static cosmic order. The result was War in Heaven, by which death entered the world. Lucifer is regarded as the "higher octave" of Saturn (Satan representing its "lower octave"), the outermost planet and polar opposite of the Sun in ancient cosmology. Because of this ongoing opposition Lucifer is still fighting the Solar Logos. The principal battlefield is our earth, which contains a negative-astral and a positive-mental sphere apart from its physical form. Saturn is seen as the great judge with scales and sword, entrusted with weight, measure and number. He is the Guardian of the Threshold, or the gateway to transcendence. Because he betrayed divine mysteries to mankind, he has been punished. His heavy, dark, leaden qualities must be transformed into gold by the magician, in an alchemical process involving the "repolarisation of lights". In this coincidence of opposites Saturn becomes the Sun, because the Solar Principle ("Chrestos Principle") was originally the inner nucleus of the Saturn Principle. Only non-initiates regard Saturn as Satan; the initiate however practices spiritual Solar service by worshipping Saturn, and contributes thus to the homecoming of the "dark brother".

Even Eastern teachings have found their way into the Fraternitas Saturni. At least in Grosche's time there was a belief in → reincarnation and karma, and the awakening of the chakras was deemed necessary for spiritual ascent. The Aquarian Age is also heralded. But in contrast to the customary → New Age view, the Fraternitas Saturni emphasizes, that Saturn was originally the astrological regent of Aquarius. Although after the discovery of Uranus in modern times, that planet is now generally regarded as its regent, one should not forget the original role of Saturn. Accordingly, in the view of the Fraternitas Saturni, the new Aquarian era is determined by both planets that is by the solitariness and hardness of the clarified Saturn as well as by the intuitive energy of Uranus.

The anti-Christian stance and sex magic of the Fraternitas Saturni have understandably provoked opposition in the churches and public media. That most Grand Masters have had a reputation for indulging in sex and drugs has made things worse. On the other hand, the Fraternitas Saturni never courted the public exhibition of theatrical satanism as with Aleister Crowley or the Church of Satan. While the Fraternitas Saturni has recruited members by means of occult magazines, it has never sought the spotlights of publicity and has always regarded itself as an elite group. It has sought to address persons who were ready for hardness, solitariness and the burden of adversity, corresponding to the character of Saturn. Thus even in its heyday it has probably never had more than 200 members. Nevertheless it has produced a comprehensive, original and varied literature, which in itself guarantees it an important place in the history of magical and occult orders.

Gregor A. Gregorius, *Magische Briefe*, 8 volumes old series, Wolfenbüttel: Verlag der Freude, 1925-1927; volumes 9-10 new series (vol. 10 Günter Helmont, ed.), Wolfenbüttel; Inveha & Berlin: Verlag der Freude, n.d.; *Saturngnosis*, 5 volumes, 1928-1930 ♦ Gregor A. Gregorius *et al., Logenschulvorträge* (14 nrs), Berlin: Inveha, n.d. (end of the 1920s) ♦ Gregor A. Gregorius *et al., Magische Einweihung*, Berlin: Inveha, n.d. (ca. 1932) ♦ *Blätter für angewandte okkulte Lebenskunst*, monthly from April 1950-December 1963 ♦ *Vita Gnosis* (3 nrs.), *Saturn Gnosis* (8 nrs.), *Sonderdrucke 1-5* (all end 1960s/beginning 1970s) ♦ Adolf

Hemberger (ed.), *Documenta et Ritualia Fraternitatis Saturni* (MS private collection; 15 parts in 17 mimeographed A 4 volumes), 1975-1977 ♦ F.W. Lehmberg (ed.), *Magische Sonderdrucke und Interna der Fraternitas Saturni* (Hiram Edition 10), München: ARW, 1980 ♦ Ordo Saturni (ed.), *60 Jahre Saturn-Loge*, n.d. [1988] ♦ Peter-Robert König (ed.), *In Nomine Demiurgi Saturni 1925-1969* (Hiram-Edition 26), München: ARW, 1998 ♦ idem, *In Nomine Demiurgi Nosferati 1970-1998* (Hiram-Edition 27), München: ARW, 1999.

Lit.: Aythos [ps. Walter Jantschik], *Die Fraternitas Saturni: Eine saturn-magische Loge* (Hiram-Edition 7), München: ARW, 1979 (with documentary appendix) ♦ Stephen Edred Flowers, *Fire & Ice: Magical Teachings of Germany's Greatest Secret Occult Order*, St. Paul: Llewellyn Publications, 1990 ♦ idem, *The Secrets of Fire & Ice: A Historical Supplement to the Text* (self-published, 1995) ♦ Friedrich-Wilhelm Haack, *Die Fraternitas Saturni (F.S.) als Beispiel für einen arkanmystogenen Geheimorden des 20. Jahrhunderts* (Hiram- Edition 1), München: ARW, 1977 (with documentary appendix) ♦ Adolf Hemberger, *Organisationsformen, Rituale, Lehren und magische Thematik der freimaurerischen und freimaurerartigen Bünde im deutsche Sprachraum Mitteleuropas: Der mystisch-magische Orden Fraternitas Saturni*, Frankfurt/Main: self-published, 1971 (in two parts) ♦ Peter-Robert König, *Das OTO-Phänomen: 100 Jahre Magische Geheimbünde und ihre Protagonisten von 1895-1994: Ein historisches Aufklärungswerk*, München: ARW, 1994 ♦ Frater V.D. ∴ (ps. Ralph Tegtmeier) (ed.), *"Die Fraternitas Saturni heute": Frater V.D. ∴ spricht mit Großmeister Thot*, Bad Münstereifel: Edition Magus, 1994.

HANS THOMAS HAKL

Freemasonry

1. FREEMASONRY AS AN ESOTERIC SOCIETY
2. ESOTERICISM AND MASONIC SYMBOLISM
3. IS THE RITUAL OF MASONIC INITIATION OF AN ESOTERIC TYPE? 4. SECRET DOCTRINES AND FREEMASONRY

The relations between Freemasonry and → esotericism are problematic. They depend essentially on the idea that freemasons generally have about their own institution: is it above all an "esoteric society", an initiatic society – and are those the same thing? –, an intellectual circle, or simply a fraternal association? Masonry has given different answers at different times and places, and the experts who study the history and sociology of this institution from the outside do not necessarily agree among themselves.

The ambiguity of the word "esotericism" is particularly salient in Masonry. Certainly it can be taken as designating a whole field of speculations, often confused, or else it may simply serve as title for a bookseller's shelves or for some publisher's series; but it seems that in masonic usage it vacillates between two special meanings. (1) First of all there is → secrecy, the notion of a hidden knowledge to be deciphered, a teaching encoded to conceal it from the profane. In this sense, masonic esotericism refers primarily to the classic *discipline of the mysteries* of which the masonic institution, as a "secret society", is a special case. (2) Alternatively, masonic esotericism, for the masons themselves, is inseparable from the initiatic dimension of the institution which is supposed to lead to an intimate experience, an inner liberation, and, to quote Mircea Eliade's apt definition, to 'an ontological mutation of the existential regime' (*Birth and Rebirth*, 1958). In this second sense, masonic esotericism has more in common with a *gnosis*, with the idea that a mystery is inherent in the things themselves, and that the penetration of this mystery occurs through a hermeneutic that is simultaneously a lived experience, capable of granting a kind of higher knowledge.

Hence, to be in a position to wonder either about the masonic "secret" or about "the initiatic" in Masonry, one has to pose certain preliminary questions. We begin with the problem of masonic symbolism. William Preston (1742-1818), in his famous definition of masonry – one among many others –, distinguishes between *allegories* that "veil" and *symbols* that "illustrate" it (*Illustrations of Masonry*, 1772). Since the 18th century, the masonic texts have often used other terms, such as *emblems* or even *hieroglyphs*. No one can deny that masonry makes lavish use of images and figures, to which it intends to give a more or less precise intellectual or spiritual meaning. But is that esotericism in either – or even both – of the two senses mentioned above? Furthermore, one of the most characteristic traits of Freemasonry is obviously the use of rituals, based on speeches that present the candidate certain legendary or mythical characters: the dramaturgy of the degrees is supposed to teach essential lessons in an allusive, indirect, and subtle manner. In this way, masonry is a kind of "esoteric theatre". Lastly, since the 19th century an important faction in masonry has claimed to reject all dogmatic thinking and to espouse "freedom of conscience"; yet many masonic systems have evidently justified their procedures by means of a more or less clearly defined doctrine.

1. Freemasonry as an Esoteric Society

Is Freemasonry essentially an esoteric society, taking this epithet in the two special senses already highlighted? Operative masonry, being that of the stonemasons' craft typically situated in the Middle Ages, is known through texts from the 12th century onwards, and much better known from the 13th. The earliest of the *Old Charges*, which are documents stemming directly from the lodges of operative masons, go back to the end of the 14th century (*Regius*, circa 1390; *Cooke*, circa 1420). They were written down by clerics, the sole possessors of the knowledge in question, who supervised the workers to keep them obedient to the rules of Christian life. Beside moral prescriptions (the "charges"), these texts merely contain a "Craft History" that is fabulous, legendary, and mythical: careless of chronology or verisimilitude, it links the work of the cathedral builders to that of the builders of the Tower of Babel or the Temple of Solomon, whose heirs and successors they are supposed to be.

Although we know almost nothing of the life and practices of the medieval builders' lodges, it seems that the induction of a new apprentice or the recognition of workers confirmed in the status of "fellow" was marked by a very simple ceremony, whose essential part was an oath taken on the Gospels. In England, the text handed down from the 17th century contains solely professional "obligations". Yet one often hears of the "builders' secret" as one of the treasures bequeathed by masonic tradition from age to age, whose source was none other than the medieval lodges. One must be clear about the nature of this secret. At a period when many crafts, notably that of the mason, were regulated by texts that were often quite restrictive, the training of workmen and their conditions of work were strictly controlled. A major concern was to protect the professional skills as far as possible, so as to reserve the privilege of their exercise to those who were worthy. Hence there was a strong tendency not to spread technical knowledge, and especially not to put it into writing, which in any case would have been of little use at a time when almost all the workers were illiterate. There was surely no other reason for the orality of the tradition, allegedly the infallible proof of an esoteric tradition understood in the sense of a "secret".

Nonetheless, these practices may explain the later appearance of an esoteric significance in the sense of a secret language, secondarily attributed to usages which were originally purely conventional and justified by professional needs. A striking example is the institution of the "Mason Word", known in Scotland from the beginning of the 17th century but certainly much older. In the Scottish operative lodges, this Mason Word was transmitted to the new masons, probably starting with the degree of Apprentice. It allowed these "regular" workmen to enjoy exclusive employment by the Masters, thus keeping out the *cowans*, who were unqualified masons and unrecognized by the lodge. The secret was a purely professional one. However, there was a practice, attested in Scotland from the beginning of the 17th century, of admitting as benefactors and honorary members certain local dignitaries ("Gentlemen Masons") by giving them also the Mason Word – of which they could make no professional use – which gradually transformed this secret into an esoteric instruction. In 1691, Robert Kirk, while describing various Scottish customs, wrote that the Mason Word is 'like a Rabbinical Tradition, in way of comment on Jachin and Boaz, the two pillars erected in Solomon's Temple with an Addition of some secret Signe delyvered from Hand to Hand'. Robert Moray (circa 1600-1673), an artilleryman, engineer, antiquarian given to esoteric speculations, and the first Gentleman Mason whose name is known to history, possessed the Mason Word as early as 1640; and this was doubtless one of the first seeds of masonic esotericism in the sense of a hidden knowledge.

The personality of Robert Moray is emblematic of the intellectual movement which led during the 17th century to the emergence of "speculative masonry", i.e., a masonry which instead of making practical use of the tools of the trade applies them to the moral life. Remarkably enough, in 1660 Moray became the first President of the Royal Society. In this milieu, from which modern science would be born, the Hermetic and Kabbalistic Renaissance still re-echoed, notably in the Rosicrucian movement [→ Rosicrucianism], as Frances Yates has well shown (1972). It was through this unexpected channel that speculations taken from an old alchemical and magical source contributed to forming the spirit of speculative masonry and giving it its esoteric tone, in the "gnostic" sense mentioned above.

In one of the foundational texts, the *Discourse* written in Paris in 1736 by André Michael de Ramsay (1686-1743), incipient French masonry proclaimed that it 'aspires to unite all men of sublime taste and agreeable humour, through love of the fine arts, where ambition becomes a virtue, where the interest of the fraternity is that of the entire human race, whence all the nations may draw solid knowledge, and where all the subjects of the differ-

ent kingdoms may act together without jealousy, without discord, and in mutual affection'. As we shall see, the affirmation of an esoteric filiation going back to the origin of humanity would come much later. In England, it was probably not until the later 18th century, with the publication of *The Spirit of Masonry* (1775) by William Hutchinson (1732-1814), that there was any acceptance of the concept of masonry as being principally the elucidation of a symbolic corpus. Even so, English rituals right up to the present day insist on the essentially moral meaning of the masonic symbols, which appear much more as conventional allegories than as mystical secrets, as Preston's definition clearly shows.

It was in 20th century France that the esoteric vision of masonry was given an impressive theoretical basis by the vast work of → René Guénon (1886-1951). He first entered the lists in the world of Parisian occultism [→ occult / occultism], especially that surrounding the magus → Papus (1865-1916), himself founder of a pseudo-masonic order around 1887. This was → Martinism, whose somewhat confused doctrine, explained in 1891 in Papus's *Traité méthodique de science occulte*, attempted a sort of synthesis between "the wisdom of the Ancients" and the infancy of modern science. The motto of the movement, inscribed on the cover of Papus's journal *L'Initiation*, was: 'The supernatural does not exist'. Guénon, soon disillusioned by the inconsistency of this kind of thinking, was next drawn to Hinduism, then attracted by the Sufi Muslim circles that had formed in Paris. In due course he received the *baraka*, and was permanently influenced by a vision of religious and world history taken from a school of thought close to the *Frères musulmans* (Muslim brothers), whose main characteristic was a blanket condemnation of the modern world. After a brief passage through masonic lodges, from which he definitively distanced himself, Guénon wrote many books and articles in which he developed his vision of the "Primordial Tradition", postulating an esotericism common to all the peoples of mankind and affirming the absolute degeneracy of the contemporary age (*La crise du monde moderne*, 1925; *Le règne de la quantité et les signes des temps*, 1945). Applying this same grid of interpretation to Freemasonry, of which he had only a very slight personal experience, he devoted many writings to it (*Écrits sur la franc-maçonnerie et le compagnonnage*, 1964), considering it to be one of the few organizations in the West that still possessed the keys to a universal esotericism. At the same time, Guénon severely criticized what he presumed to consider the deviations and disavowals of a masonry which, especially in France, had supposedly forgotten its deep roots and lost the meaning of its own symbols. Guénon stated the masonic institution, through its degrees, contains a powerful esotericism and a "spiritual influence" leading, as at Eleusis, from the "Lesser Mysteries" to the "Greater Mysteries", and opening the path to a unitive vision and to liberation of the soul. In parallel to this valuation of masonry, René Guénon constantly stressed the necessity for the initiated mason of "traditional exotericism", meaning the effective attachment to a "regular" religious tradition (predominantly one of the religions of the Book), which masonry would permit one to penetrate esoterically. René Guénon's thought has permanently influenced a faction of masonry, especially French and Italian, while meeting with much less success in Anglo-Saxon masonry, whose preference is for a purely moral or psychological reading of the masonic rituals.

2. ESOTERICISM AND MASONIC SYMBOLISM

Since one cannot avoid referring to operative masonry as the source of masonic symbolism, the question arises of whether any esoteric reflections took place in the lodges during the medieval period. The answer appears entirely negative. No evidence has ever reached us that allows one to imagine any secret teaching being dispensed to the workmen who built the cathedrals. The lodges transmitted the secrets of the craft, the art of building, which was no slight matter; it was jealously guarded and to a certain extent concealed, but not secret, for all that. Moreover, these workmen were carefully overseen by priests who were often the sponsors of the works, and we know that it was the latter who wrote down the oldest texts of the operative period. The moral prescriptions mentioned in them scarcely differ from those of the manuals in current use by the clergy for the edification of their flock.

A simple moral interpretation could certainly have been suggested to the workmen by the tools of their trade, at a time when everything, in a way, was a bearer of meaning. For example, a metal square was found inside a pile of a bridge near Limerick, Ireland, bearing the date 1507 and the inscription: 'I will strive to live with love and care, upon the level, by the square'. But it must be admitted that masonic symbolism in all its luxuriant diversity, together with its esoteric connotations, was a creation that postdated the operative period; it was introduced perhaps as early as the end of the

16th century, and certainly during the 17th, by those who wanted to found on the ancient model of the craft guilds a new society dedicated to philanthropy and later to free philosophical speculation. One can even say that masonic symbolism existed before speculative masonry, but outside any professional or operative context. Thus in the great architectural treatises of the Renaissance, which are essentially the work of educated amateurs or dilettanti, it was usual to give moral or spiritual interpretations to the three principal orders of architecture – Doric, Ionic, and Corinthian. In one of the main treatises of the French 17th century, Philibert de l'Orme's *Les Livres de l'Architecture* (published 1648), there is a whole passage about the symbolism of the cross. The portrait that Philibert draws of the ideal architect is a sort of prefiguration of the 18th-century mason: he is devoted to ancient and architectural matters, naturally, but is also a philosopher, a theologian, and even versed in the sciences and in medicine! He is the ideal polymath, such as was well represented in the membership of the Royal Society from its beginnings: a type for whom Robert Moray, as we have seen, served as model. One tributary of this current was the emblematic literature that was so popular throughout the 16th and into the 17th century, compiling hundreds of enigmatic figures, each associated with a virtue, a quality, or a short motto. Many of these "symbols" would reappear several decades later in the decoration of the masonic lodges.

Knowing as we do the identifiable sources of the masonic symbols, it is very unlikely that a secret or genuinely initiatic content would have been ascribed to them from their beginnings. As Ramsay recalled in 1737: 'We have secrets; they are figurative signs and sacred words, which comprise a language sometimes mute, sometimes most eloquent, to communicate over great distances and to recognize our Brethren no matter what their language or their native land'. It was only by playing on a much later, indeed quite recent interpretation, that these symbols assembled on the "tracing boards" could be compared to mantras, to supports for meditation opening onto an inner experience. That some minds were capable of such a development is probably due to the fact that these figures and boards play a major role during the ceremonies in which the masonic degrees are conferred.

3. IS THE RITUAL OF MASONIC INITIATION OF AN ESOTERIC TYPE?

If we consult the oldest texts, notably the Scottish manuscripts of the Haughfoot group (1696-

circa 1720), the masonic ceremonies of the pre-speculative period were quite simple. The lodge is an oriented space containing some of the objects connected with the mason's trade, into which the candidate is brought blindfold, and there receives light. Under the sanction of a solemn oath and the threat of terrible punishments, the secrets of his degree are revealed to him, in this case the Mason Word. No other teaching is given.

However, from the 1730s onwards, in England and soon after in France, a new movement arose and rapidly grew to a considerable size: that of the high degrees. All through the 18th century, many dozens of rituals containing legends most often inspired by the Bible, populated by new symbols borrowed from all quarters and loaded with words derived more or less accurately from Hebrew, plunged the masons into a strange and puzzling world. Reading the thousands of manuscripts that survive in the chief masonic archives of Europe leaves one with an ambivalent impression. Not least, history shows that a number of these degrees were invented and sold at a high price by adventurers who made a sort of commerce out of masonry.

This body of documents, however, allows us to understand that masonic ritual intends not so much to teach the candidate through discourse as to involve him in an experience: a sort of sacred drama, a mystery in the medieval sense of the word, which is supposed to awaken spiritual resonances in him. It is a masonic commonplace that the true secret of masonry does not reside in the "words, signs and tokens" taught in the degrees, but in the inner experience of their recipient. This secret is thus reputedly incommunicable and inviolable. Such a conception also justifies the apparent absurdity of certain rituals, for it is not their literal sense that matters, but the profound and exist-ential sense that the candidate lives through in his inmost being.

The exact nature of this inner experience always remains debatable. One can distinguish schemati-cally between the Guénonian concept, which sees in the process of initiation the transmission of a "spiritual influence" in harmony with the "subtle constitution" of the human being, and a more cur-rent and strongly psychologized interpretation, which associates the masonic ritual with the tech-niques used in psychoanalysis: thought-associa-tions, waking dream, and psychodrama.

This concept of masonic esotericism as ineffable initiatic experience clearly sets aside the doctrinal content of the rituals, i.e., their "catechisms" and classic "lectures". It is the lived experience that is favored here above any discursive teaching. How-ever, this approach does not exhaust the question of the esotericism at the heart of masonry, because throughout its history several masonic systems have claimed that they possess an authentic eso-teric doctrine.

4. SECRET DOCTRINES AND FREEMASONRY

Very early on, masonry integrated into its rituals various themes borrowed from esoteric currents such as → Christian theosophy and so-called spirit-ual → alchemy. It also came to include elements of a theurgical character, likewise connected with theosophy. During the extraordinary flowering of high degrees, masonic systems appeared having an overtly esoteric teaching, taking this term as referring to the currents of thought that histo-rians include under it: theosophy and alchemy (mentioned above), the kabbalah [→ Jewish Influences], arithmology [→ Number Symbolism], and several others. Here we shall mention only a few examples.

The most remarkable case is perhaps that of the → Ordre des Élus Coëns, propagated from the 1760s onward by → Martinès de Pasqually (1708/9-1774). This system, masonic in appear-ance, began with the universal masonic model of the three degrees of Apprentice, Fellow, and Mas-ter, but it pursued the specific goal of theurgy. Drawing on sources that are still partly unknown, Martinès de Pasqually offered both a doctrine (later summarized in his *Traité de la Réintégration* [Trea-tise on Reintegration]) and a practice, aimed at causing the manifestation of higher spirits by means of the order's complicated ceremonies. According to Martinès, the two approaches were connected. The doctrine explained the fall of man and the necessity of his "reconciliation" with his creator, as a prelude to the end of time when the whole universe might be "reintegrated" in the divine unity. In the course of the rituals (called "operations"), the spirits were summoned, and their presence attested that the candidate had been approved by them. The highest degree of Réau-Croix was supposed to place the candidate in the virtual state of "reconciliation".

The system of the Élus Coëns did not survive the departure of its founder in 1772 – he died in San Domingo two years later. Properly speaking, the Ordre des Élus Coëns was not masonic, but it deeply affected the Régime Ecossais Rectifié (RER) created by → J.B. Willermoz (1730-1824), one of Martinès' disciples. Beginning in 1774, Willermoz imported to France a masonic system of Templar inspiration [→ Neo-Templar Traditions] stemming from Germany: the Stricte Observance Templière (SOT). The traces were already visible there of a supposed secret doctrine inherited from the "poor knights of Christ", a theme that would inspire a whole lineage of masonic degrees up to the end of the 18th century, notably the Chevalier Kadosh. Modern historians of the Order of the Temple have never been able to present credible proof that such a secret teaching really existed among the Templars prior to their suppression in 1312. Embarrassed by this unconvincing claim of Templar filiation, Willermoz modified the system and integrated Martinesian doctrine into it, while doing away with theurgy. At the summit of the pyramid of degrees he added two secret classes, the Profès and the Grands Profès, whose reception ceremony consisted exclusively of the reading of a long instructional discourse, which summarized the main points of Martinesian doctrine and applied them to masonic symbolism. This instruction is firmly stamped with the theosophy of the period, being not only that of Martinès de Pasqually but also of → Louis-Claude de Saint-Martin. It is noteworthy that the scheme previously described is reversed here: it is now the theoretical teaching, not the initiatic experience, that transmits a theosophic content. Thus we are dealing not with something "lived", but with a "knowledge" borrowed from the particular esoteric current that is theosophy. The teaching texts of the RER stress the existence of a secret history transmitted from age to age by an unbroken line of Initiates. This history reveals that at every epoch since humanity's origins a 'primitive, essential and fundamental Order' has existed in the shadow of public history, possessing the keys that explain the origin of Man and the Universe, to which masonry – to be precise, the masonry of the Rectified Rite – is the ultimate heir. The RER, which survives to this day especially in Switzerland, France, and Belgium, was thus probably the first masonic system to present masonry as an esoteric school, whose symbols and rituals were not mere allegories and whose ultimate teaching, revealing the essential verities about the origin and destiny of man and the universe, belonged to the initiates of the highest rank. What is specifically theosophic in the high degrees of the RER is a whole "illuminated" reflection on the mysterious relationships between a complex divine world, a living Nature, and the history of man, all presented in dramaturgical fashion.

Another esoteric current greatly in favor within masonry since the 18th century was the alchemical one. By way of the Rosicrucian tradition introduced into Germany at the beginning of the 17th century and still widely re-echoing in Europe, degrees inspired by Hermeticism [→ Hermeticism and Hermetic Societies] made their appearance – e.g. the Chevalier du Soleil, circa 1750 – and sometimes structured an entire masonic system. One such can be seen in Baron Tschoudy's *L'Etoile flamboyante*, published in 1766, which describes a very imaginary Society of Unknown Philosophers; another, in the Gold- und Rosenkreuz which began in Germany in 1777 and survived for a dozen years, mingling the Templar fable with the alchemical theme. There was also the Rite Ecossais Philosophique which was quite successful in France at the end of the 18th and the first years of the 19th century.

Connections between this Hermetic masonry and "operative" alchemists were very rare. In the masonic context it was an exclusively spiritual alchemy that was envisaged. The process of masonic initiation was thus assimilated to the Great Work, and the spiritual progress of the initiate paralleled with the ripening of the Philosophic Egg in the athanor, of which the lodge was the equivalent. This was a matter of borrowing pure and simple, taking from an ancient esoteric current the explicative keys which it hoped to adapt to a new context.

Napoleon's Egyptian campaign combined with the vogue of → Egyptomany – of which Abbé Terrasson's *Sethos* (1731) had been a precursor – to create, at the start of the 19th century, the Egyptian Rites of masonry, allowing their authors to introduce into the masonic rituals a most romantic vision of the ancient Mysteries, notably as expounded by Jacques Etienne Marconis de Nègre (1796-1868) in *L'Hiérophante, développement complet des mystères maçonniques*, 1839.

From the end of the 18th century, Jewish Kabbalah inspired certain masonic systems such as the → Asiatic Brethren, founded in 1799. While this branch did not have much of a posterity, another conception of Kabbalah, often based on misinterpretations and a very vague knowledge of the sources, became a commonly acknowledged origin of masonic teachings, especially at the end of the 19th century in the high degrees of the Ancient and Accepted Scottish Rite, furnishing the rituals with symbols, tables, and instructional texts. A typical illustration of this is *Morals and Dogma of the Ancient and Accepted Scottish Rite of Freemasonry* (1871) by the great American ritualist Albert Pike (1809-1891), whose proximate source was the French occultist → Eliphas Lévi (1810-1875, author of *Dogme et rituel de la haute magie*, 1856).

In England, the motherland of masonry, the term "fringe masonry" is used to designate a masonry preoccupied with occult knowledge and hidden learning that has never had a widespread development in that country. John Yarker (1833-1913) was its most convinced and zealous propagator (author of *The Arcane Schools*, 1909). In the later 19th century, systems of high degrees emerged from this movement such as the Societas Rosicruciana in Anglia ("Soc. Ros." or SRIA, founded 1867), many of whose members gravitated to an order that was not masonic but esoteric and magical, though originally including many masons: the → Hermetic Order of the Golden Dawn (1888). In the same vein, → Annie Besant (1847-1933), the successor of → H.P. Blavatsky as head of the → Theosophical Society, introduced fringe-masonic ideas into the English-speaking branches of an Order admitting women (such orders are known as Co-masonry), Le Droit Humain. One of the dignitaries of this order, → Charles Leadbeater, a bishop of the Liberal Catholic Church, gave a long exposition of its principles in *The Hidden Life in Freemasonry*, 1926.

In France, the occult side of Freemasonry was quite popular at the end of the 19th century, although French masonry itself was undergoing a mainly secular and humanist evolution, more interested in social commitment than in mystical speculation. The work of Oswald Wirth (1860-1943) is relevant here. Wirth was the spiritual heir of → Stanislas de Guaita (1861-1897), himself one of the representatives of the Parisian occultist current of the 1880s. In a series of works that were very popular among French masons, Wirth expounded a conception of masonic symbolism inspired by a highly personal vision of alchemy and magnetism (*La franc-maçonnerie rendue intelligible à ses adeptes*, 1894-1922; *Le symbolisme hermétique dans ses rapports avec l'alchimie et la franc-maçonnerie*, 1910). His influence remained strong in the French masonic milieu, but had almost no effect outside the French-speaking countries. One should compare Wirth's production to a whole literature of esoteric pretensions influenced by the → New Age, which sees in masonry today the possible nexus of a new synthesis between the teachings of the great religious and mystical currents, indistinctly blended, and the most worrying (and often the least understood) discoveries of contemporary science.

These debates, queries, and persistent doubts serve once again to underline the extreme complexity of Freemasonry, both intellectual and moral. The first divulgation of masonic practices,

Le secret des francs-maçons (The Secret of the Freemasons), printed in Paris in 1744, playfully evokes the mystery in a way that is timely even today: 'Pour le public un franc-maçon/Sera toujours un vrai problème/Qu'il ne saurait résoudre à fond/Qu'en devenant maçon lui-même' (For the public, a freemason will always be a real problem, which cannot be resolved except by becoming a mason oneself).

Lit.: William Hutchinson, *The Spirit of Masonry*, London, 1775 ♦ *Conférences des Elus Coens de Lyon*, Du Baucens: Braine le Comte, 1975 ♦ *Les Leçons de Lyon, par Saint-Martin, Hauterive et Willermoz*, Paris: Dervy, 1999 ♦ Colin Dyer, *Symbolism in Craft Freemasonry*, London: Lewis Masonic, 1983 ♦ Antoine Faivre, *Access to Western Esotericism*, Albany: SUNY Press, 1994, 147-162, 186-193 ♦ Karl R.H. Frick, *Die Erleuchteten: Gnostisch-theosophische und alchemisch rosenkreuzerische Geheimgesellschaften bis zum Ende des 18 ♦ Jahrhunderts*, Graz: Akademische Druck- und Verlagsanstalt, 1973, 454-499 ♦ Gérard Galtier, *Franc-maçonnerie égyptienne, Rose-croix et Néo-chevalerie*, Monaco: Le Rocher, 1989 ♦ Louis Guinet, *Zacharias Werner et l'ésotérisme maçonnique*, Paris: Mouton, 1962 ♦ *Illuminisme et franc-maçonnerie (Revue des études maistriennes 5-6)*, Paris: Les Belles Lettres, 1980 ♦ *Maistre Studies*, Lanham, Md.: University Press of America, 1988 ♦ René Le Forestier, *L'occultisme et la franc-maçonnerie écossaise*, Paris: Perrin, 1928 ♦ idem, *La franc-maçonnerie templière et occultiste aux 18e et 19e siècles*, Paris: Aubier-Nauwelaerts, 1970 (Paris: reprinted La Table d'Emeraude, 1987-2003) ♦ Jean L'homme, Edouard Maisondieu, Jacob Tomaso, *Dictionnaire thématique illustré de la franc-maçonnerie*, Paris: Rocher, 1993, 12-18, 310-324, 450-452 ♦ idem, *Esotérisme et spiritualités maçonniques*, Paris, 2002 ♦ Charles Porset, *Les Philalèthes et les Convents de Paris*, Paris, Geneva: Champion-Slatkine, 1996 ♦ David Stevenson, *The Origins of Freemasonry*, Cambridge: Cambridge University Press, 1988 ♦ Henrik Bogdan, *From Darkness to Light: Western Esoteric Rituals of Initiation*: Göteborg: Göteborg University (Department of Religious Studies), 2003.

ROGER DACHEZ

Fulcanelli

As far as one can tell, the name of Fulcanelli appeared for the first time in Spring, 1926, on the cover of the first of two works published under this pseudonym: *Le Mystère des cathédrales et l'interprétation ésotérique des symboles hermétiques du Grand Œuvre* (The mystery of the cathedrals and the esoteric interpretation of the Hermetic symbols of the Great Work). Only a small number of copies was issued; the book contained a Preface by →

Eugène Canseliet (1899-1982) and plates by the painter Jean Julien Champagne (1877-1932). It was followed in 1930 by *Les demeures philosophales et le symbolisme hermétique dans ses rapports avec l'art sacré et l'ésotérisme du Grand Œuvre* (Philosophic residences and Hermetic symbolism in its relationship to sacred art and the esotericism of the Great Work), prefaced and illustrated by the same. A third work was intended to complete the trilogy, *Finis gloriae mundi* (The end of the world's glory), but for unknown reasons it was never published.

The only useful biographical information on Fulcanelli is the little that is given by his only known disciple, Eugène Canseliet, in articles, prefaces, "memoirs", and in interviews which for the most part remain unpublished. According to Canseliet, Fulcanelli was born in 1839 and educated at the École Polytechnique in Paris. He was an engineer by profession, and, like most of the other pupils from such schools, was called up to serve in the Engineers' regiments, notably during the defence of Paris in 1870-1871. Canseliet tells us nothing more precise about Fulcanelli's mundane life. Was he married? Did he have children? We have not the shadow of an answer. All that we know, and that only through Canseliet, is that during the end of the 19th and the beginning of the 20th century Fulcanelli led a divided existence: on the one hand in Parisian society, frequenting salons in which he met scientists, politicians of national importance, and artists; and on the other, devoted to the study of alchemical texts and to laboratory practice. Fulcanelli lived in Paris, but also owned a small town house in Marseille, at least in 1915 or 1916 when Canseliet first met him, where he seems to have spent several years during the First World War. The story continues that Fulcanelli attained the final alchemical "coction" and obtained the Philosopher's Stone during the 1920s, at an unspecified date but certainly after the transmutation of 1922, which Canseliet records as having taken place in the Sarcelles gas factory. At this point Fulcanelli disappeared from Canseliet's life, but the latter remained closely linked to Champagne by friendship and alchemical researches right up to the painter's death. In 1952 (or 1953), Canseliet claims to have met Fulcanelli once more in Seville, under unusual circumstances.

Despite the absence of tangible evidence, or perhaps because of that, several investigations, biographies, and articles on Fulcanelli and his presumed identity have been published from the 1960s onwards, and especially since 1980. After the second edition of Fulcanelli's works appeared, the best-seller *Le matin des magiciens* (The morning of the magicians, 1960) by Jacques Bergier (1912-1978) and Louis Pauwels (1920-1997) helped to make the alchemist a more popular figure. Bergier goes into considerable detail about → alchemy and relates his own meeting with an alchemist, presented as having been Fulcanelli, in 1937 – at the very moment when Bergier and his scientific colleagues were working on atomic energy. The purpose of the encounter was to warn the scientific world of the dangers of such manipulations. At the end of his life, Bergier confided to friends that the man he met in 1937 was → René Schwaller de Lubicz, which is impossible to verify.

Two years later, Robert Ambelain (1907-1997) published the results of his own researches and those of Jules Boucher (1902-1955): 'Jean-Julien Champagne alias Fulcanelli'. Ambelain emphasized the quasi-master-disciple relationship that existed between Champagne and Canseliet. His researches ascertained that Fulcanelli's publisher had never met anyone other than these two; the same applied to the concierge of the apartment building in Rue de Rochechouart where they had both lived from 1925 to 1932. Ambelain concluded by discerning Champagne's name in the engraving at the end of *Le Mystère des cathédrales*. Although his proofs were not totally convincing (resting as they did on unverifiable statements by people now deceased), they cannot be rejected out of hand.

Another important source for Fulcanelli's possible identity appeared in 1987, with a book on René Schwaller de Lubicz (1887-1961) by the Luxemburger-American writer André VandenBroeck. During 1959 and 1960, VandenBroeck was a frequent visitor to Schwaller, who disclosed an important and hitherto unknown fact: that at the end of the 1910s, Champagne and Schwaller had known each other. Champagne (said Schwaller) had discovered some ancient pages inserted in an alchemical book, and showed them to him: they dealt with alchemical experiments. The two worked together on them and discussed their respective researches: Schwaller had been collecting documents on the Hermetic symbolism of the cathedrals, and he confided to Champagne that he wished to publish his findings. Champagne, most interested in the manuscript, offered to read it, and perhaps to use his contacts in the world of esoteric publication to get it published. After reading it, Champagne declared that it should not be published, because it revealed too many secrets. A few years later, Schwaller was astounded to find his own work forming the substance of *Le Mystère des cathé-drales*. He guessed that Champagne had compiled it with the assistance of the erudite book-dealer Pierre Dujols (1860-1926) and of the young Eugène Canseliet, who signed the Preface. This much Schwaller told to André VandenBroeck, by the latter's account. The "Schwaller hypothesis", according to which the essential ideas of *Le Mystère des cathédrales* were supplied by Schwaller de Lubicz, developed (perhaps with further assistance from others) by Jean Julien Champagne who hid behind the pseudonym of Fulcanelli, and seen through publication by Canseliet, is supported by Geneviève Dubois, who has published a letter from Canseliet to Schwaller that confirms some of VandenBroeck's information.

The other hypotheses of Fulcanelli's identity (that he was Pierre Dujols, Camille Flammarion [F. Courjeaud 1995], Jules Violle [P. Rivière 2000], etc.) are unsupported by any documents, proofs, or concrete evidence, and as such can only appeal to opinion, not to the slightest historical validity. Given the present state of knowledge, all the evidence seems to point towards J.J. Champagne, and it seems impossible to offer an alternative hypothesis that satisfies the rules of historical method.

The importance and fascination of the question of Fulcanelli's identity should not obscure the great interest that his two works hold within the context of alchemical literature. First, they are written in a particularly fine style – supple, precise, and readable – and these qualities have favored their reception in the years since World War II by a far wider public than alchemical publications usually attract. The books belong as much to the field of erudition as to that of alchemy. They have a lofty viewpoint, a serenity, and a freedom from the polemical tendency so often found in this literature. Fulcanelli appears as a Christian Hermeticist rooted in the classic texts and especially in the French tradition, from → Nicolas Flamel to the early 19th century writer Cyliani (the manuscript reputedly discovered by Champagne, which led to his experiments with Schwaller, dated from Cyliani's time). The strongly French character of Fulcanelli's work shows in two further respects. Most of his alchemical discourses take as their starting-point the sculptural program of a Gothic cathedral or a château of the Renaissance era. Moreover, he makes great play with the *langue des oiseaux* (language of the birds): a way of phonetically interpreting words and phrases in order to discover an inner, alchemical meaning, always expressed in French even when the original words are in Latin or English. Fulcanelli's models in this were perhaps

the alchemical writer Cesare Della Riviera (*Il mondo magico de gli heroi* [The magical world of the heroes], 1605) and the antiquarian Claude-Sosthène Grasset d'Orcet (1828-1900).

The ideas that the monumental buildings of France may enshrine a secret alchemical teaching, and that the same secrets lie hidden in certain great works of literature, are immensely appealing, especially to armchair alchemists. But for the practical alchemist, the value of Fulcanelli's work (and of Canseliet's) is greater still. He describes phenomena and hints at laboratory procedures and substances in a tantalizing way, coming closer, perhaps, than any of his predecessors to giving real instruction to the aspirant. Whatever claim can be made for the reality of alchemy, and particularly for the transmutation of base metals into gold with which Fulcanelli, almost alone in the 20th century, has been credited, his writings have set in motion a renaissance of practical alchemy that shows no sign of diminishing.

In 1999, there appeared in London a book claiming to be the celebrated third volume of Fulcanelli's trilogy. Jacques d'Arès, the author of the preface, explains that the manuscript was sent to him as an attachment to an electronic mail message from "Fulcanelli", who stated that he had chosen d'Arès as being the spiritual heir of Paul Le Cour and Philéas Lebesgue. The "master" added that this manuscript was different from the first *Finis gloriae mundi*, and that its communication to the public had been forced upon him by 'compelling reasons, concerning the destiny of all mankind . . .' (23). Now aged 160(!), Fulcanelli apparently felt obliged to write a work in which he breathlessly condemns the conquest of space, experimentation on embryos, nuclear energy, etc., and predicts the fragmentation of the (currently) United States of America, then sent it to Jacques d'Arès through the latest communication channels. Thus there is repeated a pattern well known to historians of Hermeticism: that of attaching a prestigious name to one's own lucubrations – and gaining an audience thereby.

Le mystère des cathédrales et l'interprétation des symboles ésotériques du Grand Œuvre, Paris: Jean Schemit, 1926; 2nd augmented ed. Paris: Omnium Littéraire, 1957; 3rd augmented ed. with new preface, Paris: Jean-Jacques Pauvert, 1964 (frequently reprinted) ♦ Engl. transl., *Fulcanelli, Master Alchemist*, London/Jersey: Neville Spearman, 1971 (repr. Suffolk: N. Spearman, 1977); The Brotherhood of Life: Albuquerque 1984, 2000[2] ♦ *Les demeures philosophales et le symbolisme hermétique dans ses rapports avec l'art sacré*, Paris: Jean Schemit, 1930; 2nd augmented ed., with an additional chapter and new preface, Paris: Omnium Littéraire, 1960, 2 vols. ♦ Engl. trans., *The Dwellings of the Philosophers*, Boulder: Archive Press, 1999.

Lit.: Frater Albertus (= Albert Richard Riedel), *The Alchemist of the Rocky Mountains*, Salt Lake City: Paracelsus Research Society, 1976 ♦ Robert Amadou, "L'Affaire Fulcanelli", *Le Monde Inconnu* 74 (Sep. 1983), 40-45; 75 (Oct. 1983), 28-32; 76 (Nov. 1983), 44-49, 78 (Jan. 1984), 50-51 ♦ Robert Ambelain, "Dossier Fulcanelli", *Les Cahiers de la Tour Saint-Jacques* 9, n.d. [ca. 1962], 181-204 ♦ Jacques Bergier & Louis Pauwels, *Le matin des magiciens*, Paris: Gallimard, 1960 ♦ Jacques Bergier, *Je ne suis pas une légende*, Paris: Retz, 1977 (esp. ch. 12: "La très sainte alchimie", 167-180) ♦ Vincent Bridges & Jay Weidner, *A Monument to the End of Time: Alchemy, Fulcanelli, and the Great Cross of Hendaye*, Mount Gilead: Aethyrea Books, 1999 ♦ Frédéric Courjeaud, *Fulcanelli, une identité révélée*, Paris: Claire Vigne, 1995 ♦ Geneviève Dubois, *Fulcanelli dévoilé*, Paris: Dervy, 1992 (reprinted 1996) ♦ Kenneth Rayner Johnson, *The Fulcanelli Phenomenon*, London: Neville Spearman, 1980 ♦ Khaitzine, *Fulcanelli et le cabaret du chat noir: Histoire artistique, politique et secrète de Montmartre*, Villeselve: Ramuel, 1997 ♦ Luis-Miguel Martinez-Otéro, *Fulcanelli, una Biografia impossible*, Barcelona: Obelisco, 1986; French tr., *Fulcanelli, une biographie impossible*, Arista: Plazac (F-24580), 1989 ♦ Patrick Rivière, *Fulcanelli: Sa véritable identité enfin révélée. La lumière sur son œuvre*, Paris: De Vecchi, 2000 ♦ André VandenBroeck, *Al-Kemi: A Memoir. Hermetic, Occult, and Private Aspects of R.A. Schwaller de Lubicz*, Great Barrington & Rochester, Vt: Lindisfarne Press/Inner Traditions International, 1987.

RICHARD CARON

Galatino, Pietro, * ca. 1460 Galatina (Puglia), † about 1540 Roma

Galatino's surname derives from the town where he was born from a family of Albanian origin which, some time before, had reached the Italian coast under pressure of the Turkish expansion. According to one tradition, the name of the family was Colonna, according to other sources, Mongiò. While still young, Galatino joined the Observant Friars Minor in St. Catherine's monastery in Galatina; in 1515 he became Vicar of the Franciscan Observance in Puglia and in 1517 Minister, re-elected in 1536, of the St. Nicholas' district. When in Naples, in 1506, he offered his work *De optimi principis diademate* to Ferdinand the Catholic and in 1507 he wrote the *Divini nominis Tetragrammaton interpretatio contra Judaeos*. Galatino reached Rome in the last years of the pontificate of Julius II, to whom he dedicated his *Oratio "Cum ieiunatis"*. As a chaplain of the cardinal Lorenzo Pucci, he had an *Oratio de circumcisione dominica*

printed in 1515, which was dedicated to Pope Leo X. To the same Pope he dedicated, in 1519, a *Libellus de morte consolatorius*. He spent the rest of his life in Rome, becoming "artium et sacrae theologiae professor"; but whether he ever taught in the University "La Sapienza" is uncertain. His numerous works, almost all still unpublished, were collected in 1539, under licence of Paul III, in the Franciscan monastery of S. Maria in Aracoeli, and then transferred to the Vatican Library. Posterior to that date we have no information about him.

During his Roman period, Galatino came into contact with the intellectual circles interested in Hebrew culture, the kabbalist tradition and prophetism: he met → Egidio da Viterbo and Georgius Benignus Salviati (Dragišič), entered into correspondence with → Johannes Reuchlin, improved his knowledge of Hebrew mysticism under Elia Levita's guidance, and learned Ethiopian from John Potken. Urged by the cardinals Lorenzo Pucci and Adriano Castellesi, he defended Reuchlin in his *De arcanis catholicae veritatis* (12 books), written in 1515-1516, a work which earned him a high reputation. It presents a dialogue between Johannes Reuchlin and Jakob Hoogstraeten. With this work, Galatino wanted to prove that the basic tenets of the Christian religion are contained in the talmudic and kabbalistic texts. The talmudic approach leads to an allegorical interpretation of the Holy Scriptures, the kabbalistic one to an anagogic reading. The conclusion is that no Christian can afford to neglect studying the hebraic tradition. In his demonstration, Galatino made so much use of Raimundus Martini's *Pugio fidei* and Porchetus de Salvaticis' *Victoria adversus impios Hebraeos* that he was charged with plagiarism. But, even if the work does not have the value of originality, it does offer a large collection of hebraic and Christian sources. In addition one can find → Hermes Trismegistus, the moderns Egidio da Viterbo, Reuchlin, Agostino Giustiniani and → Giovanni Pico della Mirandola as parts of his project of "concordia". Galatino's work is relevant as a synthesis which had an important audience and was reprinted many times during the 17th and 18th centuries. The years after writing his *De arcanis catholicae veritatis* were spent on compiling exegetic and prophetic works: Galatino shared the hopes, widespread in this period, of a religious and political renewal; he awaited a palingenesis under the guidance of an Angelic Shepherd, who would appear flanked by a sovereign of the final times, as stated by numerous prophecies. Only at that moment the "arcana Dei" of the Scriptures would be completely revealed, going beyond the literal and allegorical meaning. Galatino wanted to make a personal contribution to this anagogic interpretation of the Scriptures and he tried to apply some kabbalistic techniques to the New Testament. Galatino tried to interpret his age by making use of prophetic texts from several epochs, particularly those belonging to the Joachimite tradition and – particularly relevant – the *Apocalyspis Nova* attributed to Beato Amadeo.

Pulcherrima divini nominis Tetragrammaton interpretatio contra Judaeos ubi divinae trinitatis mysterium distincte continetur, Granada, Abadia del Sacromonte, Ms. s. n., ff. 154-159 (see P.O. Kristeller, *Iter Italicum* IV, 507b) ◆ *Opus toti christianae Reipublicae maxime utile, de arcanis catholicae veritatis, contra obstinatissimam Judaeorum nostrae tempestatis perfidiam*, Ortonae Maris: Hieronymus Soncinus, 1518 ◆ Codices Vaticani Latini: Opera exegetica inedita, 5567-5581.

Lit.: A. Kleinhans, "De vita et operibus Petri Galatini, O.F.M., scientiarum biblicarum cultoris (c. 1460-1540)", *Antonianum* 1 (1926), 145-179, 327-356 ◆ A. Morisi, "Galatino et la Kabbale chrétienne", in: *Kabbalistes chrétiens* (Cahiers de l'Hermétisme), Paris: Albin Michel, 1979, 211-231 ◆ eadem, "The *Apocalypsis Nova*: A Plan for Reform", in: M. Reeves (ed.), *Prophetic Rome in the High Renaissance Period*, Oxford: Clarendon Press, 1992, 27-50 ◆ R. Rusconi, "An Angelic Pope before the Sack of Rome", *ibid.*, 157-187.

ANNA MORISI

Gemistos, Georgios → Plethon, Georgios Gemistos

Gichtel, Johann Georg,
* 4.3.1638 Ratisbon (Germany),
† 21.1.1710 Amsterdam

Gichtel's life can be divided into three primary sections: from 1638 to 1664, when he had problems with the clerical authorities in Ratisbon; from 1665 through 1667, when he moved about, staying for a time with Friedrich Breckling (1629-1711); and from 1668 to his death in 1710, the time during which he lived, wrote, and taught in Amsterdam. Much of our information comes from this last period, during which he established his community of the "Brethren of the Angelic Life", the *Engelsbrüder*, or "Angelic Brethren", and became more well known as a theosopher.

Gichtel's family was pious, his father was a pharmacist, and Gichtel went to study law at Strasburg. During this time he came to know → Knorr von Rosenroth, the Christian Kabbalist, and studied under Johann Schmidt, Heinrich Böckler, and Philipp Jacob Spener, all renowned historians or theologians, particularly Spener. But in 1664, at the age of 26, Gichtel's life changed radically, when he began to realize something of his spiritual calling, and began to become directly involved in the turbulent Protestant reform movements of his day.

Gichtel was always combative, as we can see in his letters, and certainly this comes through in the biography appended to his letters. There we read Gichtel's account of his ouster from Ratisbon: Ratisbon ministers denounced Gichtel as a heretic, an enthusiast, and an Anabaptist, and had him thrown in prison for thirteen weeks, though he claimed that he belonged to no sect, nor disputed with anyone. The last assertion seems unlikely. Brought before the intransigent Johann Heinrich Ursinus and his fellow clergymen, Gichtel was combative in his responses, so much so that he cowed them into silence and it was afterward said that he had a devil that knew how to handle Scripture. Even Gichtel's own mother eventually told him to leave the ministers alone (VII.35).

Although one would think Gichtel's denunciation and imprisonment would have been the low point of his life, in fact it was the turning point, for in prison he had a vision in which, while 'wrestling with Satan', he fell to earth and felt exalted into the spirit. He then saw a large serpent 'lying in a threefold coil around my heart', while in the midst of the circle appeared a light, in which the Lord appeared. Thereafter the serpent was 'cut up in innumerable pieces'. After recovering from the experience, Gichtel felt a great strength of faith and realized that this was merely the beginning of a long spiritual struggle (II.742-744). This experience was really the beginning of Gichtel's subsequent life, for after this serpent-vision he felt set free, and travelled to Switzerland and then to Holland, where he took refuge for the rest of his life – all the while engaged in the spiritual struggle he described here in its inception in prison.

In the winter of 1666, Gichtel arrived in Schwoll, Switzerland, where he was given shelter by Lutheran minister Friedrich Breckling. During this time Gichtel did preach, but saw that there was little value in mere preaching – ministers, he thought, merely flung words at their congregations. By October, 1667, Breckling was being attacked by his fellow Lutheran ministers, and while Gichtel himself tried to defend him (even though the two had already had a falling out) in a letter written 5 October 1667, Gichtel's support probably contributed to Breckling's own troubles. Gichtel left Schwoll and ended up in Amsterdam, cold and virtually penniless, where he was approached by a complete stranger who laid down six silver ducats and left. This kind of miraculous event evidently happened fairly regularly around Gichtel, whose debts were shortly paid off totally through the largesse of a Dutch book dealer. In fact, although Gichtel was to reside in Amsterdam for decades to come, he was supported all this time by friends or benefactors.

Gichtel's biography is Protestant hagiography: not for nothing is his biography in *Theosophica Practica* entitled *The Wonderful and Holy Life of the Chosen Champion and Blessèd Man of God Johann Georg Gichtel*. Readers must check their disbelief in miracles at this work's portals, for Gichtel's life apparently grew more and not less miraculous as time went on. For example, we read of how Gichtel was forced to bed for over a year since 'Breckling and his wife with their fiery prayers strove against his [Gichtel's] soul'. But after that time, an 'invisible hand' lifted Gichtel from his bed to the ground, and 'Satan's powers were broken'.

If Gichtel's friendship with Breckling ended rather nastily, his friendship with Alhart de Raedt [Raadt] ended in an equally or, if possible, even worse situation. De Raedt was a professor of theology at Harderwijk who had had to leave his chair because of another theological controversy. No doubt introduced to Gichtel by Breckling, de Raedt and Gichtel became fast friends in 1682, and in the words of Gichtel's biographer, 'they would have imparted their hearts to each other, and no one that visited them left them unmoved' (VII.185ff.).

But eventually Gichtel began to suspect that all was not well with de Raedt, that indeed a "foreign spirit" had crept into him. In a crucial incident, de Raedt prayed for a young man who had gone mad, and the more de Raedt prayed, the more insane the young man in another room became, until eventually he hanged himself. In a later such incident, a man with whom de Raedt lived for a time went quite insane and had to be chained, eventually escaping and coming to Gichtel looking 'quite wild and terrible'. Through prayer, the account goes, Gichtel was able to help restore the man to sanity again. In 1684, Gichtel invited all the Angelic Brethren to sit together at a table, and de Raedt reportedly sat apart and cried, because of his offenses – a story that reminds one of the Last Supper, with de Raedt playing the part of Judas. Thereafter, the two never met again, though de Raedt became Gichtel's bitter enemy (VII.212-213).

Between this time and Gichtel's death in 1710, his reputation spread through the Netherlands, and to England and Germany. Gichtel corresponded with numerous theosophers or aspirants, and knew what was happening in theosophical circles elsewhere in Europe. He weighed English theosopher → Jane Lead's assertion of *apocatastasis*, or universal restoration, and eventually rejected it as conflicting with → Boehme's views. As the center of the Angelic community in Amsterdam, Gichtel was a spiritual advisor to both men and women, and people not part of this group would also seek him out for advice. Gichtel saw the world as the venue for spiritual struggles between good and evil, a perspective that infuses his many volumes of letters entitled *Theosophia Practica*, and that also pervades the work of Jacob Boehme, which Gichtel edited and published under the title *Theosophia Revelata*.

In the volumes of Gichtel's *Theosophia Practica*, we find many references to paranormal or miraculous events. He wrote about how he was able through prayer to assist the soul of a friend who had committed suicide; of how he was able to help people by taking their obsessions onto himself through prayer; of how he and his "angelic brethren" were always given what they needed to survive; of how he was able to put a ghost to rest; and of how he was able to discern whether an alchemical recipe was legitimate or merely fraudulent (I.335; VII.215; V.3188, 3210-3211, 3343).

Gichtel's letters are strikingly empty of references to current events or well-known people, but instead emphasize what we may call "hierohistory". Essentially, hierohistory refers to records of the dates and times of individual spiritual events or revelations. Gichtel's letters and biography exemplify this tendency very well, and one often gets the impression that, for Gichtel, hierohistory takes absolute precedence over the progression of linear time. In a sense, Gichtel's *Theosophia Practica* is simply an extended hierohistory, the specific cycles of revelation for Gichtel and his circle being chronicled both at the beginning and at the biographic conclusion of this seven-volume magnum opus of letters.

Gichtel's death is forecast in hagiographical fashion at the end of *Theosophia Practica* by reference to archetypal cycles of time. The Divine Sophia (Wisdom) reportedly appeared to Gichtel in definite temporal cycles during his life, and these cycles culminated forty days before his death, when 'the heavenly mother of wisdom revealed herself anew in 1709, December 13'. This time of revelation was the greatest, Gichtel said, since the time of de Raedt's apostasy; and according to Johann Georg Graber, it reached its zenith in the Angelic group after Gichtel's physical death early in 1710 (VII.340-341). This cycle of revelation, Graber tells us, was renewed in subsequent years among the remaining Angelic community.

Gichtel's primary written work, as we have seen, was his voluminous collection of letters, but he left several other major works behind as well. Among these is a treatise, dated 1696, entitled *Eine kurze Eröffnung und Anweisung der dreyen Principien und Welten Im Menschen* (A Brief Revelation and Instruction on the Three Principles and Worlds in Man), published in 1723. This work – which has been reprinted several times under the erroneous title *Theosophia Practica* – includes some very important illustrations on planetary symbolism and the human microcosm, detailing the process of theosophical illumination that is discussed at length in the text. The treatise is extremely ascetic in emphasis, focusing on the "wooing" of Sophia and on advice to the aspirant on struggles against demons and temptations.

Gichtel also edited the first major collection of Boehme's writings, entitled *Theosophia Revelata*, published in three successive editions: 1682, 1715, and 1730. Between 1680 and 1682, Gichtel and his colleagues accomplished this remarkable project of collating disparate texts and producing a single, fourteen-volume edition in octavo. It was in fact the primary German edition of Boehme until the work of Werner Buddecke in the 20th century. These two multivolume series – Boehme's work in *Theosophia Revelata*, and Gichtel's own letters in *Theosophia Practica* – were deliberately complementary, Boehme offering the primary revelational paradigm of theosophy, and Gichtel concentrating on its practical implications through guiding letters.

While Gichtel certainly belongs to the tradition of Boehme, his emphasis was not on Boehmean exegesis, but upon direct spiritual experience that he details in his letters. His contributions to the Boehmean tradition include the following: (1) an emphasis on rigorous asceticism in order to "woo Sophia", or divine Wisdom personified as feminine; (2) an intense emphasis on demonic temptations in life that must be overcome (i.e., daily life as intense spiritual-ascetic struggle); (3) cycles of Sophianic revelations at specific intervals ("hierohistory"); (4) an emphasis on the androgyny of Adam prior to the Fall, and on the central role of Sophia in restoring the soul of the theosophical practitioner to primordial spiritual wholeness symbolized as androgyny; (5) explicit reference to traditions of practical and spiritual → alchemy; (6) miraculous or paranormal events, including clairvoyance. All of these themes are to be found in Boehme, though in far more symbolic form. Gichtel's work is marked above all as unique by his particularly detailed chronology of Sophianic revelation in specific temporal cycles, or hierohistory, by his practical theosophic community (the Angelic Brethren), and by his letters filled with details of his own theosophic and paranormal experiences. Gichtel's essential contribution to the theosophical tradition is his emphasis on theosophic praxis and experience.

Gichtel has been criticized by Gorceix and others as having been a misogynist, but while there is no doubt that Gichtel insisted on chastity as part of his path toward spiritual marriage with Sophia, an emphasis on chastity is not the same as hatred of women (Gorceix 1975, 125; Versluis 1999, 36-37). Gichtel wrote that he had often refused proposals of marriage from various women, but this is consistent with his worldview affirming chastity. It is also the case that he corresponded with and offered spiritual advice to women as well as to men. Gichtel was unquestionably an irascible character who argued with a great many people, but he remains among the most important of the theosophers, and his letters shed a great deal of light on Boehme and on a theosophic spiritual path. The major study remains that of Gorceix (1975); detailed discussion is also found in Hutin (1960), Thune (1948), and Versluis (1999). Translated excerpts from *Theosophia Practica* are found in Versluis (2000).

Johann Georg Gichtel, *Theosophia Practica*, 7 vols., Leipzig: n.p., 1722 ♦ *Theosophia Revelata*, 19 vols., Hamburg: Regelin, 1715, 1730-1731 ♦ *Eine kurze Eröffnung und Anweisung der dreyen Principien und Welten im Menschen* (with Johann Georg Graber), Leipzig: n.p., 1696 [mistitled as *Theosophia Practica*] Freiburg: Aurum, 1979 ♦ Some fragments translated into English in Arthur Versluis, *Wisdom's Book: The Sophia Anthology*, St. Paul: Paragon House, 2000, 129-139.

Lit.: Antoine Faivre, *Access to Western Esotericism*, Albany: SUNY Press, 1994, 64, 69, 71, 216-217 ♦ Bernard Gorceix, *Flambée et Agonie: Mystiques du XVII siècle allemand*, Sisteron: Présence, 1977, 277-294 ♦ idem, *Johann Georg Gichtel: Théosophe D'Amsterdam*, Paris: L'Age d'Homme, 1975 ♦ Serge Hutin, *Les Disciples anglais de Jacob Boehme aux XVIIe et XVIIIe siècles*, Paris: Editions Denoël, 1960, 15-25 ♦ Nils Thune, *The Behmenists and the Philadelphians: A Contribution to the Study of English Mysticism in the 17th and 18th Centuries*, Uppsala: Almquist and Wiksells, 1948, 105-130 ♦ Arthur Versluis, "Christian Theosophic Literature of the Seventeenth and Eighteenth Centuries", in: W.J. Hanegraaff and R. van den Broek (eds.), *Gnosis and Hermeticism from Antiquity to Modern Times*, Albany: SUNY Press, 1998, 217-234 ♦ idem, *Theosophia: Hidden Dimensions of Christianity*, Hudson: Lindisfarne, 1994, 67-69, 143-144 ♦

idem, *Wisdom's Children: A Christian Esoteric Tradition*, Albany: SUNY Press, 1999, 29-38.

ARTHUR VERSLUIS

Giorgio [Zorzi], Francesco, * 7.4.1466 (?) Venice, † 1.4.1540 Asolo

Giorgio was born in Venice at a date which is undocumented, but which study of his astrological nativity indicates to be April 7, 1466, thus disproving his previous identification with one Dardi Zorzi. The scarcity of sure information on his youth and early manhood prevents us from knowing about his intellectual formation or his possible places of study. We know only that he belonged to the powerful patrician family of the Zorzi, and that he was a close relative of Alberto Marino Zorzi, "Reformer" of the University of Padua, and of Marin Sanudo, the author of the *Diari* which furnish important information about him. There is an old tradition that Giorgio, like other young patricians, completed his philosophical studies at the Paduan "Studio", but it is undocumented, as is the statement that he taught before becoming a friar. Nor can one establish the exact date of his entry into the order of the Observant Friars Minor, perhaps in the Venetian monastery of San Francesco della Vigna, or whether he pursued a regular theological education in the Studio del Santo, the school of the Venetian Franciscan Province. However, Giorgio's familiarity with the Scotist doctrines that he often cites, and his reading of → Albertus Magnus and Thomas Aquinas, seems to confirm this hypothesis. His evident familiarity with the works of → Marsilio Ficino and → Giovanni Pico della Mirandola, with the Hermetic texts and the Talmudic and Kabbalistic traditions, suggests close contact with the Venetian intellectual circles influenced by the Platonic "Renaissance" and with the scholars of the Venetian Jewish community, such as Jacob Mantino, Elia Levita, Elia Menahem Halfon, as well as with the printer Gersom Soncino. Such contacts, together with the probable connections with → Egidio da Viterbo and the Venetian Augustinians engaged with editing the Joachimite and pseudo-Joachimite texts, may explain the most typical aspects of Giorgio's thought, expressed above all in the third "cantico" of *De Harmonia mundi*.

These interests, studies, and personal experiences did not hinder Giorgio from participating in the life of the Franciscan community, including a busy preaching activity and perhaps even a voyage to the Holy Land, and from maintaining excellent relations with the political institutions of Venice. In 1500 he was elected Guardian of the monastery of San Francesco della Vigna, then apostolic delegate for the celebration of the Jubilee. At the same time he found himself involved in the trial of the physician Giovanni Maria, a follower of Francesco Biondo, who had promulgated his heterodox ideas in Venice. It is unclear what Giorgio's role was in this affair, which brought him a brief excommunication; but the consequences were not serious, for in 1504 he was re-elected Guardian and continued to preach with much success in Venice, on the mainland, and also beyond the Venetian domains. He was even confessor of the Poor Clares of the monastery of Santo Sepolchro, and of the abbess, Chiara Bugni, a "visionary" and "thaumaturge" who enjoyed considerable fame in the city. The church authorities carefully investigated the ecstasies and visions of the abbess, which were then celebrated by Giorgio in his own "Life" of Bugni. A commission of theologians excluded any charge of fraud or heterodoxy, but nevertheless in 1512 the nun had to accept segregation in a sort of conventual prison, where she lived out her last years.

Not even this affair lessened the favor which Giorgio enjoyed with the Senate and Signoria, which included him among the candidates for the Patriarchate in 1504, 1508, and 1523. After the Venetian defeat at Agnadello (1509), he was their intermediary with Andrea da Capua, duke of Termoli and commander of the Spanish-Neapolitan troops stationed at Vicenza, who was considering a truce in anticipation of a shifting of alliances. The mission was unsuccessful; but again, during the war of the Holy League, Giorgio sent important confidential reports to the main Venetian institutions. In spring, 1512 he met with Francesco II Gonzaga before proceeding to Ferrara, where he stayed with Alfonso d'Este, and reported on these conversations in person to the Doge. Meanwhile Giorgio pursued his monastic career. He was superintendent of the building of the sanctuary of Motta di Livenza, and in 1513 was elected Provincial, then Provincial Vicar, a post confirmed for the next two years. As such, he took part in the general chapter of the Observants in Assisi (1514), and in 1517 in the "supreme chapter" of Rome that sanctioned the definitive separation between the Conventuals and the Observants. Giorgio was named "definitore generale cismontano" of the latter. Although he retired in 1517-1518 to the monastery of San Girolamo at Asolo to begin the laborious writing of *De Harmonia mundi*, he took part in the general chapters of Lyon (1518) and Carpi (1521), where he was re-elected Definitor General. Finally, in 1523 he became Provincial Minister, and was reconfirmed until 1525.

The exercise of these offices brought Giorgio closer to those who, reacting to the schism of the Reformation and the crisis of ecclesiastical institutions, hoped for a profound renovation of the Roman Church which would not only eliminate the corruption of the clergy, the monastic orders, and the hierarchy, but would return the Christian faith to its origins. Especially in the 1520s, Giorgio hoped that the reform of the Observants might be the example of a real Christian rebirth; and indeed in 1523, at the general chapter of Burgos, he sided with the "general" Francisco Quiñones, sharing his reforming proposals. It is not surprising that Giorgio was friendly with the Venetian supporters of the so-called "Catholic Reformation", such as Gasparo Contarini, and with personalities such as Cortese, Giberti, Fregoso, and even Carafa, who after the Sack of Rome found the Venetian environment more congenial. However, in 1523 Giorgio found himself involved in a delicate disciplinary investigation concerning some "unruly" brethren whom he had not punished sufficiently. The Cismontine Commissary General suspended him from his post of Provincial, then, because Giorgio, with other Venetian friars, had not presented himself at the chapter of Mantua, the General excommunicated him, causing him to appeal to the pontifical legate and to the Pope. This was resolved only through the direct intervention of Quiñones, who in December 1525 absolved Giorgio but punished the other brethren. We do not know whether this altercation was provoked by mere disciplinary questions, or by some heterodox attitude as was common among the Observants, made suggestible by millenarist ferments and sometimes leaning toward the acceptance of Protestant doctrines. No longer re-elected, Giorgio returned to Asolo, where he had meanwhile finished writing De Harmonia mundi, published in Venice in September, 1525.

It is difficult to sum up such a complex work, which has the form of a musical poem composed of three "songs", and in which the continuous reference to Platonic, Neoplatonic [→ Neoplatonism], and Hermetic texts [→ Hermetic Literature] is intertwined with astrological doctrines [→ Astrology] and alchemical allusions [→ Alchemy]. Long quotations from the Gospels, especially St. John's, the Apocalypse, and the Pauline Epistles cohabit with mathematical speculations of a Pythagorean and magical type [→ Number Symbolism]. Giorgio's preferred Kabbalistic doctrines [→ Jewish Influences] encounter the "Christian wisdom" of the Church Fathers (especially Origen), → Augus-

tine, and the greater Minorite masters. Such a rich erudition cannot be explained solely by the extraordinary accomplishments of → Ficino and Pico della Mirandola, but rather by the return to the Hebrew biblical tradition urged in recent works by Felice da Prato and Sante Pagnini, by the publication of writings of pure Kabbalistic inspiration such as Agostino Riccio's De motu octavae sphaerae, and by the prolific efforts of Egidio da Viterbo in his attempt to christianize the Kabbala. De Harmonia aims to be the expression of a shared "wisdom" that is at once philosophical and theological, speculative and mystical; an interpretation of the supreme divine and cosmic mystery whose "illumination" descends through all the "revelations": the Bible, the prisca theologia, the Word of Christ. Giorgio draws from these divine "springs" and their exegesis those fundamental themes which invariably influenced the religious culture of the mature Cinquecento, whether Catholic or heterodox: the "central" significance of man in the hierarchical and harmonious order of the cosmos; his liberty and dignity as a creature who comprehends the whole universe within himself; the supreme "mediating" function of Christ, the "incarnate Word" conceived as the unique "intermediary" between the eternal Monad and the infinite multiplicity of creation; the return of all to the One through the progressive reductio that every man can achieve in the privacy of his own spirit, if he follows the "path" of redemption by Christ, receives his "blessing", and "imitates" his example. Finally, in the third cantico, perhaps added later, the Franciscan – like Ficino in the Libri de Vita – comes to connect the deificatio hominis (deification of man), with the beneficial use of astrological and magical techniques that facilitate the celestial ascent, just as his Kabbalistic exegesis aims toward the millenarist expectation of the new Jerusalem and of the new Adam who will reign together with Christ.

Giorgio credits this knowledge of these eternal truths to the sages of every age and every people, who have enjoyed the secret divine "illumination" and transmitted it from the immemorial time of the prisci theologi and the poetae theologi up to the more recent meditations of the Fathers and Doctors of the Church, of Francis of Assisi and → Nicholas of Cusa. To them is due the lofty speculation on the One that is eternal and immutable but not immobile or sterile, thus the generator of every multiplicity in the infinite production of the world. From this unity and "first, most fecund mind" proceeds a "most similar offspring", the true image of the Father, who generates it with a "unique and uninterrupted" act. This "offspring" is the "Word of God" that Plato calls "son", and Orpheus sings of in the myth of Minerva born from the head of Jupiter. But the "Son" is the very principle that generates the love of divine goodness, linking every "intelligence" to the supreme Mind. Thus Giorgio proceeds to deduce the generative process from the One to the many, as conceived by the *sapientes*, and especially by Plato's *Timaeus*, Orpheus, Boethius, the Magi and the "Chaldean theologians", who have shown that the creation of the *fabrica mundi* (world-material) has been achieved following the musical and mathematical model of the perfect ternary number. The heavens and the stars have been made by the "perfect artisan" in such a way as to move with the greatest harmony and diffuse their good influences on all inferior things. Thus no calamity, mishap or catastrophe can be attributed to God, the fount of all goodness, because his celestial "ministers" operate according to his will, without ever violating human free will or disturbing the divine order of the world and the perfect reciprocal communication of all things. Christ the Word, "root" of all the "virtues" operating in the cosmos and of the "light" that forms it, attracts every earthly life and nature to himself and leads back to unity the multiplicity that is dispersed in the immense cosmic architecture. He is indeed the "redeemer" who has shown to man, placed by God between time and eternity, the finite and the infinite, how to ascend to the pure angelic intelligences and thence to return to his own origin and celestial nature. Thus the human soul, which the sacrifice of the highest cosmic and spiritual intermediary has redeemed from original sin, can again become God's favorite child; and when it has finally put off its dissonant and inharmonious "matter", it will reveal its harmony of pure spiritual and immortal substance, awaiting the last judgment when beatitude will be absolute and everything will return to its one source. As the soul pursues this journey, it will be able to enjoy all the natural energies and potencies, using the "good" magical arts of "haruspicy", chiromancy, geomancy and physiognomy [→ Divinatory Arts], which allow the "elect" to receive exceptional knowledge and powers as they approach the higher form of revelation, the "rapture" in which the omnipotent divine will reveals the mystery of the future and unveils eternity.

The publication of *De Harmonia* at a time that was so perilous for Christendom, riddled with violent religious and political conflicts, was received with great interest in the religious circles that entertained reforming notions; but it did not fail also to attract intellectuals who were later considered heretics. Not by chance did Bembo express his doubts about its ample usage of the Kabbalah, 'a most suspect and dangerous thing', while other readers distrusted its attitude toward traditional theological doctrines, harbinger of possible heretical conclusions. The book was soon diffused throughout Europe, as witness the Paris editions of 1543 and 1564 and the French version (1578, 1588) by →Guy Lefèvre de la Boderie, a disciple of → Guillaume Postel, himself an admirer of Giorgio.

During the following years, Giorgio was one of the main figures in the religious life of Venice. He was charged by the Senate in 1527 to promulgate the Jubilee conceded by Clement VII, and returned to San Francesco della Vigna as Reader in Sacred Scripture and Teacher of the Hebrew Language. In the dramatic spring of that year, on the eve of the Sack of Rome, Quiñones, on the orders of Clement VII, asked him to convince the Venetian Senate to lay down arms and support the final efforts to avoid war. Giorgio's intervention was in vain; but the following year, when he obtained the conversion of a rabbi, he was solemnly honored in San Marco in the presence of the Doge. His most dramatic effort of religious politics was his involvement in the complicated affair launched by Henry VIII's request for a divorce from Catherine of Aragon. Giorgio supported the humanist Richard Croke, sent to Italy to collect the opinions of professors, church dignitaries, biblical scholars, theologians, and even rabbis who were disposed to recognize the validity of the reasons put forth by the English king. The friar's activity succeeded in gathering support not only from various theologians of Venice, Padua, and Vicenza, but even of Elia Menahem Halfon, Baruch di Benevento, Calò Calonymos, and the converted rabbi Marco Raffaele. Not even the papal prohibition, on pain of excommunication, of writing or speaking against the validity of this marriage induced him to give up. But he did not disobey the papal brief of Clement VII (2-6-1530) which summoned him to Rome, so that with his "singular doctrine" he might assist the papacy and the Church. Even the Senate had warned Giorgio not to become further involved with the "English question", just as it refused the request of the Bishop of London, John Stokeslay, that the Paduan theologians might make their opinion known. Giorgio's stay in Rome, where it seems that he toned down his attitude, did not change the Pope's decision, after which a severe, life-threatening illness forced him to lessen his efforts. It is difficult to agree with the identification made by Roth of Giorgio as the "authoritative" Italian Franciscan present at the end of 1530 or 1531 at the English court, where, incidentally, his close associate Marco Raffaele found refuge.

Shortly after his return to Venice, and thence to Asolo – perhaps as early as March 1531, when the Signoria named him among the candidates for the diocese of Brescia – Giorgio found himself involved in a bitter conflict which set the supporters of Paolo Pisotti, General of the order, against the former Venetian Provincials and a group of young friars who supported the radical reforms of the Observants. When the future "heretic" Bernardino Ochino was sent to Venice as Pisotti's "commissary", it embittered the meeting and led to the intervention of Carafa and Gian Matteo Giberti, Bishop of Verona, in favor of the "reformers". The crisis lasted till the end of 1533, when Pisotti renounced the generalship. Giorgio, acquitted of his adversaries' accusations, could then return to dedicate himself to Kabbalistic studies, biblical exegesis, and ever bolder spiritualist meditations. Already in 1532 he had met Luca Bonfius, friend of → Heinrich Cornelius Agrippa, with whom he had a long conversation about the most important Kabbalistic themes; and the following year Agrippa, defending himself from the accusations of Corrado di Ulma, had cited Giorgio among the greatest students of the Kabbalah. The friar's fame was already widespread among European followers of the *secretior theologia* (more secret theology), whilst on the other side he regained authority in his order, becoming in 1534 Custodian, and in 1535 again Provincial and Procurator of the "fabric" of San Francesco della Vigna. The latter office allowed him to realize his idea of the canon of harmony and mathematical proportion to be used in the construction of temples, as a symbol of the universal harmony. Finally in July, 1536, he published in Venice *In Scripturam Sacram Problemata* (Problems in Holy Scripture), a work which had considerable success, especially in France where it was reprinted in 1575 and 1622.

In this book, Giorgio used a completely different procedure, tackling the "problematic" discussion of scriptural passages, of their apparent divergences and the different meanings to be attributed to them through recourse to Kabbalistic interpretation. In the dedication to Paul III he says that he has written this work solely to help the faithful, who are seeking in the divine Word the most "sweet" and solid wisdom. He points to the Bible as the source of all knowledge, from mathematics to geometry, from → music to "true and divine" astronomy, from medicine to natural philosophy

and ethics. Thus in the *Problemata* he says that he has treated not only the problems concerning the origin and order of the *fabrica mundana*, but also the creation of man, the coming of the Mosaic revelation and the history of the Law; also the themes concerning "vaticination" from the biblical prophets to the prophecies of → Hermes, → Zoroaster, Orpheus, Pythagoras, and Plato, derived from the communal divine *officina*, and thence to the more secret truths of the Gospels. Above all, he announces that he will have recourse to Kabbalistic exegesis according to the method of the *Zohar*, by which the sense of the Scripture may vary in 72 "facets", thereby revealing unknown "treasures" of wisdom. It is no surprise that in this book the most subtle theological and dogmatic arguments, subjected to Kabbalistic analysis, alternate with prophetic, messianic, and eschatological themes aimed at the expectation of the necessary *renovatio* of man and the world.

In the first section, *De mundi fabrica*, the friar revives the defence of the creationist doctrine against Averroes and the Peripatetics; but he asserts that God has created a unique, universal soul from which he has drawn the individual souls, infused in Adam and other men. Giorgio accepts the Platonic myth of the original, androgynous nature of man, which he says Plato took from → Moses, a prophet illuminated by divine wisdom. Thus Giorgio shows his intention to interpret the sacred texts in complete liberty, in search of recondite and arcane meanings foreign to traditional exegesis, and in particular of propositions that refer directly to trinitarian dogma. He emphasizes the work done by the Son-Word in the formation of the cosmos, dominating the original chaos and the dark formlessness of primordial matter. Moreover, the conception of sacred history, discussed in nine groups of problems, allows Giorgio to extend the Old Testament revelation up to the coming of Christ, the universal mediator, so as to consider the Mosaic law in close symbolic continuity with the Christian message.

The true significance of the *Problemata* appears only in the third tome, dedicated to the *Prophetarum oracula* (oracles of the prophets). While Giorgio praises the supreme value of prophecy, he considers "natural reason" and philosophy as frivolous and vain in comparison with that "divine gift" perceptible to the "spiritual senses" alone, because the true prophet must express himself in enigmatic form, presenting the divine truth only in obscure form, comprehensible by few. Moreover, when Giorgio discusses the significance of the sacraments, particularly baptism, and their "potency", he insists on their "spiritual" and "symbolic" character, whether it is a matter of penitence, baptism, or the "sacrifice" of the Mass and the Eucharist, of which Christ is the only priest. He alone who participates in complete inner purity can unite himself with God in *charitas* (love), like the grains of wheat in bread, while the false Christians, no longer his children, will be subjected to God's strict justice.

Like the *problemata* on the secret reason that God permits the evils and disasters of the world, the interpretation of the sacraments is resolved within the eschatological perspective of the war between good and evil, concluded by the coming of the "new men" reborn in Christ and the end of worldly rites and observances, necessary under the Law but now abolished by the sacrifice of Christ, "celestial man", and by faith in him. Then in the fourth tome, the friar discusses original sin and the fullness of time, which is now very close; he returns to the divine-human nature of Christ and his supreme thaumaturgic virtue, revealed by the messianic name that dismays the demons with its powers and its numeric virtue, in which the power of all the divine names is collected. Certainly, faith in the man-God is now too scarce among "worldly men", and the very "mystical body of Christ", the Church, can no longer preserve that divine "treasure", while the mystery persists of "Judaic incredulity" toward the true Messiah so long awaited. In the fourth and fifth tomes Giorgio appeals not only to Paul, Augustine and other Fathers, but to Hermes, Orpheus, Zoroaster, Pythagoras and Plato, to renew the ancient "secret wisdom", interpret the supreme mystery of the Trinity, and recognize the divine glory, conqueror of demonic cunning, which is only revealed when one despises the desires and temptations of the mortal and ephemeral body. Giorgio also discusses the Kabbalistic significance of the angelic natures; the heavens, stars, and celestial influences governed by them; and lastly the "secret" arts among which is → alchemy, often wrongly used but worthy of faith. Thus there emerges the image of the Christian "thaumaturge" to whom divine wisdom has revealed the most hidden mysteries of the cosmos, which he uses for his final identification with the Word as redeemer of his earthly and carnal nature.

The publication of the *Problemata* caused doubts and fears even among Giorgio's friends. Contarini, especially, judged severely the interpretations of trinitarian dogma as being close to the Arian heresy, and the prevalence of rabbinic and Kabbalistic exegesis over Christian theologians. Giorgio defended his work, asserting its absolute

orthodoxy; then, returning to Asolo, devoted himself to writing an unpublished commentary on the Kabbalistic Conclusions of Pico, and to the composition in Italian of the *Elegante poema* and its *Commento*, perhaps interrupted by his death. In the introductory *Argomento*, he writes that he intends to 'make clear and bright many places in Scripture that seem more occult and obscure' by 'following the poetic custom', that is, with a poem evidently imitative of Dante, on the lines of the Platonic and prophetic interpretation of the *Commedia* proposed by Ficino and Landino. The *Poema* and *Commento*, which resume the doubts and Kabbalistic exegesis of the *Problemata*, survive in a single manuscript tradition which must have circulated only among the friar's most faithful followers, among them perhaps → Giulio Camillo.

Giorgio died in Asolo in April 1, 1540, while his works were still circulating in Europe. But later, after the harsh attack by the Dominican Sisto da Siena (1566) and the drastic accusations by Bellarmino (1585), came the final condemnation of *De Harmonia* and the *Problemata*, sanctioned by the *Index romanus* of Sixtus V (1590) and repeated in the *Index librorum prohibitorum et expurgandorum* of Giovanni Maria Guazzelli (1607).

De Harmonia mundi totius Cantica tria, Venice: Bernardini de Vitalibus, 1525 ◆ *De Harmonia mundi cantica tria*, Paris: Andreas Berthelin, 1543 ◆ *Liber promptuarium rerum theologicarum et philosophicarum*, Paris: Jean Macé, 1564 ◆ *L'harmonie du monde, divisée en trois cantiques*, trans. Guy Le Fèvre de la Boderie, Paris: Jean Macé, 1578 (repr. Neuilly/Seine: Arma Artis, 1978) ◆ *In Scripturam Sacram Problemata*, Venice: Bernardus Vitalis, 1536 ◆ *In Scripturam Sacram*, Paris: Michael Somnium, 1575 ◆ *In Scripturam Sacram et philosophos tria milia problemata. Additae sunt theologicae . . . correctiones cum indice triplici*, Paris: I. Bassin & G. Alliot, 1622 ◆ *L'Elegante Poema & Commento sopra il Poema*, ed. J.F. Maillard, preface by J. Mesnard, Milan: Archè, 1991.

Lit.: Marin Sanudo, *I Diari (MCCCCXCVI-MDXXXIII)* (ed. R. Fulin, F. Stefani, M. Barozzi, G. Berchet), Venice: M. Allegri, 1879-1913 (see Indices of the various vols.) ◆ Sixtus Senensis, *Bibliotheca Sancta criticis et theologicis animadversionibus*, Venice, 1566 ◆ Roberto Bellarmino, *Disputationes de controversiis christianae fidei adversus huius temporis haereticos*, Rome, 1587 ◆ Marin Mersenne, *Observationes et emendationes ad Francisci Veneti problemata*, Paris, 1623 ◆ J. Brucker, *Historia critica philosophiae*, 4, Leipzig, 1743, 376-385 ◆ Giovanni Degli Agostini, *Notizie storico- critiche intorno alla vita e le opere degli Scrittori Veneziani*, II, Venice, 1754, 332-362 ◆ D. Kaufmann, "Jacob Mantino: Une page de l'histoire de la Renaissance", *Revue des études juives*, 27 (1893), 30-60, 207-238 ◆ U. Vicentini, "Francesco Zorzi e la

Palestina", *Le Venezie francescane* 19 (1952), 174-176 ♦ idem, "Jacopo Sansovino e Francesco Zorzi", *ibidem* 21 (1954), 33-51 ♦ idem, "Francesco Zorzi O.F.M. teologo cabbalista", *ibidem*, 21 (1954), 121-162, 174-214; *ibidem*, 24 (1957), 25-26 ♦ C. Vasoli, *Francesco Giorgio Veneto: Testi scelti*, in: E. Garin (ed.), *Testi umanistici sull'Ermetismo*, in: *Archivio di Filosofia*, 1955, 81-104 ♦ D.P. Walker, *Spiritual and Demonic Magic from Ficino to Campanella*, London, 1958 ♦ F. Secret, *Les kabbalistes chrétiens de la Renaissance*, Paris, 1964 (new ed., Milan-Paris, 1985), 126-140 ♦ idem, *Le Zôhar chez les kabbalistes chrétiens de la Renaissance*, Paris: The Hague, 1964, esp. 43-49 ♦ J.F. Maillard, "Le 'De Harmonia Mundi' de Georges de Venise: Aperçus sur la genèse et la structure de l'oeuvre", *Revue de l'Histoire des Religions* 179 (1971), 181-203 ♦ idem, "Aspects musicaux du 'De harmonia mundi' de Georges de Venise", *Revue de musicologie* 8 (1972), 162-75 ♦ idem, "Henry 8 et Georges de Venise: Documents sur l'affaire du divorce", *Revue de l'Histoire des Religions* 181 (1972), 157-186 ♦ D.P. Walker, *The Ancient Theology: Studies in Christian Platonism from the Fifteenth to the Eighteenth Century*, London, 1972 ♦ F. Secret, "Notes sur quelques kabbalistes chrétiens", *Bibliothèque d'Humanisme et Renaissance* 36 (1974), 71-74 ♦ C. Wirszubski, "Francesco Giorgio's Commentary on Giovanni Pico's Kabbalistic Theses", *Journal of the Warburg and Courtauld Institutes* 37 (1974), 145-156 ♦ F. Secret, "Franciscus Georgius Venetus et les 'Oracula chaldaica'", *Bibliothèque d'Humanisme et Renaissance* 26 (1974), 81-82 ♦ idem, "Franciscus Georgius Venetus et ses références à Proclus", *ibidem*, 78-81 ♦ J.F. Maillard, "Sous l'invocation de Dante et de Pic de la Mirandole: Les manuscrits inédits de Georges de Venise (Francesco Zorzi)", *ibidem*, 26 (1974), 47-61 ♦ C. Vasoli, *Profezia e ragione: Studi sulla cultura del Cinquecento e del Seicento*, Napoli, 1974, esp. 129-403 ♦ J.F. Maillard, "Science sacrée et science profane dans la tradition ésotérique de la Renaissance", *Cahiers de l'Université Saint-Jean de Jérusalem* I (1975), 329-347 ♦ G. Zanier, "Un frammento di Giulio Camillo Delminio su un poema italiano di Francesco Giorgio Veneto", *Giornale critico della filosofia italiana*, N. S. 30 (1976), 128-131 ♦ F.A. Yates, *The Occult Philosophy in the Elizabethan Age*, London, 1979, 29-36 ♦ M.T. Franco, "San Francesco della Vigna e Francesco Giorgi", in: L. Puppi (ed.), *Architettura e utopia nella Venezia del Cinquecento*, Milan, 1980, 410-411 ♦ C. Vasoli, "Vers la crise de l'hermétisme: le P. Mersenne et Fr. Zorzi", in: *L'Automne de la Renaissance*, Paris, 1981, 281-295 ♦ A. Rotondò, "Cultura umanistica e difficoltà di censori: Censura ecclesiastica e discussioni cinquecentesche sul platonismo", in: *Le pouvoir et la plume: Incitation, contrôle et répression dans l'Italie du XVIe siècle*, Paris, 1982, 15-50, esp. 15-33 ♦ L. Magagnato, *Istruzione e promemoria di Francesco Giorgio per S. Francesco della Vigna architettura di Jacopo Sansovino*, Milan, 1982 ♦ V. Perrone Compagni, "Una fonte di Cornelio Agrippa: il 'De harmonia mundi' di Francesco Giorgio Veneto", *Annali dell'Istituto di Filosofia dell'Università di Firenze* 4 (1982), 45-75 ♦ A. Foscari & M.A. Tafuri, *L'armonia e i conflitti:*

La Chiesa di San Francesco della Vigna nella Venezia del Cinquecento, Turin, 1983 ♦ J.F. Maillard, "L'harmonie universelle, de Georges de Venise à Marin Mersenne", in: *Musique et philosophie*, Dijon, 1985, 27-43 ♦ C. Vasoli, *Filosofia e religione nella cultura del Rinascimento*, Napoli, 1988, s.v. ♦ idem, "L'hermétisme à Venise, de Giorgio à Patrizi", in: A. Faivre (éd.), *Présence d'Hermès Trismégiste*, Paris, 1988, 120-152 ♦ L. Pierozzi, "Note su un inedito zorziano: Il 'Commento sopra il Poema' del R.P. fra Francesco Giorgio", *Rinascimento*, Ser. II, 37 (1987), 349-386 ♦ V. Marchetti, "Francesco Giorgio e la mistica del seme maschile", in: *Asmodeo* 1 (1989), 57-76 ♦ F. Bacchelli, "Di una lettera di Erasmo ed altri appunti da due codici bolognesi", *Rinascimento*, Ser. II, 30 (1990), 257-287 ♦ L. Pierozzi, "Intorno al 'Commento sopra il Poema' di Francesco Giorgio Veneto", *Rinascimento*, Ser. II, 30 (1990), 37-80 ♦ E. Scapparone, "Temi filosofici e religiosi nell''Elegante poema' di Francesco Giorgio Veneto", *Rivista di storia della filosofia* 45 (1990), 37-80 ♦ F. Secret, "L'originalité du *De occulta philosophia*", *Charis: Archives de l'Unicorne* 2 (1990), 57-87 ♦ G. Busi, "F. Zorzi, a methodical dreamer", in: J. Dan (ed.), *The Christian Kabbalah: Jewish Mystical Books and their Christian Interpreters*, Cambridge (Mass.), 1997, 97-125 ♦ S. Campanini, "Francesco Zorzi: Qabbalah cristiana e armonia del mondo", doctoral thesis, Turin, 1998 ♦ C. Vasoli, "L'ermetismo a Venezia da Francesco Giorgio ad Agostino Steuco", in: *L'ermetismo nell'antichità e nel Rinascimento*, Milan, 1998, 127-162 ♦ idem, "Il tema musicale e architettonico della 'Harmonia mundi', da Francesco Giorgio Veneto all'Accademia degli Uranici e a Gioseffo Zarlino" in: *Musica e storia* VI (1998), 193-210 ♦ idem, "Nuovi documenti sulla condanna all'Indice e la censura delle opere di Francesco Giorgio Veneto", in: *Censura ecclesiastica e cultura politica in: Italia tra Cinquecento e Seicento*, Florence, 2001, 55-78 ♦ idem, "Considerazioni sulla 'Prefatione o vero proemio' al 'Commento sopra il poema del Reverendo Padre fra Francesco Giorgio'", *Archiwum historii filozofii i myśli społeicznej* 47 (2002), 187-198.

CESARE VASOLI

Gnostic Church

The Gnostic Church (Église Gnostique), created in 1890 by Jules-Benoît Doinel (1842-1902), was born in the environment of modern → spiritualism and the → Theosophical Society. Doinel had for some years frequented esoteric and occultist circles, and, while practicing spiritualism, had attended the Swedenborgian Church [→ Swedenborgian Traditions]. In 1875 he met Léon Denis (1846-1927), for whom he would always have a great admiration. From 1882 to 1893 Doinel belonged to the sect of Guillaume Monod (1800-1896), a reformed minister who believed himself to be the new Christ, and gave lectures there which

Monod praised, considering Doinel to be his prophet, a reincarnation of Nehemias. Doinel's masonic career began in 1884. He was initiated Master in 1885 with the 'congratulations and encouragement' of Albert Pike (1809-1891). From 1886 to 1893 he was Orator of his Orléans lodge, and became its Worshipful Master in 1892. The following year, he attained the degree of Rose-Croix within the Parisian chapter "L'Étoile Polaire".

As far as the Gnostic Church is concerned, everything began as a result of a spiritualist séance held at the end of 1889 at Lady Caithness's (1832-1895). The circle of friends grouped around this lady was much concerned with spiritualism, on the one hand, and with ancient → gnosticism, on the other. During this particular séance, in which Doinel participated, the "spirit" of Guilhabert de Castres, former Bishop of Montségur, manifested to demand the creation, or re-creation, of a "Gnostic Church". Doinel became convinced that he had received a "gnostic investiture" on this occasion, and was indeed the elect appointed to head this church, which he called Nouvelle Église Gnostique Universelle (New Universal Gnostic Church). It was primarily a matter of giving new life to ancient gnosticism, broadly understood (not only → Valentinus, but also personages such as Apollonius of Tyana and → Simon Magus, and even Origen, figure as authorities here). After founding his church, Doinel consecrated its bishops, including → Papus (1865-1916). Then he joined Papus's Martinist Order [→ Martinism: Second Period], and became a member of its Supreme Council.

The goal of the Gnostic Church was to create a spiritual and elitist → Freemasonry under the sign of Gnosis. In his study of the Gnostic Church, René Le Forestier has emphasized one of its particularities, viz. that its directors wished to teach an elite: 'while the postulates of the gnostic doctrines and the dogmas of the Cathar religion had been made known to all the discipes and catechumens, . . . it was quite different with the new Gnostic Church, where the three orders of the faithful were like masonic "degrees"' (Le Forestier 1990, 50-51). A bridge was in fact established with the lodges of the Scottish Rite, thanks to the "Ordre des chevaliers faydits [the name given to the Cathar lords] de la Colombe du Paraclet", which was an imitation of a Templar Masonic System (or "Rite"), known as the Strict Observance. 'Only knights should belong to Gnosis, to Martinism, and to Kabbalah'; their password *Ad Spiritum per Helenam* 'was most significant, and the Order de la Colombe du Paraclet, creation of the Gnostic Church, was fortunate in attracting to the latter the attention of enthusiasts for the occult sciences, and bringing it proselytes' (ibid., 56-57). The ties between the Gnostic Church and Freemasonry would never be broken.

The adherence of the leaders of the Gnostic Church to the Martinist Order was a constant. This was notably the case with Doinel's successor, Synésius (Léonce Fabre des Essarts, 1848-1917), as with the neo-gnostic bishops Théophane (Léon Champrenaud, 1870-1925) and Simon (Albert de Pouvourville, 1861-1940). These last two published the periodical *La Voie* (1904-1907), and, in 1907, *Les Enseignements secrets de la Gnose* (The secret teachings of gnosis). The same adherence applied (1909-1912) to Palingenius (→ René Guénon, 1886-1951).

Doinel presided over the Très Haut Synode, i.e. the group of "bishops" who were at the head of this Gnostic Church. We have very little information on this synod's activity. Le Forestier states that within it a 'council of members of the third degree' practiced a ritual of magical character that was in favor in certain occult Orders, notably the → Élus Coëns. Doinel presided over the synod for the last time in September, 1894. At this point, in fact, he broke with his church, going so far as to denigrate it in a book that appeared in the same year (under the pseudonym of Jean Kostka), *Lucifer démasqué* (Lucifer unmasked). Yet he re-joined it at the end of his life, then holding only the simple title of bishop.

Another organization was in liaison with the Gnostic Church, thanks to → François-Charles Barlet (Albert Faucheux): the → Hermetic Brotherhood of Luxor, defined by Guénon in the review *La Gnose*, its organ, as 'one of the rare serious initiatic fraternities that currently still exist in the West' and as 'foreign to any occultist movement' (*La Gnose*, no. of November 1911). René Guénon's entrance onto the stage marked the rejection, at the heart of the Gnostic Church, of sympathy and complicity with spiritualist and reincarnationist theories. Guénon's contributions to the review *La Gnose* were his first writings, in which the seeds of his future work were already present. He there declared expressly the continuity of the lineage of Doinel, announced the publication of 'all that we have been able to collect of the printed or unpublished writings of Jules Doinel (T Valentin), who was the Restorer of Gnosis in the 19th century' (*La Gnose*, no. 1, November 1909, p. 2), and reaffirmed 'the bonds that have always united Gnosticism and Masonry, bonds which we will demonstrate all the better by reproducing some masonic discourses (already published some time before in *La Chaîne d'Union* by F. Jules Doinel [T Valentin], who was simultaneously Patriarch of the

Gnostic Church and member of the Council of the Order of the Grand Orient of France' (*La Gnose*, no. 5, March 1910, 84).

Another of the bishops consecrated by Doinel, Bardesane (Lucien Mauchel/Chamuel [1867-1936]), elected president of the Holy Synod of the Gnostic Church in 1932, extended his authority in 1934 over the Supreme Council of the Ordre Kabbalistique de la Rose-Croix. The delegate of this order to the Brussels Convention was Frère Yesir (Victor Blanchard, 1877-1953), incidentally head of the Ordre Martiniste Synarchique and of the Fraternité des Polaires, and also delegate of the Ordre Kabbalistique de la Rose-Croix de France, instituted by F. Jollivet-Castelot. At this convention, Blanchard, alias Yesir, became Imperator d'Orient, i.e. one of the three elected Emperors of the F.U.D.O.S.I. (Federatio Universalis Dirigens Omnes Ordines Societatesque Initiationis [Universal Federation Directing All Orders and Societies of Initiation]). After Doinel's departure, Fabre des Essarts took over leadership of the Gnostic Church but was faced with a secession, that of the bishop-primate of Lyon, Johannès, pseudonym of Jean/Joanny Bricaud (1881-1934).

Bricaud had already trodden a long path through the occultist milieu (Masonry, Martinism, Vintras's Church of Carmel, the Johannite Church, the Chaldeo-Latin Church) and had frequented → Maître Philippe of Lyon. In 1908, Bricaud held at Lyon the Holy Synod, which raised him to the patriarchal throne under the name of John II. He was then initiated into the Ancient and Primitive Rite of Memphis-Misraïm. In 1911 he signed, with Papus, the treaty that made the Église Gnostique Universelle the official church of the Martinist Order (along with the Gallican Church of France). Wishing to reserve initiation for an elite, he took Freemasonry as the model, 'raising the number of gnostic degrees to 33'. Very ambitious, Bricaud entered into relations with the occultist circles of Europe and the United States, and allied himself with the heads of the principal dissident organizations of the Roman church. In 1912, he instituted the "Gnostic Legates", and many personalities of the occult world received this title. Thus Charles Détré/Téder (1855-1918) became Legate for England, Spain, and the British colonies; Dr. Krauss (Grand Master of the Samaritains Inconnus), Legate for Bavaria; the famous → Theodor Reuss (Grand Master General of the → Ordo Templi Orientis and of the Ancient and Primitive Oriental Order of Memphis-Misraïm), Legate for Switzerland. The ties between the latter and Bricaud are easy to understand: Bricaud had a great admiration

for Vintras, and valued the form of sexual magic sanctioned by the latter. Theodor Reuss, co-founder with Carl Kellner of the O.T.O., became Sovereign Patriarch and Primate of the E.G.C. (Ecclesia Gnostica Catholica), and in 1918 published a "Gnostic Mass" written by → Aleister Crowley.

Upon Détré's death, Bricaud became head simultaneously of the Ancient and Primitive Rite of Memphis-Misraïm, the Martinist Order, and the Rose-Croix Kabbalistique et Gnostique. His successor Constant Chevillon (T Harmonius, 1880-1944) took over the headship of these organizations. Chevillon allied himself with Reuben Swinburne Clymer (1878-1966) and his Rosicrucian order, rival to the A.M.O.R.C. – the Rosicrucian order created by → Harvey Spencer Lewis (1883-1939) – and belonged to the F.U.D.O.F.S.I. (Fédération Universelle des Ordres Fraternités et Sociétés Initiatiques [Universal Federation of Initiatic Orders, Fraternities, and Societies]).

After the tragic death of Chevillon in 1944, the Église Gnostique Universelle was successively headed by Antoine Fayolle (T Marcos), in 1948 by Charles-Henry Dupont (T Charles-Henry, 1877-1960), and finally in 1960 by Robert Ambelain (T Jean III). The latter, head of the Martinist Order, "put to sleep" the Église Gnostique Universelle, transferring his activities to his own Église Gnostique Apostolique, founded in 1958.

J. Doinel, "Études gnostiques", *L'Initiation*, series of articles Feb. 1890 – Mar. 1893, reprinted in *Études gnostiques*, Paris: Cariscript, 1983 ♦ Jean Kostka (J. Doinel), *Lucifer démasqué*, Paris & Lyon: Delhomme & Briguet, 1895; Geneva & Paris: reprint Slatkine, 1983 ♦ Synésius (L. Fabre des Essarts), "Mandement de S.G. Synésius, Primat de l'Albigeois, évêque de Montségur, à l'occasion de son élévation aux fonctions primatiales", *Le Voile d'Isis* 186, Jan. 16, 1896 ♦ L. Fabre des Essarts, "Hymnes gnostiques", *L'Initiation* July, Dec. 1896 ♦ idem, "Les martyrs de la Gnose: Hypatie", *L'Initiation* May, June 1897 ♦ idem, "La Sainte Gnose en France: L'inscription d'Autun", *L'Initiation*, Sep. 1897 ♦ Synésius (L. Fabre des Essarts), *L'Arbre Gnostique*, Paris: Chamuel, 1899 ♦ Sophronius, Évêque de Béziers (L.S. Fugairon), *Catéchisme expliqué de l'Église Gnostique*, Paris: Chamuel, 1899-1900 (3 fascicules) ♦ J. Doinel, *Hymnarium gnosticum oratorii Electensis et Mirapiscencis dioceseos. . . .*, Carcassonne: G. Servière, 1901 ♦ L. Fabre des Essarts, *Les Hiérophantes: Étude sur les fondateurs de religions depuis la Révolution jusqu'à nos jours*, Paris: Chacornac, 1905 ♦ idem, *Sadisme, Satanisme et Gnose*, Paris: Bodin, 1906 ♦ J. Bricaud, *Catéchisme Gnostique: À l'usage des fidèles de l'Eglise Catholique Gnostique*, Lyon: Ed. du Réveil Gnostique: 1907 ♦ Simon-Théophane (L. Champrenaud & A. de Pouvourville), *Les Enseignements secrets de la Gnose*,

Avec des notes documentaires par Synésius, Société des Éditions Contemporaines – Paris: Lucien Bodin, 1907; Milan: reprinted Archè, 1999 ♦ Palingénius (René Guénon), articles in *La Gnose* Nov. 1909 – Feb. 1912 ♦ S.J. Esclarmonde (M. Chauvel de Chauvigny), *Bref exposé de la Doctrine Gnostique*, Paris: Fernand Drubay, 1913 ♦ C. Chevillon: *La Gnose de Constant Chevillon: La Tradition Universelle – Du néant à l'Être – Et Verbum caro factum est*, Paris: Éditions Traditionnelles, 1982 ♦ For a more complete documentation of the sources, see the periodicals *La Voie*, Paris: Diffusion L. Bodin, 1904-1907 (of which Perlector, in *Charis: Archives de l'Unicorne* 2 [1990], has made a review and an almost exhaustive anthology), *Le Réveil Gnostique* (1907-1914), and *La Gnose* (1909-1912).

Lit.: R. Amadou, "L'Église Gnostique: Histoire, Doctrines, Rites", in: *L'Autre Monde*, 1982 (May)-1983 (Jan.) ♦ idem, "Jules Doinel et la Franc-Maçonnerie", in: *Chroniques d'Histoire Maçonnique (Institut d'Études et de Recherches Maçonniques)*, supplement to *Humanisme* 33 (1984) ♦ J. Bois, *Les Petites églises de Paris*, Paris: Le Challey, 1894 ♦ J.P. Bonnerot, "Un aventurier de la Gnose occidentale: Jules Doinel", *Le Monde Inconnu* 1 (Dec. 1979) ♦ idem, "Déodat Roché et l'Église Gnostique", special number of *Cahiers d'Études Cathares*, 2nd series, 4:5 (1982) ♦ idem, "Constant Chevillon (1880-1944) philosophe et martyr: Sa vie, son oeuvre", special number of *L'Initiation* (1980) ♦ K.R.H. Frick, *Licht und Finsternis: Gnostisch-theosophische und freimaurerisch-okkulte Geheimgesellschaften bis an die Wende zum 20. Jahrhundert*, Graz: Akademische Druck- und Verlagsanstalt, 1978, vol. 2, 336-344 ♦ P. Geyraud (= R. Guyader), *Les Religions Nouvelles de Paris*, Paris: Émile-Paul Frères, 1937 ♦ idem, *Parmi les sectes et les rites: Les Petites Églises de Paris*, Paris: Émile-Paul Frères, 1937 ♦ idem, *Parmi les sectes et les rites: Les Sociétés Secrètes de Paris*, Paris: Émile-Paul Frères, 1939 ♦ M. Introvigne, *Il ritorno dello gnosticismo*, Carnago: Sugar Co Edizioni, 1993, 96-125, 126-148, 149-202 ♦ P.R. König, "Das OTO-Phänomen (12): Die Wandernden Bischöfe", *AHA*, vol. 4, 11, Nov. 1991 ♦ idem (ed.), *Der kleine Theodor-Reuss Reader*, Munich: Arbeitsgemeinschaft für Religions und Weltanschauungsfragen, 1993 ♦ R. Le Forestier, *L'Occultisme en France aux XIXᵉ et XXᵉ siècles: L'Église gnostique* (A. Faivre, ed. avec une ample anthologie de textes néo-gnostiques de J. Doinel, L. Fabre des Essarts, L.S. Fugairon, Paul Sédir, R. Guénon, M. Chauvel de Chauvigny et une étude complémentaire par E. Mazzolari), Milan: Archè, 1990 ♦ G. Marie, "La Voie royale de Constant Chevillon", *ARIES* 6 (1987), 27-34 ♦ A. Pédron, "Qu'est-ce l'Église Gnostique? Entretien avec T Jacques", *L'Initiation* 3, Paris: A.E.I.-OCIA, 1978 ♦ V. Soro, *La Chiesa del Paracleto: Studi sullo gnosticismo*, Todi: Atanor, 1922.

LADISLAUS TOTH

Gnosticism I: Gnostic Religion

1. The PROBLEM OF DEFINITION
2. GNOSTIC VIEWS (A. GOD AND THE DIVINE WORLD   B. FALL AND CREATION   C. SALVATION   D. ETHICS) 3. BACKGROUNDS AND RELATIONSHIPS (A. JUDAISM   B. GREEK PHILOSOPHY   C. HERMETISM   D. CHRISTIANITY) 4. CONCLUSION

1. THE PROBLEM OF DEFINITION

The term "Gnosticism" is a scholarly invention, coined by the Cambridge Platonist → Henry More (1614-1687), who used it in a pejorative sense (Layton 1995). In Antiquity, the religious phenomenon it designates was simply called "Gnosis" (Gr. *gnōsis*, "knowledge") or, by its opponents, "the Gnosis falsely so called" (already in 1 Timothy 6:20). In this connection, the word Gnosis does not refer to rational, philosophical knowledge, but to religious, spiritual insight, based on revelation. From the beginning, the modern word Gnosticism has been used in particular to indicate a special brand of Gnosis that flourished in the 2nd and 3rd centuries and was vehemently combated by several early Christian writers because of its "heretical" doctrine of creation and salvation. But even in this limited sense, it proved increasingly difficult to exactly determine its characterizing features, especially after the discovery of the Nag Hammadi Library (→ Gnosticism II). Especially in German scholarship, the words "Gnosis" and "Gnosticism" have always been used indiscriminately to indicate both the great Gnostic systems of the 2nd and 3rd centuries and the more general spiritual current they belonged to. The English-speaking world preferentially used the word "Gnosticism". The terminological obscurity was further complicated by the fact that, under the influence of early Christian anti-heretical literature, the adjective "Gnostic" was – as it still is – used almost exclusively to refer to the "Gnosticism" considered heretical by the church fathers, which gave the term a pejorative meaning. Not without reason, A.D. Nock, in his review of the first volume of Jonas's now classic *Gnosis und spätantiker Geist*, exclaimed: 'I am left in a terminological fog' (I, 444). To create more clarity on this point, the primary objective of the first great colloquium on Gnosticism, held in Messina in 1966, was to establish generally accepted definitions of the terms "Gnosis" and "Gnosticism". The final document of this colloquium (in Italian, French, English and German) was a 'Proposal for a Terminological and

Conceptual Agreement with regard to the theme of the Colloquium' (Bianchi, XXVI-XXIX, English version). It proposed to reserve the term "Gnosticism" for the movement that began 'with a certain group of systems of the Second Century A.D.' and to regard "Gnosis" as 'knowledge of the divine mysteries reserved for an élite', i.e. of an esoteric kind. The characteristics of Gnosticism 'can be summarized in the idea of a divine spark in man, deriving from the divine realm, fallen into this world of fate, birth and death, and needing to be awakened by the divine counterpart of the self in order to be finally reintegrated'. The proposal emphasized: 'Not every *Gnosis* is Gnosticism, but only that which involves . . . the idea of the divine consubstantiality of the spark that is in need of being awakened and reintegrated. This *Gnosis* of Gnosticism involves the divine identity of the *knower* (the Gnostic), the *known* (the divine substance of one's transcendent self) and the *means by which one knows* (*Gnosis* as an implicit divine faculty that is to be awakened and actualized)'. As was to be expected, the Messina definitions did not receive unanimous scholarly approval, for the description of the *Gnosis* of Gnosticism could also be applied to currents that certainly did not fit the proposed definition of Gnosticism. To mention only one influential scholar, Kurt Rudolph almost immediately (1967) rejected the separation between Gnosis and Gnosticism. In accordance with the German scholarly tradition, he continued to use both terms for the religion of salvation through Gnosis that flourished in the first centuries of our era, but later on (1985) he preferred the term Gnosis and advised to eliminate the term Gnosticism 'as far as possible, since it is not only pejorative, but also confusing' (Rudolph 1996, 34-52 [1985], 144-148 [1967]). The term Gnosticism was completely discredited by Michael Williams in his *Rethinking "Gnosticism": An Argument for Dismantling a Dubious Category* (1996). Based on a solid knowledge of the primary and secondary sources, his book contains a massive attack on what is usually understood by the terms "Gnostic", "Gnosis", "Gnosticism" and "Gnostic Religion". He rightly argues that there never existed one clearly definable religious system that could be called Gnosticism. He shows that many texts that are commonly thought to represent the "Gnostic religion" do not contain the characteristics usually ascribed to it (separation between the supreme God and the Creator, protest exegesis, anti-cosmic world rejection, hatred of the body, Gnostic ethics as either libertinist or ascetic, etc.). In his view,

terms such as "Gnosis" and "Gnostic" are so vague that they have lost any specific meaning and, therefore, should be avoided. Of course, even Williams could not deny that a number of 2nd-century texts unquestionably show the existence of a group of related and more or less coherent systems that together are usually, as in Messina, labelled "Gnosticism". The dominant idea in these systems is the assumption that the world has not been created by the supreme transcendent God, but by a lower, imperfect and even bad Demiurge, who is identified with the God of the Jews (see below). Williams proposed to speak in this connection of "biblical demiurgical" texts and traditions; but this new terminology does not bring us much further, for one still needs to specify what kind of biblical demiurgical texts and traditions are meant, that is to say, those that through a specific interpretation of biblical myths proclaim that salvation is only possible through *Gnosis*, i.e. an esoteric knowledge of the origin and destination of one's inner self.

From the above it may have become clear that an unambiguous definition of what is understood by the much-used terms "Gnosis", "Gnosticism" and "Gnostic" is impossible; but nevertheless some degree of clarification is necessary. It is undeniable that there existed in Antiquity a broad and variegated religious current characterized by a strong emphasis on esoteric knowledge (Gnosis) as the only means of salvation, which implied the return to one's divine origin. This religious current can best be referred to as the "Gnostic Movement" or "Gnostic religiosity". The great Gnostic systems of the 2nd and 3rd centuries are integral parts of this broader Gnostic movement and should not be isolated from it. The main characteristic of these systems is that their central ideas are expressed in myths, which may vary from one system to another, but as a whole display strong similarities. For that reason, and to maintain the link with the Gnostic current in general, it is preferable to speak here of mythological Gnostic texts or systems. The term "Gnosticism", if used at all, should be reserved for these more or less coherent expressions of mythological Gnosis. The people who believed and proclaimed that salvation is possible only through revealed, secret Gnosis should be called "Gnostics", i.e. "those who know". There were Gnostics who used this term as a self-designation, for instance the followers of → Prodicus and the people referred to in Irenaeus, *Adversus haereses*, I, 29 (Smith). The emphasis on secrecy alone is not decisive to label an idea or a system as Gnostic: in Greek philosophy (Pythagoreanism and Platonism) as well as in Alexandrian Christian theology (the *Sentences of Sextus*, → Clement of Alexandria, Origen, and the *Teachings of Silvanus*), there was a strong tendency to maintain secrecy about some central doctrines or mysteries (van den Broek 1996, 264-270), but nobody would classify these doctrines as "Gnostic" and their adherents as "Gnostics". Rather, the decisive criterion for designating an idea or text as Gnostic is whether or not it involves a concept of knowledge that considers Gnosis the indispensable means of salvation, indeed salvation itself. In this sense, the esoteric *Gospel of Thomas* can be labelled Gnostic, even though it shows no traces of mythological Gnosis. On the other hand, Clement of Alexandria, who always speaks of his ideal Christian as "the true Gnostic", cannot be called a Gnostic, because he declared simple faith alone sufficient for salvation. The Gnostic knows of his divine origin and destination. According to the second-century Christian Gnostic Theodotus, Gnosis is the knowledge of 'who we were and what we have become, where we were and into what we have been thrown, whither we hasten and from what we are redeemed, what is birth and what rebirth' (Clement of Alexandria, *Excerpts from Theodotus*, 78, 2). The central Gnostic idea of revealed, secret Gnosis as a gift that illuminates and liberates man's inner self is found in all periods, as is abundantly shown by the present Dictionary. For that reason, the terms "Gnosis" and "Gnostic" are applicable to all ideas and currents, from Antiquity to the present day, that stress the necessity of esoteric knowledge. The term "Gnosticism", however, should be used with respect to the Gnostic systems of Antiquity only.

2. GNOSTIC VIEWS

The Gnostic ideas of Antiquity display such an enormous variety that it is impossible to reduce them to one coherent system. However, there is a certain set of views that can be considered characteristic of the Gnostic movement, even if most of them also occur in contexts that are not Gnostic at all. To this kernel of Gnostic thought belongs the idea of a completely transcendent God, who produces a divine world, to which the human being's inner self originally belonged. Through a tragic course of events, which is often more implied than openly exposed, man became separated from his divine origin, which made him forget his high descent. Return to his place of origin is only possible though Gnosis, which in some way or another is imparted to him through revelation.

A. GOD AND THE DIVINE WORLD

The starting point of all Gnostic theology, both in its mythological and its more speculative form, is the idea of God's absolute transcendence. In a number of texts, this idea is expressed in the same terminology of negative theology that was also used by pagan philosophers and hermetists as well as by Christian theologians. God is ineffable, invisible, unbegotten, incomprehensible, immeasurable, incorruptible, unnameable, etc. Long enumerations of these negative qualifications of God are, for instance, found at the beginning of the *Apocryphon of John* (NHC II, 1), the *Tractatus Tripartitus* (NHC I, 5), and *Eugnostus the Blessed* (NHC III, 1 and V, 1). The negative theology of the Gnostics went even further than that of the Greek philosophers and most Christian theologians. The latter held that God, although unknowable in his essence, could at least partially be comprehended by the human mind (*nous*), through philosophical reasoning and contemplation of the cosmic order; but the Gnostics denied this and declared knowledge of God to be possible only through revelation.

A central theme of Hellenistic philosophy was the relationship between the One and the Many, the Monad and the infinite Dyad. In these speculations, the One was always identified with the Good, whereas evil somehow arose from the principle of duality and multiplicity, mostly associated with matter. The Middle Platonists preferred a triad of basic principles of the universe, which could be described differently by the individual philosophers (Dillon). The first principle was mostly seen as Mind, but sometimes it was thought to be above Mind and Being; in that case the second principle was considered Mind. The Platonic ideas, which formed the patterns of visible reality, were conceived of as the thoughts of God and, accordingly, located either in the first or the second principle. The third principle was often identified with primal, formless matter, which by receiving the imprints of the ideas became the created world. A detailed discussion of the complicated Middle Platonist views on the first principles of being is impossible in the present context. May it suffice to say that the Gnostic authors, who often show themselves to be rather well educated, almost inevitably made use of these philosophical speculations to express their fundamentally religious ideas. In many Gnostic systems, a triad of divine hypostases constitutes the apex of the divine world. Most of those described by Hippolytus start from three basic principles of the universe, *inter alia* → Justin the Gnostic, the →

Naasssenes, the → Perates, and the → Sethians. The Perates distinguished between the Unbegotten (*agennēton*), the Self-begotten (*autogenes*) and the Begotten (*gennēton*), which are also described as the Father, the Son and Matter (Hippolytus, *Refutatio* V, 17,1). A similar terminology is found in the *Discourse on the Ogdoad and the Ennead* (NHC VI, 57, 13-18; 63-21-23), in the Naassene system, and partly also in *Eugnostus the Blessed* (NHC III, 72, 22; 75, 6-7). The *Paraphrase of Shem* says of 'the great powers that were in existence in the beginning': 'There was Light and Darkness and there was Spirit between them' (NHC VII, 1, 25-28; the same principles occur in the Sethian system according to Hippolytus, *Refutatio* V, 19).

There is, however, an important difference between the Middle- and Neoplatonist ideas on the principles of the universe and those of the Gnostics. The latter assumed a much greater number of levels of being than the philosophers were prepared to accept. In the middle of the third century, this led to a conflict in the school of Plotinus, which was also frequented by Gnostics. In his *Against the Gnostics* (*Enneads* II, 9), Plotinus rejected the Gnostic introduction of a great number of other hypostases within and outside the three basic principles he acknowledged himself (the One, Mind and Soul). This switch from philosophical reasoning to religious mythology is clearly to be seen in *Zostrianus* (NHC VIII, 1), which Plotinus' pupil Amelius, at the master's instigation, refuted in no less than forty books (Porphyry, *Life of Plotinus*, 16). Especially the mythological Gnostic texts and systems abound in a cascade of divine entities down from the summit of Being, but both the direct and the indirect sources show that there were great differences at this point, which led to quite different pictures of the structure of the divine world. Some Gnostic texts do mention these lower entities, sometimes even by name, but without further information about their origin and mutual relationship.

The divine realm as a whole is mostly called the *Pleroma* ("Fullness"), and described as constituted of a variety of divine qualities and attributes, called *aeons*. These aeons successively develop out of God, which means that the development of the Pleroma in fact represents the self-realization of the ineffable God. The Gnostic mythological texts show a great variety of aeons and their interrelations, but some aeonic systems exerted a particular influence, especially those of the "Gnostics" behind the *Apocryphon of John* and the Valentinians (→ Valentinus and Valentinians). There were

Gnostics who indulged almost exclusively in endless speculations about the structure of the divine world. The most bewildering example of this is to be found in the *Books of Jeû* and the *Untitled Treatise* of the Bruce Codex.

Before discussing some aspects of the development of the Pleroma, a clarification of the concept of aeon may be in order. The Greek word *aiōn* means "(a long space of) time", "age", and in plural "eternity" (e.g. Romans 16:27: 'until the aeons [of aeons]'). In the Hellenistic world, infinite Time was honoured as a God under the name of Aion, especially in Alexandria. From the meaning "age" the word aeon also evolved into another word for "world" (e.g. Matthew 12:32: 'this aeon' versus the 'the coming aeon'). In some early Christian texts, God is called 'the King of the aeons' (1 Timothy 1:17), who through his Son has created the aeons (Hebrews 1:2), so that Clement of Rome (ca. 95 A.D.), in his *Letter to the Corinthians*, 35, 3, could speak about God as 'the Creator and Father of the aeons'. The exact meaning of these expressions is a matter for dispute, but it will be clear that they could easily be interpreted in a Gnostic sense. For a correct understanding of the Gnostic concept of aeons it should be realized that, just like the Pleroma as a whole, the Gnostic aeons have a distinct spatial aspect. That explains why, for instance, it is said in the *Apocryphon of John* that the race of Seth and other Gnostics are placed in specific aeons (BG 36, 1-15 parr. = Synopsis 22, 18-23, 12), and also why in the *Gospel of Truth* the aeons are often called "spaces", which are emanations of the Father (NHC I, 27, 11). The aeons are aspects of the ineffable God, but at the same time they are also forms of time and space. There may be an influence here of Greek interpretations of the Persian Zervan Akarana, the Unbegotten Time, from which the opposed gods Ormuzd and Ahriman have come forth: according to Eudemus of Rhodos (4th century B.C.) this primal principle was called both "Place" and "Time" (Frg. 150, ed. Wehrli, VIII, 71). Although there are clear similarities, the aeons differ from other → intermediary beings because of their often artificial nature (personified abstract concepts) and their functions.

As said above, the development of the Pleroma is the self-realization of God: the Unknown Father becomes conscious of himself. A well-known description of this development is that of the *Apocryphon of John*, which has a close and more original parallel in Irenaeus, *Adversus haereses* I, 29, and partly also in the *Gospel of the Egyptians*.

Other interesting pleromatic structures are those of *Eugnostus the Blessed* and the Valentinians (Irenaeus, *AH* I, 1). According to the *Apocryphon*, the Unknown Father saw himself reflected in the light-water that surrounded him, he recognized himself, and immediately his thought became an independent female entity, called Ennoia ("Thought"), who is also called Barbelo. The Father and Barbelo generate the Light, who is also called Autogenes and identified with Christ (probably a secondary addition). Then this original trinity of Father, Mother and Son expands into the spiritual, divine world of the Pleroma. The Father adds to Barbelo the aeons Prognōsis ("Foreknowledge"), Aphtharsia ("Incorruptibility") and Aeōnia Zōē ("Eternal Life"), and to the Light (Christ) he adds the aeons Nous ("Mind"), Thelēma ("Will"), and Logos ("Word"). These two tetrads are then combined into an ogdoad that consists of four pairs, which generate a number of other aeons, which in their turn do the same. The identification of the aeons with abstract concepts that together form the Fullness of God shows that this myth of the development of the Pleroma is of a clearly artificial character. Just as in the *Apocryphon of John*, the top of the Valentinian Pleroma is formed by an ogdoad that also consists of four pairs of aeons. The first pair consists of the Unknown Father, called Bythos ("Depth"), and his Ennoia ("Thought"), also called Charis ("Grace") and Sigē ("Silence"). They generate the second level of divine being: Nous ("Mind") and Aletheia ("Truth"), which produce the third level: Logos ("Word") and Zoē ("Life"), which in their turn bring forth Anthropos ("Man") and Ecclesia ("Church"). In the myth of the *Apocryphon of John* and Irenaeus, *AH* I, 29, the coming forth of the Anthropos, 'the perfect and true Man', also called Adamas, is narrated at the end of the section on the Pleroma. But in both texts the last aeon is called Sophia ("Wisdom"), who becomes responsible for the split in the Pleroma and the origin of evil and, as a corollary, the creation of the world. The insertion of many aeons between the Unknown Father and Sophia was apparently intended to make the distance between the transcendent God and the cause of evil as great as possible.

There are strong indications, however, that the complicated Gnostic myths of the Pleroma developed out of a much simpler model, which was more mythological and presented Anthropos and Sophia as the first manifestations of the transcendent God. According to *Eugnostus the Blessed*, the 'self-grown, self-created Father' conceived the idea of having 'his likeness come into being', and 'immediately the beginning of that Light manifested itself as an immortal androgynous Man' (NHC III, 76, 14-24). His female aspect is *inter alia* called 'All-wise Begettress Sophia' (III, 3-4). Immortal Man and his Sophia put forth another androgynous Man, called the Son of Man, whose female aspect is also called Sophia. This pair generates a third androgynous Man, the Son of the Son of Man, whose female name is again Sophia. In other Gnostic systems, too, the first principles are called Man and the Son of Man, for instance in those of → Monoimus, the Naassenes, and Irenaeus *AH*, I, 30, which is presupposed in the second part of the *Apocryphon of John* (see below). In Eugnostus, the addition of the second and third pairs is an obvious amplification of an originally more simple myth that only knew of one Anthropos and Sophia (Schenke 1962 [2]). The figures of Anthropos and Sophia derive from Jewish speculations about the first manifestations of God that were based on biblical texts. Wisdom herself says, in Proverbs 8:22, 'The Lord created me *the beginning* of his ways, before all else he made, long ago', which led to the idea of Wisdom as the creative agent of God: in Genesis 1:1 the words "in the beginning" were accordingly interpreted as "through Wisdom". In Wisdom of Solomon 7:25, Wisdom is described as an emanation of God, 'a pure effluence from the glory of the Almighty, . . . the reflection of everlasting light'. Speculations on the manifestation of God as a heavenly Man were triggered off by Ezekiel 1:26-28, which describes a vision of the Glory of God in 'the likeness as the appearance of a man' (King James Version), appearing in fire and light. The figure of a heavenly Man as manifestation of the transcendent God has had an enormous influence in Judaism, → Hermetism (*Poimandres*), and Gnostic and non-Gnostic Christianity. The attribution of a human shape to the radiant manifestation of God's Glory caused the heavenly Anthropos to be always associated with Light. The Jewish Alexandrian writer Ezekiel the Dramatist (2nd century B.C.) describes in his *Exodus*, 66-89, a vision by → Moses of a man (Gr. *phōs*, with another accentuation also "light"), who sat on a throne, with a diadem on his head and a sceptre in his left hand. Before the man – who is apparently God's viceregent on earth – disappears, he summons Moses to sit down on the throne and accept the *regalia*, which makes him a divine being. The association of Heavenly Man with light played an important role in Gnostic speculations about the first manifestation of God.

According to *On the Origin of the World*, NHC II, 107, 25-108, 14, the Demiurge became aware that 'an immortal Man of Light had been existing before him', which refers to the primeval light of Genesis 1:3 ('Let there be light!'). At the Demiurge's request, the radiant light manifested itself: 'As that light appeared, a likeness of Man, which was very marvellous, revealed itself in it'. The association with Genesis 1:3 (Light) and Ezekiel 1:26 (likeness of a man) is clearly visible not only in this text, but also in that of *Eugnostus the Blessed* (NHC III, 76, 14 ff.), quoted above (Fossum 1985, 266-291).

It is of interest to note that *Eugnostus* not only describes the apex of the divine world in terms of the Jewish myth of Anthropos and Sophia, but also in those of Platonic philosophy. Immortal Man is identified with Nous ("Mind"; NHC V, 6, 6-7; cf. III, 104, 8) and Sophia with Alētheia ("Truth"; NHC III, 77, 3-10; V, 6, 8-10). According to Plato, Nous and Aletheia are noetic entities produced by the Good (*Republic*, 517b; cf. also 490b). Plato already placed the Good above Mind and Being and, accordingly, the Middle Platonists identified the Good with the supreme, ineffable God. Read with the eyes of a second-century Platonist, the master himself had taught in the *Republic* that the unknowable, transcendent God puts forth two noetic entities, Nous and Aletheia. The author of *Eugnostus the Blessed* apparently knew a tradition that identified the transcendent Jewish God with the Good of Platonism, and the latter's first products, Nous and Aletheia, with the former's pre-eminent divine hypostases, Anthropos and Sophia. In the Valentinian myth of the Pleroma, Nous and Aletheia also form the second level of being, but there are some considerable differences with the tradition of *Eugnostus*, which make it probable that the priority belongs to the latter. In *Eugnostus*, the supreme, ineffable God is strictly monadic; the principle of androgynous duality is first expressed in Immortal Man and his Sophia. It is to such a conception that Plato's view of the Good as producing Nous and Aletheia could be applied. In the Valentinian system, the principle of duality and fecundity was transferred to the deepest ground of being itself, by changing its monadic essence into Bythos and Sige, Depth ands Silence (though there were Valentinians who adhered to a more monadic view of the supreme God). The Valentinian Pleroma seems ultimately based on speculations on the structure of the divine world that were closely related to those expressed in *Eugnostus the Blessed* (van den Broek 1996, 122-129).

B. FALL AND CREATION

That the human soul, or at least its higher part, was of divine origin, had somehow fallen into its earthly existence, and had to strive for its return to heaven, was a common idea in the Graeco-Roman world. It had been an integral part of Platonic philosophy since Plato's *Phaedrus*. While the Gnostic view of the origin and destination of one's inner self fits this general scheme, its elaboration was not philosophical but religious and mythological, even if use was made of philosophical categories. An important difference between the philosophical and the Gnostic views in this regard is that the Gnostics assumed a pre-cosmic Fall, which had taken place within the divine Pleroma. In many Gnostic texts this Fall is not mentioned or only vaguely hinted at: they concentrate on the bondage of human beings to the evil powers that dominate our world, and on the way to escape from it. The Gnostic, i.e. esoteric, character of these texts is apparent above all from their emphasis on revealed knowledge as the decisive means of salvation. But other writings, especially those that belong to the great systems of the 2nd century, present a full account of how evil originated within the divine Pleroma and eventually led to the creation of the material world and the body as the prison of man's real self (Dahl, Logan, van der Vliet). However, in this regard too, a clear Gnostic doctrine did not exist; there were only variations on a common theme, namely that of a fatal rupture within the Pleroma.

According to the basic text of Gnostic mythology, the *Apocryphon of John*, the split in the deity was caused by the lowest aeon, Sophia (BG 36, 16-47, 13 parr. = Synopsis 24, 1-37, 5). As the Father had brought forth Ennoia out of himself, she wanted to produce her image in the same way, without the consent of the Father and her counterpart. For that reason she is called "lascivious". As a result of her lewd thought, she produced an ugly, imperfect being: a dragon with a lion's head and fiery eyes, which she called Jaldabaoth. The etymology of this name is still disputed. For a long time, it was thought to mean "Son of Chaos"; more recent explanations are "Begetter of (S)abaoth" (also interpreted as "Begetter of the Powers") and "Son of Shame" (Black). Another name given to Jaldabaoth is Saklas, which derives from the Aramaic *Saklā'* ("Fool"). In order to hide her son, Sophia pushed him out of the Pleroma. However, he had extracted a great power from his mother and created his own world and his own aeons, 360 "angels" in all, among them the twelve signs of the zodiac and the seven planets. Having finished his creation, he said: 'I am a jealous God, there is no one except me!' (a combination of Exodus 20:5 and Isaiah 45:5). It is for that reason that he was called Saklas, for only 'the Fool says in his heart: there is no God' (Psalm 14:1 and 53:2). The myth of Irenaeus, *AH* I, 29, which is so closely related to that of the *Apocryphon* with respect to the constitution of the Pleroma, gives another account of the Fall of Sophia (29, 4). The sect of the Gnostics behind this text denied that Sophia had a pleromatic counterpart. On the contrary, she wanted to have one; and as she did not find it within the Pleroma, she sought it outside the divine realm, but did not find it there either. Realizing that she had acted against the will of the Father, she brought forth a product of herself. She did so with the best intentions, but nevertheless her son was full of ignorance and pride. Sophia repented, but had to remain outside the Pleroma, above the eighth sphere. Though it does not fit its main story, the *Apocryphon* also knows of her 'moving to and fro' outside the Pleroma (which is connected with the moving of the Spirit above the waters of Chaos in Genesis 1:2) and of her repentance and her being placed in the ninth sphere 'until she has corrected her deficiency'. Related ideas are found in *On the Origin of the World* and the *Hypostasis of the Archons* (NHC II, 4 and 5). It is of interest to note that the Valentinians spiritualized the fall of Sophia. According to them, she wanted to have the same union with the Father as Mind had, i.e. to know him, which means that, in fact, she represents the impossible search for knowledge of the depths of the Father. She would have been swallowed up by the sweetness of the Father, had she not been pushed back (Irenaeus, *AH* I, 2, 2).

The Fall of Sophia and the origin of the bad Demiurge serve as a prelude to what the Gnostics were primarily interested in: the explanation of how the divine element had come to reside in man and how it could return to its original state. The story as told by the *Apocryphon* (BG 47, 14-55,17 parr. = Synopsis 37, 6-56, 10) is not wholly coherent with the preceding section (which indicates a combination of various sources), but it has much in common with the views that Irenaeus, *AH* I, 30, ascribes to 'other people' than the "Gnostics" he described in I, 29. The incoherence is brought out by the sudden introduction of Man and the Son of Man, as the supreme God and his first manifestation. As Jaldabaoth had declared himself the only God, a voice resounded saying: 'Man exists and the Son of Man!', and 'the holy and perfect Father, the first Man' revealed himself to him in human form. The radiant image of the heavenly Man was reflected in the waters of Chaos and the Demiurge said to the powers that attended him (or they said to themselves): 'Let us create a man in the image and likeness of God' (cf. Genesis 1:26). The seven planetary powers of Jaldabaoth made up the components from which the *psychic* body of man was made, which shows a clear influence of Plato's *Timaeus* (van den Broek 1996, 67-85). The long recension of the *Apocryphon* even assigns the composition of the body to no less than 365 "angels" (demons), who are all mentioned by name. There is little doubt that this list derives from magical sources (van der Vliet, 179-237). The assistants of the Demiurge proved to be incapable of awakening and raising the motionless psychic body of Adam. Then the Father of the All sent his son Autogenes with four great lights to the world of Ialdabaoth and they advised him: 'Blow into his face something of your spirit and the artefact will arise' (cf. Genesis 2:7). The Demiurge, who is now identified with the biblical Creator, blew his Spirit, i.e. the divine power of his mother, into the body and it began to move. In this way the divine spirit entered the human being, who because of this spirit was more intelligent than the powers and the Demiurge himself. They realized that he was free from wickedness, and to imprison his divine element they made the material body. This is followed in the *Apocryphon* by the story of Paradise, which, however, is explained in a Gnostic sense: the Tree of Life is a tree of death and the command not to eat of the Tree of Knowledge of Good and Evil was meant to prevent Adam from discovering his divine descent.

Even if a Gnostic text does not presuppose a myth of the kind described above, its perception of the human condition is the same as that of the mythological texts: man's inner self is of divine origin, but he is unaware of it, because he is entangled in this material world and subjected to the passions of the body. He needs to be saved.

C. SALVATION

Living in ignorance is often compared with a state of drunkenness or a sleep haunted by nightmares, and the attainment of knowledge is compared with becoming sober again and awakening in the bright daylight (for instance *Gospel of Truth*, NHC I, 22, 16-20; 28, 24-30, 16). Gnostic salvation is not the remission of sins but the rectification of a situation of ignorance. It might be said that ignorance is the original sin or, in the words of the *Gospel of Philip*, NHC II, 34, 30-31: 'Ignorance is the mother of all evil'. In the section that precedes this statement, the author compares ignorance, the root of wickedness, with the root of a tree: if it is hidden in the earth, the tree sprouts and grows, but if it is exposed, the tree dries up and dies. And from this simile he draws the conclusion: 'As for ourselves, let each one of us dig down after the root of evil that is within one, and let one pluck it out of one's heart from the root. It will be plucked out if we recognize it. But if we are ignorant of it, it takes root in us and produces its fruit in our heart. It masters us. We are its slaves'. Gnosis is the spiritual understanding of our divine origin and the world we live in. As such, it is in fact self-knowledge, as Jesus says to his twin-brother Thomas in the *Book of Thomas the Contender*, NHC II, 138, 16-18: 'For he who has not known himself has known nothing, but he who has known himself has at the same time already achieved knowledge about the depth of the All' (a variant of the Armenian hermetic *Definitions* 9, 4; cf. *Gospel of Thomas*, 67, NHC II, 45, 19-20). But this spiritual knowledge of oneself and the All must be awakened: one must learn to understand. The spiritual leader of a Gnostic community can teach his pupils the essentials of Gnosis, but in the end his teachings derive from divine inspiration and revelation. This revelation is mostly given by a divine Revealer, who is often called the Saviour.

In Christian Gnostic texts the Saviour is identified with Christ, but in non-Christian texts, or at least those in which no Christian influence is discernible or which are only superficially Christianized, the Saviour is called by other names. In the *Paraphrase of Shem* (NHC VII, 1), the Revealer and Saviour is Derdekeas, the Son or Likeness of the Light, i.e. the second divine being, who gives his salvific revelation to a certain Shem. It has been suggested that this Shem is no other than Seth, the third Son of Adam, but there is no convincing evidence for this. However, in the *Gospel of the Egyptians* Seth appears as the Saviour, who imparts saving knowledge to those who belong to him ("the race of Seth") and who, certainly secondarily, is identified with Christ (NHC III, 64, 1-3; IV, 75, 15-17: 'Jesus the living one, he whom the great Seth has put on'). A similar doctrine about Seth was professed by the → Archontics. In the *Apocryphon of John* it is Christ who answers John's questions, like a teacher instructs his pupil, but the real saving figure is a female power, called Epinoia of the Light, who 'assists the whole creature, by toiling with him, and by restoring him to his fullness (*plērōma*) and by teaching him about the descent of his seed and

by teaching him about the way of ascent' (NHC II, 19-23 parr. = Synopsis 54, 8-13). The word *epinoia* means "thinking, reflection, thought" and is here virtually identical with *ennoia*, which in the *Apocryphon* is used as name of the Mother, the second divine being. At the end of the long version of the *Apocryphon* there is a beautiful *Hymn of Pronoia*, also called the *Providence Monologue*, in which it is not Epinoia or Ennoia but Pronoia ("Providence") who acts as the Revealer and Saviour of mankind. There is no doubt that in this case Pronoia stands for the personified Wisdom, the manifestation of God in the world according to Jewish speculations (Waldstein 1995; van den Broek 1996, 86-116).

For Christian Gnostics, Christ was the Saviour *par excellence*. The *Gospel of Truth*, NHC I, 118, 16-20, says of Jesus that 'he enlightened those who were in darkness through forgetfulness. He enlightened them and showed them a way. The way, then, is the truth which he taught them' (cf. John 14:6). He is the Saviour because he reveals the truth about the unknown Father; his death on the cross has no salvific meaning. The Gnostics usually adhered to a docetic Christology, which means that they denied that Christ had a material body of flesh and blood. For them, and also for those who ascribed to Jesus a real human body and soul, as, for instance, Justin the Gnostic did, the crucifixion was primarily the event in which Christ's pneumatic being was separated from its bodily envelope. Some Christian Gnostic texts, however, described the meaning of salvation in terms that were strongly influenced by biblical images and, for that reason, came close to those found in more "orthodox" writings. Thus the *Gospel of Philip*, NHC II, 52, 35-53, 4, uses the terminology of ransom: 'Christ came to ransom some, to save others, to redeem others. He ransomed those who were strangers and made them his own'. But in this text as well, Christ is the Revealer of the hidden mystery of the Father. The *Gospel of Truth* in particular makes use of biblical images and expressions that even suggest a salvific meaning in the crucifixion. Christ was 'nailed to a tree and became a fruit of the knowledge of the Father. It did not, however, cause destruction because it was eaten (cf. Genesis 2:17), but it gave gladness to those who ate it' (NHC I, 18, 24-28). Jesus, 'the merciful one, the faithful one, patiently accepted the sufferings . . ., since he knows that his death is life for many' (NHC I, 20, 10-14). Nevertheless, the *Gospel of Truth* is a thoroughly Gnostic work: Christ 'became a way for those who were gone astray and knowledge for those who were ignorant, a discovery for those who were searching, and a support for those who were wavering, immaculateness for those who were defiled' (NHC I, 31, 28-35). Christian Gnostics of the 2nd century could sometimes speak about Jesus with much more warmth and spiritual depth than their non-Gnostic fellow Christians.

The completion of the Gnostic's road of salvation is the return of his divine particle to the Pleroma. This happens at his death, but the salvation is in fact already enjoyed in this earthly life. The divine spark in human beings is often called the Pneuma (Spirit). The Valentinians, in particular, developed a subtle theory about the pneumatic, the psychic and the hylic (material) natures in the individual human being as well as in humankind as a whole. The treatise *On the Origin of the World*, NHC II, 122, 1-9, also distinguishes between three types of human beings: Pneumatics, Psychics and Choics (earthly people), which may point to Valentinian influence. However, many texts simply speak about the soul as the divine element in man. This is found, for instance, in the reports on the Archontics and the Naassenes, who both adhered to mythological forms of Gnosis, and also in non-mythological writings such as the *Treatise on the Soul* (NHC II, 6) and the *Authentikos Logos* (NHC VI, 3). In the *Apocryphon of John*, Christ describes three possible fates of the soul. The soul that has come to knowledge 'is saved and taken up to the repose of the aeons'. Those who have not yet come to know the All are reincarnated in the prison of the body 'until they are saved from forgetfulness and the soul acquires knowledge and thus becomes perfect and is saved'. Only those who once had Gnosis but renounced it 'will be tortured with eternal punishment' (BG 67, 18-71, 2 = Synopsis 70, 19-73, 14).

The ascent of the soul to the divine realm could only take place if it knew the passwords or possessed the seals that permitted it to pass the hostile rulers of the seven heavens. This idea was not typically Gnostic in itself, but it played an important role in the Gnostic imagination. Examples of passwords are to be found in the first *Apocalypse of James*, (NHC V, 32, 24-36, 1), the *Gospel of Mary* (BG 15, 1-17, 7), the *Gospel of Thomas*, log. 50 (NHC II, 41, 31-42, 7), and Origen's *Contra Celsum*, VI, 30-31. The two *Books of Jeû* give an elaborate description, with drawings, of the "seals" and "signs" and the many aeons the soul has to pass through on its way upwards. Finally, the soul or the pneuma arrives at the place of its origin, the Pleroma. The state of bliss that it enjoys there is often called the *Anapausis* ("rest, repose").

The *Gospel of Truth*, in which this conception plays a prominent role, says of those who have found the Anapausis of the Pleroma that 'they rest in him who is at rest, . . . and the Father is within them and they are in the Father, being perfect, being undivided in the truly Good One, being in no way deficient in anything, but they are set at rest, refreshed in the Spirit' (NHC I, 42, 21-33).

D. ETHICS

Not only the anti-Gnostic writers, but the authentic Gnostic sources as well, testify that the Gnostic believers felt themselves elected and predestined to Gnosis. They were the 'Immovable race' and belonged to the 'generation without a king' (*Apocalypse of Adam*, NHC V, 82, 19f. and 83, 1ff.), and as such they had overcome the power of evil. The anti-Gnostic writers often inferred from this possibly somewhat arrogant attitude that the Gnostics felt themselves morally free to do whatever they wanted. The accusation of moral licentiousness – a well-known means of bringing opponents into disrepute – was often raised against the Gnostic believers. This has led to the long-standing scholarly opinion that there were two different types of Gnostics: ascetics, who stuck to a thoroughly ascetic way of life, including the rejection of marriage, and libertines, who rejected asceticism and even indulged in sexual licentiousness. However, the reports of the anti-Gnostic authors contain very little information that gives colour to their allegations of immoral behaviour in Gnostic groups; and even if they seem to have a point, for instance in the case of the → Carpocratians and the → Borborites, the evidence asks for a careful interpretation. Of more weight is the fact that there are no authentic Gnostic texts that advocate immoral behaviour. On the contrary, the whole Nag Hammadi Library is thoroughly ascetic, and it may be assumed that it was because of their asceticism that some non-Gnostic writings, such as the *Teachings of Silvanus* and the *Sentences of Sextus*, were included in the collection. But even if the Gnostics themselves taught a strong asceticism and did not show any indication of immoral or non-ascetic behaviour, their opponents suggested that they simply were keeping up appearances. Examples of such negative polemics are Irenaeus on → Satornilus (*Adversus haereses*, I, 24, 2), Clement of Alexandria on the followers of Prodicus (*Stromateis*, III, 30, 2-3), and Epiphanius on the Archontics (*Panarion*, 40, 2, 4). All the evidence suggests that the adherents of the Gnostic movement propagated and practised an ascetic way of life, which, however, did not need to imply the rejection of marriage. An important group like the Valentinians, for instance, held marriage in high esteem and considered it an image of the union of the soul with its heavenly counterpart in the Pleroma. The moral ideas of Clement of Alexandria, to whom we owe this information (*Stromateis*, III, 1, 1), did not differ much from those of Valentinus. At most there may have been a relative difference of emphasis between Gnostic and non-Gnostic Christians with respect to moral ideas and practices, in so far as the former tended to have a more negative view of the material world and the body and, therefore, may have been more inclined to a strongly ascetic way of life than their non-Gnostic fellow-Christians.

3. BACKGROUNDS AND RELATIONSHIPS

The origin of the Gnostic movement has been the subject of much debate, but this has not led to any kind of scholarly consensus. The main reason for this is that actually there never existed one clearly definable "Gnosticism", but only a variety of related religious ideas and currents, which had the idea of salvific, revealed Gnosis as their common denominator. Michael Williams (1996) has convincingly argued that it is useless to continue the search for *the* origin of this complicated and variegated religious phenomenon. However, as he also pointed out, it is quite possible to clarify the origin and history of specific Gnostic traditions, such as those of Valentinianism and of what he called the "biblical demiurgical texts". The authentic Gnostic texts of the Nag Hammadi Library show that important notions derived from Judaism, Greek philosophy and Christianity had a considerable influence on the various elaborations of the central Gnostic idea of salvation through knowledge.

A. JUDAISM

There is a broad scholarly consensus that Jewish traditions played an important part in the formation of mythological Gnosis, although opinions differ about the interpretation of this phenomenon [→ Jewish influences I]. As was already pointed out above (2A), the figures of Anthropos and Sophia can only be explained from Jewish speculations about the first manifestations of the transcendent God. Traditions found in the Jewish apocrypha and pseudepigrapha, but also speculations known only from Merkavah mysticism (Gruenwald 1982) have contributed to the formation of the Gnostic myths. Close analysis of such basic mythological texts as the *Apocryphon of John*, the *Hypostasis of the Archons* and *On the Origin of the World* has brought to light such a wealth of Jewish parallels that the conclusion that they originated in a Jewish milieu is inescapable. This has raised the question of whether the emergence of the Gnostic Demiurge and his identification with the biblical Creator can also be explained from Jewish sources. Rabbinic polemics show that there were *minim*, dissident Jews, who speculated about the existence of Two Powers in heaven, God and his agent or vice-regent, who was known under various names (Angel of the Lord, the Lesser Jahweh, the Name, Shekina, Man, Wisdom, etc.) and who shared in or was wholly responsible for the creation of the world (Segal, Fossum). The rabbis were vehemently opposed to this idea, because they considered it a serious threat to Jewish monotheism. It should be noticed, however, that in the Jewish (and Samaritan) sources there is no evidence whatsoever that this divine agent or intermediary was ever placed in opposition to God. Various suggestions have been made to explain how Jews could have come to a degradation of the God of their fathers to the status of a lower and bad Demiurge, but none of them have succeeded in convincing the majority of scholars. There is no evidence that suggests the existence of a distinctly mythological Gnosis in Judaism. Nevertheless, it seems certain that the earliest myths about the origin of evil and the world were developed by Jews who were well informed about apocryphal and mystical Jewish traditions, but had apparently lost the faith of their fathers in the God of Israel as the creator of the world. This might be explained out of a deeply felt disappointment with the apparent inability of this God to prevent the tragic events that happened to the Jewish people in the first century. However this may be, there is no reason to see the whole Gnostic movement as derived directly from Judaism.

B. GREEK PHILOSOPHY

The authentic Gnostic texts demonstrate beyond doubt the influence of Greek philosophy on Gnostic thought. Hippolytus of Rome (ca. 220) already argued that the Gnostics, like all heretics, had derived their ideas and systems from Greek philosophy and → astrology (Koschorke 1975). More recently, several experts in classical philosophy have studied the complicated relationship between philosophical and Gnostic ideas, with less prejudice and more competence than Hippolytus (*inter al.* Mansfeld, Armstrong, Dillon, Turner). The central question is whether or not Greek philosophy could have given rise to the Gnostic idea of the bad world and the evil Demiurge. In Orphism and early Pythagoreanism one may find an anthropological pessimism (incarnation as punishment, the body as a tomb) of which most Gnostics would have approved, but it is neither based on nor does it correspond to an equally pessimistic cosmology. Almost all Greek philosophers were convinced of the essential goodness of the cosmos; if they accepted a Demiurge, they declared him to be good as well. Only the Epicureans held that the world is not good, but a 'random, meaningless, transitory and very badly arranged cosmos' (Armstrong); but not only did they reject the idea of a Demiurge, their whole philosophy of life was in sharp contrast with that of the Gnostics. Especially in the 2nd century, there were Platonists who in several respects came close to the position of the more radical Gnostics. Plutarch and Atticus assumed a maleficent world soul as the principle of evil in the material universe, and Numenius taught the existence of two souls, a good and a bad one, both in the universe and in man; but neither of them introduced a Gnostic kind of strict cosmic dualism. The Neoplatonists [→ Neoplatonism I], and Plotinus in particular, espoused a more positive and world-accepting attitude and strongly opposed the Gnostic view of the universe and its maker (Elsas).

The problems that were the philosophers' concern – the relationship between the One and the many, or between the supreme God and lower levels of being, and the origin of evil – were of equal interest for the Gnostic thinkers. Since the latter did not live in a vacuum, they inevitably made use of current philosophical ideas to express their religious convictions. Moreover, from Hellenistic times onward, philosophy, and later Platonism in particular, had become increasingly religious. Under these circumstances, one understands that it is often difficult to draw a sharp borderline between philosophical and Gnostic writings, especially in the case of non-mythological Gnostic texts. In general, however, one can say that the philosophers sought philosophical solutions to philosophical problems, even if their language was religiously coloured, whereas the Gnostic thinkers sought religious answers to religious problems, even if they made use of philosophical terminology. The philosophers aimed at understanding, the gnostics sought and proclaimed salvation through revealed knowledge. A good example of the relationship between (even mythological) Gnosis and philosophical speculation is provided by the Gnostic treatise *Zostrianus*, which was known in the school of Plotinus. Describing the

supreme God by means of the terminology of negative and affirmative theology (NHC VIII, 64, 11-84, 22), the author makes use of the same Middle- or Neoplatonic source that was also used by the fourth-century Christian writer Marius Victorinus in his *Adversus Arium*, I, 49-50 (Tardieu 1996). Comparison of the texts shows that the Gnostic author quotes his source literally. However, he presents its contents as a revelation, which Zostrianus has received from an angelic interpreter called Salamex, during a heavenly journey. This Salamex has revealed to him the three aeons of Barbelo, which contain numerous other aeons, who are mentioned by name. The vision ends with the words: 'Behold, Zostrianus, you have heard all these things of which the gods are ignorant'. Although the work testifies to a considerable Neoplatonic influence on third-century Gnostic speculations, its author was a fully-fledged Gnostic, who adhered to a type of "Sethian" Gnosis. Gnostic thought was not "a Platonism run wild" (Nock), nor was it a department of the "Platonic underworld" (Dillon).

c. Hermetism
The philosophical Hermetica [→ Hermetic Literature I] and Gnostic literature in general have much in common, but there are also considerable differences. The similarities between Gnosticism and Hermetism are due to the fact that both originated and developed in the same time, in the same oriental part of the Mediterranean world, Egypt, and Alexandria in particular, and in the same spiritual climate. Both Gnostics and hermetists adhered to the widespread philosophical concept of God as a completely transcendent Being, who can only be described in the terms of negative theology. An important difference, however, was that according to the hermetists, the human mind was able to know God at least partially through the contemplation of the cosmos. Although the hermetists recognized that the material world could wholly absorb the human being, the cosmos always remained for them the beautiful product, the first son, of the supreme God. They could sometimes speak of the world as the 'plenitude of vice' (C.H. VI, 4), but they never ascribed the origin of the world to an imperfect and evil Demiurge. The "Way of Hermes" implied instruction concerning the nature of the cosmos, with the help of all kinds of sciences: theories of space and movement, astronomy (which included → astrology), medicine and → magic. Its aim was to make the world transparent toward God. Gnostic cosmological instruction, especially that of the

mythological and radical type, only aimed at explaining how this world of darkness and evil had come into being. Another difference is that the abundant Gnostic mythology has no counterpart in Hermetism. The hermetic speculations about the divine world have nothing to offer that might be compared with the abundant Gnostic descriptions of the divine Pleroma. The only hermetic text that relates the origin of the world and man in the form of a myth is the *Poimandres* (C.H. I), but it is precisely this text that shows most clearly, *inter alia* by the introduction of the heavenly Anthropos, that it comes from the same background as, for instance, the *Apocryphon of John*. The *Poimandres* could be called a gnosticizing hermetic composition, but the author nevertheless remains a hermetist. He does not teach that the cosmos and the human body are bad in themselves, as the radical Gnostics did, but finds the origin of evil in sexual desire, which makes him an ascetic hermetist. In many respects, Gnosticism seems to have been a radicalization of important hermetic notions. Just like the Gnostics, the hermetists were convinced that the human soul or mind had its origin in God and that only through the gift of knowledge the original integrity could be restored, – an integrity which could already be experienced in this earthly life. Both offered a road to salvation, but this has led to two different religious systems.

D. CHRISTIANITY

The Gnostic movement did not arise as a Christian heresy. Although there are no Gnostic works that in their present form are demonstrably pre-Christian, several treatises are certainly non-Christian or so superficially Christianized that the non-Christian original is still clearly recognizable. Moreover, the Gnostic religion of the → Mandaeans ("Gnostics") cannot by any means be explained as an offshoot of early Christianity. A Gnostic work should only be called Christian if it presents Jesus or Christ as the decisive Saviour, who imparts salvific knowledge to the Gnostic believer.

In New Testament scholarship there has been much debate concerning the question of possible Gnostic influences on earliest Christianity. As an example, we may mention the discussion about the relationship between the prologue of the Gospel of John and the *Trimorphic Protennoia* (NHC XIII, 1). It has been claimed that the latter represents an earlier and better Gnostic version of the threefold descent of the Saviour than the prologue ascribes to the Logos. However, this threefold descent, which also determines the structure of the *Hymn of Pronoia* at the end of the *Apocryphon of John*, is derived from Jewish speculations about three descents of Wisdom. These speculations have apparently determined the myth of the threefold descent of the Saviour into the world of darkness, both in evidently Gnostic mythological texts and in the Gospel of John (van den Broek 1996, 86-116). Although this Gospel rejects the idea of a bad Demiurge (John 1:3, but cf. 8:44), it may nevertheless be called Gnostic too, since it puts much emphasis on the salvific meaning of Gnosis (John 1:18; 17:3). As a matter of fact, the Gospel of John easily lent itself to Gnostic exegesis (Pagels). If this Gospel had been unknown and had first come to light with the Nag Hammadi Library, it would certainly have been classified as a Gnostic or "gnosticizing" work.

The relationship between the Gnostic movement and early Christianity can be best explained from the fact that both developed in the same spiritual climate, which was strongly influenced by Jewish ideas expressed in mythical forms. As said above (section 3A), Jews must have played an important role in the formation of the Gnostic myths. From Philo we know that there were Jews in Alexandria who rejected the beliefs and practices of their paternal religion. But the deeply pessimistic view of the human condition expressed in the early Gnostic myths cannot have been limited to some apostate Jews. It apparently reflected a more general experience of alienation from the world and a longing for salvation by spiritual knowledge, which is also evident in those Gnostic writings that do not show any specific Jewish influence. The Christian anti-Gnostic works of the 2nd and 3rd centuries testify to the great attraction of Gnostic views, and of the religious experience upon which they were based, on Christian thinkers or teachers and their followers. The result was a distinct Gnostic current within the variegated world of early Christianity. The most influential Gnostic variant of Christianity seems to have been Valentinianism, which was based on older mythological constructions (see above). That Valentinus and even his pupil Ptolemy were simply well educated Christian Platonists, who did not yet teach the "Valentinian" mythological Gnostic system that was taught by their followers, as has been argued from a church-historical point of view (Markschies), is highly unlikely. In the middle of the 2nd century, ecclesiastical leaders in Rome began to define the boundaries of the Church and, accordingly, to reject views that for a time had been acceptable within the Christian communities. The Christian teachers who taught the prevalence of Gnosis over faith or ascribed the creation of the world to a lower Demiurge were expelled from the Church and vehemently fought.

4. CONCLUSION

The Gnostic movement in Antiquity has many faces, which makes an unambiguous definition virtually impossible. The scholarly term "Gnosticism" suggests a uniformity that never existed. If used at all – and then, of course, without any pejorative connotation –, the term should be reserved for the more elaborate mythological systems that were developed from the 2nd century onward. The Gnostic character of a considerable number of texts can be disputed, since their contents show a position intermediate between a distinct Gnostic and more philosophical, hermetic, or generally Christian views. The decisive criterion is whether or not esoteric knowledge is held to be indispensable for personal salvation, i.e. the return to one's divine origin. But even this criterion is not always easy to apply, because the indispensability of Gnosis is sometimes merely presupposed rather than explicitly expressed. However, all these ambiguities are no reason to deny the existence of Gnostic religiosity in the Roman world and to declare terms as "Gnostic", "Gnosticism", "Gnostic movement", etc. meaningless. The Gnostic religion, its mythological variants included, was not a degenerated form of Greek philosophy, nor did it arise as a Christian heresy. To some extent it was a religion in its own right, or at least a distinct religious mentality, which expressed itself in an almost inextricable combination of important notions derived from Jewish mysticism, Greek philosophy, and Christian theology. Its central belief found a succinct expression in the Christian Gnostic *Testimony of Truth*, NHC IX, 44,30-45, 6: 'When man comes to know himself and God who is over the truth, he will be saved, and he will crown himself with the crown unfading'.

Lit.: B. Aland (ed.), *Gnosis: Festschrift für Hans Jonas*, Göttingen: Vandenhoeck & Ruprecht, 1978 ♦ A.H. Armstrong, "Gnosis and Greek Philosophy", in: Aland, *Gnosis*, 87-12 ♦ B. Barc (ed.), *Colloque international sur les textes de Nag Hammadi (Québec, 22-25 août 1978)* (Bibliothèque Copte de Nag Hammadi, Section "Études", 1), Quebec/Louvain: Presses de l'Université Laval/Peeters, 1981 ♦ K. Berger & R. McL. Wilson, "Gnosis/Gnostizismus", *Theologische Realenzyklopädie*, XIII (1984), 519-530 ♦ H.G. Bethge *et alii* (eds.), *For the Children, Perfect Instruction: Studies in Honor of Hans-Martin Schenke on the Occasion of the Berliner Arbeitskreis für koptisch-gnostischen Schriften's Thirtieth Year*

(NHMS, LIV), Leiden: E.J. Brill, 2002 ♦ U. Bianchi (ed.), *The origins of Gnosticism: Colloquium of Messina, 13-18 April 1966* (Studies in the History of Religions, XII), Leiden: E.J. Brill, 1967 ♦ M. Black, "An Aramaic Etymology for Jaldabaoth?", in: A.H.B. Logan & A.J.M. Wedderburn (eds.), *The New Testament and Gnosis: Essays in Honour of Robert McL. Wilson*, Edinburgh: T. & T. Clark, 1983, 69-72 ♦ W. Bousset, *Hauptprobleme der Gnosis* (FRLANT, 10), Göttingen: Vandenhoeck & Ruprecht, 1907 (reprint 1973) ♦ R. van den Broek & M.J. Vermaseren, *Studies in Gnosticism and Hellenistic Religions Presented to Gilles Quispel on the Occasion of his 65th Birthday* (EPRO, 91), Leiden: E.J. Brill, 1981 ♦ R. van den Broek, "The Present State of Gnostic Studies", *Vigiliae Christianae* 37 (1983), 41-71 ♦ idem, *Studies in Gnosticsm and Alexandrian Christianity* (NHMS XXXIX), Leiden: E.J. Brill, 1996 ♦ P. Brown, *The Body and Society: Men, Women, and Sexual Renunciation in Early Christianity*, New York: Columbia University Press, 1988 ♦ G. Casadio, "From Hellenistic Aiōn to Gnostic Aiōnes", in: D. Zeller (ed.), *Religion im Wandel der Kosmologien*, Frankfurt: Peter Lang, 1999, 175-190 ♦ C. Colpe, "Gnosis II (Gnostizismus)", *RAC* 11 (1981), 537-659 ♦ N.A. Dahl, "The Arrogant Archon and the Lewd Sophia: Jewish Traditions in Gnostic Revolt", in: Layton, *Rediscovery*, II, 689-712 ♦ J. Dillon, *The Middle Platonists: A Study of Platonism, 80 B.C. to A.D. 220*, London: Duckworth, 1977 ♦ C. Elsas, *Neuplatonische und gnostische Weltablehnung in der Schule Plotins*, Berlin: De Gruyter, 1975 ♦ G. Filoramo, *A History of Gnosticism*, Cambridge (Mass.)/Oxford: Blackwell, 1990 ♦ J.E. Fossum, *The Name of God and the Angel of the Lord: Samaritan and Jewish Concepts of Intermediation and the Origin of Gnosticsm* (WUNT, 36), Tübingen: J.C.B. Mohr (Paul Siebeck), 1985 ♦ idem, *The Image of the Invisible God: Essays on the Influence of Jewish Mysticism on Early Christianity* (Novum Testamentum et Orbis Antiquus, 30), Freiburg Schweitz / Göttingen: Universitätsverlag / Vandenhoeck & Ruprecht, 1995 ♦ I. Gruenwald, "The problem of Anti-Gnostic Polemic in Rabbinic Literature", in: Van den Broek & Vermaseren, *Studies in Gnosticism*, 171-189 ♦ idem, "Jewish Merkavah Mysticism and Gnosticism", in: J. Dan & F. Talmage (eds.), *Studies in Jewish Mysticism: Proceedings of the Regional Conferences held at the University of California, Los Angeles, and McGill Universitiy in April 1978*, Cambridge, Mass.: Association for Jewish Studies, 1982, 41-55 ♦ Ch.W. Hedrick & R. Hodgson (ed.), *Nag Hammadi, Gnosticism, and Early Christianity*, Peabody, Mass.: Henrickson, 1986 ♦ J. Helderman, *Die Anapausis im Evangelium Veritatis: Eine vergleichende Untersuchung des valentinianisch-gnostischen Heilsgutes der Ruhe im Evangelium Veritatis und in anderen Schriften der Nag Hammadi-Bibliothek* (NHS 18), Leiden: E.J. Brill, 1984 ♦ M. Hengel, "Die Ursprünge der Gnosis und das Urchristentum", in: J. Ådna *et alii* (eds.), *Evangelium, Schriftauslegung, Kirche: Festschrift für P. Stuhlmacher zum 65. Geburtstag*, Göttingen: Vandenhoeck & Ruprecht,

1997, 190-223 ♦ A. Hilgenfeld, *Die Ketzergeschichte des Urchristentums urkundlich dargestellt*, Leipzig: Fues, 1884 (reprinted Darmstadt: Wissenschaftliche Buchgesellschaft, 1963) ♦ J. Holzhausen, *Der "Mythos vom Menschen" im hellenistischen Ägypten: Eine Studie zum "Poimandres" (= CH I), zu Valentin und dem gnostischen Mythos* (Theophaneia, 33), Bodenheim: Athenäum-Hain-Hanstein, 1994 ♦ H. Jonas, *Gnosis und spätantiker Geist* (FRLANT, 51), 2 vols., Göttingen: Vandenhoeck & Ruprecht, 1964-1966, reprinted 1988-1993 (4th ed. of vol. 1 [1934], 2nd ed. of vol. 2,1-2 [1954, 1964]) ♦ K.L. King, *What is Gnosticism?*, Cambridge, Mass.: Harvard University Press, 2003 ♦ B. Layton (ed.), *The Rediscovery of Gnosticism* (Studies in the History of Religions, XLI), 2 vols., Leiden: E.J. Brill, 1980 ♦ idem, "Prolegomena to the Study of Ancient Gnosticism", in: L.M. White & O.L. Yarbrough (eds.), *The Social World of the First Christians: Essays in Honor of Wayne Meeks*, Minneapolis: Fortress Press, 1995, 334-50 ♦ A.H.B. Logan, *Gnostic Truth and Christian Heresy: A Study in the History of Gnosticism*, Edinburgh: T&T Clark, 1996 ♦ J. Mansfeld, "Bad World and Demiurge: A 'Gnostic' Motif from Parmenides and Empedocles to Lucretius and Philo", in: Van den Broek & Vermaseren, *Studies in Gnosticism*, 261-314 ♦ C. Markschies, *Die Gnosis*, München: Beck 2001 (Engl. trans. *Gnosis: An Introduction*, London: T&T Clark, 2003) ♦ A.D. Nock, *Essays on Religion and the Ancient World*, 2 vols., Oxford: Oxford University Press, 1972 ♦ E.H. Pagels, *The Johannine Gospel in Gnostic Exegesis: Heracleon's Commentary on John* (Society of Biblical Literature Monograph Series, 17), Nashville: Abingdon, 1973 ♦ eadem, *The Gnostic Paul: Gnostic Exegesis of the Pauline Letters*, Philadelphia: Fortress Press, 1975 ♦ B.A. Pearson, *Gnosticism, Judaism, and Egyptian Christianity*, Minneapolis: Fortress Press, 1990 ♦ idem, *Gnosticism and Christianity in Roman and Coptic Egypt*, New York-London: T & T Clark International, 2004 ♦ G. Quispel, *Gnosis als Weltreligion*, Zurich: Origo Verlag, 1951, ²1972 ♦ idem, *Gnostic Studies* (Uitgaven van het Nederlands Historisch-Archeologisch Instituut te Istanbul, XXXIV, 1-2), 2 vols., Istanbul: Nederlands Historisch-Archeologisch Instituut, 1975 ♦ R. Roukema, *Gnosis and Faith in Early Christianity*, Harrisburg: Trinity Press, 1999 ♦ H.-Ch. Puech, *En quête de la gnose*, 2 vols., Paris: Gallimard, 1978 ♦ K. Rudolph (ed.), *Gnosis und Gnostizismus* (Wege der Forschung, 262), Darmstadt: Wissenschaftliche Buchgesellschaft, 1975 ♦ idem, *Die Gnosis: Wesen und Geschichte einer spätantiken Religion*, 2nd rev. ed., Göttingen: Vandenhoeck & Ruprecht, 1980 (English translation: *Gnosis: The Nature and History of Gnosticism*, San Francisco/Edinburgh: Harper & Row/T & T Clark, 1983) ♦ idem, *Gnosis und spätantike Religionsgeschichte* (NHMS, XLII), Leiden:

E.J. Brill, 1996 ♦ idem, "Gnosis, Gnostiker", in: *Der Neue Pauly*, 4 (1998), 1117-1125 ♦ H.-M. Schenke, *Der Gott "Mensch" in der Gnosis: Ein religionsgeschichtlicher Beitrag zur Diskussion über die paulinische Anschauung von der Kirche als Leib Christi*, Göttingen: Vandenhoeck & Ruprecht, 1962 ♦ idem [2], "Nag Hammadi Studien III: Die Spitze des dem Apocryphon Johannis und der Sophia Jesu Christi zugrundeliegenden Systems", *ZRGG 14* (1962), 352-361 ♦ A.F. Segal, *Two Powers in Heaven: Early Rabbinic Reports about Christianity and Gnosticism* (Studies in Judaism in Late Antiquity, XXV), Leiden: E.J. Brill, 1977 ♦ M. Smith, "The History of the Term Gnostikos", in: Layton, *Rediscovery*, II, 796-807 ♦ G.A.G. Stroumsa, *Another Seed: Studies in Gnostic Mythology* (NHS, XXIV), Leiden: E.J. Brill, 1984 ♦ idem, *Savoir et Salut*, Paris: Éditions du Cerf, 1992 ♦ idem, *Hidden Wisdom: Esoteric Traditions and the Roots of Christian Mysticism* (Studies in the History of Religion, LXX), Leiden: E.J. Brill, 1996 ♦ M. Tardieu & J.-D. Dubois, *Introduction à la littérature gnostique*, I: *Histoire du mot "gnostique", Instruments de travail, Collections retrouvées avant 1945*, Paris: Éditions du Cerf/Éditions du C.N.R.S., 1986 ♦ K.-W. Tröger (ed.), *Gnosis und Neues Testament: Studien aus Religionswissenschaft und Theologie*, Gütersloh: Mohn, 1973 ♦ idem (ed.), *Altes Testament, Frühjudentum, Gnosis: Neue Studien zu "Gnosis und Bibel"*, Güterloh: Mohn, 1980 ♦ J.D. Turner, *Sethian Gnosticism and the Platonic Tradition* (Bibliothèque copte de Nag Hammadi, Section "Études", 6), Quebec/Louvain: Presses de l'Université Laval/Peeters, 2001 ♦ J.D. Turner & A. McGuire (eds.), *The Nag Hammadi Library after Fifty years: Proceedings of the 1995 Society of Biblical Literature Commemoration* (NHMS XLIV), Leiden: E.J. Brill, 1997 ♦ J. van der Vliet, *L'image du mal en Égypte: Démonologie et cosmogonie d'après les textes gnostiques coptes*, Dissertation University of Leiden, 1996 ♦ M. Waldstein, "The *Providence Monologue* in the Apocryphon of John and the *Johannine Prologue*", *Journal of Early Christian Studies* 3 (1995), 369-402 ♦ idem, "The Primal Triad in the *Apocryphon of John*", in Turner & McGuire (eds.), *The Nag Hammadi Library*, 154-187 ♦ G. Widengren (ed.), *Proceedings of the International Colloquium on Gnosticism, Stockholm August 20-25, 1973* (Kungl. Vitterhets Historie och Antikvitets Akademiens Handlingar, Filologisk-filosofiska serien, 17), Stockholm: Almqvist & Wiksell, 1977 ♦ M.A. Williams, *The Immovable Race: A Gnostic Designation and the Theme of Stability in Late Antiquity* (NHS, 29), Leiden: E.J. Brill, 1985 ♦ idem, *Rethinking "Gnosticism": An Argument for Dismantling a Dubious Category*, Princeton, NJ: Princeton University Press, 1996.

ROELOF VAN DEN BROEK

Gnosticism II: Gnostic literature

1. Original Greek Texts 2. Coptic
Texts Discovered Before 1945 3. The
Nag Hammadi Library (a. Introduction
b. Non-Gnostic Writings c. Gospels
and Related Texts d. Mythological
Texts e. Apocalyptic and Polemical
Texts f. Valentinian Texts g. Ascents
to heaven) 4. The Testimony of
Anti-Gnostic Writers

1. Original Greek texts

Most of the authentic Gnostic writings have
been preserved in Coptic, but there is little doubt
that all of them were originally translated from
the Greek. The vehement opposition by the leaders of the Church against the basic ideas of →
Gnosticism led to the almost complete extinction
of the once flourishing Greek Gnostic literature.
The works of anti-Gnostic writers, such as
Irenaeus, Hippolytus and Epiphanius, have preserved many testimonies of the ideas and sometimes even the religious practices of individual
Gnostic teachers and their schools or sects. But
since these testimonies were written down by
opponents who wanted to show how heretical or
ridiculous were the ideas that they discussed, one
must always ask to what extent any report can be
trusted. However, sometimes these authors transmit extensive excerpts from original Gnostic documents, or even a complete treatise. A well-known
example of such extracts is the *Excerpts from
Theodotus* by → Clement of Alexandria, although
in this case it is not always easy to decide where
Theodotus' text ends and Clement's begins. A
complete 2nd-century text has been preserved in
Epiphanius of Salamis, *Panarion*, 33, 3-7. It is the
famous *Letter to Flora* by the Valentinian Gnostic
Ptolemy [→ Valentinus and Valentinians] about
the correct interpretation of the five books of
Moses. Making an appeal to Jesus, the author distinguishes between the Law of God, the additions
by → Moses, and the "injunctions" of the elders.
According to Ptolemy, these last two have to be
rejected. The first, however, can again be divided
into three kinds of law: the pure Law of God, i.e.
the Ten Commandments, then those laws that are
to be interpreted symbolically, and finally the
unjust law of retaliation (an eye for an eye, etc.).
Jesus has rejected the latter, introduced the symbolic interpretation, and fulfilled the pure Law of
God. In the 2nd century, the interpretation of the
Old Testament became a hotly-debated issue in
the Christian church. Considerable differences

notwithstanding, Ptolemy's ideas have much in
common with those of his contemporary Justin
Martyr († 165). His Gnostic point of view
becomes visible in his remarks about the nature of
the creator and lawgiver. Just like → Marcion's
Demiurge, he is said to be righteous; however, he
is neither the supreme God nor the devil, but a
being midway between them, neither unambigu-
ously good nor thoroughly evil. Moreover, the
Letter to Flora is obviously an exoteric writing,
for at the end Ptolemy promises his 'sister' that she
will come to a deeper understanding when she is
ready for it. Another Greek text, almost certainly
a testimony of Valentinian Gnosticism, is the epitaph for Flavia Sophe (probably 4th century).
Sophe's sorrowing husband addresses his beloved
wife as follows: 'You whose desire was for the
light of the Father, Sophe, my sister, my bride,
anointed though the bath of Christ with imperishable holy perfume, you hastened to gaze on the
divine faces of the aeons, the Angel of the Great
Counsel, the true Son, when you went to the
Bridal Chamber and rose [incorruptible] to the
Father's house' (McKechnie).

2. Coptic Texts Discovered Before 1945

In 3rd- and 4th-century Egypt, Gnosticism (and
→ Manichaeism as well) continued to attract a
considerable number of adherents, whereas elsewhere it had lost much of its influence. Especially
in the 4th century, many Gnostic works, most of
them written in the 2nd or 3rd century, were
translated from Greek into Coptic: the last stage
of the Egyptian language, which was spoken by
the Christians. Before the discovery of the Nag
Hammadi Library in 1945, only a few of these
original Gnostic texts were known, having been
discovered in the 18th and 19th centuries.

The first of these texts to become known was
the *Pistis Sophia*, preserved in the *Codex
Askewianus*, called after Antoninus Askew, who
bought it from a London antiquarian around
1750. After Askew's death (1772), it was acquired
by the British Museum in 1785. Where it was
found and how it came to London is still
unknown. The best scholarly edition of the text
was published by Carl Schmidt in 1925. This
edition remains indispensable because of its critical apparatus, which, unfortunately, was reorganized by Violet MacDermot in the reprint of
Schmidt's text that accompanied her own English
translation (1978). Schmidt had already published
an excellent, and much-used, German translation
in 1905 (4th edition by H.-M. Schenke, 1981).

The *Pistis Sophia* consists of dialogues between Jesus and his male and female disciples, among whom Mary Magdalen takes first rank. These dialogues are divided into four parts, which are clearly indicated in the text of the manuscript. The first three parts belonged together from the beginning; the fourth part may originally have been an independent treatise. The first three parts contain numerous exegeses of biblical Psalms, of five *Odes of Solomon*, and of some of the *Psalms of Solomon*; all are interpreted with respect to the salvation of Pistis Sophia, the aeon that had become the cause of evil, and its consequences for the individual soul. The fourth part is a revelation about the construction of the aeonic world and the rites that the soul needs to know in order to ascend through the heavens to the transcendent Father. The Coptic manuscript is generally dated to the middle of the 4th century; the date of the Greek original of the *Pistis Sophia* is difficult to establish, but there are reasons to assign it to the second half of the 3rd century (see below).

The second Gnostic manuscript discovered in the 18th century is the *Codex Brucianus*, called after the Scotch traveller James Bruce, who bought it in Egypt in 1773. Since 1848 it has been in the Bodleian Library, Oxford. The manuscript contains two texts, written in different hands, of which the first, in two parts, is usually called the *Books of Jeû* and the second the *Untitled Treatise*. The *Books of Jeû* are also mentioned in the *Pistis Sophia*, 99 and 134, where they are said to have been written by Enoch in Paradise; most probably this reference does indeed refer to the first two books of the Bruce Codex. The full title of this work is mentioned at the end of the first book: the *Book of the Great Initiatory Discourse (of Jeû)*. It contains enumerations of numerous heavenly beings, descriptions (with drawings) of their places or "treasures", and magical names and formulas that the soul needs to know during its ascent to its place of origin. The second part of the Bruce Codex, the *Untitled Treatise*, certainly did have a title once, but it has been lost because of the bad condition of the manuscript. Tardieu has proposed to call it the *Celestial Topography*. Like the *Books of Jeû*, it deals with the structure of the heavenly world, its places (which are often called "depths"), and the powers that dominate it. The *Books of Jeû* and the *Untitled Treatise* belong to the same spiritual world as the *Pistis Sophia*. There are correspondences with *Zostrianus* (NHC VIII,1) and other works that reflect the influence of Neoplatonism (see below), which implies that

they cannot have been written before the middle of the 3rd century.

In 1896 the papyrological department of the State Museums of Berlin acquired a Coptic codex that, shortly before, had been found in Akhmim (Upper Egypt). The codex was registered as *Papyrus Berolinensis 8502*, mostly referred to as BG (= (Codex) Berolinensis Gnosticus) in Coptic Gnostic studies. It contains three Gnostic works – the *Gospel of Mary*, the *Apocryphon of John*, and the *Sophia of Jesus Christ* – and one non-Gnostic writing, the *Act of Peter*, which belongs to the literary genre of the apocryphal Acts of the Apostles. The great Coptic scholar Carl Schmidt (1868-1938) immediately recognized the importance of this codex for Gnostic studies, but his efforts to get it published were very unsuccessful. In 1912, when Schmidt's edition was nearly ready for publication, the whole of it was destroyed by an accident. Two World Wars and personal circumstances caused the edition of the Berlin codex to be delayed further, until it was finally published by Walter C. Till in 1955. But paradoxically, by that time it might be said that the edition came too early, because meanwhile three other copies of the *Apocryphon of John* and one of the *Sophia of Jesus Christ* had been discovered at Nag Hammadi. Till could do no more than note a number of variant readings of these texts in his critical apparatus. Since these two Gnostic writings from the BG cannot be understood in isolation from the same or related texts in the Nag Hammadi Library, they will be discussed in more detail in the next section.

The *Gospel of Mary* is preserved only in a fragmentary state: pages 1-6 and 11-14 of the originally 19 pages of the manuscript are missing. A Greek fragment, which parallels BG 17, 6-19, 3, and shows considerable textual differences, is found in Papyrus Rylands 463. The first part of the preserved text starts with the closing section of a revelatory dialogue between Jesus, called the Saviour or the Lord, and his disciples, which ends with Jesus' command to go out and preach the gospel of the kingdom. The disciples are afraid of the sufferings ahead, but encouraged by Mary (Magdalen), they begin to discuss the words of the Saviour. Then Peter asks Mary: 'Sister, we know that the Saviour loved you more than the other women. Tell us the words of the Saviour which you remember and which you know; we do not know them, nor have we heard them' (BG 10, 1-6). Then Mary tells the disciples about a vision she once had and about a revelation she received from the Saviour about the ascent of the soul and the formulas it has to know in order to overcome the powers that try to prevent it from moving upwards through the heavens. The apostle Andrew doubts the authenticity of this revelation: 'I at least do not believe that the Saviour said this. For certainly these teachings are strange ideas'. Peter agrees and makes Mary cry by saying: 'Did he (the Saviour) really speak with a woman without our knowledge and not openly? Are we to turn about and all listen to her? Did he prefer her to us?'. Levi rebukes "hot-tempered" Peter: 'If the Saviour made her worthy, who are you to reject her?'. He exhorts the apostles to go forth and preach the Gospel, which they do (BG 17, 10-19, 2). This text testifies to the importance of the female disciple Mary Magdalen, and women in general, in the Gnostic communities. Andrew and Peter, however, seem to give voice to the increasing conviction in non-Gnostic circles that secret and deviant teachings should not be accepted and that women should not be active as teachers.

3. THE NAG HAMMADI LIBRARY

A. INTRODUCTION

In December 1945, Egyptian peasants found a pottery jar with Coptic manuscripts in a cave near Nag Hammadi, Upper Egypt. The jar contained at least 12 codices and eight leaves of another one that were inside the front cover of what was later called Codex VI. Through middlemen and antiquity dealers all the codices were eventually acquired by the Coptic Museum in Cairo, although it took one of them two decades to arrive there. It was smuggled out of Egypt and bought by the Jung Institute in Zurich, through the mediation of the Dutch professor Gilles Quispel. This codex became known as the Jung Codex; after the publication of its texts, it was reunited with the other codices in Cairo. Following some confusion about the classification of the codices, the scholarly world reached agreement on an internationally accepted numbering: the Jung Codex became Nag Hammadi Codex (NHC) I and the eight leaves in Codex VI were counted as NHC XIII.

Although there are many individual editions of separate tractates, two groups of scholars have set themselves the task of editing and translating the whole Nag Hammadi Library. Under the auspices of the Institute for Antiquity and Christianity at Claremont, California, a complete edition of all codices with English translations was published under the title "The Coptic Gnostic Library", in the series "Nag Hammadi [later: and Manichaean] Studies" (Brill, Leiden). A group of French speaking scholars at Laval University, Quebec, started the "Bibliothèque Copte de Nag Hammadi" (Université Laval/Peeters, Quebec/Louvain), which at present already contains editions of a considerable number of Nag Hammadi treatises, but is still on its way to completion. The Laval series is especially valuable because of the extensive introductions and commentaries that accompany the texts and French translations. The enormous increase in Gnostic studies that resulted from the discovery of the Nag Hammadi Library has been recorded in the excellent bibliographies of D.M. Scholer.

The thirteen codices of Nag Hammadi contain at least 52 texts and 46 different works, of which 40 were previously unknown. Four treatises are present in two copies (the *Gospel of Truth* [NHC I, 3 and XII, 2], the *Gospel of the Egyptians* [NHC III, 2 and IV, 2], *Eugnostus the Blessed* [NHC III, 3 and V, 1], and *On the Origin of the World* [NHC II, 5 and XIII, 2]) and one even in three copies (the *Apocryphon of John* [NHC II, 1, III, 1, and IV, 1]). In order to give an impression of the contents of the Nag Hammadi Library and the location of the individual tractates, it is useful here to enumerate all the texts (using the English titles adopted by the team of the "Coptic Gnostic Library").

Codex I: 1. *The Prayer of the Apostle Paul.* 2. *The Apocryphon of James.* 3. *The Gospel of Truth.* 4. *The Treatise on the Resurrection.* 5. *The Tripartite Tractate.*

Codex II: 1. *The Apocryphon of John.* 2. *The Gospel of Thomas.* 3. *The Gospel of Philip.* 4. *The Hypostasis of the Archons.* 5. *On the Origin of the World.* 6. *The Exegesis on the Soul.* 7. *The Book of Thomas the Contender.*

Codex III: 1. *The Apocryphon of John.* 2. *The Gospel of the Egyptians.* 3. *Eugnostus the Blessed.* 4. *The Sophia of Jesus Christ.* 5. *The Dialogue of the Saviour.*

Codex IV: 1. *The Apocryphon of John.* 2. *The Gospel of the Egyptians.*

Codex V: 1. *Eugnostus the Blessed.* 2. *The Apocalypse of Paul.* 3. *The (First) Apocalypse of James.* 4. *The (Second) Apocalypse of James.* 5. *The Apocalypse of Adam.*

Codex VI: 1. *The Acts of Peter and the Twelve Apostles.* 2. *Thunder: Perfect Mind.* 3. *Authoritative Teaching.* 4. *The Concept of our Great Power.* 5. *Plato, Republic 588a-589b.* 6. *The Discourse*

It is useless to discuss the Nag Hammadi writings in the order they appear in the codices. Therefore, to describe the rich contents of this collection, the texts will be arranged according to more or less coherent categories. References to the enormous scholarly literature on these texts are omitted; they can easily be found in the editions of the separate texts and in Scholer's bibliographies.

b. Non-Gnostic Writings

The Nag Hammadi Library contains several works that certainly did not originate in a Gnostic milieu. The most conspicuous example is NHC VI, 5, a fragment of the ninth book of Plato's Republic (588a-589b). This passage was most probably taken from a doxographical handbook, for it also occurs in Eusebius, Praeparatio evangelica, XII, 46, 2-6 and is repeatedly quoted or referred to by Neoplatonic philosophers. The text may have been slightly abridged and gnosticized before its translation into Coptic, but there is no certainty at this point, for the Coptic translator apparently had so little command of Greek that without comparison with Plato's original text the result of his work has become incomprehensible.

Other texts that are non-Gnostic, or of which the Gnostic inspiration is very dubious, are the Apocryphon of James (NHC I, 2), the Exegesis on the Soul (NHC II, 6), the Authoritative Teaching (or Authentikos Logos; NHC VI, 3), the Acts of Peter and the Twelve Apostles (NHC VI, 1),

Thunder: Perfect Mind (NHC VI, 2), the three hermetic writings of NHC VI, 6, 7 and 8 (see → Hermetic Literature I), the Teachings of Silvanus (NHC VII, 4) and the Sentences of Sextus (NHC XII, 1). One of these works, the Acts of Peter and the Twelve Apostles, though interesting in itself, does not need a separate discussion here: it belongs to the literary genre of the apocryphal Acts of the Apostles.

The Apocryphon of James purports to be a secret revelation received by James and Peter, originally written in Hebrew. The present title of this work is based on its contents; it has no title in the manuscript. A letter by James, to a recipient whose name has been lost, informs the reader that Jesus had appeared to the twelve disciples 550 days after his resurrection and selected James and Peter for the special and secret revelation that follows. The Apocryphon contains nothing that is specifically Gnostic. Although Jesus says that only 'through knowledge' the kingdom of heaven can be received (NHC I, 8, 23-27), he also puts much emphasis on the necessity of faith, even to the extent of also saying: 'But you, through faith and knowledge, have received life' (NHC I, 14, 8-10). The speeches of Jesus are often reminiscent of those in the Gospel of John. The Apocryphon is a very interesting early Christian document, but there is no reason to declare it a specimen of Gnostic literature.

The Exegesis on the Soul and the Authoritative Teaching describe the fate of the soul from its fall into matter to its return to heaven. To strengthen his arguments, the author of the Exegesis not only quotes texts from the Old and the New Testament, but also from Homer's Odyssey. The Authoritative Teaching teaches ideas on the soul that are known from Middle Platonism and the Neoplatonist philosopher Porphyry; the presence of Christian influences is disputed. A common characteristic of these two treatises is their strong emphasis on rigorous moral behaviour and continence in sexual matters. It was most probably for this reason that they were included in the Nag Hammadi Library. The same holds for the Teachings of Silvanus and the Sentences of Sextus, both of which belong to the rare early Christian sapiential literature. The Sentences were already known through the Greek original and translations in Latin and several oriental languages; they are usually dated around 200 A.D. Because of the fragmentary state of the Coptic manuscript only the sentences 157-180 and 307-397 have been preserved. The Teachings, which were previously unknown, show some influence of the Sentences, but are much more openly Christian than the latter and may, in their present form, date from the beginning of the 4th century.

The Thunder: Perfect Mind is a fascinating hymnal work, but very difficult to classify because of the absence of distinct Christian, Jewish or Gnostic features. It is a revelatory self-proclamation of an unnamed female being, whose utterances mostly begin with 'I am' and in most cases are of an antithetical and paradoxical nature, for instance: 'I am the whore and the holy one. I am the wife and the virgin. I am the mother and the daughter' (NHC VI, 13, 18-21). Similar contradictory expressions in a hymnal style are found in Gnostic, Mandaean and even Indian literature. They most probably served to emphasize the absolute transcendence of the self-revealing deity. There are also parallels in the Isis aretalogies and in Jewish Wisdom literature, but without the antitheses and paradoxes. It has been suggested that the revealer is Sophia, but for this there is no conclusive evidence.

c. Gospels and Related Texts

The Nag Hammadi Library contains four writings that are labelled as Gospels: the *Gospel of Truth* (NHC I, 3 and XII, 2), the *Gospel of Thomas* (NHC II, 2), the *Gospel of Philip* (NHC II, 3), and the *Gospel of the Egyptians* (NHC II, 2 and IV, 2). Only one of them, the *Gospel of Thomas*, can be called, at least partly, a gospel in the usual sense of the word. However, there are some other treatises that transmit traditions about words and deeds of Jesus, which for reasons of convenience will also be discussed in this section: *Thomas the Contender* (NHC II, 7) and the *Dialogue of the Saviour* (NHC III, 5).

The *Gospel of Thomas* contains 114 sayings of Jesus, but no stories about his birth, actions or death. Prior to its discovery, the existence of this gospel was known from a few references and quotations in early Christian literature. After its discovery, the famous but very fragmentary "Unknown Sayings of Jesus", which had been found in Oxyrynchus, proved to represent three different manuscripts of the Greek text of the *Gospel of Thomas*. Only half of the sayings are also found in the canonical gospels. From the beginning, scholarly discussion has concentrated on two major questions: 1. how Gnostic is the *Gospel of Thomas*, 2. does it contain a tradition of the sayings of Jesus that is independent of the canonical gospels? With respect to the first question, according to a growing scholarly consensus this Gospel cannot be called Gnostic, at least if

this term is taken in its usual sense of representing a form of mythological Gnosis; however, there are still scholars who contest this. There can be no doubt, on the other hand, that the label "Gnostic" is appropriate if it is taken in the sense of "esoteric". This is immediately clear from the opening sentences: 'These are the secret sayings that the living Jesus spoke and Didymus Judas Thomas wrote down. And he said: "Whoever finds the interpretation of these sayings will not taste death"'. About the second question opinions are still divided, but a majority of scholars now think that, on the one hand, the *Gospel of Thomas* contains at least a nucleus of independent sayings by Jesus, which can be dated around 50 A.D., and that, on the other hand, other sayings are clearly influenced by the synoptic traditions. The authenticity of the previously unknown sayings is disputed: some of them may be authentic, while others obviously presuppose later theological developments. Whatever its early development may have been, in its present form – which is mostly dated to the first half of the 2nd century – the *Gospel of Thomas* proclaims that understanding the esoteric meaning of Jesus' sayings resolves the duality that exists between God and man and within the human being itself.

The introductory words of *Thomas the Contender* are very reminiscent of those of the Gospel of Thomas: 'The secret words that the Saviour spoke to Judas Thomas, which I, even I Mataias, wrote down'. Although this shows that the work purports to have an esoteric message, there are no references to a specific Gnostic myth. It is a revelatory dialogue between Jesus and his twin brother Thomas, who is called the Contender (*athlētēs*, 'the one who struggles', i.e. against the passions). Accordingly, the main teaching of Jesus turns out to be strongly ascetic.

The *Dialogue of the Saviour* is, in its present form, the result of a complicated literary history. The greater part of it reflects its primary source: a dialogue between Jesus and his disciples Judas, Mary Magdalen and Matthew. The sayings of Jesus have parallels in the Gospels of Matthew and Luke and particularly in those of John and Thomas, but the *Dialogue* seems to reflect an independent tradition. Unfortunately, the text is very fragmentary due to the bad state of the manuscript. For that reason the Gnostic character of this work cannot be determined with certainty; it seems, however, to be rather superficial.

The *Gospel of Truth* is not a gospel in the usual sense of the word, but a Gnostic meditation on the person and work of Jesus as the revealer of salvific

Gnosis. It has no explicit title in the manuscript; its name derives from the first words of the tractate: 'The gospel of truth is joy for those who have received from the Father of truth the grace of knowing him' (NHC I, 16, 31-33). The work shows a considerable number of Valentinian notions, which, however, are not arranged according to the system that the anti-Gnostic writers ascribe to Valentinus and the Valentinians. Irenaeus, *Adversus haereses*, III, 11, 9, says that the Valentinians possessed a *Gospel of Truth*, and another anti-heretical writer, Pseudo-Tertullian, *Adversus omnes haereses*, 4, reports that Valentinus had his own gospel, but he does not mention its name. There has been much disagreement about whether the Nag Hammadi *Gospel of Truth* and the Valentinian gospel mentioned by Irenaeus are identical. Based on the sources presently at our disposal, the question cannot be settled with certainty, although the arguments in favour of the two texts being identical seem more compelling than those against it. The same holds for the question of the possible authorship of Valentinus. Whoever the author may have been, his work evinces his impressive qualities as a writer. He must have been a highly gifted person, a powerful religious thinker and a poet, who cannot have remained unnoticed by his contemporaries. He might indeed have been Valentinus himself.

The *Gospel of Philip* is not a coherent treatise but a compilation of short notes (in some modern editions numbered 1-127) about various subjects, written from a Valentinian perspective. Important subjects are, *inter alia*, the difference between Gnostic and non-Gnostic Christians and, especially, the sacraments. The author seems to know five sacraments: 'The Lord did everything in a mystery: baptism, chrism, eucharist, redemption, and bridal chamber' (NHC II, 67, 28-31). The mystery of the bridal chamber means the completion of the Gnostic's salvation: it implies the unification of the (female) soul with its "angel", its heavenly counterpart. The work also contains some previously unknown sayings of Jesus and a few stories about him that are not recorded in the canonical gospels, for instance in NHC II, 63, 25-30: 'The Lord went into the dye works of Levi. He took seventy-two different colours and threw them into the vat. He took them out all white. And he said: "Even so has the Son of Man come as a dyer"'.

The *Gospel of the Egyptians* is, in the manuscript, also called *The Holy Book of the Great Invisible Spirit*. The two copies in the Nag Hammadi Library are independent translations from the Greek. It is a mythological Gnostic work, closely related to the tradition of the *Apocryphon of John*. There is no relationship with the apocryphal *Gospel of the Egyptians*, of which fragments have been preserved in Clement of Alexandria.

D. MYTHOLOGICAL TEXTS

Various forms of Gnostic mythology have found concrete shape in a number of Nag Hammadi tractates. An important mythological tradition, to which modern scholars often attach the label "Sethian" [→ Sethians], is the one found in the *Apocryphon of John* (NHC II, 1; III, 1; IV, 1 and BG 8502, 2), the *Hypostasis of the Archons* (NHC II, 4), *On the Origin of the World* (NHC II, 5 and XIII, 2), the *Gospel of the Egyptians* (see above) and other works that are clearly influenced by the same complex of ideas. These texts show considerable differences with respect to concrete details, but they all clearly reflect the same mythological structure. *Eugnostus the Blessed* (NHC II, 3 and V, 1), which only deals with the constitution of the Pleroma, belongs to an early stage of the same tradition. It is also reflected in a part of the *Letter of Peter to Philip* (NHC VIII, 2), which for that reason will also be discussed in this connection. The final hymn in the longer recension of the *Apocryphon* (the *Hymn of Pronoia*) belongs to a tradition that has also strongly influenced the mythological structure of the *Trimorphic Protennoia* (NHC XIII, 1). The myth transmitted in the *Paraphrase of Shem* (NHC VII, 1), however, has no relationship with that of the texts just mentioned.

The *Apocryphon of John* may be called the basic text of mythological Gnosis. Two versions, a shorter and a longer one, in four manuscripts, testify to its importance. NHC III, 1 and BG 8502, 2 contain independent translations of the shorter version; NHC II, 1 and IV, 1 present, with variants, a translation of the longer version. After an introduction in which Christ reveals himself to John as the Father, the Mother and the Son, the *Apocryphon* continues with a description of the supreme God, the emanation of the Mother, called Ennoia or Barbelo, the birth of the Son and the further development of the Pleroma. This section has a close and even more original parallel in Irenaeus, *Adversus haereses*, I, 29, and partially also in the *Gospel of the Egyptians*. However, the story of the creation of Adam presupposes another tradition about the highest divine beings (Man and the Son of Man). It has a parallel in Irenaeus,

AH I, 30 and other texts, and was apparently borrowed from another source. Thereupon the first chapters of Genesis are retold from a Gnostic perspective, which takes the form of a dialogue between Christ and John. The longer version ends with a beautiful hymn by the female saviour of mankind, Pronoia, which has been suppressed in the shorter version. The esoteric character of the *Apocryphon* becomes apparent at the end of the tractate, when the Saviour says to John: 'I am saying these things to you that you might write them down and give them secretly to your fellow spirits, for this mystery is that of the immovable race' (II, 31, 29-31 parr. = Synopsis 82, 5-9). The complicated textual history of the *Apocryphon* cannot be reconstructed with certainty, and the same holds for the exact development of its myth, of which the basic elements are already ascribed to → Satornilus (ca. 120). Accordingly, it is impossible to assign an exact date to it: most probably it originated in the 2nd century and then became involved in an ongoing process of rewriting and expanding, which may have continued until the 4th century.

The *Hypostasis of the Archons* and *On the origin of the World* both present a Gnostic interpretation of the first chapters of Genesis. They are closely related, but at the same time they show so many differences that their relationship has to be explained from the use of common sources. There are also distinct parallels with the *Apocryphon of John*. Both texts are difficult to date, although they are often assigned to the 3rd century A.D. As its name indicates, the *Hypostasis* primarily deals with the threatening reality of the archons, the rulers of the world of darkness, who have enslaved the human being. But in the end the Gnostics will be saved through the gift of Gnosis, 'and they will ascend into the limitless light' (NHC II, 97, 7-8). The untitled treatise of NHC II, 5 and XIII, 2 (of which only a small fragment has been preserved), owes its title, *On the Origin of the World*, to modern scholarship, based on its contents. To describe the primeval history of the world, the author has made use of many sources, which he sometimes mentions by name. The work evinces a strong influence of Jewish apocryphal and apocalyptic traditions, whereas there are only a few superficial Christian elements, which suggests that it is basically a non-Christian Gnostic text. The process of salvation already begins with the activities of Pistis Sophia, who was also the cause of the creation of the world of darkness, and of another divine entity, Sophia Zoë. The Jewish apocalyptic influence becomes apparent in the

description of the total destruction of the world of matter and the forces of evil (NHC II, 125, 23-127, 17).

Other works belonging to the same mythological tradition, or at least influenced by it, are several tractates that were known in the school of Plotinus (see below) and also the small treatise called the *Thought of Norea* (NHC IX, 2). Norea, who in other texts is described as the daughter of Adam and Eve or as the wife of Noah or Shem, is presented here as the saved Saviour, whose vicissitudes reflect the salvation of the Gnostic. In the *Hypostasis of the Archons* (NHC II, 91, 34-92, 3) she is called 'an assistance for many generations of mankind' and 'the virgin whom the forces did not defile'.

Eugnostus the Blessed is a non-Christian Gnostic tractate with strong Jewish influences. It describes the development of the Pleroma, beginning with the transcendent 'self-grown, self-constructed Father' and his shining likeness, called Immortal Androgynous Man, whose female name is All-wise Begettress Sophia. The work only deals with the structure of the heavenly world, not with the origin of evil and the creation of the world. It has been claimed that it once was the first part of *On the Origin of the World*, which, however, must remain a (albeit well-argued) hypothesis. Corresponding ideas in Philo suggest an Alexandrian origin, possibly in the beginning of the 2nd century. A later Gnostic author christianized *Eugnostus*, by making it a dialogue between Christ and his disciples, called the *Sophia of Jesus Christ* (NHC III, 4 and BG 8502, 3). He added the figures of Sophia as the cause of evil and Christ as the Saviour who has come from heaven to break the power of the archons. A similar procedure of transforming a non-Christian Gnostic text into a Christian one may also have been applied to other Gnostic texts, such as the *Apocryphon of John* and *On the Origin of the World*.

In the *Apocryphon of John*, the appearance of Christ and the subsequent revelation is provoked by a number of anxious questions that John asks himself. A similar situation is depicted in the *Letter of Peter to Philip*. This tractate opens with a letter of Peter to Philip, in which he invites him to come together with the other apostles. Probably this letter is a later addition, perhaps inspired by the fact that Peter at the end of the text encourages his fellow apostles and sends them away to preach the gospel. A transition to the second part of the tractate is made by the information that Philip agreed and that the apostles assembled on the Mount of Olives. What follows is a revelatory discourse by Christ, in answer to questions raised by the apostles. They want to know the nature of the deficiency of the aeons and their pleroma, how they themselves have become detained in their earthly existence, and in what manner they should return to their origin. Christ answers with a short summary of the myth as told in the tradition of the *Apocryphon of John*. In addition, Christ informs them that they will have to fight the archons by preaching the Gospel and by suffering for it.

The *Trimorphic Protennoia* betrays a complicated literary development, the basis of which seems to have been three self-predications ('I am . . .') of a female Saviour, called Protennoia ("First Thought"), who reveals herself as Voice, Speech, and Word. She has descended three times from heaven to the world of darkness, to save her fallen "members". The same scheme of a threefold descent is found in the *Hymn of Pronoia* at the end of the longer version of the *Apocryphon* and in the Prologue of the Gospel of John. There has been much discussion about the question of which text can claim priority at this point; it seems certain, however, that there is no direct interrelationship between them, but that all three have been influenced by Jewish speculations on the threefold descent of Wisdom. This basic structure of the *Trimorphic Protennoia* has been expanded by the insertion of several doctrinal passages, which evince some influence from the tradition of the *Apocryphon of John* and also show a superficial christianization.

A completely different mythology is found in the *Paraphrase of Shem*. It describes a revelation which Shem (spelled Sēm) received from a divine being, Derdekeas, during his ascent to heaven. The *Paraphrase* assumes three basic principles of the universe: Light, Darkness and the Spirit between them. Hippolytus, *Refutatio*, V, 19, ascribes the same principles to the Sethians, but for the rest there are no correspondences between their ideas and those of the *Paraphrase*. This work explains how the light of the Spirit came to be held in bondage by Nature, and how the creation of heaven and earth and the subsequent history of the world are part of an attempt to save the power of the spirit. Derdekeas is the son or likeness of the Light, and as such he is both revealer and saviour. The work contains several references to biblical and Jewish traditions (the Flood, the tower of Babel), but distinct Christian elements are lacking. There is some resemblance with Manichaean traditions [→ Manichaeism], but not enough to suggest any kind of interdependency. The *Para-*

phrase has a weak composition and is difficult to interpret, perhaps partly due to an inadequate, faulty translation from the Greek into Coptic. Interesting features are the positive evaluation of the Sodomites, the polemics against water baptism, and the prominence of eschatology. As a matter of fact, it can be characterized as a Gnostic apocalypse.

e. APOCALYPTIC AND POLEMICAL TEXTS

The Nag Hammadi Library contains several tractates that present themselves as apocalypses: the *Apocalypse of Paul* (NHC V, 2), the *(First) Apocalypse of James* (NHC V, 3), the *(Second) Apocalypse of James* (NHC V, 4), the *Apocalypse of Adam* (NHC V, 5), and the *Apocalypse of Peter* (NHC VII, 3). Other apocalyptic works that must be discussed in this connection are the *Concept of our Great Power* (NHC VI, 4), *Melchizedek* (NHC IX, 1), and *Hypsiphrone* (NHC XI, 4). The *Apocalypse of Peter* contains some interesting polemics against other Christian Gnostics; this is also the case for the *Testimony of Truth* (NHC IX, 3) and the *Second Treatise of the Great Seth* (NHC VII, 2), which for this reason will also be dealt with in this section.

The *Apocalypse of Adam* is the only one of the texts just mentioned that does not show a clear Christian influence. It presents itself as a revelation, received by Adam from three heavenly visitors and narrated by him to his son Seth. Adam explains how he and Eve lost their original Gnosis at the moment they were split into two individuals by the wrathful 'god, the ruler of the aeons and the powers', i.e. when they lost their androgynous unity. The saving knowledge was transferred to the heavenly Seth, who is 'the seed of the great generation' (the Gnostics). Adam reveals to his son Seth, whom he had called after the great Seth, that the creator-god will be unable to prevent the transmission of knowledge through the generations, despite his attempts to destroy mankind by flood and fire. A saviour figure, called "the Illuminator", will prevail over the powers of darkness and save the elect. Although baptism is mentioned several times, the work does not contain explicit references to the Christian tradition. There are some correspondences with the *Gospel of the Egyptians*, the *Untitled Treatise* of the Bruce Codex, *Zostrianus* (VIII, 1) and *Trimorphic Protennoia* (NHJC XIII, 1), which *inter alia* becomes apparent by their common use of three sets of angel names: Abrasax, Sablo, Gamaliel – Micheus, Michar, Mnesonous – Iesseus, Mazareus, Iessedekeus. The emphasis on baptism in several of these texts may reflect some connection with Jewish baptist circles. According to Epiphanius, *Panarion*, 26, 8, 1, the "Gnostics" used 'apocalypses of Adam' and likewise the Cologne Mani Codex, 48, 16-50, 7 cites an *Apocalypse of Adam*, which, however, does not seem to have been identical with NHC V, 5. The absence of clear references to Christian ideas as well as the influence of Jewish apocalyptic and possibly also baptist traditions suggests an early date, probably the 2nd century.

The *Apocalypse of Paul* has no relationship with a Greek work of the same name that has been known for a long time. It relates how a little child, who is also called the (Holy) Spirit, guides Paul through nine heavens to the tenth, where he embraces his fellow spirits. Building on 2 Corinthians 12:2-4, the revelation starts with the visit to the fourth heaven, where the souls are being interrogated and sometimes sent back to another existence on earth, whereas in the fifth heaven the souls are punished. Of the other heavens only the seventh receives a more than superficial discussion. Paul sees there an old man, wearing a white garment and sitting upon a throne that was seven times brighter than the sun (cf. Daniel 7:9). It is the Demiurge, the god of the Old Testament, who does not want to let him pass to the next heaven and threatens him with his "principalities and authorities". But when Paul gives him the sign he has received from the Spirit, the old man 'turned his face downwards to his creation and to those who are his own authorities' and allows him to pass to the Ogdoad (NHC V, 22, 23-24,1). The *Apocalypse of Paul* most probably dates from the second century: Irenaeus (ca. 180), *Adversus haereses*, II, 30, 7, already knew a Gnostic tradition that ascribed to Paul an ascent to the heavens above that of the Demiurge.

In the manuscript, the tractates of NHC V, 3 and 4 are both called the *Apocalypse of James*, and it is only for reasons of convenience that modern scholars have numbered them. Both texts are revelatory discourses rather than apocalypses in the usual sense of the word. They relate the revelations Jesus gave to James the Just, the Brother of the Lord, who played an important role in Jewish Christianity. The *First Apocalypse* deals with suffering, both of Jesus and James, and with the soul's ascent to heaven. After his resurrection, Jesus, whom James always addresses as "Rabbi", informs James about the docetic nature of his crucifixion and teaches him the formulas the soul needs in order to pass by the "toll collectors" of

the various heavens. The *Second Apocalypse* is cast in the form of a two-part report to Theuda, the father of James, by a Jerusalem priest called Mareim. The first section deals with revelations James has received from Jesus; the second section, which most probably had an independent circulation at one time, deals with James's death. Especially the *Second Apocalypse* shows strong Jewish-Christian influences, but at the same time it is clearly a Gnostic composition: the author alludes to the bad, ignorant Demiurge (NHC V, 54, 7-15; 58, 2-6) and mentions the aeons (53, 8) and the archons (56, 19), and the whole work emphasizes that knowledge is indispensable for salvation. The *Apocalypses of James* are mostly ascribed to the 2nd century, but there is no certainty on this point.

The *Apocalypse of Peter* contains an account of three revelations received by the apostle Peter and explained by Jesus the Saviour. The first vision deals with the hostile Jews who try to kill Jesus and his followers: they are called 'blind ones who have no guide' and interpreted as at least six groups of opponents of the author's Gnostic views, including both orthodox believers and other Gnostics. These inner-Christian polemics take up a considerable part of the whole treatise (NHC VII, 73, 10-81,3) and seem to have been the author's main concern. The second and third revelations instruct Peter about the correct Gnostic interpretation of the crucifixion and resurrection of Jesus. On the cross he sees a glad and laughing Jesus, who is the 'Living Jesus'; the one into whose hands and feet the nails are driven is his 'physical part', the 'substitute'. Jesus' resurrection means the unification of the Living Jesus with the perfect light of the spiritual Pleroma. The work originated most probably in the 3rd century: its vehement polemics against other Christians, both Gnostic and non-Gnostic, makes a date before the end of the 2nd century improbable.

In this connection, attention must be drawn to another treatise in which polemics play an important part, the *Testimony of Truth* (NHC IX, 3). Almost half of this text has been lost because of the fragmentary state of the manuscript. Its original title being unknown, scholars have given it one that is based on its contents. The work consists of two parts: a well-constructed homily and miscellaneous additions. The homily, addressed to a Christian Gnostic congregation, warns against the erroneous ideas of non-Gnostic Christians, who, for instance, think that martyrdom leads to immediate salvation or that marriage and procreation are allowed, whereas in fact they are 'defilement'.

The homily then describes the behaviour of the true Gnostic and ends with a characteristic Gnostic confession: 'When man comes to know himself and God who is over the truth, he will be saved and he will crown himself with the crown unfading'. The miscellaneous part starts with a firm rejection of the god of the Old Testament and then continues with polemics against → Valentinus, → Basilides and his son Isidore, the Simonians (see → Simon Magus), and also against water baptism. Unfortunately, this part of the manuscript is in such a bad state that most details of the author's argumentation escape us.

The *Second Treatise of the Great Seth* is a revelation by Jesus Christ to the 'perfect and incorruptible ones'. It reveals the true story of Jesus, including his commission by the heavenly 'multitudinous assembly of the rejoicing Majesty', his descent to earth and his struggle with and victory over the powers of darkness, his seeming crucifixion, and his return to the Pleroma. In a long passage (VII, 55, 14-56, 19) apparently directed against the orthodox interpretation of the crucifixion, Christ explains that he 'did not die in reality but in appearance'. In reality 'I was rejoicing in the height over all the wealth of the archons ... And I was laughing at their ignorance'. In the second part of the treatise the author attacks the orthodox Christians who persecute the elect: they 'think that they are advancing the name of Christ, since they are vain in ignorance' (VII, 59, 19-60, 1). Christ rejects the Christology of the orthodox and their claim to be the true Church: in fact, the archons made an imitation of the ineffable union that exists among the children of light by 'proclaiming the doctrine of a dead man and falsehoods to resemble the freedom and purity of the perfect assembly' (60, 13-61, 3).

The *Concept of our Great Power* betrays a complicated literary history. It divides history into three "aeons": the 'aeon of the flesh', which ends with the Flood, then the 'psychic' aeon, in which the Saviour appears, and finally the last aeon in which al kinds of disasters occur, ending with the consummation of the world by fire and the redemption of the Gnostic believers. They will go to the 'unchangeable aeon' of the Great Power, who is the supreme God, exalted 'above all powers', including the 'Father of the flesh', i.e. the creator god of the Old Testament. The Saviour is not mentioned by name, but from what is said about him it becomes obvious that he is identified with Christ.

Melchizedek is an apocalyptic work, which derives its modern title from the fact that it purports to transmit the revelation that the Old Testament figure of Melchizedek (Genesis 14:18) had received from several heavenly beings. The tractate contains, *inter alia*, a long list of hymnal invocations of divine entities ('Holy are you, . . .') that also appear in the mythological tradition of the *Apocryphon of John* and the *Gospel of the Egyptians*. The manuscript of this tractate is severely damaged, but what is left leaves no doubt about the fact that Melchizedek is identified with Jesus Christ.

A further unknown female visionary appears in the short tractate *Hypsiphrone* (NHC XI, 4). It contains a vision that was revealed to a certain Hypsiphrone ('High-minded One') 'in the place of her virginity', but the manuscript is so badly damaged that it has become impossible to grasp the message of this short treatise.

F. VALENTINIAN TEXTS
The Nag Hammadi Library contains several works that can be classified as Valentinian, although none of them completely fits the Valentinian schools and systems described by the church fathers. Valentinian treatises are: the *Gospel of Truth* (NHC I, 3 and XII, 2), the *Treatise on Resurrection* (NHC I, 4), the *Tripartite Tractate* (NHC I, 5), the *Gospel of Philip* (NHC II, 3), the *Interpretation of Knowledge* (NHC XI, 1) and the *Valentinian Exposition* with the fragments on the Anointing, Baptism and the Eucharist (NHC XI, 2).

Although a Valentinian origin has been claimed for all five tractates of NHC I, this can only be proven with respect to its tractates 3, 4 and 5. Most probably the *Apocryphon of James* (NHC I, 2) is not a Gnostic text at all (see above), whereas for the *Prayer of the Apostle Paul* (NHC I, 1) the evidence is far from compelling. The *Prayer*, which is written on the front flyleaf of the codex, is a hymn of praise and at the same time a prayer for redemption (I, A, 22-23: 'redeem my eternal light-soul and my spirit'). The Creator is called 'the psychic God' (I, A, 31), which is in accordance with the terminology of the Western branch of Valentinianism, but not necessarily an indication that the whole prayer is of Valentinian inspiration. The general similarity to other Gnostic and hermetic hymns and prayers, and to the invocations found in magical texts as well, make it conceivable that the author simply used a term of Valentinian provenance to characterize the creator.

The *Treatise on Resurrection* deals with the question of how to interpret the Christian doctrine of the resurrection. It has the form of a doctrinal letter addressed to a certain Rheginus. For this reason the tractate was formerly also called the *Letter to Rheginus on the Resurrection*; it has no title in the manuscript. As a good Gnostic, the author says that the resurrection can already be achieved in this life: 'flee from the divisions and the fetters, and already you have the resurrection . . . why not consider yourself as risen?' (NHC I, 49, 13-24). But that does not mean that the resurrection of the dead is of less importance. As Son of God, Christ vanquished death and as Son of Man he realized the restoration of the Pleroma. He was able to do so, 'because he was originally from above, a seed of the truth', before the cosmos came into being (NHC I, 44, 21-38). This Christology betrays the author's Valentinianism. As could be expected, he denies the resurrection of the flesh: he subscribes to Paul's view that the dead will be raised in a spiritual body.

The *Tripartite Tractate* has no title in the manuscript. It received its modern title because the text is divided by scribal decoration into three parts. It is an elaborate and highly speculative theological treatise, written by an original thinker. The first part describes the transcendent Father and the aeonic world that emanated from him, the second part deals with the creation and the Fall, and the third part with the coming of the Saviour. Though the work obviously belongs to the Western branch of Valentinianism, it presents a radical revision of some important Valentinian notions. One of them is that the function of Sophia as the aeon who stirs the process of creation is taken over by the Logos. At this point, as also with respect to Christology and many other themes, the author comes close to the views of orthodox theologians from the 3rd century, such as Origen, but he has also much in common with the Valentinian Gnostic Heracleon, who wrote an influential commentary on the Gospel of John. The unknown author of the *Tripartite Tractate*, one of the longest of the Nag Hammadi Library (88 pages), was a powerful thinker who obviously did not want to hide his light under the bushel of a Valentinian minority: he wanted to address the Church as a whole.

The *Interpretation of Knowledge* is a homily probably directed at a group of Gnostic believers who were still members of a larger Christian community. The author offers an explanation of the major themes of the Christian tradition, using many terms and expressions that were current among Valentinian Gnostics. The community appears to be torn by jealousy and hatred over the issue of spiritual gifts. Gnostics should not be proud and presumptuous because of their Gnosis. Christ is the great example of unity and humility. The author takes up Paul's simile of the Church as a composite body, in which the eye and the hand and the foot each have their own function and special gift and are not jealous at each other but work together: 'be thankful that you do not exist outside the body!' (XI, 18, 33-34). This document provides a unique picture of a mixed Christian community, many of which must still have existed at the end of the 2nd and in the first half of the 3rd century.

The *Valentinian Exposition* is also unique in its kind. It presents an original Valentinian account of the origin of the Pleroma, the Fall of Sophia and the creation of the world, together with fragments of a Valentinian celebration of baptism and the eucharist. It is also of great interest because it provides inside information about theological controversies among the Valentinians themselves. The reports of the church fathers about disagreements on specific issues turn out to be right: the author repeatedly argues for certain interpretations of the Valentinian myth, rejecting the views favoured by others, for instance with respect to the cause of Sophia's suffering.

G. ASCENTS TO HEAVEN

The Nag Hammadi Library contains several Gnostic treatises that show the influence of Neoplatonism and are focused on the ascent to heaven more than on the Gnostic myth of fall and salvation. These writings are the *Three Steles of Seth* (NHC VII, 5), *Zostrianus* (VIII, 1), *Marsanes* (NHC X, 1) and *Allogenes* (NHC XI, 3). The *Books of Jeû* and the *Untitled Treatise* of the Bruce Codex belong to the same category.

In his *Life of Plotinus*, 16, Porphyry relates that in the school of Plotinus there were people who 'had abandoned the old philosophy' and held that 'Plato had not penetrated to the depths of intelligible reality'. In support of their views they appealed to 'Revelations by Zoroaster, Zostrianus, Nicotheus, Allogenes, Messos, and other people of the kind'. It is virtually certain that the Nag Hammadi writings *Zostrianus* and *Allogenes* are identical with the books of the same name mentioned by Porphyry. Moreover, the revelations described in *Allogenes* are addressed by Allogenes to his "son" Messos, who is also mentioned by Porphyry. About 265, Plotinus took the offensive against these Gnostics: not only did he himself write a full treatise against them (*Enneads* II, 9: *Against the Gnostics*), but he also induced his most faithful pupils, Amesius and Porphyry, to do the same. Amesius wrote forty treatises against *Zostrianus*, of which, unfortunately, not a single one has been preserved. Plotinus' main objections to the Gnostics are: 1. they introduce a great number of levels of being, whereas he only accepts three (the One, Mind, and Soul), and 2. they affirm that the world and its creator are bad, whereas he holds that the world is good and beautiful, originating from the divine World-Soul. There is no doubt that Plotinus reacted against what he had read in books like *Zostrianus* or the *Untitled Treatise* of the Bruce Codex. In his attack on the Gnostics' complete rejection of the visible creation and their idea that they will ascend to another, new earth, he remarks that they introduce strange hypostases such as "Exiles", "Antitypes" and "Repentances" (*Enneads*, II, 9, 6). These 'strange hypostases' are also mentioned in *Zostrianus* (NHC VIII, 4, 20-5, 29; 8, 10-20; etc.) and the *Untitled Treatise* (Baynes, 180; Schmidt-MacDermot, 263). The strong influence of later Platonism on *Zostrianus* can also be seen in the latter's description of the transcendent God (VIII, 64, 11-84, 22), which is based on the same Middle- or Neoplatonic source that was used by the fourth-century Christian writer Marius Victorinus in his *Adversus Arium*, I, 49-50. Another indication of philosophical influence is the appearance of the Neoplatonic triad Existence-Life-Thought in the *Three Steles of Seth* (VII, 122, 18-21; 125, 28-32; cf.; 123, 18-21), *Zostrianus* (VIII, 15, 10-17), and *Allogenes* (XI, 49, 26-38; 61, 33-39).

Plotinus' observation that the Gnostics are 'giving names to a multitude of intelligible realities' is abundantly confirmed by these authentic Gnostic writings. Unfortunately, the manuscripts of *Zostrianus* and *Marsanes* are so severely damaged that great portions have been lost. *Marsanes*, in particular, shows that the heavenly ascent was accompanied and effectuated by theurgic rites, which have their counterpart in magical practices and related ideas in the Neoplatonist Iamblichus. The knowledge of the divine world revealed in these texts and the invocations used are apparently sufficient for salvation. The *Three Steles of Seth* contain hymns to the three fundamental levels of divine being: the divine Son (Autogenes), the divine Mother (Barbelo), and God the Unknown Father. A short introduction in prose claims that Dositheus, traditionally seen as the predecessor of Simon Magus, has transmitted these hymns to the elect. This is followed by an interesting personal remark: 'Many times I joined in giving glory with

the powers, and I became worthy of the immeasurable majesties'. This implies that these hymns are to be said during the ascent to heaven, which is confirmed by some remarks, after the third hymn and again in prose, about how the hymns should be used. First they must be spoken one after another in ascending order, and then there should be silence: 'After the silence, they descend from the third; they bless the second and after these the first. The way of ascent is the way of descent' (NHC VII, 127, 11-21). This shows that the mystic experience of the individual was re-enacted in a liturgical celebration by the Gnostic community.

Although there may be some vague allusions to Christian ideas in *Zostrianus*, these texts are fundamentally non-Christian. As far as the entities of the aeonic world are concerned, there are clear links with the mythological tradition of the *Apocryphon of John* and the *Gospel of the Egyptians*. But the classic Gnostic myth as a whole had apparently lost its interest for Plotinus' Gnostics; they were primarily interested in the last stage of the salvation: the ascent to the divine world.

4. THE TESTIMONY OF ANTI-GNOSTIC WRITERS

Before the Berlin Gnostic Codex and the Nag Hammadi writings became known, the student of the Gnostic current in Antiquity had to rely almost exclusively on the reports about Gnostic schools and systems by anti-Gnostic writers. And this was all the more so, since the bewildering original works of the *Codex Askewianus* and the *Codex Brucianus* were generally thought to be late productions of an already declining Gnosis. Most of the anti-Gnostic writers were Christian theologians who considered the Gnostic movement a threat to the Christian Church and its doctrines. But Platonic philosophers such as Plotinus and his pupils also wrote treatises against the Gnostics, because in their view the ideas about a multitude of intelligible realities were not based on solid philosophical reasoning but on very dubious revelations.

The numerous authentic Gnostic works that are now available have made it perfectly clear that there was never one single Gnosticism. Instead, there existed a broad current of frequently inter-related ideas, expressed by individuals, schools or communities, which had one common denominator: esoteric, revealed Gnosis as the only means of salvation. Except for their common emphasis on salvific Gnosis, the author of the thoroughly

Christian *Gospel of Truth* cannot have had much in common with that of the non-Christian *Three Steles of Seth*. The church fathers, however, although admitting its variegated character, described the Gnostic movement as one coherent current, which had started with Simon Magus and through a succession of Gnostic teachers had led to the Gnostic schools, systems and communities they knew or had heard about. Since they were almost exclusively interested in the ideas of Christian Gnostics, they speak about Gnosticism as a Christian heresy – an idea that has long dominated Gnostic studies and is still defended by some church historians even today. Nevertheless, the anti-Gnostic polemics of such writers as Irenaeus, Hippolytus and Epiphanius contain so much information about the ideas of individual Gnostics, their schools or communities, and even their rituals, that they will always remain of great importance for Gnostic studies. Surprisingly, none of the Nag Hammadi writings proves to be in complete agreement with any of the many systems described by the church fathers. On the other hand, the church fathers give information about a great number of real of alleged Gnostic teachers and groups for which there is no counterpart in the authentic Gnostic writings. A discussion of many of them is to be found elsewhere in the present Dictionary (→ Archontics, Audians, Basilides, Borborites, Cainites, Carpocratians, Cerinthus, Elchasai, Justin the Gnostic, Marcion, Marcus the Magician, Menander, Monoimus, Naassenes, Ophites, Perates, Prodicus, Satornilus, Sethians, Simon Magus, Valentinus and Valentinians).

The study of the early Christian anti-Gnostic writers is beset with many problems. In a few cases they transmit an original Gnostic document (see first section, above), but mostly they give only a summary of the ideas of individual Gnostics or Gnostic groups, sometimes with a few isolated quotations from a relevant Gnostic text. The information is often so sketchy that the real meaning of the views that are being criticized remains in the dark. They use both direct and indirect sources, and the value of the latter in particular is difficult to determine. Since their goal is to fight against views that in their eyes are dangerous, the major question about these polemical writers concerns their trustworthiness. Did they really try to understand their opponents? In how far did they misunderstand their sources, or consciously manipulate them? These questions cannot be neglected in any study of the patristic evidence. They can only be answered, if at all, by carefully analyzing the information in question and evaluate it against the background of the polemic's theological intentions.

The first anti-Gnostic work we know of is the so-called *Syntagma* of Justin Martyr († 165), which he himself mentions in his first *Apology*, 26: 'We have also a treatise, written against all heresies that have arisen, which, if you wish to read it, we will give to you'. Unfortunately, this work is lost, but it is quite certain that much of it found its way into the extensive anti-Gnostic works of Irenaeus, Hippolytus and Epiphanius. According to Eusebius, *Church History*, IV, 7, 15-8,1, Justin's younger contemporary Hegesippus also fought the impious heresies, but his work is lost as well. Although there are other authors who provide first-hand information about Gnostics, such as → Clement of Alexandria and Tertullian (ca. 200), Irenaeus, Hippolytus and Epiphanius are by far the most important and, therefore, deserve a short discussion.

Irenaeus originally came from Asia Minor, where he had heard the famous bishop Polycarpus. In 178, he became bishop of Lyons and Vienne in the Rhone valley, where he witnessed the rapidly spreading influence of Christian Gnostics of the Valentinian type. In order to refute their ideas he composed an extensive work in five volumes, entitled *Refutation and Overthrow of the Gnosis Falsely so Called*, mostly referred to as *Adversus Haereses (Against Heresies)*. The work was originally written in Greek, but except for a number of fragments, it has survived completely only in a Latin translation. Irenaeus seems to have had first-hand knowledge of the Valentinian school of Ptolemy and of the teachings and liturgical practices of → Marcus the Magician, but he also gives information about other teachers and groups he considers Gnostic. Irenaeus presents this material in Book I, and in the next books he refutes the Gnostic views from various angles: in Book II from reason, in Book III from the teaching of the apostles, and in Book IV from the sayings of Jesus; Book V is mainly devoted to a defence of the resurrection of the flesh, which was generally rejected by the Gnostics. Although he sometimes demonstrably made use of excellent sources, Irenaeus does not really try to understand his opponents; he characterizes their ideas and myths as ridiculous, unreasonable, impious and contrary to the true faith of the Church.

An important aspect of Irenaeus' work, which had a great influence on later heresiology, and for a long time on the study of Gnosticism as well, is his "historical" approach to the Gnostic movement. According to him, it was a heresy that had started with Simon Magus and through a chain of teachers had been transmitted and variously elaborated up to its manifestation in the Valentinians and other Gnostics of his own days. This description of the development of Gnostic thought accords with the usual presentation of the history of Greek philosophy: as a succession of teachers within a school of thought, who provide their own interpretation and elaboration of the founder's fundamental ideas. The Greek word *hairesis* was used to indicate such a school or a faction within it, but in the Christian vocabulary of the second half of the 2nd century its meaning began to change from that of a divergent opinion that was open to discussion to that of impious "heresy". Most probably, Irenaeus already found this idea of a Gnostic genealogy in the *Syntagma* of Justin, who speaks about this work in connection with Simon Magus. Justin was a philosopher and a (Christian) school-head himself, which may have induced him to describe the variety of thought within Christianity in the same way as was usually done with respect to Greek philosophy. It is not exactly known which heresiarchs filled Irenaeus' complete list of successive teachers, but according to *AH*, I, 23-27, it comprised at least the following names: Simon Magus, Menander, Satornilus, Basilides, and Carpocrates, with whom Cerinthus and the Ebionites are connected, apparently because they taught the same doctrine about Jesus. Cerdo and his pupil Marcion are said to derive from the Simonians. There is a general scholarly consensus that this Gnostic genealogy and similar ones in later authors have no historical value whatsoever.

Hippolytus was a learned Roman priest, who around 220 became the first "anti-pope", after a conflict with his bishop Callistus on doctrinal and moral issues. He wrote two anti-heretical works, the *Syntagma against all heresies* and the *Refutation of all heresies* (*Refutatio omnium haeresium*). The former is lost, although some scholars think that it can be partly reconstructed from Pseudo-Tertullian's *Adversus omnes haereses*, Philastrius' *Liber de haeresibus* and Epiphanius' *Panarion*. The *Refutatio*, written after 222, consists of ten books, of which books II and III are lost. The first book deals with the Greek philosophical schools and opinions, the fourth with astrology and magic; books V-IX contain a refutation of 33 Gnostic sects, whereas book X, *inter alia*, gives a summary of the previous refutations. Hippolytus consistently tries to prove that the Gnostic systems and myths he describes have

simply been derived from Greek philosophy or mythology; however, his arguments are far from being convincing, and often amount to sheer nonsense.

A major problem with Hippolytus' *Refutatio* concerns the presence in his work of what, with a German term, is usually called his "Sondergut", i.e. his description of Gnostic systems for which there is no counterpart in Irenaeus or other sources. It comprises at least the whole of book V (Naassenes, Perates, Sethians, Justin the Gnostic), VI, 9-18 (the Simonian *Apophasis megalē*) and 29-37 (Valentinians), VII, 20-27 (Basilides), VIII, 8-11 (Docetists) and 12-15 (Monoimus). An intriguing feature of this "Sondergut" is that the systems it describes are characterized by evident parallels with respect to both content and wording, by frequent allegorical interpretations of Greek mythological material, and by a much more frequent and variegated use of biblical texts than is found in the authentic Nag Hammadi documents. Of the various solutions that have been proposed to explain these common characteristics, three may be mentioned here, the last one of which is most likely: 1. Hippolytus himself has adapted a collection of sources he had at his disposal, 2. this dossier had already been composed and adapted by a non-Christian Gnostic before it came into Hippolytus' possession, 3. this was done by a Christian Gnostic. In any case, the fact that the sources used by Hippolytus have obviously been manipulated often prevents firm conclusions about (details of) the systems described and refuted in his *Refutatio*.

Epiphanius of Salamis (ca. 315-403) served for thirty years as head of a monastery near Eleutheropolis in Palestine, before he was consecrated bishop of Constantia in the island of Cyprus in 367. He was famous for his learning and his zeal for ecclesiastical orthodoxy. Between 374 and 377 he wrote an extensive anti-heretical work called *Panarion* or *Medicine Chest*, intended as an antidote to those who had been bitten by the serpent of heresy. It deals with 80 heresies of which the first 20 belong to the Greek and the Jewish world. The Christian heresies start with Simon Magus and end with the 4th-century Messalians. Epiphanius' work is indispensable because of the many and sometimes excellent sources he quotes or makes use of, but at the same time its value is very much restricted by the fact that he is obviously incapable of handling his sources. His reports about the individual heresies are confused and confusing: he often misunderstands what he has read or heard; he sees connections between persons and currents that certainly did not exist; he often contradicts himself; and his explanations are seldom to the point. It is no wonder that scholars have reached sometimes completely divergent opinions about the Gnostic and other sects that are dealt with by Epiphanius. Reading his work is mostly frustrating and often unrewarding, but it cannot be ignored.

The discovery of so many original Gnostic writings at Nag Hammadi has not made the study of the testimonies of the church fathers superfluous. Notwithstanding their often scanty information and their biased attitude, the anti-Gnostic authors testify to the existence of Gnostic works and systems other than those contained in the Coptic codices. In late Antiquity, there must have circulated a great number of Gnostic books, which varied enormously with respect to both content and style. The authentic works that have been preserved are often difficult to interpret because of their obscure language and unknown presuppositions, and sometimes the testimonies of the church fathers do contribute to a better understanding. Only by careful analysis of the direct and indirect sources, combined with in-depth studies of the spiritual and social climate of late Antiquity in which the Gnostic movement originated and flourished, may we nourish hopes of reaching a better understanding of the Gnostics' experience of the divine and their interpretation of the world in which they were living.

Greek and Latin texts: W. Völker (ed.), *Quellen zur Geschichte der christlichen Gnosis* (Sammlung ausgewählter kirchen- und dogmengeschichtlicher Quellenschriften, Neue Folge, 5), Tübingen: J.C.B. Mohr (Paul Siebeck), 1932 ♦ K. Holl (ed.), *Epiphanius. Panarion haer.*, 3 vols., Leipzig: Hinrichs, 1915-1933, 2nd rev. ed. of vols. 2 and 3 by J. Dummer, Berlin: Akademie Verlag, 1980 ♦ F. Sagnard (ed.), *Clément d'Alexandrie: Extraits de Théodote* (SC 23), Paris: Les Éditions du Cerf, 1948, 1970 ♦ G. Quispel (ed.), *Ptolémée: Lettre à Flora* (SC 24 bis), Paris: Les Éditions du Cerf, 1966 ♦ A. Rousseau, L. Doutreleau *et al.* (eds.), *Irenée de Lyon: Contre les Hérésies*, 8 vols. (SC 34, 100, 152-153, 263-264, 293-294), Paris: Éditions du Cerf, 1952-1982 (with French translation) ♦ M. Marcovich (ed.), *Hippolytus: Refutatio omnium haeresium* (PTS, 25), Berlin-New York: De Gruyter, 1986 ♦ W. Foerster, *Die Gnosis*, vol 1: *Zeugnisse der Kirchenväter*, Zürich: Artemis Verlag, 1969, rev. ed. 1995 (Engl. trans. ed. by R.McL. Wilson, *Gnosis: A Selection of Gnostic Texts*, vol. 1: Patristic evidence, Oxford: Clarendon Press, 1972).

Coptic Texts: a. Texts found before 1945: C. Schmidt (ed.), *Gnostische Schriften in koptischer Sprache aus dem Codex Brucianus* (TU, 8, 1-2), Leipzig: Hinrichs, 1892 ♦ Idem (transl.), *Koptisch-gnostischen Schriften*

I: *Die Pistis Sophia, Die beiden Bücher des Jeû, Unbekanntes altgnostisches Werk* (Die griechischen christlichen Schriftsteller der ersten drei Jahrhunderte, 13), Leipzig: Hinrichs, 1905, revised editions in 1925, 1954 (by W.C. Till) and 1981 (by H.-M. Schenke) ♦ Idem (ed.), *Pistis Sophia, neu herausgegeben mit Einleitung nebst griechischem Wort- und Namenregister* (Coptica, II), Copenhagen: Gyldendalske Boghandel-Nordisk Forlag, 1925 ♦ Ch. A. Baynes (ed.), *A Coptic Gnostic Treatise Contained in the Codex Brucianus*, Cambridge: Cambridge University Press, 1933 ♦ W.C. Till (ed.), *Die gnostischen schriften des koptischen Papyrus Berolinenhsis 8502* (TU, 60), Berlin: Akademie-Verlag, 1955 (2nd, revised edition by H.-M. Schenke, 1972) ♦ R. McL. Wilson & G.W. MacRae (eds.), *The Gospel according to Mary*, BG, 1: 7,1-19,5, in: D.M. Parrott (ed.), *Nag Hammadi Codices V,2-5 and VI with Papyrus Berolinensis 8502, 1 and 4* (NHS XI), Leiden: E.J. Brill, 1979, 453-471 (with the Greek fragment) ♦ A. Pasquier (ed.), *L'Évangile selon Marie* (BG 1) (Bibliothèque Copte de Nag Hammadi, Section "textes", 10), Quebec: Presses de l'Université Laval, 1983 (with the Greek fragment) ♦ M. Tardieu, *Codex de Berlin* (Sources Gnostiques et Manichéennes, 1), Paris: Les Éditions du Cerf, 1984 (introductions, translations, commentaries) ♦ V. MacDermot (ed.), *Pistis Sophia* (NHS, IX), Leiden: E.J. Brill, 1978 (reprint of Schmidt's 1925 edition, translation and notes by MacDermot) ♦ V. MacDermot (ed.), *The Books of Jeu and the Untitled Text in the Bruce Codex* (NHC, XIII), Leiden: E.J. Brill, 1978 (reprint of Schmidt's 1892 edition, translation and notes by MacDermot).

b. The Nag Hammadi Library: J.M. Robinson (ed.), *The Facsimile Edition of the Nag Hammadi Codices*, 13 vols., Leiden: E.J. Brill, 1972-1984 ♦ *The Coptic Gnostic Library*: edition and English translation of all texts by the Claremont group, published in the NH(M)S series, Leiden: E.J. Brill, 1975-1996 (paperback edition 2000): Cod. I (H.W. Attridge *et al.*), NHS XXII, XXIII, 1985; Cod. II, 1; III, 1; IV, 1, with BG 8502, 2 (M. Waldstein & F. Wisse), NHMS XXXII, 1995; Cod. II, 2-7 (B. Layton *et al.*), NHS XX, XXI, 1989; Cod. III, 2 and IV, 2 (A. Böhlig & F. Wisse), NHS IV, 1975; Cod. III, 3-4 and V, 1 (D.M. Parrot), NHS XXVII, 1991; Cod. III, 5 (S. Emmel *et al.*), NHS XXVI, 1984; Cod. V, 2-5 and VI, with BG 8502, 1 and 4 (D.M. Parrott *et al.*), NHS XI 1979; Cod. VII (B.A. Pearson *et al.*), NHMS XXX, 1996; Cod. VIII (H. Sieber *et al.*), NHS XXXI, 1991; Cod. IX and X (B.A. Pearson *et al.*), NHS XV, 1981; Cod. XI, XII, XIII (Ch.W. Hedrick *et al.*), NHS XXVIII, 1990) ♦ English translation: J.M. Robinson (ed.), *The Nag Hammadi Library in English*, 4th, rev. ed., Leiden: E.J. Brill, 1996 ♦ *Bibliothèque Copte de Nag Hammadi, section "Textes"*: edition and French translation of all texts by the Laval group (in progress, about 35 texts published) ♦ idem, *section "Concordances"*: concordances of all Coptic codices in 8 vols. (to be completed in 2005) ♦ H.-G. Bethge, *Der Brief des Petrus an Philippus: Ein neutestamentliches Apokryphon aus dem Fund von Nag Hammadi* (NHC VIII,2) (TU, 141), Berlin: Akademie Verlag, 1997 (edition, German translation, commentary) ♦ U.-K. Plisch, *Die Auslegung der Erken-*

ntnis (Nag Hammadi-Codex XI, 1) (TU, 142), Berlin: Akademie Verlag, 1996 (edition, German translation, commentary) ♦ H.-M. Schenke, *Das Philippus-Evangelium (Nag Hammadi-Codex II,3)* (TU, 143), Berlin: Akademie Verlag, 1997 (edition, German translation, commentary) ♦ W. Foerster (transl.), *Die Gnosis*, vol. II: *Koptische und mandäische Quellen*, Zürich: Artemis Verlag, 1971, rev. ed. 1995 (Engl. trans. by R.McL. Wilson, *Gnosis: A Selection of Gnostic Texts*, vol. II: *Coptic and Mandaean Sources*, Oxford: Clarendon Press, 1974) ♦ B. Layton, *The Gnostic Scriptures. A New Translation with Annotations and Introductions*, Garden City, New York: Doubleday & Company, 1987.

Lit.: L. Abramowski, "Ein gnostischer Logostheologe: Umfang und Redaktor des gnostischen Sondergutes in Hippolyts 'Widerlegung aller Häresien'", in: eadem, *Drei christologische Untersuchungen* (Beiheft zur Zeitschrift für die neutestamentliche Wissenschaft, 45), Berlin-New York: Walter de Gruyter, 1981, 18-62 ♦ A. le Boulluec, *La notion d'hérésie dans la littérature grecque, IIe-IIIe siècles*, 2 vols., Paris: Études Augustiniennes, 1985 ♦ R. van den Broek, "Coptic Gnostic and Manichaean Literature, 1996-2000", in: M. Immerzeel & J. van der Vliet (eds.), *Coptic Studies on the Threshold of a New Millennium: Proceedings of the Seventh International Congress of Coptic Studies, Leiden, 27 August-2 September 2000* (Orientalia Lovaniensia Analecta, 133), Louvain: Peeters/ Departement Oosterse Studies, 2004, 669-693 ♦ C.A. Evans, R.L. Webb & R.A. Wiebe (eds), *Nag Hammadi Texts and the Bible: A Synopsis and Index* (New Testament Tools and Studies, 18), Leiden: E.J. Brill, 1993 ♦ P. Hadot, "Être, Vie et Pensée chez Plotin et avant Plotin", in: E.R. Dodds et alii, *Les sources de Plotin: Dix expositions et discussions* (Entretiens sur l'Antiquité Classique, 5), Geneva: Vandoeuvres, 1960, 107-157 ♦ K. Koschorke, *Hippolyt's Ketzerbekämpfung und Polemik gegen die Gnostiker*, Wiesbaden, 1975 ♦ J. Mansfeld, *Heresiography in Context: Hippolytus' Elechos as a Source for Greek Philosophy* (Philosophia Antiqua, 56), Leiden: E.J. Brill, 1992 ♦ P. McKenchie, "Flavia Sophe in Context", *Zeitschrift für Papyrologie und Epigraphik* 135 (2001), 117-124 ♦ L. Painchaud & A. Pasquier (eds.), *Les Textes de Nag Hammadi et le problème de leur classification: Actes du colloque tenu à Québec du 15 au 19 septembre 1993* (Bibliothèque copte de Nag Hammadi, "Section Études", 3), Quebec/Louvain: Presses de l'Université Laval/Peeters, 1995 ♦ B.A. Pearson, "Gnosticism 1992-1996", in: S. Emmel *et alii* (eds.), *Ägypten und Nubien in spätantiker und christlicher Zeit: Akten des 6. Internationalen Koptologenkongresses, Münster, 20-26 Juli 1996*, vol. II, Wiesbaden: Reichert, 1999, 431-452 ♦ idem, "Gnostic Ritual and Iamblichus's Treatise *On the Mysteries of Egypt*", in: idem, *Gnosticism and Christianity in Roman and Coptic Egypt*, New York, London: T&T Clark International, 2004 ♦ J.M. Robinson, "From the Cliff to Cairo: The Story of the Discoverers and the Middlemen of the Nag Hammadi Codices", in: B. Barc (ed.), *Colloque international sur les textes de Nag Hammadi (Québec, 22-25 août 1978)* (Bibliothèque copte de Nag Hammadi, Section

"Études", 1), Quebec/Louvain: Presses de l'Université Laval/Peeters, 1981, 21-58 ♦ Idem, "Nag Hammadi: the First Fifty Years", in: J.D. Turner & Anne McGuire (eds.), *The Nag Hammadi Library after Fifty Years: Proceedings of the 1995 Society of Biblical Literature Commemoration* (NHMS, 44), Leiden: E.J. Brill, 1997, 3-33 ♦ D.M. Scholer, *Nag Hammadi Bibliography 1948-1969* (NHS 1), Leiden: E.J. Brill, 1971 ♦ idem, *Nag Hammadi Bibliography 1970-1994* (NHMS 32), Leiden: E.J. Brill, 1997, continued in *Novum Testamentum* 40 (1998) and subsequent volumes ("Bibliographia Gnostica, Supplementum II") ♦ C. Scholten, "Die Nag-Hammadi-Texte als Buchbesitz der Pachomianer", *Jahrbuch für Antike und Christentum* 31 (1988), 144-172 ♦ idem, "Hippolytos II (von Rom)", *RAC* 15 (1991), 492-551 ♦ M. Tardieu, *Recherches sur la formation de l'Apocalypse de Zostrien et les sources de Marius Victorinus* (Res Orientales, 9), Bures-sur-Yvette: Groupe pour l'Étude de la Civilisation du Moyen-Orient, 1996 ♦ M. Tardieu & J.-D. Dubois, *Introduction à la littérature gnostique*, I: *Histoire du mot "gnostique", Instruments de travail, Collections retrouvées avant 1945*, Paris: Éditions du Cerf/ Éditions du C.N.R.S., 1986 ♦ G. Vallée, *A Study in Anti-Gnostic Polemics: Irenaeus, Hippolytus, and Epiphanius* (Studies in Christianity and Judaism, 1), Waterloo, Ontario: Wilfrid Laurier University Press, 1981.

ROELOF VAN DEN BROEK

Goethe, Johann Wolfgang von, * 28.8.1749 Frankfurt am Main, † 22.3.1832 Weimar

Goethe's relationship to esoteric traditions is a constant throughout his life, and its complexity reflects that of the mystical and esoteric currents as they developed from the end of the 18th century into the era of → Romanticism. As both a witness and a participant in the successive phases of interest in esotericism between 1770 and 1830, his point of view adjusted to the evolving contexts of esoteric knowledge and their changing impact on culture and society. His relation to this tradition was not free from ambivalence and was sometimes critical, giving rise to parodic and satirical expressions (e.g. in the play *Der Groß-Cophta*, 1791).

We can distinguish several main phases in Goethe's relationship to esoteric traditions, the first being that of Frankfurt (1768-69), where he was introduced into some alchemical and theosophical works. This was due to the pietist Susanna Catharina von Klettenberg (1722-1774), who was the niece of the alchemist Johann Hector von Klettenberg (1684-1720), and to her doctor, Johann Friedrich Metz (1720-1782). The famous episode told in the eighth book of Goethe's autobiography, *Dichtung und Wahrheit* (Poetry and truth), describes his reading at this time as having been marked by an eclectic approach to such works as the *Aurea catena Homeri* (Golden chain of Homer, 1723) by Anton Josef Kirchweger, the *Opus mago-cabbalisticum et theosophicum* (Magic-kabbalistic and theosophic work) of → Georg Welling (1735), and the *Eröffneter Weg zum Frieden mit Gott und allen Creaturen* (Open way to peace with God and all creatures, 1747) by Johann Conrad Dippel (1673-1734). The reception of → Paracelsus and → Paracelsianism, of → Jacob Boehme's theosophy [→ Christian Theosophy], and their continuation in the writings of → Friedrich Christoph Oetinger were decisive for Goethe's intellectual formation, while → Rosicrucianism, with the *Chemical Wedding of Christian Rosenkreuz* (1616), was also part of this background. In all his writings, Goethe shows familiarity with the main philosophical themes of Hermeticism: macrocosm and microcosm, the idea of polarity, the unity of living nature and the divine, the alchemical idea of transformation. These would remain major themes of his work until the end of his life. The young Goethe's interest in esotericism also belongs within the context of a personal religious crisis which went in parallel with the advance of collective secularization. The religious framework within which the alchemical [→ Alchemy], gnostic [→ Gnosticism], and Neoplatonic [→ Neoplatonism] traditions were transmitted to him was that of → Pietism, which, as represented by → Gottfried Arnold (1666-1714), was a bearer of the esoteric and alchemical traditions. This group of influences led Goethe to develop a "private religion", not identified with any confessional structure, which was still at the center of his preoccupations during his late period. His stay in Strasbourg in 1770, one of the European capitals of esotericism at the end of the Enlightenment, brought him into contact not only with Johann Gottfried Herder (1754-1803) but with Johann Heinrich Jung, called → Jung-Stilling (1740-1817). In the latter's presence, Goethe encountered another approach to esotericism, from which he quickly distanced himself.

This first phase was followed in the last decade of the 18th century by a more critical, even sceptical one as Goethe, now established in Weimar and exercising political functions, came into contact with the world of secret societies. Like Friedrich Schiller (1759-1805) and several of his contemporaries, Goethe was personally involved in → Freemasonry and → Illuminism. His *Groß-Cophta* presents an intrigue centered on the charlatan → Cagliostro, embroiled in the "Diamond Necklace Affair"; it is a violent satire on the mystifications to which certain "magi" resort, and a criticism of the collective forms of embracing esoteric doctrines. Goethe also expressed a sort of scepticism in the first part of *Faust* (1808), which reveals all his ambivalence towards certain aspects of the occult. But these critical positions in no way detracted from his deep convictions as a thinker, who in the course of his development took notice of Kant's doctrine and of its proclaimed limits to knowledge, but never renounced a Hermetic vision of the world and of man. Many of Goethe's works are marked by the presence of Hermetic themes. An example from his lyric poetry is *Die Geheimnisse* (The secrets, 1784), but it is above all his narrative works that reveal the presence of an esoteric anthropology. Some of them are constructed around the symbolism of the alchemical Great Work, such as his *Märchen* (Fairytale, 1795) and *Die Wahlverwandtschaften* (The elective affinities, 1809).

After 1800, Goethe's theoretical reflections and literary work were affected by contact with the romantic philosophy of nature and with its major works, such as that of → F.W. Schelling. More particularly, he was influenced by the reception of the → animal magnetism theory: by Franz Anton Mesmer, Adam Karl August von Eschenmayer (1768-1852), Josef Ennemoser (1787-1854), → Johann Wilhelm Ritter, and → Justinus Kerner, who inspired Goethe's mediumistic personages such as Odile in the *Wahlverwandtschaften* and Makarie in *Wilhelm Meisters Wanderjahre* (Wilhelm Meister's years of travel). Esotericism is present not only in the literary work but also in his scientific and aesthetic writings, with the *Farbenlehre* (Theory of colours, 1810) and the Goethean conception of the symbol. His notions of systole and diastole and the archetype of an "original" plant (*Urpflanze*), already formulated in 1790 in the *Metamorphose der Pflanzen* (Metamorphosis of plants), seek to preserve the concept of a unity of nature and of man, as against the mechanistic and mathematical model imposed by the Newtonian paradigm. On the basis of the *Bildungsroman* (novel of education) tradition, which he helped to form, Goethe wrote novels of initiation: *Wilhelm Meisters Lehrjahre* (Wilhelm Meister's apprentice years, 1795-1796), where Wilhelm is received into a mysterious "Society of the Tower"; *Wilhelm Meisters Wanderjahre* (1829), with the presence of a female initiate, Makarie; and the intrigue of the *Wahlverwandtschaften* (1809), based on alchemical symbolism.

The ultimate achievement of Goethe's esotericism was the second part of *Faust*, finished in the year of the author's death, which is a succession of "mysteries" founded on alchemical figures such as the "homunculus". Many modern interpretations of the esoteric tradition (e.g. → Carl Gustav Jung, → Rudolf Steiner) have treated Goethe, and more particularly *Faust*, as a major point of reference.

The continuity of Goethe's relationship with the esoteric traditions is visible throughout all these phases. By means of representations drawn from Hermeticism, then a philosophy of nature that follows in the same channels, he aimed at a unitary comprehension of reality, natural, human, and divine, and of Nature as a totality. His approach to Hermeticism did not rest on outmoded positions, but took notice of current developments in science, in thought, and in anthropology (e.g. the theories of Rousseau, the idea of "genius", sensualism, Kantian criticism, the Romantic philosophy of nature), and often embodied a personal response to them. Goethe's esoteric culture was also at the service of a religious aim, and marked by tension between a Christian esotericism and the vision of a religion beyond all confessional anchorage, such as presented in the doctrine of the "three respects" in *Wilhelm Meisters Wanderjahre*.

Johann Wolfgang Goethe, *Sämtliche Werke nach Epochen seines Schaffens. Münchner Ausgabe* (Karl Richter et al., ed.), 25 vols., Munich: Carl Hanser, 1985.

Lit.: Nicholas Boyle, *Goethe: The Poet and The Age*: vol. 1: *The Poetry of Desire (1749-1790)*; vol. 2: *Revolution and Renunciation (1790-1803)* Oxford, New York: Clarendon Press, 1991/1992 ♦ Antoine Faivre (eds.), *Goethe* (Cahiers de l'hermétisme), Paris: Albin Michel, 1980 ♦ Antoine Faivre/Rolf Christian Zimmermann (eds.), *Epochen der Naturmystik: Hermetische Tradition im wissenschaftlichen Fortschritt*, Berlin: E. Schmidt, 1979 ♦ Antoine Faivre, "Les lectures théosophiques du jeune Goethe d'après *Poésie et vérité*", in: Jean-Marie Valentin (ed.), *Johann Wolfgang Goethe: L'Un, l'Autre et le Tout*, Paris: Klincksieck, 2000, 491-506 ♦ *Goethe-Handbuch* (Bernd Witte etc., eds.), Stuttgart/Weimar: Metzler, 1997, 4 vols. ♦ Ronald D. Gray, *Goethe the Alchemist: A Study of Alchemical Symbolism in Goethe's Literary and Scientific Works*, Cambridge: Cambridge University Press, 1952 ♦ G.F. Hartlaub, "Goethe als Alchemist", *Euphorion: Zeitschrift für Literaturgeschichte* 48 (1954), 19-40 ♦ Bettina Knapp, "Goethe's *Die Wahlverwandtschaften*", *Symposium: A Quarterly Journal in Modern Foreign Literatures* 3 (1981), 235-250 ♦ Christian Lepinte, *Goethe et l'occultisme*, Paris: Les Belles Lettres, 1957 ♦ Maurice Marache, *Le Symbole dans la pensée et l'œuvre de Goethe*, Paris: A.G. Nizet, 1960 ♦ Alice Raphael, *Goethe and the Philosopher's Stone*, London: Routledge & Kegan Paul, 1965 ♦ G. Seibt and Oliver R. Scholz, "Zur Funktion des Mythos in *Die Wahlverwandtschaften*", *Deutsche Vierteljahresschrift für Literaturwissenschaft und Geistesgeschichte* 59 (1985), 609-634 ♦ Josef Strelka, *Esoterik bei Goethe*, Tübingen: Niemeyer, 1980 ♦ Andreas B. Wachsmuth, "Die magia naturalis im Weltbilde Goethes: Zur Frage ihrer Nachwirkungen", *Neue Folge des Jahrbuchs der Goethe-Gesellschaft* 19 (1957), 1-27 ♦ Waltraud Withölter, "Legenden: Zur Mythologie von Goethes *Wahlverwandtschaften*", *Deutsche Vierteljahresschrift für Literaturwissenschaft und Geistesgeschichte* 56 (1982), 1-64 ♦ Hugo Wernekke, *Goethe und die königliche Kunst*, Berlin: A. Unger, 1923 ♦ Daniel Wilson, *Unterirdische Gänge: Goethe, Freimaurerei und Politik*, Göttingen: Wallstein, 1999 ♦ Rolf Christian Zimmermann, *Das Weltbild des jungen Goethe: Studien zur hermetischen Tradition des 18. Jahrhunderts*, 2 vols., Munich: Wilhelm Fink, 1969/1979.

CHRISTINE MAILLARD

Gohory, Jacques (also known as Leo Suavius), * 20.1.1520 Paris, † 15.3.1576 Paris

Perhaps of Italian descent, Gohory belonged to a family of the lesser nobility that destined him to study law, then to an overly demanding career as a diplomat and lawyer. These important functions did not agree with him. He is thus seen to complain in an epistle dated 1544 about 'the fortune of his birth', that had placed him in a family whose chief members were employed in the affairs of the kingdom. Repelled by 'the Courts as much of Princes as of Justice', as he says himself in the introduction to his *Instruction sur l'herbe petum*, he retired of his own accord 'to the contemplation of Nature', in order to deal with 'only her, beyond the troubles, vices and confusions of the world' and to discover her 'beautiful secrets'. In fact, without thus renouncing his duty as a lawyer at the Parliamentary court, where he remained incumbent for thirty-two years, until his death, Gohory would devote himself mainly to literature and research and would produce many works whose diversity evinces the encyclopedic breadth of his culture. He thus translated *Le premier livre de la première decade de Tite-Live* (1548), and two works by Machiavelli, *Discours sur la première decade de Tite-Live* (1544) and *Le Prince* (1571). He further added to the last text the first French biography of the Italian philosopher; he collaborated on the translations of Colonna's *Hypnerotomachia Poliphili* (1546) and the novel *Amadis*, of which he made known books X (1553), XI (1554), XIII (1571) and XIV (1575). Beyond his taste for history, politics and literature, his writings reflect a constant interest in natural philosophy, which is

often identified in his mind with occult philosophy
[→ occult / occultism]: his interest in medicinal
plants or natural curiosities led him to defend the
therapeutic virtues of tobacco in his *Instruction
sur l'herbe Petum* (1572) or to make a French
version of *Occulta Naturae Miracula* (1567) by
Lemnius Levinus, a collection of surprising observations in which superstition, science and erudition
form an inextricable mixture. But it was especially
as the introducer of → Paracelsianism into France
that Gohory would be known in the scholarly
community of his era: as he reports it himself,
he was notably in relationship with Jean Fernel
(1497-1558), Ambroise Paré (ca. 1509-1590), Jean
Chastellan and Leonardo Botal, as many famous
interlocutors with whom he discussed his ideas on
medicine and spagyric. In the Saint-Marceau district, his "Lyceum philosophal" (1571-1576), a
botanical garden that also functioned as a little
academy, in addition often served as an outdoor
setting for his scholarly conversations.

Excepting the *Clavis totius philosophiae chymistae* by Gérard Dorn published in Lyon in the same
year 1567, the *Theophrasti Paracelsi ... universale compendium* by Gohory is the first French
work devoted to → Paracelsus. As its title indicates,
the *Compendium* is a summary of the philosophy
and therapeutic principles of the German doctor,
with his biography, a bibliographical draft, and
one of his writings: the *De Vita longa* followed
by commentaries. The tone of the text is often
polemical: Gohory criticizes notably the translations of Paracelsus furnished by Dorn in his *Clavis*;
he defends → Trithemius against the criticisms
of Charles de Bovelles (1479-1553), and Jean
Wier (1515-1588) against the censure of Cardano (1501-1576). Elsewhere he tones down the
novelty of the Paracelsian system by attaching it
to distant historical origins. Thus, its sources are
to be discovered among the ancient alchemists, and
in the works of → Roger Bacon, → Marsilio Ficino
or Joannes Valentianus. As Allen G. Debus has
emphasized, Gohory gives of the Paracelsian doctrine a representation strongly influenced by the
Philosophia ad Athenienses. He conceives of Man
as a small microcosm whose intimate functioning
is organically and analogically connected with
the laws of the natural world; he rejects the theory
of humors and insists on the need for a doctor to
have a full knowledge of chemistry and astronomy:
the first in order to prepare his remedies, and the
second to know at what propitious time to administer them. Among medications, he recommends
the use of antimony and drinkable gold. Animism,
→ magic and kabbalah [→ Jewish Influences] fur-

ther play a primary role in this work, no doubt less
faithful to the spirit of Paracelsus than to that of the
hermeticist tradition such as it was illustrated, for
example, in the occult philosophy of → Cornelius
Agrippa.

As the *Compendium* reveals, spagyric medicine,
→ alchemy and magic are fundamentally mysterious subjects for Gohory. Indeed, for him science
is combined with a secret tradition that he
traced back, as did many of his contemporaries,
to Egyptian origins. This initiatory understanding
of knowledge led him to be interested in steganog-
raphy in a short tract, *De usu et mysteriis notarum liber* (1550), strongly impregnated with the
teachings of Johannes Trithemius, or again to gloss
alchemically a series of engravings dedicated to the
quest for the Golden Fleece in *Hystoria Iasonis
Thessaliae Principis de Colchica velleris aurei
expeditione* (1563). His literary activities themselves reflect his taste for a scholarly exegesis
responsive to esoteric allusions. Also in his Commentary on the *Livre de la Fontaine Périlleuse*
(1572), he gives his readers many keys of alchemical interpretation applied to an allegory of courtly
style. In this respect, Gohory reveals himself an heir
to the lessons in hermeneutics already dispensed in
the works of the Italians Aurelio Augurelli (1456-
1530) and Giovanni Bracesco (ca. 1481-?), but
also appears as an innovator in his own country
where, before him, such an approach to literary
texts had never been taken so far. Perhaps as much
as his Paracelsian stances, his speculations as a
subtle interpreter would make a mark. Pierre Borel
(toward 1620-1671), in any case, would still
remember him in the mid-17th century, listing in
his *Bibliotheca chimica* (1654) the novel *Amadis*
and the *Hypnerotomachia Poliphili* by Colonna,
works partially translated by Gohory and that,
according to him, hid under a fabulous veil an
interesting alchemical content.

De usu et mysteriis notarum liber ..., Paris: V. Serte-
nas, 1550 ♦ *Hystoria Iasonis Thessaliae Principis de
Colchica velleris aurei expeditione: cum figuris aere
excusis, earumque expositione, versibus priscorum
poetarum*, Paris, 1563 ♦ (Translation) Lemnius Levinus, *Les Occultes merveilles et secrets de nature*, Paris
1567 ♦ *Theophrasti Paracelsi philosophiae et medicinae utriusque universale compendium, ...* Paris:
Roville, 1567 ♦ (Commentary) *Le livre de la fontaine
périlleuse avec la chartre d'Amours, autrement intitulé
le Songe du verger*, Paris: Jean Ruelle, 1572.

Lit.: W.H. Bowen, *Jacques Gohory (1520-1576)*,
unpublished thesis, Cambridge Mass.: Harvard University, 1935 ♦ A.G. Debus, *The Chemical Philosophy:
Paracelsian Science and Medicine in the Sixteenth and*

Seventeenth Centuries, vol. 1, New York: Science History Publications, 1977, 146-148 ◆ E.T. Hamy, *Un précurseur de Guy de la Brosse: Jacques Gohory et le Lyceum philosophal du faubourg saint-Marceau-lès-Paris (1571-1576)*, Paris: Nouvelles Archives du Museum d'Histoire Naturelle, 1899 ◆ D. Kahn, *Alchimie et paracelsisme en France (1567-1625)*, Geneva: Droz (forthcoming) ◆ G. Polizzi, "La fabrique de l'énigme: Lectures alchimiques du *Poli-phile* chez Gohory et Béroalde de Verville", in: J.C. Margolin & S. Matton (eds.), *Alchimie et philosophie à la Renaissance*, Paris: Vrin, 1993, 265-282 ◆ L. Thorndike, *A History of Magic and Experimental Science* (1941), vol. 5, New York: Columbia University Press, 1987, 636-638.

FRANK GREINER

Golden Dawn → Hermetic Order of the Golden Dawn

Grashof, Carl Louis Fredrik → Heindel, Max

Grail Traditions in Western Esotericism

According to most contemporary scholars, the Grail mythology in the Middle Ages was not connected to extra-Catholic esotericism, but either to a Roman Catholic eucharistic spirituality or to a literature designed for the purpose of providing (non-esoteric) entertainment. After what the Italian historian Franco Cardini called 'the eclipse of the Grail', the myth resurfaced in the 19th century in the Romantic literary and artistic milieu [→ Romanticism], particularly that of the composer Richard Wagner (1813-1883) and the painter Dante Gabriel Rossetti (1828-1882). The romantic interpretation of such artists was influential in introducing the Grail into Theosophical circles [→ Theosophical Society], in which scholars such as Charles Williams (1866-1945) and Jesse Weston (1850-1928) promoted a non-Catholic interpretation of the Grail as a universal symbol with pre-Christian origins. Within the same milieu, → Arthur Edward Waite (1857-1942) tried to reconcile the Christian and the pagan interpretation of the Grail, by establishing a "Hidden Church of the Holy Grail", the membership of which was largely drawn from the Theosophical Society and the → Hermetic Order of the Golden Dawn. In fact, one of the splinter groups of the Golden Dawn, established in Havelock North, New Zealand in 1916 by Robert William Felkin (1853-1926) and Reginald Gardiner (1872-1959), following an eso-

teric "work" started by Gardiner in 1907 before Felkin's arrival in 1916, created a cult of the Grail and an Order of the Table Round (not to be confused with the Order of the Round Table, which was a juvenile branch of the Theosophical Society). Other esoteric authors who had been members of the Golden Dawn also developed their own Grail rituals, including → Aleister Crowley (1875-1947), whose Grail was definitely anti-Christian, and → Dion Fortune (pseudonym of Violet Firth, 1890-1946), whose thinking, in turn, evolved from a Christian to a pagan interpretation of the myth within her Community of the Inner Light (the Christian element re-emerged in the Community after Fortune's death). A Christian esotericism centred on the Grail was promoted in France by Lithuanian poet → Oscar Venceslas de Lubicz Milosz (1877-1939), and it later inspired the establishment of an Order of the Grail by Auguste-Edouard Chauvet (1863-1946), James Chauvet (1885-1955, not a relative of the former), and Octave Béliard (1876-1951). A Christian-oriented esoteric reading of the Grail myth also emerged within → Anthroposophy, thanks to → Rudolf Steiner (1861-1925), whose insights were developed particularly by Walter Johannes Stein (1891-1957) and by the Italian Anthroposophist → Massimo Scaligero (pseudonym of Antonio Scabelloni, 1906-1980), whose interest in the Grail originally derived from his encounter with the pagan interpretation of the myth elaborated on by → Julius Evola (1898-1974). Although not supported by academic historians, the idea that the Grail was a symbol of the Cathar [→ Catharism] resistance to Catholicism acquired widespread support within the Neo-Cathar movement [→ Neo-Catharism] of Antonin Gadal (1877-1962) and Déodat Roché (1877-1978). Through this milieu, the alleged Cathar connection to the Grail inspired in the 1930s the mysterious activities of Otto Rahn (1904-1939), an SS officer who visited Southern France looking for the Grail reputedly hidden there by the Cathars, as also the esoteric spirituality of → Jan van Rijckenborgh (pseudonym of Jan Leene, 1896-1968) and his Lectorium Rosicrucianum, that Gadal himself eventually joined after World War II. Through these authors, the Grail continued its ubiquitous career among contemporary esoteric movements in three different incarnations: Christian (although not necessarily Catholic and eucharistic), neo-pagan, and Gnostic.

The larger esoteric movement centred on the Grail myth is the Grail Movement, founded by Oskar Ernst Bernhardt (1875-1941), a German esoteric author known under the pen name of

Abd-ru-shin ("Son of Light" in the Persian language). He was born in Bischofswerda in 1875, and from 1900 on travelled extensively in the Middle and Far East, the United States, and Europe; he also published several novels, short stories, and theatrical pieces. The outbreak of World War I found him, a German citizen, in an enemy country, the United Kingdom, and he was interned on the Isle of Man. In 1923, he circulated the first parts of *The Grail Message*, the publication of which continued through to 1937. *The Grail Message*, a complicated esoteric work, found interested readers particularly in Germany, France, the former Czechoslovakia, and Austria. Bernhardt decided, in fact, to settle in Austria, at the Vomperberg (Tyrol), together with a handful of followers of what later became known as the Grail Movement. In 1938, Austria was occupied by Nazi Germany, whereupon *The Grail Message* was banned, the Vomperberg centre closed, and Abd-ru-shin arrested. Released from jail in September 1938, he was banished firstly to Schlauroth (near Görlitz, Saxony), and then to Kipsdorf, where he died in 1941.

The Grail Message includes 168 talks, which purport to explain the structure of the whole universe and of the laws that govern it. The border between the divine and human realms is the Grail Castle, where the Holy Cup of the Grail represents God's direct irradiation. Creation is the spread of God's rays, with their consequent and gradual cooling beyond this border. This is how different planes of the universe were generated, a scheme very reminiscent of what we find in the Theosophical Society. Firstly the "original spiritual" level, then the "spiritual" level and so on down to matter, originated, it is believed, from the cooling and solidification of the divine rays. Crucial for this descent of the rays are two characters, known as Parsifal and the pristine Queen, or Mother. A Force flows down from the Holy Grail and sustains the whole of creation. Planet Earth is part of the creation's denser and lower level. Human beings, however, keep within themselves a spiritual spark capable of reminding them of their divine origin. By cultivating this spark through their subsequent reincarnations, humans can transcend the lower planes of matter, achieve a higher spiritual consciousness, and ultimately return to their heavenly home. At the Vomperberg, and in other places, the Grail Movement celebrates three spiritual feasts each year: the Feast of the Holy Ghost (Pentecost) on May 30; the Feast of the White Lily on September 7; and the Feast of the Radiant Star on December 29.

After World War II, the Vomperberg centre was re-opened and the Movement re-established under the leadership of Maria Kauffer Freyer (née Taubert, who was later adopted into the wealthy Kauffer family: 1887-1957), who was Bernhardt's second wife (his first wife, Martha Oener, her daughter Edith Nagel, and Nagel's descendants never played a role in the Movement, whilst the only male child of this first marriage died in World War I). Maria married Bernhardt in 1924, and her three children by her first marriage (Irmgard [1908-1990], Alexander [1911-1968] and Elizabeth [1912-2002] Freyer) also legally changed their last name from Freyer to Bernhardt. Maria led the movement until her death in 1957, and was succeeded first by Alexander and then by Irmgard (whose name had been changed to Irmingard by Abd-ru-shin himself, for esoteric reasons). The fact that Maria's children succeeded her, was never recognized by an important part of the large Brazilian constituency of the movement, which under the leadership of Roselis von Sass (1906-1997), who had been one of Abd-ru-shin's and Maria's most beloved disciples, created a splinter group under the name Ordem do Graal na Terra (web site: www.graal.org.br). Brazilian loyalists to Alexander and Irmingard remained in the Sociedade do Graal no Brazil, the local branch of the Movement; in 1989, after thirteen years of litigations, the Sao Paulo court ruled that the latter could not claim the exclusive copyright on Abd-ru-shin's writings in Brazil.

The most important schism occurred between 1999-2001, although its origin can be traced back to Irmingard Bernhardt's will. When Irmingard died in 1990, she left the Grail properties, including the Vomperberg, to Claudia-Maria (1961-1999), a natural child of Irmingard's adopted daughter Marga (b. 1943); both Claudia-Maria and her husband Siegfried (b. 1955) had legally adopted the surname Bernhardt, with Irmingard's blessing. The International Grail Movement, led by Siegfried Bernhardt, maintains to this date the control of the headquarters at the Vomperberg (web site www.gralswerk.org) and of the trademark "International Grail Movement", except in the English-speaking countries. Irmingard, on the other hand, left the copyrights of the Grail literature to an International Grail Foundation, led by Herbert Vollmann (1903-1999, the husband of Elizabeth Bernhardt, Irmingard's younger sister). It was Irmingard's hope that the two legal entities, the Movement and the Foundation, would peacefully cooperate. In fact, Siegfried's alleged infidelity to his invalid wife, Claudia-Maria, provoked a family crisis, and in 1999, shortly before his death, Voll-mann asked his followers to no longer acknowl-edge "the Mountain" (i.e. the Vomperberg) but to follow "the Light" (the Foundation and its litera-ture, for which he appointed Jürgen Sprick as his successor, and the Foundation's current leader). The Foundation maintains ownership of the copy-right on the founder's writings, and controls both the publishing house Stiftung Graalsbotschaft and the web site www.graal.org. In the United States, Great Britain, Australia, Canada, and Nigeria, the Foundation has maintained the "International Grail Movement" trademark, and operates under this name, thereby creating a certain amount of confusion with the International Grail Movement led by Siegfried Bernhardt from the Vomperberg. A substantial number of members followed Voll-mann in the separation from the Movement, and are currently establishing places of worship alter-native to the Vomperberg, to which they are pre-vented entry, with many unsolved legal issues remaining. The total membership of the two main branches of the Grail Movement (including the International Movement and the Foundation, but not the splinter groups, the larger of which is the Braziliam Ordem do Graal na Terra, with smaller branches in the Czech Republic and elsewhere fol-lowing local leaders, some of whom claim to receive visions and revelations from the founder) is currently 20.000. The international readership of *The Grail Message* is certainly much larger.

Jesse L. Weston, *The Quest of the Holy Grail*, London: G. Bell & Sons, 1913 ♦ Jacques Chauvet, *La Queste du Saint Graal* (Robert Amadou, ed.), Paris: Cariscript, 1988 ♦ Abd-ru-shin, *In the Light of Truth: The Grail Message* (3 vols.), Vomperberg (Tyrol): Alexander Bernhardt, 1985 ♦ John Matthews (ed.), *The House-hold of the Grail*, Wellingborough (Northampton-shire): The Aquarian Press, 1990.

Lit.: Helen Adolf, *Visio Pacis: Holy City and Grail – An Attempt at an Inner History of the Grail Legend*, State College (Pennsylvania): Pennsylvania State Uni-versity Press, 1960 ♦ *Graal et Modernité (Actes du Col-loque de Cerisy, 24-31 juillet 1995)*, Paris: Dervy, 1996 ♦ Franco Cardini, Massimo Introvigne & Marina Montesano, *Il Santo Graal*, Florence: Giunti, 1998.

MASSIMO INTROVIGNE

Grand Jeu, Le

Historians are today restoring to *Le Grand Jeu* ("The Big Game") the prominent place that it deserves in the spiritual, artistic and literary history of the first half of the 20th century. Long eclipsed

by Surrealism, the *Le Grand Jeu* group now appears in a new light that permits us to better outline its contours and appreciate its originality – particularly as regards its metaphysical perspec-tives – in relation to the endeavors of André Breton (1896-1966) and his epigones.

The adventure of *Le Grand Jeu* began at the Lycée de Reims (France) in 1922, when a few students of the class of *troisième* (Br: fourth year, US: 9th grade), about fifteen years old, excep-tionally precocious, and passionate about the absolute, began a little initiatiory society. They decided to challenge social values and break through the rational limits of the mind in order to reach the "Beyond", by means of all kinds of experiments inherited from the practice of 'der-anging all the senses' advocated by Arthur Rim-baud (1854-1891). Roger Vailland (1907-1965), Roger Gilbert-Lecomte (1907-1943), René Dau-mal (1908-1944) and Robert Meyrat (1907-1997) were trying to rediscover the holistic knowledge of the world that they believed had once been the spontaneous possession of traditional people, and still existed primarily in children today. To distinctly mark their wish of returning to the origins, and their faith in the creative virtues of child-like awareness, these young men soon called themselves the "Phrères [sic] Simplistes". Their revolt against social and intellectual shackles was exhibited by pataphysical or dadaist provocations; but on a deeper level – inspired by *La saison en enfer*, by Lautréamont (1846-1870), by Poe (1809-1849), → Nerval, → Huysmans and → Novalis – they often identified themselves with visionary angels, fallen creatures close to Satan, 'come down from heaven on a stretcher' (R. Gilbert-Lecomte). They claimed to be able to travel in other realms, to perceive the musical rhythm of the universe and to discern the expansion and metamorphoses of time. All their experiences took place in the context of what would soon become "experimental meta-physics". This included techniques for "projection of the astral body", the inhalation of carbon tetra-chloride (by Daumal), and experiments in extra-retinal vision and extrasensory perception. As early as this period, it was a matter, for them, of tran-scending the limits of the mind and gaining access to the immediate perception of another universe believed to be incommensurable with our sensory knowledge and irreducible to our understanding. The Simplists were thus engaged in a true revo-lution of consciousness, systematized and pro-claimed by *Le Grand Jeu* from 1928 on.

In Paris, in 1927, Daumal, Vailland and Gilbert-Lecomte grouped around the painter Joseph Sima

(1891-1971), an artist of Czech origin fascinated by the spiritual quest. Sima in his work was concerned with abolishing matter-spirit dualism and recovering a vision of the original unity. The Simplists were enthusiastic about such endeavours, which echoed their own aspirations and went far beyond traditional aesthetics, being presented as an authentic means of knowledge, a "clairvoyance" in Rimbaud's sense of the term; art should be a metaphysical experience, free of any hedonistic connotations. The friendship with this artist whose concerns were so close to theirs strengthened the Simplists' aspirations, and other kindred spirits soon joined them – André Rolland de Renéville (1903-1962), Monny de Boully (1904-1968), Georges Ribemont-Dessaignes (1884-1974), Maurice Henry (1907-1984), Hendrik Cramer (1884-1945), Arthur Harfaux (1906-1995), and Pierre Minet (1909-1975). Supported morally and financially by Léon-Pierre Quint (1895-1958), the Simplists published in the course of summer 1928 the first number of the review *Le Grand Jeu*. Two more would follow, one in the spring of 1929, the other in the autumn of 1930. The three issues of this review – and a few pages of a fourth that did not make it beyond the planning stage – constitute the basic referential corpus for anyone who attempts to understand the *Le Grand Jeu* enterprise and evaluate its influence, especially in relation to esoteric thought.

The inner quest of the protagonists of *Le Grand Jeu* may be compared with a mystical endeavor to attain an immediate omniscience, whose secret, lost since times immemorial, must urgently be rediscovered so that Man can attain the perfect realization of his condition. The prenatal universe, the return to origins, and the condition of childhood are as many recurrent themes in the texts of Daumal and Gilbert-Lecomte. Avid readers of → René Guénon's works on the primordial Tradition and on the *Crise du monde moderne* (1927), and aware of Lévy-Bruhl's (1857-1939) writings on primitive mentality, the poets of *Le Grand Jeu* were also vitally interested in the intuitions of hermetic thought, with the main representatives of which they were familiar. Pythagoras, Heraclitus, Plato, Plotinus, Apollonius of Tyana, → (Pseudo-) Dionysius Areopagita, → Giordano Bruno, → Swedenborg, → Louis-Claude de Saint-Martin, and → Fabre d'Olivet are cited or mentioned, sometimes several times, in the three numbers of their review. This apparently disparate list of philosophers, magi or great initiates conceals, however, a basic coherence: the idea – a true act of faith for these young explorers of thought – that the

world is a unity, that there is neither spirit nor matter, but only Spirit-Matter, and that dualism has been transcended. Coupled with this is the conviction that everything acts and reacts upon everything else, and the microcosm and the macrocosm, in line with the hermetic tradition, are in symbolic correspondence and exercise a secret power on each other.

To attain the awareness of this unity, and especially to *live* it from the inside, the mind must break through its limits, lose its individuality, transcend the narrow self, and become universalized, until it regains the primordial integrity of its nature. As Gilbert-Lecomte wrote, 'the particle of being that was assigned to our consciousness at the beginning of the world was not irremediably separated from the universal being'. In order for man to *reintegrate* himself – in the sense that theosophy confers on this term –, it is his duty to transgress all the boundaries, revolt against all conditioning and against all social, cultural, moral, ecclesiastical or religious constraints – in short, to practice a systematic 'Break-Dogma' (*Le Grand Jeu*, no. II). The goal is to shatter the principles of Aristotelian logic that, by the radical distinction of subject and object or of dream and reality, impose on us a deformed and false vision of the nature of things. The adepts of *Le Grand Jeu*, adopting Rimbaud's opinion that 'our pale reason is hiding infinity from us', wanted '. . . to tear down the colossus with a cretin's head that represents Western science' (*Grand Jeu*, no. II).

The "experimental metaphysics" put into practice by the partisans of *Le Grand Jeu* would offer a means of acceding to 'this still point in its own vibrating interior', to the '*punctum stans* of the old metaphysics' (Gilbert-Lecomte) where all contradictions are abolished. But such a breakthrough is possible only if we take leave of our habitual mental categories and dare to engage, at the risk of our annihilation, all our physical and spiritual potentials in a quest that fundamentally challenges the very act of knowing. Identification with the Vision comes at this price. *Le Grand Jeu* tells us first to establish a connection between the visible and the invisible, the separation between which is only apparent and which represents a gross limitation of our deficient and atrophied senses and ways of thinking. One has to restore unity to the body, and learn to conceive of it, not in the Cartesian manner as a substance radically different from the spirit, but rather as its symbolic image. From there on, by means of new so-called "extra-sensory" experiences, psychic states of various degrees of intensity will manifest themselves, and as many stages of knowledge; the initiatory process may finally lead to ideal omniscience. Drugs, narcotics, perception of the "subtle body", paramnesia, sleep deprivation, waking dreams, extra-retinal vision, and the experience of death itself are only means to gain access to a higher consciousness, a different plane of reality analogous to the astral plane defined by the occultists. Perhaps more precisely, this plane is the *mundus imaginalis* (the imaginal), the intermediary space of which → Henry Corbin (1903-1978) speaks in relation to the theosophies of Islam: a *mesocosm* situated between the perceptible and the intelligible, where spirits are incarnated and where bodies are spiritualized. The coveted Absolute thus has a precise and unambiguous position in relation to perceptible experience: 'The spirit is ONE', says Gilbert-Lecomte, 'and has nothing in common with the perceptible world'. Therefore "experimental metaphysics" cannot start from sensations alone. It makes use of the body only in order to escape from it. The sensory experiences that it uses like a trampoline are not directed to the acquisition of powers – which would imply magic – but toward the pursuit of Knowledge, a spiritual awakening, and a continuously expanding field of consciousness. For consciousness, at the very instant when it expands unto infinity and risks dissolving into the void of emptiness or fall into sleep, can, in 'a lightning-flash' (Gilbert-Lecomte), reconquer the lost unity. A note, composed collectively for number II of *Le Grand Jeu* (May 1929) clearly explains this point: '. . . A Man can, according to a certain so-called mystical method, attain the immediate perception of another universe, incommensurable with his senses and irreducible to his understanding . . . Knowledge of this universe belongs in common to all those who, at one period of their life, have wished desperately to pass beyond the possibilities inherent to their species and have begun the mortal departure'.

Although the adepts of *Le Grand Jeu* never spoke of the Fall in the sense of → Christian theosophy, they considered man a fallen creature. To regain his true nature and original state, man must attempt to change his current and limited mode of consciousness in order to acquire the supplement of soul that will rescue him from the "absence" here on earth and lead him to rediscover the "true life" glimpsed by Rimbaud. Although certainly desecralized, this approach remains formally faithful to the religious scheme of Christianity and its theosophical avatars. The fault that casts Man down to a status lower than his original one is strongly stigmatized by *Le Grand Jeu*. This catas-

trophe is the result, especially in the West, of the immoderate cult of reason and science; of the break of the connection that used to magically unite us to nature; and finally, of the lethal tendency among Westerners to take into account only matter, only the reign of quantity, and ignore the qualitative essence of things. Such is the original sin of our technico-scientific civilization in the eyes of Daumal and Gilbert-Lecomte.

To rise again after this Fall is possible, as we have seen, only by engaging the whole being of Man in a metaphysical adventure, fully lived and boldly risked, that involves the individual's body and soul. This adventure requires him to play a crucial game, a sort of "who loses wins", in the course of which, by venturing as far as the extreme limits of the mind, he may either glimpse the supreme illumination, or else be dramatically annihilated in insanity or death. Mere research of an intellectual nature does not suffice; a quest that remains limited to conceptual speculation will prove ineffective in restoring to consciousness the ability to embrace the infinite. While *Le Grand Jeu* finds its place in the history of modern esoteric thought, it bears rather few similarities to purely gnostic endeavors; it relates more to the alchemical process [→ Alchemy], which attempts to harmonize the different planes of being by means of a purification and transmutation of psychic and physical elements. The adepts of *Le Grand Jeu*, like the initiates of the Great Work, were aware of the dangers of this most perilous path and subscribed to the famous adage: "Nonnulli perierunt in opere nostro" (some have perished in our work). The discovery of the Philosopher's Stone, the access to the Self as a unique principle presiding over the *hierogamos* (the sacred marriage that reconciles the opposites), and the contemplation of the "circle whose center is everywhere and circumference nowhere", in short: all these hermetico-alchemical approaches account for the undertaking of *Le Grand Jeu* better than traditional metaphysical constructs can. The latter are not considered to have any truly effective impact insofar as they do not proceed to a total metamorphosis of Man seen in his double nature of incarnated creature and spiritual principle.

When the members of *Le Grand Jeu* dispersed (end of 1932) and the review ceased to appear, the two main protagonists of this dazzling odyssey took different paths and their destinies definitively separated. Gilbert-Lecomte, a modern archetype of the *poète maudit* (cursed poet), did not succeed, despite repeated efforts, to tear himself away from the deadly demands of the "black goddess" (opium). In a fatal, suicidal impulse, consumed more than ever by the desire for self-annihilation and dissolution, he pursued his asymptotic quest for the Absolute as far as the final destruction, which tragically came wearing the hideous mask of tetanus (1943). As for René Daumal, he freed himself from the grip of drugs. After his encounter with Alexandre de Salzmann (1874-1933), a disciple of → Gurdjieff whose powerful influence he experienced, he progressively gave up poetry to devote himself to a deep study of Sanskrit and the translation of Indian sacred texts. At the same time, he made ceaseless efforts at realizing his desire for integral transformation, practicing a strict asceticism to accede to the heights of spiritual simplicity (*Le Contre-Ciel*, 1936; *Le Mont analogue*, posthumous, 1950); he died prematurely of tuberculosis in 1944.

Le Grand Jeu (New edition of the three numbers published and partial reconstitution of number IV), Paris: Jean-Michel Place, 1977 ♦ René Daumal, *Le Contre-Ciel*, Paris: Gallimard, 1990 ♦ idem, *La Grande Beuverie*, Paris: Gallimard, 1986 ♦ idem, *Chaque fois que l'aube paraît*, Paris: Gallimard, 1954 ♦ idem, *Le Mont Analogue*, Paris: Gallimard, 1981 ♦ idem, *Poésie noire, poésie Blanche*, Paris: Gallimard, 1954 ♦ idem, *Correspondance*, 3 vols., Paris: Gallimard, 1992, 1993, 1996 ♦ Roger Gilbert-Lecomte, *Oeuvres complètes*, 3 vols., Paris: Gallimard, 1974/1977 ♦ idem, *Correspondance*, Paris: Gallimard, 1971.

Lit.: *Le Grand Jeu* (Cahier de l'Herne no. 10), Paris: Editions de l'Herne, 1968 ♦ Michel Random, *Le Grand Jeu*, Paris: Denoël, 1970 ♦ Alain & Odette Virmaux, *Roger Gilbert-Lecomte et le Grand Jeu*, Paris: Belfond, 1981 ♦ "Le Grand Jeu", *Europe* 782-783 (1994), 3-156 ♦ Kathleen Ferrick Rosenblatt, *René Daumal: The Life and Work of a Mystic Guide*, Albany: SUNY Press, 1999 ♦ *Grand Jeu et Surréalisme*, Reims: Ville de Reims et Éditions Ludion, 2003.

JEAN-LUC FAIVRE

Guaïta, Stanislas, Marquis de,
* 6.4.1861 Alteville (Moselle),
† 19.12.1897 Alteville

The descendant of a noble Catholic Italian family settled at the Château d'Alteville in imperial Lorraine, young Stanislas was educated at the religious boarding-school of la Malgrange, near Nancy. Here in 1878-1879 he discovered literature, in the company of the future novelists Maurice Barrès (1862-1923) and Paul Adam (1862-1920), as well as another writer, Albert de Pouvourville (1861-1940), who holds an important place in Parisian occultism [→ occult / occultism] under his

Taoist initiate's name, Matgioï. Guaïta tried his luck in Paris as a poet, publishing in 1881 *Oiseaux de passage: rimes fantastiques* . . . (Birds of passage: fantastic rhymes), followed by *La muse noir: heures de soleil* (The black muse: sunny hours, 1883) and *Rosa mystica* (Mystic rose, 1885). His reading of → Péladan's initiatic novel *La Vice Suprême* (The supreme vice, 1884) excited him by opening up new horizons; but, along with all those occultists of the period who had inherited the Romantic concept of the spiritual mission of the writer, literary expression would remain fundamental for him. Guaïta's apartment at Rue Trudaine, Paris, became a meeting-place for the esoteric world, all the more attracted by an extraordinary library that his fortune had allowed him to acquire. Associated from 1884 on with Joséphin Péladan, who claimed to be the inheritor of the initiation into a Toulouse branch of the Rose-Croix, Guaïta progressed rapidly in his knowledge of the occult. In 1886 he published a kind of historical résumé of the masters of the occult after the fashion of → Eliphas Lévi: *Au seuil du mystère* (At the threshold of the mystery), and at the end of 1887, turning to the practical side, he founded an "Ordre Kabbalistique de la Rose-Croix". This was directed by six known members (Péladan, → Papus, Paul Adam, → Barlet, then → Sédir and the Abbé Alta [1842-1933]) and six unknown ones.

The functioning of this initiatic society was chaotic, like that of the contemporary Martinist Order "reawakened" by Papus together with Guaïta. Like most of the occultist groups, they were obsessed with the idea of accomplishing an historical social mission. The themes developed in Guaïta's written work, *Le temple de Satan* (Satan's temple, 1891), *La clef de la magie noire* (The key to black magic, 1897), and his articles in *L'Initiation* confirm the fact: the great names of esoteric thought, from → Khunrath to → Boehme, → Fabre d'Olivet, and Eliphas Lévi, are utilized within the perspective of a final unveiling of the truth by means of a synthesis of the knowledge gained by science with the experience of the past transmitted by esotericism. Initiatic degrees were conferred after the model of university examinations: e.g., the "Licentiate in Kabbalah" obtained through library study. In 1887, Guaïta employed a secretary who would play an important role in the renaissance of symbolic and spiritualist → Freemasonry in France, Oswald Wirth (1860-1943). After the latter conveyed to Guaïta some papers of the Abbé Boullan (1824-1893), an occultist priest of Lyon who directed a community founded by the "prophet" Pierre-Michel Vintras (1807-1875), Guaïta embarked on a veritable "magical war", whose echoes reached the popular press. The affair ended with a spectacular duel (1893). Boullan was indirectly the model for → Huysman's character in *Là-bas*. Another typically Parisian polemic opposed Guaïta to Péladan, who quit the Rose-Croix Kabbalistique (1890-1891) to create a branch that was exclusively Catholic and oriented to artistic activities. In poor health and a great consumer of morphine, Guaïta returned home to die at age 36 in his paternal château, where his family sought to dispel the memory of his life as an occultist.

Oiseaux de passage, Paris: Berger & Levrault, 1881 ◆ *Au seuil du mystère*, Paris: Chamuel, 1896 ◆ *Essais de sciences maudites, le serpent de la Genèse*, Paris: Carré, 1890 (1st ed. 1886) ◆ *Le Temple de Satan*, Paris: Librairie du merveilleux, 1891 ◆ *La Clef de la magie noire*, Paris: Trédaniel, 1995 (1st ed. Paris, 1897).

Lit.: Jean-Pierre Laurant, "Guaïta, Stanislas de", in: *Dictionnaire de biographie française*, Paris: Letouzey & Ané, 1985 ◆ *L'Initiation*, special number, Jan. 1898 (contributions by Barlet, Papus, Marc Haven, V.E. Michelet, Jollivet-Castelot) ◆ René Philipon, *Stanislas de Guaïta et sa bibiliothèque occulte*, Paris: Dorbon, 1899 ◆ Maurice Barrès, *Un rénovateur de l'occultisme, Stanislas de Guaïta*, Paris: Chamuel, 1898 ◆ Philippe Encausse, *Sciences occultes . . .*, Paris: Ocia, 1949, 57-109 ◆ André Billy, *Stanislas de Guaïta*, Paris: Mercure de France, 1971 ◆ Jean-Pierre Laurant, *L'Esotérisme chrétien en France au XIXᵉ siècle*, Lausanne, L'Age d'Homme, 1992, chs. 4-5.

JEAN-PIERRE LAURANT

Guénon, René Jean Marie Joseph,
* 15.11.1886 Blois, † 7.1.1951 Cairo

Guénon was born in central France in the town of Blois in November 1886. His parents – and family – were strict Catholics. The strong sense of tradition found in late 19th-century French Catholicism was ingrained in Guénon during his earliest and most formative years, and was to affect his perspective throughout his life. As a boy, and again throughout his life, he was afflicted with *une santé fort délicate* (a very delicate health) – to the degree that at one point in his graduate school career it prevented him from attending classes. Education and learning were early and strong influences upon his life, owing largely to the proximity and involvement of his childless maternal aunt, Mme. Duru, who lived next door and was a primary school teacher. His father was an architect. Thus Guénon was raised in a home environment where learning generally, and mathematics and geometry specifically, were prominent.

Guénon's early education was in Jesuit-run institutions. At the age of twelve he was enrolled in Notre-Dame des Aydes, where he remained until 1901, when he was transferred by his father to the Collège Augustin-Thierry. His academic record throughout these years was exceptionally good; he won several prizes, among them two for physics and Latin. In 1902 he received his baccalaureate, and in the following year his Bachelor of Philosophy with honors. In 1904 Guénon arrived in Paris, where he enrolled in the Collège Rollin. His field was advanced mathematics, and he was studying to prepare for the *licence de mathématique*. After two years, however, he withdrew from the university for reasons which are unclear. One of his biographers, Paul Sérant, speculates that it was due either to ill health or to the seductions of the intellectual life that Paris could offer a provincial and bright, curious youth.

Regardless of the reasons for his withdrawal from the university, this action proved to be a decisive one in Guénon's life, since it was at this point, in 1906, that he began in earnest to pursue a course of study to which he had been introduced only shortly before, viz., the study of esotericism and occultism [→ occult / occultism]. It is fair to say that for the first of these years from 1906, Guénon was a protegé of Gérard Encausse (a.k.a. Papus), described by Paul Chacornac as the 'undisputed leader' of the French occult movement since 1888, the year in which Encausse became Corresponding Secretary of the → Theosophical Society in France. Guénon had first met Encausse while attending classes at the Ecole Hermétique, a school that formed the outer or public vehicle of the Parisian occult movement directed by Encausse. Guénon was admitted into all the various occult organizations controlled by Encausse, including the Ordre Martiniste. Throughout these years, while centered in Paris, Guénon both participated in and carried out research in occult and Masonic groups and esoteric religious doctrines. In 1908 he broke away from Encausse and his organizations and, until 1911 upon its dissolution by Guénon, he was head of the Ordre du Temple Renové (O.T.R.). For a period he was heavily involved in the → Gnostic Church in Paris, where he assumed the Gnostic name of Palingenius and the role of holy bishop. Upon the urging of Synesius, patriarch of the Gnostic Church, Guénon began a review called *La Gnose*, of which he was editor until 1912.

It was also in this period, around 1912, that he adopted Islam through the medium of a Swedish Theosophist named John Gustaf Aguéli, a.k.a. Abdul-Hadi, and was accepted as a pupil by Aguéli's teacher Sheikh Abder-Rahman Elish el-Kebir for preparation and initiation into a Sufi sect. Several of Guénon's biographers view 1912 as a pivotal year in his life, not only because of his new association with Islam and his corresponding break with most of the former occult organizations with which he had been associated, but also because of his marriage.

In 1912 Guénon married Berthe Loury from Tours, which marriage lasted sixteen years until he was left a widower by her untimely death in 1928. Guénon's life during the period from 1912 to 1930 was shared between Blois and Paris, except for a short interim during 1917-1918 when he was appointed instructor of philosophy at Setif, Algeria. He tried, but failed, to earn a *docteur-ès-lettres* from the Sorbonne following his short stay in Algeria. In 1923 Guénon marked the end of his investigations and interest in occultism and → spiritualism with the publication of *L'Erreur spirite* (The Spiritist Error), and turned his concentration solely on that area for which he was to become renowned: metaphysics, *la Tradition primordiale*. Beginning in 1925, Guénon began submitting articles to the journal *Le Voile d'Isis* whose editor was Paul Chacornac. Within the space of three or four years Guénon became that journal's principal contributor; he remained so through 1936 when the journal's name changed to *Études Traditionnelles*, and thereafter throughout his life.

In the Fall of 1929, Guénon met Marie Dina, the wealthy daughter of a Canadian railroad baron, and the widow of an Egyptian engineer. As a great admirer of Guénon's work she proposed to become, essentially, his patron, and offered to establish a publishing house (Véga) to serve as the vehicle for his writings. Véga was to publish Guénon's original metaphysical works in addition to all the French translations he could make of traditional Islamic texts. Guénon and Mme. Dina embarked for Cairo, Egypt on March 5, 1930, in order to obtain the first of the Sufi texts for translation and publication. They planned to be in Egypt only for three months, but circumstances changed and Mme. Dina returned to France while Guénon remained in Cairo. Mme. Dina's enthusiasm for the whole project waned, and Guénon was left in Cairo where he began a process of gradual assimilation into the Arabic culture. By the end of 1932 he had apparently decided not to return to France, and committed himself to becoming both a Muslim Sufi and an Egyptian.

Guénon remained in Cairo until his death in 1951. There he perfected his Arabic and became, in effect, a practicing Sufi and fully integrated

into Egyptian society. In 1933 Guénon met Sheikh Muhammad Ibrahim, an elderly lawyer whom he visited often. The following year he married his second wife, the Sheikh's daughter, Fatima, and they moved to Doki, a suburb of Cairo. Toward the end of his life he began to suffer continuous bouts of ill health, so he and his family moved back into central Cairo. Two daughters were born to them in 1944 and 1947; a third child – a son – was born in 1949, and another son was born four months after Guénon's death in 1951. In 1948 he officially became a naturalized Egyptian citizen, but throughout his expatriation, Guénon always kept abreast of the intellectual and political climate of France, and the West. His writings remained constant and prolific as they had been before his departure from France, during this period focusing more on the process of attaining effective metaphysical insight, though still under the same genre of "Tradition", or *sophia perennis*.

While Guénon published scores of articles and reviews in numerous journals, he is best known for his major works published in book form. Though the subjects of his books cover a relatively wide range of fields of inquiry, within the larger context of world religions and esotericism and metaphysics, there are several common themes that run through them all. There is, first, the theme of a "universal principle", which inheres in all, and of which it may be said that every other principle is derived. Then there are the related subjects of revelation, initiation, and Intellect (this last concept contains a component of "intuition", by means of which knowledge and understanding of an esoteric truth may be directly apprehended without recourse to reason and dialectic). These and certain other, related subjects such as periodicity, polarity, correspondence, and aeviternity, collectively, are referred to as "first principles". Guénon held that the first principles of the Tradition, or *philosophia perennis*, are essential, and that substance proceeds from essence; that Traditional societies were those wholly informed by these first principles and thereby unanimous and substantively reflective of the essential principles; that a key characteristic of Traditional culture is the absence of a bifurcation (or, alternatively, a fusion) of sacred and secular; that the description "Traditional" encompasses pre-modern non-literate or tribal societies as well as literate civilizations; and that due to inexorable cosmic cycles the modern world is at present virtually entirely secular and therefore the antithesis of → Tradition.

Guénon's first book, *Introduction générale à l'étude des doctrines hindoues* (unsuccesfully submitted as a thesis for the title *docteur-ès-lettres* at the Sorbonne) was published in 1921, and during the thirty-year period that began then and ended with his death in 1951, he published seventeen seminal works of metaphysics and esotericism whose lucidity and penetration have been described as mathematical in their precision and personal detachment. Two of his greatest books, *La crise du monde moderne* (The Crisis of the Modern World) and *Le règne de la quantité et les signes des temps* (The Reign of Quantity and the Signs of the Times), deal primarily with the vicissitudes of modernity in the West, *i.e.*, since the Middle Ages, and the inversions of metaphysical truths that according to Guénon form the structure of modern culture. Two of his other books, first translated into English in 2003, reflect Guénon's substantial deficiency in what he himself referred to as the "historical method" (his only two books to make an attempt in that direction): *L'erreur spirite* (The Spiritist Error) a book about the rise of spiritualism in the 19th century and the problems associated with it, and *Le Théosophisme: Histoire d'une pseudo-religion* (Theosophy: History of a Pseudo-Religion), a putative history of the Theosophical Society that purports to be an exposé of its esoteric *bona fides*. The remainder of his books are expositions of symbolism, metaphysics, and esotericism as these are expressed within the world's religions, and discussions of the primordial Tradition, in which subjects – and in the treatment of which – he excelled.

During the last three decades of his life, and especially after his immigration to Egypt, Guénon engaged in a long-term correspondence and close relationship with Ananda K. Coomaraswamy (1877-1947), the curator of the Indian and Asian collection of the Boston Museum of Fine Arts in the United States. Coomaraswamy, who had received his Ph.D. from the University of London in 1906 and who was a master of Greek, Latin, Pali, and Sanskrit, produced a tremendous published corpus of scholarly materials on the *philosophia perennis* – a term more or less interchangeable with Guénon's *Tradition primordiale* – based upon his own translations of the sacred texts of these languages. Together, Coomaraswamy and Guénon became the founders, with no prior plan or intention to do so, of what has come to be referred to as the "Traditional school" of esotericism and metaphysics in the 20th century. Another principal proponent of these Traditional views in the succeeding generation was → Frithjof Schuon, considered by many to be the preeminent expositor of the Tradition in the second half of the 20th century. The Tra-

ditional school would attract to it numerous other students and writers on the subjects of esotericism and metaphysics, including Titus Burckhardt, Martin Lings, Marco Pallis, Leo Schaya, William Stoddart, and Seyyed Hossein Nasr, to name a few.

In addition to the Traditionalists *per se*, there exist many individuals in the West who were and are to varying degrees affected by the thought of Guénon, but who were or are not part of this central core of the Traditional school. In France, for example, Guénon had a relatively significant impact on literature and contemporary thought: André Breton, Georges Vallin, Romain Rolland, René Daumal and, to a degree perhaps more apocryphal than actual, André Gide, were all influenced by the writings of Guénon.

The Italian → Julius Evola had been a spokesman for his own particular theories of political philosophy, one of which he referred to as "pagan imperialism", but in 1930 Evola turned to the concepts of Tradition and Traditional cultures as espoused by Guénon. This was the same year Guénon left France for Cairo, and it marked a significant turning point in Evola's philosophy. From this basic Traditional foundation, Evola began his assiduous critiques of liberalism, Marxism, nationalism, and even Christianity, which gained him the reputation – at least in Italy – of being a *maître à penser*.

Among the more reputable and renowned scholars in the United States who have written about and to some extent have been influenced by Guénon are Mircea Eliade, Huston Smith, and Jacob Needleman. Others, like Roger Lipsey, Seyyed Hossein Nasr, and Joseph Epes Brown, are more directly identified with the school of Traditional thought *per se*. Although the former are typically cautious not to rely excessively or even expressly on Guénon in their writings, *i.e.* with regard to citations, their reliance on Traditional perspectives is most significant. Huston Smith, more than Mircea Eliade or Jacob Needleman, expressly incorporates the works of Guénon and of Coomaraswamy, whom he cites in his publications. In *Forgotten Truth: The Primordial Tradition* (1976), Smith was careful to avoid the terms "Tradition" and *philosophia perennis* (in Latin or English), referring instead to the "primordial philosophy" and similar constructions. He nonetheless made perfectly clear to whom he was indebted and what constitutes, for him, the primordial tradition.

Guénon's influence, whether effected directly or through those who followed him in the Traditionalist forum, has continued to spread since the first half of the 20th century. Those who openly admit that their expressions are wholly or partially shaped by the Traditional perspective may be said to be within the Traditional forum. Others may not acknowledge the influence expressly but nonetheless infuse it in their oeuvre. Those in the latter category range in scope from poets like T.S. Eliot and Kathleen Raine to scholars like Mircea Eliade and → Henry Corbin to mendicants like Swami Ramdas and Thomas Merton. Many more could be added to this list by tracing in further detail the emanations of pervading influence of the Tradition as espoused by Guénon. Guénon's influence has also grown within the Muslim world. Prior to the Islamic revolution in Iran in the 1980s, Tehran was a very active center for Traditionalist thought and activity. It continues to retain strong elements of a Traditionalist interpretation of Islam, though somewhat more guarded in the present day's milieu. Another venue for the appreciation of Guénon and his Traditionalist vision of Islam is Turkey where, owing to the process of reintegrating an intellectual Islam into its post-1949 culture, the views of Guénon and Traditionalists such as S.H. Nasr have found a certain acceptance.

Introduction générale à l'étude des doctrines hindoues, Paris: Véga, 1921 ◆ *Le Théosophisme: Histoire d'une pseudo-religion*, Paris: Editions Traditionnelles, 1921 [henceforth referred to as "ET"] ◆ *L'erreur spirite*, ET 1923 ◆ *Orient et Occident*, Paris: Véga, 1924 ◆ *L'homme et son devenir selon le Vedanta*, ET 1925 ◆ *L'ésotérisme de Dante*, Paris: Gallimard, 1925 ◆ *Le roi du monde*, Paris: Gallimard, 1927 ◆ *La crise du monde moderne*, Paris: Gallimard, 1927 ◆ *Autorité spirituelle et pouvoir temporel*, Paris: Véga, 1929 ◆ *Saint Bernard*, ET 1929 ◆ *Le Symbolisme de la Croix*, Paris: Véga, 1931 ◆ *Les états multiples de l'être*, Paris: Véga, 1932 ◆ *La Métaphysique orientale*, ET 1939 ◆ *Le règne de la quantité et les signes des temps*, Paris: Gallimard, 1945 ◆ *Les principes du calcul infinitésimal*, Paris: Gallimard, 1946 ◆ *Aperçus sur l'initiation*, ET 1946 ◆ *La Grande Triade*, Paris: Gallimard, 1946.

Lit.: Christophe Andruzac, *René Guénon: La contemplation métaphysique et l'expérience du mystique*, Paris: Dervy, 1980 ◆ Marie-France James, *Esotérisme et christianisme: Autour de René Guénon*, Paris: Nouvelles Editions Latines, 1981 ◆ René Alleau & Marina Scriabine (eds.), *René Guénon et l'actualité de la pensée traditionnelle*, Milan: Archè, 1981 ◆ Paul Chacornac, *La vie simple de René Guénon*, Paris: Editions Traditionnelles, 1958 ◆ Jean-Pierre Laurant, *Le Sens caché dans l'oeuvre de René Guénon*, Lausanne: L'Age d'Homme, 1975 ◆ Lucien Meroz, *René Guénon ou la sagesse initiatique*, Paris: Plon, 1962 ◆ Paul Serant, *René Guénon*, Paris: La Colombe, 1953 ◆ Jean-Pierre Laurant (ed.), *René Guénon*, Paris: Cahiers de l'Herne, 1985 ◆ Robin Waterfield, *René Guénon and the Future of the West*, Great Britain: Crucible, 1987 ◆ Gabriel Asfar, "René Guénon: A Chapter of French Symbolist Thought in the Twentieth Century", Unpubl. Ph.D. diss. Princeton University, 1972 ◆ Marilyn Gustin, "The Nature, Role and Interpretation of Symbol in the Thought of René Guénon", unpubl. Ph.D. diss. Graduate Theological Union, Berkeley, 1987 ◆ William W. Quinn, *The Only Tradition*, Albany: SUNY Press, 1997.

WILLIAM QUINN

Gurdjieff, George Ivanovitch, * 13.1.1866 (?) Alexandropol (Russia), † 29.10.1949 Neuilly, Paris

Greco-Armenian holistic philosopher, thaumaturge, and teacher of Sacred Dances (whose ancillary personae as musicologist, therapist, hypnotist, raconteur, explorer, polyglot, and entrepreneur exercise the taxonomic mind). Gurdjieff's work comprises one ballet, some 250 Sacred Dances, 200 piano pieces composed in collaboration with his pupil Thomas Alexandrovitch de Hartmann (1886-1956), and four books, the *magnum opus* being *Beelzebub's Tales to His Grandson*. For more than 35 years he privately taught, by example and oral precept, a previously unknown doctrine styled "The Work", attracting – and often quixotically repulsing – groups of gifted disciples: Russian, English, American, and French. His system integrated a semantic critique, a social critique, an epistemology, a mythopoeic cosmogony and cosmology, a phenomenology of consciousness, and a practical *Existenzphilosophie*.

Gurdjieff's sketch of his infancy and early childhood (1866-1877) finds a modicum of corroboration in vestigial family memories, traditions, and photographs. The eldest son of a Cappadocian Greek father and an illiterate Armenian mother, he was born in the Greek quarter of Alexandropol, a Russian garrison town bordering Ottoman Turkey. In practically Old Testament conditions, Ioannas Giorgiades, a well-to-do grazier on the Shiraki Steppe, imposed on his son a character-forming, even Spartan, regime; and, as an amateur *ashokh* or bardic poet, imbued him with an inextinguishable interest in an oral tradition at once living and archaic (not least the Epic of Gilgamesh). Cattle plague (1873) impoverished the family, and the Russo-Turkish war (1877) drew them hopefully to the captured Turkish citadel town of Kars.

At this early juncture balanced encyclopaedism is baulked by Gurdjieff's cavalier burning of his personal papers in spring 1930 and by a curious absence of collateral evidence. For the ensuing thirty-three years we are, *pro tem*, chasteningly reliant on Gurdjieff's four autobiographicodidactic texts which – although innocent of consistency, Aristotelian logic, and chronological discipline – have the ring of a poetic truth. From these alone derives our notion of Gurdjieff's private tutoring by "Dean Borsh"; his unprogressed vocations as a doctor and a priest; his wonder at a succession of paranormal phenomena; and his burgeoning existential question as to the cosmic function of the biosphere and of humanity. Gurdjieff's auto-mythopoesis equally furnishes us the twenty-six adult years (1885-1911) of his long quest for, and synthesis of, valid esoteric sources. None of Gurdjieff's fifteen companions, the "Seekers of Truth", have resolved into recognisable historical entities. His apologists' attempts to differentiate and substantiate five successive expeditions – to Egypt, Crete, and the Holy Land; to Abyssinia and the Sudan; to Persia and Transoxiana; to Siberia; and finally to Afghanistan, the Pamirs, and India – display ingenuity but are necessarily compromised by self-indexicality, i.e. reliance on the correlation of purely internal evidence. Soberingly, Gurdjieff's putative decade in Central Asia (1897-1907), including his pivotal initiatic experience in the "Sarmoung Monastery", finds no support in the meticulous journals of contemporary explorers (Sven Hedin, Sir Aurel Stein, Albert Le Coq, Paul Pelliot, and Count Kozui Otani).

Yet, given the vastness of the territory, Gurdjieff's verve, and his predilection for aliases and disguise, these important caveats fall well short of conclusively invalidating his spiritual Odyssey: absence of proof is not proof of absence. Wholesale scepticism as to Gurdjieff's Central Asian venture confronts its own difficulties in accommodating his relevant linguistic command, his well-attested knowledge of the region's musical modalities and tribal carpets, and his arguably unique grasp of its dance – folk and liturgical.

With Gurdjieff's arrival in Metropolitan Russia (ca. New Year 1912), biography finally rests on defensible ground. Significant among Gurdjieff's earliest associates in Moscow is his cousin the monumental sculptor Sergei Dmitrievich Mercourov (1881-1952). In St Petersburg in 1913, while affecting the title "Prince Ozay", Gurdjieff briefly engages with his first British pupil: the young musical student Paul [later Sir Paul] Dukes (1889-1967); and in 1914 attracts the Finnish alienist Leonid Robertovich de Stjernvall (1872-1938). In November 1914, Gurdjieff enticingly advertises his prospective ballet *The Struggle of the Magicians* as 'the property of a certain Hindu'. Consequently, in April 1915 Gurdjieff attracts the

Russian journalist and polymath → Piotr Demianovich Ouspensky, successful author of the speculative metaphysical study *Tertium Organum*; and, in December 1916, the well-established Russian classical composer de Hartmann. These two crucial accessions in war-time Petrograd bracket a concentrated teaching phase, arguably the most significant and brilliant of Gurdjieff's entire ministry: certainly he will never again so explicitly exhibit his teaching's arithmosophical constituent and systemic integration, nor recruit pupils as contributive to its dissemination.

Mere days before Tsar Nicolas II is deposed (February 1917) Gurdjieff presciently goes south, soon followed by his cadre whom he shepherds through the ensuing Russian Civil War. In Essentuki he contrives two seminal "workshops" of intense psycho-somatic experimentation, which witness *inter alia* his inception of life- long work on Sacred Gymnastics (later termed "Movements" or Sacred Dance). Finally, in August-September 1918, he audaciously extricates his nucleus (excepting an increasingly disaffected Ouspensky) on foot over the Caucasus mountains, crossing Red and White lines five times.

The year 1919 in Menshevik Georgia is quadruply notable: for the accession (Easter) of Jeanne de Salzmann (1899-1990) a gifted young French-Swiss eurhythmics pupil of Emile Jaques-Dalcroze, and of her husband Alexandre Gustav de Salzmann (1874-1934) an associate of Rilke and Kandinsky; for the inaugural public demonstration of Gurdjieff's Sacred Dance in Tbilisi Opera House (22 June); for the notional founding of Gurdjieff's Institute for the Harmonious Development of Man (September); and thereafter for Gurdjieff's work (co-opting de Hartmann) on the scenario and music of *The Struggle of the Magicians*. Relatively unproductive are Gurdjieff's transitional spells in Constantinople (July 1920-July 1921) and Germany (August 1921-July 1922). The latter, however, is enlivened by Gurdjieff's extravagant prospectus for his Institute and by two brief spring visits to London, where he quarrels irretrievably with Ouspensky, but from whom he captures the allegiance of "Alfred Richard" (James Alfred) Orage (1873-1934), the mystically predisposed editor of the critical weekly *New Age*.

In July 1922, on a restricted Nansen Passport for Russian refugees, Gurdjieff relocates in France (where he will remain domiciled for twenty-seven years until his death). On 1 October he settles in his most famous seat, the Prieure des Basses Loges at Fontainebleau-Avon, and opens his Institute: thus, at 56, Gurdjieff is finally circumstanced to bring West his gleanings in the East. His Russian nucleus is soon substantially augmented by new pupils, whose preponderant British element includes Orage and Dr Henry Maurice Dunlop Nicoll (1884-1953), a former protege of → C.G. Jung. More illustrious is the terminally consumptive New Zealand short story writer "Katherine Mansfield" (Kathleen Mansfield Murry, b. 1888), whose death on 9 January 1923 undeservedly stigmatises Gurdjieff, most enduringly in France. Although, in summer 1923, "open evenings" of music and Sacred Dance in the Prieuré Study House attract some international notables, e.g. Diaghilev and Sinclair Lewis, the mixed reception given Gurdjieff's flamboyant and fully orchestrated demonstration at the Théâtre des Champs-Élysées (December 1923) predicates a decade of French indifference.

Exceptionally significant is 1924. A pivotal demonstration (2 February) at the Neighbourhood Playhouse, Greenwich Village (on the first of Gurdjieff's nine American excursions) excites the New York intelligentsia, drawing inter alia Jane Heap (1883-1964), co-editor of The Little Review, Gorham B. Munson (1896-1969), the critic, and "Jean" (Nathan Pinchback) Toomer (1894-1967), author of Cane. After founding his Institute's New York branch (April), Gurdjieff returns to France, where his work is bluntly recanalised by a near-fatal car accident (8 July). Still convalescent, Gurdjieff formally disbands his Institute (26 August); empowers Orage to supervise America; ceases teaching Movements; and – resolved henceforward to propagate his ideas more enduringly – embarks (16 December) on his vast trilogy All and Everything.

Milestones on the problematic decade 1926 to 1935 are: the death (26 June 1926) of Gurdjieff's wife Julia Osipovna Ostrowska (b. 1889); his self-sacrificial dismissal of intimate Prieuré retainers (May 1928); his effectual expulsion (June 1929) of Thomas de Hartmann; and (February 1930) of the composer's wife Olga Arkadievna (1885-1979), Gurdjieff's devoted secretary and amanuensis; his contrived break with Orage, and enturbulation of the American groups (December 1930); the closure of the Prieuré and disbandment of the Institute (May 1932); the private publication (March 1933) of Gurdjieff's imprudent tract Herald of Coming Good (hastily repudiated and suppressed); the outright loss of the Prieuré (May 1933); the deaths of Alexandre de Salzmann (March 1934) and Orage (November 1934); and, finally, Gurdjieff's irrevocable abandonment of writing (May 1935). Against these must be handsomely weighed: Gurdjieff's

unprecedented musical collaboration (July 1925-May 1927) with Thomas de Hartmann, yielding 170 new piano compositions; and, above all, his prodigious accomplishment of Beelzebub and Meetings (see bibl.).

In October 1935 Gurdjieff far-sightedly prompts Jane Heap to propagate his work in London; and from among her former expatriate associates in Paris constitutes (January 1936) "The Rope", a minuscule group of lesbian literati, with whom he constructively experiments until autumn 1937. In summer 1936 – now aged 70, and deprived, not least by his own will, of virtually all his closest companions – Gurdjieff acquires a modest Paris appartment at 6 rue des Colonels-Renard. Here in 1938 transpires his first personal contact with René Daumal (1908-1944), poet and former member of → Le Grand Jeu a prior student of Work ideas first under Alexandre de Salzmann then Jeanne de Salzmann. With World War II looming, Gurdjieff makes a brief penultimate trip to New York (spring 1939) but resists promptings to settle securely in New Jersey, and returns (May) to France; similarly he declines to vacate Colonels-Renard when the Germans invest Paris (June 1940). In October 1940 Jeanne de Salzmann (already Gurdjieff's de facto deputy) presents to him her gifted preparatory group including the journalist and photographer Henri Tracol (1909-1997) and his wife Henriette (née Lannes) (1899-1980). Despite the Occupation's hazards and rigour, Gurdjieff's Paris group progressively enlarges. At the Salle Pleyel (in morning classes supported only by piano extemporisation) Gurdjieff works indefatigably on new Movements – the "39 Series". In afternoons and evenings he supervises readings of his texts and hosts ritualistic meals featuring an inviolable succession of ceremonious "Toasts to the Idiots". VE-day (6 May 1945) heralds Gurdjieff's consumatory phase (richly documented in memoirs), as tributary streams of British and American pupils merge with the French. Momentum is lent by the death of Ouspensky (2 October 1947) and by the near death of Gurdjieff himself in a second car crash (8 August 1948). On a final visit to New York (December 1948-February 1949) Gurdjieff confides his American endeavour to Henry John Sinclair, 2nd Baron Pentland (1907-1984); and approves publication of Ouspensky's In Search of the Miraculous. In Paris in October 1949 Gurdjieff's health finally collapses: his receipt (21st) of a proof copy of Beelzebub crowns his life's work; he gives instructions to Jeanne de Salzmann (27th) for his texts' posthumous publication, and sends a message to de Hartmann requesting compositions for the 39

Series. Aged 83, Gurdjieff dies at the American Hospital at Neuilly (29th), and is buried (November 3) at Fontainebleau-Avon according to the rite of the Russian Orthodox Church.

Gurdjieff's followers view his teaching as implicated in the man himself ('the function of a master is not limited to the teaching of doctrines, but implies an actual incarnation of knowledge'). He nevertheless bequeaths posterity a free-standing critique, nourishingly, if contentiously, explanatory on three levels: individual, social and cosmic. This panoramic and triple-tiered ideology coheres, constituting a *concordia universa* which by any standards is impressive. Underpinning its integration are Gurdjieff's two axiomatic, universally interacting laws: a dialectical "Law of Three" and a more technically complex "Law of Seven" (assigning to each completing process seven *irregularly* developing phases). Tempering the high intellectuality of this model is Gurdjieff's manifest practicality: he is not offering a set of self-supportive notional abstractions – rather he is harnessing his deepest ontological findings about "world creation and world maintenance" to an eminently approachable *Existenzphilosophie*. As to axiology, Gurdjieff's *summum bonum*, his supreme intrinsic value, is the universal evolution of consciousness: all his subordinate values, ethical, psychological, aesthetic etc. are pragmatically ranked according to this exacting criterion.

Gurdjieff's mythopoeic cosmogony (see *Beelzebub*) presents the Megalocosmos as issuing by *Fiat* from God the Father, expressly to circumvent the encroachments of His holy adversary and coeval – Time. Thereafter, the laws, constants, and parameters in-built in the Megalocosmos preclude God's intervention there; Gurdjieff's is thus a classic Deism of the "absentee landlord" type, in which God, notwithstanding his intuited compassion, lacks effectuality at creation's periphery and forfeits direct transactions with earth. To this scenario Gurdjieff poignantly adds the idea of God's unassuagable sorrow at His inability to alleviate the suffering of far-removed sentient beings. Substituting the term "Absolute" for God, Gurdjieff's formal cosmology (Petrograd group 1916) elaborates in arithmosophical detail a "Ray of Creation" – a cosmicization of being, hierarchically disposed through an involutionary *solfeggio (DOminus* the Lord. *SIdera* the stars, *LActea* the Milky Way, the *SOLar* system etc.). This model of the universe aspires to bridge incrementally the discontinuity between creation and an ultra-transcendent Creator (the "Wholly Other" of Kierkegaard and Barth); to resolve the "ghost in the machine"

dilemma of Cartesian dualism; to give the broadest conceivable canvas to principles of relativism and scale; and to submit the entire natural order to a discrete principle of discontinuity with a musical analogue (redolent of certain late 20th century paradigms in quantum physics).

Overall, however, Gurdjieff's philosophy of nature issues an uncompromising challenge to the hegemony of reductionist technoscience. Gurdjieff's universe is sacred, qualitative, and dramatic: science's universe is secular, quantitative and mechanical. Gurdjieff's universe has a centrum (the "Holy Sun Absolute"): science's universe is isotropic. Gurdjieff's universe is growing in "being": science's growing in "space-time". Gurdjieff's universe is living (hylozoistic in Spinoza's sense): science's inherently inanimate. Gurdjieff's universe has an ontological dependence on the Creator, and a hierarchy of subordinate levels; science's universe is value-free. Arguably Gurdjieff's prime scientific heresy is his attribution to the moon of unsubstantiable macro-effects on the earth and its fauna and flora. Gurdjieff's "moon" transpires as a nascent body (cf. Kepler), symbiotically coupled with the biosphere, activating all organic life on earth (just as a clock's pendulum impels its mechanism), and "fed" by certain "wavicles" liberated at the death of all terrestrial life forms (cf. Posidonius).

Gurdjieff's "Ray of Creation" is not static: its key dynamic of "reciprocal feeding" anticipates, indeed extrapolates, various Green and holistic paradigms (Schweitzer's "reverence for life", Vernadsky's biosphere, and Arne Naess's "deep ecology"). At play on the cosmological level, Gurdjieff's symbiotic principle mimics a Benthamite utilitarianism, its *idée fixe* being the greatest good of the greatest entities: in the big Thrasymachean pecking order – cosmos, galaxy, sun, planets – the earth ranks poorly and its intricate and beautiful biosphere is merely epiphenomenal. Unsurprisingly, human beings en masse are dismally situated: reified on a scale not dreamt of by Adorno, they are eternally subservient to an alien solar economy and demiurgic politics – in effect (to invoke metaphor) factory-farmed for the sweet savour of their abjection and the phosphorescence of their mortality.

Gurdjieff's space-Odyssey *Beelzebub* elaborates an historical and social critique of feignedly extra-terrestrial objectivity (the literary device termed "celestial optics"). Following the three Abrahamic world religions, Gurdjieff initiates human history with a variant of The Fall which complements his favoured theodicy and axiology. Thereafter, in Manichaean temper, he models two discrete streams of human history: conscious v. unconscious; initiatic v. profane; the first current everlastingly transports true spiritual authority and morally vindicated elites (cf. Ortega y Gasset), and the second current temporal power and culturally inflected oligarchies (cf. Robert Michels).

Notwithstanding the cordiality of Gurdjieff's fraternal ideal and his abundantly attested "good Samaritanism", he never surrenders ideologically to modernity's politically correct egalitarianism; in his historiography the masses essentially constitute the genetic humus whence arise, with tragic rarity, authentically "learned beings" e.g. Leonardo da Vinci. *Beelzebub*'s Everyman, by contrast, is exhibited as deeply asleep, blindly and aimlessly struggling and suffering; torn by war and passion, fouling everything he touches; sporadically aroused from torpid preoccupation with 'digestion, mother-in-law, John Thomas, and cash', only to be duped by the Caesarism of powerful demagogues (themselves the unsuspecting dupes of planetary imperatives). In sum, man is a pitiable creature who, by virtue of malign residues of The Fall, clings ingeniously to the very instruments which wound, the patterns which betray.

In stressing 'The Terror of the Situation' Gurdjieff is neither neutral nor fatalistic: his is no perverse celebration of the socially Dadaesque but an epic lamentation at the ascendancy of paranoid forms over normative. Freighting *Beelzebub* with value-judgements (pietistic, patriarchal, traditionalist, pacifist, internationalist, holistic etc.), Gurdjieff tenders ethology as critique, with abundant *Sollen* implicit in his *Sein* (cf. Dickens & Marx). His wry bitter-sweet iconoclasm thus allies itself not to the nihilistic paradigm (as does Adorno's) but to a revolutionist paradigm of meaning; he sweeps the ground clear professedly to build a new and better world. Yet whether Gurdjieff seriously presents as a social reformer, or even entertains the possibility of esotericism's accomplishing benign and stable effects on a Weberian scale, remains highly debatable. His life evidences no political adhesion; his teaching no breath of millenarianism; and his Ray of Creation dooms all generalised humanistic utopias to wither in the chill of the cosmic *Realpolitik*.

Although Gurdjieff salutes the magnaminity and efficacy of traditional esoteric schools down the ages, he reserves to a minuscule segment of humanity the prevenient grace and spiritual hunger which plants one's feet on an authentic Way. For this small candidate-meritocracy Gurdjieff himself propounds an evolutionary, dynamic, or redemptive psychology – not cultivated in religious seclusion (still less on a psychiatrist's couch) but

in the vortex of day-to-day life. Gurdjieff's call is urgent and uncompromising: awake from your unsuspected hypnotic sleep to consciousness and conscience; struggle to attain imperishable "being"; elevate the taste of "I am" from cheap egotism to an essential presence replete with noetic content; come to know yourself – then create, by dint of 'conscious labour and intentional suffering', the soul you imagine you already possess.

In assessing this exhortatory prospectus, encyclopaedism must concede the danger of false cognates (Gurdjieff's Petrograd phase, incidentally, reveals him sharply differentiating *signifiant* from *signifié*). The key words of Gurdjieffian psychology – "self-observation", "self-remembering", "awakening", "being", "essence", "presence", "sensation", "inner work", "centres" – contest ground already colonised by multiple preconceptions and misconceptions. If the specificity of Gurdjieffian terminology is to be respected, it must be grasped that his seasoned pupils dedicated years of arduous experiential pupillage to discovering, and ceaselessly refurbishing, empirically valid referents for these expressions. *Hic labor, hic opus est.*

Abjuring lop-sided genius, Gurdjieff promotes the harmonious development of head, heart, and hand – respectively supporting the intellectual, emotional, and physical temperaments through his writings, music, and Movements. He nevertheless issues a ubiquitous demand for mobilised attention. Contemplatively deployed, this ever-refined attention builds a progressively deeper awareness of nuances of one's physical existence – approaching the Cartesian mind/body mystery in profound interior silence, while putatively opening the psyche to benign supernal influences.

Albeit Gurdjieff emerges as an agent and advocate of tradition, braiding recognisable and hallowed strands of Western and oriental esotericism, he is certainly no mere syncretist. Even jettisoning his surreal ideological provocations (e.g. that the sun neither heats nor lights), his system abounds in markedly original extrapolations and paradigms. Consider his stress on semi-tonal intervals and shocks in the diatonic scale, which differentiates his system from → Robert Fludd; or his intricate synthesis of the Laws of Three and Seven (in his key symbol the "enneagram" and in the "Food Diagram", correlating food, air, and impressions).

Gurdjieff necessarily bears his share of the irony which the 20th century's overweening currents of positivism, scientism, and structuralism reserve for esotericism *in toto*. But, beyond this generalised alienation, Gurdjieff's case is exacerbated by his emphatic individuality – a "hero" of sorts in the age of the anti-hero; an unrepentant patriarch in a phase of post-feminist sensibility; a proponent of spiritual hierarchy in a world where equality is a social shibboleth. Throughout his life Gurdjieff curiously courted opprobrium by charlatanesque role-playing (while his teaching, incidentally, has posthumously contended with ill-considered revisionism, slipshod and counter-productive advocacy, and many distorting appropriations). All in all – with the important caveat that the "missing years" may yet fall prey to investigative scholarship – Gurdjieff's emerging cultural status is impressive. His writing, music, and dance are respectively acclaimed by André Breton, Frank Lloyd Wright, and Lincoln Kirstein, while the dismissive epithets of → René Guénon, D.H. Lawrence, Wyndham Lewis, and François Mauriac seem curiously ill-considered today – eclipsed by positive and markedly better informed valuations e.g. from Peter Brook, Jerzy Grotowski, and Basarab Nicolescu.

Gurdjieff's is a life and a teaching suffused with the starkest of ontologies: 'I travail: therefore I am'. To populate this concept mythopoetically, to structure it dialectically, to loft it, level by level, towards the conceived fountainhead of consciousness – such is Gurdjieff's intellectual achievement. But heart, as well as head, begs recognition here. The noteworthy photographs of Gurdjieff in grandfatherly old age, and the poignancy of his late improvisations on the harmonium, hint at this affective dimension. Gurdjieff is palpably anguished by humanity's reeling disorientation. He abominates war. He suffers from our suffering. Full of years, full of sorrows, the "Teacher of Dancing" emanates an implacable compassion. Yet to "domesticate" him, to divest him of the sharp sting of the real, would betray fact: incontestably among the most influential 20th century esotericists, he stands formidably at the root of a potent contemporary tradition, whose vector resists scrutiny. Strange, nevertheless, that one intuits in him, finally, a benign source candidly and generously approachable.

The Struggle of the Magicians, Capetown: The Stourton Press, 1957 ♦ *Views from the Real World: Early Talks in Moscow, Essentuki, Tiflis, Berlin, London, Paris, New York and Chicago, As Recollected by His Pupils*, London: Routledge & Kegan Paul, 1973 ♦ *All and Everything* (a trilogy comprising *Beelzebub's Tales to His Grandson*, London: Routledge & Kegan Paul, 1950; *Meetings with Remarkable Men*, London: Routledge & Kegan Paul, 1963; *Life is Real Only Then, When "I AM"*, New York: Triangle Editions, 1975) ♦ *The Herald of Coming Good: First Appeal to*

Contemporary Humanity, Angers (France): La Société Anonyme des Editions de l'Ouest, 1933 ♦ *In Search of the Miraculous: Fragments of an Unknown Teaching*, London: Routledge & Kegan Paul, 1950.

Lit.: John G. Bennett & Elizabeth Bennett, *Idiots in Paris: Diaries of J.G. Bennett and Elizabeth Bennett*, Daglingworth Manor, Gloucestershire, (UK): Coombe Springs Press, 1949, 1980 ♦ J. Walter Driscoll and the Gurdjieff Foundation of California, *Gurdjieff: An Annotated Bibliography*, New York: Garland Publishing, 1985 ♦ Thomas & Olga de Hartmann (Thomas C. Daly and T.A.G. Daly, eds.), *Our Life with Mr. Gurdjief*, New York: Penguin Books, 1992 ♦ James Moore, *Gurdjieff: the Anatomy of a Myth*, Shaftesbury, (UK): Element Books, 1991 ♦ Jacob Needleman & George Baker (eds.), *Gurdjieff: Essays and Reflections on the Man and his Teaching*, New York: Continuum Publishing, 1996 ♦ Maurice Nicoll, *Psychological Commentaries on the Teaching of Gurdjieff and Ouspensky*, London: Vincent Stuart, 1952 (vols. 1, 2 & 3), 1955 (vol. 4), 1956 (vol. 5) ♦ Henri Tracol, *The Taste For Things That Are True: Essays and Talks by a pupil of G.I. Gurdjieff*, Shaftesbury: Element Books, 1994 ♦ James Webb, *The Harmonious Circle: The Lives and Works of G.I. Gurdjieff, P.D. Ouspensky, and Their Followers*, London: Thames & Hudson, 1980.

JAMES MOORE

Gurdjieff Tradition

The tradition definable as Gurdjieffian derives its specific character and inspiration from the direct teaching of → G.I. Gurdjieff. Before his death, Gurdjieff entrusted the task of transmitting the teaching to his chief pupil, Jeanne de Salzmann (1889-1990), and a small circle of other pupils in France, England and America who acknowledged her leadership. Under her guidance, the first centers of "the Work" – as the teaching calls itself, echoing alchemical terminology – were established in Paris, London, New York and Caracas. Over the past half-century other centers have radiated from them to major cities of the Western world. Most of the groups maintain close correspondence with the principal centers, usually in relationship to one or two first-generation Gurdjieff pupils who personally guide the work of these affiliated groups. The general articulation of these various groups is a cooperative one, rather than one based on strictly sanctioned jurisdictional control. There are also groups which no longer maintain close correspondence with the main body of pupils and operate independently. And there are numerous other organizations led by individuals who claim no historical lineage with either Gurdjieff or his direct pupils. We limit ourselves here to the teaching as it has been studied and transmitted by the direct Gurdjieff lineage. This teaching can historically be designated as the Gurdjieff tradition.

The theoretical teaching embraces an all-encompassing body of ideas dealing with universal laws and how they govern the whole of man's life on Earth, and in the past half century a vast body of exposition and commentary has accumulated about these ideas (see bibl.). Nevertheless, the teaching remains essentially an oral tradition, continually unfolding – without fixed doctrinal beliefs or external rites – as a way towards freeing humanity from the waking-sleep that holds man in a kind of hypnotic illusion. At the same time, Gurdjieff taught that man's possibilities are very great, and that his destiny is to actualize his true individuality as a bridge between a subtle world above and the unknown world below.

A central focus of the Gurdjieff teaching is the awakening to consciousness and the creation of proper conditions that can support this multi-leveled process. For this, a preparatory work is necessary, as stated by Jeanne de Salzmann: 'According to Gurdjieff, the truth can be approached only if all the parts which make the human being, the thought, the feeling, and the body, are touched with the same force in a particular way appropriate to each of them – failing which, development will inevitably be one-sided and sooner or later come to a stop. In the absence of an effective understanding of this principle, all work on oneself is certain to deviate from the aim. The essential conditions will be wrongly understood and one will see a mechanical repetition of the forms of effort which never surpass a quite ordinary level' (Foreword to *Life is Real Only Then, When "I Am"*).

Gurdjieff gave the name of "self-remembering" to the central state of conscious attention in which the higher force that is available within the human structure makes contact with the functions of thought, feeling and body. The individual "remembers", as it were, who and what he really is and is meant to be, over and above his ordinary sense of identity. This attention is not a function of the mind but is the active spiritual force which all the functions of man obey as the "inner master".

Consistent with the knowledge behind many contemplative traditions of the world, such as the pre-Socratics and especially the Niptic current of Hesychastic Christianity – which speaks of an "attention that comes from God" – the practice of the Gurdjieff work places chief emphasis on preparing the inner world of man to receive this higher attention. When the inner world is prepared

the spirit enters instantly – to use the language of Meister Eckhart.

Great care was taken by Gurdjieff to delineate the cosmic laws that at one and the same time govern both the processes of the universal world and the processes of man's inner life and development. Of these laws, two are fundamental – the law of three and the law of seven or the law of the octave. The law of three states that three forces – active, passive and neutralizing – are necessary for any creation, either at the cosmic level or within the process of the individual search for inner rebirth. The law of seven, for its part, governs the nature of process, stating that all processes develop in seven steps – with two intervals, as represented in the major scale in music with its two intervals of the semi-tone. Both the law of three and the law of seven are contained in the esoteric symbol of the enneagram – a symbol which has been appropriated by individuals and groups outside of the tradition and employed in ways having no correspondence with its meaning in the Gurdjieff tradition.

It is clear that from the beginning of his mission, Gurdjieff adapted the transmission of the teaching to the subjectivity of his pupils, explaining elements that corresponded to their capacities and needs, while holding back other aspects of the whole teaching until they could be received. It is therefore misleading to take any one exposition or interpretation as definitive. → P.D. Ouspensky, for example, considered his own deeply influential and faithful account as no more than '*fragments* of an unknown teaching'.

Seen in this light, and as in other spiritual teachings, the dynamic life of the tradition supports the individual search, and helps to overcome the seemingly universal impulse of resistance or inertia: the tendency toward attachment or "identification", as the Gurdjieff teaching expresses this idea, and the gradual fixing on partial aspects, institutionalized forms, dogmatic doctrines and a habitual reliance on the known rather than facing and entering the unknown. According to the Gurdjieff teaching, the forms exist only to help to discover, to incarnate, and to elaborate a formless energy of awakening, and without this understanding the forms of the teaching become an end in themselves and lose their meaning.

At present, the comparatively invariant general forms of practice in the Gurdjieff tradition may be characterized as follows:

Group Meetings: Gurdjieff taught that one man alone cannot see himself. In group meetings students regularly come together to participate in a collective atmosphere that is said to function as a principal means for the transformation of the individual state of consciousness. Although questions are shared and responded to in words, the fundamental support of the group is directed to the individual work of facing oneself and consciously suffering one's own inner lack until the descent of a new energy is possible. The leader, as part of his or her own search, strives to be sensitive, not so much to the content of the exchange, but to the process of the developing energy. In their turn group leaders just as urgently need to work in groups, albeit at a more advanced level. In this way, a redefinition of the conventional image of the spiritual leader is inevitable. At each level, what is apparently understood needs to be re-examined and verified in the movement of a dynamic living esoteric school.

The *dances and movements*, which Gurdjieff taught, were partially a result of his research in the monasteries and schools of Asia, and are of a nature that seems unique in the modern Western world. In certain respects, they are comparable to sacred dances in traditional religious systems (for example, the 'Cham dances of Tibetan Buddhism or the dervish dances of the Sufis). Like them, the Gurdjieff movements are based on the view that a series of specific postures, gestures, and movements supported by an intentional use of melody and rhythm and an essential element of right individual effort can help to evoke an inner condition which is closer to a more conscious existence, or a state of unity, which can allow an opening to the conscious energy of the Self. The movements are now regularly given at major centers of the work by specially prepared pupils who emphasize the need for exactitude and sincerity of intention, without which the movements cannot provide the help for which they were brought.

The Gurdjieffian practice of *guided meditation* is difficult to characterize in a few words apart from observing that, although it is far from being a technique or method, it corresponds in its essentials to the contemplative aspect of life that is embedded in the heart of all the religious traditions of the world. The Gurdjieffian approach to sitting meditation was gradually emphasized and developed by Jeanne de Salzmann in the 1960's. Here the pupil searches for a quality of seeing and an embodied presence that sustains and supports his attempt to know and directly experience what he is, including both his limitations and his possibilities.

Work in Life. To be able to work in life in the full sense would be considered a very high achievement. The struggle to be "present" in everyday life constitutes a major aspect of the Gurdjieff practice, a struggle which entails the question of full engagement in the duties and rewards of the life of man on Earth, now and here. In this context, Gurdjieff restored and created many inner exercises, some intended mainly for the meditative practice and others for the conditions of everyday life. Such exercises are understood as providing a structure that makes possible use of everyday life as material for self-observation and the gradual growth of self-awareness. Through repetition of such exercises, the individual may begin to come into touch with a deep sense of need which allows an opening to the spiritual energies within oneself. According to Gurdjieff, without a relationship to this more central aspect of oneself, everyday life is bound to be an existential prison, in which the individual is held captive, not so much by the so-called forces of modernity as by the parts of the self which cannot help but react automatically to the influences of the world around him. The help offered by the special conditions of the work is therefore understood not as replacing man's life in the world, but as enabling him, in the course of time, to live life with authentic understanding and full participation.

Briefly, the movement toward awakening which is meant to be supported by the ideas and these forms of practice becomes in fact an organic process in life and movement and for that reason, dogmatic approaches will inevitably fail. The movement toward awakening, then, requires an understanding not only of the constituent forces and laws which govern man's psyche and actions, but also a deep sensitivity and appreciation of individual subjective needs and conditions. In other words, for an effective guidance, the principle of relativity must be recognized in the transmission of the teaching: individuals must be approached according to their respective levels of development and experience. Gurdjieff might have stressed one view to a student at a certain level of understanding and quite another view when that student had reached another level. This might give the appearance of contradiction, but in fact it was consistent in applying only those aspects of the whole teaching truly necessary at a given moment. The same principle applies to the ideas, some of which seemed more accessible at one period while others still remained to be revealed in the unfolding life of the teaching. In this light, it is interesting to note that groups that break away at different moments to work by themselves and on their own run the risk of clinging dogmatically to certain specific forms and practices.

For example, the work of "self-observation" is given new meaning as the developing attention lets go of its effort, joining and willingly submitting to an impartial conscious seeing, resting in its vision. The action that might take place in this condition – meditation or even outer action – is held to reflect the simultaneous dual nature of an impersonal consciousness and a personal attention which has a new capacity to manifest and act in the world. The qualities of both these aspects of consciousness and attention are considered quite unknown to the ordinary mind. In this new relationship of individual attention and a divine impersonal consciousness, man is believed to become a vessel, serving another energy which can act through him, an energy which at the same time transforms the materiality of the body at the cellular level. This understanding of inner work introduced by de Salzmann has been transmitted in the oral tradition of the Gurdjieff teaching and can be found today in many of the Gurdjieff Foundation groups worldwide.

The half century that has passed since Gurdjieff's death has witnessed dramatic developments with respect to the reception of his ideas – as well as a proliferation of interpretations and applications. Louis Pauwels' derogatory *Monsieur Gurdjieff*, published in 1954, was for a time the only book about Gurdjieff, other than Ouspensky's. Although late in his life Pauwels repudiated his earlier views and spoke of the great value of Gurdjieff's teaching, the negative tone of *Monsieur Gurdjieff* strongly influenced public opinion in France and elsewhere. Starting in the early 1960s, however, numerous accounts and testimonies by pupils who were close to Gurdjieff began to present a far more comprehensive view of the ideas, as well as a positive description of Gurdjieff the teacher. The number of these accounts has continued to grow until the present day and, taken together, they offer a far more balanced and nuanced picture of the teaching and the man than was available in the first decade after his death (see Bibl.).

The broader cultural influence of the Gurdjieff teaching has also become clearer. In the field of psychology, the practice of group therapy (e.g. Skynner and Slavson) owes much to the Gurdjieff idea about the necessity of group work; and the very phrases "self-observation" and "work on oneself" have not only entered into many psychological and psychotherapeutic disciplines, but have even entered into the vernacular of the English language. The idea of consciousness as the key to spiritual development owes much to Gurdjieff's identification of this aspect of the psyche as the uniquely human element, over and above the analytic and combinatory powers of the mind.

In the arts, the insights of Gurdjieff have been acknowledged by leading figures such as Frank Lloyd Wright (architect), Thomas de Hartmann (composer), Peter Brook (theater), Lincoln Kirstein (dance) and in many other venues including literature, philosophy and the study of religion. Often, his ideas are applied without acknowledgement, and a study of this aspect of the reception of his teaching needs to be undertaken to show the surprising extent to which his ideas and terminology, in widely varying interpretations and alterations, have become a significant cultural and philosophical influence in contemporary arts, letters and various forms of therapeutic praxis, including such unexpected areas as corporate management training.

Among pupils who broke away from the main community of pupils after Gurdjieff's death and established groups of their own which continue to be active, the most significant are Willem Nyland, and J.G. Bennett. The reasons behind these breaks are not easily discernible from the outside, and are not "doctrinal" in the familiar sense of the term. Doubtless, personal issues are often prominent. During Gurdjieff's lifetime, as is known, many advanced pupils were compelled to leave by Gurdjieff himself, who rigorously resisted any tendency toward devotion or attachment to his person. This was most notably the case with Thomas de Hartmann. In many other instances, such as with P.D. Ouspensky, Gurdjieff may have considered it necessary to place strong emotional challenges before his pupils at certain key junctures in the process of their inner work, and the result was sometimes that they broke away from him. However, it is idle to speculate in this general area; it is still too early in the life of this teaching to speak in broadly familiar categories of "orthodoxy", "schisms" or "heresies". It is sufficient to note that each generation of the Work has witnessed this process of independent creation of groups, whereby individuals, after a period of membership in the mainstream tradition, leave to create their own organizations. It is impossible to estimate the number of individuals involved in these organizations, although probably all of them combined have fewer members than the main network of some 10.000 pupils worldwide.

[For more extensive bibliographical information and history, see J. Walter Driscoll and The Gurdjieff Foundation of California, *Gurdjieff: An Annotated Bibliography* and *The Gurdjieff International Review*, www.Gurdjieff.org.]

Lit.: James Moore, *Gurdjieff: The Anatomy of a Myth*, Boston, Mass.: Element Books, 1999 ♦ Jacob Needleman, "G.I. Gurdjieff and his School", in Antoine Faivre & Jacob Needleman (eds.), *Modern Esoteric Spirituality*, New York: Crossroad, 1995, 359-380 ♦ John Pentland, *Exchanges Within: Questions from Everyday Life Selected from Gurdjieff Group Meetings with John Pentland in California 1955-1984*, New York: Continuum, 1998 ♦ William Segal, *Opening: Collected Writings of William Segal 1985-1997*, New York: Continuum, 1998 ♦ A.L. Stavely, *Memories of Gurdjieff*, Aurora, Oregon: Two Rivers Press, 1978 ♦ Henri Tracol, *The Taste For Things That Are True: Essays and Talks By A Pupil of G.I. Gurdjieff*, Shaftsbury: Element Books, 1994 ♦ James Webb, *The Harmonious Circle: The Lives and Work of G.I. Gurdjieff, P.D. Ouspensky, and Their Followers*, New York: Putnam's, 1980.

JACOB NEEDLEMAN

Hahn, Michael, * 2.2.1758 Altdorf, † 20.1.1819 Sindlingen

Hahn came from a family of Pietists [→ Pietism]. He felt the presence of God within him as early as the age of twelve. Toward 1777, he received the grace of an illumination that he himself called a *Zentralschau* (Central Vision). He compensated for a neglected education by much reading. In 1784, a second illumination confirmed him in his desire to center his whole life on God and to preach his kingdom. Through his zeal and piety, he attracted to himself crowds of believers eager to hear him. His disciples, the *Michelianer*, would endeavour to continue his work. Often neglecting the theosophical [→ Christian Theosophy] aspect of his thought, they would especially retain its pietistic tendency.

This Swabian theosopher deserves particular mention for his tireless efforts to order his theosophical concepts in a coherent system, whence a certain rationality that is never absent. One cannot consider him a Pietist, a separatist or a pure mystic. His thinking always evokes these tendencies, but his insistence on demanding personal reflection from the believer makes him a son of the Aufklärung. Nevertheless, Hahn, whose faith found equal support in esoteric gnosis, was indeed a Christian theosopher even if his system can at times appear incomplete. All his thinking flowed from his "Central Vision" (*Zentralschau*), which he strove to explicate as clearly as possible.

To understand the Bible, keystone of all, erudition is less important than a personal encounter with God. Knowledge of God and knowledge of self must blend in the intimate experience that operates in the *Centralgrund* (inner Center) of man. The whole mystery of the complex relationships between God, Man and the universe is written in Man the microcosm. It is enough for a free will to be united with a deepened personal will for it to be clarified and elucidated. From then on, by sinking into the contemplation of the image of divinity, Man can "see" with the eye of God. However, the depth of thinking gives this inexpressible experience all its scope. The true Christian must think for himself. He will then grasp all the intimate motivations of the divine Economy by observing that what is in God is also in Man.

Conscious of having developed a system that was proper to himself, Hahn was nonetheless indebted to → Boehme and to → Friedrich Christoph Oetinger for elements that are part of it. The undetermined foundation of the Boehmean *Ungrund*, the unmanifest transcendent God, similar to the Father, is revealed in the Son in a plural immanence that affects all creation. In its ardent desire to know itself, the *Ungrund* gives birth to the *Urgrund*, the Son, who becomes the "Central point of God" and of all creatures. The Father is Fire, but less wrathful than in Boehme, and more harmonious even if duality inhabits Him. The Son is Light manifested, the *männliche Jungfrau* (masculine virgin) who controls, by His central position, the good and the evil activated in the creative process. A reflection of the Son, the primordial Adam was androgynous. One finds in Hahn, together with the Oetingerian idea that any spirit tends to manifest itself "in bodies" (*Geistleiblichkeit*), the theory of the double fall. Both Lucifer, who wanted to arrogate the Son's nature, and Man fell, tempted by the fallen angel and enclosed in the opaque matter of our visible world, where a few rays of the divine Light still shine through. Although Christ has redeemed the whole of undeserving humanity, the true Christian must tend to spiritual perfection for a true rebirth (*Wiedergeburt*) and not remain content with a conventional faith. God is not only merciful, he is also just: our faults are forgiven and there are no eternal punishments (*Apocatastasis*), but a purifying fire (*Läuterungsfeuer*) is necessary, the trials that accompany it being an integral part of the grace that God grants us.

The Unity of God in all his living members is the object of the quest of every true Christian community. The Roman Church and the neology rife in the Protestant milieu are far from this ideal. The Evangelical Church, by the free will that it grants the believer, is preferable. Neither a separatist nor a

Pietist, Hahn hardly got along with the members of the clergy, who saw in him an eccentric with an equivocal doctrine. Nevertheless, in his apocalyptic and eschatological considerations, he had the prudence, contrary to Johann Albrecht Bengel, not to make short-term prophecies. If the influence of Gerhard Tersteegen and German → mysticism is perceptible in his work, the influence of Boehme and Friedrich Christoph Oetinger is more so. However, the extreme tension of a Boehme seeking to circumscribe the good and evil at work in creation, and the considerations of Oetinger on → alchemy and palingenesis remain equally foreign to him. Far from straining over the insoluble problem of evil, he stresses the profound harmony of the consubstantial elements in God, Man and the universe. He considers that Boehmenism contains a good share of unresolved dualism and insists rather on the primacy of divine unity. Without beginning or end, God uses linear time as a material apt to open up eternal perspectives through the history of salvation set forth in the typology of Holy Scripture. One must ceaselessly scrutinize Holy Scripture to grasp its hidden truths, because faith does not go without understanding nor understanding without faith. Hahn's christology is too anchored in the depths of the God-filled soul for the Son, despite the theosopher's requirement that his presence be apprehended equally by reason, ever to be regarded as a mere principle exemplifying redemption and grace.

Hahn's rich personality and charisma explains the number of his admirers and disciples. Little concerned about orthodoxy, he exhorted them, on the one hand, to read the Bible and its most inspired commentators from Luther to Bengel, and, on the other hand, to exercise their personal thinking. It alone, according to him, was capable of providing answers relevant to the times in which they were living.

Hahn'sche Gemeinschaft (ed.), *Auszug aus Michael Hahns Schriften* (1857-58) & *Ausgewählte Betrachtungen* (1924-1929), 2 vols., Stuttgart, 1945 and 1959.

Lit.: Joachim Trautwein, *Die Theosophie Michael Hahns und ihre Quellen*, Stuttgart: Calwer Verlag, 1969 ◆ Gerhard Schäfer (ed.), *J. Michael Hahn: Gotteserkenntnis und Heiligung. Aus seinen Briefen, Betrachtungen, Liedern*, Metzingen: Franz, 1994.

JACQUES FABRY

Halatophilus Irenaeus → Oetinger, Friedrich Christoph

Hall, Manly Palmer, * 18.3.1901 Peterborough, Ontario, † 29.8.1990 Los Angeles

Writer, Collector, Lecturer. Hall was raised by his maternal grandmother, Mrs. Arthur Whitney Palmer, and spent a wandering childhood in San Diego, Washington, New York, Sioux Falls, and other cities of the United States. Apart from a short spell at a military school, he was without formal education. In California he came under the influence of the → Theosophical Society. He began his public career in 1920 in Santa Monica, giving a series of lectures on → reincarnation. He became a lifelong admirer of → H.P. Blavatsky and her *Secret Doctrine*. In 1921 he conceived the plan of an encyclopedic work on esoteric traditions and began to collect materials for it. In 1922 he founded a journal, *The All-Seeing Eye* (first monthly, then irregular). At about this time, he became the pastor of a church called The Church of the People, which met at Trinity Auditorium at Ninth and Grand in Los Angeles. In 1923-1924, thanks to a wealthy patron or patrons whose identity was never revealed, he was able to make an extensive tour of Europe, Egypt, and Asia, and to lay the basis for a magnificent collection of books and artefacts representing the spiritual traditions of East and West. The following years were spent writing, compiling, financing, and commissioning the illustrations for his masterwork *The Secret Teaching of All Ages* (1928). This oversized volume, often reprinted, contains 54 color plates by Augustus Knapp and hundreds of illustrations from books and manuscripts, many of them by now in Hall's library. It was designed by the eminent typographer John Henry Nash. The text is an introduction to almost every facet of Western esotericism, and, more briefly, to Eastern religions. It carries a strong atmosphere of → Freemasonry and of Theosophy.

Southern California, with its Theosophical and Rosicrucian centers [→ Rosicrucianism] and its openness to exotic religions, was a natural home to Hall's endeavors. In 1934 he founded the Philosophical Research Society, whose initials, P.R.S., stood also for the combined wisdom of Philosophy, Religion, and Science. In 1934-1935 he went to London and Paris to acquire rare books dispersed in the Lionel Hauser sale (see his *Codex Rosae Crucis*). A large building adorned with sphinxes (3910 Los Feliz Boulevard, Los Angeles) was built to house Hall's library and the lecture-room in which he gave addresses on Sunday mornings.

These long impromptu talks and other lectures continued regularly until shortly before his death, and formed the basis for innumerable publications of the P.R.S.

Hall is said to have authored over 200 books, in addition to hundreds of essays and to editing the *P.R.S. Journal* (called *Horizon* from 1940-1954). They were virtually all published by his Hall Publishing Company, then by the P.R.S. Hall was honored by the 33rd degree of Scottish Rite Freemasonry. In 1950 he married Marie Bauer, a fellow-adherent of the theory that Sir → Francis Bacon wrote the plays of Shakespeare (see her *Foundations Unearthed*, 1940). After Hall's death, there was a long lawsuit between his widow and other claimants to his estate. This was settled to Mrs. Hall's satisfaction in 1993, allowing the P.R.S. to continue its activities. Many of the library's treasures were sold, notably the collection of Japanese art and many of the alchemical books. Hall's alchemical collection, including the manuscripts of Dr. Sigismund Bacstrom which Hall had owned since 1923, was acquired by the J. Paul Getty Museum, Malibu.

Hall was a blend of the scholar-collector with the inspirational writer and speaker. He formed his own "academy" of followers and readers who appreciated the depth, sincerity, and wide sympathies of his learning. Hall's philosophy also had a strong element of → "New Thought", and he always dwelt on the positive aspect of things. From a scholarly point of view, his writing may appear inaccurate and banal, but he had a gift for making complex subjects, such as → Neoplatonism or occult anatomy, comprehensible to a lay audience. Although open to the claims of the occult sciences [→ occult/occultism], he did not promote them, and in later life moved closer to Buddhism. Hall is most comparable to G.R.S. Mead and to the American Platonists Thomas M. Johnson (1851-1919), and Kenneth Sylvan Guthrie (1871-1940). He may be remembered as the last link in the American Transcendentalist tradition.

The Secret Teaching of All Ages: An Encyclopedic Outline of Masonic, Hermetic, Qabbalistic, and Rosicrucian Symbolical Philosophy, San Francisco: H.S. Crocker, for the Author, 1928 and many re-editions ♦ *Lectures on Ancient Philosophy*, Los Angeles: Philosophical Research Society [hereafter PRS], 1929 ♦ *The Phoenix: An Illustrated Review of Occultism and Philosophy*, Los Angeles: PRS, 1931 ♦ *Man, Grand Symbol of the Mysteries*, Los Angeles: PRS, 1932 ♦ *Codex Rosae Crucis: A Rare and Curious Manuscript of Rosicrucian Interest, Now Published for the First Time in Its Original Form*, Los Angeles: PRS, 1938.

Lit.: Information on Hall's life is scarce, and the scholarly world has totally ignored him. On his relation to the Theosophical Society, see *Secret Doctrine Centenary: Report of Proceedings, October 29-30, 1988*, Pasadena: Theosophical Society, 1989, 23-27 ♦ For a romanticized early autobiography, see his *Life with Grandmother*, Los Angeles: Philosophical Research Society, 1985 ♦ On his collecting, see Ron. Charles Hogart (ed.), *Alchemy: A Comprehensive Bibliography of the Manly P. Hall Collection of Books and Manuscripts, Including Related Material on Rosicrucianism and the Writings of Jacob Boehme*, Los Angeles: Philosophical Research Society, 1986 ♦ On the scandals following Hall's death, see Bob Pool, reports in *Los Angeles Times*, May 9, 1993; December 22/23, 1994 ♦ A full-length biography of Hall by Lawrence Sahagun is in preparation.

JOSCELYN GODWIN

Hamvas, Béla, * 23.3.1897 Eperjes (today Presov in Slovakia), † 7.11.1968 Budapest

Hungarian philosopher, and one of the most comprehensive gnostic thinkers of the 20th century. Hamvas was born in a family of Lutheran pastors serving in Upper Hungary, today's Slovakia. After World War I the family moved to Budapest, where Hamvas studied classical languages, read German and Hungarian at the university, and received his MA in 1923. He started working as a journalist, but soon settled as a librarian at the Budapest Public Library, a most congenial occupation for him. In 1935 he became the co-founder of Karoly Kerenyi's circle, *Sziget* (Island), in the context of which he published essays on a wide variety of topics, including Russian mystics (Berdjaev) and existentialist philosophers (Heidegger and Jaspers). During the war he served at the Russian front, then resumed his job in the library from where in 1948 he was released because his views were incompatible with the communist regime. A particularly shocking event to him was the destruction of his manuscripts as well as his private library during a bombing attack on Budapest in 1945. From that time on a long series of afflictions followed. Georg Lukács, chief ideologue of the Hungarian communist government, prohibited the publication of his works. Being expelled from the library, Hamvas had to take a job as a stock-attendant in an industrial plant. In the 1950s he was forced to work at a power station outside Budapest and could go home only on weekends. Even after 1956 when he applied for rehabilitation, his request of being restored to his position as a librarian was refused. He retired in 1964 and spent his last years in

Budapest as a charismatic mystic around whom a growing circle a students gathered. After he died of a stroke, immediately a cult around his person began. His works were typed and passed from hand to hand as "samizdat" (illegal publications bypassing state censorship) until the late 1980s, from which time on his writings have been published in comprehensive editions. Today he is widely appreciated as one of Hungary's most original philosophers.

Hamvas's literary output is large and versatile. He excelled in *belles lettres*, and wrote a number of strange novels in which modernist and mystical elements are mixed with grotesque irony. Most famous among them is *Karneval* (Carnival, 1948-1951, published in 1985). He was an accomplished essayist, one of the finest in 20th century Hungarian literature. He put together several collections of essays during his career, such as *Láthatalan történet* (The invisible story, 1940-1941), *A bor filozófiája* (The philosophy of wine, 1947), *Silentium* (1950), and *Patmosz* (Pathmos, 1959-1966). Another genre in which he felt at home was translating and editing/annotating works of mystical philosophy from a wide range of cultures and periods, including 25 chapters of the *Vedas*, the *Upanishads*, and *The Flowers of Tao* (1943); the Apocalypse of Enoch (1944); Jakob Boehme's *Psychologia vera* (1946); the *Tabula smaragdina* (1950); and *Sefer Yetsirah* (1954). Particularly notable is his annotated anthology of "the Tradition" [→ Tradition] which was published under the title *Az ősök nagy csarnoka* (The great hall of the ancestors, 1943) and to which he added a monumental introductory essay titled "Ekstasis".

Beyond these, Hamvas also wrote major individual works in the form of carefully constructed and logically arranged monographs, none of which appeared in print during his lifetime. His "opus magnum" is *Scientia sacra: the Spiritual Tradition of the Ancients* (1943-1944, first published 1988), a compelling account of human wisdom in the midst of the madness of war. The second part of this work deals with a comparison of Christianity and "the Tradition" (*Scientia sacra II*, 1960-63), while his *Mágia szutra* (Magia sutra [1950], first published 1994) discusses the practical application of "the Tradition" in view of attaining the ideal of 'a consciously purified way of life'.

Hamvas's philosophy may be referred to as "sacral metaphysics", and his approach is related to that of → Julius Evola, → Leopold Ziegler, and → René Guénon. His main concern was the most ancient past, as remote as the lost Golden Age. As opposed to → Rudolf Steiner, he never thought of mixing the spheres of natural science with that of hermeticism, and claimed that the investigation of nature was confined to the surface material world only. For a philosopher like him, the occult relations of the universe are effective in the transcendental and supernatural spheres, to which the development of science is irrelevant.

In *Scientia sacra*, Hamvas aimed at synthetizing the Tao, the Vedas, Buddhism, the Hebrew kabbalah [→ Jewish Influences], Egyptian hermeticism, and the teachings of the Persian → Zoroaster. In the first part of the work Hamvas discusses the tradition that has preserved the memory of the Golden Age and that, according to him, may lead humankind back to the happiness of the lost antediluvian state. The second book is devoted to archaic man, who still participated in the occult knowledge. Hamvas reviews various accounts about the loss of Eden, and against that background provides a reconstruction of the major stages of man's historical existence: the primordial state – sin – the awakening – repetition (the "development" constituting the further phases of awakening) – the outer darkness (offering a choice between purposeful pilgrimage and random roaming) – and liberation. Liberation is the state towards which the magus is striving; and since occult knowledge is embedded in the analogical symbols of the ancients, the magus has to become a philologist of sorts in order to be able to analyse and interpret the esoteric tradition. The subject of the third book is "Cult and Culture". A comparison of ancient and modern cultures reveals that real knowledge is not to be gained from rational and analytical science, but belongs only to the sacral way of life.

Hamvas's personal experience of the "world crisis" of the 20th century, culminating in two World Wars, was of decisive importance to his life. He saw no other way of escaping from this apocalyptic collapse than by means of a reintegration of the individual in the community in the context of a revitalization of inspired ancient laws and wisdom. His continuing popularity proves that this program still has a strong appeal.

A világválság ("The world crisis", 1935-37), Budapest: Magvető, 1983 ♦ *Karneval* ("Carnival", 1948-51), Budapest: Magvető, 1985 ♦ *Scientia sacra, Az őskori emberiség szellemi hagyománya* ("The spiritual tradition of the Ancients", 1943-44), Budapest: Magvető, 1988 (English translation by Andrea Kibedi is as yet unpublished; Italian translation Milano 2001) ♦ *Hamvas Béla művei* ("Collected works"), Szombathely-Budapest: Életünk-Medio, 1990- ♦ *Silentium*, Szentendre: Editio M., 1999 ♦ *Philosophie des*

Weines, Szentendre: Editio M., 1999 ◆ *La philosophie du vin*, Szentendre: Editio M., 1999.

Lit.: Dúl Antal, "A sors és a szó – Hamvas Béla kísérlete" ("Fate and Words – The Experiment of Hamvas"), in: Hamvas, *A láthatatlan történet* ("The invisible story"), Budapest: Akadémiai, 1988, 7-16 ◆ György E. Szőnyi, "Occult Ascension in Troubled Times: The Ideals of Mankind in Rudolf Steiner and Béla Hamvas", in: M. Kronegger and A.-T. Tymieniecka (eds.), *Ideals of Mankind* (Analecta Husserliana 49), Dordrecht–Boston–London: Kluwer Academic Publishers, 1996, 29-43 ◆ Endre Török, "Ami teljes, és ami részleges" ("Of what is complete and what is fragmentary"), attached to Hamvas, *Scientia sacra* (1988), 547-73.

GYÖRGY E. SZŐNYI

Hardenberg, Friedrich von → Novalis

Hartmann, Franz, * 22.11.1838 Donauwörth, † 7.8.1912 Kempten

German physician, author, and leading German Theosophist. Hartmann first worked as a pharmacy assistant in Kempten. In 1859 he was enlisted as a volunteer in the 1st Artillery Regiment of Bavaria during the Austrian-Italian War. In 1860 he commenced studies in pharmacy (receiving his state qualification in 1862) and medicine at Munich University. In July 1865 he took passage as a ship's doctor on a vessel bound from Le Havre to New York and spent the next eighteen years in the United States. The same year 1865 he completed his medical training and opened a practice for eye ailments at St Louis. In 1867 he acquired U.S. citizenship; and in 1870 he travelled to New Orleans and thence by ship to Mexico, visiting Mexico City, Cordova and Orizaba, where he became acquainted with Indian tribes. He resumed medical practice at New Orleans, where he became interested in American → spiritualism, attending the seances of Mrs Rice Holmes and Kate Wentworth and studying the writings of Judge Edmonds and → Andrew Jackson Davis. In 1873 he travelled to Texas where he bought a ranch, married the sister of a neighbour but widowed after seven months. In 1878 he settled in Georgetown, Colorado, engaging in gold and silver mining besides his medical practice, and from 1882 served as coroner for Clear Creek County; he continued to be interested in spiritualism, encountered Theosophical literature, and entered into correspondence with → H.S. Olcott. In 1882 he joined the → Theosophical Society in the U.S.A. In September 1883 he left Colorado to visit the Theosophists in India, with brief visits to Japan and China en route. In December he arrived at Adyar, where he came to play a major role at Theosophical Society headquarters. In April 1885 he returned to Europe with → H.P. Blavatsky. In 1891 he became founder-director of a sanatorium at Hallein, near Salzburg, and in August 1896 President of a new German Theosophical Society at Berlin founded by Katherine Tingley of the American Theosophists. In September 1897 he founded the *Internationale Theosophische Verbrüderung* at Munich. From 1899, Hartmann collaborated with Hugo Vollrath (b. 1877) on Theosophical lecture tours and publishing. In 1906, Vollrath founded the *Theosophische Verlagshaus* in Leipzig, which systematically publishes Hartmann's works besides translations of H.P. Blavatsky, → Annie Besant and → Charles Leadbeater.

From his youth, Hartmann combined mystical and idealistic speculations with his interest in medicine and science. Following experiments with spiritualism in the United States, Hartmann discovered Theosophy, which became his life's work. While Blavatsky and Olcott were in Europe, Hartmann presided at Theosophical Society headquarters in Adyar during the investigation of the Society of Psychical Research into the Coulomb scandal in 1884. After his return to Europe in 1885, Hartmann decided that Theosophy required a new foundation to counter negative publicity. At Kempten he frequented the pietistic group around the weaver Alois Mailänder (1844-1905). In September 1889 Hartmann founded, together with Alfredo Pioda and Countess Constance Wachtmeister, a Theosophical lay-monastery at Ascona, Switzerland. His Theosophical monthly periodical *Lotusblüten* (1892-1900), later revived as *Neue Lotusblüten* (1908-1912), provided a forum for the fast-growing number of German Theosophists. Although Hartmann's collaboration with the American theosophists under Katherine Tingley in 1896 was short-lived, his *Internationale Theosophische Verbrüderung* acted as a major platform for the movement in Germany. Between 1894 and 1907 Hartmann collaborated with the German Theosophical publishers C.A. Schwetschke of Brunswick, Wilhelm Friedrich and the Theosophische Centralbuchhandlung, both at Leipzig. Their extensive book-series attracted a German readership for the writings of Hartmann and other German Theosophists such as Rudolph Böhme, Hugo Göring and Arthur Weber, together with translations of Annie Besant and Charles Leadbeater.

Besides his Theosophical activities, Hartmann was also linked with other occult and fringe-masonic orders. He was associated with Carl Kellner (1851-1905), initiator of the → Ordo Templi Orientis, who used ligno-sulphite in the manufacture of cellulose at Hallein. Hartmann used a by-product of this process for the treatment of lung ailments at his neighbouring sanatorium. Hartmann was associated in 1897 with Leopold Engel (1858-1931) in an Order of the Illuminati at Dresden, which was absorbed by → Theodor Reuss in 1902. In September 1902 Hartmann became Deputy Grand Commander General in Reuss's Rite of Memphis and Misraim; and in October 1905, following Kellner's death, Hartmann became Honorary Grand Master General. These fringe-masonic groups were succeeded by Reuss's Ordo Templi Orientis in 1906.

Hartmann was one of the most prolific writers of his generation on Theosophy, → magic and esotericism. His publications, written in both English and German, almost all follow his involvement with the Theosophical Society. Hartmann's earliest works were devoted to → Rosicrucianism, → Paracelsus, → Jacob Boehme, magic, the astrological geomancy of → Cornelius Agrippa and other topics in the Western esoteric tradition. *The Life of Jehoshua, Prophet of Nazareth* described the psychical and spiritual processes experienced on the path of initiation. From 1892 he developed his prodigious output on Theosophy. He wrote two translations in prose and verse of the *Bhagavad Gita* and was instrumental in the German translation, in collaboration with Dr Robert Froebe, of Blavatsky's *The Secret Doctrine* (1897-1901). He also translated Blavatsky's *The Voice of the Silence* and several oriental scriptures, such as the *Atma Bodha*, the *Tattwa Bodha*, and the *Tao-Teh-King*. His own publications in German number more than thirty books and hundreds of articles in his magazine. The books include commentaries on Theosophy, studies of karma and → reincarnation, the doctrine of Buddhism, as well as further studies of Paracelsus and → alchemy.

Report of Observations made during a Nine Months' Stay at the Headquarters of The Theosophical Society at Adyar (Madras), India, Madras: Scottish Press, 1884 ♦ *Magic, White and Black*, London: George Redway, 1886 ♦ *The Life of Paracelsus and the Substance of his Teachings*, London: George Redway, 1887 ♦ *An Adventure among the Rosicrucians*, Boston: Occult Pub. Co., 1887 ♦ *Cosmology or Universal Science*, Boston: Occult Pub. Co., 1888 ♦ *The Principles of Astrological Geomancy*, London: Theos. Pub. Co., 1889 ♦ *The Life and Doctrines of Jacob Boehme*, London: Kegan Paul, 1891 ♦ *Selbsterkenntnis und Wiederverkörperung*, Brunswick: C.A. Schwetschke, 1894 ♦ *Die Geheimlehre in der christlichen Religion nach den Erklärungen von Meister Eckart*, Leipzig: W. Friedrich, 1898 ♦ *Die Religionslehre der Buddhisten*, Leipzig: W. Friedrich, 1898 ♦ *Denkwürdige Erinnerungen*, Leipzig: W. Friedrich, 1898 ♦ *Kurzgefaßte Grundriß der Geheimlehre*, Leipzig: W. Friedrich, 1899 ♦ *Die Erkenntnislehre der Bhagavad Gita*, Leipzig: W. Friedrich, 1900 ♦ *Mysterien, Symbole und magisch wirkende Kräfte*, Leipzig: Lotus, 1902 ♦ *Was ist Theosophie?*, Leipzig: Theosophische Centralbuchhandlung, 1903.

Lit.: H.P. Blavatsky, *Collected Writings: 1887*, Adyar: Theosophical Publishing House, 1960, Volume VIII, 439-457 ♦ Walter Einbeck, "Leben und Wirken Dr. Franz Hartmanns", *Theosophische Kultur* 12:9 (1925), 258-266 ♦ Hugo Göring, *Dr Franz Hartmann, ein Vorkämpfer der Theosophie*, Brunswick: C.A. Schwetschke, 1894 ♦ Robert Hütwohl (ed.), *Some Fragments of the Secret History of the Theosophical Society by Franz Hartmann*, Theosophical History Occasional Papers Vol. VIII, 2000 ♦ Robert Hütwohl, *Bibliography of Franz Hartmann, M.D. with an addenda: His Stay in Georgetown, Colorado*, Santa Fe: Spirit of the Sun, 2001.

NICHOLAS GOODRICK-CLARKE

Haslmayr (or Haselmayer), Adam, * ca. 1560 Bolzano, † 1630 Augsburg (?)

Haslmayr was born around 1560 in Bolzano, South Tyrol. By 1588 he was the organist in a Cordelier convent, while teaching Latin and fulfilling the duties of an imperial secretary (*Notarius Caesareus*). In 1593, Archduke Ferdinand of the Tyrol granted him a patent of nobility. According to Haslmayr's own account, in the following year he began to discover the works of → Paracelsus. It was the latter's belief that God reveals himself to mankind both through his Word and through the marvels of Nature, which it is man's mission to discover. Thanks to → alchemy, conceived in its broadest sense, man is therefore able, and obligated, to transform the world, to realize the "new man" in himself, and to lead Nature to its perfection.

Reading this aroused Haslmayr to such enthusiasm that in 1603 he did not hesitate to address to Archduke Maximilian of Austria a compendium of Paracelsus's ideas, which, to say the least, were not completely orthodox. The Archduke apparently took notice of this: he ordered an inquiry, in consequence of which Haslmayr was summoned to Innsbruck and underwent an interrogation, in which Jesuit theologians took part. They condemned the non-Catholic ideas of his writing, but considered him more as a person of confused mind than as a true heretic, who should no longer be entrusted with educational duties.

In 1605 Haslmayr settled near Innsbruck in the town of Schwaz, where mining activity had aroused a lively interest in alchemy. After that he lived in Hall (Tyrol), where he translated medical works of the French Paracelsian Joseph Duchesne (known as Quercetanus). In 1607 he came to know the Paracelsian Benedictus Figulus, author of a *Rosarium novum,* whose thought was very close to certain ideas expressed in the *Fama Fraternitatis* (see Edighoffer 1987, II, 695). Manuscript copies of this Rosicrucian manifesto [→ Rosicrucianism] were circulating in the Tyrol from 1610 onwards. At this time, Haslmayr was in correspondence with Archduke Maximilian, to whom he had sent a Paracelsian recipe on the making of an *aurum potabile* intended to protect from poisons and to cure gout.

However, Haslmayr brought many serious troubles on himself by requesting the Archuke to ban an anti-Paracelsian book published by an emulator of the Jesuits, the official physician of Hall, Hippolyte Guarinoni. The latter immediately hit back, accusing Haslmayr of being a heretic and of preventing his own children from attending church. Haslmayr replied by accusing Guarinoni of being a "cacosopher", but his arguments were weak, seeing that he himself had ignored the obligations of the Concordat of 1605.

Denounced by his adversary, Haslmayr was imprudent enough to write a number of pamphlets explaining his position: that his absence from the sacraments was not due to any leanings toward the ideas of Luther, Calvin, or Zwingli, but to the conviction that with Paracelsus and the Rosicrucians, the time of the Holy Spirit had begun. His naïvety went so far as to bring his profession of faith in person to Vienna in July 1612, and to request an audience with Maximilian. Summoned to the Chancery, he was charged to bear to the privy councillors of the Archduke in Innsbruck a sealed letter, which in fact sealed his fate: it stated that on presentation of this document, the bearer was to be arrested and sent to the galleys in Genoa until he had repented and begged the Archduke for mercy.

On the eve of this dramatic event, Haslmayr was innocent enough to address the Archduke once again, with a letter in which he asked for a grant to go in search of the Brethren of the Rose-Cross! He thought that he could find them in the region of Montpellier, probably on the strength of the prophecy known as the "Lion of the North". On August 21, 1612, he naïvely presented this *Epistola adhortatoria humilitate demissa* (A Letter of Encouragement, Sent with Humility), together with the sealed letter, to the Chancery of the Tyrol. On interrogation, he refused to retract. Condemned to the galleys on October 15, he was sent to Genoa and chained on a trireme. His sentence would last four and a half years, because it was only in January, 1617 that Archduke Maximilian allowed him to be transferred to a hospice in Genoa.

All the same, Haslmayr seems to have had certain privileges during this period. At Genoa he was protected by the powerful Andea Grimaldi, a lover of alchemy, as well as by Antonio de' Medici, and he had kept many correspondents in Europe. Some of his friends had even suggested escaping from the galleys. He also found the time to write treatises which he dedicated to his benefactors and to Cosimo de' Medici, Grand Duke of Tuscany.

In Germany, his best defenders were Carl Widemann and Prince August von Anhalt. The former was a physician, but in practice a copyist and collector of manuscripts by Paracelsus, → Weigel, and Schwenckfeld. As for the Calvinist Prince August, he preferred a spirituality of the Weigelian type to the organized church. August had read Johann Arndt's *Vom wahren Christenthum* (On True Christianity), he venerated Paracelsus, and owned an alchemical laboratory. He had founded a press for the publication of esoteric works, and planned at one point to appoint Haslmayr as its director. Ever since 1611, August had wanted to read the manuscript of the *Fama Fraternitatis,* and it was probably he who financed the printing of Haslmayr's *Responsio,* or *Antwort An die lobwürdige Brüderschafft der Theosophen von Rosen-Creutz* (Response to the Praiseworthy Fraternity of the Theosophers of the Rosy Cross).

In March, 1612 came the first printing of this text, which would be published regularly in the editions of the first Rosicrucian writings between 1614 and 1617, with the exception of the one which contains both the Latin text and the German translation of the *Confessio Fraternitatis* (Cassel 1615). Haslmayr's encomium is marked by a large number of biblical citations; by a hope inspired by the prophet Isaiah (ch. 65) when he promises to a "small remnant" of the righteous a life of felicity on a renovated earth; and by reference to the *Theologia Germanica,* of which Luther had published two editions. But the deepest inspiration stems from Paracelsus, to whom Haslmayr often refers and whose prophecies of the Three Treasures and the Lion of the North he quotes. Haslmayr believes that the Rosicrucians are called upon to spread 'the eternal, divine and Theophrastic truth', in view of which he expects the advent of "Elias Artista" as described by Paracelsus. According to Haslmayr, the end of time is imminent: 1613 will be the year of the Judges, and 1614 that of the Judgment.

Haslmayr's vision of the Rose Cross does not, in fact, accurately reflect the spirit of this multiform and polyvalent myth. → Johann Valentin Andreae, who was its principal creator, wrote in the preface to his utopian work *Christianopolis* that the Fraternity 'offered vast and strange things for the *curiosi* to browse upon'. Haslmayr was certainly one of the first among these *curiosi*.

> *Discantus: Newe Teütsche gesang / mit vier / fünff / und sechs Stimmen*, Augsburg, 1612 ♦ *Antwort An die lobwürdige Brüderschafft der Theosophen von Rosen-Creutz N.N. . . .*, Hall, 1612 (reprinted in Carlos Gilly, *Adam Haslmayr*) ♦ *Philosophia Mystica* (collective work), Newstadt, 1618 ♦ *Nucleus sophicus* (collective work), Frankfurt am Main, 1623.

> Lit.: Anton Dörrer, "Die Tragödie des Bozner Tondichters Adam Haslmair", *Der Schlern* 20 (1946), 43-45 ♦ Roland Edighoffer, "Le Lion du septentrion", *Etudes Germaniques* 22 (1967), 161-189 ♦ idem, *Rose-Croix et société idéale selon Johann Valentin Andreae*, 2 vols., Paris, 1987 ♦ Carlos Gilly, *Adam Haslmayr: Der erste Verkünder der Manifeste der Rosenkreuzer*, Amsterdam: In de Pelikaan, 1994 ♦ Walter Senn, "Adam Haslmayr: Musiker, Philosoph und 'Ketzer'", in: *Festschrift Leonhard C. Franz*, Innsbruck, 1965, 379-400.

ROLAND EDIGHOFFER

Haugwitz, Christian (August?) (Karl?) Heinrich (Curt?), * 11.6.1752 Peucke bei Oels (?), † 9.2.1832 Venice (?)

Christian Karl Heinrich, first Baron (Freiherr) and later Count (Graf) of Haugwitz, is known as a statesman whose political career with the Prussian government in Berlin culminated in his becoming President of the Province of Silesia, Ambassador to Vienna, then, in 1791, Minister of State and member of the Cabinet. Simultaneously, he played an active and lifelong role in the world of European → Freemasonry, exemplifying the mystical and religious current that flourished in France and Germany from the 1760s onwards. Being an aristocrat and politically quite conservative, after the French Revolution he became a determined enemy of Freemasonry.

After studies at the University of Göttingen, Haugwitz emulated many wealthy young men of his time by making a long Italian journey. In Florence he frequented the Grand Duke of Tuscany, who showed a marked taste for mysterious sciences and mystical secrets. Returning to Germany, he was initiated into the Minerva Lodge of Leipzig, then affiliated to the Union Lodge of Frankfurt. Subsequently he joined lodges that were "rectified" according to the Dresden Reform, i.e., the Stricte Observance Templière. Soon he was made Chevalier Profès in the Ordre Intérieur, and took as his masonic name (*nomen ordinis*) Eques a Monte Sancto (Knight of the Holy Mountain). From then onward he displayed a somewhat muddled eclecticism, adding an affinity to the system of Zinzendorf (1700-1760) and taking part in the activities of the Provincial Lodge which represented the Swedish Rite in Silesia.

From 1777, Haugwitz was much taken with the mystical doctrines of the Swiss Christian Kauffmann (1753-1795), described in → Lavater's *Physiognomische Fragmente* as 'the apostle blest by the Divinity', and associated his master's theosophic teachings with those of the Moravian Brethren. As an ardent Pietist [→ Pietism], Haugwitz rapidly became the head of a group first called Les Confidents de Saint-Jean (The Confidents of Saint John), then Les Frères de la Croix (The Brothers of the Cross). Haugwitz and his brethren wished to 'penetrate the mysteries of the natural world and the divine world which Jehovah long ago, in his infinite goodness, revealed to Adam'. They also believed that through interior prayer, 'by uniting oneself to the Lord by virtue of the cross and the grace of Jesus Christ, initiates might receive strength, power, and domination over all earthly things, as well as a portion of the Divine Wisdom' (cited in Le Forestier, 584).

It was in this spirit that Haugwitz undertook to reinterpret, and if possible reform Freemasonry. In 1778 he came to know Duke Ferdinand of Brunswick (1721-1792), and became very close to Landgrave Charles of Hesse-Cassel (1744-1836). Thanks to these two eminent leaders of the Stricte Observance, he was able to enter into relations with → Jean Baptiste Willermoz (1730-1824), who had consigned to the two secret classes of Profès and Grand Profès, codified at the Convent of Lyon (1778), the secret and supreme teachings of what would become the Régime Ecossais Rectifié. There was an uneasy confrontation between the Silesian Pietism of Haugwitz and the esoteric Christianity of the → Chevaliers Bienfaisants de la Cité Sainte, and even more so with the → Élus Coëns, which Willermoz had inherited after the death of his master → Martinès de Pasqually (1708/9-1774).

In 1781, Charles of Hesse-Cassel informed Willermoz that Haugwitz had communicated to him 'the first degrees of true masonry', i.e., those of the Frères de la Croix – whereas Willermoz himself seemed to be hesitating to reveal to Haugwitz all the mysteries of the Grande Profession. In April of the same year, Ferdinand of Brunswick envisaged a kind of fusion between Haugwitz's system and that of Willermoz; and in August, the latter at last consented to receive Haugwitz into the Grande Profession.

The divergences soon became evident between Willermoz's system, founded on impressive ceremonies and complex teachings, and the humble and submissive prayer that Haugwitz advocated for attaining illumination. Haugwitz came to the point of demanding justifications and explanations concerning the sources of the doctrinal texts used by Willermoz – of which the latter was himself the author. Willermoz preferred to evade this problem, which highlighted two very different conceptions of mystical masonry. From the beginning of 1782, he preferred to advise Ferdinand, the Magnus Superior Ordinis, to leave it to the general Convent assembled at Wilhelmsbad. Ferdinand decided for Willermoz, provoking Haugwitz to an angry and definitive retreat. However, we still find Haugwitz involved with the preparation of the Convent of the Philalèthes, held in Paris in 1785, which ended in confusion.

When in September 1810 the aged Willermoz, after twenty years of silence, re-established contact with Charles of Hesse-Cassel in a long and moving letter, he asked the prince 'what has become of this dear and worthy Baron d'Haugwitz (a Monte sancto) of Kapitz, and the wise school that he founded on solid instructions which had been communicated to you, and of which several essential portions are in my hands? Do he and his school still exist? Has he attained the final goal of his labors? Has he been authorized to communicate them *in plenis* [fully] to prepared and selected men?' As for Haugwitz, having quit the Régime Ecossais Rectifié out of pique, he seems to have lost none of his rancor when in 1822, at the Congress of Verona, he stated against all the evidence 'that a plot against the social order and the sovereigns [was] hatched at Wilhelmsbad'. Fortunately Willermoz, who died two years later, never knew anything of this.

An meine Brüder [authorship uncertain], Breslau: Löwe, 1774 ♦ *An unsere Brüder*, Breslau: Löwe, 1779 ♦ "Fromme Erklärung von einem deutschen Meister. Erster Grad", in: *Der Signatstern, oder die entfüllten sämmtlichen sieben Grade der mystischen Freimaurerei...*, Berlin: Schöne, 1803, part 2, 152-202 (last ed.: Freiburg im Breisgau: Ambra/Aurum, 1979, 2, 181-238) ♦ "Denkschrift des Grafen von Haugwitz über die Freimaurerei, in französischer Sprache auf dem Congress zu Verona (1822) eingereicht, dann von ihm selbst ins Deutsche übersetzt", in: von Dorow (ed.), *Denkschriften und Briefe zur Charakteristik der Welt und Literatur*, Berlin: Duncker, 4 (1840), 211-221.

Lit.: René Le Forestier, *La Franc-maçonnerie templière et occultiste aux 18è et 19è siècles*, Paris: La Table d'Emeraude, 1987 (last ed. 2003), 582-592, 596-608 ♦ C.C.F.W. von Nettelbladt, *Geschichte Freimaurerischer Systeme in England, Frankreich und Deutschland*, Berlin: E.S. Mittler & Sohn, 1879 (reprinted Walluf bei Wiesbaden: M. Sändig, 1972), 422-434, etc. ♦ Charles Porset, *Les Philalèthes et les Convents de Paris: Une politique de la folie* (Nouvelle Bibliothèque Initiatique 18), Paris: H. Champion, 1996, 119-122, 564, etc.

ROGER DACHEZ

Heindel, Max (ps. of Carl Louis Fredrik Grasshof), * 23.7.1865 Aarhus (Denmark), † 6.1.1919 Oceanside (California)

According to the biography written by his second wife Frau Augusta Foss, née Voß (1865-1949) which has been taken over by almost all later authors, Heindel was a member of the aristocracy. However, according to the church register and the baptismal certificate issued at Aarhus on 15.10.1865, Heindel was the son of an immigrant baker from Germany, Frantz Ludvig Grasshof and his Danish wife, Anne Sörine Withen, the daughter of a clog-maker. When he was three years of age, Heindel lost his father through an accidental explosion. At the age of sixteen (perhaps nineteen) Heindel went to Glasgow and worked as a tobacconist, as can be inferred from the local marriage register. In 1885 he married Catherine Wallace, the daughter of a maid servant, who bore him two girls. Heindel subsequently worked as a ship's mechanic with the merchant navy at Liverpool, but he returned to Denmark, where he ran an import business with his brother. In 1896 he emigrated to the USA, first settling in Somerville near Boston and then in Los Angeles (1903). At this time he was plagued by health problems (lameness and a heart disease) and financial difficulties. In 1903 he attended a lecture of the → Theosophical Society, where he met the woman who was to become his second wife, Frau Augusta Foss, an astrologer and active Theosophist. Heindel joined the Theosophical Society and within a year he had already become vice-president in California; however he left the Society after three or four years. In 1905 his first wife had died, after what seems (according to his second wife) to have been an unhappy marriage. At a Theosophical Society lecture in Minnesota in 1907 Heindel met Frau Dr. Alma von Brandis, who gave him money for a trip to Germany, in order to make the acquaintance of → Rudolf Steiner (1861-1925). During a stay of several months in Berlin, Heindel studied Steiner's Rosicrucian teachings. Augusta Foss writes in her biography that Heindel was disappointed by Steiner's teachings and received the Rosicrucian doctrine from 'elder brothers' near Berlin, where he spent a month in their temple. However a statement of Rudolf Steiner himself and Heindel's fundamental text *The Rosicrucian Cosmo-Conception*, written after this stay and the first edition of which (1909) contains a dedication to Steiner 'for much valuable information', suggest that Heindel largely took over the ideas of Steiner (secret at the time) and published them with the financial and stylistic assistance of friends. In 1908, in Columbus, USA, Heindel founded his first Rosicrucian group [→ Rosicrucianism]. Further groups soon followed, in Seattle, North Yakina, Washington and Portland. Probably with the help of rich followers, Heindel was finally able to buy property on "Mount Ecclesia" in Oceanside, 120 km south of Los Angeles, where the headquarters of his Rosicrucian Fellowship was established. Its official dedication as such did not occur until 25 December 1920. In 1910 Heindel married Augusta Foss, and in the same year he just barely survived an acute heart problem. During the following year he built up his Rosicrucian Fellowship and wrote books on its fundamental doctrines, until his death in 1919. His wife then assumed leadership of the community until her own death in 1949. The Lectorium Rosicrucianum of Haarlem, Holland (established in 1924), is probably a schismatic group of the Rosicrucian Fellowship.

Heindel's doctrine is essentially a form of Christian esotericism, the foundations of which may be traced to the influence of Steiner. At the time of Heindel's visit, Steiner was still the head of the German section of the Theosophical Society, but was already turning against the latter's increasing emphasis on influences from the far east and looking for an alternative in Rosicrucianism. Esoteric Christianity is proclaimed by Heindel the coming world-religion. The community is characterized by a certain ecclesiastical tendency including the celebration of mass, usually without priests, in its own places of worship, decorated with a rose-decked cross. There are also specific ceremonies for weddings and funerals. Cremation is forbidden. A twelve-sided white temple stands in Mount Ecclesia itself, and there are guest-houses and a sanatorium. The community demands from its members to abstain from alcohol, tobacco and the eating of meat, because man must be purified of his bestial sympathies before his divine powers can be consecrated and employed. Higher initiates also abstain from sexual love. Prior to being received into the Rosicrucian Fellowship as a regular member one must serve as a "probationer" and practice entirely independently, while observing a rule of silence. Members living at a distance are instructed by correspondence courses. There is a special emphasis on spiritual healing, which is taught in addition to → astrology. Healing the sick, and selfless service of one's neighbour, are counted among the highest commandments of the community. Apart from the number seven (the outer symbol of the community is a cross with seven roses and a pentagram in the background, 7 + 5 = 12), the number twelve possessed a very special significance for Heindel. According to his teachings, twelve great spiritual hierarchies assist mankind in its evolution. The Rosicrucian order is said to consist of twelve brothers who congregate around a thirteenth (as the twelve apostles did around Jesus Christ), who forms the connecting link to a higher Central Council. Only seven brothers may fulfil their good deeds in the world, while the remaining five are active on an inner plane. The number twelve also refers to the zodiac, in connection with the extraordinary importance of astrology within the community. Through its continuous publication of the ephemerides since World War I, the Rosicrucian Fellowship has probably contributed significantly to the widespread practice of astrology in the USA.

Throughout, Heindel's doctrine bears the stamp of Theosophy and → Anthroposophy, including these movement's belief in → reincarnation and the law of karma. Christ (the highest initiate of the solar period) incarnated at the baptism of Jesus of Nazareth, who still had to atone for bad karma by means of his crucifixion. According to Heindel, the universe consists of seven worlds (the world of God, of primal spirits, of the spirits of life, of the Divine Spirit, of thoughts, of desires, and at the lowest level, of bodies). In addition there are four kingdoms: those of minerals, plants, animals and men. Like the cosmos as a whole, men must develop through seven periods, each one ruled by one of the seven planets. The evolution of mankind is thus achieved through a succession of higher races, reminiscent of Theosophy and Anthroposophy. In the current time-period, the germ of the last race will develop from the melting-pot of nations in the USA, which as yet has no racial spirit of its own. The representative of this new race will be marked by a special kind of perfection. Heindel's conception of God is hierarchical as well, being composed of a supreme essence followed by seven great logoi. The cosmic sphere is the lowest and consists of 823.000 hierarchies. Christian Rosenkreuz is the symbolic name of an advanced spiritual teacher, who came to Europe in the 13th century. He remained in constant incarnation (although in different bodies) and influenced people like → Francis Bacon, → Jacob Boehme, → Johann Wolfgang von Goethe and Richard Wagner.

In 1995 the Rosicrucian Fellowship reported a number of 8.000 members worldwide. Most members are found in the United States, Germany, Switzerland, Austria, the United Kingdom, and Brazil.

The Rosicrucian Cosmo-Conception, Oceanside: Rosicrucian Fellowship, 1909 ♦ *The Rosicrucian Mysteries*, Oceanside: Rosicrucian Fellowship, 1911 ♦ *The Rosicrucian Philosophy: Questions and Answers*, Oceanside: Rosicrucian Fellowship, 1922 ♦ *Letters to Students (Dec. 1910 to Jan. 1919, inclusive)*, Oceanside: Rosicrucian Fellowship, 1925 ♦ *Simplified Scientific Astrology*, Oceanside: Rosicrucian Fellowship, 1928.

Lit.: Monthly magazine *Rays from the Rosy Cross* ♦ Augusta Foss, *The Birth of the Rosicrucian Fellowship*, Rosicrucian Fellowship: Oceanside n.d. ♦ Augusta Foss, *Max Heindel, "A Short Biography"*, in: Max Heindel, *Blavatsky and the Secret Doctrine*, Los Angeles: Phoenix Press, 1933, 19-31 ♦ Augusta Foss Heindel, *Memoirs about Max Heindel and the Rosicrucian Fellowship*, Oceanside: Rosicrucian Fellowship, 1997 ♦ Christopher McIntosh, *The Rosicrucians*, York Beach: Samuel Weiser, 1997, 124-125, 132 ♦ J. Gordon Melton, *Biographical Dictionary of American Cult and Sect Leaders* (Garland Reference Library of Social Science, vol. 212), New York/London: Garland, 1986, 108-109 ♦ J. Gordon Melton, *Encyclopedia of American Religions*, Detroit: Gale, 1996 (Fifth Edition), 720 ♦ Massimo Introvigne, *Il Cappello del Mago*, Milano: SugarCo., 1990, 204-205 ♦ Harald Lamprecht, *Neue Rosenkreuzer: Ein Handbuch*, Göttingen: Vandenhoeck & Ruprecht, 2004, 205-248 ♦ Horst E. Miers, *Lexikon des Geheimwissens*, München: Goldmann, 1993, 283-284 ♦ *Mitteilungen der anthroposophischen Gesellschaft* 1 (March 1913), 23-24 ♦ Pierre Montloin & Jean-Pierre Bayard, *Les Rose-Croix*, Paris: Culture, Art, Loisir, 1971, 243-247 ♦ Horst Reller (ed.), *Handbuch Religiöse Gemeinschaften*, Gütersloh: Gütersloher Verlagshaus Gerd Mohn, 1979², 539-553 *passim* ♦ Eric Sablé, *Dictionnaire des Rose-Croix*, Paris: Dervy, 1996, 107-109, 202-203 ♦ A.A.W. Santing, "Notities bij de geschiedenis der R+Cr bewegingen in de 20ᵉ eeuw", *Das Rosenkreuz* 1 (1923), 13-16 ♦ Robert Vanloo, *Les Rose-Croix du Nouveau Monde*, Paris: Claire Vigne, 1996, 83-95 ♦ Fr. Wittemans, *Histoire des Rose-Croix*, Paris: Adyar, 1925, 166-168.

HANS THOMAS HAKL

Helmont, Franciscus Mercurius van, * 20.10.1614 Vilvorde, † 12.1698 Ter Borg

Son of → Joan Baptista van Helmont. Adviser to Prince Karl Ludwig, Elector of the Palatine (1617-1680), and Prince Christian August of Sulzbach (1622-1708). Granted patent of nobility and title of Baron by Emperor Leopold I for conciliation efforts among German princes. Imprisoned by the Roman Inquisition on the charge of "Judaizing" (1661-1663), but freed on the grounds of insufficient evidence. Famous as an alchemist, Kabbalist, Quaker convert, author, and physician. Skilled weaver, wood-worker, and tailor. Reputed to be a Rosicrucian [→ Rosicrucianism] and to posses the philosopher's stone (he denied both). Collaborated with → Christian Knorr von Rosenroth in the publication of the *Kabbala denudata* (1677, 1684). Close friend of Gottfried Wilhelm Leibniz, John Locke, → Henry More, Anne, Viscountess Conway, and Sophie, Duchess of Hanover. Authored and co-authored books on chemistry, medicine, kabbalah [→ Jewish Influences], philosophy, and theology.

Little is know about van Helmont's early life except that he was educated entirely at home by his father, the renowned chemist J.B. van Helmont, whose eclectic philosophy combined Paracelsian iatrochemistry, stoic and neoplatonic vitalism, and mystical elements. With the death of his two older brothers, van Helmont became even closer to his father, acting as his laboratory assistant. He did not attend university, probably because of his father's dissatisfaction with his own university education. Consequently the most formative influence on his early thought was that of his father. Like him, he was a vitalist and rejected material or mechanical explanations of physical events. He also rejected the galenic theory of humors and accepted his father's view that diseases are specific entities that attack specific organs and require specific chemically prepared remedies. Both the elder and younger van Helmont emphasized the psychological roots of illness, a theme emphasized in a work published toward the end of van Helmont's life, *The Spirit of Diseases* (1694). As a result of his laboratory work with his father he became a skilled chemist and gained a reputation for discovering and compounding miraculous medicines, which explains why he was sought after as a physician throughout his life.

Van Helmont was not entirely happy with his education. In the preface to the posthumous edition of his father's works, which he edited and published in 1648, he describes himself as 'not content', desiring 'thorowly to know the whole sacred Art, or Tree of Life, and to enjoy it' (*Oriatrike*, 3). To this end he taught himself Latin and German by reading the New Testament many times in both languages and traveled throughout Europe seek-ing enlightenment from a variety of unorthodox sources, which included mystics, followers of → Jakob Boehme, Kabbalists, Collegiants, and Quakers. Between 1644 when he left home after his father's death and 1648 he became acquainted with members of the Palatine family, becoming especially close in later years to the two eldest sons, Karl Ludwig (1617-1680) and Rupert (1619-1682), and to the two most distinguished and learned of the Palatine Princesses, Elizabeth (1618-1680), to whom Descartes dedicated his *Principia Philosophiae*, and Sophie (1630-1714), later the Duchess of Hanover and patron of Leibniz. In 1650 he was invited to Sulzbach by Duke Christian August (1622-1708), who asked for van Helmont's help in resolving the conflict between the Lutherans and Catholics in his territories. Van Helmont received a patent of nobility from Emperor Leopold in 1658 in recognition of the diplomatic and practical services he performed for these members of the German aristocracy.

The second major influence shaping van Helmont's mature thought were the teachings of the Jewish Kabbalah. How he became acquainted with the Kabbalah is unknown, although it is probable that he came into contact with Jewish and Christian Kabbalists in Amsterdam. By the time he published his first book in 1667 his kabbalistic philosophy was formulated in a way that would never change throughout his long life. He was convinced that the Kabbalah represented the *prisca theologia* granted by God to Adam and that it consequently offered profound insights into the natural and supernatural worlds. Through the Kabbalah mankind would come to share a single religion and obtain the philosophical basis for a complete understanding of the natural world.

Van Helmont's role as advisor to Prince Christian August of Sulzbach led to his arrest by the Roman Inquisition on the charge of "judaizing" in 1661, which suggests that his kabbalistic phi-losophy was already in place six years before the publication of his first book. Christian August's ardently Catholic cousin Philip Wilhelm, Duke of Neuburg, was convinced that van Helmont was undermining Christian August's Catholic faith by encouraging him to study Hebrew and the Kabbalah and by advocating the settlement of Protestants and Jews in the Sulzbach territories. He persuaded the Inquisition to imprison van Helmont on the grounds that van Helmont's judaizing had led him to reject the Sacraments, to interpret Christ's death and resurrection allegorically, and to claim that anyone could be saved in his own faith. Van Helmont was released after a year and half probably due to the intervention of Christian August.

While imprisoned van Helmont began work on his first book, his *Kurtzer Entwurff des eigentlichen Naturalphabets der heiligen Sprache* (Short sketch of the truly natural alphabet of the holy Hebrew language). In this work, van Helmont argued that Hebrew was the *Ursprache*, the divine language of creation in which words exactly expressed the essential natures of things. While time and ignorance had led to the corruption of Hebrew, van Helmont contended that he had rediscovered its original written form, which corresponded to the tongue movements made while pronouncing individual letters. Van Helmont was convinced this discovery would lead to the correct understanding of the biblical text and consequently provide the basis for an ecumenical religion rooted in the Jewish Kabbalah and capable of uniting Christians, Jews, and pagans. Furthermore, because it was the *Ursprache* Hebrew provided access to both the divine and natural worlds. Studying it would therefore lead to a better understanding of the natural world and to the advancement of learning in all fields, including natural science.

Van Helmont collaborated with Christian Knorr von Rosenroth in the publication of the *Kabbala denudata* (1677, 1684), a collection and translation of the largest number of kabbalistic texts (particularly Lurianic kabbalistic ones) available to the Latin-reading public until the 19th century. The first part was published in Sulzbach at the Hebrew press jointly financed by van Helmont, Knorr, and Christian August. On the basis of two kabbalistic concepts, *tikkun* (restoration) and *gilgul* (→ reincarnation), van Helmont believed he had discovered the foundation for an impregnable theodicy. By attributing the inequalities and misfortunes of life to the faults of previous existences, the Kabbalah reaffirmed God's goodness and justice. Human beings were responsible for their own sin and suffering; but God was lenient and granted every soul the necessary time and assistance to achieve redemption. On the basis of the doctrine of *tikkun* van Helmont categorically rejected the existence of an eternal hell. Punishment was "medicinal"; it was only inflicted on a creature for its own good and improvement. This was an unorthodox and unusual view at the time since the fear of hell was considered the only way to keep most people virtuous.

Like → Francis Bacon, van Helmont envisioned Solomon's Temple as a haven for the arts and sciences revealed in the Hebrew Scriptures. He was convinced he had found a key to unlock the door to this Temple in the kabbalah, an idea illustrated in the frontispiece of the *Kabbala denudata*, which shows the kabbalah as a young maiden running towards the entrance of a building marked *Palatium Arcanorum* (Palace of Secrets). This explains why the *Kabbala denudata* was dedicated not simply to the "lover of Hebrew", but also to the "lover of philosophy" and to "the lover of chemistry" (which, in this case, meant natural philosophy in general). For van Helmont science and religion, or chemistry and the Kabbalah, were two routes to recovering God's original revelation.

Van Helmont's life-long interest in reform and social progress is illustrated by two other early works he published in collaboration with Knorr, translations of Octavius Pisani's *Lycurgus Italicus* (1666) and Boethius's *Consolation of Philosophy* (1667). Pisani, a lawyer and scholar, argued that crime was the product of social inequality and to prevent it required improved education, health, and welfare, a view endorsed by van Helmont. Like Boethius, van Helmont was both a philosopher and a statesman deeply concerned with the issue of justice. He shared Boethius's neoplatonic and stoic orientation and concurred with his view that true happiness can be found only in God, who is the highest good. A constant theme in van Helmont's writing is that real evil does not exist because God is all powerful and all good. Everything that happens to an individual happens for his ultimate benefit; virtue is never unrewarded, just as vice is always punished.

When it comes to defining the key elements in van Helmont's alchemical and kabbalistic philosophy, his merging of the material and spiritual realms is crucial. His vitalistic, organic philosophy allowed no place for dead matter in the form of lifeless atoms propelled by external forces. Matter and spirit were dual aspects of a single entity, substance, and every created substance was engaged in constant transmutation and evolution towards a higher state. Van Helmont took this idea from the Lurianic kabbalah, a form of kabbalah that arose in the 16th century among the disciples of Isaac Luria (1534-1572). Luria believed that everything was alive and full of souls, and that as a result of repeated reincarnations every soul would return to its divine source. This was the message of the treatise "Concerning the Revolutions of Souls", written by his disciple Hayyim Vital, and included in a Latin translation in the *Kabbala denudata* (II, pt. 3, 244ff.). Van Helmont echoed this idea in his short treatise published in the *Kabbala denudata* (I, pt. 2, 308ff.) and later in English as *A Cabbalistical Dialogue* (1682).

Van Helmont's epistemology, which stresses the role of the → imagination, intuition, and experiment in the acquisition of knowledge, reflects his alchemical, kabbalistic, and Paracelsian background. For van Helmont, as for many of his contemporaries, imagination and illumination are powerful forces that reveal hidden levels of reality and provide access to divine knowledge. The elder van Helmont stressed this point in all his works. Like his father, van Helmont also advocated experiment. An emphasis on experimental learning and the rejection of written authority is a constant refrain among natural philosophers during the scientific revolution, although scholars have recognized it as an exaggeration of actual scientific practice.

Van Helmont was an extensive traveler and a tireless proselytizer for his kabbalistic philosophy. In 1670 he arrived in England, where he met the Cambridge Platonist Henry More, who implored him to treat his good friend Anne, Viscountess Conway for her increasingly severe and incapacitating headaches. Although van Helmont could not help Conway as a physician, he could as a kabbalist by enabling her to envision her own suffering as part of the divine redemptive process of *tikkun*. Van Helmont stayed with Conway until her death nine years later. During this period they collaborated on several kabbalistic works (*Two Hundred Queries Concerning the Doctrine of the Revolution of Humans Souls*, 1684 and *A Cabbalistical Dialogue . . .*, 1682). Conway also wrote a small treatise on her own, *The Principles of the Most Ancient and Modern Philosophy*, in which she employed kabbalistic theories to refute the theories of Hobbes, Descartes, and Spinoza.

Van Helmont's association with Conway is not only memorable for their mutual interest in the kabbalah but also for the profound effect their kabbalistic philosophy had on contemporary Quakers. The Quakers were ardent proselytizers.

But when they made their first missionary visit to Conway in 1675, they found more than they bargained for in van Helmont. A sect of "Helmontian" Quakers arose from this encounter. These Quakers found in the kabbalistic idea of reincarnation a solution to the problem posed by the fact that Christianity could not offer salvation to those who lived before Christ or in parts of the world that never heard of him. The doctrines of *tikkun* and *gilgul* solved this problem by providing individuals with the opportunity to be reincarnated until they achieved salvation. This solution was not to the liking of the Quakers as a whole. George Fox, the founder of the Quakers, was particularly critical. After Conway's death he called for a meeting to investigate van Helmont's ideas. They were eventually rejected, and van Helmont left the Society, although he spoke with admiration of the Quakers to his dying day.

Van Helmont was a close friend of both Leibniz and Locke and may have acted as an intermediary between the two. He visited Hanover, where he discussed the kabbalah, → alchemy, medicine, and natural philosophy with Leibniz and Sophie, Duchess of Hanover. The Leibniz archives in Niedersächsische Bibliothek in Hanover provide evidence that the friendship between van Helmont and Leibniz was close. They shared an interest in chemical experiments and arts and manufacturing processes, discussing at length such practical inventions as more efficient wheelbarrows, improved flax combs, shoes with springs for fast getaways, a carriage that would run on a flat surface, better cooking pots, a method of spinning with two hands, and a way to print with feet. Leibniz was interested in van Helmont's kabbalistic philosophy, encouraging him to publish his ideas and even helping him to the point of ghostwriting his last book, *Quaedam praemeditatae & consideratae cogitationes super quatuor priora capita libri primi Moysis* (1697), a kabbalistic interpretation of Genesis. Leibniz's epitaph for van Helmont is a striking tribute to their friendship: 'Here lies the other van Helmont, in no way inferior to his father./ He joined together the arts and sciences and/ Revived the sacred doctrines of Pythagoras and the Kabbalah./ Like Elaus he was able to make everything he needed with his own hands./ Had he been born in earlier centuries among the Greeks,/ He would now be numbered among the stars' (Niedersächsische Landesbibliothek, Hanover, MS Helmont, LBr 389, fol. 125).

It has been alleged that Leibniz derived the term "monad" from various philosophers, ranging from → Giordano Bruno to Henry More. However,

a strong case can be made for van Helmont as his most direct and important source. Van Helmont accepted the kabbalistic idea that every created entity progresses to an increasingly higher state as a result of repeated reincarnations. "Dull", "sluggish", or "sleepy" monads, to use van Helmont's adjectives, would eventually become "active", and "awake" monads. Leibniz adopted this scheme in his own work, expressing it more philosophically. Michael Gottlieb Hansch described Leibniz drinking a cup of café latte and speculating that the monads existing in it might one day become human souls (*Godofredi Guilielmi Leibnitii Principia Philosophiae More Geometrico Demonstrata*, Frankfurt & Leipzig, 1728, 135). Leibniz's correspondence with the Lutheran millenarian and advocate of universal salvation Johann Wilhelm Petersen reveals that by the end of his life he accepted the radical, kabbalistic idea of *tikkun* and believed that every created thing would eventually reach a state of perfection.

Van Helmont figures prominently in Locke's correspondence. He met Locke during the 1680s when Locke was in exile in Holland and visited him later in England. Locke read van Helmont's books, commented on them, and even helped to get them published. Excerpts from the *Kabbala denudata* exist among Locke's manuscripts. Locke is clearly critical of the kabbalah. He entitles one of his notes "Dubia circa philosophiam Orientalem" and brings up a point he makes so forcefully throughout his *Essay Concerning Human Understanding* about the danger of using 'words without a clear and distinct notion'. But he was clearly interested in the very same questions broached in that work: what is the nature of God, the Messiah, spirits, and matter; why was the world created, and why did souls fall; do souls preexist and are they restored to their original purity? Furthermore, Locke accepted the possibility of reincarnation (*Essay*, II.xxvii.27).

Van Helmont's medical and scientific theories also interested Locke. Locke was a member of the Royal Society and a practicing alchemist. In the journals Locke kept while in Holland, he included van Helmont's recipes for making boot polish, preparing a primitive blackboard from kid's skin, and preserving beer. Like Leibniz, Locke shared van Helmont's interest in practical inventions, which explains the presence among Locke's papers of a drawing dated 1688 illustrating a device made by van Helmont for polishing stones. Locke also recorded van Helmont's cures for gangrene, plague, and scabies and his observations on the way crystals and pebbles 'grow and nourish'.

Van Helmont's friendship with Leibniz and

Locke indicates the difficulty of making clear-cut distinctions between rationalists, empiricists, esotericists, and scientists during the 17th century. Leibniz and Locke associated with van Helmont because of their mutual interest in alchemy and natural philosophy, their sincere interest in religious issues, and their desire to restore religious peace by promoting tolerance and ecumenism. For all their philosophical differences, Leibniz and Locke shared certain unorthodox religious views that were similar in many regards to those advocated by van Helmont All three men rejected the doctrine of original sin, predestination, and the eternity of hell. Even more significantly, they rejected Christ's essential role in salvation. Orthodox Christians routinely dubbed any diminution in Christ's role as "Jewish". We have seen that van Helmont was imprisoned by the Inquisition as a "judaizer". The same label was attached to Locke, for he was accused of being, and probably was, a Socinian or Arian. The Arian Jesus is far more like the Kabbalah's *Adam Kadmon* than the Christian Christ. He is the first among creatures and the mediator between God and man, but not in any way equal or consubstantial with the Father

Van Helmont offers an example on the contribution made by heterodox and esoteric thinkers to ideas that became the hallmark of Enlightenment thought, namely a belief in scientific progress and a commitment to religious toleration. Van Helmont's published work advocates an ideal of toleration that makes inspiring reading to this day, especially towards the Jews. His philosemitism was unique because he accepted Jews as Jews and not simply as potential Christians converts. Through the process of *tikkun* anyone could and would be saved, whatever his faith. Furthermore, human beings were responsible for restoring the world to its prelapsarian perfection. Experimental science was therefore a laudable occupation and the key to progress.

Alphabeti vere naturalis Hebraici brevissima Delineatio. . . . Sulzbaci, 1657 [1667] [German edition (1667); Dutch (1697)] ♦ *Des fürtrefflichen hochweisen Herrn Sever. Boetti weil. Bürgermeisters zu Rom, christlich-vernunftgemesser Trost und Unterricht, in Widerwertigkeit und Bestürzung über dem vermeyten Wohl – oder Uebelstand der Bösen and Frommen . . .* Sultzbach, 1667 [2nd German edition (1697)] ♦ *A*

Cabbalistical Dialogue in answer to the Opinion of a learned Doctor in Philosophy and Theology, that the World was made of Nothing . . . To which is subjoined a Rabbinical and Paraphrastical Exposition of Genesis I. . . . London, 1682 [First part appeared *Kabbala denudata*, I, 308ff.] ♦ *The Divine Being and its Attributes . . .* London, 1693 [Dutch edition (1694)] ♦ *Lycurgus Italicus. . . .* Sulzbaci, 1666 [German edition (1666)] ♦ *Paradoxal Discourses of F.M. van Helmont . . .* London, 1685 [German edition (1691)] ♦ *Quaedam praemeditatae & consideratae cogitationes super quatuour priora capita libri primi Moysis . . .* Amsterlodami, 1697 [German edition 1698; Dutch (1698); English (1701)] ♦ *The Spirit of Diseases, – or Diseases from the Spirit . . .* London, 1694 [Latin and Dutch edition (1692)] ♦ *Two Hundred Queries moderately propounded concerning the Doctrine of the Revolution of Humane Souls . . .* London, 1684 [German edition (1686)].

Lit.: A. Becco, "Leibniz et F.M. van Helmont: Bagatelle pour des monads", *Studia Leibnitiana Sonderheft* 7 (1978), 119-142 ♦ S. Brown, "F.M. van Helmont: His Philosophical Connections and the Reception of his Later Cabbalistical Philosophy", in: M.A. Stewart (ed.), *Oxford Studies in the History of Philosophy*, Oxford: Clarendon Press, 1997 ♦ idem, "Some Occult Influences on Leibniz's Philosophy", in: A.P. Coudert, R.H. Popkin & G.M. Weiner (eds.), *Leibniz, Mysticism and Religion*, Dordrecht: Kluwer, 1998, 1-21 ♦ A.P. Coudert, *The Impact of the Kabbalah in the 17th Century: The Life and Thought of Francis Mercury van Helmont*, Leiden: Brill, 1999 ♦ idem, *Leibniz and the Kabbalah*, Dordrecht: Kluwer, 1994 ♦ C. Merchant, *The Death of Nature: Women, Ecology, and the Scientific Revolution*, San Francisco: Harper & Row, 1979 ♦ M.H. Nicolson, *The Conway Letters* (rev. ed., ed. Sarah Hutton), Oxford: Clarendon Press, 1992 ♦ B. Orio de Miguel, "Leibniz und 'die physischen Monaden' van Fr. M. van Helmont", in: J. Marchlewitz & A. Heinekamp (eds.), *Leibniz' Auseinandersetzung mit Vorgängern und Zeitgenossen*, Stuttgart: F. Steiner, 1990 ♦ idem, *Leibniz y la Tradicion Theosofico-Kabbalistica: Francisco Mercurio van Helmont* (Doctoral Dissertation, University of Madrid, 1993) ♦ idem, *Leibniz y el Pensamiento Hermético: A proposito de los "Cognitata in Genesim" de F.M. van Helmont*, 2 vols., Universidad Politécnica de Valencia, 2002 ♦ G.B. Sherrer, *Francis Mercury van Helmont* (Doctoral Dissertation, Western Reserve University, 1937) ♦ V. Wappmann, *Durchbruch zur Toleranz: Die Religionspolitik des Pfalzgrafen August von Sulzbach, 1622-1708*, Neustadt: Verlag Degener, 1995 ♦ C. Weir, Jr, *Francis Mercury van Helmont* (Doctoral Dissertation, Harvard University, 1941).

ALLISON P. COUDERT

Helmont, Joan Baptista van,
* 12.1.1579 Brussels, † 30.12.1644 Brussels

1. LIFE 2. PSYCHOLOGY AND
EPISTEMOLOGY 3. NATURE
4. MEDICINE 5. PHARMACOLOGY
AND ALCHEMY

1. LIFE

Joan Baptista van Helmont was the youngest child of Marie de Stassart and Christian van Helmont, who died one year after his son's birth. Van Helmont's education was considered of prime importance. At an early age he began his studies in philosophy and classics at the University of Leuven, but both the academic climate and the subjects taught left him deeply disappointed. Frustrated, he turned to astronomy, algebra and Euclidean geometry, hoping to find more truth than in scholastic logic. His enthusiasm waned when he discovered that the Ptolemaic worldview was less accurate than the Copernican; certainty concerning the world system seemed unobtainable. Van Helmont claimed that he finished his philosophical studies at the age of fourteen, but refused the title *magister artium* to express his contempt for the curriculum. He was offered a well-endowed canonry on the condition that he would read theology, but he declined on the grounds that a servant of the church should be poor. By then, the Jesuit order in Leuven had developed an alternative philosophy curriculum and van Helmont decided to take several courses. He studied with the renowned Martinus del Rio (1551-1608), who lectured on → magic and authored the *Disquisitionem magicarum*, a monumental work on → witchcraft and the occult [→ occult / occultism] in all its forms. But van Helmont could not identify with the Jesuits either and turned to Stoicism, aspiring to the strict lifestyle of silence and obedience characteristic of the Pythagoreans. Then, he had a spiritual experience; through a vision, he realized that he had taken the wrong path and, while apparently modest, had become arrogant. This episode marks the beginning of his life as a Christian mystic. He began to study the works of Thomas à Kempis and Johannes Tauler. Influenced by these writers, he yearned for God to impart the ultimate truth to him. In the same period, he developed an interest in medicinal herbals. After reading Matthioli and Dioscorides, he concluded that since late antiquity no progress had been made in the field – there had only been speculation upon the "grades" and "qualities" of herbs. He then briefly studied law, but lost interest when he discovered that human law is always subject to change. Driven by altruism and the desire to know nature, he again turned to medicine. He read Fuchs, Fernel, and other contemporary authors. He studied the complete works of Hippocrates and → Avicenna, and read Galenus twice. By his own account, he read and took notes on six hundred books on the subject. At the age of seventeen he was offered a lectureship in surgery, but after a couple of months he realized he was ill-equipped for the task – he had neither the necessary education nor the research facilities. In 1599 he earned his doctorate in medicine, but he was so disillusioned by the academic world that he abandoned it permanently. Upon graduation he started to practice a form of chemical medicine. From 1599 to 1605 he toured Europe. He visited Switzerland and Italy from 1600 to 1602, and France and England from 1602 to 1605. The ignorance and pedantry he encountered on his travels left him disappointed yet again. He rejected offers of private employment by people of influence, such as Ernest of Bavaria and Emperor → Rudolf II. In 1609 he married Margarite van Ranst, a relative of the Merode family, and retreated to their country estate in Vilvorde on the outskirts of Brussels. From 1609 to 1616 he dedicated himself to meditation and experimental research. Van Helmont was fascinated with *pyrotechnia*, which he hoped could penetrate the nature of things, and called himself *Philosophus per ignem*. To him, *pyrotechnia* specified chemical research conducted within a broad and modernized alchemistic conceptual framework. In studying the works of → Paracelsus he believed he was on the right path – but he also believed he needed divine enlightenment to discern the falsehoods in → Paracelsus' writings. Seven years later van Helmont had another mystical experience, after which he considered himself initiated as an *adeptus naturae*. By that time he had fathered four daughters, and a son who would follow in his footsteps. Believing that he had succeeded in getting gold from mercury, he baptized his son Mercurius in 1618 [→ Franciscus Mercurius van Helmont].

In 1617 van Helmont wrote a treatise that would have a dramatic impact on his life. *De magnetica vulnerum curatione* concentrated on the controversy between Rudolphus Goclenius, a protestant professor of philosophy and medicine from Germany, and Jean Roberti, a Belgian Jesuit. In his works, Goclenius had championed a magnetic weapon-salve said to cure wounds from a distance when applied to the weapon that had inflicted the wound. The cure was based on the pseudo-Paracelsic writing *Archidoxis magica*. In 1617 Roberti attacked Goclenius and accused him of idolatry, blasphemy and black magic. A number of learned men, including van Helmont, joined the discussion. Although in his treatise van Helmont declared himself both a Paracelsist and a fervent Catholic, he nevertheless found fault with both parties. He attacked Goclenius on the basis of factual evidence, Roberti for his theological approach of the matter: theologians do not know about medicine and therefore should not concern themselves with medical questions. The argument was punctuated with venomous remarks against the Jesuits. In 1621 the treatise, which until then had been distributed in small circles only, appeared in print in Paris, most likely without van Helmont's permission. Roberti reacted and the incident resulted in van Helmont's formal indictment by the Inquisition. He confessed in 1627 and 1630, and recanted, but was nevertheless arrested in 1634. His works were confiscated, and he was temporarily incarcerated and placed under house arrest until 1636. Despite his public renunciation, his letters to Marin Mersenne (written between 1630 and 1631) show clearly that his convictions had not changed significantly since 1621. This would suggest that van Helmont's most innovative works were written during the last ten years of his life. Until that he remained rather faithful to the ideas of Paracelsus. It is only in his final years, when he wrote his Opus Magnum that, for various reasons, he clearly distanced himself from his predecessor in the pyrotechnical art.

Van Helmont did not receive an ecclesiastical imprimatur for his work on fevers until 1642, the final year of legal procedures against him. He died in 1644. Two years after his death, his widow obtained official vindication of her late husband. Van Helmont's principal work, the *Ortus medicinae*, and the collected *Opuscula medica inaudita* were published posthumously in Amsterdam in 1648 by his son, Franciscus Mercurius van Helmont, and received wide international acclaim.

2. PSYCHOLOGY AND EPISTEMOLOGY

Van Helmont's psychology is integral to his theory of knowledge and was firmly rooted in the neoplatonic tradition [→ Neoplatonism]. Man alone was created in the image of God. Contrary to angels, man has a physical body, but while angels are an image of the image of God, man

is *imago Dei*. Distinguishable but not separable from the immortal *mens* is the knowing part of the highest soul, the *intellectus*. From Paracelsus, van Helmont adopted the concept of the *archeus* as the vital principle. Man is governed by the *archeus influens* situated in the *duumvirate* (stomach and spleen). The *archeus influens* moves freely through the body; the *archei institi* are secondary and govern the individual organs. Before the Fall, the human body's *archei* were governed directly by the *mens-intellectus*. After having eaten from the tree of knowledge – interpreted as a cryptic reference to sexual intercourse – the immortal mind was left in a state of shock. Then, disgusted by the animal urge to procreate, it obeyed both nature and the divine will, and withdrew into one locus, the *archeus* of the stomach, located in the cardiac orifice (*in ore stomachi*). There it curled up in the center of the sensitive soul, which took control of the body. Van Helmont believes that since the Fall man is condemned from the moment of conception: in accordance with the rest of nature, he must spend his time on earth in a "middle-life" (*media vita*), a state of reduced vitality in which the *archei* ultimately get exhausted, especially by digestion and disease. When they have finished their inner cycles they end in "ultimate life" (*ultima vita*). The lower mortal soul, which man shares with animals, is no more than a vague reflection of the *mens-intellectus* from which it receives its light. The cognitive faculty of this *anima sensitiva* is the *ratio*. The sensitive soul is governed by the *duumvirate* (the stomach and the spleen), while the light of the immortal soul radiates via the heart up to the head. Conform neoplatonic thought, the highest form and its light become less distinctive as they distance themselves from the center. (i.e.: the rational brain is less enlightened).

The sensitive soul's faculty of thought is guided by the *imaginatio* [→ Imagination]. Given that this process leads to uncertain knowledge, van Helmont opposes scholastic exaltation of the *ratio*: scholasticism should never have adopted the heathen, Aristotelian definition of man as an *animal rationale*. Traditional Aristotelian logic, expanded upon by scholasticism, provokes van Helmont to a radical, hermetically inspired skepticism. True knowledge is only obtainable through divine enlightenment of the *mens-intellectus*, and this enlightenment is only bestowed on elect Christians. God touches all forms, but only in a state of ecstasy can man reflect the light he receives back to God. Then, for a moment, Adamic knowledge is restored, and man compre-

hends the essence of things in God and in himself. To this end, man must practice a "spiritual
Paternoster". Van Helmont explains this practice
by referring to the Pseudo-Dionysian [→ Pseudo-
Dionysius Areopagita] method of *unknowing* as
elaborated in *De mystica theologia*, a method by
which thought is gradually separated from the
world of the senses. In this context, van Helmont
refutes the warnings issued by both rabbis and
schools of → mysticism that ecstasy should be
avoided because of its harmful consequences. It
should be noted that van Helmont's concept of
divine enlightenment does not imply that it will
lead to full knowledge; it only steers the pyrotech-
nician's investigations of nature in the right direction. Van Helmont constantly emphasizes the
value of experimental research, but also considers
dreams and visions of prime importance in the
quest for knowledge. The method he employed
himself was to visualize the object of research
and enter into imaginative conversation with it.
Subsequently, he would fall asleep and experience
a meaningful dream containing the answer to his
questions. Late in life, for example, he envisioned
the immortal soul of man as having no gender
traits and as therefore androgynous.

Van Helmont states that research into nature
should always serve true medicine. God has given
doctors the role of mediator; they are meant to
cure people of diseases He justly inflicts upon
them as punishment for their sins. Although
Hippocrates was a heathen, van Helmont considers him an enlightened spirit whom he values over
→ Hermes Trismegistus, and often refers to his
ideas. Van Helmont refutes mainstream medicine
as taught by the scholastics, who based their
theories on Galenus and his Arab commentators,
particularly Avicenna. Like all Paracelsists, he
exaggerates scholastic conservatism for the sake
of controversy. On the other hand, he strives to
correct several misguided opinions of Paracelsus.
Van Helmont himself was to be the first to explain
the foundations of true medicine, which he claims
were revealed to him by God.

3. NATURE

Van Helmont rejects the doctrine of the four elements and their qualities, which had dominated
western thought since Empedocles. He bases his
own doctrine of the elements on the biblical Creation story. Water, heaven and earth pre-existed the
first day of creation. God separated the higher
from the lower waters by creating the firmament
and ordained that the firmament would separate
the waters for as long as the world existed. There
are two original elements: water and air. The bible
does not mention their creation; both are referred
to cryptically by the word "heaven". Water and
air are original elements because it is impossible to
convert one into the other, as van Helmont claims
to have proven through experiment. Earth to him
was no element. God created earth simultaneously with water and air, but because earth can be
made fluid *per ignem*, it is essentially water. Given
that the elements were created before God created
the sun on the fourth day, they are cold by nature.
The creation of fire is not mentioned in Genesis
and fire is therefore not an element. In fact, van
Helmont considers this a heathen opinion. Fire
can only turn the elements inside out, so to speak,
so that objects are reduced to their smallest components. According to van Helmont, Aristotle was
mistaken in postulating the non-existence of
vacua in nature. Van Helmont lacked the proper
experimental framework to prove the existence of
a vacuum, but given the fact that air can be com-
pressed, he argues that there are many empty
spaces in air which together constitute a whole,
the *Magnale magnum*. This *Magnale magnum*
functions as the soul of the world. It is not a
lumen but a *forma adsistens*: not a constituent of
air, but co-existing with it.

The primary reason for van Helmont's lasting
reputation as a scientist is his introduction of
the term *gas*, which he most likely derived from
the word *chaos*. He identified fifteen different
gases, including (the one, now known as) carbon
dioxide, and was the first to articulate the difference between air, water-vapour and *gas*. Gases are
object-specific: they embody objects in their finest
material form. *Gas* equals the *archeus*, which is
partly spiritual and partly material although its
kernel is predominantly spiritual.

In conjunction with the concept *gas* van Helmont invented the concept of *blas*, a term derived
from the Dutch word *blazen* (to blow). Together
they form a duality in van Helmont's philosophy
of nature. *Blas* is astral in origin and functions as
the general principle of movement. Van Helmont
associates it with the Hippocratic *enhormon*. *Blas*
exists in various forms: *blas motivum*, for example, spurs things into motion and *blas alterativum*
catalyzes change. Van Helmont proposes his concept of *blas* as an alternative to Aristotle's doctrine
of movement, considered by him a heathen doctrine since the concept of God as the "unmoved
mover" curtails God's omnipotence. Instead, he
postulates that God implanted all forms of *blas*
in the original *semina*, out of which all things
come into being. This theory would explain the

possiblity of "action at distance" in the Paracelsic worldview, which is dominated by the concept of *sympathia*. All of nature is animated by a certain *sensus*. Together, the planets emanate a *blas astrorum*, which, through the *Magnale*, can spread through the whole world. Its influence, however, is limited.

Van Helmont explicitly rejects traditional → astrology: the planets do not control the movements of animals and plants, and certainly not those of men; and neither do they determine the future. They can, however, predict it, because God has preordained their movements for all eternity in conjunction with events on earth. Therefore the *blas humanum* follows the *blas stellarum*, but without the causality assumed in traditional astrology. Thus, van Helmont also rejects the analogy between macrocosm and microcosm in the Paracelsian sense. In this context, van Helmont repeatedly cites Psalm 19:2: 'The heavens declare the glory of God; and the firmament sheweth his handywork'. Knowledge of the future is primarily a question of revelation, he claims, citing Acts 2:17: '. . . and your sons and your daughters shall prophesy, and your young men shall see visions, and your old men shall dream dreams'. Here, the spleen, connected with both the *mens-intellectus* and the *anima sensitiva-ratio*, plays a crucial role. Despite his profound criticism of Aristotle, however, van Helmont maintains the entelechic principle and thinks in a wholly vitalistic way.

4. MEDICINE

Van Helmont rejects the view held by Galenic medicine that the digestive system is threefold. He describes it as sixfold, with a specific fermentation process occurring at every stage. According to van Helmont, fermentation takes place everywhere in nature and in man, and is in close connection with the *archaeus*. He derives his definition from the fermentation concept used in alchemy, though the two are not identical. After the first stage of digestion, when the acids of the spleen are blown into the stomach, the food is converted into a white gastric juice called *chylum*. In subsequent digestions (in the small intestine, the mesentery veins, and the left ventricle) the venous blood becomes more subtle. In line with the Galenic view that the heart partition is porous, van Helmont states that the venous blood is pumped from the right to the left ventricle. There, a local *fermentum* transforms it to arterial blood and it becomes spiritualized. The final digestion of the blood takes place in the individual organs. If diges-

tion processes are disrupted, various diseases can occur. It is, for instance, harmful for the gastric juice to pass the first digestion. Strangely, nothing in van Helmont's works indicates that he was familiar with Harvey's views on blood circulation. Van Helmont rejects Galenist physiology and pathology, which are based on the doctrine of the humours (blood, slime, yellow bile and black bile), and hold that an excess of any of these humours causes disease. Van Helmont considers this doctrine a malicious fiction. Van Helmont's own pathology, which he himself calls "Platonic", maintains that disease is caused by local chemical changes. Every disorder has its own form. Disease is a light that develops into an *archeus* and penetrates the body. This hostile *archeus* then attacks a vital *archeus* and tries to overpower it. Part of the vital *archeus* is subsumed, while another part continues to resist. Eventually this leads to inflammation of a larger or smaller part of the physical body. Using various anatomical, physiological and logical arguments, van Helmont tries to refute the ancient doctrine of the catarrh once and for all. The catarrh doctrine stipulated that disease occurs when food fumes rise from the stomach to the head, condense and subsequently pour throughout the body. Notwithstanding the connection with his own concept of local *semina*, van Helmont criticizes the Paracelsic idea of *Tartarus* as a catalyst of disease for being too materialistic. And he believes Paracelsus is again mistaken when explaining disease as linked to the *Tria prima* (sal, sulphur and mercury), as he does in his widely read *Archidoxis*. In accordance with his rejection of the paracelsian system of → correspondences between the macro- and microcosm, he also rejects the doctrine of signatures.

5. PHARMACOLOGY AND ALCHEMY

Adam and Solomon are believed to have been acquainted with the medicinal properties of herbs, stones and words. From the work of Flavius Josephus, van Helmont concludes that Solomon wrote many books on the power of herbs and plants; they were lost during the reign of his son Rehabiam, when a prophet ordered these books to be burned out of fear that the Jews would forget their God. Van Helmont believes that through initiation and experimentation the medicinal qualities of these herbs can be rediscovered, although the secret knowledge will only be truly revealed with the coming of Elias Artista (the mysterious "Messiah of Nature" first mentioned by Paracelsus). Van Helmont has not written an extensive Pharmacopoeia, as one might have expected. He does, however, emphasize that the medicinal qualities of naturally poisonous herbs and metals can be restored through *pyrotechnia*. Purified metals have especially powerful medicinal properties because, contrary to herbs, they are immutable. He also believes in the use of medicinal minerals, and in the therapeutic effect of words and texts. In this respect, he does not refer to kabbalah, but to certain incantations used by the catholic church.

Van Helmont's discourse on "Butler's Stone" reflects his interest in → alchemy. The treatise concerns an Irish nobleman, Butler, who for some time was detained as a prisoner at van Helmonts estate at Vilvorde. Butler had in his possession a stone with which he seemed to be able to swiftly cure all illnesses; van Helmont had read about such cures in Paracelsus but had never before witnessed one in reality. After Butler had dipped the stone in a bottle of olive oil, van Helmont found that the oil indeed cured several of his patients, although they suffered from different kinds of illness. After some time, however, the olive oil lost its healing power, and Butler refused to reveal the secret of his stone. After several years of experimentation, van Helmont was convinced he was able to reproduce the stone; he called it "Drif", and his treatise contains almost the complete formula. This universal medicine he believed reflected the unity of the immortal mens-intellectus.

In his work on the fountain of Spa, of 1624, van Helmont had described an important experiment which disproved the natural transmutation of metals: he demonstrated that iron could not be converted into copper by adding copper sulphate. Later, he claimed that although he could not produce the Philosophers' Stone himself, an initiated visitor had given him a piece of it. For him, there was no contradiction: while he remained convinced that the transmutation of metals was not possible by natural chemical reactions, he believed it could take place as a supernatural process, similar to what took place in the eucharist. In the presence of witnesses, van Helmont demonstrated this by bringing about a transmutation.

As a Paracelsist, however, he was far more interested in the elixir of life, which could be produced from the tree of life. After extensive research, van Helmont had a vision in which he experienced himself in a "timeless state". He saw the Cedars of the Lebanon, which, as he concludes in retrospect, had existed since the beginning of the world. The wood is the basic ingredient for the elixir; this "tree of life" (as he calls the Cedar) can prolong human life for up to 120 years. The key to the formula, however, was in the liquor *Alkahest*, the universal solvent, which would lead to numerous speculations well into the 18th century. Van Helmont indicated that revealing the secret would be like casting pearls before swine, and therefore withheld the formula.

Van Helmont is a transitional figure in the history of chemistry: while theories and terminologies associated with traditional alchemy are present in his work, his methodologies have more in common with those of the modern chemist. In fact, he is considered to be one of the founders of iatrochemistry, a discipline that employs chemistry for medical purposes. He is also considered the most important and original representative of the second generation of Paracelsists. While clearly taking his distance from Paracelsus in various respects, he critically developed the latter's method and concepts. Paracelsus is praised by him mostly for his pyrotechnical abilities and his arcana, but van Helmont believes to be superior to his predecessor even in these domains. It is important that van Helmont's (al)chemical, scientific experiments and his philosophical speculations be seen in the context emphasized by himself: they are parts of a new kind of medicine. Traditional school medicine is satanically inspired and based upon an uncritical copying of the heathenish Galen. Among the Christians, God has elected a small group of people to introduce a new medicine, and it has fallen to van Helmont to establish its foundations. By doing so, he opens a new era in the history of humanity.

Standard edition: *Ortus medicinae. Id est, initia physicae inaudita. Progressus medicae novus, in morborum ultionem, ad vitam longam ... Edente authoris filio, Francisco Mercurio Van Helmont, cum ejus praefatione ex Belgico translatâ*, Amsterdam, apud Ludovicum Elzevirum, 1648 ♦ *Opuscula medica inaudita*. 1: *De lithiasi*. 2: *De febribus*. 3: *De humoribus Galeni*. 4: *De peste. Editio secunda*, Amsterdam: apud Ludovicum Elzevirum, 1648; Facsimile edition: Impression Anastaltique, Culture et Civilisation, 115, Bruxelles: Avenu Gabriel Lebon, 1966.
Dageraad, oft nieuwe opkomst der geneeskonst, in verborgen grondtregulen der Nature ... Noit in 't licht gesien, en van den Autheur selve in het Nederduits beschreven, Amsterdam: Jan Jacob Schipper, 1659; Rotterdam: Johannes Naeranus, 1660 ♦ Antwerp: facsimile reprint of the Rotterdam edition by the Vlaamse Academie der Geneeskunde (Flemish Academy of Medicine), 1944; idem, Amsterdam: W.N. Schors, 1978 ♦ Letters: these are published in P. Tannery and C. de Waard (eds.), *Correspondance du P. Marin Mersenne*, vols. 1-3 (Paris, 1932-1946). Of the fourteen letters written between 1630 and

1631, three are to be found in part II and eleven in part III.

Translations of the *Ortus Medicinae*: *Aufgang der Artzney-Kunst, das ist: Noch nie erhörte Grund-Lehren von der Natur, zu einer neuen Beförderung der Artzney-Sachen, sowol die Kranckheiten zu vertreiben als ein langes Leben zu erlangen. Geschrieben von Johann Baptista von Helmont, auf Merode, Royenborch, Oorschot, Pellines etc. Erbhernn. Anitzo auf Beyrathen dessen Herrn Sohnes, Herrn H. Francisci Mercurii Freyherrn von Helmont, In die Hochteutsche Sprache übersetzet in seine rechte Ordnung gebracht, mit Beyfügung dessen, was in der Ersten auf Niederländisch gedruckten Edition, genannt Die Morgen Röhte ... auch einem vollständigen Register*, Sultzbach: Johann Andreae Endters Sel. Söhne, 1683; Reprinted and edited by W. Pagel and F. Kamp, 2 vols., Munich: Kösel, 1971. This translation by Christian Knorr von Rosenroth was made in close cooperation with Fransiscus Mercurius van Helmont. They added several previously unknown treatises to the Opera omnia and inserted supplementary passages translated from the Dageraad. This translation still stands the test of contemporary criticism.

Oriatrike, Or, Physick Refined. The Common Errors therein Refuted, And the whole Art Reformed & Rectified: Being a New Rise and Progress of Phylosophy and Medicine, for the Destruction of Diseases and Prolongation of Life ... now faithfully rendred into English, in tendency to a common good, and the increase of true Science; by J.C. Sometime of M.H. Oxon [John Chandler of Magdalen Hall, Oxford], Printed for Lodowick Loyd, 1662, London: Second edition, 1664 as *Van Helmont's Works*. This translation is useful, although sometimes incorrect.

Les Oeuvres de Jean Baptiste Van Helmont, traittant des principes de médecine et physique, pour la guérison assurée des maladies: De la traduction de M. Jean Leconte, docteur médecin, Lyons: I.A. Huguetan, 1670. An unsatisfactory selection of pieces.

Lit.: Walter Pagel, *J.B. Van Helmont: Einführung in die philosophische Medizin des Barock*, Berlin, 1930 ◆ idem, *Joan Baptista Van Helmont: Reformer of science and medicine*, Cambridge-Sydney: Cambridge University Press, 1982 ◆ idem, *The Smiling Spleen: Paracelsianism in Storm and Stress*, Basel-Sydney: S. Karger, 1984 ◆ idem, *Religion and Neoplatonism in Renaissance Medicine*, London: Variorum Reprints, 1985 ◆ idem, *From Paracelsus to Van Helmont: Studies in Renaissance Medicine and Science*, London: Variorum Reprints, 1986 ◆ Allen G. Debus, *The Chemical Philosophy: Paracelsian Science and Medicine in the Sixteenth and Seventeenth Centuries*, 2 vols., New York: Science History Publications, 1977, vol. 2, 295-379 ◆ idem, *Chemistry and the Medical Debate, van Helmont to Boerhaave*, Canton: Science History Publications, 2001 ◆ Paulo Alves Porto, *Van Helmont e o Conceito de Gas: Quimica e Medicina no secolo XVII*, Sao Paulo: Educ, 1995 ◆ Berthold Heinecke, *Wissenschaft und Mystik bei J.B. van Helmont (1579-1644)*, Bern-Wien: Peter Lang, 1996 ◆ Paul Nève de

Mévergnies, *Jean Baptist van Helmont: Philosophe par le feu*, Liège-Paris, 1935 ◆ Henri de Waele, *J.B. Van Helmont*, Office de Publicité, S.C., Anc. Etabliss. Bruxelles: J. Lebègue & C., 1947 ◆ Franz Strunz, *Johann Baptist Van Helmont (1577-1644): Ein Beitrag zur Geschichte der Naturwissenchaften*, Leipzig und Wien, 1907 ◆ Friedrich Giesecke, *Die Mystik Joh. Baptist van Helmonts (1577-1644)*, Leitmeritz: Buchdruckerei von Dr. Karl Pickert, 1908 ◆ A.J.J. Van de Velde, "Helmontania", in: *Verslagen en mededelingen der Koninklijke Vlaamse Academie voor Taal- en Letterkunde*, Ledeberg/Gent: N.V. Drukkerij Erasmus, 1929, 453-476; 715-737; 857-879; 1932, 110-122; 1936, 3-51 ◆ William R. Newman & Lawrence M. Principe, *Alchemy Tried in the Fire: Starkey, Boyle and the Fate of Helmontian Chymistry*, Chicago & London: University of Chicago Press, 2002.

ALBERT ROODNAT

Hermes Trismegistus I: Antiquity

1. THOT AND HERMES 2. HERMES TRISMEGISTUS 3. THE GENEALOGY OF HERMES 4. HERMETIC DISCIPLES AND TEACHERS

1. THOT AND HERMES

In the later Graeco-Roman world Hermes Trismegistus was seen as an Egyptian sage of remote antiquity whose knowledge of both the material and the spiritual world and their interrelationship were of great help to get some control of the vicissitudes of life and to bring the soul into harmony with its divine origin. Though his name shows that the Greeks saw some correspondences between this sage and their own god Hermes, the figure of Hermes Trismegistus was in reality firmly rooted in the religious soil of Egypt. Already in the 5th century B.C., Herodotus identified the Greek Hermes with the Egyptian god Thot, and most probably he was not the first to do so: without any comment he called the cult-centre of Thot "Hermopolis" (later Hermopolis Magna) and mentioned the existence of a temple of Hermes at Boubastis (*Histories*, II, 67 and 138, resp.). Hermes Trismegistus originated as the Greek interpretation of the god Thot (*interpretatio graeca*), just as on the Jewish side Thot was identified with → Moses (*interpretatio judaica*).

The career of the moon god Thot in the Egyptian pantheon and his complex relationship with many other gods is well known (Boylan, Kurth). His most characteristic feature, which in some way determined most of his other qualities, was that he was considered the inventor of count-

ing and writing. He was represented as an ibis
or a baboon and as an ibis-headed or baboon-
headed man. Since the moon receives its light from
the sun, he was considered the latter's nightly
representative and as such he often appears with
the sun god in the solar bark, as the "Scribe of
Re". At the same time, he was also the protector
and healer of the moon: its waning and reappearance was associated with the stolen or damaged
Eye of Horus, which on the day of the full moon
was retrieved or healed by Thot, who thus became
the restorer of cosmic order. As a god of the
moon, Thot became the chief measurer of time,
who distinguished seasons, months and years and
also determined the regnal years of the pharaohs.
Under this aspect, he became the ordering principle of civil and religious life in general, the "Lord
of laws". The institutions of temple-worship and
the plans of the temples were ascribed to him. He
was the "Lord of the divine words", i.e. of the
sacred formulae of ritual and cult, including the
invocations of the gods in magical practices, but
he was also the one who spoke for the gods. His
wisdom concerning things divine made him the
magician *par excellence*, the one "great in magic",
to whom a great number of charms and spells
were attributed. As the "One who knows", the
"All-knowing", he was considered the inventor of
script, language and literature and of all kinds of
sciences, and even, especially in the Ptolemaic
period, the creator, who had made the world by
thought and speech. Thot was also an important
god of the dead: from the earliest times to the
Greek period, he was seen as psychopompus, the
one who brought the dead to the other world,
where he also played a part in the judgment ceremony. Just as he had done in the case of Osiris,
he reconstructed the corpse of the deceased and
opened his mouth in order to give him the breath
of life. In the 4th century B.C., the main characteristics of Thot were already known to the
Greeks. Plato, who calls him Theuth, knew that he
was an Egyptian God, to whom the ibis was
sacred and who had invented numbers and counting, geometry and astronomy, draughts and
gambling, and in particular the art of writing
(the usefulness of which was questioned by king
Thamus, who is the humanized Egyptian god
Ammon; *Phaedrus*, 274c-275b).

Thot's function as psychopompus may have
been one of the reasons that prompted the Greeks
to identify him with their god Hermes. According
to the *Homeric Hymn on Hermes*, 19, he was the
son of Zeus and Maia, born on Mount Cyllene.
The name Hermes derived from the heaps of

stones (*herma, hermaion*) that served as land-
marks. From the earliest times Hermes had been
the god who guided and protected the wayfarer.
Originally a squared ithyphallic pillar with a head,
his image became gradually more anthropomorphic, which resulted in his most well-know representation, with winged sandals, a staff, and his
characteristic traveller's hat. Herms were *inter alia*
set up at crossroads, on market places, at the gate-
ways of cities and the borders of estates. As god of
the road he also became the god who guided the
dead to the underworld, which became a popular
literary motif but had firm roots in ordinary
life. Because of his inventiveness he was called
"cleverest of the gods", even "crafty", and so he
also became the god of merchants and thieves.
Having made the lyre and played it on the first day
of his life (*Homeric Hymn to Hermes*, 17, 39-61),
he became the patron of → music and the musi-
cians. He was the eloquent messenger of the gods
(cf. also Acts 14:11-12), the interpreter (*hermēneus*) of their will, which led Plato to a more
philosophical interpretation of Hermes as expressing both the positive and the negative power of
speech (*Cratylus*, 407e-408b). This view was further developed in the later philosophical, especially Stoic, tradition, in which Hermes became
identical with the Logos and so even became the
creator of the world. The anti-gnostic writer Hippolytus (ca. 225) says of the Greeks, and the gnostic → Naassenes, that they honour Hermes as the
Logos, 'because he is the interpreter (*hermēneus*)
and creator (*dēmiourgos*) of everything that has
come into being, that comes into being and that
will come into being' (*Refutatio* V, 7, 29; cf. IV,
48, 2: 'The Logos is called Hermes by the Greeks').
These Hellenistic philosophical speculations did
not yet exist when the Greeks began to identify
their Hermes with the Egyptian Thot, but they
certainly facilitated the emergence of Hermes
Trismegistus in the centuries around the beginning
of our era. In the Hellenistic period Hermes also
became a god of → magic, but it seems most likely
that this was primarily due to his merging with
Thot. The two gods came from completely different cultural and religious backgrounds, and, in
fact, their identification was only based on a
superficial resemblance. The common features
that led to their identification may have been their
role as guides to the underworld, as messengers of
the gods, and as inventors of arts and crafts.

2. HERMES TRISMEGISTUS

It would be wrong to see in Hermes Trismegistus no more than Thot in Greek disguise.

This even holds for the magical papyri, as can be seen from the prayers that are sometimes addressed to Hermes (Trismegistus), though it is in these papyri that the continuity between the Egyptian Thot and the Hellenistic Thot-Hermes is most clearly visible (Festugière, *Révélation*, I, 283-308). Nevertheless, even in the later period there remained authors who liked to describe Hermes Trismegistus with almost all the characteristic features of the Egyptian Thot, as, for instance, appears from a hermetic text quoted by Cyril of Alexandria, *Contra Julianum* I, 41. The hermetist, the same who composed 15 hermetic book in Athens, declared that Hermes, *inter alia*, had measured the land of Egypt and divided it into nomes and smaller units, had cut the irrigation canals, and that he was the maker of contracts and the inventor of all kinds of sciences and arts.

The name Trismegistus also reflects Egyptian usage. It is first attested in the late 2nd century A.D., in Athenagoras, *Legatio*, 28, 6, who says that Hermes, 'who is called Trismegistus', just like Alexander the Great linked his family with the gods (Fowden, 216-217). The closing line of the Roman satirist Martial's epigram on the gladiator Hermes (*Epigrammata*, V, 24, 15), 'Hermes, the only one who is all things, the thrice-one' (*Hermes omnia solus ter unus*), cannot be taken as proof of the existence of the term Trismegistus in the last decades of the 1st century A.D. (Versnel). In Egyptian the superlative was expressed by repeating the positive two or three times, and this was taken over in literal Greek translations: "great (*megas*) and great (*megas*) (and great [*megas*]" means "very great" or "greatest". Probably because of a Greek misunderstanding of the Egyptian writing of the superlative, already the Raffia decree of 217 B.C. calls Hermes 'the greatest (*megistos*) and the greatest (*megistos*)'. In an oracle text from Saqqara which dates from 168-164 B.C., mention is made three times of "the greatest (*megistos*) and greatest (*megistos*) and great (*megas*) god Hermes". It seems quite certain that we have here a Greek combination of two well-known divine epithets: "the greatest and the greatest" and "the great god" (Versnel, Quaegebeur). However, there existed demotic forms as "great, great, great" with an adverb indicating the superlative = "three times very great" (first attested in an inscription of 105 B.C.; in the Roman period even the title "five times very great" was used for Thot), which, in fact, simply means "the greatest" (Quaegebeur). The Greek form "greatest and greatest and greatest", which would be the exact equivalent of Trismegistus, has

not been found so far and may have never existed, but there is little doubt that the demotic expression has given rise to the Greek epithet. From its Egyptian background it should have been translated as *megistos*, "the greatest" or as *trismegas*, "the thrice-great" (which occurs in a 3rd century papyrus). However, similar abundant superlatives with the prefix *tris-* were not uncommon in later Greek: the form *trismakaristos* ("thrice-most blest" = *trismakar(ios)*, "thrice-blest"), is found in the 2nd-century writer Lucian, i.e. contemporarily with the first attestation of the epithet Trismegistus in Athenagoras.

3. THE GENEALOGY OF HERMES

There was an important difference between the Egyptian and the Greek views of Thot/Hermes: the Egyptians always considered Thot a god, whereas the Greeks mostly saw him as a human being, a teacher of divine wisdom. The latter view is predominant in the philosophical Hermetica, though there are some treatises in which Hermes distinctly appears as a god, e.g. in the *Korē Kosmou*, or suddenly becomes identical with the divine Mind, as in the *Discourse on the Ogdoad and the Ennead* (for both, see → Hermetic Literature I). Already Plato left it undecided whether Thot (Theuth) was a god or a divine man (*Philebus*, 18b), and in the discussion between Thot and king Thamus, reported in the *Phaedrus* and mentioned above, he has the king argue as if Thot, 'the father of writing', was one of his subjects. The humanization of Thot was certainly furthered by the Hellenistic theory of Euhemerism, which implied that the gods were in fact deified kings. Athenagoras, who, as we saw above, said that Alexander the Great and Hermes Trismegistus had linked their own family with the gods, as many others had done, concluded from this that 'there is no longer any reason left to doubt that they were regarded as gods because they were kings'. This euhemerist explanation became part of the more general criticism of traditional religion by the Sceptics, as can be seen in the third book of Cicero's *De natura deorum*. There the Sceptic Cotta attacks the Stoic view of religion in a long exposition, in which he *inter alia* gives a long list of gods who have the same name but according to tradition were born from different parents (e.g three different Jupiters, III, 53). There are even five gods with the name Hermes (Mercurius), of whom the third is Hermes the son of the third Jupiter and Maia and the fifth is the Egyptian Theyt (Thot), who had fled to Egypt after the murder of Argus and had given laws and the art of writing to the Egyptians (III, 56). Lactantius adopted this identification of Trismegistus and Cicero's fifth Hermes, but he also explicitly expressed the euhemerist view that this Hermes originally had been a man, who long ago had been deified (*Divinae Institutiones*, I, 6, 1-3). It seems that the Greek hermetists tried to counter the devastating effects of this criticism by introducing the idea of a lineage of Hermeses. In the *Asclepius*, 37, Hermes Trismegistus says that his grandfather, called Hermes too, resides (i.e. has been buried) in his natal city that is named after him, where 'he gives aid and protection to mortals who come to him from everywhere'. → Augustine, in a discussion of the superiority and priority of Hebrew culture even with respect to that of the Egyptians, adopted this genealogy from the *Asclepius*, but made the first Hermes the son of Jupiter and Maia. He argued, in his *City of God*, XVIII, 39, that Hermes, 'who is called Trismegistus', taught philosophy in Egypt long before the Greek philosophers, 'and yet after Abraham, Isaac, Jacob, and Joseph, and, in fact, Moses himself'. Atlas, 'the maternal grandfather of the elder Mercury', lived in the time of Moses, which implies that his grandson, 'this Mercury Trismegistus', lived three generations after Moses. It has often been suggested that Augustine transmits here information he had found in the roman writer Varro (1st century B.C.). This might be possible, but it seems more probable that he has adapted the information he found in the *Asclepius* for apologetic reasons. Notwithstanding Augustine's authority, the idea that Hermes Trismegistus was a contemporary of Moses, or even had lived before him, prevailed in the later medieval tradition (cf. the floor mosaic in the cathedral of Siena: 'Mercurius Trismegistus contemporaneus Moysi'). That Thot was 'the first Hermes' is explicitly stated in an interesting text of uncertain date, which is preserved in the Byzantine chronograph Georgius Syncellus († ca. 810) and attributed to the Egyptian historian Manetho (ca. 280 B.C.). The text is slightly corrupt, but less than is usually assumed (Fowden, 30-31; Copenhaver, xv-xvi). According to Pseudo-Manetho, Thot, the first Hermes, had engraved his wisdom on steles in the 'sacred language' and in hieroglyphs. After the Flood, 'the second Hermes', who was the son of Agathodaimon and the father of Tat, translated these texts from the sacred language into Greek and deposited them in books in the inner sanctuaries (*adyta*) of Egyptian temples (Syncellus, *Chronographia*, I, 72, ed. Dindorf; Scott, III, 491-492, with many emendations). According to *Korē Kosmou*, 5-6, which

makes no difference between a first and a second Hermes, Hermes had already engraved everything he knew on steles before the creation of the world, and left it to Tat, his son and successor, Asclepius and others to explain his teachings. However, there are authors who tell another story about how the Egyptian texts of Hermes Trismegistus had been translated into Greek. Iamblichus, *De mysteriis*, VIII, 5 and X, 7, mentions the prophet Bitys as the one who found hieroglyphic texts of Hermes in Egyptian temples and translated them into Greek, and he also aptly explains the Greek philosophical elements in the Hermetica by saying that those who made these translations were skilled in Greek philosophy (VIII, 4).

The separation between Thot, the god of Hermopolis, and Hermes Trismegistus made it easier, on the one hand, to explain how the original hermetic writings had been translated from the Egyptian into Greek and, on the other, to consider Hermes as a divine man, a teacher of divine wisdom from remote antiquity.

4. HERMETIC DISCIPLES AND TEACHERS

A curious result of the separation of Thot and Hermes Trismegistus was the re-emergence of Thot in the figure of *Tat*, as the son, pupil and successor of Hermes, to whom many tractates are addressed. The hermetic authors were apparently completely unaware of the fact that both personalities originally had been identical. In C.H. XVII it is Tat himself who instructs an unnamed king, probably Ammon.

Asclepius was another important pupil of Hermes Trismegistus. The *Perfect Discourse/Asclepius* was devoted to him, but he also acted as a teacher himself, as appears from the title of C.H. XVI, *Definitions of Asclepius to King Ammon*. In Hellenistic Egypt, the cult of the Greek god Asclepius merged with that of the Egyptian Imhotep, especially in Memphis and Thebes. The two gods had in common that they were gods of healing and medicine and had both started their career as deified men. Nevertheless, they were rarely completely identified, because Imhotep's healing capacity was only one of his qualities. In fact, he had many features in common with Thot and was seen as the personification of wisdom. In Greek literary texts he retained an independent existence as Imouthes. This state of affairs is reflected in the *Asclepius*, 37, where the two gods are clearly distinguished: Imhotep is said to be Asclepius' grandfather, just as Thot is the grandfather of Hermes Trismegistus.

King *Ammon* is a much less important hermetic figure. He is no other than the euhemerist version of the Egyptian god Amun, who was called Zeus-Ammon by the Greeks and had a great reputation as oracle god. In Plato's *Phaedrus*, 274de, already mentioned above, it is Thot himself who discusses with King Thamus, i.e. the humanized Ammon, all kinds of sciences, in particular the art of writing. Whereas C.H. XVI makes him a disciple of Asclepius, he participates, as Hammon, with Asclepius and Tat in the discussions of the *Asclepius*, and it was for him that, according to Iamblichus, the prophet Bithys had translated the teachings of Hermes into Greek (see above). This *Bithys* remains a mysterious personality, but from Iamblichus and → Zosimus we know that he was a theurgical authority (Fowden, 150-153).

The goddess *Isis* was also seen as a teacher of hermetic doctrines. In the Hellenistic and Roman period she was identified with almost every Egyptian, Greek and Oriental goddess, 'you are the One who is everything' (*una quae es omnia*). In Greek aretalogies, hymns of praise, she was hailed as 'educated by Hermes' and, *inter alia*, as having invented, together with Hermes, the hieroglyphic and demotic scripts (Bergman). She was said to have taught the medical, mantic and alchemical arts [→ Alchemy] to her son Horus (Festugière, in NF III, CXXVI-CXXVII). In Stobaeus, *Fragm.* XXIII-XXVII, she acts as the hermetic teacher of Horus, while she is supposed to have been instructed herself by Hermes Trismegistus. This is explicitly stated in Stobaeus, *Fragm.* XXIII (*Korē Kosmou*), though this writing also has another tradition about Kamephis as intermediary between Hermes and Isis (see below).

Agathodaimon (*Agathos Daimōn*), who according to Pseudo-Manetho was the father of Hermes Trismegistus, plays an unimportant part in the philosophical Hermetica, but his role in ancient magic and alchemy is all the more important and equals that of Hermes. Having started in Greece as a rather vague domestic god of luck and prosperity, he finally became associated with a variety of Greek deities and, in Hellenistic Egypt, with the Egyptian snake-god Kneph (Knephis, Chnoubis) in particular, but also with Amon, Thot, Isis, Horus, and others (Ganschinietz, 51; Copenhaver, 164-165). In *Korē Kosmou*, 32, Isis pretends to transmit to her son Horus 'a secret doctrine that my ancestor Kamephis learned from Hermes, the recorder of everything, and I from Kamephis, who is older than all of us'. It seems that Kamephis is none other than the late Egyptian god Kematef,

who was identified with Kneph and Agathodaimon (Barta; but see Festugière, NF III, CLXII-CLXVIII). Sayings of Agathodaimon are quoted in C.H. XII, 1, 8 and 13, though in the second passage Hermes deplores that Agathodaimon has not given it out in writing. Cyril of Alexandria, *Contra Julianum*, II, 30 (NF IV, 136-140, *Fragm.* 31 and 32; Ferguson, in Scott IV, 213-214), knew a *Discourse to Asclepius*, in which Hermes quotes some teachings of Agathodaimon to Osiris about the origin of the earth and the sun. It remains unclear, however, whether this information was actually found in a philosophical or alchemical treatise under the name of Agathodaimon or is simply a case of literary fiction.

Lit.: For the text edition by Nock & Festugière and the studies of Festugière, Fowden, and Scott & Ferguson, → Hermetic Literature I: Antiquity ♦ W. Barta, "Kematef", *Lexikon der Ägyptologie*, III, Wiesbaden: Harrassowitz, 1980, 382-383 ♦ G. Baudy & A. Ley, "Hermes", in: *Der Neue Pauly*, 5 (1998), 426-432 ♦ J. Bergman, *Ich bin Isis: Studien zum memphitischen Hintergund der griechischen Isis-Aretalogien* (Acta Universitatis Upsalensis, Historia religionum, 3), Uppsala, 1968 ♦ F. Daumas, "Le fonds égyptien de l'hermétisme", in J. Ries (ed.), *Gnosticisme et monde hellénistique: Actes du Colloque de Louvain-La-Neuve (11-14 mars 1980)* (Publications de l'Institut Orientaliste Louvain, 27), Louvain-La-Neuve: Université Catholique de Louvain, Institut Orientaliste, 1982, 3-25 ♦ M.-Th. Derchain-Urtel, *Thot à travers ses épithètes dans les scènes d'offrandes des temples d'époque gréco-romaine* (Rites Égyptiennes, 3), Brussels: Fondation Égyptologique Reine Élisabeth, 1981 ♦ W. Fauth, "Agathos Daimon", in: *Der Kleine Pauly*, vol. 1, München: Artemis Verlag, 1975 (paperback: München: Deutscher Taschenbuch Verlag, 1979), 121-122 ♦ idem, "Hermes", in: *Der Kleine Pauly*, vol. 2, 1069-1076 ♦ R. Ganschinietz, "Agathodaimon", in: G. Wissowa et alii, *Realencyclopädie der Classischen Altertumswissenschaft*, Supplementband 3 (1918), 37-60 ♦ D. Kurth, "Thot", *Lexikon der Ägyptologie*, VI (1986), 498-523 ♦ L.H. Martin, "Hermes", in: K. van der Toorn, B. Becking & P.W. van der Horst (eds.), *Dictionary of Deities and Demons in the Bible*, 2nd extensively revised edition, Leiden: Brill, 1999, 405-411 ♦ J. Quaegebeur, "Thot-Hermès, le Dieu le plus grand", in: H. Altenmüller et al., *Hommages à François Daumas*, Montpellier: Institut d'Égyptologie, Université Paul Valéry, 1986, 525-544 ♦ H.S. Versnel, *Ter Unus: Isis, Dionysos, Hermes. Three Studies in Henotheism* (Studies in Greek and Roman Religion, 6), Leiden: Brill, 1990 ♦ R.L. Vos, "Thoth", in: Van der Toorn, Becking & Van der Horst, *Dictionary*, 861-864 ♦ D. Wildung, "Asklepios", *Lexikon der Ägyptologie*, I (1975), 472-473 ♦ idem, "Imhotep", *Lexikon der Ägyptologie*, III (1980), 146-148.

ROELOF VAN DEN BROEK

Hermes Trismegistus II: Middle Ages

Throughout the Middle Ages the figure of Hermes Trismegistus is portrayed in a discordant manner because of disagreements over the Hermetic "revelation" among the varying interpreters within Latin culture. These disagreements concern, first, the *Asclepius*, the only philosophical-religious Hermetic text translated into Latin; second, during the 12th-13th centuries, they concern the vast technical-operational Hermetic literature (→ astrology, medicine and natural → magic, divination [→ Divinatory Arts], necromancy); and, third, the relations between philosophical concepts and operational knowledge.

But before examining the judgments concerning Hermes, in both their contrasts and their continuities, it is necessary to recall that the mythology of the *Asclepius* makes a distinction between Hermes the god, who dwells in the temples of Hermopolis and grants aid and salvation to all mortals, and his grandson Hermes Trismegistus who in his books unveils the secrets of divine wisdom. This duplication of Hermes is accepted by the first Christian writers: Lactantius in his *Divinae institutiones* and a century later → Augustine in book VIII of *De civitate Dei*. Reference is made to the two figures of Hermes by Hermann of Carinthia in his *De essentiis*, by → Daniel of Morley in his *Liber de naturis inferiorum et superiorum* in the 12th century, and by other scholars later on.

In the Christian era the figure of Hermes Trismegistus (or Mercurius) is drawn in opposing profiles by Lactantius and Augustine. In his *Divinae institutiones* (304-313) Lactantius sees Hermes as an ancient prophet of Christian revelation, who in some mysterious way, perhaps by evoking the great spirits of the past, rose to an understanding of almost the whole truth, *veritatem paene universam*, and learned the mysteries on the Father and the Son. In the pages Lactantius devotes to him, the great Egyptian seer heralds the Holy Scriptures: the eternal and ineffable divine nature, the birth of the Son, the creation of the world, providence, the creation of man, the nature of angels and devils, religious worship, the contemplation of God, and the final descent of the Son for the salvation of the righteous. But in book VIII (415-417) of *De civitate Dei* Augustine unmasks the demonic origin of Hermetic theurgy (referring to the statues that dwell in temples among men, granting good and decreeing evil) and Hermes' words are transformed, in his tirade, into the voice of evil demons: the ancestors of Hermes Trismegistus are the founders of all idolatrous cults. The "Christian" interpretation of Lactantius would nevertheless prevail over Augustine's invectives: a sermon of Quodvultdeus, bishop of Carthage, which simplifies Lactantius' perspective and brings it still closer to Christian sensibilities, was inserted in the North African collection of Augustine's *Sermons* and under his unquestioned authority came to influence the entire Middle Ages.

In the 12th century Hermes' presence becomes deeply entrenched in intellectual discussion, and the foundations are laid for a new and more complex portrayal of him. This change occurs for various reasons: due to the fragments of "Augustine" and the wide circulation of the *Asclepius* Hermes is credited with a superior wisdom not ignorant of Christian truths; the text of a famous pseudo-epigraph like the *Liber viginti quattuor philosophorum* (attributed to Hermes in many manuscripts and by the almost unanimous opinion of philosophers and theologians) places him in the perspective of the purest Christian → Neoplatonism and attributes to him an awareness of the mystery of the Trinity; the text of another apocryphal work, the *Liber de sex rerum principiis*, contains a systematic treatment of divine and natural causality, and traces this back to Hermes' philosophy; the new translations from the Greek and Arabic present him as the first inventor of both "natural" and "necromantic" → magic. If we add to all this the fact that Albumasar's *Introductorium maius*, translated by John of Seville (1133) and later by Hermann of Carinthia (1140), credits Asclepius and Hermes with a prophecy of the birth of "Jesus", we can well understand the varieties and contradictions the portrayal of Hermes will acquire in the next centuries. But in the 12th century there still persists the single powerful image of an ancient sage who by inner revelation anticipated parts of Christian teaching: the most distinguished examples are the great *magistri* of the period, Abelard and Theodoric of Chartres, → Bernard Silvester and Alain of Lille.

A very significant testimony comes from the *Glosae super Trismegistum*, written at the turn of the 13th century, perhaps a work of Alan of Lille or a disciple of his. Hermes, one reads in the prologue, is the greatest philosopher of the pagans, and we know that he composed many volumes on the supreme artificer of all things: in a book which Augustine calls *Logos tileos* (that is, in the fragments cited by Quodvultdeus) he exceeded others and himself, since in treating of the Father and the Son he seems to elevate himself to our theology (*ad nostram videtur aspirare theologiam*). In another book entitled *Trimegistrus* (namely the *Asclepius*) not only did he speak of the Creator and the creation, but in discussing the "uncreated Spirit" he did not omit the mysteries of theology: his purpose was to confute the ancient philosophers by affirming the unity of the Creator, his power, knowledge and goodness.

In the 13th century we encounter some harshly contrasting views of Hermes. While the *Asclepius* and the *Liber viginti quattuor philosophorum* enjoyed an almost universal respect, and the texts on astrology and "natural" magic received attention and respect consistent with official doctrine, the "necromantic" books (Hermes, Belenus, Toz the Greek, Germa the Babylonian) led to renewed accusations, formerly levelled by Augustine, of idolatry and trafficking with evil demons.

This debate on Hermes begins toward 1230 and lasts until the end of the century. The first to pose the problem in radical terms clearly deriving from Augustine is the bishop of Paris → William of Auvergne, who in his *De legibus* (1228) traces to Hermes the 'philosopher and sorcerer' all the idolatrous cults that are praised in the books of necromancy. This criticism of Hermetism proceeds with emphatic harshness, uniting in a single condemnation both the philosophical and the magical-astrological strands of Hermetism: in William's tirade the *Asclepius*, which had inspired and moved the philosophers of the 12th century, is transformed into an impious vehicle of errors, illusions and deceits induced by diabolical spirits. That Mercurius is the prophet of diabolical operations, seduced by "evil spirits", finds confirmation in ancient Egyptian idolatry: Egypt is in fact the country which more than any other was familiar with the cult of idols and the presence of hellish spirits, and Hermes himself calls his land *templum mundi* since all demons were worshipped there.

During the same years → Michael Scot – translator, astrologer, sorcerer – in his *Liber introductorius* (1231-1236) does not hesitate to present Hermes and other *nigromanti* as the origin of a secret knowledge that exalts man and enables his body to sense paradise. Of course, the Church condemns writings of this kind, but magical doctrine and operations, even if forbidden, are nevertheless real and possible, since they have a scientific statute and constitute a true "ars". Scot confesses that he has himself carried out magical operations for himself and his friends, and has experimented with their truth and effectiveness by applying the teachings of the Hermetic *Liber imaginum Lunae*. And moreover, despite ecclesi-

astical prohibitions Michael reproduces two texts in their entirety: the *Liber imaginum Lunae* by Belenus, 'secundum Hermetem', which sets forth the magical-astrological effectiveness of the lunar mansions; and the *De viginti quattuor horis* by Belenus, with the names of the hours of the day and night, and the operations that can be performed with images, characters and invocations.

But a new showdown of "Hermes the magus" was near at hand. First, → Roger Bacon, while recognizing in Hermes one of the first "moral" philosophers of antiquity and the author of doctrines concordant with Christian truth, rejected the necromantic texts. He declared that these *libri pessimi*, composed by demons and corrupt men, had been falsely attributed to great personalities – Adam and → Moses, Solomon, Aristotle and Hermes – to seduce the human spirit. Hermes, the author of the *Asclepius*, is thus not responsible for the books on sorcery that bear his name. Toward 1260-1265 an extremely violent condemnation was pronounced in the *Speculum astronomiae*, attributed by many to → Albertus Magnus. As part of its project of salvaging true astrology, which is defended as being in accordance with Aristotelian-Ptolemaic cosmology and Christian ethics, the text denounces the idolatrous nature of necromancy: that is to say, that part of the "science of images" which, while being associated with astrology, fashions talismans and evokes demons by means of religious rituals. The science of images based upon Hermes, Belenus, Toz the Greek and Germath the Babylonian (that is the whole Hermetic necromantic corpus), which calls for suffumigations and invocations, is *abominabilis* because idolatrous, and induces man to pay to earthly creatures the homage he owes God. Before listing them, the author recalls having read on previous occasions many necromantic books; while reading them he had experienced horror, and his mind had fled from them with dread. Thus, once again, after the accusations of Augustine and of William of Auvergne, Hermes is considered the first and the most impious of idolaters.

At this point the portrayal of Hermes, depicted as it is with such incongruous features, seems to have divided into two directions: that of the prophet of Christian truths, and that of the diabolical sorcerer. How could the author who had risen to the peaks of trinitarian contemplation have plunged into the abysses of idolatrous perdition? The *Asclepius* and the *Liber viginti quattuor philosophorum* on the one hand, and the body of necromantic writings on the other, create a split which seems irreparable. Which one is the true Hermes? How can the admiration of celebrated theologians (Alain of Lille and William of Auxerre, Alexander of Hales and Bonaventure) for the *Liber viginti quattuor philosophorum* and the unanimous respect for the *Asclepius* be reconciled with the invectives of William of Auvergne and of the *Speculum astronomiae*? Is it possible to find an interpretation that can transcend such radical oppositions?

A response to this challenge, although not without inconsistencies, is provided in the long and balanced reflection of Albertus Magnus, the medieval author who was most familiar with the full extent of the Hermetic writings. Hermes is the *primus philosophus*, who lived in Egypt in very ancient times: chief among the Greek, Egyptian, Chaldaean and Indian sages, inspirer of Pythagoras and Empedocles, Socrates and Plato, he is the prophet and forerunner of all philosophers. The most admirable aspect of Albertus' analysis is his critical attitude. He is the only one who, faced with the universal admiration for the theological maxims of the *Liber viginti quattuor philosophorum*, shows some reservation, for philological and philosophical reasons: he declares that he has never read this book, but that if in the maxim of the "generating monad" Hermes spoke of God in triadic terms, he could not have been announcing the divine Trinity and certainly meant something else. Even with respect to the *Asclepius* Albertus takes a very guarded position. Hermes has expressed great truths: the omnipotence and causality of God, His unity and ineffability, the ideal forms and the flux of forms from the first cause to being created by causation, and man in the image of God and the link between God and the world. There are open expressions of agreement: Hermes statements on fate are concordant 'with us in the same truth' and it is not difficult to trace the sayings of Trismegistus to the doctrine of Aristotle. But in his reading of the *Liber de sex rerum principiis* and of the *Asclepius* Albertus does not hesitate to identify conceptual errors: in the former the thesis of a hypostatic universal nature *non placet Aristoteli*, and in the latter the affirmation that the first principle penetrates all things and is the being in itself of all things is a *pessimus error*. In Albertus' pages, therefore, Hermes emerges as endowed with the powers of a great philosopher, but as operating within the limits of human reason. There still remained the problem of Hermes' magical writings. In his *De mineralibus*, written at a time when Albertus was not yet very familiar with talismanic literature, he

deals with necromantic images and indicates, *propter bonitatem doctrinae*, the first inventors: Toz the Greek, Germa the Babylonian and Hermes the Egyptian. At first sight this text seems to be a re-evaluation of the Hermetic science of images, contrasting with the judgment of the *Speculum astronomiae*. Actually Albertus is dealing with "astronomic" images, that is to say, with those images, produced by nature or fashioned by man, which channel the influx of the stars and acquire a marvellous power. When, later on, in his *Summa theologiae*, Albertus becomes aware of his error, he does not hesitate to condemn necromantic images, recalls that someone has associated them with idolatry, and proclaims the illusory nature of necromancy, a craft carried on by demons and wicked persons and in antiquity made popular by 'Achot Graeco et Grema Babylonico et Hermete Egyptio'. Still, even in this later judgment Hermes is not portrayed with the features of idolatry; in fact, shortly afterwards he is reaffirmed as the exponent of a pure monotheism. The result is a Hermes who did not write the *Liber viginti quattuor philosophorum*, who in the *Asclepius* proclaimed many truths and upheld some errors, who was deceived by necromantic images, but who never repudiated a philosophical and religious monotheism. A more critical and mature interpretation of Hermes Trismegistus was not possible in the Middle Ages.

The perspective opened by Albertus Magnus would inspire later investigations, which made explicit what Albertus merely implied. In the 14th century Thomas Bradwardine opens his *De causa Dei* (ca. 1335-1344) by calling attention to Hermes, who in the *Asclepius* proclaims the perfection, sanctity and eternity of God. Praised and venerated by the Greeks, master of Plato and Aristotle, Hermes, by his wisdom which was not ignorant of the Holy Spirit, is invoked along with the Prophets and Christians. Thomas Bradwardine could nevertheless not ignore the polemic about Hermetic theurgy. Like Albertus Magnus, he observes that in many pages Hermes has defined the only God in all His power, wisdom and goodness, and he adds that hence there is no point in affirming in the *Asclepius* the existence of 'other gods or another god' and in consecrating idols to evil spirits. This is reason for Thomas to rebuke Hermes for the fault of imprudence and inconsistency, but not – as opposed to Augustine, William of Auvergne and the *Speculum astronomiae* – for the sin of idolatry.

Shortly afterwards Berthold of Moosburg concludes his imposing commentary on Proclus'

Elements of Theology (ca. 1340-1360). In Berthold, too, the figure of Hermes is delineated in all its grandeur, as representing a substantial concordance between the Platonic tradition and Christian theology. The many references to the *Logos teleios*, the *Asclepius* and the *Liber viginti quattuor philosophorum*, from the Prologue throughout the commentary, confer on Hermes an unquestioned authority. However, Berthold, too, must confront the problem of the polytheistic theurgy of the *Asclepius*. His answer is founded – as previously, although with different nuances, in Albert and in Thomas Bradwardine – on the authenticity of Hermes' monotheism. Such a wise and prudent man, who stated profound truths on God, the first causes, the world and man, was deluded and is not to be believed when he glorifies idols consecrated with chants and liturgies. Hermes' polytheism is "superstitious" because it fashions idols considered to be gods through the infusion of a divine force. And yet, when Berthold describes "non-superstitious" polytheism, as found in Plato and the Platonists, he still makes reference to Hermes for the concept of "gods by participation", that conforms with the truth.

With → Nicholas of Cusa the long voyage of Hermes through the Latin Middle Ages draws to a close. An interest in the Hermetic writings runs through all his works, from *Sermo I* (1430) to *De ludo globi* (1463): the knowledge of the divine Word, the doctrine of divine names, and the concept of matter, world and man are taken from the *Asclepius*. Illustrative of his interest are the numerous glosses as well as textual corrections in Nicholas' own hand, found in the margins of the most ancient manuscript of the *Asclepius* (Brussels, Bibliothèque Royale, 10054-10056). On the matter of Hermetic polytheism he offers prudent and moderate considerations. If in *De pace fidei* (1453) he cannot avoid, for ecclesiastical reasons, condemning the consecrated idols which threaten man's salvation, philosophical reasons lead him in *De docta ignorania* (1440) to absolve Hermes of any accusation of idolatry: the ancient philosophers conceived the traditional plurality of the gods as a personification of divine attributes, "explications" of the One, and so Hermes explicates in the figures of Cupid and Venus the creative force of divine causality.

Following the contrasts between Augustine and Lactantius, which express the two different responses of Christian culture to the figure of Hermes, we see how his presence became ever more complex and indecipherable over the centuries. The appearance of celebrated apocryphal works, the translations from Greek and Arabic, and the harsh conflicts over sorcery, tended to rend the image of the Egyptian sage apart, making him into an ambiguous figure between good and evil, at once divine philosopher and idolatrous sorcerer. If William of Auvergne saw Hermes as combining the philosopher and the sorcerer, and if the *Speculum astronomiae* attacks the Hermetic science of images, Albertus Magnus arrives at an honest and critical judgment which privileges the speculative wealth of the *Asclepius* and rejects, even while condemning necromantic practice, the accusation of idolatry. This path was also trodden, with different premises and conclusions, by Thomas Bradwardine and Berthold of Moosburg. At the end of the 14th century, Hermes is once again the great philosopher of antiquity, father and forerunner of all philosophers: he committed errors, of course, but these seem more due to imprudence or inconsistency than to wickedness of spirit. Along this path, taken also by Nicholas of Cusa, the history of Hermes Trismegistus in the Middle Ages and up to the threshold of the modern era comes to an end.

Lit.: Roelof van den Broek, "Hermes and Christ: Pagan Witnesses to the Truth of Christianity", in: R. van den Broek & C. van Heertum (eds.), *From Poimandres to Jacob Böhme: Gnosis, Hermetism and the Christian Tradition* (Pimander, 4), Amsterdam: In de Pelikaan, 2000, 369-384 ◆ Charles Burnett, "The Establishment of Medieval Hermeticism", in: P. Linehan & J. Nelson (eds.), *The Medieval World*, London, New York: Routledge, 2001, 111-130 ◆ Peter Dronke, *Hermes and the Sibyls: Continuations and Creations* (Inaugural Lecture Delivered 9 march 1990), Cambridge: Cambridge University Press, 1990 ◆ Antoine Faivre, *The Eternal Hermes: from Greek God to Alchemical Magus*, Grand Rapids (Mich.): Phanes Press, 1995 ◆ Carlos Gilly, "Die Überlieferung des Asclepius im Mittelalter", in: van den Broek & van Heertum, *From Poimandres to Jacob Böhme*, 335-367 ◆ Paolo Lucentini, "L'Asclepius ermetico nel secolo XII", in: J. Westra (ed.), *From Athens to Chartres: Neoplatonism and Medieval Thought. Studies in Honour of Edouard Jaeuneau*, Leiden, New York, Köln: E.J. Brill, 1992, 397-421 ◆ idem, "L'ermetismo magico nel secolo XIII", in: M. Folkerts & R. Lorch (eds.), *Sic itur ad astra: Studien zur Geschichte der Mathematik und Naturwissenschaften. Festschrift für den Arabisten Paul Kunitzsch zum 70. Geburtstag*, Wiesbaden: Harrassowitz, 2000, 409-450 ◆ P. Lucentini, V. Perrone Compagni & I. Parri (eds.), *Hermetism from Late Antiquity to Humanism: La tradizione ermetica dal mondo tardo-antico all' Umanesimo. Atti del Convegno internazionale di studi, Napoli, 20-24 novembre 2001* (Instrumenta Patristica et Mediaevalia, 40), Turnhout: Brepols, 2003 (especially: Zénon Kaluza, "Comme une branche d'amandier en fleurs: Dieu dans Le Liber viginti quattuor philosophorum", 99-126; Pasquale Arfé, "Ermete Trismegisto e Nicola Cusano", 223-243; Vittoria Perrone Compagni, "I testi magici di Ermete", 505-533; Sylvain Matton, "Hermès Trismégiste dans la littérature alchimique médiévale", 621-649 ♦ Claudio Moreschini, *Storia dell'ermetismo cristiano*, Brescia: Morcelliana, 2000 ♦ David Pingree, "Learned Magic in the Time of Frederick II", *Micrologus* 2 (1994), 39-56 ♦ David Porreca, *The Influence of Hermetic Texts on Western European Philosophers and Theologians (1160-1300)* Ph. Diss. Warburg Institute, University of London, 2001 ♦ Antonella Sannino, "La tradizione ermetica a Oxford nei secoli XIII e XIV: Ruggero Bacone e Tommaso Bradwardine", *Studi filosofici* 18 (1995), 23-56 ♦ Paolo Siniscalco, "Ermete Trismegisto, profeta pagano della rivelazione cristiana: La fortuna di un passo ermetico (Asclepius 8) nell'interpretazione di scrittori cristiani", *Atti della Accademia delle Scienze di Torino. II. Classe di Scienze Morali, Storiche e Filologiche* 101 (1966-1967), 83-117 ♦ Loris Sturlese, "Saints et magiciens: Albert le Grand en face d'Hermès Trismégiste", *Archives de Philosophie* 43:4 (1980), 615-634.

PAOLO LUCENTINI

Hermes Trismegistus III: Modernity

The fictional personage of Hermes Trismegistus did not disappear after the end of the Middle Ages, but remained very much alive throughout the following centuries. As early as the end of the 15th century he began to enjoy a great vogue. Indeed, within the general context of a renewed interest for ancient mythology in the Renaissance, he profited from the craze for Hermes Mercurius (Mercury). Both figures were often blended together, with the result that "Hermes" entered the cultural imagination under these two forms – Hermes Mercurius and Hermes Trismegistus – to the point of serving as a sort of catch-all name.

But apart from his proximity with Hermes Mercurius, the new interest in Hermes Trismegistus had much to do, of course, with → Ficino's translation of the *Corpus Hermeticum* published in 1471 and his commentaries on it [→ Hermetic Literature IV]. Ficino gave a genealogy of Hermes Trismegistus slightly different from those proposed by authors of late Antiquity such as Lactantius and → Augustine, and by medieval authors. But like them, he held that he had lived after the time of → Moses, and considered him a major link in a chain of great philosophers. Ficino and → Giovanni Pico della Mirandola considered "Hermes" as one of the "first theologians" (for Ficino, only Zoroaster was earlier); and whereas Ficino believed Hermes to have lived after Moses, → Lodovico Lazzarelli

even concluded (from Diodorus Siculus, *Bibliotheca Historica* I, 13ff.) that Hermes lived far before Moses. Regardless of such differences, Renaissance adherents of the *prisca theologia* concurred in giving Hermes an important place in their genealogies of wisdom, consisting of lists such as e.g. Enoch – Abraham – Noah – Zoroaster – Moses – Hermes Trisgmegistus – Orpheus – Pythagoras – Plato – the Sybils.

Already in the Middle Ages Hermes Trismegistus had been represented in pictures, albeit rarely (for example, in an illuminated text of Augustine in the 14th century), but as of the 15th century such representations became more frequent. Thus he appears in Bacchio Baldini's *Florentine Picture Chronicle* as well as in several alchemical treatises (like *Aurora Consurgens*, and Thomas Norton's *Ordinall of Alchymy*). At that time and as late as the 16th century he, or sometimes Apollonius instead, is represented as a sage seated in a crypt, tomb, pyramid or temple, holding the *Emerald Tablet* in his hands. In Botticelli's *Primavera* (1482), the god Hermes is represented as looking upwards and playing with clouds, touching them lightly as if they were beneficent veils through which transcendent truths might reach the beholder; therefore, a connection could be established between that representation and Hermes Trismegistus (Wind, 122-124). Six years later, an artist inlaid the pavement of Siena Cathedral with a panel representing Hermes Trismegistus as a tall and venerable bearded man, dressed in a robe and cloak, wearing a brimmed mitre and in the company of two personages (Moses and Plato?), with the inscription "Hermes Mercurius Trismegistus Contemporaneus Moysi". Not long after, Pope Alexander VI, the protector of Pico della Mirandola, commanded Pinturiccio to paint a great fresco in the Borgia Apartments of the Vatican. It abounds with hermetic symbols and zodiacal signs, and there we see Hermes Trismegistus, young and beardless, in the company of Isis and Moses. Around 1500 he was painted on a wall of the church Sint-Walburgis in Zutphen in the Low Countries, in the company of Maria, the newly-born Jesus, angels and sibyls. On a pilaster of a Sistine room in the Biblioteca Vaticana, a painting (1587) shows him with attributes of Mercurius; the caption informs us that he is "Mercurius-Thoth, inventor of the alphabets". Other examples of his presence in Roman-Catholic buildings could be adduced.

Hermes Trismegistus occasionally served as a figure within fictional narratives, as in François Rabelais, the author of *Gargantua* and *Pantagruel*

(1532/1564). Rabelais not only evinces a good knowledge of traditions related to Hermes Mercurius, but also gives Panurge, one of the main heroes of the story, many traits of Hermes Trismegistus. Panurge refers to the latter when he claims having a "thrice greatest" codpiece and being fond of the "thrice greatest Bottle" (of wine, obviously). Through his medical knowledge, Panurge claims to possess the Philosopher's Stone; he is not only connected to the tradition of "hermetic" magic, but has also something of the Humanist Hermes, i.e. the ideal figure of the Renaissance savant.

Quite a few other commentators dealt with the figure of Hermes Trismegistus in the 16th century, not least → Francesco Patrizi, whose *Discussiones peripateticae* (1581, see vol. IV) abounds in references to him. But already in Patrizi's time – beginning in 1567 with Gilbert Genebrard – his great "antiquity", and by the same token that of the hermetic writings, had been seriously called into question; what followed was an agonizing process of reappraisal, culminating in Isaac Casaubon's demonstration, in 1614, that these writings could not have been written prior to the 2nd-3rd centuries A.D. (see Mulsow 2002, correcting Frances Yates, who had presented Casaubon as the first protagonist in the dating debate). In spite of this outcome, interest in Hermes Trismegistus did not disappear; but it occasionally took on additional forms, not least political ones. In the Elisabethan period, the figures of Hermes Trismegistus and Mercury were utilized with a view to justifying the pretension of realizing an ideal Empire. The idea that a "magical" or "Mercurian" monarch could achieve an ideal kingdom or empire seems to have first appeared in English literature with Edmund Spencer's *The Faerie Queen* (1590-1596, see Book V), written under the reign of Queen Elisabeth. Spenser identified monarchy and → magic through the figure of Mercury, more specifically of Hermes Trismegistus – considered as a channel of divine influence. Elisabeth, herself interested in magic (she consulted → John Dee), was presented therein as the sovereign who would restore the Golden Age and undo the ravages wrought by the Fall of man. Elisabeth's Protestantism was thus seen metaphorically as a return to the old "Egyptian" religion, as opposed to Catholic imperialism, understood as a perversion, to the true religion of Isis and Hermes Trismegistus. Likewise and much later, in his *Penseroso* (1645), in which Hermes is the central character, John Milton would link poetry, hermetism and Protestant reform (see Brooks-Davies 1983). Later, in Germany, one

sees Hermes Trismegistus playing a similar role in W.Chr. Kriegsmann's *Conjectaneorum de Germanicae gentis origine, ac Conditore, Hermete Trismegisto* (1684), where he appears not as a benefactor of humanity in general, but only as the patron of the "German race". Kriegsmann resorted to weighty philological demonstrations aimed at proving he had been the founder of the German people; he associated the Egyptian Thoth with "Theut" (by the same token, Hermes Trismegistus) and "Teutonic".

Hermes Trismegistus continued to play a positive role as one of the guardians or representatives of true wisdom. For example, in Heinrich Nollius' novel *Parergi philosophici speculum* (1623), which stands in the wake of early rosicrucian literature [→ Rosicrucianism], the hero, Philarethes, goes to Egypt in order to meet Hermes Trismegistus, who has been put in charge by God of instructing human beings about how to find the *arx fortunae*. Likewise, the learned Jesuit → Athanasius Kircher (notably in his *Oedipus Aegyptiacus*, 1652) saw in him the inventor of the hieroglyphs and of the truths inscribed on the stone obelisks. Alchemical treatises (*e.g.* → Michael Maier's *Symbola aureae mensa duodecim nationum*, 1617) occasionally devote an entire, laudatory chapter to him. Besides, many such books of the 17th century are rich in pictures on which Hermes Trismegistus appears, usually on the front page, either alone or in the company of personages such as Hippocrates, Galen, Aristotle, Geber, → Paracelsus.

At the dawn of the Enlightenment, in 1700, the Jesuit Joachim Bouvet, a mathematician and musician who was corresponding with Leibniz about the *I Ching*, wrote to him that this Chinese document 'is like a symbol invented by some extraordinary genius of Antiquity, such as Mercury Trismegistus, to render visible the most abstract principles of all the sciences'. According to Bouvet, Fo-Hi (the supposed inventor of the *I Ching*) is the same as Enoch, who is the same as Hermes Trismegistus; and both are prototypes of Christ. He further claimed that Enoch/Fo-Hi/Hermes taught the mathematical symbols of that divinatory instrument to men endowed with superior intelligence. We also encounter him in Michel de Ramsay's novel *Les Voyages de Cyrus* (1727). There, we learn through the discourse of a pontiff in Thebes that after a shipwreck Hermes Trismegistus' mother gave birth to him on a desert island, but died shortly after. Then a goat fed him with its milk. He passed his early years in the desert eating dates. Eventually he was gratified with an apparition of 'the First Hermes, or Mercury', who taught him and gave him the name

"Trismegistus". From that time on, he was called upon to become himself a great teacher in symbols and mysteries.

Many authors in alchemical literature followed in the footsteps of earlier ones, granting Hermes Trismegistus a distinguished place in their works. Editions of alchemical books in German show him decked out in Rococo style and decor (for example, Friedrich Roth-Scholz's *Deutsches Theatrum Chimicum*, 1728; F.J.W. Schröder's *Neue alchmyistische Bibliothek*, 1772). Nicholas Langlet-Dufresnoy (*Histoire de la philosophie hermétique*, 1742) presented him as identical with King Siphoas who reigned around 1900 B.C. In 1733 another alchemist, Ehrd de Naxagoras (*Aurum Vellus oder Güldenes Vliess*, 1733), claimed that 'a plaque of precious emerald engraved with inscriptions was made for him after his death and discovered in his tomb by a woman named Zora, in the Valley of Hebron'. → Hermann Fictuld, in one of his alchemical/theosophical books (*Turba Philosophorum*, 1763), gave a long narrative halfway between mythical history and literary fiction. It opens with a scene representing Hermes, the Egyptian priest, strolling between the Elysian Fields and the Great World Ocean. This passage is designed to introduce a dialogue between Hermes and a few other fictitious persons and is partly inspired by Michael Maier's book (see above). Such examples are all the less surprising since "hermetic science" had come to be frequently used to qualify "alchemy", with "Hermes" or "Hermes Trismegistus" designating the tutelary figure of that science.

Outside the pale of alchemy, Johann Gottfried Herder, in *Über die Älteste Urkunde der Menschheit* (About the Most Ancient Document of Mankind, 1774), presents Hermes Trismegistus and/or Thoth as the founder and inventor of numbers, letters, languages, etc., and hence as the great benefactor of humanity. In addition, in 1801 he wrote for his journal *Adrastea* a long poetical dialogue titled "Hermes and Pymander" (the two figures who appear in *Corpus Hermeticum* I). Shortly after, in his *Manière de se Récréer avec le Jeu de Cartes Nommées Tarot* (1783), → Etteilla (ps. of Jean-Baptiste Alliette) claimed that the Book of Thoth (i.e., the deck of Marseilles) had been devised by a committee of Sages presided over by Hermes Trismegistus himself in the 171st year after the Flood. Etteilla's book was to be newly edited and reprinted several times, and played an important role in encouraging further discourses about Hermes Trismegistus.

Also in the same period, he came to be identified with Hiram, mentioned in the Bible and present in the Masonic degree of Master mason. Such is the case in a German or French fringe-masonic Rite established around 1790, the "Magi of Memphis". The instructions of this Rite contain a series of drawings, one of which represents Hermes Trismegistus (instead of Hiram proper) rising from the grave and giving a statement ending with these words: 'Remember me. My true name is Mercurius for the Egyptians, Thoth for the Phoenicians, Hermes Trismegistus for the Greeks, and all over the earth I am Hiram'. Prior to that picture, and besides others on paper, there survives a coloured painting on wood panel (63 × 142 cms.), anonymous and probably made around 1740, now in the Museum of Pharmacy in Basel; it depicts Hermes Trismegistus standing alone, carrying the armillary sphere and a scroll containing the first verse of the *Emerald Tablet* (see commentary in Neugebauer-Wölk 2001).

In the Romantic period, the figure of Hermes Trismegistus receded to the background, replaced as it was by other ones, Orpheus in particular. But later, in the period of the Occultist current, → Edouard Schuré, in his influential and heavily syncretistic book *Les Grand Initiés* (1889), devoted to "Hermes" – here again, a blending of Mercurius and Hermes Trismegistus – a long chapter, which is a vibrant homage. The other chapters deal with Rama, Krishna, Moses, Orpheus, Pythagoras, Plato and Jesus — therefore, what we have here is a chain of initiates comparable to that which had flourished in the Renaissance, but now extended to include Eastern traditions.

At the same time the personage also inspired the American writer Henry W. Longfellow, whose strong interest in esoteric traditions is well documented. His drama *The Golden Legend* (1851) contains a passage of twenty-four verses in which the Nile, Geber's alchemy, and Hephaistos, are evoked in a blend of Egyptian and Arabian wisdom. His poem "Hermes Trismegistos" (written around 1881) evokes in eighty verses the existence of a forlorn Tradition to be recovered thanks to Hermes Trismegistus, with whom the author identifies himself.

The American esotericist → Manly P. Hall ranges among the authors of the 20th century who were most influential in continuing to spread Hermes Trismegistus' image, not least through his book *The Encyclopedic Outline of Masonic, Hermetic, Qabbalistic and Rosicrucian Philosophy* (1928, in fol., several new editions). Not only does it contain a chapter and many other passages devoted to him, but it also presents what seems to be the latest noteworthy "portrait". It is in colour, and shows Hermes-Thoth with his foot upon the back of

Typhon. The caption informs us that he is 'the personification of Universal Wisdom'. He wears 'the ancient Egyptian Masonic apron', and is surrounded by other symbols (like dog, caduceus, scarab).

It is evident from these examples that Hermes Trismegistus as imagined and represented since the Renaissance has served many purposes. Often considered to have been a real person, he has thus been holding an intermediate position between Olympus and Earth, which contributed to make him an axial figure of the philosophical history of mankind, notably whenever he was seen as the representative par excellence of a perennial philosophy. In this respect, his enduring existence has been fostered by the production of a neo-alexandrian hermetic literature until the present time. He also appears to have been the patron of alchemy, a welcome symbol for egyptophilian settings, a kind of logo accompanying the titles of books, a name used to legitimate political aims, and occasionally an inspirational personage for novelists and poets. The existence of Hermes Mercurius, sometimes his twin or even siamese brother, as it were, may partly account for the variety of these roles. Indeed, Hermes Trismegistus possesses several of the essential attributes of Hermes Mercurius: mobility and mutability (an eclectic figure, Hermes Trismegistus easily adapts himself to various religious creeds); a liking for discourse and interpretation (he is the "inspirer" of the variegated forms of neo-alexandrian hermeneutics); and not least, his position at crossroads (as exemplified by the irenicism of neo-alexandrian authors).

Lit.: Douglas Brooks-Davies, *The Mercurial Monarch: Magical Politics from Spenser to Pope*, Manchester: Manchester University Press, 1983 ♦ Antoine Faivre, *The Eternal Hermes: From Greek God to Alchemical Magus*, Grand Rapids (Mich.): Phanes Press, 1995 (see chapters I, III, V [V is devoted to iconographic documents]; revised and expanded version: *I volti di Ermete*, Rome: Atanor, 2001) ♦ Antoine Faivre (ed.), *Présence d'Hermès Trismégiste* (Cahiers de l'Hermétisme), Paris: Albin Michel, 1985 ♦ M. de la Garanderie (ed.), *Mercure à la Renaissance*, Paris: H. Champion, 1988 ♦ Jean-François Maillard, "Hermès théologien et philosophe", in: *Mercure à la Renaissance* (see above), 11-14 ♦ idem, "Mercure alchimiste dans la tradition mytho-hermétique", in: idem, 117-130 ♦ Martin Mulsow (ed.), *Das Ende des Hermetismus: Historische Kritik und neue Naturphilosophie in der Spätrenaissance. Dokumentation und Analyse der Debatte um die Datierung der hermetischen Schriften von Genebrard bis Casaubon (1567-1614)*, Tübingen: J.C.B. Mohr (Paul Siebeck), 2002 ♦ Monika Neugebauer-Wölk, "'Denn dis ist Müglich, Lieber Sohn!'": Zur esoterischen Übersetzungstradition des Corpus Hermeticum in der frühen Neuzeit", in: Richard Caron, Joscelyn Godwin, Wouter J. Hanegraaff, Jean-Louis Vieillard-Baron (eds.), *Esotérisme, gnoses et imaginaire symbolique: Mélanges offerts à Antoine Faivre*, Leuven: Peeters, 2001, 131-144 ♦ Mirko Sladek, "Mercurius Triplex, Mercurius Termaximus et les 'Trois Hermès'", in: Faivre, *Présence d'Hermès Trismégiste*, 88-99 ♦ Cesare Vasoli, "Mercure dans la tradition ficinienne", in: de la Garanderie, *Mercure à la Renaissance*, 27-43 ♦ Edgar Wind, *Pagan Mysteries in the Renaissance* (1958), Middlesex: Penguin Books, 1967, 121-124.

ANTOINE FAIVRE

Hermetic Brotherhood of Luxor

A short-lived secret organization devoted to practical occult work, active in England, France and the United States in the mid-1880s but possessing an influence far greater than its size and duration might suggest. It came to public notice in late 1884 in the form of a notice appended to Robert H. Fryar's republication of *The Divine Pymander*, that advised searchers after the truth and Theosophists disillusioned with "Hindoo Mahatmas'" willingness to dispense wisdom, to contact "Theon" in care of Fryar. The public propaganda continued in the pages of a journal published by the order, *The Occult Magazine* of Glasgow (February 1885-October 1886), and at that point the H.B. of L. already had corresponding members as far afield as Russia, France and the United States. The editor of the journal and Provisional Grand Master of the North (of Great Britain) was a Scotsman, Peter Davidson (1837-1915), a cabinet- and violin-maker and visionary with an interest in secret brotherhoods, Rosicrucians [→ Rosicrucianism] and magic mirrors. Associated with him in governing the H.B. of L. was Thomas Henry Burgoyne (born Thomas Henry Dalton; c. 1855-c. 1895), and beyond both of these, as Grand Master of the Exterior Circle, was → "Max Theon" (Louis Maximilian Bimstein; ca. 1848-1927), a Polish or Russian Jew. According to its own mythology (later adopted by → René Guénon and other advocates of the so-called "Hidden Hand" theory of history), the H.B. of L. was the outward manifestation of the Western branch of the Great Brotherhood of initiates and adepts, which differed from the Eastern branch (exemplified by the → Theosophical Society) in denying → reincarnation on this earth and in advocating active, practical magical and ritual work to gain individual spiritual advancement (clairvoyance and astral travel). It was this magical practice, based almost exclusively on the sexual magical teachings of → Paschal Beverly Randolph, that primarily sets the H.B. of L. apart. The order's doctrinal and practical teachings were circulated to the scattered members by mail. The H.B. of L. recruited members largely from the ranks of the Theosophical Society and for a period can be said to have constituted a practical order within the T.S. composed of most of its leading lights: W.A. Ayton, → F.-Ch. Barlet (ps. of Albert Faucheux), A. Chaboseau, → Papus (ps. of G. Encausse), J.D. Buck, T.M. Johnson, Elliott Coues, and Eliot B. Page, among others.

The order came to naught when, in October 1885, it began touting and then raising subscriptions for a Colony Scheme – a project which promised to buy a large section of land in America where the members of the order could participate in the restored mysteries of antiquity. Ayton's name was used in the promotional material without his consent. When he discovered the deception, he made enquiries, found out that Burgoyne was actually Dalton, who had been convicted of a petty fraud in 1883, and hastily wrote to all concerned to denounce the imposture. Davidson and Burgoyne then fled to America. Davidson settled down in Georgia, near the place chosen for the colony, where he instituted a new Order of the Cross and Serpent, published a journal, *The Morning Star*, and continued to be active in various French occult groups around Papus. Burgoyne settled in Colorado and then California, making his living by writing and selling lessons on occult → astrology (published as *The Light of Egypt*) and continuing to initiate groups in the western United States into the mysteries of the H.B. of L. His work survives today in the form of the Church and Order of Light, which traces its orgins back to "C.C. Zain" (Elbert Benjamin). At least some portion of the secret sexual teachings of the H.B. of L. also found their way, via Sylvester Clark Gould († 1909), into the Hermetic Brotherhood of Light and through it into the → Ordo Templi Orientis, and into the Societas Rosicruciana in America of George Winslow Plummer ("Khei"). Theon and his wife moved to Tlemcen, Algeria , where they continued the work of the H.B. of L. under the name *Tradition Cosmique* and trained, among others, Mirra Alfassa, who went on to become "the Mother" in Sri Aurobindo's ashram at Pondicherry.

Zanoni (ps. of T.H. Burgoyne), *The Light of Egypt, or, the Science of the Soul and the Stars*, vol. 1, Chicago & London: Religio-Philosophical Publ. House/ Redway, 1889; vol. 2, Denver: Astro-Philosophical Publishing Co., 1900. See also Godwin, Chanel & Deveney (under *Lit.*).

Lit.: Christian Chanel, *De la "Fraternité Hermetique de Louxor" au "Mouvement Cosmique": L'Oeuvre de Max Théon. Contribution à l'étude des courants ésotériques en Europe à la fin du XIXème siècle et au début du XXème siècle*, Diss. Doctorat d'Etat, E.P.H.E., 5e section, Paris, 1994 ◆ Joscelyn Godwin, "The Hidden Hand", *Theosophical History* 3:2-5 (April 1990-January 1991), 35-43, 66-76, 107-117, 137-148 ◆ Joscelyn Godwin, Christian Chanel & John Patrick Deveney, *The Hermetic Brotherhood of Luxor: Initiatic and Historical Documents of an Order of Practical Occultism*, New York: Weiser, 1995.

JOHN PATRICK DEVENEY

Hermetic Literature I: Antiquity

1. INTRODUCTION 2. TECHNICAL HERMETICA 3. PHILOSOPHICAL HERMETICA (A. *CORPUS HERMETICUM* B. SOME TREATISES OF THE *CORPUS HERMETICUM* C. GREEK AND LATIN FRAGMENTS D. THE *ASCLEPIUS* E. COPTIC TEXTS F. THE ARMENIAN *DEFINITIONS*) 4. "GENERAL" AND "DETAILED" DISCOURSES 5. DATE AND PLACE OF ORIGIN OF THE PHILOSOPHICAL HERMETICA

1. INTRODUCTION

The literary works attributed to → Hermes Trismegistus reflect the various activities he was thought to have deployed. In accordance with his function as a teacher of → magic, → astrology, → alchemy and philosophically coloured religious knowledge, there are under his name magical spells, astrological and alchemical treatises and religious-philosophical discourses. In recent scholarship, there has been much discussion about the relationship between the "occult" magical, astrological and alchemical works on the one hand and the more philosophical religious tracts on the other. The two great scholars who worked on the Hermetica in the 20th century, Walter Scott and André-Jean Festugière, made an almost complete separation between the two kinds of literature. Festugière's distinction between "popular Hermetism" (*hermétisme populaire*) and "learned" or "philosophical" Hermetism (*hermétisme savant/philosophique*) became almost universally accepted. In recent research, however, the more neutral term of "technical Hermetica" has become current for the magical, astrological and alchemical texts that go under the name of Hermes. This term indeed fits these texts better than the word "popular", since they present primarily techniques to achieve personal objectives. The second kind of hermetic writings is still mostly called "philosophical", and sometimes "theoretical". The latter term should be avoided since it suggests that these works provide a theoretical basis for the technical, more practical Hermetica, which is by no means certain. In the first centuries of our era, Greek philosophy became increasingly religious and thinking about religion became more and more philosophical. To find confirmation of their ideas on ultimate reality, philosophers turned to divine revelation, and religious thinkers liked to express their beliefs in terms of Greek philosophy. Therefore, the term "philosophical Hermetica" is acceptable for almost all the works that are usually covered by that name, since they are strongly influenced by Greek philosophical ideas, especially those of Platonism and Stoicism. It would be wrong, however, to consider them as primarily philosophical works. On the contrary, they are essentially religious tracts, which make free use of Greek philosophical ideas to express their views on religious knowledge and individual salvation. As a matter of fact, the word "theosophical" would provide a better term, if it could be stripped of its modern connotations.

In recent research, the sharp distinction between technical and philosophical hermetic texts has been questioned. Scott and Festugière were convinced that the authors and audiences of the two kinds of hermetic literature were almost completely different. However, Garth Fowden has convincingly argued that both the technical and the philosophical hermetic writings emanated from the same cultural and religious milieu, namely that of Graeco-Roman Egypt in the centuries around the beginning of our era. According to Fowden, the technical and the philosophical Hermetica corresponded to successive stages on 'the way of Hermes', but there is no decisive proof for this contention. In some hermetic treatises initiation into the hermetic mysteries is attended by magic and astrology, but that does not imply that all magical or astrological texts ascribed to Hermes presuppose the typical ideas about knowledge and salvation that characterize the philosophical Hermetica.

Unfortunately, an edition of all the technical Hermetica in one or more volumes does not exist, but there are two editions of the Greek and Latin philosophical Hermetica. Walter Scott made an edition in four volumes (1924-1936), with English translations and notes (the fourth volume, containing *testimonia* and fragments, was published by A.S. Ferguson). Though Scott's works remains very valuable because of its wealth of information, the text edition itself is generally considered a failure, because of its hypercritical character, which resulted into a great number of unwarranted textual emendations. The standard edition of the Greek and Latin Hermetica, also in four volumes, has become the one published by A.D. Nock and A.-J. Festugière (1946-1954).

2. TECHNICAL HERMETICA

The basic idea behind the technical Hermetica, and the philosophical as well, is the notion that all things that exist, both in the spiritual and in the material world, in some way or another are interconnected. This universal coherence or *sympatheia* could be the basis for quite different practices. It enabled the magician to bend gods or daemons to his will if he knew the appropriate divine names and the required materials to make a spell, but it also enabled the astrologer to foretell which days would be auspicious or inauspicious to take certain actions, because of the unalterable course of the heavenly bodies (*fatum*). The art of alchemy was based on two fundamental assumptions. The first is that there is a material substratum, some kind of "first matter", which forms the basis of ordinary matter, and the second that all precious metals derive from lead and therefore can be made from it by performing the right alchemical procedure. In the first volume of his *Révélation*, Festugière has collected, translated and thoroughly studied a great number of astrological, magical and alchemical texts and fragments in Greek and Latin that are ascribed to Hermes. Though most of these texts date from the first centuries of the present era, there is little doubt that similar texts already circulated in the Hellenistic (Ptolemaic) period. In his *Stromateis*, VI, 35-37, → Clement of Alexandria describes a procession of Egyptian priests, possibly derived from the Egyptian priest and Stoic philosopher Chaeremon (1st century A.D.), who each carry the symbols and books that mark their position in the hierarchy. Clement mentions forty-two books, which he all attributes to Hermes, i.e. Thot. Among them are books containing hymns and instructions concerning the cult of the gods, but also four astrological books, ten hieroglyphic books on cosmography and geography, Egypt, the Nile, the construction of temples etc., and six medical books. Similar books are mentioned in a catalogue of books, inscribed on the walls of the library of the temple of Edfu. The library, which dates from 140-124 B.C., contained, *inter alia*, magical and astrological books, such as *Spells for the averting of the evil eye*, *Knowledge of the recurrence of the two stars* (i.e. sun and moon) and *Control over the recurrence of the stars* (cf. Fowden, 57-59). Hellenistic astrology owed only a little to earlier Egyptian observations of the celestial phenomena, even though its invention was ascribed to Thot/Hermes, but the Greek magical texts continued the early Egyptian magical literature under the name of Thot, even though they show unmistakable Hellenistic features.

3. PHILOSOPHICAL HERMETICA

A. THE *CORPUS HERMETICUM*

The standard edition by Nock and Festugière has the comprehensive title *Corpus Hermeticum* on the front-page of each of the four volumes. As a matter of fact, all the hermetic philosophical texts preserved from Antiquity could indeed be said to constitute one great hermetic Corpus, for they all have the same literary structure, that of a dialogue, and the same kind of teaching. However, the title *Corpus Hermeticum* (C.H.) usually refers to a specific Byzantine collection of 17 hermetic texts, and it is in that sense that also Nock and Festugière take the term in their introductions and notes. The Byzantine scholar Michael Psellus (11th century) seems to have known the C.H. proper in roughly its present form, but there are no witnesses that attest its existence in earlier centuries. Stobaeus (5th century, see below) cited parts of C.H. II, IV, and IX in his *Anthology*, but he apparently did not yet know the C.H. as a collection. Nevertheless, the Vienna hermetic fragments, published by Mahé, show that such collections already existed at an early date. These fragments, which date from the late second or early 3rd century, were apparently part of a collection of at least 10 numbered treatises, for fragment B contains the end of treatise number 9 and the beginning of number 10. Bishop Cyril of Alexandria [ca. 440] also knew a collection of 15 books, called *Hermaika*, which had been composed by someone in Athens (*Contra Julianum* I, 41), but his quotations show that he had not the present C.H. before him. This evidence proves that the C.H. as a collection may be much older than the 11th century.

The C.H. became known in the West through → Marsilio Ficino's Latin translation (1463; pub-

lished 1471) of a Greek manuscript that had been brought to Florence by the monk Leonardo of Pistoia, who presented it to Cosimo de Medici in 1460. This manuscript of the 15th century contains only the treatises I-XIV (Biblioteca Medicea Laurenziana, Plut. 71, 33, ff. 123ʳ-145ʳ; Gentile & Gilly, 41-43). Ficino apparently did not know that the Greek cardinal Bessarion, already in 1458 and also in Florence, had acquired a more complete 14th century manuscript of the C.H., which also contained the tractates XVI-XVIII (Biblioteca Nazionale Marciana [Venice], Cod. Marc. Gr. Z. 242 [= 993]; Gilly & Van Heertum, II, 15-16). Treatise XV has never existed. Adrien Turnèbe, the first editor of the Greek text (Paris 1554; Gentile & Gilly, 126-128), made a fifteenth tractate from some hermetic excerpts by Stobaeus. This artificial treatise was left out again by later editors, who, however, retained Turnèbe's numbering, so that the C.H. contains the treatises I-XIV and XVI-XVIII. Ficino gave his 14 treatises the collective title of *Pimander* (later editors wrote *Poemander*), after the title of the first tractate, *Poimandres*. However, the writings of the C.H. are not chapters of one and the same work, as Ficino thought, but completely independent compositions. The criterion that determined their selection into one collection is unknown. It has been suggested that Byzantine scholars selected them because of their relatively pure philosophical and religious contents; according to another view, they may have expurgated them of suspicious magical and astrological elements. As a matter of fact, the Coptic treatise *On the Ogdoad and the Ennead* (see below) gives these elements a prominent place in its description of an inner religious experience, whereas they are lacking in the otherwise closely related C.H. XIII. The *Asclepius* (see below) has in chapter 37 a famous passage about the theurgical conjuration of divine powers into the statues of the gods (a related idea is expressed in C.H. XVII), but the book as a whole is an excellent summary of hermetic religious philosophy. In view of the fact that magic and astrology were integral parts of the spiritual world in which the Hermetica originated, it may be assumed that magical and astrological elements appeared in many hermetic philosophical treatises. With respect to the C.H. we can only say that some cleansing by Byzantine editors cannot be excluded, but the *Asclepius* shows that there is no need to assume that this has happened on a large scale. It is not the place here to discuss the importance of the C.H. for our knowledge of classical → Hermetism, but some of its tractates deserve a closer examination.

B. Some Treatises of the Corpus Hermeticum

C.H. I, the first tractate of the C.H., entitled *Poimandres*, is the most well-known and one of the most important hermetic writings, but at the same time it is singular because of its strongly mythological character. It is not a first-hand teaching of Hermes Trismegistus to a pupil but a report of an unnamed person about a revelation received from a divine being, who introduces himself as 'I am Poimandres, the intelligence (*nous*) of the supreme authority'. The recipient of this revelation was later identified with Hermes Trismegistus, as appears, *inter alia*, from the title in the manuscripts and C.H. XIII, 15. The idea that the divine *Nous* instructs Hermes is also found in C.H. XI. The name Poimandres has often been interpreted as "Shepherd (*poimèn*) of men (*andres*)", both in the later hermetic tradition and by modern scholars, but this is linguistically impossible. Peter Kingsley has convincingly argued that the name is a Greek form of the Egyptian *p-eime nte-rē*, 'the intelligence (or understanding) of Re', and that the rest of the introductory formula, 'the intelligence of the supreme authority (*tēs authentias nous*)', simply is a Greek translation of the name Poimandres.

After the introduction, the *Poimandres* presents, in the form of a vision, a cosmological, anthropological and eschatological myth, followed by the command to preach the hermetic message, and a final hymn. The *Poimandres* teaches a dualism between light and darkness, spirit and matter, but not an absolute dualism. Primeval matter was a watery substance that came into existence within the darkness, which somehow had originated out of the light. The light was the divine Intelligence or Mind (*nous*), and out of it appeared the Word (*logos*), which is the 'Son of God'. From this, the author immediately draws an anthropological consequence by establishing a distinct parallelism between God and man: 'That what sees and hears within you is the word of the Lord, and your mind is God the Father; they are not separate from one another, for their union is life' (I, 6). In the process of creation, the Word separated the elements, so that fire and air went on high, whereas water and earth remained below. The divine Mind, 'being androgyne and existing as light and life', gave birth to two other divine beings: a second Mind (*nous*), a craftsman, who created the seven planets 'whose government is called fate', and Man (*Anthropos*), who had his father's image and was loved by him as his own form and received from him the dominion over everything that had been made (I, 9-13). The heavenly Anthropos looked though the cosmic framework and displayed the form of God to lower nature. Nature saw his shape in the water and his shadow on the earth, and she smiled with love (similar ideas on the Anthropos in → Gnosticism). When the divine Man saw the reflection of his image, he loved it and wanted to be united with it, and nature 'enfolded him completely and they united, for they loved each other'. For this reason, man is a double being: 'mortal because of the body, immortal because of the real Man' (I, 14-15). After a period of seven androgyne generations the human beings became male and female, for which no reason is given, and they were commanded to increase and multiply. This command is clearly influenced by Gen. 1:28, but it has some negative overtones, for the dissolution of androgyny entailed sexuality, procreation, birth and death. By all this, human beings run the risk of forgetting their divine descent, and, therefore, the injunction to increase and multiply is followed by the warning not to lose sight of one's origin: 'Let him who is endowed with mind (*nous*) recognize that he himself is immortal and that sexual desire is the cause of death, and let he so know all that exists' (I, 18). Who has understood himself comes to God (I, 21), which is the basic idea of hermetic salvation. In ascending to its origin the soul leaves its characteristic (mostly bad) features to the planets from which it had received them at its descent, and then, stripped of the astral influences, its real self enters the eighth sphere and joins the hymns sung by those who are there. Finally, they all ascend to the heaven above the eighth sphere, become powers and are merged in God: 'This is the final good for those who have received knowledge (*gnosis*): to become God' (I, 26).

After the command to preach the hermetic gospel, a short description of its contents and the reaction it received (I, 26-29), the Poimandres concludes with a hymn of nine lines, which might be called a triple Trishagion since all lines begin with "Holy": "Holy is God" (3x) and "Holy are you" (6x). The hymn passes into a prayer in prose, in which "Hermes" bears witness to his salvation: 'I go to life and light. You are blessed, Father' (I, 32). This hymn has also had an independent circulation and was even included in a Christian hymn book of the 3rd century, but most probably it was part of the *Poimandres* from the beginning. The hymn and the *Poimandres* as a whole are permeated with Jewish ideas, which suggest that this writing originated in a milieu in which Jews played an important part (Dodd, Philonenko, Pearson). Other elements can be best explained from an Egyptian background, which points to

Alexandria as its place of origin. Since the large Jewish community in Alexandria was almost completely extirpated during the revolt of A.D. 117-119, it seems probable that the *Poimandres* dates from the 1st century or the beginning of the second, which would make it one of the earliest hermetic writings. It has some central themes in common with the Gospel of John, e.g. God as life and light, but there is no indication of a direct Christian influence, let alone that it would represent a "paganization" of original Christian ideas (Büchli).

– C.H. IV has a double title: *The mixing bowl (Crater) or the Monad*, which refers to the two parts of this "Discourse of Hermes to Tat". The first part (IV, 1-10) argues, contrary to the whole Greek philosophical tradition, that intelligence or mind (*nous*) is not the possession of every human being, but a heavenly gift which may be added to his reasoning capacity (*logos*). As a result the text distinguishes between two classes of men, the 'reasonable people' (*logikoi*) and those who have received *nous*. Closely related ideas are found among the Valentinian Gnostics [→ Valentinus and Valentinians]. As a matter of fact, the *nous* of this treatise identifies with the *pneuma* that characterizes the Gnostic. Though being a gift of God, the *nous* is in this treatise at the same time a prize, in the form of a mixing bowl, which has to be won in the contest of life. The crater is presented as a kind of baptismal font, in which the souls of the *logikoi* that make use of their *logos* have to immerse themselves. It has often been suggested that this passage alludes to a hermetic initiatory rite or "sacrament", which implied the drinking from a crater, as in the Greek mystery religions. The second part of this treatise, which deals with God as a Monad, the origin and root of everything, remains within the framework of Greek philosophy.

– C.H. V is also a discourse of Hermes to Tat, entitled: *God is invisible and entirely visible*. It argues that God can be known from the contemplation of his works, which in itself is a common Stoic idea. According to the author, however, this is not a "natural" knowledge of God, for God is unknowable; it is a divine gift, an act of divine grace: 'Ask him the grace to enable you to understand so great a God, to permit even one of his rays to illuminate your thinking' (IV, 2).

– C.H. VI has often been used to demonstrate that in Antiquity there existed a radical negative form of Hermetism, alongside a more positive one. Starting from the common idea that the Good is in fact identical with God, the author draws a conclusion that would have been subscribed by radical Gnostics only. It is aptly expressed in the title of the treatise: *The Good is alone in God and nowhere else*. For that reason, 'the cosmos is the plenitude (*pleroma*) of evil, as God is the plenitude of the good, or the good of God' (VI, 4).

– C.H. VII, entitled *Ignorance concerning God is the greatest evil*, is a hermetic sermon, an incitement to leave the drunkenness of ignorance behind and to seek the way to the 'gate of knowledge', where the pure light is and nobody gets drunk but all are sober and look with the heart at Him who wants to be seen, but who can only be seen by the *nous* and the heart. The human body is in the strongest terms described as an impediment to see the beauty of truth and the Good.

– C.H. X, entitled *The Key*, is a discussion of some basic hermetic tenets: God the Father as the supreme Good, the contemplation of God as a divine gift, ignorance as the greatest evil for the soul, the immortal Cosmos as the second level of being and mortal man as the third. This treatise is interesting in particular because of its doctrine of the soul and its fate after death (X, 13-25). The mind (*nous*) is enclosed within reason (*logos*), reason within the soul (*psychè*), the soul within the astral body (*pneuma*), which passes through veins, arteries and the blood and moves the living carnal body. At death the *nous* of a pious soul puts on its own garment of fire and becomes pure *Nous*, but the impious soul has to reincarnate in a new human body.

– C.H. XIII is one of the most important hermetic writings. It is a 'discourse of Hermes Trismegistus to his son Tat', entitled *A Secret Discourse on the Mountain about Rebirth and the Promise to be Silent*. As a matter of fact, it is a dialogue that is said to have taken place after Hermes and Tat had come down from a mountain. Hermes says about his own rebirth that he has come out of his former self into an immortal body, which has no colour and cannot be touched or measured; he is re-born in the divine *Nous* (XIII, 3). Tat is exhorted to turn into himself and to cleanse himself from the twelve tormenting spirits of the material world, which are somehow connected with the twelve signs of the Zodiac: ignorance, sorrow, intemperance, lust, injustice, greed, deceit, envy, treachery, anger, recklessness, and malice. They withdraw one by one from the one who receives God's mercy: 'This is the manner and meaning of rebirth' (XIII, 7 and 12). Spiritual rebirth is actualised by the arrival of ten good 'spirits': knowledge of God, joy, self-control, steadfastness, justice, generosity, truth, the good, life and light. Whoever has attained divine birth by God's mercy 'knows himself as constituted of these powers and he rejoices' (XIII, 8-10). Within the exposition of the twelve bad and the ten good powers, the tractate somewhat unexpectedly describes a spiritual experience by Tat, which apparently is the effect of his own rebirth. This experience, in which he falls together with the whole cosmos (XIII, 11), differs from that of the ascent to the ninth sphere as described in the *Poimandres* and in the *Ogdoad and the Ennead*, which shows that initiation into the hermetic mysteries could lead to quite different mystical experiences. Through his rebirth Tat has been born a god, a child of the One, and he wants to hear the hymn of praise that according to the *Poimandres* was sung in the Ogdoad (I, 26). This song, the hymn of rebirth, can be heard in silence only; it cannot be taught; it is a secret kept in silence. Then follows, after some instructions, a beautiful hymn, which celebrates the beauty of the cosmos and the glory of its creator. It is indicated in the manuscripts as 'Secret Hymn Book, Song 4', which suggest that once it was part of a collection of hymns and may have had an independent circulation. Whether this is true or not cannot be established with any certainty, but it is by no means impossible, for also the hymns at the end of both the *Poimandres* and the *Asclepius* were transmitted independent of the texts to which they now belong. C.H. XIII concludes its report of a spiritual enlightenment with the words: 'Now you have come to spiritual knowledge of both yourself and our Father'.

– Whether the last three writings (XVI-XVIII) were part of the C.H. from the beginning or were added at a later date is difficult to decide, but they certainly stand a little apart from the rest of the collection. Not Hermes Trismegistus, or the Nous through Hermes, is the teacher but Asclepius (XVI), Tat (XVII, a fragment, in which a king is exhorted to honour the statues of the gods), and an unknown panegyrist, who hardly can be called a hermetist at all (XVIII).

C.H. XVI, which presents itself as a letter of Asclepius to king Ammon, is a distinct hermetic writing. It pretends to have been written in the Egyptian language, 'which preserves the (magical) power of the words', and urges the king not to have it translated, 'in order that these mysteries do not reach the Greeks' (XVI, 1-2). In this treatise, the Creator is identified with the Sun, whose energy gives life to the whole cosmos (XVI, 5-9). The role of daemons, who are subjected to the planets, is extensively discussed: they are not only responsible for natural catastrophes, such as earthquakes and volcanic eruptions, but also for the evil deeds of human beings, while at the same time they serve to

punish them for these deeds (XVI, 10-17). The tractate concludes with a summary of a hymnal character (XVI, 18-19). It praises God the Father and the Sun as the creator of everything: 'All things are parts of God, but if all things are parts of God, then everything is God. Therefore, in making all things, he makes himself'.

c. Greek and Latin Fragments

The great number of quotations of now lost hermetic texts in authors of the 4th and 5th centuries shows that in late Antiquity many more hermetic philosophical treatises were in circulation than have been preserved today. The earliest quotation of a hermetic writing is found in Tertullian (ca. A.D. 200), *De anima*, 33, 2 (Nock & Festugière, IV, 104). Forty fragments have been preserved in the *Anthology* that John of Stobi, usually called Stobaeus, composed in the first decades of the 5th century for the instruction of his son Septimius. Ten of them derive from C.H. II, IV and IX and one from the *Asclepius*; they are valuable since they represent an earlier and better textual tradition than the preserved complete manuscripts. The other 29 fragments of Stobaeus were taken from hermetic writings that are now lost. Most of them deal with the central themes of hermetic philosophy, God, cosmos and man, but there are some remarkable exceptions. In *Fragm.* VI (NF III, 34-39), for instance, Hermes explains to his son Tat the activity of the 36 decans and their relationship with the other celestial bodies, which shows that astrology and philosophical Hermetism did not belong to completely separate areas. A very interesting fragment is Stobaeus' large excerpt from 'a holy book of Hermes Trismegistus' called *Daughter* (or *Pupil*) *of the World*, mostly indicated by its Greek title *Korē kosmou* (*Fragm.* XXIII, NF III, 1-50). In this writing, the teacher is not Hermes but Isis, who instructs her son Horus after herself having been instructed by Hermes. 'All-knowing Hermes' is said to have written down all the cosmic mysteries before the creation of the world and to have hidden the books near the secret symbols of Osiris, with a prayer and magical formulas (XXIII, 1-8). Then follows an artificial myth about the creation of the cosmos: first God made Nature, then 60 different kinds of souls of diminishing grades of purity, and the bodies of birds, fish and quadrupeds. The human body was made to imprison and punish disobedient souls (XXIII, 9-52). Ignorance reigned on earth, but Osiris and Isis, 'instructed by Hermes of the secret ordinances of God' were appointed to regulate life on earth by giving laws and teaching crafts and sciences (XXIII, 53-70).

The author has apparently used a lost hermetic treatise as one of his sources, which explains the inconsistencies that can be observed in this work (Festugière, in NF III, CXXXIII-CLXVIII).

A considerable number of important fragments have been preserved in the Christian writers Lactantius and Cyril of Alexandria. Lactantius, who was born and educated in Africa, became a professor of Latin rhetoric in Nicomedia in Bythinia by special request of the emperor Diocletian (284-304). Since he had become a Christian, he had to resign his chair in 303, when the Great Persecution began. About 317, the emperor Constantine the Great summoned him to Treves in Gaul to become the teacher of his son Crispus. In his most important work, the *Divinae Institutiones* in seven volumes, written between 304 and 314, he frequently invokes Hermes Trismegistus as a pre-Christian witness to Christ. The work contains a great number of hermetic quotations (Wlosok, 261-262), of which 13 are unknown from other sources (NF IV, 106-114). Some quotations are in Greek, which is sometimes very helpful to recover the original text, especially in the case of the Latin *Asclepius*. Lactantius himself composed an *Epitome* of his principal work, which has some value of its own, since he used the opportunity to make corrections and additions that sometimes affect his hermetic quotations.

Cyril of Alexandria, who occupied the Alexandrian see from 412-444, appealed 13 times to Hermes Trismegistus in his *Apology against Julian* (*Contra Julianum*), which was directed to emperor Julian's *Against the Galilaeans*. Cyril wrote this work between 430 and 440, when vehement polemics against Nestorius and the Nestorians, about God and man in Christ, monopolized his attention almost completely. That he nevertheless felt himself compelled to write this enormous work of at least 20 volumes, of which the first ten books have been preserved and fragments of books 11-20 exist (books 20-30 were probably never written), about 80 years after the death of Julian "the Apostat" (363), shows how dangerous he even then still considered Julian's attack on the Christians. Cyril did not embrace Hermes as wholeheartedly as Lactantius had done, but he adduced his testimony as a pre-Christian prophecy of the coming of Christ and even of the doctrine of the Trinity. Though he seems to have had a direct knowledge of hermetic sources, in some cases Cyril apparently borrowed his hermetic passages, and their interpretation as well, from a work on the Trinity, *De trinitate*, which by tradition and also by most modern scholars is ascribed to Didymus

the Blind (313-398), the last head of the famous Alexandrian School. In *Contra Julianum* I, 47, Cyril presents an alleged testimony of the Trinity by Plato and two hermetic fragments (nrs. 23 and 24, NF IV, 126-129), which, together with their interpretation, are already found in Didymus' *De trinitate*, II, 27, though not in the same order (Scott, IV, 171-173).

After the publication of the then known Greek and Latin fragments by Scott and Nock & Festugière some new material has come to light: the Greek Vienna fragments, published by Mahé (see above), and some Greek extracts, in the Bodleian Library, Oxford, published by Paramelle and Mahé, of which some derive from an otherwise unknown treatise *On the Soul* and others from a work called *Definitions*, which has been preserved in Armenian (see below). Another hermetic fragment, quoted by C. Iulius Romanus (3rd century) and preserved in Charisius (4th century), *Ars grammatica* II, 239, was noticed by I.G. Taifacos (Fowden, xvii).

D. *ASCLEPIUS*

The largest preserved hermetic treatise is the *Asclepius*, which has always had an independent existence. Its original Greek title was *Logos Teleios* (*Perfect Discourse* or *Perfect Revelation*), but the Greek text has been lost, except for a few fragments in later writers. Though some scholars prefer an earlier date, it was most probably written in the second half of the 3rd century. Augustine is the first to quote the Latin *Asclepius*, in his *City of God* (between 410 and 426), whereas Lactantius does not seem to know it, which might be an indication that the Latin translation dates from the 4th century. It survived among the works of Apuleius (ca. 150), who can hardly have been the translator of the Greek text, as has been suggested (Hunink), and it became the only known complete hermetic treatise in the West until the Renaissance.

The Latin *Asclepius* appears to be a rather free translation of the Greek *Logos Teleios*. That became apparent after the discovery of a Coptic translation of *Asclepius*, 21-29, which *inter alia* contains the famous "Hermetic Apocalypse" (24-26), in Codex VI of the Nag Hammadi Library. Comparison between the Latin and Coptic translations shows that the Latin translator took the liberty to abridge or expand the Greek original. A good example of the abridgement is offered by the description of the desolate state of the land of Egypt after the gods' withdrawal from the earth to heaven. Having said that in those days the Egyptians will be prohibited from worshipping God and even punished if they do so, the Latin text simply says, in chapter 24: 'Then this most holy land, seat of shrines and temples, will be completely filled with tombs and corpses'. The Coptic translation, however, presents this prophecy in a more elaborate form, NHC IV, 70, 30-36: 'On that day, the country that was more *pious* than all (other) countries will become *impious*. No longer will it be full of *temples* but it will be full of *tombs*, neither will it be full of *gods* but (it will be full of) *corpses*.' The Latin translator has obviously suppressed the distinct antithetic parallelism of the original (pious/impious, temples/tombs, gods/corpses); the gods are even not mentioned at all. That the Coptic translation represents the original text is confirmed by Augustine's polemics against a pagan interpretation of this prophecy, in his *City of God*, VIII, 23-27 (van den Broek [1]). The discovery of the Coptic translation has also made an end to the widespread scholarly opinion that between Lactantius and Augustine the Latin "Hermetic Apocalypse" had been interpolated with allusions to the Christian persecution of paganism. These "allusions" were already to be found in the Greek text that underlies the Coptic translation and must necessarily have been written down before the persecution of pagan religions began. As a matter of fact, the idea that strangers will occupy the land and destroy the traditional religious institutions of Egypt is one of the stock themes of ancient Egyptian prophetic and apocalyptic texts (Mahé 1982, II, 68-113).

Of the original Greek text of the Asclepius only a few fragments are left. Two of them deserve to be mentioned here separately: a very influential quotation by Lactantius and the Greek version of the final hymn of the *Asclepius*. In his *Divinae Institutiones* IV, 6, 4, Lactantius cites the Greek text of the beginning of *Asclepius* 8, about the creation of the second god, which he interprets in a Christian sense as referring to the generation of the Son by the Father. The passage was translated into Latin by Quodvultdeus († ca. 453) in his *Adversus quinque haereses*, III, 4, a work that later gained great authority because of its attribution to Augustine. In a somewhat abbreviated and occasionally Christianized form the passage became one of the most cited hermetic texts in medieval theological literature. Its best-known variant is found in the famous representation of Hermes Mercurius in the Siena floor mosaic by Giovanni di Stefano (1488; van den Broek [2], 135).

The final hymn of the *Asclepius*, in chapter 41, has had an independent circulation. The somewhat lacunal Greek text is found in a magical papyrus in Paris, the so-called Papyrus Mimaut (Pap. Louvre, N. 2391), where it is part of a longer prayer. A Coptic translation of the Greek text, usually called the *Prayer of Thanksgiving*, is found in Codex VI, 7 of the Nag Hammadi Library, where it immediately follows the *Discourse on the Ogdoad and the Ennead* (see below). Scholarly opinion is divided about the question of whether the hymn was part of the *Asclepius* from the beginning and afterwards started its independent circulation or that the process went the other way round. On the basis of the Latin, Coptic and Greek texts it has been possible to reconstruct the original Greek text to a high degree of probability. It is a beautiful hymn of thanksgiving for the gift of Gnosis, which glorifies the androgyne nature of the supreme God in such a bold language that the Latin translator thought it wise to mitigate it: 'We know you, O spiritual Light, O Life of our life. We know you, O Womb of every creature. We know you, O Womb that is pregnant by the member (*physis*) of the Father. We know you, O begetting Father who eternally exists' (NHC VI, 64, 22-29 parr.).

It is impossible to detect a detailed structure in the *Asclepius*: the subjects discussed are only loosely connected, mostly by association, and often interrupted by the insertion of other material. But that does not diminish its importance, for it is an extensive compendium of ancient Hermetism, most probably based on existing hermetic treatises, which the author extracted and abridged 'without much intelligence' (Ferguson, in Scott, IV, x-xxxiii). It has the form of a discussion between Hermes, Asclepius, Tat and Ammon, situated in the *adyton*, the inner sanctuary, of an Egyptian temple. Already before Tat and Ammon have arrived, Hermes discloses to Asclepius a fundamental hermetic idea: 'All things are part of the One, or the One is all things' (*omnia unius esse aut unum esse omnia*). In the following discussion about the structure of the universe, matter and soul, gods and demons, the position of the human being receives special attention (ch. 6-12). The section begins with what might be the most renowned statement of the *Asclepius*, which had such a great influence on the Renaissance concept of man (→ Pico della Mirandola): 'Man is a great wonder, a living being to be worshipped and honoured' (*magnum miraculum est homo, animal adorandum et honorandum*). A special human faculty, which according to the *Asclepius* shows the greatness of man, is his power to create the earthly gods by conjuring heavenly powers into their statues (37, 38, cf. 24). This view has aroused the interest, and the opposition as well, of many later writers; it shows beyond doubt that the philosophical hermetists did not shun theurgical practices.

e. Coptic Hermetic Texts

The Nag Hammadi Library presented the scholarly world with three Coptic Hermetic texts and a scribal note about other hermetic texts in his possession. The Coptic translations of two important parts of the *Asclepius*, namely chapters 21-29 (NHC VI, 65,15-78, 43; with the "Hermetic Apocalypse"), and chapter 41 (NHC VI, 63, 33-65, 7; the "Prayer of Thanksgiving") have already been discussed in the preceding section. Between these two texts there is a note (NHC VI, 65,8-14) in which the scribe directly addresses those who had commissioned him, declaring that he has only copied 'this one discourse' of the very great number of treatises that he had at his disposal, because he did not know whether his addressees already had them in their possession. It is improbable that this note was taken over from the Greek manuscript upon which the translator based his translation, but it remains undecided whether 'this one discourse' refers to the preceding hermetic text or to the subsequent translation of *Asclepius* 21-29. In any case, it shows that in the 4th century there existed much more Coptic translations of hermetic texts than the three that are extant in NHC VI. The discovery of the first of these three texts, preserved in NHC VI, 52-63, was a surprise, for it was not only completely unknown previously, but it also proved to be of great importance. It has lost its original title, but on the basis of its contents it is usually called the *Discourse on the Eighth and the Ninth (Sphere)* or *On the Ogdoad and the Ennead*. Interspersed with didactic explanations, it describes the mystical experience of a pupil who is initiated into the hermetic mystery. The first part of the treatise explains that the elevation of the pupil's mind into the eighth and the ninth sphere is not only a personal experience but at the same time the adoption into the brotherhood of the hermetic community, which makes him a son of Hermes Trismegistus. The initiate's future brothers, all sons of Hermes Trismegistus, join his prayers during the initiation (VI, 52, 1-54, 22). The vision of the eighth and the ninth spheres concludes a way of spiritual progress, which comprised a study of hermetic books (VI, 54, 6-32) and a pious life. This was apparently compared to a journey through the seven planetary spheres, VI, 56, 27-32: 'We have already advanced to the seventh sphere (the Hebdomad), since we are pious and walk in your law and always fulfil your will'. After a prayer to the supreme God, 'to whom one speaks in silence' (VI, 56, 11-12), Hermes and his pupil embrace each other (VI, 57, 26-27) and then experience the coming down of the divine Light-power. In this experi-

ence, the initiator, Hermes, somehow becomes identical with the supreme Mind that reveals itself, and the initiate attains an ecstatic state of mind: 'I see myself. I want to speak. Fear restrains me. . . . I see a fountain bubbling with life! . . . I have seen!' (VI, 58, 8-14). Language is of no use any more; to sing a hymn in silence is the only way to adore the divine Mind [→ Hymns and Prayers], just like the souls and the angels do in the Ogdoad (VI, 58, 17-21; 59, 28-32). A discussion of the importance of singing spiritual hymns in silence, with some examples of this form of mystic prayer, concludes the description of the initiation proper (VI, 58, 17-61, 17). Moreover, the initiate is exhorted to keep silence about his experience: 'Do not speak about the vision from now on. It is proper to sing a hymn to the Father until the day to quit the body' (VI, 60, 3-5). It is of interest to note that the author speaks about prayer in words that betray a distinct biblical influence. In VI, 55, 10-14, Hermes says that it is fitting 'to pray to God with all our mind and all our heart and our soul', and in 57, 18-23, he calls the hermetic prayers spiritual sacrifices, 'which we send to you with all our heart and our soul and all our strength'. It will be clear that this phraseology is strongly coloured by one of the basic texts of Judaism, Deuteronomy 6:5: 'You must love the Lord your God with all your heart and all your soul and all your strength' (cf. Mark 12:29 parr.).

One of the most interesting features of *The Ogdoad and the Ennead* is its use of magical and astrological elements. The supreme God is addressed by the same enumeration of the seven vowels that is often used in magical papyri to express the deity's hidden name. In VI, 56, 17-22, the series of vowels is preceded and followed by the magical names Zōxathazō and Zōzazōth. Each vowel is followed by a series of omegas (with scribal mistakes after the vowels i and ō): 'Zōxathazō. a ōō, ee ōōō, ēēē ōōōō, iiii ōōōōō, ooooo ōōōōōō, uuuuu ōōōōōōō, ōōōōōōō ōōōōōōōō. Zōzazōth'. A similar but not identical series is found in the prayer at VI, 61, 8-15 (with three scribal mistakes): 'I praise you. I call your name that is hidden within me: a ō, ee ōō, ēēē ōōō, iiii ōōōō, ooooo ōōōōō, uuuuu ōōōōōō, ōōōōōōō ōōōōōōō'. Immediately after this prayer, Hermes instructs the initiate to write down what had happened on turquoise steles in hieroglyphic characters and to place them in his sanctuary at Diospolis (most probably Diospolis Magna, Thebes, which possessed a temple of Thot). The steles should be guarded by the sun and eight guardians, those on the right being male and frog-faced, those on the left female and cat-faced. They have to be placed there at an astrologically important moment, when the sun is in the first half of the day and the planet Mercury (Hermes) is in the Sign of the Virgin and has passed 15 degrees, i.e. when the influence of Hermes' planet is most strongly felt (VI, 61, 18-62, 20; Mahé [1978] I, 129-130). The treatise ends with an oath to be sworn by everyone who reads the book: he has to swear by the four elements, the seven rulers of being and their creating spirit, and 'the unbegotten God and the self-begotten one and him who has been begotten'. Who keeps this oath will be reconciled with God and the deities mentioned, but who violates it will experience their wrath (VI, 22-63, 30). All this shows again that hermetic authors who described highly spiritual experiences felt no hesitation to make use of magical and astrological ideas and practices: it all belonged to their world.

F. THE ARMENIAN DEFINITIONS

The Coptic *Discourse on the Eighth and the Ninth Sphere* and the Armenian *Definitions of Hermes Trismegistus to Asclepius* are the most important hermetic texts discovered in the 20th century. The Armenian translation of the original Greek text most likely dates from the second half of the 6th century. It was first edited with a Russian translation in 1956, but it was only through Mahé's magisterial edition, translation and commentary (1982, II) that its basic importance for the study of Hermetism became clear. Some Greek fragments of the *Definitions* have been discovered in the Bodleian Library, Oxford (Mahé & Paramelle, 1990-1991), which have been integrated into Mahé's English translation of the Armenian text (1999). The *Definitions* do not have the usual form of a dialogue; they are a collection of short, often aphoristic summaries of the main points of hermetic doctrine. A similar collection has been preserved in Stobaeus' *Fragm.* XI. In C.H. XIV, 1, Hermes seems to refer to such collections, when he writes to Asclepius that he will send him a summary of the most important points (*kephalaia*) he had discussed with Tat. These short sentences apparently had a mnemonic function (Stobaeus, *Fragm.* XI, 1), which explains that, with variations, they turn up through the whole of ancient hermetic literature. At the same time, they are meant to be the object of silent meditation: 'When you keep silent, you understand; when you talk, you just talk' (*Def.* 5, 2). The *Definitions* 'as a whole can be regarded as a general outline of hermetic spiritual exercises aimed at developing individual *nous* and making the disciple worthy of undergoing mystic initiation' (Mahé 1999, 103). They deal with the three great themes of hermetic thought – God,

world and man –, which can be distinguished from one another but not completely separated: 'God is within himself, the world is in God, and man is in the world' (7, 5). The *Definitions* predominantly deal with the world (2-3) and man (4-10), but the relationship of these 'images of God' to each other and, above all, to God himself is never lost sight of.

The aphoristic nature of Stobaeus' *Fragm.* XI and the *Definitions* has led Mahé to an interesting theory about the development of hermetic literature, not in a pure chronological but in a more ideal-typical sense. According to him, the earliest form of hermetic literature was a series of independent sentences expressing the basic ideas of hermetic religious philosophy, such as still found in Stobaeus' *Fragm.* XI. The next step was the grouping together of related sentences into chapters, as in the *Definitions*. In the third stage, the sentences were linked together into a coherent treatise, which might be interspersed with reflections and didactic expositions. Even in such mythological texts as the *Poimandres* (C.H. I) the hermetic maxims appear at the key points of the myth, determining both its structure and the arrangement of the mythic elements borrowed from older sources (Mahé 1982, II, 408-436). Moreover, based on the observation that the *Poimandres* reflects a considerable number of sentences of the *Definitions*, Mahé dated the original Greek version of the latter work to the 1st century A.D. Moreover, he also tried to establish a direct link with the earlier Egyptian wisdom literature (also Mahé 1999). These views have met with strong opposition from Fowden (71-72). It should be observed, however, that the development from hermetic sentence to hermetic treatise, as described by Mahé, has a distinct and undisputed parallel in Greek gnomic literature, as can be seen from an analysis of the sententious structure of Porphyry's *Letter to Marcella* and, on the Christian side, the *Teachings of Silvanus*. Though the Egyptian connection is not to be excluded completely, it seems quite certain that the literary forms and contents of the hermetic sentences and treatises are more closely related to the Greek gnomic tradition than to Egyptian wisdom literature.

4. "GENERAL" AND "DETAILED" DISCOURSES

In the hermetic literature itself, a distinction is made between "general" and "detailed" discourses. This may be no more than a literary device, reflecting the usual practice in philosophical school teaching (Festugière, *Révélation*, II, 34-40), for there are no hermetic treatises that explicitly designate themselves as general or detailed discourses. Hermes (C.H. X, 1 and 7;

Stobaeus, *Fragm.* III, 1; Vienna, *Fragm.* B, 6; *Ogdoad and Ennead*, NHC VI, 63, 2) or his pupils (*C.H.* XIII, 1; Stobaeus, *Fragm.* VI, 1) often refer to the "General Discourses" (*genikoi logoi*), which Hermes had delivered previously. C.H. X presents itself as a summary of the general lectures Hermes had given to Tat the preceding day. The second category of hermetic discourses is mentioned by Cyril of Alexandria (*Contra Julianum*, I, 46; NF IV, 135/6, Fragm. 30), who quotes a teaching of Hermes from 'the first of the Detailed Discourses (*diexodikoi logoi*) to Tat'. The word *exodikos*, a shorter form of *diexodikos* and also meaning "detailed", most probably appears in *Asclepius* 1, when Hermes says that he has written many *physica* and *exotica* for his son Tat. Here the word *physica* seems to refer to the technical Hermetica and the word *exotica* to the "detailed discourses". An interesting passage of the Coptic *Discourse on the Ogdoad and the Ennead*, mentions both kinds of hermetic instruction, NHC VI, 62, 33-63, 8: 'And he who will not first be begotten by God should stick to the general (*genikos*) and detailed (*exōdiakos*, corruption of *exodikos*) discourses. He will not be able to read what has been written in this book, although his conscience is pure within him . . . Rather by stages he advances and enters into the way of immortality'. Most of the preserved hermetic treatises can be assigned to these two types of hermetic instruction, though it is often impossible to distinguish them clearly. They suggest that the aspirant initiate was first instructed on an elementary level and then in a more detailed and fundamental manner, as succeeding stages on the way to initiation. The initiation itself, the direct vision of God, is a personal experience, which is not described but only hinted at in the hermetic oral or written instruction. This idea is clearly expressed in the opening sentence of C.H. XIII: 'In the general lectures, O Father, you spoke in riddles and not openly about the divine nature. You have not revealed anything, saying that nobody can be saved before rebirth'. The only works that describe the initiation proper, though interspersed with didactic expositions, are C.H. XIII and the *Discourse on the Ogdoad and the Ennead*, but the quotation of the latter work, cited above, shows that the real meaning of these works can only be understood if one has been 'begotten by God', i.e. after the initiation.

5. DATE AND PLACE OF ORIGIN OF THE PHILOSOPHICAL HERMETICA

Since Hermes was thought to have lived in remote Egyptian antiquity, his works were also generally dated to a time that long preceded Graeco-Roman civilization. The hermetic writings sometimes explicitly claimed to have been translated from the Egyptian (see about C.H. XVI above), but implicitly this was suggested by all of them. The idea of the extreme old age of the hermetic literature held the field until the beginning of the 17th century. That Luther had already declared the *Asclepius* a fraud in the thirties of the preceding century remained widely unnoticed. In his *Disputations* (ed. Hermelink, Weimarer Ausgabe, 39, 1, 179-180), he argues that the Greek philosophers did not know anything about God the Creator and man made of the dust of earth. He refers briefly to Augustine, who in his *Confessiones* VII, 13-14, had said that in the books of the Platonists he had found the same ideas about the Word of God that are also to be found in the first chapter of the Gospel of John, with one exception: that the Word became flesh. Then Luther continues: 'But Hermegistus (*sic*) composed that book of Plato and stole everything from the Gospel of John. That book then came into the hands of Augustine and by its persuasive force he was deceived'. The suggestion is that Augustine's Platonists did not teach similar ideas as John in his Gospel, but that they were dependent on it. It seems that Luther with 'that book of Plato' meant the *Asclepius*, which was extensively discussed by Augustine in his *City of God*, and not only in a negative sense. But the final blow to the idea that the Hermetica were authentic writings of the Egyptian sage Hermes Trismegistus came from Isaac Casaubon (1559-1614). He was not the first to put the authenticity of the Hermetica, or at least of some parts of it, in doubt (Purnell; Mulsow), but his criticism proved to be decisive, even in the eyes of those who adhered, and continued to adhere, to the hermetic world view (Grafton). In 1614 Casaubon published his *De rebus sacris et ecclesiasticis exercitationes XVI*, in which he attacked Cardinal Cesare Baronio's *Annales ecclesiastici* (12 vols., 1588-1607). He shared with Baronio the common view that Hermes was a historical person, who had lived in Egypt before Moses and had invented the art of writing and all kinds of sciences. What provoked his reaction was Baronio's passing remark that there had been pre-Christian pagan prophets, such as Hermes Trismegistus, Hydaspes and the Sibyls, who had predicted the coming of Christ. Against this view Casaubon's main arguments were: 1) that the book *Poemander*, i.e. what we now call the C.H., was completely unknown to pre-Christian authors, which leaves little doubt about its peudepigraphic character, 2) that it could not have been written by Hermes, because it is inconceivable that God had already revealed the coming of Christ to a pagan before the Law was given to Moses, 3) that the hermetic writings 'do not contain the Egyptian doctrines of Mercurius, but ideas which are partly Greek, taken from the books of Plato and the Platonists and often with the same words, partly Christian, drawn from the Sacred Scriptures'. In his discussion of these groups of texts, Casaubon showed his great philological skill and vast knowledge. He pointed out that the style and vocabulary of the Hermetica are typical for the late Greek and Christian period, without any indication that they had been translated from the Egyptian. He found a strong Christian influence especially in the treatises I, IV and XIII of the C.H. Casaubon's criticism, especially his philological arguments, convinced all serious philologists and historians. After him, it became an established fact of classical scholarship that the Hermetic writings date from the first centuries of our era and betray a strong influence of later Platonism and Stoicism. The great hermetic studies published by Scott and Festugière in the 20th century, with their wealth of philosophical parallels, marked the culmination *and* the completion of the philological tradition that was inaugurated by Casaubon. These scholars, however, did not share his argument about the Christian inspiration of at least some of the hermetic writings, though this idea has been revived in more recent scholarship, without much success (Büchli). There is no need to doubt that the seemingly Christian elements were current in the spiritual milieu the Hermetica came from, whereas the obvious biblical expressions and ideas are due to a direct or indirect Jewish influence. After Scott and Festugière, scholars have become more sensitive to the possible and actual presence of original Egyptian elements in the Hermetica (Mahé, Fowden). There is a general scholarly consensus that the treatises that abound in biblical expressions and ideas, such as C.H. I and VII, belong to the oldest layers of Hermetic literature, probably dating from the first or the beginning of the 2nd century. There are also good reasons to date the *Asclepius* to the 3rd century, but for the bulk of the hermetic writings it is virtually impossible to go any further than to ascribe them to the first three centuries of our era.

The spiritual climate that pervades the Hermetica points to Alexandria in Egypt as the place of origin of the hermetic world-view. For that reason it is mostly assumed that the hermetic treatises were written in Egypt too. For some of them, for instance the *Poimandres* and the *Discourse on the Ogdoad and the Ennead*, an Alexandrian origin is indeed very likely, but it is quite possible that elsewhere in the Roman world adepts of the "way of Hermes" set themselves down to compose hermetic treatises as well. There is no reason to assume that the man in Athens, who according to Cyril of Alexandria composed a work called *Hermaika* in 15 books, was an exception.

Greek and Latin texts: A.D. Nock & A.-J. Festugière (eds.), *[Hermès Trismégiste:] Corpus Hermeticum*, 4 vols., Paris: Les Belles Lettres, 1946-1954 and later reprints (I. C.H. I-XII, ed. Nock, Fr. transl. Festugière [1946]; II. C.H. XIII-XVIII, *Asclepius*, ed. Nock, Fr. transl. Festugière [1946]; III. *Fragm. Stob.* I-XXII, ed. and Fr. transl. Festugière [1954]; IV. *Fragm. Stob.* XXIII-XXIX, ed. and Fr. transl. Festugière, *Fragments divers*, ed. Nock, Fr. transl. Festugière [1954]) ♦ W. Scott (ed.), *Hermetica: The Ancient Greek and Latin Writings which contain Religious or Philosophic Teachings Ascribed to Hermes Trismegistus*, 4 vols., I: *Texts and Translation*, II: *Notes on the Corpus Hermeticum*, III: *Notes on the Latin Asclepius and the Hermetic Excerpts of Stobaeus*, IV: *Testimonia*, London: Dawsons, 1924-1936 ♦ other English translations: B.P. Copenhaver, *Hermetica: The Greek Corpus Hermeticum and the Latin Asclepius in a New English Translation, with Notes and Introduction*, Cambridge: Cambridge University Press, 1992 ♦ C. Salaman *et alii*, *The Way of Hermes*, London: Duckworth, 1999, 7-98 (*The Corpus Hermeticum*) ♦ German translation: J. Holzhausen & C. Colpe, *Corpus Hermeticum deutsch: Übersetzung, Darstellung, Kommentierung*, 3 vols., Stuttgart-Bad Canstatt: Frommann-Holzboog, 1997 ♦ J.-P. Mahé, "Fragments hermétiques dans les papyri Vindobonenses graecae 29456 r° et 29828 r°", in: E. Lucchesi & H.D. Saffrey (eds.), *Mémorial André-Jean Festugière: Antiquité païenne et chrétienne* (Cahiers d'Orientalisme, X), Geneva: Patrick Cramer, 1984, 51-64 ♦ J. Paramelle & J.-P. Mahé, "Extraits hermétiques inédits dans un manuscrit d'Oxford", *Revue des Études Grecques* 104 (1991), 109-139 ♦ eidem, "Nouveaux parallèles grecs aux *Définitions hermétiques arméniennes*", *Revue des Études Arméniennes* 22 (1990-1991, 115-134). Concordance: L. Delatte, S. Govaerts & J. Denooz, *Index du Corpus Hermeticum*, Rome: Ateneo e Bizzarri, 1977.
Coptic and Armenian texts: Edition of NHC VI, 6, 7 and 8 (with introduction and Engl. transl.) by P.A. Dirkse, D.M. Parrott *et alii* (eds.), in: D.M. Parrott (ed.), *Nag Hammadi Codices V, 2-5 and VI, with Papyrus Berolinensis 8502, 1 and 4* (NHS XI), Leiden: Brill, 1979, 341-451 ♦ also by J.P. Mahé (ed., with Fr. transl. and extensive studies), *Hermès en Haute-Égypte* (Bibliothèque Copte de Nag Hammadi, Section "Textes", 3 and 7), 2 vols. (I: edition of *NHC* VI, 6 and 7; II: edition of NHC VI, 8, and the Armenian Hermetic *Definitions*), Quebec: Les Presses de l'Université Laval, 1978 and 1982 ♦ Ital. transl., with extensive introductions and notes, by A. Camplani, *Scritti ermetici in copto*, Brescia: Paideia, 2000 ♦ Engl. transl. of the *Definitions* by J.P. Mahé in C. Salamani *et alii*, *The Way of Hermes*, London: Duckworth, 1999, 99-124 (*The Definitions of Hermes Trismegistus to Asclepius*).

Lit.: R. van den Broek [1], "The Hermetic Apocalypse and other Greek Predictions of the End of Religion", in: R. van den Broek & C. van Heertum (eds.), *From Poimandres to Jacob Böhme: Gnosis, Hermetism and the Christian Tradition*, Amsterdam: In de Pelikaan, 2000, 97-113 ◆ idem [2], "Hermes and Christ: Pagan Witnesses to the Truth of Christianity", in: Van den Broek & Van Heertum, 115-144 ◆ J. Büchli, *Der Poimandres: Ein paganisiertes Evangelium* (Wissenschaftliche Untersuchungen zum NT, 2. Reihe, 27), Tübingen: Mohr, 1987 ◆ C.H. Dodd, *The Bible and the* Greeks, Hodder & Stoughton: London 1935 (repr. 1954) ◆ A.J. Festugière, *La révélation d'Hermès Trismégiste*, 4 vols., Paris: Gabalda, 1944-1954 and later reprints (I: *L'Astrologie et les sciences occultes* [1944], II: *Le dieu cosmique* [1949], III: *Les doctrines de l'âme* [1953], IV: *Le dieu inconnu et la gnose* [1954]) ◆ idem, *Hermétisme et mystique païenne*, Paris: Aubier-Montaigne, 1967 ◆ G. Fowden, *The Egyptian Hermes: A Historical Approach to the Late Pagan Mind*, Princeton: Princeton University Press, 1993 (First Princeton Paperback printing, with corrections and a new preface, of the edition Cambridge: Cambridge University Press, 1986) ◆ S. Gentile & C. Gilly (eds), *Marsilio Ficino e il ritorno di Ermete Trismegisto – Marsilo Ficino and the Return of Hermes Trismegistus*, Florence: Centro Di, 1999 ◆ G. Gilly & C. van Heertum (eds.), *Magia, alchimia, scienza dal '400 al '700 – Magic, Alchemy and Science 15th-18th Centuries*, 2 vols., Florence: Centro Di, 2002 ◆ A. Grafton, "Protestant versus Prophet: Isaac Casaubon on Hermes Trismegistus", *Journal of the Warburg and Courtauld Institutes* 46 (1983), 78-93 ◆ W.C. Grese, *Corpus Hermeticum XIII and Early Christian Literature* (Studia ad Corpus Hellenisticum Novi Testamenti, vol. 5), Leiden: Brill, 1979 ◆ Th. Hofmeier, "Philology versus Imagination: Isaac Casaubon and the Myth of Hermes Trismegistus", in: Gilly & Van Heertum, *Magia*, I, 568-572 ◆ V. Hunink, "Apuleius and the 'Asclepius'", *Vigiliae Christianae* 50 (1996), 288-308 ◆ P. Kingsley, "Poimandres: 'The Etymology of the Name and the Origins of the Hermetica'", in Van den Broek & Van Heertum (see above), 41-76 (slightly revised version of the article published in the *Journal of the Warburg and Courtauld Institutes* 56 (1993), 1-24 ◆ J.P. Mahé, "Preliminary Remarks on the Demotic *Book of Thot* and the Greek *Hermetica*", *Vigiliae Christianae* 50 (1996), 353-363 ◆ Martin Mulsow (ed.), *Das Ende des Hermetismus: Historische Kritik und neue Naturphilosophie in der Spätrenaissance. Dokumentation und Analyse der Debatte um die Datierung der hermetischen Schriften von Genebrard bis Casaubon (1567-1614)*, Tübingen: J.C.B. Mohr (Paul Siebeck) 2002 ◆ B.A. Pearson, "Jewish Elements in Corpus Hermeticum I (Poimandres)", in: R. van den Broek & M.J. Vermaseren (eds.), *Studies in Gnosticism and Hellenistic Religions Presented to Gilles Quispel on the Occasion of his 65th Birthday* (EPRO 91), Leiden: Brill, 1981, 336-348 ◆ M. Philonenko, "Le *Poimandres* et la liturgie juive", in: F. Dunand & P. Lévêque (eds.), *Les syncrétismes dans les religions de l'Antiquité*, Leiden: E.J. Brill, 1975, 204-211 ◆ idem, "Une utilisation du Shema dans le *Poimandres*",

Revue d'histoire et de philosophie religieuses, (1979), 369-372 ◆ F. Purnell Jr., "Francesco Patrizi and the Critics of Hermes Trismegistus", *Journal of Medieval and Renaissance Studies* 6 (1976), 155-178 ◆ R. Reitzenstein, *Poimandres: Studien zur griechisch-ägyptischen und frühchristlichen Literatur*, Leipzig: Teubner 1904 (reprinted Darmstadt: Wissenschaftliche Buchgesellschaft, 1966) ◆ K.W. Tröger, *Mysterienglaube und Gnosis in Corpus Hermeticum XIII* (Texte und Untersuchungen zur Geschichte der altchristlichen Literatur, vol. 110), Berlin: Akademie Verlag, 1964 ◆ A. Wlosok, *Laktanz und die philosophische Gnosis: Untersuchungen zur Geschichte und Terminologie der gnostischen Erlösungsvorstellung* (Abhandlungen der Heidelberger Akademie de Wissenschaften, Philos.-Hist. Klasse, 1960, 2), Heidelberg: Winter, 1960.

ROELOF VAN DEN BROEK

Hermetic Literature II: Latin Middle Ages

A. PHILOSOPHICAL-RELIGIOUS HERMETISM 1. THE *ASCLEPIUS* IN LATIN PATRISTICS 2. THE *ASCLEPIUS* IN THE 12TH CENTURY 3. APOCRYPHA AND TRANSLATIONS IN 12TH AND 13TH CENTURIES 4. THE INTERPRETATION OF THE *ASCLEPIUS* FROM WILLIAM OF AUVERGNE TO NICHOLAS OF CUSA 5. THE DIFFUSION OF THE *LIBER VIGINTI QUATTUOR PHILOSOPHORUM* 6. THE *LIBER DE SEX RERUM PRINCIPIIS* IN MEDIEVAL THOUGHT

B. TECHNICAL AND OPERATIVE HERMETISM 1. ASTROLOGY, MEDICINE AND NATURAL MAGIC, DIVINATION A. TRANSLATIONS FROM THE GREEK B. TRANSLATIONS FROM THE ARABIC C. LATIN ORIGINALS 2. CEREMONIAL MAGIC 3. THE FORTUNE OF HERMETIC CEREMONIAL MAGIC IN LATIN: TRANSLATIONS AND DISPUTES

A. PHILOSOPHICAL-RELIGIOUS HERMETISM

The Hermetic literature in Latin of the Middle Ages inherited from ancient → Hermetism (known just partially from Greek and Arabic versions) ambiguities and problems which would characterize it for centuries: the unresolved differences between philosophical-religious doctrines and operational techniques (→ magic, → astrology, →

alchemy); the inner tensions of the *Asclepius*, suspended in a cultural *koiné* that combines late Platonism and Stoicism with a ceremonial theurgy of Egyptian origin; and the mythological origin of → Hermes Trismegistus (Mercurius in Latin), seen as a primal source of wisdom, who appears at times as a prophet of monotheism and at times as the founder of idolatry, a source of spiritual truths and inventor of demonic liturgies. But beyond the difficulties inherited from ancient Hermetism, the Middle Ages had to face still others in its attempt to achieve a consistent exegesis: the formation of a Hermetic tradition in the Arab world; the cross-circulation of texts in different linguistic areas (Latin, Hebrew, Arabic) with complicated transitions from one area to another; and the emergence of pseudo-epigraphs and the attribution to Hermes of works by different authors, which credit him with doctrines extraneous to his tradition. And yet the most complex problem for the historian lies in the diachronic character of medieval Hermetism: while in fact the *Asclepius* was already known and commented on in late antiquity, other works were translated only in the 12th and 13th centuries, and eventually they all merged, together with famous pseudo-epigraphs – such as the *Liber viginti quattuor philosophorum* and the *Liber de sex rerum principiis* – and disparate attestations, into an ensemble, the outlines of which are confused and undefinable.

For these reasons we consider it appropriate to describe the evolution of medieval Hermetism and the reactions it produced by following a differentiated route. Up to the 12th century we will examine the entry of the *Asclepius* into Latin culture; thereafter the works that were erroneously ascribed to Hermes and the translations of the technical-operational texts in the 12th and 13th centuries; lastly, the relationships of the *Asclepius* to Hermes' other writings in the interpretations of the great medieval masters up to → Nicholas of Cusa.

1. THE *ASCLEPIUS* IN LATIN PATRISTICS

The historical precedents, that open the way for a Christian interpretation of philosophical Hermetism and condition that interpretation for centuries to come, originate in the 4th and 5th centuries. Lactantius and Quodvultdeus, on the one hand, and → Augustine, on the other, offer two opposing paradigms of response to the *Asclepius* and to the few Hermetic fragments passed down by Christian writers (Tertullian, pseudo-Justin, Arnobius and Philastrius of Brescia). It may safely be said that the long trail of philosophical Hermetism in the Middle Ages begins with Lactantius. In his

Divinae institutiones (304-313) he cites numerous fragments, which largely derive from the original Greek of the Latin *Asclepius*, known under the title of *Logos Teleios*. Hermes Trismegistus, writes Lactantius, proclaims the majesty of the supreme and only God, whom he, like the Christians, calls Lord and Father. Unbegotten, God created the universe and rules it with eternal providence; and without a name because of His unity (names are necessary only in the multiple), He is unintelligible to the mind. Man was created *ad imaginem Dei*, and if he raises his intellect up towards a knowledge of the divine he escapes the laws of fate and the power of evil demons. The "baptism" which Lactantius thus bestows on Hermes culminates in an interpretation of the universe – the "second god" of the Hermetic triad (God, world, man) – as a prophetic proclamation of the Word made flesh. The *deus sensibilis* of the *Asclepius* becomes the God made man of the Christian revelation: first-born son of the supreme God, brimming with the greatest power, He has by His wisdom been operative in the creation of the world. And in the famous "Apocalypse" of the *Asclepius*, where Hermes describes the "aging of the world" and the approaching empire of evil, he announces the dispatching of the Son onto the earth for the sake of the world's renewal and the salvation of the righteous.

A century later, in book VIII of *De civitate Dei* (415-417), Augustine proposes to the Christian conscience a different interpretation of the *Asclepius*, which had been translated into Latin toward the end of the 4th century. After having condemned the doctrine of Apuleius – who regarded demons as necessary mediators between gods and men and did not distinguish their cult from true religion – Augustine turns the arrows of his criticism against the theurgy of the *Asclepius*. Hermes the Egyptian distinguishes between the gods created by God, who animate heaven, and the "earthly gods" created by man, that is the spirits who through hymns and incantations are induced to dwell in temple statues so as to grant prayers and work good and evil. But it is ridiculous to believe that the gods, evoked and, by unknown procedures, shut inside the simulacra built by man, have a power greater than that of man, who was created in God's image. And in the Hermetic "Apocalypse", which foretells the disappearance of religion in Egypt, Hermes bewails the future triumph of Christ and the coming to grief of demons. I do not understand, writes Augustine, by what obfuscation of the heart a sage, who said many truths concerning the only and true God, the creator of the world, could be plunged into distress by the incumbent defeat of the wicked angels. Hermes, indeed, not only confesses that the art of fashioning the earthly gods was invented by his ancestors because they lived in error and ignorance of God, but despairs in view of the future disappearance of the idolatrous rites and gives voice to the terror-stricken dismay of the demonic spirits.

It is striking how the conflicting readings of Lactantius and Augustine appear to be supported by exegetic misunderstandings (just how "innocent", we do not know) of a philological and philosophical nature. On the one hand, Augustine attributes to Hermes the confession that the cult of holy statues was born from the religious ignorance of his ancestors; on the other, Lactantius interprets the created world, the second god of the Hermetic hierarchy, as the Word made flesh. The fact remains however that, although the interpretation of the *Asclepius* would continue to produce conflicting judgments in Christian culture, from the very onset these interpretations are marked by a forced and ideological position. Two such differing interpretations of Hermetism came about, in African Christianity toward the end of antiquity, because of opposing needs. Lactantius, an illustrious pagan rhetorician prior to his conversion, wanted to demonstrate the concordance of ancient wisdom with revealed truth; Augustine, a bishop and shepherd of souls, aspired to demolish the persistent forms of idolatry and superstition among the population of the faithful. If the unquestioned authority of Augustine did not prevail in Christian reflection, this did not depend on the force of his arguments, but on a literary event which originated in the preaching of Quodvultdeus, bishop of Carthage at the time of the Vandalic invasion and later exiled in 439 to Campania, by King Genseric. In his *Tractatus adversus quinque haereses* Quodvultdeus accepts the exegesis of Lactantius, simplifies it, and emphasizes the knowledge of the Son of God evident in the words of a pagan like Hermes. The Greek title *Logos teleios* is translated as *Verbum perfectum*, the divine Word, and Hermes' comments on the ineffable perfection of the Son and the immense joy of the Father are related to the Gospel of St. John and the Old Testament *Proverbs*. Thus refuting the unbelieving pagan, Quodvultdeus exclaims: 'I will not expound my authors to you, Mercurius is yours . . . Heed him, let him convince and vanquish you so that in being defeated you may yield to him and so believe me'. The *Tractatus* perhaps would never have had a decisive role in the encounter of Christian theology with Hermetic thought if his homilies had not come to be included in the African collections attributed to Augustine and placed under the high authority

of his name. So it happened that the vehement invective of the *De civitate Dei* against Hermes' demonic simulacra was countered and neutralized by the enthusiastic plea for a concordance between Hermetism and Christianity found in the *Tractatus* attributed to Augustine.

2. THE *ASCLEPIUS* IN THE 12TH CENTURY

In the many centuries that pass between the dissolution of the Roman Empire and the Renaissance of the 12th century, Hermetism seems to disappear from the scene of Latin culture. Its rare occurrences are limited to the erudite citations of Fulgentius in the 5th-6th century, a new translation of Greek fragments (mentioned by Lactantius) by Sedulius Scot in the 9th century, and lastly, in the 11th century, the criticisms by the poet Warnerius of Basel in his *Paraclitus* and above all by Adalbold of Utrecht in his commentary on Boethius: Hermes and Plato, devoid of faith and too ingrained in philosophical thinking, did not know about the generation of Wisdom which governs the universe.

It is only in the 12th century that we witness a revival of the *Asclepius*, in the wake of pseudo-Augustine's (Quodvultdeus') concordizing interpretation, and as a result of direct reading of the Hermetic dialogue. With respect to the former aspect, some authors see in the *Tractatus adversus quinque haereses* the authoritative declaration of an agreement between the *Logos Tileos* (*Logos Teleios*) and the Christian revelation of the Son: this is the case with Abelard, John of Salisbury and Robert of Melun, Alan of Lille and the *Liber Alcidi de immortalitate animae*. Abelard in particular, engaged in demonstrating the natural revelation of the trinitarian dogma, in many of his writings examines the words of the *Tractatus* and with linguistic-semantic sapience absolves Hermes regarding his lexical imprecisions: even the Scriptures, the Fathers and Boethius, he writes, sometimes spoke improperly of the eternal generation of the Word.

But it is the authors who themselves read the codices of the *Asclepius* who supply the first responses of medieval thought to the Hermetic text. Theodoric of Chartres, perhaps the subtlest thinker of the 12th century, derives from it the theme of the spirit which governs the universe (identified with the Platonic *anima mundi* and with the Holy Ghost of the Christians), the concept of destiny as causality within created order, and the hope of deification. Still more profound is the dialectical relationship he establishes between the Hermetic idea of an ineffable God and the doctrine of *unus-omnia*, between the solitary transcendence of God and His ordering presence in creation. Bernardus Silvester in his *Cosmographia* (a philosophical poem in prose and verse, which describes by means of imaginative allegories the birth of the universe and the formation of man) peoples the astral scenario of the cosmogonic myth with the *dei intelligibiles* of the *Asclepius* (Imarmene, Pantomorphos, Usiarchi). The Hermetic glorification of man, *magnum miraculum*, composed of eternal and mortal substance and placed at the center of the world to worship God and govern the earth, inspires Bernard to a bold and unusual vision of man: dweller of the upper and the lower regions, god and earth together, man is destined to love the gods and to perfect creation, to learn the secret reasons of things, and to dominate the universe as sovereign and pontifex. And with a sensitivity akin to the *Asclepius* but altogether rare in medieval consciousness, Bernard places the natural and joyous fecundity of the sexes in the earthly regality of man. Subsequently, in Alan of Lille we find a frequent use of and intimate adhesion to Hermetic theology and cosmology. In his *Summa Quoniam homines* and *Contra haereticos* Alan appeals to the Egyptian sage, mentioned among the great philosophers of the past, with respect to numerous questions: the unity of God, His omnipotent, incomprehensible and ineffable nature, the rejection of Manichaean doctrines, the denial of eternal void, the creation of man, and the immortality of the soul. But his exegesis becomes boldest and most contentious when he ascribes to the *Asclepius* (23: 'god created the eternal gods') a prophetic awareness of the trinitarian dogma: "God" designates the Father; "the eternal gods", the Son and the Holy Ghost. As Abelard had already observed elsewhere, even in the book of *Ecclesiastices* the word "create" is synonymous with "beget". In this interpretation we encounter the attempt, common in the 12th century, to perceive in the pagan authors traces of revealed truth, in line with the unequivocal message of "Augustine" in the *Tractatus adversus quinque haereses.*

An identical perspective guides the *Glosae super Trismegistum*, a lengthy commentary on the *Asclepius* (which unfortunately has survived only in part) composed around the turn of the 13th century. Considering its style, language, topics and doctrinal conclusions, the work can be attributed, if not to Alan of Lille himself, then to one of his disciples or to a *magister* of his circle. The commentary, which in the surviving manuscript treats the first four chapters, must have been quite long. The picture of Mercurius in the prologue defines the exegetic project: 'Mercurius precedes all the pagan philosophers. We know that he wrote many

volumes on the supreme creator of things, and since more than the others he reflected on the mysteries of the heavenly realities, not only was he very honored in life by the philosophers, but even after his death it is said that they honored him with a divine cult. Of his published volumes on the heavenly realities, one, as Augustine testifies, is entitled *Logos Tileos*: in this, after having surpassed all in his other volumes, he surpassed even himself, and in his speculations on the Father and the Son seems to come close to our theology. There is also another of his works, now in our possession, which is entitled Trismegistus or Mercurius'. Describing the text according to the traditional model of the *accessus*, the author illustrates its aim, subject and the reason why he wrote it. Its aim is to treat the three main causes of the world – God, the archetypal world and primordial matter – by demonstrating the harmony of the world and the relationship between creator and creature. The subject is the philosophy of nature and mathematics; but when Hermes expounds his doctrine on created spirits and the uncreated Spirit, he does not abandon the mysteries of theology. He wrote it in order to counter the materialist concepts of his time (eternity of the world, plurality of first principles, fortuitousness of reality) with the affirmation of a single God, the creator of the universe, who in His potency, wisdom and goodness brings all things into being, orders them and preserves them with His love. Therefore, merged together in the prologue and developed in a lengthy commentary are the central motifs which in the 12th century determine the fortune of Hermes, regarded as the pagan perhaps closest to Biblical revelation. And like Alan of Lille, the *Glosae* draws a distinction between *Logos Tileos* and the *Asclepius*: to the former it ascribes the knowledge of the Father and the Son, to the latter the doctrine of the Holy Ghost. In fact, in commenting on the passage 'genus ergo deorum ex se deorum facit species' (*Ascl.* 4), the author writes that by "species deorum" Mercurius means the three persons and by "genus deorum" the divine essence.

Toward the end of the 12th century → Daniel de Morley, in his *Liber de naturis inferiorum et superiorum*, likewise refers to the *Asclepius* on theological and philosophical themes: the hierarchy of being, the divine and human origin of man, intellect and deification, time and eternity.

3. APOCRYPHA AND TRANSLATIONS IN 12TH AND 13TH CENTURIES

The *Glosae super Trismegistum* concludes an epoch in the history of Hermetism which had commenced with the Latin Fathers and had witnessed a Renaissance in the 12th century. This intense flowering was manifested by the widespread circulation of the *Asclepius*, in the wake of Lactantius' *Divinae institutiones* and of Quodvultdeus' *Tractatus adversus quinque haereses*, supported by Abelard's criticism of language, nurtured at Chartres and Paris by the faith in reason and by a sort of "perennis theologia" which discovered the light of eternal truth in the sages of antiquity.

But already toward the end of the 12th century the overall physiognomy of Hermetism has profoundly changed: the appearance of theological and cosmological pseudo-epigraphs, attributed to the authoritative name of Trismegistus, and of translations from the Arabic and Greek, mark the appearance of another type of Hermetic literature, characterized by a wealth of operational knowledge (astrology, botany, medicine, magic, divination [→ Divinatory Arts] and alchemy). The new texts stimulate a variety of reflections, now full of admiration, now full of dismay. But with the sole exception of → William of Auvergne, the two "Hermetisms" never enter into conflict: they ignore one another or take separate paths. The research that would make possible a thorough diachronic reconstruction of Hermetism still needs to be done. We can, however, follow a simpler route: trace the history of "philosophical" Hermeticism as represented by its main texts, identify connections, and mention the Hermetism of an "operational" content only where necessary, while treating the latter separately elsewhere. Let us first sketch a general picture of the new documents attributed to the Egyptian sage.

(a) The *Liber viginti quattuor philosophorum* (Book of the Twenty-four Philosophers). This new writing reinforces the myth of a Hermes inwardly inspired by God or instructed by His prophets; in many codices it is attributed to Hermes Trismegistus. As the prologue explains, the book contains a summary of definitions of God, as formulated by twenty-four sages who meet in a holy convocation. Their maxims are accompanied by brief commentaries which seem to belong to the original redaction; some manuscripts, dating perhaps from the beginning of the 14th century, add a second and more extensive commentary, while others present only the maxims. The traditional line of interpretation, from C. Baeumker to M.-T. d'Alverny, saw in the text the work of a Neoplatonic Christian of the second half of the 12th century, who combined themes of late Platonism with doctrinal elements developed by the school of Chartres and by Gilbert Porreta. Recently, however, F. Hudry has suggested

a different reconstruction, which dates the work's speculative content back to the 3th century; it is seen as having appeared in the wake of Aristotelian theology and belonging to the history of the philosophical schools of Harran and Alexandria, its philosophical perspective being characterized by the "rationalistic" pretence of knowing the divine essence. However, the fine and well-documented edition by F. Hudry itself, offering a full and coherent text, nevertheless tends – through its structural, conceptual and lexical analysis of the dicta and the first commentary – to confirm the earlier hypothesis.

The structure of the work reveals strong analogies with the writings which, in the second half of the 12th century, introduced into theology the axiomatic method, which expressed a theological concept formally based upon the enunciation of intuitive truths; these truths were accepted on the basis of their evidence and exposed in an argumental form. In the first place the work repeatedly expounds – using "rational" language in the maxims and "theological" terminology in the commentary – the Christian formulation of the trinitarian dogma. If, in fact, in its definitions the life of God is expressed by triads (for example: mind-word-connection, principle-process-end, power-being-goodness, potency-wisdom-will, unity-truth-goodness) which assign common attributes to the whole divine nature and could have been intuited even by the "philosophers", the commentary resorts openly to the traditional "theological" lexicon: the dynamism of the Divine Being constitutes itself eternally in the relationship between the Progenitor, the Begotten, and the Spirit, and there was also an explicit affirmation of equal dignity among the three Persons. The hypothesis of a Christian origin gains probability by still other elements: references to the doctrine of creation *ex nihilo*, allusions to Scripture and to the dogmatic tradition, and near-verbatim quotations of writers from late antiquity and the Middle Ages. The basic theses bear the tangible mark of Christian → Neoplatonism according to a tradition which goes from Augustine to Boethius, and from → Pseudo-Dionysius Areopagita to → John Scottus Eriugena: see e.g. the themes of divine infinity, the identity of one and being, God as thought of Himself, the circularity of trinitarian motion, eternal processions and creative processions, the idea of a continuous creation, the illumination of ideal forms, negative theology, and the *vera ignorantia*. If then we consider that certain triads of the maxims are attested only from the 12th century, that the first textual quotations appear in

Alan of Lille in the years 1165-1180, and that throughout this period the axiomatic method takes shape in theology, we are allowed to conclude that the *Liber viginti quattuor philosophorum* is the work of a Christian thinker engaged in demonstrating the agreement of Neoplatonic "reason" with Biblical "revelation". The Hermetic attribution of the text, subsequent to its original composition, is certainly due to the prestige Trismegistus had gained among Christian theologians because of the *Logos Tileos* and the *Asclepius*.

(b) The *Liber de sex rerum principiis* is a pseudonymous cosmological text composed certainly after 1147, and probably before 1175. Its origin is again uncertain, but its lengthy verbatim quotations of authors such as William of Conches and Bernardus Silvester, as well as the Platonic character of its cosmology, link it with the school of Chartres. The attribution to Hermes derives mainly from the preface, which contains a mythical history known as the "Legend of the Three Hermeses", also present in different versions in other Hermetic texts. In the legend the figure of Hermes is identified with Enoch, Noah, and Mercurius Triplex, the last of whom is credited with the discovery of many occult sciences. While the legend seems to have no clear relation to the contents of the treatise, it is certain that it does not constitute a later addition: its citations of the *Virga aurea*, *Liber longitudinis et latitudinis*, *Liber electionis*, and *Liber Ezich*, which are unique to this version, are also cited periodically within the body of the treatise, as if the author were trying to reestablish his connection with the history behind the legend itself.

In our exposition we follow the clear in-depth analysis and conclusions of Mark Delp. The text begins with a metaphysical exposition of the three most important principles of things: Cause, Reason, and Nature. In subsequent chapters it develops a systematic cosmology based on the three other derivative principles: World, Mechanism of World, and Time. Although Hermes describes the metaphysical principles of the cosmos in terms of an emanative generation, Reason being produced by Cause, and Nature being produced from both – the trinitarian character of their relations constituting the only hint of the text's "Christianity" –, he does not explain the genesis of the cosmos but, rather, describes the perpetual principles of its motions and forms. The most important element in the systematic cosmology, and the one that has attracted most scholarly attention, is quality. Nature itself, emerging from Cause and Reason, is said to 'mutably obtain successive general and specific qualities'. The general quality of nature is described as the form of heaven from which earthly phenomena receive their dynamic elemental characters, whereas the specific quality is called the operational force which constitutes the particular qualitative form and motion of things here below. Thus, considered as the universally active power in the stars and planets, the quality of nature is that of "crafter", and considered as the immanent life principle of things it is "operational". The resulting cosmic vision of the text is of a perpetual, dynamic flow of qualities from things above to things below, the whole deriving its being and ordered motion from the law of the stars, which is Reason itself. Although Nature is clearly the most important principle of things in terms of the concrete operations of the cosmos, the metaphysical principles Cause and Reason are integral to the overall system as simultaneously transcendent and immanent powers granting existence, order and motion to the world as a whole. Combining Platonic and Stoic elements, Reason is at once the transcendent Divine Mind of the cosmos, the immanent source of the "same" and "different" motions of the stars and planets respectively, as well as the subtle material spirit penetrating all things. Furthermore, by incorporating the immanent operations of Reason into the descriptions of all the lower principles of things, and by conceiving of every existing form as a variation upon the "vigor" of Nature, itself an emanation from divine Cause and Reason, Hermes effectively envisions all things as essentially qualifications of divinity.

In order to address the question of this text's place in the greater Hermetic tradition, scholars must look at the Legend of the Three Hermeses in the preface. Considered together with the author's systematic omission of any direct reference to Christian doctrine, his extensive quotations from Arab and Jewish astrologers and Firmicus Maternus, and his focus upon the occult operations of nature in its celestial and earthly forms, the Legend of the Three Hermeses can be seen to set the tone for a scientific/occult work appealing to a perennial truth comparable to what is found in the books listed in the legend as composed by Hermes himself. This presentation of the legend in the preface gives the impression of an author perceiving himself as belonging to a tradition at once more ancient and more authoritative than the one into which he has been born. The name of Hermes becomes at once a sign of separation from the theological and political structures of the time, and a sign of union with a secret and more ancient society of philosophers.

(c) A brief Hermetic fragment is quoted in *De septem septenis*, a work attributed to John of Salisbury. Other philosophical fragments of uncertain origin are present in the *Liber de naturis inferiorum et superiorum* of Daniel of Morley, who attributes them to "Magnus Hermes" or "Magnus Mercurius", author of a *Liber eternorum* and ancestor of Hermes Trismegistus: the former affirms the unity, eternity and immutability of the Principle in itself, as source of universal creation, while the latter expresses a contrast between divine eternity and the temporal transience of the world.

4. THE INTERPRETATION OF THE *ASCLEPIUS* FROM WILLIAM OF AUVERGNE TO NICHOLAS OF CUSA

At the start of the 13th century, then, there emerges a much more complex picture of philosophical and religious Hermetism. To the *Asclepius* – read from the perspective indicated by Lactantius and Quodvultdeus – were added two new texts composed in Christian environments: the *Liber viginti quattuor philosophorum*, rooted in Catholic dogma and in the Neoplatonic tradition, and only later attributed to Hermes, and the *Liber de sex rerum principiis*, a systematic work on divine and natural causality, which establishes a concord between the Platonic tradition and Arab sources. Nor must it be forgotten – even if it was ignored in mediaeval discussions of Hermetism – that toward the middle of the century, at the court of Alphonse X the Wise, there was made a translation into Castilian, under the title *Bocados de Oro*, of the *Mokhtār el Hikam* (Selected Thoughts) written in 1050 by the Arab Emir, physician and philosopher, Abu'l Wefa Mubeschschir ben Fatik. The work includes the moral and spiritual maxims of twenty-two sages and ends with an anthology of other sayings; the second and third chapters are dedicated to Hermes and Tac (Thot). In the last decades of the century the Castilian version was translated into Latin, perhaps by Giovanni da Procida, under the title *Liber philosophorum moralium antiquorum* (in turn translated into French as *Livre des philosophes*, by Guillaume de Tignonville toward the end of the 14th century, and from French into English by Stebyn Scrope Squyer in 1450 and by Count Ryvers in 1474-1477).

We will trace the presence of the single Hermetic texts – ancient and modern – in medieval philosophy and theology. But we have to bear in mind the complex and contradictory lineaments taken on by Hermetism after the appearance of the operative writings. Medieval scholars often considered philosophical-religious as well as operative Hermetic texts as belonging to the same tradition. The encyclopedic works will not be examined here, even though they often contain interesting references to Hermes: Henry de Bate de Malines, for example, in his *Speculum divinorum et quorumdam naturalium* (1281-1302) mentions the *Asclepius*, the *Liber viginti quattuor philosophorum* and the *Liber de sex rerum principiis*.

(a) *William of Auvergne.* In the 13th century, one of the most tormented periods of medieval history, the first theologian who confronts Hermetic thought in its new complexity is William of Auvergne, bishop of Paris (1228-1249). A very curious and well-read man, William is familiar with the texts that have flown in from Greece and Islam, and with inexhaustible energy he fights against astrological, magical and divinatory forms of knowledge. It is certainly no accident that the severest condemnation of Hermes since Augustine comes from another bishop, shepherd of souls and strict keeper of tradition. Already in his *Tractatus secundus de bono et malo*, one of his first works, William contrasts the hidden forces of nature with the prodigies of demons and wizards, and associates idolatry with the "dei facticii" of the *Asclepius*. His overall approach derives, with wider-ranging and more closely argued criticisms, from Augustine's *De civitate Dei*: Mercurius is the primary inspirer of pagan idolatry. The broad discussion undertaken in *De legibus* (1228) begins with a classification of the "sacred" images of ancient paganism. The first type includes the portraits of historical personages, that is, mere images in memory. The second consists of the religious simulacra which demons, seduced by sacrifices and honours, have adopted in order to give responses, and which men have thought could be transformed into sacred abodes of the gods by means of impious rites. The third consists of the "dei facticii": statues produced in accordance with the astral configurations, animated with a sort of divine power by the heavenly spirits or by the heavens and the stars, and worshipped by idolaters with use of fumigations, invocations and chants 'ac si veri Dii essent'. This last invention, as William goes on to confirm by several quotations, is the work of Hermes, who erroneously perceives the glory and power of God not only in images made by ceremonial magic and astrological observations, but also in the stars and their symbols. The idolatrous cults listed and described by William thus seem to have their origin in the impious theurgy described in the *Asclepius*. The religion of the stars is nevertheless traced not only to Mercurius, who defines the world as a "deus sensibilis", but also to the philosophers from

Plato to Aristotle and from Boethius to Avicenna who consider the heavens and the stars as "animalia divina" – nobler and more powerful than mortals, wise keepers and governors of human life, worthy of divine honours and religious sacrifices. William ceaselessly fires confutations against the idols of the *Asclepius* and their progeny in order to show, often taking recourse to Aristotle's philosophy, the inconsistency and falsity of Hermetic doctrine. The attack leveled against Mercurius, *philosophus et magus*, is all the stronger for its emphasis on the link between philosophical and magical Hermetism. Again in *De universo* (1231-1236), an imposing treatise on natural philosophy, William relates the religious cantos of the *Asclepius* to the "mournful chants" intoned in the consacration of a magical ring of Saturn. It is perhaps true that, for example, the peony puts demons to flight by means of its natural virtues, but there is no analogy with the demoniac use of herbs in fashioning idols, since, as he already proved in *De legibus*, the Egyptian was deceived by evil spirits. Lastly, on another page William attacks the Hermetic doctrine of "imarmene" (fate, *heimarmene*), the 'concatenated connection of causes' which seems to refer to an order of necessity that denies the freedom of the creator and of rational spirits. Certainly, scattered throughout *De universo*, *De virtutibus et vitiis* and *De anima* there are some positive references to Hermetism, but they are rare and perfunctory, and cover themes of ancient religious thought widely embraced by Christianity: the resistance of the body which diverts the soul from the sublime and intelligible good, and the shaping of the soul in God's image.

(b) *Michael Scot, Roger Bacon*. In the same period the circulation of the *Asclepius* is attested to by → Michael Scot in his *Liber introductorius* (1228-1235) and in his commentary on John of Sacrobosco's *De sphaera*. Toward the middle of the 13th century → Roger Bacon in his *Opus maius* and in his *Metaphysica*, both completed in 1267, gives proof of a careful reading of the *Asclepius*. Bacon refers to the Hermetic text – called *Liber de divinitate* or *Liber de natura divina* or *Liber de divinis* – on themes of metaphysics and theology. In his doctrine of the creation and ideal forms Hermes is associated, as previously in Theodoric of Chartres, with St. John's Gospel; the soul is immortal and man must reject the seductions of the wicked angels, who lead him to sin and vice, and thus to the sufferings of hell; after the separation from the body, the soul is subject to the supreme judgment which assigns the pious and righteous spirits to the place of beatitude; and Hermes' prayer, which con-

cludes the *Asclepius*, is the highest example of a solemn prayer also for Christians.

(c) *Thomas of York*. An author who more extensively discusses the *Asclepius* is the English Franciscan Thomas of York in the *Sapientiale*, the first metaphysical "summa" of the 13th century, perhaps composed between the years 1250-1256. The text is still unpublished, but its focus on Hermetism has been examined in a recent contribution (Porreca 2000). Thomas' attitude is characterised by a deep respect towards Hermes' pagan wisdom, even if it is often invoked – together with other authorities – regarding problems that Thomas leaves unsolved and suspended. For example, in the discussion about the soul of the world Thomas examines the doctrines of the ancient philosophers, that appear to him obscure and blundering because sometimes they identify the soul of the world with God, while elsewhere they consider it a creature: Hermes too, according to Thomas, advocates the two opposite arguments. In Thomas' opinion this happens also because of the doctrine of the principles, or causes of the world, a doctrine that Hermes follows when he states that the first principles are two (divine will and matter); Thomas thinks that Hermes sometimes contradicts this theory when he proclaims God as the sole principle of reality. Generally, the *Asclepius* is one of the most authoritative sources of the *Sapientiale*. When it comes to theology, cosmology, morality and eschatology, Hermes' wisdom converges with Christian doctrine about main issues such as the nature and the characteristics of God, the eternal ideas, providence and fate, the harmony and beauty of creation, matter and evil, the immortality of the soul and life after death. This is not an easy concordism, because the difficulties of interpretation concerning the *Aclepius* are not eluded but confronted and discussed. The Hermetic text is even invoked, in one passage, to solve a seeming obscurity in the Scriptures, where the book of *Wisdom* seems to hint at a movement in God (*Sap.* 8:1 'Attingit ergo a fine usque ad finem fortiter'); Thomas writes that it is true that the biblical text seems to contradict divine motionlessness, but Hermes would reply that mobility is not related to God as he exists in itself, but only to his effects. The *Asclepius* is only criticised for the cult of the statues, worshipped by pagans. Thomas (following Augustine's *De Civitate Dei*) considers the cult of the statues consecrated with ceremonies and rituals inside Egyptian temples idolatrous, but seems to see it as an isolated mistake, an internal contradiction within the text that does not express the true Hermetic theology based on a unique and sovereign God. The *Ascle-*

pius' final prayer – preceded by Hermes' rejection of the use of incense 'as a sacrilege' – is therefore presented as a testimony of the true divine cult, the inner one, as opposed to the exterior cult of Aristotle's *Ethica*.

(d) *Albertus Magnus*. But it is with → Albertus Magnus that a different and more mature analysis takes shape, with the aim both of delving into the philosophical elements of the *Asclepius* and of bringing them into concord with the image of Hermes the "magus", who has unveiled the secrets of nature and affirmed the astrological correspondance between heaven and earth.

The *Asclepius* – referred to by varied titles, as *De natura deorum*, *De distinctione deorum et causarum*, *De natura dei et veneratione*, *Dehlera ad Asclepium*, *De causis* – offers, firstly, a conception of God which Albert traces in various writings to the tenets of Christian theology and considers to have been transmitted by Hermetic thought to the Platonic tradition: God is omnipotent, the Lord of gods, ineffable and incomprehensible; the paternal Intellect begets the Word, and the Word encompasses the ideal forms of all things, which Socrates and Plato will call "forms" and Dionysius the Areopagite "divine processions". Hermes is therefore credited with the creation of metaphysical idealism, the origin of a speculative tradition that goes from Socrates and Plato to Augustine's exemplarism and to the Christian Neoplatonism of Dionysius the Areopagite. Hermes, writes Albert in his *Summa theologiae* (begun after 1272 and left incomplete), declares that 'God the prince of gods is in everything', and this doctrine – like similar theories of great Greek, Christian and Islamic philosophers – encompasses the Catholic faith. To the accusation of idolatry, leveled at Hermes by 'some' (maybe William of Auvergne is intended) because of his theurgic concept, Albert replies by affirming Hermes' pure monotheism. Hermes and other philosophers who asserted a plurality of "gods and goddesses", in reality believed in a sole God: 'And they considered Him as one, since He alone is God by His essence, and of Him Plato and Trismegistus say that the human mind, when it is freed from the body, is barely able to understand what He is and is infinitely'.

In his *De causis et processu universitatis* (1263-1267) Albert adopts Hermes' opinion on the causative flux: all things overflow with the spirit, which infuses every being with the divine forms and virtues. But right after this, he points out that the first philosophers, 'Trismegistus et Apollo et Hermes Aegyptius et Asclepius' erred in their conception of the "mode" of influx, by maintaining in fact that the First principle penetrates all things and is the being in itself of all things. Hermes thus upholds that 'God is all that is', and this is a serious error, because it destroys all the ontological gradations between beings. This is the gravest accusation formulated by Albert, worried as he is by a theory which identifies the ontological foundation of beings in a first and universal being: a metaphysical pantheism which sees in God the embodied form of everything and thus obliterates the hierarchical order of the gradations of being. Subsequently, in his *Summa theologiae*, Albert, in order to refute the immanentist doctrine of God as world soul, nevertheless cites a celebrated page of the *Asclepius*, in which God's nature is proclaimed as one, eternal, infinite, perfect, stable and immutable, the center and mainstay of the universe. Even fate or the *heimarmene* of the Hermetic dialogue is the object of a long reflection. In his *Physica* (1250) Albert traces to Hermes the definition of fate as 'connection of causes dependent on the providence of the first cause', while bending the Hermetic text (which actually combines in an ambiguous manner the Platonic concept that fate is the second god with the Stoic concept that fate is the highest god) into the direction of Christian theology: in this doctrine the sayings of Trismegistus and of other philosophers, Albert proceeds, 'concur with us in the same truth'. In his *De caelo* he returns to the Hermetic triad fate-necessity-order; in his *De fato* he analyses the definition of fate as 'form of the order of being and of life in inferior beings caused by the cyclical motion of the celestial spheres'; and in his *De causis et processu universitatis* he proclaims that it is not hard to trace Hermes' words back to Aristotle. Finally, in his *Summa theologiae*, after having distinguished providence and fate as *exemplar et exemplatum*, the influencing cause and the influenced cause, Albert states that Hermes and Plato describe the world as derived from the divine exemplar and as almost a second god shaped by the God of gods: 'And there is nothing erroneous in defining fate in this manner'. The justification of Hermes is thus complete; his teaching is put in concord by Albert with Plato, Aristotle and Christian theology, while being distinguished from the opinions of Egyptians and Chaldaeans, who had an idea of fate characterized by astral determinism. Finally, the *Asclepius* seems not only to sustain but to promote Albert's reflections on the concept of man as microcosm and link between God and the world. In many of his writings Albert borrows from Hermes, for example when he declares that to gain superior sight, prophecy and divination, it is necessary to purify oneself by isolation and ascesis, and that only in detachment from the body the intellect can achieve certain knowledge of God. In his *Liber de intellectu et intelligibili* (ca. 1260) Albert introduces the theme of man as *nexus dei et mundi*, attributing this formulation to Hermes: man is the nexus between God and the world, in that the assimilative intellect unites him to God, while other intellects result merely in cognition of the sensible and intelligible world. In his *De animalibus* (ca. 1260), still drawing from Hermes, Albert repeats that man unites God and the world because he encloses in himself a divine intellect which in its ascent draws after it the body and the universe, subjugates matter, transforms things and appears to perform miracles; even in his terrestrial nature man dominates the world as "governor", and performs transmutations, spells, and enchantments. Man is in fact two men, he writes again in his *Ethica* (1262-1263): he is as though suspended, he affirms in his *Metaphysica* (1263-67), between the world and God. Man is above the world thanks to the power of his mathematical and physical knowledge, and he is close to God because he contemplates His inner beauties with the light of pure intellect.

(e) *Thomas Bradwardine*. In the first half of the 14th century, in a profoundly altered cultural milieu, Thomas Bradwardine, great mathematician and theologian of Merton College, Oxford, proves himself to be an assiduous reader of the *Asclepius*. Bradwardine is the author of *De causa Dei* (1335-1344), a theological treatise constructed "more geometrico", which rejects Aristotelian philosophy and returns to the Augustinian roots of Christian thought. He begins his reflection with a thesis, 'God is supremely perfect and good', which he confirms and substantiates in the course of a lengthy "corollary" divided into forty sections. The first authority invoked is the father of philosophers, Hermes, who in his *De verbo aeterno* (the title given to the *Asclepius*) proclaims God to be complete, perfect, holy, incorruptible, eternal. But in the corollary "Against the idolaters" Bradwardine cannot forget the terrible accusations which Augustine in *De civitate Dei* had levelled against Hermetic theurgy and the cult of the "dei facticii". Bradwardine's responds curtly: if Hermes attributes the same nature to God and to the gods, it is not hard to refute him; if instead he distinguishes them, then there is nothing to worry about, since 'it is pointless, once the truth is known, to quibble over names'. Nevertheless, Bradwardine proceeds to frame a skillful statement of accusation. Since Trismegistus affirms in many places that the one God is supremely wise, good, pious, clement,

immense, powerful and present, it makes no sense, he says reproachfully, to imagine 'other gods or another god', to confer the honour of divinity on statues, to consecrate idols to demons and evil spirits, and to lavish on creatures the worship due to God, who is the ultimate cause of every being. Arguments and confutations proceed, in this imaginary dialogue, with great dialectical and rhetorical effectiveness, but the conclusion is not, as in Augustine and in William of Auvergne, the accusation of idolatry, but censure for lack of prudence and consistency: evil demons, even if they know the future and perform wonders, must not for that reason be worshipped but must be feared as fatal enemies and shrewd seducers. In Bradwardine's treatise Hermes is respected as the highest authority of the pagan tradition, and invoked (along with many others) on several themes and issues, always in agreement with true philosophy and true theology. Divine nature is incomprehensible to natural reason; happiness resides in knowledge of God; the resurrection of the flesh is followed by eternal rewards or punishment; true philosophy consists in respect and gratitude for divine works; the world and man were created in time; at the end of time the universe will attain a state of glory; all things flow from God who preserves them in being and is the first shape of reality 'ex ipso, in ipso, per ipsum'; divine will or goodness (habitually associated with the Holy Spirit) proceeds from God, and even Hermes at times calls it "Spirit" in accordance with the many testimonies of Judaeo-Christian Revelation; the unitary order of the universe is the archetypal and intelligible world; God – efficient cause, *primum mobile* of created being, immutable stability and perfection – has a distinct consciousness of all things, events and human actions, and His will, the origin of everything, is the source of grace granted to men; all things, eternally present in the divine conscience and prescience, come about through fate (*famen divinum*), understood as an immutable, indissoluble, necessitating law which realizes the knowledge and will of God; fate, order and necessity, which govern the world, obey eternal reason, which is immobile and indissoluble. Lastly, in the *Sermo Epinicius* (1346) attributed to Bradwardine, a reference appears to Hermes' *De verbo aeterno* on the emergence of fate from God. This list certainly fails to do justice to the extent and variety of his references to the *Asclepius*, often combined with the *Liber de sex rerum principiis* and the *Liber viginti quattuor philosophorum*, nor does it provide an evaluation of Bradwardine's complex interpretation, but it does allow us to understand how themes that are central to his system are based on the ancient wisdom of the "father of philosophers".

(f) The first disciples of Albertus Magnus do not seem to take up their master's reflection on the *Asclepius*; only Ulrich of Strasbourg, in his *Summa de Summo Bono*, takes from Albert some Hermetic references, such as the doctrine of man as "nexus dei et mundi" and the comparison of Hermes with the Stoic school. But in Berthold of Moosburg, the last exponent of Albert's school and author of the *Expositio super Elementationem theologicam Procli* (an imposing commentary, composed in 1340-1360), the study of the *Asclepius*, often called *De Deo deorum*, energetically fosters the exegesis of Proclus' theology, presented in the framework of a constant comparison and association between Hermetic thought, the Platonic tradition and Christian theology. Already in the Prologue, dedicated to a famous passage of the *Letter to the Romans* (1:20 'The invisible perfections of God, since the creation of the world, are understood through His works'), Berthold, in order to explain the concept of "world", chooses as his guide the *Asclepius*. After having distinguished the macrocosm and the microcosm, the universe and man, Berthold constructs his exegesis, confirming it with Christian and pagan authorities, on the basis of two Hermetic definitions, taken as paradigms and commented at length, word for word. The first is authentic: 'the universe is the immutable work of God, a glorious construction, a good made out of a multiform variety of aspects, instrument of the will of God who sustains His work without envy' (*Ascl.* 25); the second, also attributed to Hermes, is actually taken from a page of Albertus Magnus on man as "nexus dei et mundi", governor of the world through the power conferred by physical and mathematical research and subject to God because He contemplates His inner beauties with pure intellect (*Metaphysica* I, 1,1). Berthold's recognition of Hermes' authority could not be more solemn. In the course of his *Expositio*, many and substantial quotations confirm and deepen, in diverse theoretical contexts, the value of the *Asclepius*. (i) The Hermetic text offers an extraordinary variety of doctrines and formulations which Berthold applies to Proclus' system, not without strains and at times with subtle shifts from cosmology to metaphysics. God is one, in Himself perfect and transcendent, ineffable and unknowable, the ungenerated cause and supreme end of all things, beginning without beginning and end without end. Brimming with fecundity, He freely produces in an eternal instant the chain of intelligible and sensible beings. The universe, eternally present in the creative thought, has a causal order subject to divine reason, pervaded with consonance and harmony, and manifests a triadic structure in the macrocosm (destiny, necessity, order) and in the microcosm (sense, reason, intellect). As an instrument of the divine will, begotten in the image of archetypal ideas, it is permeated, vivified and enshrouded by the spirit, the *anima mundi* shaped by God. As repository and place for all species, it returns perennially to the gods who constitute intelligible being and produce sensible being, and to the One who transcends being, by virtue of whom all things constitute a single unity. (ii) In his attempt to trace the trinitarian truth of the One in pagan thought, Berthold does not hesitate to perceive in Hermes' maxims, with reference to the *Logos Teleios* as well as the *Liber viginti quattuor philosophorum*, the 'plurality of the divine persons'. The begetting of *voluntas* from divine *consilium* (*Ascl.* 26) expresses the eternal birth of the Word from the Father, and the *spiritus* which animates all things and nurtures souls (*Ascl.* 6, 14, 18) is the Holy Spirit. (iii) Concerning the difficult problem of polytheism and Hermetic theurgy, which had already provoked the radical condemnation of William of Auvergne and the reproaches of Thomas Bradwardine, Berthold's position is at once clearcut and problematic. The many references to one God in the *Asclepius* support Berthold's certainty of Hermes' monotheistic authenticity; but the textual evidence of the theory of the "dei facticii" meets with his severe disapproval. The claim of a plurality of gods indeed may or may not be "superstitious": it is erroneous when, as in Hermes, fashioned idols are considered to be gods due to the infusion of a sacred power; but it is in conformity with truth (and superstitious only in name) when, as in Plato and in the Platonic philosophers, they are considered gods only in so far as they participate in the only true God. In Prop. 115 Berthold's censure is clearcut: the error of Hermes, this extremely prudent man – he quotes lengthy passages from the *Asclepius* – who was wise in many things but was here deluded beyond all measure, must not be believed. And yet Berthold visibly strives to limit the extent of the ancient Egyptian's error. A few pages earlier he writes that Hermes and Plato affirm that the "God of gods" is unknowable, and when he condemns Hermes' error and contrasts it with the theology of Plato (Prop. 114 and 120), he also traces the Platonic concept of "gods by participation" back to the *Asclepius*: 'Hermes affirms that many are said to be gods by participation with the supreme God, the God of gods. His book in fact is called *De Deo deorum*'.

(g) In the 15th century even the works of Nicholas of Cusa show a direct knowledge of the Hermetic dialogue. His first reference to Hermes is found in his *Sermo* I (1430): his oldest surviving work, in which Cusanus, inspired by Lactantius, credits Hermes with knowledge of the divine Word. His "Christian" interpretation of Hermetism is confirmed by numerous autographic glosses placed in the margins of the *Asclepius* (MS Bruxelles, Bibliothèque Royale 10054-56), which testify to a deeply attentive reading, probably prior to 1140. In his *De docta ignorantia* (1440) Cusanus returns on several occasions to the Hermetic doctrine of God as "one and everything", nameless (*innominis*), and at the same time expressible by all names (*omninominis*). Since He is One, God is ineffable, as names are instituted by reason to distinguish individual beings, or, since He is All, He can be designated by the names of all things and all things by His name (*Ascl.* 20). The reflection on divine names, which also occurs in subsequent writings, is probably inspired by a page of Theodoric of Chartres, but at the same time it reveals a direct awareness of the Hermetic text, which also reappears in other contexts. Again in his *De docta ignorantia* Cusanus takes from Hermes the concept of *hyle* or universal matter as *nutrix generationum*, the substratum of forms which "nourishes" all material beings; in his *De dato patris luminum* (1445-1446), the definition of the world as "sensible god"; in his *De beryllo* (1458), the idea of man as "second god", the creative and provident imitator of the divine intellect; in his *De ludo globi* (1463), the theory that the spherical totality of the world is in itself invisible and only the forms molded in matter are perceptible. Lastly, on the question of Hermetic theurgy – an obligate subject after the judgments of William of Auvergne, Albertus Magnus, Thomas Bradwardine and Berthold of Moosburg – Cusanus' considerations are prudent and moderate. According to his *De pace fidei* (1453) the statues and simulacra that are worshipped, as if 'something divine' inhabited their stone and were lodged within the idol, should be destroyed because they distract from the worship of God and the truth: their responses, ambiguous or false, are the work of the evil spirit, the enemy of human salvation. Cusanus clearly has in mind the pages of the *Asclepius* on divine statues and his condemnation of magical practices is radical. But in *De docta ignorantia*, like Albertus Magnus before him, he dissociates magic from Hermetic polytheism, which he interprets as a personification (typical in the pagan world) of divine attributes: Hermes, he writes, sees in God the cause of all

things, the *complicatio* which includes both the male and female gender, the creative force which is manifested (*explicata*) in the divine figures of Amor and Venus. The names given to God by the pagans 'are expressions of the single ineffable name which implies all names'.

(h) Along with the *Asclepius*, there circulate in the 13th and 14th centuries Hermetic fragments translated by Lactantius and reworked by Quodvultdeus. Almost all are drawn from the *Asclepius* and are gathered under the title of *Logos Teleios*, considered from the 12th century on – precisely because of his distinct Christian bias – to be another and separate work of Hermes, who by divine inspiration had come to know the mystery of the eternal Word. Acclaimed as authentic by "Augustine's" authority, the declarations of the *Logos Teleios* give credit to the image of a Hermes tending, as is written in the *Glosae super Trismegistum*, 'ad nostram theologiam', and help to reinforce the attempt to bring the *Asclepius* in line with Christian doctrine. Just a few examples of these are the quotations in *De septem septenis*, in William of Auvergne, Gilbert of Tournai, Albertus Magnus, Thomas Aquinas, Ulrich of Strasbourg, Thomas Bradwardine, Berthold of Moosburg and Nicholas of Cusa.

5. THE DIFFUSION OF THE *LIBER VIGINTI QUATTUOR PHILOSOPHORUM*

The history of the *Liber viginti quattuor philosophorum* in the philosophical and literary culture of the Middle Ages is like a long road, partly straight, partly meandering and intricate. Undoubtedly the text encountered resistance and incomprehension. Precise textual and documentary data attest to this. In the 13th century the Franciscan Thomas of York in his *Sapientiale* (1250-1256) begins a lengthy commentary which is interrupted at the third maxim. In a manuscript of the first half of the 14th century the *Liber* was violently crossed out, like the writings of the Pseudo-Aristotle, Alfarabi, → Avicenna and Adelard of Bath are also mutilated or effaced. Finally, in another codex the Parisian theologian Etienne Gaudet placed in the margins a series of highly critical notations. These interventions, self-censuring (as perhaps in the case of Thomas of York) or external, are all traceable to individual initiatives, and there is no record of official censure. Of these elements there have developed two radically divergent interpretations: some see in them the rejection of a conception closely related to an intense Neoplatonic inspiration and a radical apophatism, while others, on the contrary, see in them the rejection of a rationalistic thought which claims to reach the divine essence, the "quid est" of God by mere reason. If we wish to simplify the philosophical trajectory of the *Liber*, we may distinguish – beyond the presence and the peregrinations of the manuscripts in the libraries – two different aspects: the circulation of the text in its entirety and the autonomous circulation of the first two maxims – the most celebrated ones – which state 'God is a monad which begets a monad and in himself reflects a sole fire of love' (I) and 'God is an infinite sphere whose center is everywhere and whose circumference is nowhere' (II).

The text is mentioned for the first time in its original form (maxims and first commentary) by Thomas of York. At the beginning of the 14th century it is commented a second time, perhaps by the Dominican Nicholas Triveth. Subsequently other authors, united by a lively opposition against Christian Aristotelianism, draw from the *Liber* reflections of a philosophical and theological kind; this is the case with Meister Eckhart, Thomas Bradwardine, Berthold of Moosburg. The most intense phase of this development is the speculation of Nicholas of Cusa, who in his *De docta ignorantia* is inspired by the *Liber* to confirm or elaborate on themes of a metaphysical order, to found the method of symbolic knowledge, and to express the ontological reasons for his new cosmology. The first two maxims were more widely circulated in the 12th-15th centuries, and knew a much better fortune. Commented on by the greatest theologians and philosophers of the Middle Ages and attributed most of the time to Hermes, the "images" (as they are defined in the first commentary) of the generating monad and the infinite sphere for centuries represented one of the most favored references for discussing and reflecting upon two central themes of theology: the problem of the natural knowledge of revealed mysteries and the concept of divine infinity.

The interpretation of the generating monad seems to pass through three stages, sometimes not following upon one another chronologically. In the first stage (12th and beginning of 13th century), Alan of Lille and Alexander Nequam read the first maxim as an extraordinary testimony of an awareness of the trinitarian God among the ancient pagans. Subsequently, on the basis of the principles affirmed in Pietro Lombardo's *Sententiae* (1155-1157), the intellect was denied the possibility of such knowledge except through revelation as handed down by the sacred Books or through inner inspiration: this is the position we find, with different premises, forms and outcomes, in William of

Auxerre, Alexander of Hales, Albertus Magnus, Thomas Aquinas, John of Ripa and still others. With the advent (second half of 13th century) of a marked reaction to Christian Aristotelianism, in thinkers or mystics who turn to Augustinian and Neoplatonic sources, the image of the generating, generated and reflected monad is once again seen as manifesting a real awareness of the inner life of God, as in the writings of Marghareta Porete, Meister Eckhart, Thomas Bradwardine and Berthold of Moosburg.

In theological and cosmological meditations on the "infinite" or "intelligible" sphere, four phases can be delineated. The first commentators, Alan of Lille and Michael Scot, perceive in the constituent elements of the geometric figure – the point and the circumference – the likeness of God and of the world, but in reversed terms. Alan sees in the circumference the supreme immensity which encompasses and sustains every created point, while Michael sees in the center the immutable source of divine operation and in the circumference the created universe. The Franciscans Alexander of Hales and Bonaventura of Bagnoregio, with a language that anticipates both Meister Eckhart and Nicholas of Cusa, unify the center and the circumference in the divine nature: the circumference metaphor expresses simultaneously God's absolute simplicity and His absolute infinity, Being which is one and all, the transcendent minimum and maximum. Subsequently, Eckhart further develops the idea of the identity of the center and the circumference, projects it (with his theory of the "essential" emanation) into the uncreated "depth of the soul", while designating it as the symbol and paradigm of religious experience and the moral life, and seems finally to extend it to the totality of creation, as God's Being is the true being of finite beings. Toward the middle of the 15th century Cusanus explicitly draws from the "infinite sphere" the conceptual structure of his symbolic method: conceiving a geometric figure with its properties (and the sphere is the noblest of all), extending it to infinity, and then applying it to God. At the same time, however, another exegesis of the second maxim is taking shape, which transposes it onto the cosmological plane. So it happens that Thomas Bradwardine adopts it as a symbol of infinite space, neither created nor uncreated, a metaphysical condition of the act of creation, and Nicholas of Cusa uses it as the foundation of a new cosmology, which subverts the Aristotelian-Ptolemaic system and presents the image of a universe in total motion, 'like a wheel inside a wheel and a sphere inside a sphere', which has no motionless center, no hierarchies, no finitude.

6. The *Liber de Sex Rerum Principiis* in Medieval Thought

Other than with the *Asclepius* and the *Liber viginti quattuor philosophorum*, systematic inquiry into the spread of the *Liber de sex rerum principiis* in medieval philosophy has not yet been carried out. It is possible, however, to give a few indications.

(a) A few years after the publication of the text, its presence is attested in the *De septem septenis* attributed to John of Salisbury. The seventh *septena* attributes to "Hermes Mercurius Triplex" the description of human progress, perfected when the first sages discovered theology for the soul's salvation and physic for the health of the body; but John omits the conception, elaborated in the *Sex rerum principia*, that the spiritual development of man imitates the generation of the world carried out in the conjunctions of the Moon with the five planets and is subject to the cyclical phases of birth, progress and dissolution. He then summarizes, partly shifting and subverting – not without relevant implications – the system's original principles and hierarchy, the six "principles of things". Cause – the substantial principle which, unrelated to necessity, precedes its effect – is identified with the trinitarian God. The primordial causes are four principles: the Law of heavenly bodies or Reason, Nature (which Plato calls the soul of the world, others fate, still others divine order), the World and the Mechanism of the world. In the *De septem septenis*, then, the six principles of things are expanded to seven: three transcendent (Cause which unfolds in the Father, the Son and the Spirit) and four primordial. In this re-elaboration the author resolves the ambiguity of the "Hermetic" text and separates the transcendent triune principle from the primordial principles which mediate between the divine being and worldly being.

(b) In the 13th century the *Sex rerum principia* is quoted by Thomas of York in his *Sapientiale* (1250-1256). Thomas, when he writes about the uniqueness of the first principle of reality, rejects the distinction between the three "superior" principles (*causa-ratio-natura*); in the same way, when he comments on the *Asclepius*, he criticizes the affirmation of the two principles (divine will and matter). Since in the pseudo-Hermetic text the relations between the three principles are presented according to the model of the Christian trinity ('Ratio ex causa, et ex utraque natura'), Thomas rejects the use of the term "nature" for the Holy Ghost, and accuses the author of contradicting himself. The principle of the creative causality of God, and the theory of the archetypal ideas in the Word, are accepted, together with other cosmological doctrines: the distinction between operating nature and operated nature (that is, the power of the stars regulated by divine providence and the effects that are produced in the world), the harmony of the elements, the division of creatures in relation to matter, the union of the accidental forms with the beings, and finally, always in agreement with the Christians, the beauty and the order of the world.

The profoundest discussion dates back to Albertus Magnus who in his *Physica* (1250) refutes the thesis – attributed to the Pythagoreans, Plato and Hermes – of a "universal nature" which precedes the particular natures and divides itself into them. Hermes in particular supposedly stated that nature is a force which proceeds from the First cause by way of the movement of the heavens, and then becomes incorporated and diversified in particular beings, nobler and more effective the nearer they are to the First cause, less noble and effective the further they move away from it. But if this were so, says Albert, then it would not be a force, but 'a substance which divides itself', its universal nature would have a being constituted 'before single beings' and would not be distinct from the being of particular nature: 'Aristotle does not approve of this'. The accusation, inspired by Aristotelian metaphysics, is therefore aimed against a hypostatic and substantialist conception of nature, against the idea of a substance which precedes and is the foundation of particular substances. Albert does not mention the Hermetic text by name, but the theory contested is couched in terms taken directly from the *Sex rerum principia*. Still in the 13th century, the pseudo-Hermetic text is quoted by some writers and by the author of the *De investigatione creatoris per creaturas* (a Franciscan identified erroneously as Bertram of Ahlen).

(c) At the beginning of the next century, *Le Roman de Fauvel* by Gervais du Bus mentions 'L'auctour de Sex Principes', who described the similarity between macrocosm and microcosm, the operations of elementary qualities in the universe, and the workings of Nature in the genesis of the four human temperaments. But only Thomas Bradwardine and Berthold of Moosburg give evidence of a thorough and attentive reading of the *Sex rerum principia*. Thomas Bradwardine, who calls it *De mundo et caelo* (even though he knows the real title), in his *De causa Dei* draws from it numerous motifs, always in line with Christian tradition. All peoples, prophets and theologians, poets and philosophers before Aristotle have always affirmed that the world has had a temporal beginning: like-

wise also Hermes, when he writes that 'the world
began from eternity and will resolve itself into eternity', that the temporal world is in relation to eternity as a circle to its center, that the motions of
heaven are stable and immutable since it was
formed by the reason of the divine mind, and that
it is not easy to understand or explain the origin of
a world which cyclically dies and is reborn. And as
everything is produced by an active cause, Hermes
proclaims that all things (genera, species and individuals, matter, world and time) originate from the
divine Cause and Reason: the three supreme principles – Cause, Reason and Nature – represent the
trinitarian life, the origin and eternal model of created being. Later Bradwardine returns several time
to these themes of the *Sex rerum principia*, to prove
the absolute predestination of man, the unfaltering
order of fate, the necessity of contingent futures
and divine prescience (which does not contradict
but agrees with freedom of action), the motionless
infinite of eternity and the mobile flow of time.
In his *Sermo Epinicius* (1346) Bradwardine once
again cites the *De mundo et caelo* and the *De verbo
aeterno* to reaffirm that the series of fate descends
from God and that his 'worthy sons' Plato and
Aristotle also thought so.

In Berthold of Moosburg the *Sex rerum principia*
is an important source for his commentary on Proclus: the pages on the three first principles – Cause,
Reason, Nature – are widely cited in support of the
reflection on the One, the intelligible world and
sensible effects. The human intellect, shaped in the
image of divine life and ordained to have knowledge of the intelligible world, investigates into
the first cause – creator of all things, fullness of
thought, foundation of worldly being, place of
archetypal ideas – and into the sensible effects
of divine causes. The doctrine of the three superior principles, which occurs again and again in
Berthold's work, inspires his analysis of the
concept of *nature* referred to in the "triple principle" (Cause, Reason, Nature), and the distinction
of Nature in two different cosmological aspects:
"operative" nature, which proceeds from Cause
and Reason, is incorporated in the forces of heaven
and is the immanent principle of life, while "operated" nature consists in worldly qualities produced
by the astral constellations. The sensible world,
animated by a perennial motion, encompasses the
being of all things, and for this reason, Berthold
concludes, it is excellent and is governed by a transcendent principle. The ideal form of the universe is
"written" in Reason and is of an absolute simplicity, but the single primordial causes, which proceed
from the principal form, are in themselves mani-

fold: in this representation Hermes inspires pagan
and Christian Platonism, and Berthold can thus
confirm Proclus' thesis on the substantial nature,
one and manifold, of intelligible species.

B. Technical and Operative Hermetism

In the 12th and 13th centuries, initially in Italy
and Spain, generations of translators introduced
into libraries and Latin culture most of the philosophical and scientific knowledge of the ancient
world and of Arab civilization. Among the works
translated (such as Aristotle, Proclus, Euclid,
Ptolemy, → al-Kindī, Abū Maʿshar, → Avicenna,
Averröes) were also the technical and operative
works originally written in Greek under the names
of → Hermes Trismegistus and of mythical or historical figures linked to the tale of his revelation, as
well as a large stream of Hermetic writings handed
down by Islamic scientists and philosophers or
passed down to the Arab world from the Sabaeans
of Harran. For an understanding of the value and
significance of this tradition, the textual extent and
content of the technical-operative works attributed
to Hermes must first be examined.

1. Astrology, Medicine and Natural Magic, Divination

A. Translations from the Greek
Among the first translations from the Greek were
writings on natural magic, believed to operate
through the occult properties [→ occult / occultism]
of things. It was probably the cleric Paschalis
Romanus who, in Constantinople in 1169, translated into Latin the *Kyranides*, an ample treatise
on the medicinal and magical virtues of animals,
plants and stones. This work, defined by the translator as a 'liber medicinalis', is entitled *Liber phys-
icalium virtutum, compassionum et curationum*
and is made up of two books: the "Kyranis", which
Hermes revealed to King Kyranus of Persia (rewritten by Harpocration of Alexandria in the 4th century), and the "Short medicinal book of Hermes to
Asclepius". The Latin translation is based on the
complete re-elaboration of these two works compiled by a Byzantine editor between the 5th and the
8th century. The first Kyranis, given to mankind by
Hermes Trismegistus and carved in Syriac characters on an iron pillar, deals with twenty-four stones,
herbs, fish and birds arranged in the order of the
Greek alphabet: their powers, united and mixed
together for the cure and pleasure of the human
body, are a prodigy of nature revealed by the wisdom of almighty God. The "Short medicinal book"

consists of three bestiaries – which describe birds, animals of the land, and fish – and gives instructions on how to prepare products with medical and magical powers. The Byzantine editor arranged the three bestiaries in alphabetical order and entitled them *Kyranides* II-IV.

In the preface to his translation, Paschalis Romanus refers to two Greek books on astrological botany, which he perhaps translated into Latin as well: the Book of Alexander the Great on planetary herbs, *De septem herbis*, and the Book of Thessalos on zodiacal and planetary herbs, *Liber Thessali de virtutibus herbarum*. In the Greek tradition the *De septem herbis*, which deals with the medical-magical virtues of planetary plants, exists in two slightly different editions: the first is anonymous or attributed to Hermes and was not translated into Latin; the second is attributed to Alexander the Great and was translated into Latin. The *Liber Thessali* is the revelation of the god Asclepius to the physician Thessalos, identifiable according to some scholars as the famous Thessalos of Thralles of the 1st century. Disappointed with the teaching of Nechepsos and Petosirides, Thessalos had engaged the help of an Egyptian priest to invoke Asclepius in a temple near Thebes; after purification rituals and prayers, Asclepius indeed made his appearance, and revealed to Thessalos the medical-magical virtues of zodiacal and planetary plants. Of all the technical texts the *Liber Thessali* is the one most marked by a profound religious sentiment. The Greek original had two editions: the first and older one, attributed to Thessalos, was translated twice during the Middle Ages, and once again in 1528; the other one is attributed to Hermes, who instructs Asclepius in the wonderful properties of plants.

The *Compendium aureum* is the Latin translation of a lost Greek original. In his dedicatory letter, the author, 'Flaccus Africus discipulus Belbenis Claudio Atheniensi epilogistico', describes his rediscovery – in Troy, among the bones of the first King Kyranus – of the tract, taken from the *Kyranides*. Actually, as to their content there is no relationship between the *Compendium aureum* and the *Kyranides*. Belbenus designates Apollonius of Tyana, called by the Arab equivalent (Balīnūs, in the Latin versions referred to as Balenus, Belenus and other variants). In the manuscripts the title, taken from the text itself, is *Tractatus de septem herbis septem planetis attributis*, but actually the names of the planets are not mentioned. Each herb is linked to a month, proceeding backwards from June to December, to a number and to a metal, but the metals do not have the traditional correspon-

dances with the planets. For the most part prodigious medical-therapeutic properties are described and only in a few cases virtues which are in a proper sense magical.

The lost original of the *Liber de triginta sex decanis*, probably translated between the 12th and the 13th century, is the main text of Hermetic astrology and among the most ancient ones of Greek astrology. It reached the Latin world in a long summary composed in the 8th century. The work, which contains astronomical elements dating from the time of Hypparchus, has some very interesting features: a long account of the *sphaera barbarica*, carefully examined in comparison with other ancient documentation; the two stellar catalogues of the *sphaera graeca*, each independent of the other and edited centuries apart; astronomical observations of successive periods; and different, even contradictory, astrological doctrines and methods juxtaposed together, to which the astrological vulgate in general and the Hermetic vulgate in particular refer. The work constitutes valuable testimony of the extent to which the astronomical and astrological materials were scrutinized, first in the Byzantine period (edition of the original) and then in the Middle Ages (Latin translation), and of the abundant repertories available.

The *Iatromathematica*, an astrological text on medicine, has come down to us in two slightly different Greek editions and was translated only in the 16th century. The author follows the astrological notion of "melotesia", according to which each organ is presided over by a planet, and the conditions of the human body derive from the fortunate or unfortunate position of the planet in the zodiacal circle at the moment of conception and birth. The text examines the pathologies that occur when the Moon is in the twelve zodiacal signs in particular relationships with other planets, and proposes appropriate therapies. The medical theory is not homeopathic (as affirmed by Festugière 1944), but allopathic: *refrigerantia* substances heal illnesses originating from heat and *calefacentia* substances heal those originating from cold. Two Latin translations were made from the second Greek edition: one by David Hoeschelius (1555), and the other, anonymous and dating from before 1489, was published by Johannes Stadius as his own (1556).

A few years later the translation of a poem on earthquakes concludes the inflow of Greek *Hermetica* into Latin culture. The original of this text dates from before the Byzantine era and is attributed in the manuscript tradition both to Hermes and to Orpheus. It describes monthly omens and the meaning of earthquakes; the author traces the position of the Sun in the signs of the zodiac, starting with Aries (April). The work, translated into Latin by J.A. Baifius with the title *Orpheus seu Mercurius ter maximus, Prognostica a terrae motibus*, was published in 1586.

B. TRANSLATIONS FROM THE ARABIC

Toward the middle of the 12th century Hugo of Santalla translated from the Arabic two texts: the *Liber de spatula* and the *De secretis naturae* by pseudo-Apollonius. In the Arabic literature on scapulimancy (divination by examining the scapula of sacrificed animals), a single fragment, of North African origin, is attributed to Hermes, and seems to be the oldest document. From this fragment and from a work attributed to al-Kindī, who refers to the teachings of 'Hermes the wise and of other Greek philosophers', two translations were made: the first, with the title *Liber de spatula*, is dedicated by Hugo of Santalla to Bishop Michael of Tarragon (1119-1151); the second, entitled *Liber alius de eadem*, presents many of the same elements but is different in form and partly in content. The *Liber de secretis naturae* is the translation of an Arab work, *Kitāb sirr al-ḫalīqa* (Book of the secret of creation) attributed to Balīnūs (Apollonius of Tyana), who narrates the discovery of the text and of the *Tabula smaragdina* in Hermes' crypt. The origin of the *Sirr al-ḫalīqa* is still uncertain – according to some scholars, it is the translation of a Greek text, according to others, it is an apocryphal Arab work –, but there is general agreement concerning the attribution of the Arab edition to the reign of al-Ma'mūn in the 9th century. Several different traditions flow into the work: Greek and Syriac, Islamic and pre-Islamic, philosophical and alchemical. A discussion of the nature and names of God is followed in the treatise by a description of the birth of the cosmos and the formation of minerals and stones, vegetable and animal life, and finally man. The books closes with the *Tabula smaragdina*, the most inspired and famous of alchemical texts.

The 12th and 13th centuries see the appearance of several translations of an astrological treatise, the *Liber de stellis beibeniis*, which through various reworkings and vagaries had traveled from Greek astrology to Arab science and lastly to the Latin world. The term *stella beibenia* means fixed star, and the text describes the qualities of persons born under the influence of certain fixed stars linked to the "temperaments" or "complexions" of the planets when they are in their Ascendant or in Mid-Heaven. The Greek original is a fragment of the lost work of an Egyptian astrologer who wrote it in 379 A.D., but the doctrine of the "Thirty fixed

stars" goes back to older sources. The text was then revived by an anonymous Greek astrologer, in an edition since lost, at the beginning of the 6th century (ca. 505 A.D.). A corrupt copy of it seems to be the inspiration of Rhetorius Alexandrinus in the 7th century and the source of translations into Middle-Persian (Pahlavi) as well as, perhaps, into Neo-Persian and, finally, Arabic. The Arabic version, only partly conserved today, is attributed to Hermes. In the 8th century it is included in an abridged version in a treatise attributed to Māshā'allāh, which was translated into Latin by Hermann of Carinthia in 1141-1151 under the title *Liber Aristotilis de ducentis quinquaginta quinque Indorum voluminibus*. The original Arabic version (or a derivation of it) was translated in Toledo by Salio of Padua toward 1218, under the title *Liber de stellis beibeniis*. A Hebrew version from the Arabic also survives.

In the 12th or 13th century a translation was also made of the *Liber de quindecim stellis et de quindecim lapidibus et de quindecim herbis et de quindecim figuris*, attributed to Hermes Abhaydimon 'father of philosophers and most antique sage'. The text seems to derive from the Arab version of a Greek original, completed and reworked by the astrologer Māshā'allāh. The treatise has very interesting astronomical and astrological features and is divided, after a brief prologue by Māshā'allāh, into four sections, dedicated to fifteen fixed stars (following the order of the zodiacal signs), fifteen stones, fifteen plants, and fifteen talismans for magical operations; in some manuscrips these sections are followed by a brief appendix entitled *Dicta Messahalla*. At the same time or shortly thereafter appeared an Arabic reworking of the text, shorter than the original and attributed to the prophet Enoch, which contains in fifteen chapters the same data about the single stars, stones, plants and talismans. Lastly, Thābit ibn Qurra (9th century) is the author of yet another compendium, translated into Latin with the title *Tractatus de proprietatibus quarundam stellarum*: according to the last note of a manuscript which dates the "rectification" of the stellar coordinates, the translation is from 1360.

Possibly between the 7th and 8th centuries, a translation is made of the *Liber Antimaquis* ("This is the book of Aristotle's spiritual works and it is the *Liber Antimaquis* which is the book of the secrets of Hermes"), which derives from an ample body of Hermetic magic, with different titles and contents in the Arab manuscripts, and in which Aristotle reveals to Alexander the Great the secret knowledge of Hermes. Of the complex Arab tradition, the Latin text reproduces only a brief selection which omits the cosmic and mythological chronology and concentrates on the parts essential to the practice of magic; it conserves the passage which exalts the greatness of man and his power over all things, but its content is mainly of a practical kind. In the second part (devoted to the names of the astral "spirits" and their dominion over earthly substances) the *Liber Antimaquis* corresponds more evidently with the Arab tradition. It is not possible to establish whether the Latin edition is a direct translation or a later adaptation of a preceding version. Another translation of a brief section is conserved under the title *De amicitia vel inimicitia planetarum* and perhaps derives from a Jewish translation.

From the early 13th century (or perhaps even earlier) we have a translation of the *Liber de quattuor confectionibus ad omnia genera animalium capienda*, a short treatise which takes the form of a dialogue between Hermes and Aristoas (Aristotle). Hermes describes four different recipes, *confectiones*, made up of animal and vegetable substances; a suffumigation ritual and a prayer to the "spirit" of animals, intended to capture and dominate various types of wolves, wild beasts, birds and reptiles. The revelation is derived, according to Hermes, from a book 'with the secrets of the occult sciences' which Arod (i.e. the archangel Gabriel) taught to Ismenus (i.e. Adam).

The *Centiloquium*, together with the *Asclepius* and the *Tabula smaragdina* the most widespread work of Hermetic literature in the Latin Middle Ages, is an anthology of a hundred astrological aphorisms. The text has the form of an acrostichon, which allows us to identify the author, Stephen of Messina, and the dedicatee, King Manfred of Sicily (1258-1266). According to David Pingree, the collection – which does not follow an orderly plan and covers different areas of astrological science (birth, elections, transitions, iatromathematics, meteorology) – is taken partly or entirely from the unpublished *Liber rememorationum* by Sadan, also known as *Albumasar in Sadan*, who transmits many sayings of Abū Maʿshar gathered by his disciple.

The *Liber de accidentibus* is a collection of astrological sayings, exemplifying in a concrete form the terrestrial effects corresponding to the celestial motions described by Ptolemy in the second book of the *Tetrabiblos*. The text dates from the commentary to the *Tetrabiblos* written by ʿAlī ben Riḍwān (a physician and philosopher of the 11th century), who in his last comment to Book 2 states that it is useful to add 'the sayings by Hermes in his Book on events that happen, which can help us in

our universal prognostications'. Ptolemy's *Tetrabiblos*, in the Arab redaction and with a commentary by ʿAlī ben Riḍwān, was translated in 1271-1275 by Aegidius of Parma, with the help of an Arabic-Castilian version (possibly the work of Jehuda ben Moses), and dedicated to Alphonso X the Wise. The *Liber de accidentibus* is simply the literal transcription of the Hermetic anthology taken from a manuscript of Aegidius' version and transmitted in the form of an autonomous text.

C. LATIN ORIGINALS

Also part of the Hermetic tradition, along with translations from the Greek and Arabic, are various writings on astrological medicine and geomancy probably originally written in Latin, and placed under the authority of Hermes. A brief text on astrological medicine, the *Liber duodecim formarum*, attributed to Hermes/Enoch, describes twelve therapeutic images linked to signs of the zodiac and, in some cases, to their "decani". The image that must be carved on metal does not always correspond to the classic zodiacal portrait, nor does the subdivision of the parts of the body always reflect the traditional melotesia. The list of twelve talismans is sometimes preceded by the description of an image of the Leo talisman against kidney stones, which is different from that of the talisman described in the orderly series. This "extravagant" image became extraordinarily popular, and at times appears independently. From ca. 1300 the writing was interpolated under the title of *De ymaginibus ad calculum* in the Latin translation of the *Picatrix*. The existence of a Jewish version of the *Liber duodecim formarum*, its mention of Hermes/Enoch, and its circulation among the Jewish physicians of Montpellier suggest a Jewish origin.

The *De arbore borissa* is a brief chapter dedicated to the amazing alchemical, medical and magical virtues of a plant called "Borissa" or "Lunaria", placed under the influence of the Moon. Some of the properties described are found in later authors and texts: Joseph Flavius, Elian, the herbarium attributed to Solomon, the Hermetic texts *De septem herbis* and *Liber Thessali de virtutibus herbarum*. The *De arbore borissa*, which has come down to us from manuscripts no earlier than the 14th century, revives these traditions and adds further elements related to alchemical properties. The vagueness of the description does not allow certain and unmistakable botanical identification; but even at the time of its widest circulation (in the last centuries of the Middle Ages and during the Renaissance) numerous plants were ascribed, often by analogy, to the ever-expanding group of Lunary herbs.

The *Lectura geomantiae* is the only geomantic text attributed to Hermes. According to the brief prologue, Hermes 'the philosopher and first inventor', wishing to know whether his son far from home was dead, climbed to the top of a mountain, where an angel revealed to him the divinatory art of geomancy. The *Lectura* is a compilation, and does not enable the beginner to practice geomancy since it illustrates only the first phase of the outline of the "geomantic theme" and the definition of the first figures, without indicating how to arrive at the others and how to arrange them for a complete interpretation. The work has the appearance of a set of notes on the principal notions useful to a geomancer and has neither the structure nor the pretensions of a real treatise.

The *Tractatus de iudicio urinae* (or *Liber de iudiciis urinae sine visione eiusdem urinae*), published in a small number of manuscripts of varying length, is sometimes anonymous and sometimes attributed to Hermes, perhaps because a maxim of Hermes is quoted just at the beginning. Knowledge of the zodiacal configuration and the planetary hour makes it possible to establish the properties of a patient's urine and to proceed to a diagnosis.

2. CEREMONIAL MAGIC

(a) From the end of the 11th century to the first half of the 12th, magical literature begins to enter the West by way of Sicily and Spain. This process can be considered complete by the first half of the 13th century. Among the copious and varied materials in this domain, the most substantial part is the corpus of ceremonial writings of Arab origin attributed to Hermes or to authors linked to him: his pupil Belenus (Apollonius of Tyana), Toz the Greek and Germa the Babylonian, as well as Aristotle himself as circulator of Hermes' doctrines. Hermetic ceremonial writings present themselves in the form of mere collections of precepts, which state their theoretical basis of reference only in general terms, and conserve but few traces of their presumed dependence on Hermes' revelation. And yet, despite its shabby literary vestments, this hodge-podge of texts exerted an irresistible attraction upon Latin culture. Evidence of this are the often quite early translations signed by authoritative translators, and in some cases subjected to later revisions, in an attempt to utilize every bit of this "divine" doctrine and its "stupendous" precepts. The magic in question certainly appears stupendous in its claimed capacity to satisfy man's most disparate wishes: it caters not only to his elemen-

tary needs (nutrition, health, protection of his environment) and promises to fulfil his individual and interpersonal expectations (mastery of science, success in love, in business, or in pursuing political and social ambitions), but also makes even more unusual and extravagant claims (communication at distance, opening of locks, and optical illusions). Like all learned magic, Hermetic magic has its institutional basis in → astrology. The direct relationship between the motion of the stars and sublunary events, the existence of a specific influence of each celestial body on given aspects of worldly life, and hence the possibility of establishing causal links by calculable laws, are the theoretical assumptions borrowed by magic from astrology. Yet magic is not a mere acknowledgement of the natural relationship between heaven and earth but applies it in a practical way and bends it to its own advantage. Magic does not predict events but determines them. Thanks to this ability to transform knowledge into power, the theoretical subordination of magic to astrology does not devalue this art, which 'exalts man among the mighty' and enables him materially to get 'almost a foretaste of heaven', as written by → Michael Scot.

Nevertheless, the intense activity of translation, which in a short time makes available the entire literature of Hermetic ceremonial magic, immediately brings up the difficulty of integrating within a Christian framework a subject matter that is so radically alien and antithetical to it. The texts in fact include operative rituals such as prayers, suffumigations, and the pronunciation and writing of mysterious names. In most cases we are dealing with a liturgy calling on intelligent spiritual essences linked to the planets, who are different from the angels of Christianity and who are invoked in shapes and for ends quite different from those allowed by the Christian religion. Within the timeframe of one century, this fundamental incompatibility led to the definitive banishment of the Hermetic ceremonial tradition from the official horizon of Latin culture. The texts survived and were handed down by wayward subterranean paths, in manuscripts subjected to manipulations, abbreviations and contaminations according to the specialization and particular interests of whatever scholar was transcribing them.

(b) According to David Pingree, most of the Hermetic ceremonial texts that reached the West from the Moslem world can be traced back to the authorship of one or more Arab writers. He claims that these authors autonomously produced a pseudo-Hermetic magical literature by mixing the Greek heritage with cultural traditions of Indian and Iranian origin, as well as with local materials. According to Pingree, these falsifications have their origin in the Sabaean circles of Harran, in the period between the 9th and the 10th centuries A.D., that is to say, from the period immediately following the visit of the Caliph al-Ma'mūn to the city of Harran (around 830 A.D.). The attempt of Harranians at preserving their ancient pagan religion by adapting it to the requirements of the religions tolerated by Islam could also have led them to re-elaborate their astral magic along the lines of the Neoplatonic tradition of late antiquity, and place it under the lofty aegis of Hermes. Pingree's persuasive hypothesis finds ample confirmation in the texts, which refer mainly to the planets, attributing special importance to the Moon and utilizing spiritual essences as intermediaries and executors of magical operations. It is well-known that in the declaration of their religious credo, the Harranians had proclaimed the existence of God as transcendent and inscrutable creator who becomes pluralized in epiphanic figures of a spiritual nature. These essences of pure light, which the philosophers call intelligences and the holy law angels, are the only spiritual beings with whom man can enter into contact. The angels par excellence are those who govern the seven planets, in which they have their visible temples. It is thus necessary to turn to the star, assuming its nature in one's dress and gestures, places, astrological times, rites and requests, in order to address its angel, who in his turn will serve as mediator with God for man's material and spiritual expectations.

This quite blatant syncretism of religious, magical and astrological elements constitutes (with few exceptions) the distinctive feature of the ceremonial magical literature of Arab origin which circulates in Latin under the direct or indirect aegis of Hermes. Nevertheless, despite this basic homogeneity, Pingree suggests a generic classification, distinguishing the texts on the basis of the means used to achieve the effect: thus, there is a division between magic which makes use of amulets, on the one hand, and magic which makes use of talismans, on the other.

An amulet is a stone, usually a gem, naturally endowed with occult virtues, that is capable on its own of producing specific physical or spiritual effects. This special power originates in the planet to which the stone corresponds and can be amplified by operating at the astrological time in which the stellar position provides the greatest output of the influence desired. The principle of classifying sublunary objects (animals, plants, stones) into "sets" is of Neoplatonic derivation. Originally

it was assumed that every being possesses the essential virtue of a divine higher principle, whose imprint is only weakly present in each element but can be activated by appealing to the sympathies among all the links in the chain of beings that share the same virtue. But already in the magic of late antiquity, the stars as such had replaced the classic gods, and the sets had become entirely astrological. In its simplest form, magic which makes use of amulets can be considered strictly "natural" since it is limited to using the extraordinary powers present in sublunary beings only. A unique example of this "zero degree" magic in the corpus of Hermetic literature is the *De lapidibus Veneris*. This text lists ten stones belonging to the domain of Venus, endowed with occult medical properties (in the widest sense of the term). The virtues inherent in stones can be heightened or modified by mixing them with other ingredients, chosen by means of the principle of analogy. The *De lapidibus Veneris* is attributed to Toz the Greek, a mysterious figure whose name appears in different versions in manuscripts and in indirect testimonies. His identification with the Egyptian god Toth has recently been questioned by Pingree, who sees in it a pseudonym (Ta'us, the peacock). It serves as a *nom de plume* for one or more authors who specialized in describing operations connected to the influence of the planet Venus. That Toz belongs to the Hermetic domain is confirmed by other works, in which he appears in company with Germa the Babylonian, that is Hermes the Babylonian of the genealogy of Abū Ma'shar. And it is not improbable that Latin readers spontaneously associated Toz with Tat, the pupil of Hermes in the *Asclepius*. Because of its total absence of astrological, ritual and figurative elements, the *De lapidibus Veneris* is an anomalous text in the Hermetic magical tradition. Usually, amuletic magic also involves the engraving of a picture of the planet on the stone. As the studies of Fritz Saxl and Jean Seznec have shown, these images are connected to the iconography of the ancient stellar gods, whose survival in the West was guaranteed by the magical texts. In the *De imaginibus sive annulis septem planetarum*, attributed to or at any rate associated with Hermes, there is a description of the different planetary images that must be engraved at the suitable astrological time on gems appropriate to each planet, which will then be set in rings made of metal pertaining to the same sympathetic domain. The effectiveness of the ring in traditional activities connected to the planet depends upon the observance of certain prohibitions, which in some cases suggest religious taboos, while in other cases their intention seems to be simply to prevent mistakes in respecting the boundaries of the sympathetic domain. In the *De duodecim annulis*, which introduces Toz the Greek and Germa the Babylonian as authorities, there is a description of twelve gems to be engraved at precise astrological moments, and then set in rings, which can be worn or used as seals. The first four stones belong to the domain of Venus, confirming that this was the authors' specialization; the remaining ones are linked to the other planets, with the exception of Mars. Writing or invoking the names of God, the angels and the hours is required for all the rings; only in one case does the prescription mention merely the writing down of what is intended. The *De duodecim annulis* also contains dietary, lustral and sexual prohibitions, which are as detailed as they are far-fetched. The presence of religious elements becomes more evident in some texts of amuletic magic which include an actual sacred ceremony. In the *Liber Mercurii Hermetis* the engraving of two different images of Mercury must be preceded by a staged procession, which requires participation of the magus and a young assistant, and by a long peroration whose aim is to invoke the planetary spirit by means of listing his attributes. The fashioning of two rings is accompanied by suffumigations, invocations, songs and chants, a sacrifice and a ritual meal. An analogous ceremony is to be found in the *Liber Saturni* attributed to Hermes, translated perhaps in Chaldaean by Apollonius, "philosopher of Egypt", and from there into Latin by an otherwise unknown Theodosius archbishop "Sardiensis". The presence of planetary prayers is not at all uncommon in the magic of late antiquity; but it is interesting to note the similarity of these orations to the descriptions, known to us from other sources, of the ceremonies of the Harranians, which often coincide in gestural details and in the planet and angel names invoked. A very detailed planetary liturgy is described in the *Liber orationum planetarum septem*. Even if the *Liber* is not attributed to Hermes, its close textual affinities with Arab accounts give evidence of its belonging to the Hermetic Harranian tradition.

In talismanic magic, as distinct from amuletic magic, an image is molded or carved in metal, or in rare cases modelled in wax or clay. The material used does not contribute to the success of the operation, since it has no particular occult property and at most must respect the planet's sympathetic domain. The image, too, is hardly of influence, since it does not stand in relation to the planetary iconography but merely "represents" the pursued aim. The elements which in amuletic magic are merely added to the natural property of the stones and the planetary depictions, become pre-eminent in talismanic magic, that is to say: the choice of the astrological time and the elaborate ritual which takes place around the image (pronouncement of names, engraving of characters or symbols with appropriate types of ink, recital of a prayer, and use of suffumigations). At the end of this complex ceremony, the image must be either worn or buried with an appropriate exorcism. The words and names to be pronounced can merely be epithets of the star in various languages, or simple statements expressing the magician's wish, or, far more frequently, actual prayers of a persuasive kind which aim at attracting the spiritual force of the planet and obliging it to flow into the talisman and, through it, exert an influence on the place or the person.

An interesting collection of talismanic magic with the title of *Liber septem planetarum ex scientia Abel* spread very rapidly in the Latin world. The Arab original, which remains unidentified, was translated twice, first by Adelard of Bath and then by → Robert of Chester (after 1144). The collection consists of seven books, one for each planet, according to the sequence Moon-Sun-Mercury-Venus-Mars-Jupiter-Saturn; but Adelard's translation has come down to us with the third and fourth books missing. The first treatise, *Liber Lunae*, has an interesting prologue which reproduces, with some meaningful variants, the genealogy of the three Hermeses narrated by Abū Ma'shar. The ancient philosophers, who had foreseen the imminent flood, had carved the precepts of the sciences and the arts on marble pillars as a record for posterity. After the flood, Hermes Triplex had gone to Hebron, the city of Adam, of his son Abel, and of most of the antediluvian sages. Here he had retrieved almost all the tablets buried by the ancient philosophers; among these had come to light the stones on which Abel had relied for the survival of his talismanic doctrine, *praestigiorum scientia*, the first and most perfect of all. Hermes had tested one of the talismans, confirmed its effectiveness, and hence had decided to transcribe Abel's precepts. The effectiveness of the talismans, made of different metals, depends on the positions of the planets, on the names or symbols which are engraved on various parts of the image, on the words (specific for each talisman) which are pronounced, on suffumigations, and on the prayers which must be recited, during the various phases of the operation, to God, the zodiacal angels and the planet dominating the talisman. The operative prescriptions are preceded by highly detailed preparatory recommendations: a period of purification with daily baths, prayers, observance of daily fasting and a nightly meal with bread of wheat crushed by one's own hands and water likewise personally drawn. The physical preparation must contribute to creating a proper psychological attitude in the operator, of whom perfect moral qualities are also required.

This operative procedure is a constant feature in the texts on talismanic magic, even if certain details may vary. In Belenus' *De imaginibus septem planetarum*, the preparation of the images involves all the elements listed in the *Liber planetarum* (writing of the planet's name and seal, suffumigation and prayer to the spirits, burial), but it makes no mention of pronouncing names proper to the specific purpose, whereas it does prescribe the use of a metal appropriate to the planet. The *De imaginibus et horis*, attributed by some manuscripts to Hermes, does not talk of suffumigations and prayers, but of the need to pronounce the name of the interested party, the name of the planet, and the aim to be achieved, while the names of the day, the hour and the planet's characters have to be written on the image. The ritual dedicated to Venus in Toz's *Liber de stationibus ad cultum Veneris* and in Toz-Germa's *Liber Veneris* must have been particularly complex. Only a small fragment of *De stationibus* survives, from which can be conjectured only that the ceremony included at least five stations; but a lost manuscript divided the text into fifty chapters (therefore does this mean that there were fifty stations?). By contrast, the content of the *Liber Veneris* can be reconstructed, although it remains confused, from three manuscripts – all of which are unfortunately incomplete – corresponding to three different translations, one of which is attributed to John of Seville. Despite numerous discrepancies, it seems possible to identify three magical operations: the construction of talismans, the fashioning of rings (some coinciding with those of the *De duodecim annulis*) and the preparation of four magical mirrors (*De quattuor speculis*). All the operations involve preparatory purification rituals, determining the astrological time, choosing the material, writing the names of planets and angels, suffumigations, and invocations. As regards talismans, which predict the future and induce the angels of Venus to appear before the magus, two manuscripts speak of a three-dimensional image which must be dressed in garments of five colors. But the third manuscript refers to the fashioning of a head, *caput*. The mention of a prophetic "caput" is interesting since it seems to confirm the link between the *Liber Veneris* and the Harranian tradition

and, in particular, one of the most macabre legends of human sacrifice practised by the inhabitants of Harran. Arab historical sources report with obsessive regularity the Harranian custom of immersing a man up to his neck in a mixture of oil and spices until his head came off, which was then supposed to pronounce prophecies. In his recent study on the religion of the Harranians, Jan Hjärpe insists on the lack of neutrality of these testimonies and hypothesizes that such charges, apart from being customary in religious polemic, resulted from a malevolent and distorted interpretation of practices which were actually alchemical or magical. The *Liber Veneris* would seem to bear this out, even if the question of where the sources got the other details of the story still needs to be clarified. It should also be noted that in one of the manuscripts the list of the names of the angels of Venus and of the planets is preceded by a warning that 'these are the names of the Greek Sabaeans of Harran', that is the Harranian Neoplatonists.

Also linked to talismanic magic is the text which in the West had the greatest fortune of all, the *Liber imaginum Lunae*, available in Latin at least from the first decades of the 13th century and then widely circulated in two different translations. The *Liber imaginum Lunae* attributes the actual composing of the text to Belenus, after the doctrine of his master Hermes, and lists the talismans to be fashioned when the Moon is in one of its twenty-eight mansions (that is to say, in the star or group of stars in which the Moon appears or "makes station" each night of its monthly course). The list of lunar mansions specifies neither what image to write nor what material to use, but limits itself to indicating the name of the mansion, its color (an element referring back to Babylonian tradition), its favorable or unfavorable quality, the name of the planet which dominates it, and, lastly, the aims which can be achieved by each talisman. This Hermetic list coincides with an exclusively astrological list contained in other manuscripts, which also marks the Moon's location in the Zodiac and the design of the stars that make up the station, but contains no indication as to what initiatives should be undertaken and as to Hermes' authorship. This would suggest an Arabic adaptation of a more ancient and merely astrological doctrine derived from Indian tradition, which made use of the lunar mansions for divinatory purposes from the middle of the second millennium B.C. In some Latin manuscripts the text on mansions is preceded by a brief prologue, which gathers together all the elements typical of Greek revelation literature as analysed by Festugière. In his tireless research Hermes discovered this wondrous book hidden inside a set of coffers, each more precious than the last; he decided to translate the work into Arabic to make it available to sages, while at the same time cautioning them to keep the content secret since its extraordinary power would make it dangerous in the hands of the ignorant. In a fair number of the Latin manuscripts the list of lunar mansions is followed by two writings by Belenus, the *De viginti quattuor horis* and the *De imaginibus diei et noctis*. The first relies on an Arab reworking of a Greek original attributed to Apollonius of Tyana, which probably dates from the 3rd century and also has a Syrian parallel by the title *Testament of Adam*. The text lists the names of the twenty-four hours and specifies the classes of beings which at that hour turn their prayers to God. These elements are supplemented in the Arab translation and then in the Latin one by the indication of the talismans to fashion at each hour. The *De imaginibus diei et noctis* is an elaboration of Arab origin of Apollonius' doctrine of hours; in fact it contains precepts for fashioning the talismans of the twenty-four hours (time and purpose, material, size, weight, figure, names of hours, God and angels, suffumigations). Some talismans are purported to have been fashioned and used by Apollonius himself; these stories are similar to those found in numerous Greek writings from the 5th century on. Four other talismans, not linked to the hours, are described in a sort of brief appendix, the *De quattuor imaginibus magnis*. In the oldest Latin manuscripts the Hermetic list of lunar mansions and the two texts by Belenus are presented as a single whole. The link probably dates back to the Arab originals and seems to be confirmed by the operative introduction to the *Liber imaginum Lunae*: the consecration ritual of the talisman in fact involves elements which were traceable only in the two texts attributed to Belenus. The Greek original of the *De viginti quattuor horis* also contains the names of the seven days and of the seasons, the names of the sun and the moon, the earth, the heavens and the sea in each of the four seasons. In Latin this section is preserved with the title of *De sigillis Mercurii* or *De discretione operis differentia ex iudiciis Hermetis de intentione huius operis*, attributed to Belenus, and in some manuscripts it is placed after the three texts mentioned above.

3. THE FORTUNE OF HERMETIC CEREMONIAL MAGIC IN LATIN: TRANSLATIONS AND DISPUTES

A fascination with knowledge which is also power is evident throughout Adelard of Bath's career as a translator. In his *Quaestiones Naturales*

Adelard (ca. 1080-1155) unhesitatingly acknowledges his interest in magic and tells us how he took lessons from an aged expert in magical operations. He is a true pioneer in exploring works on magic, and has the deliberate cultural objective of introducing this "useful" and "puissant" art into the scientific curriculum and legitimizing it as the operative branch of astrology (which he and other translators strive to establish as a science as well). In addition to his translation of Abū Ma'shar's *Isagoge minor* and of the first thirty-nine aphorisms of the pseudo-Ptolemaic *Centiloquium*, Adelard puts the *Liber planetarum ex scientia Abel* into Latin. Stylistic and terminological affinities suggest he has also had a hand in translating Belenus' *Liber de imaginibus septem planetarum*. Furthermore he translates the *Liber praestigiorum Elbidis secundum Hermetem et Ptolomaeum*, a text attributed to Thābit ibn Qurra, interpolating Hermetic elements into it.

In his *De essentiis* (1143), Herman of Carinthia generically refers to Iorma the Babylonian and Tuz the Ionian as "operators of talismans", *thelesmatici*. But the references get more and more precise when the texts of the two authors are available in the translation of John of Seville. → Daniel of Morley's *Liber de naturis inferiorum et superiorum* cites Toz's 'great and universal *Liber Veneris*' as a fundamental text of the 'science of images'. The circulation of texts on magic may have aroused some reaction on the part of theologians, since John of Seville's preface to his translation of Thabit's *De Imaginibus Astrologicis* alludes to objections advanced in the name of the faith, *sub praetextu religionis*, concerning the propriety of spreading a morally reprehensible (*infamis*) doctrine. But this does not stop the circulation of Hermetic texts, all of which are probably available by the first decades of the 13th century (given the fact that the authors who discuss them from 1230 on state that they read them 'in their youth', 'long ago').

The Hermetic ceremonial texts were destined, for various reasons, to play a central role in the broad theological and scholarly debate which developed, between 1230 and the end of the century, about astrology and the operative techniques linked to it. First, they constitute a true *corpus*, quantitatively substantial, homogeneous in content and conceptually consistent with the theory of magic as expounded in the *Asclepius*. Second, they are associated with the mythical figure of Hermes Trismegistus: the progenitor of all magicians and father of idolatry according to Augustine, but also, in the interpretation of Lactantius and Quodvultdeus, a philosopher divinely inspired in his presentiment of the mysteries of the Christian God. Finally, thanks to their "extreme" operative nature, they make it possible to develop very different argumentative strategies in the general discussion of astrological magic. Taken as a prototype of *all* magic, they made it possible for some authors to radicalize their condemnation and to extend it to any kind of magical operation; taken instead as only *one* of its possible modes, they made it possible for other authors to set up a distinction between different kinds of magical operation and to utilize the condemnation of Hermetic magic in the interest of legitimizing other modes.

Pastoral concerns are behind the categorical condemnation by William of Auvergne, Bishop of Paris from 1228 to 1249, of all magical material and the very figure of Hermes Trismegistus. His goal is to cut away at its very base, *gladio et igne*, all interest in magical literature, 'which has been written either by men deceived by demons and having become in turn deceivers of other men, or directly by demons'. The Hermetic citations contained in his *De fide et legibus* (1228-30) and *De universo* (1231-36) testify to William's updatedness: they refer to Hermes' *Liber septem planetarum ex scientia Abel, De imaginibus et horis* and *Liber Saturni*, Belenus' *Liber imaginum Lunae* and *De viginti quattuor horis*, Toz's *De stationibus ad cultum Veneris, Liber Veneris* and *De quattuor speculis*. His detailed textual references accord with the works we possess today. Only one quotation remains unidentified; the story of the angels Haroc and Maros is not found in the *Liber Veneris* of the *Liber septem planetarum*; and the distinction of three kinds of magnets attributed to Hermes is in Toz's *De lapidibus Veneris*. In his *De universo* William makes a sharp distinction between two kinds of magic: on the one hand there is natural magic, which is limited to using the occult properties of physical beings, and which was bestowed by divine Providence so that men might employ it for noble ends; on the other hand, there is necromantic magic, which uses operative techniques such as images, characters and incomprehensible words. The astrological images and the figures that old women carve for evil purposes, *invultuationes vetularum*, do not act from their own intelligence or will, or from their own natural virtue, or from some specific celestial virtue captured in the moment of its making and absorbed inside the talisman. Their effectiveness therefore depends on the action of demons, who seduce men in order to lead them toward astral idolatry. William thus connects Augustine's picture of Hermes the false prophet and false philosopher with the Hermes mentioned

as author of texts on amulets and talismans: smallscale reproductions of the statues animated by demons as described in the *Asclepius*. William's overall analysis is important because of his lexical and conceptual specification of the notion of *necromantia*, which in the usage of many Latin translators and thinkers takes on the broad generic sense of "magic". The distinction between natural magic and necromantic magic, as put forth by William, was to contribute to the slow but progressive development of the latter term towards a notion of "demonic magic" in the full sense of the word.

A contemporary of William, → Michael Scot, court astrologer of Frederick II, confronts the problem of Hermetic magic from a very different stance. His *Liber Introductorius* (1228-1235), an encyclopedic manual in three books written at the request of Frederick, is an introduction into astrology, but opens with discussions of cosmology, meteorology, geography, physics and medicine. According to Scot, astrology is the noblest of the seven liberal arts because of its 'necessary veracity'; it is inferior only to the science of theology and forms the basis of numerous other branches of knowledge, among which is magic. It goes without saying that given this relationship to astrology, magic can only be judged by Scot as being true (*verax*) and highly useful. Scot repeatedly insists on the validity of its techniques and on the real, non-illusory character of the operations of the astral spirits. The stellar bodies and their ruling angels are instruments of the divine will and signs of the order which governs natural and human actions. The reduction of talismanic science to astrology makes possible a 'necromantia secundum physicam', that is an operative non-demonic technique, which is a simple practical application of the knowledge of the relationships between the stars and the events of the sublunary world. Scot writes that he has personally and successfully carried out operations of astrological magic following Hermes' *Liber imaginum Lunae*, which because of its proven utility is reproduced in its entirety in the *Liber introductorius*, together with Belenus' *De viginti quattuor horis*. But, apart from the historical value of this testimony, Scot's knowledge in the area of Hermetic magic does not seem to have been very wide. On the other hand, the ethical problem which these techniques present to the good Christian is quite evident to him. Divinatory science is 'abominable' and prohibited by the Church: not because of its content, which is true because it is founded on astrology, but rather because of the 'malice' it teaches. Magic is not included in the philosophical curriculum because of its ethically reprehensible aims, *magistra omnis iniqui-tatis*. Scot's position, halfway between recognition on the scientific level and condemnation on the religious one, reflects the difficulty of absorbing the new magical material into the traditional cultural framework.

→ Albertus Magnus' judgment of the literature of Hermetic magic is marked by a profound evolution in his thinking. In his *De mineralibus* (datable from 1255-1262 according to some, from before 1250-1252 according to others), his adherence to Hermes' magical and alchemical doctrines is far-reaching and consistent with his acceptance, in other works, of the cosmology and anthropology of the *Asclepius*. The theme of the carving of images and seals is extensively treated, even though the discussion is presented almost as a digression, meant to satisfy the curiosity of 'socii'. Albert in fact specifies that the explanation of the effects of images and seals is not the province of physics but of that 'sort of necromancy which is subordinate to astronomy', since the proof is derived from the principles of astronomy (observation of stellar configurations and movements, that is, astrology), of magic (knowledge of the occult properties inherent in a stone, that is, natural magic as William of Auvergne understands it) and of "necromantic science" (understood generically as a technique for utilizing the astrological correspondances between heaven and earth, or astrological magic). Actually, the discussion of images is not at all marginal for Albert, who is in fact very much interested in legitimizing it 'propter bonitatem doctrinae' in the context of his vision of natural causality. Admitting the relationship of obedience according to which sublunary bodies are subject to the stars, Albert explains the power of artificially carved stones in perfect analogy with the power of stones found already carved in nature, such as a marble he has seen in Venice which bore the image of a crowned king with a long beard. In both cases the figure determines the introduction of a special astral influence, a modification of the form (*forma substantialis*) of the stone, and hence the acquisition of a particular occult virtue. But while in the images carved by nature the imprint of the celestial influence is direct, in the case of artificial images it is the operator who acts as the instrument mediating between the stars and the stone. The *scientia imaginum* is therefore legitimate, since it fits into the context of normal natural causality. Albert cites Toz the Greek, Germa the Babylonian and Hermes the Egyptian as the first 'praeceptores et professores' of this discipline, which was then passed down to Ptolemy and Geber and reached its

perfection in Thabit. Toz and Hermes are most likely intended in his generic reference to the 'two great books of Venus', mentioned without any indication of authorship. But Albert's approbation of Hermetic magic requires some clarifications. The magical procedure described by *De mineralibus* mentions only three elements: the astrological phase, the figure to be engraved, and the material used (mostly gems, although he alludes in passing to the use of metal). What is being dealt with therefore is a type of amuletic and talismanic magic which cannot be strictly defined as Hermetic since there appear in it none of the ritual elements that characterize almost all the texts on Hermetic ceremonial magic. Among the Hermetic writings which have survived, only *De septem annulis septem planetarum* corresponds to the operative type outlined by Albert; but the planetary images described in *De Mineralibus* certainly do not derive from it. On the other hand, Albert explicitly rejects recourse to 'incantationes, impetrationes sive adiurationes, characteres', that is to say, to those elements which are an integral part of Toz's *Liber Veneris*. In short, the references of *De Mineralibus* do not prove with certainty that, at this time, Albert was directly familiar with the works of Hermes, Toz and Germa, but they do suggest generic information mediated from other sources, which Albert fits into his interpretation of Hermetism as an extremely ancient and primal philosophy. By contrast, in his *Summa theologiae* (begun after 1272 and left incomplete) Albert's judgment is very different. *Necromantia*, understood here in its full sense of demonic magic, is traced (at least dubitably, *secundum quosdam*) directly to the teachings of Achot the Greek, Germa the Babylonian and Hermes the Egyptian. The authors who in *De mineralibus* were cited as initiators of a natural legitimate science are now linked to necromantic texts 'de imaginibus et annulis et speculis Veneris et sigillis daemonum'. It is hard to understand the reasons for this shift in perspective toward the Hermetic texts. Albert's later perspective may have been influenced, at least in part, by the urgency of the contemporary debate on astrology and magic; and perhaps also by the *Speculum astronomiae*, which condemns Hermes' talismanic magic without appeal (see below). But it is possible that this new judgment of Albert also depends on his direct reading of the Hermetic texts, from which he could have concluded that there is a basic incompatibility between the ritual magic contained therein, and the "natural" explanation of astrological images which he sustained in *De mineralibus* and still intended to defend.

In the *Speculum astronomiae* (ca. 1255-1260), the attribution of which is still an object of debate, the bibliographical acquisitions from the Arabic are subjected to a careful adjustment which is of great philosophical and documentary interest. The aim of the *Speculum* is establishing the scientific basis of astrology, demonstrating its agreement with Aristotelian science and with Christian theology, and distinguishing it from doctrines and practices incorrectly confounded with it. After having described the various aspects of the science of the stars (astronomy and astrology, subdivided into theory and practice), in chapter 11 the anonymous author addresses the problem of the science of images, which he subdivides into three categories. The necromantic images described by the Hermetic texts are considered abominable. They adopt generic references to astrology but actually their effectiveness is based upon a religious liturgy that is different from that of Christianity and therefore idolatrous. The necromantic images described in the texts of Solomon and the Hebrew authors are less dangerous but equally detestable. They do not resort to actual ceremonials but present inscriptions of characters that are unknown and therefore suspect, since they may conceal acts contrary to the sanctity of the Christian religion. The third and last category is that of the properly astrological images described in Thābit ibn Qurra's *De imaginibus astrologicis*. These images, fashioned at an auspicious astrological time, are fully licit, since they limit themselves to utilizing stellar influxes without resorting to idolatrous rituals. Thus the classification of images rests on the analysis of the role which the single operative elements play in producing their effect. Prayers, the engraving of characters and the pronouncement of unknown words, typical of Hermetic and Solomonic necromantic magic, identify a supernatural agent as object of veneration and are therefore demonic practices. By contrast, the engraving of intelligible words – such as *amor, destructio* – and the pronouncement of the name of the thing and of the planet, which Thabit makes use of in his astrological images, refer to a natural agent, that is to say, the stellar influx. The presence of magical formulas ("may this talisman produce this effect") is not in itself suspect, since it is a mere enunciation of intent, addressed to beings of the sublunary sphere, and does not constitute an act of idolatry. Although it proceeds from William of Auvergne's distinction between natural magic and necromancy, the *Speculum* significantly modifies that distinction, broadening the notion of natural magic to the point of fully including in it astrological influence. This interpretation of magic is very close to Albertus' in *De mineralibus*, but is based on a profound knowledge of the texts. The Hermetic literature cited by the *Speculum* is nearly the same as William's: Toz-Grema's *Liber Veneris*, *De stationibus ad cultum Veneris*, *De quattuor speculis*; Hermes-Belenus' *Liber imaginum Lunae*; Belenus' *De imaginibus diei et noctis* and *De quattuor imaginibus magnis*; Hermes' *De sigillis Mercurii* (described as part of a larger collection, unknown to us, called *Liber imaginum Mercurii*), *Liber Martis, Liber Iovis* and *Liber Saturni* (that is, the last three books of the *Liber planetarum ex scientia Abel*), a text unknown to us, which would have followed the Abel series (*Tractatus octavus in magisterio imaginum*), *De imaginibus et horis, Liber Veneris* (whose incipit does not correspond to those of the surviving texts), and the *Liber praestigiorum* (actually the translation, altered by Adelard, of Thabit's text on images). The author of the *Speculum* justifies the possible gaps and lack of precision in his bibliographical references by the fact that he read these books a long time ago and by the horror caused in him by that reading, *quoniam eos abhorrui, non extat mihi perfecta memoria*. But as far as the Hermetic texts on amuletic and talismatic magic are concerned, his memory is very exact, in that he cites and condemns almost all of them. Nonetheless, if it is true that the bibliographical updating is from a fairly remote period, it is hard to accept the attribution of the *Speculum* to the Albertus Magnus who, at the time of the *De mineralibus*, i.e. not many years earlier, does not seem to have had direct knowledge of the Hermetic texts.

With the *Speculum*, the project of integrating the magus Hermes into the scientific curriculum can be considered to have failed. In his *Tractatus brevis et utilis* (1268-1270), Roger Bacon denies the authenticity of the texts on magic which circulate under Hermes' name. The whole of magical necromantic literature is written by demons or by men inspired by demons, and it has been attributed to Adam, → Moses, Solomon, Aristotle and Hermes so as to better deceive and seduce 'not only youths, but even mature adults and authoritative persons, as we unfortunately witness in our day'. Thomas Aquinas' *Summa contra Gentiles* (1269-73) and his *Summa theologiae* (begun in 1269 and left incomplete) reassert Augustine's condemnation of Hermes, who in the *Asclepius* taught the cult of statues, *imagines*, animated by demons. But in his discussion of astrological images Aquinas does not even mention Hermes. His polemical objection is to the theory of astrological magic found in Albertus' *De mineralibus* and in the *Speculum*. Artificial images acquire no special virtues by human operation, other than the natural one impressed on them by celestial bodies. Therefore their extraordinary effects do not depend on their respective substantial forms, but must be considered the work of demons. The distinction between "astrological" and "necromantic" images, carefully traced in the *Speculum*, is reduced for Aquinas to a mere distinction of the ways in which demons are invoked. While in the necromantic images the prayers and the pronouncement of names represent 'expressa pacta cum daemonibus inita', in the astronomical images the pact remains a tacit one, understood through the use of characters and figures.

Paradoxically, a treatise *De essentiis essentiarum*, with the full recognition it grants to Hermes' necromantic images, circulated as a work of Thomas Aquinas himself. The author, a Dominican Thomas who seems to have written it prior to 1309, aims at demonstrating that celestial bodies do not derive their influences from souls but from the Intelligences that govern them. To prove his thesis, he tells of having used the *Liber planetarum ex scientia Abel* to fashion a talisman inscribed with the names of the planet and its Intelligence.

In the first quarter of 14th century at the latest, the *Liber de imaginibus Lunae* was briefly commented upon by an anonymous scholar. The *Glosulae super librum imaginum Lunae*, which are preserved in an unique manuscript, explain why sympathetic rules must be respected and discuss the meaning of characters according to three different interpretations. A broad extract from Adelard's translation of the *Liber planetarum ex scientia Abel* and some shorter excerpts from Solomonic magical literature are also inserted.

→ Peter of Abano's fame as magus and necromancer derives from the attribution to him of pseudoepigraphic works close to the Judaeo-Christian magical tradition, *Heptameron seu Elementa magica* and *De annulis secundum viginti octo mansiones Lunae*, but this fame does not find confirmation in the texts of certified authorship. In his *Lucidator dubitabilium astronomiae* (1302-1310) Peter of Abano associates himself with the interpretive line of the *Speculum* and sanctions the scientific validity of astrology by distinguishing it from the vain and superstitious practices of demonic magic. He also seems to have drawn from the *Speculum* the traditional distinction between "strictly" astronomical images and necromantic images, and the customary condemnation of Hermetic literature, rather generically referred to ('imagines . . . Hermetis, Belenuz, Thozz greci, Germath Babylonensis, *Liber Lune Liberque*

Veneris et aliorum planetarum . . . libri satis obsceni ac intellectus depravativi'). On the other hand, Peter also reintroduces the legend of Hermes as inventor of all the sciences and identifies him with the biblical Enoch, thus presenting the figure of Hermes under two profoundly different identities: 'Hermes Enoch seu Mercurius', who gave rise to the scientific tradition of observation and representation of celestial images; and Hermes the necromancer, inventor of an "evil and detestable" art, dangerous to religion and rightly condemned. The invocation of spirits is heresy, declares Peter in his *Conciliator differentiarum philosophorum et praecipue medicorum* (1302-1310); but his intent is to explain the physical effectiveness of the *incantationes* as a result of the psychosomatic transitive force of the → imagination. Astronomical images do not address themselves to spiritual entities but reproduce stellar configurations, capturing the eminently physical influence determined by the various clusterings of celestial bodies, median causes, instruments of divine action and principles of motion. Upholding the validity of the astronomical images described by Ptolemy and by Thābit ibn Qurra, Peter describes how, in order to cure a case of kidney stones, he used a lion figure carved in gold under the domain of the zodiacal sign (that is, a seal described at the beginning of the *Liber formarum duodecim signorum*). But Peter does not recall the Hermetic origin of this talisman.

At the beginning of the 14th century, the Leo seal described by the *Liber formarum* is now part of a tradition of disparate attributions (Hermes, John of Seville, Andreas Cordubensis, Arnau de Vilanova) and is a commonly prescribed remedy in the Jewish medical milieu of Montpellier. In effect, in his *Speculum medicinae* Arnau de Vilanova recalls the Leo seal 'described by Hermes' and in his *Aphorismi particulares* he describes the virtues of the Pisces seal as a remedy against gout. Perhaps for these reasons the manuscript tradition often associates the *Liber formarum* with Arnau's name, indicating him as the author of the entire text or at any rate as the one responsible for the additions to the original Hermetic work. The Christian adaptation of the *Liber formarum duodecim signorum*, which was printed among Arnau's works under the title *De sigillis*, is, however, apparently not his. A *Glosa super imagines duodecim signorum Hermetis* was composed by the doctor of arts and medicine Antonius de Monte Ulmi, who flourished at Bologna between 1384 and 1390. Antonius says that he tested some Hermetic images and that they always fulfilled his expectations. But, according to the *Glosa*, their effectiveness should be increased by adding a suffumigation, inscribing the name of the zodiacal angel and pronouncing a prayer (more or less Christian in tone) to the spirits. The procedure is identical to the one which Antonius expounds in his *De occultis et manifestis artium et medicinae* or *Liber intelligentiarum*, where he gives evidence of being quite familiar with Solomonic and Hermetic ceremonial literature.

The actual contribution of Hermetism is much more difficult to determine in the case of some authors traditionally interested in demonology. We do not know the reasons for the condemnation of Cecco of Ascoli (Francesco Stabili), burnt at the stake in Florence in 1327. It was influenced possibly by the rash digressions which run throughout his comments on two canonical texts on astrology, the *Sphere* by Sacrobosco and the *Liber introductorius* by Alcabitius. In his *Commentary on the Sphere*, astrology is defined as 'glory of our mind and divinity of human nature, to be desired more than the glory of divine things, as Hermes states'. But Hermes is in fact remembered only as a writer on astrology, while there are repeated and lengthy quotations of theurgic authors and texts, not always identifiable but linked to Solomonic and Jewish magic. The hodge-podge of news and anecdotes, found in this work, never arranges itself into a systematic and theoretical exposition of necromantic magic; rather, it seems to be a pretext for expounding, while attributing them to others, heretical interpretations of important aspects of the Christian doctrine (the birth of Christ from the union of the Virgin with a demon, the eclipse which occurred during the Passion as the magical effect of the use of the heliotrope, and the horoscope of religions). In his *Commentary* on Alcabitius's text Cecco confronts the problem of astronomical images by giving them a strictly physical explanation. The astral position, *aspectus modalis*, under which the metal is melted and engraved, enables the material to gain the correct proportion of elements from which the effectiveness of the talisman derives. The example cited by Cecco (a tin talisman fashioned while Venus is in Pisces or in Taurus) recalls Toz-Germa's *De quattuor speculis*; but Cecco makes no mention of the engraving of angel names or invocations. Instead, 'Zot graecus et Germa Babilonensis' are cited, together with Evax, King of the Arabs, only with regard to the natural properties of the carbuncle; the reference is to Toz's *De lapidibus Veneris*.

As a result of its subterranean and semi-clandestine circulation, Hermetic ceremonial literature lost much of its theoretical specificity, and found itself relegated to the vague and confused realm of necromantic practice. Further research is necessary in order to provide a complete and clear picture of textual borrowings and the paths of transmission of medieval Hermetic texts as well as of the ways in which they intertwine and overlap with those belonging to other traditions.

The Hermetic texts, their commentaries and the critical bibliography are indicated in section A (Philosophical-religious Hermetism) and in section B (Technical and Operative Hermetism). The sequence of the texts is as a rule the one followed in the essay. It is preceded by a short general bibliography on the manuscripts and the latin editions. The critical editions and, in their absence, the *editio princeps*, are indicated. The following abbreviations are used: CTC = *Catalogus Translationum et Commentariorum: Mediaeval and Renaissance Latin Translations and Commentaries*, Washington: The Catholic University of America Press, 1960 (I), 1971 (II), 1976 (III); CCCM = Corpus Christianorum: Continuatio Mediaevalis, Turnhout: Brepols. For a summary presentation of the texts and of the manuscripts, see Paolo Lucentini & Vittoria Perrone Compagni, *I testi e i codici di Ermete nel Medioevo* (Appendice: Paolo Lucentini & Antonella Sannino, *Le stampe ermetiche*), Firenze: Polistampa, 2001 (hereafter: Lucentini & Perrone Compagni).

Francis J. Carmody, *Arabic Astronomical and Astrological Sciences in Latin Translation: A Critical Bibliography*, Berkeley-Los Angeles: University of California Press, 1956, 52-70 ♦ Karl. H. Dannenfeldt, "Hermetica philosophica", in: Paul O. Kristeller (ed.), *CTC* I, 137-151 (Appendix I: Marie-Thérèse d'Alverny, "Liber XXIV philosophorum", 151-154; Appendix II: Theodore Silverstein, "De VI rerum principiis", 155-156) ♦ Paul O. Kristeller, "Hermetica philosophica: Addenda et corrigenda", *CTC* II, 423 ♦ Marie-Thérèse d'Alverny, "Hermetica philosophica: Addenda et corrigenda", *CTC* III, 425-426 ♦ Hermann Diels, "Die Handschriften der antiken Ärzte. II. Die übrigen griechischen Ärzte ausser Hippokrates und Galenos", Berlin: Verlag der Königl. Akademie der Wissenschaften, 1906 (Aus den Abhandlungen der Königl. Preuss. Akademie der Wissenschaften vom Jahre 1906), 43-48 ♦ Raymond Klibansky & Franz Regen, *Die Handschriften der philosophischen Werke des Apuleius: Ein Beitrag zur Überlieferungsgeschichte*, Göttingen: Vandenhoeck & Ruprecht, 1993 ♦ Paolo Lucentini, *L'edizione critica dei testi ermetici latini*, in: Vincenzo Placella & Sebastiano Martelli (eds.), *I moderni ausili all'Ecdotica* (Atti del Convegno Internazionale di Studi, Fisciano, Vietri sul Mare, Napoli, 27-31 ottobre 1990), Napoli: Edizioni Scientifiche Italiane, 1994, 265-285 ♦ Lynn Thorndike & Pearl Kibre, *A Catalogue of Incipits of Mediaeval Scientific Writings in Latin*, Cambridge (Mass.): The Mediaeval Academy of America, 1963, passim (see Index).

New perspectives on philosophical-religious and technical and operative Hermetism are to be found in: Paolo Lucentini, Ilaria Parri, Vittoria Perrone

Compagni (eds.), *Hermetism from Late Antiquity to Humanism, La tradizione ermetica dal mondo tardo-antico all'Umanesimo: Convegno internazionale di studi, Napoli, 20-24 novembre 2001* (Instrumenta Patristica et Mediaevalia, 40), Turnhout: Brepols, 2003.

A. PHILOSOPHICAL-RELIGIOUS HERMETISM

Asclepius, ed. Paul Thomas, *Apulei Opera*, III, Leipzig: Teubner, 1908, 36-81; ed. Walter Scott, *Hermetica: The Ancient Greek and Latin Writings which Contain Religious or Philosophic Teachings Ascribed to Hermes Trismegistus*, I, Oxford: Clarendon Press, 1924, 286-377; ed. Arthur D. Nock & André-Jean Festugière, *Corpus Hermeticum*, II, Paris: Les Belles Lettres, 1945, 296-355; Claudio Moreschini (ed.), *Apulei Opera*, III, Stuttgart, Leipzig: Teubner, 1991, 39-86 ♦ *Glosae super Trismegistum*, ed. Paolo Lucentini, *Archives d'histoire doctrinale et littéraire du Moyen Âge* 62 (1995), 189-293 ♦ *Liber viginti quattuor philosophorum*, ed. Heinrich Denifle, "Meister Eckeharts lateinische Schriften und die Grundanschauung seiner Lehre", *Archiv für Literatur- und Kirchengeschichte des Mittelalters* 2 (1886), 427-429; ed. Clemens Baeumker, "Das pseudo-hermetische Buch der vierundzwanzig Meister (Liber XXIV philosophorum): Ein Beitrag zur Geschichte des Neupythagoreismus und Neuplatonismus im Mittelalter", in: *Studien und Charakteristiken zur Geschichte der Philosophie, insbesondere des Mittelalters: Gesammelte Aufsätze und Vorträge* (Beiträge zur Geschichte der Philosophie des Mittelalters, 25: 1-2), Münster, 1927, 194-214 (1st edition in *Festgabe von Hertling*, Freiburg i. B., 1913, 17-40); ed. Françoise Hudry, CCCM 143 A, 1997 ♦ *Liber de sex rerum principiis*, ed. Theodore Silverstein, *Archives d'histoire doctrinale et littéraire du Moyen Âge* 22 (1955), 217-302.

Lit.: Marie-Thérèse d'Alverny, "Un témoin muet des luttes doctrinales du XIIIᵉ siècle", *Archives d'histoire doctrinale et littéraire du Moyen Âge* 17 (1949), 223-248 ♦ Mario Bertolini, "Sul lessico filosofico dell'Asclepius", *Annali della Scuola Normale Superiore di Pisa* 15 (1985), 1151-1209 ♦ Roelof van den Broek, "Hermes and Christ: Pagan Witnesses to the Truth of Christianity", in: Roelof van den Broek & Cis van Heertum (eds.), *From Poimandres to Jacob Böhme: Gnosis, Hermetism and the Christian Tradition*, Amsterdam: In de Pelikaan, 2000, 115-144 ♦ Mark Damien Delp, *De sex rerum principiis: A Translation and a Study of a Twelfth-Century Cosmology*, Ph. Diss. University of Notre Dame, Ann Arbor (Mich.): U.M.I., 1995 ♦ Giulio D'Onofrio, "L'età boeziana della teologia", in: *Storia della teologia nel Medioevo*, II. *La grande fioritura*, Casale Monferrato: Piemme, 1996, 353-356 (Il Liber XXIV philosophorum) ♦ Peter Dronke, *Hermes and the Sibyls: Continuations and Creations*, Inaugural Lecture Delivered 9 march 1990, Cambridge: Cambridge University Press, 1990 ♦ Carlos Gilly, "Die Überlieferung des Asclepius im Mittelalter", in: van den Broek & van Heertum, *From Poimandres to Jacob Böhme*, 335-367 ♦ Françoise Hudry, *Le Livre des XXIV Philosophes*, Grenoble: Millon, 1989 ♦ eadem, "Le Liber XXIV philosophorum et le Liber de causis dans les manuscrits", *Archives d'histoire doctrinale et littéraire du Moyen Âge* 59 (1992), 63-88 ♦ Paolo Lucentini, "Il Commento all'Asclepius del Vaticano Ottoboniano lat. 811", in: Michele Ciliberto & Cesare Vasoli (eds.), *Filosofia e cultura: Per Eugenio Garin*, I, Roma: Editori Riuniti, 1991, 39-59 ♦ idem, "L'Asclepius ermetico nel secolo XII", in: Haijo J. Westra (ed.), *From Athens to Chartres: Neoplatonism and Medieval Thought. Studies in Honour of Edouard Jeauneau*, Leiden, New York, Köln: Brill, 1992, 397-421 ♦ idem, "Il corpo e l'anima nella tradizione ermetica medievale", in: Luisa Rotondi Secchi Tarugi (ed.), *L'Ermetismo nell'Antichità e nel Rinascimento*, Milano: Nuovi Orizzonti, 1998, 61-72 ♦ idem, *Il Libro dei ventiquattro filosofi*, Milano: Adelphi, 1999 ♦ idem, "Il Liber viginti quattuor philosophorum nei poemi medievali: il Roman de la Rose, il Granum sinapis, la Divina commedia", in: John Marenbon (ed.), *Poetry and Philosophy in the Middle Ages: A Festschrift for Peter Dronke*, Leiden, Boston, Köln: Brill, 2001, 131-153 ♦ Dietrich Mahnke, *Unendliche Sphäre und Allmittelpunkt: Beiträge zur Genealogie der mathematischen Mystik*, Halle: Niemeyer, 1937 ♦ Claudio Moreschini, *Storia dell'ermetismo cristiano*, Brescia: Morcelliana, 2000 ♦ Ilaria Parri, "Note sul Libro dei ventiquattro filosofi", in: Stefano Caroti & Roberto Pinzani (eds.), *Ob rogatum meorum sociorum: Studi in memoria di Lorenzo Pozzi*, Milano: Angeli, 2000, 155-170 ♦ David Porreca, *The Influence of Hermetic Texts on Western European Philosophers and Theologians (1160-1300)*, Ph. Diss. Warburg Institute, University of London, 2001 ♦ Gilles Quispel, *Asclepius: De volkomen openbaring van Hermes Trismegistus*, Amsterdam: In de Pelikaan, 1996, 211-250 ♦ Kurt Ruh, *Geschichte der abendländischen Mystik*, III. *Die Mystik des deutschen Predigerordens und ihre Grundlegung durch die Hochscholastik*, München: Beck, 1996, 33-44 (Liber XXIV philosophorum) ♦ Antonella Sannino, "La tradizione ermetica a Oxford nei secoli XIII e XIV: Ruggero Bacone e Tommaso Bradwardine", *Studi filosofici* 18 (1995), 23-56 ♦ eadem, "The Hermetic Sources in Berthold of Moosburg", *Journal of the Warburg and Courtauld Institutes* 63 (2000), 243-258 ♦ Paolo Siniscalco, "Ermete Trismegisto, profeta pagano della rivelazione cristiana: La fortuna di un passo ermetico (Asclepius 8) nell'interpretazione di scrittori cristiani", *Atti della Accademia delle Scienze di Torino. II. Classe di Scienze Morali, Storiche e Filologiche* 101 (1966-1967), 83-117 ♦ Loris Sturlese, "Saints et magiciens: Albert le Grand en face d'Hermès Trismégiste", *Archives de Philosophie* 43:4 (1980), 615-634 ♦ idem, "Proclo ed Ermete in Germania da Alberto Magno a Bertoldo di Moosburg", in: Kurt Flasch (ed.), *Von Meister Dietrich zu Meister Eckhart* (Corpus Philosophorum Teutonicorum Medii Aevi, 2), Hamburg: Meiner, 1984, 22-33 ♦ R.B. Woolsey, "Bernard Silvester and the Hermetic Asclepius", *Traditio* 6 (1948), 340-344.

B. Technical and Operative Hermetism

I. Astrology, Medicine and Natural Magic, Divination

Kyranides, ed. Louis Delatte, *Textes latins et vieux français relatifs aux Cyranides* (Bibliothèque de la Faculté de Philosophie et Lettres de l'Université de Liège, 93) Liège-Paris, 1942 (hereafter: Delatte, *Textes*), 3-206 ♦ [Alexander Magnus] *De septem herbis*, unpublished; cf. Lucentini & Perrone Compagni, 40-42 ♦ [Thessalus] *Liber de virtutibus herbarum*, ed. Hans-Veit Friedrich, *Thessalos von Tralles griechisch und lateinisch* (Beiträge zur klassischen Philologie, 28), Meisenheim am Glan: Anton Hain, 1968 ♦ [Flaccus Africus] *Compendium aureum*, ed. Delatte, *Textes*, 207-233 ♦ *De triginta sex decanis*, ed. Wilhelm Gundel, *Neue astrologische Texte des Hermes Trismegistos: Funde und Forschungen auf dem Gebiet der antiken Astronomie und Astrologie* (Abhandl. Bayer. Akad. Wiss., Philos. – histor. Abteil., N. F. 12), München, 1936, 19-111; ed. Simonetta Feraboli, CCCM 144, 1994 ♦ *Iatromathematica*, transl. David Hoeschelius, *Ratio judicandi de morbis et infirmorum decubitu ex mathematica scientia*, in: Thomas Boderius, *De ratione et usu dierum criticorum*, Parisiis: A. Wechel, 1555, ff. 52r-56v; transl. Johannes Stadius, *Iatromathematicum*, in: Johannes Stadius, *Ephemerides nouae et exactae ab Anno 1554 ad Annum 1570*, Coloniae Agrippinae: A. Birckmanns Erben, 1556, ff. a3r-b3v ♦ *Liber de quindecim stellis quindecim lapidibus quindecim herbis et quindecim imaginibus*, ed. Delatte, *Textes*, 235-275 ♦ [Enoch] *Tractatus de quindecim stellis*, ed. Delatte, *Textes*, 276-288 ♦ [Thabit ibn Qurra] *De proprietatibus quarundam stellarum*, unpublished; cf. Lucentini & Perrone Compagni, 49 ♦ [Apollonius] *De secretis naturae*, ed. Françoise Hudry, "Le De secretis nature du ps.-Apollonius de Tyane, traduction latine par Hugues de Santalla du Kitāb sirr al-ḥalīqa", *Chrysopœia* 6 (1997-1999), 1-154 ♦ *Liber de Spatula*, ed. Charles Burnett, CCCM 144 C, 2001, 251-272 ♦ *Liber alius de eadem*, ed. Charles Burnett, CCCM 144 C, 2001, 273-283 ♦ *Liber de stellis beibeniis*, ed. Paul Kunitzsch, CCCM 144 C, 2001, 9-81 ♦ *Fragmentum pseudo-Aristotelicum*, ed. Charles Burnett & David Pingree, *The Liber Aristotilis of Hugo of Santalla* (Warburg Institute Surveys and Texts, 26), London: The Warburg Institute, 1997, 48-51 (reprint in CCCM 144 C, 2001, 101-107) ♦ *Liber Antimaquis*, ed. Charles Burnett, CCCM 144 C, 2001, 177-221 ♦ *De amicitia vel inimicitia planetarum*, CCCM 144 C, 2001, 223-228 ♦ *Liber de quattuor confectionibus ad omnia genera animalium capienda*, ed. Antonella Sannino, "Ermete mago e alchimista nelle biblioteche di Guglielmo d'Alvernia e Ruggero Bacone", *Studi medievali* 41 (2000), 151-209 ♦ *Centiloquium*, in: Ptholemaeus, *Liber quadripartiti*, Venetiis: per Erhardum Ratdolt, 1484 ♦ *Liber de accidentibus*, ed. Paolo Lucentini, CCCM 144 C, 2001, 139-173 ♦ *Liber duodecim formarum*, unpublished; cf. David Pingree (ed.), *Picatrix: The Latin version of the Ghāyat al-Hakīm*, London: The Warburg Institute, 1986, 82-85 ♦ Hieronymus

Torrella, *Opus praeclarum de imaginibus astrologicis*, Valencia: apud Alphonsum de Orta, 1496, ff. miir – miiiv ♦ *Capitulum de arbore borissa*, ed. Vera Segre Rutz, "Le piante della Luna", in: Laurent Golay, Philippe Lüscher & Pierre-Alain Mariaux (eds.), *Florilegium: Scritti di storia dell'arte in onore di Carlo Bertelli*, Milano: Electa, 1995, 124-129 ♦ *Lectura geomantiae*, ed. Thérèse Charmasson, CCCM 144 C, 2001, 349-397 ♦ *Tractatus de iudicio urinae*, unpublished; cf. Lucentini & Perrone Compagni, 55.

II. Ceremonial Magic

Almost all Hermetic texts on ceremonial magic are as yet unpublished; cf. Lucentini & Perrone Compagni, 59-93 ♦ [Hermes] *De imaginibus sive annulis septem planetarum, Liber planetarum (Liber Saturni), Liber Mercurii, De imaginibus et horis, Liber septem planetarum ex scientia Abel, Liber orationum planetarum septem* ♦ [Belenus] *Liber imaginum Lunae, De viginti quattuor horis, De imaginibus diei et noctis, De quattuor imaginibus magnis, De discretione operis differentia ex iudiciis Hermetis (De sigillis Mercurii), De imaginibus septem planetarum* ♦ [Toz Graecus] *De lapidibus Veneris, De stationibus ad cultum Veneris* ♦ [Toz Graecus-Germa Babiloniensis] *Liber Veneris, De quattuor speculis, De duodecim annulis* ♦ The *Liber imaginum Lunae* and the *De viginti quattuor horis* have been published according to Michael Scot's reworked edition by Paolo Lucentini, "L'ermetismo magico nel secolo XIII", in: Menso Folkerts & Richard Lorch (eds.), *Sic itur ad astra: Studien zur Geschichte der Mathematik und Naturwissenschaften. Festschrift für den Arabisten Paul Kunitzsch zum 70. Geburtstag*, Wiesbaden: Harrassowitz, 2000, 409-450 ♦ The *Liber orationum planetarum septem* has been published according to the ms. Darmstadt 1410 by V. Perrone Compagni, "Una fonte ermetica: il Liber orationum planetarum septem", *Bruniana & Campanelliana* 7 (2001), 189-197.

Lit.: Charles Burnett, "Michael Scot and the Transmission of Scientific Culture from Toledo to Bologna via the Court of Frederick II Hohenstaufen", *Micrologus: Natura, scienze e società medievali* 12 (1994), 101-126 ♦ idem, *Magic and Divination in the Middle Ages: Texts and Techniques in the Islamic and Christian Worlds*, Aldershot: Variorum, 1996 ♦ Thérèse Charmasson, *Recherches sur une technique divinatoire: La géomancie dans l'Occident médiéval*, Paris, Genève: Droz, 1980 ♦ Claire Fanger (ed.), *Conjuring Spirits: Texts and Traditions of Late Medieval Ritual Magic*, Phoenix Mill, Stroud, Glouchestershire: Sutton, 1998 ♦ André-Jean Festugière, *La révélation d'Hermès Trismégiste*, I, Paris: Gabalda, 1950 ♦ Tamara M. Green, *The City of Moon God: Religious Traditions of Harran*, Leiden, New York, Köln: Brill, 1992 ♦ Charles H. Haskins, *Studies in the History of Medieval Science*, Cambridge (Mass.): Harvard University Press, 1924 ♦ Jan Hiärpe, *Analyse critique des traditions arabes sur les Sabéens Harraniens*, Uppsala: Skriv Service, 1972 ♦ Paul Kunitzsch, "Zum Liber Hermetis de stellis beibeniis", *Zeitschrift der Deutschen Morgenländischen Gesellschaft* 118 (1968), 62-

74 ◆ idem, "Neues zum Liber Hermetis de stellis beibeniis", *Zeitschrift der Deutschen Morgenländischen Gesellschaft* 120 (1970), 126-130 ◆ Paolo Lucentini, "L'ermetismo magico nel secolo XIII", in: Folkerts & Lorch (eds.), *Sic itur ad astra*, 409-450 ◆ idem, "Il Liber de accidentibus ermetico e il commento di Haly Abenrudianus al Tetrabiblos di Tolomeo", in: Stefano Caroti & Roberto Pinzani (eds.), *Ob rogatum meorum sociorum: Studi in memoria di Lorenzo Pozzi*, Milano: Angeli, 2000, 93-122 ◆ Vittoria Perrone Compagni, "Studiosus incantationibus: Adelardo di Bath, Ermete e Thabit", *Giornale critico della filosofia italiana* 80:1 (2001), 36-61 ◆ David Pingree, "Some of the Sources of the Ghāyat al-Ḥakīm", *Journal of the Warburg and Courtauld Institutes* 43 (1980), 1-15 ◆ idem, "The Diffusion of Arabic Magical Texts in Western Europe", in: Bianca Scarcia Amoretti (ed.), *La diffusione delle scienze islamiche nel Medio Evo europeo: Atti del Convegno Internazionale (Roma, 2-4 ottobre 1984)*, Roma: Accademia Nazionale dei Lincei, 1987, 57-102 ◆ idem, "al-Ṭabarī on the Prayers to the Planets", *Bulletin d'Études Orientales* 44 (1993), 105-117 ◆ idem, "Learned Magic in the Time of Frederick II", *Micrologus: Natura, scienze e società medievali* 2 (1994), 39-56 ◆ Antonella Sannino, "Ermete mago e alchimista nelle biblioteche di Guglielmo d'Alvernia e Ruggero Bacone", *Studi medievali* 41 (2000), 151-209 ◆ Fritz Saxl, "Beiträge zur einer Geschichte der Planetendarstellung", *Der Islam* 3 (1912) ◆ idem, *Verzeichnis astrologischer und mythologischer Illustrierter Handschriften des lateinischen Mittelalters*, Heidelberg, 1915 ◆ idem, "Rinascimento dell'antichità: Studien zu den Arbeiten A. Warburgs", *Repertorium für Kunstwissenschaft* 43 (1922), 220-272 ◆ Jean Seznec, *The Survival of the Pagan Gods* (orig. 1940), Princeton: Princeton University Press, 1981 ◆ Lynn Thorndike, *A History of Magic and Experimental Science*, II, New York, London: Columbia University Press, 214-235 ◆ idem, "Traditional Medieval Tracts concerning Engraved Images", in: *Mélanges Auguste Pelzer*, Louvain: Université de Louvain, 1947, 217-274 ◆ Pinella Travaglia, *Una cosmologia ermetica, il Kitab sirr al-ḫalīqa / De secretis naturae*, Napoli: Liguori, 2001 ◆ Nicholas Weill-Parot, *Les "images astrologiques" au Moyen Âge et à la Renaissance: Spéculations intellectuelles et pratiques magiques, XIIᵉ-XVᵉ siècle* (Sciences, techniques et civilisations du Moyen Âge à l'aube des lumières, 6), Paris: Champion, 2002.

PAOLO LUCENTINI (A & B1) &
VITTORIA PERRONE COMPAGNI (B2-3)

Hermetic Literature III: Arab

After the Arab armies conquered the largest part of the Middle East, including Egypt, Syria, and Mesopotamia, between 634 and 660 A.D., the moslem elites came into contact with a large array of religious and doctrinal trends within Christianity and Judaism, but also with remains of pagan thought and mysticism. They became progressively interested in several ancient disciplines, in the domains of astronomy and medicine, and also in philosophy and esotericism. Local scholars were invited at the caliph's and governor's courts, treatises were translated into Arabic during the 9th and 10th centuries – in some cases even earlier –, and these found a vast readership. Among the huge amount of translated Greek, Coptic or Syriac texts that were put into circulation, it is clear that those concerned with the so-called "occult sciences" aroused the earliest interest. It is not certain that we may trust our data about the Arabic translation of an alchemical treatise of → Zosimos in 658 (Sezgin 1971, 19ff.), or other translations ordered by the omeyyad prince Khâlid ibn Yazîd (d. 704) – the king Calid filius Jazichi appearing in the Latin treatise *Liber de compositione alchemiae*, and to whom the *Liber secretorum alchemiae* and the *Liber triorum verborum* are attributed (Ruska 1924; Ullmann 1978) – but they at least demonstrate the very early curiosity of Arabs towards these kinds of speculation and practice. We know that the hermetic literature composed in Egypt during late Antiquity comprises some doctrinal treatises ("hermétisme savant", according to Festugière's terminology), as well as others dealing with occult sciences such as → astrology, → alchemy and → magic ("hermétisme populaire"). The latter form of hermetism apparently aroused much more interest than the former one.

How exactly the hermetic literature in the Arabic language developed remains a puzzling question. The community of the Sabians of Harrân, with their star cult, must have played a key role in this transmission (Green 1997; Tardieu 1986). This pagan community of northern Mesopotamia, which practised a complex religion in which astrology played an important part, considered Hermes as one of their gods and as the inventor of sacred sciences and rituals. They obviously fascinated several moslem scholars who suspected the existence of a real wisdom behind the outward paganism of this community. The muslem philosopher → al-Kindî (d. 866) was supposed to have read 'a book in which these people believe, being the dialogue between Hermes and his son on theology [lit.: on God's oneness]. It was theologically so right that a philosopher, if he made an effort, could only adhere to it and profess it' (Ibn al-Nadîm, 385). The high level of their astronomers and mathematicians led some eminent personalities of their community to settle in Baghdad near to the caliphal court. There, in the political and cultural capital city of the empire, they may have made known the twofold function of Hermes, part god and part prophet, in which they believed. But the precise roads taken in the spread of hermetic conceptions remain obscure. To clarify them, we will first describe the extant remnants of this literature; and then analyse what the Arab hermetists took from the Greek literature, and how they understood it.

The Arabs never collected something like a *Corpus Hermeticum* in Arabic. The various fragments attributed to Hermes remain scattered among a large amount of treatises devoted to occult sciences, and deprived of unity. But first of all, who was Hermes according to the moslem scholars? Some considered him the inspired inventor of many arts. According to the most common version, first exposed by the astronomer Abû Ma'shar († 886) in his *Books of Thousands*, and then adopted with several changes of detail by bio-bibliographs like Ibn Juljul († 994), Sâ'id al-Andalusî († 1070), Mubashshir ibn Fâtik (11th century), Ibn Abî Usaybi'a († 1270), and others, there had actually existed three Hermeses. The oldest one, living in Egypt before the Flood, was supposed to have developed astronomy and → astrology as well as medicine and poetry. He was considered identical with the biblical Enoch and the koranic Idrîs. Foreseeing the Flood, he built the pyramids (Arabic: *haram*, etymologically associated by some authors with the name "Hermes") after having engraved in them the secrets of the sciences he had discovered. A second – Babylonian – Hermes was supposed to have restored the old sciences and developed medicine, mathematics and philosophy. A third "Hirmis" living in Egypt had practised and fostered the hidden sciences and especially alchemy and related disciplines in his country, and had been the master of Asklepios. Hence the name of "thrice great" (literally: "thrice wise", *al-muthallath bi-al-hikma*, among other titles. See Ullmann 1972 371-373; Plessner 1954). Among these authors, the Christian historian Ibn al-'Ibrî (Barhebraeus, † 1286) mentioned in his *Summary of the History of States* a link between the third Hermes and the inspirer of the *Corpus Hermeticum*. Of course, the belief in the existence of several figures called "Hermes" had been mentioned before in Greek literature. But in moslem culture, this myth acquired a new dimension. Since the ante-diluvian Hermes was often identified with the prophet Enoch (Ukhnûkh)/Idrîs, twice mentioned in the Koran (XIX 56-57 and XXI 85), the various teachings attributed to Hermes (concerning alchemy, astrology, magic, but also mathematics, medicine etc.) acquired a more orthodox status, almost of revealed sciences. As Louis Massignon put it, 'it

is thanks to Hermes-Idrîs that the hellenistic tradition reclaimed droit de cité in Islam, whereas the syllogistic method and the metaphysics of Aristotle were not yet accepted' (Massignon 1950, 385). In most hermetic texts in Arabic, the teachings of Hermes appear like a kind of revelations with a transcendent origin. In this respect, they follow the tradition of the Greek texts of the *Corpus Hermeticum* and we may rightly consider them as "hermetic literature" in the full sense of the word, even if they happen to be moulded into the framework of islamic prophetology. In this respect, Massignon went too far by listing as "hermetic" many philosophical or mystical treatises not referring expressly to Hermes nor presented as revelation (Plessner 1954). But the ancient literary context of a revelation by a Hermes (god or wise man) is often to be found in Arabic texts. In the *Book of the Secrets of Creation*, Apollonius of Tyana (Balînâs) finds the text of the *Tabula Smaragdina* in an underground place, in front of the wise Hermes himself. More dramatically, the *Book of Alexander's Treasure* was supposed to have been hidden by Hermes in an underground place, and then discovered by Apollonius, transmitted to Aristotle and from there passed on to Alexander. The Arab armies conquering the city of Amorium in 838 were believed to have finally discovered it again in a chest.

The hermetic texts in arabic language are dealing with several occult sciences, and generally mix them up. Magic and theurgy as well as alchemy are based on astrological conceptions, on the idea of the general correspondence between things, and on the theory of four elements and four qualities. We can nevertheless distinguish three main strands:

(1) Alchemy. The hermetica in Greek dealing with alchemy are rather scarce. Hence the importance of the texts which have reached us in Arabic. The role of Hermes as iniator into alchemy was known at least during the 3th/9th centuries. Ibn al-Nadîm, the famous librarian of Baghdad, reported in his *Catalogue* (finished in 987; Ibn al-Nadîm, 417-418) that people considered Hermes of Babel the first founder of alchemy, about which he had written on the walls of the pyramids after settling down in Egypt. Apparently, Ibn al-Nadîm believed that there was only one historical Hermes, and did not identify him with Enoch. In this account, quite different therefore from that of Abû Ma'shar mentioned *supra*, we notice the fundamental relationship established between the figure of Hermes and alchemy. Ibn al-Nadîm gives a list of thirteen Arabic texts by Hermes in his chapter on alchemy. But the extant works are far more numerous. Fuat

Sezgin (1971, 39-41) lists 18 known manuscripts. Of paramount importance are the *Great Treatise of the Sphere* and the *Treatise of the Secret*. The first is presented as a text by Hermes of Dendera, taught by the high priest Uwîrûs (Osiris), about the links between spirits and bodies and the transformation of metals; the second as an exchange of letters between Amnûthîsyâ (Theosebia) and the high priest Hermes Bûdashîr on the alchemical "weddings" needed for the preparation of the Stone. Both have been edited, translated into German and commented by Ingolf Vereno. We may also mention the *Book of the Sun and the Moon*, another interesting example: the sage Krates meets Hermes in a vision and discovers the secrets of the alchemical Art in a book placed in his hand. The text has been edited and translated into French by O. Houdas (Berthelot 1893, III). Ruska has suggested that it might have been written in the 9th or 10th century. In all these texts, the environment and background are clearly ancient, Greco-Egyptian, but framed in islamic formulas and ideas. The most famous of hermetic texts on alchemy is doubtless the *Tabula Smaragdina* (Ruska 1926; Plessner 1927). The question whether this short but fundamental summary of hermetic philosophy was translated from a Greek original or not is still under discussion. In any case, it was quoted by several Arab authors (Ullmann 1972, 171 gives 7 references). But the more complete and perhaps oldest mention of this text is to be found in *The Secrets of Creation* or *Book of Causes* attributed to Apollonius of Tyana (arabic: Balînâs). As said before, Hermes was supposed to have given it to Balînâs in a secret underground cave (complete edition by U. Weisser 1979). Generally speaking, Hermes plays the role of an inspirer of several other alchemical texts in Arabic, like those by Apollonius-Balînâs, Agathodaimon, "Artefius", and al-Habîb (Sezgin 1971; Ullmann 1972 index), and he is quoted by the most famous alchemical works of the time such as those ascribed to Jâbir ibn Hayyân (see Kraus 1942 chapters I, 4 and V, 5), Khâlid ibn Yazîd, Ibn Umayl, the *Turba Philosophorum*, and the great works of Aydamor Jaldakî (14th century; see Corbin 1983, 71f.).

(2) Astrology. Hermes plays a decisive role in the Arabic astrological tradition as well. As in the case of alchemy, he is often considered the founder of this science. The Jewish astrologer Mâshâ' Allâh († after 809) supposedly knew 24 treatises by Hermes on several astrological topics (Ullmann, 289). Ibn al-Nadîm (1988, 327) quotes five titles. Fuat Sezgin has recorded 23 titles of extant hermetic manuscripts on astrology (Sezgin 1971, 41-43).

Hermes' mastery of astrology is probably to be understood against the background of the koranic verses XIX, 56-57 where God says of Idrîs 'And mention in the Book Idrîs; he was a true man, a Prophet. We raised him up to a high place'; hence several legends circulated that described Hermes / Idrîs' travels through the heavens, where he stayed for several long years and could get acquainted with all the secrets of the influences of the planets and stars on the lower bodies. As the philosophical and scientific encyclopaedia *Epistles of the Brethren of Purity* (10th century) puts it: 'It is said that Hermes Trismegistus – who is Idrîs the prophet, peace be upon him – ascended to the sphere of Saturn where he turned during thirty years, until he had observed all the positions of the sphere. Afterwards he came down to earth and taught astrology to mankind. God the Exalted said: We raised him up to a high place'.

(3) Magic. Ibn al-Nadîm (373) records four treatises devoted specifically to magic. The books called *al-Istamâkhîs, al-Istamâtîs, al-Ustûtâs* or the important *Alexander's Treasure* for example are all dealing with the secret properties and influences of minerals, vegetals or animals upon other things, and with the manufacture of talismans. Other treatises are devoted to magic squares and the mystical science of letters (see Ullmann 1972, 374f.). With the exception of a few fragments, they remain unpublished, and their precise content and relation to hermetism therefore still needs to be analyzed. Hermetic themes are also present in the encyclopaedia of magic *The Purpose of the wise* (arabic: *Ghâyat al-hakîm*, latin: *Picatrix*), based on astrology and on the theory of → correspondences. In one passage, an interesting ritual for meeting one's "Perfect Nature", giving him guidance about the role of wisdom, and teaching him the truth of the secret sciences, is attributed to Hermes (*Ghâyat al-hakîm* 187f.; Corbin 1983, 51f.). But it must be noticed that the practice of magic in Islam distanced itself more and more from ancient pagan principles – found in the *Purpose of the wise*, for instance – and gradually came to focus more on literary aspects (such as words, letters, verses from the Koran).

Treatises similar in content to the Greek texts of the *Corpus Hermeticum* are scarce in arabic. This may be explained by the strong anti-pagan context of islamic spirituality. Neoplatonic [→ Neoplatonism], stoic or hermetic ideas were actually studied by numerous muslim philosophers and theologians, and many of them were adopted, but within the framework of koranic monotheism and everything that this entailed. In islamic mysticism

(Sufism) we find ideas like the correspondences between microcosmos and macrocosmos, or the contact with the inner master. But no explicit relationship is made with ancient hermetism. The case of the "illuminative philosophy" of Suhrawardî (executed in 1191), who claimed an initiatic inspiration going back to Hermes, → Zoroaster, and Plato (Corbin 1972, II and 1983, 49f.) is rather exceptional. Similarly, the andalusian mystic Ibn Sab'în (m. 1270) presented his spiritual teaching as related to that of several hellenistic sages, with Hermes as the greatest among them; his disciple Shushtarî (d. 1269) describes his own initiatic chain as starting with Hermes and ending with Suhrawardî and Ibn Sab'în. The *Epistles of the Brethren of Purity* (10th century) likewise mention Hermes as one of the great figures of ancient science and spirituality; and so do several other thinkers, notably the shî'ite philosophers of Iran like Mulla Sadra (17th century), studied by H. Corbin. But generally speaking, the hermetic influence remained implicit (sometimes linked with stories about the prophet Idrîs in sufi literature). Still, there remain some hermetic texts, the most famous of them being the treatise on the *Punishment of the Soul*, which circulated in Arabic and was even translated into Persian by Afzal al-dîn Kâshânî (13th century). It also came to be translated into Latin (*De castigatione animae*) and evoked renewed interest by Western scholars since the 18th century. This long exhortation to the human soul to take its leave from earthly desires and illusions and turn towards her own heavenly nature could have a hermetic origin; but some manuscripts attribute it to Plato or Aristotle, and its content could be acceptable to readers belonging to different philosophical trends. It must be noted that apart from these different treatises, numerous fragments attributed to Hermes, in all domains of human thought and science, are scattered through various texts of Arabic literature. See for the fragments related to alchemy Ullmann 1972, 169-170; for astrology *ibid.*, 292-293, for magic *ibid.*, 377; and for mysticism and philosophy *ibid.*, 378.

Now, all the above points towards a difficult and much-debated question: are all these texts attributed to Hermes translations of older Greek treatises – or must we see them as belonging to a huge corpus of pseudepigraphical literature? J. Ruska was among the defenders of the former interpretation. The almost complete absence of Greek parallels to the Arabic texts was, for him, proof that the latter had been written during the islamic era after the occult sciences had become popular among Muslims. But other research could lead one to the conclusion that the name of Hermes as an author on occult science was known much earlier. The hermetic treatises on *The Breadth of the Key of the Secrets of Stars* and *The Length of the Key of the Secrets of Stars* for instance were translated in 743, according to one manuscript. Besides, the discovery of the Nag Hammadi collection has adduced new material: some ideas of the Greek hermetic tradition were found in Coptic manuscripts belonging to this ancient library (→ Hermetic Literature I), and may later have passed through an Arabic translation (Plessner 1954). Fuat Sezgin has tried to sum up these several points in a dense synthesis (1971, 31-38). Particularly interesting for our concerns are the first two alchemical texts ascribed to Hermes and written in Arabic, *The Great Treatise on the Sphere* (dated 832, year of the visit of caliph al-Ma'mûn to Egypt) and the *Treatise of the Secret* (beginning of the 10th century or earlier) studied by Ingolf Vereno and mentioned *supra*. They present an obviously ancient kind of material (maybe from the 3th century): they contain details of pagan rituals, images and concepts – the date of an eclipse even refers to hellenistic Egypt. The spiritual dimension of the alchemical *opus* therefore corresponds to hellenistic alchemy (Vereno 1992, 337-339). But all these alchemical teachings are surely not translations (Vereno 1992, 332-333) but re-writings ('Bearbeitungen') by Arab authors aiming at an Arabic readership. They provide good illustrations of the transformation of the Greek hermetica during the ca. six centuries of islamic transition preceding their translation into Latin.

The conclusion of all this is that the relationship between Arabic culture and the hermetic tradition is a very strange one. It can hardly be seen as similar to the interest the Arab scholars displayed for medicine, astronomy, or philosophy. While "officially recognized" philosophers like al-Kindî, Fârâbî, or → Avicenna discussed, for instance, the ideas of Plato by comparing them to the aristotelian corpus, and tried to work out a synthesis of both, nothing like this happened in the case of hermetism. The role played by Hermes was and remained that of a source of inspiration, giver of an authorative speech, if not a revelation; the reader is placed in the position of an (ignorant but clever) disciple trying to grasp the mysteries taught to him. The very fact of Hermes' presence in a moslem milieu, where these books were read and commented – in spite of the fact that Muhammad's words were considered the final authoritative teaching in history, abrogating earlier doctrines –, seems quite revolutionary in and for itself.

Marcelin Berthelot, *La Chimie au Moyen Age*, vols. 1-3, Paris, 1983 (Osnabrück/Amsterdam: reprint Otto Zeller/Philo Press, 1967) ♦ Hermes, *Hermes Trismegistus an die menschliche Seele*, transl. by H.L. Fleischer, Leipzig 1870 and into english by W. Scott in: *Hermetica*, vol. 4, Oxford, 1936 ♦ New edition of the arabic text by A.R. Badawî in: *Al-iflâtûniyya al-muhdatha 'inda al-'Arab*, Dirâsât islâmiyya, vol. 19, Cairo, 1955 55-116 ♦ Ibn al-Nadîm, *Kitâb al-Fihrist*, ed. by Z.A. Ha'irî Mâzanderânî, Dâr al-Masîra, s.l. 1988; transl. by B. Dodge as *The Fihrist of al-Nadîm*, vols. 1-2, New York, 1970 ♦ *Kitâb ghâyat al-hakîm*, H. Ritter, ed., Studien der Bibliothek Warburg 12, Leipzig-Berlin 1933; trans. as *"Picatrix": Das Ziel des Weisen von pseudo Majrîtî* by H. Ritter and M. Plessner, Studies of the Warburg Institute 27, London, 1962 ♦ Ursula Weisser, *Buch über das Geheimnis der Schöpfung und die Darstellung der Natur (Buch der Ursachen) von Pseudo-Apollonios von Tyana*, Institute for the History of Arabic Science, Aleppo: University of Aleppo, 1979.

Lit.: Daniel Chwolsohn, *Die Ssabier und der Ssabismus*, St Petersbourg, 1856 (reprint Amsterdam, 1965) ♦ Henry Corbin, *En Islam iranien*, vols. 1-4, Paris: Gallimard, 1972 ♦ idem, *L'Homme et son Ange – Initiation et chevalerie spirituelle*, Paris: Fayard, 1983 ♦ idem, *L'alchimie comme art hiératique*, Paris: L'Herne, 1986 ♦ Tamara M. Green, *The City of the Moon God: Religious Traditions of Harran*, Leiden etc.: E.J. Brill, 1997 ♦ Paul Kraus, *Jâbir ibn Hayyân – Contribution à l'histoire des idées scientifiques dans l'Islam*, Mémoires présentés à l'Institut d'Egypte 45, Cairo, 1942 (Paris: reprint Les Belles Lettres, 1986) ♦ Pierre Lory, "Hermès/Idris dans la religion islamique" in: *Présence d'Hermès Trismégiste*, Paris: Albin Michel, 1988 ♦ Louis Massignon, "Inventaire de la littérature hermétique arabe", in: André Jean Festugière, *La Révélation d'Hermès Trismégiste*, Paris: Gabalda, 1950 (Paris: reprint Les Belles Lettres, 1983), I 384-400 ♦ Massimo Pappacena, "La figura di Ermete Trismegisto nella tradizione araba", in: Paolo Lucentini, Ilaria Parri & Vittoria Perrone Compagni (eds.), *Hermetism from Late Antiquity to Humanism: La tradizione ermetica dal mondo tardo-antico all'umanesimo. Atti del Convegno internazionale di studi, Napoli, 20-24 novembre 2001*, Turnhout: Brepols, 2003, 263-283 ♦ Martin Plessner, "Neue Materialen zur Geschichte der Tabula Smaragdina", *Der Islam* 16 (1927) ♦ idem, "Hermes Trismegistus in Arab Science", *Studia Islamica* 2 (1954) ♦ idem, entry "Hirmis", in the *Encyclopaedia of Islam*, Leiden: E.J. Brill, 1971 ♦ Julius Ruska, *Arabische Alchemisten*, Heidelberg: C. Winter, 1924 (Vaduz: reprint Sändig Reprint, 1977) ♦ idem, *Tabula Smaragdina*, Heidelberg: C. Winter, 1926 ♦ Fuat Sezgin, *Geschichte des arabischen Schrifttums*, vol. 4, Leiden: E.J. Brill, 1971 ♦ Michel Tardieu, "Sâbiens coraniques et 'Sâbiens' de Harrân'", *Journal Asiatique* 274 (1986), 1-44 ♦ Manfred Ullmann, *Die Natur- und Geheimwissenschaften im Islam* (Handbuch der Orientalistik I, Der Nahe und der Mittlere Osten, Ergänzungsband VI), vol. 2, Leiden/Köln: E.J. Brill, 1972 ♦ idem, "Khâlid ibn Yazîd und die Alchemie: Eine Legende", *Der Islam* 55-1 (1978) ♦ Ingolf Vereno, *Studien zum ältesten alchemistischen Schrifttum – Auf der Grundlage zweier erstmals edierter arabischer Hermetica* (Islamkundliche Untersuchungen, Band 155), Berlin: Klaus Schwarz Verlag, 1992.

PIERRE LORY

Hermetic Literature IV: Renaissance – Present

1. THE GOLDEN AGE (CA. 1471-1614) 2. REAPPRAISALS AND EXTENSIONS (1614-1706) 3. TESTIMONIES AT THE TIME OF THE ENLIGHTENMENT AND IN THE PRE-ROMANTIC PERIOD 4. THE OCCULTIST CONTEXT 5. SURVIVALS AND DEBATES (SECOND HALF OF THE 20TH CENTURY) & GENERAL CONSIDERATIONS

1. THE GOLDEN AGE (CA. 1471-1614)

Around the year 1450, in Florence, Cosimo de' Medici the Elder entrusted → Marsilio Ficino with the creation of a Platonic Academy. One of their intentions was to have the available writings of Plato translated into Latin. Then, ca. 1460, a collection of Greek manuscripts was brought to Florence by Leonardo da Pistoia, a monk returning from Macedonia. These texts or treatises, on which the title *Corpus Hermeticum* (now dated 2nd-3rd century A.D., henceforth referred to as C.H.) was later bestowed, belong to the genre of the so-called *Hermetica* [→ Hermetic Literature I] attributed to or related to → Hermes Trismegistus, and had been lost since Late Antiquity. Cosimo insisted that Ficino temporarily set aside his Latin translation of Platonic texts. Ficino's translation of the fourteen treatises (C.H. I-XIV) was finished in 1463 and printed at Treviso in 1471 under the title *Mercurii Trismegisti Pimander Liber de potestate et sapientia Dei*, or *Pimander*, together with a prefatory argument (*Argumentum*) by Ficino himself.

In his *Argumentum*, Ficino also called attention to another, related text: the *Asclepius*, considered by him as 'the most divine' in this kind of literature (an edition had just been printed in Rome in 1469, inserted into Apuleius's *Opera*). Unlike the C.H. proper, the *Asclepius* (originally known in Greek as *Logos Teleios*), had survived in an ancient Latin translation only (the original Greek version has never been found; a large part of it in Coptic translation surfaced only as late as the 20th century, in the Nag Hammadi Library). As of 1505 (see below), the C.H. and the *Asclepius* were combined in a great number of editions. Later, a series of other hermetic texts, from the so-called *Stobaei Anthologium* (compiled ca. 500 A.D. by Johannes Stobaeus of Macedonia) was added to that corpus (the *Anthologium* was published partly in Venice [1536], another part in Zurich [1543], the rest in Antwerp [1575]). The C.H. (often published under the title of the first treatise, *Poimandres*, rendered as *Pimander* since Ficino's 1471 translation) and the *Asclepius* enjoyed a considerable success. Up to 1641, no fewer than twenty-four editions of the C.H. appeared, not counting partial ones or translations into other European languages. They became a central element in Renaissance culture (on the presence of Hermetism in Renaissance art, see → Hermes Trismegistus III) and were most popular among the learned and prominent members of society. Throughout the Renaissance and in the following centuries they have been the subject of a great many commentaries.

Furthermore, as had already been the case prior to that period, the Hermetic treatises were considered the expression of a philosophy that had supposedly been transmitted over the sweep of centuries. Ficino called it *prisca theologia*. Later, it was also to be called, albeit in a slightly different sense, *philosophia perennis*. The latter term was introduced by an Italian Augustinian and Vatican librarian, Agostino Steuco (*De perenni philosophia*, Lyon 1540, new ed. 1590). Although staunchly attached to the Church's magisterium, he too tried to reconstruct the ancient philosophy as a foundation for restoring Christian unity (see → Tradition). The C.H., the *Asclepius*, and Hermes Trismegistus, were thus thought to belong to a far distant past: to the age of → Moses, or even earlier (on some variations in chronology, see → Tradition). Although they were of a pagan nature, they were considered to foreshadow Christian truths and be of a nature to give new depth to the Christian revelation. In his *Argumentum*, Ficino describes a "genealogy of wisdom" – explicitly referred to as *prisca theologia* – consisting of six main figures: Mercurius (Hermes) Trismegistus, Orpheus, Aglaophemus (an Orphic teacher of Pythagoras), Pythagoras, Philolaus, Plato. That list was later to undergo various changes depending on the various authors who presented it.

At the time of Ficino, → Giovanni Pico della Mirandola, whose *Oratio de hominis dignitate*

(1486) begins with a reference to the "Magnum, O Asclepi, miraculum" passage of the *Asclepius* (*Ascl.* 6), made a compound that included not only the traditions to which Ficino held, but also the kabbalah [→ Jewish Influences], which Pico believed had been entrusted to Moses on Mount Sinai. The same quest for origins prevailed in other esoteric currents. Indeed, the corpus of writings directly inspired by the C.H. and the *Asclepius* from the Renaissance until the present time itself constitutes one of these currents; it may be called Neo-alexandrian Hermetism, or Alexandrian Neo-Hermetism, but for convenience it will here be abbreviated as Hermetism (*stricto sensu*, i.e. as a term to be distinguished from "Hermeticism" [→ Hermeticism and Hermetic Societies], a much vaguer term whose connotations may refer to → alchemy, or even to esotericism in general). During these centuries, Hermetism was present in several countries, especially Italy, France, Germany and England.

Anthony Woodville's English translation of a few hermetic texts in the anthology *The dyctes or sayengis of the philosophers* (Westminster 1477, the first dated book in the history of English printing), published by William Caxton, bears witness to an early, albeit discreet presence of the C.H. in England. Woodville's anthology was later incorporated into other ones. In Italy, more than ten years before Giovanni Nesi's *Oraculum de novo saeculo* (Florence 1497), which belongs to the genre of hermetic literature, → Giovanni da Correggio had fiercely and loudly promoted a Hermetic Reformation of Christianity. He had caused sensation by appearing clad in symbolic garments in the streets of Rome in 1484, attended by servants similarly accoutered and claiming to be 'Giovanni Mercurio da Correggio, the Angel of Wisdom Pimander'.

→ Lodovico Lazzarelli, who saw in Correggio a new and divine prophet and considered him his mentor, has left us a vivid description of this event in a manifesto entitled *Epistola Enoch*, published probably in Milan ca. 1490. Another text of Lazzarelli, *Crater Hermetis* (complete title: "A Dialogue on the Supreme Dignity of Man, entitled the Way of Christ and the Mixing-Bowl of Hermes"), which he wrote probably between 1492 and 1494 (it remained unpublished until → Lefèvre d'Etaples edited it in 1505) is a fictitious conversation (very much in the form of the dialogues contained in the C.H.) between Lazzarelli himself, who plays the role of the initiator, and two other historical personalities, Ferdinand I of Aragon, king of Naples and Sicily, and his prime minister Giovanni Pontano, who are cast in the role of pupils. The *Crater*

Hermetis may be among the most interesting examples of Hermetic-Christian syncretism written during the Renaissance. It is certainly one of the most important hermetic texts of its time, if not for its direct influence, then at least with regard to the depth and originality of its contents. Furthermore, convinced of the equality of the Bible and the hermetic writings, in 1482 Lazzarelli dedicated to Correggio a manuscript in his own hand, which he had just completed. It consisted in three parts, each one opening with a dedicatory preface. The first contained Marsilio Ficino's translation of the *Pimander* (1471, i.e., *Corpus Hermeticum* I-XIV). The second contained the *Asclepius*. And the third contained the first Latin translation, by himself, of C.H. XVI-XVIII, i.e., three extra treatises which he had apparently discovered in a separate manuscript (unfortunately not preserved). He entitled this text *Diffinitiones Asclepii ad regem Ammonem*. In sum, far more even than Ficino and Pico, Lazzarelli appears to be a pure example of a "Christian hermetist" in the Renaisssance (in addition to being one of the first noteworthy authors instrumental in the early development of a Christian kabbalah [→ Jewish Influences III]). Strangely enough, he was almost completely passed over in silence by Frances A. Yates in her ground-breaking books since 1964, and not until recently has justice been done to him (in particular by Claudio Moreschini and Wouter J. Hanegraaff).

Jacques Lefèvre d'Etaples' first edition of the *Pimander* (Paris 1494) contains, besides Ficino's translation, a series of commentaries (*Argumenta*) of his own (long attributed to Ficino). The second edition (Paris 1505) was augmented with both the *Asclepius* and Lazzarelli's *Crater Hermetis* (but in an abridged version). Interestingly, it was the first time that the *Asclepius* had been published together with the C.H. As for → Symphorien Champier's *Liber de quadruplici vita: Theologia Asclepii Hermetis Trismegisti discipuli cum commentariis . . .* (Lyon, 1507), it contains Lazzarelli's translation of the *Diffinitiones Asclepii*, among other texts, but Champier substituted a commentary of his own for Lazzarelli's prefaces. He also goes as far as to include into the tradition of *prisca theologia* the doctrines of the Druids and elements drawn from the kabbalah.

As exemplified by Lefèvre and Champier, the French were generally much more cautious than their Italian or German counterparts regarding the "magical" elements of the C.H. All adherents of *prisca theologia* dealt with Hermetism from a perspective of Christian apologetics. This is reflected, for instance, in Gabriel du Préau's *Mercure Tris-*

mégiste ancient Thelogien & excellent Philosophe, de la puissance & sapience de Dieu . . . Auecq' un Dialogue de Loys Lazarel poëte chrestien intitulé le Bassin d'Hermès (Paris 1549; new ed. 1557), the first edition in French of C.H. I-XIV, of the *Asclepius* and (as the title indicates) of Lazzarelli's *Crater Hermetis*. Du Préau's book also contains abundant commentaries of his own, some of which were designed to establish parallels between the narrative of creation according to Moses and that of C.H. I.

In the wake of new scholarly publications, like the first edition of the original Greek C.H. by the French Catholic scholar Adrien Turnèbe (Paris 1554, with a preface by Angelos Vegerius), → François Foix-Candale, Bishop of Aire, near Bordeaux, published another in 1574 (C.H. I-XIV, accompanied by some other hermetic texts), and five years later produced very extensive commentaries of his own in French, in his *Le Pimandre de Mercure Trismégiste: de la Philosophie Chrestienne, Cognoissance du Verbe Divin . . .* (Bordeaux 1579, new ed. Paris 1587). In the latter book, the hermetic texts serve as supports of meditation on a great variety of questions, like those pertaining to the Soul of the World, the spirits of the elements, celestial bodies, etc. Among various sources, Foix drew on the *philosophia occulta* [→ occult/ occultism] of the Renaissance, and his book foreshadows some of the themes which → Christian Theosophy was to develop from the 17th century onward. The Huguenot Protestant Philippe du Plessis-Mornay, surnamed "the Pope of the Huguenots", who contrary to Foix gave chronological precedence to the Books of Moses over the C.H., did not proffer any passages of the latter, but wrote a number of laudatory, albeit not uncritical commentaries in his *De la vérité de la religion chrestienne . . .* (Antwerp 1581; English translation by Sir Philip Sidney, 1587). This work was published several times in a Latin translation and proved to be influential in the development of Protestantism in France.

Along with Foix, some 16th-century authors of importance, like → Giorgio, → Bruno and → Agrippa, must be counted amongst the most influential ones in later Hermetism in particular, and esoteric literature in general. → Francesco Giorgio (or Zorzi), who belonged to the Order of Friars Minor, was the author of *De Harmonia Mundi totius Cantica tria* (Venice 1525; Paris 1545, 1546; French translation by Guy Lefèvre de la Boderie, Paris 1578), and *In Sacram Scripturam Problemata* (Venice 1536; Paris 1622). These two works represent an original construction aimed at making the Ficininan hermetic *prisca theologia* coincide with → neoplatonism, kabbalah, and not least astrological [→ Astrology] and even alchemical elements. *De Harmonia mundi* was to enjoy a lasting success in several milieus, in particular among the representatives of most esoteric currents (see below). Heinrich Cornelius Agrippa and → Guillaume Postel were later to be among his enthusiastic followers. → Giordano Bruno makes frequent use of the Hermetic texts (notably in *Spaccio della bestia triomphante*, 1584). Not a Christian, unlike most other hermeticists of his time, he was all the less prone to share the hope nursed by others that a religious reconciliation might be effected by a general acceptance of Hermetism. He did not desire a reformed Christendom, but rather a return to the cults or beliefs of ancient Egypt as described in the *Hermetica*, and particularly in the *Asclepius*.

In Germany, some of Sebastian Frank's works attest to an interest in Hermetism. His *Die Güldin Arch* (Augsburg 1538) presents itself as a collection of biblical sayings and paraphrases, together with extracts from 'illuminated pagans and philosophers' like Hermes Trismegistus. In Basel (1542), Frank also made a German translation of both the *Asclepius* and C.H. I-XIV, completed by long commentaries dealing mostly with commonalities between the Bible and Nature (it remains unpublished; the manuscript is preserved in the Stadtbibliothek Augsburg). Much more esoterically oriented was another German, Cornelius Agrippa. Several writings of his are devoted to a hermeneutics of the C.H., particularly its third treatise: *Oratio in praelectionem Hermetis Trismegisti de Potestate et Sapientia Dei* (Cologne, 1535; an "oratio" given at the University of Pavia in 1515); *Liber de triplici ratione cognoscendi Dei* (1516); and *Dehortatio gentiles theologiae* (ca. 1526, a text in which, contrarily to the other two, Agrippa distances himself from Hermetism).

Not until the last two decades of the 16th century do we find two other authors of importance. First, the Italian Capuchin Hannibal Rossel, whose *Pymander Mercurii Trismegisti*, swollen to six volumes (Cracovia 1585-1590), is not so much a commentary on the C.H. as an encyclopaedic roll-call of a variety of philosophical themes, along with a presentation of C.H. I-VII and the *Asclepius*. This work was popular enough to require a second issue (in one vol., Cologne 1630). Second, → Francesco Patrizi, whose collection of hermetic texts is most extensive. His *Nova de universis philosophia* (Ferrara 1591) contains C.H. I-XIV, the *Asclepius*, and C.H. XVI-XVIII (*Diffinitiones Asclepii*), along

with the medieval so-called *Theologia Aristotelis*. Extracts were reissued under the title *Magia Philosophica* (Hamburg 1593). In the dedicatory preface, Patrizi asks Pope Gregorius XIV to place the C.H. on the academic curriculum as an alternative philosophy. Indeed, he subjected the Aristotelian philosophy to sharp criticism and wanted it to be ousted from Jesuit-run colleges. In 1592 he was appointed to the chair of Platonic philosophy at the University La Sapienza in Rom, but his attempts met with dire failure and his book was placed on the Index. Alongside such reforming plans as Patrizi's, other works continued to appear, like Mutius Pansa's *De Osculo, seu consensus ethnicae et Christianae philosophiae tractatus* (Marburg, 1605) – the "kiss" mentioned in the title being that which Hermetism and Christianity are supposed to exchange.

Any overview of modern Hermetism must also give attention to a very short text which, along with the foundational Greek texts mentioned above, pertains to the *Hermetica* and has been the object of innumerable discussions and esoteric commentaries until the present time. This is the famous *Tabula Smaragdina* (*The Emerald Tablet*, or *The Smaragdine Table of Hermes*, henceforth referred to as T.S.) Originally written in Greek (the original version is lost), its earliest known version (934 A.D.) is in Arabic, set within a small alchemical and philosophical treatise entitled *The Book of the Secrets of Creation*. A Latin translation circulated as early as the 12th century. The first printed edition, also in Latin, appeared in a compilation of alchemical texts, *De Alchemia* (Nurnberg 1541). Its brevity permits us to quote it here in full: 'True it is, without falsehood, certain and most true. That which is above is like to that which is below, and that which is below is like to that which is above, to accomplish the miracles of one thing. /And as all things were by contemplation of one, so all things arose from this one thing by a single act of adaptation./The father thereof is the Sun, the mother the Moon,/The wind carried it in its womb, the earth is the nurse thereof./It is he father of all works of wonder throughout the whole world./The power thereof is perfect./If it be cast on to the earth, it will separate the element of earth from that of fire, the subtle from the gross./With great sagacity it doth ascend gently from earth to heaven./Again it doth descent to earth, and uniteth in itself the force from things superior and things inferior./Thus thou wilt possess the glory of the brightness of the whole word, and all obscurity will fly far from thee./This thing is the strong fortitude of all strength, for it overcometh every subtle thing and doth penetrate

every solid substance./Thus was this world created./Hence will there be marvellous adaptations
achieved, of which the manner is this./For this reason I am called Hermes Trismegistus, because I
hold three parts of the wisdom of the whole world.
That which I had to say about the operation of
Sol is completed' (transl. According to Linden
2003, 27-28).

In the 16th century, fostered by the edition of
1541 (but earlier than that already), this rather
enigmatic prose poem has caused torrents of hermetic, alchemical, and theosophical ink to flow (see
Faivre, *Annuaire . . .*, 1985-1997). To mention
only a few remarkable commentaries in the esoteric
literature of that time, what might be called the
"T.S. tradition" was illustrated and enriched by
such authors as → Johannes Trithemius (see his correspondence with Germain de Ganay in 1505);
Gérard Dorn (*Artificii chymistici*, 1569; often reed-
ited as *Physica Trismegisti*, it is one of the works
of that time which foreshadows the advent of
the theosophical current); Jacques Nuysement
(*Traictez . . . du Vray Sel*, 1621), and not least →
Athanasius Kircher (in his *Oedipus Aegyptiacus*,
1653, see vol. II; see also *Mundus Subterraneus*,
1664-1665). What is known as the first German
translation (by Johan Schaubert) of the T.S. had
appeared in 1600.

2. REAPPRAISALS AND EXTENSIONS (1614-1706)

Isaac Casaubon, a Protestant minister in Geneva,
set out to prove (in a chapter of his *De rebus sacris
ecclesiasticis exercitations XVI*, London 1614) that
the C.H. had not been written prior to the 2nd or
3rd centuries A.D., and was therefore a forgery
of the early Christian Era. Although Casaubon's
name has long been attached to that new dating,
recent research (see especially Purnell 1976; Mulsow 2002) has shown that similar "discoveries"
had already been made by other philologists as
early as the 1560s. Nonetheless, the claim that the
C.H. had been erroneously dated could only deal
a heavy blow to its authority, since the authority of
a text, even at that time, was highly dependent
upon its age. But hermetism did not disappear
for all that; indeed, from then until now, many
esoterically-oriented authors and readers have
preferred to ignore or to downplay the significance
of the new dating of the Hermetic writings.

One of the first highly sympathetic exegetes
of the C.H. in early 17th-century Germany was
Heinrich Noll (*Theoria Philosophiae Hermeticae,
septem tractatibus*, Hanover 1617; *Theoria Philosophiae Hermeticae*, Copenhagen 1617; and *Pan-

ergii Philosophici Speculum, 1623, an initiatic
novel). Noteworthy too is, in Italy, Livius Galante,
who authored *Christianae theologiae cum platonica comparatio* (Bologna 1627). Furthermore, a
number of translations of the C.H. into European
languages appeared. A few extracts were presented
in German in "Verba Hermetis in Pimandro" (a
section set within the anonymous *Occulta Philosophia*, vol. II, Frankfurt 1613). More importantly,
Abraham Willemsz van Beyerland gave under the
title *Sestien boecken . . .* (Amsterdam 1643; new
ed. 1652) a Dutch version of sixteen treatises of the
C.H., based on Patrizi's text. Van Beyerland, who
was also a translator of → Jacob Boehme and himself a theosopher, added long, strongly theosophically oriented commentaries of his own. His
translation was used by the first translator into
German (1706, *cf.* below).

The first version of the C.H. in English (*The
Divine Pymander of Hermes Mercurius Trismegistus, in XVII Books. Translated formerly out of
the Arabick into Greek . . .*, London 1650; new ed.
1657) was made by John Everard. This Anglican
minister, a preacher at Kensington, had already
produced in 1640 a detailed commentary (preserved at the Bodleian Library in Oxford) of the
T.S. He also authored short translations from similar texts and some works of his own (see his *Some
Golden Treasures*, London 1653). The title, and
the preface signed J.F., attest to the ignorance of the
publishers, not least because they claim that these
books were originally in Arabic. The preface deals
mostly with the legendary figure of Hermes Trismegistus. Everard's book has proved to be very
influential in the development of Hermetism in
England (see below).

Along with → Paracelsianism, Hermetism became part of a medical debate principally illustrated by one of its proponents, the Dane Olaus
Borrichius (Olaf Borch), who composed a vibrant
apology for Hermetism and → alchemy (*Hermetis Aegyptiorum, et chemicorum sapientia . . .*,
Copenhagen 1674; see also his *De Ortu et progres-
sio chemiae* Copenhagen 1688, which contains a
detailed history of alchemical literature). This
was meant as a counter-attack against the German
Hermann Conring, in whose *De Hermetica Aegyptiorum vetere et paracelsicorum nova medicina*
(Helmstedt 1648, new ed. 1699) Hermetism and
Paracelsianism had come in for their share of harsh
criticism. In Conring's line, Johann Heinrich Ursinus also tried (in *De Zoroastre bactriano, Hermete
Trismegisto, Sanchoniatone Phoenicio, eorumque
scriptis, et aliis, contra Mosaicae scipturae antiqui-
tatem*, Nürnberg 1661) to demonstrate that the

C.H. was merely a collection of texts plagiarized from Christian sources. Both Conring's and Borrichius's works are of a particular interest here because they do not depend only on Paracelsianism and Hermetism, but also on alchemical literature. Nevertheless, the C.H. is rarely the object of commentaries in the alchemical discourses of the 17th century, although Hermes Trismegistus often appears therein as the tutelary figure of that science, for instance in → Michael Maier's *Symbola Aureae Mensae Duodecim Nationum* (Frankfurt 1617). Notwithstanding, the T.S. continued to trigger a lot of alchemical commentaries, for example those by → Isaac Newton are much developed. They are extant in the great quantity of alchemical manuscripts he had left to posterity (King's College, Cambridge), and which have recently been the object of a number of scholarly studies. Besides, Wilhelm Christoph Kriegsmann produced a most original, albeit fantastic "philological" commentary (*Hermetis Trismegisti . . . Tabula Smaragdina*, 1657).

Indeed, throughout the period, and ever after, the tendency was strong in Hermetic literature to blend Hermetism not only with alchemy, but also with Jewish or Christian Kabbalah, → Rosicrucianism, and generally with the *philosophia occulta* inherited from the Renaissance. Among Rosicrucian productions this tendency is instanced by Stellatus's (i.e. Christoph Hirsch's) *Pegasus Firmamenti, sive introductio brevis in Veterum Sapientiam . . .* (n.p., 1618), which associates Rosicrucianism with Hermetism, Paracelsianism, pansophy and alchemy. Opponents of Hermetism also often grouped these currents together. Two examples may serve to illustrate this. First, one year after the publication of Zorzi's (Giorgio's, see above) *Problemata*, the famous Catholic Priest Marin Mersenne, very much bent on orthodoxy and a famous opponent of such orientations, published his *Observationes et emendationes ad Francisci Giorgii Veneti Problemata* (Paris 1623), directed against Giorgio's work, but also Hermetism, Rosicrucianism, Robert Fludd (see below), etc. The other characteristic example is the Lutheran minister Ehregott Daniel Colberg. In his voluminous *Das Platonisch-Hermetisches* [sic] *Christenthum . . .* (Leipzig, 2 vols., 1690 and 1691, new ed. 1710), he settles scores with the C.H. as well as with Rosicrucianism, Theosophy, → mysticism, etc., reproaching them mainly for fostering a self-divinization of Man.

Within the pale of esotericism proper, → Robert Fludd, particularly in *Utriusque cosmi . . . historia* (Oppenheim 1617-1621), was instrumental in propagating the "magical" tradition which had been represented by such people as → Paracelsus, Agrippa, → John Dee, or the Rosicrucian manifestoes. He drew heavily on the hermetic writings: nearly every page of his works contains a quotation from Ficino's translation. Fludd also makes use of the *Asclepius* and of other hermetic writings, for instance in presenting his views on the creation of the world, of which he gives a "chemical" description that draws on the *Pimander* (C.H. I) as much as on the Bible and the first verses of the Gospel of John. Later on, among the so-called Cambridge platonists, → Ralph Cudworth was the one who dealt most extensively with the C.H. (even more so than → Henry More). His *The True Intellectual System of the Universe* (London 1678) contains a lengthy commentary on its treatises, with a particular emphasis on cosmogony. As against Casaubon, Cudworth stressed the presence of Egyptian elements. He also considered that treating the C.H. as one single text (whereas it is actually a collection) entails that the arguments liable to discredit the great age of some treatises do not need to discredit the rest of them (and least of all the *Asclepius*). Moreover, Hermetism had already made its way into English culture in general, with Woodville (see above), Edmund Spencer (many relevant passages in *The Fairie Queene*, London 1590-1596), and others. This process continued well into the English 17th century, as documented by works of celebrated authors who do not belong to this orientation but give it a place, albeit a modest one, like Richard Burton (*The Anatomy of Melancholy*, Oxford 1621), Sir Thomas Browne (*Religio Medici*, 1643), Sir Walter Raleigh (*History of the World*, 1614), John Milton (*Il Penseroso*, London 1645), etc. (see Shumaker, 1972, 236-247; and 1988).

As was already the case in the preceding century, but even more so now, the *Hermetica* had become part and parcel of many discourses marked by → Egyptomania. Typical of that trend are works of the Jesuit → Athanasius Kircher, notably *Oedipus Aegyptiacus* (Rome 1652-1654; but see also *Prodromus coptus*, Rome 1636), which uses the C.H., among other ingredients, to make Catholicism palatable, with a view to deterring his readers from Protestantism and/or incredulity. Kircher, however, was not a great admirer of the hermetic literature and regarded e.g. Paracelsus, the Rosicrucians, or Robert Fludd with great suspicion.

Interestingly, the French Jesuits and theologians involved in missionary activities in the Far East, particularly in China, shared a project similar to Kircher's, though hardly at all from an Egyptophile perspective. Apart from Rapine (see below), these Catholic priests were not interested in Hermetism itself, but used it as a tool for converting people to Catholicism. It was a matter of demonstrating that Confucius's teachings, for example, as well as those of Western pagan philosophers – primarily Plato and Hermes Trismegistus – were compatible with monotheism. This missionary program, often strongly hermetically tinged, is exemplified by Paschal Rapine's *Le Christianisme naissant dans la gentilité* (Paris 1655-1659), Paul Beurrier's *Perpetuitas fidei, ab origine mundi* . . . (Paris 1666; French ed. 1680); Daniel Huet's *Demonstratio evangelica* (Paris 1678; several re-eds.); Philippe Couplet's *Confucius Sinarum philosophus* (1687), and several writings by Joachim Bouvet around 1700, notably his correspondence with Leibniz.

3. Testimonies at the Time of the Enlightenment and in the pre-Romantic Period

Like Everard's English version, the first complete German translation of the seventeen treatises of the C.H. became influential on later esoteric literature. Its author, who had had at his disposal the editions of Patrizi and van Beyerland, signed himself Aletophilus (perhaps a pen name for Wolf Metternich) and entitled it *Hermetis Trismegisti Erkänntnüsz der Natur und des darin sich offenbahrenden Grossen Gottes* . . . (Hamburg 1706; reed. 1855, see below). His long introduction to the book, in which he shows himself to be a Paracelsian, is noteworthy. He endorses the main legends surrounding the C.H. and tries to marry Hermetism with alchemy, extolling the Egyptian elements of the text over the Greek ones. The T.S. is very present in Aletophilus' book and, not surprisingly, in numerous other alchemical treatises of the period. Three works in German stand out in that context, namely Ehrd de Naxagoras' *Aureum Vellus* (Frankfurt 1731-1733, 2 vols.); the anonymous *Vernünftige Erklärung der Smaragdenen Tafel* . . . (s.l. 1760); and above all → Hermann Fictuld's *Turba Philosophorum* (s.l. 1763), one of the most important works in the history of the T.S. tradition, and in which alchemy and theosophical outlooks are blended together.

The period of the Enlightenment saw new German translations of the C.H. First, Dietrich Tiedemann's (C.H. I-XVIII), entitled *Poemander, oder von der göttlichen Macht und Weisheit* (Berlin & Stettin 1781). It was published three years after the first German translation of the *Asclepius*, at the Press of Friedrich Nicolai, one of the most celebrated representatives of the *Aufklärung*. Indeed,

Tiedeman's commentaries are reflective of the intellectual orientation of the Enlightenment. They are also replete with comparisons between the C.H., Plato, → Gnosticism and Jewish Kabbalah.

Alongside these translations there appeared further erudite studies. Some were of a more or less hermetic orientation, like Hermann van der Hardt's "Poemander" (inserted in his book *Antiquitatis Gloria*, Helmstedt 1737), a long paraphrase of C.H. I, in which, for example, Jacob's dream (Gen. 28) is compared to Hermes's vision in C.H. I, 1. Other studies were definitely more scholarly oriented. Two of them stand out. First, *Bibliotheca Graeca*, by Johann Albrecht Fabricius (Hamburg 1705-1728, see vol. I, 1708, lib 1, chapters VII-XII; new, enlarged ed. 1790). Second, Jacob Brucker's *Kurze Fragen aus der philosophischen Historie* (Ulm 1730-1736) and *Historia critica philosophiae* (Leipzig 1743; see vol. I, chapters I-IV), which provided a wealth of information on theosophical, alchemical and Rosicrucian literature, not least on the C.H. and whatever Brucker knew about the *Hermetica* in general (see notably *ibid.*, vol. I, liber 3). Brucker goes as far as to deal with works appearing as late as the beginning of the 18th century. Certainly, he was not a proponent of any of these currents, but his very detailed – albeit not always unprejudiced – presentation would ensure a knowledge about them for a long time, all the more so since the book of 1743 quickly became essential to most good libraries all over Europe.

Toward the end of the 18th century, Hermetism started at the top rung of the literary ladder in Germany with two texts written by Johann Gottfried Herder. First, *Über die älteste Urkunde des Menschengeschlechts* (Riga 1774), in which he claimed to have found in ancient traditions, notably in Hermes Trismegistus, keys capable of unlocking a number of mysteries and retrieving a long lost knowledge. Second, "Hermes und Pymander" (in the journal *Adrastea*, 1801), a dialogue (inspired by C.H. I) between Pymander and his disciple, which deals with the new scientific discoveries (not least those by Isaac Newton) as well as with spiritual and material light, the Soul of the World, etc.

In Italy, although Hermetism as an esoteric current had all but ceased to manifest its presence, it was still occasionally the object of publications; see for instance a reprint in Bologna (1820) of an edition of the C.H. which C. Lenzoni had published in 1584. In the United States, Ralph Waldo Emerson's *The Dial* (see in particular the issues published from 1842 to 1844), a journal expressing the views of the Transcendentalist movement in the United

States, published (in vol. IV) a number of "ethnic Scriptures" – as it called them –, including extracts from Everard's translation of the C.H. Hermetism also seems to have left its imprint, albeit a mostly indirect one, on a number of authors of pre-Romantic and Romantic literature in England and the United States (see E.L. Tuveson 1982). The middle of the 19th century was also the time of new studies in pure scholarship (like B.J. Hilgers' *De Hermetis Trismegisti Poimandro commentario*, Bonn 1855, and particularly Gustav Parthey's *Hermetis Trismegisti Poemander* [the Greek text], Berlin 1854). Noteworthy too is the importance of the T.S. almost throughout → Franz von Baader's theosophical works (notably from 1809 to 1839). Not very interested in alchemy, nor in Hermetism for that matter, he nonetheless made a frequent use of some verses of the T.S., commenting on them and merging them with his theosophical outlooks.

4. THE OCCULTIST CONTEXT

The so-called occultist current [→ Occult/occultism] flourished from ca. 1850 to ca. 1920, and drew upon a great variety of elements pertaining to the esoteric literature of earlier centuries. Certainly, Hermetism is part of the referential corpus of the so-called occultists, for example in fringe-masonic literature. Thus → Marie Ragon de Bettignies's widely disseminated *Maçonnerie occulte, suivie de l'Initiation hermétique* (1853) is a blend of masonic symbolism, alchemy, mythology and Hermetism. But the presence of Hermetism within the occultist current appears to be very limited, except in England (see below). In France, for instance, such important representatives of occultism as → Stanislas de Guaïta or → Papus hardly referred to Hermetism. They did, however, devote many pages to their understanding of the T.S., which they, like so many other representatives of the current, took to be one of the most essential referential documents in Western esotericism (see for example → Stanislas de Guaita's *Le Serpent de la Genèse*, Book II, Paris 1897). And in Italy, for example, the occultist → Giuliano Kremmerz authored a long series of commentaries entitled "Commento alla Tvola di Smeraldo" (in *Commentarium per le Academia Ermetice . . .*, Bari 1910).

With regard to esotericism in Germany, the new edition of Aletophilus's translation of the C.H. (1706, see above) is noteworthy, along with its introduction. It appeared as *Hermetis Trismegisti Einleitung ins höchste Wissen* (Stuttgart 1855) in the semi-popular series "Das Kloster" directed by J. Scheible, which from 1849 to 1860 offered new German editions of texts by Agrippa, →

Trithemius, Paracelsus, → J.B. Van Helmont, → Eliphas Lévi, Catherine Crowe, Nostradamus et al. As for Louis Ménard's *Hermès Trismégiste: Traduction complète précedée d'une étude sur l'origine des livres hermétiques* (Paris 1866, several re-eds.), its influence should not be underestimated. It is a new French translation of C.H. I-XIV (relying on Parthey's Greek edition, see above), *Asclepius*, *Korè Kosmou* ("The Virgin of the World", part of Stobaeus' *Anthologium*), and the *Diffinitiones Asclepii* (C.H. XVI-XVIII) after Patrizi's text. The book also contains a long but sober introduction of 112 pages, in which Ménard places these texts in the perspective of a comparative approach of religions which shows him to be slightly inspired by the idea of a perennial philosophy. Triggered in part by Ménard's book, a flurry of new English editions of hermetic treatises appeared, mostly in England and in the United States, accompanied by esoterically oriented presentations and/or commentaries. Most of them have little scholarly value, but in various ways they are representative of occultism, especially since many were produced by people with a reputation in that current.

The first on this list is a reprinting of Everard's translation at the Rosicrucian Publishing Co. in Boston (*Hermes Trismegistus: His Divine Pymander. Also, the Asiatic Mystery. The Smaragdine Tablet, and the Song of Brahm*, repr. Toledo [Ohio] 1889). Its editor was the famous Rosicrucian → Paschal Beverly Randolph. The strongly Rosicrucian-oriented "Prefatory Note" is signed by Alfred E. Giles and Flora Russell (who also gives there a reprinted version of the *Asiatic Mystery*; one of Randolph's Rosicrucian manifestoes). The "Song of Brahm" is a poem by R.W. Emerson.

There followed a new reprint of Everard's translation by the Rosicrucian → Hargrave Jennings (Madras 1884, "Secret Doctrine Reference series"), who devoted his own prefatory text mostly to the personage Hermes Trismegistus and alchemical literature. Prompted by the former one, this book turns out to contain the first public mention of the esoteric Society called → The Hermetic Brotherhood of Luxor. Almost at the same time, there appeared in the same series one of the most influential books of that publishing enterprise, namely *The Virgin of the World of Hermes Mercurius Trismegistus* (London [and Madras] 1885), edited by → Anna Bonus Kingsford and Edward Maitland, which contains an English version of *Koré Kosmou*, "A treatise on initiations" (in fact, a new translation of the *Asclepius*), "The Definitions of Asclepios" (i.e., C.H. XVI-XVIII), plus further extracts from Stobaeus's *Anthologium*. In their translation and long introductions, Kingsford and Maitland drew heavily on Ménard's book. They saw in the Hermetic texts a survival of ancient Egypt and believed in a coincidence between them and Christianity, it being understood that Christianity itself represents, as they say, 'a development from or reformulation of a doctrine long pre-existent'. Along these lines, they considered their edition to be part of 'the revival of Occult Science and Mystical, or Esoteric, philosophy'. A new edition of Kingsford and Maitland's anthology soon followed (Bath 1886), with an appendix pertaining to alchemy and taken from Mary Anne Atwood's *A Suggestive Inquiry into the Hermetic Mystery* (1850). The appendix was introduced by the famous John Yarker, author of many works in such domains, particularly esoteric → Freemasonry.

Given the number of such books, it is hardly surprising that Hermetism also entered esoteric periodicals. For example, we find *Koré Kosmou* again (presented anonymously and in a different translation) in *The Occult Magazine* (Glasgow, see issues of 1885-1886). In 1894, → William Wynn Westcott, who along with → MacGregor Mathers had created the fringe-masonic → Hermetic Order of the Golden Dawn in 1887, inserted into the second volume of his series Collectanea Hermetica (1893-1896) the Everard version of the C.H., here titled *The Pymander of Hermes, with a Preface by the editor* (London, Theosophical Publishing Society). Westcott's preface, more enthusiastic that critical, emphasizes the commonalities between Hermetism, Freemasonry and Christianity.

On the scholarly side, *The Theological and Philological Work of Hermes Trismegistus, Christian Neoplatonist, Divine Pymander and other writings of Hermes Trismegistus* (Edinburgh 1882), edited by John D. Chambers, reflects a new scientific approach. But it was mostly → George R.S. Mead's enterprise that paved the way for deeper and more extensive scholarly researches. Three years before breaking with the Theosophical Society, of which he was a prominent member, he published his *Thrice Greatest Hermes: Studies in Hellenistic Theosophy and Gnosis* (London & Benares, Theosophical Publishing Society, 3 vols. 1906; German version Leipzig 1909). Never before, indeed, had such a virtually complete ensemble of *Hermetica* been gathered together, accompanied by copious notes, excerpts from *testimonia* of the Fathers, serious historical studies, etc. Mead distanced himself markedly from the aforementioned English-speaking occultists by displaying a great deal of objectivity in dealing with his material. That said, he did not

disguise the fact that he was an esotericist too ('to translate "Hermes" in Greek', he writes in the introduction, 'requires not only a good knowledge of Greek, but also a Knowledge of . . . gnosis'). Indeed, not unlike → Arthur E. Waite in the same period, Mead was both a scholar and a fully-fledged esotericist. Nevertheless, his work, even more that Chambers's, heralds the development of 20th century critical research as represented by such distinguished historians and philologists as Richard Reitzenstein, Walter Scott, A.D. Nock, A.J. Festugière, Gilles Quispel, Roelof van den Broek, Jean-Pierre Mahé, Brian P. Copenhaver et al.

The last decades of occultism saw further hermetically oriented publications, of which a few examples follow. *The Shepherd of Men: An Official Commentary on the Sermon of Hermes Trismegistos* (San Francisco, Hermetic Publishing Company 1916) is by A.D. Raleigh, who called himself "Hierophant of the Mysteries of Isis". Although the title of his book implicitly refers to the famous text of Late Antiquity, *The Shepherd of Hermas*, Raleigh's discourse is pervaded by the idea of a perennial tradition and is blended with a fantastic history of human races, echoing some of the Theosophical Society's teachings. More situated within "classical" Hermetism is the thin volume *The Divine Pymander of Hermes Trismegistus* (n.p. [London?] 1923, no publisher's name), which presents a short selection drawn from the Everard, Chambers and Mead editions, along with some commentaries. It is in fact one of the "Manuals" published by The Shrine of Wisdom, which was a ritual Order, a publishing house and a journal. The Shrine of Wisdom was largely inspired by the works of the Platonist Thomas Taylor.

In closing, we should mention → Manly Palmer Hall's oversized folio *An Encyclopaedic Outline of Masonic, Hermetic, Qabbalistic and Rosicrucian Philosophy* (Los Angeles, Philosophical Research Society 1928), another product of late occultism and one of the most popular *summae* of Western esoteric traditions. Hermetism is almost ubiquitous in that strange encyclopaedia.

5. SURVIVALS AND DEBATES (SECOND HALF OF THE 20TH CENTURY) & GENERAL CONSIDERATIONS

Most of the above editions and commentaries of the C.H. which saw the light in the period of the occultist current were reprinted in the second half of the 20th century. The latter has not been lacking in original publications, although they seem to have been decreasing in number. Among them are

The Gospel of Hermes, edited and translated from the Greek and Latin Hermetica, introduced by Duncan Greenless and published in 1949 by the Theosophical Publishing Company. More famous is → Jan van Rijckenborgh's *De Egyptische oergnosis en haar roep in het Euwige Nú . . .* (Haarlem 1960-1965), an interpretation of the C.H. in the light of the teachings of an initiatory Order (the Lectorium Rosicrucianum) of which he was the founder. Here, ancient Gnosticism, → Neo-Catharism, Paracelsianism and Boehmism are blended together in an original way. Since its first publication, van Rijckenborgh's book has gone through countless reprints and translations, fostered worldwide by the Lectorium Rosicrucianum. Noteworthy therein is the long development he devotes to the T.S. He uses the text to support the tenets of his own teachings and does not hesitate to claim that it was written ten thousand years ago.

One of the prominent members of the Lectorium Rosicrucianum in the Netherlands, Joost R. Ritman, has founded a library in Amsterdam, the *Bibliotheca Philosophica Hermetica* (open to the public since 1984), which is the richest in the world in terms of esoteric literature, including manuscripts and incunables, from the early Renaissance to the present, not to mention a wealth of more ancient materials. This remarkable institution is especially noteworthy here because Hermetic literature in the proper sense represents its most fundamental core, as demonstrated not only by its holdings, but also by the exhibitions it organizes and by its publications. Its Editorial board includes such reputable scholars as Frans A. Janssen and Carlos Gilly.

Hermetism as a specific esoteric current all but became extinct after the 17th century, having merged with so many other currents. It cannot be said to have merged with the perennialist current [→ Tradition], whose representatives are not prone to extol the interest it may present (or of that of other Western esoteric currents, for that matter). But interestingly enough, the T.S. occasionally finds entrance into the perennialist current, most likely because this short text can be read without any reference to Hermetism proper, and easily lends itself to multiple exploitations. Titus Burckhardt, an author of the perennialist persuasion, has produced one of the best known contemporary commentaries of the T.S. (in his *Alchemie – Sinn und Weltbild*, Olten/Freiburg 1960).

That said, even outside the pale of esotericism proper, Hermetism has never entirely ceased to trigger the interest of people from various orientations. Occasionally it has been revived by philosophers who see in the C.H. the paradigm of an alternative philosophy able to enrich the mainstream with new insights, or to replace it. For example, Ralph Liedtke's book *Die Hermetik: Traditionelle Philosophie der Differenz* (Paderborn 1996), purports to foster a return to other modes of thinking, among which the author considers the contents of the C.H. to be one of the best possible introductions to a desirable and drastic reappraisal with regard to mainstream contemporary trends in philosophy. Just as Renaissance Hermetism served to bring about reforms within the Churches, so now it has occasionally become a means of "reforming" philosophy. Similarly, efforts have been and are still made to extol it as a method for the fruitful completion or enrichment of psychology. For example, Lietaert Pierbolte (*Poimandres . . . vertaald met een transpersonalistische beschouwing*, Deventer 1974) presents C.H. I in Dutch and comments on it by explaining why it should be used as a method for practising the kind of transpersonal psychology that he advocates. Similarly, and along perspectives not very far from those of the → New Age movement, the T.S. is occasionally interpreted and commented as a practical guide to spiritual growth. For instance, Dennis William Hauck's *The Emerald Tablet: Alchemy for Personal Transformation* (Harmondsworth [UK] 1999) throughout expresses such a tendency.

In the post-war period, more particularly since the 1960s, most discourses on Hermetism have been of a scholarly character. Frances A. Yates' *Giordano Bruno and the Hermetic Tradition*, published in 1964, has been highly instrumental in calling attention to its importance and significance in the history of the Renaissance. Although not without forbears, Yates's work was a watershed. Many scholars whose work is dedicated to Renaissance Hermetism in general, or to one particular author, stand in its wake; even if they do not necessarily endorse Yates's views, they are directly or indirectly indebted to her writings. By the same token, Yates's work has paved the way for an ongoing academic recognition, even institutionalization, of modern Western esoteric currents as a specialty in its own right. In addition to that, it has caused a flurry of debates, first over what Robert S. Westman (1977) called the "Yates Thesis" (concerning the relation between Hermetism and the scientific revolution), and more recently over what Wouter J. Hanegraaff (2001) has referred to as "the Yates paradigm". As pointed out by the latter, Yates's works have created a "grand narrative", as it were, based on two main assumptions. First, the existence of what she calls "the Hermetic Tradition" understood as a more or less autonomous tradition based upon a covert reaction against both Christianity and the rise of scientific world-views. Secondly, and however paradoxical it may seem, the claim that the essential tradition of "magic" – which she sees as essentially non-progressive – has been an important factor in the development of the scientific revolution (i.e., the "Yates thesis", see above). Even if neither of these two tenets has proved resistant to close scrutiny, the opinions implicit in the "Yates paradigm" still causes ink to flow.

Be that as it may, such debates around Yates's work concern the early modern period. Their relevance to the later periods is of secondary importance. Indeed, Neo-Alexandrian Hermetism taken as a whole, i.e. over the sweep of a little over five centuries, is of great interest to the historian of ideas (and of literature) not least because it reflects the various contexts in which it has taken on ever-changing aspects. This is all the more so since it would not be possible to define Hermetism as a set of fixed, unchangeable beliefs. Rather, its manifold manifestations evince a spiritual attitude which contains in itself a principle of constant readjustment. Not surprisingly, it has flourished mostly in times and countries hospitable to religious tolerance. Although its representatives have been people desiring to "reform" religious systems, the reforms they had in mind were not dogmatic in character, and very rarely designed to overthrow established Churches. They rather tended to enrich the latter by prompting them to return *ad fontes*, i.e., both to ancient foundational texts and to specific forms of meditation. Indeed, far from stressing a war between Good and Evil, Light and Darkness, as is often the case in Christian thought, their discourses have expressed a generally optimistic conception of the inborn powers of Man, understood as a being able to liberate and expand his consciousness and develop his inborn powers.

As one of the several esoteric currents in modernity (i.e., from the Renaissance until the present time), Hermetism has naturally found itself historically intertwined with the others. In this respect, it is interesting to see how far and in which directions these relationships have been operating. We note, for example, that despite their commonalities, Hermetism and Christian Theosophy (which appeared later, at the beginning of the 17th century) have had few contacts and have hardly influenced each other. One of the reasons is that Hermetism, originally a branch of Humanism, always remained dependent upon ancient sources, notably Greek, whereas Theosophy is rooted,

rather, in Paracelsus and Jacob Boehme, who represent a German, "barbaric" trend all but devoid of erudite leanings. It is therefore hardly surprising that even long after the Renaissance, the foremost representatives of Theosophy, like → Louis-Claude de Saint-Martin or → Franz von Baader, practically never drew on the Hermetic writings.

Lit.: Jan Assmann, *Moses the Egyptian: The Memory of Egypt in Western Monotheism*, Cambridge Ma. & London: Harvard University Press 1997 ♦ Antonio Gonzàlez Blanco, "Hermetism: A Bibliographical Approach", in: W. Haase (ed.), *Aufstieg und Niedergang der römischen Welt . . .*, vol. 2, 4. (Teilband *Religion*), Berlin/New York: W. de Gruyter, 1984, 2240-2281 (notably 2261-2281) ♦ Roelof van den Broek & Cis van Heertum (eds.), *From Poimandres to Jacob Böhme: Gnosis, Hermetism and the Christian Tradition*, Amsterdam: In de Pelikaan, 2000 ♦ John G. Burke, "Hermetism as a Renaissance World View", in: Robert S. Kinsman (ed.), *The Darker Vision of the Renaissance*, Berkeley, Los Angeles, London: University of California Press, 1974, 95-118 ♦ Antoine Faivre, "La Table d'Emeraude", in: *Annuaire (Résumés des conférenes et travaux)*, Paris: Ecole Pratique des Hautes Etudes (Section Sciences Religieuses, Sorbonne), vol. 94-105 (1985/1986-1996/1997) ♦ Antoine Faivre & Frédérick Tristan (eds.), *Présence d'Hermès Trismégiste* (Cahiers de l'Hermétisme), Paris: Albin Michel, 1988 ♦ Antoine Faivre, *The Eternal Hermes: From Greek God to Alchemical Magus*, Grand Rapids (MI): Phanes Press, 1995 ♦ Eugenio Garin, Mirella Brini, Cesare Vasoli, Paola Zambelli (eds.), *Testi umanistici su l'Ermetismo: Testi di Ludovico Lazarelli, F. Giorgio Veneto, Cornelio Agrippa di Nettesheim*, Rome: Fratelli Bocca, 1955 ♦ Eugenio Garin, *Ermetismo del Rinascimento*, Rome: Riuniti, 1988 ♦ Carlos Gilly, "Das Bekenntnis zur Gnosis von Paracelsus bis auf die Schüler Jacob Böhmes", in: van den Broek & van Heertum, *From Poimandres to Jacob Boehme*, 385-426 ♦ Carlos Gilly & Cis van Heertum (eds.), *Magic, Alchemy and Science 15th-18th Centuries: The Influence of Hermes Trismegistus*, bilingual (English and Italian), Florence: Centro di della Edifimi, 2002, 2 vols ♦ Joscelyn Godwin, *The Pagan Dream of the Renaissance*, London: Thames & Hudson, 2002 ♦ Wouter J. Hanegraaff, "Beyond the Yates Paradigm: The Study of Western Esotericism between Counterculture and New Complexity", *Aries* 1:1 (2001), 5-37 ♦ Frans A. Janssen, "Dutch Translations of the *Corpus Hermeticum*", in: Tom Croiset van Uchelen et al. (eds.), *Theatrum Orbis Librorum*, Utrecht, HES Publications, 1989, 229-241 ♦ Didier Kahn, *Hermès Trismégiste, La Table d'Emeraude et sa tradition alchimique*, Paris: Les Belles Lettres, 1998 ♦ Paul Oskar Kristeller, "Marsilio Ficino e Lodovico Lazzarelli: Contributo alla diffusione delle idee ermetiche nel Rinascimento", *Annali della R. Scuola Normale Superiore di Pisa, Lettere, Storia e Filosofia* 2 (1938), 237-62; repr. in: Kristeller, *Studies in Renaissance Thought and Letters* 1, Roma: Edizioni di Storia e Letteratura, 1956, 221-247 ♦ F. van Lamoen, *Hermes*

Trismegistus Pater Philosophorum: Textgeschiedenis van het Corpus Hermeticum, Amsterdam: Bibliotheca Philosophica Hermetica, 1990 ♦ Stanton J. Linden, *The Alchemy Reader (From Hermes Trismegistus to Isaac Newton)*, Cambridge: Cambridge University Press, 2003 ♦ Jean-Pierre Mahé, "La Renaissance et le mirage égyptien", in: Van den Broek & Van Heertum, o.c., 369-384 ♦ Ingrid Merkel & Allen G. Debus (eds.), *Hermeticism and the Renaissance: Intellectual History and the Occult in Early Modern Europe*, London, Missisauga (Ontario): Associated University Presses, 1988 ♦ Martin Mulsow (ed.), *Das Ende des Hermetismus: Historische Kritik und neue Naturphilosophie in der Spätrenaissance. Dokumentation und Analyse der Debatte um die Datierung der hermetischen Schriften von Genebrard bis Casaubon (1567-1614)*, Tübingen: J.C.B. Mohr (Paul Siebeck), 2002 ♦ Monika Neugebauer-Wölk, "'Denn dis ist möglich, Lieber Sohn!' Zur esoterischen Übersetzungstradition des Corpus Hermeticum in der frühen Neuzeit", in: Richard Caron, Joscelyn Godwin, Wouter J. Hanegraaff & Jean-Louis Vielliard-Baron (eds.), *Esotérisme, gnoses & imaginaire symbolique: Mélanges offerts à Antoine Faivre*, Louvain: Peeters, 2001, 131-144 ♦ J. van Oort, "Gisbertus Voetius, Hermes Trismegistus en Jacob Böhme", in: Gilles Quispel (ed.), *De hermetische Gnosis in de loop der eeuwen*, Baarn (the Netherlands): Tirion, 1992, 383-394 ♦ Margaret J. Osler (ed.), *Rethinking the Scientific Revolution*, Cambridge, 2000 ♦ Frederick Purnell, Jr., "Francesco Patrizi and the Critics of Hermes Trismegistus", *Journal of Medieval and Renaissance Studies*, 6 (1976), 155-178 ♦ J. Ruska, *Tabula Smaragdina: Ein Beitrag zur Geschichte der hermetischen Literatur*, Heidelberg: C. Winter, 1926 ♦ Charles B. Schmidt, "Perennial Philosophy: From Agostino Steuco to Leibniz", *Journal of the History of Ideas* 27 (1966), 502-532 ♦ idem, "Prisca Theologia e Philosophia perennis: due temi del Rinascimento italiano e la lora fortuna", in: *Atti del V. Convegno internazionale del Centro di Studi Umanistici: Il Pensiero italiano del Rinascimento e il tempo nostro*, Florence: Olschki, 1970, 211-236 ♦ Wayne Shumaker, *The Occult Sciences in the Renaissance: A Study in Intellectual Patterns*, Berkeley/Los Angeles/London: University of California Press, 1972, 201-251 ♦ idem, "Literary Hermeticism: Some Test Cases", in: Merkel & Debus, o.c., 293-301 ♦ Mirko Sladek, *Fragmente der Hermetischen Philosophie in der Naturphilosophie der Neuzeit*, Bern: Peter Lang, 1984 (French trans. Paris: Albin Michel, 1992) ♦ Lionello Sozzi, "Nexus Caritatis: l'Ermetismo in Francia nel Cinquecento", in: Lisa Rotondi & Secchi Tarugi (eds.), *L'Ermetismo nell'Antiquità e nel Rinascimento*, Milano: Nuovi Orizzonti, 1998, 113-126 ♦ Charlott Trepp & Hartmut Lehmann (eds.), *Antike Weisheit und kulturelle Praxis: Hermetismus in der Frühen Neuzeit*, Göttingen: Vandenhoeck & Ruprecht, 2001 ♦ Ernst Lee Tuveson, *The Avatars of Thrice Greatest Hermes: An Approach to Romanticism*, Lewisburg: Bucknell University Press, 1982 ♦ Cesare Vasoli, "Ermetismo e Cabala nel tardo Rinascimento e nel Primo '600'", in: Fabio Troncarelli (ed.), *La Città dei segreti (Magia, astrologia et cultura esoterica a Roma (XV-XVIII)* (Studi e richerche storiche), Milano: Franco Angeli, 1985, 103-118 ♦ idem, "Hermetism in Venice: From Francesco Giorgio Veneto to Agostino Steuco", in: Gilly & van Heertum, o.c., I, 51-67 (Italian, 31-49) ♦ D.P. Walker, *The Ancient Theology: Studies in Christian Platonism from the 15th to the 18th century*, London: Duckworth, 1972 ♦ Robert S. Westman & James E. McGuire, *Hermeticism and the Scientific Revolution*, Los Angeles (CA): William A. Clark Memorial Library, 1977 ♦ Frances A. Yates, *Giordano Bruno and the Hermetic Tradition*, London: Routledge & Kegan Paul, 1964 (several reprints) ♦ idem, "The Hermetic tradition in Renaissance Science", in: C.S. Singleton (ed.), *Art, Science and History in the Renaissance*, Baltimore, 1967, 255-274.

ANTOINE FAIVRE

Hermetic Order of the Golden Dawn

The foremost esoteric, and later magical, initiatic Order of the late 19th and early 20th centuries. It was founded in March 1888 but its roots lie in the plethora of fringe masonic Orders and quasi-masonic societies that flourished from the 1860s onwards. Both the administrative structure of the Order and the form of its ceremonies were masonic, but the symbolism and doctrinal content of the rituals were drawn almost exclusively from Western esoteric sources, and in its essentials the Golden Dawn conformed to the definition of an esoteric Order given by → Dion Fortune: a fraternity 'wherein a secret wisdom, unknown to the generality of mankind might be learnt, and to which admission was obtained by means of an initiation in which tests and ritual played their part' (*The Esoteric Orders and their Work*, 1928, ix).

The immediate inspiration for the Golden Dawn was a masonic Rosicrucian body, the Societas Rosicruciana in Anglia, that had been established in 1867. This society worked simple rituals of initiation through its system of Grades and encouraged its members to study 'the Kabbalah and the doctrines of Hermes Trismegistus'. Each member also chose a motto, usually a Latin tag, which would – in theory – become his official name within the society. Such a combination of quasi-masonic ritual, ostensible secrecy and academic discussion was more than adequate for most of the society's members, but for some it was not enough. They wanted prescribed courses of study in various forms of occultism [→ occult/occultism] and, above all, they wished to practise → magic. They also realised that none of this could take place within the S.R.I.A. and that a new and practical body must be founded – but it was not until 1883 that the first attempt at such a foundation was made.

It was the brainchild of Frederick Holland, an industrial chemist who joined the S.R.I.A. in April 1882. Within a year he had set up his "Society of Eight" and drawn in a number of prominent masonic Rosicrucians, including Kenneth Mackenzie who described the new society as 'practical and not visionary' and as standing for '*work* and not play'. But the Society of Eight was only a stepping-stone. It had no ritual structure and no systematic teaching; for these Mackenzie and his fellows had to look elsewhere – to a minuscule, fringe masonic body, the Royal Oriental Order of Sikha and the Sat B'hai. Mackenzie had joined the Sat B'hai in 1875 and had helped to develop its rituals. It was not, in any sense, a magical Order, but it did have a curriculum of 'subjects for investigation' that covered virtually every aspect of both eastern and western occultism, and it admitted women as members. This factor was clearly very important for Mackenzie who, having completed the Sat B'hai rituals, began to construct a new series of ritual texts for a wholly new initiatic Order: androgynous, disciplined and designed to inculcate the essence of Western esotericism. This new Order was, however, only one among Mackenzie's many esoteric activities, and at the time of his death, on 3 July 1886, the ritual texts existed only in outline form in manuscript – and in cipher. Shortly afterwards these outline texts were discovered by another member of the S.R.I.A., provided with a false pedigree and transformed into the rituals of the Hermetic Order of the Golden Dawn.

The discovery was made by chance. Upon Mackenzie's death → William Wynn Westcott, a London coroner and prominent member of the S.R.I.A., took over the post of Grand Secretary of yet another small masonic body, the Swedenborgian Rite, together with his predecessor's papers. Among them he found the incomplete rituals, identified the source of the cipher (the *Polygraphiae* of → Trithemius), and translated the text. He also recognised their enormous potential and began to develop them into a complete, working system. At what point Westcott determined to launch this new Order upon the world is unknown, but his decision was probably precipitated by the closure of the Hermetic Society [→ Hermeticism and Hermetic Societies]. This was a lecture society, founded in 1884 by → Anna Kingsford and Edward Maitland with the intention of propagating the Western esoteric tradition, which they perceived as being deliberately ignored and rejected within the → Theosophical Society. Both Westcott and → Samuel Liddell Mathers, one of his closest colleagues in the S.R.I.A., were frequent lecturers at the Hermetic

Society, and when its activities ceased after Anna Kingsford's death in 1887 they felt keenly the loss of a public platform.

In October 1887 Westcott wrote to Mathers asking for his help in writing up the rituals 'with all your erudition' from the now completed translation of the cipher manuscripts. He did not, however, reveal their source to Mathers; rather, he claimed to have received them from a masonic historian, the Rev. A.F.A. Woodford who, conveniently for Westcott, had died two months later. Westcott also inserted his own note, in the Trithemius cipher, among Mackenzie's manuscripts. This confirmed the contents of a letter from Woodford to Westcott (but known only from a copy in Westcott's hand), and directed the reader to a Fräulein Sprengel, otherwise Soror Sapiens dominabitur astris – 'a chief among the members of die goldene dammerung', at an accommodation address in Stuttgart. Having created his continental adept Westcott next began a correspondence with her, producing a series of five letters that provided a spurious history of the Golden Dawn; gave him authority to found a new Temple; and authorised him to sign her motto on her behalf. Later, in August 1890, he would kill her off, but for the present he needed her alive – and invisible. It is probable that Westcott based her on Anna Kingsford, for he would have found the motto, Sapiens dominabitur astris, on the title-page of one of her last works (an edition, 1886, of → Valentin Weigel's *Astrology Theologized*) and he later gave Fräulein Sprengel the name Anna.

Westcott also created a spurious history for his Order, claiming descent from a hybrid body that conflated a genuine masonic lodge at Frankfurt with a fictitious Rosicrucian Society, and listing a number of prominent, but deceased, occultists as members. Whether or not Mathers believed, at this time, in either Anna Sprengel or the spurious history is unknown, but he acted as if he did so and willingly became a co-creator with Westcott of the Hermetic Order of the Golden Dawn. With the all-important "history" in place (Westcott was a member of the → Theosophical Society and thus was fully aware of the value to an esoteric Order of an august pedigree), and the rituals complete, all that was needed was a third Chief for the projected Temple. This was necessary not only because Soror S.D.A. required it, but because the S.R.I.A. – on which the structure of the Golden Dawn was closely modelled – also had three Chiefs.

The obvious, and willing, candidate was Dr. William Robert Woodman, Supreme Magus of the S.R.I.A., an excellent Hebraist and a learned kabbalist. Possessed between them of ritual genius, a wealth of esoteric knowledge, and a breathtaking creative imagination the three Chiefs were ready to launch their Order. On 1 March 1888, at Mark Masons' Hall in London, the Fratres Magna est Veritas (Woodman), Sapere Aude (Westcott), and 'S Rioghail Mo Dhream (Mathers) constituted and consecrated 'the Isis-Urania Temple No. 3, of the Order of the G.D. in the Outer'. By the end of the month seven members, four men and three women, had been initiated as Neophytes of the Order.

The Order was constructed in a graduated form, the Neophyte ceremony being the first in a progressive series based upon a symbolic entry into and ascent of the kabbalistic Tree of Life. It was impressive, as were the rest of the series, and followed the standard pattern of ceremonies of initiation, albeit utilising an eclectic mix of symbols drawn from both Eastern and Western esotericism. Much of this was called for in the cipher manuscripts, but the language employed and the ceremonial embellishments are evidence of Mathers's flair for the dramatic. Each stage, or Grade, of the initiate's ceremonial progress was related to one of the Sephiroth of the Tree of Life, the nature, qualities and correspondences of which were symbolically presented and explained. Each Grade was also given a specific name and number, derived, for the most part, from the structure of an 18th Century German quasi-masonic Order, the *Gold- und Rosenkreuz*. The Grade of Neophyte, in the course of which the candidate took an Obligation to maintain strict secrecy as to the affairs of the Order, stood below the Sephiroth and was thus numbered 0=0. The succeeding Grades were as follows: Zelator, 1=10 (Malkuth); Theoricus, 2=9 (Yesod); Practicus, 3=8 (Hod), and Philosophus, 4=7 (Netzach). At this point the Outer Order ended and the initiate – who might have taken several years to reach the Grade of Philosophus, as advancement through the Grades demanded proficiency in the prescribed courses of study – came to a stop. Beyond it lay the Second, or Inner Order of the Adepts, although the ceremonies for this were not constructed in detail until 1891.

Westcott and his co-chiefs were fully aware that such a complex system required sound administration and they had established an effective hierarchical structure at the outset. Ultimate authority in the Golden Dawn, at least in the material world, rested in the hands of the three founding Chiefs, while each Temple had its own Chiefs who acted as senior administrative officers. These were the Imperator, who 'compell[ed] the obedience of the Temple to the *commands* issued by the Second Order'; the Praemonstrator, who instructed the members and superintended the working of the Temple; and the Cancellarius, the Recorder, Secretary and Archivist of the Temple.

The direction of the Order ceremonies was in the hands of seven officers, who took their titles from those of functionaries of the Eleusinian Mysteries, although their roles were clearly modelled on those of the officers of a masonic Lodge. They, and their masonic parallels, were as follows: Hierophant (Worshipful Master); Hiereus (Senior Warden); Hegemon (Junior Warden); Kerux (Inner Guard); Stolistes (Senior Deacon); Dadouchos (Junior Deacon); and Sentinel (Tyler). Each officer wore distinctive robes and insignia, but the Order differed from → Freemasonry in that every office was open to both men and women.

Within twelve months of its foundation the Golden Dawn had attained a membership of sixty persons: fifty-one men and nine women. Almost two-thirds of this total were members of the Isis-Urania Temple in London, the remainder being almost equally divided between two additional Temples that had been founded in October 1888: Osiris Temple No. 4, at Weston-Super-Mare, in Somerset; and Horus Temple No. 5, at Bradford in Yorkshire. The siting of these Temples reflects the sources from which members were drawn. Weston-super-Mare was the home of the former Bristol College of the S.R.I.A., of which all of the Osiris initiates had been members, while Bradford had a thriving lodge of the Theosophical Society and was close to the headquarters of the York College of the S.R.I.A. Throughout its history very few members of the Golden Dawn would be other than theosophists or masonic Rosicrucians.

Not all theosophists approved of the Order, however, and early in 1889 → Madame Blavatsky forbade members of the Esoteric Section of the Theosophical Society from belonging to other occult orders. Westcott was soon able to allay her suspicions of the Golden Dawn, but growth was temporarily slowed – by May 1890 only another twelve men and seven women entered the Order. Thereafter expansion was steady and after ten years of active existence two further Temples of the Golden Dawn had been established – the Amen Ra Temple No. 6 at Edinburgh, in 1893, and the Ahathoor Temple No. 7, at Paris, in 1894 – and 331 men and women had entered the Order, in a ratio of approximately three to two. Not all, however, remained active: death, resignation and exclusion accounted for almost 25% of those initiated.

For those who remained there were, in addition

to the ceremonial activities of the Order, extensive, if eclectic, courses of study. The subjects to be studied were presented to the initiate in the form of "Knowledge Lectures" that became progressively more complex as he or she advanced from the Grade of Neophyte to that of Philosophus. As initiates progressed, so they were expected to become increasingly familiar with the Hebrew alphabet, the meaning of kabbalistic [→ Jewish Influences], alchemical [→ Alchemy] and → tarot symbolism, the technicalities of → astrology and other forms of divination [→ Divinatory Arts], and the names and natures of the Elemental Beings – in all of which areas of study they were duly examined. In addition, they were required to meditate and to become proficient in the Rituals of the Pentagram, but this was the sole activity that could possibly be construed as magical, everything else provided for members of the Golden Dawn in the Outer being a part of traditional Western esotericism. The study and practice of magic was the exclusive preserve of the Adepts: members of the Second, or Inner Order, the "Rosae Rubeae et Aureae Crucis".

In theory a Second Order had always existed, although its membership was confined at first to the three Chiefs, who issued the Charters (under different mottoes: Vincit Omnia Veritas for Woodman; Non Omnis Moriar for Westcott; and Deo Duce Comite Ferro for Mathers) and permitted the Temples of the Golden Dawn to function. This Order comprised the three Adept Grades that corresponded to the three sephiroth in the kabbalistic World of Briah. These were the 5=6 Grade of Adeptus Minor, corresponding to the sephira Tiphereth; the 6=5 Grade of Adeptus Major, corresponding to Geburah; and the 7=4 Grade of Adeptus Exemptus, corresponding to Chesed. Philosophi who pursued their studies successfully, proved to be able ritualists, and who showed an aptitude for teaching both the theory and practice of occultism, were encouraged to progress to the Second Order.

Technically, entrance to the Second Order began with admission to the Portal Grade that preceded the Grade of Adeptus Minor. It corresponded to the lower aspect of the sephira Tiphereth, and attaining it symbolised the initiate's parting of the veil of Paroketh (which, on the kabbalistic Tree of Life, separates the worlds of Yetzirah and Briah). In the early years of the Order, however, attainment of both the Portal and Adeptus Minor Grades was solely by way of examinations to establish the initiate's competence as an occultist. Between 1888 and 1891 sixteen prominent members of the Golden Dawn entered the Second Order in this way: ceremonial admission to the Adept Grades did not begin until December, 1891.

Neither Westcott nor Woodman had shown any great enthusiasm for a working Second Order, but Mathers was eager to develop rituals for the Adept Grades and to construct a "Vault of the Adepts" around and within which the ceremonies could be worked. The rituals, and indeed the whole ethos, of the effectively separate Ordo Rosae Rubeae et Aureae Crucis were based upon the legend of the discovery of the tomb of Christian Rosencreutz and the symbolism associated with the tomb. The ceremonies were loosely derived from those of the Adept Grades of the S.R.I.A., but Mathers was a ritualist of genius and in the Golden Dawn system they were transformed into spectacular dramas of death and resurrection, worked within a Vault that he designed and constructed.

As its name indicates, the Portal ceremony, which followed logically from those of the First Order, took place outside the Vault, and the candidate was not aware of its existence. The working of the next Grade – of Adeptus Minor – was far more dramatic and of a very different nature. It consisted of three "Points" or stages, in the first of which the candidate took a second Obligation to the Order while bound symbolically upon the "Cross of Suffering", subsequently being made aware of the Vault while the legend of Christian Rosencreutz was related. During the Second Point the candidate entered the Vault and discovered its symbolism, while being addressed by the entombed Chief Adept. For the Third Point the Vault was re-entered and the candidate found the now resurrected Chief Adept, in full regalia, who completed the explanation of the symbolism and received him (or her) as a true Adeptus Minor.

The ceremony of initiation into the Adeptus Minor Grade of the R.R. et A.C. inevitably had a powerful and often transformative effect upon the candidate – a necessary condition for his or her self-perception as a magician – but it marked only the beginning of the Adept's magical progress. The 5=6 Grade of Adeptus Minor consisted of two sub-Grades: Zelator Adeptus Minor and Theoricus Adeptus Minor, and to progress from the first to the second required two years of intensive application to the theory and practice of magic. In addition to learning and practising the various prescribed rituals, the Adept was required to study the thirty-six instructional texts known as "Flying Rolls"; to make and consecrate a personal Rose Cross lamen (the badge of the R.R. et A.C.), a magical sword, a lotus wand, and the four elemental implements; and to pass a series of examinations that would demonstrate proficiency in all of these activities. Comparatively few Adepts succeeded in attaining the second sub-Grade, but all of those who entered the Second Order considered themselves to be magicians in a meaningful sense.

By 1898 the Golden Dawn had a notional active membership of almost 250 persons, of whom about one hundred had progressed to the Second Order. But whereas the ratio of men to women in the Outer Order was two to one, the sexes were evenly divided in the R.R. et A.C. Almost all of the women had been ceremonially admitted as Adepti Minores, many of them within a comparatively short time after their initiation as Neophytes. Their success within the Golden Dawn was a reflection of both their status in society, and the social structure of the Order itself.

The founders and the earliest members had come to the Order as experienced occultists, but as public awareness of the Golden Dawn grew – carefully orchestrated by Westcott, who placed cryptic comments and letters in appropriate journals – so an increasing number of initiates proved to be enthusiastic novices. Some were drawn from aristocratic circles, although few of these remained for long, but the majority were either from the professional class or from the literary and artistic *avant garde* of the 1890s.

The first of these, chronologically, was Mina Bergson, a young art student and sister of the philosopher Henri Bergson, who was initiated in the Isis-Urania Temple in March 1888 and who became, eighteen months later, the first member of that Temple (other than the three Chiefs) to enter the Second Order. In June 1890 she further consolidated her position in the Golden Dawn by marrying Mathers. By this time there were some eighty members of the Order, but only three others who would play any significant role in its affairs: Annie Horniman, the daughter of a tea magnate; the actress Florence Farr; and the poet → W.B. Yeats. Most of the other members who entered the Order during the 1890s and who were destined to determine its history were drawn from the professional classes: lawyers (J.W. Brodie Innes, and Percy Bullock); scientists (W.F. Kirby, the entomologist, and William Peck, City Astronomer for Edinburgh); and a number of medical doctors (E.W. Berridge, George Dickson, R.W. Felkin, Henry Pullen Bury, and R.M. Theobald). Others who played decisive roles were → A.E. Waite; the Egyptologist M.W. Blackden; and the magician and *farceur* → Aleister Crowley.

At the end of 1891 Dr. Woodman died, and control of the Order was jointly maintained by his co-Chiefs, with the Outer Order effectively in Westcott's hands and Mathers in charge of the R.R. et A.C. For the most part matters progressed smoothly for some years, although there were disputes within the Horus Temple and the Osiris Temple was virtually moribund (it closed down in 1895), and new Temples were founded. Mathers and his wife had moved to Paris in 1892 and set up a sub-branch of Isis Urania, which was elevated to the status of an independent Temple, Ahathoor No. 7, in January 1894 – just over two weeks after the consecration of the Amen-Ra Temple No. 6 at Edinburgh.

By this time it was clear to the members that the real work of the Golden Dawn lay in the R.R. et A.C. Technically, those in the Outer Order were supposed to be ignorant of even the existence of an Inner Order, and the Adepti were assiduous in keeping secret its rituals and magical activities. In practice, however, all members knew that the Grade of Philosophus was not their final goal and increasing numbers sought and attained admission to the Adept Grades. Once within the Second Order they had access to the vault for their ritual work, and to an excellent library to aid them in their studies. Inevitably, their increasing knowledge and magical proficiency led them not only into the senior offices of their Temples, but also to question both the authority and wisdom of their nominal Chiefs. To Mathers, who was rigidly authoritarian, such independence was anathema and he reacted strongly against it.

In 1893 he had suspended, and later expelled, Theresa O'Connell, one of the earliest initiates of the Order, over a minor dispute, while Westcott attempted (probably at Mathers's instigation and ultimately without success) to limit the activities of female adepts in the Isis-Urania Vault. These attempts to impose discipline were followed by a more serious affair that brought to light signs of real discontent among the adepts.

Annie Horniman, who had been providing regular funds for Mathers and his wife, expressed increasing unease at both the unorthodox sexual doctrines of a fellow adept, Dr. Berridge, and his behaviour towards the lady adepts. But when, in 1896, she complained of this to Mathers he reproved her and accused her of mental imbalance, later adding accusations of insubordination and incompetence. Miss Horniman then resigned as Sub-Praemonstrator of Isis-Urania, and also ceased her funding of Mathers. He promptly expelled her from the Order and justified his action in a long and bizarre letter to the Adepti that sought their submission to his authority – which he obtained, but at the price of increasing dissension. This was further inflamed in 1897 by the sudden withdrawal of Westcott from any active role in the Golden Dawn in response to pressure from the civil authorities, who objected to a Crown official (Westcott was a coroner) being involved in a magical Order.

During the next two years resentments within the Order grew. There was increased opposition to Mathers's autocracy in both the Isis-Urania and Amen-Ra Temples, while the Horus Temple resented 'dogmatic control' from London. By 1900 some members of Isis-Urania had grown so disenchanted with the confusion that resulted from Mathers's eccentric direction of affairs that they wished to close down the Temple. Mathers's response, in a letter of March 1900 to Florence Farr, was to deny their request and to make an extraordinary claim about Westcott that undermined the integrity of the Golden Dawn and threatened to destroy the Order. Mathers claimed that he alone had ever been in communication with the Secret Chiefs and that Westcott had forged the original correspondence with Anna Sprengel. What he seems to have failed to recognise is that if the members of the Order believed him then they would realise that the Golden Dawn was an utter sham, based upon forgery and deceit.

Their immediate reaction was to demand proof from Mathers and to confront Westcott with the charges made against him. Mathers refused to offer any evidence and Westcott was evasive in the extreme. Later documents – which members of the Order never saw – give strong support to Mathers's claim about Westcott, but his own actions at the time led the Adepti from simple mistrust to an outright rejection of his authority. He had made the mistake of trusting Aleister Crowley and of admitting him to the Second Order in Paris, even though Crowley had been denied such advancement in London. In April 1900, Crowley arrived in London as Mathers's representative, charged with reclaiming the Order for its erstwhile Chief. His mission failed, partly because of his bizarre behaviour, and the Adepts in London promptly expelled Mathers and advised members of the Golden Dawn that 'a Revolution has taken place.'

Government of the Order reverted to the old system of three Chiefs, supported by a Council of ten, but the Golden Dawn faced further problems that would prove to be highly damaging. The immediate cause of Mathers's disastrous letter to Florence Farr was his conviction that he had finally met the real Anna Sprengel in the guise of one Madame Horos. He soon discovered, however, that she was a charlatan and criminal who stole copies of the

Golden Dawn rituals and decamped to London, where she set up a spurious version of the Order and aided her husband in criminal fraud and rape. Eventually, in December 1901, both husband and wife were arrested, tried, found guilty and gaoled for their crimes. But the trial was disastrous for the Golden Dawn: the Obligation and the Neophyte ritual were made public and derided by the press. With their reputations under threat many members of the Order left it in haste and those who remained were divided by long-standing factional quarrels. The most significant of these involved both the structure of the Golden Dawn and the working of the Second Order. Some, notably Florence Farr, wished to work unofficial magical ceremonies within small groups of adepts, while others – Yeats and the now reinstated Annie Horniman especially – were vehemently opposed to such groups and wished to maintain also the rigid examination structure for advancement in the Order. No compromise was achieved and in 1903 the Golden Dawn finally disintegrated.

By the beginning of that year Westcott and Yeats were inactive, and both Florence Farr and Annie Horniman had resigned. The major protagonists were now A.E. Waite, J.W. Brodie-Innes, and R.W. Felkin. After a failed attempt by Brodie-Innes to be accepted as Chief of the Order, Waite gained the support of those who looked upon the Golden Dawn as mystical rather than magical, took control of the Isis Urania Temple, and on 8 July 1903 instituted the "Independent and Rectified Rite" of the Golden Dawn (in public the name Golden Dawn was no longer used, having been altered to the German "Morgen Röthe" in the aftermath of the Horos affair). The new Rite was also avowedly Christian and, as a consequence, it was able to draw in those, such as Evelyn Underhill, who would have utterly rejected magic.

The magical faction continued under R.W. Felkin and Brodie-Innes, renaming their branch of the Order the → Stella Matutina, and establishing a new Temple, named Amoun, in London. Both men produced new rituals and new teaching which they believed to be derived from supernatural beings known as the Sun Masters. In addition Felkin had convinced himself that he was in contact with the true Anna Sprengel and that he would be able to find the real Secret Chiefs. On a more practical level they recognised the need for harmony and arrived at a concordat with Waite's Order. It did not last.

Mathers had continued to work the Golden Dawn at Paris in his Ahathoor Temple, and maintained a presence in London with the aid of Dr. Berridge and a few others who sided with him.

Their branch of the old Order took the name of Alpha et Omega, with a new Temple, named Isis. Eventually Mathers obtained further support from Brodie-Innes who had distanced himself from Felkin and, by 1910, re-founded the Amen-Ra Temple at Edinburgh. It is probable that Brodie-Innes saw himself as a potential successor, but when Mathers died, in 1918, Mina Mathers took charge of the Alpha et Omega and Brodie-Innes remained loyal to her until his own death in 1923. Her management of the Order was no less idiosyncratic and authoritarian and she alienated the most able members, among them most of her American followers and the young → Dion Fortune, who left to found the Fraternity of the Inner Light.

Felkin was rather more successful. In 1916 he emigrated to New Zealand and settled at Havelock North, Hawkes Bay, where he had founded the Smaragdum Thalasses Temple during a visit four years earlier. The Temple had a custom built vault (which still exists) in the basement of Felkin's house, Whare Ra, and this became the focal point for the work of the Stella Matutina for the next fifty years. In England the Order remained active through the Amoun Temple in London and the Hermes Temple at Bristol, despite the vitriolic attacks in print of Miss C.M. Stoddart, a former Chief of Amoun Temple who had become convinced that the Order was simply a vehicle for forces of supernatural evil.

At the other end of the esoteric spectrum Waite's Independent and Rectified Rite also had problems. The Concordat with the Stella Matutina had resulted in an uneasy harmony (in 1910 a Neophyte ritual was printed for the use of both Orders) but disputes over the interpretation of its terms brought the Concordat to an end in 1912. Waite was also becoming increasingly sceptical about the contents of the cipher manuscripts, and when Blackden, Waite's co-Chief, supported by a majority of the members, insisted that the cipher rituals were of ancient Egyptian origin, he found himself in an impossible position. Waite withdrew his own rituals and, in 1914, dissolved the Rite. Within twelve months he had created a new Order, the Fellowship of the Rosy Cross, but it was in no sense a continuation of the Golden Dawn.

The traditional Golden Dawn did survive, and still does, as a result of the actions of an errant member of the Stella Matutina: Francis Israel Regardie, who had entered the Hermes Temple in 1933 following an earlier initiation into the Societas Rosicruciana in America (a quasi-masonic body that had borrowed the Outer Order rituals of the Golden Dawn). Regardie firmly believed that the teaching and rituals of the Order should be available to all and over a four year period, from 1937 to 1940, he published the greater part of them. There was little immediate reaction, but following the reprinting of Regardie's texts in 1969, new Temples appeared claiming descent from the original body. Many of these were short-lived but a few that were authorised by Regardie himself are working at the present time. Having survived for more than a century the Golden Dawn seems destined to continue indefinitely.

But what did the Order achieve? It undoubtedly influenced the work of W.B. Yeats and it gave rise to a new, if minor, genre of fiction – that of the psychic detective. Whether it exercised any significant artistic or literary influence beyond this is doubtful, but in one area of culture it has been of great importance. The Hermetic Order of the Golden Dawn has been responsible, more than any other esoteric body, for ensuring the survival of much of Western esotericism into the 21st Century.

F.I. Regardie (ed.), *The Complete Golden Dawn System of Magic*, Phoenix: Falcon Press, 1984 ◆ F. King (ed.), *Astral Projection, Ritual Magic and Alchemy, By S.L. Mathers and others: Hitherto unpublished Golden Dawn Material* (2nd ed.), Wellingborough: Aquarian Press, 1987 ◆ D. Kuntz (ed.), *The Complete Golden Dawn Cipher Manuscript: Deciphered, translated and edited*, Edmonds, WA: Holmes Publishing Group, 1996.

Lit.: Ellic Howe, *The Magicians of the Golden Dawn: A Documentary History of a Magical Order 1887-1923*, London: Routledge & Kegan Paul, 1972 ◆ R.A. Gilbert, *The Golden Dawn Companion: A Guide to the History, Structure and Workings of the Hermetic Order of the Golden Dawn. Compiled and Introduced*, Wellingborough: Aquarian Press, 1986 ◆ D. Kuntz, *The Golden Dawn Source Works: A Bibliography. Compiled, with Notes*, Edmonds, WA: Holmes Publishing Group, 1996.

ROBERT A. GILBERT

Hermetic Society → Hermeticism and Hermetic Societies

Hermeticism and Hermetic Societies

1. HERMETICISM 2. THE KINGSFORD-MAITLAND HERMETIC SOCIETY (1884-1887) 3. THE DUBLIN HERMETIC SOCIETIES (1885-1939)

1. HERMETICISM

By the 18th century, Hermeticism had expanded well beyond its Renaissance focus on → Hermes Trismegistus and his revelation of a *prisca theologia* [→ Tradition]. Contemporary interest in encyclopaedias, universal histories, and comparative mythology created an eclectic current in which "Hermetic" denoted a wider field including → Egyptomany, Orphic mysteries, Pythagoreanism, Kabbalah [→ Jewish Influences], → Paracelsianism, → alchemy, and → Rosicrucianism. Several Enlightenment historians included an account of Hermes Trismegistus or Thoth and Hermeticism in their accounts of ancient history and religion, including Johann Jakob Brucker, *Historia critica philosophiae* (1742-67), Johann Gottfried Herder, *Die älteste Urkunde des Menschengeschlechtes* (1774) and Antoine Court de Gébelin, *Le Monde Primitif* (1773-82). This Enlightenment eclecticism, alongside the development of → Pietism, led to Hermetic imports in philosophy, medicine, and → Freemasonry. In Britain, the heritage of → Robert Fludd (1574-1637), → Elias Ashmole (1617-1692), and → Thomas Vaughan (1622-1666) chiefly passed into Freemasonry, regulated after 1717 by the English Grand Lodge. But in Germany, Pietism created a religious subculture favourable to sectarian developments, with later ramifications in a subculture of lodges, secret societies, and irregular Masonic lodges, especially among court officials and the non-commercial middle class. As early as 1690, the Lutheran theologian Ehregott Daniel Colberg had written *Das Platonisch-Hermetisches* [sic] *Christenthum* as a polemic against the pietist-enthusiastic sects mushrooming among Paracelsians, Weigelians, Behmenists, Quakers, Labadists and Quietists. From 1700 onwards a handful of philosophers and theologians emerged from sectarian isolation to articulate Hermetic ideas within the syncretic Enlightenment. Samuel Richter's *Theo-Philosophia Theoretico-Practica* (1711) exemplifies a systematic Hermeticism of theosophical provenance. Johann Konrad Dippel (1673-1734) progressed from radical Pietism to Hermetic and alchemical speculations and scientific experiment. Hermetic elements appear in the thought of Hermann Boerhaave (1668-1738), the Dutch scientist, and Friedrich Joseph Wilhelm Schröder (1733-1778), professor of medicine at Marburg and a Rosicrucian. Johann Salomo Semler (1725-1791), professor of theology at Halle and → Friedrich Christoph Oetinger (1702-1782) both embraced Hermeticism. Alchemico-hermetic writers such as Anton Joseph Kirchweger, → Georg von Welling (1652-1727), and the physician Johann Friedrich Metz (1720-1782) influenced the young Johann Wolfgang Goethe, further evidence of this widespread Hermetic subculture in Germany during the late Enlightenment.

Lodge discourse rapidly assimilated these ideas. Baron Tschoudy's *Hermetic Catechism* (1766) and the Hermetic Rite of Montpellier (c. 1770), traceable to → Antoine-Joseph Pernety and Boileau, likewise the → Illuminées d'Avignon founded in 1785, are examples of an "Hermetic" Freemasonry. The alchemico-Hermetic culture of the *Gold- und Rosenkreuzer* found its ultimate expression in the beautiful and complex coloured illustrations of the *Geheime Figuren der Rosenkreuzer* printed at Altona in 1785-1788.

The use of the adjective "Hermetic" to describe a society dates only from the modern period. The first Hermetic Society was founded in 1796 at Dortmund for the purpose of practical alchemy by Carl Arnold Kortum (1745-1824) and Friedrich Bährens (1765-1831). Kortum was born into a family of apothecaries, qualified as a physician, authored the famous comic epic poem *Jobsiade* (1786), and wrote regularly for the *Westphälischer Anzeiger*, the leading journal of Westphalia and the Rhineland. He was also associated with the radical pietistic movement of Gerhard Tersteegen (1697-1769). Bährens was the Lutheran pastor at nearby Schwerte and also a physician. The Hermetic Society continued its work on practical alchemy until 1819, attracting controversy among the new generation of post-Lavoisier chemists as the era of German Romantic → Naturphilosophie drew to a close.

In the first half of the 19th century, esoteric subjects and societies favoured the label "Rosicrucian" rather than "Hermetic" for several reasons. Rosicrucianism had connoted alchemy among 18th-century *Gold- und Rosenkreuzer*. However, once linked with Templarism [→ Neo-Templar Traditions], as in many high-degree Masonic rites, Rosicrucianism also signified a Christian, medieval, and chivalrous world, whose Orient was Jerusalem and the Holy Land. Rosicrucianism was linked with mediaevalism in Gothic literature, e.g. Percy Shelley, *St Irvyne or The Rosicrucian* (1801), Sir → Edward Bulwer-Lytton, *Zanoni: A Rosicrucian Tale* (1842). By contrast, Hermetic references signified a *philosophia perennis*, where Christianity was a single strand in a universal pansophy sometimes aligned with neo-pagan, anti-clerical Enlightenment interests. "Hermeticism" still pointed to an Orient represented by ancient Egypt, polytheism and mystery-religions. Hermeticism even combined with the cosmopolitan, Enlightenment critique of the *ancien regime* and Church before the advent of Napoleon, but its irenic vision was unsuited to German nationalism. In any case, the age of reaction or *Vormärz* period (1815-1848/67) with its conservative suppression of nationalist and democratic currents on the Continent witnessed a general decline in the numbers of initiatory high-degree rites and secret societies with some notable exceptions, e.g. Rites of Memphis and Misraim, the Ancient and Accepted Scottish Rite.

A "Rosicrucian" heritage, based on the memorials of the *Gold- und Rosenkreuzer* and Gothic references, characterised the para-masonic societies in England, which fostered esotericism from the 1850s onwards, e.g. Knights of the Red Cross of Rome and Constantine, est. 1865; Societas Rosicruciana in Anglia (Soc. Ros.), est. 1866; the Ordo Rosae Rubeae et Aureae Crucis (Second Order of the Golden Dawn), est. 1892. It is also notable that → Paschal Beverly Randolph and → Hargrave Jennings (1817-1890), major publicists of Rosicrucian mysteries in the United States and England during the 1850-1870 period, used Rosicrucianism as a portfolio term for esotericism. They both had a powerful influence on → Helena Petrovna Blavatsky.

Hermeticism subsequently entered 19th-century Masonic discourse in England with reference to Egypt, just as it had a century earlier in 18th-century France and Germany. Kenneth Robert Henderson Mackenzie (1833-1886) became the English expert on high-degree Freemasonry and para-masonic societies, documented in his *Royal Masonic Cyclopaedia* (1875-77). Largely educated on the Continent, familiar with Austria and France, Mackenzie published a translation of the *Discoveries in Egypt, Ethiopia and the Peninsula of Sinai* (1852) by K.R. Lepsius, Professor of Egyptology at the University of Berlin. After visiting → Eliphas Lévi at Paris in 1861, Mackenzie helped establish the Soc. Ros. He referred to a Hermetic Order of Egypt as early as 1874, linking it with Lévi. Mackenzie's inspiration for such para-masonic orders associated with an "Egyptian" Orient was again evident in his Order of Ishmael (est. 1872). Given his access to old *Gold- und Rosenkreuzer* sources, Mackenzie may have posthumously supplied the grade-system for the → Hermetic Order of the Golden Dawn (earliest documents, 1886).

The 1870s thus witnessed a certain revival in the use of Hermeticism as a collective term for the Western esoteric traditions with regard to their Egyptian (Hellenistic) origins. In her articles of 1874-1875, Blavatsky had discussed Kabbalah and Rosicrucianism to distinguish occultism from → spiritualism. By September 1875, however, when writing her first book *Isis Unveiled* (1877), she gave much greater prominence to Hermeticism, → Neoplatonism, and Kabbalah than Rosicrucianism in her presentation of the Western esoteric tradi-

tion. Her early travels and inspiration in Egypt and the Middle East during the 1850s led to an "Egyptian" theme in the early → Theosophical Society (TS). Her first masters, Serapis Bey and Tuitit Bey, were members of a Brotherhood of Luxor. "Hermetic", "Egyptological" and "Rosicrucian" were among the names proposed for the new Theosophical Society in September 1875. Its actual adopted name was proposed by Charles Sotheran (1847-1902), an English Freemason, U.S. representative of the Swedenborgian Rite (est. 1859), and author of a biography of → Cagliostro, the founder of Egyptian Freemasonry. Blavatsky responded to Sotheran's "Egyptian" references as more suited to her new revelation than the Christian overtones of Rosicrucianism.

2. THE KINGSFORD-MAITLAND HERMETIC SOCIETY (1884-1887)

The term "Hermetic" later served as a means of emphasising Western esoteric traditions in the vicinity of the Theosophical Society with its later, post-1880 interest in India and a revelation by Masters (*Mahatmas*) of an ancient wisdom-religion descended through Tibetan Buddhism. The first such Hermetic Society was founded in 1884 under the presidency of → Anna Bonus Kingsford (1846-1888). The origins of this Hermetic Society in Anna Kingsford's own vocation throw much light on its representation of Greek and Christian esoteric traditions.

Dr Anna Kingsford, the young wife of an Anglican clergyman, had converted to Roman Catholicism in 1870, become an outspoken advocate of vegetarianism and anti-vivisection, and went in 1874 to study medicine in Paris, as the Sorbonne had recently opened its doors to women students. Anna Kingsford was an extraordinarily beautiful woman, highly intelligent and a fluent public speaker. While residing in Paris together with her colleague, Edward Maitland (1824-1897), she had begun to have prophetic dreams in 1875-1876, later progressing in 1877 to inner illuminations and celestial visions. These illuminations, published posthumously as *"Clothed with the Sun"* (1889) involved the Graeco-Egyptian and Christian mysteries, hymns to Hermes, the Adonai, and elemental divinities, revelations regarding the meaning of sin, death, and redemption, the esoteric significance of the Creed and the Lord's Prayer, and an ecstatic cosmological vision. Kingsford learned from her illuminators that Christianity had existed among the ancients as a hidden, esoteric doctrine and thus complemented rather than supplanted pagan religions. It is noteworthy that Eliphas Lévi's literary revival of → magic (after 1856) had created in Paris a new interest in the Hermetic tradition based on Judaeo-Christian traditions, and also made French esotericists possibly less receptive later on to the Eastern wisdom of Anglo-Indian Theosophy. Marie, Countess of Caithness (1830-1895), an aristocratic supporter of spiritualism, befriended Anna Kingsford and Edward Maitland in Paris and encouraged them to read books by → Jacob Boehme and Eliphas Lévi.

Back in London, Kingsford and Maitland gave a series of private lectures in May-June 1881 on Esoteric Christianity, published anonymously as *The Perfect Way, or the Finding of Christ* (1882). Their purpose was "the restoration of the esoteric philosophy or Theosophy of the West, and the interpretation thereby of the Christian and kindred religions". Kabbalah began to feature in Kingsford's revelation: in July 1881 she had a vision of kabbalistic doctrine, soon authenticated by subsequent study of → Knorr von Rosenroth's *Kabbala Denudata*. Another friend in France, Baron Guiseppe Spedalieri, the literary heir of Lévi, also confirmed the kabbalistic nature of *The Perfect Way*.

Among their audiences were some members of the British Theosophical Society, founded in London on 27 June 1878 as a branch of the New York society. These included its chief organizer and first president, Charles Carleton Massey (1838-1905), also among the founders of the New York society; Dr George Wyld (1821-1906), an eminent medical homeopath with an interest in phrenology and → Mesmerism; the Hon. Roden Noel (1834-1894), and Isabel de Steiger (1836-1927), who had studied the Hermetic tradition with Mrs Mary Anne Atwood, *née* South (1817-1910), an elderly lady long immersed in → Christian Theosophy and author of *A Suggestive Enquiry into the Hermetic Mystery* (1850).

Friction soon developed between Kingsford and Maitland, and the (Adyar) Thesophists. In March 1881 Alfred Percy Sinnett (1840-1921) was back from India to publish his account of the Theosophists, Blavatsky's phenomena, and the mysterious Masters, as *The Occult World* (1881). Maitland thought Sinnett's initiation into (Eastern) Theosophy rather rudimentary, noting that he dilated more on mediumship than spiritual vision, and even denied → reincarnation (on the basis of *Isis Unveiled*). Kingsford and Maitland upheld the doctrine of reincarnation and thereby unleashed some confusion among the London Theosophists in the course of their 1882 lectures. Divergences of interest between their views and those of the

Theosophists in India were apparent in an ambiguous review of *The Perfect Way* in *The Theosophist* (May 1882), written either by Sinnett or Subba Row. Meanwhile, Anna Kingsford's charismatic lectures and inspired letters were winning her more friends among the English and French Theosophists. In August 1882 Maitland received a letter from Gerard Finch, a member of the British Theosophical Society, suggesting he and Kingsford play a more prominent role in the Society, as it was now languishing. After some correspondence with Massey, now president, Anna Kingsford was elected president, and Maitland vice-president, of the British Theosophical Society on 7 January 1883, which, on her suggestion, was afterwards designated the London Lodge of the Theosophical Society.

Her first public appearance as president at a reception on 17 July 1883 was attended by Sinnett, who was again over from India, this time to publish his new book, *Esoteric Buddhism* (1883), on (Eastern) Theosophical doctrine. Sinnett adhered to his exclusive revelation through a secret lodge of Himalayan adepts, an attractive marvel to many Theosophists, while Maitland and Kingsford emphasised universal access to theosophy offered by visionary experience, and were offended by the evident hostility of the Indian Theosophists towards Christianity. By November 1883, Kingsford wrote to Madame de Steiger that Sinnett sought to silence 'every other voice but that of the "Mahatmas"'. A outright schism soon developed in the London Lodge between members interested in the Kingsford-Maitland revelation of Western mysteries and those impressed by Sinnett's dogmatic insistence on the sole authority of the Himalayan Masters. At a meeting of the London Lodge on 7 April 1884, chaired by Olcott, Kingsford and Maitland were initially deposed, with Finch and Sinnett taking their respective offices. In an atmosphere charged with conflict, Blavatsky unexpectedly arrived from Paris to settle matters and took charge of the disorderly meeting. Blavatsky's Masters had already, in letters of December 1883 and January 1884, welcomed Anna Kingsford's presidency, approving of her views on animal vivisection and vegetarianism, and recognising the additional appeal of her Western mysteries to English audiences. With Blavatsky's timely intervention, it was thus agreed that Kingsford should form a new group called the Hermetic Lodge, Theosophical Society to accommodate her numerous supporters, while the London Lodge should continue. However, many members of the two lodges still wished to attend each other's meetings. As dual lodge membership had been ruled out by Olcott, the Hermetic Lodge charter was returned and Kingsford and Maitland founded an independent, extramural Hermetic Society on 9 May 1884, which any TS members were entitled to attend. Others cultivating the Western esoteric tradition also joined, including → Samuel Liddell MacGregor Mathers (1854-1918), a young Freemason, member of the Soc. Ros. since 1882, and a student of the Kabbalah. Both he and → William W. Westcott (1848-1925), subsequent co-founders of the Golden Dawn, gave lectures and became honorary members of the Hermetic Society. Its secretary, W.F. Kirby, also later joined the Golden Dawn.

The name was chosen with regard to Hermes [Trismegistus] as 'the supreme initiator into the Sacred Mysteries of existence . . .'. Its chief aim was 'to promote the comparative study of the philosophical and religious systems of the East and the West; especially of the Greek Mysteries and the Hermetic Gnosis, and its allied schools, the Kabalistic, Pythagorean, Platonic, and Alexandrian, – these being inclusive of Christianity, – with a view to the elucidation of their original esoteric and real doctrine, and the adaption of its expression to modern requirements'. Kingsford and Maitland's lecture programme focused on Hermeticism, Kabbalah, and Christian mysteries. The summer session of June and July 1884 comprised weekly lectures on the correspondence of the Christian Creed to the ancient sacred mysteries. Around this time, she expanded her commentary on the Kabbalah with complex glyphs representing the body and soul, male and female, and spiritual regeneration, based on the Seal of Solomon and the Tree of Life. In September 1884 she received a further illumination of 'The Mysteries of the Kingdoms of the Seven Spheres', which matched the verses of the Creed to correspondences with seven archangels, planets, rays, colours and Graeco-Egyptian gods. In 1885 the weekly meetings of the Hermetic Society resumed from April to July with lectures from Kingsford and Maitland on the Hermetic fragment Kore Kosmou, the symbology of the Old Testament, interpretations of the Gospels and the Communion of Saints. The third session ran from April to July 1886 with Kingsford lecturing on Bible Hermeneutics and Maitland on the "Higher Alchemy", their Hermetic view of regeneration and resurrection. In June 1886 Mathers lectured on the Kabbalah. Many lectures of the Hermetic Society were later published as The Credo of Christendom (1916). The lectures were read by the elderly Mrs Atwood, the mentor of Isabelle de Steiger, whose opinion as a Christian Hermeticist was especially valued by Maitland and Kingsford. Kingsford and Maitland pursued further Hermetic researches, publishing a translation of some Trismegistic treatises known as The Virgin of the World (1885) and a new edition of Astrology Theologized (1886) originally written by → Valentin Weigel. Both works carried lengthy introductions by their editors, placing them in the Hermetic-Christian tradition. Anna Kingsford fell ill in September 1886 and sought recovery and convalescence abroad. Her health continued to deteriorate and the session was abandoned for 1887. Following her death in February 1888, the Hermetic Society fell into abeyance. Edward Maitland devoted the rest of his life to writing The Life of Anna Kingsford (1896) and otherwise seeking to proclaim their 'new gospel of interpretation'.

Despite its brief life, the Hermetic Society highlighted the Theosophical Society's need to accommodate Hellenistic, kabbalistic, and Christian theosophy together with Oriental religions, in order to appeal to Europeans. Interest in Kabbalah had already revived among esotericists, once Blavatsky herself had drawn attention to the Kabbalah in Isis Unveiled. Mathers discussed Kabbalah with Blavatsky and was already using her book in 1883 to compile his own translation of the Sephir Zohar, published as The Kabbalah Unveiled (1887), tellingly dedicated to Kingsford and Maitland. Blavatsky and her Masters evidently recognised a risk of sectarian isolation if the Theosophical Society was identified exclusively with Oriental religion by Sinnett and other enthusiastic converts.

After the demise of the Hermetic Society, the → Hermetic Brotherhood of Luxor (est. 1884) and the Hermetic Order of the Golden Dawn (est. 1888) became the chief vehicles for Western esoteric traditions in Britain, America, and France, concentrating on practical ceremonial magic, Kabbalah, and the Hermetic sciences of → astrology and alchemy. Blavatsky founded her Esoteric Section and Inner Group to pursue studies in Eastern metaphysics and macro-microcosmic correspondences until her death in May 1891. Under the presidency of → Annie Besant, Indian (Adyar and London) Theosophy became more identified with Oriental religion, especially after its discovery of Krishnamurti as the coming messiah. Secessions by leading Theosophists from Adyar such as → George Robert Stow Mead (1909), → Rudolf Steiner (1912) and → Dion Fortune (1928) all reflect the resurgent interest in Western esoteric traditions in the Theosophical Society, thus echoing the earlier schism of the Hermetic Society.

By 1890 the word "Hermetic" was well re-launched into esoteric discourse, frequently appearing in the titles of books, editions, and articles by Westcott, Mead, and → Arthur Edward Waite, the leading author and editor of the modern occult revival. Between the two World Wars, Hermeticism continued to feature as a cognate term for alchemy, astrology, Kabbalah, and magic among Golden Dawn derivative groups and in the works of → Manley Palmer Hall. In the 1960s its usage expanded in the scholarly community following the seminal researches into Renaissance culture by Frances Yates and her students at the Warburg Institute, London. Besides its scholarly currency, "Hermeticism" presently serves to distinguish magico-esoteric traditions of Graeco-Egyptian (Hellenistic) origin from neo-pagan, nativist traditions derived from the ancient Celts, Teutons, and extra-European peoples, more current among "New Age" groups.

3. The Dublin Hermetic Societies (1885-1939)

Two further foundations also took the name Hermetic Society, both associated with Blavatskyan Theosophy in Ireland in the period 1885-1935. Their principal figures played a leading role as poets, scholars, and artists in the Irish Renaissance of the 1890s, namely the literary revival, the founding of the Irish National Theatre and Abbey Theatre, and a quickening interest in early Irish history, the great Celtic myths, folklore and the supernatural. The first (Dublin) Hermetic Society arose from the interests of the budding poet → William Butler Yeats (1865-1939) and his friend Charles Johnston (1867-1931). Johnston had been first introduced to Theosophy by reading A.P. Sinnett's *The Occult World* in November 1884 and *Esoteric Buddhism* the following spring. Another account relates that shortly after Yeats had left Erasmus Smith High School, Dublin in December 1883, he loaned his friend a copy of *Esoteric Buddhism*, which both Professor Edward Dowson of Trinity College and then his London aunt Isabella Pollexfen Varley had drawn to his attention in 1884. The son of a distinguished Irish MP, Johnston was a brilliant classical scholar. His headmaster was dismayed at this enthusiasm for Theosophy and asked Yeats to discourage this interest. However, Johnston had been completely convinced of the truth of Blavatsky's message, of the reality of the Masters, and of her position as Messenger of the Great Lodge. Yeats and Johnston now read ever more widely on esoteric subjects, including Baron von Reichenbach's Odic force and Theosophical litera-

ture. On 15 June 1885 they founded the Hermetic Society in Dublin 'to discover the wonders of Eastern Philosophy'. Other members included the 18-year old Claude Falls Wright, Charles Weekes, Hamilton Malcolm Magee, and Alaud Alihad. They conducted experiments and read papers at their York Street premises on the Vedas, the Upanishads, the Neoplatonists, and modern mystics and spiritualists. A professor of Oriental Languages at Trinity College lectured on "magicians of the East". In the spring 1885 Johnston visited the Theosophists in London, meeting both Sinnett and Mohini Chatterji (1858-1936), a personal pupil of Master Koot Hoomi and one of the most brilliant Hindu members of the early Theosophical Society. Johnson made a vigorous public defense of Blavatsky following the defamatory SPR Report on her activities in India, which had only increased his zeal for Theosophy.

In April 1886 he and several friends founded an official Dublin Lodge of the Theosophical Society, which effectively succeeded his and Yeats' Hermetic Society. Charter members included Charles Johnston, his brother L.A.M. Johnston, F.J. Gregg, Hamilton Malcolm Magee, E.A. Seale, W.F. Smeeth, and R.A. Potterton. They invited Mohini Chatterji to stay in Dublin and address the Society. Abandoning earlier plans to become a missionary, Johnston studied Sanskrit at Trinity College Dublin and took the examinations for the Indian Civil Service (ICS) in London, where he first visited Blavatsky in early 1887. Yeats left Dublin in May 1887 to live in London, and was introduced by Johnston to Blavatsky. Yeats soon joined the Blavatsky Lodge of the Theosophical Society in London, then became her personal student in the Esoteric Section, where he proposed empirical experiments involving her *Esoteric Instructions*, based on correspondences of sound, number and color. However, Yeats' interest in applied esotericism alienated the more metaphysically-minded members of the Esoteric Section, though not Blavatsky. He subsequently found more scope for his interests in the magical ceremonies of the Golden Dawn, which he joined in March 1890.

Already in 1885 Johnston had met the young painter and poet George William Russell (1867-1935), later known as → AE (derived from "Æon", a Gnostic term for the spiritual offspring of the Deity), another leading member of the Irish Renaissance. Russell had already been attracted to the sacred literature of India before meeting Johnston. Less scholarly than either Yeats or Johnston, Russell did not immediately join the Dublin Lodge on its formation, but he and Johnston shared an exploration of the Upanishads and the Bhagavad Gita over three years before Johnston passed his final ICS examinations and left for India in October 1888, after marrying Blavatky's niece. Johnston crowned his short career in the Bengali Civil Service with literary accolades. He became president of the Irish Literary Society with several works, including translations of *The Upanishads* (1896) and *The Yoga Sutras of Patanjali* (1912). Russell had met Mohini Chatterji on his Dublin visit and was greatly impressed, but he also pondered Gnostic revelations and the inner illumination of Hellenistic theosophy in the formation of his own myth of mystical and artistic creation. By 1887 he had read *Light on the Path* and *The Idyll of the White Lotus*, both by Mabel Collins, a leading Theosophist in London, and then proceeded to study Blavatsky's *Isis Unveiled*, Mohini Chatterji and Laura C. Holloway, *Man: Fragments of a Forgotten History* and Sinnett's *Esoteric Buddhism*, which he considered only partly authentic. Only in December 1890 did he finally join the Dublin Lodge.

In April 1891 the Scottish engineer, Frederick J. Dick and his wife Annie rented a row of Georgian terrace houses on Upper Ely Place which they put at the disposal of the Dublin Lodge of the Theosophical Society and a residential community of young disciples, which became known as the "Household". Members of this community included Russell, who lived there happily for the next six years, Edmund King, Daniel Nicol Dunlop, Hamilton Malcolm Magee, Arthur Dwyer, James Nolan, and Charles Johnston's sister Georgie. Though Yeats was no longer involved with the reorganized Hermetic Society, nor even with the Theosophical Society in London, he and Russell painted several symbolic murals in summer 1892 upon the walls of the new Lodge, which were signed "GWR, WBY". Irish-born William Quan Judge, President of the American Section of the Theosophical Society, was visiting Dublin at the time and wrote in his American Section journal, *The Path*: 'Bro. Russell has begun to illuminate the walls of the place with wonderful paintings symbolizing the journey of the pilgrim soul'. Russell's and Yeats' paths gradually diverged with his pursuit of → mysticism and Theosophy, and the latter's focus on magic, myth, and artistic power. Violet North, a young English Theosophist with literary and psychic gifts, and James Pryse, an American Theosophist who had run Blavatsky's printing press in London, joined the Household in early 1895. Russell and Pryse collaborated in producing the *Irish Theosophist* (1892-97), until the latter's return to the United States in December to con-

duct the affairs of the American Theosophical Society as Judge was seriously ill. Violet subsequently took over Pryse's work on the journal, romance blossomed and she and Russell married in June 1898. In 1896 the Dublin Theosophists expected the Celtic Avatar, based on prophecies of divine incarnations of a Ray of the Logos, another instance of the mutual influence of literary, esoteric and political ideas in the Irish Renaissance.

Meanwhile Annie Besant's and Olcott's dispute with William Quan Judge, running since December 1893 over allegations that the latter had forged Mahatma letters to himself, climaxed with the secession of the American Theosophists and their election of Judge as their permanent president in April 1895. At the 4 July 1895 meeting of the European Section in London, the majority of the English Theosophists supported Mrs Besant, while the Irish delegates withdrew, proclaimed themselves the Theosophical Society in Europe and also elected Judge as their president. The Irish contingent then elected its own national officers with Dunlop as president, Russell vice-president, and Dick secretary. After Judge's death, the Dublin Lodge affiliated with the American Theosophists under Katherine Tingley, but in March 1898 Russell fell out with her after she disapproved of one of his articles and he resigned from her Universal Brotherhood and Theosophical Society.

Russell then founded the (second) Hermetic Society for members of the old Dublin Lodge, a group which met weekly first at his home, after May 1900 at its own premises in Dawson Chambers, to discuss Blavatky's teachings and certain mystical classics. While still living in the Household, Russell had read much esoteric literature besides Theosophy, including Plato, the Hermetic writings, the Chaldaean Oracles, Lao Tzu, Sufi poetry, and modern texts of psychical research such as Carl Du Prel's *Philosophy of Mysticism*. His Theosophy left plenty of room for admiration of the Psalms and Prophets, and he venerated St John, St Paul and Origen. The Hermetic Society reflected this breadth of vision and attracted budding and some later renowned poets, including James Joyce, Padraic Colum, James Starkey (pseud. Seumas O'Sullivan) (1879-1958), and an overlapping membership with George Moore's literary circle. The second Hermetic Society fulfilled the promise of the first Dublin foundation, demonstrating the important imaginal contribution Hermeticism and Theosophy made to the Irish Renaissance. A copy of *The Secret Doctrine* was kept in the room, where Russell regularly spoke on the common wellsprings of literature and mysticism. The Hermetic Society came to an end in late 1904, when Russell and many of his disciples joined the Adyar Theosophical Society. On 20 October 1904, Olcott issued a charter for the revived Dublin Lodge, whose members included George and Violet Russell, James Starkey (Seumas O'Sullivan), and H.F. Norman. In 1909 Russell left the Theosophical Society again, dismayed at the leadership of Annie Besant and → Charles Leadbeater, and refounded the Hermetic Society. Its Thursday evening meetings resumed in the Leinster School of Music on Harcourt Street. The room was unadorned save for one of Russell's visionary paintings and Blavatsky's book. Russell's teachings were in fact closely based on those of *The Secret Doctrine*, illustrated with a rich fund of literary and esoteric commentaries. His political work and American lecture tours brought him an international public but he was still running the Hermetic Society until he sold his Dublin home and left for London in July 1933.

Russell entrusted the leadership of the Hermetic Society to Captain P.G. Bowen (1882-1940), whom he had first met after the latter's return to Ireland after First World War. At Russell's request, Bowen published a remarkable book on the inner life, *The Occult Way* (1933), later followed by *The Sayings of the Ancient One* (1935), based on initiation into a source of the wisdom-tradition he had discovered while working in South Africa. Bowen also published a "Back-to-Blavatsky" piece *Madame Blavatsky on How to Study Theosophy* (1932), attributed to his father Robert Bowen, allegedly a member of her circle in London. Bowen dissolved the Society at the outbreak of war.

[1a. Hermeticism:] Ehregott Daniel Colberg, *Das Platonisch-Hermetisches Christenthum*, 2 Teile, Frankfurt and Leipzig, 1690-1691 ♦ Johann Konrad Dippel, *Eröffneter Weg zum Frieden mit Gott und allen Creaturen*, Amsterdam, 1709 ♦ Anton Joseph Kirchweger, *Aurea Catena Homeri*, Franckfurt & Leipzig, 1723 ♦ Samuel Richter, *Theo-Philosophia Theoretico-Practica*, Breslau, 1711 ♦ idem, *Sinceri Renati sämtliche Philosophisch- und Chymische Schrifften*, 1741 ♦ Georg von Welling, *Opus Mago-Cabbalisticum et Theosophicum*, Homburg vor der Hohe, 1735 ♦ Johann Jakob Brucker, *Historia critica philosophiae*, 6 vols., Leipzig: Breitkopf, 1742-1767, vols. 1 & 4 ♦ Johann Gottfried Herder, *Die älteste Urkunde des Menschengeschlechtes*, 1744 ♦ Friedrich Joseph Wilhelm Schröder, *Neue alchymische Bibliothek für den Naturkundiger unsers Jahrhunderts*, Frankfurt & Leipzig: Bronner, 1772-1774 ♦ Antoine Court de Gébelin, *Le Monde Primitif, analysé et comparé avec le monde moderne*, 9 vols., Paris, 1773-1782 ♦ *Hermetisches A.B.C., deren ächten Weisen alter und neuen Zeiten von Stein der Weisen*, 4 Teile, Berlin: Christian Ulrich Ringmacher, 1778-79

[1b. Hermetic Society, Bochum (1796-1819):] Die Hermetische Gesellschaft, "Höhere Chemie", *Der Reichsanzeiger oder Allgemeines Intelligenzblatt zum Behuf der Justiz, der Polizey und der bürgerlichen Gewerbe im Teutschen Reiche wie auch zur öffentlichen Unterhaltung der Leser über gemeinnützige Gegenstände aller Art* (Gotha) (1796), Sp. 6034 ♦ C.H. Wendelin and Die Hermetische Gesellschaft, "Naturkunde", idem, (1797), Sp. 948-95 ♦ "Erste Erklärung der Hermetischen Gesellschaft fürs Publicum, nebst Antworten auf die an sie eingegangenen Briefe", idem (1797), Sp. 1032-1038 ♦ "Naturkunde. Über die Geschwindigkeit aufeinander folgender Vorstellungen in der Seele", idem (1797), Sp. 1093-1102 ♦ "Gemeinnützige Schriften: Antwort der Hermetischen Gesellschaft auf verschiedenste an sie eingegangene Briefe und Aufsätze", idem (1797), Sp. 2117-2125 ♦ "Naturkunde. Die hermetische Gesellschaft an ihre Freunde", idem (1798), Sp. 805-813, subsequent articles in idem, (1798), Sp. 841-843; (1798), Sp. 869-877; (1798), Sp. 879-881; (1798), Sp. 893-898; (1798), Sp. 3111-3117; (1799), Sp. 621-623; (1802), Sp. 3521-3525 ♦ Johann Friedrich Benzenberg, "Menschenkunde: Ueber die Hermetische Gesellschaft", *Westfälischer Anzeiger* (1802), Sp. 1121-1131 ♦ idem, "Über die Hermetische Gesellschaft", *Gilberts Annalen der Physik* 12 (1802), 493-496 ♦ "Antwort an Hrn. Benzenberg wegen seines Aufsatzes im 71. ten Stücke des W. Anzeigers die hermetische Gesellschaft betreffend", *Westfälischer Anzeiger* (1802), Sp. 1213-1215
[2. Kingsford-Maitland Hermetic Society (1884-1887):] Anna Bonus Kingsford and Edward Maitland, *The Perfect Way; or, The Finding of Christ*, fifth ed., edited and a biographical preface by S.H. Hart, London: John Watkins, 1923 (first ed. 1881) ♦ *The Hermetic Works: The Virgin of the World of Hermes Mercurius Trismegistus*, edited by Anna Kingsford and Edward Maitland, London: George Redway, 1885 ♦ *"Astrology Theologized": The Spiritual Hermeneutics of Astrology and Holy Writ by Valentin Weigel*, reprint of 1649 ed. and with prefatory essay by Anna Kingsford, London: George Redway, 1886 ♦ *"Clothed with the Sun" being the Book of the Illuminations of Anna (Bonus) Kingsford*, edited by Edward Maitland, third ed., edited by S.H. Hart, London: John Watkins, 1937 (first ed. 1889) ♦ Edward Maitland, *The Story of Anna Kingsford and Edward Maitland and of the New Gospel of Interpretation*, third and enlarged ed., edited by S.H. Hart, Birmingham: Ruskin Press, 1905 (first ed. 1893) ♦ Anna Bonus Kingsford, *The Credo of Christendom and Other Addresses and Essays on Esoteric Christianity*, biographical preface and edited by S.H. Hart, London: John Watkins, 1916 ♦ Edward Maitland (ed.), *Anna Kingsford: Her Life, Letters, Diary and Work*, 2 vols., third ed., edited by Samuel Hopgood Hart, London: John Watkins, 1913 (first ed. 1896) ♦ *The Mahatma Letters to A.P. Sinnett*, ed. A.T. Barker, third ed., Adyar, Madras: Theosophical Publishing House, 1972 (first ed. 1923)
[3. Dublin Hermetic Societies (1885-1939):] George William Russell, *The Descent of the Gods: The Mystical Writings of George W. Russell-AE*, edited by Raghavan and Nandini Iyer, (Collected Works, Part

Three) Gerrards Cross: Colin Smythe, 1988 [This volume contains A.E.'s four major works, *The Avatars* (1933), *The Candle of Vision* (1918), *The Interpreters* (1922), and *Song and its Fountains* (1932), together with his letters and other prose contributions to *Dana, Ethical Echo, The Internationalist, The Irish Theosophist, Lucifer,* and *Ourselves,* W.Y. Evans Wentz's interview with A.E. in: *The Fairy-Faith in Celtic Countries,* A.E.'s first independent publication, *To the Fellows of the Theosophical Society*] ♦ W.B. Yeats, *The Celtic Twilight,* with an introduction by Kathleen Raine, Gerrards Cross: Colin Smythe, 1981 (first ed. 1891) ♦ idem, *Autobiographies,* London: Macmillan, 1926.

Lit.: [1a. Hermeticism:] Klaus Epstein, *The Genesis of German Conservatism,* Princeton, NJ: Princeton University Press, 1966, Chapter 2 ♦ Antoine Faivre, *The Eternal Hermes: From Greek God to Alchemical Magus,* Grand Rapids, Michigan: Phanes, 1995 ♦ Karl R.H. Frick, *Die Erleuchteten,* Graz: Akademische Druck- und Verlagsanstalt, 1973 ♦ Carlos Gilly and Cis van Heertum, *Magic, Alchemy and Science, 15th-18th Centuries: The Influence of Hermes Trismegistus,* 2 vols., Amsterdam: Bibliotheca Philosophica Hermetica, 2002 ♦ Hans Grassl, *Aufbruch zur Romantik: Bayerns Beitrag zur deutschen Geistesgeschichte 1765-1785,* Munich: C.H. Beck, 1968 ♦ Ronald Gray, *Goethe the Alchemist,* Cambridge: Cambridge University Press, 1952 ♦ Wouter J. Hanegraaff, "Beyond the Yates Paradigm: The Study of Western Esotericism between Counterculture and New Complexity", *Aries* 1:1 (2001), 5-37 ♦ Ingrid Merkel & Allen G. Debus (eds.), *Hermeticism and the Renaissance: Intellectual History and the Occult in Early Modern Europe,* Washington D.C.: Folger Shakespeare Library, 1988 ♦ Ellic Howe, "Fringe Masonry in England, 1870-85", *Ars Quatuor Coronatorum* 85 (1972), 242-280 ♦ Christopher A. McIntosh, *The Rose Cross and the Age of Reason: Eighteenth-Century Rosicrucianism in Central Europe and Its Relationship to the Enlightenment,* Leiden: E.J. Brill, 1992 ♦ John M. Roberts, *The Mythology of the Secret Societies,* London: Secker and Warburg, 1972 ♦ Rolf Christian Zimmermann, *Das Weltbild des jungen Goethe: Studien zur hermetischen Tradition des deutschen 18ten Jahrhunderts,* Munich: Wilhelm Fink, 1969 [1b. Hermetic Society, Bochum (1796-1819):] ♦ Karl Frick, "Die alchemistischen Studien des Bochumer Arztes und Jobsiade-Dichters Dr. Carl Arnold Kortum", *Sudhoffs Archiv* 43 (1959), 245-274 ♦ Karl Frick, "Johann Christian Friedrich Bährens (1765-1833), ein westfälischer Pfarrer, Arzt und Alchemist", *Sudhoffs Archiv* 53 (1969), 423-439 ♦ K. Frick, "Aus dem Briefwechsel zweier rheinisch-westfälischer Ärzte und Alchemisten über den Orden der Gold- und Rosenkreuzer in der 2. Hälfte des 18. Jahrhunderts", in: *Medicinae et artibus: Festschrift für Prof. Dr. phil Dr. med. Wilhelm Katner,* Düsseldorf, 1968, 11-21 ♦ Gerhard Hallen, "Bemerkungen über die Weltanschauung des Dr. Johann Christoph Friedrich Bährens im Spiegel seiner Schriften", *Unnaer Beiträge* (1986), 98-111 ♦ Hermann Kopp, *Über den Verfall der Alchemie*

und der Hermetischen Gesellschaft, Gießen, 1847 (= Denkschrift der Gesellschaft für Wissenschaft und Kunst in Gießen, Heft 1) ♦ Irmgard Müller, "Kortum als Verteidiger der Alchemie" in: Institut für Geschichte der Medizin, Ruhr-Universität Bochum (ed.), *Dr. med. Carl Arnold Kortum (1724-1824). Arzt, Volksaufklärer, Alchemist, Dichter: Ausstellungskatalog,* Bochum, 1991, 69-91 ♦ J.A. Peddinghaus, "Der 'Stein der Weisen'. Dr. Kortum als Chemiker und Hellseher", *Bochumer Anzeiger* 19.7.1938 ♦ Ernst Schultze, *Das letzte Aufflackern der Alchemie in Deutschland vor 100 Jahren: Die Hermetische Gesellschaft 1796-1819,* Leipzig, 1897 ♦ G. Vulpius, "Ueber die Alchemisten", *Archiv der Pharmazie* (1875), 342-350 [2. Kingsford-Maitland Hermetic Society (1884-1887):] Joscelyn Godwin, *The Theosophical Enlightenment,* Albany, New York: SUNY Press, 1994 ♦ Ellic Howe, *The Magicians of the Golden Dawn: A Documentary History of a Magical Order 1887-1923,* London: Routledge & Kegan Paul, 1972 [3. Dublin Hermetic Societies (1885-1939):] Robert Bernard Davis, *George William Russell ("AE"),* Boston, Mass.: Twayne, 1977 ♦ Richard Ellmann, *Yeats: The Man and the Masks,* New York: Norton, 1978 ♦ Roy F. Foster, *W.B. Yeats: A Life,* 2 vols., Vol. 1. *The Apprentice Mage, 1865-1914,* Oxford: Oxford University Press, 1997 ♦ Michel Gomes, *The Dawning of the Theosophical Movement,* Wheaton, Illinois: Theosophical Publishing House, 1987 ♦ Monk Gibbon, "The Early Years of George Russell (AE) and His Connection with the Theosophical Movement", Ph.D. thesis, Dublin: Trinity College, 1947-1948 ♦ Robert A. Gilbert, *The Golden Dawn Scrapbook: The Rise and Fall of a Magical Order,* York Beach, Maine: Samuel Weiser, 1997 ♦ George Mills Harper, *Yeats's Golden Dawn,* London: Macmillan, 1974 ♦ Alexander Norman Jeffares, *W.B. Yeats: A New Biography,* London: Hutchinson, 1988 ♦ *Letters from AE,* selected and edited by Alan Denson; with a foreword by Dr. Monk Gibbon, London, New York, Toronto: Abelard-Schuman, 1961 ♦ Jerry Hejka-Ekins, "The Literary Art of William Butler Yeats' 'Magical Tradition'", M.A. thesis, Stanislaus: California State University, 2001 ♦ Ulick O'Connor, *Celtic Dawn: A Portrait of the Irish Literary Renaissance,* London: Hamish Hamilton, 1984 ♦ Henry Summerfield, *That Myriad-Minded Man: A Biography of George William Russell "A.E." 1867-1935,* Gerrards Cross: Colin Smythe, 1975 ♦ Frank Tuohy, *Yeats,* London: Macmillan, 1976.

NICHOLAS GOODRICK-CLARKE

Hermetism

1. THE UNITY OF THE UNIVERSE 2. GOD 3. THE COSMOS 4. MANKIND 5. INITIATION 6. RELIGIOUS PRACTICES IN HERMETIC COMMUNITIES? 7. THE CRUCIBLE OF ALEXANDRIA: GREEK PHILOSOPHY, EGYPTIAN RELIGION, JUDAISM 8. HERMETISM AND CHRISTIAN BELIEF

1. The Unity of the Universe

The term "Hermetism" is used here to indicate the specific religious worldview of the so-called philosophical Hermetica [→ Hermetic literature I]. Its most characteristic feature is the idea of an indissoluble interrelationship between God, the cosmos and man, which implies the unity of the universe. Its final aim is to lead its adepts to the worship of the supreme God as the source of being and eventually to union with him. However, the hermetic writings show a great divergence with respect to the philosophical and religious ideas that were used to argue in favour of these fundamental tenets. Hermetism never knew a coherent doctrinal system, as will become abundantly clear from the following exposition.

It was a firm hermetic conviction that everything that exists, both in the material and the spiritual world, is fundamentally one, because it derives from *the* One, God. Hermes says in the first chapters of the *Asclepius* that 'all things are part of the One, or the One is all things'; before the creation everything existed in the creator, who alone is everything. The same idea is expressed in the hymn that concludes C.H. V: 'You are everything, and there is nothing else; what is not, you are as well. You are all that has come to be; you are what has not come to be' (V, 11). And, to give one more example, Asclepius writes in his letter to king Ammon, in C.H. XVI, 19: 'If all things are parts of God, then everything is God. Therefore, in making all things, he makes himself'.

The view that all things have their unity in God was based on the fundamental idea of a close interrelationship between God, the cosmos and man. According to the Armenian *Definitions* 7, 5: 'God is within himself, the world is in God, and man in the world'. And Hermes says in *Asclepius* 10: 'God, the Lord of eternity, is the first, the world is second, man is third' (also in Stobaeus, *Fragm.* XI, 6; cf. Armenian *Definitions* 1, 1). God is the father of the cosmos; and the cosmos is the father of everything it contains (C.H. IX, 8), and is, therefore, called the second god (C.H. VIII, 2, 5). Man is called 'the third living being' but he is not explicitly said to be the third God. According to C.H. X, 14, man is the son of the son of God: 'So there are three levels of being: God the father and the good, the cosmos, and man. God holds the cosmos and the cosmos the human being. And in this way the cosmos becomes the son of God and man the son of the cosmos – a grandson of God, as it were'. A similar figure of speech occurs in the Middleplatonist and Neopythagorean philosopher Numenius (Dillon, 367). Through the intermediary of these

two all things exist, but the One is their final cause (C.H. X, 25). The cosmos and man are also called images of God: 'the second god is made by the first god in his image', and 'man, the third living being, came to be in the image of the cosmos' (C.H. VIII, 2 and 5). But as such he is himself also the image of God: the human being reveres the first image, the cosmos, 'but he is not unaware that he is himself in the image of God too, for there are two images of God, the world and man' (*Asclepius* 10). In a passage that was to have a long-lasting influence (see below, section 8), the author of the *Asclepius* says that the human being was primarily created in order to contemplate the beautiful cosmos, which the Lord of the universe loved as his own child (8).

This idea of the indissoluble interrelationship between God, cosmos and man dominates the hermetic worldview and its piety. But within this general structure of the universe the hermetists sometimes introduced subordinate divisions of the divine and the material world that were borrowed from Greek philosophy or Judaism. The idea that the world is an image of God presupposes the Middle Platonist view that the ideas, i.e. the forms after which Plato's Demiurge created the world, are enclosed in the mind (*nous*) of the supreme God, as his thoughts. All earthly things are images, reflections, of their eternal forms within God, and in this sense the world as a whole is an image of God, just as the species man is an image of the idea of mankind (*Asclepius* 4). The Middle Platonists usually made a distinction between the supreme God, called the Good and One, who was considered the (first) Mind (*Nous*), and his active mind, which contains the ideas, called the second god or second *Nous* or the *Logos* and identified with Plato's Demiurge (Dillon). This distinction is also made in the *Poimandres* (C.H. I), 9: 'The Mind who is God . . . gave birth to a second Mind, a craftsman'. In the *Asclepius* this second god is called Aiōn, i.e. living and life-giving Eternity, which always stands still along with the supreme God, 'holding within it a world that had not come to be' (30-32). According to C.H. XI, 15, Eternity (Aiōn) is the image of God, and the cosmos that of Eternity (and the sun is the image of the cosmos, and man of the sun). The hermetists could obviously adhere to different views concerning the structure of being. The *Asclepius* attributes the creative activity to a third mind, that of the cosmos, which leads the author, in 32, to distinguish between four kinds of minds: (1) God, (2) the absolute mind, Aiōn, resembling divinity and containing the archetypes of the visible world, (3) the mind of the cosmos, the receptacle of all visible forms, and (4) the human mind. This fourfold hierarchical structure of mind in the universe stands alone in hermetic literature, but it was also propagated by the *viri novi* ("modernists"), a group of hermetic Platonists with gnostic inclinations that was criticized by Arnobius of Sicca (ca. 300). They said that the rational human soul 'holds the fourth place after God, the source of everything, and after the two minds (*mentes geminas*)' (*Adversus nationes*, II, 25; cf. Festugière 1967, 260-312). The idea that there are three divine hypostases is not uncommon in Middle- and Neoplatonism (Festugière 1967, 123-125), but that they are all called "mind" is exceptional. The *viri novi* need not have been dependent on the Latin *Asclepius*, which expresses itself not very clearly on this point. Most probably both the *viri novi* and the author of the *Asclepius* borrowed this idea from an existing hermetic or platonist source. The *Asclepius* is a composite work, which explains that it also contains ideas that do not concur with those just mentioned. In chapter 14, the author repeats a common Stoic doctrine, though combined with platonist ideas, about the two principles of the universe, God and matter, of which the latter is pervaded by the divine spirit (*pneuma*). But in his wording the influence of the first verses of Genesis 1, about the spirit of God moving above the primeval chaos, is unmistakable. He says that in the beginning 'there was God and there was matter. And the spirit was with matter, or rather it was in matter, but not in the way it was in God or the principles from which the world derives were in God'. Here and also in his view, mentioned above, that man is created 'in the image of God' (Gen. 1:26), the author shows himself to be directly or indirectly influenced by a Jewish source. Scott considered the mention of the spirit a later interpolation, but that assumption is not necessary, for we know from Cyril of Alexandria that there were hermetic writings that contained speculations about the divine *pneuma* (see below).

2. GOD

The hermetists could not and would not avoid expressing their ideas about God in the philosophical language of their time, but at the same time this rather abstract language proved insufficient for giving voice to their religious feelings. A good example of this insufficiency is C.H. V, entitled *God is invisible and entirely visible*, in which the author impressively argues that the visible world reveals the greatness of the invisible God. At first sight this seems no more than the common Stoic argument

for the existence of God based on the perfection of the created world. But the author explicitly states that one cannot know this God of one's own accord. On the contrary, one has to implore him for the grace of enlightenment, 'if only by one of his rays' (V, 2). It was a profound hermetic conviction that true Gnosis was only possible though divine illumination (C.H. VI, 4; *Asclepius* 32). Adopting a term coined by Plato, the hermetist of C.H. V calls God 'the Father of All', and he adds that the creator alone fully deserves this title, because his essence exists in eternally creating everything, without which he even would not be eternal himself (cf. also C.H. II, 14-17: the only appropriate names for God are 'the Good One' and 'Father'). 'If forced to say something still more daring', the author is prepared to declare that 'God's essence is to be pregnant of all things and to produce them', which is a veiled reference to his androgyny (V, 9). That God is androgynous is repeatedly stated in the *Poimandres* (C.H. I, 9 and 15). According to the *Asclepius*, 20, God is 'completely filled with the fecundity of both sexes' (*utraque sexus fecunditate plenissimus*), which then, however, is explained in a more philosophical way: since he is 'ever pregnant with his own will, he always begets whatever he wishes to procreate'. But in the final hymn of the *Asclepius*, in its original version as preserved in the Coptic *Prayer of Thanksgiving* (NHC VI, 7), the bisexual language of procreation comes to the surface in plain terms: 'We know you, O Womb of every creature, We know you, O Womb that is pregnant by the member (*physis* = phallus) of the Father. We know you, O begetting Father who eternally exists' (VI, 25-29). In Greece, the idea of divine androgyny played a role in the Orphic theogony, according to which Phanes/Erikepaios came forth from the primordial egg as an androgynous being, but outside Orphism the idea of an androgynous deity was unknown in Greek religion. Lactantius correctly observed that Hermes and Orpheus were in agreement with respect to the bisexuality of God (*Divinae Institutiones*, IV, 8, 3ff.). He could have added that this idea also played an important role in → Gnosticism. It seems certain that we have to look to Egypt for the origin of the hermetic idea of God's androgyny, for this idea, and its expression in bold sexual terms as well, was very common in Egyptian religion. At this point and also with respect to the idea of divine self-generation, the hermetists apparently continued an ancient Egyptian tradition (Daumas, 17-20; Zandee, 120-125; Scott III, 135-138). The notion of the supreme God's androgyny led to the idea of his being born out of himself. The *Asclepius* says that God's nature has been wholly born out of itself (*Asclepius* 14: *ex se tota*), and that he is 'in himself, by himself and wholly enclosing himself' (30: *in se est et a se est et circum se totus est*). The idea of divine self-generation is also expressed in C.H. IV, 10; VIII, 2 ('if he came to be, it was by himself') and in *Korē Kosmou* 58 (Stobaeus, *Fragm.* XXIII; NF, IV, 19). That the supreme principle, or God, was "unoriginated" (*agenētos*) or "unbegotten/unborn" (*agennētos*) was a philosophical commonplace, shared by Greek philosophers and Christian theologians alike. It was a way to express the transcendence of the first principle of the universe, as was also, for instance, the assertion that God has no name or all names (C.H. V, 10; *Asclepius* 20). The terms for "self-generated/self-begotten" (*autogenēs, autogen(n)ētos, autogonos, autogenethlos, et al.*) were less common for the supreme God, but they were often applied to the second level of divine being, not only in Hermetism and Gnosticism, but in → Neoplatonism as well. In the *Discourse on the Ogdoad and the Ennead* (NHC VI, 57, 13-18 and 63, 21-23), the author distinguishes between three levels of being: the Unbegotten (*agennētos*) God, the Self-begotten (*autogenētos*) One, and the Begotten (*ge[n]nēton*), of which the second most probably is identical with the heavenly Anthropos of the *Poimandres* and several Gnostic systems. Lactantius repeatedly says that → Hermes Trismegistus called God 'without father' (*apatōr*) and 'without mother' (*amētōr*), 'since he was out of himself and by himself' (*Divinae Institutiones* I, 7, 2; IV, 13, 2; *Epitome* 4, 4, NF IV, 106-107; Augustine explicitly denied this, *De Trinitate* I, 1). The hermetic idea of the self-generation of the supreme God most probably derives from the Egyptian view on the origin of the primeval gods (Daumas, 18-20; Zandee, 123-124). A hieroglyphic text from the Persian period says of Amon-Re: 'There was no father who begot him, no mother who was pregnant by his seed', and a hymn from a Theban tomb of the 19th dynasty says of the same god that he is the one who 'spontaneously came into being, who brought forth his mother and begot his father'. Another Theban hymn to the sun-god uses the same bold language as found in the hermetic *Prayer of Thanksgiving* quoted above, but now in a negative sense: 'no vulva has brought him forth, no phallus begot him'. Also Thot, as primeval god, is called the one 'who brought himself forth'.

Of course, the hermetists did not completely reject the traditional gods and demons of Greek and Egyptian religion, but these divine beings did not play a part of any importance in hermetic piety, which was wholly directed at the mystic union with the supreme God. The role of the heavenly and earthly gods and demons will be discussed in the subsequent sections on the cosmos and mankind.

3. THE COSMOS

According to the general hermetic view, the cosmos is the second living being or the second god, who incessantly produces everything that exists. But within this general scheme, the hermetic writings show a great variety with respect to the manner in which the creation actually takes place. A few of these ideas may be mentioned here. The creation story could be told in the form of a myth, as in the *Poimandres* (C.H. I), which in its turn, together with the creation story of Genesis, apparently strongly influenced the description in C.H. III (cf. Dodd, 210-234). But at the same time, the latter treatise combined this with the view that it was the gods of the planets and the fixed stars that created plants, animals and human beings. The human soul was created 'through the course of the cycling gods', i.e. the planets (III, 3; cf. I, 19). But according to C.H. XVI it is the sun that through its energies creates and transforms all existing things. It drives the chariot of the cosmos and in order to prevent the cosmos going out of control it holds fast the reins, 'which are life and soul and spirit and immortality and becoming'. The *Asclepius*, 2-3, gives a more philosophical explanation through the introduction of the World-soul and Nature: soul and matter, embraced by Nature, reproduce the images, i.e. the ideas, into an infinite number of sensible forms. Nature imprints these forms on matter by means of the four elements and leads the whole series of beings up to the vault of heaven, 'so that they will be pleasing in the sight of God' (cf. Genesis 1:31). Borrowing from another source, the *Asclepius*, in chapter 19, presents a hierarchy of beings that control everything that exists. A distinction is made between hypercosmic, intelligible gods (*theoi noētoi*), who are called *ousiarchai*, and cosmic, sensible gods (*theoi aisthētoi*), i.e. the celestial bodies. The ousiarchs are gods who rule over divine entities of a secondary order (Festugière 1967, 121-130). Zeus/Jupiter is the ousiarch of the heaven of the fixed stars, through which he gives life to all beings; Light is the ousiarch of the sun, through which we receive the good gift of light; the ousiarch of the 36 decans of the zodiac is called Pantomorphus or Omniform, because he gives the various classes of being their own form; Fate (*heimarmenē*) is the ousiarch of the seven spheres of the planets, through which all changes occur by the immutable law of nature, etc. In this way, all things are connected and comply with the Master of the universe, God, in whom they are in fact one. The gods have lost any religious meaning here; they are mere forces that steer the creation and course of the world.

This variety of ideas shows that there was not one specific hermetic doctrine on these points. As a matter of fact, the hermetists' primary concern was the ultimate cause of the universe, God, and therefore the aim of all their discussions of cosmology and creation was to bring the reader or listener through admiration of the cosmos to the adoration of and mystical union with the supreme God. In the *Asclepius*, 12-13, Hermes even goes so far as to attach merely a relative value to the traditional sciences: they are useful only in so far as they lead us to contemplation and adoration of the godhead. In his view the sophistic scholars have corrupted true philosophy by the 'unashamed curiosity of their mind', and, therefore, he prophesizes that 'after us there will no longer be any sincere love for philosophy, which solely consists in the desire to know the deity by frequent contemplation and holy piety'.

In the first half of the 20th century it became an established scholarly opinion that in ancient Hermetism there had been two quite different currents, which adhered to two irreconcilable hermetic doctrines. According to one of them, represented by C.H. V, VIII, and IX, the world is good and beautiful, enclosed in and permeated by God, who can be attained and experienced through the contemplation of the cosmos. According to the other view, represented by C.H. I, IV, VI, VII, and XIII, the world is fundamentally bad, and for that reason cannot be the product of the completely transcendent God but must have been created by a second god. The only way to attain the supreme God and become united with him is by renouncing the world in which the enlightened man knows himself to be a stranger. Accordingly, Festugière distinguished between two kinds of Hermetism. The first, represented by C.H. I, IV, VII and XIII, knew a more or less coherent doctrine of salvation, dominated by the pessimistic world-view. The other, represented by most of the other hermetic treatises, was characterized by a general pious attitude, which tended to bring the participants in a hermetic discussion to spiritual and moral elevation and to worship of the Creator of this beautiful world (1967, 39). There is no doubt that these observations are correct in so far as the C.H. does contain quite different statements about the status of evil in the world and man. However, reading the hermetic treatises more closely, it becomes evident that the problem of evil was a serious concern for the more "optimistic" writers too (see below). Hermetism presents itself not as a coherent set of doctrines that should be believed in, but as a way of moral and spiritual progress that leads to an ever better understanding of the world we live in and to knowledge of, and even union with, the transcendent God who is its final cause. Admiration of the beauty of the cosmos is an indispensable first step on the way of Hermes, but the more one advances on this way the more it becomes clear that the world and worldly things tend to lead the human being astray, so that he no longer strives to attain knowledge of God. This experience may lead to such strong expressions as the one found in C.H. VI, 4: 'The cosmos is the plenitude of evil, as God is the plenitude of the good'. Moreover, because Hermetism was not a coherent doctrinal system and human beings are simply not all equally optimistic or pessimistic, it is only to be expected that the force of evil in the world was variously appreciated.

4. Mankind

The glory and tragedy of the human condition is that, of all living beings, man alone has a twofold nature, earthly and mortal on the one hand and divine and immortal on the other. This basic idea of hermetic anthropology underlies all discussions of the position of the human being in the created world. The explanation of this singular status of man could be given in the form of a myth or more philosophically. The mythological explanation is to be found in the *Poimandres*, though even there philosophical and "scientific" explanations are clearly discernible. According to the myth, the heavenly Man (*Anthrōpos*) and unreasoning lower Nature fell in love with each other and as a result of their union brought forth the human being: 'For this reason, of all living beings on earth, man alone is twofold, mortal because of the body, immortal because of the real Man' (15; also e.g. *Asclepius* 7 and 20; Armenian *Definitions* 6, 1). This human being is called (16) 'a wonder most wondrous' (*thauma thaumasiōtaton*), which means that man is an extremely amazing being, not 'a great miracle'. This expression must be the background of that most famous statement in the *Asclepius*, 6: 'For that reason, Asclepius, man is a great wonder (*magnum miraculum est homo*), a living being to be worshipped and honoured'. The apposition to *homo* shows that, here too, *magnum miraculum* does not mean 'great miracle' but 'something extremely amazing' (also Armenian *Definitions* 9, 6: 'God is worthy of worship, man is worthy of admiration'). In the *Poimandres*, this most wondrous wonder of the human being is presented as 'a mystery that has been kept hidden to the present day', which seems to be that from the union of Man and Nature sprang seven androgynous and upright-going beings, made by Nature after the form (*eidos*) of Man. Here, the later platonist view that man is an image of the idea of Man is obviously in the background: the life and light of the divine Anthropos respectively became the soul and mind in the human body, which was made out of the four material elements. The seven human beings most probably derive from another source. The author says that they and all other living beings remained in their primal androgynous state 'until the end of a cycle and the beginning of ages' (17). A new era began when they were sundered into two parts, one male and one female, and were ordered: 'Increase in increasing and multiply in multitude' (cf. Genesis 1:28). The author has apparently made use of a Jewish source, which has also left its traces in the Pseudo-Clementine *Recognitions*, I, 29. This text says that the first seven generations of the human race lived the sinless and sexless life of the angels and that the eighth generation, seduced by the beauty of the women, introduced intercourse and procreation, which led to the birth of giants and, finally, to the Flood (cf. Genesis 6). Similarly, the *Poimandres* emphasizes that the focus on sexuality and procreation, though necessary for the continuation of the human race, contains the danger of forgetting one's divine descent. Therefore the injunction to increase and multiply is accompanied by the following warning: 'Let him who is endowed with mind (*nous*) recognize that he himself is immortal and that sexual desire is the cause of death, let him thus know all that exists' (18). That the corporeal component of man can be a danger to its spiritual counterpart is stated explicitly: 'he who loves the body, which is born from the error of desire, remains wandering in the dark and sensibly suffers the effects of death' (19).

The author of the *Asclepius* subscribed to a more optimistic view of the human condition, but for him evil was a great problem too. According to him, the human being occupies a middle position between the gods and earthly things: he combines divinity and corporeality (6). He is so shaped that he can answer to his twofold vocation, 'wondering at heavenly beings and worshipping them, tending earthly beings and governing them' (*Asclepius* 8). Though he cares for and cherishes those who are beneath him, he 'despises the part of him that is human nature, having put his trust in the divinity of his other part' (6). Man and all living beings live through the spirit that pervades the universe, but in addition, only the human being has received a reasoning mind (*sensus* = *logos* and *nous*). According to C.H. IV, 2, man surpasses even the cosmos and the gods by his reason and mind (cf. also VIII, 5; XII, 12; *Asclepius* 22). Therefore, he may be called an ornament (*kosmos*) of the universe (*kosmos*), a well-ordered world in itself, a microcosm (*Asclepius* 10).

However, it is a fact of experience that many people evince unreasonable and impious behaviour. That observation led the hermetists to the view that not everybody has *nous*: rather, it is a divine grace bestowed on only a few people (e.g. *Asclepius* 7 and 18; C.H. I, 22; IV, 3). It should be realized that *nous*, mostly translated as "mind", is not the discursive, analytical human faculty of reason (*logos*), but the intuitive, all-embracing vision by which one understands the sense and coherence of the whole of reality. The question why apparently not all human beings have *nous*, i.e. the problem of evil, was a point of much concern for the hermetists. There was a general consensus that the cause of evil was to be sought in the lower material component of the world and man. According to the *Asclepius*, 22 (= NHC VI, 67, 12ff.), there is an important difference between the star gods and human beings: the former 'have been made from the purest part of nature (fire) and, therefore, they need not have understanding (*epistēmē*) or knowledge (*gnōsis*), for the immortality of the gods is for them understanding and knowledge'. Man, on the other hand, who was made from the lower material elements and, therefore, became subject to the passions and evil inclinations that are inherent in them, has been given the possibility of overcoming these vices through the gifts of understanding and gnosis. From this perspective, one might say that God created man as good and immortal! But that statement is based on man's ultimate potentiality, which proves to be unrealizable for most people. It can only be effectuated if man is led by his divine *nous*, lives a pious life and despises his corporeality. The hatred of the body is not only recommended in such "pessimistic" treatises as CH I, IV (6), VI and VII, but also in more optimistic writings like the *Asclepius*, which says that 'the malice that begrudges immortality prevents the soul from acknowledging its divine part' (12). That immortality can only be reached if the soul, led by the divine *nous*, devotes itself to an ascetic way of life, found a succinct expression in the Armenian *Definitions* 9, 5 (of which the Greek text has been preserved in the Oxford fragments): 'Whoever behaves well towards his body, behaves badly towards himself. Just as the body, without a soul, is a corpse, likewise soul, without Nous, is inert'. It was this gloomy view of the dangers to which the soul is exposed that led some hermetists to very negative descriptions of mankind and the world in general. Strictly speaking, nothing in our world can be called good; even what is called good by ordinary speech is in fact not good at all; God is the only one who is actually good (CH VI). According to the *Asclepius*, 16, however, it is an impious question to ask 'Was God not able to put an end to evil and banish it from nature?' As a matter of fact, we read here, the Creator has endowed man with mind (*sensus* = *nous*), knowledge (*disciplina* = *gnosis*) and understanding (*intellegentia* = *epistēmē*), which enable him 'to avoid the tricks, snares and vices of evil' (cf. C.H. XII, 12: the gifts of *nous* and *logos* are of equal value as immortality). The same idea is expressed in the final hymn of the *Asclepius*, 41 (= the *Prayer of Thanksgiving* in NHC, VI, 64, 8-14), in which the hermetic believers say that God's goodness has 'graciously given us *nous*, *logos* and *gnosis*: *nous* to understand you, *logos* to interpret you, and *gnosis* to know you. We rejoice that we have been illuminated by your *gnosis*'. However, there were also hermetists who preferred another, more mythical explanation of the origin of good or evil in man. According to C.H. IX, 3-4, the cosmos is full of *daimones*, i.e. good or bad spiritual, → intermediary beings, who sow the seeds of virtue or malice in the human mind (here used in a neutral sense, not as a divine gift of grace). A similar idea is found in C.H. XIII, 8-10, where Tat at his spiritual rebirth is cleansed from twelve tormenting spirits of the material world and filled by ten good spirits.

The good and bad *daimones* played an important role in the hermetic view of the world. The *Asclepius* contains some notorious passages about the presence of demons in the statues of the gods (23 and 37-38). The greatness of man is demonstrated by his capacity of making the gods that are worshipped in the temples (23). Originally the human beings did not even know that there were gods. They realised their existence when they discovered the art of making images, and added a magic power from the cosmos to the material from which they made the statues. Then they conjured the souls of *daimones* into the statues, which in that way received the power to be beneficent or harmful (37-38). Another important aspect of the *daimones* is that they punish the sinners and help the pious after the separation of soul and body at death. In C.H. X, it is connected with the idea of a telescopic construction of the human person: the carnal body encloses the astral body (*pneuma*, which makes it alive and moving), the soul (*psychè*) is enclosed within the astral body, reason (*logos*) within the soul, and mind (*nous*) within reason (X, 13). This view is determined by the conviction that the divine *nous* cannot be in direct contact with the body (X, 17). At death the *nous* puts on its original garment of fire and also the pious soul becomes wholly *nous* (X, 18-19), which means that they become demons. At death the bad souls are sent back to another existence in a human body. There they are punished by the demons, who, on the other hand, lead the good ones to the 'light of knowledge' (X, 21). The Latin *Asclepius*, 28, speaks about one chief demon in the air who weighs and judges the soul's merits, allowing those of the righteous to go to places that suit them while severely punishing those of evil people. But since the Latin and Coptic translations show considerable differences concerning these punishments, especially in chapter 29, the original Greek version cannot be established with cer-tainty. John Lydus († ca. 555), *De mensibus* IV, 32 and 149, reports that 'the Egyptian Hermes in his *Perfect Discourse*' mentioned three classes of demons: (1) 'avenging demons', who are present in matter and already punish criminals on earth, (2) 'cleansing demons', who live in the air and purify the bad souls that after death try to ascend, and (3) 'saving demons', who live on the moon and save the souls of the righteous. We may assume that concerning this point as well, there was not one single hermetic doctrine about the fate of the soul after death but, rather, that the hermetists could adhere to quite different ideas. However, they all shared the conviction that only the soul of the pious, who had come to knowledge of himself and of God, could escape the bonds of matter and return to its previous divine status (*Asclepius* 11).

5. INITIATION

Whether the hermetic writers subscribed to a more positive or negative evaluation of the world and man, their unanimous aim was to bring the reader to the praise and worship of the supreme God, who is 'not visible [i.e. knowable], but evident within the visible' (Armenian *Definitions* 1, 2). The authors of C.H. I (*Poimandres*), XI and XIII and NHC VI, 6 (*Discourse on the Ogdoad and the Ennead*) go even further and describe ecstatic experiences in which the hermetist leaves his earthly state behind and feels himself united with the supreme God or the universe. In C.H. XIII and NHC VI the experience is connected with a direct initiation into the hermetic mysteries. This has raised the much-debated question of whether there existed actual hermetic communities in the late antique world, in which such initiations and other religious rites were practised. This question will receive due attention in the next section; here we confine ourselves to the descriptions as given in the texts mentioned. The authors apparently wanted to bring the reader to a re-enactment of the mystic experience they described. In this sense, the hermetic mystery indeed was a 'reading mystery' (*Lese-Mysterium*), as Reitzenstein has characterized it (1927, 52; also, 64: 'literarische Mysterien').

In the *Poimandres*, 25-26, the union with God is described as a *post mortem* event: the soul of the deceased ascends through the seven planetary spheres and in each sphere leaves behind the bad qualities which it has received from that planet during its descent to earth. Then, stripped of the astral influences, the souls enters the eighth sphere 'with its own power', i.e. with its proper self. Singing hymns to the Father, he becomes like the blessed in the eighth sphere and hears the hymns that the powers above the eighth sphere sing to the praise of God. Then they all ascend to the Father and, becoming powers themselves, they are merged in God: 'This is the final good for those who have received knowledge (*gnosis*): to be made god'. Though the *Poimandres* describes this as occurring after death, later hermetists interpreted it as an ecstatic experience of Hermes himself, which could happen to every hermetist. In C.H. XIII, 15, Tat asks his father Hermes to reveal the hymn that the powers sang when he was in the Ogdoad (C.H. I, 26). Hermes agrees, 'just as Poimandres revealed the eighth sphere to me', and recites the fourth song of the Secret Hymn Book (17-20).

However, apart from this reference to the Ogdoad in the *Poimandres*, the mystic experience described in C.H. XIII is quite different from that in C.H. I (see below). The *Discourse on the Ogdoad and the Ennead* actually presents the ascent to the eighth and the ninth heavens as an ecstatic event that can be experienced during one's lifetime. The *Discourse* suggest that the initiation proper was preceded by a preparatory initiation consisting of seven grades, apparently corresponding to the seven planetary spheres, which included the study of hermetic books and required a pious way of life. After a prayer to 'the One who rules over the kingdom of Power' (NHC VI, 55, 24-26), who is addressed by magical names, Hermes and the pupil embrace each other and then experience the descent of the divine Light-power. They both get into an ecstatic state of mind and the pupil exclaims: 'I see the one that moves me through an ecstasy. You give me power. I see myself. I want to speak. Fear restrains me. I have found the origin of power that is above all powers and does not have an origin itself. I see a fountain bubbling with

life . . . I have seen! Language is not able to reveal this' (58, 6-17). After some instruction by Hermes about the Ogdoad and the hymns that the angels sing there in silence, the initiate also sings a silent hymn and then exclaims again: 'Father Trismegistus! What shall I say? We have received this light. And I myself see this same vision in you. And I see the Ogdoad and the souls that are in it and the angels singing a hymn to the Ennead and its powers. And I see him who has the power of them all, creating spiritually' (59, 24-60,1). The initiate sees himself and the Ogdoad in Hermes, which means that during the initiation Hermes changes from mystagogue into a manifestation of the divine Mind (*Nous*) itself. In the mixture of didactic instruction and ecstatic experience characteristic of this tractate and C.H. XIII, Hermes repeatedly says to the initiate: 'I am Mind' (58, 4; 14-15; 21-22; 27). He becomes the mirror, as it were, in which the initiate sees the godhead and the divine world. An exclamation similar to expressions found in the *Discourse* ('I see myself' and 'I see this vision in you'), but without the identification of Hermes with the divine Mind, is made by Tat in C.H. XIII, 13: 'Father, I see the universe and myself in *nous*', i.e. in my own mind, which participates in the divine Mind.

C.H. XIII presents another kind of initiation. At the beginning of this treatise, Hermes describes the effects of his own rebirth: he has come out of his former self into an immortal body, and in that state he is no longer what he was before, because he has been born again in the divine *Nous*. He is now without colour and cannot be touched or measured. Tat can see him, but what he really is cannot be seen with corporeal eyes. It may be assumed that it was in a form like this that the initiate of the Coptic *Discourse* saw Hermes during his ecstasy. Hermes explains that the actual rebirth is effectuated when Tat is cleansed from the twelve evil powers and is filled with the ten good powers: 'Whoever, then, by God's mercy attains a divine birth is freed from the bodily senses and knows himself, namely that he has been made whole by these powers, and he rejoices' (10). Thereupon, without any transition, Tat exclaims: 'I have been made steadfast by God; I no longer picture things with the sight of my eyes but with the mental energy that comes through the powers. I am in heaven, in earth, in water, in air; I am in animals and plants, in the womb, before the womb, after the womb; everywhere' (11). What is described here is the experience of falling together with the whole creation, a cosmic omnipresence. It was a philosophical commonplace to say that man through his mind (*nous*) was able to be present everywhere, but in the hermetic adaptation of this idea the original mental activity became a mystic experience. This is clearly demonstrated in C.H. XI, 19-20, where the divine Nous instructs Hermes about the unlimited reach of the human mind. The first part of this instruction remains within the boundaries of Greek philosophy, but then Hermes is exhorted to make himself equal to God, for like is only understood by like. Then nothing will be impossible for him: 'Conceive yourself to be in all places at the same time: in earth, in the sea, in heaven; that you are not yet born, within the womb, young, old, dead, beyond death. And when you have understood all these things at the same time – times, places, things, qualities and quantities – then you can understand God.' What started as a mental exercise becomes the revelation of the true essence of God. The same idea is expressed in the secret hymn of C.H. XIII, 20: 'O spirit-bearer, O craftsman, you are God! Your man shouts this through fire, through air, through earth, through water, through spirit, through your creatures'. Also in C.H. XIII, Tat comes to know the universe, himself and God. He exclaims that he sees the All and himself in *nous* (13, see above). His mind has been illuminated (21), so that Hermes can conclude at the end of the treatise (22): 'Now you know both yourself and our Father in a spiritual way'.

The articulations of hermetic mysticism show considerable differences, but they all have in common that the hermetist comes to an intuitive knowledge of himself, the universe and God – a knowledge that transcends the ordinary human mental faculties and is experienced as a unification with the ground of being, God.

6. RELIGIOUS PRACTICES IN HERMETIC COMMUNITIES?

There is no scholarly consensus about the existence of hermetic communities in the Graeco-Roman world. Festugière, for example, totally rejected the idea of a 'confraternity of initiates'. Because of his great influence on hermetic scholarship, it is worthwhile to quote him literally: 'In hermetic literature, there is no trace of particular ceremonies for the alleged faithful of Hermes, nothing resembling the sacraments of gnostic sects: neither baptism nor communion nor confession of sins nor laying-on of hands to ordain cult officials. There is no clergy: no evidence whatsoever of hierarchical organization or degrees of initiation' (1967, 38; 1950-1954, I, 83). This characterization is so strongly determined by the Christian view of what religious practices are that it is no wonder that Festugière did not find them in the Hermetica.

The strongest argument that can be adduced against the existence of religious rituals in Hermetism is found in chapter 41 of the *Asclepius*, where Hermes and his pupils are about to say a prayer and Asclepius suggests that they should also burn frankincense and spices. Hermes is disturbed by this suggestion and calls burning incense at prayer a kind of sacrilege. God wants nothing, because he is himself all things or all things are in him: 'rather let us worship him by giving thanks, for God finds mortal gratitude to be the best incense'. This testifies to a purely spiritual concept of God; but we saw already that elsewhere in the *Asclepius*, the author, who uses a variety of hermetic sources, defends the idea that through theurgic rites man is able to conjure divine powers into the images of the earthly gods. This at least shows that, on this point too, the hermetists could adhere to opposed views. If there were hermetic communities, their members certainly also participated in other civil and religious associations, in which rituals that involved the burning of incense were quite common. 'A religious community had to have at least a minimal set of common ideas, even if it were only the fact of honouring some god or of following the teaching of some teacher' (Belayche, 18). It seems possible that there did exist hermetic communities that answered to this minimal definition of a religious association, just as there were philosophical schools that practised religious rites to honour their founder and studied and further developed his teachings.

The hymns and prayers found in the hermetic texts, such as the final hymns of the *Poimandres* and the *Asclepius* and the fourth song of the Secret Hymn Book in C.H. XIII, 17-20, may have played a role in the gatherings of such communities. In the *Discourse on the Ogdoad and the Ennead* and also in the Coptic *Prayer of Thanksgiving*, mention is made of an embrace or kiss after prayer (NHC VI, 57, 26-28 and 65, 3-7, respectively). The only parallel to this usage is the embrace or kiss (*aspasmos*) that the early Christians also gave each other after prayer (e.g. Justin Martyr, *Apology* I, 65, 1; Tertullian, *On Prayer*, 18, 1 and 3). Since the rest of the *Discourse* does not show any Christian influence, there is no reason to assume that this particular feature reflects a Christian practice.

Another religiously inspired practice among the hermetists may have been the vegetarian meal, which is mentioned in *Asclepius* 41 ('Wishing these things, we turn to a pure meal without flesh of animals') and the corresponding passage in NHC VI, 65, 3-7 ('When they had said these things in prayer, they embraced each other and they went to eat their holy food, which had no blood in it'). Of course, this can be taken as being no more than a literary motif. On the other hand, we know that sacred meals were quite usual in all kinds of religious communities and even in secular associations, so that it would have been very strange if such a meal had been unknown among like-minded people such as the hermetists. A much-discussed text in this connection is that of C.H. IV, 4 about the mixing-bowl (*krater*) filled with *nous*, i.e. intuitive knowledge. The 'human hearts' are exhorted to immerse themselves in it, if they believe to rise up again to the One who gives *nous* and if they realise why they have come into being. Those who have merged with *nous* partake of higher knowledge and become perfect, but the others only have reason, not *nous*. This passage does not point to some kind of hermetic baptism, since it is impossible to be baptized in a mixing-bowl (for an attempt to explain it, see Festugière 1967, 100-112). It has to be read in the light of the Greek translation of Proverbs 9:1-6, about Lady Wisdom who has mixed her wine in a *krater* and invites the fools to taste it and to grow in understanding. The participation in spiritual knowledge and wisdom was often compared to drinking wine or water. It is possible that C.H. IV, 4 refers to a hermetic ritual of drinking from a mixing-bowl as an image of the imparting of knowledge and the initiation into the hermetic mystery – a ritual that is also known from the Hellenistic mystery religions. But it is also possible that the whole passage is no more than an awkwardly constructed figure of speech, which intended to emphasize that spiritual insight (*nous*) is not a common human capacity but a divine gift.

The discovery of the *Discourse on the Ogdoad and the Ennead* has given a new impetus to the debate on the existence of hermetic communities and rituals. It contains hymns and prayers, speaks about a hermetic confraternity, knows of at least eight grades of initiation and describes an initiation into the Ogdoad, which because of its stammering language of ecstasy gives the impression of authenticity (see above). As it now stands, the text is indeed a "Lese-Mysterium", a literary mystery, but there are no compelling reasons to assume that such initiations did not exist in reality. In view of the general tendency in the ancient world of forming associations of people with the same interests, it would be strange if the hermetists had not come together in meetings to discuss the way of Hermes, collectively celebrate the individual experience of initiation, send up hymns and prayers, and share a vegetarian meal. Of course, we should not assume the existence of a fixed hermetic

liturgy, comparable to that of the great cultic religions of the time, including Christianity. There may even have been hermetic groups in which the initiation did not play a role of any importance, but as a whole there is no reason to assume that it did not exist in real life.

7. THE CRUCIBLE OF ALEXANDRIA: GREEK PHILOSOPHY, EGYPTIAN RELIGION, JUDAISM

There is a general scholarly consensus that Hermetism originated in Alexandria. The combination of Egyptian, Jewish and Greek religious and philosophical elements that characterizes the hermetic writings can best be explained from an Alexandrian background. Founded by Alexander the Great in 332/31 B.C., in the 3rd and 2nd centuries Alexandria became the economic and cultural centre of the Greek world. Ptolemy I Soter (323-283) founded the Mouseion, which attracted the greatest scholars of the period and contained an enormous, continually expanding library. Another great library was founded in the temple of Sarapis: the Sarapeion, which was built under Ptolemy III Euergetes (246-222). In the Mouseion, not only all Greek literature was collected and studied but in addition translations were made of important works of Egyptian, Hebrew and Mesopotamian origin. The Alexandrian scholars devoted themselves primarily to philology and the mathematical, medical and natural sciences. They were less interested in philosophy and the disputes between the philosophical schools, and if they turned to philosophy they showed a preference for an eclectic approach. This also holds for the first Alexandrian philosopher whose work became of lasting importance, Eudorus. He was a Platonist who combined ideas of Plato with Aristotelian and Stoic elements and gave the whole a strong Neopythagorean colouring (Dillon, 114-135). He exerted a great influence on the Jewish religious philosopher Philo of Alexandria (born about 20 B.C.) and undoubtedly also on the equally eclectic religious philosophy of Hermetism.

Alexandria was a Greek city – only a small minority of its citizens was Egyptian – but the Ptolemies sought to combine the Egyptian and Greek religious traditions, which, *inter alia*, resulted in the cult of Sarapis. Scholars of Egyptian descent like Manetho (3rd century B.C.) and Charemon (1st century A.D.) did much to make the history and religious culture of Egypt known to the Greek-speaking world (Fowden, 52-57). Together with material goods from all parts of the world, there also arrived in Alexandria reliable information about the *spiritual* goods of remote peoples, for instance about Buddhism in India (Buddha was first mentioned by Clement of Alexandria, *Stromateis*, I, 71, 6).

Hermetism was one of the interesting religious phenomena that took shape in the crucible of Alexandria. The presence of Greek philosophy in the Hermetica needs no demonstration; their contents are for the greater part a mixture of Platonism and Stoicism, of the Eudorian type. The Jewish influence is undisputed, though scholars have different opinions about how far it went. Until A.D. 117, there was a very large Jewish community in Alexandria, which was mainly concentrated in two of the five districts of the city and numbered in the hundreds of thousands (Pearson, 145-151). The writings of Philo show that there were (1) Jews who strictly adhered to the religious convictions and lifestyle of their forefathers, (2) those who stuck to the observance of the Jewish law but gave an allegorical Greek interpretation to their traditional religion, and (3) others who abandoned both the observance of the Law and the Jewish religion as a whole or combined this religion so strongly with Greek or Oriental elements that the essence of Judaism was lost. Philo himself belonged to the second category, and it seems that Jews from the third group were involved in the origin and development of Hermetism (and Gnosticism as well). Hermetic writings like C.H. I and III can only have been written in a milieu that was strongly influenced by Jewish ideas and traditions (Dodd). If there ever existed some kind of a hermetic lodge in Alexandria – which is quite possible –, it must have counted some Jews among its most influential members.

The Egyptian component of Hermetism has long been a controversial topic of scholarly research. Classicists with a vast knowledge of Greek philosophy always tended to minimize the Egyptian influence. Thus, according to Festugière, Hermetism simply represents a set of popularized Greek philosophical notions with strong religious overtones, whereas the "Egyptian" elements are widespread commonplaces about Egypt: no more than a literary device, intended to suggest that Hermetism had ancient and foreign origins. Egyptologists, on the other hand, have always argued that under the Greek surface a great number of Egyptian religious ideas can be observed. A major difficulty, mostly neglected by classicists, is that the Egyptians never developed an abstract philosophical language but expressed comparable ideas in religious myths and images. In recent research, Egyptologists have presented a great number of

Egyptian religious ideas that have their counterpart in Hermetism (Derchain, Daumas, Iversen, Zandee). The fact alone that the names Trismegistus and Poimandres have their etymological origins in the Egyptian language and that some typical hermetic ideas, such as the androgyny of the supreme God, have their closest parallels in Egyptian religion, shows that Festugière's position has to be abandoned or at least qualified. The Egyptian influence must be ascribed to Hellenized Egyptians who knew their own religious traditions quite well. Perhaps there is some truth, after all, in Iamblichus' contention (*De mysteriis*, VIII, 4) that the Egyptians who, according to him, 'translated' the hermetic writings from Egyptian into Greek were skilled in Greek philosophy. What is urgently needed is an interdisciplinary study by classicists and Egyptologists of all the Egyptian parallels that have been suggested in recent research. Less problematic is the relationship between hermetic and gnostic ideas (→ Gnosticism).

8. HERMETISM AND CHRISTIAN BELIEF

The Christian doctrine of God, as developed by Christian theologians from the 2nd century onward, owed much to Platonism and, for that reason, also had much in common with Hermetism. This agreement did not escape the attention of early Christian writers who wanted to show that Christianity was not a recent religion – something that the outside world generally considered a negative point – but, rather, that its essential doctrines had already been taught in remote antiquity by the ancient Egyptian sage Hermes Trismegistus, as well as by the Sibyls, Orpheus and others (van den Broek). The authors that have to be discussed in this connection are Lactantius, Didymus the Blind and Cyril of Alexandria. → Augustine is much more critical, although even he is able to make a positive remark on Hermes.

Lactantius says of Trismegistus that he 'has investigated virtually the entire truth, I do not know how' (*Divinae Institutiones* IV, 9, 3). He is a witness of Christianity, 'who agrees with us, that is to say with the prophets whom we follow, both as to substance and verbatim' (*Div. Inst.* VI, 25, 10). Hermes has 'said about God the Father everything and about the Son much which is contained in the divine secrets (i.e. the Holy Scriptures)' (*Div. Inst.* IV, 27, 20). For Lactantius, the view that Hermes had taught the Christian doctrine of God was more than an apologetic device: it was his sincere conviction. The hermetically coloured Platonism in which he was steeped before his conversion to Christianity apparently kept its validity after that event.

If there was some justification in Lactantius' claim that Hermes and the Christians taught the same doctrine of the supreme God, his idea that Hermes had also already spoken of the Son of God, Christ, was certainly mistaken. From the *Logos Teleios*, the Greek original of the Latin *Asclepius*, he quotes in Greek the passage to be found in *Asclepius* 8: 'When the Lord and Maker of all things, whom we are used to call God, had made the second God who is visible and sensible . . .; when he, then, had made this God as the first and only and sole one, he seemed beautiful to him and entirely full of all good things, and he rejoiced and loved him very much as his own son' (*Div. Inst.* IV, 6, 4). Through the intermediary of Quodvultdeus' *Adversus quinque haereses*, III, 4, a somewhat abbreviated and occasionally more Christianized form of this text was to have a great history in the Middle Ages (→ Hermetic Literature II). However, as was already pointed out above, the passage speaks in fact about the creation of the cosmos as the first son of God. In defence of Lactantius, it might be said that his "exegesis" of this hermetic text is in no way different from the Christological reading of the Old Testament that was usual in the 4th century.

Didymus the Blind and Cyril of Alexandria found the entire doctrine of the Trinity in the works of Hermes Trismegistus. Cyril was partly dependent on Didymus, but he also had access to hermetic sources that were not used by the latter. Cyril had a low esteem of Greek philosophy and Greek culture in general, but for apologetic reasons quoted Orpheus, Pythagoras, Plato and Hermes with approval. In his view, Hermes, Pythagoras and Plato owed their doctrine of God to → Moses, who had always remained in great esteem in Egypt. Pythagoras and Plato had become acquainted with Moses' teachings when they studied with Egyptian sages. Hermes was a native Egyptian who always lived in the temples of the idols, Cyril says, but nevertheless he knew the Mosaic doctrine of God – not wholly correctly and impeccably, but at least partly.

According to Didymus and Cyril, the hermetic writings also contained clear references to the Christian doctrine of the Son and even to that of the Holy Spirit. Independent of Didymus, Cyril quotes some texts discussing the 'creative Logos of the Lord of the All', who is *inter alia* 'the first-born of the All-Perfect, his perfect, fertile Son (*Contra Julianum* I, 46; NF IV, 132-136). The nature of this 'spiritual Logos' is called 'generating and creating', which makes it probable that for the hermetist it was the creative force in the universe,

which according to the *Poimandres* (10-11) was of the same substance (*homoousios*) as the divine Nous. Didymus (*De trinitate* II, 27) and Cyril (*Contra Julianum* I, 47), who in this case depends on the former, also quote and discuss a hermetic text that in their view proved that Hermes had already spoken about the Holy Spirit. In a rather obscure language this text says that there is 'one single, eternal spiritual light, existing before the spiritual light, the light-mind (*nous*) of the mind (*nous*). And nothing else existed but the unity of this mind. It is always contained within itself and always comprises all things with its own mind (*nous*) and light and spirit (*pneuma*)'. Didymus and Cyril interpreted the 'light-mind of the mind' as 'mind from mind', i.e. the Son, who also was 'light from light', as the Nicene and Constantinopolitan Creeds of 325 and 381 put it. In their view, Hermes' remark on the spirit that comprises all things referred to the Holy Spirit. In the same connection, but in reversed order, Didymus and Cyril also quote another hermetic text, which reads *inter alia*: 'All things are in need of this spirit (*pneuma*), of which I have already often spoken. It carries everything and makes everything as much as is needed and feeds it. It is dependent on the holy source and is the helper of the spirits and the generator of life to all, even though he is still one'. There is little doubt that the hermetist conceived of this spirit as the divine creative force in the cosmos, but according to Cyril the text showed that Hermes already knew the Spirit 'as an independent hypostasis', who comes forth from God the Father by nature and takes care of creation through the mediation of the Son' (*Contra Julianum* I, 49).

Augustine did not have much to say in favour of Hermes Trismegistus; he quotes him almost exclusively in order to refute him. In *De civitate dei*, VIII, 23-26, he presents a vigorous attack on the notorious passages in the *Asclepius* (23 and 37-38) about man as the creator of the gods who are worshipped in the temples (see above). But in the same context, he also states that Hermes had much to say 'about the one true God, the creator of the world, which corresponds to the teaching of the truth' (VIII, 23). In his polemics with Faustus the Manichee, Augustine also admitted that pagan prophets such as the Sibyls, Hermes and Orpheus 'had made truthful predictions – or are said to have done so – about the Son of God and God the Father', but he warned against investing these pagans with authority (*Contra Faustum*, XIII, 15). Augustine rejected the appeal to pagan prophets as pre-Christian witnesses to the truth of Christianity, but even his great authority was unable to erase this idea from the minds of later theologians.

Lit.: N. Belaye, "En quête de marqueurs des communautés 'religieuses' gréco-romaines", in: N. Belayche & S.C. Mimouni (eds.), *Les communautés religieuses dans le monde gréco-romain: Essays de définitions* (Bibliothèque de l'École des Hautes Études, Sciences Religieuses, 117), Turnhout: Brepols, 2003, 9-20 ♦ R. van den Broek, "Religious Practices in the Hermetic 'Lodge': New Light from Nag Hammadi", in: R. van den Broek & C. van Heertum (eds.), *From Poimandres to Jacob Boehme: Gnosis, Hermetism and the Christian Tradition*, Amsterdam: In de Pelikaan, 2000, 77-113 ♦ idem, "Hermes and Christ: 'Pagan' Witnesses to the Truth of Christianity", ibidem, 115-144 ♦ F. Daumas, "Le fonds égyptienne de l'Hermétisme", in: J. Ries *et alii* (eds.), *Gnosticisme et monde hellénistique: Actes de Colloque de Louvain-La-Neuve (11-14 mars 1980)*, Louvain-La-Neuve: Université Catholique de Louvain, Institut Orientaliste, 1982, 3-25 ♦ Ph. Derchain, "L'authenticité de l'inspiration égyptienne dans la 'Corpus Hermeticum'", *Revue de l'Histoire des Religions* 161 (1962), 175-198 ♦ J. Dillon, *The Middle Platonists: A Study of Platonism, 80 B.C. to A.D. 220*, London: Duckworth, 1977 ♦ Ch. Dodd, *The Bible and the Greeks*, London: Hodder & Stoughton, 1935 (reprinted 1954), especially Part II: "Hellenistic Judaism and the Hermetica" ♦ A.J. Festugière, *La révélation d'Hermès Trismégiste*, 4 vols., Paris: Les Belles Lettres, 1950-1954 ♦ idem, *Hermétisme et mystique païenne*, Paris: Aubier-Montaigne, 1967 ♦ G. Fowden, *The Egyptian Hermes: A Historical Approach to the Late Pagan Mind*, Cambridge: Cambridge University Press, 1986 (paperback edition, with corrections and a new preface, Princeton: Princeton University Press, 1993) ♦ P.M. Fraser, *Ptolemaic Alexandria*, 3 vols., Oxford: Oxford University Press, 1972 ♦ E. Iversen, *Egyptian and Hermetic Doctrine*, Copenhagen: Museum Tusculanum Press, 1984 ♦ G. van Moorsel, *The Mysteries of Hermes Trismegistus*, Utrecht: Kemink, 1955 ♦ B.A. Pearson, "Earliest Christianity in Egypt: Some Observations", in: B.A. Pearson & J.E. Goehring (eds.), *The Roots of Egyptian Christianity*, Philadelphia: Fortress Press, 1986, 132-159 ♦ G. Quispel, *Asclepius: De volkomen openbaring van Hermes Trismegistus, ingeleid, vertaald en toegelicht*, Amsterdam: In de Pelikaan, 1996 ♦ G. Quispel (ed.), *Die hermetische Gnosis im Lauf der Jahrhunderte*, Haarlem/Birnbach: Rozekruis Pers/DRP Verlag, 2000, 98-176 (= *De Hermetische Gnosis in de loop der eeuwen*, Baarn: Tirion, 1992, ²1996, translated from the Dutch by K. Warnke & K. Dietzfeldbinger) ♦ R. Reitzenstein, *Poimandres: Studien zur griechisch-ägyptischen und frühchristlichen Literatur*, Leipzig: Teubner, 1904 (reprinted Wissenschaftliche Buchgesellschaft: Darmstadt 1966) ♦ idem, *Die hellenistischen Mysterienreligionen nach ihren Grundgedanken und Wirkungen*, 3rd ed., Stuttgart: Teubner, 1927 (reprinted Wissenschaftliche Buchgesellschaft: Darmstadt 1956), 46-52 ♦ J. Zandee, "Der Hermetismus und das alte Ägypten", in Quispel, *Hermetische Gnosis*, 98-176.

ROELOF VAN DEN BROEK

Heydon, John (Eugenius Theodidactus), * 1626 England, † ca. 1665 London?

Under this name, some of the most luminous prose of late Renaissance Hermeticism was published. Passages worthy of English writers like → Elias Ashmole, → Francis Bacon, → Henry More, Walter Raleigh, and → Thomas Vaughan and of Continental masters like → Agrippa, → Ficino, → Paracelsus, and even → Hermes Trismegistus appeared under Heydon's name or his pseudonym Eugenius Theodidactus (i.e., a gentleman taught by God) between 1655 and 1665. Indeed, the passages were first published in England under those other names, and were only then gathered into the series of "guides" that Heydon issued under the general rubric of "Rosicrucian" [→ Rosicrucianism]. Heydon's motives are hard to guess. His personal comments are usually efforts to conceal his plagiarism; he claims to have kept his works in manuscript for years and condemns his often indignant sources as plagiarists themselves. He does seek publicity, though, and encourages readers to consult him as an astrologer and as a "physician" dispensing herbal and other remedies. He also does everything possible to make a profit; he takes the same manuscripts to different publishers, under different titles, and recycles unsold sheets of an old book under a new title (all told, his books exceed six thousand pages). He is a forerunner of today's gurus and popularizers, and his ethics bode ill for the lot. The prolific occultist → A.E. Waite (1857-1942), who suffered repeated piracy in the United States, once described Heydon as 'the prototypical thief of English occult literature'.

By his own account, Heydon was born in 1629, was educated in Oxford, and became a London barrister by the age of twenty-five. A lifelong student, he added medicine to law and theology to medicine, writing on all of them. He was jailed under two governments, the Protectorate of Oliver Cromwell and the restored monarchy of Charles I, for having published subversive comments. Though he often denied it, Heydon married Alice Culpeper, the widow of the upstart physician and medical translator Nicholas Culpeper (1616-1654). His books began to appear in 1655. His first prose tract was, ironically, a book of moral instruction for Culpeper's daughter. His first specifically Rosicrucian tract was later exposed as his fantasia on a manuscript from Culpeper's library. In the exposé, Elias Ashmole described Heydon as 'an ignoramus and a cheat'. The term stuck, and Heydon was later portrayed on the stage as the main character in John Wilson's comedy *The Cheats*. His main speech in the play is plagiarized from Hermes Trismegistus. Heydon swore off writing when he experienced a religious conversion, after the death of a sister, and then he insisted that he was only an editor. The excuse seems feeble, even in the days before copyright law. Nevertheless, Heydon did a great deal to popularize the term "Rosicrucian" and to suggest in what ways Bacon's *New Atlantis* or Agrippa's *Occult Philosophy* is "Rosicrucian". Frances Yates found Heydon's reworking of Bacon, with interpolations from the Rosicrucian manifestos of 1614 and 1615, an essential text for Bacon's subsequent reputation and for her own theme of a "Rosicrucian Enlightenment".

John Heydon, *The English Physitians Tutor*, London, 1665 ♦ *The Harmony of the World*, London, 1662 ♦ *The Holy Guide*, London, 1662 ♦ *A New Method of Rosie Crucian Physick*, London, 1658 ♦ *The Rosie Crucian Infallible Axiomata*, London, 1660 ♦ *Theomagia; or, the Temple of Wisdome, Spiritual, Coelestial, and Elemental*, London, 1662 ♦ *The Wise-Mans Crown; or, The Glory of the Rosie-Cross*, London, 1664.

Lit.: F. Leigh Gardner, *A Catalogue Raisonné of the Works on the Occult Sciences*, Vol. 2: Rosicrucian Books, Privately published, 1911 ♦ A.E. Waite, *The Brotherhood of the Rosy Cross*, London: Kegan Paul, 1924, 388 ♦ Thomas Spaulding Willard, "John Heydon's satire of hermetic medicine", in: Marie Mulvey Roberts & Roy Porter (eds.), *Literature and Medicine During the Eighteenth Century*, London & New York: Routledge, 1993, 136-150 ♦ Frances A. Yates, *The Rosicrucian Enlightenment*, rev. ed. Frogmore: Paladin, 1975, 165-167.

THOMAS WILLARD

Hildegard of Bingen, * 1098 Bermersheim bei Alzey, † 17.9.1179 Rupertsberg, Bingen-am-Rhein

German Benedictine nun, founder and head of two monasteries for women, the Rupertsberg (destroyed in the Thirty Years' War) and the present-day Abbey of St. Hildegard, Eibingen. Visionary, prophet, composer, and prolific author of theological and scientific books. The tenth child of a noble family, Hildegard made her profession of virginity at 14 under the tutelage of Jutta of Sponheim, a recluse at the monastery of Disibodenberg, and in 1136 was elected mistress of the nuns there. In 1141 she received a prophetic call to 'cry out and write' what God revealed to her in the visions she had experienced from childhood, and in 1151 pub-

lished her first book, *Scivias* (Know the Ways of the Lord). Structured around a cycle of illustrated visions, the work includes extensive allegories, biblical exegesis, and liturgical lyrics. Meanwhile Hildegard felt called to leave the Disibodenberg and found her own nunnery at Mount St. Rupert (1148-1150). Other books followed: the *Liber vite meritorum* (Book of Life's Merits, 1158-1163), *Liber divinorum operum* (Book of Divine Works, 1163-1174), *Liber epistolarum* (Book of Letters), two saints' lives, a medical and scientific encyclopedia (*Physica*), and a handbook of practical and theoretical medicine (*Causae et curae* or *Causes and Cures*). Her musical compositions include 70 liturgical chants with original texts, assembled in the collection *Symphonia armonie celestium revelationum* (Symphony of the Harmony of Heavenly Revelations), and a music drama, the *Ordo virtutum* (Play of the Virtues). Known as a healer, exorcist, and apocalyptic prophet, Hildegard had a wide circle of correspondents that included powerful bishops and nobles. In her later years she travelled extensively on preaching tours, speaking at monasteries and sometimes in cathedral squares – the only medieval woman to have done so.

Orthodox in her dogmatic and sacramental theology, Hildegard developed a complex cosmology based on ideas that were current among 12th-century Platonists, but soon afterwards fell from general favor and remained central only within esoteric systems of thought. Her visionary worldview is built around a series of feminine theophanies, the *Virtutes*, who represent creative energies active in the natural world and especially in souls that willingly cooperate with God. Chief among these are Caritas (Divine Love) and Sapientia (Divine Wisdom), who function almost interchangeably as manifestations of God. Hildegard teaches the absolute predestination of Christ, i.e. the doctrine that the incarnation of the Word in human form was the original purpose of God's creation, not just a remedy for original sin. In the *Liber divinorum operum* she develops an elaborate system of → correspondences between macrocosm and microcosm, correlating celestial bodies and elemental forces with parts of the human body as well as spiritual and moral states. Speculations on the unfallen Adam and Eve underlie Hildegard's medicine, which is based on an unconventional version of humoral theory and aims to restore the physical and spiritual equilibrium lost in the Fall. Hildegard also developed an esoteric theology of → music, comparing the melody of chant to the divinity of Christ and the words to his humanity. Musical instruments, she asserts, were invented by the prophets to compensate for the lost resonance that Adam's voice had possessed in paradise.

Hildegard's style was notably obscure, in part because she lacked formal training in Latin grammar and rhetoric, but also because she was imitating the manner of the biblical prophets. Her apocalyptic prophecies, which appear in the final visions of the *Scivias* and *Liber divinorum operum* and in her letters and sermons, were couched in a deliberately vague and grandiloquent style to mask their potentially dangerous political content. These prophecies, widely studied and anthologized, kept Hildegard's reputation alive in later medieval centuries, when she was remembered as "Sibyl of the Rhine" for her speculations on the Antichrist and events of the eschaton. Her most strictly esoteric work is the *Lingua ignota* (Unknown Language), composed of about 900 words, which she may have devised to create the aura of an initiated sisterhood among her elite nuns. The *Lingua* is accompanied by an 'unknown alphabet' (*Litterae ignotae*) of 23 characters. Because of their cryptic style, Hildegard's prophecies have been diversely interpreted: she has been credited with predicting phenomena as disparate as the 13th-century fraternal orders, the Protestant Reformation, and the French Revolution. Her other works were not widely read after her lifetime, but several Renaissance esotericists took an interest in her, including → Trithemius of Sponheim and → Jacques Lefèvre d'Étaples, who published the *editio princeps* of her *Scivias*.

In the late 20th century Hildegard enjoyed a sudden surge in popularity. Most of her works were critically edited and translated into German and English, and her music has been recorded by numerous vocalists. Popularized by Matthew Fox and his movement for "creation-centered spirituality", Hildegard is now revered by adherents of → New Age spiritualities as well as traditional and feminist Catholics. Her medicine has undergone a revival among holistic health practitioners, and "Hildegard practices" have opened in a number of European and North American cities.

Scivias (Adelgundis Führkötter and Angela Carlevaris, eds.), CCCM 43-43a, Turnhout: Brepols, 1978 (English transl.: *Scivias*, New York: Paulist, 1990) ♦ *Liber vite meritorum* (Angela Carlevaris, ed.), CCCM 90, Turnhout: Brepols, 1995 (Engl.: *Book of the Rewards of Life*, New York: Oxford, 1994) ♦ *Liber divinorum operum* (Albert Derolez & Peter Dronke, eds.), CCCM 92, Turnhout: Brepols, 1996 (Engl. [abridged]: *Book of Divine Works* [Matthew Fox, ed.], Santa Fe, NM: Bear & Company, 1987) ♦ *Epistolarium* (Lieven Van Acker, ed.), CCCM 91-91b, Turnhout: Brepols, 1991, 1993, 2001 (Engl.: *Letters of Hildegard of Bin-*

gen, Oxford, 1994, 1998, 2004) ♦ *Symphonia armonie celestium revelationum* (Barbara Newman, ed. and trans.), Ithaca, NY: Cornell U. Press, 1998 ♦ *Ordo virtutum* (Peter Dronke, ed. and trans.), in: *Nine Medieval Latin Plays*, Cambridge, 1994 ♦ *Causae et curae* (Paul Kaiser, ed.), Leipzig: Teubner, 1903 (Engl. [abridged]: *Hildegard of Bingen on Natural Philosophy and Medicine*, Cambridge: D.S. Brewer, 1999) ♦ *Physica*, in: *Patrologia Latina* vol. 197 (J.-P. Migne, ed.), Paris, 1855 (Engl.: *Hildegard von Bingen's Physica*, Healing Arts Press: Rochester, VT 1998) ♦ *Wörterbuch der Unbekannten Sprache* [*Lingua ignota*] (Marie-Louise Portmann & Alois Odermatt, eds.), Basel: Basler Hildegard-Gesellschaft, 1986 ♦ *Vita Sanctae Hildegardis* (Monika Klaes, ed.), CCCM 126, Turnhout: Brepols, 1993 (Engl.: *Jutta and Hildegard: The Biographical Sources* [Anna Silvas, ed. and trans.], Turnhout: Brepols, 1998).

Lit.: Peter Dronke, *Women Writers of the Middle Ages*, Cambridge, 1984 ♦ Barbara Newman, *Sister of Wisdom: St. Hildegard's Theology of the Feminine*, Berkeley: University of California Press, 1987 ♦ Sylvain Gouguenheim, *La Sibylle du Rhin: Hildegarde de Bingen, abbesse et prophétesse rhénane*, Paris: Sorbonne, 1996 ♦ Heinrich Schipperges, *Hildegard of Bingen: Healing and the Nature of the Cosmos*, Princeton, NJ: Markus Wiener, 1997 ♦ Edeltraud Forster (ed.), *Hildegard von Bingen, Prophetin durch die Zeiten*, Freiburg: Herder, 1997 ♦ Charles Burnett & Peter Dronke (eds.), *Hildegard of Bingen: The Context of Her Thought and Art*, London: Warburg Institute, 1998 ♦ Barbara Newman (ed.), *Voice of the Living Light: Hildegard of Bingen and Her World*, Berkeley: University of California Press, 1998.

BARBARA NEWMAN

Hohenheim, Theophrastus Bombast von → Paracelsus

Human Potential Movement

1. INTELLECTUAL TRADITIONS AND FOUNDERS 2. THERAPEUTIC PREDECESSORS 3. SOCIAL SETTING 4. PRACTICES 5. AT THE FRINGES 6. THE FATE OF THE HUMAN POTENTIAL MOVEMENT

The term Human Potential Movement (HPM) arose in the 1960s as referring to a highly eclectic mix of therapies, many of which were poised on the border between a psychological and a religious framework. They must be regarded as belonging to the history of gnosis and Western esotericism both for historical reasons and because of doctrinal similarities: historically, since by mediation of the mind cure or → New Thought movements, the

intellectual foundations of the HPM may be found
in the psychologization of → Mesmerism during
the 19th century; doctrinally, since the religious
aspects of the HPM to a considerable extent can be
characterized as the search for an existential experience of the "real self" and its essential divinity – a
search for what traditionally is known as "gnosis".
This search finds expression, however, in a quintes-
sentially modern framework that emphasizes indi-
vidualism to an extent unknown in traditional
esoteric contexts.

1. INTELLECTUAL TRADITIONS AND FOUNDERS

The Human Potential Movement comprises a
variety of methods centered on a shared vision of
the human condition. Mainstream therapies up to
and including the 1950s typically saw the human
predicament in pessimistic and largely deterministic terms. Thus, orthodox psychoanalysis builds on
the idea that humans are forced to sublimate their
basic drives in order to be able to live in organized
societies. The result is said to be the widespread
occurrence of neuroses. Psychoanalytic practice
therefore saw the aim of therapy as enabling the
patient to function once more in society, especially
in the family and at work. Humanistic psychology
arose as an alternative view both of personhood
and of the goals of therapy. It presented a view of
human beings as constrained and alienated by negative social forces, living far below their natural
capacities. Humanistic psychology also carried the
seeds of a psychological utopia. If individual people were to find the ability to truly love, create and
fulfil their potentials, society would be transformed
almost beyond recognition. Social change basically
required a consciousness revolution.

The fundamental idea that we in our normal
mode of existence remain unaware of vast inner
potentials can be traced back to the period of →
Romanticism (see e.g. the somnambulic patients
investigated by → Justinus Kerner). The specific
perspectives of the HPM, however, have their more
immediate roots in the "mind cure" or → New
Thought philosophies of the 19th century. Inspired
by the gulf between our everyday existence and the
apparently supernatural abilities evinced by people
in mesmeric trance, Phineas Parkhurst Quimby
(1802-1866) and his successors suggested that we
were normally constrained by our false beliefs.

In a more academic mode, somewhat similar
ideas were being developed around the turn of the
20th century by a number of American psychologists of religion. Edwin Starbuck (1866-1947),
James Leuba (1868-1946) and others emphasized
the inner potentialities of the individual, his or her

capacity for growth and development, and the
importance of spiritual elements in that process.
However, none of these writers had an enduring
popularity to match that of William James (1842-
1910). James firmly joined religion and psychology
by understanding the subconscious mind as a link
to a spiritual realm. Exploring one's own mind
was ultimately the pathway to the divine. While
optimistic, humanistic and spiritually-oriented
psychologies continued to be formulated throughout the first half of the 20th century, James' vast
influence on the American cultural landscape provided the principal link of continuity between the
optimistic post-mesmerist esotericism of the mid-
to late 19th century and the development of the
humanistic psychologies proper, beginning in the
late 1950s.

Rollo May (1909-1994) is one of the most
important figures in the development of humanistic psychology. May, who studied theology and
philosophy as well as psychology, was critical of
Freudian thought and preferred to draw inspiration
from psychologists such as Alfred Adler (1870-
1937) and → Carl Gustav Jung. His background in
theology, particularly the influence of the existential theologian Paul Tillich (1886-1965), was a
major impetus for his desire to pursue a study of
the human condition informed by existentialist
philosophy. Carl Rogers (1902-1987) contributed
to the movement by formulating client-centered
therapy. Rogers suggested that clients in therapy
strive of their own accord towards self-actualization, and that the therapist's primary role is to facilitate this process by accepting clients as they are.
Perhaps the most overtly Jamesian of the founding
fathers of humanistic psychology was Abraham
Maslow (1908-1970). He believed that each individual possesses a true, inner nature, and that psychological health came through a quest for this
core self. Maslow, like James before him, used case
studies to support his theory of personality. By
studying exceptionally creative, "self-actualizing"
individuals, he concluded that these people had
gone through a number of peak experiences, i.e.
moments of full awareness and bliss.

Whereas the HPM was rooted in specific psychotherapeutic doctrines and methods, a considerable sector of the movement from the late 1960s
and onwards gradually shifted focus towards a
more distinctly religious point of view. Abraham
Maslow was a central figure in the emergence of
this new direction. Maslow described peak experiences in overtly religionist terms, understanding
mystical experience to be the highest form. He
came to believe that a psychology rooted in such
experiences could provide a spiritual value system

and a philosophy that was essentially identical to the core of the major world religions. Maslow and Stanislav Grof (b. 1931) jointly coined the term transpersonal psychology for this new view.

Transpersonal psychology became an established concept with the foundation in 1969 of the *Journal of Transpersonal Psychology*. The editor of this journal, Anthony Sutich, programmatically positioned the new school as a fourth force beside the three forces of classical psychoanalytic theory, behaviorism and humanistic psychology. In a frequently quoted formulation, he presented the aim of the new psychological schools as the empirically scientific study of, among other things, 'transpersonal process, values and states, unitive consciousness, meta-needs, peak experiences, ecstasy, mystical experience, being, essence, bliss, awe, wonder, transcendence of the self, spirit, sacralization of everyday life, oneness, cosmic awareness, cosmic play, individual and species-wide synergy, the theories and practices of meditation, spiritual paths, compassion, transpersonal cooperation, transpersonal realization and actualization; and related concepts, experiences and activities'. This list is surely at least as imbued with modern religious values as with psychology. That mystical experience was presented in the singular is also symptomatic of the apologetic and essentialist tenor of much transpersonal psychology.

The most influential contemporary spokesperson of transpersonal psychology, Ken Wilber (b. 1948), has further accentuated this spiritualizing trend. Different modes of consciousness are placed within an overarching hierarchical and evolutionary scheme, in which mystical states represent the highest levels. Wilber presents a vision of the human predicament as the gradual evolution of Spirit, in which individuals as well as entire cultures can gradually come to access transpersonal reaches of consciousness that go far beyond self-actualization as described by Maslow.

Humanistic and transpersonal psychology as developed by these and other psychologists largely emerged as intellectual movements. The Human Potential Movement *sensu stricto* developed a variety of practical methods devised to bring out the full capacities of the human being: not in order to elevate pathologically malfunctioning individuals to normality, but to raise normal individuals to realize their full human potential. This ambition gave the Human Potential Movement its name.

2. THERAPEUTIC PREDECESSORS
Mainstream therapies, with psychoanalysis as a paradigmatic example, typically employ conversa-

tion as the privileged therapeutic tool. Commonly, the verbal interchange between psychotherapist and patient is carried out in numerous sessions spread over a long period of time, involves relatively low levels of intervention from the therapist and is aimed, through the process of transference, at making patients increasingly aware of the structural similarities between situations and emotions experienced in their everyday lives and the interchange in the therapeutic setting. The Human Potential Movement would form a radically different view of praxis, and found inspiration in several unorthodox therapies developed from the 1920s and onward. These alternative practices often privileged bodily expression over verbalization, were emotionally powerful and required the therapist to play a considerably more active role in the therapeutic process. Two schools that particularly contributed to the development of HPM therapies were psychodrama and Reichian bodywork.

Psychodrama was developed by Jacob L. Moreno (1890-1974). Moreno was born in Bucharest, Romania, and moved to Vienna to study medicine. The beginnings of psychodrama were developed during his last years there, before his emigration to America in 1925. Moreno opened a psychodrama school in 1925, but worked in relative obscurity until the emerging HPM – in search for methodologies and historical roots – found inspiration in his work. The fundamental idea of psychodrama is to choose an emotionally intense episode from one's life and act it out together with a group of people. The role of the leader of the psychodrama group is to guide the process by suggesting ways to act out the dramatic aspects of the situation: the scene, the roles to play, ways of enhancing the emotional tenor of the interaction. The director can also suggest that members of the group switch roles with each other, or intervene to interpret the lines and actions of a protagonist.

A perhaps even more important influence on the HPM was the work of Wilhelm Reich (1897-1957). Reich's point of departure was the idea that there existed a form of vital force, orgone energy, which in a neurosis-free individual flows unhindered through the body. However, forbidden impulses or painful traumas create blocks both in the person's psyche (in Reichian terminology, the character armor) and in the body (the muscular armor). Character structure and such somatic symptoms as muscular rigidity, posture and bodily movements are thus intimately linked. By working on the physical manifestations of blocked energy, character structure could be changed and the patient would be made more capable of experiencing pleasure, especially in the form of sexuality. Among the techniques used by Reich and his followers were manipulation of the body through touch and pressure as well as controlled breathing.

3. SOCIAL SETTING

The 1960s were a period of social experimentation. This innovative mood influenced sectors of the psychotherapeutic community, and led to the development and spread of an eclectic set of new therapies, based on the generally shared vision of bringing out the hidden potential of the individual. A vital element in transforming a number of historically distinct ideas and therapies into a consolidated movement was the creation of a social setting in which practitioners of various persuasions could join forces. The paradigmatic location for the various alternative therapies was the growth center, typically a place where clients could board and lodge for a relatively short period of time while sampling a number of different methods.

One of the very first, and arguably the most influential, was Esalen Institute, at Big Sur, California. Esalen Institute (which for its first three years was known as Big Sur Hot Springs) was founded by Michael Murphy and Richard Price in 1962, as a seminar center for lectures on a variety of ideas that might appeal to the budding California counterculture. The topics discussed included mysticism, philosophy, religion, the occult [→ occult / occultism], humanistic psychology, psychedelics and Oriental cultures. Through active networking, a large number of luminaries of the 1960s spiritual counterculture agreed to appear at Esalen. Thus, famous writers and thinkers such as Gregory Bateson, Kenneth Rexroth, Abraham Maslow and Aldous Huxley endorsed the project or became actively involved in it. To sum up the vast variety of subjects addressed at the meetings, the term Human Potentiality was created. Out of the mix of elements, some were soon given a privileged place. The interest in the paranormal, in Eastern philosophies, in altered states of consciousness and in other elements of the 1960s cultic milieu gave Esalen a distinct touch of alternative religiosity. Thus, one of the first and most prominent speakers at Esalen was Alan Watts (1915-1973), a onetime clergyman, flamboyant popularizer of Zen Buddhism, philosophical entertainer and advocate of the psychedelic experience.

Esalen Institute remained a site dedicated to intellectual discussion for a year or two. By then, a gradual but profound change in direction had taken place. Rather than merely talking about the development of human potential, Esalen would now be devoted to experiential sessions designed to actively bringing out the hidden capacities of its visitors. Since Esalen was privately run, therapists were free to experiment with a variety of unorthodox methods. The most prevalent practices developed at Esalen can be roughly divided into three groups: gestalt therapy, encounter groups and body therapies.

4. PRACTICES

Gestalt therapy is primarily associated with the work of the German-American psychologist Frederick ("Fritz") Perls (1893-1970). Rather than going back to e.g. childhood memories, as would be done in many other methods, gestalt therapy emphasizes the here and now of the therapeutic setting. In particular, Perls would interpret the quality of voice, the gestures and body language of his clients, and draw their attention to any discrepancies between these cues and the overt message of what they were saying. Awareness of such subtle discrepancies was one key to a psychological breakthrough. Among the material Perls would take up in such sessions were clients' dreams and the emotionally intense issues of their everyday lives. These would be drawn into the therapeutic setting by being reenacted in the here and now. Thus, clients would not only talk about their dreams, but also act the various characters appearing in them.

Gestalt therapy shared with many other HPM therapies the insistence on the responsibility of the individual for every aspect of their lives. This method is thus based on an existential philosophy that focuses on our own active role in shaping our lives. Part of Perls' credo was that we inflict symptoms on ourselves; progress in therapy involves understanding that nobody but ourselves burdens us with our neuroses.

Perls, who became part of Esalen's resident staff, had the curious role of practicing one of the most publicized methods of Human Potential Movement, yet in a sense also one of the least representative of the direction in which the HPM was headed. Whereas other therapists were increasingly prone to invoke religious motifs in their theories and practices, Perls remained intensely skeptical of anything that was labeled "spiritual". His basic attitude was that spirituality was a refuge for people who were unwilling to take responsibility for the real issues of their lives.

The history of *encounter groups* has been traced to the philosophy of dialogue of Martin Buber (1878-1965), as well as the research on the effects of self-disclosure carried out by Sidney Jourard

(1926-1974). There have been several different versions of the encounter group. An immediate precursor of the HPM encounter group is derived from the work of Carl Rogers. Here people would sit in a circle, usually on chairs, and interact almost entirely at a verbal level. The role of the leader was simply to facilitate whatever process was taking place, and to encourage people to be more honest and more self-disclosing.

The form of encounter which would become emblematic of much of the HPM, however, was a considerably more intense form developed by William Schutz. In this version, a group of perhaps six to fifteen people would sit in a circle, usually on cushions because furniture might hamper physical action. There was much more emphasis on the body and on the emotions than on any intellectual or verbal expression. As in Gestalt, the here-and-now was considered paramount. The injunction was not to talk about one's emotions but show them. And as in so many HPM therapies, participants were strongly encouraged to accept responsibility for their own actions and feelings. Among the basic rules of the encounter group were to speak only for oneself, to speak and act directly to whatever other participant elicits an emotion, and to be specific in doing so. The basic role of the leader was to choose among an eclectic set of methods to move the group in the direction where the emotional intensity was greatest. Thus, if the group leader sensed that a technique from gestalt therapy, psychodrama, breath control, guided imagery or bodywork might enable a person to go deeper into an emotionally intense experience, he or she would initiate such an action. Encounter groups could range from a few hours to marathon sessions of several days, which would significantly lower the defenses of the participants and, it was hoped, facilitate growth through direct and uninhibited communication.

Although originally aimed at producing emotional and social rather than spiritual transformation, the encounter group would later be adopted for religious purposes. One of the most successful of these attempts was made by Bhagwan Shree Rajneesh (1931-1990), founder of a new religious movement that is today known as the Osho Movement (q.v. below).

Although *body therapies* generally build on Reich's general approach, his praxis was to be modified in a number of ways by later practitioners. One of the main schools where this has been done is bioenergetics, developed in the 1950s and 1960s by one of Reich's students, Alexander Lowen (b. 1910). Lowen believed that different

character types manifest in various forms of muscle tone, breathing, posture, and so forth. Each character type can be diagnosed by paying close attention to such somatic manifestations. Bioenergetics could, in turn, help to redress the various problems typically associated with each character type. Thus, bioenergetics lays particular emphasis on the concept of grounding, with various methods concerned with making better contact with our legs and feet. Such bodily processes were often interpreted metaphorically: being physically more aware of the lower half of our body was interpreted as making one more "grounded" also in a psychological sense.

Another visible component of the HPM scene was Rolfing, a technique named after founder Ida Rolf (1896-1979). Rolfing involves a forceful and at times painful manipulation of deep-lying muscles. The theory behind the method states that memories of physical as well as emotional traumas can be activated in the process.

Although not all body therapists saw their work in spiritual terms, several assumptions contributed to giving at least some of these practices a religious tinge. Firstly, there was a widespread understanding that some form of life force was released as therapeutic effects could be observed. Secondly, the holistic emphasis on body/mind interconnections led a number of therapists and their clients to assume that some form of spiritual attunement was also possible through manipulation of the body. Thirdly, the common interest in various forms of Eastern philosophy made it tempting to find similarities between yogic techniques and body therapies.

5. AT THE FRINGES
Many of the spokespersons of the HPM and the leaders of various growth centers were highly eclectic in their approaches. Several independent methods were in time incorporated under the general Human Potential umbrella. The success and high profile of places such as the Esalen Institute inspired others to develop new practices, some of which received considerable publicity.

Among these one could include psychosynthesis, developed by Roberto Assagioli (1888-1974). Assagioli was one of the first psychologists to introduce Freud's theories in Italy, but he was also a disciple of → Alice Bailey. He combined the two influences by attempting to devise a set of therapeutic methods to bring his clients in touch with what he understood to be their higher selves. Another parallel development was that of the Arica Method, a set of exercises inspired by the teachings of → Gurdjieff and created by Oscar Ichazo (b. 1931). Ichazo's contention was that the true self was hidden behind the false ego, which manifested in one of nine overriding drives that in his and Gurdjieff's view constitute our personalities. The attraction of these two methods for the mainstream of the 1960s HPM may have been the fact that both combined the idea that humanity lived well below its full abilities, with the conviction that the necessary awakening included a strong spiritual component with discernible roots in esoteric thought.

If the HPM generally built on the intellectual and philosophical underpinnings of humanistic psychology, a number of other therapies with similar aims of raising the individual to new levels of awareness were constructed on more speculative bases. Such therapies could, at least from a sociological point of view, be characterized as the fringe of the HPM. Some remained at the fringe because they managed to transgress even the very liberal mores of the 1960s; among these one might count nude encounter groups. Some, e.g. large group programs such as *est*, became controversial due to their strictly regimented and authoritarian ethos. Others, such as primal therapy, did so because they built on theories that were perceived by many as highly speculative.

Nude encounter groups were a short-lived radical extension of the then prevalent (clothed) encounter sessions. By stripping, it was assumed that one's defenses would come down quicker. Nude encounter groups remained marginal to the Human Potential Movement, but did cause considerable negative publicity for the entire movement by being prominently depicted in a 1968 issue of *Life* magazine.

Equally controversial, but of considerably more lasting impact, were large group programs, personal development training programs in which dozens to hundreds of people would participate in a few hours to several days of intense experiential sessions. These were aimed at helping participants begin to discover what was hindering them from achieving their full potential and living more satisfied lives. Werner Erhard's *est* – an abbreviation of Erhard Seminar Training as well as Latin for "it is" – was the most widely publicized of these programs.

Although not overtly spiritual in aim, *est* resonated with some of the mind cure-inspired tenets that would also enter the → New Age movement. Taking responsibility for your life, in the *est* world view, included assuming responsibility for every event that one is part of. Even poverty, illness and personal tragedies were thus included in the sphere of personal responsibility. As do many New Age texts, *est* claimed that each of us creates our own reality. The path to accepting the *est* philosophy – of "getting it", to use the jargon of the movement – was to submit to a strictly scripted event that included considerable verbal abuse from the leaders as well as physical hardship.

Primal therapy rests on the belief that problems in the present can be traced back to the intense, traumatic sensory stimulation supposedly occurring at birth. This belief can be traced back to the theories of Freud's pupil Otto Rank (1884-1939), who developed the concept of the birth trauma in the 1920s. Generally speaking, psychoanalysts never accorded Rank's theory any greater credibility. It was, however, revived by the founding father of primal therapy, Arthur Janov (b. 1924). The concept of the birth trauma was in Janov's book *The Primal Scream* (1970) linked to a therapeutic method based on abreaction.

6. The Fate of the Human Potential Movement

The HPM proper lost much of its credibility with mainstream society after a period of almost faddish general interest in the late 1960s and early 1970s. Part of this disaffection with the HPM had to do with the growing critique against the movement. To judge whether this critique was justified or not is a normative exercise that will not be attempted here. It may suffice to note that the criticism typically followed a few lines of attack.

(1) One common objection to the aims of the HPM was that it fostered a narcissistic attitude. HPM therapies were accused of privileging short-term experience over long-term goals, individual indulgence over social concerns, and so forth. To counter such negative assessments, spokespersons for the HPM pointed e.g. at the attempts to create interracial encounter groups. (2) Another perceived problem had to do with the clients attracted by the often emotionally highly intense methods. Although aimed at improving the healthy rather than curing the ill, some of those who attended sessions at growth centers were too psychologically fragile to go through emotionally intense encounter groups or Gestalt therapy. Thus, several suicides took place at Esalen and other growth centers, generating serious doubts about the methods employed. (3) Related to this last theme were the misgivings concerning forms of bodywork, voiced by more traditional therapists. The emphasis on touch and emotionality thus raised concerns regarding the risk of creating overly strong bonds of transference and countertransference. It was

suggested that these bonds could be psychologically harmful. (4) The eclectic and academically unaffiliated nature of much of the HPM led to the proliferation of methods, some of which were highly unorthodox. Part of the critique of the HPM concerned this "anything goes" atmosphere, which was said to attract unqualified people to take on the role of therapist. A related criticism targeted the lack of clinical and experimental validation of many of the therapies on offer. (5) The perhaps most common criticism was that HPM therapies resulted in cathartic experiences and feelings of emotional breakthrough, the effects of which largely vanished once clients returned to their everyday lives.

Despite the massive critique against the perceived ills of the HPM, some of its manifestations have survived well. Certain aspects of the HPM have approached the norms of more traditional psychotherapeutic work. Modern gestalt therapy tends to focus on individual rather than group sessions, and has adopted methods that are less emotionally challenging to clients and therefore less focused on catharsis. Encounter groups are rarer, while their ideological ancestor, psychodrama, has fragmented into several different forms. Body therapies have proliferated, and have partly become more professionally established.

Arguably, however, the very fact that much of the HPM came under such heavy attack from the media and from academic psychologists led to its affiliation with countercultural and/or spiritual concerns rather than with more traditional forms of psychotherapy. The transpersonal elements of the movement were increasingly emphasized in the mid-1970s and beyond. Furthermore, certain facets of the HPM, especially in this radicalized and spiritualized form, came to share goals and ideas with the emerging New Age movement. Health was defined by the HPM in ways that prefigure a number of contemporary systems of complementary medicine. Rather than implying freedom from disease, as standard biomedical conceptions would do, health involves a broad spectrum of positive values such as creativity, vitality and spirituality. The focus of much of the New Age on radical personal transformation also has its precursor in the ideology of the HPM. The belief in the integration of mind and body, as well as the primacy of non-intellectual means of achieving this holistic vision, also unite the HPM and the New Age.

The specific methods of the HPM have also had their successors with appeal to the New Age milieu. The body therapy techniques developed by Reich and Lowen and their followers, and

described above, could involve emotionally and physically intense activities, including hitting, kicking, screaming, hyperventilation and painful manipulation of the muscles. In contrast to this approach are the considerably gentler methods of bodywork popular among New Agers, such as body harmony. Similar aims of contacting buried traumas through memories supposedly encoded in the muscular tissue are achieved through much milder forms of bodily manipulation.

Perhaps most visible in the New Age milieu are offshoots of the radical fringe of the HPM. Although largely discredited, primal therapy inspired a popular component of the New Age scene, rebirthing, a method of controlled breathing that is claimed by its practitioners to resolve physical and mental traumas, and even prevent aging. The manipulation of the physical body prevalent in the HPM has its radicalized counterparts in New Age theories that attempt to manipulate non-physical aspects of the body, be it the chakras or the aura. The regression therapies of the HPM are radicalized in New Age techniques that attempt to go back beyond birth to purported past lives.

Many later developments of various HPM methods have increasingly embraced religious themes. There have even been attempts to integrate the decidedly anti-spiritual Gestalt therapy of Fritz Perls with religious concerns. It is, perhaps, only fitting that one of the most direct heirs of the 1960s HPM is a religious organization, the Osho movement mentioned above. The movement's main center in Koregaon Park, an affluent suburb of Pune, India, resembles a 1960s and 1970s growth center. Visitors can combine their own palette of experiential workshops, including neo-Reichian therapies and sessions that are replicas of 1960s encounter groups.

Finally, it can be noted that some of the ideas of the HPM have managed to enter the cultural mainstream. A number of facets of contemporary culture, ranging from best-selling self-help books to business management training seminars, are at times based on ideals drawn from the positive view of our hidden potential and the practices typical of the HPM.

Lit.: Walter T. Anderson, *The Upstart Spring: Esalen and the American Awakening*, Reading, Mass.: Addison-Wesley, 1983 ◆ Donald Moss (ed.), *Humanistic and Transpersonal Psychology: A Historical and Biographical Sourcebook*, Westport and London: Greenwood Press, 1999 ◆ Hendrik M. Ruitenbeek, *The New Group Therapies*, New York: Discus Books, 1970 ◆ Bruce W. Scotton et al., *Textbook of Transpersonal Psychiatry and Psychology*, New York: Basic Books/

HarperCollins, 1996 ◆ Donald Stone, "The Human Potential Movement", in: Charles Y. Glock & Robert N. Bellah (eds.), *The New Religious Consciousness*, Berkeley, Los Angeles, London: Univ. of California Press, 1976, 93-115 ◆ Charles Tart, *Transpersonal Psychologies*, New York: Harper & Row, 1975 ◆ Ronald S. Valle & Steen Halling (eds.), *Existential-Phenomenological Perspectives in Psychology*, New York: Plenum, 1989 ◆ Roy Wallis, "The Dynamics of Change in the Human Potential Movement", in: Rodney Stark (ed.), *Religious Movements: Genesis, Exodus and Numbers*, New York: Paragon House, 1985, 129-156.

OLAV HAMMER

Huysmans, Joris-Karl (Charles-Marie-Georges), * 5.2.1848 Paris, † 12.5.1904 Paris

One of the most celebrated novelists of the 19th century, Huysmans was baptized with the names Charles-Marie-Georges, but later in life adopted "Joris-Karl" as his christian name in acknowledgement of his father's Dutch origins. A civil servant, in the 1870s he publishes his first novels, abandons his family's Roman Catholicism and becomes a protégé of Emile Zola (1840-1902), the patriarch of French literary positivism. In 1884, Huysmans publishes his most famous novel, *À rebours*, and breaks with Zola. Regarded as the master of "decadentism", a neo-romantic, anti-positivistic literary school of the time, Huysmans is also interested in → spiritualism, → occultism, and the apocalyptic Roman Catholicism of his friend and fellow novelist Léon Bloy (1846-1917).

Another friend and novelist, Remy de Gourmont (1858-1915), has a lover called Berthe Courrière (1852-1917), who becomes Huysmans's guide into Paris' occult underground. Berthe tells Huysmans of her contacts with Father Louis Van Haecke (1864-1912), a Belgian priest whom she accuses of being the leader of an international Satanist ring. Huysmans decides to write a novel about → Satanism, and interviews among others journalist Jules Bois (1868-1943) and defrocked Lyon priest Joseph-Antoine Boullan (1824-1893). The latter was the leader of one among several rival branches of the Œuvre de la Miséricorde, a new religious movement founded by Bayeux visionary Eugène Vintras (1807-1875). Boullan's controversial rituals were a curious blend of Catholicism, sex magic and occultism; Huysmans regarded him as reliable, however, and echoes of Boullan's worldview are evident in Huysmans's best-selling novel *Là-bas*, a vivid portrait of French-speaking Satanism published in 1891.

Là-bas includes what was to become the standard literary depiction of a Black Mass, based on combined material Huysmans had received from Berthe Courrière, Bois, and Boullan. Paradoxically, this section of *Là-bas* (a novel intended to expose Satanism as evil) would be read as an how-to manual by later Satanists. It would also be used by Léo Taxil (pseudonym used by Marie-Joseph-Antoine-Gabriel Jogand-Pagès, 1854-1907), an imposter who would falsely claim to have evidence that Freemasons [→ Freemasonry] actually worship Satan in their lodges. Taxil would enjoy a certain popularity among Roman Catholics and other critics of Freemasonry until confessing his fraud in 1897.

It is *Là-bas* and his correspondence with Boullan and other characters of the occult fringe, that ensures Huysmans a place in the history of esotericism. This period of his life ends, however, in 1891, when Boullan dies and Berthe Courrière introduces Huysmans to Father Arthur Mugnier (1879-1939), who completes the novelist's subsequent conversion to mainstream Roman Catholicism. In later years, Huysmans would rarely speak about occult issues, and his subsequent itinerary would ultimately bring him into the field of French Catholic literature.

Huysmans defended *Là-bas*, however, as a novel that, although written by a non-Christian, could also be read both as a reliable documentary account of Satanism, and as a moral meditation on the power of evil. The assessment of the first claim depends on whether Huysmans's sources are regarded as reliable. Whether Father Van Haecke was in fact a Satanist, or a victim of libelous accusations by local enemies, or whether Berthe Courrière actually gave Huysmans real accounts of Satanic rituals or merely figments or her own imagination, are questions widely debated among Huysmans's biographers, and unlikely ever to be finally resolved. As for the second claim, there were those in the Catholic camp (including Léon Bloy) who finally accused Huysmans of exploiting spiritual themes for the sole purpose of producing best-selling novels. Others, however, including right-wing English author Robert Hugh Benson (1871-1914), claimed that they owed their conversion to Catholicism to *Là-bas*.

Be that as it may, the scarcity of sources about both 19th century Satanism in continental Europe and the Boullan movement makes Huysmans' novels and correspondence important references on these topics, although he was clearly writing as a novelist rather than as an historian.

Joris-Karl Huysmans, *Œuvres complètes*, 23 vols., Paris: Crès, 1928-1934.

Lit.: Richard Griffiths, *The Reactionary Revolution: The Catholic Revival in French Literature, 1870-1914*, London: Constable, 1966 ♦ Div. authors, "J.K. Huysmans", thematic issue of *Les Cahiers de la Tour Saint-Jacques* 8 (1963) ♦ Maurice Belval, *Des ténèbres à la lumière: Etapes de la pensée mystique de J.K. Huysmans*, Paris: Maisonneuve & Larose, 1968.

MASSIMO INTROVIGNE

Hymns and Prayers (Gnostic and Hermetic)

1. INTRODUCTION 2. GNOSTICISM
(A. PRAYERS OF PETITION; B. PRAYERS/
HYMNS OF THANKSGIVINGS; C. HYMNS OF
SELF-PROCLAMATION; D. BAPTISMAL
AND EUCHARISTIC HYMNS AND PRAYERS;
E. INVOCATIONS OF HEAVENLY BEINGS;
F. SUMMARY) 3. HERMETISM
(A. THE CLOSING PRAYER OF THE
POIMANDRES; B. HYMNS OF REBIRTH;
C. BACKGROUNDS; D. HERMETIC
COMMUNITIES?) 4. CONCLUSION

1. INTRODUCTION

In Gnostic [→ Gnosticism] and Hermetic [→ Hermetism; → Hermetic Literature] documents there are passages which can be classified as hymns and prayers, either directly (that is, quoted as such within the documents) or indirectly (that is through allusions to celestial and earthly beings praying or singing hymns). The tendency, both Gnostic and Hermetic, to appropriate and re-use traditional material of this type, is well documented. It can also be noted that, generally speaking, even the Gnostic and Hermetic "production" of hymns and prayers, when not actually drawn from earlier sources, seems in any case to be strongly influenced by other contexts. If, then, there is a tendency to depend on forms and sometimes even on content taken from other traditions, it is characteristic of Gnostics and Hermetists to be absolutely original in re-elaborating the borrowed material. They inserted it into their own religious perspectives, with meanings and functions that are completely idiosyncratic. This process is especially evident in cases where prayers or formulae of Gnostic and Hermetic literature are also attested unequivocally in other religious traditions: their re-use involves a radical re-reading and change of function within the typically Gnostic and Hermetic concepts of the relationships between the human and super-human realms.

It must be considered highly likely that an extensive and organised repertoire of prayers, hymns, invocations, litany formulae or specific expressions circulated to some extent in late antiquity. From time to time, this repertoire was appealed to in various religious contexts, which were undeniably similar in a series of aspects but still presented their specific ideological and traditional frameworks as well: from Gnosticism to Hermetism, from the complex ideology underlying magical papyri to Jewish and Christian circles. We are dealing here with a dynamic and fluid process in which adoption of common liturgical formulae did not necessarily imply the acquisition or acceptance of the same doctrinal horizons. Adapting these elements to a new context was in fact an effective means for Gnostics and Hermetists of distancing themselves from others and affirming their own originality.

In the light of all this, it will be clear that also in Gnostic and Hermetic studies, any attempt at an accurate identification and classification of prayers and hymns meets with many difficulties, since from the perspectives of terminology and form, sources of varying provenance were used; this is true for the formulation of the hymns and prayers and for the reflections on them. On the other hand, a specific aspect of the milieu discussed here can be noted: these prayers seem in fact to form a functional part of the experience of knowledge of gnosis which, in different forms, marks both the Gnostic and the Hermetic system.

2. GNOSTICISM

Both the direct Gnostic documentation provided by the Nag Hammadi Library and the documentation which has reached us through Christian heresiologists, are rich in expressions and images with respect to doxology, eulogy and hymns. These elements are sometimes so closely intertwined with the rest of the respective documents that it is difficult to determine whether they really are hymns or simply passages of "poetic prose". Serious research is hampered by the very nature of the documents, which are not conditioned by the need to set out a doctrine in a systematic way and, in particular, almost never provide explicit ritual elements and religious practices. In most cases, when prayers or hymns can be identified, we find them partially or completely without an adequate context. One is therefore forced to reconstruct the picture as a whole indirectly (and even this is possible only in a few privileged cases), and with results which, for that very reason, cannot claim to be either certain or unambiguous.

Historians of religions have thoroughly studied the phenomenon of prayer, for which they have proposed various formal classifications. These are based, for example, on the dynamics of the relationship between speakers, or on the structure and nature of the communication (who is praying, what is being prayed for, how does one pray, where does one pray, why does one pray, etc.). Due to the nature and limitations of our evidence, it is difficult to apply such a classification to Gnostic and Hermetic material. Sometimes it is possible, however, to perceive well-known formal and functional distinctions, which we will attempt to document here. This is true, for example, in the case of some texts in which prayer is closely linked with the dimension of "repentance": in such cases one can speak of prayers of petition.

A. PRAYERS OF PETITION

In the case of Gnosticism, this type of prayer is closely linked to the existential condition of the "pneumatic seed", that is of that divine spark imprisoned in man which longs to return to the divine plane from which it fell and therefore invokes the supreme god to come and save it. In our documentation, the prayer of petition of the Gnostic (that is, of the one who is aware of living in this world but of belonging ontologically, in respect of his true "self", to the divine plane) is projected into a mythological dimension which is its foundation and at the same time its prototype. This is the case in the *Exegesis of the Soul* (NHC II, 6) which relates the events of the prototypical soul that has moved away from the Father and, after experiencing every kind of abuse and sexual violence in the material world, repents and invokes him to set it free from that slavery. This document belongs to a "primeval" Gnosticism which reflects the passage from a Platonizing psychology to a full Gnostic religiosity. The prayer of petition comprises three parts: the invocation of the Father, the recalling and confession of the fall, and the final entreaty for salvation. To the same category (although inevitably with some disparities) belongs the prayer of Sophia, who also repents of her rebellion against the Father, to whom she turns to be set free from the material world and its evil demiurges (cf. *Apocryphon of John*, II, 13, 32-14, 6 and parallels; Irenaeus, *Adv. haer.* I, 2, 3-4; Hippolytus, *Ref.* VI, 30-32; *Pistis Sophia* I, 32-67). Moving from myth to anthropology, the Gnostic prayer of petition seems to be very closely connected to the moment of consciousness, that is to say, the moment when the Gnostic becomes fully aware of his own real essence. This becoming conscious is also marked by the rejection of material reality and the entrance into the "current" of salvation (cf. *The Book of Thomas*, NHC II, 138, 1; 145, 19). It should be observed that the same prayer, even if formulated and recited in the dimension of reality, does not really belong there: it is inner prayer, completely spiritual and recited by the spirit which, in the view of the Gnostics, is ontologically the same as the divine plane. Thus, for the person praying, the prayer of petition is the expression of his break with the material world and of his own aspiration for salvation.

B. PRAYERS/HYMNS OF THANKSGIVING

Besides the prayer of petition there is another type which can be defined as prayer or hymn of thanksgiving: an expression of joy about the gnosis obtained and the salvation reached as a result (cf. *Exegesis of the Soul*, NHC II, 134, 15-25; *Gospel of the Egyptians*, NHC III, 66, 22-67, 22 = NHC IV, 79, 3-80, 8; *Pistis Sophia* II, 68-76). This type of prayer occurs in various ways in our documentation. In the enthusiastic situation of praise, even heavenly beings can sing hymns and prayers: in the *Apocryphon of James* (NHC I, 15, 5-23), in the context of an ascension, James and Peter hear the prayers of praise and the hymns of rejoicing of the angels; in *On the Origin of the World* (NHC II, 105, 20-106, 3) there is a reference to an angelic church in perpetual prayer of praise; the *Letter of Peter to Philip* (NHC VIII, 136, 1-7) mentions the cosmic powers which, by mistake since they do not know the supreme god, send their prayer to the Autohades; in the *Trimorphic protennoia* (NHC XIII, 38, 22-30) the prayer of praise of the celestial Aeons is quoted. It is very likely that in all these references to a heavenly liturgy there is a projection to the extra-human level of the actual community of Gnostics who, just like the angels and superior powers, send prayers to the heavenly beings and to the supreme god.

C. HYMNS OF SELF-PROCLAMATION

In the Gnostic hymns the celebration of a particular character can occur in the form of self-proclamation, according to a model which to a high degree concurs with that of the "pagan" aretalogies, in which the god introduced himself enumerating his different attributes and numerous functions. The *Apocryphon of John* (NHC II, 30, 11-31, 27 and the parallel version NHC IV, 46, 23-49, 9) presents a self-proclamation by Pronoia who describes her repeated interventions to bring gnosis into the material world. A hymn on Eve, recited in the first person, is documented in *On the Origin of the World* (NHC II, 114, 7-15), whereas a hymn of Jesus is found in the *Second Apocalypse of James* (NHC V, 4-49, 5-15). The treatise *Thunder, Perfect Mind* (NHC VI, 2) is a complete self-proclamation of a female being; in the *Trimorphic protennoia* (NHC XIII, 1) the three different forms in which the heavenly redeemer descends are introduced by the same number of self-proclamations. The *Psalm of the Soul* ascribed to the Naassenes by Hippolytus (Hipp., *Ref.* V, 10, 2), certainly belongs to this context. In it the divine intermediary principle, here represented in his saving function and identified with Jesus, implores the Father to send him to earth and set free the soul which has become lost and so is unable to find the way back to the divine. By going down into the material world he will bring to the soul 'the mysteries of the holy way', gnosis in particular, so that it can set itself free. But the hymns can also be used to express through their poetic language visions otherwise ineffable, such as the cosmological picture described in the psalm of Valentinus (Hipp., *Ref.* VI, 37, 6-7).

D. BAPTISMAL AND EUCHARISTIC HYMNS AND PRAYERS

In some cases there is some evidence that prayers and hymns of praise and petition are connected to community-type practices, of which the heavenly liturgy is a projection. More specifically, they seem to be connected with the practice of baptism. In the *Gospel of the Egyptians* the two final hymns refer to this praxis. The first of the two hymns (NHC III, 66, 8-22 // NHC IV, 78, 10-79, 3) is addressed to a pleromatic deity and comprises six invocations alternating with an acclamation, in which there is a large number of vowel sequences interspersed with names and formulae in Greek. The addressee of the hymn is connected with the five seals, which are fundamental to the baptismal praxis. The liturgical nature of the text is emphasised by the fact that it is spoken by a collective "we", indicating that the hymn was recited or sung by a soloist whose acclamations were repeated by the whole assembly. The second hymn (NHC III, 66, 22-68, 1 // NHC IV, 79, 3-80, 15) is recited by an "I" to a "you" (sing.). It seems clear that the person who is praying praises the deity for the state he has attained: it is a praise expressed by an individual who has acquired gnosis and so has attained salvation. The hymn probably had to be recited during a ritual act that marked the individual's entry into the Gnostic community. This ritual act must have been accompanied by certain gestures. Probably the first hymn was sung during or immediately after the baptism, whereas the second was recited by the initiate. In the treatise *Trimorphic protennoia* there is a list of beings recited by Protennoia (NHC XIII, 48, 11-35); although not a hymn in the strict sense, it is close to it in structure. It has five

strophes, with an introduction that connects it with the rest of the document. In each strophe three heavenly functionaries are mentioned by name, followed by a description of the saving act performed by them.

In the treatise known as *Melchizedek* (NHC IX, 1) two hymnal sections can be identified. In the first (14, 15-18, 7) the mythical priest raises a prayer of joy, giving thanks for the salvation obtained through gnosis. The utterance of his name seems to be connected with a baptismal context. It is obviously a litany hymn, but it cannot be determined whether it was recited by the community or by a single initiate. In the second section (5, 24-6, 14) there is, on the other hand, an invocation pronounced by an angel. The hypothesis has been put forward that whereas the one being baptised is identified with Melchizedek, the mystagogue can be identified with the angel. The hymn of praise contained in 16, 16-18, 7 follows a pattern marked by the *trishagion*, followed by the title of the being invoked and its name; this structure is also found in 5, 24-6, 14, but then without the *trishagion*. There is also a *trishagion* in the *Untitled Text* of Codex Brucianus, ch. 7. *Zostrianus* (NHC VIII, 6, 5-30) recites a hymn of praise which the protagonist sends to the powers after the baptism in the name of Autogenes: in this case also there is the pattern of a title followed by a name or a name followed by a title.

In the Sethian Gnostic treatises marked by baptismal praxis the prayer of praise thus assumes peculiar characteristics: it is addressed to pleromatic and non-pleromatic beings all of whom are connected with baptism, it is uttered in the form of a litany, and accompanied by titles and names. At the same time, the content of this litany is firmly connected with the mythology underlying the document or the tradition with which the hymn itself is connected. In fact there is not always a perfect match between the religious system to which the hymn belongs and the system of which the hymn is an expression. The actual structure of the hymns is liable to vary: sometimes they are an expression of praise, sometimes a request, and sometimes a profession of faith. Also, the beings involved are not always the same: only some of them recur with a certain regularity and suggest a specific liturgical tradition, whereas the unsystematic presence of others raises important questions about their origin and role. It is likely that there were lists of them.

The doxological prayers recorded in NHC XI, 2 *On Anointing* and *On the Eucharist* (40, 1-29 and 43, 20-38) derive from a sacramental context of a Valentinian type, whereas the three prayers which

comprise the treatise *Three Steles of Seth* (NHC
VII, 5) must be considered as hymns which accompany the three different levels of mystical ascension. In the *Oration of Paul* (NHC I, A, 1-B, 10) the
aim of the prayer of invocation is the mystical elevation of the Gnostic, here represented by Paul,
who in this way succeeds in penetrating the divine
mystery.

E. Invocations of heavenly beings

The *epiclesis*, that is, the invocation of the beings
by name, has some interesting parallels in primitive
Christianity, which also attests the request for help
in a baptismal context, in order to place the initiates under the protection of the beings invoked.
Also *nomina barbara* and various sequences of
vocals belong to this context. The multiplication of
the intracosmic and pleromatic heavens in Gnostic
cosmology allows the number of beings living in
them to be expanded almost to infinity. Whereas
the beings of the intracosmic realms, such as the
heavenly Archons, are totally aggressive and negative, the pleromatic beings are beneficial, able to
assist the Gnostic who starts on the path of faith
and to support him during the whole journey of
salvation he has to complete. In the *Pistis Sophia*
IV, 136, the ritual prayer spoken by Jesus after
his resurrection is marked by vocalizations and
mysterious names, and occurs in a context in which
the spatial orientation of Jesus and his disciples
seems to play an important role. On the other
hand, the presence of *voces mysticae* and of vocalic
sequences in hymns and prayers reveals the interest
the Gnostic had in invocations of a "magical" kind.
Many of the names invoked, in fact, as well as the
series of vowels, are common to the repertoire of
the magical papyri. There, access to the deity is permitted only through knowing his "names": they
represent the deity itself and should not be revealed
to anyone. Originally only the gods knew these
names, and actually they do not belong to human
but to divine language. The secret language also
uses secret formulae, vocalic sequences, palin-
dromes, combinations of letters and numbers,
"foreign" languages, or animal language. Thus in
Gnostic circles these elements are evidently appropriated but they are given a new function within a
different religious system. Gnosticism undoubtedly
shared with the world of religious magic the need
for contact with the divine through a "different"
language (mysterious words) and a knowledge – to
some extent "secret" – of the names of the beings
invoked (*nomina mystica*) and of the system of
interrelationships between the various cosmic
levels (vocalic sequences understood as symbols
of the planets).

F. Summary

From this mass of evidence it emerges that Gnostics made wide use of prayers and hymns which
were strongly influenced by (if not indeed adopted
from) both the Jewish and the Christian world, as
well as the "pagan" tradition in the widest sense.
The Odes and Psalms of the Old Testament are
widely used, as is also the model of the *trishagion*,
and the use of a terminology comes very close to
Jewish and Christian usage. But equally, prayers
and hymns occur which are strongly influenced by
magic literature. There are also two syncretistic
"pagan" hymns to Attis that in the context of the
Naassenes form the starting point for doctrinal
speculation (Hipp., *Ref.* V, 9, 8-9). The use of mystery language is not in itself evidence of a doctrines
shared with the mystery cults, since this terminology was in fairly common use in the religious languages of late antiquity.

3. Hermetism

Hermetic prayer shows the same tendency to
make use of various sources, and the presence of
elements taken from different religious contexts is
also evident. As with Gnostic prayer, here too one
should consider a special process of reinterpretation of the material used.

As is well known, enlightenment and the resulting rebirth form the centre of Hermetic experience. The acquisition of that state by an individual
entails, on the one hand, a complete vision of the
divine world and, on the other, a transformation of
the initiate, also in ethical and intellectual respects.
He is said to attain a state of repose where he dedicates himself to perpetual praise of God. One of
the privileged tools to attain Gnosis consists precisely in prayer, through which the *mystes* succeeds
in establishing a relationship and communication
with God.

A. The closing prayer of the Poimandres

At the end of the Hermetic treatise known as
Poimandres (CH I, 30-32) a prayer is recorded
which undoubtedly refers to themes presented in
the treatise. In terms of structure it comprises a
sequence of sayings preceded by the adjective
"Holy", which in turn can be subdivided into three
groups of each three praises: in the first, God is
addressed in the third person, in the others, in the
second. This hymn is followed by the offering of a
spiritual sacrifice, a petition, a profession of faith,
a blessing and a conclusion. The Jewish inspiration
of this prayer is evident in the use of sayings preceded by "holy", the oldest antecedent of which is
the *Sanctus* of Isaiah (*Is.* 6, 3), re-written in an

apocalyptic context, which is attested both in Jewish and early Christian liturgy. In the introduction to the prayer and in the petition there are allusions to the *Shema'* (*Deuteronomy* 6, 4-5). Moreover, certain expressions of the Hermetic *Sanctus* have equivalents in the eighteen *berakoth* (blessings that have to be said three times a day), especially the *Yotser* (the morning prayer) of the Jewish liturgy and at the same time form part of the blessings which precede the *Shema'*. Other parallels can be identified in the prayers said at morning and evening by the Therapeutae, as attested by Philo (*Vita cont.* 27. 89). In addition, attention has also correctly been drawn to parallels with the "instruction" genre of Egyptian tradition, with Greek philosophical sayings as well as with a series of possible contributions from the Christian liturgy. The invocations stress the generative role of the deity and his connection with man. God carries out his will through the powers whereas gnosis is the qualifying element of the link between God and "his own". The offer consists of "pure rational (= spiritual) sacrifices" and marks the process of spiritualization of sacrifice, also documented in literary texts and "pagan" philosophers and in Jewish and Christian sources. The petition made is for remaining in the state of gnosis, followed by a profession of faith and finally the blessing and statement of the wish to share with God in the work of sanctification. In CH V 10-11, there is also a prayer at the end of the treatise, which is a celebration of the absolute essence of God.

B. Hymns of rebirth

The prayer contained in CH XIII 17-19 rehearses the experience of rebirth previously undergone by Tat. In the hymnal section are invoked the various powers which are within the *mystes*, followed by an offering of spiritual sacrifices (a speech offering) and a conclusion. The reference in the document to eulogy as an already codified formula which the *mystes* wishes to know, and the information on the ways in which it has to be recited (orientation, gestures), speak in favour of a ritual defined as and forming part of a type of initiation. Of special interest is the comparison with the morning and evening prayers in Greek religion. The hymn that is spoken at the end of the rebirth is in fact sung by the powers that have penetrated the *mystes*, defined as the instrument through which the *logos* sings. The spiritual sacri-fice referred to is the prayer itself which results in the *mystes* finding "repose", peace.

Other interesting evidence on Hermetic prayer comes from the library of Nag Hammadi. In the *Discourse on the Eight and Ninth* (NHC VI, 52, 1-63, 32), the disciple, who by now is ready to reach

the Ogdoad and the Ennead, is requested by Hermes to pray: they will pray with mind, heart and soul (53, 12). The following prayer by Hermes is characterised by the glorification of God's power, by vocalic sequences and by the request for vision (55, 4-57, 25). Then the disciple also receives the vision through silent prayer. His vision has to be kept secret, while the *mystes* continues to praise god incessantly for the rest of his days. It is a prayer requesting divine intervention, which has the structure of an invocation to god through his functions, a series of *voces mysticae* and of vocalic sequences, a petition and finally an offering, which in this case also consists of spiritual sacrifices. Here too there is an allusion to the *Shema'*, while mysterious names and sequences of vocals connect the document with the world of the magical papyri. The idea that the life of the enlightened takes the shape of a continual hymn of praise goes back to Stoicism and Judaism (cf. Epict., *Diss.* 1, 16, 15-21; Philo, *Heres.* 200).

In the *Prayer of Thanksgiving* (NHC VI, 63, 33-65, 7), the persons who are praying thank the deity who has granted them his love and given them some gifts (*nous, logos, gnosis*). It is a prayer of praise for the gnosis obtained, to which those who are praying ask to remain faithful. An intervention by the redactor at the close of the prayer portrays those who are praying as now turned towards pure nourishment without blood. It is interesting to stress that the *Prayer of Thanksgiving* is also found at the end of the *Asclepius* and in the Papyrus Mimaut. Probably this is the result of independent circulation.

C. Backgrounds

The structural similarities that can be discovered between the various prayers (the sequence: offering, petition, profession of faith, conclusion in CH I and CH XIII, or the same sequence of formulae in CH, I 31 and the *Eight and Ninth*, NHC VI, 6 56, 15-17) pose the problem of whether the Hermetists used common sources, not necessarily Hermetic, or whether these similarities derive from making use of the same liturgical model.

As for the parallels with other religious traditions, there is the reference to heavenly hymn singing in the *Eight and Ninth* and CH I. The idea of human singing based on the singing of the heavenly powers is present in Jewish apocalyptic literature and is common in Christian liturgical texts. The theme of "spiritual sacrifice" goes back to Jewish and Christian milieus, an expression that in pagan contexts has an equivalent only in Hermetic texts, in some of which it simply means prayer. Of interest for comparative purposes is the Egyptian Christian anaphora attested in *P. Strasb. Gr.* 254, one of the oldest occurrences of an anaphora, where spiritual sacrifice does not mean the sacrifice of Christ but the offering of prayers of thanksgiving. When Jewish liturgical material was transferred to the Christian liturgy, it remains difficult to determine from which of the two traditions elements of Hermetic prayers were taken. The life of the enlightened as a continual hymn of praise to the deity is a Jewish and Stoic motif. Hermetism shares with Platonic theurgy the idea that certain cultic acts, including prayer, allow the soul to complete its ascent towards the divine realm. As for the use of formulae, expressions and "mysterious" names widely attested in magical papyrological literature, the same comments apply as for Gnosticism: this material is only used after being reshaped to make it suitable for new religious meanings.

D. HERMETIC COMMUNITIES?

The role of prayer in Hermetism can be understood only in close connection with the problem of whether or not there was a Hermetic community in the strict sense. In other words, whether Hermetic practices actually existed or whether the documentary material is to be considered as a purely literary phenomenon without any ritual background (see also → Hermetism). The question still remains open, and in the past the opinions of scholars have oscillated between two extremes: on the one hand the hypothesis that a Hermetic community did exist, and on the other the hypothesis which denied the existence of Hermetic communities in the strict sense. Recent studies, while accepting that the treatises do not describe a specific historical and sociological reality, are inclined to consider them as a phenomenon which is not exclusively literary. In particular, there emerges from them the picture of one or very few disciples gathering closely around a master who transmits to them his teaching by word of mouth. The transcripts of these lessons have enabled the teachings to pass beyond the confines of these restricted circles. These written documents, which comprise a tradition parallel to the oral tradition of teacher to disciple, were considered "sacred" and therefore were kept secret. Study, instruction, dialogue, prayers, and hymns, all ultimately create a deep bond between master and disciples, who feel themselves to be part of a tradition and in a wide sense of a community. But a situation like this is extremely fluid and tied to the charisma of a single master. On the other hand, the existence of "communities" linked in some way to prayer emerges in allusive form from the documents: in the *Eight and Ninth*, initiation seems to take on a communal dimension through the reference to "brothers" who welcome the *mystes*. In the *Asclepius* spiritual prayer develops in a temple context and according to specific times and positions; it follows a structure and is recited by several persons, and thus appears to be a complex liturgical act. There is also evidence for cultic practices in CH XIII, where Hermes supplies Tat with certain instructions about the position and orientation regulating recitation of the prayer.

Gnostics and Hermetists connect prayer with enlightenment, either conceived of as a sign of conversion, understood both as "repentance" and as initiation, or considered instead as an expression of joy for the salvation which has now been acquired. However, for neither Gnostics nor Hermetists can one speak of organised churches, and the liturgical practices attested in some documents cannot be applied to all the "communities", not even to those which seem to be close to each other (among the Gnostics, for example, the Valentinian [→ Valentinus and Valentinians] or Sethian [→ Sethians] circles) since the differences at the doctrinal and liturgical levels make such generalisations difficult. In particular, the link between prayer and baptism, which emerges more or less allusively and only in a few Gnostic documents, has almost no equivalent in Hermetic literature. An exception is CH IV, 4 where, according to Hermes, god says to the human hearts to immerse themselves "in the mixing bowl". There also exists a letter (4th cent. C.E.) written by a devotee of → Hermes Trismegistus in which he speaks about 'the inexorable water of the god Hermes who protects'.

It is precisely this lack of specific information concerning the existence and operation of Hermetic circles, due to the very nature of the documents which have reached us, which makes it difficult to reach conclusions about the contexts in which the prayers and hymns were recited. In some cases they seem to be the result of personal devotion, in others they appear to have liturgical functions within circles of devotees. In Hermetism, at the highest levels of the initiation process, oration becomes internal and silent prayer, whereas in Gnosticism in some cases we find the paradox that the devotee, once he has reached the dimension of "perfect", no longer needs to pray.

4. CONCLUSION

If prayers and hymns seem to be widely documented both in Gnostic and Hermetic sources, a salient fact that is immediately obvious is the extreme variety of documentation. The common elements, which are also present, do not however allow a "typically" original Gnostic or Hermetic structure to be identified. Rather they seem to be the result of the recovery and reinterpretation of earlier or contemporary models, in terms of both language and theological content and perhaps also with respect to certain cultic acts. These processes of reinterpretation occur in milieus – and this applies to both Gnosticism and Hermetism – which in themselves exhibit extremely fluid outlines. The result of all this is that it is not possible to speak of Gnostic and Hermetic prayers or hymns except in rather general terms. A more correct and fruitful approach is to study, one by one, the references to hymns and prayers documented within each of the texts, with particular attention to the ideology – in form and substance, "original" or received – which they express.

P. Wendland (ed.), *Hippolytus Werke III: Refutatio omnium haeresium* (GCS 26), Leipzig: J.C. Hinrichs, 1916 ♦ A.D. Nock & A.-J. Festugière (eds.), *Corpus Hermeticum*, 4 Volumes, Paris: Les Belles Lettres, 1945-1954 ♦ B.R. Ree (ed.), *Papyri from Hermopolis and Other Documents of the Byzantine Period* (Greco-Roman Memoirs, 42), London: Egypt Exploration Society, 1964 ♦ A. Rousseau & L. Doutreleau (eds.), *Irénée de Lyon: Contre les Hérésies*, 10 Volumes, Paris: Les Éditions du Cerf, 1965-1982 ♦ T. Wolbergs (ed.), *Griechische religiöse Gedichte der ersten nachchristlichen Jahrunderte*. Band I: *Psalmen und Hymnen der Gnosis und des frühen Christentums*, Meisenheim am Glan: Anton Hain, 1971 ♦ J.-P. Mahé (ed.), *Hermès en Haute-Égypte*, 2 Volumes, (Biliothèque copte de Nag Hammadi, Section "Textes", 3 and 7), Québec, Canada: Les Presses de l'Université Laval, 1978-1982 ♦ V. MacDermot & C. Schmidt (eds.), *Pistis Sophia*, Leiden: E.J. Brill, 1978 ♦ V. MacDermot & C. Schmidt (eds.), *The Books of Jeu and the Untitled Text in the Bruce Codex*, Leiden: E.J. Brill, 1978 ♦ J.-M. Sevrin, *L'Exégèse de l'âme (NH II, 6)*, Québec, Canada: Les Presses de l'Université Laval, 1983 ♦ J.M. Robinson (ed.), *The Facsimile Edition of the Nag Hammadi Codices. Introduction*, Leiden: E.J. Brill, 1984 ♦ B.P. Copenhaven (ed.), *Hermetica: The Greek Corpus Hermeticum and the Latin Asclepius in a New English Translation, with Notes and Introduction*, Cambridge: Cambridge University Press, 1992 ♦ J.M. Robinson (ed.), *The Nag Hammadi Library in English*, Leiden-New York-Köln: E.J. Brill, 1996 ♦ A. Camplani (ed.), *Scritti ermetici in copto*, Brescia: Paideia, 2000.

Lit.: A.-J. Festugiére, *La révélation d'Hermès Trismégiste*, 4 Volumes, Paris: J. Gabalda et C., 1944-1954 ♦ G. Zuntz, "On the Hymns in Corpus Hermeticum XIII", *Hermes* 83 (1955), 68-92 ♦ A. Kehl, "Beiträge zum Verständnis einiger gnostischer und frühchristlicher Psalmen und Hymnen", *Jahrbuch für Antike und Christentum* 15 (1972), 92-119 ♦ M. Philonenko, "Le Poimandrès et la liturgie juive", in: F. Dunand & P. Lévêque (eds.), *Les syncrétismes dans les religions de l'antiquité. Colloque de Besançon (22-23 octobre 1973)*, Leiden: E.J. Brill, 1975, 204-234 ♦ E. Segelberg,

"Prayer among the Gnostics? The Evidence of Some Nag Hammadi Documents", in: M. Krause (ed.), *Gnosis and Gnosticism: Papers read at the Seventh International Conference on Patristic Studies (Oxford, September 8th-13th 1975)*, Leiden: E.J. Brill, 1977, 55-69 ♦ M. Philonenko, "Une utilisation du Shema dans le Poimandrès", *Revue d'histoire et de philosophie religieuse* 49 (1979), 369-372 ♦ J.-M. Sevrin, "La prière gnostique", in: H. Limet & J. Ries (eds.), *L'expérience de la prière dans les grandes religions: Actes du colloque de Louvain-la-Neuve et Liège (22-23 novembre 1978)*, Louvain-la-Neuve: Centre d'histoire des religions, 1980, 367-374 ♦ M. Marcovich, "The Naassene Psalm in Hippolytus (*Haer.* 5.10.2)", in: B. Layton (ed.), *The Rediscovery of Gnosticism: Proceedings of the International Conference on Gnosticism at Yale, New Haven, Connecticut, March 28-31, 1978*, II, Leiden: E.J. Brill, 1980, 770-778 ♦ B.A. Pearson, "Jewish Elements in Corpus Hermeticum I (*Poimandres*)", in: R. van den Broek & M.J. Vermaseren (eds.), *Studies in Gnosticism and Hellenistic Religions, presented to Gilles Quispel on the Occasion of his 65th Birthday*, Leiden: E.J. Brill, 1981, 336-348 ♦ J.-M. Sevrin, *Le dossier baptismal séthien: Études sur la sacramentaire gnostique* (Bibliothéque copte de Nag Hammadi, Section "Études", 2), Québec, Canada: Les Presses de l'Université Laval, 1986 ♦ J. Büchli, *Der Poimandres: Ein paganisiertes Evangelium* (WUNT 2, 27), Tübingen: J.C.B. Mohr (Paul Siebeck), 1987 ♦ R. Flasche, s.v. *Gebet*, in: H. Cancik, B. Gladigow, M. Laubscher, *Handbuch religionswissenschaftlicher Grundbegriffe*, Band II, Stuttgart-Berlin-Köln: W. Kohlhammer, 1990, 456-468 ♦ M. Lattke, *Hymnus: Materialen zu einer Geschichte der antiken Hymnologie* (NTOA), Göttingen: Vandenhoeck & Ruprecht, 1991 ♦ G. Fowden, *The Egyptian Hermes: A Historical Approach to the Late Pagan Mind*, Princeton: Princeton University Press, 1993 ♦ J. Holzhausen, "Ein gnostischer Psalm? Zu Valentins Psalm in Hipp. ref. VI 37, 7 (= frg. 8 Völker)", *Jahrbuch für Antike und Christentum* 36 (1993), 67-80 ♦ E. Mazza, "L'eucarestia: dalla preghiera giudaica alla preghiera cristiana", in: *La preghiera nel mondo tardo antico: Dalle origini ad Agostino. XXVII Incontro di studiosi dell'antichità cristiana, Roma 7-9 maggio 1998*, Roma: Institutum Patristicum Augustinianum, 1999, 25-51 ♦ F. García Bazán, "Dos breves plegarias gnósticas y su contexto codicológico: Oración de Pablo (NHC I, A*-B*) y Oración de acción de gracias (NHC VI, 7)", in: *ibidem*, 67-84 ♦ A.M. Mazzanti, "La preghiera nel Corpus Hermeticum" in: *ibidem*, 101-112 ♦ R. van den Broek, "Religious Practices in the Hermetic 'Lodge': New Light Form Nag Hammadi", in: R. van den Broek & C. van Heertum, *From Poimandres to Jacob Boehme: Gnosis, Hermetism and the Christian Tradition*, Amsterdam: In de Pelikaan, 2000, 77-95 ♦ A. Camplani, "Introduzione", in: idem (ed.), *Scritti ermetici in copto*, Brescia: Paideia, 2000, 13-131 ♦ M.G. Lancellotti, *The Naassenes: A Gnostic Identity Among Judaism, Christianity, Classical and Ancient Near Eastern Traditions* (Forschungen zur Anthropologie und Religionsgeschichte, 35), Münster: Ugarit, 2000.

MARIA GRAZIA LANCELLOTTI